The Heath
Introduction to
LITERATURE

The Heath Introduction to LITERATURE

Fourth Edition

Alice S. Landy

D. C. Heath and Company
Lexington, Massachusetts • Toronto

Address editorial correspondence to:
D. C. Heath
125 Spring Street
Lexington, MA 02173

Cover design: Diana Coe

Cover: Varujan Boghosian, *The World,* 1977
Collage, ink, and watercolor on paper; 9″ × 7¼″
Private Collection.

About the Cover: An artist of rare talent, whose media include watercolors, collage, and sculpture, Varujan Boghosian (b. 1926) works "with the mystery of myth and the ambiguity of form." He views the ancient myths as legacies of the past and attempts to illuminate them in a new way by combining elements that suggest both a sense of linear time and a sense of the spiritual realm beyond the constriction of time. *The World* (1977), a collage with watercolor, clearly presents these two ideas of time.

Student Edition International Standard Book Number: 0-669-24409-0

Instructor's Edition International Standard Book Number: 0-669-24410-4

Library of Congress Catalog Number: 91-65857

10 9 8 7 6 5 4

Acknowledgments

Margaret Atwood. "In Search of the Rattlesnake Plantain" from *Bluebeard's Egg* by Margaret Atwood. Copyright © 1983, 1986 by O. W. Toad, Ltd. Reprinted by permission of Houghton Mifflin Co.

W. H. Auden. "The Unknown Citizen" and "Musee des Beaux Arts" from *W. H. Auden: Collected Poems* by W. H. Auden, ed. by Edward Mendelson. Copyright 1940 and renewed 1968 by W. H. Auden. Reprinted by permission of Random House, Inc.

James Baldwin. "Sonny's Blues," copyright © 1957 by James Baldwin from *Going To Meet the Man* by James Baldwin. Used by permission of Doubleday, a division of Bantam Doubleday Dell Publishing Group, Inc.

Toni Cade Bambara. "My Man, Bovanne" from *Gorilla, My Love* by Toni Cade Bambara. Copyright © 1971 by Toni Cade Bambara. Reprinted by permission of Random House, Inc.

Amiri Baraka (LeRoi Jones). "W.W." from *Black Magic Poetry 1961–1967*, copyright © 1969 by LeRoi Jones. Reprinted by permission of Ronald Hobbs Literary Agency.

Jorge Luis Borges. "The South" by Jorge Luis Borges, translated by Anthony Kerrigan, from *Ficciones*. Copyright © 1962 by Grove Press, Inc. from the Spanish edition copyright © 1956 by Emece Editores, S.A., Buenos Aires. Used by permission of Grove Press, Inc.

Gwendolyn Brooks. "The Bean Eaters" and "We Real Cool" from *Blacks* by Gwendolyn Brooks, copyright © 1987. Reprinted by permission of Gwendolyn Brooks.

John Cheever. "The Swimmer" from *The Stories of John Cheever* by John Cheever. Copyright © 1964 by John Cheever. Reprinted by Permission of Alfred A. Knopf, Inc.

John Ciardi. "Project for a Cliff Face" by John Ciardi. Reprinted by permission of Judith Ciardi.

Arthur C. Clarke. "An Ape About the House." Reprinted by permission of the author and the author's agents, Scott Meredith Literary Agency, Inc., 845 Third Avenue, New York, New York 10022.

Countee Cullen. "For a Lady I Know" from *On These I Stand* by Countee Cullen. Copyright 1925 by Harper & Row, Publishers, Inc. Renewed 1953 by Ida M. Cullen. Reprinted by permission of Harper and Row, Publishers, Inc.

E. E. Cummings. "All in Green Went My Love Riding," "in Just," "the Cambridge ladies who live in furnished souls," and "next to god of course america i" reprinted from *Complete Poems, 1913–1962*, by E. E. Cummings, by permission of Liveright Publishing Corporation. Copyright © 1923, 1925, 1931, 1935, 1938, 1939, 1940, 1944, 1945, 1946, 1947, 1948, 1949, 1950, 1951, 1952, 1953, 1954, 1955, 1956, 1957, 1958, 1959, 1960, 1961, 1962 by the Trustees for the E. E. Cummings Trust. Copyright 1961, 1963, 1968 by Marion Morehouse Cummings.

Emily Dickinson. All selections reprinted by permission of the publishers and the Trustees of Amherst College from *The Poems of Emily Dickinson*, Thomas H. Johnson, ed., Cambridge, Mass.: The Belknap Press of Harvard University Press, copyright 1951, © 1955, 1979, 1983 by the President and Fellows of Harvard College.

Hilda Doolittle. "Heat" from *Collected Poems, 1912–1944* by Hilda Doolittle. Copyright © 1982 by the Estate of Hilda Doolittle. Reprinted by permission of New Directions Publishing Corporation.

T. S. Eliot. "The Love Song of J. Alfred Prufrock" from *Collected Poems 1909–1962*, copyright 1936 by Harcourt Brace Jovanovich, Inc., copyright © 1964, 1963 by T. S. Eliot, reprinted by permission of the publisher.

William Faulkner. "A Rose for Emily" from *Collected Stories of William Faulkner* by William Faulkner. Copyright 1930 and renewed 1958 by William Faulkner. Reprinted by permission of Random House, Inc.

Lawrence Ferlinghetti. "The pennycandy store beyond the El" from *A Coney Island of the Mind* by Lawrence Ferlinghetti. Copyright © 1958 by Lawrence Ferlinghetti. Reprinted by permission of New Directions Publishing Corporation.

Parker Fillmore. "Clever Manka" from *The Shepard's Nosegay* by Parker Fillmore, copyright © 1958 and renewed 1986 by Harcourt Brace Jovanovich, Inc., reprinted by permission of the publisher.

Robert Frost. "Design" and "Birches" from *The Poetry of Robert Frost* edited by Edward Connery Lathem. Copyright 1916, © 1969 by Holt, Rinehart and Winston. Copyright 1936, 1944 by Robert Frost. Copyright © 1964 by Lesley Frost Ballantine. Reprinted by permission of Henry Holt and Company, Inc.

Allen Ginsberg. "In Back of the Real" copyright 1954 by Allen Ginsberg and "A Supermarket in California" copyright © 1955; from *Collected Poems 1947–1980* by Allen Ginsberg. Reprinted by permission of HarperCollins Publishers.

Nikki Giovanni. "You Are There" and "Woman" from *Cotton Candy on a Rainy Day* by Nikki Giovanni. Copyright © 1978 by Nikki Giovanni. Reprinted by permission of William Morrow & Company, Inc.

Susan Glaspell. "Trifles" from *Plays* by Susan Glaspell. Copyright 1920 by Dodd, Mead & Company, Inc. Copyright renewed 1948 by Susan Glaspell. Reprinted by permission of Dodd, Mead & Company, Inc.

Robert Graves. "Down, Wanton, Down!" from *Collected Poems 1975* by Robert Graves. Copyright © by Robert Graves. Reprinted by permission of Oxford University Press, Inc.

Arthur Guiterman. "On the Vanity of Earthly Greatness" by Arthur Guiterman. From *Gaily the Troubadour.* Reprinted by permission of Louise H. Sclove.

Lorraine Hansberry. *A Raisin in the Sun* by Lorraine Hansberry. Copyright © 1958 by Robert Nemiroff, as an unpublished work. Copyright © 1959, 1966, 1984 by Robert Nemiroff. Reprinted by permission of Random House, Inc.

Robert Hayden. "Those Winter Sundays" is reprinted from *Angle of Ascent*, New and Selected Poems, by Robert Hayden, by permission of Liveright Publishing Corporation. Copyright © 1975, 1972, 1970, 1966 by Robert Hayden.

Seamus Heaney. "Docker" from *Poems 1965–1975* by Seamus Heaney. Copyright © 1966, 1969, 1972, 1975, 1980 by Seamus Heaney. Reprinted by permission of Farrar, Straus & Giroux, Inc.

Ernest Hemingway. "Hills Like White Elephants" reprinted with permission of Charles Scribner's Sons, an imprint of Macmillan Publishing Company, from *Men Without Women* by Ernest Hemingway. Copyright 1927 by Charles Scribner's Sons; copyright renewed 1955 by Ernest Hemingway.

A. E. Housman. "With Rue My Heart Is Laden," "When I Was One-and-Twenty," "Terence, This is Stupid Stuff" and "To An Athlete Dying Young" from "Shropshire Lad"—Authorised Edition—from *The Collected Poems of A. E. Housman.* Copyright 1939, 1940, © 1965 by Holt, Rinehart and Winston. Copyright © 1967, 1968 by Robert E. Symons. Reprinted by permission of Henry Holt and Company, Inc.

Langston Hughes. "Harlem" from *Selected Poems by Langston Hughes.* Copyright © 1951 by Langston Hughes. "Mother to Son" from *Selected Poems of Langston Hughes* by Langston Hughes. Copyright 1926 by Alfred A. Knopf, Inc. and renewed 1954 by Langston Hughes. Both are reprinted by permission of Alfred A. Knopf, Inc.

Ted Hughes. "Pike" from *New Selected Poems* by Ted Hughes. Copyright © 1959 by Ted Hughes. By permission of Harper & Row, Publishers, Inc.

Henrik Ibsen. *A Doll's House* by Henrik Ibsen, translation by Otto Reinert. Reprinted by permission.

Robinson Jeffers. "Love the Wild Swan" from *The Selected Poetry of Robinson Jeffers* by Robinson Jeffers. Copyright 1935 and renewed 1963 by Donnan Jeffers and Garth Jeffers. Reprinted by permission of Random House, Inc.

James Weldon Johnson. "O Black and Unknown Bards," copyright 1917 by James Weldon Johnson, from *Saint Peter Relates an Incident* by James Weldon Johnson. Used by permission of Viking Penguin, a division of Penguin Books USA Inc.

James Joyce. "Araby" from *Dubliners* by James Joyce. Copyright 1916 by B. W. Heubsch. Definitive text Copyright © 1967 by the Estate of James Joyce. Used by permission of Viking Penguin, a division of Penguin Books USA Inc.

Franz Kafka. "The Bucket Rider" from *Franz Kafka: The Complete Stories* by Franz Kafka, ed. by Nahum Glatzer. Copyright 1946, 1947, 1948, 1949, 1954, 1958, 1971 by Schocken Books, Inc. Reprinted by permission of Schocken Books, published by Pantheon Books, a division of Random House, Inc.

D. H. Lawrence. "The Horse Dealer's Daughter," copyright 1922 by Thomas B. Seltzer, Inc., renewed 1950 by Frieda Lawrence, from *Complete Short Stories of D. H. Lawrence* by D. H. Lawrence. "Piano," "Mystic" from *The Complete Poems of D. H. Lawrence* by D. H. Lawrence. Eds. de Sola Pinto & Roberts. Copyright © 1964, 1971 by Angelo Ravagli and C. M. Weekley, Executors of the estate of Frieda Lawrence Ravagli. Used by permission of Viking Penguin, a division of Penguin Books USA Inc.

Ursula Le Guin. "The Ones Who Walk Away from Omelas" from *The Wind's Twelve Quarters* by Ursula Le Guin. Copyright © 1973 by Ursula K. Le Guin; first appeared in *New Dimensions 3;* reprinted by permission of the author and the author's agent, Virginia Kidd.

Doris Lessing. "A Sunrise on the Veld" from *African Stories* by Doris Lessing. Copyright © 1951, 1953, 1954, 1957, 1958, 1962, 1963, 1964, 1965 by Doris Lessing. Reprinted by permission of Simon & Schuster, Inc.

Denise Levertov. "Six Variations" (part iii) from *Poems 1960–1967* by Denise Levertov. Copyright © 1961 by Denise Levertov Goodman. First published in *Poetry.* Reprinted by permission of New Directions Publishing Corporation.

Amy Lowell. "Wind and Silver" from *The Complete Poetical Works of Amy Lowell* by Amy Lowell. Copyright © 1955 by Houghton Mifflin Co. Copyright © 1953 renewed by Houghton Mifflin Co., Brinton P. Roberts, and G. D'Andelot Belin, Esquire. Reprinted by permission of Houghton Mifflin Co.

Robert Lowell. "The Old Flame" from *For the Union Dead* by Robert Lowell. Copyright © 1962, 1964 by Robert Lowell. Reprinted by permission of Farrar Straus and Giroux.

Archibald MacLeish. "Ars Poetica" from *New and Collected Poems 1917–1982* by Archibald MacLeish. Copyright © 1985 by the Estate of Archibald MacLeish. Reprinted by permission of Houghton Mifflin Co.

Katherine Mansfield. "Miss Brill" from *The Short Stories of Katherine Mansfield* by Katherine Mansfield. Copyright 1922 by Alfred A. Knopf, Inc. and renewed 1950 by John Middleton Murry. Reprinted by permission of Alfred A. Knopf, Inc.

Carson McCullers. "A Tree, a Rock, a Cloud" from *The Ballad of the Sad Cafe and Collected Short Stories* by Carson McCullers. Copyright 1936, 1941, 1942, 1950, © 1955 by Carson McCullers. Copyright © renewed 1979 by Floria V. Lasky. Reprinted by permission of Houghton Mifflin Co.

Edna St. Vincent Millay. "Love Is Not All . . . ," "What Lips My Lips Have Kissed," and "First Fig" by Edna St. Vincent Millay from *Collected Poems,* Harper & Row. Copyright © 1922, 1923, 1931, 1950, 1951, 1958 by Edna St. Vincent Millay and Norma Millay Ellis. Reprinted by permission of Elizabeth Barnett, Literary Executor.

Moliere. *Tartuffe,* by Moliere, copyright © 1963 by Richard Wilbur, reprinted by permission of Harcourt Brace Jovanovich, Inc. CAUTION: All rights including professional, amateur, motion picture, recitation, lecturing, performance, public reading, radio broadcasting, and television are strictly reserved. Inquiries on all rights should be addressed to Harcourt Brace Jovanovich, Inc., Orlando, FL 32887.

Marianne Moore. "The Mind Is an Enchanting Thing," reprinted with permission of Macmillan Publishing Company from *Collected Poems* by Marianne Moore. Copyright 1941, and renewed 1969, by Marianne Moore. "Poetry," reprinted with permission of Macmillan Publishing Company from *Collected Poems* by Marianne Moore. Copyright 1935, and renewed 1963, by Marianne Moore. "I May, I Might, I Must," copyright © 1959 by Marianne Moore, © renewed 1987 by Lawrence E. Brinn and Louise Crane, Executors of the estate of Marianne Moore, from *The Complete Poems of Marianne Moore* by Marianne Moore. Used by permission of Viking Penguin, a division of Penguin Books USA Inc.

Flannery O'Connor. "A Good Man Is Hard to Find" from *A Good Man Is Hard to Find and Other Stories,* copyright 1953 by Flannery O'Connor and renewed 1981 by Regina O'Connor, reprinted by permission of Harcourt Brace Jovanovich, Inc.

Tillie Olsen. "Tell Me a Riddle," excerpted from the book *Tell Me a Riddle* by Tillie Olsen. Copyright © 1956, 1957, 1960, 1961 by Tillie Olsen. Reprinted by permission of Delacorte Press/Seymour Lawrence, a division of Bantam Doubleday Dell Publishing Group, Inc.

Eugene O'Neill. "Desire Under the Elms" from *The Plays of Eugene O'Neill* by Eugene O'Neill. Copyright 1924 and renewed 1952 by Eugene O'Neill. Reprinted by permission of Random House, Inc.

Wilfred Owen. "Dulce et Decorum Est," "Anthem for Doomed Youth" from *Collected Poems.* Copyright © 1963 by Chatto & Windus, Ltd.

Dorothy Parker. "Resume" by Dorothy Parker, copyright 1926, 1928, renewed 1954, © 1956 by Dorothy Parker, from *The Portable Dorothy Parker,* Introduction by Brendan Gill. Used by permission of Viking Penguin, a division of Penguin Books USA Inc.

Sylvia Plath. "Mirror" from *The Collected Poems of Sylvia Plath,* edited by Ted Hughes, copyright © 1963 by Ted Hughes. "Metaphors" from *The Collected Poems of Sylvia Plath,* edited by Ted Hughes, copyright © 1960 by Ted Hughes. Reprinted by permission of HarperCollins Publishers.

Katherine Anne Porter. "The Jilting of Granny Weatherall" from *Flowering Judas and Other Stories,* copyright 1930 and renewed 1958 by Katherine Anne Porter, reprinted by permission of Harcourt Brace Jovanovich, Inc.

Ezra Pound. "In a Station of the Metro," "L'Art 1910," "These Fought in Any Case," "Ancient Music," and "The Seafarer" from *Personae* by Ezra Pound. Copyright 1926 by Ezra Pound. Reprinted by permission of New Directions Publishing Corporation.

Dudley Randall. "Ballad of Birmingham." Reprinted by permission of Dudley Randall.

Adrienne Rich. "Aunt Jennifer's Tigers" is reprinted from *The Fact of a Doorframe,* Poems Selected and New, 1950–84, by Adrienne Rich, by permission of W. W. Norton & Company, Inc. Copyright © 1984 by Adrienne Rich. Copyright © 1975, 1978 by W. W. Norton & Company, Inc. Copyright © 1981 by Adrienne Rich.

Theodore Roethke. "My Papa's Waltz," copyright 1942 by Hearst Magazines, Inc. "I Knew a Woman," copyright 1954 by Theodore Roethke from the book *The Collected Poems of Theodore Roethke.* Both reprinted by permission of Doubleday & Company, Inc.

Carl Sandburg. "Cool Tombs" from *Cornhuskers,* copyright 1918 by Holt, Rinehart and Winston, Inc. and renewed 1946 by Carl Sandburg. "Fog" from *Chicago Poems,* copyright 1916 by Holt, Rinehart and Winston, Inc. and renewed 1944 by Carl Sandburg. Both reprinted by permission of Harcourt Brace Jovanovich, Inc.

Anne Sexton. "Welcome, Morning" from *The Awful Rowing Toward God* by Anne Sexton. Copyright © 1975 by Loring Conant, Jr., Executor of the estate of Anne Sexton. Reprinted by permission of Houghton Mifflin Co.

William Shakespeare. "Hamlet," edited by Willard Farnham, in *The Pelican Shakespeare.* General Editor: Alfred Harbage (rev. ed.; New York: Penguin Books, 1970). Copyright © Penguin Books Inc., 1957, 1970. Reprinted by permission of Penguin Books.

Sophocles. *Oedipus Rex* translated by Dudley Fitts and Robert Fitzgerald, copyright 1949 by Harcourt Brace Jovanovich, Inc. and renewed 1977 by Cornelia Fitts and Robert Fitzgerald, reprinted by permission of the publisher. CAUTION: All rights including professional, amateur, motion picture, recitation, lecturing, performance, public reading, radio broadcasting, and television are strictly reserved. Inquiries on all rights should be addressed to Harcourt Brace Jovanovich, Inc., Orlando, FL 32887.

Sophocles. *Antigone,* translated by Dudley Fitts and Robert Fitzgerald, copyright 1939 by Harcourt Brace Jovanovich, Inc. and renewed 1967 by Dudley Fitts and Robert Fitzgerald, reprinted by permission of the publisher. CAUTION: All rights including professional, amateur, motion picture, recitation, lecturing, performance, public reading, radio broadcasting, and television are strictly reserved. Inquiries on all rights should be addressed to Harcourt Brace Jovanovich, Inc., Orlando, FL 32887.

John Steinbeck. "The Chrysanthemums," from *The Long Valley* by John Steinbeck. Copy-

CONTENTS

DRAMA   539

PREFACE

In compiling and writing *The Heath Introduction to Literature*, we began from the groundwork laid by the Heath introductions to fiction, poetry, and drama—books that themselves draw on the help and expertise of scores of teachers of English and the humanities. This book differs from those texts in bringing together all three genres within one affordable volume; in ordering its material in thematic rather than chronological fashion (except in the case of drama); and in providing introductions and study questions that make the book not just an anthology, but a unified teaching plan.

Like previous editions, the fourth edition is divided into four parts. The first part supplies a general introduction to the study of literature. Its opening chapter, on reading literature, introduces the student to the basic components of literature—plot, character, and theme—and to basic critical concepts such as unity and inevitability. This chapter also introduces the philosophy of the text: that literature is a dialogue between writer and reader, an art form whose subject is a vision of humanity and the universe. The second chapter, on writing about literature, reiterates these fundamentals and shows how they underlie the skills and techniques of writing about literature. While the first chapter is philosophical in bent, the second is practical. Work plans, lists of questions, and a diagram make the idea of writing both concrete and comprehensible, and provide "how-to's" for the assignments in the rest of the book.

Although these introductory chapters precede the structured parts on fiction, poetry, and drama, they need not be read first. The instructor who wishes to begin with short stories or poems can elicit spontaneous student responses, unguided by study questions. The questions raised in the introductory chapters can then be applied to works everyone has recently read, and the focus of the course will be clearly defined as being the reading *of* (rather than *about*) literature.

The first genre offered is fiction. Its presentation is organized around modes of narration and narrative techniques. The interplay of listener and narrator is thus highlighted, and the basic framework of the text is kept simple. Within this framework, other concepts appear as a natural outgrowth of the subject under discussion and easily become a part of the student's critical vocabulary. The presentation provides a variety of critical concepts within a firmly structured framework—a more satisfying organization than the "grasshopper" approach in which each chapter, or each story, heralds a new topic and leaves students and instructors alike negotiating the jumps between topics as best they can. Fourteen stories are new to this edition. Also, two new thematic groups, Portraits and Beyond Reality, appear in this edition.

Poetry follows fiction, this being the order preferred by most instructors. Throughout the poetry section we use well-known and highly readable works to introduce the student to the technical aspects of poetry, such as rhythm and verse form, and then to the genre's subtler concerns, among them the voice of the speaker, imagery, and the use of sound. This movement allows the student to begin with a general overview of what a poem *is*, and then to delve more deeply into the specific characteristics that *make* it a poem. For those instructors who wish to offer their students works free of critical commentary, an anthology of poems completes the part. Twenty-five poems have been added to this edition, appearing in both the introductory chapters and the poetry anthology.

Drama receives strong, chronological coverage in this edition. The section, including works from tragedy, comedy, realism, and contemporary drama, features three plays new to this edition: Molière's *Tartuffe,* Tennessee Williams' *The Glass Menagerie,* and Lorraine Hansberry's *A Raisin in the Sun.* The chronological organization of this section clearly illustrates the important structural and historical developments of this genre.

Within each section there are plentiful study aids: introductory essays, study questions, essay suggestions, and questions for further thought. Objective and subjective responses both have their place as answers to our questions; the emphasis is on knowing the difference and on achieving a judicious balance between the two. In general, questions near the beginning of a section will offer more guidance than those that come later, thus tacitly encouraging students to greater independence as their skills and familiarity with literature grow. Some sets of questions are constructed so that they form an example of how to organize an essay; others concentrate on showing how to follow a theme through a story, poem, or play; still others encourage students to look at a work from as many angles as possible.

We feel that a good textbook, like the literature it contains, must offer variety within unity, and we have done our best to achieve that goal. Our thanks to the many colleagues who have helped us, especially to Michael J. Anzelone, Nassau Community College; Phillip D. Atteberry, University of Pittsburgh at Titusville; Ethel Bonds, Virginia Western Community College; Susan Bullard, Cedar Valley College; Robert Burke, Joliet Junior College; Adele Carpenter, Lewis and Clark Community College; John Driscoll, Phoenix College; Allan Duane, Ulster County Community College; Lou Ellison, Lurleen B. Wallace State Junior College; James F. Gordon, Jr., Mississippi Delta Junior College; Maria Haman, Louisiana Technical University; Jeff Jeske, University of California, Los Angeles; Mary Lund, Henry Ford Community College; Vernon Miles, University of Arkansas; Richard M. Salamas, Henry Ford Community College; Margaret Shepherd, Surry Community College; Rebecca Shuttleworth, Mississippi Delta Junior College; Bev Smith, Lurleen B. Wallace State Junior College; Margaret Stein, University of Notre Dame; Margaret Sullivan, University of California, Los Angeles; Barry Tomkins, Hudson County Community College; John A. Weldon, Clinton Community College; and Roger Zimmerman, Lewis and Clark Community College.

Finally, we thank you, the users of this book, who have helped us revise the menu of selections and commentary, and who bring to it your own love of literature and skills in teaching. May you enjoy using this book, and may it serve you well.

ALICE S. LANDY,
Editor
PAUL A. SMITH,
Senior Editor,
D. C. Heath and Company

The Heath
Introduction to
LITERATURE

ON LITERATURE

1 _The Bases of Literature_

Literature has its roots in one of the most basic human desires—the desire for pleasure. Its writers find one source of pleasure in mastering the difficult demands of their craft. If they do well, they then reap a second delight from witnessing the pleasure their work gives to others. Readers, meanwhile, derive pleasure from literature's power to imitate life. A truly good book can speak of imaginary people so vividly that they seem more alive than people we meet on the street, and can make us care about its characters as if they were close friends.

We are always curious about each other, and usually curious about ourselves as well. Why do we behave as we do? What are the causes of our actions? Literature is far from having all the answers. But it does offer hints, suggestions, and flashes of insight. Moreover, it offers them in such a way as to refresh and encourage our own thinking, and so leads us to insights of our own. Readers have many standards for judging writers. But one enduring standard is the writers' power to interpret us, as humans, to ourselves. The greater the writers' knowledge of people seems to be, the more openly they share their knowledge with us, the higher we rate them. We speak with disdain of shallow or insincere writers; we demand truth and sincerity even in the most fantastic fiction.

Literature, then, exists because it pleases us. And it pleases us by imitating life—or, more precisely, by displaying its writers' visions of life as it is or as the writers think it should be. But how does it contrive its imitation? Its only medium is words; and we know how hard it is to make words say what we want them to say. How do writers handle their words to get such powerful effects from them? What guidelines help them make the million-and-one choices that result in a play, a poem, or a story?

The first necessities for any work of literature—and therefore the first things that writers must consider—are **plot** and **character**. These may occur to a writer in either order. That is, a writer may first imagine some characters, and then decide what actions they are to perform; or a writer may envision some action, and then decide on the people who must perform it. Every work of literature, however, must have both action and characters. It cannot please us, or hold our interest, otherwise.

It may seem that poetry is an exception to this rule. While stories and plays tend to present fully developed plots with sequences of actions with discernable beginnings, middles, and ends, poems more often plunge us into the middle of an event, and may tell us neither what came before the event nor what comes after it. Here, for instance, is a poem with no physical action at all. Yet it shows us one person, at least, and gives us some insight into his actions and feelings.

GEORGE GORDON, LORD BYRON (1788–1824)

So We'll Go No More A-Roving

So we'll go no more a-roving
   So late into the night,
Though the heart be still as loving,
   And the moon be still as bright.

5 For the sword outwears its sheath,
   And the soul wears out the breast,
And the heart must pause to breathe,
   And Love itelf have rest.

Though the night was made for loving,
10   And the day returns too soon,
Yet we'll go no more a-roving
   By the light of the moon.

We know several things about the speaker of this poem. We know that he has enjoyed "roving," and that he still thinks warmly of it, since he declares that "the night was made for loving, / And the day returns too soon." We know that he feels weary, like a sheath worn out by the motions of the sword within it. We hear him declare that his roving days are done. But we also hear him speak of pausing and resting, verbs that imply an eventual return to action. And so we begin to wonder: is he really finished with love, as he says he is? The action of the poem might thus be described as the act of the lover forswearing love. Its interest arises from our recognition of the complex emotions the renunciation reveals. It is the action, and the emotion, of a moment; but it is none the less real—and none the less action—for its momentary nature.

For now, however, let us return to the more thoroughly developed plots of drama and fiction. These, too, must find some balance between action and emotion, some method of telling us both what the characters do and how they feel. A given story may emphasize action or feeling; that choice, like so many others, is up to its writer. But it must contain some of both. We have no interest in unfeeling characters, or in characters who do nothing.

In addition to a plot and to characters who act and feel, a work of literature must have **unity** and **coherence**. It must make us believe that its characters really would have committed the actions it says they commit, and that the actions could really have taken place. At its best, the movement of a play, a poem, or a story must make us feel that the tale could have reached no other end, and that it could have reached it in no other way. When this happens, the story's ending seems inevitable. Its characters and its actions have convinced us wholly. A sense of inevitability is thus another hallmark of a fine work of literature. Works so marked tend to be moving and powerful.

The **language** of a work of literature is also important. Words have so many undercurrents of meaning that the change of one word may change our image of a scene or a character. Consider, for instance, the difference between *a thin, tense man; a thin, nervous man;* and *a thin harried man*—or the difference between *a plump woman, a well-rounded woman,* and *an overweight woman.* A writer's language must be chosen with care. It should carry overtones that enrich our sense of the story, thus adding to the pleasure we get from the tale. And it must avoid all false tones, for those would diminish our pleasure. Again, we demand at least that the words fit the actions and characters of which they tell. And again, we shall find that the best seem almost inevitable. Reading them, we cannot imagine the author having used any other words.

When we read, we don't want to be aware of these choices of words and acts and characters. We don't want to hear the author muttering behind the scenes: "I need this word, not that one. This character must say this; that description must carry this message." Rather, we want to be able to concentrate on the story itself, accepting everything within it as valid and necessary parts of its world. When we discuss and analyze works of literature, however, we do become aware of the choices the writers made in constructing them. We note who the characters are and how they relate to each other. We observe how the action begins, how it ends, and how it is carried from beginning to ending. We study the ways in which the language characterizes people and events and consider the broader or deeper meanings it suggests.

These questions, we may note, are **questions of fact.** Their answers can be found, decided, and agreed upon. We can count the characters in *Hamlet,* and we will learn that Hamlet is a prince of Denmark, that Gertrude is his mother and Claudius his stepfather, and that the ghost who appears from time to time is the ghost of Hamlet's murdered father. Similarly, we learn that eight people are killed during the course of the play (one by stabbing, one by drowning, two by beheading, one by poison, and three by some combination of sword wounds and poison) and that virtually none of the major characters is still alive when the play ends. There is no question about any of these happenings and no reason to argue about them.

Questions of fact, however, are only a beginning in thinking about a work of literature. They tell us certain choices a writer has made, but they rarely tell us why the writer has made those particular choices. To learn that, we must go on to **questions of interpretation,** questions that deal with the artistic vision underlying the work and thus with such issues as theme, pattern, message, and meaning.

Message and **meaning** are not universal to literature. They belong to one school of literature, the **didactic.** When writers or critics demand that a story carry a message to its readers, that it "mean something" to them, they are saying that literature should teach us something and that it should appeal to our sense of moral values. At its simplest, this approach ends in pat morals: "Always tell the truth; stop beating up on your fellow humans." On a more sophisticated level, however, didacticism becomes what the critic Matthew Arnold called "high seriousness" and produces literature that deals with such complex questions as the value of human life and the sources of human ideals and aspirations.

Not all literature is didactic. Some writers believe that literature does not need to make a moral statement. For these writers, a work of literature is important for its own sake, not for any message it might carry. As one modern poet put it, "A poem should not mean, but be."[1] In works like these, the concept of message does not apply; to impose it upon them is to falsify the intent of the writer.

The questions of **theme** and **pattern,** however, concern all literature. Within any work of literature that strikes us as unified and complete we will find some sort of pattern into which its parts fit or through which they are perceived. Didactic tales, for example, present acts and people in terms of a moral order. Hence the tales tend to be built around patterns of good and evil, temptation and response. In contrast, a Romantic poem

---

[1] Archibald MacLeish, "Ars Poetica," p. 609.

describing a summer day might have sensory impressions of light and shade, coolness and warmth, as its unifying vision.

There may be many patterns—patterns of action, characterization, language, or metaphor—within a single work. Sometimes each will work separately; sometimes several will be intertwined to bear on a single theme. Sometimes, too, several themes will be interwoven within one work to create a complexity of vision that no single theme could contain. But always there will be that sense of a single ordered vision embracing and unifying all the patterns or themes.

When we study literature, we first look at each story as an entity in itself, existing on its own terms. We enter the world of the story and speak of its characters and narrator as though they were living people. Eventually, however, we begin to wonder about the writers of the stories. Why did they choose to create these characters, to have them perform these actions, to tell their tales from this particular point of view?

We can never know exactly what writers had in mind when they were writing their stories. The process of writing is too complex, with too much of it hidden even from the writers themselves, to allow any sure or simple answers to that question. But we should examine our own ideas on the subject—our sense of what the writers seem to consider important and what values or feelings of ours they seem to be invoking; for our impression of the writers' values and intentions plays an important part in our response to their work.

Here interpretation becomes most individual and most varied. We all read the same words when we read a story. We observe the same characters acting out the same deeds and passions. But we each interpret them a little differently because of our individual views of life, our interests, and our experience. When we try to explain how the story works, therefore, or decide what themes are being emphasized, we read some of our own perceptions into the story.

If we realize that we are interpreting, all is well. Then we can say, "This is how it seems to me." We can look for patterns of language or imagery and details of action or characterization to support our view. We can listen to others who have other views and evaluate the support they bring for their arguments; and, in the end, we can probably come to a pretty fair idea of what the story does have to offer and how it is able to offer it.

On the other hand, if we do not recognize the extent to which we are active interpreters of what we read, we may have trouble when we try to deal with such subjective issues as theme or message. For then we may make the error of saying, "I see this. Therefore the author intended it that way and I have found the only correct interpretation this story can possibly have." Since very few works of literature will not admit some variance of interpretation, definitive statements such as this are wrong more often than not. It is true that there are limits to the range of interpretations we can apply to a work of literature if we are to read it honestly on its own terms. Within those limits, however, we must be willing to acknowledge various ways of looking at it.

We must also be willing to allow our perceptions to change. It often happens that what we notice the first time we read a story is not what seems most important to us later on. Nor would it make sense to talk or write about a poem or a story if our perception of it could not be enriched by the discussion. Too, we must be willing to use our full judgment, to read the story carefully and attentively. We must be sure we are trying to discover what it really does say rather than simply assuming that it says what we want it to say. Once we have done this, however, we should be able to feel comfortable with our judgments and our responses. Above all, we must not undervalue ourselves. We are the people for whom these stories, plays, and poems are written. If we cannot trust ourselves, we will have a hard time trusting them.

2 Writing About Literature

Literature allows writers to share their ideas and visions with their readers. Their work is not complete until someone has read it and responded to it.

As readers, we too have something to say. At the very least, we have opinions about the work itself, but we also may have other ideas to express. Perhaps we are moved to compare this story with others, or perhaps it has given us some new ideas that we want to explore further. Sometimes we share our ideas directly with others in face-to-face discussions. At other times, we become writers in order to communicate our thoughts and opinions.

The first part of writing about literature, therefore, is thinking about it. This step is perhaps the most vital part of the process, for we need to know not only what we think but why we think as we do. Which of our thoughts come from the work itself? Which have been inspired by it? Which come from our predispositions and preconceptions about literature?

We enjoy stories for many reasons. Some are intrinsic to the story itself: language artfully used, characters we believe in and care about, actions that carry significant messages for us or give us new insight into ourselves and our society. (Whether the story provides that insight by answering questions for us or by urging us into asking our own questions does not matter here. What does matter is that the impetus for question or answer comes from within the story itself.) Other causes of enjoyment are external, coming not from the artistry of the story, but from the fact that the story fits our current notions of what a story should be like, or calls forth some pleasant personal memories. In short, the external factors in our response to a story come from things we already think or feel. Intrinsic factors come from the writer's craftsmanship and art.*

When we read for pleasure alone, we need not care where our pleasure comes from. Any appeal a story may have will be welcome. When we study literature, however, we want to concentrate on the intrinsic qualities of the works we read, for they can teach us most about the craft and the workings of literature. It is a story's intrinsic qualities, therefore, and our response to them, that we want to write about when we write about literature.

When we rule out external responses to literature, and say that we are only going to talk and write about its intrinsic qualities, we are not denying the individuality of our responses. In fact, only when we escape from our prejudices and preconceptions about literature can we respond most freely to the stories we read. Even when we write most directly of the story itself and the art that created it, our writing will contain an emotional component as well as an intellectual one. Emotion and intellect together answer such questions as, "Does the hero's death seem inevitable?" and "How has it been made to seem so?"

All analysis ends in judgment. All questions of, "How is this done?" begin or end with, "Is it a success?" It would be useless to ask, "How has the writer characterized his heroine?" if we could not also ask, "Has he made me care what happens to her?" Literature appeals to mind and emotions alike; our response, therefore, must be both analytic and emotional, objective and subjective. Concentrating on those things that are intrinsic to the story does not deny the subjective component of our response. Rather, it frees us for more truly personal reactions, subjective and objective alike, even while it helps us recognize how and why we are responding.

Before we begin to write about a story, therefore, we should ask ourselves some version of the following questions:

1. Which aspects of the story had the greatest impact on me?
2. What did they seem to be saying? How did they say it? (Or what did they make me think that seemed new to me? How did they make me think it?)

---

* What is true for stories is true for plays and poems as well. For the rest of this chapter, therefore, I shall use the word "stories" to stand for all types of literature, rather than repeating the more awkward phrases "stories, plays, and poems" and "works of literature."

3. How did other aspects of the story support or contribute to my response?
4. How did these particular aspects of the story help create the story's total effect?

We start, that is, with our response to the story; we move from there to an analysis of the art that creates the response; and then we return to the overall impression or effect.

When we write, we follow the same pattern of response, analysis, and final judgment. Unless we have unlimited time and paper, however, we will not be able to write down all that we have thought about the story. Choices must be made: What shall I include? What shall I emphasize? To make those choices, we must consider not only the story and our response to it, but the purpose of our paper and the audience for which we are writing it.

Let's look at two extreme examples. Let's imagine, first, that we keep a journal or diary and that we want to record in it the fact that we read and enjoyed a story. In this case, our main interest would be our own reaction to the story; our writing, therefore, would concentrate on our subjective response. We would mention only those incidents or characters that impressed us most strongly; and we could write in whatever style we pleased, for we would be our only audience.

At the other extreme, suppose we were writing a paper for a scholarly journal. In this case, we would write in an objective, balanced style, presenting carefully worked out analyses of each aspect of the story that related to our topic. We would define our terms carefully and provide adequate illustrations to support our thesis. In fact, we would be writing almost like a debater, trying to make our points as clear, convincing, and firmly based on factual evidence as possible.

Somewhere between these extremes lie most writing assignments. Two we might look at are book reviews and English papers. Let's consider what these types of writing most often say. Then let's look at how they can go about saying it.

Book reviews tend to be frankly subjective, focusing on "What I liked and why I liked it." (Or, alternatively, "Why you shouldn't waste time or money on this book.") By its very nature, a review commits the reviewer to making judgments: the book may be "one of the year's best," or "not up to this author's usual standards," or simply "a pleasant afternoon's reading." Too, the reviewer may try to judge what type of reader would enjoy the book most: "Readers with a taste for psychological studies will enjoy . . .", or "Mystery fans will welcome the appearance of. . . ."

A brief review may contain little more than these judgments. A more thorough review will usually provide evidence to support them, by discussing some particularly outstanding character or episode or by quoting a few lines of description or dialogue as a sample of the writer's style. Readers of reviews are presumed to be asking themselves, "Is this a book I want to read?" Through judgments and illustrations supporting the judgments, reviews are designed to help readers answer that question. A review, therefore, will generally begin in one of two ways. It will either start right out with its broadest judgment to show exactly where the reviewer stands, or it will start out with a "teaser," a quote or detail from the book that seems striking enough to catch the readers' attention and "tease" them into reading at least the review, if not the book itself.

Then will come the explanation, details, and analyses. What was it that made the experience of reading the book so enjoyable? Why is the teaser a good sample of what the book has to offer? Reviews may focus on one aspect of a book, such as its characters, or they may glance at many aspects in turn. But they must maintain a balance between the personal interest of the reviewers' subjective comments and the objective analyses with which they try to convince us that they are sound judges of books whose opinions should be respected. And they must bring their comments and analyses together again in a final summary, judgment, or call to action: "Rush right out and buy this book; you won't be disappointed."

Reviewers, then, consider their audience (potential readers of the book being reviewed) and their purpose (telling their readers that the book exists and helping them decide whether or not they want to read it). They offer their own judgments, support them with relevant evidence, and draw all together to a logical conclusion.

English papers demand many of the same techniques as reviews and are often written in similar formats. They vary in scope and purpose, however, more than reviews do. The assignments in this book provide a range of possible types of papers.

Many of the assignments are quite narrowly defined. Their purpose is to make you look closely at some particular technique of the writer's— the role of the narrator in a story, for example, or the way a theme is carried through a tale. In this case your writing, too, must be tightly focused, your style almost wholly objective. Your first sentence will probably state your basic theme; and every sentence that follows, down to your final summation, will bear directly on that theme. The particular points you discuss, and the order in which you present them, may be suggested by the questions or instructions of the assignment itself. The evidence with which you support your answers will come from within the story. But the finished product will be very much your own: a tight, coherent piece of writing built on your own handling of the material given to you by the story.

Other assignments are broader, or ask that you define your own subject. (For example, "What do you think is the major theme of this story? How would you support your view?") Now your own judgments must be more boldly expressed. You must decide which aspects of the story should be

FIGURE ONE

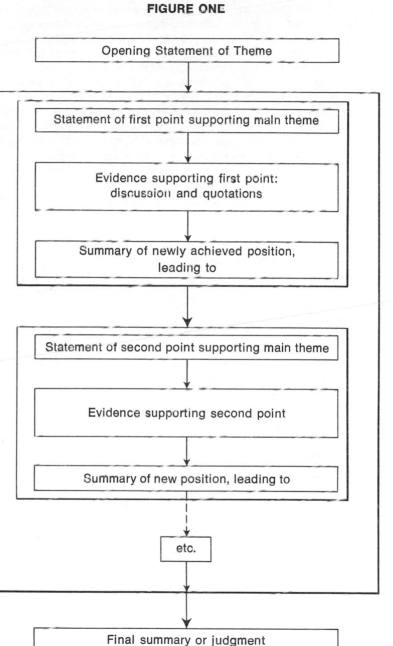

emphasized, and which are irrelevant to the question at hand. Your responsibility is not only to provide evidence to support a theory you were told to discuss, but first to set up your theory and then to support it.

Again, you will want a tightly focused paper, making full use of detailed evidence. But your opening, conclusion, and whatever general statements control your central discussion will be somewhat broader in their implications than those of the earlier assignment, and they will represent your own judgments as to what is most important to the story and to your essay. This essay, too, will follow the general format of initial response → analysis → final summary. But the analysis will be fuller and more complex than is necessary with a more narrowly defined paper.

As you can see in Figure One, the general pattern of statement → proof → summary is useful for each point within the analysis, just as it is for the essay as a whole. We use each new statement to remind ourselves and our readers just where we are in our argument, and each summary to establish our new position before proceeding to the next point. This step-by-step construction, together with a careful focusing of each point toward our main theme, will create a unified, tightly argued paper.

The act of writing about literature, by forcing us to look closely at what we have read and to analyze both the work and our own responses, can thus be seen as the final step in the act of reading. Now we are not only enjoying the words by which someone else speaks to us, we also are stretching our own minds to the task of communicating with others. Reading and writing, we take an active role and thus reassert ourselves as active, thinking, feeling beings. The opportunity to make that reassertion may well represent one of the deepest values of literature. It is certainly an opportunity well worth our taking.

FICTION

FICTION AS NARRATIVE

1

The Art of Narration: Giving Meaning to Action

Fiction is the art of the storyteller. Not only are writers of fiction storytellers themselves, but within every story they create a new storyteller, the narrator of the tale. It is the narrator's voice we hear speaking as we read a novel or short story. The narrator introduces the tale to us, keeps us amused during its telling, and dismisses us at its end. The narrator describes scenes and characters, relates events, sets the tone of the tale, and supplies whatever meanings or explanations the author sees fit to provide.

Reader and story are thus brought together by the narrator. For this reason, the study of fiction usually begins with a study of types of narrators and narrations. Let us now look at two very brief stories: first a folk tale, from one of the oldest traditions of storytelling, and then a more modern tale. Notice, in each case, the simplicity of the action and the sharp contrasts drawn among the few characters. Listen to the voices of the storytellers as they build their tales.

Clever Manka (Czechoslovakia)

There was once a rich farmer who was as grasping and unscrupulous as he was rich. He was always driving a hard bargain and always getting the better of his poor neighbors. One of these neighbors was a humble shepherd who, in return for service, was to receive from the farmer a heifer. When the time of payment came, the farmer refused to give the shepherd the heifer, and the shepherd was forced to lay the matter before the burgomaster.

The burgomaster, who was a young man and as yet not very experienced, listened to both sides, and when he had deliberated, he said:

"Instead of deciding this case, I will put a riddle to you both, and the man who makes the best answer shall have the heifer. Are you agreed?"

The farmer and the shepherd accepted this proposal and the burgomaster said:

"Well, then, here is my riddle: What is the swiftest thing in the world? What is the sweetest thing? What is the richest? Think out your answers and bring them to me at this same hour tomorrow."

The farmer went home in a temper.

"What kind of burgomaster is this young fellow!" he growled. "If he had let me keep the heifer, I'd have sent him a bushel of pears. But now I'm in a fair way of losing the heifer, for I can't think of any answer to his foolish riddle."

"What is the matter, husband?" his wife asked.

"It's that new burgomaster. The old one would have given me the heifer without any argument, but this young man thinks to decide the case by asking us riddles."

When he told his wife what the riddle was, she cheered him greatly by telling him that she knew the answers at once.

"Why, husband," said she, "our gray mare must be the swiftest thing in the world. You know yourself nothing ever passes us on the road. As for the sweetest, did you ever taste honey any sweeter than ours? And I'm sure there's nothing richer than our chest of golden ducats that we've been laying by these forty years."

The farmer was delighted.

"You're right, wife, you're right! That heifer remains ours!"

The shepherd, when he got home, was downcast and sad. He had a daughter, a clever girl named Manka, who met him at the door of his cottage and asked:

"What is it, father? What did the burgomaster say?"

The shepherd sighed.

"I'm afraid I've lost the heifer. The burgomaster set us a riddle, and I know I shall never guess it."

"Perhaps I can help you," Manka said. "What is it?"

The shepherd gave her the riddle, and the next day, as he was setting out for the burgomaster's, Manka told him what answers to make.

When he reached the burgomaster's house, the farmer was already there rubbing his hands and beaming with self-importance.

The burgomaster again propounded the riddle and then asked the farmer his answers.

The farmer cleared his throat and with a pompous air began: "The swiftest thing in the world? Why, my dear sir, that's my gray mare, of course, for no other horse ever passes us on the road. The sweetest? Honey from my beehives, to be sure. The richest? What can be richer than my chest of golden ducats!"

And the farmer squared his shoulders and smiled triumphantly.

"H'm," said the young burgomaster dryly. Then he asked:

"What answers does the shepherd make?"

The shepherd bowed politely and said:

"The swiftest thing in the world is thought, for thought can run any distance in the twinkling of an eye. The sweetest thing of all is sleep, for when a man is tired and sad, what can be sweeter? The richest thing is the earth, for out of the earth come all the riches of the world."

"Good!" the burgomaster cried. "Good! The heifer goes to the shepherd!"

Later the burgomaster said to the shepherd:

"Tell me now, who gave you those answers? I'm sure they never came out of your own head."

At first the shepherd tried not to tell, but when the burgomaster pressed him, he confessed that they came from his daughter, Manka. The burgomaster, who thought he would like to make another test of Manka's cleverness, sent for ten eggs. He gave them to the shepherd and said:

"Take these eggs to Manka and tell her to have them hatched out by tomorrow and to bring me the chicks."

When the shepherd reached home and gave Manka the burgomaster's message, Manka laughed and said: "Take a handful of millet and go right back to the burgomaster. Say to him: 'My daughter sends you this millet. She says that if you plant it, grow it, and have it harvested by tomorrow, she'll bring you the ten chicks and you can feed them the ripe grain.'"

When the burgomaster heard this, he laughed heartily.

"That's a clever girl of yours," he told the shepherd. "If she's as comely as she is clever, I think I'd like to marry her. Tell her to come to see me, but she must come neither by day nor by night, neither riding nor walking, neither dressed nor undressed."

When Manka received this message, she waited until the next dawn when night was gone and day not yet arrived. Then she wrapped herself in a fish net and, throwing one leg over a goat's back and keeping one foot on the ground, she went to the burgomaster's house.

Now I ask you: did she go dressed? No, she wasn't dressed. A fish net isn't clothing. Did she go undressed? Of course not, for wasn't she covered with a fish net? Did she walk to the burgomaster's? No, she didn't walk, for she went with one leg thrown over a goat. Then did she ride? Of course she didn't ride, for wasn't she walking on one foot?

When she reached the burgomaster's house, she called out:

"Here I am, Mr. Burgomaster, and I've come neither by day nor by night, neither riding nor walking, neither dressed nor undressed."

The young burgomaster was so delighted with Manka's cleverness and so pleased with her comely looks that he proposed to her at once and in a short time married her.

"But understand, my dear Manka," he said, "you are not to use that cleverness of yours at my expense. I won't have you interfering in any of my cases. In fact, if ever you give advice to anyone who comes to me for judgment, I'll turn you out of my house at once and send you home to your father."

All went well for a time. Manka busied herself in her housekeeping and was careful not to interfere in any of the burgomaster's cases.

Then one day two farmers came to the burgomaster to have a dispute settled. One of the farmers owned a mare that had foaled in the market-place. The colt had run under the wagon of the other farmer, and thereupon the owner of the wagon claimed the colt as his property.

The burgomaster, who was thinking of something else while the case was being presented, said carelessly:

"The man who found the colt under his wagon is, of course, the owner of the colt."

As the owner of the mare was leaving the burgomaster's house, he met Manka and stopped to tell her about the case. Manka was ashamed of her husband for making so foolish a decision, and she said to the farmer:

"Come back this afternoon with a fishing net and stretch it across the dusty road. When the burgomaster sees you, he will come out and ask you what you are doing. Say to him that you're catching fish. When he asks you how you can expect to catch fish in a dusty road, tell him it's just as easy for you to catch fish in a dusty road as it is for a wagon to foal. Then he'll see the injustice of his decision and have the colt returned to you. But remember one thing: you mustn't let him find out that it was I who told you to do this."

That afternoon, when the burgomaster chanced to look out the window, he saw a man stretching a fish net across the dusty road. He went out to him and asked:

"What are you doing?"

"Fishing."

"Fishing in a dusty road? Are you daft?"

"Well," the man said, "it's just as easy for me to catch fish in a dusty road as it is for a wagon to foal."

Then the burgomaster recognized the man as the owner of the mare, and he had to confess that what he said was true.

"Of course the colt belongs to your mare and must be returned to you. But tell me," he said, "who put you up to this? You didn't think of it yourself."

The farmer tried not to tell, but the burgomaster questioned him until he found out that Manka was at the bottom of it. This made him very angry. He went into the house and called his wife.

"Manka," he said, "did you forget what I told you would happen if you went interfering in any of my cases? Home you go this very day. I don't care to hear any excuses. The matter is settled. You may take with you the one thing you like best in my house, for I won't have people saying that I treated you shabbily."

Manka made no outcry.

"Very well, my dear husband, I shall do as you say: I shall go home to my father's cottage and take with me the one thing I like best in your house. But don't make me go until after supper. We have been very happy together and I should like to eat one last meal with you. Let us have no more words but be kind to each other as we've always been and then part as friends."

The burgomaster agreed to this, and Manka prepared a fine supper of all the dishes of which her husband was particularly fond. The burgomaster opened his choicest wine and pledged Manka's health. Then he set to, and the supper was so good that he ate and ate and ate. And the more he ate, the more he drank until at last he grew drowsy and fell sound asleep in his chair. Then without awakening him, Manka had him carried out to the wagon that was waiting to take her home to her father.

The next morning, when the burgomaster opened his eyes, he found himself lying in the shepherd's cottage.

"What does this mean?" he roared out.

"Nothing, dear husband, nothing!" Manka said. "You know you told me I might take with me the one thing I liked best in your house, so of course I took you! That's all."

For a moment the burgomaster rubbed his eyes in amazement. Then he laughed loud and heartily to think how Manka had outwitted him.

"Manka," he said, "you're too clever for me. Come on, my dear, let's go home."

So, they climbed back into the wagon and drove home.

The burgomaster never again scolded his wife, but thereafter whenever a very difficult case came up, he always said:

"I think we had better consult my wife. You know she's a very clever woman."

KATE CHOPIN (1851–1904)

The Story of an Hour

Knowing that Mrs. Mallard was afflicted with a heart trouble, great care was taken to break to her as gently as possible the news of her husband's death.

It was her sister Josephine who told her, in broken sentences; veiled hints that revealed in half concealing. Her husband's friend Richards was there, too, near her. It was he who had been in the newspaper office when intelligence of the railroad disaster was received, with Brently Mallard's name leading the list of "killed." He had only taken the time to assure himself of its truth by a second telegram, and had hastened to forestall any less careful, less tender friend in bearing the sad message.

She did not hear the story as many women have heard the same, with a paralyzed inability to accept its significance. She wept at once, with sudden, wild abandonment, in her sister's arms. When the storm of grief had spent itself she went away to her room alone. She would have no one follow her.

There stood, facing the open window, a comfortable, roomy armchair. Into this she sank, pressed down by a physical exhaustion that haunted her body and seemed to reach into her soul.

She could see in the open square before her house the tops of trees that were all aquiver with the new spring life. The delicious breath of rain was in the air. In the street below a peddler was crying his wares. The notes of a distant song which some one was singing reached her faintly, and countless sparrows were twittering in the eaves.

There were patches of blue sky showing here and there through the clouds that had met and piled one above the other in the west facing her window.

She sat with her head thrown back upon the cushion of the chair, quite motionless, except when a sob came up into her throat and shook her, as a child who has cried itself to sleep continues to sob in its dreams.

She was young, with a fair, calm face, whose lines bespoke repression and even a certain strength. But now there was a dull stare in her eyes, whose gaze was fixed away off yonder on one of those patches of blue sky. It was not a glance of reflection, but rather indicated a suspension of intelligent thought.

There was something coming to her and she was waiting for it, fearfully. What was it? She did not know; it was too subtle and elusive to name. But she felt it, creeping out of the sky, reaching toward her through the sounds, the scents, the color that filled the air.

Now her bosom rose and fell tumultuously. She was beginning to recognize this thing that was approaching to possess her, and she was striving to beat it back with her will—as powerless as her two white slender hands would have been.

When she abandoned herself a little whispered word escaped her slightly parted lips. She said it over and over under her breath: "free, free, free!" The vacant stare and the look of terror that had followed it went from her eyes. They stayed keen and bright. Her pulses beat fast, and the coursing blood warmed and relaxed every inch of her body.

She did not stop to ask if it were or were not a monstrous joy that held her. A clear and exalted perception enabled her to dismiss the suggestion as trivial.

She knew that she would weep again when she saw the kind, tender hands folded in death, the face that had never looked save with love upon her, fixed and gray and dead. But she saw beyond that bitter moment a long procession of years to come that would belong to her absolutely. And she opened and spread her arms out to them in welcome.

There would be no one to live for her during those coming years; she would live for herself. There would be no powerful will bending hers in that blind persistence with which men and women believe they have a right to impose a private will upon a fellow-creature. A kind intention or a cruel intention made the act seem no less a crime as she looked upon it in that brief moment of illumination.

And yet she had loved him—sometimes. Often she had not. What did it matter! What could love, the unsolved mystery, count for in face of this possession of self-assertion which she suddenly recognized as the strongest impulse of her being!

"Free! Body and soul free!" she kept whispering.

Josephine was kneeling before the closed door with her lips to the keyhole, imploring for admission. "Louise, open the door! I beg; open the door—you will make yourself ill. What are you doing, Louise? For heaven's sake open the door."

"Go away. I am not making myself ill." No; she was drinking in a very elixir of life through that open window.

Her fancy was running riot along those days ahead of her. Spring days, and summer days, and all sorts of days that would be her own. She breathed a quick prayer that life might be long. It was only yesterday she had thought with a shudder that life might be long.

She arose at length and opened the door to her sister's importunities. There was a feverish triumph in her eyes, and she carried herself unwittingly like a goddess of Victory. She clasped her sister's waist, and together they descended the stairs. Richards stood waiting for them at the bottom.

Some one was opening the front door with a latchkey. It was Brently Mallard who entered, a little travel-stained, composedly carrying his grip-sack and umbrella. He had been far from the scene of accident, and did not even know there had been one. He stood amazed at Josephine's piercing cry; at Richards' quick motion to screen him from the view of his wife.

But Richards was too late.

When the doctors came they said she had died of heart disease—of joy that kills.

THINKING ABOUT WHAT WE'VE READ

How can we compare these two stories we have just read? What can we say about them?

We can begin by noticing some things the two stories have in common. For instance, both are quite short. Both have women as their main characters (or protagonists); both women are loved by those who know them, and each one's marriage is an important element in her story.

Next, we can look at the ways in which the two stories differ. Before you read further, make a list—by yourselves or as a group—of the differences you notice between the two stories. Then, as we consider what steps one should take when thinking about a story, in order to discuss it (either by itself or in comparison with some other story), and how we can apply these steps to "Clever Manka" and "The Story of an Hour," you can find out how many of the ideas in the essay you yourselves discovered.

※

Let's return now to our questions: What steps should one take when thinking about a story, in order to discuss it and write about it? How can we apply these steps to "Clever Manka" and "The Story of an Hour"?

STEP 1.   Begin with your initial impressions.

The first thing to do is to jot down whatever things about the story (or stories) strike you as being most noticeable—the ideas that affect you most strongly. For example, the most striking difference I notice between these two stories is that Manka, because of her cleverness, is always triumphant—a victor—while Louise Mallard seems destined to be a victim. Manka's story ends happily, with its heroine and her husband living happily ever after, while Mrs. Mallard's tale ends, surprisingly and grimly, with her misunderstood death. I notice, too, that my mood after ending each story varies accordingly. You probably had other "first impressions," or more of them; but these will do for a sample.

STEP 2.   Consider the structure of the story.

The ordering of incidents within a story may be spoken of as its **structure**. Traditionally, a story's structure has been said to consist of four basic parts:

1. The **exposition.** The beginning of the story, which introduces the reader to the tale's setting (time and place) and to some or all of its characters.

2. The **conflict.** Every story centers on a conflict of some sort: one person, or group of people, against another; people against nature; an individual against some rule or custom of society. Generally the conflict increases in tension or in complexity until it reaches a climax.
3. The **climax.** The point of greatest tension, at which the turning-point or breaking-point is reached.
4. The **denouement** or **resolution.** The ending, which brings the tale to a close, picking up the pieces of the action and reordering the lives left disordered by the conflict and its climax.

Of these four parts, only numbers two and three, the conflict and the climax, are essential. You don't have to begin with an exposition; your first sentence can show your characters already embroiled in their conflict. You don't have to end with a resolution; you can stop your tale short at its climactic moment. But you must have some sort of conflict in your action; and it must rise to some peak of intensity somewhere between the middle and end of your story.

How can we apply this theory to our two stories? Let's find out.

> There was once a rich farmer who was as grasping and unscrupulous as he was rich. He was always driving a hard bargain and always getting the better of his poor neighbors. One of these neighbors was a humble shepherd who, in return for service, was to receive from the farmer a heifer. When the time of payment came, the farmer refused to give the shepherd the heifer, and the shepherd was forced to lay the matter before the burgomaster.

This is obviously an exposition. The opening words, "There was once," tell us immediately that this will be a "tall tale," not a realistic story. The rich farmer—"as grasping and unscrupulous as he was rich"—and the "humble shepherd" in danger of being cheated by the rich man reinforce this idea, and alert us to the coming conflict as well, setting out its themes of rich versus poor and justice versus injustice. The burgomaster—young and inexperienced—does not promise to be much help. What will happen?

The conflict develops as we hear the rich man's wife and the poor man's daughter ponder the burgomaster's riddle. The wife, like her husband, thinks of their property: "our gray mare," "our honey," "our chest of golden ducats." The shepherd's daughter thinks of essential things, in which all humans share: thought, sleep, the earth. And so, of course, the underdogs win the first round of the conflict.

But it is only the first round. The burgomaster now challenges Manka directly: he "thought he would like to make another test of Manka's cleverness." Manka wins this round as well. The burgomaster begins to think of marriage, and sets a third riddling test. Manka triumphs again, and is married. But now the burgomaster sets limits to Manka's use of her wits:

> "But understand, my dear Manka," he said, "you are not to use that cleverness of yours at my expense. I won't have you interfering in any of my cases. In fact, if ever you give advice to anyone who comes to me for

judgment, I'll turn you out of my house at once and send you home to your father."

Do we hear a husband-wife conflict starting here? We certainly do. Once again, Manka sees an injustice about to happen; once again, she prevents the injustice. But the burgomaster, holding to his warning, exiles her, allowing her only to "take with you the one thing you like best in my house." This, of course, is all Manka needs. As the climax of the story, she kidnaps her own husband, once again asserting the claim of the essential over that of mere property: "You know you told me I might take with me the one thing I liked best in your house, so of course I took you! That's all."

The resolution, of course, is reconciliation, happiness, and the firm establishment of Manka's right to use her cleverness for the general good: "I think we had better consult my wife. You know she's a very clever woman."

"The Story of an Hour" begins even more directly: "Knowing that Mrs. Mallard was afflicted with a heart trouble, great care was taken to break to her as gently as possible the news of her husband's death." We are told that there has been a death, and that the dead man's widow is herself in danger from the strain the bad news may place on her weak heart. No conflict between people here: rather, a conflict of caring people against uncaring nature and disease.

As the story develops, a second conflict grows clear: a conflict between grief and joy, between expected and actual emotions. The marriage, loving though it was, has not been happy for her: in the freedom of her widowhood, Louise expects to find happiness.

At the tale's climax, Louise emerges "like a goddess of Victory" to rejoin her sister and friend, only to die from shock at the sight, not of a dead husband, but of a live one. The kindly plan has backfired; the new shock, with its reversal of already-strong emotion, is deadlier than the originally feared shock would have been.

The tale's last sentence provides its resolution. "When the doctors came, they said she had died of heart disease—of joy that kills." Nature and illness have defeated care; and no one is left within the tale who can realize the gap between the expected emotion and the true one. Only we, the readers, know whether or not it was "joy" that killed Louise Mallard.

STEP 3.   Consider the major aspects of each story.

As this volume's opening essay on "The Bases of Literature" suggested, each work of fiction involves four key elements: action, or plot; character; setting; and language, or voice. When considering a work of fiction, we look at these various aspects; we note how they're presented and what is the balance among them. What do we find in this case?

Action, or plot: We notice substantial differences between the plots of the two tales. The action of "Clever Manka" consists of a number of brief episodes, each of which shows the heroine acting cleverly, so that she moves from triumph to triumph towards the successful climax and resolution. In

"The Story of an Hour" we have a single, more fully developed episode, in which the heroine *reacts* first to a piece of news, then to her own emotions, finally to the sight of a man believed dead. The climax of this tale represents a complete reversal of everything expected by characters and readers alike, and thus presents a classic "surprise ending"; while the resolution, with its irony, underscores the reversals that distinguish this tale.

Character: Manka is a clever, active, resourceful character; she judges situations correctly and acts decisively. Louise reacts, rather than acts; she is defined by her emotions and her illness rather than by her more active attributes. Manka is worth reading about because she does something praiseworthy; Louise is worth reading about because she is the victim of such a remarkable chain of accidents.

Setting: "Clever Manka" has almost a fairy-tale setting, with its burgomaster who wields absolute power but can yield to a wise peasant girl; "The Story of an Hour" is set in its author's own social setting.

Language, or voice: The language of "Clever Manka" is that of the traditional storyteller. Direct and to the point, it spends little time on description, but concentrates instead on the tale's action. "The Story of an Hour," in contrast, uses much more sophisticated language and takes considerable care to describe and comment upon its characters' thoughts and sensations, as when describing "a physical exhaustion that haunted her body and seemed to reach into her soul" or telling how the heroine "carried herself unwittingly like a goddess of Victory."

STEP 4.　Create a synthesis.

Now we've gathered our data. We've noted our initial reactions, and we've filled those out by checking each of the major aspects and structural elements of the stories under discussion, noting key aspects of each and strengthening our understanding of how the story creates those effects we first noted. Now it's time to put together the information thus gathered to arrive at an overall picture of the stories: a sense of the vision that informs each one, and of your interpretation of that vision. If you write a formal essay on a story, this is the point at which you write it. Even if you write only on a single theme out of the number you've noticed, it's best to have this balanced study behind you so that you're working from a firm foundation.

If I were writing an essay on these two tales, for example, I would probably choose to write on one of my first ideas. I'd call the paper something like "Victors and Victims," and concentrate on the character and fortune of the two protagonists. I'd bring in ideas from my study of action, character, setting, and conflict, to show how Manka uses her cleverness to succeed in a world where people have only other individuals as adversaries, and where individual wisdom and honesty are important and valid weapons in the perpetual combat against injustice; and I'd say that Manka's success leaves me, as a reader, feeling good about the possibility of taking action in my own world to make good things happen. Then I'd show, in contrast, how Kate Chopin's tale depicts people as well-meaning, caring creatures (in contrast to the combative types that people Manka's world), but also as creatures whose power is severely limited by the dangers inherent in living in a "real world" where physical limitations and accidents can overturn whatever people plan. I'd show how Louise Mallard is victim to all these types of dangers. And I'd admit that—although I enjoyed the story, with its study of hidden feelings—it left me less cheerful than did "Clever Manka," and did nothing to increase my sense of my own potential powers.

In doing such an essay, I'd think that I had covered some of the important points about the two stories, and particularly the key difference between the two. But many other, equally valid essays could be written, stressing other themes and ideas about the stories. Perhaps you have already thought of some such ideas. If you were to write an essay on one or both of these tales, what would you want to write?

2 The Omniscient Narrator

"Clever Manka" and "The Story of an Hour" are tales related by omniscient narrators. As the term implies, these narrators "know all" about the characters and events of which they tell. Somewhat distanced by their greater knowledge from action and actors alike, omniscient narrators project an air of authority over their material.

Their relation to the readers is a more variable matter. The anonymous narrator of "Clever Manka" treats us familiarly, sharing occasional asides with us to bring us into the story ("Now I ask you: did she go dressed?"). Chopin's narrator keeps us at the same distance that she keeps her material. She tells us of her protagonist's thoughts and feelings, so that we see the contrast between the private thoughts and the public image; but she does so with the objectivity of a reporter. Her prose carries no awareness of its audience.

This chapter contains three more stories told by omniscient narrators. Read each story through once, as you would any story, and note your reactions to its plot, characters, and style. Then read and answer the questions that follow the story, re-reading the story as necessary while you consider your answers. Note, throughout, how the narrator's voice helps shape your view of the story's action and characters.

NATHANIEL HAWTHORNE (1804–1864)

Young Goodman Brown

Young Goodman Brown came forth at sunset, into the street of Salem village, but put his head back, after crossing the threshold, to exchange a parting kiss with his young wife. And Faith, as the wife was aptly named, thrust her own pretty head into the street, letting the wind play with the pink ribbons of her cap, while she called to Goodman Brown.

"Dearest heart," whispered she, softly and rather sadly, when her lips were close to his ear, "prithee, put off your journey until sunrise, and sleep in your own bed to-night. A lone woman is troubled with such dreams and such thoughts, that she's afeard of herself, sometimes. Pray, tarry with me this night, dear husband, of all nights in the year!"

"My love and my Faith," replied young Goodman Brown, "of all nights in the year, this one night must I tarry away from thee. My journey, as thou callest it, forth and back again, must needs be done 'twixt now and sunrise. What, my sweet, pretty wife, dost thou doubt me already, and we but three months married!"

"Then God bless you!" said Faith with the pink ribbons, "and may you find all well, when you come back."

"Amen!" cried Goodman Brown. "Say thy prayers, dear Faith, and go to bed at dusk, and no harm will come to thee."

So they parted; and the young man pursued his way, until, being about to turn the corner by the meeting-house, he looked back and saw the head of Faith still peeping after him, with a melancholy air, in spite of her pink ribbons.

"Poor little Faith!" thought he, for his heart smote him. "What a wretch am I, to leave her on such an errand! She talks of dreams, too. Methought, as she spoke, there was trouble in her face, as if a dream had warned her what work is to be done to-night. But no, no! 't would kill her to think it. Well; she's a blessed angel on earth; and after this one night, I'll cling to her skirts and follow her to Heaven."

With this excellent resolve for the future, Goodman Brown felt himself justified in making more haste on his present evil purpose. He had taken a dreary road, darkened by all the gloomiest trees of the forest, which barely stood aside to let the narrow path creep through, and closed immediately behind. It was all as lonely as could be; and there is this peculiarity in such a solitude, that the traveller knows not who may be concealed by the innumerable trunks and the thick boughs overhead; so that, with lonely footsteps, he may yet be passing through an unseen multitude.

"There may be a devilish Indian behind every tree," said Goodman Brown to himself; and he glanced fearfully behind him, as he added, "What if the devil himself should be at my very elbow!"

His head being turned back, he passed a crook of the road, and looking forward again, beheld the figure of a man, in grave and decent attire, seated at the foot of an old tree. He arose at Goodman Brown's approach, and walked onward, side by side with him.

"You are late, Goodman Brown," said he. "The clock of the Old South was striking, as I came through Boston; and that is full fifteen minutes agone."

"Faith kept me back awhile," replied the young man, with a tremor in his voice, caused by the sudden appearance of his companion, though not wholly unexpected.

It was now deep dusk in the forest, and deepest in that part of it where these two were journeying. As nearly as could be discerned, the second traveller was about fifty years old, apparently in the same rank of life as Goodman Brown, and bearing a considerable resemblance to him, though perhaps more in expression than features. Still, they might have been taken for father and son. And yet, though the elder person was as simply clad as the younger, and as simple in manner too, he had an indescribable air of one who knew the world, and would not have felt abashed at the governor's dinner-table, or in King William's court, were it possible that his affairs should call him thither. But the only thing about him that could be fixed upon as remarkable, was his staff, which bore the likeness of a great black snake, so curiously wrought, that it might almost be seen to twist and wriggle itself like a living serpent. This, of course, must have been an ocular deception, assisted by the uncertain light.

"Come, Goodman Brown!" cried his fellow-traveller, "this is a dull pace for the beginning of a journey. Take my staff, if you are so soon weary."

"Friend," said the other, exchanging his slow pace for a full stop, "having kept covenant by meeting thee here, it is my purpose now to return whence I came. I have scruples, touching the matter thou wot'st of."

"Sayest thou so?" replied he of the serpent, smiling apart. "Let us walk on, nevertheless, reasoning as we go, and if I convince thee not, thou shalt turn back. We are but a little way in the forest, yet."

"Too far, too far!" exclaimed the goodman, unconsciously resuming his walk. "My father never went into the woods on such an errand, nor his father before him. We have been a race of honest men and good Christians, since the days of the martyrs. And shall I be the first of the name of Brown that ever took this path and kept—"

"Such company, thou wouldst say," observed the elder person, interrupting his pause. "Well said, Goodman Brown! I have been as well acquainted with your family as with ever a one among the Puritans; and that's no trifle to say. I helped your grandfather, the constable, when he lashed the Quaker woman so smartly through the streets of Salem. And it was I that brought your father a pitch-pine knot, kindled at my own hearth, to set fire to an Indian village, in King Philip's war. They were my good friends, both; and many a pleasant walk have we had along this path, and returned merrily after midnight. I would fain be friends with you, for their sake."

"If it be as thou sayest," replied Goodman Brown, "I marvel they never spoke of these matters. Or, verily, I marvel not, seeing that the least rumor of the sort would have driven them from New England. We are a people of prayer, and good works to boot, and abide no such wickedness."

"Wickedness or not," said the traveller with twisted staff, "I have a very general acquaintance here in New England. The deacons of many a church have drunk the communion wine with me; the selectmen, of divers towns, make me their chairman; and a majority of the Great and General Court are firm supporters of my interest. The governor and I, too—but these are state secrets."

"Can this be so!" cried Goodman Brown, with a stare of amazement at his undisturbed companion. "Howbeit, I have nothing to do with the governor and council; they have their own ways, and are no rule for a simple husbandman like me. But, were I to go on with thee, how should I meet the eye of that good old man, our minister, at Salem village? Oh, his voice would make me tremble, both Sabbath-day and lecture-day!"

Thus far, the elder traveller had listened with due gravity, but now burst into a fit of irrepressible mirth, shaking himself so violently, that his snakelike staff actually seemed to wriggle in sympathy.

"Ha! ha! ha!" shouted he, again and again; then composing himself, "Well, go on, Goodman Brown, go on; but, prithee, don't kill me with laughing!"

"Well, then, to end the matter at once," said Goodman Brown, considerably nettled, "there is my wife, Faith. It would break her dear little heart; and I'd rather break my own!"

"Nay, if that be the case," answered the other, "e'en go thy ways, Goodman Brown. I would not, for twenty old women like the one hobbling before us, that Faith should come to any harm."

As he spoke, he pointed his staff at a female figure on the path, in whom Goodman Brown recognized a very pious and exemplary dame, who had taught him his catechism in youth, and was still his moral and spiritual adviser, jointly with the minister and Deacon Gookin.

"A marvel, truly, that Goody Cloyse should be so far in the

wilderness, at nightfall!" said he. "But, with your leave, friend, I shall take a cut through the woods, until we have left this Christian woman behind. Being a stranger to you, she might ask whom I was consorting with, and whither I was going."

"Be it so," said his fellow-traveller. "Betake you to the woods, and let me keep the path."

Accordingly, the young man turned aside, but took care to watch his companion, who advanced softly along the road, until he had come within a staff's length of the old dame. She, meanwhile, was making the best of her way, with singular speed for so aged a woman, and mumbling some indistinct words, a prayer, doubtless, as she went. The traveller put forth his staff, and touched her withered neck with what seemed the serpent's tail.

"The devil!" screamed the pious old lady.

"Then Goody Cloyse knows her old friend?" observed the traveller, confronting her, and leaning on his writhing stick.

"Ah, forsooth, and is it your worship, indeed?" cried the good dame. "Yea, truly is it, and in the very image of my old gossip, Goodman Brown, the grandfather of the silly fellow that now is. But, would your worship believe it? my broomstick hath strangely disappeared, stolen, as I suspect, by that unhanged witch, Goody Cory, and that, too, when I was all anointed with the juice of smallage and cinque-foil and wolf's-bane—"

"Mingled with fine wheat and the fat of a new-born babe," said the shape of old Goodman Brown.

"Ah, your worship knows the recipe," cried the old lady, cackling aloud. "So, as I was saying, being all ready for the meeting, and no horse to ride on, I made up my mind to foot it, for they tell me there is a nice young man to be taken into communion to-night. But now your good worship will lend me your arm, and we shall be there in a twinkling."

"That can hardly be," answered her friend. "I may not spare you my arm, Goody Cloyse, but here is my staff, if you will."

So saying, he threw it down at her feet, where, perhaps, it assumed life, being one of the rods which its owner had formerly lent to the Egyptian Magi. Of this fact, however, Goodman Brown could not take cognizance. He had cast up his eyes in astonishment, and looking down again, beheld neither Goody Cloyse nor the serpentine staff, but his fellow-traveller alone, who waited for him as calmly as if nothing had happened.

"That old woman taught me my catechism!" said the young man; and there was a world of meaning in this simple comment.

They continued to walk onward, while the elder traveller exhorted his companion to make good speed and persevere in the path, discoursing so aptly, that his arguments seemed rather to spring up in the bosom of his auditor, than to be suggested by himself. As they went he plucked a branch of maple, to serve for a walking-stick, and began to strip it of the twigs and little boughs, which were wet with evening dew. The moment his fingers touched them, they became strangely withered and dried up, as with a week's sunshine. Thus the pair proceeded, at a good free pace, until suddenly, in a gloomy hollow of the road, Goodman Brown sat himself down on the stump of a tree, and refused to go any farther.

"Friend," said he, stubbornly, "my mind is made up. Not another step will I budge on this errand. What if a wretched old woman do choose to go to the devil, when I thought she was going to Heaven! Is that any reason why I should quit my dear Faith, and go after her?"

"You will think better of this by and by," said his acquaintance, composedly. "Sit here and rest yourself awhile; and when you feel like moving again, there is my staff to help you along."

Without more words, he threw his companion the maple stick, and was as speedily out of sight as if he had vanished into the deepening gloom. The young man sat a few moments by the roadside, applauding himself greatly, and thinking with how clear a conscience he should meet the minister, in his morning walk, nor shrink from the eye of good old Deacon Gookin. And what calm sleep would be his, that very night, which was to have been spent so wickedly, but purely and sweetly now, in the arms of Faith! Amidst these pleasant and praiseworthy meditations, Goodman Brown heard the tramp of horses along the road, and deemed it advisable to conceal himself within the verge of the forest, conscious of the guilty purpose that had brought him thither, though now so happily turned from it.

On came the hoof-tramps and the voices of the riders, two grave old voices, conversing soberly as they drew near. These mingled sounds appeared to pass along the road, within a few yards of the young man's hiding-place; but owing, doubtless, to the depth of the gloom, at that particular spot, neither the travellers nor their steeds were visible. Though their figures brushed the small boughs by the wayside, it could not be seen that they intercepted, even for a moment, the faint gleam from the strip of bright sky, athwart which they must have passed. Goodman Brown alternately crouched and stood on tiptoe, pulling aside the branches, and thrusting forth his head as far as he durst, without discerning so much as a shadow. It vexed him the more, because he could have sworn, were such a thing possible, that he recognized the voices of the minister and Deacon Gookin, jogging along quietly, as they were wont to do, when bound to some ordination or ecclesiastical council. While yet within hearing, one of the riders stopped to pluck a switch.

"Of the two, reverend Sir," said the voice like the deacon's, "I had rather miss an ordination dinner than to-night's meeting. They tell me that some of our community are to be here from Falmouth and beyond, and others from Connecticut and Rhode Island; besides several of the Indian powwows, who, after their fashion, know almost as much deviltry as the best of us. Moreover, there is a goodly young woman to be taken into communion."

"Mighty well, Deacon Gookin!" replied the solemn old tones of the minister. "Spur up, or we shall be late. Nothing can be done, you know, until I get on the ground."

The hoofs clattered again, and the voices, talking so strangely in the empty air, passed on through the forest, where no church had ever been gathered, nor solitary Christian prayed. Whither, then, could these holy men be journeying, so deep into the heathen wilderness? Young Goodman Brown caught hold of a tree, for support, being ready to sink down on the ground, faint and over-burthened with the heavy sickness of his heart. He looked up to the sky, doubting whether there really was a Heaven above him. Yet, there was the blue arch, and the stars brightening in it.

"With Heaven above, and Faith below, I will yet stand firm against the devil!" cried Goodman Brown.

While he still gazed upward, into the deep arch of the firmament, and had lifted his hands to pray, a cloud, though no wind was stirring, hurried across the zenith, and hid the brightening stars. The blue sky was still visible, except directly overhead, where this black mass of cloud was sweeping swiftly northward. Aloft in the air, as if from the depths of the cloud, came a confused and doubtful sound of voices. Once, the listener fancied that he could distinguish the accents of town's-people of his own, men and women, both pious and ungodly, many of whom he had met at the communion-table, and had seen others rioting at the tavern. The next moment, so indistinct were the sounds, he doubted whether he had heard aught but the murmur of the old forest, whispering without a wind. Then came a stronger swell of those familiar tones, heard daily in the sunshine, at Salem village, but never, until now, from a cloud at night. There was one voice, of a young woman, uttering lamentations, yet with an uncertain sorrow, and entreating for some favor, which, perhaps, it would grieve her to obtain. And all the unseen multitude, both saints and sinners, seemed to encourage her onward.

"Faith!" shouted Goodman Brown, in a voice of agony and desperation; and the echoes of the forest mocked him, crying—"Faith! Faith!" as if bewildered wretches were seeking her, all through the wilderness.

The cry of grief, rage, and terror was yet piercing the night, when the unhappy husband held his breath for a response. There was a scream, drowned immediately in a louder murmur of voices fading into far-off laughter, as the dark cloud swept away, leaving the clear and silent sky above Goodman Brown. But something fluttered lightly down through the air, and caught on the branch of a tree. The young man seized it and beheld a pink ribbon. "My Faith is gone!" cried he, after one stupefied moment. "There is no good on earth, and sin is but a name. Come, devil! for to thee is this world given."

And maddened with despair, so that he laughed loud and long, did Goodman Brown grasp his staff and set forth again, at such a rate, that he seemed to fly along the forest path, rather than to walk or run. The road grew wilder and drearier, and more faintly traced, and vanished at length, leaving him in the heart of the dark wilderness, still rushing onward, with the instinct that guides mortal man to evil. The whole forest was peopled with frightful sounds; the creaking of the trees, the howling of wild beasts, and the yell of Indians; while, sometimes, the wind tolled like a distant church bell, and sometimes gave a broad roar around the traveller, as if all Nature were laughing him to scorn. But he was himself the chief horror of the scene, and shrank not from its other horrors.

"Ha! ha! ha!" roared Goodman Brown, when the wind laughed at him. "Let us hear which will laugh loudest! Think not to frighten me with your deviltry! Come witch, come wizard, come Indian powwow, come devil himself! and here comes Goodman Brown. You may as well fear him as he fear you!"

In truth, all through the haunted forest, there could be nothing more frightful than the figure of Goodman Brown. On he flew, among the black pines, brandishing his staff with frenzied gestures, now giving vent to an inspiration of horrid blasphemy, and now shouting forth such laughter, as set all the echoes of the forest laughing like demons around him. The fiend in his own shape is less hideous, than when he rages in the breast of man. Thus sped the demoniac on his course, until, quivering among the trees, he saw a red light before him, as when the felled trunks and branches of a clearing have been set on fire, and throw up their lurid blaze against the sky, at the hour of midnight. He paused, in a lull of the tempest that had driven him onward, and heard the swell of what seemed a hymn, rolling solemnly from a distance, with the weight of many voices. He knew the tune. It was a familiar one in the choir of the village meeting-house. The verse died heavily away, and was lengthened by a chorus, not of human voices, but of all the sounds of the benighted wilderness, pealing in awful harmony together. Goodman Brown cried out; and his cry was lost to his own ear, by its unison with the cry of the desert.

In the interval of silence, he stole forward, until the light glared full upon his eyes. At one extremity of an open space, hemmed in by the dark wall of the forest, arose a rock, bearing some rude, natural resemblance either to an altar or a pulpit, and surrounded by four blazing pines, their tops aflame, their stems untouched, like candles at an evening meeting. The mass of foliage, that had overgrown the summit of the rock, was all on fire, blazing high into the night, and fitfully illuminating the whole field. Each pendent twig and leafy festoon was in a blaze. As the red light arose and fell, a numerous congregation alternately shone forth, then disappeared in shadow, and again grew, as it were, out of the darkness, peopling the heart of the solitary woods at once.

"A grave and dark-clad company!" quoth Goodman Brown.

In truth, they were such. Among them, quivering to-and-fro, between gloom and splendor, appeared faces that would be seen, next day, at the council board of the province, and others which, Sabbath after Sabbath, looked devoutly heavenward, and benignantly over the crowded pews, from the holiest pulpits in the land. Some affirm that the lady of the governor was there. At least, there were high dames well known to her, and wives of honored husbands, and widows a great multitude, and ancient maidens, all of excellent repute, and fair young girls, who trembled lest their mothers should espy them. Either the sudden gleams of light, flashing over the obscure field, bedazzled Goodman Brown, or he recognized a score of the church members of Salem village, famous for their especial sanctity. Good old Deacon Gookin had arrived, and waited at the skirts of that venerable saint, his reverend pastor. But, irreverently consorting with these grave, reputable, and pious people, these elders of the church, these chaste dames and dewy virgins, there were men of dissolute lives and women of spotted fame, wretches given over to all mean and filthy vice, and suspected even of horrid crimes. It was strange to see, that the good shrank not from the wicked, nor were the sinners abashed by the saints. Scattered, also, among their pale-faced enemies, were the Indian priests, or powwows, who had often scared their native forest with more hideous incantations than any known to English witchcraft.

"But, where is Faith?" thought Goodman Brown; and, as hope came into his heart, he trembled.

Another verse of the hymn arose, a slow and mournful strain, such as the pious love, but joined to words which expressed all that our nature can conceive of sin, and darkly hinted at far more. Unfathomable to mere mortals is the lore of fiends. Verse after verse was sung, and still the chorus of the desert swelled between, like the deepest tone of a mighty organ. And, with the final peal of that dreadful anthem, there came a sound, as if the roaring wind, the rushing streams, the howling beasts, and every other voice of the unconverted wilderness were mingling and according with the voice of guilty man, in homage to the prince of all. The four blazing pines threw up a loftier flame, and obscurely discovered shapes and visages of horror on the smoke-wreaths, above the impious assembly. At the same moment, the fire on the rock shot redly forth, and formed a glowing arch above its base, where now appeared a figure. With reverence be it spoken, the apparition bore no slight similitude, both in garb and manner, to some grave divine of the New England churches.

"Bring forth the converts!" cried a voice, that echoed through the field and rolled into the forest.

At the word, Goodman Brown stepped forth from the shadow of the trees, and approached the congregation, with whom he felt a loathful brotherhood, by the sympathy of all that was wicked in his heart. He could have well-nigh sworn, that the shape of his own dead father beckoned him to advance, looking downward from a smoke-wreath, while a woman, with dim features of despair, threw out her hand to warn him back. Was it his mother? But he had no power to retreat one step, nor to resist, even in thought, when the minister and good old Deacon Gookin seized his arms, and led him to the blazing rock. Thither came also the slender form of a veiled female, led between Goody Cloyse, that pious teacher of the catechism, and Martha Carrier, who had received the devil's promise to be queen of hell. A rampant hag was she! And there stood the proselytes, beneath the canopy of fire.

"Welcome, my children," said the dark figure, "to the communion of your race! Ye have found, thus young, your nature and your destiny. My children, look behind you!"

They turned; and flashing forth, as it were, in a sheet of flame, the fiend-worshippers were seen; the smile of welcome gleamed darkly on every visage.

"There," resumed the sable form, "are all whom ye have reverenced from youth. Ye deemed them holier than yourselves, and shrank from your own sin, contrasting it with their lives of righteousness and prayerful aspirations heavenward. Yet, here are they all, in my worshipping assembly! This night it shall be granted you to know their secret deeds; how hoary-bearded elders of the church have whispered wanton words to the young maids of their households; how many a woman, eager for widow's weeds, has given her husband a drink at bedtime, and let him sleep his last sleep in her bosom; how beardless youths have made haste to inherit their father's wealth; and how fair damsels—blush not, sweet ones!—have dug little graves in the garden, and bidden me, the sole guest, to an infant's funeral. By the sympathy of your human hearts for sin, ye shall scent out all the places—whether in church, bed-chamber, street, field, or forest— where crime has been committed, and shall exult to behold the whole earth one stain of guilt, one mighty blood-spot. Far more than this! It shall be yours to penetrate, in every bosom, the deep mystery of sin, the fountain of all wicked arts, and which inexhaustibly supplies more evil impulses than human power—than my power, at its utmost!—can make manifest in deeds. And now, my children, look upon each other."

They did so; and, by the blaze of the hell-kindled torches, the wretched man beheld his Faith, and the wife her husband, trembling before that unhallowed altar.

"Lo! there ye stand, my children," said the figure, in a deep and solemn tone, almost sad, with its despairing awfulness, as if his once angelic nature could yet mourn for our miserable race. "Depending upon one another's hearts, ye had still hoped that virtue were not all a dream! Now are ye undeceived!—Evil is the nature of mankind. Evil must be your only happiness. Welcome, again, my children, to the communion of your race!"

"Welcome!" repeated the fiend-worshippers, in one cry of despair and triumph.

And there they stood, the only pair, as it seemed, who were yet hesitating on the verge of wickedness, in this dark world. A basin was hollowed, naturally, in the rock. Did it contain water, reddened by the lurid light? or was it blood? or, perchance, a liquid flame? Herein did the Shape of Evil dip his hand, and prepare to lay the mark of baptism upon their foreheads, that they might be partakers of the mystery of sin, more conscious of the secret guilt of others, both in deed and thought, than they could now be of their own. The husband cast one look at his pale wife, and Faith at him. What polluted wretches would the next glance show them to each other, shuddering alike at what they disclosed and what they saw!

"Faith! Faith!" cried the husband. "Look up to Heaven, and resist the Wicked One!"

Whether Faith obeyed, he knew not. Hardly had he spoken, when he found himself amid calm night and solitude, listening to a roar of the wind, which died heavily away through the forest. He staggered against the rock, and felt it chill and damp, while a hanging twig, that had been all on fire, besprinkled his cheek with the coldest dew.

The next morning, young Goodman Brown came slowly into the street of Salem village staring around him like a bewildered man. The good old minister was taking a walk along the grave-yard, to get an appetite for breakfast and meditate his sermon, and bestowed a blessing, as he passed, on Goodman Brown. He shrank from the venerable saint, as if to avoid an anathema. Old Deacon Gookin was at domestic worship, and the holy words of his prayer were heard through the open window. "What God doth the wizard pray to?" quoth Goodman Brown. Goody Cloyse, that excellent old Christian, stood in the early sunshine, at her own lattice, catechising a little girl, who had brought her a pint of morning's milk. Goodman Brown snatched away the child, as from the grasp of the fiend himself. Turning the corner by the meeting-house, he spied the head of Faith, with the pink ribbons, gazing anxiously forth, and bursting into such joy at sight of him that she skipt along the street, and almost kissed her husband before the whole village. But Goodman Brown looked sternly and sadly into her face, and passed on without a greeting.

Had Goodman Brown fallen asleep in the forest, and only dreamed a wild dream of a witch-meeting?

Be it so, if you will. But, alas! it was a dream of evil omen for young Goodman Brown. A stern, a sad, a darkly meditative, a distrustful, if not a desperate man did he become, from the night of that fearful dream. On the Sabbath day, when the congregation were singing a holy psalm, he could not listen, because an anthem of sin rushed loudly upon his ear, and drowned all the blessed strain. When the minister spoke from the pulpit, with power and fervid eloquence, and with his hand on the open Bible, of the sacred truths of our religion, and of saint-like lives and triumphant deaths, and of future bliss or misery unutterable, then did Goodman Brown turn pale, dreading lest the roof should thunder down upon the gray blasphemer and his hearers. Often, awaking suddenly at midnight, he shrank from the bosom of Faith, and at morning or eventide, when the family knelt down at prayer, he scowled, and muttered to himself, and gazed sternly at his wife, and turned away. And when he had lived long, and was borne to his grave, a hoary corpse, followed by Faith, an aged woman, and children and grandchildren, a goodly procession, besides neighbors not a few, they carved no hopeful verse upon his tombstone; for his dying hour was gloom.

QUESTIONS

1. Though the main action of "Young Goodman Brown" takes place in the woods outside Salem, the story begins and ends inside Salem village. What is gained by organizing the story in this way?
2. In the opening scene, we might particularly notice the introduction of Goodman Brown's wife, Faith. Why does the narrator say she is "aptly named"? How do Faith's talk of her "fears" and Brown's emphasis on the newness of their marriage set the stage for the story that follows?
3. How does the narrator's description of the forest and of Brown's thoughts (pp. 30–31) establish the atmosphere of the story? How would you describe the atmosphere thus created?
4. On pp. 31–35, what sort of argument is going on within young Goodman Brown, or between him and his companion? What people does he encounter

during this time? What significance do these people have for him? What do you notice about the order in which he meets them?

5. On p. 36, the narrator remarks that "the fiend in his own shape is less hideous, than when he rages in the breast of man." Why does he place such a comment at this point in the story? What development of action or characterization docs it emphasize?

6. In the scene on pp. 38–39, with what is the fiend tempting Faith and Goodman Brown? What sort of faith is he trying to get them to renounce? With what would he replace it?

7. On p. 40, the narrator enters the story again to raise (and dismiss) the question of whether Brown's experience had been real or only a dream. Why should he raise the question if he does not intend to answer it? What is your reaction to the passage? (Had the notion that Brown's adventures might be a dream already entered your mind? If it had, what clues had put it there?)

8. Another way to read the story, already hinted at by the narrator in the opening scene, is as an **allegory,** a tale that has not only a literal but also a metaphorical meaning. The central figure in an allegory most often represents any or every person, while the action usually presents a struggle between good and evil forces anxious to save or damn the central character. Since the battleground for this struggle is the mind or soul of the disputed character, this type of allegory is called a **psychomachia,** or soul-battle. How would you interpret "Young Goodman Brown" as allegory? If it is a battle, who has won?

9. Is there one reading of the story—either as the tale of an actual happening, as a tale of a dream, or as an allegory—that seems most satisfactory to you? (If so, what reading is it, and why? If not, what is there in the story that keeps you from deciding?) How does the narrator seem to regard the story? How do his attempts to interpret it and the choice of interpretations he forces on you affect your response to the tale?

AMBROSE BIERCE   (1842–1914)

Chickamauga[1]

One sunny autumn afternoon a child strayed away from its rude home in a small field and entered a forest unobserved. It was happy in a new sense of freedom from control—happy in the opportunity of exploration and adventure; for this child's spirit, in bodies of its ancestors, had for many thousands of years been trained to memorable feats of discovery and conquest—victories in battles whose critical moments were centuries, whose victors' camps were cities of hewn stone. From the cradle of its race it had conquered its way through two continents, and, passing a great sea, had penetrated a third, there to be born to war and dominance as a heritage.

The child was a boy, aged about six years, the son of a poor planter. In his younger manhood the father had been a soldier, had fought against naked savages, and followed the flag of his country into the capital of a civilized race to the far South. In the peaceful life of a planter the warrior-fire survived; once kindled it is never extinguished. The man loved military books and pictures, and the boy had understood enough to make himself a wooden sword, though even the eye of his father would hardly have known it for what it was. This weapon he now bore bravely, as became the son of an heroic race, and, pausing now and again in the sunny spaces of the forest, assumed, with some exaggeration, the postures of aggression and defense that he had been taught by the engraver's art. Made reckless by the ease with which he overcame invisible foes attempting to stay his advance, he committed the common enough military error of pushing the pursuit to a dangerous extreme, until he found himself upon the margin of a wide but shallow brook, whose rapid waters barred his direct advance against the flying foe who had crossed with illogical ease. But the intrepid victor was not to be baffled; the spirit of the race which had passed the great sea burned unconquerable in that small breast and would not be denied. Finding a place where some bowlders in the bed of the stream lay but a step or a leap apart, he made his way across and fell again upon the rear guard of his imaginary foe, putting all to the sword.

Now that the battle had been won, prudence required that he withdraw to his base of operations. Alas! like many a mightier conquerer, and like one, the mightiest, he could not

---

[1] The Battle of Chickamauga Creek took place in Tennessee on September 19–20, 1863. Casualties in the first four hours of battle ran to over fifty percent on both sides. There were nearly 40,000 casualties in all, making it one of the most confusing and deadly battles of the Civil War.

curb the lust for war,
Nor learn that tempted Fate will leave the loftiest star.[2]

Advancing from the bank of the creek, he suddenly found himself confronted with a new and more formidable enemy; in the path that he was following, bolt upright, with ears erect and paws suspended before it, sat a rabbit. With a startled cry the child turned and fled, he knew not in what direction, calling with inarticulate cries for his mother, weeping, stumbling, his tender skin cruelly torn by brambles, his little heart beating hard with terror—breathless, blind with tears—lost in the forest! Then, for more than an hour, he wandered with erring feet through the tangled undergrowth, till at last, overcome with fatigue, he lay down in a narrow space between two rocks, within a few yards of the stream, and, still grasping his toy sword, no longer a weapon but a companion, sobbed himself to sleep. The wood birds sang merrily above his head; the squirrels, whisking their bravery of tail, ran barking from tree to tree, unconscious of the pity of it, and somewhere far away was a strange, muffled thunder, as if the partridges were drumming in celebration of nature's victory over the son of her immemorial enslavers. And back at the little plantation, where white men and black were hastily searching the fields and hedgerows in alarm, a mother's heart was breaking for her missing child.

Hours passed, and then the little sleeper rose to his feet. The chill of the evening was in his limbs, the fear of the gloom in his heart. But he had rested, and he no longer wept. With some blind instinct which impelled to action, he struggled through the undergrowth about him and came to a more open ground—on his right the brook, to the left a gentle acclivity studded with infrequent trees; over all the gathering gloom of twilight. A thin, ghostly mist rose along the water. It frightened and repelled him; instead of recrossing, in the direction whence he had come, he turned his back upon it and went forward toward the dark inclosing wood. Suddenly he saw before him a strange moving object which he took to be some large animal—a dog, a pig—he could not name it; perhaps it was a bear. He had seen pictures of bears, but knew of nothing to their discredit, and had vaguely wished to meet one. But something in form or movement of this object—something in the awkwardness of its approach—told him that it was not a bear, and curiosity was stayed by fear. He stood still, and as it came slowly on, gained courage every moment, for he saw that at least it had not the long, menacing ears of the rabbit. Possibly his impressionable mind was half conscious of something familiar in its shambling, awkward gait. Before it had approached near enough to resolve his doubts, he saw

---

[2] From *Childe Harold's Pilgrimage* by Lord Byron. Byron's "conqueror" is Napoleon.

that it was followed by another and another. To right and to left were many more; the whole open space about him was alive with them—all moving forward toward the brook.

They were men. They crept upon their hands and knees. They used their hands only, dragging their legs. They used their knees only, their arms hanging useless at their sides. They strove to rise to their feet, but fell prone in the attempt. They did nothing naturally, and nothing alike, save only to advance foot by foot in the same direction. Singly, in pairs, and in little groups, they came on through the gloom, some halting now and again while others crept slowly past them, then resuming their movement. They came by dozens and by hundreds; as far on either hand as one could see in the deepening gloom they extended, and the black wood behind them appeared to be inexhaustible. The very ground seemed in motion toward the creek. Occasionally one who had paused did not again go on, but lay motionless. He was dead. Some, pausing, made strange gestures with their hands, erected their arms and lowered them again, clasped their heads; spread their palms upward, as men are sometimes seen to do in public prayer.

Not all of this did the child note; it is what would have been noted by an older observer; he saw little but that these were men, yet crept like babes. Being men, they were not terrible, though some of them were unfamiliarly clad. He moved among them freely, going from one to another and peering into their faces with childish curiosity. All their faces were singularly white and many were streaked and gouted with red. Something in this—something too, perhaps, in their grotesque attitudes and movements—reminded him of the painted clown whom he had seen last summer in the circus, and he laughed as he watched them. But on and ever on they crept, these maimed and bleeding men, as heedless as he of the dramatic contrast between his laughter and their own ghastly gravity. To him it was a merry spectacle. He had seen his father's negroes creep upon their hands and knees for his amusement—had ridden them so, "making believe" they were his horses. He now approached one of these crawling figures from behind and with an agile movement mounted it astride. The man sank upon his breast, recovered, flung the small boy fiercely to the ground as an unbroken colt might have done, then turned upon him a face that lacked a lower jaw—from the upper teeth to the throat was a great red gap fringed with hanging shreds of flesh and splinters of bone. The unnatural prominence of nose, the absence of chin, the fierce eyes, gave this man the appearance of a great bird of prey crimsoned in throat and breast by the blood of its quarry. The man rose to his knees, the child to his feet. The man shook his fist at the child; the child, terrified at last, ran to a tree near by, got upon the farther side of it, and took a more serious view of the situation. And so the uncanny multitude dragged itself slowly and painfully along in hideous pantomime—

moved forward down the slope like a swarm of great black beetles, with never a sound of going— in silence profound, absolute.

Instead of darkening, the haunted landscape began to brighten. Through the belt of trees beyond the brook shone a strange red light, the trunks and branches of the trees making a black lacework against it. It struck the creeping figures and gave them monstrous shadows, which caricatured their movements on the lit grass. It fell upon their faces, touching their whiteness with a ruddy tinge, accentuating the stains with which so many of them were freaked and maculated. It sparkled on buttons and bits of metal in their clothing. Instinctively the child turned toward the growing splendor and moved down the slope with his horrible companions; in a few moments had passed the foremost of the throng—not much of a feat, considering his advantages. He placed himself in the lead, his wooden sword still in hand, and solemnly directed the march, conforming his pace to theirs and occasionally turning as if to see that his forces did not straggle. Surely such a leader never before had such a following.

Scattered about upon the ground now slowly narrowing by the encroachment of this awful march to water, were certain articles to which, in the leader's mind, were coupled no significant associations; an occasional blanket, tightly rolled lengthwise, doubled and the ends bound together with a string; a heavy knapsack here, and there a broken musket—such things, in short, as are found in the rear of retreating troops, the "spoor" of men flying from their hunters. Everywhere near the creek, which here had a margin of lowland, the earth was trodden into mud by the feet of men and horses. An observer of better experience in the use of his eyes would have noticed that these footprints pointed in both directions; the ground had been twice passed over—in advance and in retreat. A few hours before, these desperate, stricken men, with their more fortunate and now distant comrades, had penetrated the forest in thousands. Their successive battalions, breaking into swarms and reforming in lines, had passed the child on every side—had almost trodden on him as he slept. The rustle and murmur of their march had not awakened him. Almost within a stone's throw of where he lay they had fought a battle; but all unheard by him were the roar of the musketry, the shock of the cannon, "the thunder of the captains and the shouting."[3] He had slept through it all, grasping his little wooden sword with perhaps a tighter clutch in unconscious sympathy with his martial environment, but as heedless of the grandeur of the struggle as the dead who died to make the glory.

The fire beyond the belt of woods on the farther side of the creek, reflected to earth from the canopy of its own smoke, was now suffusing

---

[3] Job 39:25 "He saith among the trumpets, Ha, ha! and he smelleth the battle afar off, the thunder of the captains, and the shouting."

the whole landscape. It transformed the sinuous line of mist to the vapor of gold. The water gleamed with dashes of red, and red, too, were many of the stones protruding above the surface. But that was blood; the less desperately wounded had stained them in crossing. On them, too, the child now crossed with eager steps; he was going to the fire. As he stood upon the farther bank, he turned about to look at the companions of his march. The advance was arriving at the creek. The stronger had already drawn themselves to the brink and plunged their faces in the flood. Three or four who lay without motion appeared to have no heads. At this the child's eyes expanded with wonder; even his hospitable understanding could not accept a phenomenon implying such vitality as that. After slaking their thirst these men had not the strength to back away from the water, nor to keep their heads above it. They were drowned. In rear of these the open spaces of the forest showed the leader as many formless figures of his grim command as at first; but not nearly so many were in motion. He waved his cap for their encouragement and smilingly pointed with his weapon in the direction of the guiding light—a pillar of fire to this strange exodus.[4]

Confident of the fidelity of his forces, he now entered the belt of woods, passed through it easily in the red illumination, climbed a fence, ran across a field, turning now and again to coquette with his responsive shadow, and so approached the blazing ruin of a dwelling. Desolation everywhere. In all the wide glare not a living thing was visible. He cared nothing for that; the spectacle pleased, and he danced with glee in imitation of the wavering flames. He ran about collecting fuel, but every object that he found was too heavy for him to cast in from the distance to which the heat limited his approach. In despair he flung in his sword—a surrender to the superior forces of nature. His military career was at an end.

Shifting his position, his eyes fell upon some outbuildings which had an oddly familiar appearance, as if he had dreamed of them. He stood considering them with wonder, when suddenly the entire plantation, with its inclosing forest, seemed to turn as if upon a pivot. His little world swung half around; the points of the compass were reversed. He recognized the blazing building as his own home!

For a moment he stood stupefied by the power of the revelation, then ran with stumbling feet, making a half circuit of the ruin. There, conspicuous in the light of the conflagration, lay the dead body of a woman—the white face turned upward, the hands thrown out and clutched full of grass, the clothing deranged, the long dark hair in tangles and full of clotted blood. The greater part of the forehead was torn away, and from the jagged hole the brain protruded, overflowing

---

[4] Exodus 13:21 During the flight from Egypt, God led the Israelites with a pillar of fire lighting the night.

the temple, a frothy mass of gray, crowned with clusters of crimson bubbles—the work of a shell!

The child moved his little hands, making wild, uncertain gestures. He uttered a series of inarticulate and indescribable cries— something between the chattering of an ape and the gobbling of a turkey—a startling, soulless, unholy sound, the language of a devil. The child was a deaf mute.

Then he stood motionless, with quivering lips, looking down upon the wreck.

QUESTIONS

Action, setting, and character are all crucial in creating Chickamauga; and they are all somewhat unusual. For example, when we speak of the tale's "action," we must talk of two things: the battle of Chickamauga itself, and the acts of a small deaf-mute who became caught up in the battle's horrifying aftermath: an actor who, moving through his personal drama, cannot begin to comprehend the larger action being waged around him. Similarly, the tale's setting is both the fringes of a battlefield and the woods near the child's home. As for the protagonist himself, he is the most helpless and vulnerable that any storyteller could have imagined for the setting; the distinction between his realizations and our own, plus the immensity of the gap between the events that surround him and his ability to respond to them, account for much of the story's impact.

When discussing Chickamauga, therefore, you will want to take all these elements into consideration. When writing about the story, however, you can either discuss the interactions of the three or focus on one of the elements. Thus, an essay might discuss one of the following topics:

1. What is the effect of having such a young protagonist in the story? How does the narrator play off the child's limited understanding against the reader's greater understanding?
2. Note that one method by which Bierce heightens his story's impact is by having the tale's only explicit vision of warfare be the view of military glory learned by the protagonist from his father. In contrast, the actual battle is presented only by glimpses of its effects. Discuss how Bierce plays off the vision and reality of warfare during the course of the story: how does it affect the exposition, the main action, and the climax?
3. Discuss Bierce's use of the "surprise ending" in Chickamauga.
4. "Chickamauga" and "Young Goodman Brown" both present characters who leave their homes temporarily for the nearby woods, and there encounter a devastating experience. Discuss the use of woods as a setting in these two stories.
5. Whatever else Bierce may have intended in this tale, he did not intend his readers to remain unmoved by it.
   a. Describe your reaction to the story.
   b. If you had been its author, is this a reaction you would have wanted? Why or why not?
   c. What reaction do you think Bierce was likely to have been looking for? Why do you think so?

ERNEST HEMINGWAY (1898–1961)

Hills like White Elephants

The hills across the valley of the Ebro were long and white. On this side there was no shade and no trees and the station was between two lines of rails in the sun. Close against the side of the station there was the warm shadow of the building and a curtain, made of strings of bamboo beads, hung across the open door into the bar, to keep out flies. The American and the girl with him sat at a table in the shade, outside the building. It was very hot and the express from Barcelona would come in forty minutes. It stopped at this junction for two minutes and went on to Madrid.[1]

"What should we drink?" the girl asked. She had taken off her hat and put it on the table.

"It's pretty hot," the man said.

"Let's drink beer."

"Dos cervezas," the man said into the curtain.

"Big ones?" a woman asked from the doorway.

"Yes. Two big ones."

The woman brought two glasses of beer and two felt pads. She put the felt pads and the beer glasses on the table and looked at the man and the girl. The girl was looking off at the line of hills. They were white in the sun and the country was brown and dry.

"They look like white elephants," she said.

"I've never seen one," the man drank his beer.

"No, you wouldn't have."

"I might have," the man said. "Just because you say I wouldn't have doesn't prove anything."

The girl looked at the bead curtain. "They've painted something on it," she said. "What does it say?"

"Anis del Toro. It's a drink."

"Could we try it?"

The man called "Listen" through the curtain. The woman came out from the bar.

"Four reales."[2]

"We want two Anis del Toro."

"With water?"

"Do you want it with water?"

"I don't know," the girl said. "Is it good with water?"

---

[1] The references to the Ebro River and the cities of Barcelona and Madrid identify the setting as Spain.

[2] Spanish coins.

48

"It's all right."

"You want them with water?" asked the woman.

"Yes, with water."

"It tastes like licorice," the girl said and put the glass down.

"That's the way with everything."

"Yes," said the girl. "Everything tastes of licorice. Especially all the things you've waited so long for, like absinthe."

"Oh, cut it out."

"You started it," the girl said. "I was being amused. I was having a fine time."

"Well, let's try and have a fine time."

"All right. I was trying. I said the mountains looked like white elephants. Wasn't that bright?"

"That was bright."

"I wanted to try this new drink. That's all we do, isn't it—look at things and try new drinks?"

"I guess so."

The girl looked across at the hills.

"They're lovely hills," she said. "They don't really look like white elephants. I just meant the coloring of their skin through the trees."

"Should we have another drink?"

"All right."

The warm wind blew the bead curtain against the table.

"The beer's nice and cool," the man said.

"It's lovely," the girl said.

"It's really an awfully simple operation, Jig," the man said. "It's not really an operation at all."

The girl looked at the ground the table legs rested on.

"I know you wouldn't mind it, Jig. It's really not anything. It's just to let the air in."

The girl did not say anything.

"I'll go with you and I'll stay with you all the time. They just let the air in and then it's all perfectly natural."

"Then what will we do afterward?"

"We'll be fine afterward. Just like we were before."

"What makes you think so?"

"That's the only thing that bothers us. It's the only thing that's made us unhappy."

The girl looked at the bead curtain, put her hand out and took hold of two of the strings of beads.

"And you think then we'll be all right and be happy."

"I know we will. You don't have to be afraid. I've known lots of people that have done it."

"So have I," said the girl. "And afterward they were all so happy."

"Well," the man said, "if you don't want to you don't have to. I wouldn't have you do it if you didn't want to. But I know it's perfectly simple."

"And you really want to?"

"I think it's the best thing to do. But I don't want you to do it if you don't really want to."

"And if I do it you'll be happy and things will be like they were and you'll love me?"

"I love you now. You know I love you."

"I know. But if I do it, then it will be nice again if I say things are like white elephants, and you'll like it?"

"I'll love it. I love it now but I just can't think about it. You know how I get when I worry."

"If I do it you won't ever worry?"

"I won't worry about that because it's perfectly simple."

"Then I'll do it. Because I don't care about me."

"What do you mean?"

"I don't care about me."

"Well, I care about you."

"Oh, yes. But I don't care about me. And I'll do it and then everything will be fine."

"I don't want you to do it if you feel that way."

The girl stood up and walked to the end of the station. Across, on the other side, were fields of grain and trees along the banks of the Ebro. Far away, beyond the river, were mountains. The shadow of a cloud moved across the field of grain and she saw the river through the trees.

"And we could have all this," she said. "And we could have everything and every day we make it more impossible."

"What did you say?"

"I said we could have everything."

"We can have everything."

"No, we can't."

"We can have the whole world."

"No, we can't."

"We can go everywhere."

"No, we can't. It isn't ours any more."

"It's ours."

"No, it isn't. And once they take it away, you never get it back."

"But they haven't taken it away."

"We'll wait and see."

"Come on back in the shade," he said. "You mustn't feel that way."

"I don't feel any way," the girl said. "I just know things."

"I don't want you to do anything that you don't want to do—"

"Nor that isn't good for me," she said. "I know. Could we have another beer?"

"All right. But you've got to realize—"

"I realize," the girl said. "Can't we maybe stop talking?"

They sat down at the table and the girl looked across at the hills on the dry side of the valley and the man looked at her and at the table.

"You've got to realize," he said, "that I don't want you to do it if you don't want to. I'm perfectly willing to go through with it if it means anything to you."

"Doesn't it mean anything to you? We could get along."

"Of course it does. But I don't want anybody but you. I don't want any one else. And I know it's perfectly simple."

"Yes, you know it's perfectly simple."

"It's all right for you to say that, but I do know it."

"Would you do something for me now?"

"I'd do anything for you."

"Would you please please please please please please please stop talking?"

He did not say anything but looked at the bags against the wall of the station. There were labels on them from all the hotels where they had spent nights.

"But I don't want you to," he said, "I don't care anything about it."

"I'll scream," the girl said.

The woman came out through the curtains with two glasses of beer and put them down on the damp felt pads. "The train comes in five minutes," she said.

"What did she say?" asked the girl.

"That the train is coming in five minutes."

The girl smiled brightly at the woman, to thank her.

"I'd better take the bags over to the other side of the station," the man said. She smiled at him.

"All right. Then come back and we'll finish the beer."

He picked up the two heavy bags and carried them around the station to the other tracks. He looked up the tracks but could not see the train. Coming back, he walked through the barroom, where people waiting for the train were drinking. He drank an Anis at the bar and looked at the people. They were all waiting reasonably for the train. He went out through the bead curtain. She was sitting at the table and smiled at him.

"Do you feel better?" he asked.

"I feel fine," she said. "There's nothing wrong with me. I feel fine."

QUESTIONS

1. In contrast to the vivid action of "Young Goodman Brown" and "Chickamauga," "Hills Like White Elephants" seems to contain almost no action whatever. Nor do the characters at its end seem to have changed, or been changed, from what they were at its beginning. For many years, in fact, critics

questioned whether "static" stories like this one deserved the title of "story" at all. What do you think? "Hills Like White Elephants" is generally regarded as an excellent example of twentieth-century fiction. Do you agree that it merits this regard? If it is a fine example of the art of fiction, in what lies its artistry?

2. Discuss the mechanics of the story.
   a. How are the characters created? Do you find them clearly drawn? recognizable? or not?
   b. By what means is the tale's conflict defined? How completely is it defined? Is it resolved by the tale's end? What sense do you have regarding its ultimate resolution? Why?
   c. How is the setting described? Is it important? Why or why not?
   d. What amount of time does the story cover? How does this affect your perception of characters, conflict, and setting?
3. How do the elements listed in Question 2 work together to create coherence and vision within the story?
4. Hawthorne, in "Young Goodman Brown," not only described events but interpreted them. Bierce, in "Chickamauga," gave us considerable background at the start of the tale, then shifted to a more reportorial tone as events themselves became more compelling; but not till the tale's end did he stop explaining something of what was in his protagonist's mind. Hemingway, in contrast, is wholly reportorial, relying wholly on description and dialogue to carry the story. How does this affect the story's power? How does it affect your reaction to it?

3 The First-Person Narrator

Omniscient narrators stand somewhat apart from their stories. Having no role in the action themselves, they can interpret its events and characters impartially. Even when an omniscient narrator shows us most of the story through one central character's eyes, as does the narrator of "Young Goodman Brown," he can still give us glimpses into minds and actions that the character cannot see, as when Hawthorne's narrator tells us that Brown's townsmen "carved no hopeful verse upon his tombstone." Moreover, he can still interpret the events he relates from his own point of view, even when his view of the matter conflicts with his central character's: "Had Goodman Brown fallen asleep in the forest . . . ?"

First-person narrators, on the other hand, are participants in their own stories. They are telling us of something that happened to them, and are telling their tale from their own point of view. They cannot see into the minds of the other characters; indeed, they may hardly understand their own actions. In contrast to the total knowledge of the omniscient narrator, the first-person narrator's powers of interpretation may be slight indeed.

As the narrator's knowledge shrinks, the reader's role expands. If we cannot trust the narrator as an omniscient, final authority, then our own wisdom and judgment must come into play. We must weigh the narrator's perceptions against our own and so create our own understanding of the actions and characters within the story.

Often, therefore, first-person narratives are rich in **irony,** with the narrators describing what they think they see and the readers interpreting the descriptions to discover what "really" happened. In these stories the relationship between reader and narrator is completely reversed. Now we are the wise ones, the ones with the fullest perception of what's going on. If we could only speak to these narrators, as they seem to be speaking to us, how much we could tell them!

In other stories, however, first-person narrators retain the full authority of the storyteller. Indeed, if the tales they tell are set far enough in their pasts, the narrators may view themselves as nearly omniscient. They know what they were thinking and feeling when the events took place, so they can take us into their major character's mind; they know how events turned out, so they feel that they can interpret the patterns within them. Moreover, they may feel that they have grown considerably wiser since the time of the actions they are relating and can therefore combine past feelings and present understanding to interpret events and emotions as no one else could.

In either case, and in less extreme cases as well, we often feel closer to first-person narrators than we feel either to omniscient narrators or to the characters they describe. The limitations of human knowledge and insight within which the first-person narrators work, the blend of attempted objectivity and personal involvement their voices convey, and their apparent openness in telling their own stories appeal to our sympathy and our sense of fellowship. In telling us, as they often do, of their dreams and desires, first-person narrators speak eloquently of human aspirations; in confessing (consciously or unconsciously) their shortcomings, they speak no less eloquently of human limitations.

The narrators of "Bartleby the Scrivener" and "My Man Bovanne" are storytellers in the grand tradition. They catch our attention from the opening sentence, and share with us both facts and feelings as they move from incident to incident towards a well-crafted climax. Their voices, however, are very different. Melville's narrator, deliberately telling a formal tale, sets a leisurely pace. His tale is rich in detail and reflection; his vocabulary and tone attest to his position as a solid and educated citizen; and he is conscientious in telling his story as fully as he can and in admitting the limits of his knowledge. Bambara's narrator, in contrast, seems to be carrying on a conversation with people she already knows. Her tone and opinions are direct, and mix humor with insight and common sense; her pace is relatively rapid, as befits an active woman with a strong sense of her own priorities.

"The Yellow Wall-Paper" represents a second tradition in first-person narrative: the creation of a tale in the shape of a journal or diary. Unlike the first two stories, which claim clear descent from the oral tradition of tale-telling, this story comes from a purely written tradition. You must have journals—and hence writing—before you can create a story that pretends to be a group of entries from somebody's journal.

Stories written in this "diary-like" tradition share several interesting features. First, they allow their narrators to ponder and reveal things the narrators would shrink from saying aloud. As the narrator of "The Yellow Wall-

Paper" says, "I would not say it to a living soul, of course, but this is dead paper and a great relief to my mind." We, however, do read this "dead paper"; and we thus gain a closeness to the narrator that his or her closest friends might not have.

Second, the diary like tale assumes that each event within it is chronicled on the day it occurs. It thus makes possible an immediacy which few other types of writing allow.

There is little room for hindsight in this sort of writing, little chance for the narrator to fit events into a pattern. We, as readers, must provide the pattern ourselves, just as we must come to our own understanding of the narrator by observing how her feelings and perceptions change during the course of the narrative. Caught up in the flow of events, the narrator may or may not be able to interpret them. We, standing outside those events, are challenged to do so.

Somewhat less traditional is "In Search of the Rattlesnake Plantain." Again there is immediacy, as the narrator speaks in the present tense, and sometimes seems to address us directly. But the episodes she describes happened, for the most part, in the past; her story moves among them—not always in consecutive steps—in the half-logical, half-random way that memory often moves; and her reflections are as deeply personal as any diary would be. It's a technique that requires a bit of care from us as readers to keep the episodes straight in our own minds; but it repays this care by offering us a sense of personal acquaintance with the narrator, and by creating in her a wholly recognizable and believable character.

Each of these stories is well worth reading for its own sake. Taken together, they remind us, once again, of the range of style and effect available to writers, and of the uniqueness of each voice that we hear speaking to us from literature.

HERMAN MELVILLE (1819–1891)

Bartleby the Scrivener

I am a rather elderly man. The nature of my avocations, for the last thirty years, has brought me into more than ordinary contact with what would seem an interesting and somewhat singular set of men, of whom, as yet, nothing, that I know of, has ever been written—I mean, the law-copyists, or scriveners. I have known very many of them, professionally and privately, and, if I pleased, could relate divers histories, at which good-natured gentlemen might smile, and sentimental souls might weep. But I waive the biographies of all other scriveners, for a few passages in the life of Bartleby, who was a scrivener, the strangest I ever saw, or heard of. While, of other law-copyists, I might write the complete life, of Bartleby nothing of that sort can be done. I believe that no materials exist, for a full and satisfactory biography of this man. It is an irreparable loss to literature. Bartleby was one of those beings of whom nothing is ascertainable, except from the original sources, and, in his case, those are very small. What my own astonished eyes saw of Bartleby, *that* is all I know of him, except, indeed, one vague report, which will appear in the sequel.

Ere introducing the scrivener, as he first appeared to me, it is fit I make some mention of myself, my *employés,* my business, my chambers, and general surroundings; because some such description is indispensable to an adequate understanding of the chief character about to be presented. Imprimis: I am a man who, from his youth upwards, has been filled with a profound conviction that the easiest way of life is the best. Hence, though I belong to a profession prover-bially energetic and nervous, even to turbulence, at times, yet noth-ing of that sort have I ever suffered to invade my peace. I am one of those unambitious lawyers who never addresses a jury, or in any way draws down public applause; but, in the cool tranquillity of a snug retreat, do a snug business among rich men's bonds, and mortgages, and title-deeds. All who know me, consider me an eminently *safe* man. The late John Jacob Astor,[1] a personage little given to poetic enthusiasm, had no hesitation in pronouncing my first grand point to be prudence; my next, method. I do not speak it in vanity, but simply record the fact, that I was not unemployed in my profession by the late John Jacob Astor, a name which, I admit, I love to repeat; for it hath a rounded and orbicular sound to it, and rings like unto bullion. I will freely add, that I was not insensible to the late John Jacob Astor's good opinion.

Some time prior to the period at which this little history begins, my avocations had been largely increased. The good old office, now extinct in the State of New York, of a Master in Chancery, had been conferred upon me. It was not a very arduous office, but very pleas-antly remunerative. I seldom lose my temper; much more seldom indulge in dangerous indignation at wrongs and outrages; but, I must be permitted to be rash here, and declare, that I consider the sudden and violent abrogation of the office of Master in Chancery, by the new Constitution, as a —— premature act; inasmuch as I had counted upon a life-lease of the profits, whereas I only received those of a few short years. But this is by the way.

My chambers were up stairs, at No. — Wall Street. At one end, they looked upon the white wall of the interior of a spacious sky-light shaft, penetrating the building from top to bottom.

This view might have been considered rather tame than otherwise, deficient in what landscape painters call "life." But, if so, the view from the other end of my chambers offered, at least, a contrast, if nothing more. In that direction, my windows commanded an unob-structed view of a lofty brick wall, black by age and everlasting shade; which wall required no spy-glass to bring out its lurking beauties, but, for the benefit of all near-sighted spectators, was pushed up to within ten feet of my window panes. Owing to the great height of the surrounding buildings, and my chambers being on the second floor, the interval between this wall and mine not a little resembled a huge square cistern.

At the period just preceding the advent of Bartleby, I had two persons as copyists in my employment, and a promising lad as an

---

[1] *John Jacob Astor* (1763–1848), an American fur trader and financier.

office-boy. First, Turkey; second, Nippers; third, Ginger Nut. These may seem names, the like of which are not usually found in the Directory. In truth, they were nicknames, mutually conferred upon each other by my three clerks, and were deemed expressive of their respective persons or characters. Turkey was a short, pursy Englishman, of about my own age—that is, somewhere not far from sixty. In the morning, one might say, his face was of a fine florid hue, but after twelve o'clock, meridian—his dinner hour—it blazed like a grate full of Christmas coals; and continued blazing—but, as it were, with a gradual wane—till six o'clock, P.M., or thereabouts; after which, I saw no more of the proprietor of the face, which, gaining its meridian with the sun, seemed to set with it, to rise, culminate, and decline the following day, with the like regularity and undiminished glory. There are many singular coincidences I have known in the course of my life, not the least among which was the fact, that, exactly when Turkey displayed his fullest beams from his red and radiant countenance, just then, too, at that critical moment, began the daily period when I considered his business capacities as seriously disturbed for the remainder of the twenty-four hours. Not that he was absolutely idle, or averse to business, then; far from it. The difficulty was, he was apt to be altogether too energetic. There was a strange, inflamed, flurried, flighty recklessness of activity about him. He would be incautious in dipping his pen into his inkstand. All his blots upon my documents were dropped there after twelve o'clock, meridian. Indeed, not only would he be reckless, and sadly given to making blots in the afternoon, but, some days, he went further, and was rather noisy. At such times, too, his face flamed with augmented blazonry, as if cannel coal had been heaped on anthracite. He made an unpleasant racket with his chair; spilled his sand-box; in mending his pens, impatiently split them all to pieces, and threw them on the floor in a sudden passion; stood up, and leaned over his table, boxing his papers about in a most indecorous manner, very sad to behold in an elderly man like him. Nevertheless, as he was in many ways a most valuable person to me, and all the time before twelve o'clock, meridian, was the quickest, steadiest creature, too, accomplishing a great deal of work in a style not easily to be matched—for these reasons, I was willing to overlook his eccentricities, though, indeed, occasionally, I remonstrated with him. I did this very gently, however, because, though the civilest, nay, the blandest and most reverential of men in the morning, yet, in the afternoon, he was disposed, upon provocation, to be slightly rash with his tongue—in fact, insolent. Now, valuing his morning services as I did, and resolved not to lose them—yet, at the same time, made uncomfortable by his inflamed ways after twelve o'clock—and being a man of peace, unwilling by my admonitions to call forth unseemly retorts from him, I took upon me, one Saturday noon (he was always worse on Saturdays) to hint to him, very kindly, that, perhaps, now that he was growing old, it might be well to abridge his labors; in short, he need not come to my chambers after twelve o'clock, but, dinner over, had best go home to his lodgings, and rest himself till tea-time. But no; he insisted upon his afternoon devotions. His countenance became intolerably fervid, as he oratorically assured me—gesticulating with a long ruler at the other end of the room—that if his services in the morning were useful, how indispensable, then, in the afternoon?

"With submission, sir," said Turkey, on this occasion, "I consider myself your right-hand man. In the morning I but marshal and deploy my columns; but in the afternoon I put myself at their head, and gallantly charge the foe, thus"—and he made a violent thrust with the ruler.

"But the blots, Turkey," intimated I.

"True; but, with submission, sir, behold these hairs! I am getting old. Surely, sir, a blot or two of a warm afternoon is not to be severely urged against gray hairs. Old age—even if it blot the page—is honorable. With submission, sir, we *both* are getting old."

This appeal to my fellow-feeling was hardly to be resisted. At all events, I saw that go he would not. So, I made up my mind to let him stay, resolving, nevertheless, to see to it that, during the afternoon, he had to do with my less important papers.

Nippers, the second on my list, was a whiskered, sallow, and, upon the whole, rather piratical-looking young man, of about five and twenty. I always deemed him the victim of two evil powers—ambition and indigestion. The ambition was evinced by a certain impatience of the duties of a mere copyist, an unwarrantable usurpation of strictly professional affairs, such as the original drawing up of legal documents. The indigestion seemed betokened in an occasional nervous testiness and grinning irritability, causing the teeth to audibly grind together over mistakes committed in copying; unnecessary maledictions, hissed, rather than spoken, in the heat of business; and especially by a continual discontent with the height of the table where he worked. Though of a very ingenious mechanical turn, Nippers could never get this table to suit him. He put chips under it, blocks of various sorts, bits of pasteboard, and at last went so far as to attempt an exquisite adjustment, by final pieces of folded blotting-paper. But no invention would answer. If, for the sake of easing his back, he brought the table lid at a sharp angle well up towards his chin, and wrote there like a man using the steep roof of a Dutch house for his desk, then he declared that it stopped the circulation in his arms. If now he lowered the table to his waistbands, and stooped over it in writing, then there was a sore aching in his back. In short, the truth of the matter was, Nippers knew not what he wanted. Or, if he wanted anything, it was to be rid of a scrivener's table altogether. Among the manifestations of his diseased ambition was a fondness he had for receiving visits from certain ambiguous-looking fellows in seedy coats, whom he called his clients. Indeed, I was aware that not only was he, at times, considerable of a ward-politician, but he occasionally did a little business at the Justices' courts, and was not unknown on the steps of the Tombs. I have good reason to believe, however, that one individual who called upon him at my chambers, and who, with a grand air, he insisted was his client, was no other than a dun, and the alleged title-deed, a bill. But, with all his failings, and the annoyances he caused me, Nippers, like his compatriot Turkey, was a very useful man to me; wrote a neat, swift hand; and, when he chose, was not deficient in a gentlemanly sort of deportment. Added to this, he always dressed in a gentlemanly sort of way; and so, incidentally, reflected credit upon my chambers. Whereas, with respect to Turkey, I had much ado to keep him from being a reproach to me. His clothes were apt to look oily, and smell of eating-houses. He wore his pantaloons very loose and baggy in summer. His coats were execrable; his hat not to be handled. But while the hat was a thing of indifference to me, inasmuch as his natural civility and deference, as a dependent Englishman, always led him to doff it the moment he entered the room, yet his coat was another matter. Concerning his coats, I reasoned with him; but with no effect. The truth was, I suppose, that a man with so small an income could not afford to sport such a lustrous face and a lustrous coat at one and the same time. As Nippers once observed, Turkey's money went chiefly for red ink. One winter day, I presented Turkey with a highly respectable-looking coat of my own—a padded gray coat, of a most comfortable warmth, and which buttoned straight up from the knee to the neck. I thought Turkey would appreciate the favor, and abate his rashness and obstreperousness of afternoons. But no; I verily believe that buttoning himself up in so downy and blanket-like a coat had a pernicious effect upon him—upon the same principle that too much oats are bad for horses. In fact, precisely as a rash, restive horse is said to feel his oats, so Turkey felt his coat. It made him insolent. He was a man whom prosperity harmed.

Though, concerning the self-indulgent habits of Turkey, I had my own private surmises, yet, touching Nippers, I was well persuaded that, whatever might be his faults in other respects, he was, at least, a temperate young man. But, indeed, nature herself seemed to have been his vintner, and, at his birth, charged him so thoroughly with an irritable, brandy-like disposition, that all subsequent potations were needless. When I consider how, amid the stillness of my chambers, Nippers would sometimes impatiently rise from his seat, and stooping over his table, spread his arms wide apart, seize the whole desk, and move it, and jerk it, with a grim, grinding motion on the floor, as if the table were a perverse voluntary agent, intent on thwarting and vexing him, I plainly perceive that, for Nippers, brandy-and-water were altogether superfluous.

It was fortunate for me that, owing to its peculiar cause—indigestion—the iritability and consequent nervousness of Nippers were mainly observable in the morning, while in the afternoon he was comparatively mild. So that, Turkey's paroxysms only coming on about twelve o'clock, I never had to do with their eccentricities at one time. Their fits relieved each other, like guards. When Nippers' was on, Turkey's was off; and *vice versa*. This was a good natural arrangement, under the circumstances.

Ginger Nut, the third on my list, was a lad, some twelve years old. His father was a car-man, ambitious of seeing his son on the bench instead of a cart, before he died. So he sent him to my office, as student at law, errand-boy, cleaner and sweeper, at the rate of one dollar a week. He had a little desk to himself, but he did not use it much. Upon inspection, the drawer exhibited a great array of the shells of various sorts of nuts. Indeed, to this quick-witted youth, the whole noble science of the law was contained in a nut-shell. Not the least among the employments of Ginger Nut, as well as one which he discharged with the most alacrity, was his duty as cake and apple purveyor for Turkey and Nippers. Copying law-papers being proverbially a dry, husky sort of business, my two scriveners were fain to moisten their mouths very often with Spitzenbergs, to be had at the numerous stalls nigh the Custom House and Post Office. Also, they sent Ginger Nut very frequently for that peculiar cake—small, flat, round, and very spicy—after which he had been named by them. Of a cold morning, when business was but dull, Turkey would gobble up scores of these cakes, as if they were mere wafers—indeed, they sell them at the rate of six or eight for a penny—the scrape of his pen blending with the crunching of the crisp particles in his mouth. Of all the fiery afternoon blunders and flurried rashnesses of Turkey, was his once moistening a ginger-cake between his lips, and clapping it on to a mortgage, for a seal. I came within an ace of dismissing him then. But he mollified me by making an oriental bow, and saying—

"With submission, sir, it was generous of me to find you in stationery on my own account."

Now my original business—that of a conveyancer and title hunter, and drawer-up of recondite documents of all sorts—was considerably increased by receiving the master's office. There was now great work for scriveners. Not only must I push the clerks already with me, but I must have additional help.

In answer to my advertisement, a motionless young man one morning stood upon my office threshold, the door being open, for it was summer. I can see that figure now—pallidly neat, pitiably respectable, incurably forlorn! It was Bartleby.

After a few words touching his qualifications, I engaged him, glad to have among my corps of copyists a man of so singularly sedate an aspect, which I thought might operate beneficially upon the flighty temper of Turkey, and the fiery one of Nippers.

I should have stated before that ground glass folding-doors divided my premises into two parts, one of which was occupied by my scriveners, the other by myself. According to my humor, I threw open these doors, or closed them. I resolved to assign Bartleby a corner by the folding-doors, but on my side of them, so as to have this quiet man within easy call, in case any trifling thing was to be done. I placed his desk close up to a small side-window in that part of the room, a window which originally had afforded a lateral view of certain grimy backyards and bricks, but which, owing to subsequent erections, commanded at present no view at all, though it gave some light. Within three feet of the panes was a wall, and the light came down from far above, between two lofty buildings, as from a very small opening in a dome. Still further to a satisfactory arrangement, I procured a high green folding screen, which might entirely isolate Bartleby from my sight, though not remove him from my voice. And thus, in a manner, privacy and society were conjoined.

At first, Bartleby did an extraordinary quantity of writing. As if long famishing for something to copy, he seemed to gorge himself on my documents. There was no pause for digestion. He ran a day and night line, copying by sun-light and by candle-light. I should have been quite delighted with his application, had he been cheerfully industrious. But he wrote on silently, palely, mechanically.

It is, of course, an indispensable part of a scrivener's business to verify the accuracy of his copy, word by word. Where there are two or more scriveners in an office, they assist each other in this examination, one reading from the copy, the other holding the original. It is a very dull, wearisome, and lethargic affair. I can readily imagine that, to some sanguine temperaments, it would be altogether intolerable. For example, I cannot credit that the mettlesome poet, Byron, would have contentedly sat down with Bartleby to examine a law document of, say five hundred pages, closely written in a crimpy hand.

Now and then, in the haste of business, it had been my habit to assist in comparing some brief document myself, calling Turkey or Nippers for this purpose. One object I had, in placing Bartleby so handy to me behind the screen, was, to avail myself of his services on such trivial occasions. It was on the third day, I think, of his being with me, and before any necessity had arisen for having his own writing examined, that, being much hurried to complete a small affair I had in hand, I abruptly called to Bartleby. In my haste and natural expectancy of instant compliance, I sat with my head bent over the original on my desk, and my right hand sideways, and somewhat nervously extended with the copy, so that, immediately upon emerging from his retreat, Bartleby might snatch it and proceed to business without the least delay.

In this very attitude did I sit when I called to him, rapidly stating what it was I wanted him to do—namely, to examine a small paper with me. Imagine my surprise, nay, my consternation, when, without moving from his privacy, Bartleby, in a singularly mild, firm voice, replied, "I would prefer not to."

I sat awhile in perfect silence, rallying my stunned faculties. Immediately it occurred to me that my ears had deceived me, or Bartleby had entirely misunderstood my meaning. I repeated my request in the clearest tone I could assume; but in quite as clear a one came the previous reply, "I would prefer not to."

"Prefer not to," echoed I, rising in high excitement, and crossing the room with a stride. "What do you mean? Are you moon-struck? I want you to help me compare this sheet here—take it," and I thrust it towards him.

"I would prefer not to," said he.

I looked at him steadfastly. His face was leanly composed; his gray eye dimly calm. Not a wrinkle of agitation rippled him. Had there been the least uneasiness, anger, impatience or impertinence in his manner; in other words, had there been any thing ordinarily human about him, doubtless I should have violently dismissed him from the premises. But as it was, I should have as soon thought of turning my pale plaster-of-paris bust of Cicero out of doors. I stood gazing at him awhile, as he went on with his own writing, and then reseated myself at my desk. This is very strange, thought I. What had one best do? But my business hurried me. I concluded to forget the matter for the present, reserving it for my future leisure. So calling Nippers from the other room, the paper was speedily examined.

A few days after this, Bartleby concluded four lengthy documents, being quadruplicates of a week's testimony taken before me in my High Court of Chancery. It became necessary to examine them. It was an important suit, and great accuracy was imperative. Having all things arranged, I called Turkey, Nippers, and Ginger Nut, from the next room, meaning to place the four copies in the hands of my four clerks, while I should read from the original. Accordingly, Turkey, Nippers, and Ginger Nut had taken their seats in a row, each with his document in his hand, when I called to Bartleby to join this interesting group.

"Bartleby! quick, I am waiting."

I heard a slow scrape of his chair legs on the uncarpeted floor, and soon he appeared standing at the entrance of his hermitage.

"What is wanted?" said he, mildly.

"The copies, the copies," said I, hurriedly. "We are going to examine them. There"—and I held towards him the fourth quadruplicate.

"I would prefer not to," he said, and gently disappeared behind the screen.

For a few moments I was turned into a pillar of salt, standing at the head of my seated column of clerks. Recovering myself, I advanced towards the screen, and demanded the reason for such extraordinary conduct.

"*Why* do you refuse?"

"I would prefer not to."

With any other man I should have flown outright into a dreadful passion, scorned all further words, and thrust him ignominiously from my presence. But there was something about Bartleby that not only strangely disarmed me, but, in a wonderful manner, touched and disconcerted me. I began to reason with him.

"These are your own copies we are about to examine. It is labor saving to you, because one examination will answer for your four papers. It is common usage. Every copyist is bound to help examine his copy. Is it not so? Will you not speak? Answer!"

"I prefer not to," he replied in a flutelike tone. It seemed to me that, while I had been addressing him, he carefully revolved every statement that I made; fully comprehended the meaning; could not gainsay the irresistible conclusion; but, at the same time, some paramount consideration prevailed with him to reply as he did.

"You are decided, then, not to comply with my request—a request made according to common usage and common sense?"

He briefly gave me to understand, that on that point my judgment was sound. Yes: his decision was irreversible.

It is not seldom the case that, when a man is browbeaten in some unprecedented and violently unreasonable way, he begins to stagger in his own plainest faith. He begins, as it were, vaguely to surmise that, wonderful as it may be, all the justice and all the reason is on the other side. Accordingly, if any disinterested persons are present, he turns to them for some reinforcement of his own faltering mind.

"Turkey," said I, "what do you think of this? Am I not right?"

"With submission, sir," said Turkey, in his blandest tone, "I think that you are."

"Nippers," said I, "what do *you* think of it?"

"I think I should kick him out of the office."

(The reader, of nice perceptions, will here perceive that, it being morning, Turkey's answer is couched in polite and tranquil terms, but Nippers' replies in ill-tempered ones. Or, to repeat a previous sentence, Nippers' ugly mood was on duty, and Turkey's off.)

"Ginger Nut," said I, willing to enlist the smallest suffrage in my behalf, "what do *you* think of it?"

"I think, sir, he's a little *luny*," replied Ginger Nut, with a grin.

"You hear what they say," said I, turning towards the screen, "come forth and do your duty."

But he vouchsafed no reply. I pondered a moment in sore perplexity. But once more business hurried me. I determined again to postpone the consideration of this dilemma to my future leisure. With a little trouble we made out to examine the papers without Bartleby, though at every page or two Turkey deferentially dropped his opinion, that this proceeding was quite out of the common; while Nippers, twitching in his chair with a dyspeptic nervousness, ground out, between his set teeth, occasional hissing maledictions against the stubborn oaf behind the screen. And for his (Nippers') part, this was the first and the last time he would do another man's business without pay.

Meanwhile Bartleby sat in his hermitage, oblivious to everything but his own peculiar business there.

Some days passed, the scrivener being employed upon another lengthy work. His late remarkable conduct led me to regard his ways narrowly. I observed that he never went to dinner; indeed, that he never went anywhere. As yet I had never, of my personal knowledge, known him to be outside of my office. He was a perpetual sentry in the corner. At about eleven o'clock though, in the morning, I noticed that Ginger Nut would advance toward the opening in Bartleby's screen, as if silently beckoned thither by a gesture invisible to me where I sat. The boy would then leave the office, jingling a few pence, and reappear with a handful of ginger-nuts, which he delivered in the hermitage, receiving two of the cakes for his trouble.

He lives, then, on ginger-nuts, thought I; never eats a dinner, properly speaking; he must be a vegetarian, then; but no; he never eats even vegetables, he eats nothing but ginger-nuts. My mind then ran on in reveries concerning the probable effects upon the human constitution of living entirely on ginger-nuts. Ginger-nuts are so called, because they contain ginger as one of their peculiar constituents, and the final flavoring one. Now, what was ginger? A hot, spicy thing. Was Bartleby hot and spicy? Not at all. Ginger, then, had no effect upon Bartleby. Probably he preferred it should have none.

Nothing so aggravates an earnest person as a passive resistance. If the individual so resisted be of a not inhumane temper, and the resisting one perfectly harmless in his passivity, then, in the better moods of the former, he will endeavor charitably to construe to his imagination what proves impossible to be solved by his judgment. Even so, for the most part, I regarded Bartleby and his ways. Poor fellow! thought I, he means no mischief; it is plain he intends no insolence; his aspect sufficiently evinces that his eccentricities are involuntary. He is useful to me. I can get along with him. If I turn him away, the chances are he will fall in with some less-indulgent employer, and then he will be rudely treated, and perhaps driven forth miserably to starve. Yes. Here I can cheaply purchase a delicious self-approval. To befriend Bartleby; to humor him in his strange willfulness, will cost me little or nothing, while I lay up in my soul what will eventually prove a sweet morsel for my conscience. But this mood was not invariable with me. The passiveness of Bartleby sometimes irritated me. I felt strangely goaded on to encounter him in new opposition—to elicit some angry spark from him answerable to my own. But, indeed, I might as well have essayed to strike fire with my knuckles against a bit of Windsor soap. But one afternoon the evil impulse in me mastered me, and the following little scene ensued:

"Bartleby," said I, "when those papers are all copied, I will compare them with you."

"I would prefer not to."

"How? Surely you do not mean to persist in that mulish vagary?" No answer.

I threw open the folding-doors near by, and, turning upon Turkey and Nippers, exclaimed:

"Bartleby a second time says, he won't examine his papers. What do you think of it, Turkey?"

It was afternoon, be it remembered. Turkey sat glowing like a brass boiler; his bald head steaming; his hands reeling among his blotted papers.

"Think of it?" roared Turkey; "I think I'll just step behind his screen, and black his eyes for him!"

So saying, Turkey rose to his feet and threw his arms into a pugilistic position. He was hurrying away to make good his promise, when I detained him, alarmed at the effect of incautiously rousing Turkey's combativeness after dinner.

"Sit down, Turkey," said I, "and hear what Nippers has to say. What do you think of it, Nippers? Would I not be justified in immediately dismissing Bartleby?"

"Excuse me, that is for you to decide, sir. I think his conduct quite unusual, and, indeed, unjust, as regards Turkey and myself. But it may only be a passing whim."

"Ah," exclaimed I, "you have strangely changed your mind, then —you speak very gently of him now."

"All beer," cried Turkey; "gentleness is effects of beer—Nippers and I dined together to-day. You see how gentle *I* am, sir. Shall I go and black his eyes?"

"You refer to Bartleby, I suppose. No, not to-day, Turkey," I replied; "pray, put up your fists."

I closed the doors, and again advanced towards Bartleby. I felt additional incentives tempting me to my fate. I burned to be rebelled against again. I remember that Bartleby never left the office.

"Bartleby," said I, "Ginger Nut is away; just step around to the Post Office, won't you? (it was but a three minutes' walk), and see if there is anything for me."

"I would prefer not to."

"You *will* not?"

"I *prefer* not."

I staggered to my desk, and sat there in a deep study. My blind inveteracy returned. Was there any other thing in which I could procure myself to be ignominiously repulsed by this lean, penniless wight?—my hired clerk? What added thing is there, prefectly reasonable, that he will be sure to refuse to do?

"Bartleby!"

No answer.

"Bartleby," in a louder tone.

No answer.

"Bartleby," I roared.

Like a very ghost, agreeably to the laws of magical invocation, at the third summons, he appeared at the entrance of his hermitage.

"Go to the next room, and tell Nippers to come to me."

"I prefer not to," he respectfully and slowly said, and mildly disappeared.

"Very good, Bartleby," said I, in a quiet sort of serenely-severe self-possessed tone, intimating the unalterable purpose of some terrible retribution very close at hand. But upon the whole, as it was drawing towards my dinner-hour, I thought it best to put on my hat and walk home for the day, suffering much from perplexity and distress of mind.

Shall I acknowledge it? The conclusion of this whole business was, that it soon became a fixed fact of my chambers, that a pale young scrivener, by the name of Bartleby, had a desk there; that he copied for me at the usual rate of four cents a folio (one hundred words); but he was permanently exempt from examining the work done by him, that duty being transferred to Turkey and Nippers, out of compliment, doubtless, to their superior acuteness; moreover, said Bartleby was never, on any account, to be dispatched on the most trivial errand of any sort; and that even if entreated to take upon him such a matter, it was generally understood that he would "prefer not to"—in other words, that he would refuse point-blank.

As days passed on, I became considerably reconciled to Bartleby. His steadiness, his freedom from all dissipation, his incessant industry (except when he chose to throw himself into a standing revery behind his screen), his great stillness, his unalterableness of demeanor under all circumstances, made him a valuable acquisition. One prime thing was this—*he was always there*—first in the morning, continually through the day, and the last at night. I had a singular confidence in his honesty. I felt my most precious papers perfectly safe in his hands. Sometimes, to be sure, I could not, for the very soul of me, avoid falling into sudden spasmodic passions with him. For it was exceeding difficult to bear in mind all the time those strange peculiarities, privileges, and unheard of exemptions, forming the tacit stipulations on Bartleby's part under which he remained in my office. Now and then, in the eagerness of dispatching pressing business, I would inadvertently summon Bartleby, in a short, rapid tone, to put his finger, say, on the incipient tie of a bit of red tape with which I was about compressing some papers. Of course, from behind the screen the usual answer, "I prefer not to," was sure to come; and then, how could a human creature, with the common infirmities of our nature, refrain from bitterly exclaiming upon such perverseness—such unreasonableness. However, every added repulse of this sort which I received only tended to lessen the probability of my repeating the inadvertence.

Here it must be said, that according to the custom of most legal gentlemen occupying chambers in densely-populated law buildings, there were several keys to my door. One was kept by a woman residing in the attic, which person weekly scrubbed and daily swept and dusted my apartments. Another was kept by Turkey for convenience sake. The third I sometimes carried in my own pocket. The fourth I knew not who had.

Now, one Sunday morning I happened to go to Trinity Church, to hear a celebrated preacher, and finding myself rather early on the ground I thought I would walk around to my chambers for a while. Luckily I had my key with me; but upon applying it to the lock, I found it resisted by something inserted from the inside. Quite surprised, I called out; when to my consternation a key was turned from within; and thrusting his lean visage at me, and holding the door ajar, the apparition of Bartleby appeared, in his shirt sleeves, and otherwise in a strangely tattered deshabille, saying quietly that he was sorry, but he was deeply engaged just then, and—preferred not admitting me at present. In a brief word or two, he moreover added, that perhaps I had better walk around the block two or three times, and by that time he would probably have concluded his affairs.

Now, the utterly unsurmised appearance of Bartleby, tenanting my law-chambers of a Sunday morning, with his cadaverously gentlemanly *nonchalance,* yet withal firm and self-possessed, had such a strange effect upon me, that incontinently I slunk away from my own door, and did as desired. But not without sundry twinges of impotent rebellion against the mild effrontery of this unaccountable scrivener. Indeed, it was his wonderful mildness chiefly, which not only disarmed me, but unmanned me as it were. For I consider that one, for the time, is somehow unmanned when he tranquilly permits his hired clerk to dictate to him, and order him away from his own premises. Furthermore, I was full of uneasiness as to what Bartleby could possibly be doing in my office in his shirt sleeves, and in an otherwise dismantled condition of a Sunday morning. Was anything amiss going on? Nay, that was out of the question. It was not to be thought of for a moment that Bartleby was an immoral person. But what could he be doing there?—copying? Nay again, whatever might be his eccentricities, Bartleby was an eminently decorous person. He would be the last man to sit down to his desk in any state approaching to nudity. Besides, it was Sunday; and there was something about Bartleby that forbade the supposition that he would by any secular occupation violate the proprieties of the day.

Nevertheless, my mind was not pacified; and full of a restless curiosity, at last I returned to the door. Without hindrance I inserted my key, opened it, and entered. Bartleby was not to be seen. I looked round anxiously, peeped behind his screen; but it was very plain that he was gone. Upon more closely examining the place, I surmised that for an indefinite period Bartleby must have ate, dressed, and slept in my office, and that, too, without plate, mirror, or bed. The cushioned seat of a rickety old sofa in one corner bore the faint impression of a lean, reclining form. Rolled away under his desk, I found a blanket; under the empty grate, a blacking box and brush; on a chair, a tin basin, with soap and a ragged towel; in a newspaper a few crumbs of ginger-nuts and a morsel of cheese. Yes, thought I, it is evident enough that Bartleby has been making his home here, keeping bachelor's hall all by himself. Immediately then the thought came sweeping across me, what miserable friendlessness and loneliness are here revealed! His poverty is great; but his solitude, how horrible! Think of it. Of a Sunday, Wall Street is deserted as Petra;[2] and every night of every day it is an emptiness. This building, too, which of week-days hums with industry and life, at nightfall echoes with sheer vacancy, and all through Sunday is forlorn. And here Bartleby makes his home; sole spectator of a solitude which he has seen all populous —a sort of innocent and transformed Marius brooding among the ruins of Carthage!

For the first time in my life a feeling of over-powering stinging

---

[2] *Petra,* ancient city in Syria.

melancholy seized me. Before, I had never experienced aught but a not unpleasing sadness. The bond of a common humanity now drew me irresistibly to gloom. A fraternal melancholy! For both I and Bartleby were sons of Adam. I remembered the bright silks and sparkling faces I had seen that day, in gala trim, swan-like sailing down the Mississippi of Broadway; and I contrasted them with the pallid copyist, and thought to myself, Ah, happiness courts the light, so we deem the world is gay; but misery hides aloof, so we deem that misery there is none. These sad fancyings—chimeras, doubtless, of a sick and silly brain—led on to other and more special thoughts, concerning the eccentricities of Bartleby. Presentiments of strange discoveries hovered round me. The scrivener's pale form appeared to me laid out, among uncaring strangers, in its shivering winding sheet.

Suddenly I was attracted by Bartleby's closed desk, the key in open sight left in the lock.

I mean no mischief, seek the gratification of no heartless curiosity, thought I; besides, the desk is mine, and its contents, too, so I will make bold to look within. Everything was methodically arranged, the papers smoothly placed. The pigeon holes were deep, and removing the files of documents, I groped into their recesses. Presently I felt something there, and dragged it out. It was an old bandanna handkerchief, heavy and knotted. I opened it, and saw it was a saving's bank.

I now recalled all the quiet mysteries which I had noted in the man. I remembered that he never spoke but to answer; that, though at intervals he had considerable time to himself, yet I had never seen him reading—no, not even a newspaper; that for long periods he would stand looking out, at his pale window behind the screen, upon the dead brick wall; I was quite sure he never visited any refectory or eating house; while his pale face clearly indicated that he never drank beer like Turkey, or tea and coffee even, like other men; that he never went anywhere in particular that I could learn; never went out for a walk, unless, indeed, that was the case at present; that he had declined telling who he was, or whence he came, or whether he had any relatives in the world; that though so thin and pale, he never complained of ill health. And more than all, I remembered a certain unconscious air of pallid—how shall I call it?—of pallid haughtiness, say, or rather an austere reserve about him, which had positively awed me into my tame compliance with his eccentricities, when I had feared to ask him to do the slightest incidental thing for me, even though I might know, from his long-continued motionlessness, that behind his screen he must be standing in one of those dead-wall reveries of his.

Revolving all these things, and coupling them with the recently discovered fact, that he made my office his constant abiding place and home, and not forgetful of his morbid moodiness; revolving all these things, a prudential feeling began to steal over me. My first emotions had been those of pure melancholy and sincerest pity; but just in proportion as the forlornness of Bartleby grew and grew to my imagination, did that same melancholy merge into fear, that pity into repulsion. So true it is, and so terrible, too, that up to a certain point the thought or sight of misery enlists our best affections; but, in certain special cases, beyond that point it does not. They err who would assert that invariably this is owing to the inherent selfishness of the human heart. It rather proceeds from a certain hopelessness of remedying excessive and organic ill. To a sensitive being, pity is not seldom pain. And when at last it is perceived that such pity cannot lead to effectual succor, common sense bids the soul be rid of it. What I saw that morning persuaded me that the scrivener was the victim of inate and incurable disorder. I might give alms to his body; but his body did not pain him; it was his soul that suffered, and his soul I could not reach.

I did not accomplish the purpose of going to Trinity Church that morning. Somehow, the things I had seen disqualified me for the time from church-going. I walked homeward, thinking what I would do with Bartleby. Finally, I resolved upon this—I would put certain calm questions to him the next morning, touching his history, etc., and if he declined to answer them openly and unreservedly (and I supposed he would prefer not), then to give him a twenty dollar bill over and above whatever I might owe him, and tell him his services were no longer required; but that, if in any other way I could assist him, I would be happy to do so, especially if he desired to return to his native place, wherever that might be, I would willingly help to defray the expenses. Moreover, if, after reaching home, he found himself at any time in want of aid, a letter from him would be sure of a reply.

The next morning came.

"Bartleby," said I, gently calling to him behind his screen.

No reply.

"Bartleby," said I, in a still gentler tone, "come here; I am not going to ask you to do anything you would prefer not to do—I simply wish to speak to you."

Upon this he noiselessly slid into view.

"Will you tell me, Bartleby, where you were born?"

"I would prefer not to."

"Will you tell me *anything* about yourself?"

"I would prefer not to."

"But what reasonable objection can you have to speak to me? I feel friendly towards you."

He did not look at me while I spoke, but kept his glance fixed upon my bust of Cicero, which, as I then sat, was directly behind me, some six inches above my head.

"What is your answer, Bartleby," said I, after waiting a considerable time for a reply, during which his countenance remained immovable, only there was the faintest conceivable tremor of the white attenuated mouth.

"At present I prefer to give no answer," he said, and retired into his hermitage.

It was rather weak in me I confess, but his manner, on this occasion, nettled me. Not only did there seem to lurk in it a certain calm disdain, but his perverseness seemed ungrateful, considering the undeniable good usage and indulgence he had received from me.

Again I sat ruminating what I should do. Mortified as I was at his behavior, and resolved as I had been to dismiss him when I entered my office, nevertheless I strangely felt something superstitious knocking at my heart, and forbidding me to carry out my purpose, and denouncing me for a villain if I dared to breathe one bitter word against this forlornest of mankind. At last, familiarly drawing my chair behind his screen, I sat down and said: "Bartleby, never mind, then, about revealing your history; but let me entreat you, as a friend, to comply as far as may be with the usages of this office. Say now, you will help to examine papers to-morrow or next day: in short, say now, that in a day or two you will begin to be a little reasonable:—say so, Bartleby."

"At present I would prefer not to be a little reasonable," was his mildly cadaverous reply.

Just then the folding-doors opened, and Nippers approached. He seemed suffering from an unusually bad night's rest, induced by severer indigestion than common. He overheard those final words of Bartleby.

"*Prefer not,* eh?" gritted Nippers—"I'd *prefer* him, if I were you, sir," addressing me—"I'd *prefer* him; I'd give him preferences, the stubborn mule! What is it, sir, pray, that he *prefers* not to do now?"

Bartleby moved not a limb.

"Mr. Nippers," said I, "I'd prefer that you would withdraw for the present."

Somehow, of late, I had got into the way of involuntarily using this word "prefer" upon all sorts of not exactly suitable occasions. And I trembled to think that my contact with the scrivener had already and seriously affected me in a mental way. And what further and deeper aberration might it not yet produce? This apprehension had not been without efficacy in determining me to summary measures.

As Nippers, looking very sour and sulky, was departing, Turkey blandly and deferentially approached.

"With submission, sir," said he, "yesterday I was thinking abut Bartleby here, and I think that if he would but prefer to take a quart of good ale every day, it would do much towards mending him, and enabling him to assist in examining his papers."

"So you have got the word, too," said I, slightly excited.

"With submission, what word, sir," asked Turkey, respectfully crowding himself into the contracted space behind the screen, and by so doing, making me jostle the scrivener. "What word, sir?"

"I would prefer to be left alone here," said Bartleby, as if offended at being mobbed in his privacy.

"*That's* the word, Turkey," said I—"*that's* it."

"Oh, *prefer?* oh yes—queer word. I never use it myself. But, sir, as I was saying, if he would but prefer—"

"Turkey," interrupted I, "you will please withdraw."

"Oh, certainly, sir, if you prefer that I should."

As he opened the folding-door to retire, Nippers at his desk caught a glimpse of me, and asked whether I would prefer to have a certain paper copied on blue paper or white. He did not in the least roguishly accent the word prefer. It was plain that it involuntarily rolled from his tongue. I thought to myself, surely I must get rid of a demented man, who already has in some degree turned the tongues, if not the heads of myself and clerks. But I thought it prudent not to break the dismission at once.

The next day I noticed that Bartleby did nothing but stand at his window in his dead-wall revery. Upon asking him why he did not write, he said that he had decided upon doing no more writing.

"Why, how now? what next?" exclaimed I, "do no more writing?"

"No more."

"And what is the reason?"

"Do you not see the reason for yourself," he indifferently replied.

I looked steadfastly at thim, and perceived that his eyes looked dull and glazed. Instantly it occurred to me, that his unexampled diligence in copying by his dim window for the first few weeks of his stay with me might have temporarily impaired his vision.

I was touched. I said something in condolence with him. I hinted that of course he did wisely in abstaining from writing for a while; and urged him to embrace that opportunity of taking wholesome exercise in the open air. This, however, he did not do. A few days after this, my other clerks being absent, and being in a great hurry to dispatch certain letters by the mail, I thought that, having nothing else earthly to do, Bartleby would surely be less inflexible than usual, and carry these letters to the post-office. But he blankly declined. So, much to my inconvenience, I went myself.

Still added days went by. Whether Bartleby's eyes improved or not, I could not say. To all appearance, I thought they did. But when I asked him if they did, he vouchsafed no answer. At all events, he would do no copying. At last, in reply to my urgings, he informed me that he had permanently given up copying.

"What!" exclaimed I; "suppose your eyes should get entirely well—better than ever before—would you not copy then?"

"I have given up copying," he answered, and slid aside.

He remained as ever, a fixture in my chamber. Nay—if that were possible—he became still more of a fixture than before. What was to be done? He would do nothing in the office; why should he stay there? In plain fact, he had now become a millstone to me, not only useless as a necklace, but afflictive to bear. Yet I was sorry for him. I speak less than truth when I say that, on his own account, he occasioned me uneasiness. If he would but have named a single relative or friend, I would instantly have written, and urged their taking the poor fellow away to some convenient retreat. But he seemed alone, absolutely alone in the universe. A bit of wreck in the mid Atlantic. At length, necessities connected with my business tyrannized over all other considerations. Decently as I could, I told Bartleby that in six days time he must unconditionally leave the office. I warned him to take measures, in the interval, for procuring some other abode. I offered to assist him in this endeavor, if he himself would but take the first step towards a removal. "And when you finally quit me, Bartleby," added I, "I shall see that you go not away entirely unprovided. Six days from this hour, remember."

At the expiration of that period, I peeped behind the screen, and lo! Bartleby was there.

I buttoned up my coat, balanced myself; advanced slowly towards him, touched his shoulder, and said, "The time has come; you must quit this place; I am sorry for you; here is money; but you must go."

"I would prefer not," he replied, with his back still towards me.

"You *must*."

He remained silent.

Now I had an unbounded confidence in this man's common honesty. He had frequently restored to me sixpences and shillings carelessly dropped upon the floor, for I am apt to be very reckless in such shirt-button affairs. The proceeding, then, which followed will not be deemed extraordinary.

"Bartleby," said I, "I owe you twelve dollars on account; here are thirty-two; the odd twenty are yours—Will you take it?" and I handed the bills towards him.

But he made no motion.

"I will leave them here, then," putting them under a weight on the table. Then taking my hat and cane and going to the door, I tranquilly turned and added—"After you have removed your things from these offices, Bartleby, you will of course lock the door—since every one is now gone for the day but you—and if you please, slip your key underneath the mat, so that I may have it in the morning. I shall not see you again; so good-by to you. If, hereafter, in your new place of abode, I can be of any service to you, do not fail to advise me by letter. Good-by, Bartleby, and fare you well."

But he answered not a word; like the last column of some ruined temple, he remained standing mute and solitary in the middle of the otherwise deserted room.

As I walked home in a pensive mood, my vanity got the better of my pity. I could not but highly plume myself on my masterly management in getting rid of Bartleby. Masterly I call it, and such it must appear to any dispassionate thinker. The beauty of my procedure seemed to consist in its perfect quietness. There was no vulgar bullying, no bravado of any sort, no choleric hectoring, and striding to and fro across the apartment, jerking out vehement commands for Bartleby to bundle himself off with his beggarly traps. Nothing of the kind. Without loudly bidding Bartleby depart—as an inferior genius might have done—I *assumed* the ground that depart he must; and upon that assumption built all I had to say. The more I thought over my procedure, the more I was charmed with it. Nevertheless, next morning, upon awakening, I had my doubts—I had somehow slept off the fumes of vanity. One of the coolest and wisest hours a man has, is just after he awakes in the morning. My procedure seemed as sagacious as ever—but only in theory. How it would prove in practice—there was the rub. It was truly a beautiful thought to have assumed Bartleby's departure; but, after all, that assumption was simply my own, and none of Bartleby's. The great point was, not whether I had assumed that he would quit me, but whether he would prefer so to do. He was more a man of preferences than assumptions.

After breakfast, I walked down town, arguing the probabilities *pro* and *con*. One moment I thought it would prove a miserable failure, and Bartleby would be found all alive at my office as usual; the next moment it seemed certain that I should find his chair empty. And so I kept veering about. At the corner of Broadway and Canal Street, I saw quite an excited group of people standing in earnest conversation.

"I'll take odds he doesn't," said a voice as I passed.

"Doesn't go?—done!" said I, "put up your money."

I was instinctively putting my hand in my pocket to produce my own, when I remembered that this was an election day. The words I had overheard bore no reference to Bartleby, but to the success or nonsuccess of some candidate for the mayoralty. In my intent frame of mind, I had, as it were, imagined that all Broadway shared in my excitement, and were debating the same question with me. I passed on, very thankful that the uproar of the street screened my momentary absent-mindedness.

As I had intended, I was earlier than usual at my office door. I stood listening for a moment. All was still. He must be gone. I tried the knob. The door was locked. Yes, my procedure had worked to a charm; he indeed must be vanished. Yet a certain melancholy mixed with this: I was almost sorry for my brilliant success. I was fumbling under the door mat for the key, which Bartleby was to have left there for me, when accidentally my knee knocked against a panel, producing a summoning sound, and in response a voice came to me from within—"Not yet; I am occupied."

It was Bartleby.

I was thunderstruck. For an instant I stood like the man who, pipe in mouth, was killed one cloudless afternoon long ago in Virginia, by summer lightning; at his own warm open window he was killed, and remained leaning out there upon the dreamy afternoon, till some one touched him, when he fell.

"Not gone!" I murmured at last. But again obeying that wondrous ascendancy which the inscrutable scrivener had over me, and from which ascendancy, for all my chafing, I could not completely escape, I slowly went down stairs and out into the street, and while walking round the block, considered what I should next do in this unheard-of perplexity. Turn the man out by an actual thrusting I could not; to drive him away by calling him hard names would not do; calling in the police was an unpleasant idea; and yet, permit him to enjoy his cadaverous triumph over me—this, too, I could not think of. What was to be done? or, if nothing could be done, was there anything further that I could *assume* in the matter? Yes, as before I had prospectively assumed that Bartleby would depart, so now I might retrospectively assume that departed he was. In the legitimate carrying out of this assumption, I might enter my office in a great hurry, and pretending not to see Bartleby at all, walk straight against him as if he were air. Such a proceeding would in a singular degree have the appearance of a home-thrust. It was hardly possible that Bartleby could withstand such an application of the doctrine of assumptions. But upon second thoughts the success of the plan seemed rather dubious. I resolved to argue the matter over with him again.

"Bartleby," said I, entering the office, with a quietly severe expression, "I am seriously displeased. I am pained, Bartleby. I had thought better of you. I had imagined you of such a gentlemanly organization, that in any delicate dilemma a slight hint would suffice—in short, an assumption. But it appears I am deceived. Why," I added, unaffectedly starting, "you have not even touched that money yet," pointing to it, just where I had left it the evening previous.

He answered nothing.

"Will you, or will you not, quit me?" I now demanded in a sudden passion, advancing close to him.

"I would prefer *not* to quit you," he replied, gently emphasizing the *not*.

"What earthly right have you to stay here? Do you pay any rent? Do you pay my taxes? Or is this property yours?"

He answered nothing.

"Are you ready to go on and write now? Are your eyes recovered? Could you copy a small paper for me this morning? or help examine a few lines? or step round to the post-office? In a word, will you do anything at all, to give a coloring to your refusal to depart the premises?"

He silently retired into his hermitage.

I was now in such a state of nervous resentment that I thought it but prudent to check myself at present from further demonstrations. Bartleby and I were alone. I remembered the tragedy of the unfortunate Adams and the still more unfortunate Colt in the solitary office of the latter; and how poor Colt, being dreadfully incensed by Adams, and imprudently permitting himself to get wildly excited, was at unawares hurried into his fatal act—an act which certainly no man could possibly deplore more than the actor himself. Often it had occurred to me in my ponderings upon the subject, that had that altercation taken place in the public street, or at a private residence, it would not have terminated as it did. It was the circumstance of being alone in a solitary office, up stairs, of a building entirely unhallowed by humanizing domestic associations—an uncarpeted office, doubtless, of a dusty, haggard sort of appearance—this it must have been, which greatly helped to enhance the irritable desperation of the hapless Colt.[3]

But when this old Adam of resentment rose in me and tempted me concerning Bartleby, I grappled him and threw him. How? Why, simply by recalling the divine injunction: "A new commandment give I unto you, that ye love one another." Yes, this it was that saved me. Aside from higher considerations, charity often operates as a vastly wise and prudent principle—a great safeguard to its possessor. Men have committed murder for jealousy's sake, and anger's sake, and hatred's sake, and selfishness' sake, and spiritual pride's sake; but no man, that ever I heard of, ever committed a diabolical murder for

---

[3] *Adams . . . Colt*, a widely publicized murder-case in which John C. Colt killed Samuel Adams, in New York City, in January, 1842.

sweet charity's sake. Mere self-interest, then, if no better motive can be enlisted, should, especially with high-tempered men, prompt all beings to charity and philanthropy. At any rate, upon the occasion in question, I strove to drown my exasperated feelings towards the scrivener by benevolently construing his conduct. Poor fellow, poor fellow! thought I, he don't mean anything; and besides, he has seen hard times, and ought to be indulged.

I endeavored, also, immediately to occupy myself, and at the same time to comfort my despondency. I tried to fancy, that in the course of the morning, at such time as might prove agreeable to him, Bartleby, of his own free accord, would emerge from his hermitage and take up some decided line of march in the direction of the door. But no. Half-past twelve o'clock came; Turkey began to glow in the face, overturn his inkstand, and become generally obstreperous; Nippers abated down into quietude and courtesy; Ginger Nut munched his noon apple; and Bartleby remained standing at his window in one of his profoundest dead-wall reveries. Will it be credited? Ought I to acknowledge it? That afternoon I left the office without saying one further word to him.

Some days now passed, during which, at leisure intervals I looked a little into "Edwards on the Will," and "Priestly on Necessity." Under the circumstances, those books induced a salutary feeling. Gradually I slid into the persuasion that these troubles of mine, touching the scrivener, had been all predestinated from eternity, and Bartleby was billeted upon me for some mysterious purpose of an allwise Providence, which it was not for a mere mortal like me to fathom. Yes, Bartleby, stay there behind your screen, thought I; I shall persecute you no more; you are harmless and noiseless as any of these old chairs; in short, I never feel so private as when I know you are here. At last I see it, I feel it; I penetrate to the predestinated purpose of my life. I am content. Others may have loftier parts to enact; but my mission in this world, Bartleby, is to furnish you with office-room for such period as you may see fit to remain.

I believe that this wise and blessed frame of mind would have continued with me, had it not been for the unsolicited and uncharitable remarks obtruded upon me by my professional friends who visited the rooms. But thus it often is, that the constant friction of illiberal minds wears out at last the best resolves of the more generous. Though to be sure, when I reflected upon it, it was not strange that people entering my office should be struck by the peculiar aspect of the unaccountable Bartleby, and so be tempted to throw out some sinister observations concerning him. Sometimes an attorney, having business with me, and calling at my office, and finding no one but the scrivener there, would undertake to obtain some sort of precise information from him touching my whereabouts;

but without heeding his idle talk, Bartleby would remain standing immovable in the middle of the room. So after contemplating him in that position for a time, the attorney would depart, no wiser than he came.

Also, when a reference was going on, and the room full of lawyers and witnesses, and business driving fast, some deeply-occupied legal gentleman present, seeing Bartleby wholly unemployed, would request him to run round to his (the legal gentleman's) office and fetch some papers for him. Thereupon, Bartleby would tranquilly decline, and yet remain idle as before. Then the lawyer would give a great stare, and turn to me. And what could I say? At last I was made aware that all through the circle of my professional acquaintance, a whisper of wonder was running round, having reference to the strange creature I kept at my office. This worried me very much. And as the idea came upon me of his possibly turning out a long-lived man, and keep occupying my chambers, and denying my authority; and perplexing my visitors; and scandalizing my professional reputation; and casting a general gloom over the premises; keeping soul and body together to the last upon his savings (for doubtless he spent but half a dime a day), and in the end perhaps outlive me, and claim possession of my office by right of his perpetual occupancy: as all these dark anticipations crowded upon me more and more, and my friends continually intruded their relentless remarks upon the apparition in my room; a great change was wrought in me. I resolved to gather all my faculties together, and forever rid me of this intolerable incubus.

Ere revolving any complicated project, however, adapted to this end, I first simply suggested to Bartleby the propriety of his permanent departure. In a calm and serious tone, I commended the idea to his careful and mature consideration. But, having taken three days to meditate upon it, he apprised me, that his original determination remained the same; in short, that he still preferred to abide with me.

What shall I do? I now said to myself, buttoning up my coat to the last button. What shall I do? what ought I to do? what does conscience say I *should* do with this man, or, rather, ghost. Rid myself of him, I must; go, he shall. But how? You will not thrust him, the poor, pale, passive mortal—you will not thrust such a helpless creature out of your door? you will not dishonor yourself by such cruelty? No, I will not, I cannot do that. Rather would I let him live and die here, and then mason up his remains in the wall. What, then, will you do? For all your coaxing, he will not budge. Bribes he leaves under your own paper-weight on your table; in short, it is quite plain that he prefers to cling to you.

Then something severe, something unusual must be done. What! surely you will not have him collared by a constable, and commit his innocent pallor to the common jail? And upon what ground could you procure such a thing to be done?—a vagrant, is he? What! he a vagrant, a wanderer, who refuses to budge? It is because he will *not* be a vagrant, then, that you seek to count him *as* a vagrant. That is too absurd. No visible means of support: there I have him. Wrong again: for indubitably he *does* support himself, and that is the only unanswerable proof that any man can show of his possessing the means so to do. No more, then. Since he will not quit me, I must quit him. I will change my offices; I will move elsewhere, and give him fair notice, that if I find him on my new premises I will then proceed against him as a common trespasser.

Acting accordingly, next day I thus addressed him: "I find these chambers too far from the City Hall; the air is unwholesome. In a word, I propose to remove my offices next week, and shall no longer require your services. I tell you this now, in order that you may seek another place."

He made no reply, and nothing more was said.

On the appointed day I engaged carts and men, proceeded to my chambers, and, having but little furniture, everything was removed in a few hours. Throughout, the scrivener remained standing behind the screen, which I directed to be removed the last thing. It was withdrawn; and, being folded up like a huge folio, left him the motionless occupant of a naked room. I stood in the entry watching him a moment, while something from within me upbraided me.

I re-entered, with my hand in my pocket—and—and my heart in my mouth.

"Good-by, Bartleby; I am going—good-by, and God some way bless you; and take that," slipping something in his hand. But it dropped upon the floor, and then—strange to say—I tore myself from him whom I had so longed to be rid of.

Established in my new quarters, for a day or two I kept the door locked, and started at every footfall in the passages. When I returned to my rooms, after any little absence, I would pause at the threshold for an instant, and attentively listen, ere applying my key. But these fears were needless. Bartleby never came nigh me.

I thought all was going well, when a perturbed-looking stranger visited me, inquiring whether I was the person who had recently occupied rooms at No. — Wall Street.

Full of forebodings, I replied that I was.

"Then, sir," said the stranger, who proved a lawyer, "you are responsible for the man you left there. He refuses to do any copying; he refuses to do anything; he says he prefers not to; and he refuses to quit the premises."

"I am very sorry, sir," said I, with assumed tranquillity, but an inward tremor, "but, really, the man you allude to is nothing to me—he is no relation or apprentice of mine, that you should hold me responsible for him."

"In mercy's name, who is he?"

"I certainly cannot inform you. I know nothing about him. Formerly I employed him as a copyist; but he has done nothing for me now for some time past."

"I shall settle him, then—good morning, sir."

Several days passed, and I heard nothing more; and, though I often felt a charitable prompting to call at the place and see poor Bartleby, yet a certain squeamishness, of I know not what, withheld me.

All is over with him, by this time, thought I, at last, when, through another week, no further intelligence reached me. But, coming to my room the day after, I found several persons waiting at my door in a high state of nervous excitement.

"That's the man—here he comes," cried the foremost one, whom I recognized as the lawyer who had previously called upon me alone.

"You must take him away, sir, at once," cried a portly person among them, advancing upon me, and whom I knew to be the landlord of No. — Wall Street. "These gentlemen, my tenants, cannot stand it any longer; Mr. B——," pointing to the lawyer, "has turned him out of his room, and he now persists in haunting the building generally, sitting upon the banisters of the stairs by day, and sleeping in the entry by night. Everybody is concerned; clients are leaving the offices; some fears are entertained of a mob; something you must do, and that without delay."

Aghast at this torrent, I fell back before it, and would fain have locked myself in my new quarters. In vain I persisted that Bartleby was nothing to me—no more than to any one else. In vain—I was the last person known to have anything to do with him, and they held me to the terrible account. Fearful, then, of being exposed in the papers (as one person present obscurely threatened), I considered the matter, and, at length, said, that if the lawyer would give me a confidential interview with the scrivener, in his (the lawyer's) own room, I would, that afternoon, strive my best to rid them of the nuisance they complained of.

Going up stairs to my old haunt, there was Bartleby silently sitting upon the banister at the landing.

"What are you doing here, Bartleby?" said I.

"Sitting upon the banister," he mildly replied.

I motioned him into the lawyer's room, who then left us.

"Bartleby," said I, "are you aware that you are the cause of great tribulation to me, by persisting in occupying entry after being dismissed from the office?"

No answer.

"Now one of two things must take place. Either you must do something, or something must be done to you. Now what sort of business would you like to engage in? Would you like to re-engage in copying for some one?"

"No; I would prefer not to make any change."

"Would you like a clerkship in a dry-goods store?"

"There is too much confinement about that. No, I would not like a clerkship; but I am not particular."

"Too much confinement," I cried, "why you keep yourself confined all the time!"

"I would prefer not to take a clerkship," he rejoined, as if to settle that little item at once.

"How would a bar-tender's business suit you? There is no trying of the eye-sight in that."

"I would not like it at all; though, as I said before, I am not particular."

His unwonted wordiness inspirited me. I returned to the charge.

"Well, then, would you like to travel through the country collecting bills for the merchants? That would improve your health."

"No, I would prefer to be doing something else."

"How, then, would going as a companion to Europe, to entertain some young gentleman with your conversation—how would that suit you?"

"Not at all. It does not strike me that there is anything definite about that. I like to be stationary. But I am not particular."

"Stationary you shall be, then," I cried, now losing all patience, and, for the first time in all my exasperating connection with him, fairly flying into a passion. "If you do not go away from these premises before night, I shall feel bound—indeed, I *am* bound—*to—to—to* quit the premises myself!" I rather absurdly concluded, knowing not with what possible threat to try to frighten his immobility into compliance. Despairing of all further efforts, I was precipitately leaving him, when a final thought occurred to me—one which had not been wholly unindulged before.

"Bartleby," said I, in the kindest tone I could assume under such exciting circumstances, "will you go home with me now—not to my office, but my dwelling—and remain there till we can conclude upon some convenient arrangement for you at our leisure? Come, let us start now, right away."

"No: at present I would prefer not to make any change at all."

I answered nothing; but, effectually dodging every one by the suddenness and rapidity of my flight, rushed from the building, ran up Wall Street towards Broadway, and, jumping into the first omnibus, was soon removed from pursuit. As soon as tranquillity returned, I distinctly perceived that I had now done all that I possibly could, both in respect to the demands of the landlord and his tenants, and with regard to my own desire and sense of duty, to benefit Bartleby, and shield him from rude persecution. I now strove to be entirely care-free and quiescent; and my conscience justified me in the attempt; though, indeed, it was not so successful as I could have wished. So fearful was I of being again hunted out by the incensed landlord and his exasperated tenants, that, surrendering my business to Nippers, for a few days, I drove about the upper part of the town and through the suburbs, in my rockaway; crossed over to Jersey City and Hoboken, and paid fugitive visits to Manhattanville and Astoria. In fact, I almost lived in my rockaway for the time.

When again I entered my office, lo, a note from the landlord lay upon the desk. I opened it with trembling hands. It informed me that the writer had sent to the police, and had Bartleby removed to the Tombs as a vagrant. Moreover, since I knew more about him than any one else, he wished me to appear at that place, and make a suitable statement of the facts. These tidings had a conflicting effect upon me. At first I was indignant; but, at last, almost approved. The landlord's energetic, summary disposition, had led him to adopt a procedure which I do not think I would have decided upon myself; and yet, as a last resort, under such peculiar circumstances, it seemed the only plan.

As I afterwards learned, the poor scrivener, when told that he must be conducted to the Tombs, offered not the slightest obstacle, but, in his pale, unmoving way, silently acquiesced.

Some of the compassionate and curious bystanders joined the party; and headed by one of the constables arm in arm with Bartleby, the silent procession filed its way through all the noise, and heat, and joy of the roaring thoroughfares at noon.

The same day I received the note, I went to the Tombs, or, to speak more properly, the Halls of Justice. Seeking the right officer, I stated the purpose of my call, and was informed that the individual I described was, indeed, within. I then assured the functionary that Bartleby was a perfectly honest man, and greatly to be compassionated, however unaccountably eccentric. I narrated all I knew, and closed by suggesting the idea of letting him remain in as indulgent confinement as possible, till something less harsh might be done— though, indeed, I hardly knew what. At all events, if nothing else could be decided upon, the almshouse must receive him. I then begged to have an interview.

Being under no disgraceful charge, and quite serene and harmless in all his ways, they had permitted him freely to wander about the prison, and, especially, in the inclosed grass-platted yards thereof. And so I found him there, standing all alone in the quietest of the yards, his face towards a high wall, while all around, from the narrow slits of the jail windows, I thought I saw peering out upon him the eyes of murderers and thieves.

"Bartleby!"

"I know you," he said without looking round—"and I want nothing to say to you."

"It was not I that brought you here, Bartleby," said I, keenly pained at his implied suspicion. "And to you, this should not be so vile a place. Nothing reproachful attaches to you by being here. And see, it is not so sad a place as one might think. Look, there is the sky, and here is the grass."

"I know where I am," he replied, but would say nothing more, and so I left him.

As I entered the corridor again, a broad meat-like man, in an apron, accosted me, and, jerking his thumb over his shoulder, said—"Is that your friend?"

"Yes."

"Does he want to starve? If he does, let him live on the prison fare, that's all."

"Who are you?" asked I, not knowing what to make of such an unofficially speaking person in such a place.

"I am the grub-man. Such gentlemen as have friends here, hire me to provide them with something good to eat."

"Is this so?" said I, turning to the turnkey.

He said it was.

"Well, then," said I, slipping some silver into the grub-man's hands (for so they called him), "I want you to give particular attention to my friend there; let him have the best dinner you can get. And you must be as polite to him as possible."

"Introduce me, will you?" said the grub-man, looking at me with an expression which seemed to say he was all impatience for an opportunity to give a specimen of his breeding.

Thinking it would prove of benefit to the scrivener, I acquiesced; and, asking the grub-man his name, went up with him to Bartleby.

"Bartleby, this is a friend; you will find him very useful to you."

"Your sarvant, sir, your sarvant," said the grub-man, making a low salutation behind his apron. "Hope you find it pleasant here, sir; nice grounds—cool apartments—hope you'll stay with us some time— try to make it agreeable. What will you have for dinner to-day?"

"I prefer not to dine to-day," said Bartleby, turning away. "It would disagree with me; I am unused to dinners." So saying, he slowly moved to the other side of the inclosure, and took up a position fronting the dead-wall.

"How's this?" said the grub-man, addressing me with a stare of astonishment, "He's odd, ain't he?"

"I think he is a little deranged," said I, sadly.

"Deranged? deranged is it? Well, now, upon my word, I thought that friend of yourn was a gentleman forger; they are always pale and genteel-like, them forgers. I can't help pity 'em—can't help it, sir. Did you know Monroe Edwards?" he added, touchingly, and paused. Then, laying his hand piteously on my shoulder, sighed, "he died of consumption at Sing-Sing. So you weren't acquainted with Monroe?"

"No, I was never socially acquainted with any forgers. But I cannot stop longer. Look to my friend yonder. You will not lose by it. I will see you again."

Some few days after this, I again obtained admission to the Tombs, and went through the corridors in quest of Bartleby; but without finding him.

"I saw him coming from his cell not long ago," said a turnkey, "may be he's gone to loiter in the yards."

So I went in that direction.

"Are you looking for the silent man?" said another turnkey, passing me. "Yonder he lies—sleeping in the yard there. 'Tis not twenty minutes since I saw him lie down."

The yard was entirely quiet. It was not accessible to the common prisoners. The surrounding walls, of amazing thickness, kept off all sounds behind them. The Egyptian character of the masonry weighed upon me with its gloom. But a soft imprisoned turf grew under foot. The heart of the eternal pyramids, it seemed, wherein, by some strange magic, through the clefts, grass-seed, dropped by birds, had sprung.

Strangely huddled at the base of the wall, his knees drawn up, and lying on his side, his head touching the cold stones, I saw the wasted Bartleby. But nothing stirred. I paused; then went close up to him; stooped over, and saw that his dim eyes were open; otherwise he seemed profoundly sleeping. Something prompted me to touch him. I felt his hand, when a tingling shiver ran up my arm and down my spine to my feet.

The round face of the grub-man peered upon me now. "His dinner is ready. Won't he dine to-day, either? Or does he live without dining?"

"Lives without dining," said I, and closed the eyes.

"Eh!—He's asleep, ain't he?"

"With kings and counselors," murmured I.

⌘

There would seem little need for proceeding further in this history. Imagination will readily supply the meagre recital of poor Bartleby's interment. But, ere parting with the reader, let me say, that if this little narrative has sufficiently interested him, to awaken curiosity as to who Bartleby was, and what manner of life he led prior to the present narrator's making his acquaintance, I can only reply, that in such curiosity I fully share, but am wholly unable to gratify it. Yet here I hardly know whether I should divulge one little item of rumor, which came to my ear a few months after the scrivener's decease. Upon what basis it rested, I could never ascertain; and hence, how true it is I cannot now tell. But, inasmuch as this vague report has not been without a certain suggestive interest to me, however sad, it may prove the same with some others; and so I will briefly mention it. The report was this: that Bartleby had been a subordinate clerk in the Dead Letter Office at Washington, from which he had been suddenly removed by a change in the administration. When I think over this rumor, hardly can I express the emotions which seize me. Dead letters! does it not sound like dead men? Conceive a man by nature and misfortune prone to a pallid hopelessness, can any business seem more fitted to heighten it than that of continually handling these dead letters, and assorting them for the flames? For by the cartload they are annually burned. Sometimes from out the folded paper the pale clerk takes a ring—the finger it was meant for, perhaps, moulders in the grave; a bank-note sent in swiftest charity—he whom it would relieve, nor eats nor hungers any more; pardon for those who died despairing; hope for those who died unhoping; good tidings for those who died stifled by unrelieved calamities. On errands of life, these letters speed to death.

Ah, Bartleby! Ah, humanity!

QUESTIONS

1. The narrator of "Bartleby the Scrivener" begins his narration with the word *I* and ends it with the word *humanity*. We may wonder, therefore, if the events that form the conflict and climax of the story have altered the narrator's vision to allow his attention to shift from himself to others. If so, how did this happen? The following questions may help you develop your answer.

2. We note that the narrator begins his tale by introducing himself. Why does he do so? What does he reveal as his goals? What things does he seem to value most highly?

3. We might ask what tone of voice the narrator is using in this early part of the story. (Paragraph five may be especially helpful here.)

4. We then look at his introduction of his office and of his first staff member, Turkey. How does the lawyer/narrator act toward Turkey? What reasons does he give for acting as he does? Do his actions seem to match his reasons? What impression of the lawyer's character do we receive?

5. We then look at his introductions of Nippers and Ginger Nut, and end our study of the tale's introductory section by asking how the narrator's characterization of his three employees, and our impression of his interactions

with them, prepare the way for the introduction of Bartleby and for the narrator's response to him and to his behavior.

6. Having seen how the narrator prepares the way for the introduction of his main character, we now look at the first episodes involving that character (pp. 62–67). How well does Bartleby fit into our picture of the office? What does this do for our sense of him and of his relationship with his employer?

7. We next ask, what is the turning point of the story? How does it change the narrator's view of Bartleby? What emotions does it raise in him? What action does it prompt him to take? What are the results of that action?

8. We then examine the story's progress from this turning-point to Bartleby's death. We ask ourselves, what changes are taking place in the tone of the narrative? the actions? the characterizations? We examine our reactions to these changes and developments. Have we been prepared for them? Can we accept them, or do we find them out of character or hard to believe? How do we react to Bartleby's death? Has the death been made to seem inevitable? Does it seem appropriate that the narrator be the one to discover it? How do we feel now about the narrator's relation to Bartleby?

9. At this point, too, we might notice the use of walls to set scenes throughout the story. This will let us glance at the whole story once more and will give us a good key for discussing some of the shifts in tone and atmosphere that occur as the story progresses. It will also let us sum up some of our impressions of Bartleby, since he is the character most closely associated with these walls. What is the effect on us of the combination of walls and Bartleby?

10. Similarly, we might look at mentions of money throughout the story. What character is most closely associated with them? What characterization do we draw from this association?

11. We must look as well at the after-note that ends the story, and ask what it adds to our sense of Bartleby, the narrator, and the story.

12. And then we must sum up our thoughts for ourselves. Has the narrator changed during the story? And, if he has, what do we make of the change?

13. Another way to approach the story would be to look at the effects of keeping Bartleby so sketchily characterized. We might ask how essential this pared-down characterization is to the story; how the narrator's sense of his own lack of knowledge about Bartleby affects him; and how it affects our feelings toward Bartleby, toward the narrator, and toward the relationship that develops between the two men. We might also ask whether the characterization given Bartleby suggests any symbolic values for Bartleby, the narrator, or their relationship; or whether you feel the story is better dealt with as a realistic tale.

CHARLOTTE PERKINS GILMAN (1860–1935)

The Yellow Wall-Paper

It is very seldom that mere ordinary people like John and myself secure ancestral halls for the summer.

A colonial mansion, a hereditary estate, I would say a haunted house, and reach the height of romantic felicity—but that would be asking too much of fate!

Still I will proudly declare that there is something queer about it.

Else, why should it be let so cheaply? And why have stood so long untenanted?

John laughs at me, of course, but one expects that in marriage.

John is practical in the extreme. He has no patience with faith, an intense horror of superstition, and he scoffs openly at any talk of things not to be felt and seen and put down in figures.

John is a physician, and *perhaps*—(I would not say it to a living soul, of course, but this is dead paper and a great relief to my mind)—*perhaps* that is one reason I do not get well faster.

You see he does not believe I am sick!

And what can one do?

If a physician of high standing, and one's own husband, assures friends and relatives that there is really nothing the matter with one but temporary nervous depression—a slight hysterical tendency—what is one to do?

My brother is also a physician, and also of high standing, and he says the same thing.

So I take phosphates or phosphites—whichever it is, and tonics, and journeys, and air, and exercise, and am absolutely forbidden to "work" until I am well again.

Personally, I disagree with their ideas.

Personally, I believe that congenial work, with excitement and change, would do me good.

But what is one to do?

I did write for a while in spite of them; but it *does* exhaust me a good deal—having to be so sly about it, or else meet with heavy opposition.

I sometimes fancy that in my condition if I had less opposition and more society and stimulus—but John says the very worst thing I can do is to think about my condition, and I confess it always makes me feel bad.

So I will let it alone and talk about the house.

The most beautiful place! It is quite alone, standing well back from the road, quite three miles from the village. It makes me think of English places that you read about, for there are hedges and walls and gates that lock, and lots of separate little houses for the gardeners and people.

There is a *delicious* garden! I never saw such a garden—large and shady, full of box-bordered paths, and lined with long grape-covered arbors with seats under them.

There were greenhouses, too, but they are all broken now.

There was some legal trouble, I believe, something about the heirs and coheirs; anyhow, the place has been empty for years.

That spoils my ghostliness, I am afraid, but I don't care—there is something strange about the house—I can feel it.

I even said so to John one moonlight evening, but he said what I felt was a *draught*, and shut the window.

I get unreasonably angry with John sometimes. I'm sure I never used to be so sensitive. I think it is due to this nervous condition.

But John says if I feel so, I shall neglect proper self-control; so I take pains to control myself—before him, at least, and that makes me very tired.

I don't like our room a bit. I wanted one downstairs that opened on the piazza and had roses all over the window, and such pretty old-fashioned chintz hangings! but John would not hear of it.

He said there was only one window and not room for two beds, and no near room for him if he took another.

He is very careful and loving, and hardly lets me stir without special direction.

I have a schedule prescription for each hour in the day; he takes all care from me, and so I feel basely ungrateful not to value it more.

He said we came here solely on my account, that I was to have perfect rest and all the air I could get. "Your exercise depends on your strength, my dear," said he, "and your food somewhat on your appetite; but air you can absorb all the time." So we took the nursery at the top of the house.

It is a big, airy room, the whole floor nearly, with windows that look all ways, and air and sunshine galore. It was nursery first and then playroom and gymnasium, I should judge; for the windows are barred for little children, and there are rings and things in the walls.

The paint and paper look as if a boys' school had used it. It is stripped off—the paper—in great patches all around the head of my bed, about as far as I can reach, and in a great place on the other side of the room low down. I never saw a worse paper in my life.

One of those sprawling flamboyant patterns committing every artistic sin.

It is dull enough to confuse the eye in following, pronounced enough to constantly irritate and provoke study, and when you follow the lame uncertain curves for a little distance they suddenly commit suicide—plunge off at outrageous angles, destroy themselves in unheard of contradictions.

The color is repellent, almost revolting; a smouldering unclean yellow, strangely faded by the slow-turning sunlight.

It is a dull yet lurid orange in some places, a sickly sulphur tint in others.

No wonder the children hated it! I should hate it myself if I had to live in this room long.

There comes John, and I must put this away,—he hates to have me write a word.

We have been here two weeks, and I haven't felt like writing before, since that first day.

I am sitting by the window now, up in this atrocious nursery, and there is nothing to hinder my writing as much as I please, save lack of strength.

John is away all day, and even some nights when his cases are serious.

I am glad my case is not serious!

But these nervous troubles are dreadfully depressing.

John does not know how much I really suffer. He knows there is no *reason* to suffer, and that satisfies him.

Of course it is only nervousness. It does weigh on me so not to do my duty in any way!

I meant to be such a help to John, such a real rest and comfort, and here I am a comparative burden already!

Nobody would believe what an effort it is to do what little I am able,—to dress and entertain, and order things.

It is fortunate Mary is so good with the baby. Such a dear baby!

And yet I *cannot* be with him, it makes me so nervous.

I suppose John never was nervous in his life. He laughs at me so about this wall-paper!

At first he meant to repaper the room, but afterwards he said that I was letting it get the better of me, and that nothing was worse for a nervous patient than to give way to such fancies.

He said that after the wall-paper was changed it would be the heavy bedstead, and then the barred windows, and then that gate at the head of the stairs, and so on.

"You know the place is doing you good," he said, "and really, dear, I don't care to renovate the house just for a three months' rental."

"Then do let us go downstairs," I said, "there are such pretty rooms there."

Then he took me in his arms and called me a blessed little goose, and said he would go down to the cellar, if I wished, and have it whitewashed into the bargain.

But he is right enough about the beds and windows and things.

It is an airy and comfortable room as any one need wish, and, of course, I would not be so silly as to make him uncomfortable just for a whim.

I'm really getting quite fond of the big room, all but that horrid paper.

Out of one window I can see the garden, those mysterious deep-shaded arbors, the riotous old-fashioned flowers, and bushes and gnarly trees.

Out of another I get a lovely view of the bay and a little private wharf belonging to the estate. There is a beautiful shaded lane that runs down there from the house. I always fancy I see people walking in these numerous paths and arbors, but John has cautioned me not to give way to fancy in the least. He says that with my imaginative power and habit of story-making, a nervous weakness like mine is sure to lead to all manner of excited fancies, and that I ought to use my will and good sense to check the tendency. So I try.

I think sometimes that if I were only well enough to write a little it would relieve the press of ideas and rest me.

But I find I get pretty tired when I try.

It is so discouraging not to have any advice and companionship about my work. When I get really well, John says we will ask Cousin Henry and Julia down for a long visit; but he says he would as soon put fireworks in my pillow-case as to let me have those stimulating people about now.

I wish I could get well faster.

But I must not think about that. This paper looks to me as if it *knew* what a vicious influence it had!

There is a recurrent spot where the pattern lolls like a broken neck and two bulbous eyes stare at you upside down.

I get positively angry with the impertinence of it and the everlasting-ness. Up and down and sideways they crawl, and those absurd, unblinking eyes are everywhere. There is one place where two breadths didn't match, and the eyes go all up and down the line, one a little higher than the other.

I never saw so much expression in an inanimate thing before, and we all know how much expression they have! I used to lie awake as a child and get more entertainment and terror out of blank walls and plain furniture than most children could find in a toy-store.

I remember what a kindly wink the knobs of our big, old bureau used to have, and there was one chair that always seemed like a strong friend.

I used to feel that if any of the other things looked too fierce I could always hop into that chair and be safe.

The furniture in this room is no worse than inharmonious, however, for we had to bring it all from downstairs. I suppose when this was used as a playroom they had to take the nursery things out, and no wonder! I never saw such ravages as the children have made here.

The wall-paper, as I said before, is torn off in spots, and it sticketh closer than a brother—they must have had perseverance as well as hatred.

Then the floor is scratched and gouged and splintered, the plaster itself is dug out here and there, and this great heavy bed which is all we found in the room, looks as if it had been through the wars.

But I don't mind it a bit—only the paper.

There comes John's sister. Such a dear girl as she is, and so careful of me! I must not let her find me writing.

She is a perfect and enthusiastic housekeeper, and hopes for no better profession. I verily believe she thinks it is the writing which made me sick!

But I can write when she is out, and see her a long way off from these windows.

There is one that commands the road, a lovely shaded winding road, and one that just looks off over the country. A lovely country, too, full of great elms and velvet meadows.

This wall-paper has a kind of sub-pattern in a different shade, a particularly irritating one, for you can only see it in certain lights, and not clearly then.

But in the places where it isn't faded and where the sun is just so—I can see a strange, provoking, formless sort of figure, that seems to skulk about behind that silly and conspicuous front design.

There's sister on the stairs!

Well, the Fourth of July is over! The people are all gone and I am tired out. John thought it might do me good to see a little company, so we just had mother and Nellie and the children down for a week.

Of course I didn't do a thing. Jennie sees to everything now.

But it tired me all the same.

John says if I don't pick up faster he shall send me to Weir Mitchell in the fall.

But I don't want to go there at all. I had a friend who was in his hands once, and she says he is just like John and my brother, only more so!

Besides, it is such an undertaking to go so far.

I don't feel as if it was worth while to turn my hand over for anything, and I'm getting dreadfully fretful and querulous.

I cry at nothing, and cry most of the time.

Of course I don't when John is here, or anybody else, but when I am alone.

And I am alone a good deal just now. John is kept in town very often by serious cases, and Jennie is good and lets me alone when I want her to.

So I walk a little in the garden or down that lovely lane, sit on the porch under the roses, and lie down up here a good deal.

I'm getting really fond of the room in spite of the wall-paper. Perhaps *because* of the wall-paper.

It dwells in my mind so!

I lie here on this great immovable bed—it is nailed down, I believe—and follow that pattern about by the hour. It is as good as gymnastics, I assure you. I start, we'll say, at the bottom, down in the corner over there where it has not been touched, and I determine for the thousandth time that I *will* follow that pointless pattern to some sort of a conclusion.

I know a little of the principle of design, and I know this thing was not arranged on any laws of radiation, or alternation, or repetition, or symmetry, or anything else that I ever heard of.

It is repeated, of course, by the breadths, but not otherwise.

Looked at in one way each breadth stands alone, the bloated curves and flourishes—a kind of "debased Romanesque" with *delirium tremens*—go waddling up and down in isolated columns of fatuity.

But, on the other hand, they connect diagonally, and the sprawling outlines run off in great slanting waves of optic horror, like a lot of wallowing seaweeds in full chase.

The whole thing goes horizontally, too, at least it seems so, and I exhaust myself in trying to distinguish the order of its going in that direction.

They have used a horizontal breadth for a frieze, and that adds wonderfully to the confusion.

There is one end of the room where it is almost intact, and there, when the crosslights fade and the low sun shines directly upon it, I can almost fancy radiation after all,—the interminable grotesques seem to form around a common centre and rush off in headlong plunges of equal distraction.

It makes me tired to follow it. I will take a nap I guess.

I don't know why I should write this.

I don't want to.

I don't feel able.

And I know John would think it absurd. But I *must* say what I feel and think in some way—it is such a relief!

But the effort is getting to be greater than the relief.

Half the time now I am awfully lazy, and lie down ever so much.

John says I mustn't lose my strength, and has me take cod liver oil and lots of tonics and things, to say nothing of ale and wine and rare meat.

Dear John! He loves me very dearly, and hates to have me sick. I tried to have a real earnest reasonable talk with him the other day, and tell him how I wish he would let me go and make a visit to Cousin Henry and Julia.

But he said I wasn't able to go, nor able to stand it after I got there; and I did not make out a very good case for myself, for I was crying before I had finished.

It is getting to be a great effort for me to think straight. Just this nervous weakness I suppose.

And dear John gathered me up in his arms, and just carried me upstairs and laid me on the bed, and sat by me and read to me till it tired my head.

He said I was his darling and his comfort and all he had, and that I must take care of myself for his sake, and keep well.

He says no one but myself can help me out of it, that I must use my will and self-control and not let any silly fancies run away with me.

There's one comfort, the baby is well and happy, and does not have to occupy this nursery with the horrid wall-paper.

If we had not used it, that blessed child would have! What a fortunate escape! Why, I wouldn't have a child of mine, an impressionable little thing, live in such a room for worlds.

I never thought of it before, but it is lucky that John kept me here after all, I can stand it so much easier than a baby, you see.

Of course I never mention it to them any more—I am too wise,—but I keep watch of it all the same.

There are things in that paper that nobody knows but me, or ever will.

Behind that outside pattern the dim shapes get clearer every day.

It is always the same shape, only very numerous.

And it is like a woman stooping down and creeping about behind that pattern. I don't like it a bit. I wonder—I begin to think—I wish John would take me away from here!

It is so hard to talk with John about my case, because he is so wise, and because he loves me so.

But I tried it last night.

It was moonlight. The moon shines in all around just as the sun does.

I hate to see it sometimes, it creeps so slowly, and always comes in by one window or another.

John was asleep and I hated to waken him, so I kept still and watched the moonlight on that undulating wall-paper till I felt creepy.

The faint figure behind seemed to shake the pattern, just as if she wanted to get out.

I got up softly and went to feel and see if the paper *did* move, and when I came back John was awake.

"What is it, little girl?" he said. "Don't go walking about like that—you'll get cold."

I thought it was a good time to talk, so I told him that I really was not gaining here, and that I wished he would take me away.

"Why darling!" said he, "our lease will be up in three weeks, and I can't see how to leave before.

"The repairs are not done at home, and I cannot possibly leave town just now. Of course if you were in any danger, I could and would, but you really are better, dear, whether you can see it or not. I am a doctor, dear, and I know. You are gaining flesh and color, your appetite is better, I feel really much easier about you."

"I don't weigh a bit more," said I, "nor as much; and my appetite may be better in the evening when you are here, but it is worse in the morning when you are away!"

"Bless her little heart!" said he with a big hug, "she shall be as sick as she pleases! But now let's improve the shining hours by going to sleep, and talk about it in the morning!"

"And you won't go away?" I asked gloomily.

"Why, how can I, dear? It is only three weeks more and then we will take a nice little trip of a few days while Jennie is getting the house ready. Really dear you are better!"

"Better in body perhaps—" I began, and stopped short, for he sat up straight and looked at me with such a stern, reproachful look that I could not say another word.

"My darling," said he, "I beg of you, for my sake and for our child's sake, as well as for your own, that you will never for one instant let that idea enter your mind! There is nothing so dangerous, so fascinating, to a temperament like yours. It is a false and foolish fancy. Can you not trust me as a physician when I tell you so?"

So of course I said no more on that score, and we went to sleep before long. He thought I was asleep first, but I wasn't, and lay there for hours trying to decide whether that front pattern and the back pattern really did move together or separately.

On a pattern like this, by daylight, there is a lack of sequence, a defiance of law, that is a constant irritant to a normal mind.

The color is hideous enough, and unreliable enough, and infuriating enough, but the pattern is torturing.

You think you have mastered it, but just as you get well underway in following, it turns a back-somersault and there you are. It slaps you in the face, knocks you down, and tramples upon you. It is like a bad dream.

The outside pattern is a florid arabesque, reminding one of a fungus. If you can imagine a toadstool in joints, an interminable string of toadstools, budding and sprouting in endless convolutions—why, that is something like it.

That is, sometimes!

There is one marked peculiarity about this paper, a thing nobody seems to notice but myself, and that is that it changes as the light changes.

When the sun shoots in through the east window—I always watch for that first long, straight ray—it changes so quickly that I never can quite believe it.

That is why I watch it always.

By moonlight—the moon shines in all night when there is a moon—I wouldn't know it was the same paper.

At night in any kind of light, in twilight, candle light, lamplight, and worst of all by moonlight, it becomes bars! The outside pattern I mean, and the woman behind it is as plain as can be.

I didn't realize for a long time what the thing was that showed behind, that dim sub-pattern, but now I am quite sure it is a woman.

By daylight she is subdued, quiet. I fancy it is the pattern that keeps her so still. It is so puzzling. It keeps me quiet by the hour.

I lie down ever so much now. John says it is good for me, and to sleep all I can.

Indeed he started the habit by making me lie down for an hour after each meal.

It is a very bad habit I am convinced, for you see I don't sleep.

And that cultivates deceit, for I don't tell them I'm awake—O no!

The fact is I am getting a little afraid of John.

He seems very queer sometimes, and even Jennie has an inexplicable look.

It strikes me occasionally, just as a scientific hypothesis,—that perhaps it is the paper!

I have watched John when he did not know I was looking, and come into the room suddenly on the most innocent excuses, and I've caught him several times *looking at the paper!* And Jennie too. I caught Jennie with her hand on it once.

She didn't know I was in the room, and when I asked her in a quiet, a very quiet voice, with the most restrained manner possible, what she was doing with the paper—she turned around as if she had been caught stealing, and looked quite angry—asked me why I should frighten her so!

Then she said that the paper stained everything it touched, that she had found yellow smooches on all my clothes and John's, and she wished we would be more careful!

Did not that sound innocent? But I know she was studying that pattern, and I am determined that nobody shall find it out but myself!

Life is very much more exciting now than it used to be. You see I have something more to expect, to look forward to, to watch. I really do eat better, and am more quiet than I was.

John is so pleased to see me improve! He laughed a little the other day, and said I seemed to be flourishing in spite of my wall-paper.

I turned it off with a laugh. I had no intention of telling him it was *because* of the wall-paper—he would make fun of me. He might even want to take me away.

I don't want to leave now until I have found it out. There is a week more, and I think that will be enough.

I'm feeling ever so much better! I don't sleep much at night, for it is so interesting to watch developments; but I sleep a good deal in the daytime.

In the daytime it is tiresome and perplexing.

There are always new shoots on the fungus, and new shades of yellow all over it. I cannot keep count of them, though I have tried conscientiously.

It is the strangest yellow, that wall-paper! It makes me think of all the yellow things I ever saw—not beautiful ones like buttercups, but old foul, bad yellow things.

But there is something else about that paper—the smell! I noticed it the moment we came into the room, but with so much air and sun it was not bad. Now we have had a week of fog and rain, and whether the windows are open or not, the smell is here.

It creeps all over the house.

I find it hovering in the dining-room, skulking in the parlor, hiding in the hall, lying in wait for me on the stairs.

It gets into my hair.

Even when I go to ride, if I turn my head suddenly and surprise it—there is that smell!

Such a peculiar odor, too! I have spent hours in trying to analyze it, to find what it smelled like.

It is not bad—at first, and very gentle, but quite the subtlest, most enduring odor I ever met.

In this damp weather it is awful, I wake up in the night and find it hanging over me.

It used to disturb me at first. I thought seriously of burning the house—to reach the smell.

But now I am used to it. The only thing I can think of that it is like is the *color* of the paper! A yellow smell.

There is a very funny mark on this wall, low down, near the mopboard. A streak that runs round the room. It goes behind every piece of furniture, except the bed, a long, straight, even *smooch*, as if it had been rubbed over and over.

I wonder how it was done and who did it, and what they did it for. Round and round and round—round and round and round—it makes me dizzy!

I really have discovered something at last.

Through watching so much at night, when it changes so, I have finally found out.

The front pattern *does* move—and no wonder! The woman behind shakes it!

Sometimes I think there are a great many women behind, and sometimes only one, and she crawls around fast, and her crawling shakes it all over.

Then in the very bright spots she keeps still, and in the very shady spots she just takes hold of the bars and shakes them hard.

And she is all the time trying to climb through. But nobody could climb through that pattern—it strangles so; I think that is why it has so many heads.

They get through, and then the pattern strangles them off and turns them upside down, and makes their eyes white!

If those heads were covered or taken off it would not be half so bad.

I think that woman gets out in the daytime!

And I'll tell you why—privately—I've seen her!

I can see her out of every one of my windows!

It is the same woman, I know, for she is always creeping, and most women do not creep by daylight.

I see her on that long road under the trees, creeping along, and when a carriage comes she hides under the blackberry vines.

I don't blame her a bit. It must be very humiliating to be caught creeping by daylight!

I always lock the door when I creep by daylight. I can't do it at night, for I know John would suspect something at once.

And John is so queer now, that I don't want to irritate him. I wish he would take another room! Besides, I don't want anybody to get that woman out at night but myself.

I often wonder if I could see her out of all the windows at once.

But, turn as fast as I can, I can only see out of one at one time.

And though I always see her, she *may* be able to creep faster than I can turn!

I have watched her sometimes away off in the open country, creeping as fast as a cloud shadow in a high wind.

If only that top pattern could be gotten off from the under one! I mean to try it, little by little.

I have found out another funny thing, but I shan't tell it this time! It does not do to trust people too much.

There are only two more days to get this paper off, and I believe John is beginning to notice. I don't like the look in his eyes.

And I heard him ask Jennie a lot of professional questions about me. She had a very good report to give.

She said I slept a good deal in the daytime.

John knows I don't sleep very well at night, for all I'm so quiet!

He asked me all sorts of questions, too, and pretended to be very loving and kind.

As if I couldn't see through him!

Still, I don't wonder he acts so, sleeping under this paper for three months.

It only interests me, but I feel sure John and Jennie are secretly affected by it.

Hurrah! This is the last day, but it is enough. John is to stay in town over night, and won't be out until this evening.

Jennie wanted to sleep with me—the sly thing! but I told her I should undoubtedly rest better for a night all alone.

That was clever, for really I wasn't alone a bit! As soon as it was moonlight and that poor thing began to crawl and shake the pattern, I got up and ran to help her.

I pulled and she shook, I shook and she pulled, and before morning we had peeled off yards of that paper.

A strip about as high as my head and half around the room.

And then when the sun came and that awful pattern began to laugh at me, I declared I would finish it to-day!

We go away to-morrow, and they are moving all my furniture down again to leave things as they were before.

Jennie looked at the wall in amazement, but I told her merrily that I did it out of pure spite at the vicious thing.

She laughed and said she wouldn't mind doing it herself, but I must not get tired.

How she betrayed herself that time!

But I am here, and no person touches this paper but me,—not *alive!*

She tried to get me out of the room—it was too patent! But I said it was so quiet and empty and clean now that I believed I would lie down again and sleep all I could; and not to wake me even for dinner—I would call when I woke.

So now she is gone, and the servants are gone, and the things are gone, and there is nothing left but that great bedstead nailed down, with the canvas mattress we found on it.

We shall sleep downstairs to-night, and take the boat home to-morrow.

I quite enjoy the room, now it is bare again.

How those children did tear about here!

This bedstead is fairly gnawed!

But I must get to work.

I have locked the door and thrown the key down into the front path.

I don't want to go out, and I don't want to have anybody come in, till John comes.

I want to astonish him.

I've got a rope up here that even Jennie did not find. If that woman does get out, and tries to get away, I can tie her!

But I forgot I could not reach far without anything to stand on!

This bed will *not* move!

I tried to lift and push it until I was lame, and then I got so angry I bit off a little piece at one corner—but it hurt my teeth.

Then I peeled off all the paper I could reach standing on the floor. It sticks horribly and the pattern just enjoys it! All those strangled heads and bulbous eyes and waddling fungus growths just shriek with derision!

I am getting angry enough to do something desperate. To jump out of the window would be admirable exercise, but the bars are too strong even to try.

Besides I wouldn't do it. Of course not. I know well enough that a step like that is improper and might be misconstrued.

I don't like to *look* out of the windows even—there are so many of those creeping women, and they creep so fast.

I wonder if they all come out of that wall-paper as I did?

But I am securely fastened now by my well-hidden rope—you don't get *me* out in the road there!

I suppose I shall have to get back behind the pattern when it comes night, and that is hard!

It is so pleasant to be out in this great room and creep around as I please!

I don't want to go outside. I won't, even if Jennie asks me to.

For outside you have to creep on the ground, and everything is green instead of yellow.

But here I can creep smoothly on the floor, and my shoulder just fits in that long smooch around the wall, so I cannot lose my way.

Why there's John at the door!

It is no use, young man, you can't open it!

How he does call and pound!

Now he's crying for an axe.

It would be a shame to break down that beautiful door!

"John dear!" said I in the gentlest voice, "the key is down by the front steps, under a plantain leaf!"

That silenced him for a few moments.

Then he said—very quietly indeed, "Open the door, my darling!"

"I can't," said I. "The key is down by the front door under a plantain leaf!"

And then I said it again, several times, very gently and slowly, and said it so often that he had to go and see, and he got it of course, and came in. He stopped short by the door.

"What is the matter?" he cried. "For God's sake, what are you doing!"

I kept on creeping just the same, but I looked at him over my shoulder.

"I've got out at last," said I, "in spite of you and Jennie. And I've pulled off most of the paper, so you can't put me back!"

Now why should that man have fainted? But he did, and right across my path by the wall, so that I had to creep over him every time!

total breakdown

QUESTIONS

1. Obviously, the yellow wall-paper is the central image in the story. One way to analyze the story, therefore, would be to trace the narrator's impressions of the wall-paper throughout the tale. We might ask how large a part the paper plays in her narration of each episode; how her description of the paper itself changes from scene to scene; how she describes the effect the paper has on her; and how those descriptions change. We might also ask how we respond to each change, each new description. How do we use the changing descriptions to interpret the narrator's state of mind? What feelings toward her do we have, and how do they change (or develop) as the story progresses?

2. For a brief paper, you might concentrate on the wall-paper as part of the tale's setting. Notice how the surroundings narrow for the narrator, from her description of the house and its grounds on the first day to her description of her path around the room on the final day. How has this narrowing been accomplished? What does it symbolize?

3. Another approach might be to ask why the wall-paper is in the narrator's room at all? What does her explanation of its presence tell you about her marriage—about her feelings about herself and her husband, and about his feelings about himself and her? How is this theme developed throughout the story? How does it end? (Make sure you take note of the tone of the story's final sentence!)

4. "The Yellow Wall-Paper" is certainly a tale that demands much participation from its readers. The narrator and her husband disagree about her needs and her health; and we feel ourselves called on to decide who is right. The wife also describes herself in solitude (particularly with reference to the wall-paper); and again we must decide how far to believe what she says, or how to reinterpret it. You might write a paper, therefore, discussing the narrative style of the tale, explaining where your sympathies lie at various points and describing the means by which the narrative shifts you from being a listener in the first scene (which is a fairly straightforward description) to being the only person who really understands what is going on in the final scene, the one who could answer the narrator's final question.

QUESTIONS FOR FURTHER THOUGHT

Unlike the central character of "Young Goodman Brown," who seems to have withdrawn from his fellow humans at least partly of his own volition, the narrators of "Bartleby the Scrivener" and "The Yellow Wall-Paper" want to communicate with other people, but are prevented from doing so. What would you say is blocking communication for them? Who or what is to be blamed for the miseries all three characters endure?

TONI CADE BAMBARA (1939–   )

My Man Bovanne

Blind people got a hummin jones if you notice. Which is understandable completely once you been around one and notice what no eyes will force you into to see people, and you get past the first time, which seems to come out of nowhere, and it's like you in church again with fat-chest ladies and old gents gruntin a hum low in the throat to whatever the preacher be saying. Shakey Bee bottom lip all swole up with Sweet Peach and me explainin how come the sweet-potato bread was a dollar-quarter this time stead of dollar regular and he say uh hunh he understand, then he break into this *thizzin* kind of hum which is quiet, but fiercesome just the same, if you ain't ready for it. Which I wasn't. But I got used to it and the onliest time I had to say somethin bout it was when he was playin checkers on the stoop one time and he commenst to hummin quite churchy seem to me. So I says, "Look here Shakey Bee, I can't beat you and Jesus too." He stop.

So that's how come I asked My Man Bovanne to dance. He ain't my man mind you, just a nice ole gent from the block that we all know cause he fixes things and the kids like him. Or used to fore Black Power[1] got hold their minds and mess em around till they can't be civil to ole folks. So we at this benefit for my niece's cousin who's runnin for somethin with this Black party somethin or other behind her. And I press up close to dance with Bovanne who blind and I'm hummin and he hummin, chest to chest like talkin. Not jammin my breasts into the man. Wasn't bout tits. Was bout vibrations. And he dug it and asked me what color dress I had on and how my hair was fixed and how I was doin without a man, not nosy but nice-like, and who was at this affair and was the canapés dainty-stingy or healthy enough to get hold of proper. Comfy and cheery is what I'm tryin to get across. Touch talkin like the heel of the hand on the tambourine or on a drum.

But right away Joe Lee come up on us and frown for dancin so close to the man. My own son who knows what kind of warm I am about; and don't grown men call me long distance and in the middle of the night for a little Mama comfort? But he frown. Which ain't right since Bovanne can't see and defend himself. Just a nice old man who fixes toasters and busted irons and bicycles and things and changes the lock on my door when my men friends get messy. Nice man. Which is not why they invited him. Grass roots you see. Me and Sister Taylor and the woman who does heads[2] at Mamies and the man from the barber

---

[1] Black Power was a slogan of certain Civil Rights groups during the 1960s and 70s.
[2] Hairdresser.

shop, we all there on account of we grass roots.[3] And I ain't never been souther than Brooklyn Battery[4] and no more country than the window box on my fire escape. And just yesterday my kids tellin me to take them countrified rags off my head and be cool. And now can't get Black enough to suit em. So everybody passin sayin My Man Bovanne. Big deal, keep steppin and don't even stop a minute to get the man a drink or one of them cute sandwiches or tell him what's goin on. And him standin there with a smile ready case someone do speak he want to be ready. So that's how come I pull him on the dance floor and we dance squeezin past the tables and chairs and all them coats and people standin round up in each other face talkin bout this and that but got no use for this blind man who mostly fixed skates and skooters for all these folks when they was just kids. So I'm pressed up close and we touch talkin with the hum. And here come my daughter cuttin her eye at me like she do when she tell me about my "apolitical" self like I got hoof and mouf disease and there ain't no hope at all. And I don't pay her no mind and just look up in Bovanne shadow face and tell him his stomach like a drum and he laugh. Laugh real loud. And here come my youngest, Task, with a tap on my elbow like he the third grade monitor and I'm cuttin up on the line to assembly.

"I was just talkin on the drums," I explained when they hauled me into the kitchen. I figured drums was my best defense. They can get ready for drums what with all this heritage business. And Bovanne stomach just like that drum Task give me when he come back from Africa. You just touch it and it hum thizzm, thizzm. So I stuck to the drum story. "Just drummin that's all."

"Mama, what are you talkin about?"

"She had too much to drink," say Elo to Task cause she don't hardly say nuthin to me direct no more since that ugly argument about my wigs.

"Look here Mama," say Task, the gentle one. "We just tryin to pull your coat. You were makin a spectacle of yourself out there dancing like that."

"Dancin like what?"

Task run a hand over his left ear like his father for the world and his father before that.

"Like a bitch in heat," say Elo.

"Well uhh, I was goin to say like one of them sex-starved ladies gettin on in years and not too discriminating. Know what I mean?"

I don't answer cause I'll cry. Terrible thing when your own children talk to you like that. Pullin me out the party and hustlin me into some stranger's kitchen in the back of a bar just like the damn police. And

---

[3] "Grass roots" refers to the common people.
[4] Brooklyn Battery is a section of Brooklyn, New York.

ain't like I'm old old. I can still wear me some sleeveless dresses without the meat hangin off my arm. And I keep up with some thangs through my kids. Who ain't kids no more. To hear them tell it. So I don't say nuthin.

"Dancin with that tom,"[5] say Elo to Joe Lee, who leanin on the folks' freezer. "His feet can smell a cracker a mile away and go into their shuffle number post haste. And them eyes. He could be a little considerate and put on some shades. Who wants to look into them blown-out fuses that—"

"Is this what they call the generation gap?" I say.

"Generation gap," spits Elo, like I suggested castor oil and fricassee possum in the milk-shakes or somethin. "That's a white concept for a white phenomenon. There's no generation gap among Black people. We are a col—"

"Yeh, well never mind," says Joe Lee. "The point is Mama . . . well, it's pride. You embarrass yourself and us too dancin like that."

"I wasn't shame." Then nobody say nuthin. Them standin there in they pretty clothes with drinks in they hands and gangin up on me, and me in the third-degree chair and nary a olive to my name. Felt just like the police got hold to me.

"First of all," Task say, holdin up his hand and tickin off the offenses, "the dress. Now that dress is too short, Mama, and too low-cut for a woman your age. And Tamu's going to make a speech tonight to kick off the campaign and will be introducin you and expecting you to organize the council of elders—"

"Me? Didn nobody ask me nuthin. You mean Nisi? She change her name?"

"Well, Norton was supposed to tell you about it. Nisi wants to introduce you and then encourage the older folks to form a Council of the Elders to act as an advisory—"

"And you going to be standing there with your boobs out and that wig on your head and that hem up to your ass. And people'll say, 'Ain't that the horny bitch that was grindin with the blind dude?' "

"Elo, be cool a minute," say Task, gettin to the next finger. "And then there's the drinkin. Mama, you know you can't drink cause next thing you know you be laughin loud and carryin on," and he grab another finger for the loudness. "And then there's the dancin. You been tattooed on the man for four records straight and slow draggin even on the fast numbers. How you think that look for a woman your age?"

"What's my age?"

"What?"

---

[5] "Tom" is short for "Uncle Tom," the central character in Harriet Beecher Stowe's novel *Uncle Tom's Cabin*. Uncle Tom is a term of derision used against Blacks who act in a subservient manner to Whites.

"I'm axin you all a simple question. You keep talkin bout what's proper for a woman my age. How old am I anyhow?" And Joe Lee slams his eyes shut and squinches up his face to figure. And Task run a hand over his ear and stare into his glass like the ice cubes goin calculate for him. And Elo just starin at the top of my head like she goin rip the wig off any minute now.

"Is your hair braided up under that thing? If so, why don't you take it off? You always did do a neat cornroll."

"Uh huh," cause I'm thinking how she couldn't undo her hair fast enough talking bout cornroll so countrified. None of which was the subject. "How old, I say?"

"Sixtee-one or—"

"You a damn lie Joe Lee Peoples."

"And that's another thing," say Task on the fingers.

"You know what you all can kiss," I say, gettin up and brushin the wrinkles out my lap.

"Oh, Mama," Elo say, puttin a hand on my shoulder like she hasn't done since she left home and the hand landin light and not sure it supposed to be there. Which hurt me to my heart. Cause this was the child in our happiness fore Mr. Peoples die. And I carried that child strapped to my chest till she was nearly two. We was close is what I'm trying to tell you. Cause it was more me in the child than the others. And even after Task it was the girlchild I covered in the night and wept over for no reason at all less it was she was a chub-chub like me and not very pretty, but a warm child. And how did things get to this, that she can't put a sure hand on me and say Mama we love you and care about you and you entitled to enjoy yourself cause you a good woman?

"And then there's Reverend Trent," say Task, glancin from left to right like they hatchin a plot and just now lettin me in on it. "You were suppose to be talkin with him tonight, Mama, about giving us his basement for campaign headquarters and—"

"Didn nobody tell me nuthin. If grass roots mean you kept in the dark I can't use it. I really can't. And Reven Trent a fool anyway the way he tore into the widow man up there on Edgecomb cause he wouldn't take in three of them foster children and the woman not even comfy in the ground yet and the man's mind messed up and—"

"Look here," say Task. "What we need is a family conference so we can get all this stuff cleared up and laid out on the table. In the meantime I think we better get back into the other room and tend to business. And in the meantime, Mama, see if you can't get to Reverend Trent and—"

"You want me to belly rub with the Reven, that it?"

"Oh damn," Elo say and go through the swingin door.

"We'll talk about all this at dinner. How's tomorrow night, Joe Lee?" While Joe Lee being self-important I'm wonderin who's doin the cookin and how come no body ax me if I'm free and do I get a corsage and things like that. Then Joe nod that it's O.K. and he go through the swingin door and just a little hubbub come through from the other room. Then Task smile his smile, lookin just like his daddy and he leave. And it just me in this stranger's kitchen, which was a mess I wouldn't never let my kitchen look like. Poison you just to look at the pots. Then the door swing the other way and it's My Man Bovanne standin there sayin Miss Hazel but lookin at the deep fry and then at the steam table, and most surprised when I come up on him from the other direction and take him on out of there. Pass the folks pushin up towards the stage, where Nisi and some other people settin and ready to talk, and folks gettin to the last of the sandwiches and the booze fore they settle down in one spot and listen serious. And I'm thinkin bout tellin Bovanne what a lovely long dress Nisi got on and the earrings and her hair piled up in a cone and the people bout to hear how we all gettin screwed and gotta form our own party[6] and everybody there listenin and lookin. But instead I just haul the man on out of there, and Joe Lee and his wife look at me like I'm terrible, but they ain't said boo to the man yet. Cause he blind and old and don't nobody there need him since they grown up and don't need they skates fixed no more.

"Where we goin, Miss Hazel?" Him knowin all the time.

"First we gonna buy you some dark sunglasses. Then you comin with me to the supermarket so I can pick up tomorrow's dinner, which is goin to be a grand thing proper and you invited. Then we goin to my house."

"That be fine. I surely would like to rest my feet." Bein cute, but you got to let men play out they little show, blind or not. So he chat on bout how tired he is and how he appreciate me takin him in hand this way. And I'm thinkin I'll have him change the lock on my door first thing. Then I'll give the man a nice warm bath with jasmine leaves in the water and a little Epsom salt on the sponge to do his back. And then a good rubdown with rose water and olive oil. Then a cup of lemon tea with a taste in it. And a little talcum, some of that fancy stuff Nisi mother sent over last Christmas. And then a massage, a good face massage round the forehead which is the worryin part. Cause you gots to take care of the older folks. And let them know they still needed to run the mimeo machine and keep the spark plugs clean and fix the mailboxes for folks who might help us get the breakfast program goin, and the school for the little kids and the campaign and all. Cause old folks is the nation. That what Nisi was sayin and I mean to do my part.

"I imagine you are a very pretty woman, Miss Hazel."

"I surely am," I say just like the hussy my daughter always say I was.

---

[6] Political party.

QUESTIONS

The narrator in "Bartleby the Scrivener" is a classic storyteller. The narrator in "The Yellow Wall-Paper" is a diarist. Both speak a careful, polished, "literary" English.

In contrast, the narrator of "My Man Bovanne" is a conversationalist. She speaks to us directly— "if you notice," "mind you"—and she speaks with the words and rhythm of her natural, conversational, speech. She is not an uneducated woman: she can use phrases like "generation gap" and "apolitical"; and she is, in her "grass roots" way, one of her community's leaders. But, as her story points out, she insists on recognition for her own and others' individuality: and her voice is an important part of that individuality.

It is an important element in the story as well. Consider:

1. How do the narrator's voice and her idiom lend humor to her portrayal of the benefit evening? How does it help put her children's concerns in perspective?
2. How does Bambara draw a portrait of this woman who "mean[s] to do [her] part" for the "little kids" and the "old folks"? What elements stand out? How are they blended into a coherent portrait?
3. How do the family conflict and the larger social issues illuminate each other? What ideas and emotions does the narrator bring to each?
4. What are your feelings about the narrator at the different stages of the story?
5. If you were to project this story into the future, would you expect things to work out well? Why or why not?

MARGARET ATWOOD (1939–   )

In Search of the Rattlesnake Plantain

We start in from the shore, through the place where there are a lot of birches. The woods are open, the ground covered with a mat of leaves, dry on the top, pressed down into a damp substratum beneath, threaded through (I know, though I don't look, I have looked before, I have a history of looking) with filaments, strands, roots, and skeins of leaf mould laid through it like fuses, branched like the spreading arteries of watercolour blue in certain kinds of cheese.

Against the dun colour of the fallen leaves, which recedes before us, the birches stand out, or lie. Birches have only a set time to live, and die while standing. Then the tops rot and fall down, or catch and dangle—widow-makers, the loggers used to call them—and the lopped trunks remain upright, hard fungi with undersides like dewed velvet sprouting from them. This patch of woods, with its long vistas and silent pillars, always gives me the same feeling: not fright, not sadness; a muted feeling. The light diffuses here, as through a window high up, in a vault.

"Should have brought a bag," says my mother, who is behind me. We go in single file, my father first, of course, though without his axe, Joanne second so he can explain things to her. I come next and my mother last. In this forest you have to be close to a person to hear what they say. The trees, or more probably the leaves, blot up sound.

"We can come back," I say. Both of us are referring to the birch bark, curls of which lie all around us. They ought to be gathered and used for starting the fire in the wood stove. With dead birches, the skin outlasts the centre, which is the opposite from the way we do it. There is no moment of death for anything, really; only a slow fade, like a candle or an icicle. With anything, the driest parts melt last.

"Should have used your brain," says my father, who has somehow heard her. They have the ability to hear one another, even at a distance, even through obstacles, even though they're in their seventies. My father raises his head without turning his voice, and continues to stomp forward, over the dun leaves and the pieces of Greek temple that litter the ground. I watch his feet, and Joanne's, ahead of me. Really I watch the ground: I'm looking for puffballs. I too have brought no bag, but I can take off my top shirt and make a bundle with it, if I find any.

"Never had one," says my mother cheerfully. "A ball of fluff. Just a little button at the top of my spine, to keep my head from falling off." She rustles along behind me. "Where's he going?" she says.

What we're doing is looking for a bog. Joanne, who writes nature articles, is doing a piece on bogs, and my father knows where there is one. A kettle bog: no way in for the water, and no way out. Joanne has her camera, around her neck on one of those wide embroidered straps like a yodeler's braces, and her binoculars, and her waterproof jacket that folds up into its own pocket and straps around the waist. She is always so well equipped.

She brought her portable one person kayak up for this visit, assembled it, and whips around over the water in it like a Jesus bug, which is what they used to call those whirligig water beetles you find sheltering in the calm places behind logs, in bays, on stormy days, black and shiny like Joanne's curious eyes.

Yesterday Joanne stepped the wrong way into her kayak and rolled, binoculars and all. Luckily not the camera. We dried her out as well as we could; the binoculars are more or less all right. I knew then that this is the reason I am not as well equipped as Joanne: I am afraid of loss. You shouldn't have a kayak or binoculars or anything else, unless you're prepared to let it sink.

Joanne, who is bright and lives by herself and by her wits, is ready for anything despite her equipment. "They're only binoculars," she said, laughing, as she squelched ashore. She knew the address of the place where she would take them to get them dried out professionally, if all else failed. Also she had a spare pair of hiking boots. She's the kind of woman who can have conversations with strangers on trains, with impunity. They never turn out to be loonies, like the ones I pick, and if they were she would ditch them soon enough. "Shape up or ship out" is a phrase I learned from Joanne.

Up ahead my father stops, looks down, stoops, and pokes. Joanne stoops too but she doesn't uncork the lens of her camera. My father scuffles impatiently among the dried leaves.

"What's he got there?" says my mother, who has caught up with me.

"Nothing," says my father, who has heard her. "No dice. I don't know what's happened to them. They must be disappearing."

My father has a list in his head of things that are disappearing: leopard frogs, certain species of wild orchid, loons, possibly. These are just the things around here. The list for the rest of the world is longer, and lengthening all the time. Tigers, for instance, and whooping cranes. Whales. Redwoods. Strains of wild maize. One species of plant a day. I have lived with this list all my life, and it makes me uncertain about the solidity of the universe. I clutch at things, to stop them, keep them here. If those had been my binoculars, there would have been a fuss.

But right now, right at this moment, I can't remember which thing it is that must be disappearing, or why we are looking for it in the first place.

We're looking for it because this isn't the whole story. The reason I can't remember isn't creeping senility: I could remember perfectly well at the time. But that was *at the time*, and this is a year later. In the meantime, the winter, which is always the meantime, the time during which things happen that you have to know about but would rather skip, my father had a stroke.

He was driving his car, heading north. The stroke happened as he turned from a feeder lane onto an eight-lane highway. The stroke paralyzed his left side, his left hand dragged the wheel over, and the car went across all four lanes of the westbound half of the highway and slid into the guard rail on the other side. My mother was in the car with him.

"The death seat," she said. "It's a miracle we weren't mashed to a pulp."

"That's right," I say. My mother can't drive. "What did you do?"

This is all going on over long-distance telephone, across the Atlantic, the day after the stroke. I am in a phone booth in an English village, and it's drizzling. There's a sack of potatoes in the phone booth too. They don't belong to me. Someone must be storing them in here.

My mother's voice fades in and out, as mine must, for her. I have already said, "Why didn't you call me as soon as it happened?" and she has already said, "No point in upsetting you." I am still a child, from whom the serious, grown-up things must be concealed.

"I didn't want to get out of the car," my mother said. "I didn't want to leave him. He didn't know what had happened. Luckily a nice young man stopped and asked if we were having any trouble, and drove on and called the ambulance."

She was shaken up; how could she not be? But she didn't want me to fly back. Everything was under control, and if I were to fly back it would be a sign that everything was not under control. My father was in the hospital, under control too. The stroke was what they called a transient one. "He can talk again," said my mother. "They say he has a good chance of getting most of it back."

"Most of what?" I said.

"Most of what he lost," said my mother.

After a while I got a letter from my father. It was written in the hospital, where they were doing tests on him. During the brain scan, he overheard one doctor say to another, "Well, there's nothing in there, anyway." My father reported this with some glee. He likes it when people say things they haven't intended to say.

We are past the stand of dying birch, heading inland, where the undergrowth is denser. The bog is somewhere back in there, says my father.

"He doesn't remember," says my mother in a low voice to me. "He's lost."

"I never get lost," says my father, charging ahead now through the saplings. We aren't on a path of any sort, and the trees close in and begin to resemble one another, as they have a habit of doing, away from human markings. But lost people go around in circles, and we are going in a straight line. I remember now what is disappearing, what it is we're supposed to be looking for. It's the rattlesnake plantain, which is a short plant with a bunch of leaves at the base and knobs up the stem. I think it's a variety of orchid. It used to be thick around here, my father has said. What could be causing it to disappear? He doesn't want one of these plants for anything; if he found a rattlesnake plantain, all he would do is look at it. But it would be reassuring, something else that is still with us. So I keep my eyes on the ground.

We find the bog, more or less where it was supposed to be, according to my father. But it's different; it's grown over. You can hardly tell it's a bog, apart from the water that oozes up through the sphagnum moss underfoot. A bog should have edges of moss and sedge that quake when you walk on them, and a dark pool in the centre, of water brown with peat juice. It should remind you of the word *tarn*. This bog has soaked up its water, covered it over and grown trees on it, balsam six feet high by now. We look for pitcher plants, in vain.

This bog is not photogenic. It is mature. Joanne takes a few pictures, with her top-of-the-line camera and neverfail close-up lens. She focusses on the ground, the moss; she takes a footprint filling with water. We stand around, slapping mosquitoes, while she does it. We all know that these aren't the pictures she'll end up using. But she is a good guest.

There are no rattlesnake plantains here. The rattlesnake plantain does not grow in bogs.

⌘

It's summer again and I'm back home. The Atlantic lies behind me, like a sheet of zinc, like a time warp. As usual in this house I get more tired than I should; or not tired, sleepy. I read murder mysteries I've read before and go to sleep early, never knowing what year I'll wake up in. Will it be twenty years ago, or twenty years from now? Is it before I got married, is my child—ten and visiting a friend—grown up and gone? There's a chip in the plaster of the room where I sleep, shaped like a pig's head in profile. It's always been there, and each time I come back here I look for it, to steady myself against the current of time that is flowing past and over me, faster and faster. These visits of mine blur together.

This one though is different. Something has been changed, something has stopped. My father, who recovered almost completely from the stroke, who takes five kinds of pills to keep from having another one, who squeezes a woollen ball in his left hand, who however is not paying as much attention to his garden as he used to—my father is ill. I've been here four days and he's been ill the whole time. He lies on the living room sofa in his dressing gown and does not eat or even drink. He sips water, but nothing more.

There have been whispered consultations with my mother, in the kitchen. Is it the pills, is it a virus of some kind? Has he had another stroke, a tiny one, when no one was looking? He's stopped talking much. There's something wrong with his voice, you have to listen very carefully or you can't catch what he's saying.

My mother, who has always handled things, doesn't seem to know what to do. I tell her I'm afraid he'll get dehydrated. I go down to the cellar, where the other phone is, and telephone the doctor who is hard to reach. I don't want my father to hear me doing this: he will be annoyed, he'll say there's nothing wrong with him, he'll rebel.

I go back upstairs and take his temperature, using the thermometer I used to check my fertility when I was trying to get pregnant. He opens his mouth passively to let me do this; he seems uninterested in the results. His face, a little one-sided from the stroke, appears to have shrunk and fallen in upon itself. His eyes, under his white eyebrows, are almost invisible. The temperature is too high.

"You have a temperature," I tell him. He doesn't seem surprised. I bring a bowl of ice cubes to him, because he says he can't swallow. The ice cubes are something I remember from my childbirth classes, or could it be my husband's ulcer operation? All crisis is one crisis, an improvisation. You seize what is at hand.

"Did he eat the ice cubes?" says my mother, in the kitchen. He doesn't hear her, as he would have once. He doesn't say no.

Later, after dinner, when I am re-reading a bad Agatha Christie dating from the war, my mother comes into my room.

"He says he's going to drive up north," she tells me. "He says there are some trees he has to finish cutting."

"It's the temperature," I say. "He's hallucinating."

"I hope so," says my mother. "He can't drive up there." Maybe she's afraid it isn't the temperature, that this is permanent.

I go with her to their bedroom, where my father is packing. He's put on his clothes, shorts and a white short-sleeved shirt, and shoes and socks. I can't imagine how he got all of this on, because he can hardly stand up. He's in the centre of the room, holding his folded pyjamas as if unsure what to do with them. On the chair is an open rucksack, beside it a package of flashlight batteries.

"You can't drive at night," I say. "It's dark out."

He turns his head from side to side, like a turtle, as if to hear me better. He looks baffled.

"I don't know what's holding you up," he says to my mother. "We have to get up there." Now that he has a temperature, his voice is stronger. I know what it is: he doesn't like the place he finds himself in, he wants to be somewhere else. He wants out, he wants to drive, away from all this illness.

"You should wait till tomorrow," I say.

He sets down the pyjamas and starts looking through his pockets.

"The car keys," he says to my mother.

"Did you give him an aspirin?" I ask her.

"He can't swallow," she says. Her face is white; suddenly she too looks old.

My father has found something in his pocket. It's a folded-up piece of paper. Laboriously he unfolds it, peers at it. It looks like an old grocery list. "The rattlesnake plantain is making a comeback," he says to me. I understand that, from somewhere in there, from underneath the fever, he's trying to send out some good news. He knows things have gone wrong, but it's only part of a cycle. This was a bad summer for wood mice, he told me earlier. He didn't mean that there were a lot of them, but that there were hardly any. The adjective was from the point of view of the mice.

"Don't worry," I say to my mother. "He won't go."

If the worst comes to the worst, I think, I can back my car across the bottom of the driveway. I remember myself, at the age of six, after I'd had my tonsils out. I heard soldiers, marching. My father is afraid.

"I'll help you take off your shoes," my mother says. My father sits down at the edge of the bed, as if tired, as if defeated. My mother kneels. Mutely he holds out a foot.

We're making our way back. My father and mother are off in the woods somewhere, trudging through the undergrowth, young balsam and hazelnut and moose maple, but Joanne and I (why? how did we get separated from them?) are going along the shore, on the theory that, if you're on an island, all you have to do is go along the shore and sooner or later you'll hit the point you started out from. Anyway, this is a short cut, or so we have told each other.

Now there's a steep bank, and a shallow bay where a lot of driftwood has collected—old logs, big around as a hug, their ends sawn off clean. These logs are from the time when they used to do the logging in the winter, cross to the islands by the frozen lakes, cut the trees and drag them to the ice with a team of horses, and float them in the spring to the chute and the mill in log booms, the logs corralled in a floating fence of other logs chained together. The logs in this bay were once escapees. Now they lie like basking whales, lolling in the warmed inshore water, Jesus bugs sheltering behind them, as they turn gradually back to earth. Moss grows on them, and sundew, raising its round leaves like little greenish moons, the sticky hairs standing out from them in rays of light.

Along these sodden and sprouting logs Joanne and I walk, holding on to the shoreside branches for balance. They do the logging differently now; they use chain saws, and trucks to carry the logs out, over gravel roads bulldozed in a week. They don't touch the shoreline though, they leave enough for the eye; but the forest up here is becoming more and more like a curtain, a backdrop behind which is emptiness, or a shambles. The landscape is being hollowed out. From this kind of logging, islands are safer.

Joanne steps on the next log, chocolate brown and hoary with lichen. It rolls in slow motion, and throws her. There goes her second pair of hiking boots, and her pants up to the knees, but luckily not the camera.

"You can't never trust nobody," says Joanne, who is laughing. She wades the rest of the way, to where the shore slopes down and she can squelch up onto dry land. I pick a different log, make a safe crossing, and follow. Despite our short cut my parents get back first.

⌘

In the morning, the ambulance comes for my father. He's lucid again, that's the term. It makes me think of *lucent:* light comes out of him again, he is no longer opaque. In his husky, obscure voice he even jokes with the ambulance attendants, who are young and reassuring, as they strap him in.

"In case I get violent," he says.

The ambulance doesn't mean a turn for the worse. The doctor has said to take him to Emergency, because there are no beds available in the regular wards. It's summer, and the highway accidents are coming in, and one wing of the hospital is closed, incredibly, for the holidays. But whatever is or is not wrong with him, at least they'll give him an intravenous, to replace the lost fluids.

"He's turning into a raisin," says my mother. She has a list of everything he's failed to eat and drink over the past five days.

I drive my mother to the hospital in my car, and we are there in time to see my father arrive in the ambulance. They unload him, still on the wheeled stretcher, and he is made to disappear through swinging doors, into a space that excludes us.

My mother and I sit on the leatherette chairs, waiting for someone to tell us what is supposed to happen next. There's nothing to read except a couple of outdated copies of *Scottish Life.* I look at a picture of wool-dying. A policeman comes in, talks with a nurse, goes out again.

My mother does not read *Scottish Life.* She sits bolt upright, on the alert, her head swivelling like a periscope. "There don't seem to be any mashed-up people coming in," she says after a while.

"It's the daytime," I say. "I think they come in more at night." I can't tell whether she's disappointed or comforted by this absence. She watches the swinging doors, as if my father will come stomping out through them at any minute, cured and fully dressed, jingling his car keys in his hand and ready to go.

"What do you suppose he's up to in there?" she says.

QUESTIONS

Although this entire story is written in the present tense, it actually contains three separate episodes, each about six months apart The first, which opens the story and to which the narrator returns at intervals throughout the story, is a trip on an island through birch woods. During the second, which happens in winter—"the time when things happen that you have to know about but would rather skip"—the narrator learns that her father has had a stroke. The third incident, which happens during the following summer, concerns another illness suffered by the father and the actions taken in response by his wife and daughter. The incidents are tied together not only by the way they are interwoven in the narration, but also by the themes of time, of endangered and disappearing things (in nature and in family life), of loss and the fear of loss.

Potential topics for discussion and/or essays, therefore, might center on any of these three themes, or on the narrative voice moving among them, mixing personal revelation with family anecdote. For example:

1. Discuss the narrator's self-proclaimed fear of loss. ("I am afraid of loss"; "I clutch at things to stop them, keep them here"; "I look for [a chip in the plaster] to steady myself against the current of time that is flowing past and over me, faster and faster.") How does this theme, and its pronouncements, spoken as if directly to us, help shape and unify the story?

2. How are the two themes of love and concern for the environment and love and concern for family woven together in the story?

3. What is the significance of the story's title?

4. The trick of telling a story in disjoint sections, out of chronological order, is relatively new in story-telling. Discuss its effectiveness in this tale. Does it work well for you as a reader? Why or why not?

4 Portraits

So far, in our study of fiction, we've discussed the narrative voice; the basic structure of fiction (introduction, conflict, climax, and resolution); and the importance of character, action, and setting. While studying particular stories, we've noticed the use of themes and imagery to help set the mood or present the message of a story. We have certainly seen a variety of tales. We've seen stories, like "Bartleby the Scrivener" and "The Search for the Rattlesnake Plantain," that cover years, and others, like "My Man Bovanne" and "The Story of an Hour," that cover only an hour or so. We've read stories like "Young Goodman Brown," in which the action changed someone's life, and stories like "Hills like White Elephants" that seemed almost to deny the possibility of change.

Now, as a way of combining the themes we've discussed, let's look at three stories in which the writers have chosen a single basic pattern. Each of these stories centers on a single protagonist, almost to the exclusion of other characters. Each covers less than a day. And in each, the action consists of the protagonist's making some excursion on foot.

This is a very simple theme indeed, and a very common action—not one that lends itself to exciting action or dramatic conflicts. Most of us walk somewhere and return every day, and find nothing noticeable about it. Yet the chance does remain that at some time, for some people, the excursion may take on sufficient meaning to be worth recounting.

Here, then, are the stories. Notice what the three writers can do with this minimal material. Notice the portraits they can paint, the hidden dramas they can reveal.

KATHERINE MANSFIELD (1888–1923)

Miss Brill

Although it was so brilliantly fine—the blue sky powdered with gold and great spots of light like white wine splashed over the Jardins Publiques[1]—Miss Brill was glad that she had decided on her fur. The air was motionless, but when you opened your mouth there was just a faint chill, like a chill from a glass of iced water before you sip, and now and again a leaf came drifting—from nowhere, from the sky. Miss Brill put up her hand and touched her fur. Dear little thing! It was nice to feel it again. She had taken it out of its box that afternoon, shaken out the moth powder, given it a good brush, and rubbed the life back into the dim little eyes. "What has been happening to me?" said the sad little eyes. Oh, how sweet it was to see them snap at her again from the red eiderdown! [2] . . . But the nose, which was of some black composition, wasn't at all firm. It must have had a knock, somehow. Never mind—a little dab of black sealing-wax when the time came—when it was absolutely necessary . . . Little rogue! Yes, she really felt like that about it. Little rogue biting its tail just by her left ear. She could have taken it off and laid it on her lap and stroked it. She felt a tingling in her hands and arms, but that came from walking, she supposed. And when she breathed, something light and sad—no, not sad, exactly—something gentle seemed to move in her bosom.

There were a number of people out this afternoon, far more than last Sunday. And the band sounded louder and gayer. That was because the Season had begun. For although the band played all the year round on Sundays, out of season it was never the same. It was like some one playing with only the family to listen; it didn't care how it played if there weren't any strangers present. Wasn't the conductor wearing a new coat, too? She was sure it was new. He scraped with his foot and flapped his arms like a rooster about to crow, and the bandsmen sitting in the green rotunda blew out their cheeks and glared at the music. Now there came a little "flutey" bit—very pretty!

---

1 *Jardins Publiques,* public gardens.
2 *eiderdown,* a quilt stuffed with the down of the eider duck.

—a little chain of bright drops. She was sure it would be repeated. It was; she lifted her head and smiled.

Only two people shared her "special" seat: a fine old man in a velvet coat, his hands clasped over a huge carved walking-stick, and a big old woman, sitting upright, with a roll of knitting on her embroidered apron. They did not speak. This was disappointing, for Miss Brill always looked forward to the conversation. She had become really quite expert, she thought, at listening as though she didn't listen, at sitting in other people's lives just for a minute while they talked round her.

She glanced, sideways, at the old couple. Perhaps they would go soon. Last Sunday, too, hadn't been as interesting as usual. An Englishman and his wife, he wearing a dreadful Panama hat and she button boots. And she'd gone on the whole time about how she ought to wear spectacles; she knew she needed them; but that it was no good getting any; they'd be sure to break and they'd never keep on. And he'd been so patient. He'd suggested everything—gold rims, the kind that curved round your ears, little pads inside the bridge. No, nothing would please her. "They'll always be sliding down my nose!" Miss Brill had wanted to shake her.

The old people sat on the bench, still as statues. Never mind, there was always the crowd to watch. To and fro, in front of the flower beds and the band rotunda, the couples and groups paraded, stopped to talk, to greet, to buy a handful of flowers from the old beggar who had his tray fixed to the railings. Little children ran among them, swooping and laughing; little boys with big white silk bows under their chins, little girls, little French dolls, dressed up in velvet and lace. And sometimes a tiny staggerer came suddenly rocking into the open from under the trees, stopped, stared, as suddenly sat down "flop," until its small high-stepping mother, like a young hen, rushed scolding to its rescue. Other people sat on the benches and green chairs, but they were nearly always the same, Sunday after Sunday, and—Miss Brill had often noticed—there was something funny about nearly all of them. They were odd, silent, nearly all old, and from the way they stared they looked as though they'd just come from dark little rooms or even—even cupboards!

Behind the rotunda the slender trees with yellow leaves down drooping, and through them just a line of sea, and beyond the blue sky with gold-veined clouds.

Tum-tum-tum tiddle-um! tiddle-um! tum tiddley-um tum ta! blew the band.

Two young girls in red came by and two young soldiers in blue met them, and they laughed and paired and went off arm-in-arm. Two peasant women with funny straw hats passed, gravely, leading beautiful smoke-colored donkeys. A cold, pale nun hurried by. A beautiful

woman came along and dropped her bunch of violets, and a little boy
ran after to hand them to her, and she took them and threw them
away as if they'd been poisoned. Dear me! Miss Brill didn't know
whether to admire that or not! And now an ermine toque[3] and a
gentleman in gray met just in front of her. He was tall, stiff, dignified,
and she was wearing the ermine toque she'd bought when her hair
was yellow. Now everything, her hair, her face, even her eyes, was the
same color as the shabby ermine, and her hand, in its cleaned glove,
lifted to dab her lips, was a tiny yellowish paw. Oh, she was so pleased
to see him—delighted! She rather thought they were going to meet
that afternoon. She described where she'd been—everywhere, here,
there, along by the sea. The day was so charming—didn't he agree?
And wouldn't he, perhaps? . . . But he shook his head, lighted a
cigarette, slowly breathed a great deep puff into her face, and, even
while she was still talking and laughing, flicked the match away and
walked on. The ermine toque was alone; she smiled more brightly
than ever. But even the band seemed to know what she was feeling
and played more softly, played tenderly, and the drum beat, "The
Brute! The Brute!" over and over. What would she do? What was
going to happen now? But as Miss Brill wondered, the ermine toque
turned, raised her hand as though she'd seen some one else, much
nicer, just over there, and pattered away. And the band changed
again and played more quickly, more gayly than ever, and the old
couple on Miss Brill's seat got up and marched away, and such a
funny old man with long whiskers hobbled along in time to the
music and was nearly knocked over by four girls walking abreast.

Oh, how fascinating it was! How she enjoyed it! How she loved
sitting here, watching it all! It was like a play. It was exactly like a
play. Who could believe the sky at the back wasn't painted? But it
wasn't till a little brown dog trotted on solemn and then slowly
trotted off, like a little "theater" dog, a little dog that had been
drugged, that Miss Brill discovered what it was that made it so exciting. They were all on the stage. They weren't only the audience, not
only looking on; they were acting. Even she had a part and came
every Sunday. No doubt somebody would have noticed if she hadn't
been there; she was a part of the performance after all. How strange
she'd never thought of it like that before! And yet it explained why
she made such a point of starting from home at just the same time
each week—so as not to be late for the performance—and it also explained why she had quite a queer, shy feeling at telling her English
pupils how she spent her Sunday afternoons. No wonder! Miss Brill
nearly laughed out loud. She was on the stage. She thought of the

---

3 *toque*, a woman's small, round, close-fitting hat—in this case, such a hat made
from the white fur of the ermine.

old invalid gentleman to whom she read the newspaper four afternoons a week while he slept in the garden. She had got quite used to the frail head on the cotton pillow, the hollowed eyes, the open mouth and the high pinched nose. If he'd been dead she mightn't have noticed for weeks; she wouldn't have minded. But suddenly he knew he was having the paper read to him by an actress! "An actress!" The old head lifted; two points of light quivered in the old eyes. "An actress—are ye?" And Miss Brill smoothed the newspaper as though it were the manuscript of her part and said gently: "Yes, I have been an actress for a long time."

The band had been having a rest. Now they started again. And what they played was warm, sunny, yet there was just a faint chill— a something, what was it?—not sadness—no, not sadness—a something that made you want to sing. The tune lifted, lifted, the light shone; and it seemed to Miss Brill that in another moment all of them, all the whole company, would begin singing. The young ones, the laughing ones who were moving together, they would begin, and the men's voices, very resolute and brave, would join them. And then she too, she too, and the others on the benches—they would come in with a kind of accompaniment—something low, that scarcely rose or fell, something so beautiful—moving . . . And Miss Brill's eyes filled with tears and she looked smiling at all the other members of the company. Yes, we understand, we understand, she thought—though what they understood she didn't know.

Just at that moment a boy and a girl came and sat down where the old couple had been. They were beautifully dressed; they were in love. The hero and heroine, of course, just arrived from his father's yacht. And still soundlessly singing, still with that trembling smile, Miss Brill prepared to listen.

"No, not now," said the girl. "Not here, I can't."

"But why? Because of that stupid old thing at the end there?" asked the boy. "Why does she come here at all—who wants her? Why doesn't she keep her silly old mug at home?"

"It's her fu-fur which is so funny," giggled the girl. "It's exactly like a fried whiting." [4]

"Ah, be off with you!" said the boy in an angry whisper. Then: "Tell me, ma petite chère—" [5]

"No, not here," said the girl. "Not yet."

On her way home she usually bought a slice of honeycake at the baker's. It was her Sunday treat. Sometimes there was an almond in her slice, sometimes not. It made a great difference. If there was an almond it was like carrying home a tiny present—a surprise—some-

---

4 *whiting,* a food fish related to cod.
5 *ma petite chère,* my dear little one.

thing that might very well not have been there. She hurried on the almond Sundays and struck the match for the kettle in quite a dashing way.

But today she passed the baker's by, climbed the stairs, went into the little dark room—her room like a cupboard—and sat down on the red eiderdown. She sat there for a long time. The box that the fur came out of was on the bed. She unclasped the necklet quickly; quickly, without looking, laid it inside. But when she put the lid on she thought she heard something crying.

QUESTIONS

Katherine Mansfield's style in "Miss Brill" concentrates on details—details seen, heard, and interpreted by her highly observant and imaginative heroine. Note how the story is built and shaped by these details.

1. During the first part of the story, notice how the accumulation of details sets the scene. Note how observation mixes with imagination. For example, how does Miss Brill see or describe her fur piece? The bandmaster? The people on benches? The woman in the ermine toque?
2. The climax of the tale turns on a "discovery" made by Miss Brill, which tries to impose a unity on the scene and its many details. The climax itself, however, builds up in three stages. The first begins with the sentence, "Oh, how fascinating it was!" and ends with the sentence, "Yes, I have been an actress for a long time." The second begins with "The band had been having a rest" and continues through "Yes, we understand, we understand, she thought—though what they understood she didn't know." The third begins with "Just at that moment a boy and girl came" and closes with " 'No, not here,' said the girl. 'Not yet.' "
   a. What is the theme of each of these three stages? What part do observation, imagination, and feeling play in each? How fully do you accept each discovery? To what extent do you believe it to be true or feel in sympathy with it?
   b. What progression and/or contrast is created by the three stages? How do you react to it?
3. What does Mansfield do with her heroine after the climax? How does the story finish? Note again the use of details observed and imagined; how does the end tie in with the story's beginning and climax? How effective a means is this for rounding off the story?

DORIS LESSING (1919–)

A Sunrise on the Veld

Every night that winter he said aloud into the dark of the pillow: Half-past four! Half-past four! till he felt his brain had gripped the words and held them fast. Then he fell asleep at once, as if a shutter had fallen; and lay with his face turned to the clock so that he could see it first thing when he woke.

It was half-past four to the minute, every morning. Triumphantly pressing down the alarm-knob of the clock, which the dark half of his mind had outwitted, remaining vigilant all night and counting the hours as he lay relaxed in sleep, he huddled down for a last warm moment under the clothes, playing with the idea of lying abed for this once only. But he played with it for the fun of knowing that it was a weakness he could defeat without effort; just as he set the alarm each night for the delight of the moment when he woke and stretched his limbs, feeling the muscles tighten, and thought: Even my brain—even that! I can control every part of myself.

Luxury of warm rested body, with the arms and legs and fingers waiting like soldiers for a word of command! Joy of knowing that the precious hours were given to sleep voluntarily!—for he had once stayed awake three nights running, to prove that he could, and then worked all day, refusing even to admit that he was tired; and now sleep seemed to him a servant to be commanded and refused.

The boy stretched his frame full-length, touching the wall at his head with his hands, and the bedfoot with his toes; then he sprung out, like a fish leaping from water. And it was cold, cold.

He always dressed rapidly, so as to try and conserve his night-warmth till the sun rose two hours later; but by the time he had on his clothes his hands were numbed and he could scarcely hold his shoes. These he could not put on for fear of waking his parents, who never came to know how early he rose.

As soon as he stepped over the lintel, the flesh of his soles contracted on the chilled earth, and his legs began to ache with cold. It was night: the stars were glittering, the trees standing black and still. He looked for signs of day, for the greying of the edge of a stone, or a lightening in the sky where the sun would rise, but there was nothing yet. Alert as an animal he crept past the dangerous window, standing poised with his hand on the sill for one proudly fastidious moment, looking in at the stuffy blackness of the room where his parents lay.

Feeling for the grass-edge of the path with his toes, he reached inside another window further along the wall, where his gun had been set in readiness the night before. The steel was icy, and numbed fingers slipped along it, so that he had to hold it in the crook of his arm for safety. Then he tiptoed to the room where the dogs slept, and was fearful that they might have been tempted to go before him; but they were waiting, their haunches crouched in reluctance at the cold, but ears and swinging tails greeting the gun ecstatically. His warning undertone kept them secret and silent till the house was a hundred yards back: then they bolted off into the bush, yelping excitedly. The boy imagined his parents turning in their beds and muttering: Those dogs again! before they were dragged back in sleep; and he smiled scornfully. He always looked back over his shoulder at the house before he passed a wall of trees that shut it from sight. It looked so low and small, crouching there under a tall and brilliant sky. Then he turned his back on it, and on the frowsting sleepers, and forgot them.

He would have to hurry. Before the light grew strong he must be four miles away; and already a tint of green stood in the hollow of a leaf, and the air smelled of morning and the stars were dimming.

He slung the shoes over his shoulder, veld *skoen* that were crinkled and hard with the dews of a hundred mornings. They would be necessary when the ground became too hot to bear. Now he felt the chilled dust push up between his toes, and he let the muscles of his feet spread and settle into the shapes of the earth; and he thought: I could walk a hundred miles on feet like these! I could walk all day, and never tire!

He was walking swiftly through the dark tunnel of foliage that in day-time was a road. The dogs were invisibly ranging the lower travelways of the bush, and he heard them panting. Sometimes he felt a cold muzzle on his leg before they were off again, scouting for a trail to follow. They were not trained, but free-running companions of the hunt, who often tired of the long stalk before the final shots, and went off on their own pleasure. Soon he could see them, small and wild-looking in a wild strange light, now that the bush stood trembling on the verge of colour, waiting for the sun to paint earth and grass afresh.

The grass stood to his shoulders; and the trees were showering a faint silvery rain. He was soaked; his whole body was clenched in a steady shiver.

Once he bent to the road that was newly scored with animal trails, and regretfully straightened, reminding himself that the pleasure of tracking must wait till another day.

He began to run along the edge of a field, noting jerkily how it was filmed over with fresh spiderweb, so that the long reaches of great black clods seemed netted in glistening grey. He was using the steady lope he had learned by watching the natives, the run that is a dropping of the weight of the body from one foot to the next in a slow balancing movement that never tires, nor shortens the breath; and he felt the blood pulsing down his legs and along his arms, and the exultation and pride of body mounted in him till he was shutting his teeth hard against a violent desire to shout his triumph.

Soon he had left the cultivated part of the farm. Behind him the bush was low and black. In front was a long vlei, acres of long pale grass that sent back a hollowing gleam of light to a satiny sky. Near him thick swathes of grass were bent with the weight of water, and diamond drops sparkled on each frond.

The first bird woke at his feet and at once a flock of them sprang into the air calling shrilly that day had come; and suddenly, behind him, the bush woke into song, and he could hear the guinea fowl calling far ahead of him. That meant they would now be sailing down from their trees into thick grass, and it was for them he had come: he was too late. But he did not mind. He forgot he had come to shoot. He set his legs wide, and balanced from foot to foot, and swung his gun up and down in both hands horizontally, in a kind of improvised exercise, and let his head sink back till it was pillowed in his neck muscles, and watched how above him small rosy clouds floated in a lake of gold.

Suddenly it all rose in him: it was unbearable. He leapt up into the air, shouting and yelling wild, unrecognisable noises. Then he began to run, not carefully, as he had before, but madly, like a wild thing. He was clean crazy, yelling mad with the joy of living and a superfluity of youth. He rushed down the vlei under a tumult of crimson and gold, while all the birds of the world sang about him. He ran in great leaping strides, and shouted as he ran, feeling his body rise into the crisp rushing air and fall back surely onto sure feet; and thought briefly, not believing that such a thing could happen to him, that he could break his ankle any moment, in this thick tangled grass. He cleared bushes like a duiker, leapt over rocks; and finally came to a dead stop at a place where the ground fell abruptly away below him to the river. It had been a two-mile-long dash through waist-high growth, and he was breathing hoarsely and could no longer sing. But he poised on a rock and looked down at stretches of water that gleamed through stooping trees, and thought suddenly, I am fifteen! Fifteen! The words came new to him; so that he kept repeating them wonderingly, with swelling excitement; and he felt the years of his life with his hands, as if he were counting marbles, each one hard and separate and compact, each one a wonderful shining thing. That was what he was: fifteen years of this rich soil, and this slow-moving water, and air that smelt like a challenge whether it was warm and sultry at noon, or as brisk as cold water, like it was now.

There was nothing he couldn't do, nothing! A vision came to him, as he stood there, like when a child hears the word "eternity" and tries to understand it, and time takes possession of the mind. He felt his life ahead of him as a great and wonderful thing, something that was his;

and he said aloud, with the blood rising to his head: all the great men of the world have been as I am now, and there is nothing I can't become, nothing I can't do; there is no country in the world I cannot make part of myself, if I choose. I contain the world. I can make of it what I want. If I choose, I can change everything that is going to happen: it depends on me, and what I decide now.

The urgency, and the truth and the courage of what his voice was saying exulted him so that he began to sing again, at the top of his voice, and the sound went echoing down the river gorge. He stopped for the echo, and sang again: stopped and shouted. That was what he was!—he sang, if he chose; and the world had to answer him.

And for minutes he stood there, shouting and singing and waiting for the lovely eddying sound of the echo; so that his own new strong thoughts came back and washed round his head, as if someone were answering him and encouraging him; till the gorge was full of soft voices clashing back and forth from rock to rock over the river. And then it seemed as if there was a new voice. He listened, puzzled, for it was not his own. Soon he was leaning forward, all his nerves alert, quite still: somewhere close to him there was a noise that was no joyful bird, nor tinkle of falling water, nor ponderous movement of cattle.

There it was again. In the deep morning hush that held his future and his past, was a sound of pain, and repeated over and over: it was a kind of shortened scream, as if someone, something, had no breath to scream. He came to himself, looked about him, and called for the dogs. They did not appear: they had gone off on their own business, and he was alone. Now he was clean sober, all the madness gone. His heart beating fast, because of that frightened screaming, he stepped carefully off the rock and went towards a belt of trees. He was moving cautiously, for not so long ago he had seen a leopard in just this spot.

At the edge of the trees he stopped and peered, holding his gun ready; he advanced, looking steadily about him, his eyes narrowed. Then, all at once, in the middle of a step, he faltered, and his face was puzzled. He shook his head impatiently, as if he doubted his own sight.

There, between two trees, against a background of gaunt black rocks, was a figure from a dream, a strange beast that was horned and drunken-legged, but like something he had never even imagined. It seemed to be ragged. It looked like a small buck that had black ragged tufts of fur standing up irregularly all over it, with patches of raw flesh beneath . . . but the patches of rawness were disappearing under moving black and came again elsewhere; and all the time the creature screamed, in small gasping screams, and leaped drunkenly from side to side, as if it were blind.

Then the boy understood: it *was* a buck. He ran closer, and again stood still, stopped by a new fear. Around him the grass was whispering and alive. He looked wildly about, and then down. The ground was black with ants, great energetic ants that took no notice of him, but hurried and scurried towards the fighting shape, like glistening black water flowing through the grass.

And, as he drew in his breath and pity and terror seized him, the beast fell and the screaming stopped. Now he could hear nothing but one bird singing, and the sound of the rustling, whispering ants.

He peered over at the writhing blackness that jerked convulsively with the jerking nerves. It grew quieter. There were small twitches from the mass that still looked vaguely like the shape of a small animal.

It came into his mind that he should shoot it and end its pain; and he raised the gun. Then he lowered it again. The buck could no longer feel; its fighting was a mechanical protest of the nerves. But it was not that which made him put down the gun. It was a swelling feeling of rage and misery and protest that expressed itself in the thought: if I had not come it would have died like this: so why should I interfere? All over the bush things like this happen; they happen all the time; this is how life goes on, by living things dying in anguish. He gripped the gun between his knees and felt in his own limbs the myriad swarming pain of the twitching animal that could no longer feel, and set his teeth, and said over and over again under his breath: I can't stop it. I can't stop it. There is nothing I can do.

He was glad that the buck was unconscious and had gone past suffering so that he did not have to make a decision to kill it even when he was feeling with his whole body: this is what happens, this is how things work.

It was right—that was what he was feeling. *It was right and nothing could alter it.*

The knowledge of fatality, of what has to be, had gripped him and for the first time in his life; and he was left unable to make any movement of brain or body, except to say: "Yes, yes. That is what living is." It had entered his flesh and his bones and grown in to the furthest corners of his brain and would never leave him. And at that moment he could not have performed the smallest action of mercy, knowing as he did, having lived on it all his life, the vast unalterable, cruel veld, where at any moment one might stumble over a skull or crush the skeleton of some small creature.

Suffering, sick, and angry, but also grimly satisfied with his new stoicism, he stood there leaning on his rifle, and watched the seething black mound grow smaller. At his feet, now, were ants trickling back with pink fragments in their mouths, and there was a fresh acid smell in his nostrils. He sternly controlled the uselessly convulsing muscles of his empty stomach, and reminded himself: the ants must eat too! At the same time he found that the tears were streaming down his face, and his clothes were soaked with the sweat of that other creature's pain.

The shape had grown small. Now it looked like nothing recognisable.

He did not know how long it was before he saw the blackness thin, and bits of white showed through, shining in the sun—yes, there was the sun, just up, glowing over the rocks. Why, the whole thing could not have taken longer than a few minutes.

He began to swear, as if the shortness of the time was in itself unbearable, using the words he had heard his father say. He strode forward, crushing ants with each step, and brushing them off his clothes, till he stood above the skeleton, which lay sprawled under a small bush. It was clean-picked. It might have been lying there years, save that on the white bone were pink fragments of gristle. About the bones ants were ebbing away, their pincers full of meat.

The boy looked at them, big black ugly insects. A few were standing and gazing up at him with small glittering eyes.

"Go away!" he said to the ants, very coldly. "I am not for you—not just yet, at any rate. Go away." And he fancied that the ants turned and went away.

He bent over the bones and touched the sockets in the skull; that was where the eyes were, he thought incredulously, remembering the liquid dark eyes of a buck. And then he bent the slim foreleg bone, swinging it horizontally in his palm.

That morning, perhaps an hour ago, this small creature had been stepping proud and free through the bush, feeling the chill on its hide even as he himself had done, exhilarated by it. Proudly stepping the earth, tossing its horns, frisking a pretty white tail, it had sniffed the cold morning air. Walking like kings and conquerors it had moved through this free-held bush, where each blade of grass grew for it alone, and where the river ran pure sparkling water for its slaking.

And then—what had happened? Such a swift surefooted thing could surely not be trapped by a swarm of ants?

The boy bent curiously to the skeleton. Then he saw that the back leg that lay uppermost and strained out in the tension of death, was snapped midway in the thigh, so that broken bones jutted over each other uselessly. So that was it! Limping into the ant-masses it could not escape, once it had sensed the danger. Yes, but how had the leg been broken? Had it fallen, perhaps? Impossible, a buck was too light and graceful. Had some jealous rival horned it?

QUESTIONS

1. There are two ways in which you can look at the structure of this story. You can divide it simply into the times before and after the boy encounters the dying buck; or you can divide the story by the stages of the boy's emotions, using as your guidelines such sentences as "and the exultation and pride of body mounted in him till he was shutting his teeth hard against a violent

desire to shout his triumph" (p. 124). What structural progression do you get in the second case? How does it build your sense of the boy's character?

2. Discuss the use and importance of setting in this story.

3. Note the protagonist's statement on p. 125, "I contain the world," and the passage in which it occurs. Is the statement more or less effective for being spoken in a story in which the speaker is the only character? What does the statement mean to the protagonist as he says it? What overtones has it taken on by the end of the story? What would it mean to you if you made such a statement?

EUDORA WELTY (1909–   )

A Worn Path

It was December—a bright frozen day in the early morning. Far out in the country there was an old Negro woman with her head tied in a red rag, coming along a path through the pinewoods. Her name was Phoenix Jackson. She was very old and small and she walked slowly in the dark pine shadows, moving a little from side to side in her steps, with the balanced heaviness and lightness of a pendulum in a grandfather clock. She carried a thin, small cane made from an umbrella, and with this she kept tapping the frozen earth in front of her. This made a grave and persistent noise in the still air, that seemed meditative like the chirping of a solitary little bird.

She wore a dark striped dress reaching down to her shoetops, and an equally long apron of bleached sugar sacks, with a full pocket; all neat and tidy, but every time she took a step she might have fallen over her shoe-laces, which dragged from her unlaced shoes. She looked straight ahead. Her eyes were blue with age. Her skin had a pattern all its own of numberless branching wrinkles and as though a whole little tree stood in the middle of her forehead, but a golden color ran underneath, and the two knobs of her cheeks were illuminated by a yellow burning under the dark. Under the red rag her hair came down on her neck in the frailest of ringlets, still black, and with an odor like copper.

Now and then there was a quivering in the thicket. Old Phoenix said, "Out of my way, all you foxes, owls, beetles, jack rabbits, coons, and wild animals! . . . Keep out from under these feet, little bob-whites. . . . Keep the big wild hogs out of my path. Don't let none of those come running my direction. I got a long way." Under her small black-freckled hand her cane, limber as a buggy whip, would switch at the brush as if to rouse up any hiding things.

On she went. The woods were deep and still. The sun made the pine needles almost too bright to look at, up where the wind rocked. The cones dropped as light as feathers. Down in the hollow was the mourning dove—it was not too late for him.

The path ran up a hill. "Seems like there is chains about my feet, time I get this far," she said, in the voice of argument old people keep to use with themselves. "Something always take a hold on his hill—pleads I should stay."

After she got to the top she turned and gave a full, severe look behind her where she had come. "Up through pines," she said at length. "Now down through oaks."

Her eyes opened their widest and she started down gently. But before she got to the bottom of the hill a bush caught her dress.

Her fingers were busy and intent, but her skirts were full and long, so that before she could pull them free in one place they were caught in another. It was not possible to allow the dress to tear. "I in the thorny bush," she said. "Thorns, you doing your appointed work. Never want to let folks pass—no sir. Old eyes thought you was a pretty little green bush."

Finally, trembling all over, she stood free, and after a moment dared to stoop for her cane.

"Sun so high!" she cried, leaning back and looking, while the thick tears went over her eyes. "The time getting all gone here."

At the foot of this hill was a place where a log was laid across the creek.

"Now comes the trial," said Phoenix.

Putting her right foot out, she mounted the log and shut her eyes. Lifting her skirt, levelling her cane fiercely before her, like a festival figure in some parade, she began to march across. Then she opened her eyes and she was safe on the other side.

"I wasn't as old as I thought," she said.

But she sat down to rest. She spread her skirts on the bank around her and folded her hands over her knees. Up above her was a tree in a pearly cloud of mistletoe. She did not dare to close her eyes, and when a little boy brought her a little plate with a slice of marble-cake on it she spoke to him. "That would be acceptable," she said. But when she went to take it there was just her own hand in the air.

So she left that tree, and had to go through a barbed-wire fence. There she had to creep and crawl, spreading her knees and stretching her fingers like a baby trying to climb the steps. But she talked loudly to herself: she could not let her dress be torn now, so late in the day, and she could not pay for having her arm or her leg sawed off if she got caught fast where she was.

At last she was safe through the fence and risen up out in the clearing. Big dead trees, like black men with one arm, were standing in the purple stalks of the withered cotton field. There sat a buzzard.

"Who you watching?"

In the burrow she made her way along.

"Glad this not the season for bulls," she said, looking sideways, "and the good Lord made his snakes to curl up and sleep in the winter. A pleasure I don't see no two-headed snake coming around that tree, where it come once. It took a while to get by him, back in the summer."

She passed through the old cotton and went into a field of dead corn. It whispered and shook, and was taller than her head. "Through the maze now," she said, for there was no path.

Then there was something tall, black, and skinny there, moving before her.

At first she took it for a man. It could have been a man dancing in the field. But she stood still and listened, and it did not make a sound. It was as silent as a ghost.

"Ghost," she said sharply, "who be you the ghost of? For I have heard of nary death close by."

But there was no answer, only the ragged dancing in the wind.

She shut her eyes, reached out her hand, and touched a sleeve. She found a coat and inside that an emptiness, cold as ice.

"You scarecrow," she said. Her face lighted. "I ought to be shut up for good," she said with laughter. "My senses is gone. I too old. I the oldest people I ever know. Dance, old scarecrow," she said, "while I dancing with you."

She kicked her foot over the furrow, and with mouth drawn down shook her head once or twice in a little strutting way. Some husks blew down and whirled in streamers about her skirts.

Then she went on, parting her way from side to side with the cane, through the whispering field. At last she came to the end, to a wagon track, where the silver grass blew between the red ruts. The quail were walking around like pullets, seeming all dainty and unseen.

"Walk pretty," she said. "This the easy place. This the easy going."

She followed the track, swaying through the quiet bare fields, through the little strings of trees silver in their dead leaves, past cabins silver from weather, with the doors and windows boarded shut, all like old women under a spell sitting there. "I walking in their sleep," she said, nodding her head vigorously.

In a ravine she went where a spring was silently flowing through a hollow log. Old Phoenix bent and drank. "Sweetgum makes the water sweet," she said, and drank more. "Nobody knows who made this well, for it was here when I was born."

The track crossed a swampy part where the moss hung as white as lace from every limb. "Sleep on, alligators, and blow your bubbles." Then the track went into the road.

Deep, deep the road went down between the high green-colored banks. Overhead the live-oaks met, and it was as dark as a cave.

A black dog with a lolling tongue came up out of the weeds by the ditch. She was meditating, and not ready, and when he came at her she only hit him a little with her cane. Over she went in the ditch, like a little puff of milk-weed.

Down there, her senses drifted away. A dream visited her, and she reached her hand up, but nothing reached down and gave her a pull.

So she lay there and presently went to talking. "Old woman," she said to herself, "that black dog came up out of the weeds to stall you off, and now there he sitting on his fine tail, smiling at you."

A white man finally came along and found her—a hunter, a young man, with his dog on a chain.

"Well, Granny!" he laughed. "What are you doing there?"

"Lying on my back like a June-bug waiting to be turned over, mister," she said, reaching up her hand.

He lifted her up, gave her a swing in the air, and set her down, "Anything broken, Granny?"

"No sir, them old dead weeds is springy enough," said Phoenix, when she had got her breath. "I thank you for your trouble."

"Where do you live, Granny?" he asked, while the two dogs were growling at each other.

"Away back yonder, sir, behind the ridge. You can't even see it from here."

"On your way home?"

"No, sir, I going to town."

"Why, that's too far! That's as far as I walk when I come out myself, and I get something for my trouble." He patted the stuffed bag he carried, and there hung down a little closed claw. It was one of the bobwhites, with its beak hooked bitterly to show it was dead. "Now you go on home, Granny!"

"I bound to go to town, mister," said Phoenix. "The time come around."

He gave another laugh, filling the whole landscape. "I know you colored people! Wouldn't miss going to town to see Santa Claus!"

But something held Old Phoenix very still. The deep lines in her face went into a fierce and different radiation. Without warning she had seen with her own eyes a flashing nickel fall out of the man's pocket on to the ground.

"How old are you, Granny?" he was saying.

"There is no telling, mister," she said, "no telling."

Then she gave a little cry and clapped her hands, and said, "Git on away from here, dog! Look at that dog!" She laughed as if in admiration. "He ain't scared of nobody. He a big black dog." She whispered, "Sick him!"

"Watch me get rid of that cur," said the man. "Sick him, Pete! Sick him!"

Phoenix heard the dogs fighting and heard the man running and throwing sticks. She even heard a gunshot. But she was slowly bending forward by that time, further and further forward, the lids stretched down over her eyes, as if she were doing this in her sleep. Her chin was lowered almost to her knees. The yellow palm of her hand came out from the fold of her apron. Her fingers slid down and along the ground under the piece of money with the grace and care they would have in lifting an egg from under a sitting hen. Then she slowly straightened up, she stood erect, and the nickel was in her apron pocket. A bird flew by. Her lips moved. "God watching me the whole time. I come to stealing."

The man came back, and his own dog panted about them. "Well, I scared him off that time," he said, and then he laughed and lifted his gun and pointed it at Phoenix.

She stood straight and faced him.

"Doesn't the gun scare you?" he said, still pointing it.

"No, sir, I seen plenty go off closer by, in my day, and for less than what I done," she said, holding utterly still.

He smiled, and shouldered the gun. "Well, Granny," he said, "you must be a hundred years old and scared of nothing. I'd give you a dime if I had any money with me. But you take my advice and stay home, and nothing will happen to you."

"I bound to go on my way, mister," said Phoenix. She inclined her head in the red rag. Then they went in different directions, but she could hear the gun shooting again and again over the hill.

She walked on. The shadows hung from the oak trees to the road like curtains. Then she smelled wood-smoke, and smelled the river, and she saw a steeple and the cabins on their steep steps. Dozens of little black children whirled around her. There ahead was Natchez shining. Bells were ringing. She walked on.

In the paved city it was Christmas time. There were red and green electric lights strung and crisscrossed everywhere, and all turned on in the daytime. Old Phoenix would have been lost if she had not distrusted her eyesight and depended on her feet to know where to take her.

She paused quietly on the sidewalk, where people were passing by. A lady came along in the crowd, carrying an armful of red-, green-, and silver-wrapped presents; she gave off perfume like the red roses in hot summer, and Phoenix stopped her.

"Please, missy, will you lace up my shoe?" She held up her foot.

"What do you want, Grandma?"

"See my shoe," said Phoenix. "Do all right for out in the country, but wouldn't look right to go in a big building."

"Stand still then, Grandma," said the lady. She put her packages down carefully on the sidewalk beside her and laced and tied both shoes tightly.

"Can't lace 'em with a cane," said Phoenix. "Thank you, missy. I doesn't mind asking a nice lady to tie up my shoe when I gets out on the street."

Moving slowly and from side to side, she went into the stone building and into a tower of steps, where she walked up and around and around until her feet knew to stop.

She entered a door, and there she saw nailed up on the wall the document that had been stamped with the gold seal and framed in the gold frame which matched the dream that was hung up in her head.

"Here I be," she said. There was a fixed and ceremonial stiffness over her body.

"A charity case, I suppose," said an attendant who sat at the desk before her.

But Phoenix only looked above her head. There was sweat on her face; the wrinkles shone like a bright net.

"Speak up, Grandma," the woman said. "What's your name? We must have your history, you know. Have you been here before? What seems to be the trouble with you?"

Old Phoenix only gave a twitch to her face as if a fly were bothering her.

"Are you deaf?" cried the attendant.

But then the nurse came in.

"Oh, that's just old Aunt Phoenix," she said. "She doesn't come for herself—she has a little grandson. She makes these trips just as regular as clockwork. She lives away back off the Old Natchez Trace." She bent down. "Well, Aunt Phoenix, why don't you just take a seat? We won't keep you standing after your long trip." She pointed.

The old woman sat down, bolt upright in the chair.

"Now, how is the boy?" asked the nurse.

Old Phoenix did not speak.

"I said, how is the boy?"

But Phoenix only waited and stared straight ahead, her face very solemn and withdrawn into rigidity.

"Is his throat any better?" asked the nurse. "Aunt Phoenix, don't you hear me? Is your grandson's throat any better since the last time you came for the medicine?"

With her hand on her knees, the old woman waited, silent, erect and motionless, just as if she were in armor.

"You mustn't take up our time this way, Aunt Phoenix," the nurse said. "Tell us quickly about your grandson, and get it over. He isn't dead, is he?"

At last there came a flicker and then a flame of comprehension across her face, and she spoke.

"My grandson. It was my memory had left me. There I sat and forgot why I made my long trip."

"Forgot?" The nurse frowned. "After you came so far?"

Then Phoenix was like an old woman begging a dignified forgiveness for waking up frightened in the night. "I never did go to school

—I was too old at the Surrender," she said in a soft voice. "I'm an old woman without an education. It was my memory fail me. My little grandson, he is just the same, and I forgot it in the coming."

"Throat never heals, does it?" said the nurse, speaking in a loud, sure voice to Old Phoenix. By now she had a card with something written on it, a little list. "Yes. Swallowed lye. When was it—January —two—three years ago—"

Phoenix spoke unasked now. "No, missy, he not dead, he just the same. Every little while his throat begin to close up again, and he not able to swallow. He not get his breath. He not able to help himself. So the time come around, and I go on another trip for the soothing-medicine."

"All right. The doctor said as long as you came to get it you could have it," said the nurse. "But it's an obstinate case."

"My little grandson, he sit up there in the house all wrapped up, waiting by himself," Phoenix went on. "We is the only two left in the world. He suffer and it don't seem to put him back at all. He got a sweet look. He going to last. He wear a little patch quilt and peep out, holding his mouth open like a little bird. I remembers so plain now. I not going to forget him again, no, the whole enduring time. I could tell him from all the others in creation."

"All right." The nurse was trying to hush her now. She brought her a bottle of medicine. "Charity," she said, making a check mark in a book.

Old Phoenix held the bottle close to her eyes and then carefully put it into her pocket.

"I thank you," she said.

"It's Christmas time, Grandma," said the attendant. "Could I give you a few pennies out of my purse?"

"Five pennies is a nickel," said Phoenix stiffly.

"Here's a nickel," said the attendant.

Phoenix rose carefully and held out her hand. She received the nickel and then fished the other nickel out of her pocket and laid it beside the new one. She stared at her palm closely, with her head on one side.

Then she gave a tap with her cane on the floor.

"This is what come to me to do," she said. "I going to the store and buy my child a little windmill they sells, made out of paper. He going to find it hard to believe there such a thing in the world. I'll march myself back where he waiting, holding it straight up in this hand."

She lifted her free hand, gave a little nod, turned round, and walked out of the doctor's office. Then her slow step began on the stairs, going down.

QUESTIONS

1. How much of the story takes place with Granny Phoenix as its only character? What happens in this first part of the tale? What effect does it have on you, the reader?

2. Describe Granny's first meeting with another person. What new information do we learn from it?

3. The story's climax comes at the point of the scene in the clinic. Here we finally learn why Granny has made her long journey. What is your reaction to this scene? How have the story and its narrator brought you to feel as you do?

CHARACTER STUDY AND SOCIAL COMMENT

5 *Looking Inward and Outward*

In the last chapter, we looked at fiction that focussed tightly on its protagonist and on a single moment in time. In this chapter, we look at three stories that maintain a wider focus, looking not at a moment, but at days, weeks, or even years; and not at protagonists in isolation, but at protagonists who, whatever their private struggles, are members of some larger group or society.

Human beings are both individuals and social beings. Fiction, throughout its history, has concerned itself with that duality. One of fiction's most fascinating characteristics, in fact, is its ability to look in two directions at once. Fictional narrators can look into their characters, revealing their minds and feelings to us, exploring their personalities. And they can look out at the society to which the characters belong. Looking inward, they seem to ask, "What sort of people are these?" Looking outward, they seem to ask, "What has made them that way?"

Writers of fiction have long felt that their form's unique ability to deal with the common reality of everyday life made it an ideal vehicle for examining the interaction of individuals with their society. We find that concern reflected in nearly all forms of fiction, from old and traditional tales such as "Bartleby the Scrivener" to some of the most experimental contemporary works. Many Americans in the latter half of the twentieth century are deeply concerned with questions of society's influence and power over the individual and of the individual's own power to shape his or her own personality and future. Contemporary fiction reflects these concerns.

The four stories that follow are all works that engage our concern for some central character or characters, while forcing upon us some realization of or comment on the society in which these characters live. In these stories, as in others we have read, the physical settings often become metaphors for the social settings. The influence of society, and the characters' reactions to it, thus form an important part of each tale.

As you read these stories, therefore, take note of their physical and social settings, and of how these settings are used to define the characters' actions and personalities. Take note, too—as always when dealing with fiction—of the narrators' voices. What tones of voice do you hear in these stories? What attitudes do they convey? How do the narrators blend their stories' dual focus on individual and society into a concern for the fulfillment or happiness of their central characters? What moods do they leave you in at the stories' ends? How do they get you there?

WILLIAM FAULKNER (1897–1962)

A Rose for Emily

I

When Miss Emily Grierson died, our whole town went to her funeral: the men through a sort of respectful affection for a fallen monument, the women mostly out of curiosity to see the inside of her house, which no one save an old man-servant—a combined gardener and cook—had seen in at least ten years.

It was a big, squarish frame house that had once been white, decorated with cupolas and spires, and scrolled balconies in the heavily lightsome style of the seventies, set on what had once been our most select street. But garages and cotton gins had encroached and obliterated even the august names of that neighborhood; only Miss Emily's house was left, lifting its stubborn and coquettish decay above the cotton wagons and the gasoline pumps—an eyesore among eyesores. And now Miss Emily had gone to join the representatives of those august names where they lay in the cedar-bemused cemetery among the ranked and anonymous graves of Union and Confederate soldiers who fell at the battle of Jefferson.

Alive, Miss Emily had been a tradition, a duty, and a care; a sort of hereditary obligation upon the town, dating from that day in 1894 when Colonel Sartoris, the mayor—he who fathered the edict that no Negro woman should appear on the street without an apron—remitted her taxes, the dispensation dating from the death of her father on into perpetuity. Not that Miss Emily would have accepted charity. Colonel Sartoris invented an involved tale to the effect that Miss Emily's father had loaned money to the town, which the town, as a matter of business, preferred this way of repaying. Only a man of Colonel Sartoris' generation and thought could have invented it, and only a woman could have believed it.

When the next generation, with its more modern ideas, became mayors and aldermen, this arrangement created some little dissatisfaction. On the first of the year they mailed her a tax notice. February came, and there was no reply. They wrote her a formal letter, asking her to call at the sheriff's office at her convenience. A week later the mayor wrote her himself, offering to call or to send his car for her, and received in reply a note on paper of an archaic shape, in a thin, flowing calligraphy in faded ink, to the effect that she no longer went out at all. The tax notice was also enclosed, without comment.

They called a special meeting of the Board of Aldermen. A deputation waited upon her, knocked at the door through which no visitor had passed since she ceased giving china-painting lessons eight or ten years earlier. They were admitted by the old Negro into a dim hall from which a stairway mounted into still more shadow. It smelled of dust and disuse—a close, dank smell. The Negro led them into the parlor. It was furnished in heavy, leather-covered furniture. When the Negro opened the blinds of one window, they could see that the leather was cracked; and when they sat down, a faint dust rose sluggishly about their thighs, spinning with slow motes in the single sun-ray. On a tarnished gilt easel before the fireplace stood a crayon portrait of Miss Emily's father.

They rose when she entered—a small, fat woman in black, with a thin gold chain descending to her waist and vanishing into her belt, leaning on an ebony cane with a tarnished gold head. Her skeleton was small and spare; perhaps that was why what would have been merely plumpness in another was obesity in her. She looked bloated, like a body long submerged in motionless water, and of that pallid hue. Her eyes, lost in the fatty ridges of her face, looked like two small pieces of coal pressed into a lump of dough as they moved from one face to another while the visitors stated their errand.

She did not ask them to sit. She just stood in the door and listened quietly until the spokesman came to a stumbling halt. Then they could hear the invisible watch ticking at the end of the gold chain.

Her voice was dry and cold. "I have no taxes in Jefferson. Colonel Sartoris explained it to me. Perhaps one of you can gain access to the city records and satisfy yourselves."

"But we have. We are the city authorities, Miss Emily. Didn't you get a notice from the sheriff, signed by him?"

"I received a paper, yes," Miss Emily said. "Perhaps he considers himself the sheriff . . . I have no taxes in Jefferson."

"But there is nothing on the books to show that, you see. We must go by the—"

"See Colonel Sartoris. I have no taxes in Jefferson."

"But Miss Emily—"

"See Colonel Sartoris." (Colonel Sartoris had been dead almost ten years.) "I have no taxes in Jefferson. Tobe!" The Negro appeared. "Show these gentlemen out."

II

So she vanquished them, horse and foot, just as she had vanquished their fathers thirty years before about the smell. That was two years after her father's death and a short time after her sweetheart—the one we believed would marry her—had deserted her. After her father's death she went out very little; after her sweetheart went away, people hardly saw her at all. A few of the ladies had the temerity to call, but were not received, and the only sign of life about the place was the Negro man—a young man then—going in and out with a market basket.

"Just as if a man—any man—could keep a kitchen properly," the ladies said; so they were not surprised when the smell developed. It was another link between the gross, teeming world and the high and mighty Griersons.

A neighbor, a woman, complained to the mayor, Judge Stevens, eighty years old.

"But what will you have me do about it, madam?" he said.

"Why, send her word to stop it," the woman said. "Isn't there a law?"

"I'm sure that won't be necessary," Judge Stevens said. "It's probably just a snake or a rat that nigger of hers killed in the yard. I'll speak to him about it."

The next day he received two more complaints, one from a man who came in diffident deprecation. "We really must do something about it, Judge. I'd be the last one in the world to bother Miss Emily, but we've got to do something." That night the Board of Aldermen met—three graybeards and one younger man, a member of the rising generation.

"It's simple enough," he said. "Send her word to have her place cleaned up. Give her a certain time do it in, and if she don't . . ."

"Dammit, sir," Judge Stevens said, "will you accuse a lady to her face of smelling bad?"

So the next night, after midnight, four men crossed Miss Emily's lawn and slunk about the house like burglars, sniffing along the base of the brickwork and at the cellar openings while one of them performed a regular sowing motion with his hand out of a sack slung from his shoulder. They broke open the cellar door and sprinkled lime there, and in all the outbuildings. As they recrossed the lawn, a window that had been dark was lighted and Miss Emily sat in it, the light behind her, and her upright torso motionless as that of an idol. They crept quietly across the lawn and into the shadow of the locusts that lined the street. After a week or two the smell went away.

That was when people had begun to feel really sorry for her. People in our town, remembering how old lady Wyatt, her great-aunt, had gone completely crazy at last, believed that the Griersons held themselves a little too high for what they really were. None of the young men were quite good enough for Miss Emily and such. We had long thought of them as a tableau, Miss Emily a slender figure in white in the background, her father a spraddled silhouette in the foregound, his back to her and clutching a horsewhip, the two of them framed by the backflung front door. When she got to be thirty and was still single, we were not pleased exactly, but vindicated; even with insanity in the family she wouldn't have turned down all of her chances if they had really materialized.

When her father died, it got about that the house was all that was left to her; and in a way, people were glad. At last they could pity Miss Emily. Being left alone, and a pauper, she had become humanized. Now she too would know the old thrill and the old despair of a penny more or less.

The day after his death all the ladies prepared to call at the house and offer condolence and aid, as is our custom. Miss Emily met them at the door, dressed as usual and with no trace of grief on her face. She told them that her father was not dead. She did that for three days, with the ministers calling on her, and the doctors, trying to persuade her to let them dispose of the body. Just as they were about to resort to law and force, she broke down, and they buried her father quickly.

We did not say she was crazy then. We believed she had to do that. We remembered all the young men her father had driven away, and we knew that with nothing left, she would have to cling to that which had robbed her, as people will.

III

She was sick for a long time. When we saw her again, her hair was cut short, making her look like a girl, with a vague resemblance to those angels in colored church windows—sort of tragic and serene.

The town had just let the contracts for paving the sidewalks, and in the summer after her father's death they began the work. The construction company came with niggers and mules and machinery, and a foreman named Homer Barron, a Yankee—a big, dark, ready man, with a big voice and eyes lighter than his face. The little boys would follow in groups to hear him cuss the niggers, and the niggers singing in time to the rise and fall of picks. Pretty soon he knew everybody in town. Whenever you heard a lot of laughing anywhere about the square, Homer Barron would be in the center of the group.

Presently we began to see him and Miss Emily on Sunday afternoons driving in the yellow-wheeled buggy and the matched team of bays from the livery stable.

At first we were glad that Miss Emily would have an interest, because the ladies all said, "Of course a Grierson would not think seriously of a Northerner, a day laborer." But there were still others, older people, who said that even grief could not cause a real lady to forget *noblesse oblige*—without calling it *noblesse oblige*. They just said, "Poor Emily. Her kinsfolk should come to her." She had some kin in Alabama; but years ago her father had fallen out with them over the estate of old Lady Wyatt, the crazy woman, and there was no communication between the two families. They had not even been represented at the funeral.

And as soon as the old people said, "Poor Emily," the whispering began. "Do you suppose it's really so?" they said to one another. "Of course it is. What else could . . ." This behind their hands; rustling of craned silk and satin behind jalousies closed upon the sun of Sunday afternoon as the thin, swift clop-clop-clop of the matched team passed: "Poor Emily."

She carried her head high enough—even when we believed that she was fallen. It was as if she demanded more than ever the recognition of her dignity as the last Grierson; as if it had wanted that touch of earthiness to reaffirm her imperviousness. Like when she bought the rat poison, the arsenic. That was over a year after they had begun to say "Poor Emily," and while the two female cousins were visiting her.

"I want some poison," she said to the druggist. She was over thirty then, still a slight woman, though thinner than usual, with cold, haughty black eyes in a face the flesh of which was strained across the temples and about the eye sockets as you imagine a lighthouse-keeper's face ought to look. "I want some poison," she said.

"Yes, Miss Emily. What kind? For rats and such? I'd recom—"

"I want the best you have. I don't care what kind."

The druggist named several. "They'll kill anything up to an elephant. But what you want is—"

"Arsenic," Miss Emily said. "Is that a good one?"

"Is . . . arsenic? Yes, ma'am. But what you want—"

"I want arsenic."

The druggist looked down at her. She looked back at him, erect, her face like a strained flag. "Why, of course," the druggist said. "If that's what you want. But the law requires you to tell what you are going to use it for."

Miss Emily just stared at him, her head tilted back in order to look him eye for eye, until he looked away and went and got the arsenic and wrapped it up. The Negro delivery boy brought her the package; the druggist didn't come back. When she opened the package at home there was written on the box, under the skull and bones: "For rats."

IV

So the next day we all said, "She will kill herself"; and we said it would be the best thing. When she had first begun to be seen with Homer Barron, we had said, "She will marry him." Then we said, "She will persuade him yet," because Homer himself had remarked— he liked men, and it was known that he drank with the younger men in the Elks' Club—that he was not a marrying man. Later we said, "Poor Emily" behind the jalousies as they passed on Sunday afternoon in the glittering buggy, Miss Emily with her head high and Homer Barron with his hat cocked and cigar in his teeth, reins and whip in a yellow glove.

Then some of the ladies began to say that it was a disgrace to the town and a bad example to the young people. The men did not want to interfere, but at last the ladies forced the Baptist minister— Miss Emily's people were Episcopal—to call upon her. He would never divulge what happened during that interview, but he refused to go back again. The next Sunday they again drove about the streets, and the following day the minister's wife wrote to Miss Emily's relations in Alabama.

So she had blood-kin under her roof again and we sat back to watch developments. At first nothing happened. Then we were sure that they were to be married. We learned that Miss Emily had been to the jeweler's and ordered a man's toilet set in silver, with the letters H. B. on each piece. Two days later we learned that she had bought a complete outfit of men's clothing, including a nightshirt, and we said, "They are married." We were really glad. We were glad because the two female cousins were even more Grierson than Miss Emily had ever been.

So we were not surprised when Homer Barron—the streets had been finished some time since—was gone. We were a little disappointed that there was not a public blowing-off, but we believed that he had gone on to prepare for Miss Emily's coming, or to give her a chance to get rid of the cousins. (By that time it was a cabal, and we were all Miss Emily's allies to help circumvent the cousins.) Sure enough, after another week they departed. And, as we had expected all along, within three days Homer Barron was back in town. A neighbor saw the Negro man admit him at the kitchen door at dusk one evening.

And that was the last we saw of Homer Barron. And of Miss Emily for some time. The Negro man went in and out with the market basket, but the front door remained closed. Now and then we would see her at a window for a moment, as the men did that night when they sprinkled the lime, but for almost six months she did not appear on the streets. Then we knew that this was to be expected too; as if that quality of her father which had thwarted her woman's life so many times had been too virulent and too furious to die.

When we next saw Miss Emily, she had grown fat and her hair was turning gray. During the next few years it grew grayer and grayer until it attained an even pepper-and-salt iron-gray, when it ceased turning. Up to the day of her death at seventy-four it was still that vigorous iron-gray, like the hair of an active man.

From that time on her front door remained closed, save for a period of six or seven years, when she was about forty, during which she gave lessons in china-painting. She fitted up a studio in one of the downstairs rooms, where the daughters and granddaughters of Colonel Sartoris' contemporaries were sent to her with the same regularity and in the same spirit that they were sent to church on Sunday with a twenty-five-cent piece for the collection plate. Meanwhile her taxes had been remitted.

Then the newer generation became the backbone and the spirit of the town, and the painting pupils grew up and fell away and did not send their children to her with boxes of color and tedious brushes and pictures cut from the ladies' magazines. The front door closed upon the last one and remained closed for good. When the town got free postal delivery, Miss Emily alone refused to let them fasten the metal numbers above her door and attach a mailbox to it. She would not listen to them.

Daily, monthly, yearly we watched the Negro grow grayer and more stooped, going in and out with the market basket. Each December we sent her a tax notice, which would be returned by the post office a week later, unclaimed. Now and then we would see her in one of the downstairs windows—she had evidently shut up the top floor of the house—like the carven torso of an idol in a niche, looking or not looking at us, we could never tell which. Thus she passed from generation to generation—dear, inescapable, impervious, tranquil, and perverse.

And so she died. Fell ill in the house filled with dust and shadows, with only a doddering Negro man to wait on her. We did not even know she was sick; we had long since given up trying to get any information from the Negro. He talked to no one, probably not even to her, for his voice had grown harsh and rusty, as if from disuse.

She died in one of the downstairs rooms, in a heavy walnut bed with a curtain, her gray head propped on a pillow yellow and moldy with age and lack of sunlight.

V

The Negro met the first of the ladies at the front door and let them in, with their hushed, sibilant voices and their quick, curious glances, and then he disappeared. He walked right through the house and out the back and was not seen again.

The two female cousins came at once. They held the funeral on the second day, with the town coming to look at Miss Emily beneath a mass of bought flowers, with the crayon face of her father musing profoundly above the bier and the ladies sibilant and macabre; and the very old men—some in their brushed Confederate uniforms—on the porch and the lawn, talking of Miss Emily as if she had been a contemporary of theirs, believing that they had danced with her and courted her perhaps, confusing time with its mathematical progression, as the old do, to whom all the past is not a diminishing road but, instead, a huge meadow which no winter ever quite touches, divided from them now by the narrow bottle-neck of the most recent decade of years.

Already we knew that there was one room in that region above stairs which no one had seen in forty years, and which would have to be forced. They waited until Miss Emily was decently in the ground before they opened it.

The violence of breaking down the door seemed to fill this room with pervading dust. A thin, acrid pall of the tomb seemed to lie everywhere upon this room decked and furnished as for a bridal: upon the valance curtains of faded rose color, upon the rose-shaded lights, upon the dressing table, upon the delicate array of crystal and the man's toilet things backed with tarnished silver, silver so tarnished that the monogram was obscured. Among them lay a collar and tie, as if they had just been removed, which, lifted, left upon the surface a pale crescent in the dust. Upon a chair hung the suit, carefully folded; beneath it the two mute shoes and the discarded socks.

The man himself lay in the bed.

For a long while we just stood there, looking down at the profound and fleshless grin. The body had apparently once lain in the attitude of an embrace, but now the long sleep that outlasts love, that conquers even the grimace of love, had cuckolded him. What was left of him, rotted beneath what was left of the nightshirt, had become inextricable from the bed in which he lay; and upon him and upon the pillow beside him lay that even coating of the patient and biding dust.

Then we noticed that in the second pillow was the indentation of a head. One of us lifted something from it, and leaning forward, that faint and invisible dust dry and acrid in the nostrils, we saw a long strand of iron-gray hair.

QUESTIONS

1. Part of the effectiveness of "A Rose for Emily" comes from its surprise ending. How effective do you find the ending? Why?
2. How do the narrator and the townsfolk view the young Miss Emily? How does Miss Emily change with time? How does the town? How does the narrator's view of Miss Emily change? How does yours?

JAMES BALDWIN (1924–1987)

Sonny's Blues

I read about it in the paper, in the subway, on my way to work. I read it, and I couldn't believe it, and I read it again. Then perhaps I just stared at it, at the newsprint spelling out his name, spelling out the story. I stared at it in the swinging lights of the subway car, and in the faces and bodies of the people, and in my own face, trapped in the darkness which roared outside.

It was not to be believed and I kept telling myself that as I walked from the subway station to the high school. And at the same time I couldn't doubt it. I was scared, scared for Sonny. He became real to me again. A great block of ice got settled in my belly and kept melting there slowly all day long, while I taught my classes algebra. It was a special kind of ice. It kept melting, sending trickles of ice water all up and down my veins, but it never got less. Sometimes it hardened and seemed to expand until I felt my guts were going to come spilling out or that I was going to choke or scream. This would always be at a moment when I was remembering some specific thing Sonny had once said or done.

When he was about as old as the boys in my classes his face had been bright and open, there was a lot of copper in it; and he'd had wonderfully direct brown eyes, and great gentleness and privacy. I wondered what he looked like now. He had been picked up, the evening before, in a raid on an apartment downtown, for peddling and using heroin.

I couldn't believe it: but what I mean by that is that I couldn't find any room for it anywhere inside me. I had kept it outside me for a long time. I hadn't wanted to know. I had had suspicions, but I didn't name them, I kept putting them away. I told myself that Sonny was wild, but he wasn't crazy. And he'd always been a good boy, he hadn't ever turned hard or evil or disrespectful, the way kids can, so quick, so quick, especially in Harlem. I didn't want to believe that I'd ever see my brother going down, coming to nothing, all that light in his face gone out, in the condition I'd already seen so many others. Yet it had happened and here I was, talking about algebra to a lot of boys who might, every one of them for all I knew, be popping off needles every time they went to the head. Maybe it did more for them than algebra could.

I was sure that the first time Sonny had ever had horse, he couldn't have been much older than these boys were now. These boys, now, were living as we'd been living then, they were growing up with a rush and their heads bumped abruptly against the low ceiling of their actual possibilities. They were filled with rage. All they really knew were two darknesses, the darkness of their lives, which was now closing in on them, and the darkness of the movies, which had blinded them to that other darkness, and in which they now, vindictively, dreamed, at once more together than they were at any other time, and more alone.

When the last bell rang, the last class ended, I let out my breath. It seemed I'd been holding it for all that time. My clothes were wet—I may have looked as though I'd been sitting in a steam bath, all dressed up, all afternoon. I sat alone in the classroom a long time. I listened to the boys outside, downstairs, shouting and cursing and laughing. Their laughter struck me for perhaps the first time. It was not the joyous laughter which—God knows why—one associates with children. It was mocking and insular, its intent was to denigrate. It was disenchanted, and in this, also, lay the authority of their curses. Perhaps I was listening to them because I was thinking about my brother and in them I heard my brother. And myself.

One boy was whistling a tune, at once very complicated and very simple, it seemed to be pouring out of him as though he were a bird, and it sounded very cool and moving through all that harsh, bright air, only just holding its own through all those other sounds.

I stood up and walked over to the window and looked down into the courtyard. It was the beginning of the spring and the sap was rising in the boys. A teacher passed through them every now and again, quickly, as though he or she couldn't wait to get out of that courtyard, to get those boys out of their sight and off their minds. I started collecting my stuff. I thought I'd better get home and talk to Isabel.

The courtyard was almost deserted by the time I got downstairs. I saw this boy standing in the shadow of a doorway, looking just like Sonny. I almost called his name. Then I saw that it wasn't Sonny, but somebody we used to know, a boy from around our block. He'd been Sonny's friend. He'd never been mine, having been too young for me, and, anyway, I'd never liked him. And now, even though he was a grown-up man, he still hung around that block, still spent hours on the street corner, was always high and raggy. I used to run into him from time to time and he'd often work around to asking me for a quarter or fifty cents. He always had some real good excuse, too, and I always gave it to him, I don't know why.

But now, abruptly, I hated him. I couldn't stand the way he looked at me, partly like a dog, partly like a cunning child. I wanted to ask him what the hell he was doing in the school courtyard.

He sort of shuffled over to me, and he said, "I see you got the papers. So you already know about it."

"You mean about Sonny? Yes, I already know about it. How come they didn't get you?"

He grinned. It made him repulsive and it also brought to mind what he'd looked like as a kid. "I wasn't there. I stay away from them people."

"Good for you." I offered him a cigarette and I watched him through the smoke. "You come all the way down here just to tell me about Sonny?"

"That's right." He was sort of shaking his head and his eyes looked strange, as though they were about to cross. The bright sun deadened his damp dark brown skin and it made his eyes look yellow and showed up the dirt in his conked hair. He smelled funky. I moved a little away from him and I said, "Well, thanks. But I already know about it and I got to get home."

"I'll walk you a little ways," he said. We started walking. There were a couple of kids still loitering in the courtyard and one of them said good night to me and looked strangely at the boy beside me.

"What're you going to do?" he asked me. "I mean, about Sonny?"

"Look. I haven't seen Sonny for over a year, I'm not sure I'm going to do anything. Anyway, what the hell *can* I do?"

"That's right," he said quickly, "ain't nothing you can do. Can't much help old Sonny no more, I guess."

It was what I was thinking and so it seemed to me he had no right to say it.

"I'm surprised at Sonny, though," he went on—he had a funny way of talking, he looked straight ahead as though he were talking to himself—"I thought Sonny was a smart boy, I thought he was too smart to get hung."

"I guess he thought so too," I said sharply, "and that's how he got hung. And how about you? You're pretty goddamn smart, I bet."

Then he looked directly at me, just for a minute. "I ain't smart," he said. "If I was smart, I'd have reached for a pistol a long time ago."

"Look. Don't tell *me* your sad story, if it was up to me, I'd give you one." Then I felt guilty—guilty, probably, for never having supposed that the poor bastard *had* a story of his own, much less a sad one, and I asked, quickly, "What's going to happen to him now?"

He didn't answer this. He was off by himself some place. "Funny thing," he said, and from his tone we might have been discussing the quickest way to get to Brooklyn, "when I saw the papers this morning, the first thing I asked myself was if I had anything to do with it. I felt sort of responsible."

I began to listen more carefully. The subway station was on the corner, just before us, and I stopped. He stopped, too. We were in front of a bar and he ducked slightly, peering in, but whoever he was looking for didn't seem to be there. The juke box was blasting away with something black and bouncy and I half watched the barmaid as she danced her way from the juke box to her place behind the bar. And I watched her face as she laughingly responded to something someone said to her, still keeping time to the music. When she smiled one saw the little girl, one sensed the doomed, still-struggling woman beneath the battered face of the semi-whore.

"I never *give* Sonny nothing," the boy said finally, "but a long time ago I come to school high and Sonny asked me how it felt." He paused, I couldn't bear to watch him, I watched the barmaid, and I listened to the music which seemed to be causing the pavement to shake. "I told him it felt great." The music stopped, the barmaid paused and watched the juke box until the music began again. "It did."

All this was carrying me some place I didn't want to go. I certainly didn't want to know how it felt. It filled everything, the people, the houses, the music, the dark, quicksilver barmaid, with menace; and this menace was their reality.

"What's going to happen to him now?" I asked again.

"They'll send him away some place and they'll try to cure him." He shook his head. "Maybe he'll even think he's kicked the habit. Then they'll let him loose"—he gestured, throwing his cigarette into the gutter. "That's all."

"What do you mean, that's *all?*"

But I knew what he meant.

"I *mean*, that's *all*." He turned his head and looked at me, pulling down the corners of his mouth. "Don't you know what I mean?" he asked softly.

"How the hell *would* I know what you mean?" I almost whispered it, I don't know why.

"That's right," he said to the air, "how would *he* know what I mean?" He turned toward me again, patient and calm, and yet I somehow felt him shaking, shaking as though he were going to fall apart. I felt that ice in my guts again, the dread I'd felt all afternoon; and again I watched the barmaid, moving about the bar, washing glasses, and singing. "Listen. They'll let him out and then it'll just start all over again. That's what I mean."

"You mean—they'll let him out. And then he'll just start working his way back in again. You mean he'll never kick the habit. Is that what you mean?"

"That's right," he said, cheerfully. *"You* see what I mean."

"Tell me," I said at last, "why does he want to die? He must want to die, he's killing himself, why does he want to die?"

He looked at me in surprise. He licked his lips. "He don't want to die. He wants to live. Don't nobody want to die, ever."

Then I wanted to ask him—too many things. He could not have answered, or if he had, I could not have borne the answers. I started walking. "Well, I guess it's none of my business."

"It's going to be rough on old Sonny," he said. We reached the subway station. "This is your station?" he asked. I nodded. I took one step down. "Damn!" he said, suddenly. I looked up at him. He grinned again. "Damn if I didn't leave all my money home. You ain't got a dollar on you, have you? Just for a couple of days, is all."

All at once something inside gave and threatened to come pouring out of me. I didn't hate him any more. I felt that in another moment I'd start crying like a child.

"Sure," I said. "Don't sweat." I looked in my wallet and didn't have a dollar, I only had a five. "Here," I said. "That hold you?"

He didn't look at it—he didn't want to look at it. A terrible, closed look came over his face, as though he were keeping the number on the bill a secret from him and me. "Thanks," he said, and now he was dying to see me go. "Don't worry about Sonny. Maybe I'll write him or something."

"Sure," I said. "You do that. So long."

"Be seeing you," he said. I went on down the steps.

And I didn't write Sonny or send him anything for a long time. When I finally did, it was just after my little girl died, he wrote me back a letter which made me feel like a bastard.

Here's what he said:

Dear Brother,

You don't know how much I needed to hear from you. I wanted to write you many a time but I dug how much I must have hurt you and so I didn't write. But now I feel like a man who's been trying to climb up out of some deep, real deep and funky hole and just saw the sun up there, outside. I got to get outside.

I can't tell you much about how I got here. I mean I don't know how to tell you. I guess I was afraid of something or I was trying to escape from something and you know I have never been very strong in the head (smile). I'm glad Mama and Daddy are dead and can't see what's happened to their son and I swear if I'd known what I was doing I would never have hurt you so, you and a lot of other fine people who were nice to me and who believed in me.

I don't want you to think it had anything to do with me being a musician. It's more than that. Or maybe less than that. I can't get anything straight in my head down here and I try not to think about what's going to happen to me when I get outside again. Sometime I think I'm going to flip and *never* get outside and sometime I think I'll come straight back. I tell you one thing, though, I'd rather blow my brains out than go through this again. But that's what they all say, so they tell me. If I tell you when I'm coming to New York and if you could meet me, I sure would appreciate it. Give my love to Isabel and the kids and I was sorry to hear about little Gracie. I wish I could be like Mama and say the Lord's will be done, but I don't know it seems to me that trouble is the one thing that never does get stopped and I don't know what good it does to blame it on the Lord. But maybe it does some good if you believe it.

Your brother,

SONNY

Then I kept in constant touch with him and I sent him whatever I could and I went to meet him when he came back to New York. When I saw him many things I thought I had forgotten came flooding back to me. This was because I had begun, finally, to wonder about Sonny, about the life that Sonny lived inside. This life, whatever it was, had made him older and thinner and it had deepened the distant stillness in which he had always moved. He looked very unlike my baby brother. Yet, when he smiled, when we shook hands, the baby brother I'd never known looked out from the depths of his private life, like an animal waiting to be coaxed into the light.

"How you been keeping?" he asked me.

"All right. And you?"

"Just fine." He was smiling all over his face. "It's good to see you again."

"It's good to see you."

The seven years' difference in our ages lay between us like a chasm: I wondered if these years would ever operate between us as a bridge. I was remembering, and it made it hard to catch my breath, that I had been there when he was born; and I had heard the first words he had ever spoken. When he started to walk, he walked from our mother straight to me. I caught him just before he fell when he took the first steps he ever took in this world.

"How's Isabel?"

"Just fine. She's dying to see you."

"And the boys?"

"They're fine, too. They're anxious to see their uncle."

"Oh, come on. You know they don't remember me."

"Are you kidding? Of course they remember you."

He grinned again. We got into a taxi. We had a lot to say to each other, far too much to know how to begin.

As the taxi began to move, I asked, "You still want to go to India?"

He laughed. "You still remember that. Hell, no. This place is Indian enough for me."

"It used to belong to them," I said.

And he laughed again. "They damn sure knew what they were doing when they got rid of it."

Years ago, when he was around fourteen, he'd been all hipped on the idea of going to India. He read books about people sitting on rocks, naked, in all kinds of weather, but mostly bad, naturally, and walking barefoot through hot coals and arriving at wisdom. I used to say that it sounded to me as though they were getting away from wisdom as fast as they could. I think he sort of looked down on me for that.

"Do you mind," he asked, "if we have the driver drive alongside the park? On the west side—I haven't seen the city in so long."

"Of course not," I said. I was afraid that I might sound as though I were humoring him, but I hoped he wouldn't take it that way.

So we drove along, between the green of the park and the stony, lifeless elegance of hotels and apartment buildings, toward the vivid, killing streets of our childhood. These streets hadn't changed, though housing projects jutted up out of them now like rocks in the middle of a boiling sea. Most of the houses in which we had grown up had vanished, as had the stores from which we had stolen, the basements in which we had first tried sex, the rooftops from which we had hurled tin cans and bricks. But houses exactly like the houses of our past yet dominated the landscape, boys exactly like the boys we once had been found themselves smothering in these houses, came down into the streets for light and air and found themselves encircled by disaster. Some escaped the trap, most didn't. Those who got out always left something of themselves behind, as some animals amputate a leg and leave it in the trap. It might be said, perhaps, that I had escaped, after all, I was a school teacher; or that Sonny had, he hadn't lived in Harlem for years. Yet, as the cab moved uptown through streets which seemed, with a rush, to darken with dark people, and as I covertly studied Sonny's face, it came to me that what we both were seeking through our separate cab windows was that part of ourselves which had been left behind. It's always at the hour of trouble and confrontation that the missing member aches.

We hit 110th Street and started rolling up Lenox Avenue. And I'd known this avenue all my life, but it seemed to me again, as it had seemed on the day I'd first heard about Sonny's trouble, filled with a hidden menace which was its very breath of life.

"We almost there," said Sonny.

"Almost." We were both too nervous to say anything more.

We live in a housing project. It hasn't been up long. A few days after it was up it seemed uninhabitably new, now, of course, it's already run-down. It looks like a parody of the good, clean, faceless life—God knows the people who live in it do their best to make it a parody. The beat-looking grass lying around isn't enough to make their lives green, the hedges will never hold out the streets, and they know it. The big windows fool no one, they aren't big enough to make space out of no space. They don't bother with the windows, they watch the TV screen instead. The playground is most popular with the children who don't play at jacks, or skip rope, or roller skate, or swing, and they can be found in it after dark. We moved in partly because it's not too far from where I teach, and partly for the kids; but it's really just like the houses in which Sonny and I grew up. The same things happen, they'll have the same things to remember. The moment Sonny and I started into the house I had the feeling that I was simply bringing him back into the danger he had almost died trying to escape.

Sonny has never been talkative. So I don't know why I was sure he'd be dying to talk to me when supper was over the first night. Everything went fine, the oldest boy remembered him, and the youngest boy liked him, and Sonny had remembered to bring something for each of them; and Isabel, who is really much nicer than I am, more open and giving, had gone to a lot of trouble about dinner and was genuinely glad to see him. And she's always been able to tease Sonny in a way that I haven't. It was nice to see her face so vivid again and to hear her laugh and watch her make Sonny laugh. She wasn't, or, anyway, she didn't seem to be, at all uneasy or embarrassed. She chatted as though there were no subject which had to be avoided and she got Sonny past his first, faint stiffness. And thank God she was there, for I was filled with that icy dread again. Everything I did seemed awkward to me, and everything I said sounded freighted with hidden meaning. I was trying to remember everything I'd heard about dope addiction and I couldn't help watching Sonny for signs. I wasn't doing it out of malice. I was trying to find out something about my brother. I was dying to hear him tell me he was safe.

"Safe!" my father grunted, whenever Mama suggested trying to move to a neighborhood which might be safer for children. "Safe, hell! Ain't no place safe for kids, nor nobody."

He always went on like this, but he wasn't, ever, really as bad as he sounded, not even on weekends, when he got drunk. As a matter of fact, he was always on the lookout for "something a little better," but he died before he found it. He died suddenly, during a drunken weekend in the middle of the war, when Sonny was fifteen. He and Sonny hadn't ever got on too well. And this was partly because Sonny was the apple of his father's eye. It was because he loved Sonny so much and was frightened for him, that he was always fighting with him. It doesn't do any good to fight with Sonny. Sonny just moves back, inside himself, where he can't be reached. But the principal reason that they never hit it off is that they were so much alike. Daddy was big and rough and loud-talking, just the opposite of Sonny, but they both had—that same privacy.

Mama tried to tell me something about this, just after Daddy died. I was home on leave from the army.

This was the last time I ever saw my mother alive. Just the same, this picture gets all mixed up in my mind with pictures I had of her when she was younger. The way I always see her is the way she used to be on a Sunday afternoon, say, when the old folks were talking after the big Sunday dinner. I always see her wearing pale blue. She'd be sitting on the sofa. And my father would be sitting in the easy chair, not far from her. And the living room would be full of church folks and relatives. There they sit, in chairs all around the living room, and the night is creeping up outside, but nobody knows it yet. You can see the darkness growing against the window-panes and you hear the street noises every now and again, or maybe the jangling beat of a tambourine from one of the churches close by, but it's real quiet in the room. For a moment nobody's talking, but every face looks darkening, like the sky outside. And my mother rocks a little from the waist, and my father's eyes are closed. Everyone is looking at something a child can't see. For a minute they've forgotten the children. Maybe a kid is lying on the rug half asleep. Maybe somebody's got a kid on his lap and is absent-mindedly stroking the kid's head. Maybe there's a kid, quiet and big-eyed, curled up in a big chair in the corner. The silence, the darkness coming, and the darkness in the faces frightens the child obscurely. He hopes that the hand which strokes his forehead will never stop—will never die. He hopes that there will never come a time when the old folks won't be sitting around the living room, talking about where they've come from, and what they've seen, and what's happened to them and their kinfolk.

But something deep and watchful in the child knows that this is bound to end, is already ending. In a moment someone will get up and turn on the light. Then the old folks will remember the children and they won't talk any more that day. And when light fills the room, the child is filled with darkness. He knows that every time this happens he's moved just a little closer to that darkness outside. The darkness outside is what the old folks have been talking about. It's what they've come from. It's what they endure. The child knows that they won't talk any more because if he knows too much about what's happened to *them,* he'll know too much too soon, about what's going to happen to *him.*

The last time I talked to my mother, I remember I was restless. I wanted to get out and see Isabel. We weren't married then and we had a lot to straighten out between us.

There Mama sat, in black, by the window. She was humming an old church song, *Lord, you brought me from a long ways off.* Sonny was out somewhere. Mama kept watching the streets.

"I don't know," she said, "if I'll ever see you again, after you go off from here. But I hope you'll remember the things I tried to teach you."

"Don't talk like that," I said, and smiled. "You'll be here a long time yet."

She smiled, too, but she said nothing. She was quiet for a long time. And I said, "Mama, don't you worry about nothing. I'll be writing all the time, and you be getting the checks. . . ."

"I want to talk to you about your brother," she said, suddenly. "If anything happens to me he ain't going to have nobody to look out for him."

"Mama," I said, "ain't nothing going to happen to you or Sonny. Sonny's all right. He's a good boy and he's got good sense."

"It ain't a question of his being a good boy," Mama said, "nor of his having good sense. It ain't only the bad ones, nor yet the dumb ones that gets sucked under." She stopped, looking at me. "Your Daddy once had a brother," she said, and she smiled in a way that made me feel she was in pain. "You didn't never know that, did you?"

"No," I said, "I never knew that," and I watched her face.

"Oh, yes," she said, "your Daddy had a brother." She looked out of the window again. "I know you never saw your Daddy cry. But *I* did—many a time, through all these years."

I asked her, "What happened to his brother? How come nobody's ever talked about him?"

This was the first time I ever saw my mother look old.

"His brother got killed," she said, "when he was just a little younger than you are now. I knew him. He was a fine boy. He was maybe a little full of the devil, but he didn't mean nobody no harm."

Then she stopped and the room was silent, exactly as it had sometimes been on those Sunday afternoons. Mama kept looking out into the streets.

"He used to have a job in the mill," she said, "and, like all young folks, he just liked to perform on Saturday nights. Saturday nights, him and your father would drift around to different places, go to dances and things like that, or just sit around with people they knew, and your father's brother would sing, he had a fine voice, and play along with himself on his guitar. Well, this particular Saturday night, him and your father was coming home from some place, and they were both a little drunk and there was a moon that night, it was bright like day. Your father's brother was feeling kind of good, and he was whistling to himself, and he had his guitar slung over his shoulder. They was coming down a hill and beneath them was a road that turned off from the highway. Well, your father's brother, being always kind of frisky, decided to run down this hill, and he did, with that guitar banging and clanging behind him, and he ran across the road, and he was making water behind a tree. And your father was sort of amused at him and he was still coming down the hill, kind of slow. Then he heard a car motor and that same minute his brother stepped from behind the tree, into the road, in the moonlight. And he started to cross the road. And your father started to run down the hill, he says he don't know why. This car was full of white men. They was all drunk, and when they seen your father's brother they let out a great whoop and holler and they aimed the car straight at him. They was having fun, they just wanted to scare him, the way they do sometimes, you know. But they was drunk. And I guess the boy, being drunk, too, and scared, kind of lost his head. By the time he jumped it was too late. Your father says he heard his brother scream when the car rolled over him, and he heard the wood of that guitar when it give, and he heard them strings go flying, and he heard them white men shouting, and the car kept on a-going and it ain't stopped till this day. And, time your father got down the hill, his brother weren't nothing but blood and pulp."

Tears were gleaming on my mother's face. There wasn't anything I could say.

"He never mentioned it," she said, "because I never let him mention it before you children. Your Daddy was like a crazy man that night and for many a night thereafter. He says he never in his life seen anything as dark as that road after the lights of that car had gone away. Weren't nothing, weren't nobody on that road, just your Daddy and his brother and that busted guitar. Oh, yes. Your Daddy never did really get right again. Till the day he died he weren't sure but that every white man he saw was the man that killed his brother."

She stopped and took out her handkerchief and dried her eyes and looked at me.

"I ain't telling you all this," she said, "to make you scared or bitter or to make you hate nobody. I'm telling you this because you got a brother. And the world ain't changed."

I guess I didn't want to believe this. I guess she saw this in my face. She turned away from me, toward the window again, searching those streets.

"But I praise my Redeemer," she said at last, "that He called your Daddy home before me. I ain't saying it to throw no flowers at myself, but, I declare, it keeps me from feeling too cast down to know I helped your father get safely through this world. Your father always acted like he was the roughest, strongest man on earth. And everybody took him to be like that. But if he hadn't had *me* there—to see his tears!"

She was crying again. Still, I couldn't move. I said, "Lord, Lord, Mama, I didn't know it was like that."

"Oh, honey," she said, "there's a lot that you don't know. But you are going to find it out." She stood up from the window and came over to me. "You got to hold on to your brother," she said, "and don't let him fall, no matter what it looks like is happening to him and no matter how evil you gets with him. You going to be evil with him many a time. But don't you forget what I told you, you hear?"

"I won't forget," I said. "Don't you worry, I won't forget. I won't let nothing happen to Sonny."

My mother smiled as though she were amused at something she saw in my face. Then, "You may not be able to stop nothing from happening. But you got to let him know you's *there*."

Two days later I was married, and then I was gone. And I had a lot of things on my mind and I pretty well forgot my promise to Mama until I got shipped home on a special furlough for her funeral.

And, after the funeral, with just Sonny and me alone in the empty kitchen, I tried to find out something about him.

"What do you want to do?" I asked him.

"I'm going to be a musician," he said.

For he had graduated, in the time I had been away, from dancing to the juke box to finding out who was playing what, and what they were doing with it, and he had bought himself a set of drums.

"You mean, you want to be a drummer?" I somehow had the feeling that being a drummer might be all right for other people but not for my brother Sonny.

"I don't think," he said, looking at me very gravely, "that I'll ever be a good drummer. But I think I can play a piano."

I frowned. I'd never played the role of the older brother quite so seriously before, had scarcely ever, in fact, *asked* Sonny a damn thing. I sensed myself in the presence of something I didn't really know how to handle, didn't understand. So I made my frown a little deeper as I asked: "What kind of musician do you want to be?"

He grinned. "How many kinds do you think there are?"

"Be *serious*," I said.

He laughed, throwing his head back, and then looked at me. "I *am* serious."

"Well, then, for Christ's sake, stop kidding around and answer a serious question. I mean, do you want to be a concert pianist, you want to play classical music and all that, or—or what?" Long before I finished he was laughing again. "For Christ's *sake*, Sonny!"

He sobered, but with difficulty. "I'm sorry. But you sound so— *scared!*" and he was off again.

"Well, you may think it's funny now, baby, but it's not going to be so funny when you have to make your living at it, let me tell you *that*." I was furious because I knew he was laughing at me and I didn't know why.

"No," he said, very sober now, and afraid, perhaps, that he'd hurt me, "I don't want to be a classical pianist. That isn't what interests me. I mean"—he paused, looking hard at me, as though his eyes would help me to understand, and then gestured helplessly, as though perhaps his hand would help—"I mean, I'll have a lot of studying to do, and I'll have to study *everything*, but I mean, I want to play *with*—jazz musicians." He stopped. "I want to play jazz," he said.

Well, the word had never before sounded as heavy, as real, as it sounded that afternoon in Sonny's mouth. I just looked at him and I was probably frowning a real frown by this time. I simply couldn't see why on earth he'd want to spend his time hanging around night clubs, clowning around on bandstands, while people pushed each other around a dance floor. It seemed—beneath him, somehow. I had never thought about it before, had never been forced to, but I suppose I had always put jazz musicians in a class with what Daddy called "good-time people."

"Are you *serious*?"

"Hell, *yes*, I'm serious."

He looked more helpless than ever, and annoyed, and deeply hurt.

I suggested, helpfully: "You mean—like Louis Armstrong?"

His face closed as though I'd struck him. "No. I'm not talking about none of that old-time, down home crap."

"Well, look, Sonny, I'm sorry, don't get mad. I just don't altogether get it, that's all. Name somebody—you know, a jazz musician you admire."

"Bird."

"Who?"

"Bird! Charlie Parker! Don't they teach you nothing in the goddamn army?"

I lit a cigarette. I was surprised and then a little amused to discover that I was trembling. "I've been out of touch," I said, "You'll have to be patient with me. Now. Who's this Parker character?"

"He's just one of the greatest jazz musicians alive," said Sonny, sullenly, his hands in his pockets, his back to me. "Maybe *the* greatest," he added, bitterly, "that's probably why *you* never heard of him."

"All right," I said, "I'm ignorant. I'm sorry. I'll go out and buy all the cat's records right away, all right?"

"It don't," said Sonny, with dignity, "make any difference to me. I don't care what you listen to. Don't do me no favors."

I was beginning to realize that I'd never seen him so upset before. With another part of my mind I was thinking that this would probably turn out to be one of those things kids go through and that I shouldn't make it seem important by pushing it too hard. Still, I didn't think it would do any harm to ask: "Doesn't all this take a lot of time? Can you make a living at it?"

He turned back to me and half leaned, half sat, on the kitchen table. "Everything takes time," he said, "and—well, yes, sure, I can make a living at it. But what I don't seem to be able to make you understand is that it's the only thing I want to do."

"Well Sonny," I said, gently, "you know people can't always do exactly what they *want* to do—"

"*No*, I don't know that," said Sonny, surprising me. "I think people *ought* to do what they want to do, what else are they alive for?"

"You getting to be a big boy," I said desperately, "it's time you started thinking about your future."

"I'm thinking about my future," said Sonny, grimly. "I think about it all the time."

I gave up. I decided, if he didn't change his mind, that we could always talk about it later. "In the meantime," I said, "you got to finish school." We had already decided that he'd have to move in with Isabel and her folks. I knew this wasn't the ideal arrangement because Isabel's folks are inclined to be dicty and they hadn't especially wanted Isabel to marry me. But I didn't know what else to do. "And we have to get you fixed up at Isabel's."

There was a long silence. He moved from the kitchen table to the window. "That's a terrible idea. You know it yourself."

"Do you have a *better* idea?"

He just walked up and down the kitchen for a minute. He was as tall as I was. He had started to shave. I suddenly had the feeling that I didn't know him at all.

He stopped at the kitchen table and picked up my cigarettes. Looking at me with a kind of mocking, amused defiance, he put one between his lips. "You mind?"

"You smoking already?"

He lit the cigarette and nodded, watching me through the smoke. "I just wanted to see if I'd have the courage to smoke in front of you." He grinned and blew a great cloud of smoke to the ceiling. "It was easy." He looked at my face. "Come on, now. I bet you was smoking at my age, tell the truth."

I didn't say anything but the truth was on my face, and he laughed. But now there was something very strained in his laugh. "Sure. And I bet that ain't all you was doing."

He was frightening me a little. "Cut the crap," I said. "We already decided that you was going to go and live at Isabel's. Now what's got into you all of a sudden?"

"You decided it," he pointed out. *"I* didn't decide nothing." He stopped in front of me, leaning against the stove, arms loosely folded. "Look, brother. I don't want to stay in Harlem no more, I really don't." He was very earnest. He looked at me, then over toward the kitchen window. There was something in his eyes I'd never seen before, some thoughtfulness, some worry all his own. He rubbed the muscle of one arm. "It's time I was getting out of here."

"Where do you want to *go,* Sonny?"

"I want to join the army. Or the navy, I don't care. If I say I'm old enough they'll believe me."

Then I got mad. It was because I was so scared. "You must be crazy. You goddamn fool, what the hell do you want to go and join the *army* for?"

"I just told you. To get out of Harlem."

"Sonny, you haven't even finished *school.* And if you really want to be a musician, how do you expect to study if you're in the *army?"*

He looked at me, trapped, and in anguish. "There's ways. I might be able to work out some kind of deal. Anyway, I'll have the G.I. Bill when I come out."

"If you come out." We stared at each other. "Sonny, please. Be reasonable. I know the setup is far from perfect. But we got to do the best we can."

"I ain't learning nothing in school," he said. "Even when I go." He turned away from me and opened the window and threw his cigarette out into the narrow alley. I watched his back. "At least, I ain't learning nothing you'd want me to learn." He slammed the window so hard I thought the glass would fly out, and turned back to me. "And I'm sick of the stink of these garbage cans!"

"Sonny," I said, "I know how you feel. But if you don't finish school now, you're going to be sorry later that you didn't." I grabbed him by the shoulders. "And you only got another year. It ain't so bad. And I'll come back and I swear I'll help you do *whatever* you want to do. Just try to put up with it till I come back. Will you please do that? For me?"

He didn't answer and he wouldn't look at me.

"Sonny. You hear me?"

He pulled away. "I hear you. But you never hear anything *I* say."

I didn't know what to say to that. He looked out of the window and then back at me. "OK," he said, and sighed. "I'll try."

Then I said, trying to cheer him up a little, "They got a piano at Isabel's. You can practice on it."

And as a matter of fact, it did cheer him up for a minute. "That's right," he said to himself. "I forgot that." His face relaxed a little. But the worry, the thoughtfulness, played on it still, the way shadows play on a face which is staring into the fire.

But I thought I'd never hear the end of that piano. At first, Isabel would write me, saying how nice it was that Sonny was so serious about his music and how, as soon as he came in from school, or wherever he had been when he was supposed to be at school, he went straight to that piano and stayed there until suppertime. And, after supper, he went back to that piano and stayed there until everybody went to bed. He was at the piano all day Saturday and all day Sunday. Then he bought a record player and started playing records. He'd play one record over and over again, all day long sometimes, and he'd improvise along with it on the piano. Or he'd play one section of the record, one chord, one change, one progression, then he'd do it on the piano. Then back to the record. Then back to the piano.

Well, I really don't know how they stood it. Isabel finally confessed that it wasn't like living with a person at all, it was like living with sound. And the sound didn't make any sense to her, didn't make any sense to any of them—naturally. They began, in a way, to be afflicted by this presence that was living in their home. It was as though Sonny were some sort of god, or monster. He moved in an atmosphere which wasn't like theirs at all. They fed him and he ate, he washed himself, he walked in and out of their door; he certainly wasn't nasty or unpleasant or rude, Sonny isn't any of those things; but it was as though he were all wrapped up in some cloud, some fire, some vision all his own; and there wasn't any way to reach him.

At the same time, he wasn't really a man yet, he was still a child, and they had to watch out for him in all kinds of ways. They certainly couldn't throw him out. Neither did they dare to make a great scene about that piano because even they dimly sensed, as I sensed, from so many thousands of miles away, that Sonny was at that piano playing for his life.

But he hadn't been going to school. One day a letter came from the school board and Isabel's mother got it—there had, apparently, been other letters but Sonny had torn them up. This day, when Sonny came in, Isabel's mother showed him the letter and asked where he'd been spending his time. And she finally got it out of him that he'd been down in Greenwich Village, with musicians and other characters, in a white girl's apartment. And this scared her and she started to scream at him and what came up, once she began—though she denies it to this day—was what sacrifices they were making to give Sonny a decent home and how little he appreciated it.

Sonny didn't play the piano that day. By evening, Isabel's mother had calmed down but then there was the old man to deal with, and Isabel herself. Isabel says she did her best to be calm but she broke down and started crying. She says she just watched Sonny's face. She could tell, by watching him, what was happening with him. And what was happening was that they penetrated his cloud, they had reached him. Even if their fingers had been a thousand times more gentle than human fingers ever are, he could hardly help feeling that they had stripped him naked and were spitting on that nakedness. For he also had to see that his presence, that music, which was life or death to him, had been torture for them and that they had endured it, not at all for his sake, but only for mine. And Sonny couldn't take that. He can take it a little better today than he could then but he's still not very good at it and, frankly, I don't know anybody who is.

The silence of the next few days must have been louder than the sound of all the music ever played since time began. One morning, before she went to work, Isabel was in his room for something and she suddenly realized that all of his records were gone. And she knew for certain that he was gone. And he was. He went as far as the navy would carry him. He finally sent me a postcard from some place in Greece and that was the first I knew that Sonny was still alive. I didn't see him any more until we were both back in New York and the war had long been over.

He was a man by then, of course, but I wasn't willing to see it. He came by the house from time to time, but we fought almost every time we met. I didn't like the way he carried himself, loose and dreamlike all the time, and I didn't like his friends, and his music seemed to be merely an excuse for the life he led. It sounded just that weird and disordered.

Then we had a fight, a pretty awful fight, and I didn't see him for months. By and by I looked him up, where he was living, in a furnished room in the Village, and I tried to make it up. But there were lots of other people in the room and Sonny just lay on his bed, and he wouldn't come downstairs with me, and he treated these other people as though they were his family and I weren't. So I got mad and then he got mad, and then I told him that he might just as well be dead as live the way he was living. Then he stood up and he told me not to worry about him any more in life, that he *was* dead as far as I was concerned. Then he pushed me to the door and the other people looked on as though nothing were happening, and he slammed the door behind me. I stood in the hallway, staring at the door. I heard somebody laugh in the room and then the tears came to my eyes. I started down the steps, whistling to keep from crying, I kept whistling to myself, *You going to need me, baby, one of these cold, rainy days.*

I read about Sonny's trouble in the spring. Little Grace died in the fall. She was a beautiful little girl. But she only lived a little over two years. She died of polio and she suffered. She had a slight fever for a couple of days, but it didn't seem like anything and we just kept her in bed. And we would certainly have called the doctor, but the fever dropped, she seemed to be all right. So we thought it had just been a cold. Then, one day, she was up, playing, Isabel was in the kitchen fixing lunch for the two boys when they'd come in from school, and she heard Grace fall down in the living room. When you have a lot of children you don't always start running when one of them falls, unless they start screaming or something. And, this time, Grace was quiet. Yet, Isabel says that when she heard that *thump* and then that silence, something happened in her to make her afraid. And she ran to the living room and there was little Grace on the floor, all twisted up and the reason she hadn't screamed was that she couldn't get her breath. And when she did scream, it was the worst sound, Isabel says, that she'd ever heard in all her life, and she still hears it sometimes in her dreams. Isabel will sometimes wake me up with a low, moaning, strangled sound and I have to be quick to awaken her and hold her to me and where Isabel is weeping against me seems a mortal wound.

I think I may have written Sonny the very day that little Grace was buried. I was sitting in the living room in the dark, by myself, and I suddenly thought of Sonny. My trouble made his real.

One Saturday afternoon, when Sonny had been living with us, or, anyway, been in our house, for nearly two weeks, I found myself wandering aimlessly about the living room, drinking from a can of beer, and trying to work up the courage to search Sonny's room. He was out, he was usually out whenever I was home, and Isabel had taken the children to see their grandparents. Suddenly I was standing still in front of the living room window, watching Seventh Avenue. The idea of searching Sonny's room made me still. I scarcely dared to admit to myself what I'd be searching for. I didn't know what I'd do if I found it. Or if I didn't.

On the sidewalk across from me, near the entrance to a barbecue joint, some people were holding an old-fashioned revival meeting. The barbecue cook, wearing a dirty white apron, his conked hair reddish and metallic in the pale sun, and a cigarette between his lips, stood in the doorway, watching them. Kids and older people paused in their errands and stood there, along with some older men and a couple of very tough-looking women who watched everything that happened on the avenue, as though they owned it, or were maybe owned by it. Well, they were watching this, too. The revival was being carried on by three sisters in black, and a brother. All they had were their voices and their Bibles and a tambourine. The brother was testifying and while he testified two of the sisters stood together, seeming to say, Amen, and the third sister walked around with the tambourine outstretched and a couple of people dropped coins into it. Then the brother's testimony ended and the sister who had been taking up the collection dumped the coins into her palm and transferred them to the pocket of her long black robe. Then she raised both hands, striking the tambourine against the air, and then against one hand, and she started to sing. And the two other sisters and the brother joined in.

It was strange, suddenly, to watch, though I had been seeing these street meetings all my life. So, of course, had everybody else down there. Yet, they paused and watched and listened and I stood still at the window. *"Tis the old ship of Zion,"* they sang, and the sister with the tambourine kept a steady, jangling beat, *"It has rescued many a thousand!"* Not a soul under the sound of their voices was hearing this song for the first time, not one of them had been rescued. Nor had they seen much in the way of rescue work being done around them. Neither did they especially believe in the holiness of the three sisters and the brother, they knew too much about them, knew where they lived, and how. The woman with the tambourine, whose voice dominated the air, whose face was bright with joy, was divided by very little from the woman who stood watching her, a cigarette between her heavy, chapped lips, her hair a cuckoo's nest, her face scarred and swollen from many beatings, and her black eyes glittering like coal. Perhaps they both knew this, which was why, when, as rarely, they addressed each other, they addressed each other as Sister. As the singing filled the air the watching, listening faces underwent a change, the eyes focusing on something within; the music seemed to soothe a poison out of them; and time seemed, nearly, to fall away from the sullen, belligerent, battered faces, as though they were fleeing back to their first condition, while dreaming of their last. The barbecue cook half shook his head and smiled, and dropped his cigarette and disappeared into his joint. A man fumbled in his pockets for change and stood holding it in his hand impatiently, as though he had just remembered a pressing appointment further up the avenue. He looked furious. Then I saw Sonny, standing on the edge of the crowd. He was carrying a wide, flat notebook with a green cover, and it made him look, from where I was standing, almost like a schoolboy. The coppery sun brought out the copper in his skin, he was very faintly smiling, standing very still. Then the singing stopped, the tambourine turned into a collection plate again. The furious man dropped in his coins and vanished, so did a couple of the women, and Sonny dropped some change in the plate, looking directly at the woman with a little smile. He started across the avenue, toward the house. He has a slow, loping walk, something like the way Harlem hipsters walk, only he's imposed on this his own halfbeat. I had never really noticed it before.

I stayed at the window, both relieved and apprehensive. As Sonny disappeared from my sight, they began singing again. And they were still singing when his key turned in the lock.

"Hey," he said.

"Hey, yourself. You want some beer?"

"No. Well, maybe." But he came up to the window and stood beside me, looking out. "What a warm voice," he said.

They were singing *If I could only hear my mother pray again!*

"Yes," I said, "and she can sure beat that tambourine."

"But what a terrible song," he said, and laughed. He dropped his notebook on the sofa and disappeared into the kitchen. "Where's Isabel and the kids?"

"I think they went to see their grandparents. You hungry?"

"No." He came back into the living room with his can of beer. "You want to come some place with me tonight?"

I sensed, I don't know how, that I couldn't possibly say No. "Sure. Where?"

He sat down on the sofa and picked up his notebook and started leafing through it. "I'm going to sit in with some fellows in a joint in the Village."

"You mean, you're going to play, tonight?"

"That's right." He took a swallow of his beer and moved back to the window. He gave me a sidelong look. "If you can stand it."

"I'll try," I said.

He smiled to himself and we both watched as the meeting across the way broke up. The three sisters and the brother, heads bowed, were singing *God be with you till we meet again*. The faces around them were very quiet. Then the song ended. The small crowd dispersed. We watched the three women and the lone man walk slowly up the avenue.

"When she was singing before," said Sonny, abruptly, "her voice reminded me for a minute of what heroin feels like sometimes—when it's in your veins. It makes you feel sort of warm and cool at the same time. And distant. And—and sure." He sipped his beer, very deliberately not looking at me. I watched his face. "It makes you feel—in control. Sometimes you've got to have that feeling."

"Do you?" I sat down slowly in the easy chair.

"Sometimes." He went to the sofa and picked up his notebook again. "Some people do."

"In order," I asked, "to play?" And my voice was very ugly, full of contempt and anger.

"Well"—he looked at me with great, troubled eyes, as though, in fact, he hoped his eyes would tell me things he could never otherwise say—"they *think* so. And *if* they think so—!"

"And what do *you* think?" I asked.

He sat on the sofa and put his can of beer on the floor. "I don't know," he said, and I couldn't be sure if he were answering my question or pursuing his thoughts. His face didn't tell me. "It's not so much to *play*. It's to *stand* it, to be able to make it at all. On any level." He frowned and smiled: "In order to keep from shaking to pieces."

"But these friends of yours," I said, "they seem to shake themselves to pieces pretty goddamn fast."

"Maybe." He played with the notebook. And something told me that I should curb my tongue, that Sonny was doing his best to talk, that I should listen. "But of course you only know the ones that've gone to pieces. Some don't—or at least they haven't *yet* and that's just about all *any* of us can say." He paused. "And then there are some who just live, really, in hell, and they know it and they see what's happening and they go right on. I don't know." He sighed, dropped the notebook, folded his arms. "Some guys, you can tell from the way they play, they on something *all* the time. And you can see that, well, it makes something real for them. But of course," he picked up his beer from the floor and sipped it and put the can down again, "they *want* to, too, you've got to see that. Even some of them that say they don't—*some,* not all."

"And what about you?" I asked—I couldn't help it. "What about you? Do *you* want to?"

He stood up and walked to the window and remained silent for a long time. Then he sighed. "Me," he said. Then: "While I was downstairs before, on my way here, listening to that woman sing, it struck me all of a sudden how much suffering she must have had to go through—to sing like that. It's *repulsive* to think you have to suffer that much."

I said: "But there's no way not to suffer—is there, Sonny?"

"I believe not," he said, and smiled, "but that's never stopped anyone from trying." He looked at me. "Has it?" I realized, with this mocking look, that there stood between us, forever, beyond the power of time or forgiveness, the fact that I had held silence—so long!—when he had needed human speech to help him. He turned back to the window. "No, there's no way not to suffer. But you try all kinds of ways to keep from drowning in it, to keep on top of it, and to make it seem—well, like *you*. Like you did something, all right, and now you're suffering for it. You know?" I said nothing. "Well you know," he said, impatiently, "why *do* people suffer? Maybe it's better to do something to give it a reason, *any* reason."

"But we just agreed," I said, "that there's no way not to suffer. Isn't it better, then, just to—take it?"

"But nobody just takes it," Sonny cried, "that's what I'm telling you! *Everybody* tries not to. You're just hung up on the *way* some people try—it's not *your* way!"

The hair on my face began to itch, my face felt wet. "That's not true," I said, "that's not true. I don't give a damn what other people do, I don't even care how they suffer. I just care how *you* suffer." And he looked at me. "Please believe me," I said, "I don't want to see you—die—trying not to suffer."

"I won't," he said, flatly, "die trying not to suffer. At least, not any faster than anybody else."

"But there's no need," I said, trying to laugh, "is there? in killing yourself."

I wanted to say more, but I couldn't. I wanted to talk about will power and how life could be—well, beautiful. I wanted to say that it was all within; but was it? or, rather, wasn't that exactly the trouble? And I wanted to promise that I would never fail him again. But it would all have sounded—empty words and lies.

So I made the promise to myself and prayed that I would keep it.

"It's terrible sometimes, inside," he said, "that's what's the trouble. You walk these streets, black and funky and cold, and there's not really a living ass to talk to, and there's nothing shaking, and there's no way of getting it out—that storm inside. You can't talk it and you can't make love with it, and when you finally try to get with it and play it, you realize *nobody's* listening. So *you've* got to listen. You got to find a way to listen."

And then he walked away from the window and sat on the sofa again, as though all the wind had suddenly been knocked out of him.

"Sometimes you'll do *anything* to play, even cut your mother's throat." He laughed and looked at me. "Or your brother's." Then he sobered. "Or your own." Then: "Don't worry. I'm all right now and I think I'll *be* all right. But I can't forget—where I've been. I don't mean just the physical place I've been, I mean where I've *been*. And *what* I've been."

"What have you been, Sonny?" I asked.

He smiled—but sat sideways on the sofa, his elbow resting on the back, his fingers playing with his mouth and chin, not looking at me. "I've been something I didn't recognize, didn't know I could be. Didn't know anybody could be." He stopped, looking inward, looking helplessly young, looking old. "I'm not talking about it now because I feel *guilty* or anything like that—maybe it would be better if I did, I don't know. Anyway, I can't really talk about it. Not to you, not to anybody," and now he turned and faced me. "Sometimes, you know, and it was actually when I was most *out* of the world, I felt that I was in it, and that I was *with* it, really, and I could play or I didn't really have to *play*, it just came out of me, it was there. And I don't know how I played, thinking about it now, but I know I did awful things, those times, sometimes, to people. Or it wasn't that I *did* anything to them—it was that they weren't real." He picked up the beer can; it was empty; he rolled it between his palms: "And other times—well, I needed a fix, I needed to find a place to lean, I needed to clear a space to *listen*—and I couldn't find it, and I—went crazy, I did terrible things to *me*, I was terrible *for* me." He began pressing the beer can between his hands, I watched the metal begin to give. It glittered, as he played with it, like a knife, and I was afraid he would cut himself, but I said nothing. "Oh well. I can never tell you. I was all by myself at the bottom of something, stinking and sweating and crying and shaking, and I smelled it, you know? *my* stink, and I thought I'd die if I couldn't get away from it and yet, all the same, I knew that everything I was doing was just locking me in with it. And I didn't know," he paused, still flattening the beer can, "I didn't know, I still *don't* know, something kept telling me that maybe it was good to smell your own stink, but I didn't think that *that* was what I'd been trying to do—and—who can stand it?" and he abruptly dropped the ruined beer can, looking at me with a small, still smile, and then rose, walking to the window as though it were the lodestone rock. I watched his face, he watched the avenue. "I couldn't tell you when Mama died—but the reason I wanted to leave Harlem so bad was to get away from drugs. And then, when I ran away, that's what I was running from—really. When I came back, nothing had changed, *I* hadn't changed, I was just—older." And he stopped, drumming with his fingers on the windowpane. The sun had vanished, soon darkness would fall. I watched his face. "It can come again," he said, almost as though speaking to himself. Then he turned to me. "It can come again," he repeated. "I just want you to know that."

"All right," I said, at last. "So it can come again. All right."

He smiled, but the smile was sorrowful. "I had to try to tell you," he said.

"Yes," I said. "I understand that."

"You're my brother," he said, looking straight at me, and not smiling at all.

"Yes," I repeated, "yes. I understand that."

He turned back to the window, looking out. "All that hatred down there," he said, "all that hatred and misery and love. It's a wonder it doesn't blow the avenue apart."

We went to the only night club on a short, dark street, downtown. We squeezed through the narrow, chattering, jam-packed bar to the entrance of the big room, where the bandstand was. And we stood there for a moment, for the lights were very dim in this room and we couldn't see. Then, "Hello, boy," said a voice and an enormous black man, much older than Sonny or myself, erupted out of all that atmospheric lighting and put an arm around Sonny's shoulder. "I been sitting right here," he said, "waiting for you."

He had a big voice, too, and heads in the darkness turned toward us.

Sonny grinned and pulled a little away, and said, "Creole, this is my brother. I told you about him."

Creole shook my hand. "I'm glad to meet you, son," he said, and it was clear that he was glad to meet me *there*, for Sonny's sake. And he smiled, "You got a real musician in *your* family," and he took his arm from Sonny's shoulder and slapped him, lightly, affectionately, with the back of his hand.

"Well. Now I've heard it all," said a voice behind us. This was another musician, and a friend of Sonny's, a coal-black, cheerful-looking man, built close to the ground. He immediately began confiding to me, at the top of his lungs, the most terrible things about Sonny, his teeth gleaming like a lighthouse and his laugh coming up out of him like the beginning of an earthquake. And it turned out that everyone at the bar knew Sonny, or almost everyone; some were musicians, working there, or nearby, or not working, some were simply hangers-on, and some were there to hear Sonny play. I was introduced to all of them and they were all very polite to me. Yet, it was clear that, for them, I was only Sonny's brother. Here, I was in Sonny's world. Or, rather: his kingdom. Here, it was not even a question that his veins bore royal blood.

They were going to play soon and Creole installed me, by myself, at a table in a dark corner. Then I watched them, Creole, and the little black man, and Sonny, and the others, while they horsed around, standing just below the bandstand. The light from the bandstand spilled just a little short of them and, watching them laughing and gesturing and moving about, I had the feeling that they, nevertheless, were being most careful not to step into that circle of light too suddenly: that if they moved into the light too suddenly, without thinking, they would perish in flame. Then, while I watched, one of them, the small, black man, moved into the light and crossed the bandstand and started fooling around with his drums. Then—being funny and being, also, extremely ceremonious—Creole took Sonny by the arm and led him to the piano. A woman's voice called Sonny's name and a few hands started clapping. And Sonny, also being funny and being ceremonious, and so touched, I think, that he could have cried, but neither hiding it nor showing it, riding it like a man, grinned, and put both hands to his heart and bowed from the waist.

Creole then went to the bass fiddle and a lean, very bright-skinned brown man jumped up on the bandstand and picked up his horn. So there they were, and the atmosphere on the bandstand and in the room began to change and tighten. Someone stepped up to the microphone and announced them. Then there were all kinds of murmurs. Some people at the bar shushed others. The waitress ran around, frantically getting in the last orders, guys and chicks got closer to each other, and the lights on the bandstand, on the quartet, turned to a kind of indigo. Then they all looked different there. Creole looked about him for the last time, as though he were making certain that all his chickens were in the coop, and then he—jumped and struck the fiddle. And there they were.

All I know about music is that not many people ever really hear it. And even then, on the rare occasions when something opens within, and the music enters, what we mainly hear, or hear corroborated, are personal private, vanishing evocations. But the man who creates the music is hearing something else, is dealing with the roar rising from the void and imposing order on it as it hits the air. What is evoked in him, then, is of another order, more terrible because it has no words, and triumphant, too, for that same reason. And his triumph, when he triumphs, is ours. I just watched Sonny's face. His face was troubled, he was working hard, but he wasn't with it. And I had the feeling that, in a way, everyone on the bandstand was waiting for him, both waiting for him and pushing him along. But as I began to watch Creole, I realized that it was Creole who held them all back. He had them on a short rein. Up there, keeping the beat with his whole body, wailing on the fiddle, with his eyes half closed, he was listening to everything, but he was listening to Sonny. He was having a dialogue with Sonny. He wanted Sonny to leave the shore line and strike out for the deep water. He was Sonny's witness that deep water and drowning were not the same thing—he had been there, and he knew. And he wanted Sonny to know. He was waiting for Sonny to do the things on the keys which would let Creole know that Sonny was in the water.

And, while Creole listened, Sonny moved, deep within, exactly like someone in torment. I had never before thought of how awful the relationship must be between the musician and his instrument. He has to fill it, this instrument, with the breath of life, his own. He has to make it do what he wants it to do. And a piano is just a piano. It's made out of so much wood and wires and little hammers and big ones, and ivory. While there's only so much you can do with it, the only way to find this out is to try and make it do everything.

And Sonny hadn't been near a piano for over a year. And he wasn't on much better terms with his life, not the life that stretched before him now. He and the piano stammered, started one way, got scared, stopped; started another way, panicked, marked time, started again; then seemed to have found a direction, panicked again, got stuck. And the face I saw on Sonny I'd never seen before. Everything had been burned out of it, and, at the same time, things usually hidden were being burned in, by the fire and fury of the battle which was occurring in him up there.

Yet, watching Creole's face as they neared the end of the first set, I had the feeling that something had happened, something I hadn't heard. Then they finished, there was scattered applause, and then, without an instant's warning, Creole started into something else, it was almost sardonic, it was *Am I Blue*. And, as though he commanded, Sonny began to play. Something began to happen. And Creole let out the reins. The dry, low, black man said something awful on the drums, Creole answered, and the drums talked back. Then the horn insisted, sweet and high, slightly detached perhaps, and Creole listened, commenting now and then, dry, and driving, beautiful and calm and old. Then they all came together again, and Sonny was part of the family again. I could tell this from his face. He seemed to have found, right there beneath his fingers, a damn brand-new piano. It seemed that he couldn't get over it. Then, for awhile, just being happy with Sonny, they seemed to be agreeing with him that brand-new pianos certainly were a gas.

Then Creole stepped forward to remind them that what they were playing was the blues. He hit something in all of them, he hit something in me, myself, and the music tightened and deepened, apprehension began to beat the air. Creole began to tell us what the blues were all about. They were not about anything very new. He and his boys up there were keeping it new, at the risk of ruin, destruction, madness, and death, in order to find new ways to make us listen. For, while the tale of how we suffer, and how we are delighted, and how we may triumph is never new, it always must be heard. There isn't any other tale to tell, it's the only light we've got in all this darkness.

And this tale, according to that face, that body, those strong hands on those strings, has another aspect in every country, and a new depth in every generation. Listen, Creole seemed to be saying, listen. Now these are Sonny's blues. He made the little black man on the drums know it, and the bright, brown man on the horn. Creole wasn't trying any longer to get Sonny in the water. He was wishing him Godspeed. Then he stepped back, very slowly, filling the air with the immense suggestion that Sonny speak for himself.

Then they all gathered around Sonny and Sonny played. Every now and again one of them seemed to say, Amen. Sonny's fingers filled the air with life, his life. But that life contained so many others. And Sonny went all the way back, he really began with the spare, flat statement of the opening phrase of the song. Then he began to make it his. It was very beautiful because it wasn't hurried and it was no longer a lament. I seemed to hear with what burning he had made it his, with what burning we had yet to make it ours, how we could cease lamenting. Freedom lurked around us and I understood, at last, that he could help us to be free if we would listen, that he would never be free until we did. Yet, there was no battle in his face now. I heard what he had gone through, and would continue to go through until he came to rest in earth. He had made it his: that long line, of which we knew only Mama and Daddy. And he was giving it back, as everything must be given back, so that, passing through death, it can live forever. I saw my mother's face again, and felt, for the first time, how the stones of the road she had walked on must have bruised her feet. I saw the moonlit road where my father's brother died. And it brought something else back to me, and carried me past it, I saw my little girl again and felt Isabel's tears again, and I felt my own tears begin to rise. And I was yet aware that this was only a moment, that the world waited outside, as hungry as a tiger, and that trouble stretched above us, longer than the sky.

Then it was over. Creole and Sonny let out their breath, both soaking wet, and grinning. There was a lot of applause and some of it was real. In the dark, the girl came by and I asked her to take drinks to the bandstand. There was a long pause, while they talked up there in the indigo light and after awhile I saw the girl put a Scotch and milk on top of the piano for Sonny. He didn't seem to notice it, but just before they started playing again, he sipped from it and looked toward me, and nodded. Then he put it back on top of the piano. For me, then, as they began to play again, it glowed and shook above my brother's head like the very cup of trembling.

QUESTIONS

1. Explore the use of music as a metaphor in "Sonny's Blues." How many types of music do you find in the story? What meanings does the narrator give them?

2. The narrator says that he and Sonny, riding through the streets of New York, "both were seeking through our separate cab windows . . . that part of ourselves which had been left behind. It's always at the hour of trouble and confrontation that the missing member aches." What has been amputated? For each of these characters, write a stream-of-consciousness monologue in which you describe or narrate what they are seeing and thinking as they look out their separate windows.

3. "He wanted Sonny to leave the shore line and strike out for the deep water. He was Sonny's witness that deep water and drowning were not the same thing—he had been there, and he knew." Discuss this metaphor. Notice the word *witness*. It could come from legal terminology, but in this story it has a different connotation. Discuss.

ALICE WALKER (1944–   )

A Sudden Trip Home in the Spring

For the Wellesley Class

Sarah walked slowly off the tennis court, fingering the back of her head, feeling the sturdy dark hair that grew there. She was popular. As she walked along the path toward Talfinger Hall her friends fell into place around her. They formed a warm jostling group of six. Sarah, because she was taller than the rest, saw the messenger first.

"Miss Davis," he said, standing still until the group came abreast of him, "I've got a telegram for ye." Brian was Irish and always quite respectful. He stood with his cap in his hand until Sarah took the telegram. Then he gave a nod that included all the young ladies before he turned away. He was young and good-looking, though annoyingly servile, and Sarah's friends twittered.

"Well, open it!" someone cried, for Sarah stood staring at the yellow envelope, turning it over and over in her hand.

"Look at her," said one of the girls, "isn't she beautiful! Such eyes, and hair, and *skin!*"

Sarah's tall, caplike hair framed a face of soft brown angles, high cheekbones and large dark eyes. Her eyes enchanted her friends because they always seemed to know more, and to find more of life amusing, or sad, than Sarah cared to tell.

Her friends often teased Sarah about her beauty; they loved dragging her out of her room so that their boyfriends, naive and worldly young men from Princeton and Yale, could see her. They never guessed she found this distasteful. She was gentle with her friends, and her outrage at their tactlessness did not show. She was most often inclined to pity them, though embarrassment sometimes drove her to fraudulent expressions. Now she smiled and raised eyes and arms to heaven. She acknowledged their unearned curiosity as a mother endures the prying impatience of a child. Her friends beamed love and envy upon her as she tore open the telegram.

"He's dead," she said.

Her friends reached out for the telegram, their eyes on Sarah.

"It's her father," one of them said softly. "He died yesterday. Oh, Sarah," the girl whimpered, "I'm so sorry!"

"Me too." "So am I." "Is there anything we can do?"

But Sarah had walked away, head high and neck stiff.

"So graceful!" one of her friends said.

"Like a proud gazelle" said another. Then they all trooped to their dormitories to change for supper.

Talfinger Hall was a pleasant dorm. The common room just off the entrance had been made into a small modern art gallery with some very good original paintings, lithographs and collages. Pieces were constantly being stolen. Some of the girls could not resist an honest-to-God Chagall, signed (in the plate) by his own hand, though they could have afforded to purchase one from the gallery in town. Sarah Davis's room was next door to the gallery, but her walls were covered with inexpensive Gauguin reproductions, a Rubens ("The Head of a Negro"), a Modigliani and a Picasso. There was a full wall of her own drawings, all of black women. She found black men impossible to draw or to paint; she could not bear to trace defeat onto blank pages. Her women figures were matronly, massive of arm, with a weary victory showing in their eyes. Surrounded by Sarah's drawings was a red SNCC poster of a man holding a small girl whose face nestled in his shoulder. Sarah often felt she was the little girl whose face no one could see.

To leave Talfinger even for a few days filled Sarah with fear. Talfinger was her home now; it suited her better than any home she'd ever known. Perhaps she loved it because in winter there was a fragrant fireplace and snow outside her window. When hadn't she dreamed of fireplaces that really warmed, snow that almost pleasantly froze? Georgia seemed far away as she packed; she did not want to leave New York, where, her grandfather had liked to say, "the devil hung out and caught young gals by the front of their dresses." He had always believed the South the best place to live on earth (never mind that certain people invariably marred the landscape), and swore he expected to die no more than a few miles from where he had been born. There was tenacity even in the gray frame house he lived in, and in scrawny animals on his farm who regularly reproduced. He was the first person Sarah wanted to see when she got home.

There was a knock on the door of the adjoining bathroom, and Sarah's suite mate entered, a loud Bach concerto just finishing behind her. At first she stuck just her head into the room, but seeing Sarah fully dressed she trudged in and plopped down on the bed. She was a heavy blonde girl with large milk-white legs. Her eyes were small and her neck usually gray with grime.

"My, don't you look gorgeous," she said.

"Ah, Pam," said Sarah, waving her hand in disgust. In Georgia she knew that even to Pam she would be just another ordinarily attractive *colored* girl. In Georgia there were a million girls better looking. Pam wouldn't know that, of course; she'd never been to Georgia; she'd never even seen a black person to speak to, that is, before she met Sarah. One of her first poetic observations about Sarah was that she was "a poppy in a field of winter roses." She had found it weird that Sarah did not own more than one coat.

"Say listen, Sarah," said Pam, "I heard about your father. I'm sorry. I really am."

"Thanks," said Sarah.

"Is there anything we can do? I thought, well, maybe you'd want my father to get somebody to fly you down. He'd go himself but he's taking Mother to Madeira this week. You wouldn't have to worry about trains and things."

Pamela's father was one of the richest men in the world, though no one ever mentioned it. Pam only alluded to it at times of crisis, when a friend might benefit from the use of a private plane, train, or ship; or, if someone wanted to study the characteristics of a totally secluded village, island or mountain, she might offer one of theirs. Sarah could not comprehend such wealth, and was always annoyed because Pam didn't look more like a billionaire's daughter. A billionaire's daughter, Sarah thought, should really be less horsey and brush her teeth more often.

"Gonna tell me what you're brooding about?" asked Pam.

Sarah stood in front of the radiator, her fingers resting on the window seat. Down below girls were coming up the hill from supper.

"I'm thinking," she said, "of the child's duty to his parents after they are dead."

"Is that all?"

"Do you know," asked Sarah, "about Richard Wright and his father?"

Pamela frowned. Sarah looked down at her.

"Oh, I forgot," she said with a sigh, "they don't teach Wright here. The poshest school in the U.S., and the girls come out ignorant." She looked at her watch, saw she had twenty minutes before her train. "Really," she said almost inaudibly, "why Tears Eliot, Ezratic Pound, and even Sara Teacake, and no Wright?" She and Pamela thought e.e. cummings very clever with his perceptive spelling of great literary names.

"Is he a poet then?" asked Pam. She adored poetry, all poetry. Half of America's poetry she had, of course, not read, for the simple reason that she had never heard of it.

"No," said Sarah, "he wasn't a poet." She felt weary. "He was a man who wrote, a man who had trouble with his father." She began to walk about the room, and came to stand below the picture of the old man and the little girl.

"When he was a child," she continued, "his father ran off with another woman, and one day when Richard and his mother went to ask him for money to buy food he laughingly rejected them. Richard, being very young, thought his father Godlike. Big, omnipotent, unpredictable, undependable and cruel. Entirely in control of his universe. Just like a god. But, many years later, after Wright had become a famous writer, he went down to Mississippi to visit his father. He found, instead of God, just an old watery-eyed field hand, bent from plowing, his teeth gone, smelling of manure. Richard realized that the most daring thing his 'God' had done was run off with that other woman."

"So?" asked Pam. "What 'duty' did he feel he owed the old man?"

"So," said Sarah, "that's what Wright wondered as he peered into that old shifty-eyed Mississippi Negro face. What was the duty of the son of a destroyed man? The son of a man whose vision had stopped at the edge of fields that weren't even his. Who was Wright without his father? Was he Wright the great writer? Wright the Communist? Wright the French farmer? Wright whose white wife could never accompany him to Mississippi? Was he, in fact, still his father's son? Or was he freed by his father's desertion to be nobody's son, to be his own father? Could he disavow his father and live? And if so, live as what? As whom? And for what purpose?"

"Well," said Pam, swinging her hair over her shoulders and squinting her small eyes, "if his father rejected him I don't see why Wright even bothered to go see him again. From what you've said, Wright earned the freedom to be whoever he wanted to be. To a strong man a father is not essential."

"Maybe not," said Sarah, "but Wright's father was one faulty door in a house of many ancient rooms. Was that one faulty door to shut him off forever from the rest of the house? That was the question. And though he answered this question eloquently in his work, where it really counted, one can only wonder if he was able to answer it satisfactorily— or at all—in his life."

"You're thinking of his father more as a symbol of something, aren't you?" asked Pam.

"I suppose," said Sarah, taking a last look around her room. "I see him as a door that refused to open, a hand that was always closed. A fist."

Pamela walked with her to one of the college limousines, and in a few minutes she was at the station. The train to the city was just arriving.

"Have a nice trip," said the middle-aged driver courteously, as she took her suitcase from him. But for about the thousandth time since she'd seen him, he winked at her.

Once away from her friends she did not miss them. The school was all they had in common. How could they ever know her if they were not allowed to know Wright, she wondered. She was interesting, "beautiful," only because they had no idea what made her, charming only because they had no idea from where she came. And where they came from, though she glimpsed it—in themselves and in F. Scott Fitzgerald—she was never to enter. She hadn't the inclination or the proper ticket.

2

Her father's body was in Sarah's old room. The bed had been taken down to make room for the flowers and chairs and casket. Sarah looked for a long time into the face, as if to find some answer to her questions written there. It was the same face, a dark Shakespearean head framed by gray, woolly hair and split almost in half by a short, gray mustache. It was a completely silent face, a shut face. But her father's face also looked fat, stuffed, and ready to burst. He wore a navy-blue suit, white shirt and black tie. Sarah bent and loosened the tie. Tears started behind her shoulder blades but did not reach her eyes.

"There's a rat here under the casket," she called to her brother, who apparently did not hear her, for he did not come in. She was alone with her father, as she had rarely been when he was alive. When he was alive she had avoided him.

"Where's that girl at?" her father would ask. "Done closed herself up in her room again," he would answer himself.

For Sarah's mother had died in her sleep one night. Just gone to bed tired and never got up. And Sarah had blamed her father.

Stare the rat down, thought Sarah, surely that will help. *Perhaps it doesn't matter whether I misunderstood or never understood.*

"We moved so much looking for crops, a place to *live*," her father had moaned, accompanied by Sarah's stony silence. "The moving killed her. And now we have a real house, with *four* rooms, and a mailbox on the *porch*, and it's too late. She gone. *She* ain't here to see it." On very bad days her father would not eat at all. At night he did not sleep.

Whatever had made her think she knew what love was or was not?

Here she was, Sarah Davis, immersed in Camusian philosophy, versed in many languages, a poppy, of all things, among winter roses. But before she became a poppy she was a native Georgian sunflower, but still had not spoken the language they both knew. Not to him.

Stare the rat down, she thought, and did. The rascal dropped his bold eyes and slunk away. Sarah felt she had, at least, accomplished something.

Why did she have to see the picture of her mother, the one on the mantel among all the religious doodads, come to life? Her mother had stood stout against the years, clean gray braids shining across the top of her head, her eyes snapping, protective. Talking to her father.

"He called you out your name, we'll leave this place today. Not tomorrow. That be too late. Today!" Her mother was magnificent in her quick decisions.

"But what about your garden, the children, the change of schools?" Her father would be holding, most likely, the wide brim of his hat in nervously twisting fingers.

"He called you out your name, we go!"

And go they would. Who knew exactly where, before they moved? Another soundless place, walls falling down, roofing gone; another face to please without leaving too much of her father's pride at his feet. But to Sarah then, no matter with what alacrity her father moved, footdragging alone was visible.

The moving killed her, her father had said, *but the moving was also love.*

Did it matter now that often he had threatened their lives with the rage of his despair? That once he had spanked the crying baby violently, who later died of something else altogether . . . and that the next day they moved?

"No," said Sarah aloud, "I don't think it does."

"Huh?" It was her brother, tall, wiry, black, deceptively calm. As a child he'd had an irrepressible temper. As a grown man he was tensely smooth, like a river that any day will overflow its bed.

He had chosen a dull gray casket. Sarah wished for red. Was it Dylan Thomas who had said something grand about the dead offering "deep, dark defiance"? It didn't matter; there were more ways to offer defiance than with a red casket.

"I was just thinking," said Sarah, "that with us Mama and Daddy were saying NO with capital letters."

"I don't follow you," said her brother. He had always been the activist in the family. He simply directed his calm rage against any obstacle that might exist, and awaited the consequences with the same serenity he awaited his sister's answer. Not for him the philosophical confusions and poetic observations that hung his sister up.

"That's because you're a radical preacher," said Sarah, smiling up at him. "You deliver your messages in person with your own body." It excited her that her brother had at last imbued their childhood Sunday sermons with the reality of fighting for change. And saddened her that no matter how she looked at it this seemed more important than Medieval Art, Course 201.

3

"Yes, Grandma," Sarah replied. "Cresselton is for girls only, and *no*, Grandma, I am not pregnant."

Her grandmother stood clutching the broad wooden handle of her black bag, which she held, with elbows bent, in front of her stomach. Her eyes glinted through round wire-framed glasses. She spat into the grass outside the privy. She had insisted that Sarah accompany her to the toilet while the body was being taken into the church. She had leaned heavily on Sarah's arm, her own arm thin and the flesh like crepe.

"I guess they teach you how to really handle the world," she said. "And who knows, the Lord is everywhere. I would like a whole lot to see a Great-Grand. You don't specially have to be married, you know. That's why I felt free to ask." She reached into her bag and took out a Three Sixes bottle, which she proceeded to drink from, taking deep swift swallows with her head thrown back.

"There are very few black boys near Cresselton," Sarah explained, watching the corn liquor leave the bottle in spurts and bubbles. "Besides, I'm really caught up now in my painting and sculpting. . . ." Should she mention how much she admired Giacometti's work? No, she decided. Even if her grandmother had heard of him, and Sarah was positive she had not, she would surely think his statues much too thin. This made Sarah smile and remember how difficult it had been to convince her grandmother that even if Cresselton had not given her a scholarship she would have managed to go there anyway. Why? Because she wanted somebody to teach her to paint and to sculpt, and Cresselton had the best teachers. Her grandmother's notion of a successful granddaughter was a married one, pregnant the first year.

"Well," said her grandmother, placing the bottle with dignity back into her purse and gazing pleadingly into Sarah's face, "I sure would 'preshate a Great-Grand." Seeing her granddaughter's smile, she heaved a great sigh, and, walking rather haughtily over the stones and grass, made her way to the church steps.

As they walked down the aisle, Sarah's eyes rested on the back of her grandfather's head. He was sitting on the front middle bench in front of the casket, his hair extravagantly long and white and softly kinked. When she sat down beside him, her grandmother sitting next to him on the other side, he turned toward her and gently took her hand in his. Sarah briefly leaned her cheek against his shoulder and felt like a child again.

4

They had come twenty miles from town, on a dirt road, and the hot spring sun had drawn a steady rich scent from the honeysuckle vines along the way. The church was a bare, weather-beaten ghost of a building with hollow windows and a sagging door. Arsonists had once burned it to the ground, lighting the dry wood of the walls with the flames from the crosses they carried. The tall spreading red oak tree under which Sarah had played as a child still dominated the churchyard, stretching its branches widely from the roof of the church to the other side of the road.

After a short and eminently dignified service, during which Sarah and her grandfather alone did not cry, her father's casket was slid into the waiting hearse and taken the short distance to the cemetery, an overgrown wilderness whose stark white stones appeared to be the small ruins of an ancient civilization. There Sarah watched her grandfather from the corner of her eye. He did not seem to bend under the grief of burying a son. His back was straight, his eyes dry and clear. He was simply and solemnly heroic; a man who kept with pride his family's trust and his own grief. *It is strange,* Sarah thought, *that I never thought to paint him like this, simply as he stands; without anonymous meaningless people hovering beyond his profile; his face turned proud and brownly against the light.* The defeat that had frightened her in the faces of black men was the defeat of black forever defined by white. But that defeat was nowhere on her grandfather's face. He stood like a rock, outwardly calm, the comfort and support of the Davis family. The family alone defined him, and he was not about to let them down.

"One day I will paint you, Grandpa," she said, as they turned to go. "Just as you stand here now, with just"—she moved closer and touched his face with her hand—"just the right stubborn tenseness of your cheek. Just that look of Yes and No in your eyes."

"You wouldn't want to paint an old man like me," he said, looking deep into her eyes from wherever his mind had been. "If you want to make me, make me up in stone."

The completed grave was plump and red. The wreaths of flowers were arranged all on one side so that from the road there appeared to be only a large mass of flowers. But already the wind was tugging at the rose petals and the rain was making dabs of faded color all over the green foam frames. In a week the displaced honeysuckle vines, the wild roses, the grapevines, the grass, would be back. Nothing would seem to have changed.

5

"What do you mean, come *home?*" Her brother seemed genuinely amused. "We're all proud of you. How many black girls are at that school? Just *you?* Well, just one more besides you, and she's from the North. That's really something!"

"I'm glad you're pleased," said Sarah.

"Pleased! Why, it's what Mama would have wanted, a good education for little Sarah; and what Dad would have wanted too, if he could have wanted anything after Mama died. You were always smart. When you were two and I was five you showed me how to eat ice cream without getting it all over me. First, you said, nip off the bottom of the cone with your teeth, and suck the ice cream down. I never knew *how* you were supposed to eat the stuff once it began to melt."

"I don't know," she said, "sometimes you can want something a whole lot, only to find out later that it wasn't what you *needed* at all."

Sarah shook her head, a frown coming between her eyes. "I sometimes spend *weeks*," she said, "trying to sketch or paint a face that is unlike every other face around me, except, vaguely, for one. Can I help but wonder if I'm in the right place?"

Her brother smiled. "You mean to tell me you spend *weeks* trying to draw one face, and you still wonder whether you're in the right place? You must be kidding!" He chucked her under the chin and laughed out loud. "You learn how to draw the face," he said, "then you learn how to paint me and how to make Grandpa up in stone. Then you can come home or go live in Paris, France. It'll be the same thing."

It was the unpreacherlike gaiety of his affection that made her cry. She leaned peacefully into her brother's arms. She wondered if Richard Wright had had a brother.

"You are my door to all the rooms," she said. "Don't ever close."

And he said, "I won't," as if he understood what she meant.

6

"When will we see you again, young woman?" he asked later, as he drove her to the bus stop.

"I'll sneak up one day and surprise you," she said.

At the bus stop, in front of a tiny service station, Sarah hugged her brother with all her strength. The white station attendant stopped his work to leer at them, his eyes bold and careless.

"Did you ever think," said Sarah, "that we are a very old people in a very young place?"

She watched her brother from a window of the bus; her eyes did not leave his face until the little station was out of sight and the big Greyhound lurched on its way toward Atlanta. She would fly from there to New York.

7

She took the train to the campus.

"My," said one of her friends, "you look wonderful! Home sure must agree with you!"

"Sarah was home?" Someone who didn't know asked. "Oh, *great*, how was it?"

"Well, how was it?" went an echo in Sarah's head. The noise of the echo almost made her dizzy.

"How was it?" she asked aloud, searching for, and regaining, her balance.

"How was it?" She watched her reflection in a pair of smiling hazel eyes.

"It was fine," she said slowly, returning the smile, thinking of her grandfather. "Just fine."

The girl's smile deepened. Sarah watched her swinging along toward the back tennis courts, hair blowing in the wind.

Stare the rat down, thought Sarah; *and whether it disappears or not, I am a woman in the world. I have buried my father, and shall soon know how to make my grandpa up in stone.*

QUESTIONS

1. The contrasts of family versus school, Georgia versus New York are obvious and important in this story. Discuss what part each plays in creating the portrait of the protagonist? What does she need and accept from each? What does she reject?
2. Discuss the use of imagery in this story. Two important examples are images drawn from art (painting, sculpture, etc.) and from housing (doors, houses, rooms).
3. Note the reference to Richard Wright on pages 178–179. How is this discussion fitted into the story?

FOR FURTHER DISCUSSION, OR AS ESSAY TOPICS

1. Early in the story, the narrator comments that Sarah "found black men impossible to draw or to paint; she could not bear to trace defeat onto blank pages." At the end of the story, Sarah says "I am a woman in the world. I have buried my father, and shall soon know how to make my grandpa up in stone." Trace Sarah's journey from the first of these positions to the second.
2. Compare "A Sudden Trip Home in the Spring" with "Sonny's Blues." How does each handle the theme of the black creative artist in a primarily white society?

6 *Beyond Reality*

In the last two chapters, we studied 20th-century fiction that used realistic techniques to draw portraits and to study the interactions of individuals within contemporary society. In this chapter, we look at two other styles that have flowered within 20th-century fiction: surrealism and science fiction.

Surrealism presents tales in which either the protagonists' perception of reality or the narrator's depiction of reality depart from commonly accepted norms. Sometimes, just to add to the fun, the writer makes it difficult to tell which of the two is occurring; and sometimes, to add yet another dimension, the narrator manages to question reality itself by bringing the supernatural into the picture.

We saw something of this approach to fiction in Hawthorne's "Young Goodman Brown," where the narration was straightforward but the protagonist's actions and perceptions left open the question, was this a dream or reality? We saw it again in Gilman's "The Yellow Wall-Paper," where the narration itself depicted progressively less of external reality, more of reality seen through the eyes of a woman who was becoming insane. We will see it again in this chapter in Kafka's "The Bucket-Rider" and Cheever's "The Swimmer": and I leave it to your reading to determine what techniques the authors use to give a surreal quality to these two stories.

Surreal stories, then, are set within everyday society but depict that society, or some of those who live in it, in a non-realistic manner. Science fiction, on the other hand, tends to use realistic methods of presenting its stories, but sets them within societies that differ from our everyday society in time, in place, or by the inclusion of intelligent non-human beings.

Both types of story thus place one or more individuals in a situation (or a world) that is or becomes radically unfamiliar to them, and thus demands from them responses of a sort they never have had to make before. In many cases, the situation or world is also new to the readers: and thus we, like the protagonists, must adjust our perceptions to meet the new situation. At its best, non-realistic fiction then turns these new perceptions back onto our normal world: the insights we gain through fantasy give us a clearer vision of ourselves and our society.

Fantasy is often considered escapist, and put at the opposite end of a continuum from science. Yet science and fantasy both draw their energy from the human desire to understand the universe and to find in it more order and meaning than is easily seen on the surface. Science fiction uses this desire to encourage us to look at our thoughts, actions, and society in a new light by reminding us that we can change reality—for everyday life has changed greatly because of human explorations and inventions, and may change again—and thus encouraging us to ask two questions: First, in what directions may future changes take us, and what new challenges will that present to us? And, second, which things in our thoughts and behaviors are based on external and variable things—and thus should be subject to change as necessary—and which represent things that are basic and fundamental, essential parts of our humanity?

This chapter presents two science fiction stories: Arthur C. Clarke's "An Ape about the House" and Ursula LeGuin's "Those Who Walk Away from Omelas." As with all literature we present in this book, we hope not only that you enjoy studying these stories but also that you enjoy the stories themselves!

FRANZ KAFKA (1883–1924)

The Bucket-Rider

Coal all spent; the bucket empty, the shovel useless; the stove breathing out cold; the room freezing; the leaves outside the window rigid, covered with rime; the sky a silver shield against anyone who looks for help from it. I must have coal; I cannot freeze to death; behind me is the pitiless stove, before me the pitiless sky, so I must ride out between them and on my journey seek aid from the coal-dealer. But he has already grown deaf to ordinary appeals; I must prove irrefutably to him that I have not a single grain of coal left, and that he means to me the very sun in the firmament. I must approach like a beggar who, with the death-rattle already in his throat, insists on dying on the doorstep, and to whom the grand people's cook accordingly decides to give the dregs of the coffee-pot; just so must the coal-dealer, filled with rage, but acknowledging the command, "Thou shalt not kill," fling a shovelful of coal into my bucket.

My mode of arrival must decide the matter; so I ride off on the bucket. Seated on the bucket, my hands on the handle, the simplest kind of bridle, I propel myself with difficulty down the stairs; but once down below my bucket ascends, superbly, superbly; camels humbly squatting on the ground do not rise with more dignity, shaking themselves under the sticks of their drivers. Through the hard frozen streets we go at a regular canter; often I am upraised as high as the first story of a house; never do I sink as low as the house doors. And at last I float at an extraordinary height above the vaulted cellar of the dealer, whom I see far below crouching over his table, where he is writing; he has opened the door to let out the excessive heat.

"Coal-dealer!" I cry in a voice burned hollow by the frost and muffled in the cloud made by my breath, "please, coal-dealer, give me a little coal. My bucket is so light that I can ride on it. Be kind. When I can I'll pay you."

The dealer puts his hand to his ear. "Do I hear rightly?" He throws the question over his shoulder to his wife. "Do I hear rightly? A customer."

"I hear nothing," says his wife, breathing in and out peacefully while she knits on, her back pleasantly warmed by the heat.

"Oh, yes, you must hear," I cry. "It's me; an old customer; faithful and true; only without means at the moment."

"Wife," says the dealer, "it's some one, it must be; my ears can't have deceived me so much as that; it must be an old, a very old customer, that can move me so deeply."

"What ails you, man?" says his wife, ceasing from her work for a moment and pressing her knitting to her bosom. "It's nobody, the street is empty, all our customers are provided for; we could close down the shop for several days and take a rest."

"But I'm sitting up here on the bucket," I cry, and unfeeling frozen tears dim my eyes, "please look up here, just once; you'll see me directly; I beg you, just a shovelful; and if you give me more it'll make me so happy that I won't know what to do. All the other customers are provided for. Oh, if I could only hear the coal clattering into the bucket!"

"I'm coming," says the coal-dealer, and on his short legs he makes to climb the steps of the cellar, but his wife is already beside him, holds him back by the arm and says: "You stay here; seeing you persist in your fancies I'll go myself. Think of the bad fit of coughing you had during the night. But for a piece of business, even if it's one you've only fancied in your head, you're prepared to forget your wife and child and sacrifice your lungs. I'll go."

"Then be sure to tell him all the kinds of coal we have in stock; I'll shout out the prices after you."

"Right," says his wife, climbing up to the street. Naturally she sees me at once. "Frau Coal-dealer," I cry, "my humblest greetings; just one shovelful of coal; here in my bucket; I'll carry it home myself. One shovelful of the worst you have. I'll pay you in full for it, of course, but not just now, not just now." What a knell-like sound the words "not just now" have, and how bewilderingly they mingle with the evening chimes that fall from the church steeple nearby!

"Well, what does he want?" shouts the dealer. "Nothing," his wife shouts back, "there's nothing here; I see nothing, I hear nothing; only six striking, and now we must shut up the shop. The cold is terrible; tomorrow we'll likely have lots to do again."

She sees nothing and hears nothing; but all the same she loosens her apron-strings and waves her apron to waft me away. She succeeds, unluckily. My bucket has all the virtues of a good steed except powers of resistance, which it has not; it is too light; a woman's apron can make it fly through the air.

"You bad woman!" I shout back, while she, turning into the shop, half-contemptuous, half-reassured, flourishes her fist in the air. "You bad woman! I begged you for a shovelful of the worst coal and you would not give me it." And with that I ascend into the regions of the ice mountains and am lost forever.

QUESTIONS

The plot of this story is simple and all too realistic: a man who has no money to buy fuel tries unsuccessfully to buy some on credit. How does Kafka's device of giving his protagonist the notion—and the ability—to ride to the coal seller's on his coal bucket enrich the story? (Note, for example, that because of the attention paid to the bucket, Kafka can now keep the rest of the story pared down to its essentials.) What effect does the story now have? How do you respond to it?

JOHN CHEEVER (1912–1982)

The Swimmer

It was one of those midsummer Sundays when everyone sits around saying, "I *drank* too much last night." You might have heard it whispered by the parishioners leaving church, heard it from the lips of the priest himself, struggling with his cassock in the *vestiarium*, heard it from the golf links and the tennis courts, heard it from the wildlife preserve where the leader of the Audubon group was suffering from a terrible hangover. "I *drank* too much," said Donald Westerhazy. "We all *drank* too much," said Lucinda Merrill. "It must have been the wine," said Helen Westerhazy. "I *drank* too much of that claret." *Expensive wine*

This was at the edge of the Westerhazys' pool. The pool, fed by an artesian well with a high iron content, was a pale shade of green. It was a fine day. In the west there was a massive stand of cumulus cloud so like a city seen from a distance—from the bow of an approaching ship—that it might have had a name. Lisbon. Hackensack. The sun was hot. Neddy Merrill sat by the green water, one hand in it, one around a glass of gin. He was a slender man—he seemed to have the especial slenderness of youth—and while he was far from young he had slid down his banister that morning and given the bronze backside of Aphrodite on the hall table a smack, as he jogged toward the smell of coffee in his dining room. He might have been compared to a summer's day, particularly the last hours of one, and while he lacked a tennis racket or a sail bag the impression was definitely one of youth, sport, and clement weather. He had been swimming and now he was breathing deeply, stertorously as if he could gulp into his lungs the components of that moment, the heat of the sun, the intenseness of his pleasure. It all seemed to flow into his chest. His own house stood in Bullet Park, eight miles to the south, where his four beautiful daughters would have had their lunch and might be playing tennis. Then it occurred to him that by taking a dogleg to the southwest he could reach his home by water.

His life was not confining and the delight he took in this observation could not explained by its suggestion of escape. He seemed to see, with a cartographer's eye, that string of swimming pools, that quasi-subterranean stream that curved across the county. He had made a discovery, a contribution to modern geography; he would name the stream Lucinda after his wife. He was not a practical joker nor was he a fool but he was determinedly original and had a vague and modest idea of himself as a legendary figure. The day was beautiful and it seemed to him that a long swim might enlarge and celebrate its beauty.

He took off a sweater that was hung over his shoulders and dove in. He had an inexplicable contempt for men who did not hurl themselves into pools. He swam a choppy crawl, breathing either with every stroke or every fourth stroke and counting somewhere well in the back of his mind the one-two one-two of a flutter kick. It was not a serviceable stroke for long distances but the domestication of swimming had saddled the sport with some customs and in his part of the world a crawl was customary. To be embraced and sustained by the light green water was less a pleasure, it seemed, than the resumption of a natural condition, and he would have liked to swim without trunks, but this was not possible, considering his project. He hoisted himself up on the far curb—he never used the ladder—and started across the lawn. When Lucinda asked where he was going he said he was going to swim home.

The only map and charts he had to go by were remembered or imaginary but these were clear enough. First there were the Grahams, the Hammers, the Lears, the Howlands, and the Crosscups. He would cross Ditmar Street to the Bunkers and come, after a short portage, to the Levys, the Welchers, and the public pool in Lancaster. Then there were the Hallorans, the Sachses, the Biswangers, Shirley Adams, the Gilmartins, and the Clydes. The day was lovely, and that he lived in a world so generously supplied with water seemed like a clemency, a beneficence. His heart was high and he ran across the grass. Making his way home by an uncommon route gave him the feeling that he was a pilgrim, an explorer, a man with a destiny, and he knew that he would find friends all along the way; friends would line the banks of the Lucinda River.

He went through a hedge that separated the Westerhazys' land from the Grahams', walked under some flowering apple trees, passed the shed that housed their pump and filter, and came out at the Grahams' pool. "Why, Neddy," Mrs. Graham said, "what a marvelous surprise. I've been trying to get you on the phone all morning. Here, let me get you a drink. " He saw then, like any explorer, that the hospitable customs and traditions of the natives would have to be handled with diplomacy if he was ever going to reach his destination. He did not want to mystify or seem rude to the Grahams nor did he have the time to linger there. He swam the length of their pool and joined them in the sun and was rescued, a few minutes later, by the arrival of two carloads of friends from Connecticut. During the uproarious reunions he was able to slip away. He went down by the front of the Grahams' house, stepped over a thorny hedge, and crossed a vacant lot to the Hammers'. Mrs. Hammer, looking up from her roses, saw him swim by although she wasn't quite sure who it was. The Lears heard him splashing past the open windows of their living room. The Howlands and the Crosscups were away. After leaving the Howlands' he crossed Ditmar Street and started for the Bunkers', where he could hear, even at that distance, the noise of a party.

The water refracted the sound of voices and laughter and seemed to suspend it in midair. The Bunkers' pool was on a rise and he climbed some stairs to a terrace where twenty-five or thirty men and women were drinking. The only person in the water was Rusty Towers, who floated there on a rubber raft. Oh, how bonny and lush were the banks of the Lucinda River! Prosperous men and women gathered by the sapphire-coloured waters while caterer's men in white coats passed them cold gin. Overhead a red de Haviland trainer was circling around and around and around in the sky with something like the glee of a child in a swing. Ned felt a passing affection for the scene, a tenderness for the gathering, as if it was something he might touch. In the distance he heard thunder. As soon as Enid Bunker saw him she began to scream: "Oh, look who's here! What a marvelous surprise! When Lucinda said that you couldn't come I thought I'd *die.*" She made her way to him through the crowd, and when they had finished kissing she led him to the bar, a progress that was slowed by the fact that he stopped to kiss eight or ten other women and shake the hands of as many men. A smiling bartender he had seen at a hundred parties gave him a gin and tonic and he stood by the bar for a moment, anxious not to get stuck in any conversation that would delay his voyage. When he seemed about to be surrounded he dove in and swam close to the side to avoid colliding with Rusty's raft. At the far end of the pool he bypassed the Tomlinsons with a broad smile and jogged up the garden path. The gravel cut his feet but this was the only unpleasantness. The party was confined to the pool, and as he went toward the house he heard the brilliant, watery sound of voices fade, heard the noise of a radio from the Bunkers' kitchen, where someone was listening to a ball game. Sunday afternoon. He made his way through the parked cars and down the grassy border of their driveway to Alewives Lane. He did not want to be seen on the road in his bathing trunks but there was no traffic and he made the short distance to the Levy's driveway, marked with a PRIVATE PROPERTY sign and a green tube for *The New York Times.* All the doors and windows of the big house were open but there were no signs of life; not even a dog barked. He went around the side of the house to the pool and saw that the Levys had only recently left. Glasses and bottles and dishes of nuts were on a table at the deep end, where there was a bathhouse or gazebo, hung with Japanese lanterns. After swimming the pool he got himself a glass and poured a drink. It was his fourth or fifth drink and he had swum nearly half the length of the Lucinda River. He felt tired, clean, and pleased at that moment to be alone; pleased with everything.

It would storm. The stand of cumulus cloud—that city—had risen and darkened, and while he sat there he heard the percussiveness of thunder again. The de Haviland trainer was still circling overhead and it seemed to Ned that he could almost hear the pilot laugh with pleasure in the afternoon; but when there was another peal of thunder he took off for home. A train whistle blew and he wondered what time it had gotten to be. Four? Five? He thought of the provincial station at that hour, where a waiter, his tuxedo concealed by a raincoat, a dwarf with some flowers wrapped in newspaper, and a woman who had been crying would be waiting for the local. It was suddenly growing dark; it was that moment when the pinheaded birds seem to organize their song into some acute and knowledgeable recognition of the storm's approach. Then there was a fine noise of rushing water from the crown of an oak at his back, as if a spigot there had been turned. Then the noise of fountains came from the crowns of all the tall trees. Why did he love storms, what was the meaning of his excitement when the door sprang open and the rain wind fled rudely up the stairs, why had the simple task of shutting the windows of an old house seemed fitting and urgent, why did the first watery notes of a storm wind have for him the unmistakable sound of good news, cheer, glad tidings? Then there was an explosion, a smell of cordite, and rain lashed the Japanese lanterns that Mrs. Levy had bought in Kyoto the year before last, or was it the year before that?

He stayed in the Levys' gazebo until the storm had passed. The rain had cooled the air and he shivered. The force of the wind had stripped a maple of its red and yellow leaves and scattered them over the grass and the water. Since it was midsummer the tree must be blighted, and yet he felt a peculiar sadness at this sign of autumn. He braced his shoulders, emptied his glass, and started for the Welchers' pool. This meant crossing the Lindleys' riding ring and he was surprised to find it overgrown with grass and all the jumps dismantled. He wondered if the Lindleys had sold their horses or gone away for the summer and put them out to board. He seemed to remember having heard something about the Lindleys and their horses but the memory was unclear. On he went, barefoot through the wet grass, to the Welchers', where he found their pool was dry.

This breach in his chain of water disappointed him absurdly, and he felt like some explorer who seeks a torrential headwater and finds a dead stream. He was disappointed and mystified. It was common enough to go away for the summer but no one ever drained his pool. The Welchers had definitely gone away. The pool furniture was folded, stacked, and covered with a tarpaulin. The bathhouse was locked. All the windows of the house were shut, and when he went around to the driveway in front he saw a FOR SALE sign nailed to a tree. When had he last heard from the Welchers—when, that is, had he and Lucinda last regretted an invitation to dine with them? It seemed only a week or so ago. Was his memory failing or had he so disciplined it in the repression of unpleasant facts that he had damaged his sense of the truth? Then in the distance he heard the sound of a tennis game. This cheered him, cleared away all his apprehensions and let him regard the overcast sky and the cold air with indifference. This was the day that Neddy Merrill swam across the county. That was the day! He started off then for his most difficult portage.

Had you gone for a Sunday afternoon ride that day you might have seen him, close to naked, standing on the shoulders of Route 424, waiting for a chance to cross. You might have wondered if he was the victim of foul play, had his car broken down, or was he merely a fool. Standing barefoot in the deposits of the highway—beer cans, rags, and blowout patches—exposed to all kinds of ridicule, he seemed pitiful. He had known when he started that this was a part of his journey—it had been on his maps—but confronted with the lines of traffic, worming through the summery light, he found himself unprepared. He was laughed at, jeered at, a beer can was thrown at him, and he had no dignity or humor to bring to the situation. He could have gone back, back to the Westerhazys', where Lucinda would still be sitting in the sun. He had signed nothing, vowed nothing, pledged nothing, not even to himself. Why, believing as he did, that all human obduracy was susceptible to common sense, was he unable to turn back? Why was he determined to complete his journey even if it meant putting his life in danger? At what point had this prank, this joke, this piece of horseplay become serious? He could not go back, he could not even recall with any clearness the green water at the Westerhazys', the sense of inhaling the day's components, the friendly and relaxed voices saying that they had *drunk* too much. In the space of an hour, more or less, he had covered a distance that made his return impossible.

An old man, tooling down the highway at fifteen miles an hour, let him get to the middle of the road, where there was a grass divider. Here he was exposed to the ridicule of the northbound traffic, but after ten or fifteen minutes he was able to cross. From here he had a only a short walk to the Recreation Center at the edge of the village of Lancaster, where there were some handball courts and a public pool.

The effect of the water on voices, the illusion of brilliance and suspense, was the same here as it had been at the Bunkers' but the sounds here were louder, harsher, and more shrill, and as soon as he entered the crowded enclosure he was confronted with regimentation. "ALL SWIMMERS MUST TAKE A SHOWER BEFORE USING THE POOL. ALL SWIMMERS MUST USE THE FOOTBATH. ALL SWIMMERS MUST WEAR THEIR IDENTIFICATION DISKS." He took a shower, washed his feet in a cloudy and bitter solution, and made his way to the edge of the water. It stank of chlorine and looked to him like a sink. A pair of lifeguards in a pair of towers blew police whistles at what seemed to be regular intervals and abused the swimmers through a public address system. Neddy remembered the sapphire water at the Bunkers' with longing and thought that he might contaminate himself—damage his own prosperousness and charm—by swimming in this murk, but he reminded himself that he was an explorer, a pilgrim, and that this was merely a stagnant bend in the Lucinda River. He dove, scowling with distaste, into the chlorine and had to swim with his head above water to avoid collisions, but even so he was bumped into, splashed, and jostled. When he got to the shallow end both lifeguards were shouting at him: "Hey, you, you without the identification disk, get outa the water." He did, but they had no way of pursuing him and he went through the reek of suntan oil and chlorine out through the hurricane fence and passed the handball courts. By crossing the road he entered the wooded part of the Halloran estate. The woods were not cleared and the footing was treacherous and difficult until he reached the lawn and the clipped beech hedge that encircled their pool.

The Hallorans were friends, an elderly couple of enormous wealth who seemed to bask in the suspicion that they might be Communists. They were zealous reformers but they were not Communists, and yet when they were accused, as they sometimes were, of subversion, it seemed to gratify and excite them. Their beech hedge was yellow and he guessed this had been blighted like the Levys' maple. He called hullo, hullo, to warn the Hallorans of his approach, to palliate his invasion of their privacy. The Hallorans, for reasons that had never been explained to him, did not wear bathing suits. No explanations were in order, really. Their nakedness was a detail in their uncompromising zeal for reform and he stepped politely out of his trunks before he went through the opening in the hedge.

Mrs. Halloran, a stout woman with white hair and a serene face, was reading the *Times*. Mr. Halloran was taking beech leaves out of the water with a scoop. They seemed not surprised or displeased to see him. Their pool was perhaps the oldest in the country, a fieldstone rectangle, fed by a brook. It had no filter or pump and its waters were the opaque gold of the stream.

"I'm swimming across the county," Ned said.

"Why, I didn't know one could," exclaimed Mrs. Halloran.

"Well, I've made it from the Westerhazys'," Ned said. "That must be about four miles."

He felt his trunks at the deep end, walked to the shallow end, and swam this stretch. As he was pulling himself out of the water he heard Mrs. Halloran say, "We've been *terribly* sorry to hear about all your misfortunes, Neddy."

"My misfortunes?" Ned asked. "I don't know what you mean."

"Why, we heard that you'd sold the house and that your poor children . . ."

"I don't recall having sold the house," Ned said, "and the girls are at home."

"Yes," Mrs. Halloran sighed. "Yes . . ." Her voice filled the air with an unseasonable melancholy and Ned spoke briskly. "Thank you for the swim."

"Well, have a nice trip," said Mrs. Halloran.

Beyond the hedge he pulled on his trunks and fastened them. They were loose and he wondered if, during the space of an afternoon, he could have lost some weight. He was cold and he was tired and the naked Hallorans and their dark water had depressed him. The swim was too much for his strength but how could he have guessed this, sliding down the banister that morning and sitting in the Westerhazys' sun? His arms were lame. His legs felt rubbery and ached at the joints. The worst of it was the cold in his bones and the feeling that he might never be warm again. Leaves were falling down around him and he smelled wood smoke on the wind. Who would be burning wood at this time of year?

He needed a drink. Whiskey would warm him, pick him up, carry him through the last of his journey, refresh his feeling that it was original and valorous to swim across the county. Channel swimmers took brandy. He needed a stimulant. He crossed the lawn in front of the Hallorans' house and went down a little path to where they had built a house for their only daughter, Helen, and her husband, Eric Sachs. The Sachses' pool was small and he found Helen and her husband there.

"Oh, *Neddy*," Helen said. "Did you lunch at Mother's?"

"Not *really*," Ned said. "I *did* stop to see your parents." This seemed to be explanation enough. "I'm terribly sorry to break in on you like this but I've taken a chill and I wonder if you'd give me a drink."

"Why, I'd *love* to," Helen said, "but there hasn't been anything in this house to drink since Eric's operation. That was three years ago."

Was he losing his memory, had his gift for concealing painful facts let him forget that he had sold his house, that his children were in trouble, and that his friend had been ill? His eyes slipped from Eric's face to his abdomen, where he saw three pale, sutured scars, two of them at least a foot long. Gone was his navel, and what, Neddy thought, would the roving hand, bed-checking one's gifts at 3 A.M., make of a belly with no navel, no link to birth, this breach in the succession?

"I'm sure you can get a drink at the Biswangers'," Helen said. "They're having an enormous do. You can hear it from here. Listen!"

She raised her head and from across the road, the lawns, the gardens, the woods, the fields, he heard again the brilliant noise of voices over water. "Well, I'll get wet," he said, still feeling that he had no freedom of choice about his means of travel. He dove into the Sachses' cold water and, gasping, close to drowning, made his way from one end of the pool to the other. "Lucinda and I want *terribly* to see you," he said over his shoulder, his face set toward the Biswangers'. "We're sorry it's been so long and we'll call you *very* soon."

He crossed some fields to the Biswangers' and the sounds of revelry there. They would be honored to give him a drink, they would be happy to give him a drink. The Biswangers invited him and Lucinda for dinner four times a year, six weeks in advance. They were always rebuffed and yet they continued to send out their invitations, unwilling to comprehend the rigid and undemocratic realities of their society. They were the sort of people who discussed the price of things at cocktails, exchanged market tips during dinner, and after dinner told dirty stories to mixed company. They did not belong to Neddy's set—they were not even on Lucinda's Christmas-card list. He went toward their pool with feelings of indifference, charity, and some unease, since it seemed to be getting dark and these were the longest days of the year. The party when he joined it was noisy and large. Grace Biswanger was the kind of hostess who asked the optometrist, the veterinarian, the real-estate dealer, and the dentist. No one was swimming and the twilight, reflected on the water of the pool, had a wintry gleam. There was a bar and he started for this. When Grace Biswanger saw him she came toward him, not affectionately as he had every right to expect, but bellicosely.

"Why, this party has everything," she said loudly, "including a gate crasher."

She could not deal him a social blow—there was no question about this and he did not flinch. "As a gate crasher," he asked politely, "do I rate a drink?"

"Suit yourself," she said. "You don't seem to pay much attention to invitations."

She turned her back on him and joined some guests, and he went to the bar and ordered a whiskey. The bartender served him but he served him rudely. His was a world in which the caterer's men kept the social score, and to be rebuffed by a part-time barkeep meant that he had suffered some loss of social esteem. Or perhaps the man was new and uninformed. Then he heard Grace at his back say: "They went for broke overnight—nothing but income—and he showed up drunk one Sunday and asked us to loan him five thousand dollars. . . ." She was always talking about money. It was worse than eating your peas off a knife. He dove into the pool, swam its length and went away.

The next pool on his list, the last but two, belonged to his old mistress, Shirley Adams. If he had suffered any injuries at the Biswangers' they would be cured here. Love—sexual roughhouse in fact—was the supreme elixir, the pain killer, the brightly colored pill that would put the spring back into his step, the joy of life in his heart. They had had an affair last week, last month, last year. He couldn't remember. It was he who had broken it off, his was the upper hand, and he stepped through the gate of the wall that surrounded her pool with nothing so considered as self-confidence. It seemed in a way to be his pool, as the lover, particularly the illicit lover, enjoys the possessions of his mistress with an authority unknown to holy matrimony. She was there, her hair the color of brass, but her figure, at the edge of the lighted, cerulean water, excited in him no profound memories. It had been, he thought, a lighthearted affair, although she had wept when he broke it off. She seemed confused to see him and he wondered if she was still wounded. Would she, God forbid, weep again?

"What do you want?" she asked.

"I'm swimming across the county."

"Good Christ. Will you ever grow up?"

"What's the matter?"

"If you've come here for money," she said, "I won't give you another cent."

"You could give me a drink."

"I could but I won't. I'm not alone."

"Well, I'm on my way."

He dove in and swam the pool, but when he tried to haul himself up onto the curb he found that the strength in his arms and shoulders had gone, and he paddled to the ladder and climbed out. Looking over his shoulder he saw, in the lighted bathhouse, a young man. Going out onto the dark lawn he smelled chrysanthemums or marigolds—some stubborn autumnal fragrance—on the night air, strong as gas. Looking overhead he saw that the stars had come out, but why should he seem to see Andromeda, Cepheus, and Cassiopeia? What had become of the constellations of midsummer? He began to cry.

It was probably the first time in his adult life that he had ever cried, certainly the first time in his life that he had ever felt so miserable, cold, tired, and bewildered. He could not understand the rudeness of the caterer's barkeep or the rudeness of a mistress who had come to him on her knees and showered his trousers with tears. He had swum too long, he had been immersed too long, and his nose and his throat were sore from the water. What he needed then was a drink, some company, and some clean, dry clothes, and while he could have cut directly across the road to his house he went on to the Gilmartins' pool. Here, for the first time in his life, he did not dive but went down the steps into the icy water and swam a hobbled sidestroke that he might have learned as a youth. He staggered with fatigue on his way to the Clydes' and paddled the length of their pool, stopping again and again with his hand on the curb to rest. He climbed up the ladder and wondered if he had the strength to get home. He had done what he wanted, he had swum the county, but he was so stupefied with exhaustion that his triumph seemed vague. Stooped, holding on to the gateposts for support, he turned up the driveway of his own house.

The place was dark. Was it so late that they had all gone to bed? Had Lucinda stayed at the Westerhazys' for supper? Had the girls joined her there or gone someplace else? Hadn't they agreed, as they usually did on Sunday, to regret all their inviations and stay at home? He tried the garage doors to see what cars were in but the doors were locked and rust came off the handles onto his hands. Going toward the house, he saw that the force of the thunderstorm had knocked one of the rain gutters loose. It hung down over the front door like an umbrella rib, but it could be fixed in the morning. The house was locked, and he thought that the stupid cook or the stupid maid must have locked the place up until he remembered that it had been some time since they had employed a maid or a cook. He shouted, pounded on the door, tried to force it with his shoulder, and then, looking in at the windows, saw that the place was empty.

QUESTIONS

1. "Young Goodman Brown" presented a tale in which the protagonist might have been dreaming or might have had an encounter with the supernatural. And its narrator, presenting both possibilities, refused to decide. "The Swimmer" presents us with a similar dilemma, but its narrator is himself the perplexed protagonist and the author barely does us the courtesy of hinting that something strange is happening. Rather, he lets the tale slide from a realistic tale of suburbia to a surrealistic one with no break in the scene or the action whatever.

   We, therefore, must decide: Is the swimmer out of touch with reality in the early part of the story and accepting it (or forced to accept it) only at the end? Or has time really stretched, so that the swimmer begins his trip on a summer day and ends it late in the year some unknown number of years later?

   Which do you think is the case? Or do you want to propose some mixture or overlaying of the two?

2. How would you describe the protagonist of this story? How does the tale's physical and social setting contribute to your sense of his character? How does the surreal use of time enhance this?

3. We said that "Young Goodman Brown" might be considered an allegory. If you accept the second interpretation listed above for "The Swimmer," then that tale too might be considered to be, not so much the true "record of a day" as an allegory of some longer period of the protagonist's life?

   Do you think this could be an acceptable reading of the story? If so, how would you define and/or interpret the allegory?

ARTHUR C. CLARKE (1917–   )

An Ape about the House

Granny thought it a perfectly horrible idea; but then, she could remember the days when there were *human* servants.

"If you imagine," she snorted, "that I'll share the house with a monkey, you're very much mistaken."

"Don't be so old-fashioned," I answered. "Anyways, Dorcas isn't a monkey."

"Then what is she—it?"

I flipped through the pages of the Biological Engineering Corporation's guide. "Listen to this, Gran," I said. " 'The Superchimp (Registered Trade-mark) *Pan Sapiens* is an intelligent anthropoid, derived by selective breeding and genetic modification from basic chimpanzee stock—' "

"Just what I said! A monkey!"

" '—and with a large-enough vocabulary to understand simple orders. It can be trained to perform all types of domestic work or routine manual labor and is docile, affectionate, housebroken, and particularly good with children—' "

"Children! Would you trust Johnnie and Susan with a—a *gorilla?*"

I put the handbook down with a sigh.

"You've got a point there. Dorcas *is* expensive, and if I find the little monsters knocking her about—"

At this moment, fortunately, the door buzzer sounded. "Sign, please," said the delivery man. I signed, and Dorcas entered our lives.

"Hello, Dorcas," I said. "I hope you'll be happy here."

Her big, mournful eyes peered out at me from beneath their heavy ridges. I'd met much uglier humans, though she was rather an odd shape, being only about four feet tall and very nearly as wide. In her neat, plain uniform she looked just like a maid from one of those early twentieth-century movies; her feet, however, were bare and covered an astonishing amount of floor space.

"Morning, Ma'am," she answered, in slurred but perfectly intelligible accents.

"She can speak!" squawked Granny.

"Of course," I answered. "She can pronounce over fifty words, and can understand two hundred. She'll learn more as she grows used to us, but for the moment we must stick to the vocabulary on pages forty-two and forty-three of the handbook." I passed the instruction manual over to Granny; for once, she couldn't find even a single word to express *her* feelings.

Dorcas settled down very quickly. Her basic training—Class A Domestic, plus Nursery Duties—had been excellent, and by the end of the first month there were very few jobs around the house that she couldn't do, from laying the table to changing the children's clothes. At first she had an annoying habit of picking up things with her feet; it seemed as natural to her as using her hands, and it took a long time to break her of it. One of Granny's cigarette butts finally did the trick.

She was good-natured, conscientious, and didn't answer back. Of course, she was not terribly bright, and some jobs had to be explained to her at great length before she got the point. It took several weeks before I discovered her limitations and allowed for them; at first it was quite hard to remember that she was not exactly human, and that it was no good engaging her in the sort of conversations we women occupy ourselves with when we get together. Or not many of them; she did have an interest in clothes, and was fascinated by colors. If I'd let her dress the way she wanted, she'd have looked like a refugee from Mardi gras.

The children, I was relieved to find, adored her. I know what people say about Johnnie and Sue, and admit that it contains some truth. It's so hard to bring up children when their father's away most of the time, and to make matters worse, Granny spoils them when I'm not looking. So indeed does Eric, whenever his ship's on Earth, and I'm left to cope with the resulting tantrums. Never marry a spaceman if you can possibly avoid it; the pay may be good, but the glamour soon wears off.

By the time Eric got back from the Venus run, with three weeks' accumulated leave, our new maid had settled down as one of the family. Eric took her in his stride; after all, he'd met much odder creatures on the planets. He grumbled about the expense, of course, but I pointed out that now that so much of the housework was taken off my hands, we'd be able to spend more time together and do some of the visiting that had proved impossible in the past. I looked forward to having a little social life again, now that Dorcas could take care of the children.

For there was plenty of social life at Port Goddard, even though we were stuck in the middle of the Pacific. (Ever since what happened to Miami, of course, all major launching sites have been a long, long way from civilization.) There was a constant flow of distinguished visitors and travelers from all parts of the Earth—not to mention remoter points.

Every community has its arbiter of fashion and culture, its *grande dame* who is resented yet copied by all her unsuccessful rivals. At Port Goddard it was Christine Swanson; her husband was Commodore of the Space Service, and she never let us forget it. Whenever a liner touched down, she would invite all the officers on Base to a reception at her stylishly antique nineteenth-century mansion. It was advisable to go, unless you had a very good excuse, even though that meant looking at Christine's paintings. She fancied herself as an artist, and the walls were hung with multicolored daubs. Thinking of polite remarks to make about them was one of the major hazards of Christine's parties; another was her meter-long cigarette holder.

There was a new batch of paintings since Eric had been away: Christine had entered her "square" period. "You see, my dears," she explained to us, "the old-fashioned oblong pictures are terribly dated—they just don't go with the Space Age. There's no such thing as up or down, horizontal or vertical out *there*, so no really modern picture should have one side longer than another. And ideally, it should look *exactly* the same whichever way you hang it—I'm working on that right now."

"That seems very logical," said Eric tactfully. (After all, the Commodore was his boss.) But when our hostess was out of earshot, he added, "I don't know if Christine's pictures are hung the right way up, but I'm sure they're hung the wrong side to the wall."

I agreed; before I got married I spent several years at the art school and considered I knew something about the subject. Given as much cheek as Christine, I could have made quite a hit with my own canvases, which were now gathering dust in the garage.

"You know, Eric," I said a little cattily, "I could teach Dorcas to paint better than this."

He laughed and answered, "It might be fun to try it some day, if Christine gets out of hand." Then I forgot all about the matter—until a month later, when Eric was back in space.

The exact cause of the fight isn't important; it arose over a community development scheme on which Christine and I took opposing view points. She won, as usual, and I left the meeting breathing fire and brimstone. When I got home, the first thing I saw was Dorcas, looking at the colored pictures in one of the weeklies—and I remembered Eric's words.

I put down my handbag, took off my hat, and said firmly: "Dorcas—come out to the garage."

It took some time to dig out my oils and easel from under the pile of discarded toys, old Christmas decorations, skindiving gear, empty packing cases, and broken tools (it seemed that Eric never had time to tidy up before he shot off into space again). There were several unfinished canvases buried among the debris, which would do for a start. I set up a landscape which had got as far as one skinny tree, and said: "Now, Dorcas—I'm going to teach you to paint."

My plan was simple and not altogether honest. Although apes had, of course, splashed paint on canvas often enough in the past, none of them had created a genuine, properly composed work of art. I was sure that Dorcas couldn't either, but no one need know that mine was the guiding hand. She could get all the credit.

I was not actually going to lie to anyone, however. Though I would create the design, mix the pigments, and do most of the execution, I would let Dorcas tackle just as much of the work as she could handle. I hoped that she could fill in the areas of solid color, and perhaps develop a characteristic style of brushwork in the process. With any luck, I estimated, she might be able to do perhaps a quarter of the actual work. Then I could claim it was all hers with a reasonably clear conscience—for hadn't Michelangelo and Leonardo signed paintings that were largely done by their assistants? I'd be Dorcas' "assistant."

I must confess that I was a little disappointed. Though Dorcas quickly got the general idea, and soon understood the use of brush and palette, her execution was very clumsy. She seemed unable to make up her mind which hand to use, but kept transferring the brush from one to the other. In the end I had to do almost all the work, and she merely contributed a few dabs of paint.

Still, I could hardly expect her to become a master in a couple of lessons, and it was really of no importance. If Dorcas was an artistic flop, I would just have to stretch the truth a little farther when I claimed that it was all her own work.

I was in no hurry; this was not the sort of thing that could be rushed. At the end of a couple of months, the School of Dorcas had produced a dozen paintings, all of them on carefully chosen themes that would be familiar to a Superchimp at Port Goddard. There was a study of the lagoon, a view of our house, an impression of a night launching (all glare and explosions of light), a fishing scene, a palm grove—clichés, of course, but anything else would rouse suspicion. Before she came to us, I don't suppose Dorcas had seen much of the world outside the labs where she had been reared and trained.

The best of these paintings (and some of them *were* good—after all, I should know) I hung around the house in places where my friends could hardly fail to notice them. Everything worked perfectly; admiring queries were followed by astonished cries of "You don't say!" when I modestly disclaimed responsibility. There was some skepticism, but I soon demolished that by letting a few privileged friends see Dorcas at work. I chose the viewers for their ignorance of art, and the picture was an abstraction in red, gold, and black which no one dared to criticize. By this time, Dorcas could fake it quite well, like a movie actor pretending to play a musical instrument.

Just to spread the news around, I gave away some of the best paintings, pretending that I considered them no more than amusing novelties—yet at the same time giving just the barest hint of jealousy. "I've hired Dorcas," I said testily, "to work for me—not for the Museum of Modern Art." And I was *very* careful not to draw any comparisons between her paintings and those of Christine: our mutual friends could be relied upon to do that.

When Christine came to see me, ostensibly to discuss our quarrel "like two sensible people," I knew that she was on the run. So I capitulated gracefully as we took tea in the drawing room, beneath one of Dorcas' most impressive productions. (Full moon rising over the lagoon—very cold, blue, and mysterious. I was really quite proud of it.) There was not a word about the picture, or about Dorcas; but Christine's eyes told me all I wanted to know. The next week, an exhibition she had been planning was quietly canceled.

Gamblers say that you should quit when you're ahead of the game. If I had stopped to think, I should have known that Christine would not let the matter rest there. Sooner or later, she was bound to counterattack.

She chose her time well, waiting until the kids were at school, Granny was away visiting, and I was at the shopping center on the other side of the island. Probably she phoned first to check that no one was at home—no one human, that is. We had told Dorcas not to answer calls; though she'd done so in the early days, it had not been a success. A Superchimp on the phone sounds exactly like a drunk, and this can lead to all sorts of complications.

I can reconstruct the whole sequence of events: Christine must have driven up to the house, expressed acute disappointment at my absence, and invited herself in. She would have wasted no time in getting to work on Dorcas, but luckily I'd taken the precaution of briefing my anthropoid colleague. "Dorcas make," I'd said, over and over again, each time one of our productions was finished. "Not Missy make— *Dorcas* make." And, in the end, I'm sure she believed this herself.

If my brainwashing, and the limitations of a fifty-word vocabulary, baffled Christine, she did not stay baffled for long. She was a lady of direct action, and Dorcas was a docile and obedient soul. Christine, determined to expose fraud and collusion, must have been gratified by the promptness with which she was led into the garage studio; she must also have been just a little surprised.

I arrived home about half an hour later, and knew that there was trouble afoot as soon as I saw Christine's car parked at the curb. I could only hope I was in time, but as soon as I stepped into the uncannily silent house, I realized that it was too late. *Something* had happened; Christine would surely be talking, even if she had only an ape as audience. To her, any silence was as great a challenge as a blank canvas; it had to be filled with the sound of her own voice.

The house was utterly still; there was no sign of life. With a sense of mounting apprehension, I tiptoed through the drawing room, the dining room, the kitchen, and out into the back. The garage door was open, and I peered cautiously through.

It was a bitter moment of truth. Finally freed from my influence, Dorcas had at last developed a style of her own. She was swiftly and confidently painting—but not in the way *I* had so carefully taught her. And as for her subject . . .

I was deeply hurt when I saw the caricature that was giving Christine such obvious enjoyment. After all that I had done for Dorcas, this seemed sheer ingratitude. Of course, I know now that no malice was involved, and that she was merely expressing herself. The psychologists, and the critics who wrote those absurd program notes for her exhibition at the Guggenheim, say that her portraits cast a vivid light on man-animal relationships, and allow us to look for the first time at the human race from outside. But I did not see it *that* way when I ordered Dorcas back into the kitchen.

For the subject was not the only thing that upset me: what really rankled was the thought of all the time I had wasted improving her technique—and her manners. She was ignoring everything I had ever told her, as she sat in front of the easel with her arms folded motionless on her chest.

Even then, at the very beginning of her career as an independent artist, it was painfully obvious that Dorcas had more talent in either of her swiftly moving feet than I had in both my hands.

QUESTIONS

1. Note the sentence above, "The psychologists . . . say that her portraits cast a vivid light on man-animal relationships. . . ." How does the story itself present relationships, not only between man and animal, but also among its human characters? How do the two types of relationships reflect each other?
2. We talked, in Chapter 2, of insights and blind spots that a reader can expect a first-person narrator to display, and of the dynamics that can result from a reader recognizing these blind spots and thus taking up the job of interpretation when the narrator's perceptions halt. To what extent does that happen in this story?
3. Given your response to Question 2, to what extent was the tale's ending a surprise to you? to the narrator? In what way is the ending a reversal, in what way a fitting conclusion to the tale's action? Do you find it effective? Amusing?
4. What, if anything, do you think Clarke has achieved by casting the story in the future, and using a superchimp as a character, that he could not have achieved through a realistic tale?

URSULA K. LE GUIN (1929–)

The Ones Who Walk Away from Omelas[1]

With a clamor of bells that set the swallows soaring, the Festival of Summer came to the city Omelas, bright-towered by the sea. The rigging of the boats in harbor sparkled with flags. In the streets between houses with red roofs and painted walls, between old moss-grown gardens and under avenues of trees, past great parks and public buildings, processions moved. Some were decorous: old people in long stiff robes of mauve and gray, grave master workmen, quiet, merry women carrying their babies and chatting as they walked. In other streets the music beat faster, a shimmering of gong and tambourine, and the people went dancing, the procession was a dance. Children dodged in and out, their high calls rising like the swallows' crossing flights over the music and the singing. All the processions wound towards the north side of the city, where on the great water-meadow called the Green Fields boys and girls, naked in the bright air, with mud-stained feet and ankles and long, lithe arms, exercised their restive horses before the race. The horses wore no gear at all but a halter without bit. Their manes were braided with streamers of silver, gold, and green. They flared their nostrils and pranced and boasted to one another; they were vastly excited, the horse being the only animal who has adopted our ceremonies as his own. Far off to the north and west the mountains stood up half encircling Omelas on her bay. The air of morning was so clear that the snow still crowning the Eighteen Peaks burned with white-gold fire across the miles of sunlit air, under the dark blue of the sky. There was just enough wind to make the banners that marked the racecourse snap and flutter now and then. In the silence of the broad green meadows one could hear the music winding through the city streets, farther and nearer and ever approaching, a cheerful faint sweetness of the air from time to time trembled and gathered together and broke out into the great joyous clanging of the bells.

Joyous! How is one to tell about joy? How describe the citizens of Omelas?

They were not simple folk, you see, though they were happy. But we do not say the words of cheer much any more. All smiles have become archaic. Given a description such as this one tends to make certain assumptions. Given a description such as this one tends to look next for the King, mounted on a splendid stallion and surrounded by his noble

---

[1] The author says the name comes from "a road sign: Salem (Oregon) backwards. . . . Salem equals schelomo equals salaam equals Peace. Melas. O melas. Omelas. Homme hélas." The last phrase equals "Man, alas."

knights, or perhaps in a golden litter borne by great-muscled slaves. But there was no king. They did not use swords, or keep slaves. They were not barbarians, I do not know the rules and laws of their society, but I suspect that they were singularly few. As they did without monarchy and slavery, so they also got on without the stock exchange, the advertisement, the secret police, and the bomb. Yet I repeat that these were not simple folk, not dulcet shepherds, noble savages, bland utopians. They were not less complex than us. The trouble is that we have a bad habit, encouraged by pedants and sophisticates, of considering happiness as something rather stupid. Only pain is intellectual, only evil interesting. This is the treason of the artist: a refusal to admit the banality of evil and the terrible boredom of pain. If you can't lick 'em, join 'em. If it hurts, repeat it. But to praise despair is to condemn delight, to embrace violence is to lose hold of everything else. We have almost lost hold; we can no longer describe a happy man, nor make any celebration of joy. How can I tell you about the people of Omelas? They were not naïve and happy children—though their children were, in fact, happy. They were mature, intelligent, passionate adults whose lives were not wretched. O miracle! but I wish I could describe it better. I wish I could convince you. Omelas sounds in my words like a city in a fairy tale, long ago and far away, once upon a time. Perhaps it would be best if you imagined it as your own fancy bids, assuming it will rise to the occasion, for certainly I cannot suit you all. For instance, how about technology? I think that there would be no cars or helicopters in and above the steets; this follows from the fact that the people of Omelas are happy people. Happiness is based on a just discrimination of what is necessary, what is neither necessary nor destructive, and what is destructive. In the middle category, however—that of the unnecessary but undestructive, that of comfort, luxury, exuberance, etc.—they could perfectly well have central heating, subway trains, washing machines, and all kinds of marvelous devices not yet invented here, floating light-sources, fuelless power, a cure for the common cold. Or they could have none of that: it doesn't matter. As you like it. I incline to think that people from towns up and down the coast have been coming in to Omelas during the last days before the Festival on very fast little trains and double-decked trams, and that the train station of Omelas is actually the handsomest building in town, though plainer than the magnificent Farmers' Market. But even granted trains, I fear that Omelas so far strikes some of you as goody-goody. Smiles, bells, parades, horses, bleh. If so, please add an orgy. If an orgy would help, don't hesitate. Let us not, however, have temples from which issue beautiful nude priests and priestesses already half in ecstasy and ready to copulate with any man or woman, lover or stranger, who desires union with the deep godhead of the blood, although that was my first idea. But really it would be better not to have any temples in Omelas—at least, not manned temples. Religion yes, clergy no. Surely the beautiful nudes can just wander about, offering themselves like divine soufflés to the hunger of the needy and the rapture of the flesh. Let them join the processions. Let tambourines be struck above the copulations, and the glory of desire be proclaimed upon the gongs, and (a not unimportant point) let the offspring of these delightful rituals be beloved and looked after by all. One thing I know there is none of in Omelas is guilt. But what else should there be? I thought at first there were no drugs, but that is puritanical. For those who like it, the faint insistent sweetness of *drooz* may perfume the ways of the city, *drooz* which first brings a great lightness and brilliance to the mind and limbs, and then after some hours a dreamy languor, and wonderful visions at last of the very arcana and inmost secrets of the Universe, as well as exciting the pleasure of sex beyond all belief; and it is not habit-forming. For more modest tastes I think there ought to be beer. What else, what else belongs in the joyous city? The sense of victory, surely, the celebration of courage. But as we did without clergy, let us do without soldiers. The joy built upon successful slaughter is not the right kind of joy; it will not do; it is fearful and it is trivial. A boundless and generous contentment, a magnanimous triumph felt not against some outer enemy but in communion with the finest and fairest in the souls of all men everywhere and the splendor of the world's summer: this is what swells the hearts of the people of Omelas, and the victory they celebrate is that of life. I really don't think many of them need to take *drooz*.

Most of the processions have reached the Green Fields by now. A marvelous smell of cooking goes forth from the red and blue tents of the provisioners. The faces of small children are amiably sticky; in the benign gray beard of a man a couple of crumbs of rich pastry are entangled. The youths and girls have mounted their horses and are beginning to group around the starting line of the course. An old woman, small, fat, and laughing, is passing out flowers from a basket, and tall young men wear her flowers in their shining hair. A child of nine or ten sits at the edge of the crowd, alone, playing on a wooden flute. People pause to listen, and they smile, but they do not speak to him, for he never ceases playing and never sees them, his dark eyes wholly rapt in the sweet, thin magic of the tune.

He finishes, and slowly lowers his hands holding the wooden flute.

As if that little private silence were the signal, all at once a trumpet sounds from the pavilion near the starting line: imperious, melancholy, piercing. The horses rear on their slender legs, and some of them neigh in answer. Sober-faced, the young riders stroke the horses' necks and soothe them, whispering. "Quiet, quiet, there my beauty, my hope. . . . " They begin to form in rank along the starting line. The crowds along the racecourse are like a field of grass and flowers in the wind. The Festival of Summer has begun.

Do you believe? Do you accept the festival, the city, the joy? No? Then let me describe one more thing.

In a basement under one of the beautiful public buildings of Omelas, or perhaps in the cellar of one of its spacious private homes, there is a room. It has one locked door, and no window. A little light seeps in dustily between cracks in the boards, secondhand from a cobwebbed window somewhere across the cellar. In one corner of the little room a couple of mops, with stiff, clotted, foul-smelling heads, stand near a rusty bucket. The floor is dirt, a little damp to the touch, as cellar dirt usually is. The room is about three paces long and two wide: a mere broom closet or disused tool room. In the room a child is sitting. It could be a boy or a girl. It looks about six, but actually is nearly ten. It is feeble-minded. Perhaps it was born defective, or perhaps it has become imbecile through fear, malnutrition, and neglect. It picks its nose and occasionally fumbles vaguely with its toes or genitals, as it sits hunched in the corner farthest from the bucket and the two mops. It is afraid of the mops. It finds them horrible. It shuts its eyes, but it knows the mops are still standing there; and the door is locked; and nobody will come. The door is always locked; and nobody ever comes, except that sometimes—the child has no understanding of time or interval—sometimes the door rattles terribly and opens, and a person, or several people, are there. One of them may come in and kick the child to make it stand up. The others never come close, but peer in at it with fright-ened, disgusted eyes. The food bowl and the water jug are hastily filled, the door is locked; the eyes disappear. The people at the door never say anything, but the child, who has not always lived in the tool room, and can remember sunlight and its mother's voice, sometimes speaks. "I will be good," it says. "Please let me out. I will be good!" They never answer. The child used to scream for help at night, and cry a good deal, but now it only makes a kind of whining, "eh-haa, eh-haa," and it speaks less and less often. It is so thin there are no calves to its legs; its belly protrudes; it lives on a half-bowl of corn meal and grease a day. It is naked. Its buttocks and thighs are a mass of festered sores, as it sits in its own excrement continually.

They all know it is there, all the people of Omelas. Some of them have come to see it, others are content merely to know it is there. They all know that it has to be there. Some of them understand why, and some do not, but they all understand that their happiness, ·the beauty of their city, the tenderness of their friendships, the health of their children, the wisdom of their scholars, the skill of their makers, even the abundance of their harvest and the kindly weathers of their skies, depend wholly on this child's abominable misery.

This is usually explained to children when they are between eight and twelve, whenever they seem capable of understanding; and most of those who come to see the child are young people, though often enough an adult comes, or comes back, to see the child. No matter how well the matter has been explained to them, these young spectators are always shocked and sickened at the sight. They feel disgust, which they had thought themselves superior to. They feel anger, outrage, impotence, despite all the explanations. They would like to do something for the child. But there is nothing they can do. If the child were brought up into the sunlight out of that vile place, if it were cleaned and fed and comforted, that would be a good thing, indeed; but if it were done, in that day and hour all the prosperity and beauty and delight of Omelas would wither and be destroyed. Those are the terms. To exchange all the goodness and grace of every life in Omelas for that single, small improvement: to throw away the happiness of thousands for the chance of the happiness of one: that would be to let guilt within the walls indeed.

The terms are strict and absolute; there may not even be a kind word spoken to the child.

Often the young people go home in tears, or in a tearless rage, when they have seen the child and faced this terrible paradox. They may brood over it for weeks or years. But as time goes on they begin to realize that even if the child could be released, it would not get much good of its freedom: a little vague pleasure of warmth and food, no doubt, but little more. It is too degraded and imbecile to know any real joy. It has been afraid too long ever to be free of fear. Its habits are too uncouth for it to respond to humane treatment. Indeed, after so long it would probably be wretched without walls about it to protect it, and darkness for its eyes, and its own excrement to sit in. Their tears at the bitter injustice dry when they begin to perceive the terrible justice of reality, and to accept it. Yet it is their tears and anger, the trying of their generosity and the acceptance of their helplessness, which are perhaps the true source of the splendor of their lives. Theirs is no vapid, irresponsible happiness. They know that they, like the child, are not free. They know compassion. It is the existence of the child, and their knowledge of its existence, that makes possible the nobility of their architecture, the poignancy of their music, the profundity of their science. It is because of the child that they are so gentle with children. They know that if the wretched one were not there sniveling in the dark, the other one, the flute-player, could make no joyful music as the young riders line up in their beauty for the race in the sunlight of the first morning of summer.

Now do you believe in them? Are they not more credible? But there is one more thing to tell, and this is quite incredible.

At times one of the adolescent girls or boys who go to see the child does not go home to weep or rage, does not, in fact, go home at all. Sometimes also a man or woman much older falls silent for a day or two, and then leaves home. These people go out into the street, and walk down the street alone. They keep walking, and walk straight out of the city of Omelas, through the beautiful gates. They keep walking across the farmlands of Omelas. Each one goes alone, youth or girl, man or woman. Night falls; the traveler must pass down village streets, between the houses with yellow-lit windows, and on out into the darkness of the fields. Each alone, they go west or north, towards the mountains. They go on. They leave Omelas, they walk ahead into the darkness, and they do not come back. The place they go towards is a place even less imaginable to most of us than the city of happiness. I cannot describe it at all. It is possible that it does not exist. But they seem to know where they are going, the ones who walk away from Omelas.

QUESTIONS

1. What is the effect of the discussion with the reader that precedes the story? Does it add to or detract from your understanding and/or enjoyment of the story?
2. Notice the narrator's discussion of how difficult it is to describe happiness. What relationship does that have with the rest of the story? With your reaction to the story?
3. What is the effect of the narrator's inviting your participation in imagining what Omelas is like? Why do you think the invitation stops once the narrator begins describing the scapegoat and the Omelans' reaction to him?
4. What do you think happens to "the ones who walk away from Omelas"?

OPTIONAL CREATIVE WRITING ASSIGNMENT

Write a short story in which a person from a different "world" arrives in your town or college, and (1) asks you to explain things he/she/it does not understand, or (2) writes home about the curious things he/she/it sees in this new place.

AN ANTHOLOGY OF
SHORT STORIES

EDGAR ALLAN POE (1809–1849)

The Purloined Letter

Nil sapientae odiosius acumine nimio.

—Seneca[1]

At Paris, just after dark one gusty evening in the autumn of 18—, I was enjoying the twofold luxury of meditation and a meerschaum, in company with my friend C. Auguste Dupin, in his little back library, or book-closet, *au troisième, No. 33, Rue Dunôt, Faubourg St. Germain.*[2] For one hour at least we had maintained a profound silence; while each, to any casual observer, might have seemed intently and exclusively occupied with the curling eddies of smoke that oppressed the atmosphere of the chamber. For myself, however, I was mentally discussing certain topics which had formed matter for conversation between us at an earlier period of the evening; I mean the affair of the Rue Morgue, and the mystery attending the murder of Marie Rogêt.[3] I looked upon it, therefore, as something of a coincidence, when the door of our apartment was thrown open and admitted our old acquaintance, Monsieur G——, the Prefect of the Parisian police.

We gave him a hearty welcome; for there was nearly half as much of the entertaining as of the contemptible about the man, and we had not seen him for several years. We had been sitting in the dark, and Dupin now arose for the purpose of lighting a lamp, but sat down again, without doing so, upon G.'s saying that he had called to consult us, or rather to ask the opinion of my friend, about some official business which had occasioned a great deal of trouble.

"If it is any point requiring reflection," observed Dupin, as he forbore to enkindle the wick, "we shall examine it to better purpose in the dark."

"That is another of your odd notions," said the Prefect, who had a fashion of calling every thing "odd" that was beyond his comprehension, and thus lived amid an absolute legion of "oddities."

---

[1] "Nothing is more distasteful to good sense than too much cunning"; Lucius Annaeus Seneca (4 B.C.–65 A.D.), Roman poet and philosopher.

[2] Fashionable quarter of Paris. The "troisième" is literally the third floor, but is equivalent to the fourth floor in North America.

[3] "The Mystery of Marie Rogêt" and "The Murders in the Rue Morgue" are titles of earlier Dupin tales by Poe.

"Very true," said Dupin, as he supplied his visitor with a pipe, and rolled towards him a comfortable chair.

"And what is the difficulty now?" I asked. "Nothing more in the assassination way, I hope?"

"Oh no; nothing of that nature. The fact is, the business is *very* simple indeed, and I make no doubt that we can manage it sufficiently well ourselves; but then I thought Dupin would like to hear the details of it, because it is so excessively *odd*."

"Simple and odd," said Dupin.

"Why, yes; and not exactly that either. The fact is, we have all been a good deal puzzled because the affair *is* so simple, and yet baffles us altogether."

"Perhaps it is the very simplicity of the thing which puts you at fault," said my friend.

"What nonsense you *do* talk!" replied the Prefect, laughing heartily.

"Perhaps the mystery is a little *too* plain," said Dupin.

"Oh, good heavens! who ever heard of such an idea?"

"A little *too* self-evident."

"Ha! ha! ha!—ha! ha! ha!—ho! ho! ho!"—roared our visitor, profoundly amused, "oh, Dupin, you will be the death of me yet!"

"And what, after all, *is* the matter on hand?" I asked.

"Why, I will tell you," replied the Prefect, as he gave a long, steady, and contemplative puff, and settled himself in his chair. "I will tell you in a few words; but, before I begin, let me caution you that this is an affair demanding the greatest secrecy, and that I should most probably lose the position I now hold, were it known that I confided it to any one."

"Proceed," said I.

"Or not," said Dupin.

"Well, then; I have received personal information, from a very high quarter, that a certain document of the last importance has been purloined from the royal apartments. The individual who purloined it is known; this beyond a doubt; he was seen to take it. It is known, also, that it still remains in his possession."

"How is this known?" asked Dupin.

"It is clearly inferred," replied the Prefect, "from the nature of the document, and from the non-appearance of certain results which would at once arise from its passing *out* of the robber's possession;—that is to say, from his employing it as he must design in the end to employ it."

"Be a little more explicit," I said.

"Well, I may venture so far as to say that the paper gives its holder a certain power in a certain quarter where such power is immensely valuable." The Prefect was fond of the cant of diplomacy.

"Still I do not quite understand," said Dupin.

"No? Well; the disclosure of the document to a third person, who shall be nameless, would bring in question the honour of a personage of most exalted station; and this fact gives the holder of the document an ascendancy over the illustrious personage whose honour and peace are so jeopardized."

"But this ascendancy," I interposed, "would depend upon the robber's knowledge of the loser's knowledge of the robber. Who would dare—"

"The thief," said G., "is the Minister D———, who dares all things, those unbecoming as well as those becoming a man. The method of the theft was not less ingenious than bold. The document in question—a letter, to be frank—had been received by the personage robbed while alone in the royal *boudoir*. During its perusal she was suddenly interrupted by the entrance of the other exalted personage from whom especially it was her wish to conceal it. After a hurried and vain endeavour to thrust it in a drawer, she was forced to place it, open it was, upon a table. The address, however, was uppermost, and, the contents thus unexposed, the letter escaped notice. At this juncture enters the Minister D———. His lynx eye immediately perceives the paper, recognizes the handwriting of the address, observes the confusion of the personage addressed, and fathoms her secret. After some business transactions, hurried through in his ordinary manner, he produces a letter somewhat similar to the one in question, opens it, pretends to read it, and then places it in close juxtaposition to the other. Again he converses, for some fifteen minutes, upon the public affairs. At length, in taking leave, he takes also from the table the letter to which he had no claim. Its rightful owner saw, but, of course, dared not call attention to the act, in the presence of the third personage who stood at her elbow. The minister decamped; leaving his own letter—one of no importance—upon the table."

"Here, then," said Dupin to me, "you have precisely what you demand to make the ascendancy complete—the robber's knowledge of the loser's knowledge of the robber."

"Yes," replied the Prefect; "and the power thus attained has, for some months past, been wielded, for political purposes, to a very dangerous extent. The personage robbed is more thoroughly convinced, every day, of the necessity of reclaiming her letter. But this, of course, cannot be done openly. In fine, driven to despair, she has committed the matter to me."

"Than whom," said Dupin, amid a perfect whirlwind of smoke, "no more sagacious agent could, I suppose, be desired, or even imagined."

"You flatter me," replied the Prefect; "but it is possible that some such opinion may have been entertained."

"It is clear," said I, "as you observe, that the letter is still in the possession of the minister; since it is this possession, and not any employment of the letter, which bestows the power. With the employment the power departs."

"True," said G.; "and upon this conviction I proceeded. My first care was to make thorough search of the minister's hotel;[4] and here my chief embarrassment lay in the necessity of searching without his knowledge. Beyond all things, I have been warned of the danger which would result from giving him reason to suspect our design."

"But," said I, "you are quite *au fait*[5] in these investigations. The Parisian police have done this thing often before."

"O yes; and for this reason I did not despair. The habits of the minister gave me, too, a great advantage. He is frequently absent from home all night. His servants are by no means numerous. They sleep at a distance from their master's apartment, and being chiefly Neapolitans, are readily made drunk. I have keys, as you know, with which I can open any chamber or cabinet in Paris. For three months a night has not passed, during the greater part of which I have not been engaged, personally, in ransacking the D——— Hôtel. My honour is interested, and, to mention a great secret, the reward is enormous. So I did not abandon the search until I had become fully satisfied that the thief is a more astute man than myself. I fancy that I have investigated every nook and corner of the premises in which it is possible that the paper can be concealed."

"But is it not possible," I suggested, "that although the letter may be in the possession of the minister, as it unquestionably is, he may have concealed it elsewhere than upon his own premises?"

"This is barely possible," said Dupin. "The present peculiar condition of affairs at court, and especially of those intrigues in which D——— is known to be involved, would render the instant availability of the document—its susceptibility of being produced at a moment's notice—a point of nearly equal importance with its possession."

"Its susceptibility of being produced?" said I.

"That is to say, of being *destroyed*," said Dupin.

"True," I observed; "the paper is clearly then upon the premises. As for its being upon the person of the minister, we may consider that as out of the question."

"Entirely," said the Prefect. "He had been twice waylaid, as if by footpads, and his person rigorously searched under my own inspection."

"You might have spared yourself this trouble," said Dupin. "D———, I presume, is not altogether a fool, and, if not, must have anticipated these waylayings, as a matter of course."

"Not *altogether* a fool," said G., "but then he is a poet, which I take to be only one remove from a fool."

---

[4] *hotel*, town house.

[5] *au fait*, adept.

"True," said Dupin, after a long and thoughtful whiff from his meerschaum, "although I have been guilty of certain doggerel myself."

"Suppose you detail," said I, "the particulars of your search."

"Why the fact is, we took our time, and we searched *every where*. I have had long experience in these affairs. I took the entire building, room by room; devoting the nights of a whole week to each. We examined, first, the furniture of each apartment. We opened every possible drawer; and I presume you know that, to a properly trained police agent, such a thing as a *secret* drawer is impossible. Any man is a dolt who permits a 'secret' drawer to escape him in a search of this kind. The thing is *so* plain. There is a certain amount of bulk—of space—to be accounted for in every cabinet. Then we have accurate rules.[6] The fiftieth part of a line could not escape us. After the cabinets we took the chairs. The cushions we probed with the fine long needles you have seen me employ. From the tables we removed the tops."

"Why so?"

"Sometimes the top of a table, or other similarly arranged piece of furniture, is removed by the person wishing to conceal an article; then the leg is excavated, the article deposited within the cavity, and the top replaced. The bottoms and tops of bedposts are employed in the same way."

"But could not the cavity be detected by sounding?" I asked.

"By no means, if, when the article is deposited, a sufficient wadding of cotton be placed around it. Besides, in our case, we were obliged to proceed without noise."

"But you could not have removed—you could not have taken to pieces *all* articles of furniture in which it would have been possible to make a deposit in the manner you mention. A letter may be compressed into a thin spiral roll, not differing much in shape or bulk from a large knitting-needle, and in this form it might be inserted into the rung of a chair, for example. You did not take to pieces all the chairs?"

"Certainly not; but we did better—we examined the rungs of every chair in the hotel, and indeed the jointings of every description of furniture, by the aid of a most powerful microscope.[7] Had there been any traces of recent disturbance we should not have failed to detect it instantly. A single grain of gimlet-dust, for example, would have been as obvious as an apple. Any disorder in the glueing—any unusual gaping in the joints—would have sufficed to insure detection."

"I presume you looked to the mirrors, between the boards and the plates, and you probed the beds and the bed-clothes, as well as the curtains and carpets."

---

[6] *rules*, rulers.
[7] *microscope*, magnifying glass.

"That of course; and when we had absolutely completed every particle of the furniture in this way, then we examined the house itself. We divided its entire surface into compartments, which we numbered, so that none might be missed; then we scrutinized each individual square inch throughout the premises, including the two houses immediately adjoining, with the microscope as before."

"The two houses adjoining!" I exclaimed; "you must have had a great deal of trouble."

"We had; but the reward offered is prodigious."

"You include the *grounds* about the houses?"

"All the grounds are paved with brick. They gave us comparatively little trouble. We examined the moss between the bricks, and found it undisturbed."

"You looked among D———'s papers, of course, and into the books of the library?"

"Certainly; we opened every package and parcel; we not only opened every book, but we turned over every leaf in each volume, not contenting ourselves with a mere shake, according to the fashion of some of our police officers. We also measured the thickness of every book-*cover,* with the most accurate admeasurement, and applied to each the most jealous scrutiny of the microscope. Had any of the bindings been recently meddled with, it would have been utterly impossible that the fact should have escaped observation. Some five or six volumes, just from the hands of the binder, we carefully probed, longitudinally, with the needles."

"You explored the floors beneath the carpets?"

"Beyond doubt. We removed every carpet, and examined the boards with the microscope."

"And the paper on the walls?"

"Yes."

"You looked into the cellars?"

"We did."

"Then," I said, "you have been making a miscalculation, and the letter is *not* upon the premises as you suppose."

"I fear you are right there," said the Prefect. "And now, Dupin, what would you advise me to do?"

"To make a thorough re-search of the premises."

"That is absolutely needless," replied G———. "I am not more sure that I breathe than I am that the letter is not at the Hôtel."

"I have no better advice to give you," said Dupin. "You have, of course, an accurate description of the letter?"

"Oh, yes!"—And here the Prefect, producing a memorandum-book, proceeded to read aloud a minute account of the internal, and especially of the external, appearance of the missing document. Soon after finishing the perusal of this description, he took his departure, more entirely depressed in spirits than I had ever known the good gentleman before.

In about a month afterward he paid us another visit, and found us occupied very nearly as before. He took a pipe and a chair and entered into some ordinary conversation. At length I said; —

"Well, but G———, what of the purloined letter? I presume you have at last made up your mind that there is no such thing as overreaching the Minister?"

"Confound him, say I—yes; I made the re-examination, however, as Dupin suggested—but it was all labour lost, as I knew it would be."

"How much was the reward offered, did you say?" asked Dupin.

"Why, a very great deal—a *very* liberal reward—I don't like to say how much, precisely; but one thing I *will* say, that I wouldn't mind giving my individual check for fifty thousand francs to any one who could obtain me that letter. The fact is, it is becoming of more and more importance every day; and the reward has been lately doubled. If it were trebled, however, I could do no more than I have done."

"Why, yes," said Dupin, drawlingly, between the whiffs of his meerschaum, "I really—think, G———, you have not exerted yourself— to the utmost in this matter. You might—do a little more, I think, eh?"

"How?—in what way?"

"Why—puff, puff,—you might—puff, puff—employ counsel in the matter, eh?—puff, puff, puff. Do you remember the story they tell of Abernethy?"

"No; hang Abernethy!"

"To be sure! hang him and welcome. But, once upon a time, a certain rich miser conceived the design of spunging upon this Abernethy for a medical opinion. Getting up, for this purpose, an ordinary conversation in a private company, he insinuated his case to the physician, as that of an imaginary individual.

" 'We will suppose,' said the miser, 'that his symptoms are such and such; now, doctor, what would *you* have directed him to take?"

" 'Take!' said Abernethy, 'why, take *advice*, to be sure.' "

"But," said the Prefect, a little discomposed, "I am *perfectly* willing to take advice, and to pay for it. I would *really* give fifty thousand francs to any one who would aid me in the matter."

"In that case," replied Dupin, opening a drawer, and producing a check-book, "you may as well fill me up a check for the amount you mentioned. When you have signed it, I will hand you the letter."

I was astounded. The Prefect appeared absolutely thunderstricken. For some minutes he remained speechless and motionless, looking incredulously at my friend with open mouth, and eyes that seemed starting from their sockets; then, apparently recovering himself in some measure, he seized a pen, and after several pauses and vacant stares, finally filled up and signed a check for fifty thousand francs, and handed it across the table to Dupin. The latter examined it carefully and deposited it in his pocket-book; then, unlocking an *escritoire*,[8] took thence a letter and gave it to the Prefect. This functionary grasped it in a perfect agony of joy, opened it with a trembling hand, cast a rapid glance at its contents, and then, scrambling and struggling to the door, rushed at length unceremoniously from the room and from the house, without having uttered a syllable since Dupin had requested him to fill up the check.

When he had gone, my friend entered into some explanations.

"The Parisian police," he said, "are exceedingly able in their way. They are persevering, ingenious, cunning, and thoroughly versed in the knowledge which their duties seem chiefly to demand. Thus, when G—— detailed to us his mode of searching the premises at the Hôtel D——, I felt entire confidence in his having made a satisfactory investigation—so far as his labours extended."

"So far as his labours extended?" said I.

"Yes," said Dupin. "The measures adopted were not only the best of their kind, but carried out to absolute perfection. Had the letter been deposited within the range of their search, these fellows would, beyond a question, have found it."

I merely laughed—but he seemed quite serious in all that he said.

"The measures, then," he continued, "were good in their kind, and well executed; their defect lay in their being inapplicable to the case, and to the man. A certain set of highly ingenious resources are, with the Prefect, a sort of Procrustean bed,[9] to which he forcibly adapts his designs. But he perpetually errs by being too deep or too shallow, for the matter in hand; and many a schoolboy is a better reasoner than he. I knew one about eight years of age, whose success at guessing in the game of 'even and odd' attracted universal admiration. This game is simple, and is played with marbles. One player holds in his hand a number of these toys, and demands of another whether that number is even or odd. If the guess is right, the guesser wins one; if wrong, he loses one. The boy to whom I allude won all the marbles of the school. Of course he had some principle of guessing; and this lay in mere observation and admeasurement of the astuteness of his opponents. For example, an arrant simpleton is his opponent, and, holding up his closed hand, asks: 'Are they even or odd?' Our schoolboy replies, 'Odd,' and loses; but upon the second trial he wins, for he then says to himself, 'The simpleton had them even upon the first trial, and his amount of

---

[8] *escritoire*, a writing table.
[9] In Greek mythology the giant Procrustes tied travelers to an iron bed and made them fit it by either stretching or amputating their limbs.

cunning is just sufficient to make him have them odd upon the second; I will therefore guess odd;'—he guesses odd, and wins. Now, with a simpleton a degree above the first, he would have reasoned thus: 'This fellow finds that in the first instance I guessed odd, and, in the second, he will propose to himself upon the first impulse, a simple variation from even to odd, as did the first simpleton; but then a second thought will suggest that this is too simple a variation, and finally he will decide upon putting it even as before. I will therefore guess even';—he guesses even, and wins. Now this mode of reasoning in the schoolboy, whom his fellows termed 'lucky,'—what, in its last analysis, is it?"

"It is merely," I said, "an identification of the reasoner's intellect with that of his opponent."

"It is," said Dupin; "and, upon inquiring of the boy by what means he effected the *thorough* identification in which his success consisted, I received answer as follows: 'When I wish to find out how wise, or how stupid, or how good, or how wicked is any one, or what are his thoughts at the moment, I fashion the expression on my face, as accurately as possible, in accordance with the expression of his, and then wait to see what thoughts or sentiments arise in my mind or heart, as if to match or correspond with the expression.' This response of the schoolboy lies at the bottom of all the spurious profundity which has been attributed to Rochefoucault, to La Bougive, to Machiavelli, and to Campanella."[10]

"And the identification," I said, "of the reasoner's intellect with that of his opponent, depends, if I understand you aright, upon the accuracy with which the opponent's intellect is admeasured."

"For its practical value it depends upon this," replied Dupin; "and the Prefect and his cohort fail so frequently, first, by default of this identification, and secondly, by ill-admeasurement, or rather through non-admeasurement, of the intellect with which they are engaged. They consider only their *own* ideas of ingenuity; and, in searching for anything hidden, advert only to the modes in which *they* would have hidden it. They are right in this much— that their own ingenuity is a faithful representative of that of *the mass;* but when the cunning of the individual felon is diverse in character from their own, the felon foils them, of course. This always happens when it is above their own, and very usually when it is below. They have no variation of principle in their investigations; at best, when urged by some unusual emergency—by some extraordinary reward—they extend or exaggerate their old modes of *practice,* without touching their principles. What, for example, in this case of D———, has been done to vary the principle of action? What is all this

---

[10] François, Duc de la Rochefoucauld (1613–1680), French moralist and courtier; La Bougive is probably Jean de la Bruyere (1645–1696); Niccolò Machiavelli (1469–1527), Italian statesman and writer; Tommaso Campanella (1568–1639), Italian philosopher and Dominican monk.

boring, and probing, and sounding, and scrutinizing with the microscope, and dividing the surface of the building into registered square
inches—what is it all but an exaggeration *of the application* of one principle or set of principles of search, which are based upon the one set of
notions regarding human ingenuity, to which the Prefect, in the long
routine of his duty, has been accustomed? Do you not see he has taken it
for granted that *all* men proceed to conceal a letter,—not exactly in a
gimlet-hole bored in a chair-leg—but, at least, in *some* out-of-the-way
hole or corner suggested by the same tenor or thought which would
urge a man to secrete a letter in a gimlet-hole bored in a chair-leg? And
do you not see also, that such *recherchés*[11] nooks for concealment are
adapted only for ordinary occasions, and would be adopted only by
ordinary intellects; for, in all cases of concealment, a disposal of the
article concealed—a disposal of it in this *recherché* manner—is, in the
very first instance, presumable and presumed; and thus its discovery
depends, not at all upon the acumen, but altogether upon the mere
care, patience, and determination of the seekers; and where the case is
of importance—or, what amounts to the same thing in the political eyes,
when the reward is of magnitude,—the qualities in question have *never*
been known to fail. You will now understand what I meant in suggesting
that, had the purloined letter been hidden anywhere within the limits of
the Prefect's examination—in other words, had the principle of its concealment been comprehended within the principles of the Prefect—its
discovery would have been a matter altogether beyond question. This
functionary, however, has been thoroughly mystified; and the remote
source of his defeat lies in the supposition that the Minister is a fool,
because he has acquired renown as a poet. All fools are poets; this the
Prefect *feels;* and he is merely guilty of a *non distributio medii*[12] in thence
inferring that all poets are fools.

"But is this really the poet?" I asked. "There are two brothers, I know;
and both have attained reputation in letters. The Minister I believe has
written learnedly on the Differential Calculus. He is a mathematician,
and no poet."

"You are mistaken; I know him well: he is both. As poet *and* mathematician, he would reason well; as mere mathematician, he could not
have reasoned at all, and thus would have been at the mercy of the
Prefect."

"You surprise me," I said, "by these opinions, which have been con-
tradicted by the voice of the world. You do not mean to set at naught the
well-digested idea of centuries. The mathematical reason has long been
regarded as *the* reason *par excellence*."

---

[11] *recherchés,* excessively cunning.
[12] *non distributio medii,* the undistributed middle, an error in logic.

" '*Il y a à parier,*' " replied Dupin, quoting from Chamfort, " '*que toute idée publique, toute convention reçue, est une sottise, car elle a convenu au plus grand nombre.*'[13] The mathematicians, I grant you, have done their best to promulgate the popular error to which you allude, and which is none the less an error for its promulgation as truth. With an art worthy a better cause, for example, they have insinuated the term 'analysis' into application to algebra. The French are the originators of this particular deception; but if a term is of any importance—if words derive any value from applicability—then 'analysis' conveys 'algebra' about as much as, in Latin, '*ambitus*' implies 'ambition,' '*religio*' 'religion,' or '*homines honesti,*' a set of *honourable* men."

"You have a quarrel on hand, I see," said I, "with some of the algebraists of Paris; but proceed."

"I dispute the availability, and thus the value, of that reason which is cultivated in any especial form other than the abstractly logical. I dispute, in particular, the reason educed by mathematical study. The mathematics are the science of form and quantity; mathematical reasoning is merely logic applied to observation upon form and quantity. The great error lies in supposing that even the truths of what is called *pure* algebra, are abstract or general truths. And this error is so egregious that I am confounded at the universality with which it has been received. Mathematical axioms are *not* axioms of general truth. What is true of *relation*—of form and quantity—is often grossly false in regard to morals, for example. In this latter science it is very usually *un*true that the aggregated parts are equal to the whole. In chemistry also the axiom fails. In the consideration of motive it fails; for two motives, each of a given value, have not, necessarily, a value when united, equal to the sum of their values apart. There are numerous other mathematical truths which are only truths within the limits of *relation*. But the mathematician argues from his *finite truths*, through habit, as if they were of an absolutely general applicability—as the world indeed imagines them to be. Bryant, in his very learned 'Mythology,'[14] mentions an analogous source of error, when he says that 'although the Pagan fables are not believed, yet we forget ourselves continually, and make inferences from them as existing realities.' With the algebraists, however, who are Pagans themselves, the 'Pagan fables' *are* believed, and the inferences are made, not so much through lapse of memory as through an unaccountable addling of the brains. In short, I never yet encountered the mere mathematician who could be trusted out of equal roots, or one who did not clandes-

---

[13] "The odds are that every popular idea, every accepted convention is nonsense, because it has suited itself to the majority"; from *Maximes et Pensées* by Sébastian Chamfort (1741–1794).

[14] *A New System, or an Analysis of Antient Mythology,* by Jacob Bryant (1715–1804), an English scholar.

tinely hold it as a point of his faith that $x^2 + px$ was absolutely and unconditionally equal to q. Say to one of these gentlemen, by way of experiment, if you please, that you believe occasions may occur where $x^2 + px$ is *not* altogether equal to q, and having made him understand what you mean, get out of his reach as speedily as convenient, for, beyond doubt, he will endeavour to knock you down.

"I mean to say," continued Dupin, while I merely laughed at his last observations, "that if the Minister had been no more than a mathematician, the Prefect would have been under no necessity of giving me this check. I knew him, however, as both mathematician and poet, and my measures were adapted to his capacity, with reference to the circumstances by which he was surrounded. I knew him as a courtier, too, and as a bold *intriguant*.[15] Such a man, I considered, could not fail to be aware of the ordinary political modes of action. He could not have failed to anticipate—and events have proved that he did not fail to anticipate—the waylayings to which he was subjected. He must have foreseen, I reflected, the secret investigations of his premises. His frequent absences from home at night, which were hailed by the Prefect as certain aids to his success, I regarded only as *ruses*, to afford opportunity for thorough search to the police, and thus the sooner to impress them with the conviction to which G———, in fact, did finally arrive—the conviction that the letter was not upon the premises. I felt, also, that the whole train of thought, which I was at some pains in detailing to you just now, concerning the invariable principle of political action in searches for articles concealed—I felt that this whole train of thought would necessarily pass through the mind of the Minister. It would imperatively lead him to despise all the ordinary *nooks* of concealment. *He* could not, I reflected, be so weak as not to see that the most intricate and remote recess of his hotel would be as open as his commonest closets to the eyes, to the probes, to the gimlets, and to the microscopes of the Prefect. I saw, in fine, that he would be driven, as a matter of course, to simplicity, if not deliberately induced to it as a matter of choice. You will remember, perhaps, how desperately the Prefect laughed when I suggested, upon our first interview, that it was just possible this mystery troubled him so much on account of its being so *very* self-evident."

"Yes," said I, "I remember his merriment well. I really thought he would have fallen into convulsions."

"The material world," continued Dupin, "abounds with very strict analogies to the immaterial; and thus some color of truth has been given to the rhetorical dogma, that metaphor, or simile, may be made to strengthen an argument as well as to embellish a description. The principle of the *vis inertiae*,[16] for example, seems to be identical in physics

---

[15] *intriguant*, intriguer.
[16] *vis inertiae*, the power of inertia.

and metaphysics. It is not more true in the former, that a large body is with more difficulty set in motion than a smaller one, and that its subsequent *momentum* is commensurate with this difficulty, than it is, in the latter, that intellects of the vaster capacity, while more forcible, more constant, and more eventful in their movements than those of inferior grade, are yet the less readily moved, and more embarrassed and full of hesitation in the first few steps of their progress. Again: have you ever noticed which of the street signs, over the shop doors, are the most attractive of attention?"

"I have never given the matter a thought," I said.

"There is a game of puzzles," he resumed, "which is played upon a map. One party playing requires another to find a given word—the name of town, river, state, or empire—any word, in short, upon the motley and perplexed surface of the chart. A novice in the game generally seeks to embarrass his opponents by giving them the most minutely lettered names; but the adept selects such words as stretch, in large characters, from one end of the chart to the other. These, like the over-largely lettered signs and placards of the street, escape observation by the dint of being excessively obvious; and here the physical oversight is precisely analogous with the moral inapprehension by which the intellect suffers to pass unnoticed those considerations which are too obtrusively and too palpably self-evident. But this is a point, it appears, somewhat above or beneath the understanding of the Prefect. He never once thought it probable, or possible, that the Minister had deposited the letter immediately beneath the nose of the whole world, by way of best preventing any portion of that world from perceiving it.

"But the more I reflected upon the daring, dashing, and discriminating ingenuity of D———; upon the fact that the document must always have been *at hand,* if he intended to use it to good purpose; and upon the decisive evidence, obtained by the Prefect, that it was not hidden within the limits of that dignitary's ordinary search—the more satisfied I became that, to conceal this letter, The Minister had resorted to the comprehensive and sagacious expedient of not attempting to conceal it at all.

"Full of these ideas, I prepared myself with a pair of green spectacles, and called one fine morning, quite by accident, at the Ministerial hotel. I found D——— at home, yawning, lounging, and dawdling, as usual, and pretending to be in the last extremity of *ennui.* He is, perhaps, the most really energetic human being now alive—but that is only when nobody sees him.

"To be even with him, I complained of my weak eyes, and lamented the necessity of the spectacles, under cover of which I cautiously and thoroughly surveyed the whole apartment, while seemingly intent only upon the conversation of my host.

"I paid especial attention to a large writing-table near which he sat, and upon which lay confusedly, some miscellaneous letters and other papers, with one or two musical instruments and a few books. Here, however, after a long and very deliberate scrutiny, I saw nothing to excite particular suspicion.

"At length my eyes, in going the circuit of the room, fell upon a trumpery filigree card-rack of pasteboard, that hung dangling by a dirty blue ribbon, from a little brass knob just beneath the middle of the mantel-piece. In this rack, which had three or four compartments, were five or six visiting cards and a solitary letter. This last was much soiled and crumpled. It was torn nearly in two, across the middle—as if a design, in the first instance, to tear it entirely up as worthless, had been altered, or stayed, in the second. It had a large black seal, bearing the D———— cipher *very* conspicuously, and was addressed, in a diminutive female hand, to D————, the minister, himself. It was thrust carelessly, and even, as it seemed, contemptuously, into one of the upper divisions of the rack.

"No sooner had I glanced at this letter than I concluded it to be that of which I was in search. To be sure, it was, to all appearance, radically different from the one of which the Prefect had read us so minute a description. Here the seal was large and black, with the D———— cipher; there it was small and red, with the ducal arms of the S———— family. Here, the address, to the Minister, was diminutive and feminine; there the superscription, to a certain royal personage, was markedly bold and decided; the size alone formed a point of correspondence. But, then, the *radicalness* of these differences, which was excessive; the dirt; the soiled and torn condition of the paper, so inconsistent with the *true* methodical habits of D————, and so suggestive of a design to delude the beholder into an idea of the worthlessness of the document; these things, together with the hyperobtrusive situation of this document, full in the view of every visitor, and thus exactly in accordance with the conclusions to which I had previously arrived; these things, I say, were strongly corroborative of suspicion, in one who came with the intention to suspect.

"I protracted my visit as long as possible, and, while I maintained a most animated discussion with the Minister, upon a topic which I knew well had never failed to interest and excite him, I kept my attention really riveted upon the letter. In this examination, I committed to memory its external appearance and arrangement in the rack; and also fell, at length, upon a discovery which set at rest whatever trivial doubt I might have entertained. In scrutinizing the edges of the paper, I observed them to be more *chafed* than seemed necessary. They presented the *broken* appearance which is manifested when a stiff paper, having been once folded and pressed with a folder, is refolded in a reversed direction, in the same creases or edges which had formed the original fold. This discovery was sufficient. It was clear to me that the letter had been turned, as a glove, inside out, re-directed, and re-sealed. I bade the Minister good morning, and took my departure at once, leaving a gold snuff-box upon the table.

"The next morning I called for the snuff-box, when we resumed, quite eagerly, the conversation of the preceding day. While thus engaged, however, a loud report, as if of a pistol, was heard immediately beneath the windows of the hotel, and was succeeded by a series of fearful screams, and the shoutings of a mob. D——— rushed to a casement, threw it open, and looked out. In the meantime I stepped to the card-rack, took the letter, put it in my pocket, and replaced it by a *facsimile*, (so far as regards externals) which I had carefully prepared at my lodgings; imitating the D——— cipher, very readily, by means of a seal formed of bread.

"The disturbance in the street had been occasioned by the frantic behaviour of a man with a musket. He had fired it among a crowd of women and children. It proved, however, to have been without ball, and the fellow was suffered to go his way as a lunatic or a drunkard. When he had gone, D——— came from the window, whither I had followed him immediately upon securing the object in view. Soon afterward I bade him farewell. The pretended lunatic was a man in my own pay."

"But what purpose had you," I asked, "in replacing the letter by a *facsimile?* Would it not have been better, at the first visit, to have seized it openly, and departed?"

"D———," replied Dupin, "is a desperate man, and a man of nerve. His hotel, too, is not without attendants devoted to his interests. Had I made the wild attempt you suggest, I might never have left the Ministerial presence alive. The good people of Paris might have heard of me no more. But I had an object apart from these considerations. You know my political prepossessions. In this matter, I act as a partisan of the lady concerned. For eighteen months the Minister has had her in his power. She has now him in hers; since, being unaware that the letter is not in his possession, he will proceed with his exactions as if it was. Thus will he inevitably commit himself, at once, to his political destruction. His downfall, too, will not be more precipitate than awkward. It is all very well to talk about the *facilis descensus Averni;*[17] but in all kinds of climbing, as Catalani[18] said of singing, it is far more easy to get up than to come down. In the present instance I have no sympathy—at least no pity—for him who descends. He is that *monstrum horrendum,*[19] an unprincipled man of genius. I confess, however, that I should like very

---

[17] "Easy is the descent into hell . . . but to recall thy steps and issue to upper air, this is the task, this the burden"; *Aeneid* 6.126, by Virgil (70–19 B.C.), Roman poet.

[18] Angelica Catalani (1780–1844), Italian singer.

[19] The description of Polyphemus the Cyclops after his one eye had been put out by Ulysses; *Aeneid* 3.658.

well to know the precise character of his thoughts, when, being defied by her whom the Prefect terms 'a certain personage,' he is reduced to opening the letter which I left for him in the card-rack."

"How? did you put any thing particular in it?"

"Why—it did not seem altogether right to leave the interior blank— that would have been insulting. D————, at Vienna once, did me an evil turn, which I told him, quite good-humouredly, that I should remember. So, as I knew he would feel some curiosity in regard to the identity of the person who had outwitted him, I thought it a pity not to give him a clue. He is well acquainted with my MS., and I just copied into the middle of the blank sheet the words—

> ————*Un dessein si funeste,*
> *S'il n'est digne d'Atrée, est digne*
> *de Thyeste.*

They are to be found in Crébillon's 'Atrée.' "[20]

---

[20] "So baneful a plot, if not worthy of Atreus, is worthy of Thyestes"; from *Atrée et Thyeste* by Prosper Jolyot de Crébillon (1674–1762).

HENRY JAMES (1843–1916)

The Real Thing

I

When the porter's wife, who used to answer the house-bell, announced "A gentleman and a lady, sir," I had, as I often had in those days—the wish being father to the thought—an immediate vision of sitters. Sitters my visitors in this case proved to be; but not in the sense I should have preferred. There was nothing at first however to indicate that they mightn't have come for a portrait. The gentleman, a man of fifty, very high and very straight, with a moustache slightly grizzled and a dark grey walking-coat admirably fitted, both of which I noted profession-ally—I don't mean as a barber or yet a tailor—would have struck me as a celebrity if celebrities often were striking. It was a truth of which I had for some time been conscious that a figure with a good deal of frontage was, as one might say, almost never a public institution. A glance at the lady helped to remind me of this paradoxical law: she also looked too distinguished to be a "personality." Moreover one would scarcely come across two variations together.

Neither of the pair immediately spoke—they only prolonged the pre-liminary gaze suggesting that each wished to give the other a chance. They were visibly shy; they stood there letting me take them in—which, as I afterwards perceived, was the most practical thing they could have done. In this way their embarrassment served their cause. I had seen people painfully reluctant to mention that they desired anything so gross as to be represented on canvas; but the scruples of my new friends appeared almost insurmountable. Yet the gentleman might have said "I should like a portrait of my wife," and the lady might have said "I should like a portrait of my husband." Perhaps they weren't husband and wife—this naturally would make the matter more delicate. Perhaps they wished to be done together—in which case they ought to have brought a third person to break the news.

"We come from Mr. Rivet," the lady finally said with a dim smile that had the effect of a moist sponge passed over a "sunk" piece of painting, as well as of a vague allusion to vanished beauty. She was as tall and straight, in her degree, as her companion, and with ten years less to carry. She looked as sad as a woman could look whose face was not charged with expression; that is her tinted oval mask showed waste as an exposed surface shows friction. The hand of time had played over her freely, but to an effect of elimination. She was slim and stiff, and so well-dressed, in dark blue cloth, with lappets and pockets and but-tons, that it was clear she employed the same tailor as her husband. The couple had an indefinable air of prosperous thrift—they evidently got a good deal of luxury for their money. If I was to be one of their luxuries it would behove me to consider my terms.

"Ah Claude Rivet recommended me?" I echoed; and I added that it was very kind of him, though I could reflect that, as he only painted landscape, this wasn't a sacrifice.

The lady looked very hard at the gentleman, and the gentleman looked round the room. Then staring at the floor a moment and stroking his moustache, he rested his pleasant eyes on me with the remark; "He said you were the right one."

"I try to be, when people want to sit."

"Yes, we should like to," said the lady anxiously.

"Do you mean together?"

My visitors exchanged a glance. "If you could do anything with *me* I suppose it would be double," the gentleman stammered.

"Oh yes, there's naturally a higher charge for two figures than for one."

"We should like to make it pay," the husband confessed.

"That's very good of you," I returned, appreciating so unwonted a sympathy—for I supposed he meant pay the artist.

A sense of strangeness seemed to dawn on the lady. "We mean for the illustrations—Mr. Rivet said you might put one in."

"Put in—an illustration?" I was equally confused.

"Sketch her off, you know," said the gentleman, colouring.

It was only then that I understood the service Claude Rivet had rendered me; he had told them how I worked in black-and-white, for magazines, for story-books, for sketches of contemporary life, and consequently had copious employment for models. These things were true, but it was not less true—I may confess it now; whether because the aspiration was to lead to everything or to nothing I leave the reader to guess—that I couldn't get the honours, to say nothing of the emoluments, of a great painter of portraits out of my head. My "illustrations" were my pot-boilers; I looked to a different branch of art—far and away the most interesting it had always seemed to me—to perpetuate my fame. There was no shame in looking to it also to make my fortune; but that fortune was by so much further from being made from the moment my visitors wished to be "done" for nothing. I was disappointed; for in the pictorial sense I had immediately *seen* them. I had seized their type—I had already settled what I would do with it. Something that wouldn't absolutely have pleased them, I afterwards reflected.

"Ah you're—you're—a—?" I began as soon as I had mastered my surprise. I couldn't bring out the dingy word "models": it seemed so little to fit the case.

"We haven't had much practice," said the lady.

"We've got to *do* something, and we've thought that an artist in your line might perhaps make something of us," her husband threw off. He further mentioned that they didn't know many artists and that they had gone first, on the off-chance—he painted views of course, but sometimes put in figures; perhaps I remembered—to Mr. Rivet, whom they had met a few years before at a place in Norfolk where he was sketching.

"We used to sketch a little ourselves," the lady hinted.

"It's very awkward, but we absolutely *must* do something," her husband went on.

"Of course we're not so *very* young," she admitted with a wan smile.

With the remark that I might as well know something more about them the husband had handed me a card extracted from a neat new pocket-book—their appurtenances were all of the freshest—and inscribed with the words "Major Monarch." Impressive as these words were they didn't carry my knowledge much further; but my visitor presently added: "I've left the army and we've had the misfortune to lose our money. In fact our means are dreadfully small."

"It's awfully trying—a regular strain," said Mrs. Monarch.

They evidently wished to be discreet—to take care not to swagger because they were gentlefolk. I felt them willing to recognize this as something of a drawback, at the same time that I guessed at an underlying sense—their consolation in adversity—that they *had* their points. They certainly had; but these advantages struck me as preponderantly social; such for instance as would help to make a drawing-room look well. However, a drawing-room was always, or ought to be, a picture.

In consequence of his wife's allusion to their age Major Monarch observed: "Naturally it's more for the figure that we thought of going in. We can still hold ourselves up." On the instant I saw that the figure was indeed their strong point. His "naturally" didn't sound vain, but it lighted up the question. "*She* has the best one," he continued, nodding at his wife with a pleasant after-dinner absence of circumlocution. I could only reply, as if we were in fact sitting over our wine, that this didn't prevent his own from being very good; which led him in turn to make answer: "We thought that if you ever have to do people like us we might be something like it. *She* particularly—for a lady in a book, you know."

I was so amused by them that, to get more of it, I did my best to take their point of view; and though it was an embarrassment to find myself appraising physically, as if they were animals on hire or useful blacks, a pair whom I should have expected to meet only in one of the relations in which criticism is tacit, I looked at Mrs. Monarch judicially enough to be able to exclaim after a moment with conviction: "Oh yes, a lady in a book!" She was singularly like a bad illustration.

"We'll stand up, if you like," said the Major; and he raised himself before me with a really grand air.

I could take his measure at a glance—he was six feet two and a perfect gentleman. It would have paid any club in process of formation and in want of a stamp to engage him at a salary to stand in the principal window. What struck me at once was that in coming to me they had rather missed their vocation; they could surely have been turned to better account for advertising purposes. I couldn't of course see the thing in detail, but I could see them make somebody's fortune—I don't mean their own. There was something in them for a waistcoat-maker, an hotel-keeper or a soap-vendor. I could imagine "We always use it" pinned on their bosoms with the greatest effect; I had a vision of the brilliancy with which they would launch a table d'hôte.

Mrs. Monarch sat still, not from pride but from shyness, and presently her husband said to her: "Get up, my dear, and show how smart you are." She obeyed, but she had no need to get up to show it. She walked to the end of the studio and then came back blushing, her fluttered eyes on the partner of her appeal. I was reminded of an incident I had accidentally had a glimpse of in Paris—being with a friend there, a dramatist about to produce a play, when an actress came to him to ask to be entrusted with a part. She went through her paces before him, walked up and down as Mrs. Monarch was doing. Mrs. Monarch did it quite as well, but I abstained from applauding. It was very odd to see such people apply for such poor pay. She looked as if she had ten thousand a year. Her husband had used the word that described her: she was in the London current jargon essentially and typically "smart." Her figure was, in the same order of ideas, conspicuously and irreproachably "good." For a woman of her age her waist was surprisingly small; her elbow moreover had the orthodox crook. She held her head at the conventional angle, but why did she come to *me*? She ought to have tried on jackets at a big shop. I feared my visitors were not only destitute but "artistic"—which would be a great complication. When she sat down again I thanked her, observing that what a draughtsman most valued in his model was the faculty of keeping quiet.

"Oh *she* can keep quiet," said Major Monarch. Then he added jocosely: "I've always kept her quiet."

"I'm not a nasty fidget, am I?" It was going to wring tears from me, I felt, the way she hid her head, ostrich-like, in the other broad bosom.

The owner of this expanse addressed his answer to me. "Perhaps it isn't out of place to mention—because we ought to be quite business-like, oughtn't we?—that when I married her she was known as the Beautiful Statue."

"Oh dear!" said Mrs. Monarch ruefully.

"Of course I should want a certain amount of expression," I rejoined.

"Of *course*!"—and I had never heard such unanimity.

"And then I suppose you know that you'll get awfully tired."

"Oh we *never* get tired!" they eagerly cried.

"Have you had any kind of practice?"

They hesitated—they looked at each other. "We've been photographed—*immensely*," said Mrs. Monarch.

"She means the fellows have asked us themselves," added the Major.

"I see—because you're so good-looking."

"I don't know what they thought, but they were always after us."

"We always got our photographs for nothing," smiled Mrs. Monarch.

"We might have brought some, my dear," her husband remarked.

"I'm not sure we have any left. We've given quantities away," she explained to me.

"With our autographs and that sort of thing," said the Major.

"Are they to be got in the shops?" I enquired as a harmless pleasantry.

"Oh yes, *hers*—they used to be."

"Not now," said Mrs. Monarch with her eyes on the floor.

II

I could fancy the "sort of thing" they put on the presentation copies of their photographs, and I was sure they wrote a beautiful hand. It was odd how quickly I was sure of everything that concerned them. If they were now so poor as to have to earn shillings and pence they could never have had much of a margin. Their good looks had been their capital, and they had good-humouredly made the most of the career that this resource marked out for them. It was in their faces, the blankness, the deep intellectual repose of the twenty years of country-house visiting that had given them pleasant intonations. I could see the sunny drawing rooms, sprinkled with periodicals she didn't read, in which Mrs. Monarch had continuously sat; I could see the wet shrubberies in which she had walked, equipped to admiration for either exercise. I could see the rich covers the Major had helped to shoot and the wonderful garments in which, late at night, he repaired to the smoking-room to talk about them. I could imagine their leggings and waterproofs, their knowing tweeds and rugs, their rolls of sticks and cases of tackle and neat umbrellas; and I could evoke the exact appearance of their servants and the compact variety of their luggage on the platforms of country stations.

They gave small tips, but they were liked; they didn't do anything themselves, but they were welcome. They looked so well everywhere; they gratified the general relish for stature, complexion and "form." They knew it without fatuity or vulgarity, and they respected themselves in consequence. They weren't superficial; they were thorough and kept themselves up—it had been their line. People with such a taste for activity had to have some line. I could feel how even in a dull house they could have been counted on for the joy of life. At present something had happened—it didn't matter what, their little income had grown less, it had grown least—and they had to do something for pocket-money. Their friends could like them, I made out, without liking to support them. There was something about them that represented credit—their clothes, their manners, their type; but if credit is a large empty pocket in which an occasional chink reverberates, the chink at least must be audible. What they wanted of me was to help to make it so. Fortunately they had no children—I soon divined that. They would also perhaps wish our relations to be kept secret: this was why it was "for the figure"—the reproduction of the face would betray them.

I liked them—I felt, quite as their friends must have done—they were so simple; and I had no objection to them if they would suit. But somehow with all their perfections I didn't easily believe in them. After all they were amateurs, and the ruling passion of my life was the detestation of the amateur. Combined with this was another perversity—an innate preference for the represented subject over the real one: the defect of the real one was so apt to be a lack of representation. I liked things that appeared; then one was sure. Whether they *were* or not was a subordinate and almost always a profitless question. There were other considerations, the first of which was that I already had two or three recruits in use, notably a young person with big feet, in alpaca, from Kilburn, who for a couple of years had come to me regularly for my illustrations and with whom I was still—perhaps ignobly—satisfied. I frankly explained to my visitors how the case stood, but they had taken more precautions than I supposed. They had reasoned out their opportunity, for Claude Rivet had told them of the projected *édition de luxe* of one of the writers of our day—the rarest of the novelists—who, long neglected by the multitudinous vulgar and dearly prized by the attentive (need I mention Philip Vincent?), had had the happy fortune of seeing, late in life, the dawn and then the full light of a higher criticism; an estimate in which on the part of the public there was something really of expiation. The edition preparing, planned by a publisher of taste, was practically an act of high reparation; the wood-cuts with which it was to be enriched were the homage of English art to one of the most independent representatives of English letters. Major and Mrs. Monarch confessed to me they had hoped I might be able to work *them* into my branch of the enterprise. They knew I was to do the first of the books, "Rutland Ramsay," but I had to make clear to them that my participation in the rest of the affair—this first book was to be a test— must depend on the satisfaction I should give. If this should be limited my employers would drop me with scarce common forms. It was therefore a crisis for me, and naturally I was making special preparations, looking about for new people, should they be necessary, and securing the best types. I admitted however that I should like to settle down to two or three good models who would do for everything.

"Should we have often to—a—put on special clothes?" Mrs. Monarch timidly demanded.

"Dear yes—that's half the business."

"And should we be expected to supply our own costumes?"

"Oh no; I've got a lot of things. A painter's models put on—or put off—anything he likes."

"And you mean—a—the same?"

"The same?"

Mrs. Monarch looked at her husband again.

"Oh she was just wondering," he explained, "if the costumes are in *general* use." I had to confess that they were, and I mentioned further that some of them—I had a lot of genuine greasy last-century things—had served their time, a hundred years ago, on living world-stained men and women; on figures not perhaps so far removed, in that vanished world, from *their* type, the Monarchs', *quoi!* of a breeched and bewigged age. "We'll put on anything that *fits*," said the Major.

"Oh I arrange that—they fit in the pictures."

"I'm afraid I should do better for the modern books. I'd come as you like," said Mrs. Monarch.

"She has got a lot of clothes at home; they might do for contemporary life," her husband continued.

"Oh I can fancy scenes in which you'd be quite natural." And indeed I could see the slipshod rearrangements of stale properties—the stories I tried to produce pictures for without the exasperation of reading them—whose sandy tracts the good lady might help to people. But I had to return to the fact that for this sort of work—the daily mechanical grind—I was already equipped: the people I was working with were fully adequate.

"We only thought we might be more like *some* characters," said Mrs. Monarch mildly, getting up.

Her husband also rose; he stood looking at me with a dim wistfulness that was touching in so fine a man. "Wouldn't it be rather a pull sometimes to have—a—to have—?" He hung fire; he wanted me to help him by phrasing what he meant. But I couldn't—I didn't know. So he brought it out awkwardly: "The *real* thing; a gentleman, you know, or a lady." I was quite ready to give a general assent—I admitted that there was a great deal in that. This encouraged Major Monarch to say, following up his appeal with an unacted gulp: "It's awfully hard—we've tried everything." The gulp was communicative; it proved too much for his wife. Before I knew it Mrs. Monarch had dropped again upon a divan and burst into tears. Her husband sat down beside her, holding one of her hands; whereupon she quickly dried her eyes with the other, while I felt embarrassed as she looked up at me. "There isn't a confounded job I haven't applied for—waited for—prayed for. You can fancy we'd be pretty bad first. Secretaryships and that sort of thing? You might as well ask for a peerage. I'd be *anything*—I'm strong; a messenger or a coal-heaver. I'd put on a gold-laced cap and open carriage-doors in front of the haberdasher's; I'd hang about a station to carry portmanteaux; I'd be a postman. But they won't *look* at you; there are thousands as good as yourself already on the ground. *Gentlemen*, poor beggars, who've drunk their wine, who've kept their hunters!"

I was as reassuring as I knew how to be, and my visitors were presently on their feet again while, for the experiment, we agreed on an hour. We were discussing it when the door opened and Miss Churm came in with a wet umbrella. Miss Churm had to take the omnibus to Maida Vale and then walk half a mile. She looked a trifle blowsy and slightly splashed. I scarcely ever saw her come in without thinking afresh how odd it was that, being so little in herself, she should yet be so much in others. She was a meagre little Miss Churm, but was such an ample heroine of romance. She was only a freckled cockney,[1] but she could represent everything, from a fine lady to a shepherdess; she had the faculty as she might have had a fine voice or long hair. She couldn't spell and she loved beer, but she had two or three "points," and practice, and a knack, and mother-wit, and a whimsical sensibility, and a love of the theatre, and seven sisters, and not an ounce of respect, especially for the "h." The first thing my visitors saw was that her umbrella was wet, and in their spotless perfection they visibly winced at it. The rain had come on since their arrival.

"I'm all in a soak; there *was* a mess of people in the 'bus. I wish you lived near a stytion," said Miss Churm. I requested her to get ready as quickly as possible, and she passed into the room in which she always changed her dress. But before going out she asked me what she was to get into this time.

"It's the Russian princess, don't you know?" I answered; "the one with the 'golden eyes,' in black velvet, for the long thing in the *Cheapside*."[2]

"Golden eyes? I *say!*" cried Miss Churm, while my companions watched her with intensity as she withdrew. She always arranged herself, when she was late, before I could turn round; and I kept my visitors a little on purpose, so that they might get an idea, from seeing her, what would be expected of themselves. I mentioned that she was quite my notion of an excellent model—she was really very clever.

"Do you think she looks like a Russian princess?" Major Monarch asked with lurking alarm.

"When I make her, yes."

"Oh if you have to *make* her—!" he reasoned, not without point.

"That's the most you can ask. There are so many who are not makeable."

---

[1] A native of the East End of London, speaking a local dialect marked by the dropping of the letter *h*. Usually a contemptuous or bantering term, implying lower-class origins.

[2] The name of the journal is suggestive. Cheapside, a thoroughfare in the City of London, was originally a marketplace with an area set aside for popular entertainment.

"Well now, *here's* a lady"—and with a persuasive smile he passed his arm into his wife's—"who's already made!"

"Oh I'm not a Russian princess," Mrs. Monarch protested a little coldly. I could see she had known some and didn't like them. There at once was a complication of a kind I never had to fear with Miss Churm.

This young lady came back in black velvet—the gown was rather rusty and very low on her lean shoulders—and with a Japanese fan in her red hands. I reminded her that in the scene I was doing she had to look over some one's head. "I forget whose it is; but it doesn't matter. Just look over a head."

"I'd rather look over a stove," said Miss Churm; and she took her station near the fire. She fell into position, settled herself into a tall attitude, gave a certain backward inclination to her head and a certain forward droop to her fan, and looked, at least to my prejudiced sense, distinguished and charming, foreign and dangerous. We left her looking so while I went downstairs with Major and Mrs. Monarch.

"I believe I could come about as near it as that," said Mrs. Monarch.

"Oh you think she's shabby, but you must allow for the alchemy of art."

However, they went off with an evident increase of comfort founded on their demonstrable advantage in being the real thing. I could fancy them shuddering over Miss Churm. She was very droll about them when I went back, for I told her what they wanted.

"Well, if *she* can sit I'll tyke to bookkeeping," said my model.

"She's very ladylike," I replied as an innocent form of aggravation.

"So much the worse for *you.* That means she can't turn round."

"She'll do for the fashionable novels."

"Oh yes, she'll *do* for them!" my model humorously declared. "Ain't they bad enough without her?" I had often sociably denounced them to Miss Churm.

III

It was for the elucidation of a mystery in one of these works that I first tried Mrs. Monarch. Her husband came with her, to be useful if necessary—it was sufficiently clear that as a general thing he would prefer to come with her. At first I wondered if this were for "propriety's" sake—if he were going to be jealous and meddling. The idea was too tiresome, and if it had been confirmed it would speedily have brought our acquaintance to a close. But I soon saw there was nothing in it and that if he accompanied Mrs. Monarch it was—in addition to the chance of being wanted—simply because he had nothing else to do. When they were separate his occupation was gone and they never *had* been separate. I judged rightly that in their awkward situation their close union was their main comfort and that this union had no weak spot. It was a real marriage, an encouragement to the hesitating, a nut for pessimists to crack. Their address was humble—I remember afterwards thinking it had been the only thing about them that was really professional—and I could fancy the lamentable lodgings in which the Major would have been left alone. He could sit there more or less grimly with his wife—he couldn't sit there anyhow without her.

He had too much tact to try and make himself agreeable when he couldn't be useful; so when I was too absorbed in my work to talk he simply sat and waited. But I liked to hear him talk—it made my work, when not interrupting it, less mechanical, less special. To listen to him was to combine the excitement of going out with the economy of staying at home. There was only one hindrance—that I seemed not to know any of the people this brilliant couple had known. I think he wondered extremely, during the term of our intercourse, whom the deuce I *did* know. He hadn't a stray sixpence of an idea to fumble for, so we didn't spin it very fine; we confined ourselves to questions of leather and even of liquor—saddlers and breeches-makers and how to get excellent claret cheap—and matters like "good trains" and the habits of small game. His lore on these last subjects was astonishing—he managed to interweave the station-master with the ornithologist. When he couldn't talk about greater things he could talk cheerfully about smaller, and since I couldn't accompany him into reminiscences of the fashionable world he could lower the conversation without a visible effort to my level.

So earnest a desire to please was touching in a man who could so easily have knocked one down. He looked after the fire and had an opinion on the draught of the stove without my asking him, and I could see that he thought many of my arrangements not half knowing. I remember telling him that if I were only rich I'd offer him a salary to come and teach me how to live. Sometimes he gave a random sigh of which the essence might have been: "Give me even such a bare old barrack as *this,* and I'd do something with it!" When I wanted to use him he came alone; which was an illustration of the superior courage of women. His wife could bear her solitary second floor, and she was in general more discreet; showing by various small reserves that she was alive to the propriety of keeping our relations markedly professional—not letting them slide into sociability. She wished it to remain clear that she and the Major were employed, not cultivated, and if she approved of me as a superior, who could be kept in his place, she never thought me quite good enough for an equal.

She sat with great intensity, giving the whole of her mind to it, and was capable of remaining for an hour almost as motionless as before a photographer's lens. I could see she had been photographed often, but somehow the very habit that made her good for that purpose unfitted her for mine. At first I was extremely pleased with her ladylike air, and it was a satisfaction, on coming to follow her lines, to see how good they were and how far they could lead the pencil. But after a little skirmishing I began to find her too insurmountably stiff; do what I would with it my drawing looked like a photograph or a copy of a photograph. Her figure had no variety of expression—she herself had no sense of variety. You may say that this was my business and was only a question of placing her. Yet I placed her in every conceivable position and she managed to obliterate their differences. She was always a lady certainly, and into the bargain was always the same lady. She was the real thing, but always the same thing. There were moments when I rather writhed under the serenity of her confidence that she *was* the real thing. All her dealings with me and all her husband's were an implication that this was lucky for *me*. Meanwhile I found myself trying to invent types that approached her own, instead of making her own transform itself—in the clever way that was not impossible for instance to poor Miss Churm. Arrange as I would and take the precautions I would, she always came out, in my pictures, too tall—landing me in the dilemma of having represented a fascinating woman as seven feet high, which (out of respect perhaps to my own very much scantier inches) was far from my idea of such a personage.

The case was worse with the Major—nothing I could do would keep *him* down, so that he became useful only for the representation of brawny giants. I adored variety and range, I cherished human accidents, the illustrative note; I wanted to characterise closely, and the thing in the world I most hated was the danger of being ridden by a type. I had quarrelled with some of my friends about it; I had parted company with them for maintaining that one *had* to be, and that if the type was beautiful—witness Raphael and Leonardo—the servitude was only a gain. I was neither Leonardo nor Raphael—I might only be a presumptuous young modern searcher; but I held that everything was to be sacrificed sooner than character. When they claimed that the obsessional form could easily *be* character I retorted, perhaps superficially, "Whose?" It couldn't be everybody's—it might end in being nobody's.

After I had drawn Mrs. Monarch a dozen times I felt surer even than before that the value of such a model as Miss Churm resided precisely in the fact that she had no positive stamp, combined of course with the other fact that what she did have was a curious and inexplicable talent for imitation. Her usual appearance was like a curtain which she could draw up at request for a capital performance. This performance was simply suggestive; but it was a word to the wise—it was vivid and pretty. Sometimes even I thought it, though she was plain herself, too insipidly pretty; I made it a reproach to her that the figures drawn from her were monotonously (*bêtement*,[3] as we used to say) graceful. Nothing made her more angry: it was so much her pride to feel she could sit for characters

---

[3] "Foolishly" or "stupidly."

that had nothing in common with each other. She would accuse me at such moments of taking away her "reputytion."

It suffered a certain shrinkage, this queer quantity, from the repeated visits of my new friends. Miss Churm was greatly in demand, never in want of employment, so I had no scruple in putting her off occasionally, to try them more at my ease. It was certainly amusing at first to do the real thing—it was amusing to do Major Monarch's trousers. They *were* the real thing, even if he did come out colossal. It was amusing to do his wife's back hair—it was so mathematically neat—and the particular "smart" tension of her tight stays. She lent herself especially to positions in which the face was somewhat averted or blurred; she abounded in ladylike back views and *profils perdus*.[4] When she stood erect she took naturally one of the attitudes in which court-painters represent queens and princesses; so that I found myself wondering whether, to draw out this accomplishment, I couldn't get the editor of the *Cheapside* to publish a really royal romance, "A Tale of Buckingham Palace." Sometimes however the real thing and the make-believe came into contact; by which I mean that Miss Churm, keeping an appointment or coming to make one on days when I had much work in hand, encountered her invidious rivals. The encounter was not on their part, for they noticed her no more than if she had been the housemaid; not from intentional loftiness, but simply because as yet, professionally, they didn't know how to fraternise, as I could imagine they would have liked—or at least that the Major would. They couldn't talk about the omnibus—they always walked; and they didn't know what else to try—she wasn't interested in good trains or cheap claret. Besides, they must have felt—in the air—that she was amused at them, secretly derisive of their ever knowing how. She wasn't a person to conceal the limits of her faith if she had had a chance to show them. On the other hand Mrs. Monarch didn't think her tidy; for why else did she take pains to say to me—it was going out of the way, for Mrs. Monarch—that she didn't like dirty women?

One day when my young lady happened to be present with my other sitters—she even dropped in, when it was convenient, for a chat—I asked her to be so good as to lend a hand in getting tea, a service with which she was familiar and which was one of a class that, living as I did in a small way, with slender domestic resources, I often appealed to my models to render. They liked to lay hands on my property, to break the sitting, and sometimes the china—it made them feel Bohemian. The next time I saw Miss Churm after this incident she surprised me greatly by making a scene about it—she accused me of having wished to humiliate her. She hadn't resented the outrage at the time, but had seemed obliging and amused, enjoying the comedy of asking Mrs. Mon-

---

[4] Oblique views "losing" most of the profile.

arch, who sat vague and silent, whether she would have cream and sugar, and putting an exaggerated simper into the question. She had tried intonations—as if she too wished to pass for the real thing—till I was afraid my other visitors would take offence.

Oh they were determined not to do this, and their touching patience was the measure of their great need. They would sit by the hour, uncomplaining, till I was ready to use them; they would come back on the chance of being wanted and would walk away cheerfully if it failed. I used to go to the door with them to see in what magnificent order they retreated. I tried to find other employment for them—I introduced them to several artists. But they didn't "take," for reasons I could appreciate, and I became rather anxiously aware that after such disappointments they fell back upon me with a heavier weight. They did me the honour to think me most *their* form. They weren't romantic enough for the painters, and in those days there were few serious workers in black-and-white. Besides, they had an eye to the great job I had mentioned to them—they had secretly set their hearts on supplying the right essence for my pictorial vindication of our fine novelist. They knew that for this undertaking I should want no costume-effects, none of the frippery of past ages—that it was a case in which everything would be contemporary and satirical and presumably genteel. If I could work them into it their future would be assured, for the labour would of course be long and the occupation steady.

One day Mrs. Monarch came without her husband—she explained his absence by his having had to go to the City. While she sat there in her usual relaxed majesty there came at the door a knock which I immediately recognised as the subdued appeal of a model out of work. It was followed by the entrance of a young man whom I at once saw to be a foreigner and who proved in fact an Italian acquainted with no English word but my name, which he uttered in a way that made it seem to include all others. I hadn't then visited his country, nor was I proficient in his tongue; but as he was not so meanly constituted—what Italian is?—as to depend only on that member for expression he conveyed to me, in familiar but graceful mimicry, that he was in search of exactly the employment in which the lady before me was engaged. I was not struck with him at first, and while I continued to draw I dropped few signs of interest or encouragement. He stood his ground however—not importunately, but with a dumb dog-like fidelity in his eyes that amounted to innocent impudence, the manner of a devoted servant—he might have been in the house for years—unjustly suspected. Suddenly it struck me that this very attitude and expression made a picture; whereupon I told him to sit down and wait till I should be free. There was another picture in the way he obeyed me, and I observed as I worked that there were others still in the way he looked wonderingly, with his head thrown back, about the high studio. He might have been crossing himself in Saint Peter's. Before I finished I said to myself "The fellow's a bankrupt orangemonger, but a treasure."

When Mrs. Monarch withdrew he passed across the room like a flash to open the door for her, standing there with the rapt pure gaze of the young Dante spellbound by the young Beatrice. As I never insisted, in such situations, on the blankness of the British domestic, I reflected that he had the making of a servant—and I needed one, but couldn't pay him to be only that—as well as of a model; in short I resolved to adopt my bright adventurer if he would agree to officiate in the double capacity. He jumped at my offer, and in the event my rashness—for I had really known nothing about him—wasn't brought home to me. He proved a sympathetic though a desultory ministrant, and had in a wonderful degree the *sentiment de la pose*.[5] It was uncultivated, instinctive, a part of the happy instinct that had guided him to my door and helped him to spell out my name on the card nailed to it. He had had no other introduction to me than a guess, from the shape of my high north window, seen outside, that my place was a studio and that as a studio it would contain an artist. He had wandered to England in search of fortune, like other itinerants, and had embarked, with a partner and a small green hand-cart, on the sale of penny ices. The ices had melted away and the partner had dissolved in their train. My young man wore tight yellow trousers with reddish stripes and his name was Oronte. He was sallow but fair, and when I put him into some old clothes of my own he looked like an Englishman. He was as good as Miss Churm, who could look, when requested, like an Italian.

IV

I thought Mrs. Monarch's face slightly convulsed when, on her coming back with her husband, she found Oronte installed. It was strange to have to recognise in a scrap of a lazzarone[6] a competitor to her magnificent Major. It was she who scented danger first, for the Major was anecdotically unconscious. But Oronte gave us tea, with a hundred eager confusions—he had never been concerned in so queer a process—and I think she thought better of me for having at last an "establishment." They saw a couple of drawings that I had made of the establishment, and Mrs. Monarch hinted that it never would have struck her he had sat for them. "Now the drawings you make from *us*, they look exactly like us," she reminded me, smiling in triumph; and I recognised that this was indeed just their defect. When I drew the Monarchs I couldn't anyhow get away from them—get into the character I wanted to represent; and I hadn't the least desire my model should be dis-

---

[5] "Feeling for a correct pose (or position)."
[6] Neapolitan street-lounger, who lives by means of odd jobs and begging.

coverable in my picture. Miss Churm never was, and Mrs. Monarch thought I hid her, very properly, because she was vulgar; whereas if she was lost it was only as the dead who go to heaven are lost—in the gain of an angel the more.

By this time I had got a certain start with "Rutland Ramsay," the first novel in the great projected series; that is I had produced a dozen drawings, several with the help of the Major and his wife, and I had sent them in for approval. My understanding with the publishers, as I have already hinted, had been that I was to be left to do my work, in this particular case, as I liked, with the whole book committed to me; but my connexion with the rest of the series was only contingent. There were moments when, frankly, it *was* a comfort to have the real thing under one's hand; for there were characters in "Rutland Ramsay" that were very much like it. There were people presumably as erect as the Major and women of as good a fashion as Mrs. Monarch. There was a great deal of country-house life—treated, it is true, in a fine fanciful ironical generalised way—and there was a considerable implication of knickerbockers and kilts. There were certain things I had to settle at the outset; such things for instance as the exact appearance of the hero and the particular bloom and figure of the heroine. The author of course gave me a lead, but there was a margin for interpretation. I took the Monarchs into my confidence, I told them frankly what I was about, I mentioned my embarrassments and alternatives. "Oh take *him!*" Mrs. Monarch murmured sweetly, looking at her husband; and "What could you want better than my wife?" the Major enquired with the comfortable candour that now prevailed between us.

I wasn't obliged to answer these remarks—I was only obliged to place my sitters. I wasn't easy in mind, and I postponed a little timidly perhaps the solving of my question. The book was a large canvas, the other figures were numerous, and I worked off at first some of the episodes in which the hero and the heroine were not concerned. When once I had set *them* up I should have to stick to them—I couldn't make my young man seven feet high in one place and five feet nine in another. I inclined on the whole to the latter measurement, though the Major more than once reminded me that *he* looked about as young as any one. It was indeed quite possible to arrange him, for the figure, so that it would have been difficult to detect his age. After the spontaneous Oronte had been with me a month, and after I had given him to understand several times over that his native exuberance would presently constitute an insurmountable barrier to our further intercourse, I waked to a sense of his heroic capacity. He was only five feet seven, but the remaining inches were latent. I tried him almost secretly at first, for I was really rather afraid of the judgement my other models would pass on such a choice. If they regarded Miss Churm as little better than a snare what would they think of the representation by a person so little the real thing as an Italian street-vendor of a protagonist formed by a public school?

If I went a little in fear of them it wasn't because they bullied me, because they had got an oppressive foothold, but because in their really pathetic decorum and mysteriously permanent newness they counted on me so intensely. I was therefore very glad when Jack Hawley came home: he was always of such good counsel. He painted badly himself, but there was no one like him for putting his finger on the place. He had been absent from England for a year; he had been somewhere—I don't remember where—to get a fresh eye. I was in a good deal of dread of any such organ, but we were old friends; he had been away for months and a sense of emptiness was creeping into my life. I hadn't dodged a missile for a year.

He came back with a fresh eye, but with the same old black velvet blouse, and the first evening he spent in my studio we smoked cigarettes till the small hours. He had done no work himself, he had only got the eye; so the field was clear for the production of my little things. He wanted to see what I had produced for the *Cheapside,* but he was disappointed in the exhibition. That at least seemed the meaning of two or three comprehensive groans which, as he lounged on my big divan, his leg folded under him, looking at my latest drawings, issued from his lips with the smoke of the cigarette.

"What's the matter with you?" I asked.

"What's the matter with *you?*"

"Nothing save that I'm mystified."

"You are indeed. You're quite off the hinge. What's the meaning of this new fad?" And he tossed me, with visible irreverence, a drawing in which I happened to have depicted both my elegant models. I asked if he didn't think it good, and he replied that it struck him as execrable, given the sort of thing I had always represented myself to him as wishing to arrive at; but I let that pass—I was so anxious to see exactly what he meant. The two figures in the picture looked colossal, but I supposed this was *not* what he meant, inasmuch as, for aught he knew to the contrary, I might have been trying for some such effect. I maintained that I was working exactly in the same way as when he last had done me the honour to tell me I might do something some day. "Well, there's a screw loose somewhere," he answered; "wait a bit and I'll discover it." I depended upon him to do so: where else was the fresh eye? But he produced at last nothing more luminous than "I don't know—I don't like your types." This was lame for a critic who had never consented to discuss with me anything but the question of execution, the direction of strokes and the mystery of values.

"In the drawings you've been looking at I think my types are very handsome."

"Oh they won't do!"

"I've been working with new models."

"I see you have. *They* won't do."

"Are you very sure of that?"

"Absolutely—they're stupid."

"You mean *I* am—for I ought to get round that."

"You *can't*—with such people. Who are they?"

I told him, so far as was necessary, and he concluded heartlessly: *"Ce sont des gens qu'il faut mettre à la porte."*[7]

"You've never seen them; they're awfully good"—I flew to their defence.

"Not seen them? Why all this recent work of yours drops to pieces with them. It's all I want to see of them."

"No one else has said anything against it—the *Cheapside* people are pleased."

"Every one else is an ass, and the *Cheapside* people the biggest asses of all. Come, don't pretend at this time of day to have pretty illusions about the public, especially about publishers and editors. It's not for *such* animals you work—it's for those who know, *coloro che sanno;*[8] so keep straight for *me* if you can't keep straight for yourself. There was a certain sort of thing you used to try for—and a very good thing it was. But this twaddle isn't *in* it." When I talked with Hawley later about "Rutland Ramsay" and its possible successors he declared that I must get back into my boat again or I should go to the bottom. His voice in short was the voice of warning.

I noted the warning, but I didn't turn my friends out of doors. They bored me a good deal; but the very fact that they bored me admonished me not to sacrifice them—if there was anything to be done with them—simply to irritation. As I looked back at this phase they seem to me to have pervaded my life not a little. I have a vision of them as most of the time in my studio, seated against the wall on an old velvet bench to be out of the way, and resembling the while a pair of patient courtiers in a royal ante-chamber. I'm convinced that during the coldest weeks of the winter they held their ground because it saved them fire. Their newness was losing its gloss, and it was impossible not to feel them objects of charity. Whenever Miss Churm arrived they went away, and after I was fairly launched in "Rutland Ramsay" Miss Churm arrived pretty often. They managed to express to me tacitly that they supposed I wanted her for the low life of the book, and I let them suppose it, since they had attempted to study the work—it was lying about the studio—without discovering that it dealt only with the highest circles.

---

[7] "They are the sort of people one must get rid of (show to the door)."

[8] In the *Inferno* (4:131) Dante refers to Aristotle as *il maestro di color che sanno* ("the master of those that know").

They had dipped into the most brilliant of our novelists without deciphering many passages. I still took an hour from them, now and again, in spite of Jack Hawley's warning: it would be time enough to dismiss them, if dismissal should be necessary, when the rigour of the season was over. Hawley had made their acquaintance—he had met them at my fireside—and thought them a ridiculous pair. Learning that he was a painter they tried to approach him, to show him too that they were the real thing; but he looked at them, across the big room, as if they were miles away: they were a compendium of everything he most objected to in the social system of his country. Such people as that, all convention and patent-leather, with ejaculations that stopped conversation, had no business in a studio. A studio was a place to learn to see, and how could you see through a pair of feather-beds?

The main inconvenience I suffered at their hands was that at first I was shy of letting it break upon them that my artful little servant had begun to sit to me for "Rutland Ramsay." They knew I had been odd enough—they were prepared by this time to allow oddity to artists—to pick a foreign vagabond out of the streets when I might have had a person with whiskers and credentials; but it was some time before they learned how high I rated his accomplishments. They found him in an attitude more than once, but they never doubted I was doing him as an organ-grinder. There were several things they never guessed, and one of them was that for a striking scene in the novel, in which a footman briefly figured, it occurred to me to make use of Major Monarch as the menial. I kept putting this off, I didn't like to ask him to don the livery—besides the difficulty of finding a livery to fit him. At last, one day late in the winter, when I was at work on the despised Oronte, who caught one's idea on the wing, and was in the glow of feeling myself go very straight, they came in, the Major and his wife, with their society laugh about nothing (there was less and less to laugh at); came in like country-callers—they always reminded me of that— who have walked across the park after church and are presently persuaded to stay to luncheon. Luncheon was over, but they could stay to tea—I knew they wanted it. The fit was on me, however, and I couldn't let my ardour cool and my work wait, with the fading daylight, while my model prepared it. So I asked Mrs. Monarch if she would mind laying it out—a request which for an instant brought all the blood to her face. Her eyes were on her husband's for a second, and some mute telegraphy passed between them. Their folly was over the next instant; his cheerful shrewdness put an end to it. So far from pitying their wounded pride, I must add, I was moved to give it as complete a lesson as I could. They bustled about together and got out the cups and saucers and made the kettle boil. I know they felt as if they were waiting on my servant, and when the tea was prepared I said: "He'll have a cup, please—he's tired." Mrs. Monarch brought him one where he stood, and he took it from her as if he had been a gentleman at a party squeezing a crush-hat with an elbow.

Then it came over me that she had made a great effort for me—made it with a kind of nobleness—and that I owed her a compensation. Each time I saw her after this I wondered what the compensation could be. I couldn't go on doing the wrong thing to oblige them. Oh it *was* the wrong thing, the stamp of the work for which they sat—Hawley was not the only person to say it now. I sent in a large number of the drawings I had made for "Rutland Ramsey," and I received a warning that was more to the point than Hawley's. The artistic adviser of the house for which I was working was of opinion that many of my illustrations were not what had been looked for. Most of these illustrations were the subjects in which the Monarchs had figured. Without going into the question of what *had* been looked for, I had to face the fact that at this rate I shouldn't get the other books to do. I hurled myself in despair on Miss Churm—I put her through all her paces. I not only adopted Oronte publicly as my hero, but one morning when the Major looked in to see if I didn't require him to finish a *Cheapside* figure for which he had begun to sit the week before, I told him I had changed my mind—I'd do the drawing from my man. At this my visitor turned pale and stood looking at me. "Is *he* your idea of an English gentleman?" he asked.

I was disappointed, I was nervous, I wanted to get on with my work; so I replied with irritation: "Oh my dear Major—I can't be ruined for *you!*"

It was a horrid speech, but he stood another moment—after which, without a word, he quitted the studio. I drew a long breath, for I said to myself that I shouldn't see him again. I hadn't told him definitely that I was in danger of having my work rejected, but I was vexed at his not having felt the catastrophe in the air, read with me the moral of our fruitless collaboration, the lesson that in the deceptive atmosphere of art even the highest respectability may fail of being plastic.

I didn't owe my friends money, but I did see them again. They reappeared together three days later, and, given all the other facts, there was something tragic in that one. It was a clear proof they could find nothing else in life to do. They had threshed the matter out in a dismal conference—they had digested the bad news that they were not in for the series. If they weren't useful to me even for the *Cheapside* their function seemed difficult to determine, and I could only judge at first that they had come, forgivingly, decorously, to take a last leave. This made me rejoice in secret that I had little leisure for a scene; for I had placed both my other models in position together and I was pegging away at a drawing from which I hoped to derive glory. It had been suggested by the passage in which Rutland Ramsay, drawing up a chair to Artemisia's piano-stool, says extraordinary things to her while she ostensibly fingers out a difficult piece of music. I had done Miss Churm at the piano before—it was an attitude in which she knew how to take on an absolutely poetic grace. I wished the two figures to "compose" together with intensity, and my little Italian had entered perfectly into my conception. The pair were vividly before me, the piano had been pulled out; it was a charming show of blended youth and murmured love, which I had only to catch and keep. My visitors stood and looked at it, and I was friendly to them over my shoulder.

They made no response, but I was used to silent company and went on with my work, only a little disconcerted—even though exhilarated by the sense that *this* was at least the ideal thing—at not having got rid of them after all. Presently I heard Mrs. Monarch's sweet voice beside or rather above me: "I wish her hair were a little better done." I looked up and she was staring with a strange fixedness at Miss Churm, whose back was turned to her. "Do you mind my just touching it?" she went on—a question which made me spring up for an instant as with the instinctive fear that she might do the young lady a harm. But she quieted me with a glance I shall never forget—I confess I should like to have been able to paint *that*—and went for a moment to my model. She spoke to her softly, laying a hand on her shoulder and bending over her; and as the girl, understanding, gratefully assented, she disposed her rough curls, with a few quick passes, in such a way as to make Miss Churm's head twice as charming. It was one of the most heroic personal services I've ever seen rendered. Then Mrs. Monarch turned away with a low sigh and, looking about her as if for something to do, stooped to the floor with a noble humility and picked up a dirty rag that had dropped out of my paint-box.

The Major meanwhile had also been looking for something to do, and, wandering to the other end of the studio, saw before him my breakfast-things neglected, unremoved, "I say, can't I be useful *here?*" he called out to me with an irrepressible quaver. I assented with a laugh that I fear was awkward, and for the next ten minutes, while I worked, I heard the light clatter of china and the tinkle of spoons and glass. Mrs. Monarch assisted her husband—they washed up my crockery, they put it away. They wandered off into my little scullery, and I afterwards found that they had cleaned my knives and that my slender stock of plate had an unprecedented surface. When it came over me, the latent eloquence of what they were doing, I confess that my drawing was blurred for a moment—the picture swam. They had accepted their failure, but they couldn't accept their fate. They had bowed their heads in bewilderment to the perverse and cruel law in virtue of which the real thing could be so much less precious than the unreal; but they didn't want to starve. If my servants were my models, then my models might be my servants. They would reverse the parts—the others would sit for the ladies and gentlemen and *they* would do the work. They would still be in the studio—it was an intense dumb appeal to me not to turn them out. "Take us on," they wanted to say—"we'll do anything."

My pencil dropped from my hand; my sitting was spoiled and I got rid of my sitters, who were also evidently rather mystified and awestruck. Then, alone with the Major and his wife I had a most uncomfortable moment. He put their prayer into a single sentence: "I say, you know—just let *us* do for you, can't you?" I couldn't—it was dreadful to see them emptying my slops; but I pretended I could, to oblige them, for about a week. Then I gave them a sum of money to go away, and I never saw them again. I obtained the remaining books, but my friend Hawley repeats that Major and Mrs. Monarch did me a permanent harm, got me into false ways. If it be true I'm content to have paid the price—for the memory.

STEPHEN CRANE (1871–1900)

The Bride Comes to Yellow Sky

I

The great Pullman was whirling onward with such dignity of motion that a glance from the window seemed simply to prove that the plains of Texas were pouring eastward. Vast flats of green grass, dull-hued spaces of mesquite and cactus, little groups of frame houses, woods of light and tender trees, all were sweeping into the east, sweeping over the horizon, a precipice.

A newly married pair had boarded this coach at San Antonio. The man's face was reddened from many days in the wind and sun, and a direct result of his new black clothes was that his brick-colored hands were constantly performing in a most conscious fashion. From time to time he looked down respectfully at his attire. He sat with a hand on each knee, like a man waiting in a barber's shop. The glances he devoted to other passengers were furtive and shy.

The bride was not pretty, nor was she very young. She wore a dress of blue cashmere, with small reservations of velvet here and there and with steel buttons abounding. She continually twisted her head to regard her puff sleeves, very stiff, straight, and high. They embarrassed her. It was quite apparent that she had cooked, and that she expected to cook, dutifully. The blushes caused by the careless scrutiny of some passengers as she had entered the car were strange to see upon this plain, under-class countenance, which was drawn in placid, almost emotionless lines.

They were evidently very happy. "Ever been in a parlor-car before?" he asked, smiling with delight.

"No," she answered. "I never was. It's fine, ain't it?"

"Great! And then after a while we'll go forward to the diner and get a big layout. Finest meal in the world. Charge a dollar."

"Oh, do they?" cried the bride. "Charge a dollar? Why, that's too much—for us—ain't it, Jack?"

"Not this trip, anyhow," he answered bravely. "We're going to go the whole thing."

Later, he explained to her about the trains. "You see, it's a thousand miles from one end of Texas to the other, and this train runs right across it and never stops but four times." He had the pride of an owner. He pointed out to her the dazzling fittings of the coach, and in truth her eyes opened wider as she contemplated the sea-green figured velvet, the shining brass, silver, and glass, the wood that gleamed as darkly brilliant as the surface of a pool of oil. At one end a bronze figure sturdily held a support for a separated chamber, and at convenient places on the ceiling were frescoes in olive and silver.

To the minds of the pair, their surroundings reflected the glory of their marriage that morning in San Antonio. This was the environment of their new estate, and the man's face in particular beamed with an elation that made him appear ridiculous to the negro porter. This individual at times surveyed them from afar with an amused and superior grin. On other occasions he bullied them with skill in ways that did not make it exactly plain to them that they were being bullied. He subtly used all the manners of the most unconquerable kind of snobbery. He oppressed them, but of this oppression they had small knowledge, and they speedily forgot that infrequently a number of travelers covered them with stares of derisive enjoyment. Historically there was supposed to be something infinitely humorous in their situation.

"We are due in Yellow Sky at 3.42," he said, looking tenderly into her eyes.

"Oh, are we?" she said, as if she had not been aware of it. To evince surprise at her husband's statement was part of her wifely amiability. She took from a pocket a little silver watch, and as she held it before her and stared at it with a frown of attention, the new husband's face shone.

"I bought it in San Anton' from a friend of mine," he told her gleefully.

"It's seventeen minutes past twelve," she said, looking up at him with a kind of shy and clumsy coquetry. A passenger, noting this play, grew excessively sardonic, and winked at himself in one of the numerous mirrors.

At last they went to the dining-car. Two rows of negro waiters, in glowing white suits, surveyed their entrance with the interest and also the equanimity of men who had been forewarned. The pair fell to the lot of a waiter who happened to feel pleasure in steering them through their meal. He viewed them with the manner of a fatherly pilot, his countenance radiant with benevolence. The patronage, entwined with the ordinary deference, was not plain to them. And yet, as they returned to their coach, they showed in their faces a sense of escape.

To the left, miles down a long purple slope, was a little ribbon of mist where moved the keening Rio Grande. The train was approaching it at an angle, and the apex was Yellow Sky. Presently it was apparent that, as the distance from Yellow Sky grew shorter, the husband became commensurately restless. His brick-red hands were more insistent in their prominence. Occasionally he was even rather absent-minded and far-away when the bride leaned forward and addressed him.

As a matter of truth, Jack Potter was beginning to find the shadow of a deed weigh upon him like a leaden slab. He, the town marshal of Yellow Sky, a man known, liked, and feared in his corner, a prominent person, had gone to San Antonio to meet a girl he believed he loved, and there, after the usual prayers, had actually induced her to marry him, without consulting Yellow Sky for any part of the transaction. He was now bringing his bride before an innocent and unsuspecting community.

Of course, people in Yellow Sky married as it pleased them, in accordance with a general custom; but such was Potter's thought of his duty to his friends, or of their idea of his duty, or of an unspoken form which does not control men in these matters, that he felt he was heinous. He had committed an extraordinary crime. Face to face with this girl in San Antonio, and spurred by his sharp impulse, he had gone headlong over all the social hedges. At San Antonio he was like a man hidden in the dark. A knife to sever any friendly duty, any form, was easy to his hand in that remote city. But the hour of Yellow Sky, the hour of daylight, was approaching.

He knew full well that his marriage was an important thing to his town. It could only be exceeded by the burning of the new hotel. His friends could not forgive him. Frequently he had reflected on the advisability of telling them by telegraph, but a new cowardice had been upon him. He feared to do it. And now the train was hurrying him toward a scene of amazement, glee, and reproach. He glanced out of the window at the line of haze swinging slowly in towards the train.

Yellow Sky had a kind of brass band, which played painfully, to the delight of the populace. He laughed without heart as he thought of it. If the citizens could dream of his prospective arrival with his bride, they would parade the band at the station and escort them, amid cheers and laughing congratulations, to his adobe home.

He resolved that he would use all the devices of speed and plains-craft in making the journey from the station to his house. Once within that safe citadel, he could issue some sort of a vocal bulletin, and then not go among the citizens until they had time to wear off a little of their enthusiasm.

The bride looked anxiously at him. "What's worrying you, Jack?"

He laughed again, "I'm not worrying, girl. I'm only thinking of Yellow Sky."

She flushed in comprehension.

A sense of mutual guilt invaded their minds and developed a finer tenderness. They looked at each other with eyes softly aglow. But Potter often laughed the same nervous laugh. The flush upon the bride's face seemed quite permanent.

The traitor to the feelings of Yellow Sky narrowly watched the speeding landscape. "We're nearly there," he said.

Presently the porter came and announced the proximity of Potter's home. He held a brush in his hand and, with all his airy superiority gone, he brushed Potter's new clothes as the latter slowly turned this way and that way. Potter fumbled out a coin and gave it to the porter, as he had seen others do. It was a heavy and muscle-bound business, as that of a man shoeing his first horse.

The porter took their bag, and as the train began to slow they moved forward to the hooded platform of the car. Presently the two engines and their long string of coaches rushed into the station of Yellow Sky.

"They have to take water here," said Potter, from a constricted throat and in mournful cadence, as one announcing death. Before the train stopped, his eye had swept the length of the platform, and he was glad and astonished to see there was none upon it but the station-agent, who, with a slightly hurried and anxious air, was walking toward the water-tanks. When the train had halted, the porter alighted first and placed in position a little temporary step.

"Come on, girl," said Potter hoarsely. As he helped her down they each laughed on a false note. He took the bag from the negro, and bade his wife cling to his arm. As they slunk rapidly away, his hang-dog glance perceived that they were unloading the two trunks, and also that the station-agent far ahead near the baggage-car had turned and was running toward him, making gestures. He laughed, and groaned as he laughed, when he noted the first effect of his marital bliss upon Yellow Sky. He gripped his wife's arm firmly to his side, and they fled. Behind them the porter stood chuckling fatuously.

II

The California Express on the Southern Railway was due at Yellow Sky in twenty-one minutes. There were six men at the bar of the "Weary Gentleman" saloon. One was a drummer who talked a great deal and rapidly; three were Texans who did not care to talk at that time; and two were Mexican sheep-herders who did not talk as a general practice in the "Weary Gentleman" saloon. The barkeeper's dog lay on the board walk that crossed in front of the door. His head was on his paws, and he glanced drowsily here and there with the constant vigilance of a dog that is kicked on occasion. Across the sandy street were some vivid green grass plots, so wonderful in appearance amid the sands that burned near them in a blazing sun that they caused a doubt in the mind. They exactly resembled the grass mats used to represent lawns on the stage. At the cooler end of the railway station a man without a coat sat in a tilted chair and smoked his pipe. The fresh-cut bank of the Rio Grande circled near the town, and there could be seen beyond it a great, plum-colored plain of mesquite.

Save for the busy drummer and his companions in the saloon, Yellow Sky was dozing. The new-comer leaned gracefully upon the bar, and recited many tales with the confidence of a bard who has come upon a new field.

"——and at the moment that the old man fell down stairs with the bureau in his arms, the old woman was coming up with two scuttles of coal, and, of course—"

The drummer's tale was interrupted by a young man who suddenly appeared in the open door. He cried: "Scratchy Wilson's drunk, and has turned loose with both hands." The two Mexicans at once set down their glasses and faded out of the rear entrance of the saloon.

The drummer, innocent and jocular, answered: "All right, old man. S'pose he has. Come in and have a drink, anyhow."

But the information had made such an obvious cleft in every skull in the room that the drummer was obliged to see its importance. All had become instantly solemn. "Say," said he, mystified, "what is this?" His three companions made the introductory gesture of eloquent speech, but the young man at the door forestalled them.

"It means, my friend," he answered, as he came into the saloon, "that for the next two hours this town won't be a health resort."

The barkeeper went to the door and locked and barred it. Reaching out of the window, he pulled in heavy wooden shutters and barred them. Immediately a solemn, chapel-like gloom was upon the place. The drummer was looking from one to another.

"But, say," he cried, "what is this, anyhow? You don't mean there is going to be a gun-fight?"

"Don't know whether there'll be a fight or not," answered one man grimly. "But there'll be some shootin'—some good shootin'."

The young man who had warned them waved his hand. "Oh, there'll be a fight fast enough, if anyone wants it. Anybody can get a fight out there in the street. There's a fight just waiting."

The drummer seemed to be swayed between the interest of a foreigner and a perception of personal danger.

"What did you say his name was?" he asked.

"Scratchy Wilson," they answered in chorus.

"And will he kill anybody? What are you going to do? Does this happen often? Does he rampage around like this once a week or so? Can he break in that door?"

"No, he can't break down that door," replied the barkeeper. "He's tried it three times. But when he comes you'd better lay down on the floor, stranger. He's dead sure to shoot at it, and a bullet may come through."

Thereafter the drummer kept a strict eye upon the door. The time had not yet been called for him to hug the floor, but, as a minor precaution, he sidled near to the wall. "Will he kill anybody?" he said again.

The men laughed low and scornfully at the question.

"He's out to shoot, and he's out for trouble. Don't see any good in experimentin' with him."

"But what do you do in a case like this? What do you do?"

A man responded: "Why, he and Jack Potter—"

"But," in chorus, the other men interrupted, "Jack Potter's in San Anton'."

"Well, who is he? What's he got to do with it?"

"Oh, he's the town marshal. He goes out and fights Scratchy when he gets on one of these tears."

"Wow," said the drummer, mopping his brow. "Nice job he's got."

The voices had toned away to mere whisperings. The drummer wished to ask further questions which were born of an increasing anxiety and bewilderment; but when he attempted them, the men merely looked at him in irritation and motioned him to remain silent. A tense waiting hush was upon them. In the deep shadows of the room their eyes shone as they listened for sounds from the street. One man made three gestures at the barkeeper, and the latter, moving like a ghost, handed him a glass and a bottle. The man poured a full glass of whisky, and set down the bottle noiselessly. He gulped the whisky in a swallow, and turned again toward the door in immovable silence. The drummer saw that the barkeeper, without a sound, had taken a Winchester from beneath the bar. Later he saw this individual beckoning to him, so he tiptoed across the room.

"You better come with me back of the bar."

"No, thanks," said the drummer, perspiring. "I'd rather be where I can make a break for the back door."

Whereupon the man of bottles made a kindly but peremptory gesture. The drummer obeyed it, and finding himself seated on a box with his head below the level of the bar, balm was laid upon his soul at sight of various zinc and copper fittings that bore a resemblance to armorplate. The barkeeper took a seat comfortably upon an adjacent box.

"You see," he whispered, "this here Scratchy Wilson is a wonder with a gun—a perfect wonder—and when he goes on the war trail, we hunt our holes—naturally. He's about the last one of the old gang that used to hang out along the river here. He's a terror when he's drunk. When he's sober he's all right—kind of simple—wouldn't hurt a fly—nicest fellow in town. But when he's drunk—whoo!"

There were periods of stillness. "I wish Jack Potter was back from San Anton'," said the barkeeper. "He shot Wilson up once—in the leg—and he would sail in and pull out the kinks in this thing."

Presently they heard from a distance the sound of a shot, followed by three wild yowls. It instantly removed a bond from the men in the darkened saloon. There was a shuffling of feet. They looked at each other. "Here he comes," they said.

III

A man in a maroon-colored flannel shirt, which had been purchased for purposes of decoration and made, principally, by some Jewish women on the east side of New York, rounded a corner and walked into the middle of the main street of Yellow Sky. In either hand the man held a long, heavy, blue-black revolver. Often he yelled, and these cries rang through a semblance of a deserted village, shrilly flying over the roofs in a volume that seemed to have no relation to the ordinary vocal strength of a man. It was as if the surrounding stillness formed the arch of a tomb over him. These cries of ferocious challenge rang against walls of silence. And his boots had red tops with gilded imprints, of the kind beloved in winter by little sledding boys on the hillsides of New England.

The man's face flamed in a rage begot of whisky. His eyes, rolling and yet keen for ambush, hunted the still doorways and windows. He walked with the creeping movement of the midnight cat. As it occurred to him, he roared menacing information. The long revolvers in his hands were as easy as straws; they were moved with an electric swiftness. The little fingers of each hand played sometimes in a musician's way. Plain from the low collar of the shirt, the cords of his neck straightened and sank, straightened and sank, as passion moved him. The only sounds were his terrible invitations. The calm adobes preserved their demeanor at the passing of this small thing in the middle of the street.

There was no offer of fight; no offer of fight. The man called to the sky. There were no attractions. He bellowed and fumed and swayed his revolvers here and everywhere.

The dog of the barkeeper of the "Weary Gentleman" saloon had not appreciated the advance of events. He yet lay dozing in front of his master's door. At sight of the dog, the man paused and raised his revolver humorously. At sight of the man, the dog sprang up and walked diagonally away, with a sullen head, and growling. The man yelled, and the dog broke into a gallop. As it was about to enter an alley, there was a loud noise, a whistling, and something spat the ground directly before it. The dog screamed, and, wheeling in terror, galloped headlong in a new direction. Again there was a noise, a whistling, and sand was kicked viciously before it. Fear-stricken, the dog turned and flurried like an animal in a pen. The man stood laughing, his weapons at his hips.

Ultimately the man was attracted by the closed door of the "Weary Gentleman" saloon. He went to it, and hammering with a revolver, demanded drink.

The door remaining imperturbable, he picked up a bit of paper from the walk and nailed it to the framework with a knife. He then turned his back contemptuously upon this popular resort, and walking to the opposite side of the street, and spinning there on his heel quickly and lithely, fired at the bit of paper. He missed it by a half inch. He swore at himself, and went away. Later, he comfortably fusilladed the windows of his most intimate friend. The man was playing with this town. It was a toy for him.

But still there was no offer of fight. The name of Jack Potter, his ancient antagonist, entered his mind, and he concluded that it would be a glad thing if he should go to Potter's house and by bombardment induce him to come out and fight. He moved in the direction of his desire, chanting Apache scalp-music.

When he arrived at it, Potter's house presented the same still front as had the other adobes. Taking up a strategic position, the man howled a challenge. But this house regarded him as might a great stone god. It gave no sign. After a decent wait, the man howled further challenges, mingling with them wonderful epithets.

Presently there came the spectacle of a man churning himself into deepest rage over the immobility of a house. He fumed at it as the winter wind attacks a prairie cabin in the North. To the distance there should have gone the sound of a tumult like the fighting of 200 Mexicans. As necessity bade him, he paused for breath or to reload his revolvers.

IV

Potter and his bride walked sheepishly and with speed. Sometimes they laughed together shamefacedly and low.

"Next corner, dear," he said finally.

They put forth the efforts of a pair walking bowed against a strong wind. Potter was about to raise a finger to point the first appearance of the new home when, as they circled the corner, they came face to face with a man in a maroon-colored shirt who was feverishly pushing cartridges into a large revolver. Upon the instant the man dropped his revolver to the ground, and, like lightning, whipped another from its holster. The second weapon was aimed at the bridegroom's chest.

There was a silence. Potter's mouth seemed to be merely a grave for his tongue. He exhibited an instinct to at once loosen his arm from the woman's grip, and he dropped the bag to the sand. As for the bride, her face had gone as yellow as old cloth. She was a slave to hideous rites gazing at the apparitional snake.

The two men faced each other at a distance of three paces. He of the revolver smiled with a new and quiet ferocity.

"Tried to sneak up on me," he said. "Tried to sneak up on me!" His eyes grew more baleful. As Potter made a slight movement, the man thrust his revolver venomously forward. "No, don't you do it, Jack Potter. Don't you move a finger toward a gun just yet. Don't you move an eyelash. The time has come for me to settle with you, and I'm goin' to do it my own way and loaf along with no interferin'. So if you don't want a gun bent on you, just mind what I tell you."

Potter looked at his enemy. "I ain't got a gun on me, Scratchy," he said. "Honest, I ain't." He was stiffening and steadying, but yet somewhere at the back of his mind a vision of the Pullman floated, the sea-green figured velvet, the shining brass, silver, and glass, the wood that gleamed as darkly brilliant as the surface of a pool of oil—all the glory of the marriage, the environment of the new estate. "You know I fight when it comes to fighting, Scratchy Wilson, but I ain't got a gun on me. You'll have to do all the shootin' yourself."

His enemy's face went livid. He stepped forward and lashed his weapon to and fro before Potter's chest. "Don't you tell me you ain't got no gun on you, you whelp. Don't tell me no lie like that. There ain't a man in Texas ever seen you without no gun. Don't take me for no kid." His eyes blazed with light, and his throat worked like a pump.

"I ain't takin' you for no kid," answered Potter. His heels had not moved an inch backward. "I'm takin' you for a——fool. I tell you I ain't got a gun, and I ain't. If you're goin' to shoot me up, you better begin now. You'll never get a chance like this again."

So much enforced reasoning had told on Wilson's rage. He was calmer. "If you ain't got a gun, why ain't you got a gun?" he sneered. "Been to Sunday-school?"

"I ain't got a gun because I've just come from San Anton' with my wife. I'm married," said Potter. "And if I'd thought there was going to be any galoots like you prowling around when I brought my wife home, I'd had a gun, and don't you forget it."

"Married!" said Scratchy, not at all comprehending.

"Yes, married. I'm married," said Potter distinctly.

"Married?" said Scratchy. Seemingly for the first time he saw the drooping, drowning woman at the other man's side. "No!" he said. He was like a creature allowed a glimpse of another world. He moved a pace backward, and his arm with the revolver dropped to his side. "Is this the lady?" he asked.

"Yes, this is the lady," answered Potter.

There was another period of silence.

"Well," said Wilson at last, slowly, "I s'pose it's all off now."

"It's all off if you say so, Scratchy. You know I didn't make the trouble." Potter lifted his valise.

"Well, I 'low it's off, Jack," said Wilson. He was looking at the ground. "Married!" He was not a student of chivalry; it was merely that in the presence of this foreign condition he was a simple child of the earlier plains. He picked up his starboard revolver, and placing both weapons in their holsters, he went away. His feet made funnel-shaped tracks in the heavy sand.

ANTON CHEKHOV (1860–1904)

Gooseberries

The sky had been covered with rain-clouds ever since the early morning, it was a still day, cool and dull, one of those misty days when the clouds have long been lowering overhead and you keep thinking it is just going to rain, and the rain holds off. Ivan Ivanich, the veterinary surgeon, and Burkin, the high-school teacher, had walked till they were tired, and the way over the fields seemed endless to them. Far ahead they could just make out the windmill of the village of Mironositskoye, and what looked like a range of low hills at the right extending well beyond the village, and they both knew that this range was really the bank of the river, and that further on were meadows, green willow-trees, country-estates; if they were on top of these hills, they knew they would see the same boundless fields and telegraph-posts, and the train, like a crawling caterpillar in the distance, while in fine weather even the town would be visible. On this still day, when the whole of nature seemed kindly and pensive, Ivan Ivanich and Burkin felt a surge of love for this plain, and thought how vast and beautiful their country was.

"The last time we stayed in Elder Prokofy's hut," said Burkin, "you said you had a story to tell me."

"Yes. I wanted to tell you the story of my brother."

Ivan Ivanich took a deep breath and lighted his pipe as a preliminary to his narrative, but just then the rain came. Five minutes later it was coming down in torrents and nobody could say when it would stop. Ivan Ivanich and Burkin stood still, lost in thought. The dogs, already soaked, stood with drooping tails, gazing at them wistfully.

"We must try and find shelter," said Burkin. "Let's go to Alekhin's. It's quite near."

"Come on, then."

They turned aside and walked straight across the newly reaped field, veering to the right till they came to a road. Very soon poplars, an orchard, and the red roofs of barns came into sight. The surface of a river gleamed, and they had a view of an extensive reach of water, a windmill and a whitewashed bathing-shed. This was Sofyino, where Alekhin lived.

The mill was working, and the noise made by its sails drowned the sound of the rain; the whole dam trembled. Horses, soaking wet, were standing near some carts, their heads drooping, and people were moving about with sacks over their heads and shoulders. It was wet, muddy, bleak, and the water looked cold and sinister. Ivan Ivanich and Burkin were already experiencing the misery of dampness, dirt, physical discomfort, their boots were caked with mud, and when, having passed the mill-dam, they took the upward path to the landowner's barns, they fell silent, as if vexed with one another.

The sound of winnowing[1] came from one of the barns; the door was open, and clouds of dust issued from it. Standing in the doorway was Alekhin himself, a stout man of some forty years, with longish hair, looking more like a professor or an artist than a landed proprietor. He was wearing a white shirt, greatly in need of washing, belted with a piece of string, and long drawers with no trousers over them. His boots, too, were caked with mud and straw. His eyes and nose were ringed with dust. He recognized Ivan Ivanich and Burkin, and seemed glad to see them.

"Go up to the house, gentlemen," he said, smiling. "I'll be with you in a minute."

It was a large two-storey house. Alekhin occupied the ground floor, two rooms with vaulted ceilings and tiny windows, where the stewards had lived formerly. They were poorly furnished, and smelled of rye-bread, cheap vodka, and harness. He hardly ever went into the upstairs rooms, excepting when he had guests. Ivan Ivanich and Burkin were met by a maid-servant, a young woman of such beauty that they stood still involuntarily and exchanged glances.

"You have no idea how glad I am to see you here, dear friends," said Alekhin, overtaking them in the hall. "It's quite a surprise! Pelageya," he said, turning to the maid, "find the gentlemen a change of clothes. And I might as well change, myself. But I must have a wash first, for I don't believe I've had a bath since the spring. Wouldn't you like to go and have a bathe while they get things ready here?"

The beauteous Pelageya, looking very soft and delicate, brought them towels and soap, and Alekhin and his guests set off for the bathing-house.

"Yes, it's a long time since I had a wash," he said, taking off his clothes. "As you see I have a nice bathing-place, my father had it built, but somehow I never seem to get time to wash."

He sat on the step, soaping his long locks and his neck, and all round him the water was brown.

---

1 *winnowing*, the separation of the chaff, or husks, from grain.

"Yes, you certainly..." remarked Ivan Ivanich, with a significant glance at his host's head.

"It's a long time since I had a wash..." repeated Alekhin, somewhat abashed, and he soaped himself again, and now the water was dark-blue, like ink.

Ivan Ivanich emerged from the shed, splashed noisily into the water, and began swimming beneath the rain, spreading his arms wide, making waves all round him, and the white water-lilies rocked on the waves he made. He swam into the very middle of the river and then dived, a moment later came up at another place and swam further, diving constantly, and trying to touch the bottom. "Ah, my God," he kept exclaiming in his enjoyment. "Ah, my God...." He swam up to the mill, had a little talk with some peasants there and turned back, but when he got to the middle of the river, he floated, holding his face up to the rain. Burkin and Alekhin were dressed and ready to go, but he went on swimming and diving.

"God! God!" he kept exclaiming. "Dear God!"

"Come out!" Burkin shouted to him.

They went back to the house. And only after the lamp was lit in the great drawing-room on the upper floor, and Burkin and Ivan Ivanich, in silk dressing-gowns and warm slippers, were seated in arm-chairs, while Alekhin, washed and combed, paced the room in his new frock-coat, enjoying the warmth, the cleanliness, his dry clothes and comfortable slippers, while the fair Pelageya, smiling benevolently, stepped noiselessly over the carpet with her tray of tea and preserves, did Ivan Ivanich embark upon his yarn, the ancient dames, young ladies, and military gentlemen looking down at them severely from the gilded frames, as if they, too, were listening.

"There were two of us brothers," he began. "Ivan Ivanich (me), and my brother Nikolai Ivanich, two years younger than myself. I went in for learning and became a veterinary surgeon, but Nikolai started working in a government office when he was only nineteen. Our father, Chimsha-Himalaisky, was educated in a school for the sons of private soldiers, but was later promoted to officer's rank, and was made a hereditary nobleman and given a small estate. After his death the estate had to be sold for debts, but at least our childhood was passed in the freedom of the country-side, where we roamed the fields and the woods like peasant children, taking the horses to graze, peeling bark from the trunks of lime-trees, fishing, and all that sort of thing. And anyone who has once in his life fished for perch, or watched the thrushes fly south in the autumn, rising high over the village on clear, cool days, is spoilt for town life, and will long for the country-side for the rest of his days. My brother pined in his government office. The years passed and he sat in the same place every day, writing out the same documents and thinking all the

time of the same thing—how to get back to the country. And these
longings of his gradually turned into a definite desire, into a dream
of purchasing a little estate somewhere on the bank of a river or the
shore of a lake.

"He was a meek, good-natured chap, I was fond of him, but could
feel no sympathy with the desire to lock oneself up for life in an
estate of one's own. They say man only needs six feet of earth. But
it is a corpse, and not man, which needs these six feet. And now
people are actually saying that it is a good sign for our intellectuals
to yearn for the land and try to obtain country-dwellings. And yet
these estates are nothing but those same six feet of earth. To escape
from the town, from the struggle, from the noise of life, to escape
and hide one's head on a country-estate, is not life, but egoism,
idleness, it is a sort of renunciation, but renunciation without faith.
It is not six feet of earth, not a country-estate, that man needs, but
the whole globe, the whole of nature, room to display his qualities
and the individual characteristics of his soul.

"My brother Nikolai sat at his office-desk, dreaming of eating soup
made from his own cabbages, which would spread a delicious smell
all over his own yard, of eating out of doors, on the green grass, of
sleeping in the sun, sitting for hours on a bench outside his gate,
and gazing at the fields and woods. Books on agriculture, and all
those hints printed on calendars were his delight, his favourite spiritual nourishment. He was fond of reading newspapers, too, but all
he read in them was advertisements of the sale of so many acres of
arable and meadowland, with residence attached, a river, an orchard,
a mill, and ponds fed by springs. His head was full of visions of
garden paths, flowers, fruit, nesting-boxes, carp-ponds, and all that
sort of thing. These visions differed according to the advertisements
he came across, but for some reason gooseberry bushes invariably
figured in them. He could not picture to himself a single estate or
picturesque nook that did not have gooseberry bushes in it.

" 'Country life has its conveniences,' he would say. 'You sit on the
verandah, drinking tea, with your own ducks floating on the pond,
and everything smells so nice, and . . . and the gooseberries ripen on
the bushes.'

"He drew up plans for his estate, and every plan showed the
same features: a) the main residence, b) the servant's wing, c) the
kitchen-garden, d) gooseberry bushes. He lived thriftily, never ate
or drank his fill, dressed anyhow, like a beggar, and saved up all
his money in the bank. He became terribly stingy. I could hardly
bear to look at him, and whenever I gave him a little money, or
sent him a present on some holiday, he put that away, too. Once a
man gets an idea into his head, there's no doing anything with him.

"The years passed, he was sent to another gubernia,[2] he was over forty, and was still reading advertisements in the papers, and saving up. At last I heard he had married. All for the same purpose, to buy himself an estate with gooseberry bushes on it, he married an ugly elderly widow, for whom he had not the slightest affection, just because she had some money. After his marriage he went on living as thriftily as ever, half-starving his wife, and putting her money in his own bank account. Her first husband had been a postmaster, and she was used to pies and cordials, but with her second husband she did not even get enough black bread to eat. She began to languish under such a regime, and three years later yielded up her soul to God. Of course my brother did not for a moment consider himself guilty of her death. Money, like vodka, makes a man eccentric. There was a merchant in our town who asked for a plate of honey on his deathbed and ate up all his bank-notes and lottery tickets with the honey, so that no one else should get it. And one day when I was examining a consignment of cattle at a railway station, a drover fell under the engine and his leg was severed from his body. We carried him all bloody into the waiting-room, a terrible sight, and he did nothing but beg us to look for his leg, worrying all the time—there were twenty rubles in the boot, and he was afraid they would be lost."

"You're losing the thread," put in Burkin.

Ivan Ivanich paused for a moment, and went on: "After his wife's death my brother began to look about for an estate. You can search for five years, of course, and in the end make a mistake and buy something quite different from what you dreamed of. My brother Nikolai bought three hundred acres, complete with gentleman's house, servants' quarters, and a park, as well as a mortgage to be paid through an agent, but there were neither an orchard, gooseberry bushes, nor a pond with ducks on it. There was a river, but it was as dark as coffee, owing to the fact that there was a brick-works on one side of the estate, and bone-kilns on the other. Nothing daunted, however, my brother Nikolai Ivanich ordered two dozen gooseberry bushes and settled down as a landed proprietor.

"Last year I paid him a visit. I thought I would go and see how he was getting on there. In his letters my brother gave his address as Chumbaroklova Pustosh or Himalaiskoye. I arrived at Himalais-koye in the afternoon. It was very hot. Everywhere were ditches, fences, hedges, rows of fir-trees, and it was hard to drive into the yard and find a place to leave one's carriage. As I went a fat ginger-coloured

---

2 *gubernia*, a province.

dog, remarkably like a pig, came out to meet me. It looked as if it would have barked if it were not so lazy. The cook, who was also fat and like a pig, came out of the kitchen, barefoot, and said her master was having his after-dinner rest. I made my way to my brother's room, and found him sitting up in bed, his knees covered by a blanket. He had aged, and grown stout and flabby. His cheeks, nose and lips protruded—I almost expected him to grunt into the blanket.

"We embraced and wept—tears of joy, mingled with melancholy—because we had once been young and were now both grey-haired and approaching the grave. He put on his clothes and went out to show me over his estate.

" 'Well, how are you getting on here?' I asked.

" 'All right, thanks be, I'm enjoying myself.' "

"He was no longer the poor, timid clerk, but a true proprietor, a gentleman. He had settled down, and was entering with zest into country life. He ate a lot, washed in the bath-house, and put on flesh. He had already got into litigation with the village commune, the brick-works and the bone-kilns, and took offence if the peasants failed to call him 'Your Honour.' He went in for religion in a solid, gentlemanly way, and there was nothing casual about his pretentious good works. And what were these good works? He treated all the diseases of the peasants with bicarbonate of soda and castor-oil, and had a special thanksgiving service held on his name-day, after which he provided half a pail of vodka, supposing that this was the right thing to do. Oh, those terrible half pails! Today the fat landlord hauls the peasants before the Zemstvo representative[3] for letting their sheep graze on his land, tomorrow, on the day of rejoicing, he treats them to half a pail of vodka, and they drink and sing and shout hurrah, prostrating themselves before him when they are drunk. Any improvement in his conditions, anything like satiety or idleness, develops the most insolent complacency in a Russian. Nikolai Ivanich, who had been afraid of having an opinion of his own when he was in the government service, was now continually coming out with axioms, in the most ministerial manner: 'Education is essential, but the people are not ready for it yet,' 'corporal punishment is an evil, but in certain cases it is beneficial and indispensable.'

" 'I know the people and I know how to treat them,' he said. 'The people love me. I only have to lift my little finger, and the people will do whatever I want.'

"And all this, mark you, with a wise, indulgent smile. Over and

---

3 *Zemstvo representative,* a law-enforcing official of the Zemstvo, the elective council responsible for the local administration of a province.

over again he repeated: 'We the gentry,' or 'speaking as a gentleman,' and seemed to have quite forgotten that our grandfather was a peasant, and our father a common soldier. Our very surname—Chimsha-Himalaisky—in reality so absurd, now seemed to him a resounding, distinguished, and euphonious name.

"But it is of myself, and not of him, that I wish to speak. I should like to describe to you the change which came over me in those few hours I spent on my brother's estate. As we were drinking tea in the evening, the cook brought us a full plate of gooseberries. These were not gooseberries bought for money, they came from his own garden, and were the first fruits of the bushes he had planted. Nikolai Ivanich broke into a laugh and gazed at the gooseberries, in tearful silence for at least five minutes. Speechless with emotion, he popped a single gooseberry into his mouth, darted at me the triumphant glance of a child who has at last gained possession of a longed-for toy, and said:

" 'Delicious!'

"And he ate them greedily, repeating over and over again:

" 'Simply delicious! You try them.' "

"They were hard and sour, but, as Pushkin says: 'The lie which elates us is dearer than a thousand sober truths.' I saw before me a really happy man, one whose dearest wish had come true, who had achieved his aim in life, got what he wanted, and was content with his lot and with himself. There had always been a tinge of melancholy in my conception of human happiness, and now, confronted by a happy man, I was overcome by a feeling of sadness bordering on desperation. This feeling grew strongest of all in the night. A bed was made up for me in the room next to my brother's bedroom, and I could hear him moving about restlessly, every now and then getting up to take a gooseberry from a plate. How many happy, satisfied people there are, after all, I said to myself! What an overwhelming force! Just consider this life—the insolence and idleness of the strong, the ignorance and bestiality of the weak, all around intolerable poverty, cramped dwellings, degeneracy, drunkenness, hypocrisy, lying.... And yet peace and order apparently prevail in all those homes and in the streets. Of the fifty thousand inhabitants of a town, not one will be found to cry out, to proclaim his indignation aloud. We see those who go to the market to buy food, who eat in the day-time and sleep at night, who prattle away, marry, grow old, carry their dead to the cemeteries. But we neither hear nor see those who suffer, and the terrible things in life are played out behind the scenes. All is calm and quiet, only statistics, which are dumb, protest: so many have gone mad, so many barrels of drink have been consumed, so many children died of malnutrition.... And apparently this is as it should be. Apparently those who are happy can only enjoy themselves because the unhappy bear their burdens in silence, and but for this silence happiness would be impossible. It is a kind of universal hypnosis. There ought to be a man with a hammer behind the door of every happy man, to remind him by his constant knocks that there are unhappy people, and that happy as he himself may be, life will sooner or later show him its claws, catastrophe will overtake him—sickness, poverty, loss—and nobody will see it, just as he now neither sees nor hears the misfortunes of others. But there is no man with a hammer, the happy man goes on living and the petty vicissitudes of life touch him lightly, like the wind in an aspen-tree, and all is well.

"That night I understood that I, too, was happy and content," continued Ivan Ivanich, getting up. "I, too, while out hunting, or at the dinner table, have held forth on the right way to live, to worship, to manage the people. I, too, have declared that without knowledge there can be no light, that education is essential, but that bare literacy is sufficient for the common people. Freedom is a blessing, I have said, one can't get on without it, any more than without air, but we must wait. Yes, that is what I said, and now I ask: In the name of what must we wait?" Here Ivan Ivanich looked angrily at Burkin. "In the name of what must we wait, I ask you. What is there to be considered? Don't be in such a hurry, they tell me, every idea materializes gradually, in its own time. But who are they who say this? What is the proof that it is just? You refer to the natural order of things, to the logic of facts, but according to what order, what logic do I, a living, thinking individual, stand on the edge of a ditch and wait for it to be gradually filled up, or choked with silt, when I might leap across it or build a bridge over it? And again, in the name of what must we wait? Wait, when we have not the strength to live, though live we must and to live we desire!

"I left my brother early the next morning, and ever since I have found town life intolerable. The peace and order weigh on my spirits, and I am afraid to look into windows, because there is now no sadder spectacle for me than a happy family seated around the tea-table. I am old and unfit for the struggle, I am even incapable of feeling hatred. I can only suffer inwardly, and give way to irritation and annoyance, at night my head burns from the rush of thoughts, and I am unable to sleep. . . . Oh, if only I were young!"

Ivan Ivanich began pacing backwards and forwards, repeating:

"If only I were young still!"

Suddenly he went up to Alekhin and began pressing first one of his hands, and then the other.

"Pavel Konstantinich," he said in imploring accents. "Don't *you* fall into apathy, don't *you* let your conscience be lulled to sleep! While you are still young, strong, active, do not be weary of well-doing. There is no such thing as happiness, nor ought there to be, but if there is any sense or purpose in life, this sense and purpose are to be found not in our own happiness, but in something greater and more rational. Do good!"

Ivan Ivanich said all this with a piteous, imploring smile, as if he were asking for something for himself.

Then they all three sat in their armchairs a long way apart from one another, and said nothing. Ivan Ivanich's story satisfied neither Burkin or Alekhin. It was not interesting to listen to the story of a poor clerk who ate gooseberries, when from the walls generals and fine ladies, who seemed to come to life in the dark, were looking down from their gilded frames. It would have been much more interesting to hear about elegant people, lovely women. And the fact that they were sitting in a drawing-room in which everything—the swathed chandeliers, the arm-chairs, the carpet on the floor, proved that the people now looking out of the frames had once moved about here, sat in the chairs, drunk tea, where the fair Pelageya was now going noiselessly to and fro, was better than any story.

Alekhin was desperately sleepy. He had got up early, at three o'clock in the morning, to go about his work on the estate, and could now hardly keep his eyes open. But he would not go to bed, for fear one of his guests would relate something interesting after he was gone. He could not be sure whether what Ivan Ivanich had just told them was wise or just, but his visitors talked of other things besides grain, hay, or tar, of things which had no direct bearing on his daily life, and he liked this, and wanted them to go on. . . .

"Well, time to go to bed," said Burkin, getting up. "Allow me to wish you a good night."

Alekhin said good night and went downstairs to his own room, the visitors remaining on the upper floor. They were allotted a big room for the night, in which were two ancient bedsteads of carved wood, and an ivory crucifix in one corner. There was a pleasant smell of freshly laundered sheets from the wide, cool beds which the fair Pelageya made up for them.

Ivan Ivanich undressed in silence and lay down.

"Lord have mercy on us, sinners," he said, and covered his head with the sheet.

There was a strong smell of stale tobacco from his pipe, which he put on the table, and Burkin lay awake a long time, wondering where the stifling smell came from.

The rain tapped on the window-panes all night.

JAMES JOYCE (1882–1941)

Araby

North Richmond Street, being blind, was a quiet street except at the hour when the Christian Brothers' School set the boys free. An uninhabited house of two stories stood at the blind end, detached from its neighbours in a square ground. The other houses of the street, conscious of decent lives within them, gazed at one another with brown imperturbable faces.

The former tenant of our house, a priest, had died in the back drawing-room. Air, musty from having been long enclosed, hung in all the rooms, and the waste room behind the kitchen was littered with old useless papers. Among these I found a few paper-covered books, the pages of which were curled and damp: *The Abbot,* by Walter Scott, *The Devout Communicant,* and *The Memoirs of Vidocq.* I liked the last best because its leaves were yellow. The wild garden behind the house contained a central apple tree and a few straggling bushes under one of which I found the late tenant's rusty bicycle pump. He had been a very charitable priest; in his will he had left all his money to institutions and the furniture of his house to his sister.

When the short days of winter came dusk fell before we had well eaten our dinners. When we met in the street the houses had grown sombre. The space of sky above us was the colour of ever-changing violet and towards it the lamps of the street lifted their feeble lanterns. The cold air stung us and we played till our bodies glowed. Our shouts echoed in the silent street. The career of our play brought us through the dark muddy lanes behind the houses where we ran the gauntlet of the rough tribes from the cottages, to the back doors of the dark dripping gardens where odours arose from the ash-pits, to the dark odorous stables where a coachman smoothed and combed the horse or shook music from the buckled harness. When we returned to the street, light from the kitchen windows had filled the areas. If my uncle was seen turning the corner we hid in the shadow until we had seen him safely housed. Or if Mangan's sister came out on the doorstep to call her brother in to his tea we watched her from our shadow peer up and down the street. We waited to see whether she would remain or go in and, if she remained, we left our shadow and walked up to Mangan's steps resignedly. She was waiting for us, her figure defined by the light from the half-opened door. Her brother always teased her before he obeyed and I stood by the railings looking at her. Her dress swung as she moved her body and the soft rope of her hair tossed from side to side.

Every morning I lay on the floor in the front parlour watching her door. The blind was pulled down to within an inch of the sash so that I could not be seen. When she came out on the doorstep my heart leaped. I ran to the hall, seized my books and followed her. I kept her brown figure always in my eye and, when we came near the point at which our ways diverged, I quickened my pace and passed her. This happened morning after morning. I had never spoken to her, except for a few casual words, and yet her name was like a summons to all my foolish blood.

Her image accompanied me even in places the most hostile to romance. On Saturday evenings when my aunt went marketing I had to go to carry some of the parcels. We walked through the flaring streets, jostled by drunken men and bargaining women, amid the curses of labourers, the shrill litanies of shop-boys who stood on guard by the barrels of pigs' cheeks, the nasal chanting of street-singers, who sang a *come-all-you* about O'Donovan Rossa, or a ballad about the troubles in our native land. These noises converged in a single sensation of life for me: I imagined that I bore my chalice safely through a throng of foes. Her name sprang to my lips at moments in strange prayers and praises which I myself did not understand. My eyes were often full of tears (I could not tell why) and at times a flood from my heart seemed to pour itself out into my bosom. I thought little of the future. I did not know whether I would ever speak to her or not or, if I spoke to her, how I could tell her of my confused adoration. But my body was like a harp and her words and gestures were like fingers running upon the wires.

One evening I went into the back drawing-room in which the priest had died. It was a dark rainy evening and there was no sound in the house. Through one of the broken panes I heard the rain impinge upon the earth, the fine incessant needles of water playing in the sodden beds. Some distant lamp or lighted window gleamed below me. I was thankful that I could see so little. All my senses seemed to desire to veil themselves and, feeling that I was about to slip from them, I pressed the palms of my hands together until they trembled, murmuring: *"O love! O love!"* many times.

At last she spoke to me. When she addressed the first words to me I was so confused that I did not know what to answer. She asked me was I going to *Araby*. I forgot whether I answered yes or no. It would be a splendid bazaar, she said she would love to go.

"And why can't you?" I asked.

While she spoke she turned a silver bracelet round and round her wrist. She could not go, she said, because there would be a retreat that week in her convent. Her brother and two other boys were fighting for their caps and I was alone at the railings. She held one of the spikes, bowing her head towards me. The light from the lamp opposite our door caught the white curve of her neck, lit up her hair that rested there and, falling, lit up the hand upon the railing. It fell over one side of her dress and caught the white border of a petticoat, just visible as she stood at ease.

"It's well for you," she said.

"If I go," I said, "I will bring you something."

What innumerable follies laid waste my waking and sleeping thoughts after the evening! I wished to annihilate the tedious intervening days. I chafed against the work of school. At night in my bedroom and by day in the classroom her image came between me and the page I strove to read. The syllables of the word *Araby* were called to me through the silence in which my soul luxuriated and cast an Eastern enchantment over me. I asked for leave to go to the bazaar on Saturday night. My aunt was surprised and hoped it was not some Freemason affair. I answered few questions in class. I watched my master's face pass from amiability to sternness; he hoped I was not beginning to idle, I could not call my wandering thoughts together. I had hardly any patience with the serious work of life which, now that it stood between me and my desire, seemed to me child's play, ugly monotonous child's play.

On Saturday morning I reminded my uncle that I wished to go to the bazaar in the evening. He was fussing at the hall-stand, looking for the hat brush, and answered me curtly:

"Yes, boy, I know."

As he was in the hall I could not go into the front parlour and lie at the window. I left the house in bad humour and walked slowly towards the school. The air was pitilessly raw and already my heart misgave me.

When I came home to dinner my uncle had not yet been home. Still it was early. I sat staring at the clock for some time and, when its ticking began to irritate me, I left the room. I mounted the staircase and gained the upper part of the house. The high cold empty gloomy rooms liberated me and I went from room to room singing. From the front window I saw my companions playing below in the street. Their cries reached me weakened and indistinct and, leaning my forehead against the cool glass, I looked over at the dark house where she lived. I may have stood there for an hour, seeing nothing but the brown-clad figure cast by my imagination, touched discreetly by the lamplight at the curved neck, at the hand upon the railings and at the border below the dress.

When I came downstairs again I found Mrs. Mercer sitting at the fire. She was an old garrulous woman, a pawnbroker's widow, who collected used stamps for some pious purpose. I had to endure the gossip of the tea-table. The meal was prolonged beyond an hour and still my uncle did not come. Mrs. Mercer stood up to go: she was sorry she couldn't wait any longer, but it was after eight o'clock and she did not like to be out late, as the night air was bad for her. When she had gone I began to walk up and down the room, clenching my fists. My aunt said:

"I'm afraid you may put off your bazaar for this night of Our Lord."

At nine o'clock I heard my uncle's latchkey in the hall-door. I heard him talking to himself and heard the hall-stand rocking when it had received the weight of his overcoat. I could interpret these signs. When he was midway through his dinner I asked him to give me the money to go to the bazaar. He had forgotten.

"The people are in bed and after their first sleep now," he said.

I did not smile. My aunt said to him energetically:

"Can't you give him the money and let him go? You've kept him late enough as it is."

My uncle said he was very sorry he had forgotten. He said he believed in the old saying: "All work and no play makes Jack a dull boy." He asked me where I was going and, when I had told him a second time, he asked me did I know *The Arab's Farewell to his Steed*. When I left the kitchen he was about to recite the opening lines of the piece to my aunt.

I held a florin tightly in my hand as I strode down Buckingham Street towards the station. The sight of the streets thronged with buyers and glaring with gas recalled to me the purpose of my journey. I took my seat in a third-class carriage of a deserted train. After an intolerable delay the train moved out of the station slowly. It crept onward among ruinous houses and over the twinkling river. At Westland Row Station a crowd of people pressed to the carriage doors; but the porters moved them back, saying that it was a special train for the bazaar. I remained alone in the bare carriage. In a few minutes the train drew up beside an improvised wooden platform. I passed out on the road and saw by the lighted dial of a clock that it was ten minutes to ten. In front of me was a large building which displayed the magical name.

I could not find any sixpenny entrance and, fearing that the bazaar would be closed, I passed in quickly through a turnstile, handing a shilling to a weary-looking man. I found myself in a big hall girdled at half its height by a gallery. Nearly all the stalls were closed and the greater part of the hall was in darkness. I recognized a silence like that which pervades a church after a service. I walked into the center of the bazaar timidly. A few people were gathered about the stalls which were still open. Before a curtain, over which the words *Café Chantant* were written in coloured lamps, two men were counting money on a salver. I listened to the fall of the coins.

Remembering with difficulty why I had come I went over to one of the stalls and examined porcelain vases and flowered tea-sets. At the door of the stall a young lady was talking and laughing with two young gentlemen. I remarked their English accents and listened vaguely to their conversation.

"O, I never said such a thing!"

"O, but you did!"

"O, but I didn't!"

"Didn't she say that?"

"Yes. I heard her."

"O, there's a . . . fib!"

Observing me, the young lady came over and asked me did I wish to buy anything. The tone of her voice was not encouraging; she seemed to have spoken to me out of a sense of duty. I looked humbly at the great jars that stood like eastern guards at either side of the dark entrance to the stall and murmured:

"No, thank you."

The young lady changed the position of one of the vases and went back to the two young men. They began to talk of the same subject. Once or twice the young lady glanced at me over her shoulder.

I lingered before her stall, though I knew my stay was useless, to make my interest in her wares seem the more real. Then I turned away slowly and walked down the middle of the bazaar. I allowed the two pennies to fall against the sixpence in my pocket. I heard a voice call from one end of the gallery that the light was out. The upper part of the hall was now completely dark.

Gazing up into the darkness I saw myself as a creature driven and derided by vanity; and my eyes burned with anguish and anger.

D. H. LAWRENCE (1885–1930)

The Horse Dealer's Daughter

"Well, Mabel, and what are you going to do with yourself?" asked Joe, with foolish flippancy. He felt quite safe himself. Without listening for an answer, he turned aside, worked a grain of tobacco to the tip of his tongue, and spat it out. He did not care about anything, since he felt safe himself.

The three brothers and the sister sat round the desolate breakfast-table, attempting some sort of desultory consultation. The morning's post had given the final tap to the family fortunes, and all was over. The dreary dining-room itself, with its heavy mahogany furniture, looked as if it were waiting to be done away with.

But the consultation amounted to nothing. There was a strange air of ineffectuality about the three men, as they sprawled at table, smoking and reflecting vaguely on their own condition. The girl was alone, a rather short, sullen-looking young woman of twenty-seven. She did not share the same life as her brothers. She would have been good-looking, save for the impressive fixity of her face, 'bulldog,' as her brothers called it.

There was a confused tramping of horses' feet outside. The three men all sprawled round in their chairs to watch. Beyond the dark holly bushes that separated the strip of lawn from the high-road, they could see a cavalcade of shire horses swinging out of their own yard, being taken for exercise. This was the last time. These were the last horses that would go through their hands. The young men watched with critical, callous look. They were all frightened at the collapse of their lives, and the sense of disaster in which they were involved left them no inner freedom.

Yet they were three fine, well-set fellows enough. Joe, the eldest, was a man of thirty-three, broad and handsome in a hot, flushed way. His face was red, he twisted his black moustache over a thick finger, his eyes were shallow and restless. He had a sensual way of uncovering his teeth when he laughed, and his bearing was stupid. Now he watched the horses with a glazed look of helplessness in his eyes, a certain stupor of downfall.

The great draught-horses swung past. They were tied head to tail, four of them, and they heaved along to where a lane branched off from the high-road, planting their great hoofs floutingly in the fine black mud, swinging their great rounded haunches sumptuously, and trotting a few sudden steps as they were led into the lane, round the corner. Every movement showed a massive, slumbrous strength, and a stupidity which held them in subjection. The groom at the head looked back, jerking the leading rope. And the cavalcade moved out of sight up the lane, the tail of the last horse, bobbed up tight and stiff, held out taut from the swinging great haunches as they rocked behind the hedges in a motion-like sleep.

Joe watched with glazed hopeless eyes. The horses were almost like his own body to him. He felt he was done for now. Luckily he was engaged to a woman as old as himself, and therefore her father, who was steward of a neighbouring estate, would provide him with a job. He would marry and go into harness. His life was over, he would be a subject animal now.

He turned uneasily aside, the retreating steps of the horses echoing in his ears. Then, with foolish restlessness, he reached for the scraps of bacon-rind from the plates, and making a faint whistling sound, flung them to the terrier that lay against the fender. He watched the dog swallow them, and waited till the creature looked into his eyes. Then a faint grin came on his face, and in a high, foolish voice he said:

"You won't get much more bacon, shall you, you little b——?"

The dog faintly and dismally wagged its tail, then lowered its haunches, circled round, and lay down again.

There was another helpless silence at the table. Joe sprawled uneasily in his seat, not willing to go till the family conclave was dissolved. Fred Henry, the second brother, was erect, clean-limbed, alert. He had watched the passing of the horses with more *sang-froid*. If he was an animal, like Joe, he was an animal which controls, not one which is controlled. He was master of any horse, and he carried himself with a well-tempered air of mastery. But he was not master of the situations of life. He pushed his coarse brown moustache upwards, off his lip, and glanced irritably at his sister, who sat impassive and inscrutable.

"You'll go and stop with Lucy for a bit, shan't you?" he asked. The girl did not answer.

"I don't see what else you can do," persisted Fred Henry.

"Go as a skivvy,"[1] Joe interpolated laconically.

The girl did not move a muscle.

"If I was her, I should go in for training for a nurse," said Malcolm, the youngest of them all. He was the baby of the family, a young man of twenty-two, with a fresh, jaunty *museau*.[2]

But Mabel did not take any notice of him. They had talked at her and round her for so many years, that she hardly heard them at all.

The marble clock on the mantelpiece softly chimed the half-hour, the dog rose uneasily from the hearth-rug and looked at the party at the breakfast-table. But still they sat on in ineffectual conclave.

---

[1] A depreciatory term for a domestic servant.
[2] Slang for face or mug.

"Oh, all right," said Joe suddenly, apropos of nothing. "I'll get a move on."

He pushed back his chair, straddled his knees with a downward jerk, to get them free, in horsey fashion, and went to the fire. Still he did not go out of the room; he was curious to know what the others would do or say. He began to charge his pipe, looking down at the dog and saying in a high, affected voice:

"Going wi' me? Going wi' me are ter?[3] Tha'rt goin' further than tha counts on just now, dost hear?"

The dog faintly wagged its tail, the man stuck out his jaw and covered his pipe with his hands, and puffed intently, losing himself in the tobacco, looking down all the while at the dog with an absent brown eye. The dog looked up at him in mournful distrust. Joe stood with his knees stuck out, in real horsey fashion.

"Have you had a letter from Lucy?" Fred Henry asked of his sister.

"Last week," came the neutral reply.

"And what does she say?"

There was no answer.

"Does she *ask* you to go and stop there?" persisted Fred Henry.

"She says I can if I like."

"Well, then, you'd better. Tell her you'll come on Monday."

This was received in silence.

"That's what you'll do then, is it?" said Fred Henry, in some exasperation.

But she made no answer. There was a silence of futility and irritation in the room. Malcolm grinned fatuously.

"You'll have to make up your mind between now and next Wednesday," said Joe loudly, "or else find yourself lodgings on the kerbstone."

The face of the young woman darkened, but she sat on immutable.

"Here's Jack Fergusson!" exclaimed Malcolm, who was looking aimlessly out of the window.

"Where?" exclaimed Joe loudly.

"Just gone past."

"Coming in?"

Malcolm craned his neck to see the gate.

"Yes," he said.

There was a silence. Mabel sat on like one condemned, at the head of the table. Then a whistle was heard from the kitchen. The dog got up and barked sharply. Joe opened the door and shouted:

"Come on."

After a moment a young man entered. He was muffled up in overcoat and a purple woollen scarf, and his tweed cap, which he did not remove,

---

[3] "Going with me are you?"

was pulled down on his head. He was of medium height, his face was rather long and pale, his eyes looked tired.

"Hello, Jack! Well, Jack!" exclaimed Malcolm and Joe. Fred Henry merely said: "Jack."

"What's doing?" asked the newcomer, evidently addressing Fred Henry.

"Same. We've got to be out by Wednesday. Got a cold?"

"I have—got it bad, too."

"Why don't you stop in?"

"*Me* stop in? When I can't stand on my legs, perhaps I shall have a chance." The young man spoke huskily. He had a slight Scotch accent.

"It's a knock-out, isn't it," said Joe, boisterously, "if a doctor goes round croaking with a cold. Looks bad for the patients, doesn't it?"

The young doctor looked at him slowly.

"Anything the matter with *you*, then?" he asked sarcastically.

"Not as I know of. Damn your eyes, I hope not. Why?"

"I thought you were very concerned about the patients, wondered if you might be one yourself."

"Damn it, no, I've never been patient to no flaming doctor, and hope I never shall be," returned Joe.

At this point Mabel rose from the table, and they all seemed to become aware of her existence. She began putting the dishes together. The young doctor looked at her, but did not address her. He had not greeted her. She went out of the room with the tray, her face impassive and unchanged.

"When are you off then, all of you?" asked the doctor.

"I'm catching the eleven-forty," replied Malcolm. "Are you goin' down wi' th' trap,[4] Joe?"

"Yes, I've told you I'm going down wi' th' trap, haven't I?"

"We'd better be getting her in then. So long, Jack, if I don't see you before I go," said Malcolm, shaking hands.

He went out, followed by Joe, who seemed to have his tail between his legs.

"Well, this is the devil's own," exclaimed the doctor, when he was left alone with Fred Henry. "Going before Wednesday, are you?"

"That's the orders," replied the other.

"Where, to Northampton?"

"That's it."

"The devil!" exclaimed Fergusson, with quiet chagrin.

And there was silence between the two.

"All settled up, are you?" asked Fergusson.

"About."

There was another pause.

---

[4] A small carriage.

"Well, I shall miss yer, Freddy, boy," said the young doctor.

"And I shall miss thee, Jack," returned the other.

"Miss you like hell," mused the doctor.

Fred Henry turned aside. There was nothing to say. Mabel came in again, to finish clearing the table.

"What are *you* going to do, then, Miss Pervin?" asked Fergusson. "Going to your sister's, are you?"

Mabel looked at him with her steady, dangerous eyes, that always made him uncomfortable, unsettling his superficial ease.

"No," she said.

"Well, what in the name of fortune *are* you going to do? Say what you mean to do," cried Fred Henry, with futile intensity.

But she only averted her head, and continued her work. She folded the white table-cloth, and put on the chenille cloth.

"The sulkiest bitch that ever trod!" muttered her brother.

But she finished her task with perfectly impassive face, the young doctor watching her interestedly all the while. Then she went out.

Fred Henry stared after her, clenching his lips, his blue eyes fixing in sharp antagonism, as he made a grimace of sour exasperation.

"You could bray her into bits, and that's all you'd get out of her," he said, in a small, narrowed tone.

The doctor smiled faintly.

"What's she *going* to do, then?" he asked.

"Strike me if *I* know!" returned the other.

There was a pause. Then the doctor stirred.

"I'll be seeing you to-night, shall I?" he said to his friend.

"Ay—where's it to be? Are we going over to Jessdale?"

"I don't know. I've got such a cold on me. I'll come round to the 'Moon and Stars,' anyway."

"Let Lizzie and May miss their night for once, eh?"

"That's it—if I feel as I do now."

"All's one——"

The two young men went through the passage and down to the back door together. The house was large, but it was servant-less now, and desolate. At the back was a small bricked houseyard and beyond that a big square, gravelled fine and red, and having stables on two sides. Sloping, dank, winter-dark fields stretched away on the open sides.

But the stables were empty. Joseph Pervin, the father of the family, had been a man of no education, who had become a fairly large horse dealer. The stables had been full of horses, there was a great turmoil and come-and-go of horses and of dealers and grooms. Then the kitchen was full of servants. But of late things had declined. The old man had married a second time, to retrieve his fortunes. Now he was dead and everything was gone to the dogs, there was nothing but debt and threatening.

For months, Mabel had been servant-less in the big house, keeping the home together in penury for her ineffectual brothers. She had kept house for ten years. But previously it was with unstinted means. Then, however brutal and coarse everything was, the sense of money had kept her proud, confident. The men might be foul-mouthed, the women in the kitchen might have bad reputations, her brothers might have illegitimate children. But so long as there was money, the girl felt herself established, and brutally proud, reserved.

No company came to the house, save dealers and coarse men. Mabel had no associates of her own sex, after her sister went away. But she did not mind. She went regularly to church, she attended to her father. And she lived in the memory of her mother, who had died when she was fourteen, and whom she had loved. She had loved her father, too, in a different way, depending upon him, and feeling secure in him, until at the age of fifty-four he married again. And then she had set hard against him. Now he had died and left them all hopelessly in debt.

She had suffered badly during the period of poverty. Nothing, however, could shake the curious, sullen, animal pride that dominated each member of the family. Now, for Mabel, the end had come. Still she would not cast about her. She would follow her own way just the same. She would always hold the keys of her own situation. Mindless and persistent, she endured from day to day. Why should she think? Why should she answer anybody? It was enough that this was the end, and there was no way out. She need not pass any more darkly along the main street of the small town, avoiding every eye. She need not demean herself any more, going into the shops and buying the cheapest food. This was at an end. She thought of nobody, not even of herself. Mindless and persistent, she seemed in a sort of ecstasy to be coming nearer to her fulfillment, her own glorification, approaching her dead mother, who was glorified.

In the afternoon she took a little bag, with shears and sponge and a small scrubbing-brush, and went out. It was a grey, wintry day, with saddened, dark green fields and an atmosphere blackened by the smoke of foundries not far off. She went quickly, darkly along the causeway, heeding nobody, through the town to the churchyard.

There she always felt secure, as if no one could see her, although as a matter of fact she was exposed to the state of everyone who passed along under the churchyard wall. Nevertheless, once under the shadow of the great looming church, among the graves, she felt immune from the world, reserved within the thick churchyard wall as in another country.

Carefully she clipped the grass from the grave, and arranged the pinky white, small chrysanthemums in the tin cross. When this was done, she took an empty jar from a neighbouring grave, brought water, and carefully, most scrupulously sponged the marble headstone and the coping-stone.[5]

It gave her sincere satisfaction to do this. She felt in immediate contact with the world of her mother. She took minute pains, went through the park in a state bordering on pure happiness, as if in performing this task she came into a subtle, intimate connection with her mother. For the life she followed here in the world was far less real than the world of death she inherited from her mother.

The doctor's house was just by the church. Fergusson, being a mere hired assistant, was slave to the country-side. As he hurried now to attend to the out-patients in the surgery, glancing across the graveyard with his quick eye, he saw the girl at her task at the grave. She seemed so intent and remote, it was like looking into another world. Some mystical element was touched in him. He slowed down as he walked, watching her as if spellbound.

She lifted her eyes, feeling him looking. Their eyes met. And each looked again at once, each feeling, in some way, found out by the other. He lifted his cap and passed on down the road. There remained distinct in his consciousness, like a vision, the memory of her face, lifted from the tombstone in the churchyard, and looking at him with slow, large, portentous eyes. It *was* portentous, her face. It seemed to mesmerise him. There was a heavy power in her eyes which laid hold of his whole being, as if he had drunk some powerful drug. He had been feeling weak and done before. Now the life came back into him, he felt delivered from his own fretted, daily self.

He finished his duties at the surgery as quickly as might be, hastily filling up the bottles of the waiting people with cheap drugs. Then, in perpetual haste, he set off again to visit several cases in another part of his round, before tea-time. At all times he preferred to walk if he could, but particularly when he was not well. He fancied the motion restored him.

The afternoon was falling. It was grey, deadened, and wintry, with a slow, moist, heavy coldness sinking in and deadening all the faculties. But why should he think or notice? He hastily climbed the hill and turned across the dark green fields, following the black cinder-track. In the distance, across a shallow dip in the country, the small town was clustered like smouldering ash, a tower, a spire, a heap of low, raw, extinct houses. And on the nearest fringe of the town, sloping into the dip, was Oldmeadow, the Pervins' house. He could see the stables and the outbuildings distinctly, as they lay towards him on the slope. Well, he would not go there many more times! Another resource would be lost to him, another place gone: the only company he cared for in the

---

[5] The stone covering the headstone.

alien, ugly little town he was losing. Nothing but work, drudgery, constant hastening from dwelling to dwelling among the colliers[6] and the iron-workers. It wore him out, but at the same time he had a craving for it. It was a stimulant to him to be in the homes of the working people, moving, as it were, through the innermost body of their life. His nerves were excited and gratified. He could come so near, into the very lives of the rough, inarticulate, powerfully emotional men and women. He grumbled, he said he hated the hellish hole. But as a matter of fact it excited him, the contact with the rough, strongly-feeling people was a stimulant applied direct to his nerves.

Below Oldmeadow, in the green, shallow, soddened hollow of field, lay a square, deep pond. Roving across the landscape, the doctor's quick eye detected a figure in black passing through the gate of the field, down towards the pond. He looked again. It would be Mabel Pervin. His mind suddenly became alive and attentive.

Why was she going down there? He pulled up on the path on the slope above, and stood staring. He could just make sure of the small black figure moving in the hollow of the failing day. He seemed to see her in the midst of such obscurity, that he was like a clairvoyant, seeing rather with the mind's eye than with ordinary sight. Yet he could see her positively enough, whilst he kept his eye attentive. He felt, if he looked away from her, in the thick, ugly falling dusk, he would lose her altogether.

He followed her minutely as she moved, direct and intent, like something transmitted rather than stirring in voluntary activity, straight down the field towards the pond. There she stood on the bank for a moment. She never raised her head. Then she waded slowly into the water.

He stood motionless as the small black figure walked slowly and deliberately towards the centre of the pond, very slowly, gradually moving deeper into the motionless water, and still moving forward as the water got up to her breast. Then he could see her no more in the dusk of the dead afternoon.

"There!" he exclaimed. "Would you believe it?"

And he hastened straight down, running over the wet, soddened fields, pushing through the hedges, down into the depression of callous wintry obscurity. It took him several minutes to come to the pond. He stood on the bank, breathing heavily. He could see nothing. His eyes seemed to penetrate the dead water. Yes, perhaps that was the dark shadow of her black clothing beneath the surface of the water.

He slowly ventured into the pond. The bottom was deep, soft clay, he sank in, and the water clasped dead cold round his legs. As he stirred he could smell the cold, rotten clay that fouled up into the water. It was

---

[6] Coal miners.

objectionable in his lungs. Still, repelled and yet not heeding, he moved deeper into the pond. The cold water rose over his thighs, over his loins, upon his abdomen. The lower part of his body was all sunk in the hideous cold element. And the bottom was so deeply soft and uncertain, he was afraid of pitching with his mouth underneath. He could not swim, and was afraid.

He crouched a little, spreading his hands under the water and moving them round, trying to feel for her. The dead cold pond swayed upon his chest. He moved again, a little deeper, and again, with his hands underneath, he felt all around under the water. And he touched her clothing. But it evaded his fingers. He made a desperate effort to grasp it.

And so doing he lost his balance and went under, horribly, suffocating in the foul earthy water, struggling madly for a few moments. At last, after what seemed an eternity, he got his footing, rose again into the air and looked around. He gasped, and knew he was in the world. Then he looked at the water. She had risen near him. He grasped her clothing, and drawing her nearer, turned to take his way to land again.

He went very slowly, carefully, absorbed in the slow progress. He rose higher, climbing out of the pond. The water was now only about his legs; he was thankful, full of relief to be out of the clutches of the pond. He lifted her and staggered on to the bank, out of the horror of wet, grey clay.

He laid her down on the bank. She was quite unconscious and running with water. He made the water come from her mouth, he worked to restore her. He did not have to work very long before he could feel the breathing begin again in her; she was breathing naturally. He worked a little longer. He could feel her live beneath his hands; she was coming back. He wiped her face, wrapped her in his overcoat, looked round into the dim, dark grey world, then lifted her and staggered down the bank and across the fields.

It seemed an unthinkably long way, and his burden so heavy he felt he would never get to the house. But at last he was in the stable-yard, and then in the house-yard. He opened the door and went into the house. In the kitchen he laid her down on the hearth-rug and called. The house was empty. But the fire was burning in the grate.

Then again he kneeled to attend to her. She was breathing regularly, her eyes were wide open and as if conscious, but there seemed something missing in her look. She was conscious in herself, but unconscious of her surroundings.

He ran upstairs, took blankets from a bed, and put them before the fire to warm. Then he removed her saturated, earthy-smelling clothing, rubbed her dry with a towel, and wrapped her naked in the blankets. Then he went into the dining-room, to look for spirits. There was a little whisky. He drank a gulp himself, and put some into her mouth.

The effect was instantaneous. She looked full into his face, as if she had been seeing him for some time, and yet had only just become conscious of him.

"Dr. Fergusson?" she said.

"What?" he answered.

He was divesting himself of his coat, intending to find some dry clothing upstairs. He could not bear the smell of the dead, clayey water, and he was mortally afraid for his own health.

"What did I do?" she asked.

"Walked into the pond," he replied. He had begun to shudder like one sick, and could hardly attend to her. Her eyes remained full on him, he seemed to be going dark in his mind, looking back at her helplessly. The shuddering became quieter in him, his life came back to him, dark and unknowing, but strong again.

"Was I out of my mind?" she asked, while her eyes were fixed on him all the time.

"Maybe, for the moment," he replied. He felt quiet, because his strength had come back. The strange fretful strain had left him.

"Am I out of my mind now?" she asked.

"Are you?" he reflected a moment. "No," he answered truthfully, "I don't see that you are." He turned his face aside. He was afraid now, because he felt dazed, and felt dimly that her power was stronger than his, in this issue. And she continued to look at him fixedly all the time. "Can you tell me where I shall find some dry things to put on?" he asked.

"Did you dive into the pond for me?" she asked.

"No," he answered. "I walked in. But I went in overhead as well."

There was silence for a moment. He hesitated. He very much wanted to go upstairs to get into dry clothing. But there was another desire in him. And she seemed to hold him. His will seemed to have gone to sleep, and left him, standing there slack before her. But he felt warm inside himself. He did not shudder at all, though his clothes were sodden on him.

"Why did you?" she asked.

"Because I didn't want you to do such a foolish thing," he said.

"It wasn't foolish," she said, still gazing at him as she lay on the floor, with a sofa cushion under her head. "It was the right thing to do. *I* knew best, then."

"I'll go and shift these wet things," he said. But still he had not the power to move out of her presence, until she sent him. It was as if she had the life of his body in her hands, and he could not extricate himself. Or perhaps he did not want to.

Suddenly she sat up. Then she became aware of her own immediate condition. She felt the blankets about her, she knew her own limbs. For a moment it seemed as if her reason were going. She looked round, with wild eye, as if seeking something. He stood still with fear. She saw her clothing lying scattered.

"Who undressed me?" she asked, her eyes resting full and inevitable on his face.

"I did," he replied, "to bring you round."

For some moments she sat and gazed at him awfully, her lips parted.

"Do you love me, then?" she asked.

He only stood and stared at her, fascinated. His soul seemed to melt.

She shuffled forward on her knees, and put her arms round him, round his legs, as he stood there, pressing her breasts against his knees and thighs, clutching him with strange, convulsive certainty, pressing his thighs against her, drawing him to her face, her throat, as she looked up at him with flaring, humble eyes of transfiguration, triumphant in first possession.

"You love me," she murmured, in strange transport, yearning and triumphant and confident. "You love me. I know you love me, I know."

And she was passionately kissing his knees, through the wet clothing, passionately and indiscriminately kissing his knees, his legs, as if unaware of everything.

He looked down at the tangled wet hair, the wild, bare, animal shoulders. He was amazed, bewildered, and afraid. He had never thought of loving her. He had never wanted to love her. When he rescued her and restored her, he was a doctor, and she was a patient. He had had no single personal thought of her. Nay, this introduction of the personal element was very distasteful to him, a violation of his professional honour. It was horrible to have her there embracing his knees. It was horrible. He revolted from it, violently. And yet—and yet—he had not the power to break away.

She looked at him again, with the same supplication of powerful love, and that same transcendent, frightening light of triumph. In view of the delicate flame which seemed to come from her face like a light, he was powerless. And yet he had never intended to love her. He had never intended. And something stubborn in him could not give way.

"You love me," she repeated, in a murmur of deep, rhapsodic assurance. "You love me."

Her hands were drawing him, drawing him down to her. He was afraid, even a little horrified. For he had, really, no intention of loving her. Yet her hands were drawing him towards her. He put out his hand quickly to steady himself, and grasped her bare shoulder. A flame seemed to burn the hand that grasped her soft shoulder. He had no intention of loving her: his whole will was against his yielding. It was horrible. And yet wonderful was the touch of her shoulders, beautiful the shining of her face. Was she perhaps mad? He had a horror of yielding to her. Yet something in him ached also.

He had been staring away at the door, away from her. But his hand remained on her shoulder. She had gone suddenly very still. He looked down at her. Her eyes were now wide with fear, with doubt, the light was dying from her face, a shadow of terrible greyness was returning. He could not bear the touch of her eyes' question upon him, and the look of death behind the question.

With an inward groan he gave way, and let his heart yield towards her. A sudden gentle smile came on his face. And her eyes, which never left his face, slowly, slowly filled with tears. He watched the strange water rise in her eyes, like some slow fountain coming up. And his heart seemed to burn and melt away in his breast.

He could not bear to look at her any more. He dropped on his knees and caught her head with his arms and pressed her face against his throat. She was very still. His heart, which seemed to have broken, was burning with a kind of agony in his breast. And he felt her slow, hot tears wetting his throat. But he could not move.

He felt the hot tears wet his neck and the hollows of his neck, and he remained motionless, suspended through one of man's eternities. Only now it had become indispensable to him to have her face pressed close to him; he could never let her go again. He could never let her head go away from the close clutch of his arm. He wanted to remain like that for ever, with his heart hurting him in a pain that was also life to him. Without knowing, he was looking down on her damp, soft brown hair.

Then, as it were suddenly, he smelt the horrid stagnant smell of that water. And at the same moment she drew away from him and looked at him. Her eyes were wistful and unfathomable. He was afraid of them, and he fell to kissing her, not knowing what he was doing. He wanted her eyes not to have that terrible, wistful, unfathomable look.

When she turned her face to him again, a faint delicate flush was glowing, and there was again dawning that terrible shining of joy in her eyes, which really terrified him, and yet which he now wanted to see, because he feared the look of doubt still more.

"You love me?" she said, rather faltering.

"Yes." The word cost him a painful effort. Not because it wasn't true. But because it was too newly true, the *saying* seemed to tear open again his newly-torn heart. And he hardly wanted it to be true, even now.

She lifted her face to him, and he bent forward and kissed her on the mouth, gently, with the one kiss that is an eternal pledge. And as he kissed her his heart strained again in his breast. He never intended to love her. But now it was over. He had crossed over the gulf to her, and all that he had left behind had shrivelled and become void.

After the kiss, her eyes again slowly filled with tears. She sat still, away from him, with her face drooped aside, and her hands folded in her lap. The tears fell very slowly. There was complete silence. He too sat there motionless and silent on the hearth-rug. The strange pain of his heart that was broken seemed to consume him. That he should love her? That this was love! That he should be ripped open in this way! Him, a doctor! How they would all jeer if they knew! It was agony to him to think they might know.

In the curious naked pain of the thought he looked again to her. She was sitting there drooped into a muse. He saw a tear fall, and his heart flared hot. He saw for the first time that one of her shoulders was quite uncovered, one arm bare, he could see one of her small breasts; dimly, because it had become almost dark in the room.

"Why are you crying?" he asked, in an altered voice.

She looked up at him, and behind her tears the consciousness of her situation for the first time brought a dark look of shame to her eyes.

"I'm not crying, really," she said, watching him, half frightened.

He reached his hand, and softly closed it on her bare arm.

"I love you! I love you!" he said in a soft, low vibrating voice, unlike himself.

She shrank, and dropped her head. The soft, penetrating grip of his hand on her arm distressed her. She looked up at him.

"I want to go," she said. "I want to go and get you some dry things."

"Why?" he said. "I'm all right."

"But I want to go," she said. "And I want you to change your things."

He released her arm, and she wrapped herself in the blanket, looking at him rather frightened. And still she did not rise.

"Kiss me," she said wistfully.

He kissed her, but briefly, half in anger.

Then, after a second, she rose nervously, all mixed up in the blanket. He watched her in her confusion as she tried to extricate herself and wrap herself up so that she could walk. He watched her relentlessly, as she knew. And as she went, the blanket trailing, and as he saw a glimpse of her feet and her white leg, he tried to remember her as she was when he had wrapped her in the blanket. But then he didn't want to remember, because she had been nothing to him then, and his nature revolted from remembering her as she was when she was nothing to him.

A tumbling, muffled noise from within the dark house startled him. Then he heard her voice: "There are clothes." He rose and went to the foot of the stairs, and gathered up the garments she had thrown down. Then he came back to the fire, to rub himself down and dress. He grinned at his own appearance when he had finished.

The fire was sinking, so he put on coal. The house was now quite dark, save for the light of a street-lamp that shone in faintly from beyond the holly trees. He lit the gas with matches he found on the mantelpiece. Then he emptied the pockets of his own clothes, and threw all his wet things in a heap into the scullery. After which he gathered up her sodden clothes, gently, and put them in a separate heap on the coppertop in the scullery.

It was six o'clock on the clock. His own watch had stopped. He ought to go back to the surgery. He waited, and still she did not come down. So he went to the foot of the stairs and called:

"I shall have to go."

Almost immediately he heard her coming down. She had on her best dress of black voile, and her hair was tidy, but still damp. She looked at him—and in spite of herself, smiled.

"I don't like you in those clothes," she said.

"Do I look a sight?" he answered.

They were shy of one another.

"I'll make you some tea," she said.

"No, I must go."

"Must you?" And she looked at him again with the wide, strained, doubtful eyes. And again, from the pain of his breast, he knew how he loved her. He went and bent to kiss her, gently, passionately, with his heart's painful kiss.

"And my hair smells so horrible," she murmured in distraction. "And I'm so awful, I'm so awful! Oh no, I'm too awful." And she broke into bitter, heartbroken sobbing. "You can't want to love me, I'm horrible."

"Don't be silly, don't be silly," he said, trying to comfort her, kissing her, holding her in his arms. "I want you, I want to marry you, we're going to be married, quickly, quickly—to-morrow if I can."

But she only sobbed terribly, and cried:

"I feel awful. I feel awful. I feel I'm horrible to you."

"No, I want you, I want you," was all he answered, blindly, with that terrible intonation which frightened her almost more than her horror lest he should *not* want her.

KATHERINE ANNE PORTER (1890–1980)

The Jilting of Granny Weatherall

She flicked her wrist neatly out of Doctor Harry's pudgy careful fingers and pulled the sheet up to her chin. The brat ought to be in knee breeches. Doctoring around the country with spectacles on his nose! "Get along now, take your schoolbooks and go. There's nothing wrong with me."

Doctor Harry spread a warm paw like a cushion on her forehead where the forked green vein danced and made her eyelids twitch. "Now, now, be a good girl, and we'll have you up in no time."

"That's no way to speak to a woman nearly eighty years old just because she's down. I'd have you respect your elders, young man."

"Well, Missy, excuse me." Doctor Harry patted her cheek. "But I've got to warn you, haven't I? You're a marvel, but you must be careful or you're going to be good and sorry."

"Don't tell me what I'm going to be. I'm on my feet now, morally speaking. It's Cornelia. I had to go to bed to get rid of her."

Her bones felt loose, and floated around in her skin, and Doctor Harry floated like a balloon around the foot of the bed. He floated and pulled down his waistcoat and swung his glasses on a cord. "Well, stay where you are, it certainly can't hurt you."

"Get along and doctor your sick," said Granny Weatherall. "Leave a well woman alone. I'll call for you when I want you. . . . Where were you forty years ago when I pulled through milk-leg[1] and double pneumonia? You weren't even born. Don't let Cornelia lead you on," she shouted, because Doctor Harry appeared to float up to the ceiling and out. "I pay my own bills, and I don't throw my money away on nonsense!"

She meant to wave good-by, but it was too much trouble. Her eyes closed of themselves, it was like a dark curtain drawn around the bed. The pillow rose and floated under her, pleasant as a hammock in a light wind. She listened to the leaves rustling outside the window. No, somebody was swishing newspapers: no, Cornelia and Doctor

---

[1] *milk-leg,* a painful swelling of the legs sometimes occurring in women after childbirth.

Harry were whispering together. She leaped broad awake, thinking they whispered in her ear.

"She was never like this, *never* like this!" "Well, what can we expect?" "Yes, eighty years old. . . ."

Well, and what if she was? She still had ears. It was like Cornelia to whisper around doors. She always kept things secret in such a public way. She was always being tactful and kind. Cornelia was dutiful; that was the trouble with her. Dutiful and good: "So good and dutiful," said Granny, "that I'd like to spank her." She saw herself spanking Cornelia and making a fine job of it.

"What'd you say, Mother?"

Granny felt her face tying up in hard knots.

"Can't a body think, I'd like to know?"

"I thought you might want something."

"I do. I want a lot of things. First off, go away and don't whisper."

She lay and drowsed, hoping in her sleep that the children would keep out and let her rest a minute. It had been a long day. Not that she was tired. It was always pleasant to snatch a minute now and then. There was always so much to be done, let me see: tomorrow.

Tomorrow was far away and there was nothing to trouble about. Things were finished somehow when the time came; thank God there was always a little margin over for peace: then a person could spread out the plan of life and tuck in the edges orderly. It was good to have everything clean and folded away, with the hair brushes and tonic bottles sitting straight on the white embroidered linen: the day started without fuss and the pantry shelves laid out with rows of jelly glasses and brown jugs and white stone-china jars with blue whirligigs and words painted on them: coffee, tea, sugar, ginger, cinnamon, allspice: and the bronze clock with the lion on top nicely dusted off. The dust that lion could collect in twenty-four hours! The box in the attic with all those letters tied up, well, she'd have to go through that tomorrow. All those letters—George's letters and John's letters and her letters to them both—lying around for the children to find afterwards made her uneasy. Yes, that would be tomorrow's business. No use to let them know how silly she had been once.

While she was rummaging around she found death in her mind and it felt clammy and unfamiliar. She had spent so much time preparing for death there was no need for bringing it up again. Let it take care of itself now. When she was sixty she had felt very old, finished, and went around making farewell trips to see her children and grandchildren, with a secret in her mind: This is the very last of your mother, children! Then she made her will and came down with a long fever. That was all just a notion like a lot of other things, but it was lucky too, for she had once for all got over the idea of dying for a long time. Now she couldn't be worried. She hoped she had better sense now. Her father had lived to be one hundred and two years old and had drunk a noggin[2] of strong hot toddy[3] on his last birthday. He told the reporters it was his daily habit, and he owed his long life to that. He had made quite a scandal and was very pleased about it. She believed she'd just plague Cornelia a little.

"Cornelia! Cornelia!" No footsteps, but a sudden hand on her cheek. "Bless you, where have you been?"

"Here, mother."

"Well, Cornelia, I want a noggin of hot toddy."

"Are you cold, darling?"

"I'm chilly, Cornelia. Lying in bed stops the circulation. I must have told you that a thousand times."

Well, she could just hear Cornelia telling her husband that Mother was getting a little childish and they'd have to humor her. The thing that most annoyed her was that Cornelia thought she was deaf, dumb, and blind. Little hasty glances and tiny gestures tossed around her and over her head saying, "Don't cross her, let her have her way, she's eighty years old," and she sitting there as if she lived in a thin glass cage. Sometimes Granny almost made up her mind to pack up and move back to her own house where nobody could remind her every minute that she was old. Wait, wait, Cornelia, till your own children whisper behind your back!

In her day she had kept a better house and had got more work done. She wasn't too old yet for Lydia to be driving eighty miles for advice when one of the children jumped the track, and Jimmy still dropped in and talked things over: "Now, Mammy, you've a good business head, I want to know what you think of this? . . ." Old. Cornelia couldn't change the furniture around without asking. Little things, little things! They had been so sweet when they were little. Granny wished the old days were back again with the children young and everything to be done over. It had been a hard pull, but not too much for her. When she thought of all the food she had cooked, and all the clothes she had cut and sewed, and all the gardens she had made—well, the children showed it. There they were, made out of her, and they couldn't get away from that. Sometimes she wanted to see John again and point to them and say, Well, I didn't do so badly, did I? But that would have to wait. That was for tomorrow. She used to think of him as a man, but now all the children were older than their father, and he would be a child beside her if she saw him now. It seemed strange and there was something wrong in the idea. Why, he couldn't possibly recognize her. She had fenced in a hundred

---

[2] *noggin,* a small mug.
[3] *hot toddy,* a drink consisting of brandy or other liquor mixed with hot water, lemon, sugar, and spices.

acres once, digging the post holes herself and clamping the wires with just a Negro boy to help. That changed a woman. John would be looking for a young woman with the peaked Spanish comb in her hair and the painted fan. Digging post holes changed a woman. Riding country roads in the winter when women had their babies was another thing: sitting up nights with sick horses and sick Negroes and sick children and hardly ever losing one. John, I hardly ever lost one of them! John would see that in a minute, that would be something he could understand, she wouldn't have to explain anything!

It made her feel like rolling up her sleeves and putting the whole place to rights again. No matter if Cornelia was determined to be everywhere at once, there were a great many things left undone on this place. She would start tomorrow and do them. It was good to be strong enough for everything, even if all you made melted and changed and slipped under your hands, so that by the time you finished you almost forgot what you were working for. What was it I set out to do? she asked herself intently, but she could not remember. A fog rose over the valley, she saw it marching across the creek swallowing the trees and moving up the hill like an army of ghosts. Soon it would be at the near edge of the orchard, and then it was time to go in and light the lamps. Come in, children, don't stay out in the night air.

Lighting the lamps had been beautiful. The children huddled up to her and breathed like little calves waiting at the bars in the twilight. Their eyes followed the match and watched the flame rise and settle in a blue curve, then they moved away from her. The lamp was lit, they didn't have to be scared and hang on to mother any more. Never, never, never more. God, for all my life I thank Thee. Without Thee, my God, I could never have done it. Hail, Mary, full of grace.

I want you to pick all the fruit this year and see that nothing is wasted. There's always someone who can use it. Don't let good things rot for want of using. You waste life when you waste good food. Don't let things get lost. It's bitter to lose things. Now, don't let me get to thinking, not when I am tired and taking a little nap before supper. . . .

The pillow rose about her shoulders and pressed against her heart and the memory was being squeezed out of it: oh, push down the pillow, somebody: it would smother her if she tried to hold it. Such a fresh breeze blowing and such a green day with no threats in it. But he had not come, just the same. What does a woman do when she has put on the white veil and set out the white cake for a man and he doesn't come? She tried to remember. No, I swear he never harmed me but in that. He never harmed me but in that . . . and what if he did? There was the day, the day, but a whirl of dark smoke rose and covered it, crept up and over into the bright field where everything was planted so carefully in orderly rows. That was hell, she knew hell when she saw it. For sixty years she had prayed against remembering him and against losing her soul in the deep pit of hell, and now the two things were mingled in one and the thought of him was a smoky cloud from hell that moved and crept in her head when she had just got rid of Doctor Harry and was trying to rest a minute. Wounded vanity, Ellen, said a sharp voice in the top of her mind. Don't let your wounded vanity get the upper hand of you. Plenty of girls get jilted. You were jilted, weren't you? Then stand up to it. Her eyelids wavered and let in streamers of blue-gray light like tissue paper over her eyes. She must get up and pull the shades down or she'd never sleep. She was in bed again and the shades were not down. How could that happen? Better turn over, hide from the light, sleeping in the light gave you nightmares. "Mother, how do you feel now?" and a stinging wetness on her forehead. But I don't like having my face washed in cold water!

Hapsy? George? Lydia? Jimmy? No, Cornelia, and her features were swollen and full of little puddles. "They're coming, darling, they'll all be here soon." Go wash your face, child, you look funny.

Instead of obeying, Cornelia knelt down and put her head on the pillow. She seemed to be talking but there was no sound. "Well, are you tongue-tied? Whose birthday is it? Are you going to give a party?"

Cornelia's mouth moved urgently in strange shapes. "Don't do that, you bother me, daughter."

"Oh, no, Mother. Oh, no. . . ."

Nonsense. It was strange about children. They disputed your every word. "No what, Cornelia?"

"Here's Doctor Harry."

"I won't see that boy again. He just left five minutes ago."

"That was this morning, Mother. It's night now. Here's the nurse."

"This is Doctor Harry, Mrs. Weatherall. I never saw you look so young and happy!"

"Ah, I'll never be young again—but I'd be happy if they'd let me lie in peace and get rested."

She thought she spoke up loudly, but no one answered. A warm weight on her forehead, a warm bracelet on her wrist, and a breeze went on whispering, trying to tell her something. A shuffle of leaves in the everlasting hand of God, He blew on them and they danced and rattled. "Mother, don't mind, we're going to give you a little hypodermic." "Look here, daughter, how do ants get in this bed? I saw sugar ants yesterday." Did you send for Hapsy too?

It was Hapsy she really wanted. She had to go a long way back through a great many rooms to find Hapsy standing with a baby on her arm. She seemed to herself to be Hapsy also, and the baby on Hapsy's arm was Hapsy and himself and herself, all at once, and there was no surprise in the meeting. Then Hapsy melted from within and turned flimsy as gray gauze and the baby was a gauzy shadow, and Hapsy came up close and said, "I thought you'd never come," and looked at her very searchingly and said, "You haven't changed a bit!" They leaned forward to kiss, when Cornelia began whispering from a long way off, "Oh, is there anything you want to tell me? Is there anything I can do for you?"

Yes, she had changed her mind after sixty years and she would like to see George. I want you to find George. Find him and be sure to tell him I forgot him. I want him to know I had my husband just the same and my children and my house like any other woman. A good house too and a good husband that I loved and fine children out of him. Better than I hoped for even. Tell him I was given back everything he took away and more. Oh, no, oh, God, no, there was something else besides the house and the man and the children. Oh, surely they were not all? What was it? Something not given back. . . . Her breath crowded down under her ribs and grew into a monstrous frightening shape with cutting edges; it bored up into her head, and the agony was unbelievable: Yes, John, get the Doctor now, no more talk, my time has come.

When this one was born it should be the last. The last. It should have been born first, for it was the one she had truly wanted. Everything came in good time. Nothing left out, left over. She was strong, in three days she would be as well as ever. Better. A woman needed milk in her to have her full health.

"Mother, do you hear me?"

"I've been telling you—"

"Mother, Father Connolly's here."

"I went to Holy Communion only last week. Tell him I'm not so sinful as all that."

"Father just wants to speak to you."

He could speak as much as he pleased. It was like him to drop in and inquire about her soul as if it were a teething baby, and then stay on for a cup of tea and a round of cards and gossip. He always had a funny story of some sort, usually about an Irishman who made his little mistakes and confessed them, and the point lay in some absurd thing he would blurt out in the confessional showing his struggles between native piety and original sin. Granny felt easy about her soul. Cornelia, where are your manners? Give Father Connolly a chair. She had her secret comfortable understanding with a few favorite saints who cleared a straight road to God for her. All as surely signed and sealed as the papers for the new Forty Acres. Forever . . . heirs and assigns forever. Since the day the wedding cake was not cut, but thrown out and wasted. The whole bottom dropped out of the world, and there she was blind and sweating with nothing under her feet and the walls falling away. His hand had caught her under the breast, she had not fallen, there was the freshly polished floor with the green rug on it, just as before. He had cursed like a sailor's parrot and said, "I'll kill him for you." Don't lay a hand on him, for my sake leave something to God. "Now, Ellen, you must believe what I tell you. . . ."

So there was nothing, nothing to worry about any more, except sometimes in the night one of the children screamed in a nightmare, and they both hustled out shaking and hunting for the matches and calling, "There, wait a minute, here we are!" John, get the doctor now, Hapsy's time has come. But there was Hapsy standing by the bed in a white cap. "Cornelia, tell Hapsy to take off her cap. I can't see her plain."

Her eyes opened very wide and the room stood out like a picture she had seen somewhere. Dark colors with the shadows rising towards the ceiling in long angles. The tall black dresser gleamed with nothing on it but John's picture, enlarged from a little one, with John's eyes very black when they should have been blue. You never saw him, so how do you know how he looked? But the man insisted the copy was perfect, it was very rich and handsome. For a picture, yes, but it's not my husband. The table by the bed had a linen cover and a candle and a crucifix. The light was blue from Cornelia's silk lampshades. No sort of light at all, just frippery. You had to live forty years with kerosene lamps to appreciate honest electricity. She felt very strong and she saw Doctor Harry with a rosy nimbus around him.

"You look like a saint, Doctor Harry, and I vow that's as near as you'll ever come to it."

"She's saying something."

"I heard you, Cornelia. What's all this carrying-on?"

"Father Connolly's saying—"

Cornelia's voice staggered and bumped like a cart in a bad road. It rounded corners and turned back again and arrived nowhere. Granny stepped up in the cart very lightly and reached for the reins, but a man sat beside her and she knew him by his hands, driving the cart. She did not look in his face, for she knew without seeing, but looked instead down the road where the trees leaned over and bowed to each other and a thousand birds were singing a Mass. She felt like singing too, but she put her hand in the bosom of her dress and pulled out a rosary, and Father Connolly murmured Latin in a very solemn voice and tickled her feet. My God, will you stop that nonsense? I'm a married woman. What if he did run away and leave me to face the priest by myself? I found another a whole world better. I wouldn't have exchanged my husband for anybody except St. Michael himself, and you may tell him that for me with a thank you in the bargain.

Light flashed on her closed eyelids, and a deep roaring shook her. Cornelia, is that lightning? I hear thunder. There's going to be a storm. Close all the windows. Call the children in. . . . "Mother, here we are, all of us." "Is that you, Hapsy?" "Oh, no, I'm Lydia. We drove as fast as we could." Their faces drifted above her, drifted away. The rosary fell out of her hands and Lydia put it back. Jimmy tried to help, their hands fumbled together, and Granny closed two fingers around Jimmy's thumb. Beads wouldn't do, it must be something alive. She was so amazed her thoughts ran round and round. So, my dear Lord, this is my death and I wasn't even thinking about it. My children have come to see me die. But I can't, it's not time. Oh, I always hated surprises. I wanted to give Cornelia the amethyst set— Cornelia, you're to have the amethyst set, but Hapsy's to wear it when she wants, and, Doctor Harry, do shut up. Nobody sent for you. Oh, my dear Lord, do wait a minute. I meant to do something about the Forty Acres, Jimmy doesn't need it and Lydia will later on, with that worthless husband of hers. I meant to finish the altar cloth and send six bottles of wine to Sister Borgia for her dyspepsia.[4] I want to send six bottles of wine to Sister Borgia, Father Connolly, now don't let me forget.

Cornelia's voice made short turns and tilted over and crashed. "Oh, Mother, oh, Mother, oh, Mother. . . ."

"I'm not going, Cornelia. I'm taken by surprise. I can't go."

You'll see Hapsy again. What about her? "I thought you'd never come." Granny made a long journey outward, looking for Hapsy. What if I don't find her? What then? Her heart sank down and down, there was no bottom to death, she couldn't come to the end of it. The blue light from Cornelia's lampshade drew into a tiny point in the center of her brain, it flickered and winked like an eye, quietly it fluttered and dwindled. Granny lay curled down within herself, amazed and watchful, staring at the point of light that was herself; her body was now only a deeper mass of shadow in an endless darkness and this darkness would curl around the light and swallow it up. God, give a sign!

For the second time there was no sign. Again no bridegroom and the priest in the house. She could not remember any other sorrow because this grief wiped them all away. Oh, no, there's nothing more cruel than this—I'll never forgive it. She stretched herself with a deep breath and blew out the light.

---

[4] *dyspepsia,* indigestion.

JAMES THURBER (1894–1961)

The Catbird Seat

Mr. Martin bought the pack of Camels on Monday night in the most crowded cigar store on Broadway.[1] It was theater time and seven or eight men were buying cigarettes. The clerk didn't even glance at Mr. Martin, who put the pack in his overcoat pocket and went out. If any of the staff at F & S had seen him buy the cigarettes, they would have been astonished, for it was generally known that Mr. Martin did not smoke, and never had. No one saw him.

It was just a week to the day since Mr. Martin had decided to rub out Mrs. Ulgine Barrows. The term "rub out" pleased him because it suggested nothing more than the correction of an error—in this case an error of Mr. Fitweiler. Mr. Martin had spent each night of the past week working out his plan and examining it. As he walked home now he went over it again. For the hundredth time he resented the element of imprecision, the margin of guesswork that entered into the business. The project as he had worked it out was casual and bold, the risks were considerable. Something might go wrong anywhere along the line. And therein lay the cunning of his scheme. No one would ever see in it the cautious, painstaking hand of Erwin Martin, head of the filing department at F & S, of whom Mr. Fitweiler had once said, "Man is fallible but Martin isn't." No one would see his hand, that is, unless it were caught in the act.

Sitting in his apartment, drinking a glass of milk, Mr. Martin reviewed his case against Mrs. Ulgine Barrows, as he had every night for seven nights. He began at the beginning. Her quacking voice and braying laugh had first profaned the halls of F & S on March 7, 1941 (Mr. Martin had a head for dates). Old Roberts, the personnel chief, had introduced her as the newly appointed special adviser to the president of the firm, Mr. Fitweiler. The woman had appalled Mr. Martin instantly, but he hadn't shown it. He had given her his dry hand, a look of studious concentration, and a faint smile. "Well," she had said, looking at the papers on his desk, "are you lifting the oxcart out of the ditch?" As Mr. Martin recalled that moment, over his milk, he squirmed slightly. He must keep his mind on her crimes as a special adviser, not on her peccadillos as a personality. This he found difficult to do, in spite of entering an objection and sustaining it. The faults of the woman as a woman kept chattering on in his mind like an unruly witness. She had, for almost two years now, baited him. In the halls, in the elevator,

---

[1] A major thoroughfare in New York City that extends the entire length of Manhattan Island.

even in his own office, into which she romped now and then like a
circus horse, she was constantly shouting these silly questions at him.
"Are you lifting the oxcart out of the ditch? Are you tearing up the pea
patch? Are you hollering down the rain barrel? Are you scraping
around the bottom of the pickle barrel? Are you sitting in the catbird
seat?"

It was Joey Hart, one of Mr. Martin's two assistants, who had explained what the gibberish meant. "She must be a Dodger fan," he had
said. "Red Barber announces the Dodger games over the radio[2] and he
uses those expressions—picked 'em up down South." Joey had gone on
to explain one or two. "Tearing up the pea patch" meant going on a
rampage; "sitting in the catbird seat" meant sitting pretty, like a batter
with three balls and no strikes on him. Mr. Martin dismissed all this
with an effort. It had been annoying, it had driven him near to distraction, but he was too solid a man to be moved to murder by anything so
childish. It was fortunate, he reflected as he passed on to the important
charges against Mrs. Barrows, that he had stood up under it so well.
He had maintained always an outward appearance of polite tolerance.
"Why, I even believe you like the woman," Miss Paird, his other assistant, had once said to him. He had simply smiled.

A gavel rapped in Mr. Martin's mind and the case proper was resumed. Mrs. Ulgine Barrows stood charged with willful, blatant, and
persistent attempts to destroy the efficiency and system of F & S. It was
competent, material, and relevant to review her advent and rise to
power. Mr. Martin had got the story from Miss Paird, who seemed
always able to find things out. According to her, Mrs. Barrows had met
Mr. Fitweiler at a party, where she had rescued him from the embraces
of a powerfully built drunken man who had mistaken the president of
F & S for a famous retired Middle Western football coach. She had led
him to a sofa and somehow worked upon him a monstrous magic. The
aging gentleman had jumped to the conclusion there and then that this
was a woman of singular attainments, equipped to bring out the best in
him and in the firm. A week later he had introduced her into F & S as
his special adviser. On that day confusion got its foot in the door. After
Miss Tyson, Mr. Brundage, and Mr. Bartlett had been fired and Mr.
Munson had taken his hat and stalked out, mailing in his resignation
later, old Roberts had been emboldened to speak to Mr. Fitweiler. He
mentioned that Mr. Munson's department had been "a little disrupted"
and hadn't they perhaps better resume the old system there? Mr. Fitweiler had said certainly not. He had the greatest faith in Mrs. Barrows'
ideas. "They require a little seasoning, a little seasoning, is all," he had
added. Mr. Roberts had given it up. Mr. Martin reviewed in detail all

---

[2] Red Barber was the "voice" of the Brooklyn baseball Dodgers between 1939 and 1954.
The Dodgers left Ebbets Field after the 1957 season and moved to Los Angeles.

the changes wrought by Mrs. Barrows. She had begun chipping at the cornices of the firm's edifice and now she was swinging at the foundation stones with a pickaxe.

Mr. Martin came now, in his summing up, to the afternoon of Monday, November 2, 1942—just one week ago. On that day, at 3 P.M., Mrs. Barrows had bounced into his office. "Boo!" she had yelled. "Are you scraping around the bottom of the pickle barrel?" Mr. Martin had looked at her from under his green eyeshade, saying nothing. She had begun to wander about the office, taking it in with her great, popping eyes. "Do you really need *all* these filing cabinets?" she had demanded suddenly. Mr. Martin's heart had jumped. "Each of these files," he had said, keeping his voice even, "plays an indispensable part in the system of F & S." She had brayed at him, "Well, don't tear up the pea patch!" and gone to the door. From there she had bawled, "But you sure have got a lot of fine scrap in here!" Mr. Martin could no longer doubt that the finger was on his beloved department. Her pickaxe was on the upswing, poised for the first blow. It had not come yet; he had received no blue memo from the enchanted Mr. Fitweiler bearing nonsensical instructions deriving from the obscene woman. But there was no doubt in Mr. Martin's mind that one would be forthcoming. He must act quickly. Already a precious week had gone by. Mr. Martin stood up in his living room, still holding his milk glass. "Gentlemen of the jury," he said to himself, "I demand the death penalty for this horrible person."

The next day Mr. Martin followed his routine, as usual. He polished his glasses more often and once sharpened an already sharp pencil, but not even Miss Paird noticed. Only once did he catch sight of his victim; she swept past him in the hall with a patronizing "Hi!" At five-thirty he walked home, as usual, and had a glass of milk, as usual. He had never drunk anything stronger in his life—unless you could count ginger ale. The late Sam Schlosser, the S of F & S, had praised Mr. Martin at a staff meeting several years before for his temperate habits. "Our most efficient worker neither drinks nor smokes," he had said. "The results speak for themselves." Mr. Fitweiler had sat by, nodding approval.

Mr. Martin was still thinking about that red-letter day as he walked over to the Schrafft's[3] on Fifth Avenue near Forty-sixth Street. He got there, as he always did, at eight o'clock. He finished his dinner and the financial page of the *Sun* at a quarter to nine, as he always did. It was his custom after dinner to take a walk. This time he walked down Fifth Avenue at a casual pace. His gloved hands felt moist and warm, his forehead cold. He transferred the Camels from his overcoat to a jacket pocket. He wondered, as he did so, if they did not represent an unneces-

---

[3] The well-known New York restaurant.

sary note of strain. Mrs. Barrows smoked only Luckies. It was his idea to puff a few puffs on a Camel (after the rubbing-out), stub it out in the ashtray holding her lipstick-stained Luckies, and thus drag a small red herring across the trail. Perhaps it was not a good idea. It would take time. He might even choke, too loudly.

Mr. Martin had never seen the house on West Twelfth Street where Mrs. Barrows lived, but he had a clear enough picture of it. Fortunately, she had bragged to everybody about her ducky first-floor apartment in the perfectly darling three-story red-brick. There would be no doorman or other attendants; just the tenants of the second and third floors. As he walked along, Mr. Martin realized that he would get there before nine-thirty. He had considered walking north on Fifth Avenue from Schrafft's to a point from which it would take him until ten o'clock to reach the house. At that hour people were less likely to be coming in or going out. But the procedure would have made an awkward loop in the straight thread of his casualness, and he had abandoned it. It was impossible to figure when people would be entering or leaving the house, anyway. There was a great risk at any hour. If he ran into anybody, he would simply have to place the rubbing-out of Ulgine Barrows in the inactive file forever. The same thing would hold true if there were someone in her apartment. In that case he would just say that he had been passing by, recognized her charming house and thought to drop in.

It was eighteen minutes after nine when Mr. Martin turned into Twelfth Street. A man passed him, and a man and a woman talking. There was no one within fifty paces when he came to the house, halfway down the block. He was up the steps and in the small vestibule in no time, pressing the bell under the card that said "Mrs. Ulgine Barrows." When the clicking in the lock started, he jumped forward against the door. He got inside fast, closing the door behind him. A bulb in a lantern hung from the hall ceiling on a chain seemed to give a monstrously bright light. There was nobody on the stair, which went up ahead of him along the left wall. A door opened down the hall in the wall on the right. He went toward it swiftly, on tiptoe.

"Well, for God's sake, look who's here!" bawled Mrs. Barrows, and her braying laugh rang out like the report of a shotgun. He rushed past her like a football tackle, bumping her. "Hey, quit shoving!" she said, closing the door behind them. They were in her living room, which seemed to Mr. Martin to be lighted by a hundred lamps. "What's after you?" she said. "You're as jumpy as a goat." He found he was unable to speak. His heart was wheezing in his throat. "I—yes," he finally brought out. She was jabbering and laughing as she started to help him off with his coat. "No, no," he said. "I'll put it here." He took it off and put it on a chair near the door. "Your hat and gloves, too," she said. "You're in a lady's house." He put his hat on top of the coat. Mrs.

Barrows seemed larger than he had thought. He kept his gloves on. "I was passing by," he said. "I recognized—is there anyone here?" She laughed louder than ever. "No," she said, "we're all alone. You're as white as a sheet, you funny man. Whatever *has* come over you? I'll mix you a toddy." She started toward a door across the room. "Scotch-and-soda be all right? But say, you don't drink, do you?" She turned and gave him her amused look. Mr. Martin pulled himself together. "Scotch-and-soda will be all right," he heard himself say. He could hear her laughing in the kitchen.

Mr. Martin looked quickly around the living room for the weapon. He had counted on finding one there. There were andirons and a poker and something in a corner that looked like an Indian club. None of them would do. It couldn't be that way. He began to pace around. He came to a desk. On it lay a metal paper knife with an ornate handle. Would it be sharp enough? He reached for it and knocked over a small brass jar. Stamps spilled out of it and it fell to the floor with a clatter. "Hey," Mrs. Barrows yelled from the kitchen, "are you tearing up the pea patch?" Mr. Martin gave a strange laugh. Picking up the knife, he tried its point against his left wrist. It was blunt. It wouldn't do.

When Mrs. Barrows reappeared, carrying two highballs, Mr. Martin, standing there with his gloves on, became acutely conscious of the fantasy he had wrought. Cigarettes in his pocket, a drink prepared for him—it was all too grossly improbable. It was more than that; it was impossible. Somewhere in the back of his mind a vague idea stirred, sprouted. "For heaven's sake, take off those gloves," said Mrs. Barrows. "I always wear them in the house," said Mr. Martin. The idea began to bloom, strange and wonderful. She put the glasses on a coffee table in front of a sofa and sat on the sofa. "Come over here, you odd little man," she said. Mr. Martin went over and sat beside her. It was difficult getting a cigarette out of the pack of Camels, but he managed it. She held a match for him, laughing. "Well," she said, handing him his drink, "this is perfectly marvelous. You with a drink and a cigarette."

Mr. Martin puffed, not too awkwardly, and took a gulp of the highball. "I drink and smoke all the time," he said. He clinked his glass against hers. "Here's nuts to that old windbag, Fitweiler," he said, and gulped again. The stuff tasted awful, but he made no grimace. "Really, Mr. Martin," she said, her voice and posture changing, "you are insulting our employer." Mrs. Barrows was now all special adviser to the president. "I am preparing a bomb," said Mr. Martin, "which will blow the old goat higher than hell." He had only had a little of the drink, which was not strong. It couldn't be that. "Do you take dope or something?" Mrs. Barrows asked coldly. "Heroin," said Mr. Martin. "I'll be coked to the gills when I bump that old buzzard off." "Mr. Martin!"

she shouted, getting to her feet. "That will be all of that. You must go at once." Mr. Martin took another swallow of his drink. He tapped his cigarette out in the ashtray and put the pack of Camels on the coffee table. Then he got up. She stood glaring at him. He walked over and put on his hat and coat. "Not a word about this," he said, and laid an index finger against his lips. All Mrs. Barrows could bring out was "Really!" Mr. Martin put his hand on the doorknob. "I'm sitting in the catbird seat," he said. He stuck his tongue out at her and left. Nobody saw him go.

Mr. Martin got to his apartment, walking, well before eleven. No one saw him go in. He had two glasses of milk after brushing his teeth, and he felt elated. It wasn't tipsiness, because he hadn't been tipsy. Anyway, the walk had worn off all effects of the whisky. He got in bed and read a magazine for a while. He was asleep before midnight.

Mr. Martin got to the office at eight-thirty the next morning, as usual. At a quarter to nine, Ulgine Barrows, who had never before arrived at work before ten, swept into his office. "I'm reporting to Mr. Fitweiler now!" she shouted. "If he turns you over to the police, it's no more than you deserve!" Mr. Martin gave her a look of shocked surprise. "I beg your pardon?" he said. Mrs. Barrows snorted and bounced out of the room, leaving Miss Paird and Joey Hart staring after her. "What's the matter with that old devil now?" asked Miss Paird. "I have no idea," said Mr. Martin, resuming his work. The other two looked at him and then at each other. Miss Paird got up and went out. She walked slowly past the closed door of Mr. Fitweiler's office. Mrs. Barrows was yelling inside, but she was not braying. Miss Paird could not hear what the woman was saying. She went back to her desk.

Forty-five minutes later, Mrs. Barrows left the president's office and went into her own, shutting the door. It wasn't until half an hour later that Mr. Fitweiler sent for Mr. Martin. The head of the filing department, neat, quiet, attentive, stood in front of the old man's desk. Mr. Fitweiler was pale and nervous. He took his glasses off and twiddled them. He made a small, bruffing sound in his throat. "Martin," he said, "you have been with us more than twenty years." "Twenty-two, sir," said Mr. Martin. "In that time," pursued the president, "your work and your—uh—manner have been exemplary." "I trust so, sir," said Mr. Martin. "I have understood, Martin," said Mr. Fitweiler, "that you have never taken a drink or smoked." "That is correct, sir," said Mr. Martin. "Ah, yes." Mr. Fitweiler polished his glasses. "You may describe what you did after leaving the office yesterday, Martin," he said. Mr. Martin allowed less than a second for his bewildered pause. "Certainly, sir," he said. "I walked home. Then I went to Schrafft's for dinner. Afterward I walked home again. I went to bed early, sir, and read a magazine for a while. I was asleep before eleven." "Ah, yes," said Mr. Fitweiler again. He was silent for a moment, searching for the proper words to say to the head of the filing department. "Mrs. Barrows," he said finally, "Mrs. Barrows has worked hard, Martin, very hard. It grieves me to report that she has suffered a severe breakdown. It has taken the form of a persecution complex accompanied by distressing hallucinations." "I am very sorry, sir," said Mr. Martin. "Mrs. Barrows is under the delusion," continued Mr. Fitweiler, "that you visited her last evening and behaved yourself in an—uh—unseemly manner." He raised his hand to silence Mr. Martin's little pained outcry. "It is the nature of these psychological diseases," Mr. Fitweiler said, "to fix upon the least likely and most innocent party as the uh source of persecution. These matters are not for the lay mind to grasp, Martin. I've just had my psychiatrist, Dr. Fitch, on the phone. He would not, of course, commit himself, but he made enough generalizations to substantiate my suspicions. I suggested to Mrs. Barrows when she had completed her—uh—story to me this morning, that she visit Dr. Fitch, for I suspected a condition at once. She flew, I regret to say, into a rage, and demanded—uh—requested that I call you on the carpet. You may not know, Martin, but Mrs. Barrows had planned a reorganization of your department—subject to my approval, of course, subject to my approval. This brought you, rather than anyone else, to her mind—but again that is a phenomenon for Dr. Fitch and not for us. So, Martin, I am afraid Mrs. Barrows' usefulness here is at an end." "I am dreadfully sorry, sir," said Mr. Martin.

It was at this point that the door to the office blew open with the suddenness of a gas-main explosion and Mrs. Barrows catapulted through it. "Is the little rat denying it?" she screamed. "He can't get away with that!" Mr. Martin got up and moved discreetly to a point beside Mr. Fitweiler's chair. "You drank and smoked at my apartment," she bawled at Mr. Martin, "and you know it! You called Mr. Fitweiler an old windbag and said you were going to blow him up when you got coked to the gills on your heroin!" She stopped yelling to catch her breath and a new glint came into her popping eyes. "If you weren't such a drab, ordinary little man," she said, "I'd think you'd planned it all. Sticking your tongue out at me, saying you were sitting in the catbird seat, because you thought no one would believe me when I told it! My God, it's really too perfect!" She brayed loudly and hysterically, and the fury was on her again. She glared at Mr. Fitweiler. "Can't you see how he has tricked us, you old fool? Can't you see his little game?" But Mr. Fitweiler had been surreptitiously pressing all the buttons under the top of his desk and employees of F & S began pouring into the room. "Stockton," said Mr. Fitweiler, "you and Fishbein will take Mrs. Barrows to her home. Mrs. Powell, you will go with them." Stockton, who had played a little football in high school, blocked Mrs. Barrows as she made for Mr. Martin. It took him and Fishbein together to force her out of the door into the hall, crowded with stenographers and office boys. She was still screaming imprecations at Mr. Martin, tangled and contradictory imprecations. The hubbub finally died out down the corridor.

"I regret that this has happened," said Mr. Fitweiler. "I shall ask you to dismiss it from your mind, Martin." "Yes, sir," said Mr. Martin, anticipating his chief's "That will be all" by moving to the door. "I will dismiss it." He went out and shut the door, and his step was light and quick in the hall. When he entered his department he had slowed down to his customary gait, and he walked quietly across the room to the W20 file, wearing a look of studious concentration.

JORGE LUIS BORGES (1899–1986)

The South

The man who landed in Buenos Aires in 1871 bore the name of Johannes Dahlmann and he was a minister in the Evangelical Church. In 1939, one of his grandchildren, Juan Dahlmann, was secretary of a municipal library on Calle Córdoba, and he considered himself profoundly Argentinian. His maternal grandfather had been that Francisco Flores, of the Second Line-Infantry Division, who had died on the frontier of Buenos Aires, run through with a lance by Indians from Catriel; in the discord inherent between his two lines of descent, Juan Dahlmann (perhaps driven to it by his Germanic blood) chose the line represented by his romantic ancestor, his ancestor of the romantic death. An old sword, a leather frame containing the daguerreotype of a blank-faced man with a beard, the dash and grace of certain music, the familiar strophes of *Martin Fierro*, the passing years, boredom and solitude, all went to foster this voluntary, but never ostentatious nationalism. At the cost of numerous small privations, Dahlmann had managed to save the empty shell of a ranch in the South which had belonged to the Flores family; he continually recalled the image of the balsamic eucalyptus trees and the great rose-colored house which had once been crimson. His duties, perhaps even indolence, kept him in the city. Summer after summer he contented himself with the abstract idea of possession and with the certitude that his ranch was waiting for him on a precise site in the middle of the plain. Late in February, 1939, something happened to him.

Blind to all fault, destiny can be ruthless at one's slightest distraction. Dahlmann had succeeded in acquiring, on that very afternoon, an imperfect copy of Weil's edition of *The Thousand and One Nights*. Avid to examine this find, he did not wait for the elevator but hurried up the stairs. In the obscurity, something brushed by his forehead: a bat, a bird? On the face of the woman who opened the door to him he saw horror engraved, and the hand he wiped across his face came away red with blood. The edge of a recently painted door which someone had forgotten to close had caused this wound. Dahlmann was able to fall asleep, but from the moment he awoke at dawn the savor of all things was atrociously poignant. Fever wasted him and the pictures in *The Thousand and One Nights* served to illustrate nightmares. Friends and relatives paid him visits and, with exaggerated smiles, assured him that they thought he looked fine. Dahlmann listened to them with a kind of feeble stupor and he marveled at their not knowing that he was in hell. A week, eight days passed, and they were like eight centuries. One afternoon, the usual doctor appeared, accompanied by a new doctor, and they carried him off to a sanitarium on the Calle Ecuador, for it was necessary to X-ray him. Dahlmann, in the hackney coach which bore them away, thought that he would, at last, be able to sleep in a room different from his own. He felt happy and communicative. When he arrived at his destination, they undressed him, shaved his head, bound him with metal fastenings to a stretcher; they shone bright lights on him until he was blind and dizzy, auscultated him, and a masked man stuck a needle into his arm. He awoke with a feeling of nausea, covered with a bandage, in a cell with something of a well about it; in the days and nights which followed the operation he came to realize that he had merely been, up until then, in a suburb of hell. Ice in his mouth did not leave the least trace of freshness. During these days Dahlmann hated himself in minute detail: he hated his identity, his bodily necessities, his humiliation, the beard which bristled upon his face. He stoically endured the curative measures, which were painful, but when the surgeon told him he had been on the point of death from septicemia, Dahlmann dissolved in tears of self-pity for his fate. Physical wretchedness and the incessant anticipation of horrible nights had not allowed him time to think of anything so abstract as death. On another day, the surgeon told him he was healing and that, very soon, he would be able to go to his ranch for convalescence. Incredibly enough, the promised day arrived.

Reality favors symmetries and slight anachronisms: Dahlmann had arrived at the sanitarium in a hackney coach and now a hackney coach was to take him to the Constitución station. The first fresh tang of autumn, after the summer's oppressiveness, seemed like a symbol in nature of his rescue and release from fever and death. The city, at seven in the morning, had not lost that air of an old house lent it by the night; the streets seemed like long vestibules, the plazas were like patios. Dahlmann recognized the city with joy on the edge of vertigo: a second before his eyes registered the phenomena themselves, he recalled the corners, the billboards, the modest variety of Buenos Aires. In the yellow light of the new day, all things returned to him.

Every Argentine knows that the South begins at the other side of Rivadavia. Dahlmann was in the habit of saying that this was no mere convention, that whoever crosses this street enters a more ancient and sterner world. From inside the carriage he sought out, among the new buildings, the iron grill window, the brass knocker, the arched door, the entrance way, the intimate patio.

At the railroad station he noted that he still had thirty minutes. He quickly recalled that in a café on the Calle Brazil (a few dozen feet from Yrigoyen's house) there was an enormous cat which allowed itself to be caressed as if it were a disdainful divinity. He entered the café. There was the cat, asleep. He ordered a cup of coffee, slowly stirred the sugar, sipped it (this pleasure had been denied him in the clinic), and thought, as he smoothed the cat's black coat, that this contact was an illusion and that the two beings, man and cat, were as good as separated by a glass, for man lives in time, in succession, while the magical animal lives in the present, in the eternity of the instant.

Along the next to the last platform the train lay waiting. Dahlmann walked through the coaches until he found one almost empty. He arranged his baggage in the network rack. When the train started off, he took down his valise and extracted, after some hesitation, the first volume of *The Thousand and One Nights*. To travel with this book, which was so much a part of the history of his ill-fortune, was a kind of affirmation that his ill-fortune had been annulled; it was a joyous and secret defiance of the frustrated forces of evil.

Along both sides of the train the city dissipated into suburbs; this sight, and then a view of the gardens and villas, delayed the beginning of his reading. The truth was that Dahlmann read very little. The magnetized mountain and the genie who swore to kill his benefactor are—who would deny it?—marvelous, but not so much more than the morning itself and the mere fact of being. The joy of life distracted him from paying attention to Scheherezade and her superfluous miracles. Dahlmann closed his book and allowed himself to live.

Lunch—the bouillon served in shining metal bowls, as in the remote summers of childhood—was one more peaceful and rewarding delight.

Tomorrow I'll wake up at the ranch, he thought, and it was as if he was two men at a time: the man who traveled through the autumn day and across the geography of the fatherland, and the other one, locked up in a sanitarium and subject to methodical servitude. He saw unplastered brick houses, long and angled, timelessly watching the trains go by; he saw horsemen along the dirt roads; he saw gullies and lagoons and ranches; he saw great luminous clouds that resembled marble; and all these things were accidental, casual, like dreams of the plain. He also thought he recognized trees and crop fields; but he would not have been able to name them, for his actual knowledge of the countryside was quite inferior to his nostalgic and literary knowledge.

From time to time he slept, and his dreams were animated by the impetus of the train. The intolerable white sun of high noon had already become the yellow sun which precedes nightfall, and it would not be long before it would turn red. The railroad car was now also different; it was not the same as the one which had quit the station siding at Constitución; the plain and the hours had transfigured it. Outside, the moving shadow of the railroad car stretched toward the horizon. The elemental earth was not perturbed either by settlements or other signs of humanity. The country was vast but at the same time intimate and, in some measure, secret. The limitless country sometimes contained only a solitary bull. The solitude was perfect, perhaps hostile, and it might have occurred to Dahlmann that he was traveling into the past and not merely south. He was distracted from these considerations by the railroad inspector who, on reading his ticket, advised him that the train would not let him off at the regular station but at another: an earlier stop, one scarcely known to Dahlmann. (The man added an explanation which Dahlmann did not attempt to understand, and which he hardly heard, for the mechanism of events did not concern him.)

The train laboriously ground to a halt, practically in the middle of the plain. The station lay on the other side of the tracks; it was not much more than a siding and a shed. There was no means of conveyance to be seen, but the station chief supposed that the traveler might secure a vehicle from a general store and inn to be found some ten or twelve blocks away.

Dahlmann accepted the walk as a small adventure. The sun had already disappeared from view, but a final splendor exalted the vivid and silent plain, before the night erased its color. Less to avoid fatigue than to draw out his enjoyment of these sights, Dahlmann walked slowly, breathing in the odor of clover with sumptuous joy.

The general store at one time had been painted a deep scarlet, but the years had tempered this violent color for its own good. Something in its poor architecture recalled a steel engraving, perhaps one from an old edition of *Paul et Virginie*. A number of horses were hitched up to the paling. Once inside, Dahlmann thought he recognized the shopkeeper. Then he realized that he had been deceived by the man's resemblance to one of the male nurses in the sanitarium. When the shopkeeper heard Dahlmann's request, he said he would have the shay made up. In order to add one more event to that day and to kill time, Dahlmann decided to eat at the general store.

Some country louts, to whom Dahlmann did not at first pay any attention, were eating and drinking at one of the tables. On the floor, and hanging on to the bar, squatted an old man, immobile as an object. His years had reduced and polished him as water does a stone or the generations of men do a sentence. He was dark, dried up, diminutive, and seemed outside time, situated in eternity. Dahlmann noted with satisfaction the kerchief, the thick poncho, the long *chiripá,* and the colt boots, and told himself, as he recalled futile discussions with people from the Northern counties or from the province of Entre Rios, that gauchos like this no longer existed outside the South.

Dahlmann sat down next to the window. The darkness began overcoming the plain, but the odor and sound of the earth penetrated the iron bars of the window. The shop owner brought him sardines, followed by some roast meat. Dahlmann washed the meal down with several glasses of red wine. Idling, he relished the tart savor of the wine, and let his gaze, now grown somewhat drowsy, wander over the shop. A kerosene lamp hung from a beam. There were three customers at the other table: two of them appeared to be farm workers; the third man, whose features hinted at Chinese blood, was drinking with his hat on. Of a sudden, Dahlmann felt something brush lightly against his face. Next to the heavy glass of turbid wine, upon one of the stripes in the table cloth, lay a spit ball of breadcrumb. That was all: but someone had thrown it there.

The men at the other table seemed totally cut off from him. Perplexed, Dahlmann decided that nothing had happened, and he opened the volume of *The Thousand and One Nights,* by way of suppressing reality. After a few moments another little ball landed on his table, and now the *peones* laughed outright. Dahlmann said to himself that he was not frightened, but he reasoned that it would be a major blunder if he, a convalescent, were to allow himself to be dragged by strangers into some chaotic quarrel. He determined to leave, and had already gotten to his feet when the owner came up and exhorted him in an alarmed voice:

"*Señor* Dahlmann, don't pay any attention to those lads; they're half high."

Dahlmann was not surprised to learn that the other man, now, knew his name. But he felt that these conciliatory words served only to aggravate the situation. Previous to this moment, the *peones'* provocation was directed against an unknown face, against no one in particular, almost against no one at all. Now it was an attack against him, against his name, and his neighbors knew it. Dahlmann pushed the owner aside, confronted the *peones,* and demanded to know what they wanted of him.

The tough with a Chinese look staggered heavily to his feet. Almost in Juan Dahlmann's face he shouted insults, as if he had been a long way off. His game was to exaggerate his drunkenness, and this extravagance constituted a ferocious mockery. Between curses and obscenities, he threw a long knife into the air, followed it with his eyes, caught and juggled it, and challenged Dahlmann to a knife fight. The owner objected in a tremulous voice, pointing out that Dahlmann was unarmed. At this point, something unforeseeable occurred.

From a corner of the room, the old ecstatic gaucho—in whom Dahlmann saw a summary and cipher of the South (his South)—threw him a naked dagger, which landed at his feet. It was as if the South had resolved that Dahlmann should accept the duel. Dahlmann bent over to pick up the dagger, and felt two things. The first, that this almost instinctive act bound him to fight. The second, that the weapon, in his torpid hand, was no defense at all, but would merely serve to justify his murder. He had once played with a poniard, like all men, but his idea of fencing and knife-play did not go further than the notion that all strokes should be directed upwards, with the cutting edge held inwards. *They would not have allowed such things to happen to me in the sanitarium,* he thought.

"Let's get on our way," said the other man.

They went out and if Dahlmann was without hope, he was also without fear. As he crossed the threshold, he felt that to die in a knife fight, under the open sky, and going forward to the attack, would have been a liberation, a joy, and a festive occasion, on the first night in the sanitarium, when they stuck him with the needle. He felt that if he had been able to choose, then, or to dream his death, this would have been the death he would have chosen or dreamt.

Firmly clutching his knife, which he perhaps would not know how to wield, Dahlmann went out into the plain.

JOHN STEINBECK (1902–1968)

The Chrysanthemums

The high gray-flannel fog of winter closed off the Salinas Valley[1] from the sky and from all the rest of the world. On every side it sat like a lid on the mountains and made of the great valley a closed pot. On the broad, level land floor the gang plows bit deep and left the black earth shining like metal where the shares had cut. On the foothill ranches across the Salinas River, the yellow stubble fields seemed to be bathed in pale cold sunshine, but there was no sunshine in the valley now in December. The thick willow scrub along the river flamed with sharp and positive yellow leaves.

It was a time of quiet and of waiting. The air was cold and tender. A light wind blew up from the southwest so that the farmers were mildly hopeful of a good rain before long; but fog and rain do not go together.

Across the river, on Henry Allen's foothill ranch there was little work to be done, for the hay was cut and stored and the orchards were plowed up to receive the rain deeply when it should come. The cattle on the higher slopes were becoming shaggy and rough-coated.

Elisa Allen, working in her flower garden, looked down across the yard and saw Henry, her husband, talking to two men in business suits. The three of them stood by the tractor shed, each man with one foot on the side of the little Fordson.[2] They smoked cigarettes and studied the machine as they talked.

Elisa watched them for a moment and then went back to her work. She was thirty-five. Her face was lean and strong and her eyes were as clear as water. Her figure looked blocked and heavy in her gardening costume, a man's black hat pulled down over her eyes, clodhopper shoes, a figured print dress almost completely covered by a big corduroy apron with four big pockets to hold the snips, the trowel and scratcher, the seeds and the knife she worked with. She wore heavy leather gloves to protect her hands while she worked.

She was cutting down the old year's chrysanthemum stalks with a pair of short and powerful scissors. She looked down toward the men by the tractor shed now and then. Her face was eager and mature and handsome; even her work with the scissors was over-eager, over-powerful. The chrysanthemum stems seemed too small and easy for her energy.

She brushed a cloud of hair out of her eyes with the back of her glove, and left a smudge of earth on her cheek in doing it. Behind

---

[1] The Salinas Valley, south of the town of Salinas in central California, is one of the state's richest agricultural areas.
[2] A two-door Ford car, or coupe.

her stood the neat white farm house with red geraniums close-banked around it as high as the windows. It was a hard-swept looking little house, with hard-polished windows, and a clean mud-mat on the front steps.

Elisa cast another glance toward the tractor shed. The strangers were getting into their Ford coupe. She took off a glove and put her strong fingers down into the forest of new green chrysanthemum sprouts that were growing around the old roots. She spread the leaves and looked down among the close-growing stems. No aphids were there, no sow-bugs or snails or cutworms. Her terrier fingers[3] destroyed such pests before they could get started.

Elisa started at the sound of her husband's voice. He had come near quietly, and he leaned over the wire fence that protected her flower garden from cattle and dogs and chickens.

"At it again," he said. "You've got a strong new crop coming."

Elisa straightened her back and pulled on the gardening glove again. "Yes. They'll be strong this coming year." In her tone and on her face there was a little smugness.

"You've got a gift with things," Henry observed. "Some of those yellow chrysanthemums you had this year were ten inches across. I wish you'd work out in the orchard and raise some apples that big."

Her eyes sharpened. "Maybe I could do it, too. I've a gift with things, all right. My mother had it. She could stick anything in the ground and make it grow. She said it was having planters' hands that knew how to do it."

"Well, it sure works with flowers," he said.

"Henry, who were those men you were talking to?"

"Why, sure, that's what I came to tell you. They were from the Western Meat Company. I sold them those thirty head of three-year-old steers. Got nearly my own price, too."

"Good," she said. "Good for you."

"And I thought," he continued, "I thought how it's Saturday afternoon, and we might go into Salinas for dinner at a restaurant, and then to a picture show—to celebrate, you see."

"Good," she repeated. "Oh, yes. That will be good."

Henry put on his joking tone. "There's fights tonight. How'd you like to go to the fights?"

"Oh, no," she said breathlessly. "No, I wouldn't like fights."

"Just fooling, Elisa. We'll go to a movie. Let's see. It's two now. I'm going to take Scotty and bring down those steers from the hill. It'll take us maybe two hours. We'll go in town about five and have dinner at the Cominos Hotel. Like that?"

---

[3] Terriers (which take their name from a word meaning "earth") were originally bred for hunting out animals living under the ground in burrows.

"Of course I'll like it. It's good to eat away from home."

"All right, then, I'll go get up a couple of horses."

She said, "I'll have plenty of time to transplant some of these sets, I guess."

She heard her husband calling Scotty down by the barn. And a little later she saw the two men ride up the pale yellow hillside in search of the steers.

There was a little square sandy bed kept for rooting the chrysanthemums. With her trowel she turned the soil over and over, and smoothed it and patted it firm. Then she dug ten parallel trenches to receive the sets. Back at the chrysanthemum bed she pulled out the little crisp shoots, trimmed off the leaves of each one with her scissors and laid it on a small orderly pile.

A squeak of wheels and plod of hoofs came from the road. Elisa looked up. The country road ran along the dense bank of willows and cottonwoods that bordered the river, and up this road came a curious vehicle, curiously drawn. It was an old spring-wagon, with a round canvas top on it like the cover of a prairie schooner. It was drawn by an old bay horse and a little gray-and-white burro. A big stubble-bearded man sat between the cover flaps and drove the crawling team. Underneath the wagon, between the hind wheels, a lean and rangy mongrel dog walked sedately. Words were painted on the canvas, in clumsy, crooked letters. "Pots, pans, knives, sisors, lawn mores, Fixed." Two rows of articles, and the triumphantly definitive "Fixed" below. The black paint had run down in little sharp points beneath each letter.

Elisa, squatting on the ground, watched to see the crazy, loose-jointed wagon pass by. But it didn't pass. It turned into the farm road in front of her house, crooked old wheels skirling and squeaking. The rangy dog darted from between the wheels and ran ahead. Instantly the two ranch shepherds flew out at him. Then all three stopped and with stiff and quivering tails, with taut straight legs, with ambassadorial dignity, they slowly circled, sniffing daintily. The caravan pulled up to Elisa's wire fence and stopped. Now the newcomer dog, feeling out-numbered, lowered his tail and retired under the wagon with raised hackles and bared teeth.

The man on the wagon seat called out, "That's a bad dog in a fight when he gets started."

Elisa laughed. "I see he is. How soon does he generally get started?"

The man caught up her laughter and echoed it heartily. "Sometimes not for weeks and weeks," he said. He climbed stiffly down, over the wheel. The horse and the donkey drooped like unwatered flowers.

Elisa saw that he was a very big man. Although his hair and beard were graying, he did not look old. His worn black suit was wrinkled and spotted with grease. The laughter had disappeared from his face and eyes the moment his laughing voice ceased. His eyes were dark, and they were full of the brooding that gets in the eyes of teamsters[4] and of sailors. The calloused hands he rested on the wire fence were cracked, and every crack was a black line. He took off his battered hat.

"I'm off my general road, ma'am," he said. "Does this dirt road cut over across the river to the Los Angeles highway?"

Elisa stood up and shoved the thick scissors in her apron pocket. "Well, yes, it does, but it winds around and then fords the river. I don't think your team could pull through the sand."

He replied with some asperity, "It might surprise you what them beasts can pull through."

"When they get started?" she asked.

He smiled for a second. "Yes. When they get started."

"Well," said Elisa, "I think you'll save time if you go back to the Salinas road and pick up the highway there."

He drew a big finger down the chicken wire and made it sing. "I ain't in any hurry, ma'am. I go from Seattle to San Diego and back every year. Takes all my time. About six months each way. I aim to follow nice weather."

Elisa took off her gloves and stuffed them in the apron pocket with the scissors. She touched the under edge of her man's hat, searching for fugitive hairs. "That sounds like a nice kind of way to live," she said.

He leaned confidentially over the fence. "Maybe you noticed the writing on my wagon. I mend pots and sharpen knives and scissors. You got any of them things to do?"

"Oh, no," she said quickly. "Nothing like that." Her eyes hardened with resistance.

"Scissors is the worst thing," he explained. "Most people just ruin scissors trying to sharpen 'em, but I know how. I got a special tool. It's a little bobbit kind of thing, and patented. But it sure does the trick."

"No. My scissors are all sharp."

"All right, then. Take a pot," he continued earnestly, "a bent pot, or a pot with a hole. I can make it like new so you don't have to buy no new ones. That's a saving for you."

"No," she said shortly. "I tell you I have nothing like that for you to do."

His face fell to an exaggerated sadness. His voice took on a whining undertone. "I ain't had a thing to do today. Maybe I won't have no supper tonight. You see I'm off my regular road. I know folks on the highway clear from Seattle to San Diego. They save their things for me to sharpen up because they know I do it so good and save them money."

"I'm sorry," Elisa said irritably. "I haven't anything for you to do."

His eyes left her face and fell to searching the ground. They roamed

---

[4] Truckdrivers.

about until they came to the chrysanthemum bed where she had been working. "What's them plants, ma'am?"

The irritation and resistance melted from Elisa's face. "Oh, those are chrysanthemums, giant whites and yellows. I raise them every year, bigger than anybody around here."

"Kind of a long-stemmed flower? Looks like a quick puff of colored smoke?" he asked.

"That's it. What a nice way to describe them."

"They smell kind of nasty till you get used to them," he said.

"It's a good bitter smell," she retorted, "not nasty at all."

He changed his tone quickly. "I like the smell myself."

"I had ten-inch blooms this year," she said.

The man leaned farther over the fence. "Look. I know a lady down the road a piece, has got the nicest garden you ever seen. Got nearly every kind of flower but no chrysanthemums. Last time I was mending a copper-bottom washtub for her (that's a hard job but I do it good), she said to me, 'If you ever run acrost some nice chrysanthemums I wish you'd try to get me a few seeds.' That's what she told me."

Elisa's eyes grew alert and eager. "She couldn't have known much about chrysanthemums. You *can* raise them from seed, but it's much easier to root the little sprouts you see there."

"Oh," he said. "I s'pose I can't take none to her, then."

"Why yes you can," Elisa cried. "I can put some in damp sand, and you can carry them right along with you. They'll take root in the pot if you keep them damp. And then she can transplant them."

"She'd sure like to have some, ma'am. You say they're nice ones?"

"Beautiful," she said. "Oh, beautiful." Her eyes shone. She tore off the battered hat and shook out her dark pretty hair. "I'll put them in a flower pot, and you can take them right with you. Come into the yard."

While the man came through the picket gate Elisa ran excitedly along the geranium-bordered path to the back of the house. And she returned carrying a big red flower pot. The gloves were forgotten now. She kneeled on the ground by the starting bed and dug up the sandy soil with her fingers and scooped it into the bright new flower pot. Then she picked up the little pile of shoots she had prepared. With her strong fingers she pressed them into the sand and tamped around them with her knuckles. The man stood over her. "I'll tell you what to do," she said. "You remember so you can tell the lady."

"Yes, I'll try to remember."

"Well, look. These will take root in about a month. Then she must set them out, about a foot apart in good rich earth like this, see?" She lifted a handful of dark soil for him to look at. "They'll grow fast and tall. Now remember this: In July tell her to cut them down, about eight inches from the ground."

"Before they bloom?" he asked.

"Yes, before they bloom." Her face was tight with eagerness. "They'll grow right up again. About the last of September the buds will start."

She stopped and seemed perplexed. "It's the budding that takes the most care," she said hesitantly. "I don't know how to tell you." She looked deep into his eyes, searchingly. Her mouth opened a little, and she seemed to be listening. "I'll try to tell you," she said. "Did you ever hear of planting hands?"

"Can't say I have, ma'am."

"Well, I can only tell you what it feels like. It's when you're picking off the buds you don't want. Everything goes right down into your fingertips. You watch your fingers work. They do it themselves. You can feel how it is. They pick and pick the buds. They never make a mistake. They're with the plant. Do you see? Your fingers and the plant. You can feel that, right up your arm. They know. They never make a mistake. You can feel it. When you're like that you can't do anything wrong. Do you see that? Can you understand that?"

She was kneeling on the ground looking up at him. Her breast swelled passionately.

The man's eyes narrowed. He looked away self-consciously. "Maybe I know," he said. "Sometimes in the night in the wagon there——"

Elisa's voice grew husky. She broke in on him, "I've never lived as you do, but I know what you mean. When the night is dark—why, the stars are sharp-pointed, and there's quiet. Why, you rise up and up! Every pointed star gets driven into your body. It's like that. Hot and sharp and—lovely."

Kneeling there, her hand went out toward his legs in the greasy black trousers. Her hesitant fingers almost touched the cloth. Then her hand dropped to the ground. She crouched low like a fawning dog.

He said, "It's nice, just like you say. Only when you don't have no dinner, it ain't."

She stood up then, very straight, and her face was ashamed. She held the flower pot out to him and placed it gently in his arms. "Here. Put it in your wagon, on the seat, where you can watch it. Maybe I can find something for you to do."

At the back of the house she dug in the can pile and found two old and battered aluminum saucepans. She carried them back and gave them to him. "Here, maybe you can fix these."

His manner changed. He became professional. "Good as new I can fix them." At the back of his wagon he set a little anvil, and out of an oily tool box dug a small machine hammer. Elisa came through the gate to watch him while he pounded out the dents in the kettles. His mouth grew sure and knowing. At a difficult part of the work he sucked his underlip.

"You sleep right in the wagon?" Elisa asked.

"Right in the wagon, ma'am. Rain or shine I'm dry as a cow in there."

"It must be nice," she said. "It must be very nice. I wish women could do such things."

"It ain't the right kind of a life for a woman."

Her upper lip raised a little, showing her teeth. "How do you know? How can you tell?" she said.

"I don't know, ma'am," he protested. "Of course I don't know. Now here's your kettles, done. You don't have to buy no new ones."

"How much?"

"Oh, fifty cents'll do. I keep my prices down and my work good. That's why I have all them satisfied customers up and down the highway."

Elisa brought him a fifty-cent piece from the house and dropped it in his hand. "You might be surprised to have a rival some time. I can sharpen scissors, too. And I can beat the dents out of little pots. I could show you what a woman might do."

He put his hammer back in the oily box and shoved the little anvil out of sight. "It would be a lonely life for a woman, ma'am, and a scary life, too, with animals creeping under the wagon all night." He climbed over the singletree,[5] steadying himself with a hand on the burro's white rump. He settled himself in the seat, picked up the lines. "Thank you kindly, ma'am," he said. "I'll do like you told me; I'll go back and catch the Salinas road."

"Mind," she called, "if you're long in getting there, keep the sand damp."

"Sand, ma'am? . . . Sand? Oh, sure. You mean around the chrysanthemums. Sure I will." He clucked his tongue. The beasts leaned luxuriously into their collars. The mongrel dog took his place between the back wheels. The wagon turned and crawled out the entrance road and back the way it had come, along the river.

Elisa stood in front of her wire fence watching the slow progress of the caravan. Her shoulders were straight, her head thrown back, her eyes half-closed, so that the scene came vaguely into them. Her lips moved silently, forming the words "Good-bye—good-bye." Then she whispered, "That's a bright direction. There's a glowing there." The sound of her whisper startled her. She shook herself free and looked about to see whether anyone had been listening. Only the dogs had heard. They lifted their heads toward her from their sleeping in the dust, and then stretched out their chins and settled asleep again. Elisa turned and ran hurriedly into the house.

In the kitchen she reached behind the stove and felt the water tank. It was full of hot water from the noonday cooking. In the bathroom

---

[5] The horizontal crossbar on a wagon to which the draft animals are attached.

she tore off her soiled clothes and flung them into the corner. And then she scrubbed herself with a little block of pumice, legs and thighs, loins and chest and arms, until her skin was scratched and red. When she had dried herself she stood in front of a mirror in her bedroom and looked at her body. She tightened her stomach and threw out her chest. She turned and looked over her shoulder at her back.

After a while she began to dress slowly. She put on her newest under-clothing and her nicest stockings and the dress which was the symbol of her prettiness. She worked carefully on her hair, penciled her eye-brows and rouged her lips.

Before she was finished she heard the little thunder of hoofs and the shouts of Henry and his helper as they drove the red steers into the corral. She heard the gate bang shut and set herself for Henry's arrival.

His steps sounded on the porch. He entered the house calling, "Elisa, where are you?"

"In my room dressing. I'm not ready. There's hot water for your bath. Hurry up. It's getting late."

When she heard him splashing in the tub, Elisa laid his dark suit on the bed, and shirt and socks and tie beside it. She stood his polished shoes on the floor beside the bed. Then she went to the porch and sat primly and stiffly down. She looked toward the river road where the willow-line was still yellow with frosted leaves so that under the high gray fog they seemed a thin band of sunshine. This was the only color in the gray afternoon. She sat unmoved for a long time. Her eyes blinked rarely.

Henry came banging out of the door, shoving his tie inside his vest as he came. Elisa stiffened and her face grew tight. Henry stopped short and looked at her. "Why—why, Elisa. You look so nice!"

"Nice? You think I look nice? What do you mean by 'nice'?"

Henry blundered on. "I don't know. I mean you look different, strong and happy."

"I am strong? Yes, strong. What do you mean 'strong'?"

He looked bewildered. "You're playing some kind of a game," he said helplessly. "It's a kind of a play. You look strong enough to break a calf over your knee, happy enough to eat it like a watermelon."

For a second she lost her rigidity. "Henry! Don't talk like that. You didn't know what you said." She grew complete again. "I'm strong," she boasted. "I never knew before how strong."

Henry looked down toward the tractor shed, and when he brought his eyes back to her, they were his own again. "I'll get out the car. You can put on your coat while I'm starting."

Elisa went into the house. She heard him drive to the gate and idle down his motor, and then she took a long time to put on her hat. She pulled it here and pressed it there. When Henry turned the motor off she slipped into her coat and went out.

The little roadster bounced along on the dirt road by the river, raising the birds and driving the rabbits into the brush. Two cranes flapped heavily over the willow-line and dropped into the riverbed.

Far ahead on the road Elisa saw a dark speck. She knew.

She tried not to look as they passed it, but her eyes would not obey. She whispered to herself sadly, "He might have thrown them off the road. That wouldn't have been much trouble, not very much. But he kept the pot," she explained. "He had to keep the pot. That's why he couldn't get them off the road."

The roadster turned a bend and she saw the caravan ahead. She swung full around toward her husband so she could not see the little covered wagon and the mismatched team as the car passed them.

In a moment it was over. The thing was done. She did not look back.

She said loudly, to be heard above the motor, "It will be good, tonight, a good dinner."

"Now you're changed again," Henry complained. He took one hand from the wheel and patted her knee. "I ought to take you in to dinner oftener. It would be good for both of us. We get so heavy out on the ranch."

"Henry," she asked, "could we have wine at dinner?"

"Sure we could. Say! That will be fine."

She was silent for a while; then she said, "Henry, at those prize fights, do the men hurt each other very much?"

"Sometimes a little, not often. Why?"

"Well, I've read how they break noses, and blood runs down their chests. I've read how the fighting gloves get heavy and soggy with blood."

He looked around at her. "What's the matter, Elisa? I didn't know you read things like that." He brought the car to a stop, then turned to the right over the Salinas River bridge.

"Do any women ever go to the fights?" she asked.

"Oh, sure, some. What's the matter, Elisa? Do you want to go? I don't think you'd like it, but I'll take you if you really want to go."

She relaxed limply in the seat. "Oh, no. No. I don't want to go. I'm sure I don't." Her face was turned away from him. "It will be enough if we can have wine. It will be plenty." She turned up her coat collar so he could not see that she was crying weakly—like an old woman.

RICHARD WRIGHT (1908–1960)

The Man Who Was Almost a Man

Dave struck out across the fields, looking homeward through paling light. Whut's the use talkin wid em niggers in the field? Anyhow, his mother was putting supper on the table. Them niggers can't understan nothing. One of these days he was going to get a gun and practice shooting, then they couldn't talk to him as though he were a little boy. He slowed, looking at the ground. Shucks, Ah ain scareda them even ef they are biggern me! Aw, Ah know whut Ahma do. Ahm going by ol Joe's sto n git that Sears Roebuck catlog n look at them guns. Mebbe Ma will lemme buy one when she gits mah pay from ol man Hawkins. Ahma beg her t gimme some money. Ahm ol ernough to hava gun. Ahm seventeen. Almost a man. He strode, feeling his long loose-jointed limbs. Shucks, a man oughta hava little gun aftah he done worked hard all day.

He came in sight of Joe's store. A yellow lantern glowed on the front porch. He mounted steps and went through the screen door, hearing it bang behind him. There was a strong smell of coal oil and mackerel fish. He felt very confident until he saw fat Joe walk in through the rear door, then his courage began to ooze.

"Howdy, Dave! Whutcha want?"

"How yuh, Mistah Joe? Aw, Ah don wanna buy nothing. Ah jus wanted t see ef yuhd lemme look at tha catlog erwhile."

"Sure! You wanna see it here?"

"Nawsuh. Ah wans t take it home wid me. Ah'll bring it back termorrow when Ah come in from the fiels."

"You plannin on buying something?"

"Yessuh."

"Your ma lettin you have your own money now?"

"Shucks. Mistah Joe, Ahm gittin t be a man like anybody else!"

Joe laughed and wiped his greasy white face with a red bandanna. "Whut you plannin on buyin?"

Dave looked at the floor, scratched his head, scratched his thigh, and smiled. Then he looked up shyly.

"Ah'll tell yuh, Mistah Joe, ef yuh promise yuh won't tell."

"I promise."

"Waal, Ahma buy a gun."

"A gun? Whut you want with a gun?"

"Ah wanna keep it."

"You ain't nothing but a boy. You don't need a gun."

"Aw, lemme have the catlog, Mistah Joe. Ah'll bring it back."

Joe walked through the rear door. Dave was elated. He looked around at barrels of sugar and flour. He heard Joe coming back. He craned his neck to see if he were bringing the book. Yeah, he's got it. Gawddog, he's got it!

"Here, but be sure you bring it back. It's the only one I got."

"Sho, Mistah Joe."

"Say, if you wanna buy a gun, why don't you buy one from me? I gotta gun to sell."

"Will it shoot?"

"Sure it'll shoot."

"Whut kind is it?"

"Oh, it's kinda old . . . a left-hand Wheeler. A pistol. A big one."

"Is it got bullets in it?"

"It's loaded."

"Kin Ah see it?"

"Where's your money?"

"Whut yuh wan fer it?"

"I'll let you have it for two dollars."

"Just two dollahs? Shucks, Ah could buy tha when Ah git mah pay."

"I'll have it here when you want it."

"Awright, suh. Ah be in fer it."

He went through the door, hearing it slam again behind him. *Ahma git some money from Ma n buy me a gun! Only two dollahs!* He tucked the thick catalogue under his arm and hurried.

"Where yuh been, boy?" His mother held a steaming dish of black-eyed peas.

"Aw, Ma, Ah jus stopped down the road t talk wid the boys."

"Yuh know bettah t keep suppah waitin."

He sat down, resting the catalogue on the edge of the table.

"Yuh git up from there and git to the well n wash yoself! Ah ain feedin no hogs in mah house!"

She grabbed his shoulder and pushed him. He stumbled out of the room, then came back to get the catalogue.

"Whut this?"

"Aw, Ma, it's jusa catlog."

"Who yuh git it from?"

"From Joe, down at the sto."

"Waal, thas good. We kin use it in the outhouse."

"Naw, Ma." He grabbed for it. "Gimme ma catlog, Ma."

She held onto it and glared at him.

"Quit hollerin at me! Whut's wrong wid yuh? Yuh crazy?"

"But Ma, please. It ain mine! It's Joe's! He tol me t bring it back t im termorrow."

She gave up the book. He stumbled down the back steps, hugging the thick book under his arm. When he had splashed water on his face and hands, he groped back to the kitchen and fumbled in a corner for the towel. He bumped into a chair; it clattered to the floor. The catalogue sprawled at his feet. When he had dried his eyes he snatched up the book and held it again under his arm. His mother stood watching him.

"Now, ef yuh gonna act a fool over that ol book, Ah'll take it n burn it up."

"Naw, Ma, please."

"Waal, set down n be still!"

He sat down and drew the oil lamp close. He thumbed page after page, unaware of the food his mother set on the table. His father came in. Then his small brother.

"Whutcha got there, Dave?" his father asked.

"Jusa catlog," he answered, not looking up.

"Yeah, here they is!" His eyes glowed at blue-and-black revolvers. He glanced up, feeling sudden guilt. His father was watching him. He eased the book under the table and rested it on his knees. After the blessing was asked, he ate. He scooped up peas and swallowed fat meat without chewing. Buttermilk helped to wash it down. He did not want to mention money before his father. He would do much better by cornering his mother when she was alone. He looked at his father uneasily out of the edge of his eye.

"Boy, how come yuh don quit foolin wid tha book n eat yo suppah?"

"Yessuh."

"How you n ol man Hawkins gitten erlong?"

"Suh?"

"Can't yuh hear? Why don yuh lissen? Ah ast yu how wuz yuh n ol man Hawkins gittin erlong?"

"Oh, swell, Pa. Ah plows mo lan than anybody over there."

"Waal, yuh oughta keep yo mind on whut yuh doin."

"Yessuh."

He poured his plate full of molasses and sopped it up slowly with a chunk of cornbread. When his father and brother had left the kitchen, he still sat and looked again at the guns in the catalogue, longing to muster courage enough to present his case to his mother. Lawd, ef Ah only had tha pretty one! He could almost feel the slickness of the weapon with his fingers. If he had a gun like that he would polish it and keep it shining so it would never rust. N Ah'd keep it loaded, by Gawd!

"Ma?" His voice was hesitant.

"Hunh?"

"Ol man Hawkins give yuh mah money yit?"

"Yeah, but ain no usa yuh thinking bout throwin nona it erway. Ahm keepin tha money sos yuh kin have cloes t go to school this winter."

He rose and went to her side with the open catalogue in his palms. She was washing dishes, her head bent low over a pan. Shyly he raised the book. When he spoke, his voice was husky, faint.

"Ma, Gawd knows Ah wans one of these."

"One of whut?" she asked, not raising her eyes.

"One of these," he said again, not daring even to point. She glanced up at the page, then at him with wide eyes.

"Nigger, is yuh gone plumb crazy?"

"Aw, Ma—"

"Git outta here! Don yuh talk t me bout no gun! Yuh a fool!"

"Ma, Ah kin buy one fer two dollahs."

"Not ef Ah knows it, yuh ain!"

"But yuh promised me one—"

"Ah don care whut Ah promised! Yuh ain nothing but a boy yit!"

"Ma, ef yuh lemme buy one Ah'll *never* ast yuh fer nothing no mo."

"Ah tol yuh t git outta here! Yuh ain gonna toucha penny of tha money fer no gun! Thas how come Ah has Mistah Hawkins t pay yo wages t me, cause Ah knows yuh ain got no sense."

"But, Ma, we needa gun. Pa ain got no gun. We needa gun in the house. Yuh kin never tell whut might happen."

"Now don yuh try to maka fool outta me, boy! Ef we did hava gun, yuh wouldn't have it!"

He laid the catalogue down and slipped his arm around her waist.

"Aw, Ma, Ah done worked hard alla summer n ain ast yuh fer nothin, is Ah, now?"

"Thas whut yuh spose t do!"

"But Ma, Ah wans a gun. Yuh kin lemme have two dollahs outta mah money. Please, Ma. I kin give it to Pa . . . Please, Ma! Ah loves yuh, Ma."

When she spoke her voice came soft and low.

"Whut yu wan wida gun, Dave? Yuh don need no gun. You'll git in trouble. N ef yo pa jus thought Ah let yuh have money t buy a gun he'd hava fit."

"Ah'll hide it, Ma. It ain but two dollahs."

"Lawd, chil, whut's wrong wid yuh?"

"Ain nothin wrong, Ma. Ahm almos a man now. Ah wans a gun."

"Who gonna sell yuh a gun?"

"Ol Joe at the sto."

"N it don cos but two dollahs?"

"Thas all, Ma. Jus two dollahs. Please, Ma."

She was stacking the plates away; her hands moved slowly, reflectively. Dave kept an anxious silence. Finally, she turned to him.

"Ah'll let yuh git tha gun ef yuh promise me one thing."

"Whut's tha, Ma?"

"Yuh bring it straight back t me, yuh hear? It be fer Pa."

"Yessum! Lemme go now, Ma."

She stooped, turned slightly to one side, raised the hem of her dress, rolled down the top of her stocking, and came up with a slender wad of bills.

"Here," she said. "Lawd knows yuh don need no gun. But yer pa does. Yuh bring it right back t me, yuh hear? Ahma put it up. Now ef yuh don, Ahma have yuh pa lick yuh so hard yuh won fergit it."

"Yessum."

He took the money, ran down the steps, and across the yard.

"Dave! Yuuuuuh Daaaaave!"

He heard, but he was not going to stop now. "Naw, Lawd!"

The first movement he made the following morning was to reach under his pillow for the gun. In the gray light of dawn he held it loosely, feeling a sense of power. Could kill a man with a gun like this. Kill anybody, black or white. And if he were holding his gun in his hand, nobody could run over him; they would have to respect him. It was a big gun, with a long barrel and a heavy handle. He raised and lowered it in his hand, marveling at its weight.

He had not come straight home with it as his mother had asked; instead he had stayed out in the fields, holding the weapon in his hand, aiming it now and then at some imaginary foe. But he had not fired it; he had been afraid that his father might hear. Also he was not sure he knew how to fire it.

To avoid surrendering the pistol he had not come into the house until he knew that they were all asleep. When his mother had tiptoed to his bedside late that night and demanded the gun, he had first played possum; then he had told her that the gun was hidden outdoors, that he would bring it to her in the morning. Now he lay turning it slowly in his hands. He broke it, took out the cartridges, felt them, and then put them back.

He slid out of bed, got a long strip of old flannel from a trunk, wrapped the gun in it, and tied it to his naked thigh while it was still loaded. He did not go in to breakfast. Even though it was not yet daylight, he started for Jim Hawkins' plantation. Just as the sun was rising he reached the barns where the mules and plows were kept.

"Hey! That you, Dave?"

He turned. Jim Hawkins stood eying him suspiciously.

"What're yuh doing here so early?"

"Ah didn't know Ah wuz gittin up so early, Mistah Hawkins. Ah wuz fixin t hitch up ol Jenny n take her t the fiels."

"Good. Since you're so early, how about plowing that stretch down by the woods?"

"Suits me, Mistah Hawkins."

"O.K. Go to it!"

He hitched Jenny to a plow and started across the fields. Hot dog! This was just what he wanted. If he could get down by the woods, he could shoot his gun and nobody would hear. He walked behind the plow, hearing the traces creaking, feeling the gun tied tight to his thigh.

When he reached the woods, he plowed two whole rows before he decided to take out the gun. Finally, he stopped, looked in all directions, then untied the gun and held it in his hand. He turned to the mule and smiled.

"Know whut this is, Jenny? Naw, yuh wouldn know! Yuhs jusa ol mule! Anyhow, this is a gun, n it kin shoot, by Gawd!"

He held the gun at arm's length. Whut t hell, Ahma shoot this thing! He looked at Jenny again.

"Lissen here, Jenny! When Ah pull this ol trigger, Ah don wan yuh t run n acka fool now!"

Jenny stood with head down, her short ears pricked straight. Dave walked off about twenty feet, held the gun far out from him at arm's length, and turned his head. Hell, he told himself, Ah ain afraid. The gun felt loose in his fingers; he waved it wildly for a moment. Then he shut his eyes and tightened his forefinger. Bloom! A report half deafened him and he thought his right hand was torn from his arm. He heard Jenny whinnying and galloping over the field, and he found himself on his knees squeezing his fingers hard between his legs. His hand was numb; he jammed it into his mouth, trying to warm it, trying to stop the pain. The gun lay at his feet. He did not quite know what had happened. He stood up and stared at the gun as though it were a living thing. He gritted his teeth and kicked the gun. Yuh almos broke mah arm! He turned to look for Jenny; she was far over the fields, tossing her head and kicking wildly.

"Hol on there, ol mule!"

When he caught up with her she stood trembling, walling her big white eyes at him. The plow was far away; the traces had broken. Then Dave stopped short, looking, not believing. Jenny was bleeding. Her left side was red and wet with blood. He went closer. Lawd, have mercy! Wondah did Ah shoot this mule? He grabbed for Jenny's mane. She flinched, snorted, whirled, tossing her head.

"Hol on now! Hol on."

Then he saw the hole in Jenny's side, right between the ribs. It was round, wet, red. A crimson stream streaked down the front leg, flowing fast. Good Gawd! Ah wuzn't shootin at tha mule. He felt panic. He knew he had to stop that blood, or Jenny would bleed to death. He had never seen so much blood in all his life. He chased the mule for half a mile, trying to catch her. Finally she stopped, breathing hard, stumpy tail half arched. He caught her mane and led her back to where the plough and gun lay. Then he stooped and grabbed handfuls of damp black earth and tried to plug the bullet hole. Jenny shuddered, whinnied, and broke from him.

"Hol on! Hol on now!"

He tried to plug it again, but blood came anyhow. His fingers were hot and sticky. He rubbed dirt into his palms, trying to dry them. Then again he attempted to plug the bullet hole, but Jenny shied away, kicking her heels high. He stood helpless. He had to do something. He ran at Jenny; she dodged him. He watched a red stream of blood flow down Jenny's leg and form a bright pool at her feet.

"Jenny . . . Jenny," he called weakly.

His lips trembled. She's bleeding t death! He looked in the direction of home, wanting to go back, wanting to get help. But he saw the pistol lying in the damp black clay. He had a queer feeling that if he only did something, this would not be; Jenny would not be there bleeding to death.

When he went to her this time, she did not move. She stood with sleepy, dreamy eyes; and when he touched her she gave a low-pitched whinny and knelt to the ground, her front knees slopping in blood.

"Jenny . . . Jenny . . ." he whispered.

For a long time she held her neck erect; then her head sank, slowly. Her ribs swelled with a mighty heave and she went over.

Dave's stomach felt empty, very empty. He picked up the gun and held it gingerly between his thumb and forefinger. He buried it at the foot of a tree. He took a stick and tried to cover the pool of blood with dirt—but what was the use? There was Jenny lying with her mouth open and her eyes walled and glassy. He could not tell Jim Hawkins he had shot his mule. But he had to tell something. Yeah, Ah'll tell em Jenny started gittin wil n fell on the joint of the plow. . . . But that would hardly happen to a mule. He walked across the field slowly, head down.

It was sunset. Two of Jim Hawkins' men were over near the edge of the woods digging a hole in which to bury Jenny. Dave was surrounded by a knot of people, all of whom were looking down at the dead mule.

"I don't see how in the world it happened," said Jim Hawkins for the tenth time.

The crowd parted and Dave's mother, father, and small brother pushed into the center.

"Where Dave?" his mother called.

"There he is," said Jim Hawkins.

His mother grabbed him.

"Whut happened, Dave? Whut yuh done?"

"Nothin."

"C mon, boy, talk," his father said.

Dave took a deep breath and told the story he knew nobody believed.

"Waal," he drawled. "Ah brung ol Jenny down here sos Ah could do mah plowin. Ah plowed bout two rows, just like yuh see." He stopped and pointed at the long rows of upturned earth. "Then somethin musta been wrong wid ol Jenny. She wouldn ack right a-tall. She started snortin n kickin her heels. Ah tried t hol her, but she pulled erway, rearin n goin in. Then when the point of the plow was stickin up in the air, she swung erroun n twisted herself back on it . . . She stuck herself n started t bleed. N fo Ah could do anything, she wuz dead."

"Did you ever hear of anything like that in all your life?" asked Jim Hawkins.

There were white and black standing in the crowd. They murmured. Dave's mother came close to him and looked hard into his face. "Tell the truth, Dave," she said.

"Looks like a bullet hole to me," said one man.

"Dave, whut yuh do wid the gun?" his mother asked.

The crowd surged in, looking at him. He jammed his hands into his pockets, shook his head slowly from left to right, and backed away. His eyes were wide and painful.

"Did he hava gun?" asked Jim Hawkins.

"By Gawd, Ah tol him tha wuz a gun wound," said a man, slapping his thigh.

His father caught his shoulders and shook him till his teeth rattled.

"Tell whut happened, yuh rascal! Tell whut . . ."

Dave looked at Jenny's stiff legs and began to cry.

"Whut yuh do wid tha gun?" his mother asked.

"Whut wuz he doin wida gun?" his father asked.

"Come on and tell the truth," said Hawkins. "Ain't nobody going to hurt you . . ."

His mother crowded close to him.

"Did yuh shoot tha mule, Dave?"

Dave cried, seeing blurred white and black faces.

"Ahh ddinn gggo tt sshooot hher . . . Ah ssswear ffo Gawd Ahh ddin. . . . Ah wuz a-tryin t sssee ef the old gggun would sshoot—"

"Where yuh git the gun from?" his father asked.

"Ah got it from Joe, at the sto."

"Where yuh git the money?"

"Ma give it t me."

"He kept worryin me, Bob. Ah had t. Ah tol im t bring the gun right back t me . . . It was fer yuh, the gun."

"But how yuh happen to shoot that mule?" asked Jim Hawkins.

"Ah wuzn shootin at the mule, Mistah Hawkins. The gun jumped when Ah pulled the trigger . . . N for Ah knowed anythin Jenny was there a-bleedin."

Somebody in the crowd laughed. Jim Hawkins walked close to Dave and looked into his face.

"Well, looks like you have bought a mule, Dave."

"Ah swear to Gawd, Ah didn go t kill the mule, Mistah Hawkins!"

"But you killed her!"

All the crowd was laughing now. They stood on tiptoe and poked heads over one another's shoulders.

"Well, boy, looks like yuh done bought a dead mule! Hahaha!"

"Ain tha ershame."

"Hohohohoho."

Dave stood, head down, twisting his feet in the dirt.

"Well, you needn't worry about it, Bob," said Jim Hawkins to Dave's father. "Just let the boy keep on working and pay me two dollars a month."

"Whut yuh wan fer yo mule, Mistah Hawkins?"

Jim Hawkins screwed up his eyes.

"Fifty dollars."

"Whut yuh do wid tha gun?" Dave's father demanded.

Dave said nothing.

"Yuh wan me t take a tree n beat yuh till yuh talk!"

"Nawsuh!"

"Whut yuh do wid it?"

"Ah throwed it erway."

"Where?"

"Ah . . . Ah throwed it in the creek."

"Waal, c mon home. N firs thing in the mawnin git to tha creek n fin tha gun."

"Yessuh."

"Whut yuh pay fer it?"

"Two dollahs."

"Take tha gun n git yu money back n carry it t Mistah Hawkins, yuh hear? N don fergit Ahma lam you black bottom good fer this! Now march yosef on home, suh!"

Dave turned and walked slowly. He heard people laughing. Dave glared, his eyes welling with tears. Hot anger bubbled in him. Then he swallowed and stumbled on.

That night Dave did not sleep. He was glad that he had gotten out of killing the mule so easily, but he was hurt. Something hot seemed to turn over inside him each time he remembered how they had laughed. He tossed on his bed, feeling his hard pillow. N Pa says he's gonna beat me . . . He remembered other beatings, and his back quivered. Naw, naw. Ah sho don wan im t beat me tha way no mo. Dam em all! Nobody ever gave him anything. All he did was work. They treat me like a mule, n then they beat me. He gritted his teeth. N Ma had t tell on me.

Well, if he had to, he would take old man Hawkins that two dollars. But that meant selling the gun. And he wanted to keep that gun. Fifty dollars for a dead mule.

He turned over, thinking how he had fired the gun. He had an itch to fire it again. Ef other men kin shoota gun, by Gawd, Ah kin! He was still, listening. Mebbe they all sleepin now. The house was still. He heard the soft breathing of his brother. Yes, now! He would go down and get that gun and see if he could fire it! He eased out of bed and slipped into overalls.

The moon was bright. He ran almost all the way to the edge of the woods. He stumbled over the ground, looking for the spot where he had buried the gun. Yeah, here it is. Like a hungry dog scratching for a bone, he pawed it up. He puffed his black cheeks and blew dirt from the trigger and barrel. He broke it and found four cartridges unshot. He looked around; the fields were filled with silence and moonlight. He clutched the gun stiff and hard in his fingers. But, as soon as he wanted to pull the trigger, he shut his eyes and turned his head. Naw, Ah can't shoot wid mah eyes closed n mah head turned. With effort he held his eyes open; then he squeezed. *Bloooom!* He was stiff, not breathing. The gun was still in his hands. Dammit, he'd done it! He fired again. *Blooooom!* He smiled. *Blooooom! Blooooom! Click, click*. There! It was empty. If anybody could shoot a gun, he could. He put the gun into his hip pocket and started across the fields.

When he reached the top of a ridge he stood straight and proud in the moonlight, looking at Jim Hawkins' big white house, feeling the gun sagging in his pocket. Lawd, ef Ah had just one mo bullet Ah'd taka shot at tha house. Ah'd like t scare ol man Hawkins jusa little . . . Jusa enough t let im know Dave Saunders is a man.

To his left the road curved, running to the tracks of the Illinois Central. He jerked his head, listening. From far off came a faint *hoooof-hoooof; hoooof-hoooof; hoooof-hoooof*. . . . He stood rigid. Two dollahs a mont. Les see now . . . Tha means it'll take bout two years. Shucks! Ah'll be dam!

He started down the road, toward the tracks. Yeah, here she comes! He stood beside the track and held himself stiffly. Here she comes, erroun the ben . . . C mon, yuh slow poke! C mon! He had his hand on his gun; something quivered in his stomach. Then the train thundered past, the gray and brown box cars rumbling and clinking. He gripped the gun tightly; then he jerked his hand out of his pocket. Ah betcha Bill wouldn't do it! Ah-betcha . . . The cars slid past, steel grinding upon steel. Ahm ridin yuh ternight, so hep me Gawd! He was hot all over. He hesitated just a moment; then he grabbed, pulled atop of a car, and lay flat. He felt his pocket; the gun was still there. Ahead the long rails were glinting in the moonlight, stretching away, away to somewhere, somewhere where he could be a man . . .

CARSON McCULLERS (1917–1967)

A Tree, a Rock, a Cloud

It was raining that morning, and still very dark. When the boy reached the streetcar café he had almost finished his route and he went in for a cup of coffee. The place was an all-night café owned by a bitter and stingy man called Leo. After the raw, empty street, the café seemed friendly and bright; along the counter there were a couple of soldiers, three spinners from the cotton mill, and in a corner a man who sat hunched over with his nose and half his face down in a beer mug. The boy wore a helmet such as aviators wear. When he went into the café he unbuckled the chin strap and raised the right flap up over his pink little ear; often as he drank his coffee someone would speak to him in a friendly way. But this morning Leo did not look into his face and none of the men were talking. He paid and was leaving the café when a voice called out to him:

"Son! Hey Son!"

He turned back and the man in the corner was crooking his finger and nodding to him. He had brought his face out of the beer mug and he seemed suddenly very happy. The man was long and pale, with a big nose and faded orange hair.

"Hey Son!"

The boy went toward him. He was an undersized boy of about twelve, with one shoulder drawn higher than the other because of the weight of the paper sack. His face was shallow, freckled, and his eyes were round child eyes.

"Yeah Mister?"

The man laid one hand on the paper boy's shoulders, then grasped the boy's chin and turned his face slowly from one side to the other. The boy shrank back uneasily.

"Say! What's the big idea?"

The boy's voice was shrill; inside the café it was suddenly very quiet.

The man said slowly, "I love you."

All along the counter the men laughed. The boy, who had scowled and sidled away, did not know what to do. He looked over the counter at Leo, and Leo watched him with a weary, brittle jeer. The boy tried to laugh also. But the man was serious and sad.

"I did not mean to tease you, Son," he said. "Sit down and have a beer with me. There is something I have to explain."

Cautiously, out of the corner of his eye, the paper boy questioned the men along the counter to see what he should do. But they had gone back to their beer or their breakfast and did not notice him. Leo put a cup of coffee on the counter and a little jug of cream.

"He is a minor," Leo said.

The paper boy slid himself up onto the stool. His ear beneath the upturned flap of the helmet was very small and red. The man was nodding at him soberly. "It is important," he said. Then he reached in his hip pocket and brought out something which he held up in the palm of his hand for the boy to see.

"Look very carefully," he said.

The boy stared, but there was nothing to look at very carefully. The man held in his big, grimy palm a photograph. It was the face of a woman, but blurred, so that only the hat and the dress she was wearing stood out clearly.

"See?" the man asked.

The boy nodded and the man placed another picture in his palm. The woman was standing on a beach in a bathing suit. The suit made her stomach very big, and that was the main thing you noticed.

"Got a good look?" He leaned over closer and finally asked: "You ever seen her before?"

The boy sat motionless, staring slantwise at the man. "Not so I know of."

"Very well." The man blew on the photographs and put them back into his pocket. "That was my wife."

"Dead?" the boy asked.

Slowly the man shook his head. He pursed his lips as though about to whistle and answered in a long-drawn way: "Nuuu—" he said. "I will explain."

The beer on the counter before the man was in a large brown mug. He did not pick it up to drink. Instead he bent down and, putting his face over the rim, he rested there for a moment. Then with both hands he tilted the mug and sipped.

"Some night you'll go to sleep with your big nose in a mug and drown," said Leo. "Prominent transient drowns in beer. That would be a cute death."

The paper boy tried to signal to Leo. While the man was not looking he screwed up his face and worked his mouth to question soundlessly: "Drunk?" But Leo only raised his eyebrows and turned away to put some pink strips of bacon on the grill. The man pushed the mug away from him, straightened himself, and folded his loose crooked hands on the counter. His face was sad as he looked at the paper boy. He did not blink, but from time to time the lids closed down with delicate gravity over his pale green eyes. It was nearing dawn and the boy shifted the weight of the paper sack.

"I am talking about love," the man said. "With me it is a science."

The boy half slid down from the stool. But the man raised his forefinger, and there was something about him that held the boy and would not let him go away.

"Twelve years ago I married the woman in the photograph. She was my wife for one year, nine months,' three days, and two nights. I loved her. Yes. . . ." He tightened his blurred, rambling voice and said again: "I loved her. I thought also that she loved me. I was a railroad engineer. She had all home comforts and luxuries. It never crept into my brain that she was not satisfied. But do you know what happened?"

"Mgneeow!" said Leo.

The man did not take his eyes from the boy's face. "She left me. I came in one night and the house was empty and she was gone. She left me."

"With a fellow?" the boy asked.

Gently the man placed his palm down on the counter. "Why, naturally, Son. A woman does not run off like that alone."

The café was quiet, the soft rain black and endless in the street outside. Leo pressed down the frying bacon with the prongs of his long fork. "So you have been chasing the floozie for eleven years. You frazzled old rascal!"

For the first time the man glanced at Leo. "Please don't be vulgar. Besides, I was not speaking to you." He turned back to the boy and said in a trusting and secretive undertone, "Let's not pay any attention to him. O.K.?"

The paper boy nodded doubtfully.

"It was like this," the man continued. "I am a person who feels many things. All my life one thing after another has impressed me. Moonlight. The leg of a pretty girl. One thing after another. But the point is that when I had enjoyed anything there was a peculiar sensation as though it was laying around loose in me. Nothing seemed to finish itself up or fit in with the other things. Women? I had my portion of them. The same. Afterwards laying around loose in me. I was a man who had never loved."

Very slowly he closed his eyelids, and the gesture was like a curtain drawn at the end of a scene in a play. When he spoke again his voice was excited and the words came fast—the lobes of his large, loose ears seemed to tremble.

"Then I met this woman. I was fifty-one years old and she always said she was thirty. I met her at a filling station and we were married within three days. And do you know what it was like? I just can't tell you. All I had ever felt was gathered together around this woman.

Nothing lay around loose in me any more but was finished up by her."

The man stopped suddenly and stroked his long nose. His voice sank down to a steady and reproachful undertone: "I'm not explaining this right. What happened was this. There were these beautiful feelings and loose little pleasures inside me. And this woman was something like an assembly line for my soul. I run these little pieces of myself through her and I come out complete. Now do you follow me?"

"What was her name?" the boy asked.

"Oh," he said. "I called her Dodo. But that is immaterial."

"Did you try to make her come back?"

The man did not seem to hear. "Under the circumstances you can imagine how I felt when she left me."

Leo took the bacon from the grill and folded two strips of it between a bun. He had a gray face, with slitted eyes, and a pinched nose saddled by faint blue shadows. One of the mill workers signaled for more coffee and Leo poured it. He did not give refills on coffee free. The spinner ate breakfast there every morning, but the better Leo knew his customers the stingier he treated them. He nibbled his own bun as though he grudged it to himself.

"And you never got hold of her again?"

The boy did not know what to think of the man, and his child's face was uncertain with mingled curiosity and doubt. He was new on the paper route; it was still strange to him to be out in the town in the black, queer early morning.

"Yes," the man said. "I took a number of steps to get her back. I went around trying to locate her. I went to Tulsa where she had folks. And to Mobile. I went to every town she had ever mentioned to me, and I hunted down every man she had formerly been connected with. Tulsa, Atlanta, Chicago, Cheehaw, Memphis. . . . For the better part of two years I chased around the country trying to lay hold of her."

"But the pair of them had vanished from the face of the earth!" said Leo.

"Don't listen to him," the man said confidentially. "And also just forget those two years. They are not important. What matters is that around the third year a curious thing begun to happen to me."

"What?" the boy asked.

The man leaned down and tilted his mug to take a sip of beer. But as he hovered over the mug his nostrils fluttered slightly; he sniffed the staleness of the beer and did not drink. "Love is a curious thing to begin with. At first I thought only of getting her back. It was a kind of mania. But then as time went on I tried to remember her. But do you know what happened?"

"No," the boy said.

"When I laid myself down on a bed and tried to think about her my mind became a blank. I couldn't see her. I would take out her pictures and look. No good. Nothing doing. A blank. Can you imagine it?"

"Say Mac!" Leo called down the counter. "Can you imagine this bozo's mind a blank?"

Slowly, as though fanning away flies, the man waved his hand. His green eyes were concentrated and fixed on the shallow little face of the paper boy.

"But a sudden piece of glass on a sidewalk. Or a nickel tune in a music box. A shadow on a wall at night. And I would remember. It might happen in a street and I would cry or bang my head against a lamppost. You follow me?"

"A piece of glass . . ." the boy said.

"Anything. I would walk around and I had no power of how and when to remember her. You think you can put up a kind of shield. But remembering don't come to a man face forward—it corners around sideways. I was at the mercy of everything I saw and heard. Suddenly instead of me combing the countryside to find her she began to chase me around in my very soul. *She* chasing *me*, mind you! and in my soul."

The boy asked finally: "What part of the country were you in then?"

"Ooh," the man groaned, "I was a sick mortal. It was like smallpox. I confess, Son, that I boozed. I fornicated. I committed any sin that suddenly appealed to me. I am loath to confess it but I will do so. When I recall that period it is all curdled in my mind, it was so terrible."

The man leaned his head down and tapped his forehead on the counter. For a few seconds he stayed bowed over in this position, the back of his stringy neck covered with orange furze, his hands with their long warped fingers held palm to palm in an attitude of prayer. Then the man straightened himself; he was smiling and suddenly his face was bright and tremulous and old.

"It was in the fifth year that it happened," he said. "And with it I started my science."

Leo's mouth jerked with a pale, quick grin. "Well none of we boys are getting any younger," he said. Then with sudden anger he balled up a dishcloth he was holding and threw it down hard on the floor. "You draggle-tailed old Romeo!"

"What happened?" the boy asked.

The old man's voice was high and clear: "Peace," he answered.

"Huh?"

"It is hard to explain scientifically, Son," he said. "I guess the logical explanation is that she and I had fleed around from each other for so long that finally we just got tangled up together and lay down and quit. Peace. A queer and beautiful blankness. It was spring in Portland and the rain came every afternoon. All evening I just stayed there on my bed in the dark. And that is how the science come to me."

The windows in the streetcar were pale blue with light. The two soldiers paid for their beers and opened the door—one of the soldiers combed his hair and wiped off his muddy puttees before they went outside. The three mill workers bent silently over their breakfasts. Leo's clock was ticking on the wall.

"It is this. And listen carefully. I meditated on love and reasoned it out. I realized what is wrong with us. Men fall in love for the first time. And what do they fall in love with?"

The boy's soft mouth was partly open and he did not answer.

"A woman," the old man said. "Without science, with nothing to go by, they undertake the most dangerous and sacred experience in God's earth. They fall in love with a woman. Is that correct, Son?"

"Yeah," the boy said faintly.

"They start at the wrong end of love. They begin at the climax. Can you wonder it is so miserable? Do you know how men should love?"

The old man reached over and grasped the boy by the collar of his leather jacket. He gave him a gentle shake and his green eyes gazed down unblinking and grave.

"Son, do you know how love should be begun?"

The boy sat small and listening and still. Slowly he shook his head. The old man leaned closer and whispered:

"A tree. A rock. A cloud."

It was still raining outside in the street: a mild, gray, endless rain. The mill whistle blew for the six o'clock shift and the three spinners paid and went away. There was no one in the café but Leo, the old man, and the little paper boy.

"The weather was like this in Portland," he said. "At the time my science was begun. I meditated and I started very cautious. I would pick up something from the street and take it home with me. I bought a goldfish and I concentrated on the goldfish and I loved it. I graduated from one thing to another. Day by day I was getting this technique. On the road from Portland to San Diego——"

"Aw shut up!" screamed Leo suddenly. "Shut up! Shut up!"

The old man still held the collar of the boy's jacket; he was trembling and his face was earnest and bright and wild. "For six years now I have gone around by myself and built up my science. And now I am a master. Son, I can love anything. No longer do I have to think about it even. I see a street full of people and a beautiful light comes in me. I watch a bird in the sky. Or I meet a traveler on the road. Everything, Son. And anybody. All strangers and all loved! Do you realize what a science like mine can mean?"

The boy held himself stiffly, his hands curled tight around the counter edge. Finally he asked: "Did you ever really find that lady?"

"What? What say, Son?"

"I mean," the boy asked timidly. "Have you fallen in love with a woman again?"

The old man loosened his grasp on the boy's collar. He turned away and for the first time his green eyes had a vague and scattered look. He lifted his mug from the counter, drank down the yellow beer. His head was shaking slowly from side to side. Then finally he answered: "No, Son. You see that is the last step in my science. I go cautious. And I am not quite ready yet."

"Well!" said Leo. "Well well well!"

The old man stood in the open doorway. "Remember," he said. Framed there in the gray damp light of the early morning he looked shrunken and seedy and frail. But his smile was bright. "Remember I love you," he said with a last nod. And the door closed quietly behind him.

The boy did not speak for a long time. He pulled down the bangs on his forehead and slid his grimy little forefinger around the rim of his empty cup. Then without looking at Leo he finally asked:

"Was he drunk?"

"No," said Leo shortly.

The boy raised his clear voice higher. "Then was he a dope fiend?"

"No."

The boy looked up at Leo, and his flat little face was desperate, his voice urgent and shrill. "Was he crazy? Do you think he was a lunatic?" The paper boy's voice dropped suddenly with doubt. "Leo? Or not?"

But Leo would not answer him. Leo had run a night café for fourteen years, and he held himself to be a critic of craziness. There were the town characters and also the transients who roamed in from the night. He knew the manias of all of them. But he did not want to satisfy the questions of the waiting child. He tightened his pale face and was silent.

So the boy pulled down the right flap of his helmet and as he turned to leave he made the only comment that seemed safe to him, the only remark that could not be laughed down and despised:

"He sure has done a lot of traveling."

FLANNERY O'CONNOR (1925–1964)

A Good Man Is Hard to Find

The grandmother didn't want to go to Florida. She wanted to visit some of her connections in east Tennessee and she was seizing at every chance to change Bailey's mind. Bailey was the son she lived with, her only boy. He was sitting on the edge of his chair at the table, bent over the orange sports section of the *Journal*. "Now look here, Bailey," she said, "see here, read this," and she stood with one hand on her thin hip and the other rattling the newspaper at his bald head. "Here this fellow that calls himself The Misfit is aloose from the Federal Pen and headed toward Florida and you read here what it says he did to these people. Just you read it. I wouldn't take my children in any direction with a criminal like that aloose in it. I couldn't answer to my conscience if I did."

Bailey didn't look up from his reading so she wheeled around then and faced the children's mother, a young woman in slacks, whose face was as broad and innocent as a cabbage and was tied round with a green head-kerchief that had two points on the top like rabbit's ears. She was sitting on the sofa, feeding the baby his apricots out of a jar. "The children have been to Florida before," the old lady said. "You all ought to take them somewhere else for a change so they would see different parts of the world and be broad. They never have been to east Tennessee."

The children's mother didn't seem to hear her but the eight-year-old boy, John Wesley, a stocky child with glasses, said, "If you don't want to go to Florida, why dontcha stay at home?" He and the little girl, June Star, were reading the funny papers on the floor.

"She wouldn't stay at home to be queen for a day," June Star said without raising her yellow head.

"Yes and what would you do if this fellow, The Misfit, caught you?" the grandmother asked.

"I'd smack his face," John Wesley said.

"She wouldn't stay at home for a million bucks," June Star said. "Afraid she'd miss something. She has to go everywhere we go."

"All right, Miss," the grandmother said. "Just remember that the next time you want me to curl your hair."

June Star said her hair was naturally curly.

The next morning the grandmother was the first one in the car, ready to go. She had her big black valise that looked like the head of a hippopotamus in one corner, and underneath it she was hiding a basket with Pitty Sing, the cat, in it. She didn't intend for the cat to be left alone in the house for three days because he would miss her too much and she was afraid he might brush against one of the gas burners and accidentally asphyxiate himself. Her son, Bailey, didn't like to arrive at a motel with a cat.

She sat in the middle of the back seat with John Wesley and June Star on either side of her. Bailey and the children's mother and the baby sat in the front and they left Atlanta at eight forty-five with the mileage on the car at 55890. The grandmother wrote this down because she thought it would be interesting to say how many miles they had been when they got back. It took them twenty minutes to reach the outskirts of the city.

The old lady settled herself comfortably, removing her white cotton gloves and putting them up with her purse on the shelf in front of the back window. The children's mother still had on slacks and still had her head tied up in a green kerchief, but the grandmother had on a navy blue straw sailor hat with a bunch of white violets on the brim and a navy blue dress with a small white dot in the print. Her collar and cuffs were white organdy trimmed with lace and at her neckline she had pinned a purple spray of cloth violets containing a sachet. In case of an accident, anyone seeing her dead on the highway would know at once that she was a lady.

She said she thought it was going to be a good day for driving, neither too hot nor too cold, and she cautioned Bailey that the speed limit was fifty-five miles an hour and that the patrolmen hid themselves behind billboards and small clumps of trees and sped out after you before you had a chance to slow down. She pointed out interesting details of the scenery: Stone Mountain; the blue granite that in some places came up to both sides of the highway; the brilliant red clay banks slightly streaked with purple; and the various crops that made rows of green lace-work on the ground. The trees were full of silver-white sunlight and the meanest of them sparkled. The children were reading comic magazines and their mother had gone back to sleep.

"Let's go through Georgia fast so we won't have to look at it much," John Wesley said.

"If I were a little boy," said the grandmother, "I wouldn't talk about my native state that way. Tennessee has the mountains and Georgia has the hills."

"Tennessee is just a hillbilly dumping ground," John Wesley said, "and Georgia is a lousy state too."

"You said it," June Star said.

"In my time," said the grandmother, folding her thin veined fingers, "children were more respectful of their native states and their parents and everything else. People did right then. Oh look at the cute little pickaninny!" she said and pointed to a Negro child standing in the door of a shack. "Wouldn't that make a picture, now?" she asked and they all turned and looked at the little Negro out of the back window. He waved.

"He didn't have any britches on," June said.

"He probably didn't have any," the grandmother explained. "Little niggers in the country don't have things like we do. If I could paint, I'd paint that picture," she said.

The children exchanged comic books.

The grandmother offered to hold the baby and the children's mother passed him over the front seat to her. She set him on her knee and bounced him and told him about the things they were passing. She rolled her eyes and screwed up her mouth and stuck her leathery thin face into his smooth bland one. Occasionally he gave her a faraway smile. They passed a large cotton field with five or six graves fenced in the middle of it, like a small island. "Look at the graveyard!" the grandmother said, pointing it out. "That was the old family burying ground. That belonged to the plantation."

"Where's the plantation?" John Wesley asked.

"Gone With the Wind," said the grandmother. "Ha. Ha."

When the children finished all the comic books they had brought, they opened the lunch and ate it. The grandmother ate a peanut butter sandwich and an olive and would not let the children throw the box and the paper napkins out the window. When there was nothing else to do they played a game by choosing a cloud and making the other two guess what shape it suggested. John Wesley took one the shape of a cow and June Star guessed a cow and John Wesley said, no, an automobile, and June Star said he didn't play fair, and they began to slap each other over the grandmother.

The grandmother said she would tell them a story if they would keep quiet. When she told a story, she rolled her eyes and waved her head and was very dramatic. She said once when she was a maiden lady she had been courted by a Mr. Edgar Atkins Teagarden from Jasper, Georgia. She said he was a very good-looking man and a gentleman and that he brought her a watermelon every Saturday afternoon with his initials cut in it, E. A. T. Well, one Saturday, she said, Mr. Teagarden brought the watermelon and there was nobody at home and he left it on the front porch and returned in his buggy to Jasper, but she never got the watermelon, she said, because a nigger boy ate it when he saw the initials, E. A. T.! This story tickled John Wesley's funny bone and he giggled and giggled but June Star didn't think it was any good. She said she wouldn't marry a man that just brought her a watermelon on Saturday. The grandmother said she would have done well to marry Mr. Teagarden because he was a gentleman and had bought Coca-Cola stock when it first came out and that he had died only a few years ago, a very wealthy man.

They stopped at The Tower for barbecued sandwiches. The Tower was a part stucco and part wood filling station and dance hall set in a clearing outside of Timothy. A fat man named Red Sammy Butts ran it and there were signs stuck here and there on the building and for miles up and down the highway saying, TRY RED SAMMY'S FAMOUS BARBECUE. NONE LIKE FAMOUS RED SAMMY'S! RED SAM! THE FAT BOY WITH THE HAPPY LAUGH. A VETERAN! SAMMY'S YOUR MAN!

Red Sammy was lying on the bare ground outside The Tower with his head under a truck while a gray monkey about a foot high, chained to a small chinaberry tree, chattered nearby. The monkey sprang back into the tree and got on the highest limb as soon as he saw the children jump out of the car and run toward him.

Inside, The Tower was a long dark room with a counter at one end and tables at the other and dancing space in the middle. They all sat down at a broad table next to the nickelodeon and Red Sam's wife, a tall burnt-brown woman with hair and eyes lighter than her skin, came and took their order. The children's mother put a dime in the machine and played "The Tennessee Waltz," and the grandmother said that tune always made her want to dance. She asked Bailey if he would like to dance but he only glared at her. He didn't have a naturally sunny disposition like she did and trips made him nervous. The grandmother's brown eyes were very bright. She swayed her head from side to side and pretended she was dancing in her chair. June Star said play something she could tap to so the children's mother put in another dime and played a fast number and June Star stepped out onto the dance floor and did her tap routine.

"Ain't she cute?" Red Sam's wife said, leaning over the counter. "Would you like to come be my little girl?"

"No I certainly wouldn't," June Star said. "I wouldn't live in a broken-down place like this for a million bucks!" and she ran back to the table.

"Ain't she cute?" the woman repeated, stretching her mouth politely.

"Aren't you ashamed?" hissed the grandmother.

Red Sam came in and told his wife to quit lounging on the counter and hurry with these people's order. His khaki trousers reached just to his hip bones and his stomach hung over them like a sack of meal swaying under his shirt. He came over and sat down at a table nearby and let out a combination sigh and yodel. "You can't win," he said. "You can't win," and he wiped his sweating red face off with a gray handkerchief. "These days you don't know who to trust," he said. "Ain't that the truth?"

"People are certainly not nice like they used to be," said the grandmother.

"Two fellers come in here last week," Red Sammy said, "driving a Chrysler. It was a old beat-up car but it was a good one and these boys looked all right to me. Said they worked at the mill and you know I let them fellers charge the gas they bought? Now why did I do that?"

"Because you're a good man!" the grandmother said at once.

"Yes'm, I suppose so," Red Sam said as if he were struck with the answer.

His wife brought the orders, carrying the five plates all at once without a tray, two in each hand and one balanced on her arm. "It isn't a soul in this green world of God's that you can trust," she said. "And I don't count anybody out of that, not nobody," she repeated, looking at Red Sammy.

"Did you read about that criminal, The Misfit, that's escaped?" asked the grandmother.

"I wouldn't be a bit surprised if he didn't attact this place right here," said the woman. "If he hears about it being here, I wouldn't be none surprised to see him. If he hears it's two cent in the cash register, I wouldn't be a tall surprised if he . . ."

"That'll do," Red Sam said. "Go bring these people their Co'Colas," and the woman went off to get the rest of the order.

"A good man is hard to find," Red Sammy said. "Everything is getting terrible. I remember the day you could go off and leave your screen door unlatched. Not no more."

He and the grandmother discussed better times. The old lady said that in her opinion Europe was entirely to blame for the way things were now. She said the way Europe acted you would think we were made of money and Red Sam said it was no use talking about it, she was exactly right. The children ran outside into the white sunlight and looked at the monkey in the lacy chinaberry tree. He was busy catching fleas on himself and biting each one carefully between his teeth as if it were a delicacy.

They drove off again into the hot afternoon. The grandmother took cat naps and woke up every few minutes with her own snoring. Outside of Toombsboro she woke up and recalled an old plantation that she had visited in this neighborhood once when she was a young lady. She said the house had six white columns across the front and that there was an avenue of oaks leading up to it and two little wooden trellis arbors on either side in front where you sat down with your suitor after a stroll in the garden. She recalled exactly which road to turn off to get to it. She knew that Bailey would not be willing to lose any time looking at an old house, but the more she talked about it, the more she wanted to see it once again and find out if the little twin arbors were still standing. "There was a secret panel in this house," she said craftily, not telling the truth but wishing that she were, "and the story went that all the family silver was hidden in it when Sherman came through but it was never found . . ."

"Hey!" John Wesley said. "Let's go see it! We'll find it! We'll poke all the woodwork and find it! Who lives there? Where do you turn off at? Hey Pop, can't we turn off there?"

"We never have seen a house with a secret panel!" June Star shrieked. "Let's go to the house with the secret panel! Hey, Pop, can't we go see the house with the secret panel!"

"It's not far from here, I know," the grandmother said. "It wouldn't take over twenty minutes."

Bailey was looking straight ahead. His jaw was as rigid as a horseshoe. "No," he said.

The children began to yell and scream that they wanted to see the house with the secret panel. John Wesley kicked the back of the front seat and June Star hung over her mother's shoulder and whined desperately into her ear that they never had any fun even on their vacation, and that they could never do what THEY wanted to do. The baby began to scream and John Wesley kicked the back of the seat so hard that his father could feel the blows in his kidney.

"All right!" he shouted, and drew the car to a stop at the side of the road. "Will you all shut up? Will you all just shut up for one second? If you don't shut up, we won't go anywhere."

"It would be very educational for them," the grandmother murmured.

"All right," Bailey said, "but get this: this is the only time we're going to stop for anything like this. This is the one and only time."

"The dirt road that you have to turn down is about a mile back," the grandmother directed. "I marked it when we passed."

"A dirt road," Bailey groaned.

After they had turned around and were headed toward the dirt road, the grandmother recalled other points about the house, the beautiful glass over the front doorway and the candle-lamp in the hall. John Wesley said that the secret panel was probably in the fireplace.

"You can't go inside this house," Bailey said. "You don't know who lives there."

"While you all talk to the people in front, I'll run around behind and get in a window," John Wesley suggested.

"We'll all stay in the car," his mother said.

They turned onto the dirt road and the car raced roughly along in a swirl of pink dust. The grandmother recalled the times when there were no paved roads and thirty miles was a day's journey. The dirt road was hilly and there were sudden washes in it and sharp curves on dangerous embankments. All at once they would be on a hill, looking down over the blue tops of trees for miles around, then the next minute, they would be in a red depression with the dust-coated trees looking down on them.

"This place had better turn up in a minute," Bailey said, "or I'm going to turn around."

The road looked as if no one had traveled on it in months.

"It's not much farther," the grandmother said and just as she said it, a horrible thought came to her. The thought was so embarrassing that she turned red in the face and her eyes dilated and her feet jumped up, upsetting her valise in the corner. The instant the valise moved, the newspaper top she had over the basket under it rose with a snarl and Pitty Sing, the cat, sprang onto Bailey's shoulder.

The children were thrown to the floor and their mother, clutching the baby, was thrown out the door onto the ground, the old lady was thrown into the front seat. The car turned over once and landed right-side-up in a gulch on the side of the road. Bailey remained in the driver's seat with the cat—gray-striped with a broad white face and an orange nose—clinging to his neck like a caterpillar.

As soon as the children saw they could move their arms and legs, they scrambled out of the car, shouting. "We've had an ACCIDENT!" The grandmother was curled up under the dashboard, hoping she was injured so that Bailey's wrath would not come down on her all at once. The horrible thought she had had before the accident was that the house she had remembered so vividly was not in Georgia but in Tennessee.

Bailey removed the cat from his neck with both hands and flung it out the window against the side of a pine tree. Then he got out of the car and started looking for the children's mother. She was sitting against the side of the red gutted ditch, holding the screaming baby, but she only had a cut down her face and a broken shoulder. "We've had an ACCIDENT!" the children screamed in a frenzy of delight.

"But nobody's killed," June Star said with disappointment as the grandmother limped out of the car, her hat still pinned to her head but the broken front brim standing up at a jaunty angle and the violet spray hanging off the side. They all sat down in the ditch, except the children, to recover from the shock. They were all shaking.

"Maybe a car will come along," said the children's mother hoarsely.

"I believe I have injured an organ," said the grandmother, pressing her side, but no one answered her. Bailey's teeth were clattering.

He had on a yellow sport shirt with bright blue parrots designed in it and his face was as yellow as the shirt. The grandmother decided that she would not mention that the house was in Tennessee.

The road was about ten feet above and they could see only the tops of the trees on the other side of it. Behind the ditch they were sitting in there were more woods, tall and dark and deep. In a few minutes they saw a car some distance away on top of a hill, coming slowly as if the occupants were watching them. The grandmother stood up and waved both arms dramatically to attract their attention. The car continued to come on slowly, disappeared around a bend and appeared again, moving even slower, on top of the hill they had gone over. It was a big black battered hearse-like automobile. There were three men in it.

It came to a stop just over them and for some minutes, the driver looked down with a steady expressionless gaze to where they were sitting, and didn't speak. Then he turned his head and muttered something to the other two and they got out. One was a fat boy in black trousers and a red sweat shirt with a silver stallion embossed on the front of it. He moved around on the right side of them and stood staring, his mouth partly open in a kind of loose grin. The other had on khaki pants and a blue striped coat and a gray hat pulled down very low, hiding most of his face. He came around slowly on the left side. Neither spoke.

The driver got out of the car and stood by the side of it, looking down at them. He was an older man than the other two. His hair was just beginning to gray and he wore silver-rimmed spectacles that gave him a scholarly look. He had a long creased face and didn't have on any shirt or undershirt. He had on blue jeans that were too tight for him and was holding a black hat and a gun. The two boys also had guns.

"We've had an ACCIDENT!" the children screamed.

The grandmother had the peculiar feeling that the bespectacled man was someone she knew. His face was as familiar to her as if she had known him all her life but she could not recall who he was. He moved away from the car and began to come down the embankment, placing his feet carefully so that he wouldn't slip. He had on tan and white shoes and no socks, and his ankles were red and thin. "Good afternoon," he said. "I see you all had you a little spill."

"We turned over twice!" said the grandmother.

"Oncet," he corrected. "We seen it happen. Try their car and see will it run, Hiram," he said quietly to the boy with the gray hat.

"What you got that gun for?" John Wesley asked. "Whatcha gonna do with that gun?"

"Lady," the man said to the children's mother, "would you mind calling them children to sit down by you? Children make me nervous. I want all you all to sit down right together there where you're at."

"What are you telling us what to do for?" June Star asked.

Behind them the line of woods gaped like a dark open mouth. "Come here," said their mother.

"Look here now," Bailey began suddenly, "we're in a predicament! We're in . . ."

The grandmother shrieked. She scrambled to her feet and stood staring. "You're The Misfit!" she said. "I recognized you at once."

"Yes'm," the man said, smiling slightly as if he were pleased in spite of himself to be known, "but it would have been better for all of you, lady, if you hadn't of reckernized me."

Bailey turned his head sharply and said something to his mother that shocked even the children. The old lady began to cry and The Misfit reddened.

"Lady," he said, "don't you get upset. Sometimes a man says things he don't mean. I don't reckon he meant to talk to you thataway."

"You wouldn't shoot a lady, would you?" the grandmother said and removed a clean handkerchief from her cuff and began to slap at her eyes with it.

The Misfit pointed the toe of his shoe into the ground and made a little hole and then covered it up again. "I would hate to have to," he said.

"Listen," the grandmother almost screamed, "I know you're a good man. You don't look a bit like you have common blood. I know you must come from nice people!"

"Yes mam," he said, "finest people in the world." When he smiled he showed a row of strong white teeth. "God never made a finer woman than my mother and my daddy's heart was pure gold," he said. The boy with the red sweat shirt had come around behind them and was standing with his gun at his hip. The Misfit squatted down on the ground. "Watch them children, Bobby Lee," he said. "You know they make me nervous." He looked at the six of them huddled together in front of him and he seemed to be embarrassed as if he couldn't think of anything to say. "Ain't a cloud in the sky," he remarked, looking up at it. "Don't see no sun but don't see no cloud neither."

"Yes, it's a beautiful day," said the grandmother. "Listen," she said, "you shouldn't call yourself The Misfit because I know you're a good man at heart. I can just look at you and tell."

"Hush!" Bailey yelled. "Hush! Everybody shut up and let me handle this!" He was squatting in the position of a runner about to sprint forward but he didn't move.

"I pre-chate that, lady," The Misfit said and drew a little circle in the ground with the butt of his gun.

"It'll take a half a hour to fix this here car," Hiram called, looking over the raised hood of it.

"Well, first you and Bobby Lee get him and that little boy to step over yonder with you," The Misfit said, pointing to Bailey and John Wesley. "The boys want to ask you something," he said to Bailey. "Would you mind stepping back in them woods there with them?"

"Listen," Bailey began, "we're in a terrible predicament. Nobody realizes what this is," and his voice cracked. His eyes were as blue and intense as the parrots in his shirt and he remained perfectly still.

The grandmother reached up to adjust her hat brim as if she were going to the woods with him but it came off in her hand. She stood staring at it and after a second she let it fall on the ground. Hiram pulled Bailey up by the arm as if he were assisting an old man. John Wesley caught hold of his father's hand and Bobby Lee followed. They went off toward the woods and just as they reached the dark edge, Bailey turned and supporting himself against a gray naked pine trunk, he shouted, "I'll be back in a minute, Mamma, wait on me!"

"Come back this instant!" his mother shrilled but they all disappeared into the woods.

"Bailey Boy!" the grandmother called in a tragic voice but she found she was looking at The Misfit squatting on the ground in front of her. "I just know you're a good man," she said desperately. "You're not a bit common!"

"Nome, I ain't a good man," The Misfit said after a second as if he had considered her statement carefully, "but I ain't the worst in the world neither. My daddy said I was different breed of dog from my brothers and sisters. 'You know,' Daddy said, 'it's some that can live their whole life out without asking about it and it's others has to know why it is, and this boy is one of the latters. He's going to be into everything!'" He put on his black hat and looked up suddenly and then away deep into the woods as if he were embarrassed again. "I'm sorry I don't have on a shirt before you ladies," he said, hunching his shoulders slightly. "We buried our clothes that we had on when we escaped and we're just making do until we can get better. We borrowed these from some folks we met," he explained.

"That's perfectly all right," the grandmother said. "Maybe Bailey has an extra shirt in his suitcase."

"I'll look and see terrectly," The Misfit said.

"Where are they taking him?" the children's mother screamed.

"Daddy was a card himself," the Misfit said. "You couldn't put anything over on him. He never got in trouble with the Authorities though. Just had the knack of handling them."

"You could be honest too if you'd only try," said the grandmother. "Think how wonderful it would be to settle down and live a comfortable life and not have to think about somebody chasing you all the time."

The Misfit kept scratching in the ground with the butt of his gun as if he were thinking about it. "Yes'm, somebody is always after you," he murmured.

The grandmother noticed how thin his shoulder blades were just behind his hat because she was standing up looking down on him. "Do you ever pray?" she asked.

He shook his head. All she saw was the black hat wiggle between his shoulder blades. "Nome," he said.

There was a pistol shot from the woods, followed closely by another. Then silence. The old lady's head jerked around. She could hear the wind move through the tree tops like a long satisfied insuck of breath. "Bailey Boy!" she called.

"I was a gospel singer for a while," The Misfit said. "I been most everything. Been in the arm service, both land and sea, at home and abroad, been twict married, been an undertaker, been with the railroads, plowed Mother Earth, been in a tornado, seen a man burnt alive oncet," and he looked up at the children's mother and the little girl who were sitting close together, their faces white and their eyes glassy; "I even seen a woman flogged," he said.

"Pray, pray," the grandmother began, "pray, pray . . ."

"I never was a bad boy that I remember of," The Misfit said in an almost dreamy voice, "but somewheres along the line I done something wrong and got sent to the penitentiary. I was buried alive," and he looked up and held her attention to him by a steady stare.

"That's when you should have started to pray," she said. "What did you do to get sent to the penitentiary that first time?"

"Turn to the right, it was a wall," The Misfit said, looking up again at the cloudless sky. "Turn to the left, it was a wall. Look up it was a ceiling, look down it was a floor. I forgot what I done, lady. I set there and set there, trying to remember what it was I done and I ain't recalled it to this day. Oncet in a while, I would think it was coming to me, but it never come."

"Maybe they put you in by mistake," the old lady said vaguely.

"Nome," he said. "It wasn't no mistake. They had the papers on me."

"You must have stolen something," she said.

The Misfit sneered slightly. "Nobody had nothing I wanted," he said. "It was a head-doctor at the penitentiary said what I had done was kill my daddy but I know that for a lie. My daddy died in nineteen ought nineteen of the epidemic flu and I never had a thing to do with it. He was buried in the Mount Hopewell Baptist churchyard and you can go there and see for yourself."

"If you would pray," the old lady said, "Jesus would help you."

"That's right," The Misfit said.

"Well then, why don't you pray?" she asked trembling with delight suddenly.

"I don't want no hep," he said. "I'm doing all right by myself."

Bobby Lee and Hiram came ambling back from the woods. Bobby Lee was dragging a yellow shirt with bright blue parrots in it.

"Throw me that shirt, Bobby Lee," The Misfit said. The shirt came flying at him and landed on his shoulder and he put it on. The grandmother couldn't name what the shirt reminded her of. "No, lady," The Misfit said while he was buttoning it up. "I found out the crime don't matter. You can do one thing or you can do another, kill a man or take a tire off his car, because sooner or later you're going to forget what it was you done and just be punished for it."

The children's mother had begun to make heaving noises as if she couldn't get her breath. "Lady," he asked, "would you and that little girl like to step off yonder with Bobby Lee and Hiram and join your husband?"

"Yes, thank you," the mother said faintly. Her left arm dangled helplessly and she was holding the baby, who had gone to sleep, in the other. "Hep that lady up, Hiram," The Misfit said as she struggled to climb out of the ditch, "and Bobby Lee, you hold onto that little girl's hand."

"I don't want to hold hands with him," June Star said. "He reminds me of a pig."

The fat boy blushed and laughed and caught her by the arm and pulled her off into the woods after Hiram and her mother.

Alone with The Misfit, the grandmother found that she had lost her voice. There was not a cloud in the sky nor any sun. There was nothing around her but woods. She wanted to tell him that he must pray. She opened and closed her mouth several times before anything came out. Finally she found herself saying, "Jesus, Jesus," meaning Jesus will help you, but the way she was saying it, it sounded as if she might be cursing.

"Yes'm," The Misfit said as if he agreed. "Jesus thown everything off balance. It was the same case with Him as with me except He hadn't committed any crime and they could prove I had committed one because they had the papers on me. Of course," he said, "they never shown me any papers. That's why I sign myself now. I said long ago, you get you a signature and sign everything you do and keep a copy of it. Then you'll know what you done and you can hold up the crime to the punishment and see do they match and in the end you'll have something to prove you ain't been treated right. I call myself The Misfit," he said, "because I can't make what all I done wrong fit what all I gone through in punishment."

There was a piercing scream from the woods, followed closely by a pistol report. "Does it seem right to you, lady, that one is punished a heap and another ain't punished at all?"

"Jesus!" the old lady cried. "You've got good blood! I know you wouldn't shoot a lady! I know you come from nice people! Pray! Jesus, you ought not to shoot a lady. I'll give you all the money I've got!"

"Lady," The Misfit said, looking beyond her far into the woods, "there never was a body that give the undertaker a tip."

There were two more pistol reports and the grandmother raised her head like a parched old turkey hen crying for water and called, "Bailey Boy, Bailey Boy!" as if her heart would break.

"Jesus was the only One that ever raised the dead," The Misfit continued, "and He shouldn't have done it. He thown everything off balance. If He did what He said, then it's nothing for you to do but thow away everything and follow Him, and if He didn't, then it's nothing for you to do but enjoy the few minutes you got left the best way you can—by killing somebody or burning down his house or doing some other meanness to him. No pleasure but meanness," he said and his voice had become almost a snarl.

"Maybe He didn't raise the dead," the old lady mumbled, not knowing what she was saying and feeling so dizzy that she sank down in the ditch with her legs twisted under her.

"I wasn't there so I can't say He didn't," The Misfit said. "I wisht I had of been there," he said, hitting the ground with his fist. "It ain't right I wasn't there because if I had of been there I would of known. Listen lady," he said in a high voice, "if I had of been there I would of known and I wouldn't be like I am now." His voice seemed about to crack and the grandmother's head cleared for an instant. She saw the man's face twisted close to her own as if he were going to cry and she murmured, "Why you're one of my babies. You're one of my own children!" She reached out and touched him on the shoulder. The Misfit sprang back as if a snake had bitten him and shot her three times through the chest. Then he put his gun down on the ground and took off his glasses and began to clean them.

Hiram and Bobby Lee returned from the woods and stood over the ditch, looking down at the grandmother who half sat and half lay in a puddle of blood with her legs crossed under her like a child's and her face smiling up at the cloudless sky.

Without his glasses, The Misfit's eyes were red-rimmed and pale and defenseless-looking. "Take her off and thow her where you thown the others," he said, picking up the cat that was rubbing itself against his leg.

"She was a talker, wasn't she?" Bobby Lee said, sliding down the ditch with a yodel.

"She would of been a good woman," The Misfit said, "if it had been somebody there to shoot her every minute of her life."

"Some fun!" Bobby Lee said.

"Shut up, Bobby Lee," The Misfit said. "It's no real pleasure in life."

POETRY

1 Reading Poetry

Poetry may well be the oldest of all literary forms. Certainly, a great deal of the oldest literature of which we have written records is in verse. Yet today poetry is often regarded as the most sophisticated or difficult of literary forms. What has happened to cause the change? Why should something that seems so difficult to us today have seemed so natural to our ancestors? There are two answers to these questions. The first deals with music; the second with memory.

Poetry is musical, or at least rhythmic, speech. It is also usually a harmonious speech, employing words whose sounds echo each other or blend well. It may even be set to music, to be chanted or sung rather than simply spoken.

Because of its musical nature, poetry is easily remembered. Everyone knows how much easier it is to memorize the words to a song than to memorize even a few paragraphs from a newspaper or textbook. Poetry can thus serve as an aid to memory. If you must remember something, and have no written notes to help you, you can make a song of what you need to remember, and your chances of keeping it in your head will improve.

In almost any society, the desire to keep records, remember events, or tell stories precedes the invention of writing. Poetry, being pleasant and memorable, is then the natural first form for histories and tales. Once the art of writing develops, however, poetry is no longer essential. But it is still pleasing and has by now a tradition of use behind it. Prose takes over for record keeping and for transmitting technical information, but poetry keeps its hold on certain important affairs. Songs are still written to celebrate victories and loves, to mourn deaths, and to worship.

The printing of books, which gave so many people access to written words, has been one factor in the promotion of prose in our society. The invention of radio and television—whose announcers universally speak in the blandest, least musical cadences possible—has been another factor. After the age of nursery rhymes, most of us live in a world where the cadences of poetry are no longer part of our everyday life. Moreover, we live in a society where so many written and spoken words bombard us that we learn to skim through them quickly for whatever information they carry. We take no time to look for the beauty of words or for rhythm—neither of which is very likely to be there anyway.

Poetry, however, cannot be read rapidly. Newspapers can be, and, in fact, are meant to be. Fiction can be. And, again, some of it is meant for the quick, careless reader, though most good fiction improves with slow, thoughtful reading. Drama, in general, must be read more slowly, if we are to catch the sound of the individual speeches. But poetry must be read most slowly of all. It requires not only that we read it silently at the same pace that we would read it aloud, but also that we pause after we read it, to think about it for a few moments at least, to savor the mood the poem has created before we go on to something else.

It is no wonder, then, that poetry sometimes seems strange or difficult. Almost every other influence in our environment is telling us, "Hurry up! Grab the central fact or idea I'm selling and run!" Poetry is saying, "Slow down! Enjoy the music; let yourself become part of the emotion. I have many suggestions to make. Take time to let them unfold for you." In today's rush of prepackaged ideas, the stubborn individualism and refusal to be hurried that poetry represents are indeed unusual.

But anything that lets us think for ourselves, that offers us a chance to find our own feelings, ideas, and emotions, is worth pursuing. And poetry certainly encourages this kind of thinking and reflection. Moreover, once we agree to slow down enough to savor a poem completely, we discover that poetry is very similar to the literature we've been enjoying all along. Like fiction and drama, poetry tells us of people, of what it means to them and to us to be human. And, like the other forms of literature, it relays this information through the sound of human voices.

So closely related are poetry, fiction, and drama, in fact, that it is sometimes hard to tell which is which. Some poetic dramas seem better suited for reading than for performance. Should they be classed as poetry or as plays? Similarly, there are narratives that tell a complete story in verse. Should they be considered fiction as well as poetry? Or shall we simply ignore the classifications and enjoy each work for what we like best in it, whether that be a supposedly "poetic" quality, such as rhythm, or a supposedly "fictional" or "dramatic" one, such as plot, characterization, or dramatic irony?

We must, then, read poetry with the same close attention we give to all our readings in this course. Poetry, too, demands these basic questions:

1. Who is speaking?
2. What kind of person is he or she? In what mood? Thinking what thoughts? Feeling what emotions?
3. Of whom or what is he or she speaking?
4. How is this person or object being described?
5. What attitudes are being projected?
6. Are we led to share the attitudes and emotions in sympathy, or to rebel against them with feelings of anger or irony?

But, since poetry is both the most structured and the most subjective of literary forms, we may also ask questions about its forms and its sounds, to learn how they contribute to the poem's effect on us. In doing this, we may get some sense of what qualities we want to consider poetic.

Because poetry is a genre of great variety, it cannot be easily defined. Only by reading a variety of poems can we create our knowledge of poetry, enhance our enjoyment of it, and gain a sense of what it has to offer us.

Let us begin, therefore, by reading some traditional ballads. Ballads are tales told in song. Traditional ballads (or folk ballads) are songs that have been passed from one singer to another, not by having been written down but by having been sung, heard, and resung.* Ballads are thus very like folk tales in their mode of creation and in their sense of the audience. So we may expect that the voices within the ballads will be like the voices of those archetypal storytellers we first met when reading fiction. And yet ballads are sung. Their creators are singers, not speakers. How, then, will these tales sung in verse differ from tales told in prose? How will their stories be told? What will we hear that we have not heard before?

Read the ballads, and then decide what you think are the characteristics of ballads and how you think they differ from tales told in prose. To clarify your thinking, you may want to consider how the tales sung by these ballads would be told if they were written as stories, or how some story would be changed if it were turned into a ballad. You might even try your hand at writing a ballad yourself.

---

* This oral tradition accounts for the number of variations ballads possess. A singer may repeat a ballad just as he or she first heard it; or he or she may change the ballad slightly, either on purpose or accidentally. A third singer then learns this new version, and either preserves or changes it. Thus a ballad of any great age may exist in many versions, each being sung by a different group of singers.

ANONYMOUS

Get Up and Bar the Door

It fell about the Martinmas[1] time,
   And a gay time it was then,
When our good wife got puddings[2] to make,
   And she's boild them in the pan.

5 The wind sae cauld blew south and north,
   And blew into the floor;
Quoth our goodman to our goodwife,
   "Gae out and bar the door."

"My hands is in my hussyfskap,[3]
10   Goodman, as ye may see;
An it shoud nae be barrd this hundred year,
   It's no be barrd for me."

They made a paction tween them twa,
   They made it firm and sure,
15 That the first word whaeer shoud speak,
   Shoud rise and bar the door.

Then by there came two gentlemen,
   At twelve oclock at night,
And they could neither see house nor hall,
20   Nor coal nor candle-light.

"Now whether is this a rich man's house,
   Or whether is it a poor?"
But neer a word wad ane o them speak,
   For barring of the door.

25 And first they ate the white puddings,
   And then they ate the black;
Tho muckle[4] thought the goodwife to hersel,
   Yet neer a word she spake.

Then said the one unto the other,
30   "Here, man, tak ye my knife;

---

[1] November 11.
[2] Sausages.
[3] Household chores.
[4] Much.

Do ye tak aff the auld man's beard,
  And I'll kiss the goodwife."

"But there's nae water in the house,
  And what shall we do than?"
35 "What ails ye at the pudding-broo,
  That boils into the pan?"

O up then started our goodman,
  An angry man was he:
"Will ye kiss my wife before my een,
40   And scad me wi pudding-bree?"

Then up and started our goodwife,
  Gied three skips on the floor:
"Goodman, you've spoken the foremost word,
  Get up and bar the door."

Lord Randal

"O where ha you been, Lord Randal, my son?
And where ha you been, my handsome young man?"
"I ha been at the greenwood; mother, mak my bed soon,
For I'm wearied wi hunting, and fain wad lie down."

5 "An wha met ye there, Lord Randal, my son?
An wha met you there, my handsome young man?"
"O I met wi my true-love; mother, mak my bed soon,
For I'm wearied wi hunting, and fain wad lie down."

"And what did she give you, Lord Randal, my son?
10 And what did she give you, my handsome young man?"
"Eels fried in a pan; mother, mak my bed soon,
For I'm wearied wi huntin, and fain wad lie down."

"And wha gat your leavins, Lord Randal, my son?
And wha gat your leavins, my handsome young man?"
15 "My hawks and my hounds; mother, mak my bed soon,
For I'm wearied wi hunting, and fain wad lie down."

"And what becam of them, Lord Randal, my son?
And what becam of them, my handsome young man?"
"They stretched their legs out and died; mother, mak my bed soon,
20 For I'm wearied wi huntin, and fain wad lie down."

"O I fear you are poisoned, Lord Randal, my son!
I fear you are poisoned, my handsome young man!"
"O yes, I am poisoned: mother, mak my bed soon,
For I'm sick at the heart, and I fain wad lie down."

25 "What d'ye leave to your mother, Lord Randal, my son?
What d'ye leave to your mother, my handsome young man?"
"Four and twenty milk kye;[1] mother, mak my bed soon,
For I'm sick at the heart, and I fain wad lie down."

"What d'ye leave to your sister, Lord Randal, my son?
30 What d'ye leave to your sister, my handsome young man?"
"My gold and my silver; mother, mak my bed soon,
For I'm sick at the heart, an I fain wad lie down."

"What d'ye leave to your brother, Lord Randal, my son?
What d'ye leave to your brother, my handsome young man?"
35 "My houses and my lands; mother, mak my bed soon,
For I'm sick at the heart, and I fain wad lie down."

"What d'ye leave to your true-love, Lord Randal, my son?
What d'ye leave to your true-love, my handsome young man?"
"I leave her hell and fire; mother, mak my bed soon,
40 For I'm sick at the heart, and I fain wad lie down."

Sir Patrick Spens

The king sits in Dumferling town,
    Drinking the blude-reid wine:
"O whar will I get guid sailor,
    To sail this ship of mine?"

5 Up and spak an eldern knicht,
    Sat at the king's richt knee:
"Sir Patrick Spens is the best sailor
    That sails upon the sea."

The king has written a braid letter
10   And signed it wi' his hand,
And sent it to Sir Patrick Spens,
    Was walking on the sand.

---

[1] Kine = cows.

    The first line that Sir Patrick read,
      A loud lauch[1] lauched he;
15 The next line that Sir Patrick read,
      The tear blinded his ee.[2]

    "O wha is this has done this deed,
      This ill deed done to me,
    To send me out this time o' the year,
20   To sail upon the sea?

    "Mak haste, mak haste, my mirry men all,
      Our guid ship sails the morn."
    "O say na sae, my master dear,
      For I fear a deadly storm.

25 "Late, late yestre'en I saw the new moon
      Wi' the auld moon in hir arm,
    And I fear, I fear, my dear master,
      That we will come to harm."

    O our Scots nobles were richt laith[3]
30   To weet[4] their cork-heeled shoon,[5]
    But lang or[6] a' the play were played
      Their hats they swam aboon.[7]

    O lang, lang may their ladies sit,
      Wi' their fans into their hand,
35 Or ere they see Sir Patrick Spens
      Come sailing to the land.

    O lang, lang may the ladies stand
      Wi' their gold kems[8] in their hair,
    Waiting for their ain dear lords,
40   For they'll see them na mair.

---

[1] Laugh.
[2] Eye.
[3] Loath.
[4] Wet.
[5] Shoes.
[6] Before.
[7] Above.
[8] Combs.

Half o'er, half o'er to Aberdour[9]
    It's fifty fadom[10] deep,
And there lies guid Sir Patrick Spens
    Wi' the Scots lords at his feet.

The Cherry-Tree Carol

Joseph was an old man,
    and an old man was he,
When he wedded Mary,
    in the land of Galilee.

5 Joseph and Mary walked
    through an orchard good,
Where was cherries and berries,
    so red as any blood.

Joseph and Mary walked
10   through an orchard green,
Where was berries and cherries,
    as thick as might be seen.

O then bespoke Mary,
    so meek and so mild:
15 "Pluck me one cherry, Joseph,
    for I am with child."

O then bespoke Joseph:
    with words most unkind:
"Let him pluck thee a cherry
20   that brought thee with child."

O then bespoke the babe,
    within his mother's womb:
"Bow down then the tallest tree,
    for my mother to have some."

25 Then bowed down the highest tree
    unto his mother's hand;
Then she cried, "See, Joseph,
    I have cherries at command."

---

[9] Halfway back to Aberdour, on the Firth of Forth.
[10] Fathoms.

O then bespoke Joseph:
30   "I have done Mary wrong;
But cheer up, my dearest,
    and be not cast down."

Then Mary plucked a cherry,
    as red as the blood,
35 Then Mary went home
    with her heavy load.

Then Mary took her babe,
    and sat him on her knee,
Saying, "My dear son, tell me
40   what this world will be."

"O I shall be as dead, mother,
    as the stones in the wall;
O the stones in the streets, mother,
    shall mourn for me all.

45 "Upon Easter-day, mother,
    my uprising shall be;
O the sun and the moon, mother,
    shall both rise with me."

DUDLEY RANDALL (1914–   )

Ballad of Birmingham

(*On the bombing of a church in Birmingham,
    Alabama, 1963*)

"Mother dear, may I go downtown
Instead of out to play,
And march the streets of Birmingham
In a Freedom March today?"

5 "No, baby, no, you may not go,
For the dogs are fierce and wild,
And clubs and hoses, guns and jails
Aren't good for a little child."

"But, mother, I won't be alone,
10 Other children will go with me,
And march the streets of Birmingham
To make our country free."

"No, baby, no, you may not go,
For I fear those guns will fire.
15 But you may go to church instead
And sing in the children's choir."

She has combed and brushed her night-dark hair.
And bathed rose petal sweet,
And drawn white gloves on her small brown hands,
20 And white shoes on her feet.

The mother smiled to know her child
Was in the sacred place,
But that smile was the last smile
To come upon her face.

25 For when she heard the explosion,
Her eyes grew wet and wild.
She raced through the streets of Birmingham
Calling for her child.

She clawed through bits of glass and brick,
30 Then lifted out a shoe.
"O, here's the shoe my baby wore,
But, baby, where are you?"

QUESTIONS

Although "Ballad of Birmingham" was written by a twentieth-century poet, both its form and its content qualify it as a true ballad in the folk tradition. Discuss the various elements in the poem that make this so. What special power or perspective does Randall give to his telling of this historical incident by putting it in ballad form?

ELEMENTS OF POETRY

2 Repetition and Rhythm

Two elements prominent in ballads are **repetition** and **rhythm**. Sometimes single words or phrases are repeated for emphasis, as in "Lord Randal": "O where ha you been. . . . And where ha you been." Sometimes one or more lines appear in every verse as a refrain: "Mother, mak my bed soon,/For I'm wearied wi hunting, and fain wad lie down." In each case, the repetition emphasizes both the content and the rhythm of the ballad, calling our attention to the meter (that is, to the rhythmic pattern of each line) or to the grouping of lines into stanzas.

Of the three ballads printed in the previous chapter, "Lord Randal" is easily the most repetitive. In fact, it is built on a technique known as **incremental repetition.** At least half of each line is repeated from stanza to stanza, and the pattern of question and answer never varies. Yet the changes that occur reveal and develop the dying lord's story.

Repetition is important not only in ballads, but in lyric poetry in general. It is most pronounced in songs, as in the next example. But it appears frequently (and often quite subtly) in spoken lyrics as well. Let us look at some poems in which repetition plays an important role, and let us see what effects are being gained by it.

WILLIAM SHAKESPEARE (1564–1616)

It Was a Lover and His Lass

It was a lover and his lass,
   With a hey, and a ho, and hey nonino,
That o'er the green corn-field did pass
   In the spring time, the only pretty ring time,
5 When birds do sing, hey ding a ding, ding:
Sweet lovers love the spring.

Between the acres of the rye,
   With a hey, and a ho, and a hey nonino,
These pretty country folk would lie,
10   In the spring time, the only pretty ring time,
When birds do sing, hey ding a ding, ding:
Sweet lovers love the spring.

This carol they began that hour,
   With a hey, and a ho, and a hey nonino,
15 How that a life was but a flower
   In the spring time, the only pretty ring time,
When birds do sing, hey ding a ding, ding:
Sweet lovers love the spring.

And therefore take the present time,
20   With a hey, and a ho, and a hey nonino,
For love is crownèd with the prime
   In the spring time, the only pretty ring time,
When birds do sing, hey ding a ding, ding:
Sweet lovers love the spring.

QUESTIONS

1. How would you characterize this song? What is its mood?
2. How does the refrain help set the mood of the song?
3. What other repetitions of sounds do you find in the poem? What do they contribute? (Note: Two important categories here are **rhyme**—the use of words that end with the same sound, like *rye* and *lie*—and **alliteration,** the use of words that begin with the same sound, like *lover* and *lass; hey, ho,* and *hey.*)
4. Discuss the progression of thought and feeling from the first stanza to the final one. What sense of completeness does the progression impart to Shakespeare's song?

THOMAS HARDY (1840–1928)

The Ruined Maid

"O 'Melia, my dear, this does everything crown!
Who could have supposed I should meet you in Town?
And whence such fair garments, such prosperi-ty?"—
"O didn't you know I'd been ruined?" said she.

5 —"You left us in tatters, without shoes or socks,
Tired of digging potatoes, and spudding up docks;[1]
And now you've gay bracelets and bright feathers three!"—
"Yes: that's how we dress when we're ruined," said she.

—"At home in the barton[2] you said 'thee' and 'thou,'
10 And 'thik oon,' and 'theäs oon,' and 't'other'; but now
Your talking quite fits 'ee for high compa-ny!"—
"Some polish is gained with one's ruin," said she.

—"Your hands were like paws then, your face blue and bleak
But now I'm bewitched by your delicate cheek,
15 And your little gloves fit as on any la-dy!"—
"We never do work when we're ruined," said she.

—"You used to call home-life a hag-ridden dream,
And you'd sigh, and you'd sock; but at present you seem
To know not of megrims[3] or melancho-ly!"—
20 "True. One's pretty lively when ruined," said she.

—"I wish I had feathers, a fine sweeping gown,
And a delicate face, and could strut about Town!"—
"My dear—a raw country girl, such as you be,
Cannot quite expect that. You ain't ruined," said she.

QUESTIONS

1. How does Hardy use question and answer to characterize the two women?
2. What balance exists here between the two sides of the dialogue? What is the effect of the repetitions in the final line of each stanza?
3. What sort of tone or consciousness would you expect to find in a poem about a "ruined maid" that is absent from this poem? What effect does this have on the tone of the poem and on the characterization of the speakers? On the poet's apparent attitude toward them?

---

[1] Digging up weeds.
[2] Farmyard.
[3] Low spirits.

WILLIAM BLAKE (1757–1827)

From **Songs of Innocence**

The Lamb

   Little Lamb, who made thee?
   Dost thou know who made thee?
Gave thee life & bid thee feed,
By the stream & o'er the mead;
5 Gave thee clothing of delight,
Softest clothing wooly bright;
Gave thee such a tender voice,
Making all the vales rejoice!
   Little Lamb who made thee?
10   Dost thou know who made thee?

   Little Lamb I'll tell thee,
   Little Lamb I'll tell thee!
He is callèd by thy name,
For he calls himself a Lamb:
15 He is meek & he is mild,
He became a little child:
I a child & thou a lamb,
We are callèd by his name.
   Little Lamb God bless thee.
20   Little Lamb God bless thee.

From **Songs of Experience**

The Tyger

Tyger! Tyger! burning bright
In the forests of the night,
What immortal hand or eye
Could frame thy fearful symmetry?

5 In what distant deeps or skies
Burnt the fire of thine eyes?
On what wings dare he aspire?
What the hand, dare seize the fire?

And what shoulder, & what art,
10 Could twist the sinews of thy heart?
And when thy heart began to beat,
What dread hand? & what dread feet?

What the hammer? what the chain?
In what furnace was thy brain?
15 What the anvil? what dread grasp
Dare its deadly terrors clasp?

When the stars threw down their spears,
And water'd heaven with their tears,
Did he smile his work to see?
20 Did he who made the Lamb make thee?

Tyger! Tyger! burning bright
In the forests of the night,
What immortal hand or eye
Dare frame thy fearful symmetry?

QUESTIONS

If you were to write an essay on "The Lamb" and "The Tyger," you might start with the following question:

1. Both "The Lamb" and "The Tyger" are essentially religious poems. Yet they seem to describe two different aspects of religious feeling. How would you characterize each aspect? How does the first fit the conception of "innocence," the second of "experience"? How are the animals, and the feelings they represent, characterized within the poem?

To develop the answer, you could then look at the following aspects of each poem:

2. "The Lamb" and "The Tyger" have almost the same rhythm, being based on a seven-syllable line with the odd-numbered syllables accented: Ty-ger! Ty-ger! burn-ing bright. But "The Lamb" varies this meter in places, while "The Tyger" holds to it firmly throughout. Look at the rhythm and repetitions carefully in each poem, and then explain how they reinforce each other. Why is the effect so different for each poem?
3. "The Lamb" and "The Tyger" both make use of repeated questions. How does their use in "The Lamb" differ from their use in "The Tyger"? How do these differences help create the contrasting tones of the two poems?
4. What images are connected with the lamb? With the tiger? How are they related? How contrasted?
5. What attitude does the speaker seem to have toward each animal? With what evidence would you support your answer to this question?

The next two poems show what can happen to the ballad form in the hands of highly sophisticated poets who are concerned less with relating incidents than with conveying emotion and demonstrating the various effects that can be gained by a concentration on the sounds and rhythms of words. We may note that these poems provide freer and more self-consciously artistic variations on balladic themes than do any we have previously read. In contrast to folk ballads or to modern ballads that adhere closely to the folk tradition, such as Randall's "Ballad of Birmingham," these freer adaptations of the ballad form are known as **literary ballads.** We will read one nineteenth-century and one twentieth-century example.

EDGAR ALLAN POE (1809–1849)

Annabel Lee

It was many and many a year ago,
      In a kingdom by the sea,
That a maiden there lived whom you may know
      By the name of Annabel Lee;—
5 And this maiden she lived with no other thought
      Than to love and be loved by me.

She was a child and *I* was a child,
      In this kingdom by the sea,
But we loved with a love that was more than love—
10   I and my Annabel Lee—
With a love that the wingèd seraphs of Heaven
      Coveted her and me.

And this was the reason that, long ago,
      In this kingdom by the sea,
15 A wind blew out of a cloud by night
      Chilling my Annabel Lee;
So that her highborn kinsmen came
      And bore her away from me,
To shut her up in a sepulchre
20   In this kingdom by the sea.

The angels, not half so happy in Heaven,
      Went envying her and me—
Yes!—that was the reason (as all men know,
      In this kingdom by the sea)
25 That the wind came out of the cloud chilling
      And killing my Annabel Lee.

But our love it was stronger by far than the love
      Of those who were older than we—
      Of many far wiser than we—

30 And neither the angels in Heaven above,
Nor the demons down under the sea,
Can ever dissever my soul from the soul
Of the beautiful Annabel Lee:—

For the moon never beams without bringing me dreams
35 Of the beautiful Annabel Lee;
And the stars never rise but I see the bright eyes
Of the beautiful Annabel Lee;
And so, all the night-tide, I lie down by the side
Of my darling, my darling, my life and my bride,
40 In her sepulchre there by the sea—
In her tomb by the side of the sea.

QUESTIONS

1. What elements in "Annabel Lee" come from the ballad tradition? What elements have been added or altered? In developing your answer, consider the basic use of rhythm and rhyme, repetition, refrain, alliteration, vocabulary, and so on.

2. Consider the story told by the poem, and the emotions it evokes. Is the story one that fits well into the ballad form? Again, what elements harmonize well with the ballad tradition? Which suggest a more sophisticated speaker and audience?

E. E. CUMMINGS (1894–1963)

All in green went my love riding

All in green went my love riding
on a great horse of gold
into the silver dawn.

four lean hounds crouched low and smiling
5 the merry deer ran before.

Fleeter be they than dappled dreams
the swift sweet deer
the red rare deer.

Four red roebuck[1] at a white water
10 the cruel bugle sang before.

---

[1] Male roe deer.

Horn at hip went my love riding
riding the echo down
into the silver dawn.

four lean hounds crouched low and smiling
15 the level meadows ran before.

Softer be they than slippered sleep
the lean lithe deer
the fleet flown deer.

Four fleet does at a gold valley
20 the famished arrow sang before.

Bow at belt went my love riding
riding the mountain down
into the silver dawn.

four lean hounds crouched low and smiling
25 the sheer peaks ran before.

Paler be they than daunting death
the sleek slim deer
the tall tense deer.

Four tall stags at a green mountain
30 the lucky hunter sang before.

All in green went my love riding
on a great horse of gold
into the silver dawn.

four lean hounds crouched low and smiling
35 my heart fell dead before.

QUESTIONS

1. Incremental repetition is used in this modern poem for an almost balladlike
   effect. But how would you describe the way stanzas are linked in this poem?
2. What effects would you say the poem achieves? How would you distinguish
   between its effects and those of traditional ballads?

3
Compression and Verse Forms

To write a short story based on the tale told in "Lord Randal" or "Get Up and Bar the Door" would require at least one thousand words. (That would be roughly the length of "Miss Brill"—quite a short story, as stories go.) These two ballads, however, have less than five hundred words each, including refrains and repetitions. And even though the ballads are much shorter than a very short story, they seem long and loosely constructed when they are compared with such tightly written lyrics as "The Tyger."

Verse, then, is a highly compressed form. Eliminating inessentials—the name of Lord Randal's sweetheart, the reason she killed him—it takes us directly to the heart of a situation, to the one or two moments most highly charged with emotion. In the case of "Lord Randal," this technique reduces the ballad to a single moment, that in which mother and son discover that the son has been poisoned. In the case of "Get Up and Bar the Door," it produces a ballad centering on two episodes: the one that begins the quarrel and the one that ends it.

Time becomes flexible in these ballads, as one memorable moment is juxtaposed with the next, ignoring all that may have gone between: "Then by there came two gentlemen,/At twelve oclock at night." We can imagine that the lateness of the hour would have made the silent house seem even stranger than it was to the "gentlemen," and we may also suspect that quite a few hours must have passed since the feuding couple made their pact. But all the singer gives us is the crucial hour—"twelve"—and the number of intruders. The time between incidents is not important. The conflict between the couple is.

Similarly, "The Cherry-Tree Carol" moves with almost no consciousness of elapsed time from the wedding of Joseph and Mary to the scene in the orchard to a final scene between Mary and her infant son. In each case, a simple "then" defines the sequence, whether the incidents follow each other instantly, as in "then bespoke the babe," "then bowed down the highest tree," and "O then bespoke Joseph," or whether a gap of several months is indicated: "Then Mary took her babe." The passage of time, which affects everyone, is of no concern to the singer. The unique situation of parents confronted with their child's divinity engrosses all the attention, linking together the unusual circumstances of Joseph's marriage, the miracle in the orchard, and Christ's prophecy of his death and resurrection. "The Cherry-Tree Carol" assumes that its hearers are all familiar with the story of Christ's birth and death; it therefore feels free to concentrate on those aspects of the legend that bear on its central theme, leaving us to place them in chronological time if we wish.

Poetic form demands **compression.** A line of eight or ten syllables, a stanza of two, four, or six lines will not allow any wasted words. The poet must pare away all the needless background and inessential details in order to fit the essential ones into those brief stanzas.

Yet this strictness of form also helps the hearer to accept the compression it produces. We would not accept so few details as "Lord Randal" gives us in a prose account of his death. Nor could the information given in "The Lamb" or "The Tyger" stand alone as prose. Ballad and lyric alike need the cadence of their verse—the rhyme, the rhythm, the rounded-off pattern formed by the stanzas—to give our ear and mind the sense of completeness and satisfaction that allows us to enjoy the brief, tightly focused statements their poetry makes.

Compression, then, is another technique that allows the material presented and the form of its presentation to reinforce each other, providing for the reader not only a satisfying unity, but also one that seems notably poetic. Let us now examine that technique in action by looking at a few types of poetry that have compression as their most notable feature, beginning with the oldest of these forms, the **epigram.**

Epigrams may be serious or humorous, flattering or insulting. But they are usually descriptive of a person, animal, or object; and they are invariably brief. Probably the most popular type today is the **satiric epigram,** a form that can be described as a description with a sting. Here is an example:

COUNTEE CULLEN (1903–1946)

For a Lady I Know

She even thinks that up in heaven
Her class lies late and snores,
While poor black cherubs rise at seven
To do celestial chores.

QUESTIONS

1. What single fact do the four lines of this poem tell us about the "Lady" who is their subject?
2. What further facts do they suggest about her?
3. How do words like *her class* and *poor black cherubs* characterize the lady and the attitudes that the poet suggests she holds?
4. What do words like *snores* and *celestial chores* do for the poem? What do they suggest about the poet's attitude?

Not all brief poems with a punch are epigrams, however. The following poem has a sting of its own and is as highly compressed in technique as any poem you will see. Yet its structure is not that of the epigram. How would you define it?

GWENDOLYN BROOKS (1917–   )

We Real Cool

The Pool Players.
Seven at the Golden Shovel.

We real cool. We
Left school. We

5 Lurk late. We
Strike straight. We

Sing sin. We
Thin gin. We

Jazz June. We
10 Die soon.

QUESTIONS

1. What does the subtitle tell us about the speakers of the poem?
2. How do the speakers characterize themselves?
3. Discuss the use of repetition in the poem.
4. Note also the breaks in the pattern. Why has Brooks placed the word *We* at the end of each line rather than letting it come at the beginning as it does in the first line? Is the word *We* stressed more heavily, less heavily, or just as heavily at the end of the line as it would be at the beginning? What happens to the verbs? Does placing them at the beginning of the line give them any extra stress? What happens to the length of the last line? What effect does it produce?
5. What does Brooks seem to be saying in this poem about the "Seven" or about people like them? How does the form of her poem express or emphasize her feelings?

Here are two more brief, pointed poems. How do these poems combine serious and humorous elements? What makes them enjoyable to read?

ARTHUR GUITERMAN (1871–1943)

On the Vanity of Earthly Greatness

The tusks that clashed in mighty brawls
Of mastodons, are billiard balls.

The sword of Charlemagne the Just
Is ferric oxide, known as rust.

5   The grizzly bear whose potent hug
Was feared by all, is now a rug.

Great Caesar's bust is on the shelf,
And I don't feel so well myself.

MARIANNE MOORE (1887–1972)

I May, I Might, I Must

If you will tell me why the fen
appears impassable, I then
will tell you why I think that I
can get across it if I try.

Another extremely brief form, which was introduced to English and American poetry in the twentieth century, is the **imagist** poem. Imagist poetry grew out of an interest in Oriental poetry, especially in the brief, seventeen-syllable form known as **haiku.** (The poems by Pound that follow are sometimes called haiku.) As the word *imagist* implies, this poetry focuses on a single sensory image—a sight, sound, or feeling—and presents it in as brief and vivid a form as the writer can manage. Read the following four poems, and then ask what image each poem starts from and what further images it uses to reinforce the first one. How are the images combined? How would you contrast the form and effect of these poems with the form and effect of the epigrams you have just read, or with the effect and form of Blake's lyrics?

EZRA POUND (1885–1972)

In a Station of the Metro

The apparition of these faces in the crowd;
Petals on a wet, black bough.

AMY LOWELL (1874–1925)

Wind and Silver

Greatly shining,
The Autumn moon floats in the thin sky;
And the fish-ponds shake their backs and flash their
    dragon scales
As she passes over them.

DENISE LEVERTOV (1923–   )

Six Variations (Part iii)

Shlup, shlup, the dog
as it laps up
water
makes intelligent
5 music, resting
now and then to take breath in irregular
measure.

H. D. (HILDA DOOLITTLE) (1886–1961)

Heat

O wind, rend open the heat,
cut apart the heat,
rend it to tatters.

Fruit cannot drop
5 through this thick air—
fruit cannot fall into heat
that presses up and blunts
the points of pears
and rounds the grapes.

10 Cut the heat—
plough through it,
turning it on either side
of your path.

Here is one more poem by Pound, who was one of the founders of imagist poetry. What does this poem do with imagist techniques? How does it differ from the preceding poems? To what extent does its effectiveness depend on your having read these poems, or others like them?

EZRA POUND (1885–1972)

L'Art 1910

Green arsenic smeared on an egg-white cloth,
Crushed strawberries! Come, let us feast our eyes.

So far, we have looked at poems that achieved effectiveness through spareness, using as few words as possible and choosing very tight verse forms. But compression can also be achieved within other verse forms. Note, for instance, the richness of words and images that William Carlos Williams manages to crowd into "The Dance," so that the poetic form seems almost too small for the magnitude of the sounds and motions it contains. Notice too, in the poem that follows, the intensity of argument and feeling that William Wordsworth fits gracefully into the fourteen lines of a sonnet.

WILLIAM CARLOS WILLIAMS (1883–1963)

The Dance

In Breughel's[1] great picture, The Kermess,[2]
the dancers go round, they go round and
around, the squeal and the blare and the
tweedle of bagpipes, a bugle and fiddles
5 tipping their bellies (round as the thick-
sided glasses whose wash they impound)
their hips and their bellies off balance
to turn them. Kicking and rolling about
the Fair Grounds, swinging their butts, those
10 shanks must be sound to bear up under such
rollicking measures, prance as they dance
in Breughel's great picture, The Kermess.

QUESTIONS

1. Although you might expect a poem describing a painting to concentrate on color or form, Williams's poem concentrates at least as heavily on motion and sound. What words or phrases describe the sounds of the scene? Which describe shapes or forms? Which describe motion? What sorts of music and dancers does Williams seem to be portraying with these terms?
2. How do the poem's rhythm and shape support the sense of sound and motion? Note particularly the large number of heavily stressed monosyllables. What effect do they provide? How have sentence structure and grammar been reshaped to contribute to the sensation of noise and speed?
3. Note the plays on words within the poem: "bellies" for both fiddles and dancers, legs called "sound" in a poem much concerned with musical sounds. How does such wordplay help unify the scene? Note also the use of repetition: how does it help shape the poem?
4. If you are able to find a print of *The Kermess*, decide how well you think Williams has caught the spirit of the painting. What aspects of the poem stand out for you as being particularly apt?

WILLIAM WORDSWORTH (1770–1850)

The World Is Too Much with Us

The world is too much with us; late and soon,
Getting and spending, we lay waste our powers:
Little we see in Nature that is ours;

---

[1] Peter Breughel, or Brueghel (1525?–1569), a Flemish painter.
[2] A kermess is a carnival or fair.

We have given our hearts away, a sordid boon!
5 This Sea that bares her bosom to the moon;
The winds that will be howling at all hours,
And are up-gathered now like sleeping flowers;
For this, for everything, we are out of tune;
It moves us not.—Great God! I'd rather be
10 A Pagan suckled in a creed outworn;
So might I, standing on this pleasant lea,
Have glimpses that would make me less forlorn;
Have sight of Proteus rising from the sea;
Or hear old Triton blow his wreathèd horn.[1]

QUESTIONS

1. What is the argument of this poem?
2. How does Wordsworth's invocation of Triton and Proteus fit in with the argument of the poem?
3. What words or images in the poem do you find most striking? How do they support the poem's argument?
4. Note the poem's movement from "us" and "we" in the first lines to "I" at the end. At what line does the change take place? How is it marked or signaled? What changes of tone of voice and of mood go with it? What change of imagery?
5. What qualities in the poem make it suitable as a study in compression? Alternatively, if you disagree with this classification, why do you challenge the poem's placement in this chapter?

Finally, we should look at some poems by Emily Dickinson. No study of compression in poetry would be complete without a consideration of the work of this American poet, who was far ahead of her time in the concentration and spareness of her verse. Description and argument blend in Dickinson's poetry into a remarkable unity of vision and idea. Notice, in the following two poems, how images of light and motion bridge the gap between the physical and spiritual worlds and between our own physical and spiritual responses to these worlds.

EMILY DICKINSON (1830–1886)

There's a Certain Slant of Light (#258)

There's a certain Slant of light,
Winter Afternoons—
That oppresses, like the Heft
Of Cathedral Tunes—

---

[1] In Greek mythology Proteus was a prophetic sea god who, when seized, changed shape to try to escape prophesying. Triton, the son of the sea god Poseidon, played a trumpet made of a conch shell.

5 Heavenly Hurt, it gives us—
We can find no scar,
But internal difference,
Where the Meanings, are—

None may teach it—Any—
10 'Tis the Seal Despair—
An imperial affliction
Sent us of the Air—

When it comes, the Landscape listens—
Shadows—hold their breath—
15 When it goes, 'tis like the Distance
On the look of Death

Tell All the Truth but Tell It Slant (#1129)

Tell all the Truth but tell it slant—
Success in Circuit lies
Too bright for our infirm Delight
The Truth's superb surprise
5 As Lightning to the Children eased
With explanation kind
The Truth must dazzle gradually
Or every man be blind—

QUESTIONS

1. Give examples of images of light and motion in these poems. How are the two types of images connected?
2. Give examples of lines or phrases that you think are particularly good examples of compression. How is Dickinson creating this effect? For what purpose is she using it?
3. What does being human seem to mean in these poems? What aspects of our nature are being emphasized? (Note that we as readers are definitely included in these descriptions of what being human entails. How are we brought into them?)

4 Word Choice: Meanings and Suggestions

Common Phrases and New Meanings

Our study of ballads gave us insight into the use of repetition and selectivity in poetry, and thus into poetry's balance of narrative and rhythmic patterns. We saw that poetry is based on the combination of satisfying sounds and sharply focused content. And we saw how the pattern of sounds and words created by the skillful use of rhythm, repetition, and word-sound can be used to heighten the effect of compression or to set a mood.

But ballads could not tell us a great deal about word choice in poetry. For ballads, like other oral poetry, tend to rely on a shared vocabulary of predictable phrases and stock epithets. Hearing ballads, we recognize in them traditional terms, pairings, and comparisons: "my true-love," "my hawks and my hounds," "the sun and the moon," "as red as the blood," and "as dead as the stones." We are not meant to linger on any of them, or on any particular line. Rather, we let each recognized phrase add its bit to mood or situation, while we reserve our main attention for the pattern made by the story as it unfolds.

In written poetry, on the other hand, word choice is all-important. The play on words by which Shakespeare blends spring, songs, and rings to create an atmosphere (p. 366); the indelicate verb *snores* with which Cullen mocks his "lady's pretensions to gentility (p. 375); and even the archaic spelling "tyger," which gives Blake's beast its first hint of strangeness and mystery, all testify to the power of the well-chosen word. The words themselves are not unusual ones; but they surprise us when they appear, nonetheless. They call on us to pay attention and reward us for our attention by bringing their overtones of meaning and suggestion into the poem, enriching our enjoyment and understanding.

The language of poetry, then, is not necessarily composed of strange, unusual, or uniquely "poetic" words. More often, poetry gains its effects through unexpected juxtapositions of common words, bringing new meaning into the ordinary. Look, for instance, at this poem by Emily Dickinson, and consider how the poet gives significance to the simplest language.

The Bustle in a House (#1078)

The Bustle in a House
The Morning after Death
Is solemnest of industries
Enacted upon Earth—

5 The Sweeping up the Heart
And putting Love away
We shall not want to use again
Until Eternity.

The language of the first stanza is almost like prose. A few extra words, and it would be a simple prose statement: The bustle that takes place in a house, the day after someone who lived there has died, represents one of the most solemn tasks on earth. (The word *industries* may seem a bit strange in this context. At the time this poem was written, however, it was used to denote any sort of labor, just as the word *industrious* does today.)

In the second stanza, however, we notice a change. Here the poet is amplifying her first statement. She is explaining that the "bustle" is caused by the housecleaning that takes place between a death and the funeral, and that it is "solemn" because the workers must reconcile themselves to the loss of a loved one. In fact, the workers are coming to grips with their emotions even as they do the chores.

She does not, however, resort to wordy explanations. Rather, she combines housework and emotions in a tightly compressed pair of images. The verbs of the second stanza speak of housecleaning matters; the nouns, of love. It is not dust that is swept up, but "the heart"; not blankets to be put away, but "love." The combination conveys the sense of loss. "The sweeping up the heart," in particular, suggests that the heart is broken, is in pieces; and the thought of a broken heart, in turn, suggests grief.

But the poet also says that the grief and loss are not permanent. "Love" is not thrown away, but rather "put away" to be used again on a future occasion. "Until eternity": the phrase suggests a fearfully long wait, but insists, nonetheless, that the waiting will end. "Eternity" thus balances "earth," tempering the present sense of loss with faith in restoration. And in that balance the poem ends and rests.

Here is another poem by Dickinson that is notable for its unusual use of words. How would you analyze it?

EMILY DICKINSON (1830–1886)

Because I Could Not Stop for Death (#712)

Because I could not stop for Death—
He kindly stopped for me—
The Carriage held but just Ourselves—
And Immortality.

5 We slowly drove—He knew no haste
And I had put away
My labor and my leisure too,
For His Civility—

We passed the School, where Children strove
10 At Recess—in the Ring—
We passed the Fields of Gazing Grain—
We passed the Setting Sun—

Or rather—He passed Us—
The Dews drew quivering and chill—
15 For only Gossamer, my Gown—
My Tippet[1]—only Tulle[2]—

We paused before a House that seemed
A Swelling of the Ground—
The Roof was scarcely visible—
20 The Cornice—in the Ground—

---

[1] A shoulder cape.
[2] A stiff, sheer fabric.

Since then—'tis Centuries—and yet
Feels shorter than the Day
I first surmised the Horses' Heads
Were toward Eternity—

Suggestion and Interpretation

The language of Blake's "The Tyger" is stranger and more complex than Dickinson's. The description of the tiger as "Burning bright/In the forests of the night" links notions of burning passion, glowing cat-eyes, dark trees, and forests of stars to create, from words that literally are near nonsense, a beast half earthly and half unearthly, combining in his "fearful symmetry" brutal ferocity and supernatural beauty.

"The Tyger" again brings us to realize that word choice in poetry often means choosing words that can carry many meanings at once and then combining those words for the greatest power of suggestion. Blake's tiger is more than mere animal. The striking images and the strong sense of awe that pervade the poem insist that the tiger stands for something special in its questioner's eyes. But they will not tell us specifically what that something is. In this the language of the poem is poetic —it moves always toward greater suggestiveness, never toward a narrowing of meaning. As a result, the tiger symbolizes many things for many people, with all readers bringing their own experiences to this "Song of Experience" and coming away with their own visions of what the tiger can mean for them.

Sound, sense, and suggestion all blend in poetry. Words gain new relevance, new connections. They carry several meanings, suggest several more, and join with other words to suggest yet further meanings. Word choice, the craft of selecting and joining words to enrich their power to communicate, is one of the basic skills of the poet's craft.

Since the rhythms of the following two poems are smoother than those of "The Bustle in the House," and their rhymes are more satisfyingly matched, they have a more traditional sound. Yet their use of language resembles that in Dickinson's poem in that their words and syntax, basically simple and straightforward, are highlighted by a few unexpected words or images. Discuss what you think the highlights in these poems are, and how you think they function.

WILLIAM WORDSWORTH (1770–1850)

She Dwelt Among the Untrodden Ways

She dwelt among the untrodden ways
　Beside the springs of Dove.

A Maid whom there were none to praise
　　And very few to love;

5 A violet by a mossy stone
　　Half hidden from the eye!
　—Fair as a star, when only one
　　Is shining in the sky.

She lived unknown, and few could know
10　　When Lucy ceased to be;
　But she is in her grave, and, oh,
　　The difference to me!

ROBERT HERRICK (1591–1674)

Upon Julia's Clothes

Whenas in silks my Julia goes,
Then, then, methinks, how sweetly flows
The liquefaction of her clothes.

Next, when I cast mine eyes and see
5 The brave vibration each way free,
O how that glittering taketh me!

Again, the following poem presents a straightforward statement. But here the language is slightly richer, the play on words is more pronounced, and the words take on more resonance of meaning. Discuss the poem and its language. How does the choice of words give the poem more impact than its main statement, "Many friends of mine have died," would have?

A. E. HOUSMAN (1859–1936)

With Rue My Heart Is Laden

With rue my heart is laden
　　For golden friends I had,
For many a rose-lipt maiden
　　And many a lightfoot lad.

5 By brooks too broad for leaping
　　The lightfoot boys are laid;
The rose-lipt girls are sleeping
　　In fields where roses fade.

QUESTIONS

1. What repetitions do you find in the poem? How does the second stanza develop the images begun in the first stanza?
2. How does the word *golden* in line 2 fit into the mood and imagery?
3. Note the heavy use of "r" and "l" sounds. What effect does the alliteration of these sounds produce? What other examples of alliteration can you find in the poem? How would you summarize your view of Housman's choice of words for sound and sense?

Each of the next two poems presents a wish or desire and paints a scene representing the fulfillment of the wish. Note how these poems create simple and direct, yet powerful evocations of scene and mood: note the use of details, of images that appeal to sight and hearing, touch and motion, and the use of rhyme, rhythm, and alliteration.

GERARD MANLEY HOPKINS (1844–1889)

Heaven–Haven

A Nun Takes the Veil

> I have desired to go
> > Where springs not fail,
> To fields where flies no sharp and sided hail
> And a few lilies blow.
>
> 5   And I have asked to be
> > Where no storms come,
> Where the green swell is in the havens dumb,
> And out of the swing of the sea.

QUESTIONS

1. Can you explain the poem's title? Is the subtitle necessary for an understanding of the poem?
2. Each stanza in this poem describes a different scene, a different location. What links the two together? How do these scenes develop the subject set out in the poem's title?
3. Notice the differences between the structure of these sentences and that of normal English; notice also the spareness of the form and imagery (even down to the "few lilies" in the fourth line) and the relatively heavy use of alliteration. How do these contribute to the poem's effect?

ELINOR WYLIE (1885–1928)

Velvet Shoes

Let us walk in the white snow
  In a soundless space;
With footsteps quiet and slow,
  At a tranquil pace,
5   Under veils of white lace.

I shall go shod in silk,
  And you in wool,
White as a white cow's milk,
  More beautiful
10   Than the breast of a gull.

We shall walk through the still town
  In a windless peace;
We shall step upon white down,
  Upon silver fleece,
15   Upon softer than these.

We shall walk in velvet shoes:
  Wherever we go
Silence will fall like dews
  On white silence below.
20   We shall walk in the snow.

QUESTIONS

1. To what does the title of this poem refer? Are the "velvet shoes" actual shoes, or something else?
2. In contrast to the sparely drawn imaginary landscapes of "Heaven–Haven," "Velvet Shoes" presents an actual scene in a highly imaginative manner, through a multiplicity of images. Look closely at these images.
   a. Which of them describe the things they name? Which use the named things to describe something else?
   b. Notice that the images fall into four groups: softness, whiteness, silence, and peace. How are these intermingled in the course of the poem? What effect does this mingling produce?
3. How would you describe the sound of the poem—its use of rhyme, rhythm, alliteration, and repetition?
4. How would you describe the poem's overall effect?

The next two poems are written in **free verse,** a verse form invented in the early twentieth century. Free verse is marked by uneven line lengths and often by the absence of rhyme, as well. Note how these poems mix repetition and compression to create their very different effects.

CARL SANDBURG (1878–1967)

Cool Tombs

When Abraham Lincoln was shoveled into the tombs, he forgot the
    copperheads and the assassin . . . in the dust, in the cool tombs.
And Ulysses Grant lost all thought of con men and Wall Street, cash
5   and collateral turned ashes . . . in the dust, in the cool tombs.
Pocahontas' body, lovely as a poplar, sweet as a red haw in November
    or a pawpaw in May, did she wonder? does she remember? . . . in
10   the dust, in the cool tombs?
Take any streetful of people buying clothes and groceries, cheering a
    hero or throwing confetti and blowing tin horns . . . tell me if the
    lovers are losers . . . tell me if any get more than the lovers . . . in
    the dust . . . in the cool tombs.

QUESTIONS

1. What images are associated with each person? Why have they been chosen? What do they suggest?
2. Is there a message to the poem? If so, what is it? How does the poem travel from its opening statements to its final suggestions?
3. How would you describe the sound of this poem? The rhythm? How do sound and rhythm fit the meaning of the poem? How do they create its mood?

EZRA POUND (1885–1972)

These Fought in Any Case[1]

These fought in any case,
and some believing,
         pro domo,[2] in any case . . .

Some quick to arm,
5 some for adventure,
  some from fear of weakness,
  some from fear of censure,
  some for love of slaughter, in imagination,
  learning later . . .
10 some in fear, learning love of slaughter;

---

[1] Section IV from "E. P. Ode pour L'Election de Son Sépulcre" ("E. P. Ode on the Selection of His Tomb").
[2] "For homeland."

Died some, pro patria,
                non "dulce" non "et decor"[3] . . .
walked eye-deep in hell
believing in old men's lies, then unbelieving
15 came home, home to a lie,
     home to many deceits,
     home to old lies and new infamy;
     usury age-old and age-thick
     and liars in public places.

20 Daring as never before, wastage as never before.
     Young blood and high blood,
       fair cheeks, and fine bodies;

     fortitude as never before

     frankness as never before,
25 disillusions as never told in the old days,
     hysterias, trench confessions,
     laughter out of dead bellies.

QUESTIONS

1. How would you describe the tone of voice in this poem? What do the repetitions contribute to it? The word choice? (Be sure you give examples to prove your assertions.)
2. What attitude does the poem suggest towards the soldiers of which it speaks? Is the attitude simple or complex? How is it suggested?
3. What of the poem's attitude to war in general?
4. An **ode** is a poem of irregular form. How does Pound use irregularity of form to reinforce the suggestions his poem makes?
5. Although "Cool Tombs" and "These Fought in Any Case" are both written in free verse and make heavy use of repetition, the **tone** and **pace** of the two poems are completely different. Why?

The words in this final poem deserve special notice. Their underlying tone and syntax are more casual and friendly than any we have met so far. And yet Cummings has taken enormous liberties with words and syntax alike, even to the point of inventing new words and positioning each word individually on the page. To what new responses does the resulting poem seem to invite you?

---

[3] An ironic allusion to the famous line of Horace: "Dulce et decorum est pro patria mori" ("It is sweet and fitting to die for one's country").

E. E. CUMMINGS (1894–1963)

in Just-

in Just-
spring   when the world is mud-
luscious the little
lame balloonman

5 whistles   far   and wee

and eddieandbill come
running from marbles and
piracies and it's
spring

10 when the world is puddle-wonderful

the queer
old balloonman whistles
far   and   wee
and bettyandisbel come dancing

15 from hop-scotch and jump-rope and

it's
spring
and
    the
20   goat-footed

balloonMan   whistles
far
and
wee

QUESTIONS

1. In analyzing this poem, we may begin with its wordplay. How do compound words such as *mud-luscious* and *puddle-wonderful* affect the sound and meaning of the lines in which they occur? How many meanings does the word *wee* have, and what is the effect of using it? The balloon-man is described through incremental repetition, beginning as "lame" and ending as "goat-footed." Why goat-footed?
2. We may then note two unusual rhythmic devices: the breaking of lines in the middle of words or phrases, and the spacing out or running together of words.

And we may ask how these affect the sound and mood of the poem, and our sense of the scene it describes.

3. Then we may put this play with words and rhythms together with the poem's use of names and detail, and ask how Cummings creates and enhances his description. What does the intent of the poem seem to be? What message does it seem to carry? How do the sound and word choices create the tone and the message?

THE SPEAKER IN THE POEM

5 *The Speaker's Voice*

We have said that ballads, being traditional, oral poetry, rely on common words and images rather than on the unique images of written poetry. We may now make one final distinction by remarking that this stylization of ballads leaves these songs lacking uniquely memorable voices. A deserted lover in one ballad, for instance, sounds much like a deserted lover in any other ballad. They will speak at least some of the same words in the same tones and rhythms. This is not the case in written poetry, where we would take the appearance of a lover who sounds like any other lover as the sign of a second-rate poem. If we read twenty lyrics about love—or even twenty lyrics about lost love—we expect to hear twenty different voices.

This reflection brings us to one of the basic paradoxes of poetry. Because of its use of rhythm and sound patterns, the language of poetry may be the farthest of all literary languages from everyday speech. Yet the voices within poems are the most intimate of literary voices, speaking to us most vividly and directly and conveying to us most openly the speakers' deepest and most immediate emotions. No other form of literature demands so much care and craft in its writing as poetry; yet no other form can seem to present the spontaneous flow of emotion as convincingly as poetry can.

Because poetry can so thoroughly convince us that in responding to it we are sharing a genuine, strongly felt emotion, it can attract our strongest response. Subjectively, this is good; it represents poetry doing what it should do. Objectively, however, poetry's seeming frankness raises the critical danger that we may mistake the voice within the poem for the voice of the poet. The further danger then arises that we may generalize from a single poem, slipping from the critically acceptable statement, "Blake's 'Tyger' presents the tiger as a beautiful but terrifying creature" to the unacceptable, "As 'The Tyger' shows, Blake was afraid of tigers."

We cannot fall into this error so easily in drama or fiction, where the number of characters and the abundance of circumstantial detail continually warn us of the distance between author and work. Poetry, however, often has but one voice in a poem. The voice often speaks in the first person: "Oh, how that glittering taketh me!" And the intensity of emotion that is felt only in the climatic scenes of fiction and drama may illuminate an entire lyric. This combination of single voice, first person, and unflagging intensity of emotion often obliterates the distance between the poet and speaker. If the speaker then gives us the slightest hint that he or she may represent the poet, we become all too willing to make the identification.

But we must not make the identification so simply. We can speak of a poet's voice—can compare Blake's voice to Dickinson's, for example. But when we do this we must compare all the voices from at least a dozen of Blake's poems to all the voices from an equal number of Dickinson's. We can then speak either of a range of voices that seems typical of each poet or of some specific characteristics that remain constant through all their individual voices. Moreover, we may equally well make comparisons between voices belonging to a single poet—comparing the voices of Blake's early poems to those of his later poems, for instance—which we could not do if the voice in each poem were the poet's only voice.

To further emphasize this distance between speaker and poet, we may look again at poems such as "We Real Cool" and "Sir Patrick Spens." They seem to speak to us as directly and to be as immediately felt as any other poems, but we know no author for "Sir Patrick Spens" and are sure that Gwendolyn Brooks is not seven adolescents in a pool hall.

The poem is the poet's vision, nothing more. Its speakers may be inside the action (as in "Upon Julia's Clothes") or outside it (as in "The Cherry-Tree Carol"). They may have elements of the poet's own situation or emotions in them, or they may not. But they are speakers and not writers; they are the poet's creations and not the poet's self.

For discussing speakers who do seem to mirror their poets, we have the useful critical term **persona**. The speakers of "The Lamb" and "The Tyger," of "There's a Certain Slant of Light," and of "Upon Julia's Clothes" may be called their poets' personae. Personae represent one aspect of their poet's personality or experience, isolated from the rest of the poet's life, dramatized, and re-created through art. Poets—like all human beings—are complex and changeable. Personae are simpler: fixed, changeless, and slightly exaggerated. Unlike their makers, who must respond to the many demands of the everyday world in which they live, personae exist only within their poems and respond only to the thoughts and sensations that gave the poems birth.

Here, for the further study of speakers in poetry, are three groups of poems. Most of these poems employ speakers who might well be spoken of as personae, but at least one has a speaker who cannot be so described. Be aware, as you read these poems, of sound and language and total effect. But pay most attention to the characterization of the speakers and to the varying voices with which they speak.

THEODORE ROETHKE (1908–1963)

My Papa's Waltz

The whiskey on your breath
Could make a small boy dizzy;
But I hung on like death:
Such waltzing was not easy.

5 We romped until the pans
Slid from the kitchen shelf;
My mother's countenance
Could not unfrown itself.

The hand that held my wrist
10 Was battered on one knuckle;
At every step you missed
My right ear scraped a buckle.

You beat time on my head
With a palm caked hard by dirt,
15 Then waltzed me off to bed
Still clinging to your shirt.

I Knew a Woman

I knew a woman, lovely in her bones,
When small birds sighed, she would sigh back at them;
Ah, when she moved, she moved more ways than one:
The shapes a bright container can contain!
5 Of her choice virtues only gods should speak,
Or English poets who grew up on Greek
(I'd have them sing in chorus, cheek to cheek).

How well her wishes went! She stroked my chin,
She taught me Turn, and Counter-turn, and Stand;[1]
10 She taught me Touch, that undulant white skin;
I nibbled meekly from her proffered hand;
She was the sickle; I, poor I, the rake,
Coming behind her for her pretty sake
(But what prodigious mowing we did make).

15 Love likes a gander, and adores a goose:
Her full lips pursed, the errant note to seize;
She played it quick, she played it light and loose;
My eyes, they dazzled at her flowing knees;
Her several parts could keep a pure repose,
20 Or one hip quiver with a mobile nose
(She moved in circles, and those circles moved).

Let seed be grass, and grass turn into hay:
I'm martyr to a motion not my own;
What's freedom for? To know eternity.
25 I swear she cast a shadow white as stone.
But who would count eternity in days?
These old bones live to learn her wanton ways:
(I measure time by how a body sways).

QUESTIONS

1. What is the subject of each of these poems? What is the emotional state of the speaker?
2. How does the language of the two poems compare? What sort of images does each use? How does the language match the subject and mood in each?
3. How would you characterize the speaker of each poem? What would you have to say to move from a characterization of the speakers to a characterization of the poet?

WILLIAM BUTLER YEATS (1865–1939)

An Irish Airman Foresees His Death[1]

I know that I shall meet my fate
Somewhere among the clouds above;
Those that I fight I do not hate,

---

[1] Terms for the three parts of a Pindaric ode.

---

[1] Major Robert Gregory, son of Yeats's friend and patroness Lady Augusta Gregory, was killed in action in 1918.

Those that I guard I do not love;
5 My country is Kiltartan Cross,[2]
My countrymen Kiltartan's poor,
No likely end could bring them loss
Or leave them happier than before.
Nor law, nor duty bade me fight,
10 Nor public men, nor cheering crowds,
A lonely impulse of delight
Drove to this tumult in the clouds;
I balanced all, brought all to mind,
The years to come seemed waste of breath,
15 A waste of breath the years behind
In balance with this life, this death.

WILFRED OWEN (1893–1918)

Dulce Et Decorum Est

Bent double, like old beggars under sacks,
Knock-kneed, coughing like hags, we cursed through
     sludge,
Till on the haunting flares we turned our backs
And towards our distant rest began to trudge.
5 Men marched asleep. Many had lost their boots
But limped on, blood-shod. All went lame; all blind;
Drunk with fatigue; deaf even to the hoots
Of tired, outstripped Five-Nines that dropped behind.

Gas! Gas! Quick, boys!—An ecstasy of fumbling,
10 Fitting the clumsy helmets just in time;
But someone still was yelling out and stumbling
And flound'ring like a man in fire or lime . . .
Dim, through the misty panes and thick green light,
As under a green sea, I saw him drowning.

15 In all my dreams, before my helpless sight,
He plunges at me, guttering, choking, drowning.

If in some smothering dreams you too could pace
Behind the wagon that we flung him in,
And watch the white eyes writhing in his face,
20 His hanging face, like a devil's sick of sin;

---

[2] Kiltartan is an Irish village near Coole Park, the estate of the Gregorys.

If you could hear, at every jolt, the blood
Come gargling from the froth-corrupted lungs,
Obscene as cancer, bitter as the cud
Of vile, incurable sores on innocent tongues,—
25   My friend, you would not tell with such high zest
To children ardent for some desperate glory,
The old Lie: Dulce et decorum est
Pro patria mori.

QUESTIONS

1. What theme is common to these two poems?
2. How would you compare the two speakers?
3. How would you characterize the tone of each poem? The language? (Note the use of repetition. What effect does it produce in Owen's poem? In Yeats's? How does it help characterize each speaker?)
4. How does the difference in character and mood of the two speakers contribute to the difference in overall effect of the two poems? (What reaction does each poet seem to want from you? What message—if any—does his poem seem to carry?)

ANONYMOUS—MIDDLE ENGLISH LYRIC

Western Wind

Western wind, when will thou blow,
    The small rain down can rain?
Christ, if my love were in my arms
    And I in my bed again.

SIR THOMAS WYATT (1503–1542)

To a Lady to Answer Directly
with Yea or Nay

Madame, withouten many words,
Once I am sure you will or no;
And if you will, then leave your boords[1]
And use your wit, and shew[2] it so,
5   For with a beck[3] you shall me call.
And if of one that burns alway

---

[1] Jokes.
[2] Show.
[3] Gesture.

Ye have pity or ruth[4] at all,
Answer him fair[5] with yea or nay.
If it be yea, I shall be fain;[6]
10 If it be nay, friends as before.
You shall another man obtain,
And I mine own, and yours no more.

SIR PHILIP SIDNEY (1554–1586)

From **Astrophil and Stella**

Sonnet 31

With how sad steps, O moon,[1] thou climb'st the skies!
  How silently, and with how wan a face!
  What! may it be that even in heavenly place
  That busy archer his sharp arrows tries?
5 Sure, if that long-with-love-acquainted eyes
  Can judge of love, thou feel'st a lover's case;
  I read it in thy looks—thy languished grace
  To me, that feel the like, thy state descries.
Then, even of fellowship, O moon, tell me,
10   Is constant love deemed there but want of wit?
  Are beauties there as proud as here they be?
Do they above love to be loved, and yet
  Those lovers scorn whom that love doth possess?
  Do they call virtue there ungratefulness?

EDMUND WALLER (1606–1687)

Go, Lovely Rose

  Go, lovely rose,
Tell her that wastes her time and me
  That now she knows,
When I resemble her to thee,
5   How sweet and fair she seems to be.

  Tell her that's young
And shuns to have her graces spied
  That hadst thou sprung

---

[4] Compassion.
[5] Clearly, honestly.
[6] Glad, delighted.

---

[1] The technique of having the speaker seem to address someone or something within a poem is called **apostrophe.**

In deserts where no men abide,
10 Thou must have uncommended died.

Small is the worth
Of beauty from the light retired;
Bid her come forth,
Suffer herself to be desired,
15 And not blush so to be admired.

Then die, that she
The common fate of all things rare
May read in thee:
How small a part of time they share
20 That are so wondrous sweet and fair!

WILLIAM BUTLER YEATS (1865–1939)

The Folly of Being Comforted

One that is ever kind said yesterday:
"Your well-belovèd's hair has threads of gray,
And little shadows come about her eyes;
Time can but make it easier to be wise
5 Though now it seem impossible, and so
All that you need is patience."
                                        Heart cries, "No,
I have not a crumb of comfort, not a grain.
Time can but make her beauty over again:
Because of that great nobleness of hers
10 The fire that stirs about her, when she stirs,
Burns but more clearly. O she had not these ways
When all the wild summer was in her gaze."

O heart! O heart! if she'd but turn her head,
You'd know the folly of being comforted.

QUESTIONS

These five poems are spoken by five unhappy lovers. How would you compare
and contrast them?

1. To whom does each speak?
2. In what situation does each find himself? What is his reaction to the situation?
   What emotions and/or thoughts does he express?
3. How do the form and language of each poem, together with the emotion
   and situation represented, create your picture of each of these lovers?

The final poem in this chapter represents a form known as **dramatic monologue.** After you have read the poem, answer the following questions:

1. Who is the speaker?
2. To whom is he speaking? On what occasion?
3. What does the speaker tell you about his own character? How does he do so?
4. What do you think happened to the "last duchess"?
5. If you were the person being addressed, how would you feel at the end of the monologue?

ROBERT BROWNING (1812–1889)

My Last Duchess

Ferrara

That's my last duchess painted on the wall,
Looking as if she were alive. I call
That piece a wonder, now: Frà Pandolf's[1] hands
Worked busily a day, and there she stands.
5 Will't please you sit and look at her? I said
"Frà Pandolf" by design, for never read
Strangers like you that pictured countenance,
The depth and passion of its earnest glance,
But to myself they turned (since none puts by
10 The curtain I have drawn for you, but I)
And seemed as they would ask me, if they durst,
How such a glance came there; so, not the first
Are you to turn and ask thus. Sir, 'twas not
Her husband's presence only, called that spot
15 Of joy into the Duchess' cheek: perhaps
Frà Pandolf chanced to say "Her mantle laps
"Over my lady's wrist too much," or "Paint
"Must never hope to reproduce the faint
"Half-flush that dies along her throat": such stuff
20 Was courtesy, she thought, and cause enough
For calling up that spot of joy. She had
A heart—how shall I say?—too soon made glad,
Too easily impressed; she liked whate'er
She looked on, and her looks went everywhere.
25 Sir, 'twas all one! My favor at her breast,
The dropping of the daylight in the West,

---

[1] A fictitious artist, as is Claus of Innsbruck in the last line.

The bough of cherries some officious fool
Broke in the orchard for her, the white mule
She rode with round the terrace—all and each
30 Would draw from her alike the approving speech,
Or blush, at least. She thanked men—good! but thanked
Somehow—I know not how—as if she ranked
My gift of a nine-hundred-years-old name
With anybody's gift. Who'd stoop to blame
35 This sort of trifling? Even had you skill
In speech—which I have not—to make your will
Quite clear to such an one, and say, "Just this
"Or that in you disgusts me; here you miss,
"Or there exceed the mark"—and if she let
40 Herself be lessoned so, nor plainly set
Her wits to yours, forsooth, and made excuse,
—E'en then would be some stooping; and I choose
Never to stoop. Oh sir, she smiled, no doubt,
Whene'er I passed her; but who passed without
45 Much the same smile? This grew; I gave commands;
Then all smiles stopped together. There she stands
As if alive. Will 't please you rise? We'll meet
The company below, then. I repeat,
The Count your master's known munificence
50 Is ample warrant that no just pretense
Of mine for dowry will be disallowed;
Though his fair daughter's self, as I avowed
At starting, is my object. Nay, we'll go
Together down, sir. Notice Neptune, though,
55 Taming a sea-horse, thought a rarity,
Which Claus of Innsbruck cast in bronze for me!

6

The Speaker's Vision

Like other writers, poets find their visions in three basic sources: the world around them, their own experiences, and their inner vision of what is or might be. The speakers of their poems, who are charged with communicating these visions, may therefore be observers, recording scenes and experiences for our mutual pleasure and insight; or they may be visionaries, recasting real or imagined scenes to produce a new vision for our sharing.

We can see the distinction clearly enough in poems we have already read. For instance, we have already seen two types of reporters at work. The speakers in "Get Up and Bar the Door" and "The Cherry-Tree Carol" are most obviously reporters; they simply tell us what occurred and let us draw our own conclusions about it. The speakers of "We Real Cool" and "For a Lady I Know" are also reporters but are less obviously so, because we sense that the poets are not as objective as their speakers. The speakers provide no interpretation and show no emotion. But the poets' attitudes come through, nonetheless. Indeed, much of the effectiveness of these poems comes from the disparity between the speakers' objectivity and the poets' concern, a disparity felt by the reader as irony. But that is a subject we will speak of more thoroughly in the next chapter.

We can also recall poems in which the speaker was primarily a visionary. Dickinson's poems come to mind here, and Blake's. "The Lamb" and "The Tyger" are far more concerned with the religious visions the animals arouse in Blake's speakers than they are with the animals themselves; and "Tell All the Truth" is pure vision, having no objective scene or experience whatever as its starting point. Another visionary is the speaker of Pound's "These Fought in Any Case," who draws on visions of so many real or imagined soldiers that we soon lose all sense of individuals in the more compelling vision of the war itself.

These, then, are poems that mark the two extremes of the speaker's stance: the objective extreme and the visionary extreme. Between them come those poems (probably typical of the majority of poems) in which the speaker is reporter and interpreter both. These poems balance what is seen and what is felt, allowing neither to overwhelm the other. Their speakers report on what is happening while explaining or suggesting its implications. Thus, "There's a Certain Slant of Light" conveys its atmospheric sensation most vividly by interpreting its spiritual overtones. And poems such as "in Just-," and "I Knew a Woman" blend recollection and response so perfectly that it's hard to say where one stops and the other begins. Through the speaker's emotional response, the vision is made real for us; reporter, responder, and interpreter are one.

The poems we shall look at in this chapter blend objective and visionary stances, observation and interpretation. Take careful note of the speaker's character and stance within each poem. Before you answer any of the questions, make sure you know what sort of person is speaking, to what the speaker is responding, and how much of the speaker's response is to things outside himself or herself and how much to inner visions or emotions.

The common factor in the first two poems is memory. Read each poem, and then discuss:

1. The details by which the memories are presented.
2. The comparisons and contrasts created between the memories and the speaker's present circumstances or emotional state.
3. Any sense of movement through time the poem may create, and the way in which it creates it.
4. What we are told in the poem's conclusion, and what sense of the speaker's feelings or attitudes the conclusion gives us.

D. H. LAWRENCE (1885–1930)

Piano

Softly, in the dusk, a woman is singing to me;
Taking me back down the vista of years, till I see
A child sitting under the piano, in the boom of the tingling strings
And pressing the small, poised feet of a mother who smiles as she
   sings.

5 In spite of myself, the insidious mastery of song
  Betrays me back, till the heart of me weeps to belong
  To the old Sunday evenings at home, with winter outside
  And hymns in the cozy parlor, the tinkling piano our guide.

  So now it is vain for the singer to burst into clamor
10 With the great black piano appassionato. The glamour
  Of childish days is upon me, my manhood is cast
  Down in the flood of remembrance, I weep like a child for the past.

EDNA ST. VINCENT MILLAY (1892–1950)

What Lips My Lips Have Kissed, and Where, and Why

What lips my lips have kissed, and where, and why,
I have forgotten, and what arms have lain
Under my head till morning; but the rain
Is full of ghosts tonight, that tap and sigh
5 Upon the glass and listen for reply,
And in my heart there stirs a quiet pain
For unremembered lads that not again
Will turn to me at midnight with a cry.
Thus in the winter stands the lonely tree,
10 Nor knows what birds have vanished one by one,
Yet knows its boughs more silent than before:
I cannot say what loves have come and gone,
I only know that summer sang in me
A little while, that in me sings no more.

   In contrast, the next poem looks to the future. What vision of that future does the speaker see and create? How does she do so? (After you consider this poem on its own, you might want to contrast it with Millay's "What Lips My Lips Have Kissed." Note the differences in images and mood that accompany the loss or assurance of the memory of a particularly valued lover.)

NIKKI GIOVANNI (1943–   )

You Are There

  i shall save my poems
  for the winter of my dreams
  i look forward to huddling
  in my rocker with my life
5 i wonder what i'll contemplate
  lovers—certainly those

i can remember
and knowing my life
you'll be there

10   you'll be there in the cold
like a Siamese on my knee
proud purring when you let me stroke you

you'll be there in the rain
like an umbrella over my head
15   sheltering me from the damp mist

you'll be there in the dark
like a lighthouse in the fog
seeing me through troubled waters

you'll be there in the sun
20   like coconut oil on my back
to keep me from burning

i shall save a special poem
for you to say
you always made me smile
25   and even though i cried sometimes
you said i will not let you
down

my rocker and i on winter's porch
will never be sad if you're gone
30   the winter's cold has been stored
against
you will always be
there

The next group of poems presents speakers considering their own relationships to the natural world, to other humans, to their work, or to some combination of the three. Notice the range of stances between solitariness and connectedness presented by these visions and the role that nature and thought play in each.

WILLIAM WORDSWORTH (1770–1850)

I Wandered Lonely As a Cloud

I wandered lonely as a cloud
That floats on high o'er vales and hills,
When all at once I saw a crowd,

A host, of golden daffodils;
5   Beside the lake, beneath the trees,
Fluttering and dancing in the breeze.

Continuous as the stars that shine
And twinkle on the Milky Way,
They stretched in never-ending line
10   Along the margin of a bay:
Ten thousand saw I at a glance,
Tossing their heads in sprightly dance.

The waves beside them danced; but they
Outdid the sparkling waves in glee:
15   A poet could not but be gay,
In such a jocund company:
I gazed—and gazed— but little thought
What wealth the show to me had brought:

For oft, when on my couch I lie
20   In vacant or in pensive mood,
They flash upon that inward eye
Which is the bliss of solitude;
And then my heart with pleasure fills,
And dances with the daffodils.

QUESTIONS

1. The major presence in this poem is that of the "host of golden daffodils"
seen by the poet-speaker. How does the speaker describe and characterize
the daffodils? What words and images does he use for them? How many of
these words and images would normally be used for people?
   How active a role do the daffodils play in this vision—in the original scene
and in their repeated appearances?
2. How does the speaker describe himself? What images does he use? In what
activities does he depict himself? How active is his role in his relationship
with the daffodils? in relation to the poem itself?

JOHN KEATS (1795–1821)

When I Have Fears

When I have fears that I may cease to be
   Before my pen has gleaned my teeming brain,
Before high-piled books, in charactery,[1]
   Hold like rich garners the full ripened grain;

---
[1] Characters, writing.

5 When I behold, upon the night's starred face,
  Huge cloudy symbols of a high romance,
And think that I may never live to trace
  Their shadows, with the magic hand of chance;
And when I feel, fair creature of an hour,
10   That I shall never look upon thee more,
Never have relish in the faery power
  Of unreflecting love;—then on the shore
Of the wide world I stand alone, and think
Till love and fame to nothingness do sink.

QUESTIONS

1. Since the whole poem is one sentence, its syntax gets a bit complicated. Let's start, therefore, by examining it clause by clause, beginning with the three "when" clauses that make up the first eleven-and-a-half lines of the poem: What are the first four lines concerned with? The second four? The third? How are the three tied together? (Who is the "fair creature of an hour"? Why might the speaker call her so at this point in the poem?)
2. What overtones do words like *rich, romance, magic* and *faery* give to the poem? What contrast do they suggest between the poet's wishes and his sense of reality?
3. Then look at the final clause of the sentence—the last two-and-a-half lines. What action does it show the speaker taking? How explicit are his feelings made? What are you left to fill in?

WALT WHITMAN (1819–1892)

A Noiseless Patient Spider

A noiseless patient spider,
I mark'd where on a little promontory it stood isolated,
Mark'd how to explore the vacant vast surrounding,
It launch'd forth filament, filament, filament, out of itself,
5 Ever unreeling them, ever tirelessly speeding them.

And you O my soul where you stand,
Surrounded, detached, in measureless oceans of space,
Ceaselessly musing, venturing, throwing, seeking the spheres to
    connect them,
Till the bridge you will need be form'd, till the ductile anchor hold,
10 Till the gossamer thread you fling catch somewhere, O my soul.

QUESTIONS

1. Note how this poem is balanced between the first stanza, describing the speaker's vision of the spider, and the second stanza, describing his vision of

his own soul. What comparison is made between the two? What characteristics and activities do they share?

2. Note that the speaker describes the spider as "isolated" and as needing or wishing "to explore the vacant vast surrounding." How apt is this as a description of an actual spider? How does it prepare the reader for the depiction of the speaker in the second stanza?

   Similarly, how apt or evocative is the description of the spider's activity? How does it complete the picture of the spider and prepare for the speaker's invocation to his soul?

3. With what words, images, and ideas does the speaker extend his vision of the spider so that it becomes a vision of his own soul's needs?

4. The poem's final lines speak of "the bridge you will need" and "the ductile anchor." What do you think these images represent? What is needed? What does the lack of detailed definition here and in the last line's "somewhere" do for your sense of the speaker's vision?

ROBERT FROST (1874–1963)

Two Tramps in Mud Time

Out of the mud two strangers came
And caught me splitting wood in the yard.
And one of them put me off my aim
By hailing cheerily "Hit them hard!"
5   I knew pretty well why he dropped behind
And let the other go on a way.
I knew pretty well what he had in mind:
He wanted to take my job for pay.

Good blocks of oak it was I split,
10 As large around as the chopping block;
And every piece I squarely hit
Fell splinterless as a cloven rock.
The blows that a life of self-control
Spares to strike for the common good,
15 That day, giving a loose to my soul,
I spent on the unimportant wood.

The sun was warm but the wind was chill.
You know how it is with an April day
When the sun is out and the wind is still,
20 You're one month on in the middle of May.
But if you so much as dare to speak,
A cloud comes over the sunlit arch,
A wind comes off a frozen peak,
And you're two months back in the middle of March.

25 A bluebird comes tenderly up to alight
    And turns to the wind to unruffle a plume,
    His song so pitched as not to excite
    A single flower as yet to bloom.
    It is snowing a flake: and he half knew
30 Winter was only playing possum.
    Except in color he isn't blue,
    But he wouldn't advise a thing to blossom.

    The water for which we may have to look
    In summertime with a witching wand,
35 In every wheelrut's now a brook,
    In every print of a hoof a pond.
    Be glad of water, but don't forget
    The lurking frost in the earth beneath
    That will steal forth after the sun is set
40 And show on the water its crystal teeth.

    The time when most I loved my task
    These two must make me love it more
    By coming with what they came to ask.
    You'd think I never had felt before
45 The weight of an ax-head poised aloft,
    The grip on earth of outspread feet,
    The life of muscles rocking soft
    And smooth and moist in vernal heat.

    Out of the woods two hulking tramps
50 (From sleeping God knows where last night,
    But not long since in the lumber camps).
    They thought all chopping was theirs of right.
    Men of the woods and lumberjacks,
    They judged me by their appropriate tool.
55 Except as a fellow handled an ax
    They had no way of knowing a fool.

    Nothing on either side was said.
    They knew they had but to stay their stay
    And all their logic would fill my head:
60 As that I had no right to play
    With what was another man's work for gain.
    My right might be love but theirs was need.
    And where the two exist in twain
    Theirs was the better right—agreed.

65   But yield who will to their separation,
     My object in living is to unite
     My avocation and my vocation
     As my two eyes make one in sight.
     Only where love and need are one,
70   And the work is play for mortal stakes,
     Is the deed ever really done
     For Heaven and the future's sakes.

QUESTIONS

Frost's poem begins with a detailed description of an incident, and ends with as explicit a vision of the speaker's "goal in living" as we've met yet. How does this final vision grow out of the incident?

1. Consider how the speaker presents the incident: how he describes the physical scene, the tramps, his own emotions and sensations.
2. Notice the particular descriptions of the wood, sun and wind, bluebird, and water, and of the speaker himself in the sixth stanza. How do these create a sense of "love" to buttress the speaker's claim to love in the sixth and final stanzas?
3. Consider the speaker's voice: its rhythms and phrasings, its appeal to common knowledge with its audience, its blend of detailed observation and of interpretation, of seriousness and humor. What role does the voice play in determining your reaction to the poem?
4. Consider the speaker's proclamation in the final verse. How would you paraphrase it? Does it seem a fitting vision to close this poem? Is it a vision with which you yourself might be comfortable? Why or why not?

7 Beyond the Speaker: The Double Vision of Irony

Irony exists whenever we say one thing and mean the opposite. "An exam? What fun!" is an ironic statement. More generally, irony exists whenever we feel a disparity between what someone says or thinks and what we know to be the truth. Irony can be intentional or unintentional, depending on whether the speaker means the statement to be ironic or not. A student who says, "A test today? What fun!" is almost certainly indulging in deliberate irony: he or she neither thinks of the test as fun nor expects others to think of it in that manner.

Suppose, however, that we are fellow students; suppose that you know (but I don't) that an English test has been scheduled for today; and suppose that I now say something like, "Boy, am I tired! I think I'll sleep through English class today!" This is unintentional irony. I am seriously planning to sleep. You know, however, that I will *not* be sleeping through English class. Instead, I will be cudgeling my tired brain, trying to pass an unexpected exam. In this case, it is your perception (as audience) that creates the irony. You know (as I, the innocent speaker, cannot know) how far from reality my words and expectations are.

The emotions of irony arise from our perceptions of a conflict between intent or ideal and reality. The technique of irony consists of creating a parallel disparity in words, by creating an opposition between the apparent meaning of the words and their ironic significance. Always there is some hint of pain in irony, some overtone of pity or anger. And always the emotion is a shared one: shared between reader and speaker if the irony is intentional, shared between reader and writer if it is not.

In responding to irony, then, we are aligning ourselves with someone whose perceptions we share, having been invited—as one right-thinking person by another—to share both the ironist's view of the subject and the emotions of scorn or pity or rage that go with it. Always, therefore, there will be some hint of argument (implicit or explicit) in an ironic poem. And always, the use of irony will produce some distancing of effect, as we stand back and judge the presented disparity.

Beyond these basic facts, however, we will see that irony is a technique that allows many variations of meaning, tone, and effect. As with most definitions, when we have defined a poem as ironic, we have only begun to talk about its construction, its meaning, and its power to touch us.

When you have read the poems that follow, review them in order to write about the following questions:

1. What disparity is being highlighted?
2. What ideals or beliefs that you hold are being appealed to? Is the appeal explicit or implicit?
3. Is the speaker conscious or unconscious of the irony of his or her speech?
4. If there is more than one voice in the poem, how are they contrasted? What part does the contrast play in your sense of the poem's irony?
5. What range of feelings does the poem suggest?

Then discuss each poem more fully, making whatever points you think are most helpful in deciding what role the irony plays in your appreciation of the poem as a whole.

ADRIENNE RICH (1929   )

Aunt Jennifer's Tigers

Aunt Jennifer's tigers prance across a screen,
Bright topaz denizens of a world of green.
They do not fear the men beneath the tree;
They pace in sleek chivalric certainty.

5 Aunt Jennifer's fingers fluttering through her wool
Find even the ivory needle hard to pull.
The massive weight of Uncle's wedding band
Sits heavily upon Aunt Jennifer's hand.

When Aunt is dead, her terrified hands will lie
10 Still ringed with ordeals she was mastered by.
The tigers in the panel that she made
Will go on prancing, proud and unafraid.

ARTHUR HUGH CLOUGH (1819–1861)

The Latest Decalogue

Thou shalt have one God only; who
Would be at the expense of two?
No graven images may be
Worshiped, except the currency:
5 Swear not at all; for for thy curse
Thine enemy is none the worse:
At church on Sunday to attend
Will serve to keep the world thy friend:
Honour thy parents; that is, all
10 From whom advancement may befall:
Thou shalt not kill; but need'st not strive
Officiously to keep alive:
Do not adultery commit;
Advantage rarely comes of it:
15 Thou shalt not steal; an empty feat,
When it's so lucrative to cheat:
Bear not false witness; let the lie
Have time on its own wings to fly:
Thou shalt not covet; but tradition
20 Approves all forms of competition.

The sum of all is, thou shalt love,
If any body, God above:
At any rate shall never labour
More than thyself to love thy neighbour.

A. E. HOUSMAN (1859–1936)

From **A Shropshire Lad**

When I Was One-and-Twenty

When I was one-and-twenty
    I heard a wise man say,
"Give crowns and pounds and guineas
    But not your heart away;

5 Give pearls away and rubies
    But keep your fancy free."
But I was one-and-twenty,
    No use to talk to me.

When I was one-and-twenty
10   I heard him say again,

"The heart out of the bosom
  Was never given in vain;

'Tis paid with sighs a plenty
  And sold for endless rue."
15 And I am two-and-twenty,
  And oh, 'tis true, 'tis true.

DOROTHY PARKER (1893–1967)

Résumé

Razors pain you;
Rivers are damp;
Acids stain you;
And drugs cause cramp.
5 Guns aren't lawful;
Nooses give;
Gas smells awful;
You might as well live.

JOHN CIARDI (1916–1986)

Project for a Cliff Face

Before I die (said the self-riddling
stonecutter) I mean to practice a
whim on a cliff face, if I can find
an unused extrusion to be the page
5 for the following text I shall carve
in the pure practice of nothing but
the art and pleasure of my lettering:

THERE WAS A TIME BEFORE MAN.
THERE WILL BE A TIME AFTER.
10 I SPEAK ONLY WHAT IS EVIDENT,
BUT AS LONG AS THERE REMAINS
ANY MAN WHO CAN READ THESE
WORDS, NONE WILL BELIEVE THEM,
AND AFTER, NO ONE WILL KNOW
15 WHETHER TO BELIEVE THEM OR NOT.

PERCY BYSSHE SHELLEY (1792–1822)

Ozymandias

I met a traveler from an antique land
Who said: Two vast and trunkless legs of stone

Stand in the desert . . . Near them, on the sand,
Half sunk, a shattered visage lies, whose frown,
5 And wrinkled lip, and sneer of cold command,
Tell that its sculptor well those passions read
Which yet survive, stamped on these lifeless things,
The hand that mocked them, and the heart that fed:
And on the pedestal these words appear:
10 "My name is Ozymandias, king of kings:
Look on my works, ye Mighty, and despair!"
Nothing beside remains. Round the decay
Of that colossal wreck, boundless and bare
The lone and level sands stretch far away.

W. H. AUDEN (1907–1973)

The Unknown Citizen

(To JS/07/M/378
This Marble Monument
Is Erected by the State)

He was found by the Bureau of Statistics to be
One against whom there was no official complaint,
And all the reports on his conduct agree
That, in the modern sense of an old-fashioned word, he was
    a saint,
5 For in everything he did he served the Greater Community.
Except for the War till the day he retired
He worked in a factory and never got fired,
But satisfied his employers, Fudge Motors Inc.
Yet he wasn't a scab or odd in his views,
10 For his Union reports that he paid his dues,
(Our report on his Union shows it was sound)
And our Social Psychology workers found
That he was popular with his mates and liked a drink.
The Press are convinced that he bought a paper every day
15 And that his reactions to advertisements were normal in every
    way.
Policies taken out in his name prove that he was fully insured,
And his Health-card shows he was once in hospital but left it
    cured.
Both Producers Research and High-Grade Living declare
He was fully sensible to the advantages of the Instalment Plan
20 And had everything necessary to the Modern Man,
A phonograph, a radio, a car, and a frigidaire.

Our researchers into Public Opinion are content
That he held the proper opinions for the time of year;
When there was peace, he was for peace; when there was war, he
    went.
25   He was married and added five children to the population,
Which our Eugenist says was the right number for a parent of his
    generation,
And our teachers report that he never interfered with their
    education.
Was he free? Was he happy? The question is absurd:
Had anything been wrong, we should certainly have heard.

IMAGERY

8

Similes, Metaphors, and Personification

The three basic elements of any poem are the vision it embodies, the speaker who gives voice to the vision, and the language that creates voice and vision alike. (By stretching the terminology a bit, we could call them the three V's: voice, vision, and vocabulary.) In the preceding chapters, we examined the ways in which the language of a poem—its vocabulary, its connotations, its sounds—created and characterized the poem's speaker. Now it is time to look at the ways in which the language creates the vision.

Vision in literature always implies a shared vision. Originating in the writer's mind, the vision is first translated into words and then re-created in our minds, to be felt by us as it was felt by its writer. When we come to the end of a poem, therefore, the feeling we experience is likely to be a blend of recognition and surprise. We will have seen something familiar —perhaps even something of ourselves—as we have never seen it before.

There are two ways in which poets can go about creating this feeling. The first is to word their vision so precisely that we feel we are seeing things with a new closeness and clearness. This is the method chosen by Levertov in "Six Variations (part iii)" and Lawrence in "Piano."

The second method relies on figures of speech or on unexpected comparisons to lead us into making connections we may not have made before. This is Pound's method in "In a Station of the Metro," where human "faces in the crowd" are seen as "petals on a wet black bough," beauty and impersonality mingling. It is Dickinson's method, too, when she describes her "certain slant of light" as being one that "oppresses, like the weight/Of cathedral tunes."

This trick of mingling appeals to different senses in a single image—of describing a sound in terms of color, or a sight in terms of sound or feel —is called **synaesthesia.** Rather than trying to define a type of light in terms of its appearance, Dickinson compares it to a sound. But she speaks of both in terms of weight that presses down physically or spiritually. The word *cathedral,* meanwhile, not only defines the solemn, religious music that parallels the "slant of light," but also prepares us for the image of "heavenly hurt" introduced in the next line. Thus the poem weaves its pattern of imagery.

We have, then, already met poems that make use of both the literal and the figurative styles of imagery. To make sure the contrast is clear, however, let's look at two poems on one subject and see how the language works in each.

WALT WHITMAN (1819–1892)

The Dalliance of the Eagles

Skirting the river road, (my forenoon walk, my rest,)
Skyward in air a sudden muffled sound, the dalliance of the eagles,
The rushing amorous contact high in space together,
The clinching interlocking claws, a living, fierce, gyrating wheel,
5 Four beating wings, two beaks, a swirling mass tight grappling,
In tumbling turning clustering loops, straight downward falling,
Till o'er the river pois'd, the twain yet one, a moment's lull,
A motionless still balance in the air, then parting, talons loosing,
Upward again on slow-firm pinions slanting, their separate diverse
    flight,
10 She hers, he his, pursuing.

ALFRED, LORD TENNYSON (1809–1892)

The Eagle

He clasps the crag with crooked hands;
Close to the sun in lonely lands,
Ringed with the azure world, he stands.

The wrinkled sea beneath him crawls;
5 He watches from his mountain walls,
And like a thunderbolt he falls.

Obviously, these are very dissimilar poems. One, talking of a single eagle that remains unmoving throughout most of the poem, creates an atmosphere of space and solitude. The other, speaking of two eagles, seems a constant rush of motion. In part, it is the sound of the words the poets have chosen that creates these different atmospheres. Tennyson's words, lines, and sentences are all short, and the stop at the end of each line is strongly marked. Whitman uses longer lines, with less pronounced breaks between them; and his sentences are so involved and complex that they keep the reader's mind and voice in almost constant motion as dizzying as that of the eagles themselves. Yet the basic difference in the way these eagles are shown to us lies not in their motion or motionlessness, but rather in the imagery in which they are described.

If we go through each poem, noting carefully each descriptive term used, we will discover a marked contrast. Whitman relies heavily on adjectives, particularly on participles (adjectives formed from verbs). *Clinching, interlocking, living, gyrating, beating, swirling, grappling, tumbling, turning, clustering, falling*—from these comes the poem's sense of action, as well as much of its power of description. The poet's stance is primarily that of the observer. Taking a walk, he has been startled first by the "sudden muffled sound" and then by the sight of the eagles; and he describes sight and sound alike as carefully and vividly as he can:

> The clinching interlocking claws, a living, fierce, gyrating
>   wheel,
> Four beating wings, two beaks, a swirling mass tight
>   grappling,
> In tumbling turning clustering loops, straight downward
>   falling.

Tennyson's fragment, too, is pure description. But its phrasing and its imagery come as much from the poet's imagination as from his powers of observation. Where Whitman uses no words that could not, in sober prose, be applied to an eagle, Tennyson uses almost none that could. His eagle is presented largely in terms that compare it to other things: an old man, grown crooked with age; an explorer in "lonely lands"; a thunderbolt. By calling our attention to these other things, he draws on our feelings about them (respect, for instance, or awe) and uses those feelings to influence our feelings about the eagle itself. Thus, instead of a bird's "clinching . . . claws," Tennyson's eagle has "crooked hands." He "stands"—which, to some readers, may sound more human than birdlike— and "watches," as men and birds both do. Later, he "falls"—an ambiguous verb. The landscape in which he is pictured is similarly humanized. The lands are "lonely," the sea is "wrinkled" and "crawls." There is exaggeration (or **hyperbole**) as well. The eagle's perch is "close to the sun"; the sky against which he is seen is an entire "azure world"; the eagle falls "like a thunderbolt." High and remote, yet somehow in his very remoteness human, Tennyson's eagle presents a striking image of a being in lofty isolation.

By linking disparate things, by forcing us to think of one thing in terms of another, poets make us see those things in new ways, creating new images, calling forth unexpected emotions, fostering new insights. With homely and familiar images, they bring strange things closer to us, while with exotic images they cast new light on everyday things. Abstract ideas are given vivid life by concrete images, while more abstract imagery suggests new significance for particular items or experiences. Poets can speak of their subjects in the most precise, closely fitting words they can find; or they can seek out unexpected startling terms that will call our own imaginations and creative impulses into play. Since it is so largely this choice of how language will be handled in any given poem that determines our sense of that poem, our first or final reaction to it—the totally different feelings that Whitman's torrent of precisely denotative adjectives and Tennyson's careful balance of connotations of humanity, space, and isolation provoke—it will be worth our while to examine some of the techniques that poets use in the creation of imagery. Let us look, therefore, at some of the commoner forms of imagery found in poetry. Since comparisons are often the result of figurative speech, we will start with figures that are forms of comparison: the explicit comparisons, the simile and the metaphor; and the implicit ones, implied metaphor and personification.

Simile

A **simile** is a comparison and is always stated as such. You will always find *like, as, so,* or some such word of comparison within it. Usually, the things it compares resemble each other in only one or two ways, differing in all other respects. An eagle and a thunderbolt are not really much alike; yet the fact that both go from the sky to the ground can allow Tennyson to declare that "like a thunderbolt he falls." In the differences between the two lies the simile's power. The fact that a thunderbolt is so much swifter, so much more powerful and dangerous than the eagle, lends a sense of speed and power and danger to the eagle's fall. A simile may be as brief as the traditional "red as blood," or it may be considerably more complicated, as in this example from "Tell All the Truth":

> As Lightning to the Children eased
> With explanation kind
> The Truth must dazzle gradually
> Or every man be blind—

Notice the use of similes in the following poem.

LANGSTON HUGHES (1902–1967)

Harlem

What happens to a dream deferred?

Does it dry up
like a raisin in the sun?
Or fester like a sore—
5 And then run?
Does it stink like rotten meat?
Or crust and sugar over—
like a syrupy sweet?

Maybe it just sags
10 like a heavy load.

Or does it explode?

QUESTIONS

1. What relationship do the various similes have to each other and to the subject of the poem, as defined by the title and first line?
2. What has been done with the last simile? Why?

Metaphor and Implied Metaphor

Like similes, **metaphors** are direct comparisons of one object with another. In metaphors, however, the fusion between the two objects is more complete, for metaphor uses no "as" or "like" to separate the two things being compared. Instead, a metaphor simply declares that *A* "is" *B;* one element of the comparison becomes, for the moment at least, the other.

Some metaphors go even farther and omit the "is." They simply talk about *A* as if it were *B,* using terms appropriate to *B.* They may not even name *B* at all but rather let us guess what it is from the words being used. In this case, the metaphor becomes an **implied metaphor.**

Since a simile merely says that *A* is "like" *B,* it needs to find only one point or moment of similarity between two otherwise dissimilar objects in order to achieve its effect. (For example, the cherry that is "red as the blood" resembles blood in no other way.) Metaphors, in contrast, tend to make more detailed claims for closer likenesses between the subjects of their comparisons. Notice, for instance, how many points of similarity are suggested by the metaphors in the next two poems. Ask yourself, in each case, what points of comparison the metaphor makes openly or explicitly and what further points of comparison it suggests to you.

JOHN KEATS (1795–1821)

On First Looking into Chapman's Homer

Much have I travelled in the realms of gold,
 And many goodly states and kingdoms seen;
 Round many western islands have I been
Which bards in fealty to Apollo hold.
5 Oft of one wide expanse had I been told
 That deep-browed Homer ruled as his demesne;
 Yet did I never breathe its pure serene
Till I heard Chapman speak out loud and bold:
Then felt I like some watcher of the skies
10 When a new planet swims into his ken;
Or like stout Cortez when with eagle eyes
 He stared at the Pacific—and all his men
Looked at each other with a wild surmise—
 Silent, upon a peak in Darien.

QUESTIONS

1. The vocabulary in the first eight lines of this poem is taken mostly from the Middle Ages and its system of feudalism: *realms* for *kingdoms,* for example; *bards* for *poets; fealty* for the system under which a nobleman would rule part of a country, being himself ruled by a king or a greater nobleman; and *demesne* for the nobleman's domain, the part of the country he ruled. (*Oft* for *often, serene* for *air,* and *ken* for *knowledge* are also old words that are no longer in daily use.) Apollo, on the other hand, comes from classical mythology, and is the god of poets. (He's also the god of the sun, but that doesn't particularly enter into this poem.) Homer is an ancient Greek poet and Chapman a sixteenth-century English poet who translated Homer's *Iliad* into English verse. The question therefore arises: why should Keats use the language of the Middle Ages and the metaphor of traveling to talk about his joy in reading poetry and the great delight he felt when his discovery of Chapman's translation let him feel that he was really hearing Homer for the first time?
2. When Keats does discover Chapman's translation, two new similes occur to him that support the traveler metaphor. What is the first (ll. 9–10)? What sort of progression has been made: how does the new identity the poet feels resemble his earlier identity as traveler? How is it different? What sort of feelings go with each identity? (Note the phrase "a new planet"; why *new?*)
3. In lines 11–14, the second simile is set out. Whom does Keats feel like now? What kinds of feelings go with this third identity? How do they form a climax for the poem? (It was really Balboa, and not Cortez, who was the first European to see the Pacific Ocean. Does this make any difference to your enjoyment of the poem?)

CARL SANDBURG (1878–1967)

Fog

The fog comes
on little cat feet.
It sits looking
over harbor and city
5 on silent haunches
and then moves on.

Personification

Implied metaphors, being more compact and requiring the reader to share in their creation slightly more than regular metaphors do, are frequent in poetry. But one type appears so frequently that it has a name of its own. This is **personification,** the trick of talking about some non-human thing as if it were human. We saw personification used in Blake's "When the stars threw down their spears" and in the "crooked hands" of Tennyson's "Eagle."

The poems in the rest of this chapter are notable for their figures of speech. They can thus serve both as exercises in identifying metaphors, similes, and implied metaphors, and as poems illustrating how these figures of speech can help create tone and meaning in poetry. Read each of the poems through at least once. Then go through the poem and note the figures of speech you find in it. Identify each one: is it a simile, a metaphor, an implied metaphor, a personification? Decide what elements make up the comparison: what is being compared to what? And jot down your ideas on why the poet might have wanted his or her readers to think about that comparison.

When you have done this, read the poem through once more. Then look again at the figures of speech you have found. Decide how each relates to the subject of the poem, and how each contributes to your sense of the speaker's feelings toward that subject. Decide, too, how many subjects of comparison there are. Is each subject compared to one other thing, or is one subject compared to several things?

If one subject is compared to one other thing, is that comparison developed at any length? If it is, what does its development lend your sense of the poem and its progression?

If one subject is compared to more than one other thing, or if several subjects of comparison exist, how are the different images fitted together? Are unrelated images juxtaposed for you to fit into some total picture; or does the speaker suggest some relationship of similarity or contrast between them? How does the pattern thus created of related or juxtaposed images help create your sense of the speaker's vision, of the poem's meaning or movement?

Finally, read the poem through once again to see whether you are satisfied with the conclusions you have come to, or whether you think there are other things that should be said about the poem or its imagery.

This may sound like a very complicated procedure. But the method of reading through, looking closely, and reading through again allows you to give attention to details of technique without losing your grip on the poem as a whole. When dealing with relatively simple poems, it's a handy practice. When dealing with more complex poetry, it's essential.

WILLIAM WORDSWORTH (1770–1850)

Composed upon Westminster Bridge, September 3, 1802

Earth has not anything to show more fair;
Dull would he be of soul who could pass by
A sight so touching in its majesty;
This City now doth, like a garment, wear
5   The beauty of the morning; silent, bare,
Ships, towers, domes, theaters, and temples lie
Open unto the fields, and to the sky;
All bright and glittering in the smokeless air.
Never did sun more beautifully steep
10 In his first splendor, valley, rock, or hill;
Ne'er saw I, never felt, a calm so deep!
The river glideth at his own sweet will:
Dear God! the very houses seem asleep;
And all that mighty heart is lying still!

EMILY DICKINSON (1830–1886)

I Like to See It Lap the Miles (#585)

I like to see it lap the Miles—
And lick the Valleys up—
And stop to feed itself at Tanks—
And then—prodigious step

5 Around a Pile of Mountains—
And supercilious peer
In Shanties—by the sides of Roads—
And then a Quarry pare

To fit its sides
10 And crawl between
Complaining all the while

In horrid—hooting stanza—
Then chase itself down Hill—

And neigh like Boanerges[1]—
15 Then—prompter than a Star
Stop—docile and omnipotent
At its own stable door—

NIKKI GIOVANNI (1943–   )

Woman

she wanted to be a blade
of grass amid the fields
but he wouldn't agree
to be the dandelion

5 she wanted to be a robin singing
through the leaves
but he refused to be
her tree

she spun herself into a web
10 and   looking for a place to rest
turned to him
but he stood straight
declining to be her corner

she tried to be a book
15 but he wouldn't read

she turned herself into a bulb
but he wouldn't let her grow

she decided to become
a woman
20 and though he still refused
to be a man
she decided it was all
right

---

[1] Jesus' name for his apostles John and James; also used to refer to a loud-voiced
preacher or speaker.

SEAMUS HEANEY (1939–   )

Docker

There, in the corner, staring at his drink.
The cap juts like a gantry's crossbeam,
Cowling plated forehead and sledgehead jaw.
Speech is clamped in the lips' vice.

5 That fist would drop a hammer on a Catholic—
Oh yes, that kind of thing could start again;
The only Roman collar he tolerates
Smiles all round his sleek pint of porter.[1]

Mosaic imperatives bang home like rivets;
10 God is a foreman with certain definite views
Who orders life in shifts of work and leisure.
A factory horn will blare the Resurrection.

He sits, strong and blunt as a Celtic cross,
Clearly used to silence and an armchair:
15 Tonight the wife and children will be quiet
At slammed door and smoker's cough in the hall.

ROBERT FROST (1875–1963)

The Silken Tent

She is as in a field a silken tent
At midday when a sunny summer breeze
Has dried the dew and all its ropes relent,
So that in guys it gently sways at ease,
5 And its supporting central cedar pole,
That is its pinnacle to heavenward
And signifies the sureness of the soul,
Seems to owe naught to any single cord,
But strictly held by none, is loosely bound
10 By countless silken ties of love and thought
To everything on earth the compass round,
And only by one's going slightly taut
In the capriciousness of summer air
Is of the slightest bondage made aware.

---

[1] Short for porter's beer—a dark beer resembling light stout.

SYLVIA PLATH (1932–1963)

Mirror

I am silver and exact. I have no preconceptions.
Whatever I see I swallow immediately
Just as it is, unmisted by love or dislike.
I am not cruel, only truthful—
5   The eye of a little god, four-cornered.
Most of the time I meditate on the opposite wall.
It is pink, with speckles. I have looked at it so long
I think it is a part of my heart. But it flickers.
Faces and darkness separate us over and over.

10   Now I am a lake. A woman bends over me,
Searching my reaches for what she really is.
Then she turns to those liars, the candles or the moon.
I see her back, and reflect it faithfully.
She rewards me with tears and an agitation of hands.
15   I am important to her. She comes and goes.
Each morning it is her face that replaces the darkness.
In me she has drowned a young girl, and in me an old woman
Rises toward her day after day, like a terrible fish.

Most metaphors and similes have a certain timelessness to them. Wordsworth's vision of London asleep and Hughes's picture of energy turning
angry in Harlem are both visions of something real and, therefore, enduring. In the following poem, however, the metaphorical vision is transitory
and illusory. Nonetheless, it illuminates the speaker's view of the world.
Note the movement of the imagery from metaphorical to literal within the
poem. Consider how it expresses and develops the statement made by the
poem's title. (Note particularly the "difficult balance" in the last line.
What meanings does that phrase have here at the end of the poem?) Then
discuss how the metaphor's statement and development create both the
specific picture of the waking man and the wider vision that fills the
speaker's mind.

RICHARD WILBUR (1921–   )

Love Calls Us to the Things of This World

The eyes open to a cry of pulleys,
And spirited from sleep, the astounded soul
Hangs for a moment bodiless and simple
As false dawn.

5   Outside the open window
       The morning air is all awash with angels.

          Some are in bed-sheets, some are in blouses,
          Some are in smocks: but truly there they are.
          Now they are rising together in calm swells
10   Of halcyon feeling, filling whatever they wear
          With the deep joy of their impersonal breathing;

          Now they are flying in place, conveying
          The terrible speed of their omnipresence, moving
          And staying like white water; and now of a sudden
15   They swoon down into so rapt a quiet
          That nobody seems to be there.
                                    The soul shrinks

          From all that it is about to remember,
          From the punctual rape of every blessèd day,
20   And cries,
                    "Oh, let there be nothing on earth but laundry,
          Nothing but rosy hands in the rising steam
          And clear dances done in the sight of heaven."

          Yet, as the sun acknowledges
25   With a warm look the world's hunks and colors,
          The soul descends once more in bitter love
          To accept the waking body, saying now
          In a changed voice as the man yawns and rises,

          "Bring them down from their ruddy gallows;
30   Let there be clean linen for the backs of thieves;
          Let lovers go fresh and sweet to be undone,
          And the heaviest nuns walk in a pure floating
          Of dark habits,
                              keeping their difficult balance."

9

Symbol and Allegory

Similes and metaphors make their comparisons quickly and explicitly. They occupy a line or two; and then they are set, ready for further development, but equally ready to be superseded by another simile or metaphor. How the poet uses them, or how many are used within a poem, is up to the poet. The range of possibilities is wide.

Symbol and allegory, however, tend to dominate the poems in which they are used. Moreover, they usually stand alone: one symbol or allegory is usually the most any given poem can support.

Similes and metaphors are used to make us look more attentively at the poem's subject: at the beauty of an evening or early morning scene, at laundry on a clothesline, at a mirror. They appeal directly to our senses: "a cry of pulleys," a "cowling plated forehead." Often, they illuminate some larger question: "What happens to a dream deferred?" What does it mean to be a woman or a lover? Yet they illuminate the larger question by keeping our attention on the things they describe: the rotten meat and the clean laundry.

Symbols and allegories, on the other hand, urge us to look beyond the literal significance of the poem's statements or action. "The Tyger" does not call our attention to tigers so much as to the awesome qualities suggested by the tiger's fierce beauty and to the godlike powers involved in the beast's creation. If we wish, in fact, "The Tyger" can take us even further, to the question of the existence of evil, as symbolized by the tiger's murderous nature. How far we wish to pursue the questionings begun by the poem is up to us.

When we meet with imagery that seems to be calling to us to look beyond the immediate event and its emotional ramifications, we may suspect we are dealing with symbol or allegory. But how are we to distinguish which we are dealing with?

An **allegory** always tells of an action. The events of that action should make sense literally but make more profound sense through a second, allegorical, interpretation. Usually that second interpretation will have a spiritual or a psychological significance; for allegories are particularly good at using physical actions to describe the workings of the human mind and spirit. "Young Goodman Brown," we recall, was an allegory of this type. On the literal level, it described a young man's encounter with witchcraft (or his dream of witchcraft). On the allegorical level, it described the process by which a person (who can be anyone, male or female) loses faith in human goodness.

In allegory, then, we are given a story that presents a one-to-one correspondence between some physical action (most often an encounter of some kind) and some second action (usually psychological or spiritual), with each step in the literal tale corresponding to a parallel step on the allegorical level. **Symbolism** may likewise present us with a tale or an action. But it may equally well present us with a description of some unchanging being or object. And it is more likely to suggest several possible interpretations than it is to insist on a single one.

In "Ozymandias," for instance, the whole tale of the power and fall of the king is symbolic. But the most striking symbol within it is the broken statue with its vainly boastful inscription. (For many of us, it's the sight of that statue that leaps to mind when anyone says "Ozymandias." The full tale tends to come as an afterthought.)

And how do we explain the tale's symbolism? Does the king's fall symbolize the fall of the proud (which would give the poem a moral interpretation), the fall of tyranny (which would give it a political one), or merely the inevitable destruction by time of human lives and civilizations? May we not, in fact, read overtones of all three types of meaning into the traveler's tale? Certainly the tyrant, with his "sneer of cold command," seems unpleasant enough for us to rejoice in his overthrow. But the sculptor, he with "the hand that mocked" the sneer, is dead as well; and even his longer-enduring work is half destroyed. How do we feel about that? The picture the sonnet paints is straightforward enough; its tone and message are somewhat more complicated.

Some symbols are conventional; and these will suggest a single interpretation. "The Lamb," relying on the traditional association of the lamb as

Christ, is an example of conventional symbolism in poetry. Alternatively, the poet may invent a symbol and provide its interpretation as well. In general, however, symbols in poetry ask the reader to interpret them. The interaction between poet and reader thus admits the greatest possible freedom of suggestion and response.

As you read the following poems, decide whether you think them better interpreted symbolically or allegorically. How would you discuss the poem's language, imagery, and progression to support your interpretation?

GEORGE HERBERT (1593–1633)

Love (III)

Love bade me welcome; yet my soul drew back,
    Guilty of dust and sin.
But quick-eyed Love, observing me grow slack
    From my first entrance in,
5 Drew nearer to me, sweetly questioning
    If I lacked anything.

"A guest," I answered, "worthy to be here."
    Love said, "You shall be he."
"I, the unkind, ungrateful? Ah my dear,
10   I cannot look on Thee."
Love took my hand, and smiling, did reply,
    "Who made the eyes but I?"

"Truth, Lord, but I have marred them; let my shame
    Go where it doth deserve."
15 "And know you not," says Love, "who bore the blame?"
    "My dear, then I will serve."
"You must sit down," says Love, "and taste my meat."
    So I did sit and eat.

RALPH WALDO EMERSON (1803–1882)

Days

Daughters of Time, the hypocritic Days,
Muffled and dumb like barefoot dervishes,
And marching single in an endless file,
Bring diadems and fagots in their hands.
5 To each they offer gifts after his will,
Bread, kingdoms, stars, and sky that holds them all.

I, in my pleached garden, watched the pomp,
Forgot my morning wishes, hastily
Took a few herbs and apples, and the Day
10 Turned and departed silent. I, too late,
Under her solemn fillet saw the scorn.

EDNA ST. VINCENT MILLAY (1892–1950)

First Fig

My candle burns at both ends;
    It will not last the night;
But ah, my foes, and oh, my friends –
    It gives a lovely light!

STEPHEN CRANE (1871–1900)

The Heart

.In the desert
I saw a creature, naked, bestial,
Who, squatting on the ground,
Held his heart in his hands,
5 And ate of it.

I said, "Is it good, friend?"
"It is bitter—bitter," he answered;
"But I like it
Because it is bitter,
10 And because it is my heart."

ALLEN GINSBERG (1926–   )

In back of the real

railroad yard in San Jose
    I wandered desolate
in front of a tank factory
    and sat on a bench
5 near the switchman's shack.

A flower lay on the hay on
    the asphalt highway

—the dread hay flower
    I thought—It had a
10 brittle black stem and
    corolla of yellowish dirty
spikes like Jesus' inchlong
    crown, and a soiled
dry center cotton tuft
15   like a used shaving brush
that's been lying under
    the garage for a year.

Yellow, yellow flower, and
    flower of industry,
20 tough spikey ugly flower,
    flower nonetheless,
with the form of the great yellow
    Rose in your brain!
This is the flower of the World.

LANGSTON HUGHES (1902–1967)

Mother to Son

Well, son, I'll tell you:
Life for me ain't been no crystal stair.
It's had tacks in it,
And splinters,
5   And boards torn up,
And places with no carpet on the floor—
Bare.
But all the time
I'se been a-climbin' on,
10   And reachin' landin's,
And turnin' corners,
And sometimes goin' in the dark
Where there ain't been no light.
So boy, don't you turn back
15   Don't you set down on the steps
'Cause you finds it's kinder hard.
Don't you fall now—
For I'se still goin', honey,
I'se still climbin',
20   And life for me ain't been no crystal stair.

JOHN KEATS (1795–1821)

Ode on a Grecian Urn

I

Thou still unravished bride of quietness,
   Thou foster-child of silence and slow time,
Sylvan historian, who canst thus express
   A flowery tale more sweetly than our rhyme:
5 What leaf-fringed legend haunts about thy shape
   Of deities or mortals, or of both,
      In Tempe or the dales of Arcady?[1]
   What men or gods are these? What maidens loath?
What mad pursuit? What struggle to escape?
10   What pipes and timbrels? What wild ecstasy?

2

Heard melodies are sweet, but those unheard
   Are sweeter; therefore, ye soft pipes, play on;
Not to the sensual ear, but, more endeared,
   Pipe to the spirit ditties of no tone:
15 Fair youth, beneath the trees, thou canst not leave
   Thy song, nor ever can those trees be bare;
      Bold Lover, never, never canst thou kiss,
Though winning near the goal—yet, do not grieve;
      She cannot fade, though thou hast not thy bliss,
20   Forever wilt thou love, and she be fair!

3

Ah, happy, happy boughs! that cannot shed
   Your leaves, nor ever bid the Spring adieu;
And, happy melodist, unwearièd,
   Forever piping songs forever new;
25 More happy love! more happy, happy love!
   Forever warm and still to be enjoyed,
      Forever panting, and forever young;
All breathing human passion far above,
      That leaves a heart high-sorrowful and cloyed,
30   A burning forehead, and a parching tongue.

---

[1] The vale of Tempe and Arcady (Arcadia) in Greece are symbolic of pastoral beauty.

4

Who are these coming to the sacrifice?
  To what green altar, O mysterious priest,
Lead'st thou that heifer lowing at the skies,
  And all her silken flanks with garlands dressed?
35 What little town by river or sea shore,
  Or mountain-built with peaceful citadel,
    Is emptied of this folk, this pious morn?
And, little town, thy streets for evermore
  Will silent be; and not a soul to tell
40   Why thou art desolate, can e'er return.

5

O Attic² shape! Fair attitude! with brede³
  Of marble men and maidens overwrought,
With forest branches and the trodden weed;
  Thou, silent form, dost tease us out of thought
45 As doth eternity: Cold Pastoral!
  When old age shall this generation waste,
    Thou shalt remain, in midst of other woe
Than ours, a friend to man, to whom thou say'st,
  "Beauty is truth, truth beauty,—that is all
50   Ye know on earth, and all ye need to know."

WILLIAM BUTLER YEATS (1865–1939)

The Circus Animals' Desertion

1

I sought a theme and sought for it in vain,
I sought it daily for six weeks or so.
Maybe at last, being but a broken man,
I must be satisfied with my heart, although
5 Winter and summer till old age began
My circus animals were all on show,
Those stilted boys, that burnished chariot,
Lion and woman and the Lord knows what.

---

² Grecian, especially Athenian.
³ Embroidery.

2

What can I but enumerate old themes?
10 First that sea-rider Oisin[1] led by the nose
Through three enchanted islands, allegorical dreams,
Vain gaiety, vain battle, vain repose,
Themes of the embittered heart, or so it seems,
That might adorn old songs or courtly shows;
15 But what cared I that set him on to ride,
I, starved for the bosom of his faery bride?

And then a counter-truth filled out its play,
The Countess Cathleen[2] was the name I gave it;
She, pity-crazed, had given her soul away,
20 But masterful Heaven had intervened to save it.
I thought my dear must her own soul destroy,
So did fanaticism and hate enslave it,
And this brought forth a dream and soon enough
This dream itself had all my thought and love.

25 And when the Fool and Blind Man stole the bread
Cuchulain[3] fought the ungovernable sea;
Heart-mysteries there, and yet when all is said
It was the dream itself enchanted me:
Character isolated by a deed
30 To engross the present and dominate memory.
Players and painted stage took all my love,
And not those things that they were emblems of.

3

Those masterful images because complete
Grew in pure mind, but out of what began?

---

[1] In Irish legend, Oisin was a bard who married a fairy and travelled throughout fairyland with her. *The Wanderings of Oisin and Other Poems,* published in 1889, was Yeats' first volume of verse.

[2] Yeats' first published play, written in 1891 and inspired in part by Yeats' love for Maud Gonne and his concern over the intensity of her involvement in political activism. Cathleen, a figure from Irish folk tale, sold her soul to the devil to save the lives and souls of her tenants during a famine.

[3] Various poems throughout Yeats' career mention Cuchulain, a legendary Irish king who became for Yeats a symbol of Ireland's heroic past. "Cuchulain's Fight with the Sea" appeared in 1893. ("The Circus Animals' Desertion" itself was written in the 1930's.)

35 A mound of refuse or the sweeping of a street,
   Old kettles, old bottles, and a broken can,
   Old iron, old bones, old rags, that raving slut
   Who keeps the till. Now that my ladder's gone,
   I must lie down where all the ladders start,
40 In the foul rag-and-bone shop of the heart.

ROBERT HAYDEN (1913–1980)

Those Winter Sundays

Sundays too my father got up early
and put his clothes on in the blueblack cold,
then with cracked hands that ached
from labor in the weekday weather made
5 banked fires blaze. No one ever thanked him.

I'd wake and hear the cold splintering, breaking.
When the rooms were warm, he'd call,
and slowly I would rise and dress,
fearing the chronic angers of that house,

10 Speaking indifferently to him,
   who had driven out the cold
   and polished my good shoes as well.
   What did I know, what did I know
   of love's austere and lonely offices?

10
Conceits and Allusions

Metaphors and similes, because of their instant appeal, are usually the first types of figurative speech to catch our attention. Symbols and allegories, which develop as their poems progress, require more preparation from us if we are to enjoy them fully. They offer themselves only to those who are willing not only to read closely and well, but also to go beyond the poem's literal meaning into a realm of wider suggestion. Conceits and allusions may be brief or extensive in scope; but they are the most demanding figures of all, requiring extreme alertness and some outside knowledge in order to be unraveled.

Conceits

A **conceit** could be defined as an outrageous metaphor, but a more traditional definition is a comparison between two highly dissimilar objects. Conceits are often developed at some length, revealing and weighing point after point of comparison or contrast between their two objects. In love poetry, they often grow out of Renaissance traditions that depict the man as a warrior and the woman as a walled town; he attacks, she defends herself or surrenders. Or the man might be a hunter and the woman a wild animal. Or she might be the warrior, wounding him with sharp looks or sharper words. Or, if she were kinder, she might be a treasure mine or a goddess of love. (The list could go on and on.) Some

Renaissance poets take the conceits seriously; others play with them, making use of the surprise that can come from turning an expected cliché upside down.

With the metaphysical poets of the seventeenth century, the unexpected becomes a key ingredient in the conceit. The metaphysical poets used conceits not only in love poetry, but in religious poetry as well, thereby creating for both types of poetry conceits of unparalleled complexity and ingenuity. Physics, astronomy, navigation—any science, any intellectual endeavor—might yield a conceit that viewed the soul's progress and passions as parallels to the workings of the universe it inhabited. The resulting poetry tends to be remarkably tough intellectually (you read this poetry *very* slowly the first few times), but also remarkably free, self-assured, and optimistic in its visions.

Here is an example of conceits in metaphysical poetry. Note that there are two main clusters of imagery in the poem. The first turns on maps and voyages, the second on the image of Christ as "the second Adam." And note also that the two are connected by the concept of the soul's journey to salvation as an annihilation of time and space and by the physical image of the sick man, flat on his back in bed and sweating heavily with fever.

JOHN DONNE (1572–1631)

Hymn to God My God, in My Sickness

Since I am coming to that holy room,
    Where, with thy choir of Saints for evermore,
I shall be made thy music; as I come
    I tune the instrument here at the door,
5   And what I must do then, think now before.

Whilst my physicians by their love are grown
    Cosmographers, and I their map, who lie
Flat on this bed, that by them may be shown
    That this is my Southwest discovery
10   *Per fretum febris*,[1] by these straits to die,

I joy, that in these straits, I see my west;[2]
    For, though their currents yield return to none,
What shall my west hurt me? As west and east
    In all flat maps (and I am one) are one,
15   So death doth touch the Resurrection.

---

[1] Through the straits of fever.
[2] My death.

Is the Pacific Sea my home? Or are
  The eastern riches? Is Jerusalem?
Anyan,[3] and Magellan, and Gibraltàr,
  All straits, and none but straits, are ways to them,
20   Whether where Japhet dwelt, or Cham, or Shem.[4]

We think that Paradise and Calvary,
  Christ's Cross, and Adam's tree, stood in one place;
Look Lord, and find both Adams met in me;
  As the first Adam's sweat surrounds my face,
25   May the last Adam's blood my soul embrace.

So, in his purple wrapped receive me, Lord,
  By these his thorns give me his other crown;
And as to others' souls I preached thy word,
  Be this my text, my sermon to mine own,
30   Therefore that he may raise, the Lord throws down.

Allusions

Conceits ask that we bring some knowledge to our reading if we are to understand their implications. For example, we must understand the distortions of space involved in making a flat map represent a round world if we are to understand Donne's hymn. An **allusion** likewise asks us to bring some knowledge to our reading. For an allusion may be defined as a reference to some work of art or literature, or to some well-known person, event, or story. If we do not catch the reference, then we will miss the point of the allusion.

Here is a frequently anthologized Middle English poem that celebrates spring. Following that poem is a "celebration" of winter by a twentieth-century poet who, knowing of the earlier poem's popularity, felt free to burlesque it. Note that Pound's poem can stand on its own, and that it makes no direct reference to the lyric to which it alludes. But note also how much more effective its irascible tone becomes when set off in its reader's mind against the cheerfulness of its medieval model.

---

[3] Modern Annam, then thought of as a strait between Asia and America.
[4] Sons of Noah, said to have settled Europe, Asia, and Africa after the flood.

ANONYMOUS—MIDDLE ENGLISH LYRIC

Sumer Is Icumen In [1]

Sumer is icumen in,
  Lhude sing cuccu!
Groweth sed and bloweth med
  And springth the wude nu.
5   Sing cuccu!

Awe bleteth after lomb,
  Lhouth after calve cu,
Bulluc sterteth, bucke verteth;
  Murie sing cuccu!
10   Cuccu! cuccu!
Wel sings thu cuccu.
Ne swik thu naver nu!

Sing cuccu nu, Sing cuccu!
Sing cuccu, Sing cuccu nu!

EZRA POUND (1885–1972)

Ancient Music

Winter is icumen in,
Lhude sing Goddamm,
Raineth drop and staineth slop,
And how the wind doth ramm!
5   Sing : Goddamm.
Skiddeth bus and sloppeth us,
An ague hath my ham.
Freezeth river, turneth liver,
        Damn you, sing : Goddamm.

---

[1] *Translation:*

Spring has come in,
  Loudly sing cuckoo!
Grows seed and blooms mead
  And springs the wood now.
    Sing cuckoo!

Ewe bleats after lamb,
  Lows after calf the cow,

Bullock starts, buck farts;
  Merrily sing cuckoo!
    Cuckoo! cuckoo!
Well sing thou cuckoo.
Cease thou never now!

Sing cuckoo now etc.

10 Goddamm, Goddamm, 'tis why I am, Goddamm,
    So 'gainst the winter's balm.
Sing goddamm, damm, sing Goddamm,
Sing goddamm, sing goddam, DAMM.

Discuss how the speakers of the following three poems use conceits or allusions to praise the women they love and to enlarge on the benefits of love. (You will want to concentrate on the poems' imagery; but note also the use of apostrophe, or direct address, and the different tones and logical progressions within each poem. Use the questions that follow each poem to help you.)

EDMUND SPENSER (1552?–1599)

From Amoretti

Sonnet 15

Ye tradefull Merchants, that with weary toyle,
Do seeke most pretious things to make your gain,
And both the Indias of their treasure spoile,
What needeth you to seeke so farre in vaine?
5 For loe, my Love doth in her selfe containe
All this worlds riches that may farre be found:
If saphyres, loe her eies be saphyres plaine;
If rubies, loe hir lips be rubies sound;
If pearles, hir teeth be pearles both pure and round;
10 If yvorie, her forhead yvory weene;
If gold, her locks are finest gold on ground;
If silver, her faire hands are silver sheene:
    But that which fairest is but few behold:—
    Her mind, adornd with vertues manifold.

QUESTIONS

1. To whom is the poet speaking in the opening four lines (and, by implication, in the rest of the poem as well)? Why should he select this audience? How do the merchants differ from the poet? What do the words *weary* and *in vain* suggest about them or their activities?
2. What similarities do you find among the successive metaphors that occupy lines 7–12?
3. How does the conclusion continue the theme of treasure? How does it alter it? (Note especially the phrase "adorned with virtues manifold.") What new questions does the conclusion raise about the usefulness of the merchants' search for precious things?

WILLIAM SHAKESPEARE (1564–1616)

Sonnet 18

Shall I compare thee to a summer's day?
Thou art more lovely and more temperate:
Rough winds do shake the darling buds of May,
And summer's lease hath all too short a date:
5 Sometime too hot the eye of heaven shines,
And often is his gold complexion dimmed;
And every fair from fair sometime declines,
By chance or nature's changing course untrimmed:
But thy eternal summer shall not fade
10 Nor lose possession of that fair thou ow'st,[1]
Nor shall Death brag thou wand'rest in his shade,
When in eternal lines to time thou grow'st.
So long as men can breathe or eyes can see,
So long lives this, and this gives life to thee.

QUESTIONS

This sonnet, too, starts with a question relating to physical qualities—beauty and temperature—and ends up dealing with intangible ones. By what contrasts and what train of logic does it achieve this progression? (Note in particular the "summer's day" of line 1, "the eye of heaven" in line 5, and "eternal summer" in line 9. These phrases mark the starting points of three stages in the argument, with the last two lines marking the final stage. And be warned that "fair" has three meanings. It's a noun meaning "a lovely thing," an adjective meaning "lovely", and a noun meaning "beauty.")

JOHN DONNE (1572–1631)

The Sun Rising

Busy old fool, unruly sun,
    Why dost thou thus
Through windows and through curtains call on us?
Must to thy motions lovers' seasons run?
5   Saucy, pedantic wretch, go chide
    Late schoolboys and sour 'prentices,
  Go tell court huntsmen that the king will ride,
  Call country ants to harvest offices.
Love, all alike, no season knows nor clime,
10 Nor hours, days, months, which are the rags of time.

---

[1] Ownest.

Thy beams, so reverend and strong
  Why shouldst thou think?
I could eclipse and cloud them with a wink,
But that I would not lose her sight so long.
15   If her eyes have not blinded thine,
  Look, and tomorrow late tell me
  Whether both th' Indias of spice and mine
  Be where thou left'st them, or lie here with me;
Ask for those kings whom thou saw'st yesterday,
20 And thou shalt hear: All here in one bed lay.

She's all states, and all princes I;
  Nothing else is.
Princes do but play us; compared to this,
All honor's mimic, all wealth alchemy.
25   Thou, sun, art half as happy as we,
  In that the world's contracted thus;
  Thine age asks ease, and since thy duties be
To warm the world, that's done in warming us.
Shine here to us, and thou art everywhere;
30 This bed thy center is, these walls thy sphere.

QUESTIONS

1 This poem falls into the category of **aubades,** or "dawn songs." What dramatic value does this placement in time give it?
2. Note that here again earthly riches are first equated with the woman's beauty and then devalued by it, and that time is forced to yield to timelessness. How does Donne's treatment of these conceits differ from those of Shakespeare and Spenser?
3. In general, how would you compare this love poem with those two earlier ones?

The next three poems are spoken by discontented lovers. What could you say about the ways in which they use conceits or allusions to describe their predicaments or to convince themselves or their hearers that some change should be made?

SIR PHILIP SIDNEY (1554–1586)

From **Astrophil and Stella**

Leave Me, O Love

Leave me, O Love, which reachest but to dust,
And thou, my mind, aspire to higher things.

Grow rich in that which never taketh rust.
Whatever fades but fading pleasure brings.

5 Draw in thy beams and humble all thy might
To that sweet yoke where lasting freedoms be,
Which breaks the clouds and opens forth the light
That doth both shine and give us sight to see.

O take fast hold; let that light be thy guide
10 In this small course which birth draws out to death,
And think how evil becometh him to slide
Who seeketh heaven and comes of heavenly breath.
    Then farewell, world! Thy uttermost I see!
    Eternal Love, maintain thy life in me.

ANDREW MARVELL (1621–1678)

To His Coy Mistress

Had we but world enough, and time,
This coyness, lady, were no crime.
We would sit down, and think which way
To walk, and pass our long love's day.
5 Thou by the Indian Ganges' side
Shouldst rubies find; I by the tide
Of Humber would complain. I would
Love you ten years before the Flood,
And you should, if you please, refuse
10 Till the conversion of the Jews.
My vegetable love should grow
Vaster than empires, and more slow;
An hundred years should go to praise
Thine eyes and on thy forehead gaze,
15 Two hundred to adore each breast,
But thirty thousand to the rest:
An age at least to every part,
And the last age should show your heart.
For, lady, you deserve this state,
20 Nor would I love at lower rate.
    But at my back I always hear
Time's wingèd chariot hurrying near;
And yonder all before us lie
Deserts of vast eternity.
25 Thy beauty shall no more be found,
Nor in thy marble vault shall sound

My echoing song; then worms shall try
That long preserved virginity,
And your quaint honor turn to dust,
30 And into ashes all my lust.
The grave's a fine and private place,
But none, I think, do there embrace.
　　Now, therefore, while the youthful hue
　　Sits on thy skin like morning dew,
35 And while thy willing soul transpires
At every pore with instant fires,
Now let us sport us while we may,
And now, like amorous birds of prey,
Rather at once our time devour
40 Than languish in his slow-chapped power.
Let us roll all our strength and all
Our sweetness up into one ball,
And tear our pleasures with rough strife
Thorough the iron gates of life.
45 Thus, though we cannot make our sun
Stand still, yet we will make him run.

ROBERT GRAVES (1895–1985)

Down, Wanton, Down!

Down, wanton, down! Have you no shame
That at the whisper of Love's name,
Or Beauty's, presto! up you raise
Your angry head and stand at gaze?

5 Poor bombard-captain, sworn to reach
The ravelin and effect a breach—
Indifferent what you storm or why,
So be that in the breach you die!

Love may be blind, but Love at least
10 Knows what is man and what mere beast;
Or Beauty wayward, but requires
More delicacy from her squires.

Tell me, my witless, whose one boast
Could be your staunchness at the post,
15 When were you made a man of parts
To think fine and profess the arts?

Will many-gifted Beauty come
Bowing to your bald rule of thumb,
Or Love swear loyalty to your crown?
20 Be gone, have done! Down, wanton, down!

Although it is the work of a twentieth-century poet, "Down, Wanton, Down!" contains conceits that are very much in the fashion of the seventeenth century. Graves chooses one central comparison and then elaborates it and varies it throughout the poem. (The theme of love and the use of the word *wanton* to describe an overeager lover are also well within the seventeenth-century tradition.) In the next poem, the twentieth-century poet Marianne Moore adapts the use of conceits to her own equally playful and thoughtful but more kaleidoscopic style. What theme do the conceits in "The Mind Is an Enchanting Thing" combine to create? How do they do so? How are such disparate images fitted together?

MARIANNE MOORE (1887–1972)

The Mind Is an Enchanting Thing

is an enchanted thing
    like the glaze on a
katydid-wing
        subdivided by sun
5   till the nettings are legion.
Like Gieseking[1] playing Scarlatti;[2]

like the apteryx-awl [3]
    as a beak, or the
kiwi's rain-shawl
10   of haired feathers, the mind
        feeling its way as though blind,
walks along with its eyes on the ground.

It has memory's ear
    that can hear without

---

[1] Walter Gieseking (1895–1956), eminent German pianist.
[2] Domenico Scarlatti (1685–1757), Italian composer of brilliant keyboard sonatas.
[3] A flightless bird with a long, slender beak resembling the shape of an awl.

15 having to hear.
                Like the gyroscope's fall,
                truly unequivocal
        because trued by regnant certainty,

        it is a power of
20   strong enchantment. It
        is like the dove-
                neck animated by
                        sun; it is memory's eye;
        it's conscientious inconsistency.

25 It tears off the veil; tears
                the temptation, the
        mist the heart wears,
                        from its eyes,—if the heart
                        has a face; it takes apart
30 dejection. It's fire in the dove-neck's

        iridescence; in the
                inconsistencies
        of Scarlatti.
                Unconfusion submits
35 its confusion to proof; it's
        not a Herod's oath⁴ that cannot change.

---

⁴ See Matthew 2:1–16.

11 *Patterns of Imagery*

So far, we have spoken of different figures of speech in isolation. In practice, however, the various figures are almost always found in combination with each other. "Days," for instance, is an allegory. But the various gifts the Days carry are symbolic; and the phrase "morning wishes" is metaphorical. Moreover, just as form and meaning reinforce each other, so a poem's figures of speech reinforce each other to create the poem's overall patterns of meaning and imagery. When we discuss a poem, we may start by discussing some particularly striking aspect; and that may mean a particular use of imagery. But eventually we will want to talk of the complete poem; and that will mean talking of the patterns it contains.

The poems in the last chapter were heavily patterned. The Renaissance poems tended to be static, stating a position and then elaborating on it. The metaphysical poems showed more movement, following the speaker's mind through the ramifications of an idea or situation. The poems in this chapter will also display carefully worked-out patterns of imagery. And, as most of them are somewhat longer poems, the patterns will be even more complex. But these poems will also show a freer and more passionate movement, for they come either from the Romantic poetry of the nineteenth century or from twentieth-century poetry that was influenced by that movement. In the more melodious rhythms and harmonies of these poems, we find a vivid sense of immediacy, of unfolding memories or emotions, of minds and spirits caught up in vision and experience. Flowing sound and richly suggestive imagery create the sense of intense experience that was a trademark of the Romantic movement and that still provides some overtones of meaning to the common use of the word *romantic*.

As you read the following poems, be prepared for shifts of emotion as much as for shifts of thought. Note how these more modern poets create scenes, moods, and speakers through sound and imagery.

PERCY BYSSHE SHELLEY (1792–1822)

Ode to the West Wind

I

O wild West Wind, thou breath of Autumn's being,
Thou, from whose unseen presence the leaves dead
Are driven, like ghosts from an enchanter fleeing,

Yellow, and black, and pale, and hectic red,
5 Pestilence-stricken multitudes: O thou,
Who chariotest to their dark wintry bed

The wingèd seeds, where they lie cold and low,
Each like a corpse within its grave, until
Thine azure sister of the Spring shall blow

10 Her clarion o'er the dreaming earth, and fill
(Driving sweet buds like flocks to feed in air)
With living hues and odors plain and hill:

Wild Spirit, which art moving everywhere;
Destroyer and preserver; hear, oh, hear!

2

15 Thou on whose stream, mid the steep sky's commotion,
Loose clouds like earth's decaying leaves are shed,
Shook from the tangled boughs of Heaven and Ocean,

Angels of rain and lightning: there are spread
On the blue surface of thine aery surge,
20 Like the bright hair uplifted from the head

Of some fierce Maenad,[1] even from the dim verge
Of the horizon to the zenith's height,
The locks of the approaching storm. Thou dirge

Of the dying year, to which this closing night
25 Will be the dome of a vast sepulcher,
Vaulted with all thy congregated might

Of vapors, from whose solid atmosphere
Black rain, and fire, and hail will burst: oh, hear!

3

Thou who didst waken from his summer dreams
30 The blue Mediterranean, where he lay,
Lulled by the coil of his crystàlline streams,

Beside a pumice isle in Baiae's[2] bay,
And saw in sleep old palaces and towers
Quivering within the wave's intenser day,

35 All overgrown with azure moss and flowers
So sweet, the sense faints picturing them! Thou
For whose path the Atlantic's level powers

Cleave themselves into chasms, while far below
The sea-blooms and the oozy woods which wear
40 The sapless foliage of the ocean, know

Thy voice, and suddenly grow gray with fear,
And tremble and despoil themselves: oh, hear!

4

If I were a dead leaf thou mightest bear;
If I were a swift cloud to fly with thee;
45 A wave to pant beneath thy power, and share

The impulse of thy strength, only less free
Than thou, O uncontrollable! If even
I were as in my boyhood, and could be

The comrade of thy wanderings over Heaven,
50 As then, when to outstrip thy skiey speed
Scarce seemed a vision; I would ne'er have striven

---

[1] A female attendant of Dionysus.
[2] Ancient Roman resort whose submerged ruins can be seen north of Naples.

As thus with thee in prayer in my sore need.
Oh, lift me as a wave, a leaf, a cloud!
I fall upon the thorns of life! I bleed!

55 A heavy weight of hours has chained and bowed
One too like thee: tameless, and swift, and proud.

5

Make me thy lyre, even as the forest is:
What if my leaves are falling like its own!
The tumult of thy mighty harmonies

60 Will take from both a deep, autumnal tone,
Sweet though in sadness. Be thou, Spirit fierce,
My spirit! Be thou me, impetuous one!

Drive my dead thoughts over the universe
Like withered leaves to quicken a new birth!
65 And, by the incantation of this verse,

Scatter, as from an unextinguished hearth
Ashes and sparks, my words among mankind!
Be through my lips to unawakened earth

The trumpet of a prophecy! O Wind,
70 If Winter comes, can Spring be far behind?

JOHN KEATS (1795–1821)

Ode to a Nightingale

I

My heart aches, and a drowsy numbness pains
    My sense, as though of hemlock I had drunk,
Or emptied some dull opiate to the drains
    One minute past, and Lethe-wards[1] had sunk:
5 'Tis not through envy of thy happy lot,
    But being too happy in thine happiness—
        That thou, light-wingèd Dryad of the trees,
            In some melodious plot
Of beechen green, and shadows numberless,
10   Singest of summer in full-throated ease.

---

[1] Towards the river Lethe, in the underworld.

2

O, for a draught of vintage! that hath been
　　Cooled a long age in the deep-delvèd earth,
Tasting of Flora[2] and the country green,
　　Dance, and Provençal song, and sunburnt mirth!
15 O for a beaker full of the warm South,
　　Full of the true, the blushful Hippocrene,[3]
　　　　With beaded bubbles winking at the brim,
　　　　　　And purple-stainèd mouth;
　　That I might drink, and leave the world unseen,
20　　　And with thee fade away into the forest dim:

3

Fade far away, dissolve, and quite forget
　　What thou among the leaves hast never known,
The weariness, the fever, and the fret
　　Here, where men sit and hear each other groan;
25 Where palsy shakes a few, sad, last gray hairs,
　　Where youth grows pale, and spectre-thin, and dies,
　　　　Where but to think is to be full of sorrow
　　　　　　And leaden-eyed despairs,
　　Where Beauty cannot keep her lustrous eyes,
30　　　Or new Love pine at them beyond tomorrow.

4

Away! away! for I will fly to thee,
　　Not charioted by Bacchus and his pards,[4]
But on the viewless wings of Poesy,
　　Though the dull brain perplexes and retards:
35 Already with thee! tender is the night,
　　And haply the Queen-Moon is on her throne,
　　　　Clustered around by all her starry Fays;
　　　　　　But here there is no light,
　　Save what from heaven is with the breezes blown
40　　　Through verdurous glooms and winding mossy ways.

5

I cannot see what flowers are at my feet,
　　Nor what soft incense hangs upon the boughs,

---

[2] Goddess of flowers.
[3] Fountain of the Muses on Mt. Helicon.
[4] Leopards drawing the chariot of Bacchus, god of wine.

But, in embalmèd darkness, guess each sweet
  Wherewith the seasonable month endows
45 The grass, the thicket, and the fruit-tree wild;
    White hawthorn, and the pastoral eglantine;
      Fast fading violets covered up in leaves;
        And mid-May's eldest child,
    The coming musk-rose, full of dewy wine,
50   The murmurous haunt of flies on summer eves.

6

Darkling[5] I listen; and for many a time
  I have been half in love with easeful Death,
Called him soft names in many a musèd rhyme,
  To take into the air my quiet breath;
55 Now more than ever seems it rich to die,
    To cease upon the midnight with no pain,
      While thou art pouring forth thy soul abroad
        In such an ecstasy!
  Still wouldst thou sing, and I have ears in vain—
60   To thy high requiem become a sod.

7

Thou wast not born for death, immortal Bird!
  No hungry generations tread thee down;
The voice I hear this passing night was heard
  In ancient days by emperor and clown:
65 Perhaps the selfsame song that found a path
    Through the sad heart of Ruth, when, sick for home,
      She stood in tears amid the alien corn:
        The same that oft-times hath
  Charmed magic casements, opening on the foam
70   Of perilous seas, in faery lands forlorn.

8

Forlorn! the very word is like a bell
  To toll me back from thee to my sole self!
Adieu! the fancy cannot cheat so well
  As she is famed to do, deceiving elf.

---

[5] In the darkness.

75 Adieu! adieu! thy plaintive anthem fades
  Past the near meadows, over the still stream,
   Up the hill side; and now 'tis buried deep
    In the next valley-glades:
  Was it a vision, or a waking dream?
  Fled is that music:—Do I wake or sleep?

MATTHEW ARNOLD (1822–1888)

Dover Beach

The sea is calm tonight.
The tide is full, the moon lies fair
Upon the straits;—on the French coast the light
Gleams and is gone; the cliffs of England stand,
5 Glimmering and vast, out in the tranquil bay.
Come to the window, sweet is the night-air!
Only, from the long line of spray
Where the sea meets the moon-blanched land,
Listen! you hear the grating roar
10 Of pebbles which the waves draw back, and fling,
At their return, up the high strand,
Begin, and cease, and then again begin,
With tremulous cadence slow, and bring
The eternal note of sadness in.

15 Sophocles long ago
Heard it on the Aegean, and it brought
Into his mind the turbid ebb and flow
Of human misery; we
Find also in the sound a thought,
20 Hearing it by this distant northern sea.

The Sea of Faith
Was once, too, at the full, and round earth's shore
Lay like the folds of a bright girdle furled.
But now I only hear
25 Its melancholy, long, withdrawing roar,
Retreating, to the breath
Of the night-wind, down the vast edges drear
And naked shingles of the world.

Ah, love, let us be true
30 To one another! for the world, which seems

To lie before us like a land of dreams,
So various, so beautiful, so new,
Hath really neither joy, nor love, nor light,
Nor certitude, nor peace, nor help for pain;
35 And we are here as on a darkling plain
Swept with confused alarms of struggle and flight,
Where ignorant armies clash by night.

WILLIAM BUTLER YEATS (1865–1939)

Sailing to Byzantium

1

That is no country for old men. The young
In one another's arms, birds in the trees
—Those dying generations—at their song,
The salmon-falls, the mackerel-crowded seas,
5 Fish, flesh, or fowl, commend all summer long
Whatever is begotten, born, and dies.
Caught in that sensual music all neglect
Monuments of unageing intellect.

2

An aged man is but a paltry thing,
10 A tattered coat upon a stick, unless
Soul clap its hands and sing, and louder sing
For every tatter in its mortal dress,
Nor is there singing school but studying
Monuments of its own magnificence;
15 And therefore I have sailed the seas and come
To the holy city of Byzantium.

3

O sages standing in God's holy fire
As in the gold mosaic of a wall,
Come from the holy fire, perne in a gyre,
20 And be the singing-masters of my soul.
Consume my heart away; sick with desire
And fastened to a dying animal
It knows not what it is; and gather me
Into the artifice of eternity.

4

25 Once out of nature I shall never take
My bodily form from any natural thing,
But such a form as Grecian goldsmiths make
Of hammered gold and gold enamelling
To keep a drowsy Emperor awake;
30 Or set upon a golden bough to sing
To lords and ladies of Byzantium
Of what is past, or passing, or to come.

DYLAN THOMAS (1914–1953)

Fern Hill

Now as I was young and easy under the apple boughs
About the lilting house and happy as the grass was green,
    The night above the dingle starry,
      Time let me hail and climb
5   Golden in the heydays of his eyes,
And honored among wagons I was prince of the apple towns
And once below a time I lordly had the trees and leaves
    Trail with daisies and barley
    Down the rivers of the windfall light.

10 And as I was green and carefree, famous among the barns
About the happy yard and singing as the farm was home,
    In the sun that is young once only,
      Time let me play and be
    Golden in the mercy of his means,
15 And green and golden I was huntsman and herdsman, the calves
Sang to my horn, the foxes on the hills barked clear and cold,
    And the sabbath rang slowly
    In the pebbles of the holy streams.

All the sun long it was running, it was lovely, the hay
20 Fields high as the house, the tunes from the chimneys, it was air
    And playing, lovely and watery
      And fire green as grass.
    And nightly under the simple stars
As I rode to sleep the owls were bearing the farm away,
25 All the moon long I heard, blessed among stables, the night-jars
    Flying with the ricks, and the horses
      Flashing into the dark.

And then to awake, and the farm, like a wanderer white
With the dew, come back, the cock on his shoulder: it was all
30   Shining, it was Adam and maiden,
          The sky gathered again
And the sun grew round that very day.
So it must have been after the birth of the simple light
In the first, spinning place, the spellbound horses walking warm
35   Out of the whinnying green stable
          On to the fields of praise.

And honored among foxes and pheasants by the gay house
Under the new made clouds and happy as the heart was long,
      In the sun born over and over,
40   I ran my heedless ways,
          My wishes raced through the house high hay
And nothing I cared, at my sky blue trades, that time allows
In all his tuneful turning so few and such morning songs
      Before the children green and golden
45   Follow him out of grace,

Nothing I cared, in the lamb white days, that time would take me
Up to the swallow thronged loft by the shadow of my hand,
      In the moon that is always rising,
          Nor that riding to sleep
50   I should hear him fly with the high fields
And wake to the farm forever fled from the childless land.
Oh as I was young and easy in the mercy of his means,
          Time held me green and dying
          Though I sang in my chains like the sea.

SOUND

12 *Meter and Its Variations*

Sound in poetry is a function of two elements: the rhythm of a poem's lines, and the sounds of its words. Throughout our study of poetry, we have been aware of the important part sound and rhythm play in establishing our sense of a poem. But we have been more concerned with recognizing how the sounds of a given poem reinforce its ideas or emotions than with classifying the sounds themselves; and so we have not paused to build up a vocabulary of technical terms for meter and versification. Now it is time to learn that vocabulary, so that we may supplement our discussions of character and language in poetry with more detailed comments on the techniques of sound that reinforce them. Since rhythm is perhaps the most basic element of sound in a poem, and meter the most basic element of rhythm, we will start with meter.

Meter is the term used to describe the underlying rhythm of a poem, based on the number and the placement of stressed syllables in each line. In most poetry, these **stresses** will fall into a pattern and the pattern will have a particular name: **iambic pentameter,** for instance, to name one of the most common. When we learn to **scan** a poem, therefore, to find out the rhythm or meter in which it is written, these stresses and their patterns are what we will be looking at.

What do we mean by a **stress** or a **stressed syllable?** We mean that the word or syllable involved is one to which our voice will give greater emphasis than to its neighbors. Every word of more than one syllable in English has one accented, or stressed, syllable and one or more unaccented or unstressed ones. Thus, in the word *human* we stress the first syllable: *hú - man;* while in the word *humane* we stress the second: *hu - máne.* When we speak a sentence, these natural accents, or stresses, will be heard. Usually they will be joined by a second type of stress, one used for emphasis. If I say, "Is she coming?," for instance, and leave the strongest stress on the first syllable of *coming* ("Is she *coming?*"), there will be nothing startling in the sentence. If, however, I move the accent to the word *is* ("*Is* she coming?"), I sound doubtful or surprised that she'd come; while if I accent the word *she* (" Is *she* coming?") the stressed word suggests that "she" is the last person I would have expected (or perhaps wanted) to come. The emphasis may fall in an expected or an unexpected place. But it is sure to fall somewhere, for English is a heavily accented language; it sounds neither normal nor natural without the contrast of its stressed and unstressed syllables.

The number of stresses in a line of poetry, therefore, is the number of syllables on which our voice naturally tends to put a stronger emphasis. The emphasis must be natural; it must come either from the sound of the words themselves or from the meaning and emphasis of the lines. Thus, we must be able to find the meter by reading naturally; we should not distort either the sense or the natural rhythm of the lines to make them fit some preconceived meter.

So basic is this matter of stresses, in fact, that line lengths receive their names according to the number of stressed syllables they contain. One simply counts up the stressed syllables, translates the resulting number into Greek, and adds the word *meter* to finish out the term, as follows:

1. **Dimeter:** two stresses per line

   Díe soón

2. **Trimeter:** three stresses

   Dóst thou knów who máde thee?

3. **Tetrameter:** four stresses

   Tell all the truth but tell it slánt

4. **Pentameter:** five stresses:

   Leáve me, O Lóve, which reáches bút to dúst

5. **Hexameter:** six stresses (also known as an **alexandrine**)

   Which, like a wóunded snáke, drágs its slow léngth alóng

By counting the number of stresses per line, we thus discover the skeleton of a poem's rhythm. The question then becomes how those stresses are linked. In **accentual poetry,** they are linked by **alliteration** or **assonance.** There will be (usually) four stressed syllables per line; and two or three of them will start with the same sound or contain the same vowel. Here is an example, from a poem you will meet again at the chapter's end:

> Bitter breást-cares have Í abíded,
> Knówn on my kéel many a cáre's hóld,
> And díre seá-súrge, and there I oft spent
> Nárrow níghtwatch nígh the ship's héad
> While she tóssed close to cliffs. Cóldly afflicted,
> My féet wére by fróst benúmbed.

The first line is marked by the alliteration of *bitter* and *breast* and the assonance of *I* and *abided*. The second is similarly linked by the alliteration of the *k* sound in *keel* and *care* and the assonance of the *o* sound in *known* and *hold*. But the other lines are all marked by the alliteration of one sound each: *s* in the third line, *n* in the fourth, *c* in the fifth, and *f* in the sixth. This is the patterning of Old English poetry, a patterning used for several hundred years before the Norman Conquest brought French influences and rhymed verse to England. Since that time, accentual poetry has been relatively rare. One nineteenth-century poet, Gerard Manley Hopkins, however, worked out an accentual style of his own, which he called **sprung rhythm.** His style reflects the Old English influence in its irregular placement of stresses and its marked use of alliteration and assonance.

Most English and American verse is **accentual syllabic.** This means that its rhythm depends not only on the number of stressed syllables, but also on the total number of syllables per line, and on the placement of the stresses within that totality. Tetrameter lines, for instance, vary in length from the four stressed syllables of "We real cool. We," to the eight syllables, half of them stressed, of "Tell all the truth but tell it slant," to the eleven or twelve syllables (every third syllable stressed) of "You left us in tatters, without shoes or socks,/Tired of digging potatoes and spudding up docks."

To define its various combinations of stressed and unstressed syllables, therefore, accentual-syllabic meters divide each line of poetry into **feet,** a **foot** consisting of one stressed syllable with its attendant unstressed syllables. Each type of foot—that is, each pattern of syllables—is given a name. An unstressed syllable followed by a stressed one, for instance (*the wórd*) is an **iamb;** two unstressed syllables followed by a stressed one (*that she heárd*) make an **anapest.** The meter of the poem thus consists of the *name of the foot* most frequently found in the poem joined to the basic *line length.* "There's a certain slant of light" thus becomes **iambic trimeter,** despite the fact that not all its feet are iambs and not all its lines have three feet.

With this background in mind, let us chart the types of feet most commonly found in English poetry. One of the most common **duple meters** is the **iambic,** which has two syllables, the second stressed.

> Tell áll | the trúth | but téll | it slánt

The **trochaic** has two syllables, the first stressed.

> Dóst thou | knów who | máde thee?

One of the two most common **triple meters** is the **anapestic:** with three syllables, the last stressed.

> And thére | was my Ró- | land to béar | the whole weíght

The **dactylic** has three syllables, the first stressed.

> Táking me | báck down the | vísta of | yéars, till I | sée

One should also know the **spondee,** a two-syllable foot with both sylla bles accented. The spondee is used only to lend particular emphasis or variety to poetry written in other meters; there is no "spondaic meter." The **amphibrach** is a three-syllable foot with the accent on the middle syllable. Unlike the spondee, the amphibrach can be used as a sustained meter; but it's not an easy meter to work with and isn't often used for an entire poem. The **monosyllabic foot** has one syllable, accented; Gwendolyn Brooks's "We Real Cool" is an example of this foot in action. The **paeon** is a four-syllable foot. It may be called first paeon, second paeon, third paeon, or fourth paeon, depending on whether the accented syllable comes first, second, third, or fourth. There may also be a secondary accent within the foot. Traditional ballads are often written in paeonic meters.

Meter, then, will create the basic rhythm of a poem, setting up a pattern to be repeated or varied with each line. Seldom does the pattern remain perfectly regular, for to hold too closely to a meter in spoken verse is to risk monotony and boredom.

How does a poet avoid monotony? By shifting stresses, so that a poem written in iambic meter will have some feet that are trochees and some that are spondees. By adding syllables, so that an iambic line will contain an occasional dactyl or anapest. By dropping syllables, substituting a pause for the expected sound, or laying greater stress on the remaining syllables, as when a spondee is substituted for an anapest.

More importantly, poets vary their meters by making the sense of the poem, and the cadence of the speaker's voice, move in counterpoint to the rhythm.

> The sea is calm tonight.
> The tide is full, the moon lies fair
> Upon the straits;—on the French coast the light
> Gleams and is gone; the cliffs of England stand,
> Glimmering and vast, out in the tranquil bay.

The first statement fits the first line perfectly. But the next overlaps the second line, so that your voice cannot stop on "fair" but must continue with "Upon the straits." A pause, then, and the thought continues through that line and half of the next; then pauses more briefly, finishes the line with a slight pause, and comes to rest at the end of the fifth line. Because your voice stops at the end of them, the first and fifth lines are called **end-stopped lines.** Because the movement of thought and phrase forces your voice to continue past their ends, the second, third, and fourth lines are called **run-on lines.** Both end-stopped and run-on lines may contain internal pauses. We find one such pause after "full" in the second line, one after "straits" in the third," one after "gone" in the fourth, and one after "vast" in the fifth. These pauses are called **cesuras;** and their use and placement are vital in breaking the rhythms of poetry to create the sound of a speaking voice.

In contrast to "Dover Beach" (which you might want to reread in its entirety, to notice how flexible the lines are throughout), recall Blake's poems "The Lamb" and "The Tyger." Notice that many of their lines are end-stopped and that the regularity of the rhythm, with its procession of end-stopped lines and repeated questions, gives these poems almost the sound of incantations, sounds far removed from the wistful accents of Arnold's speaker. But notice, too, that even here, although each phrase is strongly separated from its fellows and heavily accented, the length of the phrases still varies, and cesuras and occasional run-on lines are still found:

> What the hammer? what the chain?
> In what furnace was thy brain?
> What the anvil? what dread grasp
> Dare its deadly terrors clasp?

We may notice, too, that Blake restricts himself to seven-syllable lines in "The Tyger," and to a patterned alternation between trimeter and tetrameter lines in "The Lamb," while Arnold varies his line lengths in "Dover Beach," the lines growing longer as the speaker warms to his topic. And, finally, we notice that all the lines quoted from Blake and Arnold end with stressed syllables. Your voice rises slightly to the stress at the end of these lines, and they are therefore said to have a **rising rhythm.** In contrast, lines that end on unstressed syllables—"O wild West Wind, thou breath of Autumn's being"—are said to have a **falling rhythm.** It's a small thing, but it can create subtle variations in tone.

These, then, are the basic meters of accentual-syllabic verse and the most common devices used to lend them variety. You will no doubt find many other devices at work as you continue your study of poetry. And you will also find that in much modern verse, such as that of Whitman and Cummings, the rules of accentual-syllabic verse have been replaced by the uncharted techniques and devices of **free verse.** Pauses and phrasings in free verse tend to be visual devices as well as rhythmic ones; line lengths and stress placement vary at the poet's will. Sounds are still being shaped with care, but the writers of free verse are being equally careful to avoid setting up rules to which critics can then bind them. In free verse, as in all verse, ultimately the total effect is the sole criterion.

Here are a modern translation of an Old English poem and an example of Hopkins's sprung rhythm. How would you compare and contrast the two types of verse?

ANONYMOUS (Eighth Century)

The Seafarer (modern version by Ezra Pound)

May I for my own self song's truth reckon,
Journey's jargon, how I in harsh days
Hardship endured oft.
Bitter breast-cares have I abided,
5 Known on my keel many a care's hold,
And dire sea-surge, and there I oft spent
Narrow nightwatch nigh the ship's head
While she tossed close to cliffs. Coldly afflicted,
My feet were by frost benumbed.
10 Chill its chains are; chafing signs
Hew my heart round and hunger begot.
Mere-weary mood. Lest man know not
That he on dry land loveliest liveth,
List how I, care-wretched, on ice-cold sea,
15 Weathered the winter, wretched outcast
Deprived of my kinsmen;
Hung with hard ice-flakes, where hail-scur flew,
There I heard naught save the harsh sea
And ice-cold wave, at whiles the swan cries,
20 Did for my games the gannet's clamor,
Sea-fowls' loudness was for me laughter,
The mews' singing all my mead-drink.
Storms, on the stone-cliffs beaten, fell on the stern
In icy feathers; full oft the eagle screamed
25 With spray on his pinion.
                    Not any protector
May make merry man faring needy.
This he little believes, who aye in winsome life
Abides 'mid burghers some heavy business,
Wealthy and wine-flushed, how I weary oft

30 Must bide above brine.
Neareth nightshade, snoweth from north,
Frost froze the land, hail fell on earth then,
Corn of the coldest. Nathless there knocketh now
The heart's thought that I on high streams
35 The salt-wavy tumult traverse alone.
Moaneth alway my mind's lust
That I fare forth, that I afar hence
Seek out a foreign fastness.
For this there's no mood-lofty man over earth's midst,
40 Not though he be given his good, but will have in his youth greed;
Nor his deed to the daring, nor his king to the faithful
But shall have his sorrow for sea-fare
Whatever his lord will.
He hath not heart for harping, nor in ring-having
45 Nor winsomeness to wife, nor world's delight
Nor any whit else save the wave's slash,
Yet longing comes upon him to fare forth on the water.
Bosque taketh blossom, cometh beauty of berries,
Fields to fairness, land fares brisker,
50 All this admonisheth man eager of mood,
The heart turns to travel so that he then thinks
On flood-ways to be far departing.
Cuckoo calleth with gloomy crying,
He singeth summerward, bodeth sorrow,
55 The bitter heart's blood. Burgher knows not—
He the prosperous man—what some perform
Where wandering them widest draweth.
So that but now my heart burst from my breastlock,
My mood 'mid the mere-flood,
60 Over the whale's acre, would wander wide.
On earth's shelter cometh oft to me,
Eager and ready, the crying lone-flyer,
Whets for the whale-path the heart irresistibly,
O'er tracks of ocean; seeing that anyhow
65 My lord deems to me this dead life
On loan and on land, I believe not
That any earth-weal eternal standeth
Save there be somewhat calamitous
That, ere a man's tide go, turn it to twain.
70 Disease or oldness or sword-hate
Beats out the breath from doom-gripped body.
And for this, every earl whatever, for those speaking after—
Laud of the living, boasteth some last word,

That he will work ere he pass onward,
75 Frame on the fair earth 'gainst foes his malice,
Daring ado, . . .
So that all men shall honor him after
And his laud beyond them remain 'mid the English,
Aye, for ever a lasting life's-blast,
80 Delight 'mid the doughty.
       Days little durable,
And all arrogance of earthen riches,
There come now no kings nor Caesars
Nor gold-giving lords like those gone.
Howe'er in mirth most magnified,
85 Whoe'er lived in life most lordliest,
Drear all this excellence, delights undurable!
Waneth the watch, but the world holdeth.
Tomb hideth trouble. The blade is layed low.
Earthly glory ageth and seareth.
90 No man at all going the earth's gait,
But age fares against him, his face paleth,
Grey-haired he groaneth, knows gone companions,
Lordly men, are to earth o'ergiven,
Nor may he then the flesh-cover, whose life ceaseth,
95 Nor eat the sweet nor feel the sorry,
Nor stir hand nor think in mid heart,
And though he strew the grave with gold,
His born brothers, their buried bodies
Be an unlikely treasure hoard.

QUESTIONS

Notice the movement of the speaker's mood and thought. How does he characterize himself? What response does he seek from his audience?

GERARD MANLEY HOPKINS (1844–1889)

Felix Randal

Felix Randal the farrier, O he is dead then? my duty all ended
Who have watched his mould of man, big-boned and
  hardy-handsome
Pining, pining, till time when reason rambled in it and some
Fatal four disorders, fleshed there, all contended?

⟋ 5   Sickness broke him. Impatient he cursed at first, but mended
       Being anointed and all; though a heavenlier heart began some
       Months earlier, since I had our sweet reprieve and ransom
       Tendered to him. Ah well, God rest him all road ever he offended!

       This seeing the sick endears them to us, us too it endears.
10   My tongue had taught thee comfort, touch had quenched thy tears,
       Thy tears that touched my heart, child, Felix, poor Felix Randal;

       How far from then forethought of, all thy more boisterous years,
       When thou at the random grim forge, powerful amidst peers,
       Didst fettle for the great grey drayhorse his bright and
               battering sandal!

QUESTIONS

1. Again, how does the speaker portray himself? How does he portray the
   blacksmith, Felix Randal?
2. Note the movement of the poem, from present to past. Why might Hopkins
   have chosen this organization for this poem?

Now read these two examples of accentual-syllabic verse. Note the metrical techniques that make the first sound like a song. The second is like the
voice of a man arguing with himself.

ALFRED, LORD TENNYSON (1809–1892)

The Splendor Falls on Castle Walls

       The splendor falls on castle walls
           And snowy summits old in story:
       The long light shakes across the lakes,
           And the wild cataract leaps in glory.
5   Blow, bugle, blow, set the wild echoes flying,
    Blow, bugle; answer, echoes, dying, dying, dying.

       O hark, O hear! how thin and clear,
           And thinner, clearer, farther going!
       O sweet and far from cliff and scar
10   The horns of Elfland faintly blowing!
    Blow, let us hear the purple glens replying:
    Blow, bugle; answer, echoes, dying, dying, dying.

       O love, they die in yon rich sky,
           They faint on hill or field or river;

15   Our echoes roll from soul to soul,
        And grow for ever and for ever.
    Blow, bugle, blow, set the wild echoes flying,
    And answer, echoes, answer, dying, dying, dying.

QUESTIONS

1. What is the meter of the main part of the poem? What is the meter of the refrain? What has been achieved by combining the two?
2. What does Tennyson mean by the phrase "our echoes" (line 15)? How do these echoes differ from the other "echoes" of which the poem speaks?
3. Fairyland and fairy things are usually pictured in literature as being immortal and unchanging, in contrast to human affairs, which are transitory. Why does Tennyson reverse that contrast in this poem?
4. How do sound and imagery combine in this poem to reinforce the speaker's message?

GEORGE HERBERT (1593–1633)

The Collar[1]

    I struck the board[2] and cried, "No more!
            I will abroad!
    What, shall I ever sigh and pine?
    My lines and life are free: free as the road,
5   Loose as the wind, as large as store.
            Shall I be still in suit?[3]
    Have I no harvest but a thorn
    To let me blood, and not restore
    What I have lost with cordial[4] fruit?
10   Sure there was wine
    Before my sighs did dry it; there was corn
            Before my tears did drown it.
    Is the year only lost to me?
            Have I no bays[5] to crown it,
15 No flowers, no garlands gay? all blasted?
            All wasted?
    Not so, my heart; but there is fruit,
            And thou hast hands.

---

[1] The iron band encircling the neck of a prisoner or slave; also perhaps a pun on "choler" as "rebellious anger."
[2] Dining table.
[3] Always petitioning.
[4] Restorative.
[5] Laurels.

Recover all thy sigh-blown age
20 On double pleasures. Leave thy cold dispute
Of what is fit and not. Forsake thy cage,
      Thy rope of sands,
Which petty thoughts have made and made to thee
    Good cable, to enforce and draw,
25   And be thy law,
While thou didst wink and wouldst not see.
      Away! take heed!
      I will abroad!
Call in thy death's-head there! Tie up thy fears!
30   He that forbears
    To suit and serve his need,
     Deserves his load."
But as I raved, and grew more fierce and wild
    At every word,
35 Methought I heard one calling, "Child!"
    And I replied, "My Lord."

QUESTIONS

Discuss how the movement of sound in "The Collar" helps create the sound of the speaker arguing with himself. (Note the addition of a second voice near the end of the poem. How do the speech of this second voice and the speaker's response to it bring the poem to its resolution?)

Finally, here are two examples of iambic pentameter by two masters of that meter. Note that even the use of the identical meter does not give these poems identical sounds. The rhythm of Shakespeare's sonnet, for all its basic regularity, is flexible and almost conversational; the rhythm of Milton's poem is as firm and regular as the marble tomb he uses as his poem's chief conceit. Read the two poems and then answer the following questions:

1. How does each poet handle his meter? How are phrasing and sentence structure fitted to the pentameter? How is the progression of the speaker's thought emphasized?
2. How does each poem's rhythm enhance or emphasize its imagery? Give examples.

WILLIAM SHAKESPEARE (1564–1616)

Sonnet 29

When, in disgrace with Fortune and men's eyes,
I all alone beweep my outcast state,
And trouble deaf heaven with my bootless cries,

And look upon myself and curse my fate,
5 Wishing me like to one more rich in hope,
Featured like him, like him with friends possessed,
Desiring this man's art, and that man's scope,
With what I most enjoy contented least;
Yet in these thoughts myself almost depising,
10 Haply I think on thee, and then my state,
Like to the lark at break of day arising
From sullen earth, sings hymns at heaven's gate;
    For thy sweet love remembered such wealth brings
    That then I scorn to change my state with kings.

JOHN MILTON (1608–1674)

On Shakespeare

What needs my Shakespeare for his honored bones
The labor of an age in pilèd stones?
Or that his hallowed reliques should be hid
Under a star-ypointing[1] pyramid?
5 Dear son of memory, great heir of fame,
What need'st thou such weak witness of thy name?
Thou in our wonder and astonishment
Has built thyself a livelong monument.
For whilst, to the shame of slow-endeavoring art,
10 Thy easy numbers flow, and that each heart
Hath from the leaves of thy unvalued[2] book
Those Delphic[3] lines with deep impression took,
Then thou, our fancy of itself bereaving,
Dost make us marble with too much conceiving,[4]
15 And so sepùlchred in such pomp dost lie
That kings for such a tomb would wish to die.

QUESTIONS

Look back at the poems you have read in this book. Select several that you especially like. Analyze the meter in each, and consider the techniques by which it is varied. Then discuss how these metrical techniques enhance your enjoyment of each poem.

---

[1] Milton added the "y" for the sake of rhythm.
[2] Invaluable.
[3] Inspired—as by the oracle at Delphi.
[4] Thinking.

13 Rhyme Schemes and Verse Forms

Although rhyme is not found in all poetry written in English, it has been so important in the history of English and American verse that we often first divide poetry into two categories—rhymed and unrhymed—and then divide further from there. Accepting that categorization for the moment, we will note that unrhymed poems tend to fall into one of three major divisions: accentual verse, which has existed from Old English times and which we met in "The Seafarer" and "Pied Beauty"; blank verse (unrhymed iambic pentameter), a sixteenth-century invention of which Hamlet's soliloquies are classic examples; or free verse, sometimes called by the French name **vers libre,** a modern (and not always unrhymed) form that we met in the works of such diverse poets as Whitman, Cummings, Pound, and Levertov.

Rhymed Verse

Rhymed verse is harder to classify. There are so many ways of combining rhymed lines! Still, one can distinguish between those forms of rhymed verse that have a fixed total length (such as the **limerick,** with five lines; the **sonnet,** with fourteen; and the **villanelle,** with nineteen) and those that do not. Rhymed verse with no fixed length is usually composed of **stanzas.** Each stanza usually has a fixed length; but the number of stanzas, and hence the length of the poem as a whole, remain variable.

Underlying both types of rhymed verse, however, stand the basic combinations of rhyme. These embrace two-, three-, and four-line patterns, called the couplet, triplet, terza rima, and the quatrain. The **couplet** has two consecutive lines that rhyme:

> So long as men can breathe or eyes can see,
> So long lives this, and this gives life to thee.

The **tercet** or **triplet** has three lines that rhyme:

> He clasps the crag with crooked hands;
> Close to the sun in lonely lands,
> Ringed with the azure world, he stands.

The **terza rima** also has three lines, but only the first and last rhyme. When terza rima stanzas are linked together, the middle line of one stanza rhymes with the first and third lines of the stanza that follows.

> O wild West Wind, thou breath of Autumn's being,
> Thou, from whose unseen presence the leaves dead
> Are driven, like ghosts from an enchanter fleeing,
>
> Yellow, and black, and pale, and hectic red,
> Pestilence-stricken multitudes: O thou
> Who chariotest to their dark wintry bed

The **quatrain** has four lines joined by any one of the following rhyme schemes:

1. Second and fourth lines rhyming (*abcb*):

> When I was one-and-twenty
> I heard a wise man say,
> "Give crowns and pounds and guineas
> But not your heart away;

2. First and third, second and fourth lines rhyming (*abab*):

> She even thinks that up in heaven
> Her class lies late and snores,
> While poor black cherubs rise at seven
> To do celestial chores.

3. First and fourth, second and third lines rhyming (*abba*):

> Earth hath not anything to show more fair!
> Dull would he be of soul who could pass by
> A sight so touching in its majesty.
> The city now doth, like a garment, wear

4. First and second, third and fourth lines rhyming (*aabb*):

"O 'Melia, my dear, this does everything crown!
Who could have supposed I should meet you in Town?
And whence such fair garments, such prosperi-ty?"—
"O didn't you know I'd been ruined?" said she.

Any of these patterns can stand alone as a stanza. Or, patterns may be added to or combined to produce more complicated stanzas, such as the **rime royale** in which the following poem is written. Notice, in this poem, not only the stanzaic pattern, but also the change of tone and of tense in each stanza. What progression of argument and emotion occurs in this poem? What is its effect?

SIR THOMAS WYATT (1503–1542)

They Flee from Me

They flee from me that sometime did me seek
With naked foot stalking in my chamber.
I have seen them gentle, tame, and meek
That now are wild and do not remember
5 That sometime they put themselves in danger
To take bread at my hand; and now they range
Busily seeking with a continual change.

Thankèd be Fortune, it hath been otherwise
Twenty times better; but once in special,
10 In thin array after a pleasant guise,
When her loose gown from her shoulders did fall,
And she me caught in her arms long and small;
And therewithall sweetly did me kiss,
And softly said, "Dear heart, how like you this?"

15 It was no dream; I lay broad waking.
But all is turned thorough my gentleness
Into a strange fashion of forsaking;
And I have leave to go of her goodness,
And she also to use newfangleness.
20 But since that I so kindely am served,
I fain would know what she hath deserved.

Limericks and Villanelles

Let us now look at two rhymed forms of fixed length: the limerick and the villanelle. (We will consider a third fixed-length form, the sonnet, in the next chapter.)

Limericks have five lines. The rhyme scheme is *aabba,* with all *a* lines having three feet, and all *b* lines two feet. The meter is usually anapestic.

Limericks are humorous verse, frequently employing puns, off-color humor, or deliberately tortured rhymes or rhythms. As one anonymous writer and critic remarks,

> The limerick packs laughs anatomical,
> Into space that is quite economical.
> But the good ones I've seen
> So seldom are clean,
> And the clean ones so seldom are comical.

More serious, but equally tightly controlled in form, is the **villanelle.** Entire lines, as well as rhyme sounds, are repeated in the villanelle to make up its prescribed pattern. Here is one of the finest twentieth-century villanelles. Analyze its form and discuss what the poet has done with it.

DYLAN THOMAS (1914–1953)

Do Not Go Gentle Into That Good Night

Do not go gentle into that good night,
Old age should burn and rave at close of day;
Rage, rage against the dying of the light.

Though wise men at their end know dark is right,
5 Because their words had forked no lightning they
Do not go gentle into that good night.

Good men, the last wave by, crying how bright
Their frail deeds might have danced in a green bay,
Rage, rage against the dying of the light.

10 Wild men who caught and sang the sun in flight,
And learn, too late, they grieved it on its way,
Do not go gentle into that good night.

Grave men, near death, who see with blinding sight
Blind eyes could blaze like meteors and be gay,
15 Rage, rage against the dying of the light.

And you, my father, there on the sad height,
Curse, bless, me now with your fierce tears, I pray.
Do not go gentle into that good night.
Rage, rage against the dying of the light.

Ballades, Ballads, and Odes

Three forms without fixed length are the **ballade, ballad,** and **ode.**

The **ballade** was popular during the Middle Ages. It uses seven- or eight-line stanzas, usually in groups of three. Each stanza ends with the same line, the **refrain.** The ballade itself ends with a shorter stanza, the **envoy** or **envoi.** The envoy is addressed directly to the person for whom the ballade is being written. It, too, ends with the refrain.

Here is a nineteenth-century translation of a medieval French ballade. Note how the envoy provides both a personal note and a conclusion to a catalog that might otherwise have no logical ending.

DANTE GABRIEL ROSSETTI (1828–1882)

The Ballad of Dead Ladies[1]

François Villon, 1450

Tell me now in what hidden way is
　Lady Flora[2] the lovely Roman?
Where's Hipparchia,[3] and where is Thaïs,[4]
　Neither of them the fairer woman?
5　Where is Echo, beheld of no man,
Only heard on river and mere,—
　She whose beauty was more than human? . . .
But where are the snows of yester-year?

Where's Héloïse, the learned nun,
10　For whose sake Abeillard, I ween,

---

[1] This is a translation of the "Ballade des Dames de Temps Jadis" by François Villon (b. 1431).

[2] A famous Roman courtesan.

[3] A Greek courtesan.

[4] An Athenian courtesan.

Lost manhood and put priesthood on?[5]
   (From Love he won such dule and teen!)
   And where, I pray you, is the Queen[6]
Who willed that Buridan should steer
15   Sewed in a sack's mouth down the Seine? . . .
But where are the snows of yester-year?

White Queen Blanche, like a queen of lilies,[7]
   With a voice like any mermaiden,—
Bertha Broadfoot, Beatrice, Alice,[8]
20   And Ermengarde the lady of Maine,[9]—
   And that good Joan[10] whom Englishmen
At Rouen doomed and burned her there,—
   Mother of God, where are they then? . . .
But where are the snows of yester-year?

25 Nay, never ask this week, fair lord,
   Where they are gone, nor yet this year,
Except with this for an overword,—
   But where are the snows of yester-year?

In contrast to the tightly defined ballade, the term **ballad** (without the final **e**) may be used for any poem that is, or can be, sung, and that has regular stanzas. Usually, the poems we refer to as ballads have four-line stanzas. Frequently, like the ballade, they make use of repeated lines or refrains. Note, in this next poem, how thoroughly and skillfully William Morris uses the battle cry he has chosen for his refrain, hammering it home at the end of each short stanza until it almost takes on the sound of the speaker's own pulse pounding in his temples.

---

[5] Héloïse, the beautiful niece of a church official, fell in love with her teacher, the famous philosopher Abelard (1079–1142). They eloped, and the uncle was so incensed that he caused Abelard to be set upon and emasculated. As a result Abelard became a monk and Héloïse a nun, and the reward of their love was sorrow and pain.

[6] Queen Margaret of Burgundy who used to have her lovers, among whom was the scholar Buridan, sewn in sacks and thrown into the Seine.

[7] Perhaps Blanche of Castile, or perhaps a figment of Villon's imagination.

[8] Bertha Broadfoot, in epic accounts is the mother of Charlemagne. The identity of Beatrice and Alice is uncertain.

[9] The countess of Anjou in France.

[10] Joan of Arc.

WILLIAM MORRIS (1834–1896)

The Gillyflower of Gold

A golden gillyflower today
I wore upon my helm alway,
And won the prize of this tourney.
    Hah! hah! la belle jaune giroflée.[1]

5 However well Sir Giles might sit,
His sun was weak to wither it;
Lord Miles's blood was dew on it.
    Hah! hah! la belle jaune giroflée.

Although my spear in splinters flew,
10 From John's steel-coat, my eye was true;
I wheeled about, and cried for you,
    Hah! hah! la belle jaune giroflée.

Yea, do not doubt my heart was good,
Though my sword flew like rotten wood,
15 To shout, although I scarcely stood,
    Hah! hah! la belle jaune giroflée.

My hand was steady too, to take,
My ax from round my neck, and break
John's steel-coat up for my love's sake.
20   *Hah! hah! la belle jaune giroflée—*

When I stood in my tent again,
Arming afresh, I felt a pain
Take hold of me, I was so fain—
    Hah! hah! la belle jaune giroflée—

25 To hear *Honneur aux fils des preux!*[2]
Right in my ears again, and shew
The gillyflower blossomed new.
    Hah! hah! la belle jaune giroflée.

The Sieur Guillaume against me came,
30 His tabard[3] bore three points of flame

---

[1] The beautiful yellow gillyflower.
[2] Honor to the sons of valiant knights!
[3] A kind of cloak or mantle worn by knights.

From a red heart; with little blame[4]—
    Hah! hah! la belle jaune giroflée—

Our tough spears crackled up like straw;
He was the first to turn and draw
35 His sword, that had nor speck nor flaw;
    Hah! hah! la belle jaune giroflée.

But I felt weaker than a maid,
And my brain, dizzied and afraid,
Within my helm a fierce tune played,
40   *Hah! hah! la belle jaune giroflée,*

Until I thought of your dear head,
Bowed to the gillyflower bed,
The yellow flowers stained with red;
    Hah! hah! la belle jaune giroflée.

45 Crash! how the swords met—*giroflée!*
The fierce tune in my helm would play,
La belle! la belle! jaune giroflée!
    Hah! hah! la belle jaune giroflée.

Once more the great swords met again;
50 *"La belle! la belle!"* but who fell then?
Le Sieur Guillaume, who struck down ten;
    Hah! hah! la belle jaune giroflée.

And as with mazed and unarmed face
Toward my own crown and the Queen's place,
55 They led me at a gentle pace—
    Hah! hah! la belle jaune giroflée—

I almost saw your quiet head
Bowed o'er the gillyflower bed,
The yellow flowers stained with red.
60   *Hah! hah! la belle jaune giroflée.*

---

[4] Damage.

Among the rhymed poetic forms, the **ode** is unique in leaving both the rhyme scheme and the length of each individual line to the poet's discretion. The one constant feature of odes in English poetry, in fact, is their elevated tone. In Keats's "Ode on a Grecian Urn" and "Ode to a Nightingale," and in Shelley's "Ode to the West Wind," we saw three different stanzaic patterns. Look back at these odes now (on pages 435, 453, and 451) and define their patterns. Note, too, that in each case the stanzaic form is constant throughout the ode. For this reason, these are sometimes called **Horatian odes.**

To conclude this chapter, we will read one further ode, this one of the type called the **irregular ode.** This particular ode, written by the early Romantic poet William Wordsworth, makes skillful use of rhyme and rhythm both. Yet, for all its careful contrivance, it maintains a remarkable freshness of tone, in keeping with its subject of early joys and maturer delights. Because it is an irregular ode, the stanzas in this poem vary among themselves, changing shape to follow the motions of the poet's mind. The basic meter remains iambic throughout, but line lengths and rhyme schemes shift constantly. The result is an unusual blend of patterning and fluidity that sometimes mutes its tone to a thoughtful expression of philosophy and sometimes rises to a hymn of joyful praise.

The ode deals with the relations between the human soul, nature, and immortality. In it, Wordsworth suggests not only that we know immortality after death, but that we know it before birth as well: "trailing clouds of glory do we come, / From God, who is our home." The ode thus celebrates the heavenlike joy the young child sees in the natural world; and it laments the dulling of that joy that occurs when the child, responding to the novelty of his mundane existence, turns his mind more fully upon earthly things. Yet the final tone is not sorrow but a greater joy, as Wordsworth passes beyond mourning this early loss into celebrating the fully human joys and loves that are the gift of the mature soul.

As you read the ode, pay careful attention to the way Wordsworth develops this train of thought, and notice how the sound and shape of the stanzas convey the changing emotions the speaker feels.

WILLIAM WORDSWORTH (1770–1850)

Ode

Intimations of Immortality from Recollections
of Early Childhood

The Child is father of the Man;
And I could wish my days to be
Bound each to each by natural piety.

I

There was a time when meadow, grove, and stream,
The earth, and every common sight,
    To me did seem
    Apparelled in celestial light,
5 The glory and the freshness of a dream.
It is not now as it hath been of yore;—
    Turn wheresoe'er I may,
    By night or day,
The things which I have seen I now can see no more.

2

10   The Rainbow comes and goes,
    And lovely is the Rose,
    The Moon doth with delight
Look round her when the heavens are bare;
    Waters on a starry night
15   Are beautiful and fair;
The sunshine is a glorious birth;
But yet I know, where'er I go,
That there hath past away a glory from the earth.

3

Now, while the birds thus sing a joyous song,
20   And while the young lambs bound
    As to the tabor's sound,
To me alone there came a thought of grief:
A timely utterance gave that thought relief,
    And I again am strong:
25 The cataracts blow their trumpets from the steep;
No more shall grief of mine the season wrong;
I hear the Echoes through the mountains throng,
The Winds come to me from the fields of sleep,
    And all the earth is gay;
30   Land and sea
Give themselves up to jollity,
    And with the heart of May
Doth every Beast keep holiday;—
    Thou Child of Joy,
35 Shout round me, let me hear thy shouts, thou happy Shepherd-boy!

4

Ye blessèd Creatures, I have heard the call
　Ye to each other make; I see
The heavens laugh with you in your jubilee;
　My heart is at your festival,
40　　My head hath its coronal,
The fulness of your bliss, I feel—I feel it all.
　　Oh evil day! if I were sullen
　　While Earth herself is adorning,
　　　This sweet May-morning,
45　　And the Children are culling
　　　On every side,
　　In a thousand valleys far and wide,
　　Fresh flowers; while the sun shines warm,
And the Babe leaps up on his Mother's arm:—
50　　I hear, I hear, with joy I hear!
　—But there's a Tree, of many, one,
A single Field which I have looked upon,
Both of them speak of something that is gone:
　　The Pansy at my feet
55　　Doth the same tale repeat:
Whither is fled the visionary gleam?
Where is it now, the glory and the dream?

5

Our birth is but a sleep and a forgetting:
The Soul that rises with us, our life's Star,
60　　Hath had elsewhere its setting,
　　And cometh from afar:
　　Not in entire forgetfulness,
　　And not in utter nakedness,
But trailing clouds of glory do we come
65　　From God, who is our home:
Heaven lies about us in our infancy!
Shades of the prison-house begin to close
　　Upon the growing Boy,
　　　But He
70 Beholds the light, and whence it flows,
　　He sees it in his joy;
The Youth, who daily farther from the east
　　Must travel, still is Nature's Priest,
　　And by the vision splendid

75   Is on his way attended;
At length the Man perceives it die away,
And fade into the light of common day.

6

Earth fills her lap with pleasures of her own;
Yearnings she hath in her own natural kind,
80 And, even with something of a Mother's mind,
      And no unworthy aim,
      The homely Nurse doth all she can
To make her Foster-child, her Inmate Man,
      Forget the glories he hath known,
85 And that imperial palace whence he came.

7

Behold the Child among his new-born blisses,
A six years' Darling of a pigmy size!
See, where 'mid work of his own hand he lies,
Fretted by sallies of his mother's kisses,
90 With light upon him from his father's eyes!
See, at his feet, some little plan or chart,
Some fragment from his dream of human life,
Shaped by himself with newly-learnèd art;
      A wedding or a festival,
95   A mourning or a funeral;
       And this hath now his heart,
       And unto this he frames his song:
        Then will he fit his tongue
To dialogues of business, love, or strife;
100   But it will not be long
       Ere this be thrown aside,
       And with new joy and pride
The little Actor cons another part;
Filling from time to time his "humorous stage"
105 With all the Persons, down to palsied Age,
That Life brings with her in her equipage;
       As if his whole vocation
       Were endless imitation.

8

Thou, whose exterior semblance doth belie
110   Thy Soul's immensity;

Thou best Philosopher, who yet dost keep
Thy heritage, thou Eye among the blind,
That, deaf and silent, read'st the eternal deep,
Haunted for ever by the eternal mind,—
115   Mighty Prophet! Seer blest!
       On whom those truths do rest,
Which we are toiling all our lives to find,
In darkness lost, the darkness of the grave;
Thou, over whom thy Immortality
120 Broods like the Day, a Master o'er a Slave,
A Presence which is not to be put by;
Thou little Child, yet glorious in the might
Of heaven-born freedom on thy being's height,
Why with such earnest pains dost thou provoke
125 The years to bring the inevitable yoke,
Thus blindly with thy blessedness at strife?
Full soon thy Soul shall have her earthly freight,
And custom lie upon thee with a weight,
Heavy as frost, and deep almost as life!

9

130   O joy! that in our embers
      Is something that doth live,
      That nature yet remembers
      What was so fugitive!
The thought of our past years in me doth breed
135 Perpetual benediction: not indeed
For that which is most worthy to be blest;
Delight and liberty, the simple creed
Of Childhood, whether busy or at rest,
With new-fledged hope still fluttering in his breast:—
140   Not for these I raise
       The song of thanks and praise;
    But for those obstinate questionings
    Of sense and outward things,
    Falling from us, vanishings;
145   Blank misgivings of a Creature
Moving about in worlds not realised,
High instincts before which our mortal Nature
Did tremble like a guilty Thing surprised:
      But for those first affections,
150   Those shadowy recollections,
    Which, be they what they may,
Are yet the fountain-light of all our day,

Are yet a master-light of all our seeing;
   Uphold us, cherish, and have power to make
155 Our noisy years seem moments in the being
   Of the eternal Silence: truths that wake,
      To perish never:
   Which neither listlessness, nor mad endeavor,
      Nor Man nor Boy,
160 Nor all that is at enmity with joy,
   Can utterly abolish or destroy!
     Hence in a season of calm weather
      Though inland far we be,
   Our Souls have sight of that immortal sea
165   Which brought us hither,
     Can in a moment travel thither,
   And see the Children sport upon the shore,
   And hear the mighty waters rolling evermore.

10

   Then sing, ye Birds, sing, sing a joyous song!
170   And let the young Lambs bound
     As to the tabor's sound!
   We in thought will join your throng,
     Ye that pipe and ye that play,
     Ye that through your hearts to-day
175   Feel the gladness of the May!
   What though the radiance which was once so bright
   Be now for ever taken from my sight,
    Though nothing can bring back the hour
   Of splendor in the grass, of glory in the flower;
180   We will grieve not, rather find
     Strength in what remains behind;
     In the primal sympathy
     Which having been must ever be;
     In the soothing thoughts that spring
185   Out of human suffering;
     In the faith that looks through death,
   In years that bring the philosophic mind.

11

   And O, ye Fountains, Meadows, Hills, and Groves,
   Forebode not any severing of our loves!
190 Yet in my heart of hearts I feel your might;

I only have relinquished one delight
To live beneath your more habitual sway.
I love the Brooks which down their channels fret,
Even more than when I tripped lightly as they;
195 The innocent brightness of a new-born Day
        Is lovely yet;
The Clouds that gather round the setting sun
Do take a sober coloring from an eye
That hath kept watch o'er man's mortality;
200 Another race hath been, and other palms are won.
Thanks to the human heart by which we live,
Thanks to its tenderness, its joys, and fears,
To me the meanest flower that blows can give
Thoughts that do often lie too deep for tears.

14 *The Sonnet*

Without a doubt, the most popular of the defined forms in English and American poetry is the **sonnet.** Sonnets are always fourteen lines long. Traditionally, they are divided into two main forms. The **Petrarchan sonnet** consists of an octet, rhymed *abba abba,* and a sestet, rhymed either *cdcdcd* or *cdecde;* and the **Shakespearean sonnet,** with three quatrains, usually rhymes *abab cdcd efef,* and a couplet at the end, *gg.* Less standard rhyme forms do, of course, exist. Notice, for example, the rhyme scheme in Cummings's "the Cambridge ladies who live in furnished souls," at the end of this chapter.

Of the two traditional forms, the Shakespearean usually seems the more emphatic. Because no sound needs to be used more than twice, it is also slightly easier to write. It was the favored form during the Renaissance. The Petrarchan sonnet, on the other hand, tends to have a somewhat smoother flow and often seems more graceful. It was therefore preferred by the Romantic poets of the nineteenth century.

The sonnet came into English as a love poem: we have read love sonnets by Shakespeare, Sidney, and Spenser. But the sonnet has proved capable of handling almost any subject and of expressing many moods and tones. Look back, for example, at "Ozymandias" (p. 415) and "Composed upon Westminster Bridge" (p. 425). And look, too, at the following examples of what can be done with the sonnet form.

WILLIAM SHAKESPEARE (1564–1616)

Sonnet 116

Let me not to the marriage of true minds
Admit impediments. Love is not love
Which alters when it alteration finds,
Or bends with the remover to remove.
5 O no! it is an ever-fixèd mark
That looks on tempests and is never shaken;
It is the star to every wand'ring bark,
Whose worth's unknown, although his height be taken.
Love's not Time's fool, though rosy lips and cheeks
10 Within his bending sickle's compass come.
Love alters not with his brief hours and weeks,
But bears it out even to the edge of doom.
    If this be error, and upon me proved,
    I never writ, nor no man ever loved.

JOHN DONNE (1572–1631)

Sonnet 10

Death, be not proud, though some have callèd thee
Mighty and dreadful, for thou art not so;
For those whom thou think'st thou dost overthrow
Die not, poor Death, nor yet canst thou kill me.
5 From rest and sleep, which but thy pictures be,
Much pleasure; then from thee much more must flow;
And soonest our best men with thee do go,
Rest of their bones and souls' delivery.
Thou'rt slave to fate, chance, kings, and desperate men,
10 And dost with poison, war, and sickness dwell;
And poppy or charms can make us sleep as well
And better than thy stroke. Why swell'st thou then?
One short sleep past, we wake eternally,
And Death shall be no more: Death, thou shalt die.

JOHN MILTON (1608–1674)

On His Blindness

When I consider how my light is spent,
Ere half my days, in this dark world and wide,
And that one talent which is death to hide

Lodged with me useless, though my soul more bent
5 To serve therewith my Maker, and present
My true account, lest he returning chide,
"Doth God exact day labor, light denied?"
I fondly ask; but Patience, to prevent
That murmur, soon replies: "God doth not need
10 Either man's work or his own gifts; who best
Bear his mild yoke, they serve him best. His state
Is kingly: thousands at his bidding speed
And post o'er land and ocean without rest.
They also serve who only stand and wait."

GERARD MANLEY HOPKINS (1844–1889)

God's Grandeur

The world is charged with the grandeur of God.
    It will flame out, like shining from shook foil;[1]
    It gathers to a greatness, like the ooze of oil
Crushed. Why do men then now not reck his rod?[2]
5 Generations have trod, have trod, have trod;
    And all is seared with trade; bleared, smeared with toil;
    And wears man's smudge and shares man's smell: the soil
Is bare now, nor can foot feel, being shod.

And for all this, nature is never spent;
10   There lives the dearest freshness deep down things;
And though the last lights off the black West went
    Oh, morning, at the brown brink eastward, springs—
Because the Holy Ghost over the bent
    World broods with warm breast and with ah! bright wings.

ROBERT FROST (1874–1963)

Design

I found a dimpled spider, fat and white,
On a white heal-all, holding up a moth
Like a white piece of rigid satin cloth—
Assorted characters of death and blight
5 Mixed ready to begin the morning right,
Like the ingredients of a witches' broth—

---

[1] Tinsel, goldfoil.
[2] Acknowledge his discipline.

A snow-drop spider, a flower like a froth,
And dead wings carried like a paper kite.

What had that flower to do with being white,
10   The wayside blue and innocent heal-all?
What brought the kindred spider to that height,
Then steered the white moth thither in the night?
What but design of darkness to appall?—
If design govern in a thing so small.

EDNA ST. VINCENT MILLAY (1892–1950)

Love Is Not All: It Is Not Meat nor Drink

Love is not all: it is not meat nor drink
Nor slumber nor a roof against the rain;
Nor yet a floating spar to men that sink
And rise and sink and rise and sink again;
5   Love can not fill the thickened lung with breath,
Nor clean the blood, nor set the fractured bone;
Yet many a man is making friends with death
Even as I speak, for lack of love alone.
It well may be that in a difficult hour,
10   Pinned down by pain and moaning for release,
Or nagged by want past resolution's power,
I might be driven to sell your love for peace,
Or trade the memory of this night for food.
It well may be. I do not think I would.

WILFRED OWEN (1893–1918)

Anthem for Doomed Youth

What passing-bells for these who die as cattle?
    Only the monstrous anger of the guns.
    Only the stuttering rifles' rapid rattle
Can patter out their hasty orisons.
5 No mockeries now for them; no prayers nor bells,
    Nor any voice of mourning save the choirs—
The shrill, demented choirs of wailing shells;
    And bugles calling for them from sad shires.

What candles may be held to speed them all?
10   Not in the hands of boys, but in their eyes

Shall shine the holy glimmers of good-byes.
    The pallor of girls' brows shall be their pall;
Their flowers the tenderness of patient minds,
And each slow dusk a drawing-down of blinds.

E. E. CUMMINGS (1894–1963)

the Cambridge ladies who live in furnished souls

the Cambridge ladies who live in furnished souls
are unbeautiful and have comfortable minds
(also, with the church's protestant blessings,
daughters, unscented shapeless spirited)
5 they believe in Christ and Longfellow, both dead,
are invariably interested in so many things—
at the present writing one still finds
delighted fingers knitting for the is it Poles?
perhaps. While permanent faces coyly bandy
10 scandal of Mrs. N and Professor D
    . . . . the Cambridge ladies do not care, above
Cambridge if sometimes in its box of
sky lavender and cornerless, the
moon rattles like a fragment of angry candy

AN ANTHOLOGY OF
POEMS

CHRISTOPHER MARLOWE (1564–1593)

The Passionate Shepherd to His Love

Come live with me, and be my love,
And we will all the pleasures prove
That hills and valleys, dales and fields,
Woods, or steepy mountain yields.

5 And we will sit upon the rocks,
Seeing the shepherds feed their flocks,
By shallow rivers, to whose falls
Melodious birds sings madrigals.

And I will make thee beds of roses
10 And a thousand fragrant posies.
A cap of flowers, and a kirtle
Embroidered all with leaves of myrtle;

A gown made of the finest wool,
Which from our pretty lambs we pull,
15 Fair linèd slippers, for the cold,
With buckles of the purest gold;

A belt of straw and ivy-buds
With coral clasps and amber studs.
And if these pleasures may thee move,
20 Come live with me, and be my love.

The shepherds' swains shall dance and sing
For thy delight each May morning.
If these delights thy mind may move,
Then live with me, and be my love.

SIR WALTER RALEIGH (1552?–1618)

The Nymph's Reply to the Shepherd

If all the world and love were young,
And truth in every shepherd's tongue,
These pretty pleasures might me move
To live with thee and be thy love.

5 Time drives the flocks from field to fold
When rivers rage and rocks grow cold,
And Philomel becometh dumb;
The rest complains of cares to come.

The flowers do fade, and wanton fields
10 To wayward winter reckoning yields;
A honey tongue, a heart of gall,
Is fancy's spring, but sorrow's fall.

Thy gowns, thy shoes, thy beds of roses,
Thy cap, thy kirtle, and thy posies
15 Soon break, soon wither, soon forgotten—
In folly ripe, in reason rotten.

Thy belt of straw and ivy buds,
Thy coral clasps and amber studs,
All these in me no means can move
20 To come to thee and be thy love.

But could youth last and love still breed,
Had joys no date nor age no need,
Then these delights my mind might move
To live with thee and be thy love.

WILLIAM SHAKESPEARE (1564–1616)

Sonnet 55

Not marble nor the gilded monuments
Of princes shall outlive this powerful rime;
But you shall shine more bright in these contents
Than unswept stone, besmeared with sluttish time.
5 When wasteful war shall statues overturn,
And broils root out the work of masonry,

Nor Mars his sword nor war's quick fire shall burn
The living record of your memory.
'Gainst death and all oblivious enmity
10 Shall you pace forth; your praise shall still find room
Even in the eyes of all posterity
That wear this world out to the ending doom.
   So, till the Judgment that yourself arise,
   You live in this, and dwell in lovers' eyes.

JOHN DONNE (1572–1631)

Sonnet 7

At the round earth's imagined corners, blow
Your trumpets, angels, and arise, arise
From death, you numberless infinities
Of souls, and to your scattered bodies go;
5 All whom the flood did, and fire shall o'erthrow;
All whom war, dearth, age, agues, tyrannies,
Despair, law, chance, hath slain, and you whose eyes
Shall behold God, and never taste death's woe.
But let them sleep, Lord, and me mourn a space,
10 For if above all these my sins abound,
'Tis late to ask abundance of thy grace
When we are there; here on this lowly ground
Teach me how to repent; for that's as good
As if thou hadst sealed my pardon with thy blood.

ROBERT HERRICK (1591–1674)

The Night-Piece, to Julia

Her eyes the glowworm lend thee;
The shooting stars attend thee;
   And the elves also,
   Whose little eyes glow
5 Like the sparks of fire, befriend thee.

No will-o'-the-wisp mislight thee;
Nor snake or slowworm bite thee;
   But on, on thy way,
   Not making a stay,
10 Since ghost there's none to affright thee.

Let not the dark thee cumber;
What though the moon does slumber?
    The stars of the night
    Will lend thee their light,
15 Like tapers clear without number.

Then, Julia, let me woo thee,
Thus, thus to come unto me;
    And when I shall meet
    Thy silvery feet,
20 My soul I'll pour into thee.

SIR JOHN SUCKLING (1609–1642)

The Constant Lover

Out upon it! I have loved
    Three whole days together;
And am like to love three more,
    If it prove fair weather!

5 Time shall moult away his wings,
    Ere he shall discover
In the whole wide world again
    Such a constant lover.

But the spite on't is, no praise
10   Is due at all to me:
Love with me had made no stays,
    Had it any been but she.

THOMAS CAREW (1594?–1639?)

Ingrateful Beauty Threatened

Know, Celia (since thou art so proud)
    'Twas I that gave thee thy renown;
Thou hadst in the forgotten crowd
    Of common beauties lived unknown,
5 Had not my verse exhaled thy name,
And with it imped[1] the wings of fame.

---

[1] Repaired, made stronger.

That killing power is none of thine,
   I gave it to thy voice and eyes;
Thy sweets, thy graces, all are mine;
10   Thou art my star, shin'st in my skies;
Then dart not from thy borrowed sphere[2]
Lightning on him that fixed thee there.

Tempt me with such affrights[3] no more,
   Lest what I made, I uncreate;
15 Let fools thy mystic forms adore,
   I know thee in thy mortal state;
Wise poets, that wrapped truth in tales,
Knew her themselves, through all her veils.

ALEXANDER POPE (1688–1744)

Ode on Solitude

Happy the man whose wish and care
   A few paternal acres bound,
Content to breathe his native air,
         In his own ground.

5 Whose herds with milk, whose fields with bread,
   Whose flocks supply him with attire,
Whose trees in summer yield him shade,
         In winter fire.

Blest, who can unconcernedly find
10   Hours, days, and years slide soft away,
In health of body, peace of mind,
         Quiet by day,

Sound sleep by night; study and ease,
   Together mixed; sweet recreation;
15 And innocence, which most does please
         With meditation.

Thus let me live, unseen, unknown;
   Thus unlamented let me die;
Steal from the world, and not a stone
20   Tell where I lie.

---

[2] The place (or orbit) in the sky to which my verses have raised you.
[3] Frights.

WILLIAM BLAKE (1757–1827)

London

I wander thro' each charter'd street,
Near where the charter'd Thames does flow,
And mark in every face I meet
Marks of weakness, marks of woe.

5 In every cry of every Man,
In every Infant's cry of fear,
In every voice, in every ban,
The mind-forg'd manacles I hear.

How the Chimney-sweeper's cry
10 Every blackning Church appalls;
And the hapless Soldier's sigh
Runs in blood down Palace walls.

But most thro' midnight streets I hear
How the youthful Harlot's curse
15 Blasts the new-born Infant's tear,
And blights with plagues the Marriage hearse.

SAMUEL TAYLOR COLERIDGE (1772–1834)

Kubla Khan

In Xanadu did Kubla Kahn
A stately pleasure-dome decree:
Where Alph, the sacred river, ran
Through caverns measureless to man
5   Down to a sunless sea.
So twice five miles of fertile ground
With walls and towers were girdled round:
And there were gardens bright with sinuous rills,
Where blossomed many an incense-bearing tree;
10 And here were forests ancient as the hills,
Enfolding sunny spots of greenery.

But oh! that deep romantic chasm which slanted
Down the green hill athwart a cedarn cover!
A savage place! as holy and enchanted
15 As e'er beneath a waning moon was haunted
By woman wailing for her demon-lover!

And from this chasm, with ceaseless turmoil seething,
As if this earth in thick pants were breathing,
A mighty fountain momently was forced:
20 Amid whose swift half-intermitted burst
Huge fragments vaulted like rebounding hail,
Or chaffy grain beneath the thresher's flail:
And 'mid these dancing rocks at once and ever
It flung up momently the sacred river.
25 Five miles meandering with a mazy motion
Through wood and dale the sacred river ran,
Then reached the caverns measureless to man,

And sank in tumult to a lifeless ocean:
And 'mid this tumult Kubla heard from far
30 Ancestral voices prophesying war!

The shadow of the dome of pleasure
Floated midway on the waves;
Where was heard the mingled measure
From the fountain and the caves.

35 It was a miracle of rare device,
A sunny pleasure-dome with caves of ice!

A damsel with a dulcimer
In a vision once I saw:
It was an Abyssinian maid,
40 And on her dulcimer she played,
Singing of Mount Abora.
Could I revive within me
Her symphony and song,
To such a deep delight 'twould win me,

45 That with music loud and long,
I would build that dome in air,
That sunny dome! those caves of ice!
And all who heard should see them there,
And all should cry, Beware! Beware!
50 His flashing eyes, his floating hair!
Weave a circle round him thrice,
And close your eyes with holy dread,
For he on honey-dew hath fed,
And drunk the milk of Paradise.

ALFRED, LORD TENNYSON (1809–1892)

Ulysses

It little profits that an idle king,
By this still hearth, among these barren crags,
Matched with an aged wife, I mete and dole
Unequal laws unto a savage race,
5 That hoard, and sleep, and feed, and know not me.
I cannot rest from travel; I will drink
Life to the lees. All times I have enjoyed
Greatly, have suffered greatly, both with those
That loved me, and alone; on shore, and when
10 Through scudding drifts the rainy Hyades[1]
Vexed the dim sea: I am become a name;
For always roaming with a hungry heart
Much have I seen and known—cities of men
And manners, climates, councils, governments,
15 Myself not least, but honored of them all;
And drunk delight of battle with my peers,
Far on the ringing plains of windy Troy.
I am a part of all that I have met;
Yet all experience is an arch wherethrough
20 Gleams that untraveled world whose margin fades
For ever and for ever when I move.
How dull it is to pause, to make an end,
To rust unburnished, not to shine in use!
As though to breathe were life! Life piled on life
25 Were all too little, and of one to me
Little remains; but every hour is saved
From that eternal silence, something more,
A bringer of new things; and vile it were
For some three suns to store and hoard myself,
30 And this gray spirit yearning in desire
To follow knowledge like a sinking star,
Beyond the utmost bound of human thought.

This is my son, mine own Telemachus,
To whom I leave the scepter and the isle—
35 Well-loved of me, discerning to fulfil
This labor, by slow prudence to make mild
A rugged people, and through soft degrees

---

[1] A group of stars in the constellation Taurus, whose rise with the sun heralded the spring rains.

Subdue them to the useful and the good.
Most blameless is he, centered in the sphere
40 Of common duties, decent not to fail
In offices of tenderness, and pay
Meet adoration to my household gods,
When I am gone. He works his work, I mine.

There lies the port; the vessel puffs her sail;
45 There gloom the dark, broad seas. My mariners,
Souls that have toiled, and wrought, and thought with me—
That ever with a frolic welcome took
The thunder and the sunshine, and opposed
Free hearts, free foreheads—you and I are old;
50 Old age hath yet his honor and his toil.
Death closes all; but something ere the end,
Some work of noble note, may yet be done,
Not unbecoming men that strove with Gods.
The lights begin to twinkle from the rocks:
55 The long day wanes: the slow moon climbs: the deep
Moans round with many voices. Come, my friends,
'Tis not too late to seek a newer world.
Push off, and sitting well in order smite
The sounding furrows; for my purpose holds
60 To sail beyond the sunset, and the baths
Of all the western stars, until I die.
It may be that the gulfs will wash us down;
It may be we shall touch the Happy Isles,
And see the great Achilles, whom we knew.
65 Though much is taken, much abides; and though
We are not now that strength which in old days
Moved earth and heaven, that which we are, we are;
One equal temper of heroic hearts,
Made weak by time and fate, but strong in will
70 To strive, to seek, to find, and not to yield.

ROBERT BROWNING (1812–1889)

The Bishop Orders His Tomb at Saint Praxed's Church

Rome, 15—

Vanity, saith the preacher, vanity!
Draw round my bed: is Anselm keeping back?

Nephews[1]—sons mine . . . ah God, I know not! Well—
She, men would have to be your mother once,
5 Old Gandolf envied me, so fair she was!
What's done is done, and she is dead beside,
Dead long ago, and I am Bishop since,
And as she died so must we die ourselves,
And thence ye may perceive the world's a dream.
10 Life, how and what is it? As here I lie
In this state-chamber, dying by degrees,
Hours and long hours in the dead night, I ask
"Do I live, am I dead?" Peace, peace seems all.
Saint Praxed's ever was the church for peace;
15 And so, about this tomb of mine. I fought
With tooth and nail to save my niche, ye know:
—Old Gandolf cozened me, despite my care;
Shrewd was that snatch from out the corner South
He graced his carrion with, God curse the same!
20 Yet still my niche is not so cramped but thence
One sees the pulpit o' the epistle side,[2]
And somewhat of the choir, those silent seats,
And up into the aery dome where live
The angels, and a sunbeam's sure to lurk:
25 And I shall fill my slab of basalt there,
And 'neath my tabernacle take my rest,
With those nine columns round me, two and two,
The odd one at my feet where Anselm stands:
Peach-blossom marble all, the rare, the ripe
30 As fresh-poured red wine of a mighty pulse.
—Old Gandolf with his paltry onion-stone,
Put me where I may look at him! True peach,
Rosy and flawless: how I earned the prize!
Draw close: that conflagration of my church
35 —What then? So much was saved if aught were missed!
My sons, ye would not be my death? Go dig
The white-grape vineyard where the oil-press stood,
Drop water gently till the surface sink,
And if ye find . . . Ah God, I know not, I! . . .
40 Bedded in store of rotten fig-leaves soft,
And corded up in a tight olive-frail,
Some lump, ah God, of *lapis lazuli,*

---

[1] Euphemism for illegitimate sons.
[2] The right-hand side, as one faces the altar.

Big as a Jew's head cut off at the nape,
Blue as a vein o'er the Madonna's breast . . .
45 Sons, all have I bequeathed you, villas, all,
That brave Frascati villa with its bath,
So, let the blue lump poise between my knees,
Like God the Father's globe on both his hands
Ye worship in the Jesu Church so gay,
50 For Gandolf shall not choose but see and burst!
Swift as a weaver's shuttle fleet our years:
Man goeth to the grave, and where is he?
Did I say basalt for my slab, sons? Black—
'Twas ever antique-black I meant! How else
55 Shall ye contrast my frieze to come beneath?
The bas-relief in bronze ye promised me,
Those Pans and Nymphs ye wot of, and perchance
Some tripod,[3] thyrsus,[4] with a vase or so,
The Saviour at his sermon on the mount,
60 Saint Praxed in a glory, and one Pan
Ready to twitch the Nymph's last garment off,
And Moses with the tables . . . but I know
Ye mark me not! What do they whisper thee,
Child of my bowels, Anselm? Ah, ye hope
65 To revel down my villas while I gasp
Bricked o'er with beggar's moldy travertine
Which Gandolf from his tomb-top chuckles at!
Nay, boys, ye love me—all of jasper, then!
'Tis jasper ye stand pledged to, lest I grieve
70 My bath must needs be left behind, alas!
One block, pure green as a pistachio nut,
There's plenty jasper somewhere in the world—
And have I not Saint Praxed's ear to pray
Horses for ye, and brown Greek manuscripts,
75 And mistresses with great smooth marbly limbs?
—That's if ye carve my epitaph aright,
Choice Latin, picked phrase, Tully's[5] every word,
No gaudy ware like Gandolf's second line—
Tully, my masters? Ulpian[6] serves his need!
80 And then how I shall lie through centuries,
And hear the blessed mutter of the mass,
And see God made and eaten all day long,

---

[3] Three-legged stool used by the oracle at Delphi.
[4] Staff carried by Dionysus and his followers.
[5] Marcus Tullius Cicero, master of Latin prose style.
[6] Domitius Ulpianus, third century Roman jurist, noted for bad prose.

And feel the steady candle-flame, and taste
Good strong thick stupefying incense-smoke!
85 For as I lie here, hours of the dead night,
Dying in state and by such slow degrees,
I fold my arms as if they clasped a crook,
And stretch my feet forth straight as stone can point,
And let the bedclothes, for a mortcloth, drop
90 Into great laps and folds of sculptor's-work:
And as yon tapers dwindle, and strange thoughts
Grow, with a certain humming in my ears,
About the life before I lived this life,
And this life too, popes, cardinals, and priests,
95 Saint Praxed at his sermon on the mount,[7]
Your tall pale mother with her talking eyes,
And new-found agate urns as fresh as day,
And marble's language, Latin pure, discreet
—Aha, ELUCESCEBAT[8] quoth our friend?
100 No Tully, said I, Ulpian at the best!
Evil and brief hath been my pilgrimage.
All *lapis*, all, sons! Else I give the Pope
My villas! Will ye ever eat my heart?
Ever your eyes were as a lizard's quick,
105 They glitter like your mother's for my soul,
Or ye would heighten my impoverished frieze,
Piece out its starved design, and fill my vase
With grapes, and add a vizor and a Term,[9]
And to the tripod you would tie a lynx
110 That in his struggle throws the thyrsus down,
To comfort me on my entablature
Whereon I am to lie till I must ask
"Do I live, am I dead?" There, leave me, there!
For ye have stabbed me with ingratitude
115 To death—ye wish it—God, ye wish it! Stone—
Gritstone, a-crumble! Clammy squares which sweat
As if the corpse they keep were oozing through—
And no more *lapis* to delight the world!
Well go! I bless ye. Fewer tapers there,
120 But in a row: and, going, turn your backs
—Aye, like departing altar-ministrants,
And leave me in my church, the church for peace,

---

[7] The bishop's failing mind attributes the Sermon on the Mount to Saint Praxed (a woman) instead of Christ.
[8] "He was illustrious," an example of Ulpian Latin.
[9] A mask and bust on a pedestal.

That I may watch at leisure if he leers—
Old Gandolf, at me, from his onion-stone,
125 As still he envied me, so fair she was!

ROBERT BROWNING (1812–1889)

Home-Thoughts, from Abroad

1

Oh, to be in England
Now that April's there,
And whoever wakes in England
Sees, some morning, unaware,
5 That the lowest boughs and the brushwood sheaf
Round the elm-tree bole are in tiny leaf,
While the chaffinch sings on the orchard bough
In England—now!

2

And after April, when May follows,
10 And the whitethroat builds, and all the swallows!
Hark, where my blossomed pear-tree in the hedge
Leans to the field and scatters on the clover
Blossoms and dewdrops—at the bent spray's edge—
That's the wise thrush; he sings each song twice over,
15 Lest you should think he never could recapture
The first fine careless rapture!
And though the fields look rough with hoary dew,
All will be gay when noontide wakes anew
The buttercups, the little children's dower
20 —Far brighter than this gaudy melon-flower!

WALT WHITMAN (1819–1892)

Out of the Cradle Endlessly Rocking

Out of the cradle endlessly rocking,
Out of the mocking-bird's throat, the musical shuttle,
Out of the Ninth-month midnight,
Over the sterile sands and the fields beyond, where the child leaving
his bed wander'd alone, bareheaded, barefoot,

5 Down from the shower'd halo,
Up from the mystic play of shadows twining and twisting as if they
    were alive,
Out from the patches of briers and blackberries,
From the memories of the bird that chanted to me,
From your memories sad brother, from the fitful risings and fallings
    I heard,
10 From under that yellow half-moon late-risen and swollen as if with
    tears,
From those beginning notes of yearning and love there in the mist,
From the thousand responses of my heart never to cease,
From the myriad thence-arous'd words,
From the word stronger and more delicious than any,
15 From such as now they start the scene revisiting,
As a flock, twittering, rising, or overhead passing,
Borne hither, ere all eludes me, hurriedly,
A man, yet by these tears a little boy again,
Throwing myself on the sand, confronting the waves,
20 I, chanter of pains and joys, uniter of here and hereafter,
Taking all hints to use them, but swiftly leaping beyond them,
A reminiscence sing.

Once Paumanok,[1]
When the lilac-scent was in the air and Fifth-month grass was grow-
    ing,
25 Up this seashore in some briers,
Two feather'd guests from Alabama, two together,
And their nest, and four light-green eggs spotted with brown,
And every day the he-bird to and fro near at hand,
And every day the she-bird crouch'd on her nest, silent, with bright
    eyes,
30 And every day I, a curious boy, never too close, never disturbing
    them,
Cautiously peering, absorbing, translating.

Shine! shine! shine!
Pour down your warmth, great sun!
While we bask, we two together.

35 *Two together!*
Winds blow south, or winds blow north,

---

[1] The Indian name for Long Island.

Day come white, or night come black,
Home, or rivers and mountains from home,
Singing all time, minding no time,
40 *While we two keep together.*

Till of a sudden,
May be kill'd unknown to her mate,
One forenoon, the she-bird crouch'd not on the nest,
Nor return'd that afternoon, nor the next,
45 Nor ever appear'd again.

And thenceforward all summer in the sound of the sea,
And at night under the full of the moon in calmer weather,
Over the hoarse surging of the sea,
Or flitting from brier to brier by day,
50 I saw, I heard at intervals the remaining one, the he-bird,
The solitary guest from Alabama.

Blow! blow! blow!
Blow up sea-winds along Paumanok's shore;
I wait and I wait till you blow my mate to me.

55 Yes, when the stars glisten'd,
All night long on the prong of a moss-scallop'd stake,
Down almost amid the slapping waves,
Sat the lone singer wonderful causing tears.

He call'd on his mate,
60 He pour'd forth the meanings which I of all men know.

Yes my brother I know,
The rest might not, but I have treasur'd every note,
For more than once dimly down to the beach gliding,
Silent, avoiding the moonbeams, blending myself with the shadows,
65 Recalling now the obscure shapes, the echoes, the sounds and sights
       after their sorts,
The white arms out in the breakers tirelessly tossing,
I, with bare feet, a child, the wind wafting my hair,
Listen'd long and long.

Listen'd to keep, to sing, now translating the notes,
70 Following you my brother.

Soothe! soothe! soothe!
Close on its wave soothes the wave behind,

And again another behind embracing and lapping, every one close,
But my love soothes not me, not me.

75 *Low hangs the moon, it rose late,*
    It is lagging—O I think it is heavy with love, with love.

O madly the sea pushes upon the land,
With love, with love.

O night! do I not see my love fluttering out among the breakers?
80 *What is that little black thing I see there in the white?*

Loud! loud! loud!
Loud I call to you, my love!
High and clear I shoot my voice over the waves,
Surely you must know who is here, is here,
85 *You must know who I am, my love.*

Low-hanging moon!
What is that dusky spot in your brown yellow?
O it is the shape, the shape of my mate!
O moon do not keep her from me any longer.

90 *Land! land! O land!*
    Whichever way I turn, O I think you could give me my mate back
        again if you only would,
    For I am almost sure I see her dimly whichever way I look.

O rising stars!
Perhaps the one I want so much will rise, will rise with some of you.

95 *O throat! O trembling throat!*
    Sound clearer through the atmosphere!
    Pierce the woods, the earth,
    Somewhere listening to catch you must be the one I want.

Shake out carols!
100 *Solitary here, the night's carols!*
    Carols of lonesome love! death's carols!
    Carols under that lagging, yellow, waning moon!
    O under that moon where she droops almost down into the sea!
    O reckless despairing carols.

105 *But soft! sink low!*
    Soft! let me just murmur,

And do you wait a moment you husky-nois'd sea,
For somewhere I believe I heard my mate responding to me,
So faint, I must be still, be still to listen,
110 But not altogether still, for then she might not come immediately
    to me.

Hither my love!
Here I am! here!
With this just-sustain'd note I announce myself to you,
This gentle call is for you my love, for you.

115 Do not be decoy'd elsewhere,
    That is the whistle of the wind, it is not my voice,
    That is the fluttering, the fluttering of the spray,
    Those are the shadows of leaves.

O darkness! O in vain!
120 O I am very sick and sorrowful.

O brown halo in the sky near the moon, drooping upon the sea!
O troubled reflection in the sea!
O throat! O throbbing heart!
And I singing uselessly, uselessly all the night.

125 O past! O happy life! O songs of joy!
    In the air, in the woods, over fields,
    Loved! loved! loved! loved! loved!
    But my mate no more, no more with me!
    We two together no more.

130 The aria sinking,
    All else continuing, the stars shining,
    The winds blowing, the notes of the bird continuous echoing,
    With angry moans the fierce old mother incessantly moaning,
    On the sands of Paumanok's shore gray and rustling,
135 The yellow half-moon enlarged, sagging down, drooping, the face of
    the sea almost touching,
    The boy ecstatic, with his bare feet the waves, with his hair the
    atmosphere dallying,
    The love in the heart long pent, now loose, now at last tumultuously
    bursting,
    The aria's meaning, the ears, the soul, swiftly depositing,
    The strange tears down the cheeks coursing,
140 The colloquy there, the trio, each uttering,

The undertone, the savage old mother incessantly crying,
To the boy's soul's questions sullenly timing, some drown'd secret hissing,
To the outsetting bard.

Demon or bird! (said the boy's soul,)
145 Is it indeed toward your mate you sing? or is it really to me?
For I, that was a child, my tongue's use sleeping, now I have heard you,
Now in a moment I know what I am for, I awake,
And already a thousand singers, a thousand songs, clearer, louder and more sorrowful than yours,
A thousand warbling echoes have started to life within me, never to die.

150 O you singer solitary, singing by yourself, projecting me,
O solitary me listening, never more shall I cease perpetuating you,
Never more shall I escape, never more the reverberations,
Never more the cries of unsatisfied love be absent from me,
Never again leave me to be the peaceful child I was before what there in the night,
155 By the sea under the yellow and sagging moon,
The messenger there arous'd, the fire, the sweet hell within,
The unknown want, the destiny of me.

O give me the clew! (it lurks in the night here somewhere,)
O if I am to have so much, let me have more!

160 A word then, (for I will conquer it,)
The word final, superior to all,
Subtle, sent up—what is it?—I listen;
Are you whispering it, and have been all the time, you sea-waves?
Is that it from your liquid rims and wet sands?

165 Whereto answering, the sea,
Delaying not, hurrying not,
Whisper'd me through the night, and very plainly before daybreak,
Lisp'd to me the low and delicious word death,
And again death, death, death, death,
170 Hissing melodious, neither like the bird nor like my arous'd child's heart,
But edging near as privately for me rustling at my feet,
Creeping thence steadily up to my ears and laving me softly all over,
Death, death, death, death, death.

Which I do not forget,
175 But fuse the song of my dusky demon and brother,
That he sang to me in the moonlight on Paumanok's gray beach,
With the thousand responsive songs at random,
My own songs awaked from that hour,
And with them the key, the word up from the waves,
180 The word of the sweetest song and all songs,
That strong and delicious word which, creeping to my feet,
(Or like some old crone rocking the cradle, swathed in sweet gar-
ments, bending aside,)
The sea whisper'd me.

EMILY DICKINSON (1830–1886)

The Poets Light but Lamps (#883)

The Poets light but Lamps—
Themselves—go out—
The Wicks they stimulate—
If vital Light

5 Inhere as do the Suns—
Each Age a Lens
Disseminating their
Circumference—

A. E. HOUSMAN (1859–1936)

"Terence, This Is Stupid Stuff . . ."

"Terence, this is stupid stuff:
You eat your victuals fast enough;
There can't be much amiss, 'tis clear,
To see the rate you drink your beer.
5 But oh, good Lord, the verse you make,
It gives a chap the belly-ache.
The cow, the old cow, she is dead;
It sleeps well, the hornèd head:
We poor lads, 'tis our turn now
10 To hear such tunes as killed the cow.
Pretty friendship 'tis to rhyme
Your friends to death before their time
Moping melancholy mad:
Come, pipe a tune to dance to, lad."

15   Why, if 'tis dancing you would be,
      There's brisker pipes than poetry.
      Say, for what were hop-yards meant,
      Or why was Burton built on Trent?[1]
      Oh many a peer of England brews
20   Livelier liquor than the Muse,
      And malt does more than Milton can
      To justify God's ways to man.
      Ale, man, ale's the stuff to drink
      For fellows whom it hurts to think:
25   Look into the pewter pot
      To see the world as the world's not.
      And faith, 'tis pleasant till 'tis past:
      The mischief is that 'twill not last.
      Oh I have been to Ludlow fair
30   And left my necktie God knows where,
      And carried half-way home, or near,
      Pints and quarts of Ludlow beer:
      Then the world seemed none so bad,
      And I myself a sterling lad;
35   And down in lovely muck I've lain,
      Happy till I woke again.
      Then I saw the morning sky:
      Heigho, the tale was all a lie;
      The world, it was the old world yet,
40   I was I, my things were wet,
      And nothing now remained to do
      But begin the game anew.

      Therefore, since the world has still
      Much good, but much less good than ill,
45   And while the sun and moon endure
      Luck's a chance, but trouble's sure,
      I'd face it as a wise man would,
      And train for ill and not for good.
      'Tis true, the stuff I bring for sale
50   Is not so brisk a brew as ale:
      Out of a stem that scored the hand
      I wrung it in a weary land.
      But take it: if the smack is sour,
      The better for the embittered hour;

---

[1] A town noted for its breweries.

55 It should do good to heart and head
   When your soul is in my soul's stead;
   And I will friend you, if I may,
   In the dark and cloudy day.

   There was a king reigned in the East:
60 There, when kings will sit to feast,
   They get their fill before they think
   With poisoned meat and poisoned drink.
   He gathered all that springs to birth
   From the many-venomed earth;
65 First a little, thence to more,
   He sampled all her killing store;
   And easy, smiling, seasoned sound,
   Sate the king when healths went round.
   They put arsenic in his meat
70 And stared aghast to watch him eat;
   They poured strychnine in his cup
   And shook to see him drink it up:
   They shook, they stared as white's their shirt:
   Them it was their poison hurt.
75 —I tell the tale that I heard told.
   Mithridates,[2] he died old.

A. E. HOUSMAN (1859–1936)

To an Athlete Dying Young

The time you won your town the race
We chaired you through the market-place;
Man and boy stood cheering by,
And home we brought you shoulder-high.

5 To-day, the road all runners come,
  Shoulder-high we bring you home,
  And set you at your threshold down,
  Townsman of a stiller town.

  Smart lad, to slip betimes away
10 From fields where glory does not stay
   And early though the laurel grows
   It withers quicker than the rose.

---

[2] King of Pontus in the first century B.C., who made himself immune to certain
poisons by taking them frequently in small doses.

Eyes the shady night has shut
Cannot see the record cut,
15 And silence sounds no worse than cheers
After earth has stopped the ears:

Now you will not swell the rout
Of lads that wore their honors out,
Runners whom renown outran
20 And the name died before the man.

So set, before its echoes fade,
The fleet foot on the sill of shade,
And hold to the low lintel up
The still-defended challenge-cup.

25 And round that early-laurelled head
Will flock to gaze the strengthless dead,
And find unwithered on its curls
The garland briefer than a girl's.

EDWIN ARLINGTON ROBINSON (1869–1935)

Mr. Flood's Party

Old Eben Flood, climbing alone one night
Over the hill between the town below
And the forsaken upland hermitage
That held as much as he should ever know
5 On earth again of home, paused warily.
The road was his with not a native near;
And Eben, having leisure, said aloud,
For no man else in Tilbury Town to hear:

"Well, Mr. Flood, we have the harvest moon
10 Again, and we may not have many more;
The bird is on the wing, the poet says,[1]
And you and I have said it here before.
Drink to the bird." He raised up to the light
The jug that he had gone so far to fill,
15 And answered huskily: "Well, Mr. Flood,
Since you propose it, I believe I will."

---

[1] A reference to stanza 7 of *The Rubáiyát of Omar Khayyám*.

Alone, as if enduring to the end
A valiant armor of scarred hopes outworn,
He stood there in the middle of the road
20 Like Roland's ghost winding a silent horn.[2]
Below him, in the town among the trees,
Where friends of other days had honored him,
A phantom salutation of the dead
Rang thinly till old Eben's eyes were dim.

25 Then, as a mother lays her sleeping child
Down tenderly, fearing it may awake,
He set the jug down slowly at his feet
With trembling care, knowing that most things break;
And only when assured that on firm earth
30 It stood, as the uncertain lives of men
Assuredly did not, he paced away,
And with his hand extended paused again:

"Well, Mr. Flood, we have not met like this
In a long time; and many a change has come
35 To both of us, I fear, since last it was
We had a drop together. Welcome home!"
Convivially returning with himself,
Again he raised the jug up to the light;
And with an acquiescent quaver said:
40 "Well, Mr. Flood, if you insist, I might.

"Only a very little, Mr. Flood—
For auld lang syne. No more, sir; that will do."
So, for the time, apparently it did,
And Eben evidently thought so too;
45 For soon amid the silver loneliness
Of night he lifted up his voice and sang,
Secure, with only two moons listening,
Until the whole harmonious landscape rang—

"For auld lang syne." The weary throat gave out,
50 The last word wavered; and the song being done,
He raised again the jug regretfully

---

[2] In the medieval *Song of Roland,* the hero refuses to blow his horn for help at the Battle of Roncevaux and loses his life.

And shook his head, and was again alone.
There was not much that was ahead of him,
And there was nothing in the town below—
55 Where strangers would have shut the many doors
That many friends had opened long ago.

JAMES WELDON JOHNSON (1871–1938)

O Black and Unknown Bards

O black and unknown bards of long ago,
How came your lips to touch the sacred fire?
How, in your darkness, did you come to know
The power and beauty of the minstrel's lyre?
5 Who first from midst his bonds lifted his eyes?
Who first from out the still watch, lone and long,
Feeling the ancient faith of prophets rise
Within his dark-kept soul, burst into song?

Heart of what slave poured out such melody
10 As "Steal away to Jesus"? On its strains
His spirit must have nightly floated free,
Though still about his hands he felt his chains.
Who heard great "Jordan roll"? Whose starward eye
Saw chariot "swing low"? And who was he
15 That breathed that comforting, melodic sigh,
"Nobody knows de trouble I see"?

What merely living clod, what captive thing,
Could up toward God through all its darkness grope,
And find within its deadened heart to sing
20 These songs of sorrow, love and faith, and hope?
How did it catch that subtle undertone,
That note in music heard not with the ears?
How sound the elusive reed so seldom blown,
Which stirs the soul or melts the heart to tears?

25 Not that great German master[1] in his dream
Of harmonies that thundered amongst the stars

---

[1] Beethoven.

At the creation, ever heard a theme
Nobler than "Go down, Moses." Mark its bars,
How like a mighty trumpet-call they stir
30　The blood. Such are the notes that men have sung
Going to valorous deeds; such tones there were
That helped make history when Time was young.

There is a wide, wide wonder in it all,
That from degraded rest and servile toil
35　The fiery spirit of the seer should call
These simple children of the sun and soil.
O black slave singers, gone, forgot, unfamed,
You— you alone, of all the long, long line
Of those who've sung untaught, unknown, unnamed,
40　Have stretched out upward, seeking the divine.

You sang not deeds of heroes or of kings;
No chant of bloody war, no exulting paean
Of arms-won triumphs; but your humble strings
You touched in chord with music empyrean.
45　You sang far better than you knew; the songs
That for your listeners' hungry hearts sufficed
Still live—but more than this to you belongs:
You sang a race from wood and stone to Christ.

ROBERT FROST (1874–1963)

Birches

When I see birches bend to left and right
Across the lines of straighter darker trees,
I like to think some boy's been swinging them.
But swinging doesn't bend them down to stay
5　As ice-storms do. Often you must have seen them
Loaded with ice a sunny winter morning
After a rain. They click upon themselves
As the breeze rises, and turn many-colored
As the stir cracks and crazes their enamel.
10　Soon the sun's warmth makes them shed crystal shells
Shattering and avalanching on the snowcrust—
Such heaps of broken glass to sweep away
You'd think the inner dome of heaven had fallen.
They are dragged to the withered bracken by the load,

15   And they seem not to break; though once they are bowed
So low for long, they never right themselves:
You may see their trunks arching in the woods
Years afterwards, trailing their leaves on the ground
Like girls on hands and knees that throw their hair
20   Before them over their heads to dry in the sun.
But I was going to say when Truth broke in
With all her matter of fact about the ice-storm,
I should prefer to have some boy bend them
As he went out and in to fetch the cows—
25   Some boy too far from town to learn baseball,
Whose only play was what he found himself,
Summer or winter, and could play alone.
One by one he subdued his father's trees
By riding them down over and over again
30   Until he took the stiffness out of them,
And not one but hung limp, not one was left
For him to conquer. He learned all there was
To learn about not launching out too soon
And so not carrying the tree away
35   Clear to the ground. He always kept his poise
To the top branches, climbing carefully
With the same pains you use to fill a cup
Up to the brim, and even above the brim.
Then he flung outward, feet first, with a swish,
40   Kicking his way down through the air to the ground.
So was I once myself a swinger of birches.
And so I dream of going back to be.
It's when I'm weary of considerations,
And life is too much like a pathless wood
45   Where your face burns and tickles with the cobwebs
Broken across it, and one eye is weeping
From a twig's having lashed across it open.
I'd like to get away from earth awhile
And then come back to it and begin over.
50   May no fate willfully misunderstand me
And half grant what I wish and snatch me away
Not to return. Earth's the right place for love:
I don't know where it's likely to go better.
I'd like to go by climbing a birch tree,
55   And climb black branches up a snow-white trunk
Toward heaven, till the tree could bear no more,
But dipped its top and set me down again.
That would be good both going and coming back.
One could do worse than be a swinger of birches.

WALLACE STEVENS (1879–1955)

Thirteen Ways of Looking at a Blackbird

I

Among twenty snowy mountains,
The only moving thing
Was the eye of the blackbird.

II

I was of three minds,
5 Like a tree
In which there are three blackbirds.

III

The blackbird whirled in the autumn winds.
It was a small part of the pantomime.

IV

A man and a woman
10 Are one.
A man and a woman and a blackbird
Are one.

V

I do not know which to prefer,
The beauty of inflections,
15 Or the beauty of innuendoes,
The blackbird whistling
Or just after.

VI

Icicles filled the long window
With barbaric glass.
20 The shadow of the blackbird
Crossed it, to and fro.
The mood
Traced in the shadow
An indecipherable cause.

VII

25 O thin men of Haddam,[1]
Why do you imagine golden birds?

---

[1] A town in Connecticut; Stevens liked its name.

Do you not see how the blackbird
Walks around the feet
Of the women about you?

VIII

30 I know noble accents
And lucid, inescapable rhythms;
But I know, too,
That the blackbird is involved
In what I know.

IX

35 When the blackbird flew out of sight,
It marked the edge
Of one of many circles.

X

At the sight of blackbirds
Flying in a green light,
40 Even the bawds of euphony
Would cry out sharply.

XI

He rode over Connecticut
In a glass coach.
Once, a fear pierced him,
45 In that he mistook
The shadow of his equipage
For blackbirds.

XII

The river is moving.
The blackbird must be flying.

XIII

50 It was evening all afternoon.
It was snowing
And it was going to snow.
The blackbird sat
In the cedar-limbs.

WILLIAM BUTLER YEATS (1865–1939)

Leda and the Swan[1]

A sudden blow: the great wings beating still
Above the staggering girl, her thighs caressed
By the dark webs, her nape caught in his bill,
He holds her helpless breast upon his breast.

5 How can those terrified vague fingers push
The feathered glory from her loosening thighs?
And how can body, laid in that white rush,
But feel the strange heart beating where it lies?

A shudder in the loins engenders there
10 The broken wall, the burning roof and tower
And Agamemnon dead.
                                    Being so caught up,
So mastered by the brute blood of the air,
Did she put on his knowledge with his power
Before the indifferent beak could let her drop?

ROBINSON JEFFERS (1887–1962)

Love the Wild Swan

"I hate my verses, every line, every word.
Oh pale and brittle pencils ever to try
One grass-blade's curve, or the throat of one bird
That clings to twig, ruffled against white sky.
5 Oh cracked and twilight mirrors ever to catch
One color, one glinting flash, of the splendor of things.
Unlucky hunter, Oh bullets of wax,
The lion beauty, the wild-swan wings, the storm of the wings."
—This wild swan of a world is no hunter's game.
10 Better bullets than yours would miss the white breast,
Better mirrors than yours would crack in the flame.
Does it matter whether you hate your . . . self? At least
Love your eyes that can see, your mind that can
Hear the music, the thunder of the wings. Love the wild swan.

---

[1] Zeus, in the form of a swan, violated *Leda*, who gave birth to Helen and Clytemnestra. Helen's flight with Paris to Troy, leaving her husband Menelaus, Agamemnon's brother, caused the war between the Greeks and the Trojans. Clytemnestra murdered her husband Agamemnon on his return from victory at Troy.

MARIANNE MOORE (1887–1972)

Poetry

I, too, dislike it: there are things that are important beyond all this
      fiddle.
Reading it, however, with a perfect contempt for it, one discovers
      in
it after all, a place for the genuine.
      Hands that can grasp, eyes
5   that can dilate, hair that can rise
        if it must, these things are important not because a

high-sounding interpretation can be put upon them but because they
      are
useful. When they become so derivative as to become unintelligble,
the same thing may be said for all of us, that we
10   do not admire what
      we cannot understand: the bat
        holding on upside down or in quest of something to

eat, elephants pushing, a wild horse taking a roll, a tireless wolf
      under
a tree, the immovable critic twitching his skin like a horse that
      feels a flea, the base-
15   ball fan, the statistician—
      nor is it valid
        to discriminate against "business documents and

school-books";[1] all these phenomena are important. One must make
      a distinction
however: when dragged into prominence by half poets, the result
      is not poetry,
20   nor till the poets among us can be
      "literalists of
      the imagination" [2]—above
        insolence and triviality and can present

for inspection, "imaginary gardens with real toads in them," shall we
      have
25   it. In the meantime, if you demand on the one hand,

---

[1] Moore's note cites the Diary of Tolstoy: "poetry is everything with the exception
of business documents and school books."
[2] From Yeats, *Ideas of Good and Evil.*

the raw material of poetry in
  all its rawness and
  that which is on the other hand
    genuine, you are interested in poetry.

D. H. LAWRENCE (1885–1930)

Mystic

They call all experience of the senses *mystic*, when the experience is
  considered.
So an apple becomes *mystic* when I taste in it
the summer and the snows, the wild welter of earth
and the insistence of the sun.
5 All of which things I can surely taste in a good apple.
  Though some apples taste preponderantly of water, wet and sour
and some of too much sun, brackish sweet
like lagoon-water, that has been too much sunned.

If I say I taste these things in an apple, I am called *mystic*, which
  means a liar.
10 The only way to eat an apple is to hog it down like a pig
and taste nothing
that is *real*.

But if I eat an apple, I like to eat it with all my senses awake.
Hogging it down like a pig I call the feeding of corpses.

T. S. ELIOT (1888–1965)

The Love Song of J. Alfred Prufrock

S'io credesse che mia risposta fosse
A persona che mai tornasse al mondo,
Questa fiamma staria senza piu scosse.
Ma perciocche giammai di questo fondo
Non torno vivo alcun, s'i'odo il vero,
Senza tema d'infamia ti rispondo.[1]

---

[1] "If I thought that my response were given to one who would ever return to the
world, this flame would move no more. But since never from this depth has man
returned alive, if what I hear is true, without fear of infamy I answer thee." In
Dante's *Inferno* these words are addressed to the poet by the spirit of Guido da
Montefeltro.

Let us go then, you and I,
When the evening is spread out against the sky
Like a patient etherized upon a table;
Let us go, through certain half-deserted streets,
5 The muttering retreats
Of restless nights in one-night cheap hotels
And sawdust restaurants with oyster-shells:
Streets that follow like a tedious argument
Of insidious intent
10 To lead you to an overwhelming question . . .

Oh, do not ask, "What is it?"
Let us go and make our visit.

In the room the women come and go
Talking of Michelangelo.

15 The yellow fog that rubs its back upon the window-panes
The yellow smoke that rubs its muzzle on the window-panes
Licked its tongue into the corners of the evening,
Lingered upon the pools that stand in drains,
Let fall upon its back the soot that falls from chimneys,
20 Slipped by the terrace, made a sudden leap,
And seeing that it was a soft October night,
Curled once about the house, and fell asleep.

And indeed there will be time
For the yellow smoke that slides along the street,
25 Rubbing its back upon the window-panes;
There will be time, there will be time
To prepare a face to meet the faces that you meet;
There will be time to murder and create,
And time for all the works and days of hands
30 That lift and drop a question on your plate;
Time for you and time for me,
And time yet for a hundred indecisions,
And for a hundred visions and revisions,
Before the taking of a toast and tea.

35 In the room the women come and go
Talking of Michelangelo.

And indeed there will be time
To wonder, "Do I dare?" and, "Do I dare?"
Time to turn back and descend the stair,

40 With a bald spot in the middle of my hair—
  [They will say: "How his hair is growing thin!"]
  My morning coat, my collar mounting firmly to the chin,
  My necktie rich and modest, but asserted by a simple pin—
  [They will say: "But how his arms and legs are thin!"]
45 Do I dare
  Disturb the universe?
  In a minute there is time
  For decisions and revisions which a minute will reverse.

  For I have known them all already, known them all:
50 Have known the evenings, mornings, afternoons,
  I have measured out my life with coffee spoons;
  I know the voices dying with a dying fall
  Beneath the music from a farther room.
     So how should I presume?

55 And I have known the eyes already, known them all—
  The eyes that fix you in a formulated phrase,
  And when I am formulated, sprawling on a pin,
  When I am pinned and wriggling on the wall,
  Then how should I begin
60 To spit out all the butt-ends of my days and ways?
     And how should I presume?

  And I have known the arms already, known them all—
  Arms that are braceleted and white and bare
  [But in the lamplight, downed with light brown hair!]
65 Is it perfume from a dress
  That makes me so digress?
  Arms that lie along a table, or wrap about a shawl.
     And should I then presume?
     And how should I begin?

               .   .   .   .   .

70 Shall I say, I have gone at dusk through narrow streets
  And watched the smoke that rises from the pipes
  Of lonely men in shirt-sleeves, leaning out of windows? . . .

  I should have been a pair of ragged claws
  Scuttling across the floors of silent seas.

               .   .   .   .   .

75 And the afternoon, the evening, sleeps so peacefully!
  Smoothed by long fingers,
  Asleep . . . tired . . . or it malingers,
  Stretched on the floor, here beside you and me.

Should I, after tea and cakes and ices,
80 Have the strength to force the moment to its crisis?
But though I have wept and fasted, wept and prayed,
Though I have seen my head [grown slightly bald] brought in upon a
    platter,
I am no prophet—and here's no great matter;
I have seen the moment of my greatness flicker,
85 And I have seen the eternal Footman hold my coat, and snicker,
And in short, I was afraid.

And would it have been worth it, after all,
After the cups, the marmalade, the tea,
Among the porcelain, among some talk of you and me,
90 Would it have been worth while,
To have bitten off the matter with a smile,
To have squeezed the universe into a ball
To roll it toward some overwhelming question,

To say: "I am Lazarus, come from the dead,
95 Come back to tell you all, I shall tell you all"—
If one, settling a pillow by her head,
    Should say: "That is not what I meant at all.
    That is not it, at all."

And would it have been worth it, after all,
100 Would it have been worth while,
After the sunsets and the dooryards and the sprinkled streets,
After the novels, after the teacups, after the skirts that trail along the
    floor—
And this, and so much more?—
It is impossible to say just what I mean!
105 But as if a magic lantern threw the nerves in patterns on a screen:
Would it have been worth while
If one, settling a pillow or throwing off a shawl,
And turning toward the window, should say:
    "That is not it at all,
110   That is not what I meant, at all."

                    . . . . . .

No! I am not Prince Hamlet, nor was meant to be;
Am an attendant lord, one that will do
To swell a progress, start a scene or two,
Advise the prince; no doubt, an easy tool,
115 Deferential, glad to be of use,
    Politic, cautious, and meticulous;
    Full of high sentence, but a bit obtuse;

At times, indeed, almost ridiculous—
Almost, at times, the Fool.

120 I grow old . . . I grow old . . .
I shall wear the bottoms of my trousers rolled.

Shall I part my hair behind? Do I dare to eat a peach?
I shall wear white flannel trousers, and walk upon the beach.
I have heard the mermaids singing, each to each.

125 I do not think that they will sing to me.

I have seen them riding seaward on the waves
Combing the white hair of the waves blown back
When the wind blows the water white and black.

We have lingered in the chambers of the sea
130 By sea-girls wreathed with seaweed red and brown
Till human voices wake us, and we drown.

ARCHIBALD MacLEISH (1892–1982)

Ars Poetica

A poem should be palpable and mute
As a globed fruit,

Dumb
As old medallions to the thumb,

5 Silent as the sleeve-worn stone
Of casement ledges where the moss has grown—

A poem should be wordless
As the flight of birds.

A poem should be motionless in time
10 As the moon climbs,

Leaving, as the moon releases
Twig by twig the night-entangled trees,

Leaving, as the moon behind the winter leaves
Memory by memory the mind—

15 A poem should be motionless in time
As the moon climbs.

A poem should be equal to:
Not true.

For all the history of grief
20 An empty doorway and a maple leaf.

For love
The leaning grasses and two lights above the sea—

A poem should not mean
But be.

E. E. CUMMINGS (1894–1963)

"next to of course god america i

"next to of course god america i
love you land of the pilgrims' and so forth oh
say can you see by the dawn's early my
country 'tis of centuries come and go
5 and are no more what of it we should worry
in every language even deafanddumb
thy sons acclaim your glorious name by gorry
by jingo by gee by gosh by gum
why talk of beauty what could be more beaut-
10 iful than these heroic happy dead
who rushed like lions to the roaring slaughter
they did not stop to think they died instead
then shall the voice of liberty be mute?"

He spoke. And drank rapidly a glass of water

W. H. AUDEN (1907–1973)

Musée des Beaux Arts[1]

About suffering they were never wrong,
The Old Masters: how well they understood
Its human position; how it takes place

---

[1] The Museum of Fine Arts in Brussels, where Brueghel's *Landscape with the Fall of Icarus* hangs.

While someone else is eating or opening a window or just walking
    dully along;
5 How, when the aged are reverently, passionately waiting
For the miraculous birth, there always must be
Children who did not specially want it to happen, skating
On a pond at the edge of the wood:
They never forgot
10 That even the dreadful martyrdom must run its course
Anyhow in a corner, some untidy spot
Where the dogs go on with their doggy life and the torturer's horse
Scratches its innocent behind on a tree.

In Brueghel's *Icarus*,[2] for instance: how everything turns away
15 Quite leisurely from the disaster; the plowman may
Have heard the splash, the forsaken cry,
But for him it was not an important failure; the sun shone
As it had to on the white legs disappearing into the green
Water; and the expensive delicate ship that must have seen
20 Something amazing, a boy falling out of the sky,
Had somewhere to get to and sailed calmly on.

DYLAN THOMAS (1914–1953)

In My Craft or Sullen Art

In my craft or sullen art
Exercised in the still night
When only the moon rages
And the lovers lie abed
5 With all their griefs in their arms,
I labor by singing light
Not for ambition or bread
Or the strut and trade of charms
On the ivory stages
10 But for the common wages
Of their most secret heart.

Not for the proud man apart
From the raging moon I write
On these spindrift pages
15 Nor for the towering dead

---

[2] In Greek mythology Icarus falls into the sea and drowns when he flies too close
to the sun on his wings of wax. In Brueghel's painting Icarus is an insignificant
part of the picture.

With their nightingales and psalms
But for the lovers, their arms
Round the griefs of the ages,
Who pay no praise or wages
20 Nor heed my craft or art.

GWENDOLYN BROOKS (1917–　　)

The Bean Eaters

They eat beans mostly, this old yellow pair .
Dinner is a casual affair.
Plain chipware on a plain and creaking wood,
Tin flatware.

5 Two who are Mostly Good.
Two who have lived their day,
But keep on putting on their clothes
And putting things away.

And remembering . . .
10 Remembering, with twinklings and twinges,
As they lean over the beans in their rented back room that is full of
beads and receipts and dolls and clothes, tobacco crumbs, vases
and fringes.

ROBERT LOWELL (1917–1977)

The Old Flame

My old flame, my wife!
Remember our lists of birds?
One morning last summer, I drove
by our house in Maine. It was still
5 on top of its hill—

Now a red ear of Indian maize
was splashed on the door.
Old Glory with thirteen stripes
hung on a pole. The clapboard
10 was old-red schoolhouse red.

Inside, a new landlord,
a new wife, a new broom!
Atlantic seaboard antique shop
pewter and plunder
15 shone in each room.

A new frontier!
No running next door
now to phone the sheriff
for his taxi to Bath
20   and the State Liquor Store!

No one saw your ghostly
imaginary lover
stare through the window,
and tighten
25   the scarf at his throat.

Health to the new people,
health to their flag, to their old
restored house on the hill!
Everything had been swept bare,
30   furnished, garnished and aired.

Everything's changed for the best—
how quivering and fierce we were,
there snowbound together,
simmering like wasps
35   in our tent of books!

Poor ghost, old love, speak
with your old voice
of flaming insight
that kept us awake all night.
40   In one bed and apart,

we heard the plow
groaning up hill—
a red light, then a blue,
as it tossed off the snow
45   to the side of the road.

LAWRENCE FERLINGHETTI (1919–   )

The pennycandystore beyond the El

The pennycandystore beyond the El
is where I first
            fell in love
                        with unreality
5 Jellybeans glowed in the semi-gloom
of that september afternoon

A cat upon the counter moved among
                         the licorice sticks
                and tootsie rolls
10   and Oh Boy Gum

Outside the leaves were falling as they died

A wind had blown away the sun
A girl ran in
Her hair was rainy
15 Her breasts were breathless in the little room

Outside the leaves were falling
                and they cried
                         Too soon! too soon!

ALLEN GINSBERG (1926–   )

A Supermarket in California

What thoughts I have of you tonight, Walt Whitman, for I walked
down the sidestreets under the trees with a headache self-conscious
looking at the full moon.

In my hungry fatigue, and shopping for images, I went into the
5 neon fruit supermarket, dreaming of your enumerations!

What peaches and what penumbras! Whole families shopping at
night! Aisles full of husbands! Wives in the avocados, babies in the
tomatoes!—and you, Garcia Lorca,[1] what were you doing down by the
watermelons?

10   I saw you, Walt Whitman, childless, lonely old grubber, poking
among the meats in the refrigerator and eyeing the grocery boys.

I heard you asking questions of each: Who killed the pork chops?
What price bananas? Are you my Angel?

I wandered in and out of the brilliant stacks of cans following you,
15 and followed in my imagination by the store detective.

We strode down the open corridors together in our solitary fancy
tasting artichokes, possessing every frozen delicacy, and never passing
the cashier.

---

[1] Federico García Lorca (1899–1936), Spanish poet and playwright. He was murdered at the start of the Spanish Civil War; his works were suppressed by the Franco
government.

Where are we going, Walt Whitman? The doors close in an hour.
20   Which way does your beard point tonight?

(I touch your book and dream of our odyssey in the supermarket
and feel absurd.)

Will we walk all night through solitary streets? The trees add shade
to shade, lights out in the houses, we'll both be lonely.

25   Will we stroll dreaming of the lost America of love past blue auto-
mobiles in driveways, home to our silent cottage?

Ah, dear father, graybeard, lonely old courage-teacher, what
America did you have when Charon quit poling his ferry and you got
out on a smoking bank and stood watching the boat disappear on the
30   black waters of Lethe?[2]

ANNE SEXTON (1928–1974)

Welcome Morning

There is joy
in all:
in the hair I brush each morning,
in the Cannon towel, newly washed,
5   that I rub my body with each morning,
in the chapel of eggs I cook
each morning,
in the outcry from the kettle
that heats my coffee,
10   each morning,
in the spoon and the chair,
that cry "hello there, Anne"
each morning,
in the godhead of the table
15   that I set my silver, plate, cup upon,
each morning.

All this is God,
right here in my pea green house,
each morning
20   and I mean,
though often forget,
to give thanks,
to faint down by the kitchen table

---

[2] Charon, in Greek myth, ferried the shades of the dead to Hades across Lethe, River
of Forgetfulness.

in a prayer of rejoicing
25   as the holy birds at the kitchen window
peck into their marriage of seeds.

So while I think of it,
let me paint a thank you on my palm
for this God, this laughter of the morning,
30   lest it go unspoken.

The Joy that isn't shared, I've heard,
dies young.

TED HUGHES (1930–   )

Pike

Pike, three inches long, perfect
Pike in all parts, green tigering the gold.
Killers from the egg: the malevolent aged grin.
They dance on the surface among the flies.

5   Or move, stunned by their own grandeur,
Over a bed of emerald, silhouette
Of submarine delicacy and horror.
A hundred feet long in their world.

In ponds, under the heat-struck lily pads—
10   Gloom of their stillness:
Logged on last year's black leaves, watching upwards.
Or hung in an amber cavern of weeds

The jaw's hooked clamp and fangs
Not to be changed at this date;
15   A life subdued to its instrument;
The gills kneading quietly, and the pectorals.

Three we kept behind glass,
Jungled in weed: three inches, four,
And four and a half: fed fry to them—
20   Suddenly there were two. Finally one

With a sag belly and the grin it was born with.
And indeed they spare nobody.
Two, six pounds each, over two feet long,
High and dry and dead in the willow-herb—

25 One jammed past its gills down the other's gullet:
   The outside eye stared: as a vice locks—
   The same iron in this eye
   Though its film shrank in death.

   A pond I fished, fifty yards across,
30 Whose lilies and muscular tench
   Had outlasted every visible stone
   Of the monastery that planted them—

   Stilled legendary depth:
   It was as deep as England. It held
35 Pike too immense to stir, so immense and old
   That past nightfall I dared not cast

   But silently cast and fished
   With the hair frozen on my head
   For what might move, for what eye might move.
40 The still splashes on the dark pond,

   Owls hushing the floating woods
   Frail on my ear against the dream
   Darkness beneath night's darkness had freed,
   That rose slowly towards me, watching.

SYLVIA PLATH (1932–1963)

Metaphors

   I'm a riddle in nine syllables,
   An elephant, a ponderous house,
   A melon strolling on two tendrils.
   O red fruit, ivory, fine timbers!
5 This loaf's big with its yeasty rising.
   Money's new-minted in this fat purse.
   I'm a means, a stage, a cow in calf.
   I've eaten a bag of green apples,
   Boarded the train there's no getting off.

AMIRI BARAKA (LeROI JONES) (1934–   )

W.W.

   Back home the black women are all beautiful,
   and the white ones fall back, cutoff from 1000
   years stacked booty, and Charles of the Ritz

where jooshladies turn into billy burke in blueglass
5 kicks. With wings, and jingly bew-teeful things.
The black women in Newark are fine. Even with all that grease
in their heads. I mean even the ones where the wigs
slide around, and they coming at you 75 degrees off course.
I could talk to them. Bring them around. To something.
10 Some kind of quick course, on the sidewalk, like Hey baby
why don't you take that thing off yo' haid. You look like
Miss Muffet in a runaway ugly machine. I mean. Like that.

DRAMA

1

Reading Drama

Analyzing Greek drama around 330 B.C., the philosopher Aristotle found each play to be composed of six parts: plot, character, thought, diction, spectacle, and music. Of these, he considered the plot—the putting together of diverse happenings to create a complete and unified action—to be the most important. Without plot, he says, there can be no play; for the chief purpose of drama is the acting-out of an action.

Characters come next in importance for Aristotle. Thought—by which he seems to mean not only the ideas expressed by the various speakers, but also their use of speech to sway the emotions of the audience—comes third. Diction, the choice of words, is fourth. Music and scenery, being pleasant and often impressive, but not essential, come last.

With the exception of music and spectacle, which apply only to plays in performance, Aristotle's categories are essentially the same categories we've been using in discussing fiction. The further we read in Aristotle, the more similarities we find: Aristotle warns would-be authors that their plots, to be complete, must have a natural beginning, middle, and end; that they must provide scope for their heroes to pass from happiness to unhappiness, or from unhappiness to happiness; and that they must be unified, containing nothing that could be taken away without leaving the drama incomplete.

In addition, Aristotle points out that the most important moments in the plot are those concerned with **reversals** and **recognition.** A reversal occurs when an action that is expected to have one result produces the opposite result instead. A recognition occurs when a character suddenly "recognizes" some fact or person, thus moving from a state of ignorance to a state of knowledge. In the best plays, the two events are joined and form the turning point of the play: the hero suddenly learns something of great personal importance, either by being informed of some facts by another character or by coming to a realization or insight himself. In either case, the result of the hero's enlightenment is a reversal, changing the course of the play's action and of the hero's life (from happiness to unhappiness or vice versa).

In discussing characterization Aristotle reminds us that all characters must be people basically like ourselves, though some may be better and some worse. And again, he insists that consistency and probability are the two most important standards of judgment. The writer must make sure that the characters' actions are consistent with their natures, and that their natures remain consistent throughout the drama.

If we have not already discussed all of these ideas, at least we have no difficulty in applying them to the fiction we've read. To discuss consistency of character, for instance, we need only look at the narrator of "Bartleby the Scrivener," with his deep and basically kindly desire for tranquility in human relations and his persistent and misplaced faith in money as a means of attaining that tranquility, or at the narrator of "My Man Bovanne," with her caring nature and her strong concern for individual dignity. The basic elements of drama, then, are the same as those of fiction. It is the method of presentation that differs.

Fiction is the telling of tales. Its roots go back to the archetypal figure of the storyteller, rehearsing old legends and inventing new marvels for the listeners who surround him. The importance of voice in fiction, therefore, can hardly be overemphasized. Indeed, as fiction has become a more silent experience, writers seem to have attached increasing importance to the question of what voice would speak through their works. Listening to stories is still enjoyable. Any good story can be read aloud and be enjoyed the better for it. But our society seems to feel that listening to tales is a pleasure most proper for children and for those who cannot read to themselves. For most of us, therefore, fiction is something read silently and alone. It involves one book, one writer, one reader. We discuss stories in company, but we tend to read them in solitude.

Drama—in performance, at least—is wholly different. It is not written for one voice, but for many. It depends not on storytellers but on actors, men and women who impersonate their tale's characters not only in voice, but also in motion, gesture, and appearance, making them live for our eyes as well as our ears. Moreover, it is written for many viewers, for only in the midst of an audience can we appreciate fully the magic of drama. Laughing alone at a joke in print is enjoyable; being one laughing person among a hundred people can be hilarious.

Actors know this well. They know how fully they must bring their characters alive for their audience. They know, too, how dependent they are on the audience's response if they are to perform well. Many actors have declared that the best performances are those during which the emotions portrayed on stage are caught and sent back by the audience until audience and actors alike are caught up in the atmosphere they have created between them, and the illusion of the play becomes more real than the realities of the world outside. Similarly, many have said that acting in films, where no audience is present to reflect the emotional impact of the scene, is a more difficult and less enjoyable form of acting than acting on the stage. Playgoers and filmgoers, in their turn, agree that the experience of attending a live performance has an electric quality not to be found in viewing a film.

The fervor with which most of us discuss a really good play or film we've just seen, as opposed to the milder delight with which we discuss a really good book, testifies to the power of drama to move and delight us. A knowledge of the origins of drama, about which we shall speak in the next chapter, may help explain the intensity of our response. Within this course, however, we are readers rather than viewers of drama. And so the very power of drama in performance is likely to raise questions for us. "Here we are," we say, "with no stage, no actors—nothing but a playscript in front of us. What can we expect from this experience?"

Reading drama is certainly different from reading fiction. Drama generally gives us no narrator to describe scenes and characters, to comment on the significance of the action, to tie scenes together, or to provide a unifying viewpoint. Instead, drama gives us several characters, distinguished in the text only by their names, talking mostly to each other instead of to us, intent on their own affairs, entering and leaving the scene in bewildering succession.

If we were watching a play, we would recognize the characters by their appearance, mannerisms, and voices. Knowing the characters, we would then find it easy to follow the action. When we read a play, however, we must do without these visual clues. Or, rather, we must supply them for ourselves. We must use the text as the play's director would, judging from its words and from the actions they describe how the play would look and sound on stage.

Reading plays, in fact, gives our imagination free rein. How would I stage this scene? What sort of actor would I want for this role? What kind of stage setting would I use? Or, what kind of camera work would I use in a film? Which would be my long shots, which my close-ups? What emotions would my filming be trying to capture?

Most of all, perhaps, you will think of the various characters as they are revealed in the text. What characteristics will each one exhibit? How will they carry themselves on stage? What tones of voice will they use in their speeches? How will they act toward each other?* The more clearly you can visualize the play's action and characters, the more readily the text will come alive for you.

Don't be afraid to experiment in your thinking. Actors, directors, and scene designers all allow themselves some freedom of interpretation when they put on a play. You can read for days about famous actors who have played Hamlet, each applying a very personal interpretation to emphasize one aspect or another of the prince's complex personality. Why should not we, as readers, enjoy the same freedom to visualize the play, interpreting and fitting together its parts to develop our vision of its conflicts and its meanings?

The text of a play will supply us with plenty of help. Since drama does depend so largely on the art of the actor, dramatists must create characters who can carry the play by their speeches and actions. Everything the actors (and readers) need must be contained in the speeches and stage directions. Here are some of the things we can look for.

We can look for characters who, like first-person narrators in fiction, reveal in their speech information about their habits, personalities, and thinking—information they do not always know they are giving us. We can expect to be wiser than most of these characters because we have the ability to stand apart from the action in which they participate, to see it fully or judge it objectively.

We can look for patterns in characterization and for conflicts between characters. We can look for characters who support each other and characters who oppose each other. We can expect to see strong characters opposed to weak ones, inflexible characters opposed to reasonable ones, good characters opposed to evil ones.

The speeches of the actors, therefore, set down in the play's text, will describe the play's characters for us, develop the action and conflict of the play, and contain the play's themes. The conflict between the ideas expressed in speeches will often be basic to the conflict of the play. Thus, in *Oedipus Rex,* much of the play's conflict centers around the question of whether it is wise or foolish for Oedipus to seek the truth about Laios' murder. And in *Hamlet,* the conflict between Hamlet and Claudius over who shall rule Denmark becomes almost secondary to the mental conflicts between Hamlet and other characters (and within Hamlet himself) on the moral and practical issues arising from the political conflict.

Patterns of speech, characterization, and thought, then, are as important in drama as they are in fiction. Patterns of language and of imagery, too, are important. Some plays, such as *A Doll's House,* try to imitate everyday speech patterns in their language. Others shift those patterns. *The Impor-*

---

* A handy device for keeping track of a play's characters, in fact, is to "cast" the play for yourself with actors you'd enjoy watching in it. Then you can follow those actors through each scene, imagining how they would interpret the roles.

tance of Being Earnest, while keeping a fairly close semblance of natural speech rhythms and vocabulary, permits its characters a greater fluency of speech and aptness of comic rejoinder than ordinary conversation would show. Still other plays, such as *Hamlet* or *Oedipus Rex,* use the full power of poetry in their speeches. Dialogue in these plays can move in a few lines from the accents of everyday speech to those of extreme poetic passion, as the playwrights draw from the rhythms of poetry a capacity for dignity and grandeur and openness of expression that the limits of everyday speech deny them.

Patterns of imagery, too, can be used to great effect in these poetic plays. But imagery, as we have seen already in our work with fiction, is not restricted to poetry. Certainly, *Hamlet* is the richest in imagery of the ten plays presented here. But all make some use of imagery, such as the imagery of physical and mental blindness in *Oedipus Rex.*

Reading drama, therefore, can offer an intensification of the pleasure provided by reading fiction. More richly patterned in action, language, and characterization than most short stories, allowing its readers more scope for interpretation and for the visual imagination, drama offers us a chance to be actors, director, and audience in one.

2 *Greek Tragedy*

Western drama is often said to have originated in ancient Greece. Certainly its two most outstanding forms, tragedy and comedy, began there.

About the beginnings of this drama, little is known, for few records have survived. We do know, however, that it began at festivals honoring Dionysus, or Bacchus, a god who was supposed to have taught men to cultivate grapes and make wine. Song and dance were the means by which this god was worshipped. At early festivals, choruses of fifty men dressed in tattered garments with wine-smeared faces or disguised as Dionysus' mythical companions, the satyrs, sang hymns praising the god's deeds while they half-danced, half-mimed his exploits. Eventually one man stepped out of the chorus and engaged his fellows in dialogue. Later still, the soloist began impersonating the god, thus dramatizing the events of which he was singing.

Sometime during this process, the content of the songs also shifted. Some still pertained to Dionysus, but some dealt with other, human, heroes. Although worshippers were reportedly shocked at the first introduction of the new tales, asking, "What has this to do with Dionysus?", the novelty soon became the rule. By 530 B.C., the performances were being called tragedies and were competing in Athens for an annual prize.

In the next hundred years, tragedy reached what Aristotle considered its full form. A second actor was added, and then a third. Episodes of dialogue among the actors, with the chorus occasionally joining in, became as important as the choric songs and dances with which they alternated. Painted backdrops, stage machinery, and special effects were introduced.

For all its developments, however, Greek drama remained a religious event. Plays were performed only at Dionysus' festivals; actors were considered his servants. Performances took place three times a year: twice at Athens, once at various rural festivals. The older of the Athenian festivals, the *Lenaea,* became the festival for comedy; but the *City Dionysia,* which drew visitors from all over Greece, was the festival for tragedy.

For this festival, three playwrights were chosen by Athenian authorities. Each was given a chorus and actors, who were paid and costumed by some rich citizen as a public service; each was allotted one day of the festival on which to perform. The performance would consist of three tragedies (sometimes on the same subject, sometimes not), followed by a satyr play, an obscene or satiric parody of some legendary event. At the end of the three days of playing, a jury of ten citizens, chosen by lot, judged the plays and awarded the prizes.* Any Athenian was welcome to attend these plays, which were held in a natural amphitheater that seated some 30,000 people. Since the theater was reported to be crowded at every performance, we may assume that virtually everybody who could attend, did.

All in all, drama in ancient Athens seems to have been regarded almost as a public possession. Looked on with a mixture of religious devotion, civic pride, and open enjoyment, it maintained a great and general popularity that seems to have declined only with the decline of Athens itself. And still the plays remained influential, both in themselves and in the theory of drama that Aristotle's comments on them provided. First the Romans copied them. Then, some 1500 years later, Renaissance playwrights took ideas from both Greek and Roman drama. We will discuss that development in the next chapter.

Tragedy and Comedy

Greek drama segregated its forms carefully. Tragedy dealt with the noble, the heroic, the sacrificial. In performance, three tragedies would be followed by a satyr play, which turned heroic figures into tricksters or clowns and often mocked the very legends that had supplied the day's

---

* Sophocles, the author of *Oedipus Rex,* held the all-time record of eighteen first prizes and is said never to have won less than second prize. Yet *Oedipus Rex* itself, which was praised by Aristotle and is still considered one of the finest of Greek tragedies, won only second prize when it was first produced.

tragedies. Comedy had its own festival, in which it could deal with the more practical aspirations of everyday people—good food, warm beds, and peaceful households and cities. The heroes of comedy battle such unheroic opponents as thieves, con men, unreasonable parents, and crooked politicians. Often, they must resort to trickery to outwit these unsavory sorts, who may very well be tricksters themselves. A happy ending is guaranteed.

Oedipus Rex and *Antigonê*

Oedipus Rex is, in many ways, the embodiment of Greek tragedy. It deals with a somewhat idealized, larger-than-life hero, a man caught in a dilemma between his ideals and his personal safety and fighting his way towards a terrifying knowledge. "Ah," cries the Shepherd in one climactic scene, "I am on the brink of dreadful speech." "And I of dreadful hearing," replies Oedipus. "Yet I must hear." This insistence on following through in a search, an action, the pursuit of an ideal has always attracted readers, perhaps because we all know how difficult that sort of courage is to sustain. It is the one force that is constant in tragedy.

The sad or terrible ending, incidentally, is not essential to tragedy. Some Greek tragedies end happily, in a reconciliation of their opposed forces, new knowledge having created new peace. The essentials of tragedy are the protagonist's own insistence on action or enlightenment and the ability of the play, however it ends, to arouse a sympathetic "fear and pity" (Aristotle's terms) in the audience as they watch the working-out of the hero's quest. *Oedipus Rex,* which begins on p. 637, clearly has these essentials.

Oedipus Rex gains much of its power from the unwavering intensity of its focus on the central character. But this focus, though not uncommon in tragedy, is also not essential to it. Many Greek tragedies have more than one central character. *The Trojan Women,* for example, has as heroines all the famous women who were caught up in the sack of Troy. *Antigonê,* which follows *Oedipus Rex* in this chapter, concentrates not so much on a single character as on the clash of wills between two characters. One of these characters is Kreon, Oedipus' uncle, now the ruler of Thebes; the other is Antigonê, Oedipus' daughter.

The action of *Antigonê* takes place some years after that of *Oedipus Rex*. In the time between the two plays, Oedipus' two sons have quarreled. In fact, just before *Antigonê* opens, one of the brothers (Polyneicês) has gathered a group of supporters and has attacked both his brother (Eteoclês) and the city of Thebes itself. In the battle, the two brothers have killed each other. Kreon, now ruling Thebes, has ordered a hero's funeral for Eteoclês, the defender of Thebes, but has refused burial to Polyneicês, Thebes's attacker. Antigonê's response to this proclamation, and Kreon's reaction to her response, form the action of the tragedy.

Throughout the play, Kreon's concern is for public welfare and order; he speaks most frequently as the voice of public authority, the defender of the public good. Antigonê's concern is for piety and for family ties. She speaks most often from her own conscience, as a private person. When she does speak of public matters, it is generally to contrast social law with divine law. Between these two forces of public and private good lies the play's tension. This is a play in which *thought,* Aristotle's third element of tragedy, is predominant. Yet, as with *Oedipus,* it is the strong-willed, dedicated nature of the antagonists that makes the play a true tragedy, not merely an argument. The issues involved are still argued; their expression here in tragedy is unique.

SOPHOCLES (496–406 B.C.)

Oedipus Rex

An English version by Dudley Fitts and Robert Fitzgerald

CHARACTERS

OEDIPUS, *King of Thebes, supposed son of Polybos and Meropê,*
    King and Queen of Corinth
IOKASTÊ, *wife of Oedipus and widow of the late King Laïos*
KREON, *brother of Iokastê, a prince of Thebes*
TEIRESIAS, *a blind seer who serves Apollo*
PRIEST
MESSENGER, *from Corinth*
SHEPHERD, *former servant of Laïos*
SECOND MESSENGER, *from the palace*
CHORUS OF THEBAN ELDERS
CHORAGOS, *leader of the Chorus*
ANTIGONÊ and ISMENÊ, *young daughters of Oedipus and*
    Iokastê. They appear in the Exodos but do not speak.
SUPPLIANTS, GUARDS, SERVANTS

THE SCENE. *Before the palace of* OEDIPUS, *King of Thebes. A central door and two lateral doors open onto a platform which runs the length of the façade. On the platform, right and left, are altars; and three steps lead down into the* orchestra *or chorus-ground. At the beginning of the action these steps are crowded by suppliants who have brought branches and chaplets of olive leaves and who sit in various attitudes of despair.* OEDIPUS *enters.*

PROLOGUE

OEDIPUS My children, generations of the living
    In the line of Kadmos,[1] nursed at his ancient hearth:
    Why have you strewn yourselves before these altars
5   In supplication, with your boughs and garlands?

---

[1] *Kadmos* founder of Thebes

The breath of incense rises from the city
With a sound of prayer and lamentation.
Children,
I would not have you speak through messengers,
5   And therefore I have come myself to hear you—
I, Oedipus, who bear the famous name.
(*To a* PRIEST) You, there, since you are eldest in the company,
Speak for them all, tell me what preys upon you,
Whether you come in dread, or crave some blessing:
10   Tell me, and never doubt that I will help you
In every way I can; I should be heartless
Were I not moved to find you suppliant here.

PRIEST   Great Oedipus, O powerful king of Thebes!
You see how all the ages of our people
15   Cling to your altar steps: here are boys
Who can barely stand alone, and here are priests
By weight of age, as I am a priest of God,
And young men chosen from those yet unmarried;
As for the others, all that multitude,
20   They wait with olive chaplets in the squares,
At the two shrines of Pallas, and where Apollo
Speaks in the glowing embers.
Your own eyes
Must tell you: Thebes is tossed on a murdering sea
25   And can not lift her head from the death surge.
A rust consumes the buds and fruits of the earth;
The herds are sick; children die unborn,
And labor is vain. The god of plague and pyre
Raids like detestable lightning through the city,
30   And all the house of Kadmos is laid waste,
All emptied, and all darkened: Death alone
Battens upon the misery of Thebes.

You are not one of the immortal gods, we know;
Yet we have come to you to make our prayer
35   As to the man surest in mortal ways
And wisest in the ways of God. You saved us
From the Sphinx, that flinty singer, and the tribute
We paid to her so long; yet you were never
Better informed than we, nor could we teach you:
40   A god's touch, it seems, enabled you to help us.

Therefore, O mighty power, we turn to you:
Find us our safety, find us a remedy,

Whether by counsel of the gods or of men.
A king of wisdom tested in the past
Can act in a time of troubles, and act well.
Noblest of men, restore

5   Life to your city! Think how all men call you
Liberator for your boldness long ago;
Ah, when your years of kingship are remembered,
Let them not say *We rose, but later fell*—
Keep the State from going down in the storm!

10   Once, years ago, with happy augury,
You brought us fortune; be the same again!
No man questions your power to rule the land:
But rule over men, not over a dead city!
Ships are only hulls, high walls are nothing,

15   When no life moves in the empty passageways.

OEDIPUS   Poor children! You may be sure I know
All that you longed for in your coming here.
I know that you are deathly sick; and yet,
Sick as you are, not one is as sick as I.

20   Each of you suffers in himself alone
His anguish, not another's; but my spirit
Groans for the city, for myself, for you.

I was not sleeping, you are not waking me.
No, I have been in tears for a long while

25   And in my restless thought walked many ways.
In all my search I found one remedy,
And I have adopted it: I have sent Kreon,
Son of Menoikeus, brother of the queen,
To Delphi, Apollo's place of revelation,

30   To learn there, if he can,
What act or pledge of mine may save the city.
I have counted the days, and now, this very day,
I am troubled, for he has overstayed his time.
What is he doing? He has been gone too long.

35   Yet whenever he comes back, I should do ill
Not to take any action the god orders.

PRIEST   It is a timely promise. At this instant
They tell me Kreon is here.

OEDIPUS   O Lord Apollo!

40   May his news be fair as his face is radiant!

PRIEST   Good news, I gather! he is crowned with bay,
The chaplet is thick with berries.

OEDIPUS   We shall soon know;
He is near enough to hear us now.

(*Enter* KREON.)

                                    O prince:
5   Brother: son of Menoikeus:
What answer do you bring us from the god?
KREON   A strong one. I can tell you, great afflictions
Will turn out well, if they are taken well.
OEDIPUS   What was the oracle? These vague words
10 Leave me still hanging between hope and fear.
KREON   Is it your pleasure to hear me with all these
Gathered around us? I am prepared to speak,
But should we not go in?
OEDIPUS   Speak to them all,
15 It is for them I suffer, more than for myself.
KREON   Then I will tell you what I heard at Delphi.
In plain words
The god commands us to expel from the land of Thebes
An old defilement we are sheltering.
20 It is a deathly thing, beyond cure;
We must not let it feed upon us longer.
OEDIPUS   What defilement? How shall we rid ourselves of it?
KREON   By exile or death, blood for blood. It was
Murder that brought the plague-wind on the city.
25 OEDIPUS   Murder of whom? Surely the god has named him?
KREON   My lord: Laïos once ruled this land,
Before you came to govern us.
OEDIPUS   I know;
I learned of him from others; I never saw him.
30 KREON   He was murdered; and Apollo commands us now
To take revenge upon whoever killed him.
OEDIPUS   Upon whom? Where are they? Where shall we find a clue
To solve that crime, after so many years?
KREON   Here in this land, he said. Search reveals
35 Things that escape an inattentive man.
OEDIPUS   Tell me: Was Laïos murdered in his house,
Or in the fields, or in some foreign country?
KREON   He said he planned to make a pilgrimage.
He did not come home again.
40 OEDIPUS   And was there no one,
No witness, no companion, to tell what happened?
KREON   They were all killed but one, and he got away

So frightened that he could remember one thing only.

OEDIPUS   What was the one thing? One may be the key
To everything, if we resolve to use it.

KREON   He said that a band of highwaymen attacked them,

5   Outnumbered them, and overwhelmed the king.

OEDIPUS   Strange, that a highwayman should be so daring—
Unless some faction here bribed him to do it.

KREON   We thought of that. But after Laïos' death
New troubles arose and we had no avenger.

10   OEDIPUS   What troubles could prevent your hunting down
the killers?

KREON   The riddling Sphinx's song
Made us deaf to all mysteries but her own.

OEDIPUS   Then once more I must bring what is dark to light.

15   It is most fitting that Apollo shows,
As you do, this compunction for the dead.
You shall see how I stand by you, as I should,
Avenging this country and the god as well,
And not as though it were for some distant friend,

20   But for my own sake, to be rid of evil.
Whoever killed King Laïos might—who knows?—
Lay violent hands even on me—and soon.
I act for the murdered king in my own interest.

Come, then, my children: leave the altar steps,

25   Lift up your olive boughs!
One of you go
And summon the people of Kadmos to gather here.
I will do all that I can; you may tell them that.

(*Exit a* PAGE.)

30   So, with the help of God,
We shall be saved—or else indeed we are lost.

PRIEST   Let us rise, children. It was for this we came,
And now the king has promised it.
Phoibos[1] has sent us an oracle; may he descend

35   Himself to save us and drive out the plague.

(*Exeunt* OEDIPUS *and* KREON *into the palace by the central door. The*
PRIEST *and the* SUPPLIANTS *disperse R and L. After a short pause the*
CHORUS *enters the* orchestra.)

---

[1] *Phoibos* Apollo

PÁRODOS [1]

Strophe 1

CHORUS   What is God singing in his profound
Delphi of gold and shadow?
5   What oracle for Thebes, the sunwhipped city?
Fear unjoints me, the roots of my heart tremble.
Now I remember, O Healer, your power, and wonder:
Will you send doom like a sudden cloud, or weave it
Like nightfall of the past?
10   Speak to me, tell me, O
Child of golden Hope, immortal Voice.

Antistrophe 1

Let me pray to Athené, the immortal daughter of Zeus,
And to Artemis her sister
15   Who keeps her famous throne in the market ring,
And to Apollo, archer from distant heaven—
O gods, descend! Like three streams leap against
The fires of our grief, the fires of darkness;
Be swift to bring us rest!
20   As in the old time from the brilliant house
Of air you stepped to save us, come again!

Strophe 2

Now our afflictions have no end,
Now all our stricken host lies down
25   And no man fights off death with his mind;
The noble plowland bears no grain,
And groaning mothers can not bear—
See, how our lives like birds take wing,

---

[1] *Párodos* the song or ode chanted by the chorus on its entry. It is accompanied by dancing and music played on a flute. The chorus in this play represents elders of the city of Thebes. Chorus members remain on stage (on a level lower than the principal actors) for the remainder of the play. The choral odes and dances serve to separate one scene from another (there was no curtain in Greek theater) as well as to comment on the action, reinforce the emotion, and interpret the situation. The chorus also performs dance movements during certain portions of the scenes themselves. *Strophe* and *antistrophe* are terms denoting the movement and counter-movement of the chorus from one side of its playing area to the other. When the chorus participates in dialogue with the other characters, its lines are spoken by the Choragos, its leader.

Like sparks that fly when a fire soars,
To the shore of the god of evening.

Antistrophe 2

The plague burns on, it is pitiless,
5   Though pallid children laden with death
Lie unwept in the stony ways,
And old gray women by every path
Flock to the strand about the altars
There to strike their breasts and cry
10   Worship of Phoibos in wailing prayers:
Be kind, God's golden child!

Strophe 3

There are no swords in this attack by fire,
No shields, but we are ringed with cries.
15   Send the besieger plunging from our homes
Into the vast sea-room of the Atlantic
Or into the waves that foam eastward of Thrace—
For the day ravages what the night spares—
Destroy our enemy, lord of the thunder!
20   Let him be riven by lightning from heaven!

Antistrophe 3

Phoibos Apollo, stretch the sun's bowstring,
That golden cord, until it sing for us,
Flashing arrows in heaven!
25   Artemis, Huntress,
Race with flaring lights upon our mountains!
O scarlet god, O golden-banded brow,
O Theban Bacchos in a storm of Maenads,

(*Enter* OEDIPUS, *C.*)

30   Whirl upon Death, that all the Undying hate!
Come with blinding torches, come in joy!

SCENE I

OEDIPUS   Is this your prayer? It may be answered. Come,
Listen to me, act as the crisis demands,
35   And you shall have relief from all these evils.

Until now I was a stranger to this tale,
As I had been a stranger to the crime.

Could I track down the murderer without a clue?
But now, friends,
As one who became a citizen after the murder,
I make this proclamation to all Thebans:
5   If any man knows by whose hand Laïos, son of Labdakos,
Met his death, I direct that man to tell me everything,
No matter what he fears for having so long withheld it.
Let it stand as promised that no further trouble
Will come to him, but he may leave the land in safety.

10   Moreover: If anyone knows the murderer to be foreign,
Let him not keep silent: he shall have his reward from me.
However, if he does conceal it; if any man
Fearing for his friend or for himself disobeys this edict,
Hear what I propose to do:

15   I solemnly forbid the people of this country,
Where power and throne are mine, ever to receive that man
Or speak to him, no matter who he is, or let him
Join in sacrifice, lustration, or in prayer.
I decree that he be driven from every house,
20   Being, as he is, corruption itself to us: the Delphic
Voice of Apollo has pronounced this revelation.
Thus I associate myself with the oracle
And take the side of the murdered king.

As for the criminal, I pray to God—
25   Whether it be a lurking thief, or one of a number—
I pray that that man's life be consumed in evil and wretchedness.
And as for me, this curse applies no less
If it should turn out that the culprit is my guest here,
Sharing my hearth.
30   You have heard the penalty.
I lay it on you now to attend to this
For my sake, for Apollo's, for the sick
Sterile city that heaven has abandoned.
Suppose the oracle had given you no command:
35   Should this defilement go uncleansed for ever?
You should have found the murderer: your king,
A noble king, had been destroyed!
               Now I,
Having the power that he held before me,
40   Having his bed, begetting children there
Upon his wife, as he would have, had he lived—
Their son would have been my children's brother,

> If Laïos had had luck in fatherhood!
> (And now his bad fortune has struck him down)—
> I say I take the son's part, just as though
> I were his son, to press the fight for him
> 5   And see it won! I'll find the hand that brought
> Death to Labdakos' and Polydoros' child,
> Heir of Kadmos' and Agenor's line.[1]
> And as for those who fail me,
> May the gods deny them the fruit of the earth,
> 10   Fruit of the womb, and may they rot utterly!
> Let them be wretched as we are wretched, and worse!
>
> For you, for loyal Thebans, and for all
> Who find my actions right, I pray the favor
> Of justice, and of all the immortal gods.

15 CHORAGOS   Since I am under oath, my lord, I swear
> I did not do the murder, I can not name
> The murderer. Phoibos ordained the search;
> Why did he not say who the culprit was?

OEDIPUS   An honest question. But no man in the world
20   Can make the gods do more than the gods will.

CHORAGOS   There is an alternative, I think—

OEDIPUS   Tell me.
> Any or all, you must not fail to tell me.

CHORAGOS·   A lord clairvoyant to the lord Apollo,
25   As we all know, is the skilled Teiresias.
> One might learn much about this from him, Oedipus.

OEDIPUS   I am not wasting time:
> Kreon spoke of this, and I have sent for him—
> Twice, in fact; it is strange that he is not here.

30 CHORAGOS   The other matter—that old report—seems useless.

OEDIPUS   What was that? I am interested in all reports.

CHORAGOS   The king was said to have been killed by highwaymen.

OEDIPUS   I know. But we have no witnesses to that.

CHORAGOS   If the killer can feel a particle of dread,
35   Your curse will bring him out of hiding!

OEDIPUS   No.
> The man who dared that act will fear no curse.

(*Enter the blind seer* TEIRESIAS, *led by a* PAGE.)

CHORAGOS   But there is one man who may detect the criminal.

---

[1] *Labdakos, Polydoros, Kadmos,* and *Agenor* father, grandfather, great-grand-father, and great-great-grandfather of Laïos

This is Teiresias, this is the holy prophet
In whom, alone of all men, truth was born.

OEDIPUS   Teiresias: seer: student of mysteries,
Of all that's taught and all that no man tells,

5   Secrets of Heaven and secrets of the earth:
Blind though you are, you know the city lies
Sick with plague; and from this plague, my lord,
We find that you alone can guard or save us.

Possibly you did not hear the messengers?

10   Apollo, when we sent to him,
Sent us back word that this great pestilence
Would lift, but only if we established clearly
The identity of those who murdered Laïos.
They must be killed or exiled.

15   Can you use
Birdflight[1] or any art of divination
To purify yourself, and Thebes, and me
From this contagion? We are in your hands.
There is no fairer duty

20   Than that of helping others in distress.

TEIRESIAS   How dreadful knowledge of the truth can be
When there's no help in truth! I knew this well,
But did not act on it: else I should not have come.

OEDIPUS   What is troubling you? Why are your eyes so cold?

25 TEIRESIAS   Let me go home. Bear your own fate, and I'll
Bear mine. It is better so: trust what I say.

OEDIPUS   What you say is ungracious and unhelpful
To your native country. Do not refuse to speak.

TEIRESIAS   When it comes to speech, your own is neither temperate

30   Nor opportune. I wish to be more prudent.

OEDIPUS   In God's name, we all beg you—

TEIRESIAS   You are all ignorant.
No; I will never tell you what I know.
Now it is my misery; then, it would be yours.

35 OEDIPUS   What! You do know something, and will not tell us?
You would betray us all and wreck the State?

TEIRESIAS   I do not intend to torture myself, or you.
Why persist in asking? You will not persuade me.

OEDIPUS   What a wicked old man you are! You'd try a stone's

40   Patience! Out with it! Have you no feeling at all?

---

[1] *Birdflight* Prophets predicted the future or divined the unknown by observing the flight of birds.

TEIRESIAS   You call me unfeeling. If you could only see
The nature of your own feelings . . .

OEDIPUS   Why,
Who would not feel as I do? Who could endure
5   Your arrogance toward the city?

TEIRESIAS   What does it matter?
Whether I speak or not, it is bound to come.

OEDIPUS   Then, if "it" is bound to come, you are bound to tell me.

TEIRESIAS   No, I will not go on. Rage as you please.

10   OEDIPUS   Rage? Why not!
                              And I'll tell you what I think:
You planned it, you had it done, you all but
Killed him with your own hands: if you had eyes,
I'd say the crime was yours, and yours alone.

15   TEIRESIAS   So? I charge you, then,
Abide by the proclamation you have made:
From this day forth
Never speak again to these men or to me;
You yourself are the pollution of this country.

20   OEDIPUS   You dare say that! Can you possibly think you have
Some way of going free, after such insolence?

TEIRESIAS   I have gone free. It is the truth sustains me.

OEDIPUS   Who taught you shamelessness? It was not your craft.

TEIRESIAS   You did. You made me speak. I did not want to.

25   OEDIPUS   Speak what? Let me hear it again more clearly.

TEIRESIAS   Was it not clear before? Are you tempting me?

OEDIPUS   I did not understand it. Say it again.

TEIRESIAS   I say that you are the murderer whom you seek.

OEDIPUS   Now twice you have spat out infamy. You'll pay for it!

30   TEIRESIAS   Would you care for more? Do you wish to be
really angry?

OEDIPUS   Say what you will. Whatever you say is worthless.

TEIRESIAS   I say you live in hideous shame with those
Most dear to you. You can not see the evil.

35   OEDIPUS   Can you go on babbling like this for ever?

TEIRESIAS   I can, if there is power in truth.

OEDIPUS   There is:
But not for you, not for you,
You sightless, witless, senseless, mad old man!

40   TEIRESIAS   You are the madman. There is no one here
Who will not curse you soon, as you curse me.

OEDIPUS   You child of total night! I would not touch you;
Neither would any man who sees the sun.

TEIRESIAS   True: it is not from you my fate will come.

That lies within Apollo's competence,
⸰As it is his concern.
OEDIPUS   Tell me, who made
⸰These fine discoveries? Kreon? or someone else?
5 TEIRESIAS   Kreon is no threat. You weave your own doom.
⸰OEDIPUS   Wealth, power, craft of statesmanship!
⸰Kingly position, everywhere admired!
⸰What savage envy is stored up against these,
⸰If Kreon, whom I trusted, Kreon my friend,
10 For this great office which the city once
⸰Put in my hands unsought—if for this power
⸰Kreon desires in secret to destroy me!

He has bought this decrepit fortune-teller, this
⸰Collector of dirty pennies, this prophet fraud—
15 Why, he is no more clairvoyant than I am!
⸰   Tell us:
⸰Has your mystic mummery ever approached the truth?
⸰When that hellcat the Sphinx was performing here,
⸰What help were you to these people?
⸰Her magic was not for the first man who came along:
20 It demanded a real exorcist. Your birds—
⸰What good were they? or the gods, for the matter of that?
⸰But I came by,
⸰Oedipus, the simple man, who knows nothing—
⸰I thought it out for myself, no birds helped me!
25 And this is the man you think you can destroy,
⸰That you may be close to Kreon when he's king!
⸰Well, you and your friend Kreon, it seems to me,
⸰Will suffer most. If you were not an old man,
⸰You would have paid already for your plot.
30 CHORAGOS   We can not see that his words or yours
⸰Have been spoken except in anger, Oedipus,
⸰And of anger we have no need. How to accomplish
⸰The god's will best: that is what most concerns us.
⸰TEIRESIAS   You are a king. But where argument's concerned
35 I am your man, as much a king as you.
⸰I am not your servant, but Apollo's.
⸰I have no need of Kreon or Kreon's name.

Listen to me. You mock my blindness, do you?
⸰But I say that you, with both your eyes, are blind:
40 You can not see the wretchedness of your life,
⸰Nor in whose house you live, no, nor with whom.
⸰Who are your father and mother? Can you tell me?

You do not even know the blind wrongs
That you have done them, on earth and in the world below.
But the double lash of your parents' curse will whip you
Out of this land some day, with only night
5   Upon your precious eyes.
Your cries then—where will they not be heard?
What fastness of Kithairon[1] will not echo them?
And that bridal-descant of yours—you'll know it then,
The song they sang when you came here to Thebes
10   And found your misguided berthing.
All this, and more, that you can not guess at now,
Will bring you to yourself among your children.

Be angry, then. Curse Kreon. Curse my words.
I tell you, no man that walks upon the earth
15   Shall be rooted out more horribly than you.
OEDIPUS   Am I to bear this from him?—Damnation
Take you! Out of this place! Out of my sight!
TEIRESIAS   I would not have come at all if you had not asked me.
OEDIPUS   Could I have told that you'd talk nonsense, that
20   You'd come here to make a fool of yourself, and of me?
TEIRESIAS   A fool? Your parents thought me sane enough.
OEDIPUS   My parents again!—Wait: who were my parents?
TEIRESIAS   This day will give you a father, and break your heart.
OEDIPUS   Your infantile riddles! Your damned abracadabra!
25   TEIRESIAS   You were a great man once at solving riddles.
OEDIPUS   Mock me with that if you like; you will find it true.
TEIRESIAS   It was true enough. It brought about your ruin.
OEDIPUS   But if it saved this town?
TEIRESIAS   (*to the* PAGE)   Boy, give me your hand.
30   OEDIPUS   Yes, boy; lead him away.
                         —While you are here
We can do nothing. Go; leave us in peace.
TEIRESIAS   I will go when I have said what I have to say.
How can you hurt me? And I tell you again:
35   The man you have been looking for all this time,
The damned man, the murderer of Laïos,
That man is in Thebes. To your mind he is foreign-born,
But it will soon be shown that he is a Theban,
A revelation that will fail to please.
40   A blind man,

---

[1] *Kithairon* the mountain where Oedipus was taken to be exposed as an infant

Who has his eyes now; a penniless man, who is rich now;
And he will go tapping the strange earth with his staff.
To the children with whom he lives now he will be
Brother and father—the very same; to her
5 Who bore him, son and husband—the very same
Who came to his father's bed, wet with his father's blood.

Enough. Go think that over.
If later you find error in what I have said,
You may say that I have no skill in prophecy.

10 (*Exit* TEIRESIAS, *led by his* PAGE. OEDIPUS *goes into the palace.*)

ODE I

Strophe 1

CHORUS The Delphic stone of prophecies
Remembers ancient regicide
15 And a still bloody hand.
That killer's hour of flight has come.
He must be stronger than riderless
Coursers of untiring wind,
For the son[1] of Zeus armed with his father's thunder
20 Leaps in lightning after him;
And the Furies hold his track, the sad Furies.

Antistrophe 1

Holy Parnassos'[2] peak of snow
Flashes and blinds that secret man,
25 That all shall hunt him down:
Though he may roam the forest shade
Like a bull gone wild from pasture
To rage through glooms of stone.
Doom comes down on him; flight will not avail him;
30 For the world's heart calls him desolate,
And the immortal voices follow, for ever follow.

Strophe 2

But now a wilder thing is heard
From the old man skilled at hearing Fate in the wing-beat
35   of a bird.

---

[1] *son* Apollo
[2] *Parnassos* mountain sacred to Apollo

Bewildered as a blown bird, my soul hovers and can not find
Foothold in this debate, or any reason or rest of mind.
But no man ever brought—none can bring
Proof of strife between Thebes' royal house,
5   Labdakos' line, and the son of Polybos;
And never until now has any man brought word
Of Laïos' dark death staining Oedipus the King.

Antistrophe 2

Divine Zeus and Apollo hold
10   Perfect intelligence alone of all tales ever told;
And well though this diviner works, he works in his own night;
No man can judge that rough unknown or trust in second sight,
For wisdom changes hands among the wise.
Shall I believe my great lord criminal
15   At a raging word that a blind old man let fall?
I saw him, when the carrion woman[1] faced him of old,
Prove his heroic mind. These evil words are lies.

SCENE II

KREON   Men of Thebes:
20   I am told that heavy accusations
Have been brought against me by King Oedipus.

I am not the kind of man to bear this tamely.

If in these present difficulties
He holds me accountable for any harm to him
25   Through anything I have said or done—why, then,
I do not value life in this dishonor.
It is not as though this rumor touched upon
Some private indiscretion. The matter is grave.
The fact is that I am being called disloyal
30   To the State, to my fellow citizens, to my friends.
CHORAGOS   He may have spoken in anger, not from his mind.
KREON   But did you not hear him say I was the one
Who seduced the old prophet into lying?
CHORAGOS   The thing was said; I do not know how seriously.
35   KREON   But you were watching him! Were his eyes steady?
Did he look like a man in his right mind?
CHORAGOS   I do not know.

---

[1] *woman* the Sphinx

I can not judge the behavior of great men.
But here is the king himself.

(*Enter* OEDIPUS.)

OEDIPUS   So you dared come back.
5   Why? How brazen of you to come to my house,
You murderer!
                    Do you think I do not know
That you plotted to kill me, plotted to steal my throne?
Tell me, in God's name: am I coward, a fool,
10   That you should dream you could accomplish this?
A fool who could not see your slippery game?
A coward, not to fight back when I saw it?
You are the fool, Kreon, are you not? hoping
Without support or friends to get a throne?
15   Thrones may be won or bought: you could do neither.
KREON   Now listen to me. You have talked; let me talk, too.
You can not judge unless you know the facts.
OEDIPUS   You speak well: there is one fact; but I find it hard
To learn from the deadliest enemy I have.
20   KREON   That above all I must dispute with you.
OEDIPUS   That above all I will not hear you deny.
KREON   If you think there is anything good in being stubborn
Against all reason, then I say you are wrong.
OEDIPUS   If you think a man can sin against his own kind
25   And not be punished for it, I say you are mad.
KREON   I agree. But tell me: What have I done to you?
OEDIPUS   You advised me to send for that wizard, did you not?
KREON   I did. I should do it again.
OEDIPUS   Very well. Now tell me:
30   How long has it been since Laïos—
KREON   What of Laïos?
OEDIPUS   Since he vanished in that onset by the road?
KREON   It was long ago, a long time.
OEDIPUS   And this prophet,
35   Was he practicing here then?
KREON   He was; and with honor, as now.
OEDIPUS   Did he speak of me at that time?
KREON   He never did,
At least, not when I was present.
40   OEDIPUS   But . . . the enquiry?
I suppose you held one?
KREON   We did, but we learned nothing.

OEDIPUS   Why did the prophet not speak against me then?
KREON   I do not know; and I am the kind of man
Who holds his tongue when he has no facts to go on.
OEDIPUS   There's one fact that you know, and you could tell it.
5 KREON   What fact is that? If I know it, you shall have it.
OEDIPUS   If he were not involved with you, he could not say
That it was I who murdered Laïos.
KREON   If he says that, you are the one that knows it!—
But now it is my turn to question you.
10 OEDIPUS   Put your questions. I am no murderer.
KREON   First, then: You married my sister?
OEDIPUS   I married your sister.
KREON   And you rule the kingdom equally with her?
OEDIPUS   Everything that she wants she has from me.
15 KREON   And I am the third, equal to both of you?
OEDIPUS   That is why I call you a bad friend.
KREON   No. Reason it out, as I have done.
Think of this first: Would any sane man prefer
Power, with all a king's anxieties,
20 To that same power and the grace of sleep?
Certainly not I.
I have never longed for the king's power—only his rights.
Would any wise man differ from me in this?
As matters stand, I have my way in everything
25 With your consent, and no responsibilities.
If I were king, I should be a slave to policy.

How could I desire a scepter more
Than what is now mine—untroubled influence?
No, I have not gone mad; I need no honors,
30 Except those with the perquisites I have now.
I am welcome everywhere; every man salutes me,
And those who want your favor seek my ear,
Since I know how to manage what they ask.
Should I exchange this ease for that anxiety?
35 Besides, no sober mind is treasonable.
I hate anarchy
And never would deal with any man who likes it.
Test what I have said. Go to the priestess
At Delphi, ask if I quoted her correctly.
40 And as for this other thing: if I am found
Guilty of treason with Teiresias,
Then sentence me to death. You have my word

It is a sentence I should cast my vote for—
But not without evidence!

            You do wrong
When you take good men for bad, bad men for good.

5   A true friend thrown aside—why, life itself
Is not more precious!

                  In time you will know this well:
For time, and time alone, will show the just man,
Though scoundrels are discovered in a day.

10 CHORAGOS   This is well said, and a prudent man would ponder it.
Judgments too quickly formed are dangerous.

OEDIPUS   But is he not quick in his duplicity?
And shall I not be quick to parry him?
Would you have me stand still, hold my peace, and let

15   This man win everything, through my inaction?

KREON   And you want—what is it, then? To banish me?

OEDIPUS   No, not exile. It is your death I want,
So that all the world may see what treason means.

KREON   You will persist, then? You will not believe me?

20 OEDIPUS   How can I believe you?

KREON   Then you are a fool.

OEDIPUS   To save myself?

KREON   In justice, think of me.

OEDIPUS   You are evil incarnate.

25 KREON   But suppose that you are wrong?

OEDIPUS   Still I must rule.

KREON   But not if you rule badly.

OEDIPUS   O city, city!

KREON   It is my city, too!

30 CHORAGOS   Now, my lords, be still. I see the queen,
Iokastê, coming from her palace chambers;
And it is time she came, for the sake of you both.
This dreadful quarrel can be resolved through her.

(*Enter* IOKASTÊ.)

35 IOKASTÊ   Poor foolish men, what wicked din is this?
With Thebes sick to death, is it not shameful
That you should rake some private quarrel up?
(*To* OEDIPUS) Come into the house.

                    — And you, Kreon, go now:
40   Let us have no more of this tumult over nothing.

KREON   Nothing? No, sister: what your husband plans for me
Is one of two great evils: exile or death.

OEDIPUS   He is right.
>   Why, woman I have caught him squarely
> Plotting against my life.

KREON   No! Let me die
5   Accurst if ever I have wished you harm!

IOKASTÊ   Ah, believe it, Oedipus!
> In the name of the gods, respect this oath of his
> For my sake, for the sake of these people here!

Strophe 1

10   CHORAGOS   Open your mind to her, my lord. Be ruled by her, I beg
>   you!

OEDIPUS   What would you have me do?

CHORAGOS   Respect Kreon's word. He has never spoken like a fool,
> And now he has sworn an oath.

15   OEDIPUS   You know what you ask?

CHORAGOS   I do.

OEDIPUS   Speak on, then.

CHORAGOS   A friend so sworn should not be baited so,
> In blind malice, and without final proof.

20   OEDIPUS   You are aware, I hope, that what you say
> Means death for me, or exile at the least.

Strophe 2

CHORAGOS   No, I swear by Helios, first in Heaven!
> May I die friendless and accurst,
25   The worst of deaths, if ever I meant that!
>   It is the withering fields
>   That hurt my sick heart:
>   Must we bear all these ills,
>   And now your bad blood as well?

30   OEDIPUS   Then let him go. And let me die, if I must,
> Or be driven by him in shame from the land of Thebes.
> It is your unhappiness, and not his talk,
> That touches me.
>   As for him—
35   Wherever he goes, hatred will follow him.

KREON   Ugly in yielding, as you were ugly in rage!
> Natures like yours chiefly torment themselves.

OEDIPUS   Can you not go? Can you not leave me?

KREON   I can.
40   You do not know me; but the city knows me,
> And in its eyes I am just, if not in yours.

(*Exit* KREON.)

Antistrophe 1

CHORAGOS   Lady Iokastê, did you not ask the King to go to
his chambers?
5   IOKASTÊ   First tell me what has happened.
CHORAGOS   There was suspicion without evidence; yet it rankled
As even false charges will.
IOKASTÊ   On both sides?
CHORAGOS   On both.
10   IOKASTÊ   But what was said?
CHORAGOS.   Oh let it rest, let it be done with!
Have we not suffered enough?
OEDIPUS   You see to what your decency has brought you:
You have made difficulties where my heart saw none.

15   Antistrophe 2

CHORAGOS   Oedipus, it is not once only I have told you—
You must know I should count myself unwise
To the point of madness, should I now forsake you——
You, under whose hand,
20   In the storm of another time,
Our dear land sailed out free.
But now stand fast at the helm!
IOKASTÊ   In God's name, Oedipus, inform your wife as well:
Why are you so set in this hard anger?
25   OEDIPUS   I will tell you, for none of these men deserves
My confidence as you do. It is Kreon's work,
His treachery, his plotting against me.
IOKASTÊ   Go on, if you can make this clear to me.
OEDIPUS   He charges me with the murder of Laïos.
30   IOKASTÊ   Has he some knowledge? Or does he speak from hearsay?
OEDIPUS   He would not commit himself to such a charge,
But he has brought in that damnable soothsayer
To tell his story.
IOKASTÊ   Set your mind at rest.
35   If it is a question of soothsayers, I tell you
That you will find no man whose craft gives knowledge
Of the unknowable.
                    Here is my proof:
An oracle was reported to Laïos once
40   (I will not say from Phoibos himself, but from
His appointed ministers, at any rate)

That his doom would be death at the hands of his own son—
His son, born of his flesh and of mine!

Now, you remember the story: Laïos was killed
By marauding strangers where three highways meet;
5   But his child had not been three days in this world
Before the king had pierced the baby's ankles
And left him to die on a lonely mountainside.

Thus, Apollo never caused that child
To kill his father, and it was not Laïos' fate
10   To die at the hands of his son, as he had feared.
This is what prophets and prophecies are worth!
Have no dread of them.
                           It is God himself
Who can show us what he wills, in his own way.

15   OEDIPUS   How strange a shadowy memory crossed my mind,
Just now while you were speaking; it chilled my heart.
IOKASTÊ   What do you mean? What memory do you speak of?
OEDIPUS   If I understand you, Laïos was killed
At a place where three roads meet.
20   IOKASTÊ   So it was said;
We have no later story.
OEDIPUS   Where did it happen?
IOKASTÊ   Phokis, it is called: at a place where the Theban Way
Divides into the roads toward Delphi and Daulia.
25   OEDIPUS   When?
IOKASTÊ   We had the news not long before you came
And proved the right to your succession here.
OEDIPUS   Ah, what net has God been weaving for me?
IOKASTÊ   Oedipus! Why does this trouble you?
30   OEDIPUS   Do not ask me yet.
First, tell me how Laïos looked, and tell me
How old he was.
IOKASTÊ   He was tall, his hair just touched
With white; his form was not unlike your own.
35   OEDIPUS   I think that I myself may be accurst
By my own ignorant edict.
IOKASTÊ   You speak strangely.
It makes me tremble to look at you, my king.
OEDIPUS   I am not sure that the blind man can not see.
40   But I should know better if you were to tell me—
IOKASTÊ   Anything—though I dread to hear you ask it.

OEDIPUS   Was the king lightly escorted, or did he ride
With a large company, as a ruler should?

IOKASTÊ   There were five men with him in all: one was a herald.
And a single chariot, which he was driving.

5   OEDIPUS   Alas, that makes it plain enough!

But who—
Who told you how it happened?

IOKASTÊ   A household servant,
The only one to escape.

10   OEDIPUS   And is he still
A servant of ours?

IOKASTÊ   No; for when he came back at last
And found you enthroned in the place of the dead king,
He came to me, touched my hand with his, and begged
15   That I would send him away to the frontier district
Where only the shepherds go—
As far away from the city as I could send him.
I granted his prayer; for although the man was a slave,
He had earned more than this favor at my hands.

20   OEDIPUS   Can he be called back quickly?

IOKASTÊ   Easily.
But why?

OEDIPUS   I have taken too much upon myself
Without enquiry; therefore I wish to consult him.

25   IOKASTÊ   Then he shall come.

But am I not one also
To whom you might confide these fears of yours?

OEDIPUS   That is your right; it will not be denied you,
Now least of all; for I have reached a pitch
30   Of wild foreboding. Is there anyone
To whom I should sooner speak?

Polybos of Corinth is my father.
My mother is a Dorian: Meropê
I grew up chief among the men of Corinth
35   Until a strange thing happened—
Not worth my passion, it may be, but strange.
At a feast, a drunken man maundering in his cups
Cries out that I am not my father's son! [1]

---

[1] *not my father's son* Oedipus perhaps interprets this as an allegation that
he is a bastard, the son of Meropê but not of Polybos. The implication, at
any rate, is that he is not of royal birth, not the legitimate heir to the
throne of Corinth.

I contained myself that night, though I felt anger
And a sinking heart. The next day I visited
My father and mother, and questioned them. They stormed,
Calling it all the slanderous rant of a fool;
5   And this relieved me. Yet the suspicion
Remained always aching in my mind;
I knew there was talk; I could not rest;
And finally, saying nothing to my parents,
I went to the shrine at Delphi.

10   The god dismissed my question without reply;
He spoke of other things.
                   Some were clear,
Full of wretchedness, dreadful, unbearable:
As, that I should lie with my own mother, breed
15   Children from whom all men would turn their eyes;
And that I should be my father's murderer.

I heard all this, and fled. And from that day
Corinth to me was only in the stars
Descending in that quarter of the sky,
20   As I wandered farther and farther on my way
To a land where I should never see the evil
Sung by the oracle. And I came to this country
Where, so you say, King Laïos was killed.

I will tell you all that happened there, my lady.

25   There were three highways
Coming together at a place I passed;
And there a herald came towards me, and a chariot
Drawn by horses, with a man such as you describe
Seated in it. The groom leading the horses
30   Forced me off the road at his lord's command;
But as this charioteer lurched over towards me
I struck him in my rage. The old man saw me
And brought his double goad down upon my head
As I came abreast.
35   He was paid back, and more!
Swinging my club in this right hand I knocked him
Out of his car, and he rolled on the ground.
                          I killed him.

I killed them all.
40   Now if that stranger and Laïos were—kin,
Where is a man more miserable than I?
More hated by the gods? Citizen and alien alike

Must never shelter me or speak to me—
I must be shunned by all.
                    And I myself
Pronounced this malediction upon myself!

5   Think of it: I have touched you with these hands,
These hands that killed your husband. What defilement!

Am I all evil, then? It must be so,
Since I must flee from Thebes, yet never again
See my own countrymen, my own country,
10   For fear of joining my mother in marriage
And killing Polybos, my father.
                              Ah,
If I was created so, born to this fate,
Who could deny the savagery of God?

15   O holy majesty of heavenly powers!
May I never see that day! Never!
Rather let me vanish from the race of men
Than know the abomination destined me!
CHORAGOS   We too, my lord, have felt dismay at this.
20   But there is hope: you have yet to hear the shepherd.
OEDIPUS   Indeed, I fear no other hope is left me.
IOKASTÊ   What do you hope from him when he comes?
OEDIPUS   This much:
If his account of the murder tallies with yours,
25   Then I am cleared.
IOKASTÊ   What was it that I said
Of such importance?
OEDIPUS   Why, "marauders," you said,
Killed the king, according to this man's story.
30   If he maintains that still, if there were several,
Clearly the guilt is not mine: I was alone.
But if he says one man, singlehanded, did it,
Then the evidence all points to me.
IOKASTÊ   You may be sure that he said there were several;
35   And can he call back that story now? He can not.
The whole city heard it as plainly as I.
But suppose he alters some detail of it:
He can not ever show that Laïos' death
Fulfilled the oracle: for Apollo said
40   My child was doomed to kill him; and my child—
Poor baby!—it was my child that died first.

No. From now on, where oracles are concerned,
I would not waste a second thought on any.
OEDIPUS   You may be right.

But come: let someone go
5   For the shepherd at once. This matter must be settled.
IOKASTÊ   I will send for him.

I would not wish to cross you in anything,
And surely not in this.—Let us go in.

(Exeunt into the palace.)

10   ODE II

Strophe 1

CHORUS   Let me be reverent in the ways of right,
Lowly the paths I journey on;
Let all my words and actions keep
15   The laws of the pure universe
From highest Heaven handed down.
For Heaven is their bright nurse,
Those generations of the realms of light;
Ah, never of mortal kind were they begot,
20   Nor are they slaves of memory, lost in sleep:
Their Father is greater than Time, and ages not.

Antistrophe 1

The tyrant is a child of Pride
Who drinks from his great sickening cup
25   Recklessness and vanity,
Until from his high crest headlong
He plummets to the dust of hope.
That strong man is not strong.
But let no fair ambition be denied;
30   May God protect the wrestler for the State
In government, in comely policy,
Who will fear God, and on His ordinance wait.

Strophe 2

Haughtiness and the high hand of disdain
35   Tempt and outrage God's holy law;
And any mortal who dares hold
No immortal Power in awe
Will be caught up in a net of pain:

The price for which his levity is sold.
Let each man take due earnings, then,
And keep his hands from holy things,
And from blasphemy stand apart—
5 Else the crackling blast of heaven
Blows on his head, and on his desperate heart.
Though fools will honor impious men,
In their cities no tragic poet sings.

Antistrophe 2

10 Shall we lose faith in Delphi's obscurities,
We who have heard the world's core
Discredited, and the sacred wood
Of Zeus at Elis praised no more?
The deeds and the strange prophecies
15 Must make a pattern yet to be understood.
Zeus, if indeed you are lord of all,
Throned in light over night and day,
Mirror this in your endless mind:
Our masters call the oracle
20 Words on the wind, and the Delphic vision blind!
Their hearts no longer know Apollo,
And reverence for the gods has died away.

SCENE III

(*Enter* IOKASTÊ.)

25 IOKASTÊ   Princes of Thebes, it has occurred to me
To visit the altars of the gods, bearing
These branches as a suppliant, and this incense.
Our king is not himself: his noble soul
Is overwrought with fantasies of dread,
30 Else he would consider
The new prophecies in the light of the old.
He will listen to any voice that speaks disaster,
And my advice goes for nothing.

(*She approaches the altar, R.*)

35   To you, then, Apollo,
Lycéan lord, since you are nearest, I turn in prayer.
Receive these offerings, and grant us deliverance
From defilement. Our hearts are heavy with fear

When we see our leader distracted, as helpless sailors
Are terrified by the confusion of their helmsman.

(*Enter* MESSENGER.)

MESSENGER   Friends, no doubt you can direct me:
5   Where shall I find the house of Oedipus,
Or, better still, where is the king himself?
CHORAGOS   It is this very place, stranger; he is inside.
This is his wife and mother of his children.
MESSENGER   I wish her happiness in a happy house,
10   Blest in all the fulfillment of her marriage.
IOKASTÊ   I wish as much for you: your courtesy
Deserves a like good fortune. But now, tell me:
Why have you come? What have you to say to us?
MESSENGER   Good news, my lady, for your house and your husband.
15 IOKASTÊ   What news? Who sent you here?
MESSENGER   I am from Corinth.
The news I bring ought to mean joy for you,
Though it may be you will find some grief in it.
IOKASTÊ   What is it? How can it touch us in both ways?
20 MESSENGER   The word is that the people of the Isthmus
Intend to call Oedipus to be their king.
IOKASTÊ   But old King Polybos—is he not reigning still?
MESSENGER   No. Death holds him in his sepulchre.
IOKASTÊ   What are you saying? Polybos is dead?
25 MESSENGER   If I am not telling the truth, may I die myself.
IOKASTÊ (*to a* MAIDSERVANT)   Go in, go quickly; tell this to
your master.

O riddlers of God's will, where are you now!
This was the man whom Oedipus, long ago,
30   Feared so, fled so, in dread of destroying him—
But it was another fate by which he died.

(*Enter* OEDIPUS, *C.*)

OEDIPUS   Dearest Iokastê, why have you sent for me?
IOKASTÊ   Listen to what this man says, and then tell me
35   What has become of the solemn prophecies.
OEDIPUS   Who is this man? What is his news for me?
IOKASTÊ   He has come from Corinth to announce your
father's death!
OEDIPUS   Is it true, stranger? Tell me in your own words.
40 MESSENGER   I can not say it more clearly: the king is dead.

OEDIPUS   Was it by treason? Or by an attack of illness?

MESSENGER   A little thing brings old men to their rest.

OEDIPUS   It was sickness, then?

MESSENGER   Yes, and his many years.

5 OEDIPUS   Ah!

Why should a man respect the Pythian hearth,[1] or
Give heed to the birds that jangle above his head?
They prophesied that I should kill Polybos,
Kill my own father; but he is dead and buried,
10 And I am here—I never touched him, never,
Unless he died of grief for my departure,
And thus, in a sense, through me. No. Polybos
Has packed the oracles off with him underground.
They are empty words.

15 IOKASTÊ   Had I not told you so?

OEDIPUS   You had; it was my faint heart that betrayed me.

IOKASTÊ   From now on never think of those things again.

OEDIPUS   And yet—must I not fear my mother's bed?

IOKASTÊ   Why should anyone in this world be afraid,
20 Since Fate rules us and nothing can be foreseen?
A man should live only for the present day.

Have no more fear of sleeping with your mother:
How many men, in dreams, have lain with their mothers!
No reasonable man is troubled by such things.

25 OEDIPUS   That is true; only—
If only my mother were not still alive!
But she is alive. I can not help my dread.

IOKASTÊ   Yet this news of your father's death is wonderful.

OEDIPUS   Wonderful. But I fear the living woman.

30 MESSENGER   Tell me, who is this woman that you fear?

OEDIPUS   It is Meropê, man; the wife of King Polybos.

MESSENGER   Meropê? Why should you be afraid of her?

OEDIPUS   An oracle of the gods, a dreadful saying.

MESSENGER   Can you tell me about it or are you sworn to silence?

35 OEDIPUS   I can tell you, and I will.
Apollo said through his prophet that I was the man
Who should marry his own mother, shed his father's blood
With his own hands. And so, for all these years
I have kept clear of Corinth, and no harm has come—
40 Though it would have been sweet to see my parents again.

---

[1] *Pythian hearth* Delphi

MESSENGER   And is this the fear that drove you out of Corinth?

OEDIPUS   Would you have me kill my father?

MESSENGER   As for that
You must be reassured by the news I gave you.

5   OEDIPUS   If you could reassure me, I would reward you.

MESSENGER   I had that in mind, I will confess: I thought
I could count on you when you returned to Corinth.

OEDIPUS   No: I will never go near my parents again.

MESSENGER   Ah, son, you still do not know what you are doing—

10   OEDIPUS   What do you mean? In the name of God tell me!

MESSENGER   —if these are your reasons for not going home.

OEDIPUS   I tell you, I fear the oracle may come true.

MESSENGER   And guilt may come upon you through your parents?

OEDIPUS   That is the dread that is always in my heart.

15   MESSENGER   Can you not see that all your fears are groundless?

OEDIPUS   Groundless? Am I not my parents' son?

MESSENGER   Polybos was not your father.

OEDIPUS   Not my father?

MESSENGER   No more your father than the man speaking to you.

20   OEDIPUS   But you are nothing to me!

MESSENGER   Neither was he.

OEDIPUS   Then why did he call me son?

MESSENGER   I will tell you:
Long ago he had you from my hands, as a gift.

25   OEDIPUS   Then how could he love me so, if I was not his?

MESSENGER   He had no children, and his heart turned to you.

OEDIPUS   What of you? Did you buy me? Did you find me by
chance?

MESSENGER   I came upon you in the woody vales of Kithairon.

30   OEDIPUS   And what were you doing there?

MESSENGER   Tending my flocks.

OEDIPUS   A wandering shepherd?

MESSENGER   But your savior, son, that day.

OEDIPUS   From what did you save me?

35   MESSENGER   Your ankles should tell you that.

OEDIPUS   Ah, stranger, why do you speak of that childhood pain?

MESSENGER   I pulled the skewer that pinned your feet together.

OEDIPUS   I have had the mark as long as I can remember.

MESSENGER   That was why you were given the name you bear.

40   OEDIPUS   God! Was it my father or my mother who did it?
Tell me!

MESSENGER   I do not know. The man who gave you to me
Can tell you better than I.

OEDIPUS   It was not you that found me, but another?

MESSENGER   It was another shepherd gave you to me.

OEDIPUS   Who was he? Can you tell me who he was?

MESSENGER   I think he was said to be one of Laïos' people.

OEDIPUS   You mean the Laïos who was king here years ago?

5   MESSENGER   Yes; King Laïos; and the man was one of his
    herdsmen.

OEDIPUS   Is he still alive? Can I see him?

MESSENGER   These men here
    Know best about such things.

10   OEDIPUS   Does anyone here
    Know this shepherd that he is talking about?
    Have you seen him in the fields, or in the town?
    If you have, tell me. It is time things were made plain.

CHORAGOS   I think the man he means is that same shepherd

15   You have already asked to see. Iokastê perhaps
    Could tell you something.

OEDIPUS   Do you know anything
    About him, Lady? Is he the man we have summoned?
    Is that the man this shepherd means?

20   IOKASTÊ   Why think of him?
    Forget this herdsman. Forget it all.
    This talk is a waste of time.

OEDIPUS   How can you say that,
    When the clues to my true birth are in my hands?

25   IOKASTÊ   For God's love, let us have no more questioning!
    Is your life nothing to you?
    My own is pain enough for me to bear.

OEDIPUS   You need not worry. Suppose my mother a slave,
    And born of slaves: no baseness can touch you.

30   IOKASTÊ   Listen to me, I beg you: do not do this thing!

OEDIPUS   I will not listen; the truth must be made known.

IOKASTÊ   Everything that I say is for your own good!

OEDIPUS   My own good
    Snaps my patience, then! I want none of it.

35   IOKASTÊ   You are fatally wrong! May you never learn who you are!

OEDIPUS   Go, one of you, and bring the shepherd here.
    Let us leave this woman to brag of her royal name.

IOKASTÊ   Ah, miserable!
    That is the only word I have for you now.

40   That is the only word I can ever have.

(Exit into the palace.)

CHORAGOS   Why has she left us, Oedipus? Why has she gone

In such a passion of sorrow? I fear this silence:
Something dreadful may come of it.

OEDIPUS   Let it come!
However base my birth, I must know about it.
5   The Queen, like a woman, is perhaps ashamed
To think of my low origin. But I
Am a child of Luck; I can not be dishonored.
Luck is my mother; the passing months, my brothers,
Have seen me rich and poor.
10   If this is so,
How could I wish that I were someone else?
How could I not be glad to know my birth?

ODE III

Strophe

15   CHORUS   If ever the coming time were known
To my heart's pondering,
Kithairon, now by Heaven I see the torches
At the festival of the next full moon,
And see the dance, and hear the choir sing
20   A grace to your gentle shade:
Mountain where Oedipus was found,
O mountain guard of a noble race!
May the god [1] who heals us lend his aid,
And let that glory come to pass
25   For our king's cradling-ground.

Antistrophe

Of the nymphs that flower beyond the years,
Who bore you,[2] royal child,
To Pan of the hills or the timberline Apollo,
30   Cold in delight where the upland clears,
Or Hermês for whom Kyllenê's heights are piled?
Or flushed as evening cloud,
Great Dionysos, roamer of mountains,
He—was it he who found you there,

---

[1] *god* Apollo
[2] *Who bore you* The chorus is suggesting that perhaps Oedipus is the son
of one of the immortal nymphs and of a god—Pan, Apollo, Hermes, or
Dionysos. The "sweet god-ravisher" (below) is the presumed mother.

And caught you up in his own proud
Arms from the sweet god-ravisher
Who laughed by the Muses' fountains?

SCENE IV

5   OEDIPUS Sirs: though I do not know the man,
I think I see him coming, this shepherd we want:
He is old, like our friend here, and the men
Bringing him seem to be servants of my house.
But you can tell, if you have ever seen him.

10   (*Enter* SHEPHERD *escorted by* SERVANTS.)

CHORAGOS I know him, he was Laïos' man. You can trust him.
OEDIPUS Tell me first, you from Corinth: is this the shepherd
We were discussing?
MESSENGER This is the very man.
15   OEDIPUS (*to* SHEPHERD) Come here. No, look at me. You must answer
Everything I ask.—You belonged to Laïos?
SHEPHERD Yes: born his slave, brought up in his house.
OEDIPUS Tell me: what kind of work did you do for him?
20   SHEPHERD I was a shepherd of his, most of my life.
OEDIPUS Where mainly did you go for pasturage?
SHEPHERD Sometimes Kithairon, sometimes the hills near-by.
OEDIPUS Do you remember ever seeing this man out there?
SHEPHERD What would he be doing there? This man?
25   OEDIPUS This man standing here. Have you ever seen him before?
SHEPHERD No. At least, not to my recollection.
MESSENGER And that is not strange, my lord. But I'll refresh
His memory: he must remember when we two
Spent three whole seasons together, March to September,
30   On Kithairon or thereabouts. He had two flocks;
I had one. Each autumn I'd drive mine home
And he would go back with his to Laïos' sheepfold.—
Is this not true, just as I have described it?
SHEPHERD True, yes; but it was all so long ago.
35   MESSENGER Well, then: do you remember, back in those days,
That you gave me a baby boy to bring up as my own?
SHEPHERD What if I did? What are you trying to say?
MESSENGER King Oedipus was once that little child.
SHEPHERD Damn you, hold your tongue!
40   OEDIPUS   No more of that!
It is your tongue needs watching, not this man's.

SHEPHERD   My king, my master, what is it I have done wrong?
OEDIPUS   You have not answered his question about the boy.
SHEPHERD   He does not know . . . He is only making trouble . . .
OEDIPUS   Come, speak plainly, or it will go hard with you.
5   SHEPHERD   In God's name, do not torture an old man!
OEDIPUS   Come here, one of you; bind his arms behind him.
SHEPHERD   Unhappy king! What more do you wish to learn?
OEDIPUS   Did you give this man the child he speaks of?
SHEPHERD   I did.
10   And I would to God I had died that very day.
OEDIPUS   You will die now unless you speak the truth.
SHEPHERD   Yet if I speak the truth, I am worse than dead.
OEDIPUS (*to* ATTENDANT)   He intends to draw it out, apparently—
SHEPHERD   No! I have told you already that I gave him the boy.
15   OEDIPUS   Where did you get him? From your house? From
       somewhere else?
SHEPHERD   Not from mine, no. A man gave him to me.
OEDIPUS   Is that man here? Whose house did he belong to?
SHEPHERD   For God's love, my king, do not ask me any more!
20   OEDIPUS   You are a dead man if I have to ask you again.
SHEPHERD   Then . . . Then the child was from the palace of Laïos.
OEDIPUS   A slave child? or a child of his own line?
SHEPHERD   Ah, I am on the brink of dreadful speech!
OEDIPUS   And I of dreadful hearing. Yet I must hear.
25   SHEPHERD   If you must be told, then . . .
                                        They said it was Laïos' child;
       But it is your wife who can tell you about that.
OEDIPUS   My wife!—Did she give it to you?
SHEPHERD   My lord, she did.
30   OEDIPUS   Do you know why?
SHEPHERD   I was told to get rid of it.
OEDIPUS   Oh heartless mother!
SHEPHERD   But in dread of prophecies . . .
OEDIPUS   Tell me.
35   SHEPHERD   It was said that the boy would kill his own father.
OEDIPUS   Then why did you give him over to this old man?
SHEPHERD   I pitied the baby, my king,
       And I thought that this man would take him far away
       To his own country.
40   He saved him—but for what a fate!
       For if you are what this man says you are,
       No man living is more wretched than Oedipus.
OEDIPUS   Ah God!
       It was true!

All the prophecies!
                              — Now,
O Light, may I look on you for the last time!
I, Oedipus,

5   Oedipus, damned in his birth, in his marriage damned,
Damned in the blood he shed with his own hand!

(*He rushes into the palace.*)   .

ODE IV

Strophe 1

10 CHORUS   Alas for the seed of men.
What measure shall I give these generations
That breathe on the void and are void
And exist and do not exist?
Who bears more weight of joy
15 Than mass of sunlight shifting in images,
Or who shall make his thought stay on
That down time drifts away?
Your splendor is all fallen.
O naked brow of wrath and tears,
20 O change of Oedipus!
I who saw your days call no man blest—
Your great days like ghosts gone.

Antistrophe 1

That mind was a strong bow.
25 Deep, how deep you drew it then, hard archer,
At a dim fearful range,
And brought dear glory down!
You overcame the stranger[1]—
The virgin with her hooking lion claws—
30 And though death sang, stood like a tower
To make pale Thebes take heart.
Fortress against our sorrow!
True king, giver of laws,
Majestic Oedipus!
35 No prince in Thebes had ever such renown,
No prince won such grace of power.

---

[1] *stranger* the Sphinx

Strophe 2

And now of all men ever known
Most pitiful is this man's story:
His fortunes are most changed, his state
5   Fallen to a low slave's
Ground under bitter fate.
O Oedipus, most royal one!
The great door[1] that expelled you to the light
Gave at night—ah, gave night to your glory:
10   As to the father, to the fathering son.
All understood too late.
How could that queen whom Laïos won,
The garden that he harrowed at his height,
Be silent when that act was done?

15 **Antistrophe 2**

But all eyes fail before time's eye,
All actions come to justice there.
Though never willed, though far down the deep past,
Your bed, your dread sirings,
20   Are brought to book at last.
Child by Laïos doomed to die,
Then doomed to lose that fortunate little death,
Would God you never took breath in this air
That with my wailing lips I take to cry:
25   For I weep the world's outcast.
I was blind, and now I can tell why:
Asleep, for you had given ease of breath
To Thebes, while the false years went by.

EXODOS [2]

30   (*Enter, from the palace,* Second Messenger.)

Second Messenger   Elders of Thebes, most honored in this land,
What horrors are yours to see and hear, what weight
Of sorrow to be endured, if, true to your birth,
You venerate the line of Labdakos!
35   I think neither Istros nor Phasis, those great rivers,
Could purify this place of all the evil

---

[1] *door* Iokastê's womb
[2] *Exodos* final scene

It shelters now, or soon must bring to light—
Evil not done unconsciously, but willed.

The greatest griefs are those we cause ourselves.
CHORAGOS   Surely, friend, we have grief enough already;
5   What new sorrow do you mean?
SECOND MESSENGER   The queen is dead.
CHORAGOS   O miserable queen! But at whose hand?
SECOND MESSENGER   Her own.
The full horror of what happened you can not know,
10   For you did not see it; but I, who did, will tell you
As clearly as I can how she met her death.

When she had left us,
In passionate silence, passing through the court,
She ran to her apartment in the house,
15   Her hair clutched by the fingers of both hands.
She closed the doors behind her; then, by that bed
Where long ago the fatal son was conceived—
That son who should bring about his father's death—
We heard her call upon Laïos, dead so many years,
20   And heard her wail for the double fruit of her marriage,
A husband by her husband, children by her child.

Exactly how she died I do not know:
For Oedipus burst in moaning and would not let us
Keep vigil to the end: it was by him
25   As he stormed about the room that our eyes were caught.
From one to another of us he went, begging a sword,
Hunting the wife who was not his wife, the mother
Whose womb had carried his own children and himself.
I do not know: it was none of us aided him,
30   But surely one of the gods was in control!
For with a dreadful cry
He hurled his weight, as though wrenched out of himself,
At the twin doors: the bolts gave, and he rushed in.
And there we saw her hanging, her body swaying
35   From the cruel cord she had noosed about her neck.
A great sob broke from him, heartbreaking to hear,
As he loosed the rope and lowered her to the ground.

I would blot out from my mind what happened next!
For the king ripped from her gown the golden brooches
40   That were her ornament, and raised them, and plunged
        them down

Straight into his own eyeballs, crying, "No more,
No more shall you look on the misery about me,
The horrors of my own doing! Too long you have known
The faces of those whom I should never have seen,
5   Too long been blind to those for whom I was searching!
From this hour, go in darkness!" And as he spoke,
He struck at his eyes—not once, but many times;
And the blood spattered his beard,
Bursting from his ruined sockets like red hail.

10   So from the unhappiness of two this evil has sprung,
A curse on the man and woman alike. The old
Happiness of the house of Labdakos
Was happiness enough: where is it today?
It is all wailing and ruin, disgrace, death—all
15   The misery of mankind that has a name—
And it is wholly and for ever theirs.

CHORAGOS   Is he in agony still? Is there no rest for him?
SECOND MESSENGER   He is calling for someone to open the
      doors wide
20   So that all the children of Kadmos may look upon
His father's murderer, his mother's—no,
I can not say it!
                  And then he will leave Thebes,
Self-exiled, in order that the curse
25   Which he himself pronounced may depart from the house.
He is weak, and there is none to lead him,
So terrible is his suffering.
                     But you will see:
Look, the doors are opening; in a moment
30   You will see a thing that would crush a heart of stone.

(The central door is opened; OEDIPUS, *blinded, is led in.)*

CHORAGOS   Dreadful indeed for men to see.
Never have my own eyes
Looked on a sight so full of fear.

35   Oedipus!
What madness came upon you, what daemon
Leaped on your life with heavier
Punishment than a mortal man can bear?
No: I can not even
40   Look at you, poor ruined one.
And I would speak, question, ponder,

If I were able. No.
You make me shudder.
OEDIPUS   God. God.
Is there a sorrow greater?
5   Where shall I find harbor in this world?
My voice is hurled far on a dark wind.
What has God done to me?
CHORAGOS   Too terrible to think of, or to see.

Strophe 1

10   OEDIPUS   O cloud of night,
Never to be turned away: night coming on,
I can not tell how: night like a shroud!
My fair winds brought me here.
                                    O God. Again
15   The pain of the spikes where I had sight,
The flooding pain
Of memory, never to be gouged out.
CHORAGOS   This is not strange.
You suffer it all twice over, remorse in pain,
20   Pain in remorse.

Antistrophe 1

OEDIPUS   Ah dear friend
Are you faithful even yet, you alone?
Are you still standing near me, will you stay here,
25   Patient, to care for the blind?
                                    The blind man!
Yet even blind I know who it is attends me,
By the voice's tone—
Though my new darkness hide the comforter.
30   CHORAGOS   Oh fearful act!
What god was it drove you to rake black
Night across your eyes?

Strophe 2

OEDIPUS   Apollo. Apollo. Dear
35   Children, the god was Apollo.
He brought my sick, sick fate upon me.
But the blinding hand was my own!
How could I bear to see
When all my sight was horror everywhere?
40   CHORAGOS   Everywhere; that is true.

OEDIPUS   And now what is left?
Images? Love? A greeting even,
Sweet to the senses? Is there anything?
Ah, no, friends: lead me away.
5   Lead me away from Thebes.

                            Lead the great wreck
And hell of Oedipus, whom the gods hate.
CHORAGOS   Your misery, you are not blind to that.
Would God you had never found it out!

10   **Antistrophe 2**

OEDIPUS   Death take the man who unbound
My feet on that hillside
And delivered me from death to life! What life?
If only I had died,
15   This weight of monstrous doom
Could not have dragged me and my darlings down.
CHORAGOS   I would have wished the same.
OEDIPUS   Oh never to have come here
With my father's blood upon me! Never
20   To have been the man they call his mother's husband!
Oh accurst! Oh child of evil,
To have entered that wretched bed—

                            the selfsame one!
More primal than sin itself, this fell to me.
25   CHORAGOS   I do not know what words to offer you.
You were better dead than alive and blind.

OEDIPUS   Do not counsel me any more. This punishment
That I have laid upon myself is just.
If I had eyes,
30   I do not know how I could bear the sight
Of my father, when I came to the house of Death,
Or my mother: for I have sinned against them both
So vilely that I could not make my peace
By strangling my own life.
35   Or do you think my children,
Born as they were born, would be sweet to my eyes?
Ah never, never! Nor this town with its high walls,
Nor the holy images of the gods.
                            For I,
40   Thrice miserable!—Oedipus, noblest of all the line
Of Kadmos, have condemned myself to enjoy

These things no more, by my own malediction
Expelling that man whom the gods declared
To be a defilement in the house of Laïos.
After exposing the rankness of my own guilt,
5   How could I look men frankly in the eyes?
No, I swear it,
If I could have stifled my hearing at its source,
I would have done it and made all this body
A tight cell of misery, blank to light and sound:
10   So I should have been safe in my dark mind
Beyond external evil.

                  Ah Kithairon!
Why did you shelter me? When I was cast upon you,
Why did I not die? Then I should never
15   Have shown the world my execrable birth.

Ah Polybos! Corinth, city that I believed
The ancient seat of my ancestors: how fair
I seemed, your child! And all the while this evil
Was cancerous within me!
20   For I am sick
In my own being, sick in my origin.

O three roads, dark ravine, woodland and way
Where three roads met: you, drinking my father's blood,
My own blood, spilled by my own hand: can you remember
25   The unspeakable things I did there, and the things
I went on from there to do?
                 O marriage, marriage!
That act that engendered me, and again the act
Performed by the son in the same bed—
30   Ah, the net
Of incest, mingling fathers, brothers, sons,
With brides, wives, mothers: the last evil
That can be known by men: no tongue can say
How evil!
35   No. For the love of God, conceal me
Somewhere far from Thebes; or kill me; or hurl me
Into the sea, away from men's eyes for ever.

Come, lead me. You need not fear to touch me.
Of all men, I alone can bear this guilt.

40   (*Enter* KREON.)

CHORAGOS   Kreon is here now. As to what you ask,
He may decide the course to take. He only
Is left to protect the city in your place.
OEDIPUS   Alas, how can I speak to him? What right have I
5   To beg his courtesy whom I have deeply wronged?
KREON   I have not come to mock you, Oedipus,
Or to reproach you, either. (*To* ATTENDANTS)
                              —You, standing there:
If you have lost all respect for man's dignity,
10   At least respect the flame of Lord Helios:
Do not allow this pollution to show itself
Openly here, an affront to the earth
And Heaven's rain and the light of day. No, take him
Into the house as quickly as you can.
15   For it is proper
That only the close kindred see his grief.
OEDIPUS   I pray you in God's name, since your courtesy
Ignores my dark expectation, visiting
With mercy this man of all men most execrable:
20   Give me what I ask—for your good, not for mine.
KREON   And what is it that you turn to me begging for?
OEDIPUS   Drive me out of this country as quickly as may be
To a place where no human voice can ever greet me.
KREON   I should have done that before now—only,
25   God's will had not been wholly revealed to me.
OEDIPUS   But his command is plain: the parricide
Must be destroyed. I am that evil man.
KREON   That is the sense of it, yes; but as things are,
We had best discover clearly what is to be done.
30   OEDIPUS   You would learn more about a man like me?
KREON   You are ready now to listen to the god.
OEDIPUS   I will listen. But it is to you
That I must turn for help. I beg you, hear me.

The woman in there—
35   Give her whatever funeral you think proper:
She is your sister.
                    —But let me go, Kreon!
Let me purge my father's Thebes of the pollution
Of my living here, and go out to the wild hills,
40   To Kithairon, that has won such fame with me,
The tomb my mother and father appointed for me,
And let me die there, as they willed I should.

And yet I know
Death will not ever come to me through sickness
Or in any natural way: I have been preserved
For some unthinkable fate. But let that be.

5   As for my sons, you need not care for them.
They are men, they will find some way to live.
But my poor daughters, who have shared my table,
Who never before have been parted from their father—
Take care of them, Kreon; do this for me.

10   And will you let me touch them with my hands
A last time, and let us weep together?
Be kind, my lord,
Great prince, be kind!
                  Could I but touch them,
15   They would be mine again, as when I had my eyes.

(*Enter* ANTIGONÊ *and* ISMENÊ, *attended.*)

Ah, God!
Is it my dearest children I hear weeping?
Has Kreon pitied me and sent my daughters?
20 KREON   Yes, Oedipus: I knew that they were dear to you
In the old days, and know you must love them still.
  OEDIPUS   May God bless you for this—and be a friendlier
Guardian to you than he has been to me!

Children, where are you?
25 Come quickly to my hands: they are your brother's—
Hands that have brought your father's once clear eyes
To this way of seeing —
               Ah dearest ones,
I had neither sight nor knowledge then, your father
30 By the woman who was the source of his own life!
And I weep for you—having no strength to see you—,
I weep for you when I think of the bitterness
That men will visit upon you all your lives.
What homes, what festivals can you attend
35 Without being forced to depart again in tears?
And when you come to marriageable age,
Where is the man, my daughters, who would dare
Risk the bane that lies on all my children?
Is there any evil wanting? Your father killed
40 His father; sowed the womb of her who bore him;
Engendered you at the fount of his own existence!

That is what they will say of you.

                        Then, whom
Can you ever marry? There are no bridegrooms for you,
And your lives must wither away in sterile dreaming.

5   O Kreon, son of Menoikeus!
You are the only father my daughters have,
Since we, their parents, are both of us gone for ever.
They are your own blood: you will not let them
Fall into beggary and loneliness;
10   You will keep them from the miseries that are mine!
Take pity on them; see, they are only children,
Friendless except for you. Promise me this,
Great prince, and give me your hand in token of it.

(KREON *clasps his right hand.*)

15   Children:
I could say much, if you could understand me,
But as it is, I have only this prayer for you:
Live where you can, be as happy as you can—
Happier, please God, than God has made your father.

20   KREON   Enough. You have wept enough. Now go within.
     OEDIPUS   I must; but it is hard.
     KREON   Time eases all things.
     OEDIPUS   You know my mind, then?
     KREON   Say what you desire.
25   OEDIPUS   Send me from Thebes!
     KREON   God grant that I may!
     OEDIPUS   But since God hates me . . .
     KREON   No, he will grant your wish.
     OEDIPUS   You promise?
30   KREON   I can not speak beyond my knowledge.
     OEDIPUS   Then lead me in.
     KREON   Come now, and leave your children.
     OEDIPUS   No! Do not take them from me!
     KREON   Think no longer
35   That you are in command here, but rather think
How, when you were, you served your own destruction.

(*Exeunt into the house all but the* CHORUS; *the* CHORAGOS *chants directly to the audience.*)

CHORAGOS   Men of Thebes: look upon Oedipus.

40   This is the king who solved the famous riddle
And towered up, most powerful of men.

No mortal eyes but looked on him with envy,
Yet in the end ruin swept over him.

Let every man in mankind's frailty
Consider his last day; and let none
5   Presume on his good fortune until he find
Life, at his death, a memory without pain.

QUESTIONS

According to Aristotle, tragedies such as *Oedipus Rex* succeed by arousing pity and fear in their audiences—pity for the suffering the plays' heroes endure, fear that we might sometime face similar agonies. How does *Oedipus Rex* call forth these feelings? In thinking out your answer, you might want to consider the following.

1. What sort of person do you think Oedipus is? What are his strengths and weaknesses? How is he different from the other characters in the play?
2. What sorts of tensions are built up (for Oedipus, for the other characters, and for the audience) by the gradual unfolding of the truth about Laïos' murder and Oedipus' history?
3. How does your knowledge of the story of Oedipus, and hence your knowledge of how the play will end, affect your reaction to such scenes as those with Teiresias and the shepherds?
4. How are the images of sight and blindness used throughout the play?

SOPHOCLES (496–406 B.C.)

Antigonê

An English version by Dudley Fitts and Robert Fitzgerald

C H A R A C T E R S

ANTIGONÊ
ISMENÊ
EURYDICÊ
KREON
HAIMON
TEIRESIAS
A SENTRY
A MESSENGER
CHORUS

SCENE. *Before the palace of* KREON, *King of Thebes. A central double door, and two lateral doors. A platform extends the length of the façade, and from this platform three steps lead down into the "orchestra," or chorus-ground.*

TIME. *Dawn of the day after the repulse of the Argive army from the assault on Thebes.*

PROLOGUE

(ANTIGONÊ *and* ISMENÊ *enter from the central door of the palace.*)

ANTIGONÊ   Ismenê, dear sister,
You would think that we had already suffered enough
5   For the curse on Oedipus.
I cannot imagine any grief
That you and I have not gone through. And now—
Have they told you of the new decree of our King Kreon?
ISMENÊ   I have heard nothing: I know
10   That two sisters lost two brothers, a double death
In a single hour; and I know that the Argive army
Fled in the night; but beyond this, nothing.

ANTIGONÊ   I thought so. And that is why I wanted you
　　To come out here with me. There is something we must do.
ISMENÊ   Why do you speak so strangely?
ANTIGONÊ   Listen, Ismenê:
5　　Kreon buried our brother Eteoclês
　　With military honors, gave him a soldier's funeral,
　　And it was right that he should; but Polyneicês,
　　Who fought as bravely and died as miserably,—
　　They say that Kreon has sworn
10　　No one shall bury him, no one mourn for him,
　　But his body must lie in the fields, a sweet treasure
　　For carrion birds to find as they search for food.
　　That is what they say, and our good Kreon is coming here
　　To announce it publicly; and the penalty—
15　　Stoning to death in the public square!
　　　　　　　　　　　　　　　　　There it is,
　　And now you can prove what you are:
　　A true sister, or a traitor to your family.
ISMENÊ   Antigonê, you are mad! What could I possibly do?
20　　ANTIGONÊ   You must decide whether you will help me or not.
ISMENÊ   I do not understand you. Help you in what?
ANTIGONÊ   Ismenê, I am going to bury him. Will you come?
ISMENÊ   Bury him! You have just said the new law forbids it.
ANTIGONÊ   He is my brother. And he is your brother, too.
25　　ISMENÊ   But think of the danger! Think what Kreon will do!
ANTIGONÊ   Kreon is not strong enough to stand in my way.
ISMENÊ   Ah sister!
　　Oedipus died, everyone hating him
　　For what his own search brought to light, his eyes
30　　Ripped out by his own hand; and Iokastê died,
　　His mother and wife at once: she twisted the cords
　　That strangled her life; and our two brothers died,
　　Each killed by the other's sword. And we are left:
　　But oh, Antigonê,
35　　Think how much more terrible than these
　　Our own death would be if we should go against Kreon
　　And do what he has forbidden! We are only women,
　　We cannot fight with men, Antigonê!
　　The law is strong, we must give in to the law
40　　In this thing, and in worse. I beg the Dead
　　To forgive me, but I am helpless: I must yield
　　To those in authority. And I think it is dangerous business
　　To be always meddling.
ANTIGONÊ　　　　　　　If that is what you think,
45　　I should not want you, even if you asked to come.

You have made your choice, you can be what you want to be.
But I will bury him; and if I must die,
I say that this crime is holy: I shall lie down
With him in death, and I shall be as dear
5   To him as he to me.
                              It is the dead,
Not the living, who make the longest demands:
We die for ever . . .
                              You may do as you like,
10   Since apparently the laws of the gods mean nothing to you.
    ISMENÊ   They mean a great deal to me; but I have no strength
        To break laws that were made for the public good.
    ANTIGONÊ   That must be your excuse, I suppose. But as for me,
        I will bury the brother I love.
15   ISMENÊ   Antigonê,
        I am so afraid for you!
    ANTIGONÊ   You need not be:
        You have yourself to consider, after all.
    ISMENÊ   But no one must hear of this, you must tell no one!
20   I will keep it a secret, I promise!
    ANTIGONÊ   O tell it! Tell everyone!
        Think how they'll hate you when it all comes out
        If they learn that you knew about it all the time!
    ISMENÊ   So fiery! You should be cold with fear.
25   ANTIGONÊ   Perhaps. But I am doing only what I must.
    ISMENÊ   But can you do it? I say that you cannot.
    ANTIGONÊ   Very well: when my strength gives out,
        I shall do no more.
    ISMENÊ   Impossible things should not be tried at all.
30   ANTIGONÊ   Go away, Ismenê:
        I shall be hating you soon, and the dead will too,
        For your words are hateful. Leave me my foolish plan:
        I am not afraid of the danger; if it means death,
        It will not be the worst of deaths—death without honor.
35   ISMENÊ   Go then, if you feel that you must.
        You are unwise,
        But a loyal friend indeed to those who love you.

(*Exit into the palace.* ANTIGONÊ *goes off, left. Enter the* CHORUS.)

PÁRODOS

40   **Strophe 1**

    CHORUS   Now the long blade of the sun, lying
        Level east to west, touches with glory

Thebes of the Seven Gates. Open, unlidded
Eye of golden day! O marching light
Across the eddy and rush of Dircê's stream,[1]
Striking the white shields of the enemy
5   Thrown headlong backward from the blaze of morning!
CHORAGOS[2]   Polyneicês their commander
Roused them with windy phrases,
He the wild eagle screaming
Insults above our land,
10   His wings their shields of snow,
His crest their marshalled helms.

Antistrophe 1

CHORUS   Against our seven gates in a yawning ring
The famished spears came onward in the night;
15   But before his jaws were sated with our blood,
Or pinefire took the garland of our towers,
He was thrown back; and as he turned, great Thebes—
No tender victim for his noisy power—
Rose like a dragon behind him, shouting war.
20   CHORAGOS   For God hates utterly
The bray of bragging tongues;
And when he beheld their smiling,
Their swagger of golden helms,
The frown of his thunder blasted
25   Their first man from our walls.

Strophe 2

CHORUS   We heard his shout of triumph high in the air
Turn to a scream; far out in a flaming arc
He fell with his windy torch, and the earth struck him.
30   And others storming in fury no less than his
Found shock of death in the dusty joy of battle.
CHORAGOS   Seven captains at seven gates
Yielded their clanging arms to the god
That bends the battle-line and breaks it.
35   These two only, brothers in blood,
Face to face in matchless rage,
Mirroring each the other's death,
Clashed in long combat.

---

[1] *Dircês stream* a stream to the west of Thebes
[2] *Choragos* the leader of the Chorus

Antistrophe 2

CHORUS   But now in the beautiful morning of victory
    Let Thebes of the many chariots sing for joy!
    With hearts for dancing we'll take leave of war:
5   Our temples shall be sweet with hymns of praise,
    And the long nights shall echo with our chorus.

SCENE I

CHORAGOS   But now at last our new King is coming:
    Kreon of Thebes, Menoikeus' son.
10   In this auspicious dawn of his rein
    What are the new complexities
    That shifting Fate has woven for him?
    What is his counsel? Why has he summoned
    The old men to hear him?

15   (*Enter* KREON *from the palace, center. He addresses the* CHORUS *from the top step.*)

KREON   Gentlemen: I have the honor to inform you that our Ship of State, which recent storms have threatened to destroy, has come safely to harbor at last, guided by the merciful wisdom of Heaven. 20 I have summoned you here this morning because I know that I can depend upon you: your devotion to King Laïos was absolute; you never hesitated in your duty to our late ruler Oedipus; and when Oedipus died, your loyalty was transferred to his children. Unfortunately, as you know, his two sons, the princes Eteoclês 25 and Polyneicês, have killed each other in battle; and I, as the next in blood, have succeeded to the full power of the throne.

    I am aware, of course, that no Ruler can expect complete loyalty from his subjects until he has been tested in office. Nevertheless, I say to you at the very outset that I have nothing but 30 contempt for the kind of Governor who is afraid, for whatever reason, to follow the course that he knows is best for the State; and as for the man who sets private friendship above the public welfare,—I have no use for him, either. I call God to witness that if I saw my country headed for ruin, I should not be afraid 35 to speak out plainly; and I need hardly remind you that I would never have any dealings with an enemy of the people. No one values friendship more highly than I; but we must remember that friends made at the risk of wrecking our Ship are not real friends at all.

40   These are my principles, at any rate, and that is why I have made the following decision concerning the sons of Oedipus:

Eteoclês, who died as a man should die, fighting for his country,
is to be buried with full military honors, with all the ceremony
that is usual when the greatest heroes die; but his brother Polyneicês, who broke his exile to come back with fire and sword
5   against his native city and the shrines of his fathers' gods, whose
one idea was to spill the blood of his blood and sell his own
people into slavery—Polyneicês, I say, is to have no burial: no
man is to touch him or say the least prayer for him; he shall lie
on the plain, unburied; and the birds and the scavenging dogs
10 can do with him whatever they like.

This is my command, and you can see the wisdom behind it.
As long as I am King, no traitor is going to be honored with the
loyal man. But whoever shows by word and deed that he is on
the side of the State,—he shall have my respect while he is living
15 and my reverence when he is dead.

CHORAGOS   If that is your will, Kreon son of Menoikeus,
You have the right to enforce it: we are yours.

KREON   That is my will. Take care that you do your part.

CHORAGOS   We are old men: let the younger ones carry it out.

20 KREON   I do not mean that: the sentries have been appointed.

CHORAGOS   Then what is it that you would have us do?

KREON   You will give no support to whoever breaks this law.

CHORAGOS   Only a crazy man is in love with death!

KREON   And death it is; yet money talks, and the wisest
25 Have sometimes been known to count a few coins too many.

(*Enter* SENTRY *from left.*)

SENTRY   I'll not say that I'm out of breath from running, King,
because every time I stopped to think about what I have to tell
you, I felt like going back. And all the time a voice kept saying,
30 "You fool, don't you know you're walking straight into trouble?";
and then another voice: "Yes, but if you let somebody else get
the news to Kreon first, it will be even worse than that for you!"
But good sense won out, at least I hope it was good sense, and
here I am with a story that makes no sense at all; but I'll tell it
35 anyhow, because, as they say, what's going to happen's going to
happen and—

KREON   Come to the point. What have you to say?

SENTRY   I did not do it. I did not see who did it. You must not
punish me for what someone else has done.

40 KREON   A comprehensive defense! More effective, perhaps,
If I knew its purpose. Come: what is it?

SENTRY   A dreadful thing . . . I don't know how to put it—

KREON   Out with it!

SENTRY   Well, then;
   The dead man—
            Polyneicês—

(Pause. The SENTRY *is overcome, fumbles for words.* KREON *waits*
5   *impassively.)*

                       out there—
                             someone,—
New dust on the slimy flesh!

(Pause. No sign from KREON.)

10   Someone has given it burial that way, and
   Gone . . .

(Long pause. KREON *finally speaks with deadly control.)*

KREON   And the man who dared do this?
SENTRY   I swear I
15   Do not know! You must believe me!
                    Listen:
The ground was dry, not a sign of digging, no,
Not a wheeltrack in the dust, no trace of anyone.
It was when they relieved us this morning: and one of them,
20   The corporal, pointed to it.
                   There it was,
The strangest—
        Look:
The body, just mounded over with light dust: you see?
25   Not buried really, but as if they'd covered it
Just enough for the ghost's peace. And no sign
Of dogs or any wild animal that had been there.

And then what a scene there was! Every man of us
Accusing the other: we all proved the other man did it,
30   We all had proof that we could not have done it.
We were ready to take hot iron in our hands,
Walk through fire, swear by all the gods,
It was not I!
I do not know who it was, but it was not I!

35   *(*KREON's *rage has been mounting steadily, but the* SENTRY *is too intent*
upon his story to notice it.)

And then, when this came to nothing, someone said
A thing that silenced us and made us stare
Down at the ground: you had to be told the news,
40   And one of us had to do it! We threw the dice,

And the bad luck fell to me. So here I am,
No happier to be here than you are to have me:
Nobody likes the man who brings bad news.

CHORAGOS　I have been wondering, King: can it be that the gods
5　have done this?

KREON (*furiously*)　Stop!
Must you doddering wrecks
Go out of your heads entirely? "The gods"!
Intolerable!

10　The gods favor this corpse? Why? How had he served them?
Tried to loot their temples, burn their images,
Yes, and the whole State, and its laws with it!
Is it your senile opinion that the gods love to honor bad men?
A pious thought!—

15　　　　　　　　No, from the very beginning
There have been those who have whispered together,
Stiff-necked anarchists, putting their heads together,
Scheming against me in alleys. These are the men,
And they have bribed my own guard to do this thing.

20　(*Sententiously.*)　Money!
There's nothing in the world so demoralizing as money.
Down go your cities,
Homes gone, men gone, honest hearts corrupted,
Crookedness of all kinds, and all for money!

25　(*To* SENTRY.)　　　　　　　　But you—!
I swear by God and by the throne of God,
The man who has done this thing shall pay for it!
Find that man, bring him here to me, or your death
Will be the least of your problems: I'll string you up

30　Alive, and there will be certain ways to make you
Discover your employer before you die;
And the process may teach you a lesson you seem to have
　　missed:
The dearest profit is sometimes all too dear:

35　That depends on the source. Do you understand me?
A fortune won is often misfortune.

SENTRY　King, may I speak?

KREON　　　　　　　　Your very voice distresses me.

SENTRY　Are you sure that it is my voice, and not your conscience?

40　KREON　By God, he wants to analyze me now!

SENTRY　It is not what I say, but what has been done, that hurts
you.

KREON　You talk too much.

SENTRY　　　　　　　Maybe; but I've done nothing.

45　KREON　Sold your soul for some silver: that's all you've done.

SENTRY   How dreadful it is when the right judge judges wrong!
KREON   Your figures of speech
    May entertain you now; but unless you bring me the man,
    You will get little profit from them in the end.

5   (*Exit* KREON *into the palace.*)

SENTRY   "Bring me the man"—!
    I'd like nothing better than bringing him the man!
    But bring him or not, you have seen the last of me here.
    At any rate, I am safe!

10   (*Exit* SENTRY.)

ODE I

Strophe 1

CHORUS   Numberless are the world's wonders, but none
    More wonderful than man; the stormgray sea
15   Yields to his prows, the huge crests bear him high;
    Earth, holy and inexhaustible, is graven
    With shining furrows where his plows have gone
    Year after year, the timeless labor of stallions.

Antistrophe 1

20   The lightboned birds and beasts that cling to cover,
    The lithe fish lighting their reaches of dim water,
    All are taken, tamed in the net of his mind;
    The lion on the hill, the wild horse windy-maned,
    Resign to him; and his blunt yoke has broken
25   The sultry shoulders of the mountain bull.

Strophe 2

    Words also, and thought as rapid as air,
    He fashions to his good use; statecraft is his,
    And his the skill that deflects the arrows of snow,
30   The spears of winter rain: from every wind
    He has made himself secure—from all but one:
    In the late wind of death he cannot stand.

Antistrophe 2

    O clear intelligence, force beyond all measure!
35   O fate of man, working both good and evil!
    When the laws are kept, how proudly his city stands!
    When the laws are broken, what of his city then?
    Never may the anárchic man find rest at my hearth,
    Never be it said that my thoughts are his thoughts.

SCENE II

(*Reenter* SENTRY *leading* ANTIGONÊ.)

CHORAGOS   What does this mean? Surely this captive woman
Is the Princess, Antigonê. Why should she be taken?

5   SENTRY   Here is the one who did it! We caught her
In the very act of burying him.—Where is Kreon?
CHORAGOS   Just coming from the house.

(*Enter* KREON, *center.*)

KREON   What has happened?
10   Why have you come back so soon?
SENTRY (*expansively*)   O King,
A man should never be too sure of anything:
I would have sworn
That you'd not see me here again: your anger
15   Frightened me so, and the things you threatened me with;
But how could I tell then
That I'd be able to solve the case so soon?
No dice-throwing this time: I was only too glad to come!
Here is this woman. She is the guilty one:
20   We found her trying to bury him.
Take her, then; question her; judge her as you will.
I am through with the whole thing now, and glad of it.
KREON   But this is Antigonê! Why have you brought her here?
SENTRY   She was burying him, I tell you!
25   KREON (*severely*)   Is this the truth?
SENTRY   I saw her with my own eyes. Can I say more?
KREON   The details: come, tell me quickly!
SENTRY   It was like this:
After those terrible threats of yours, King,
30   We went back and brushed the dust away from the body.
The flesh was soft by now, and stinking,
So we sat on a hill to windward and kept guard.
No napping this time! We kept each other awake.
But nothing happened until the white round sun
35   Whirled in the center of the round sky over us:
Then, suddenly,
A storm of dust roared up from the earth, and the sky
Went out, the plain vanished with all its trees
In the stinging dark. We closed our eyes and endured it.
40   The whirlwind lasted a long time, but it passed;
And then we looked, and there was Antigonê!
I have seen
A mother bird come back to a stripped nest, heard

Her crying bitterly a broken note or two
For the young ones stolen. Just so, when this girl
Found the bare corpse, and all her love's work wasted,
She wept, and cried on heaven to damn the hands

5   That had done this thing.
                    And then she brought more dust
And sprinkled wine three times for her brother's ghost.

We ran and took her at once. She was not afraid,
Not even when we charged her with what she had done.

10   She denied nothing.
                    And this was a comfort to me,
And some uneasiness: for it is a good thing
To escape from death, but it is no great pleasure
To bring death to a friend.

15   Yet I always say
There is nothing so comfortable as your own safe skin!
KREON (*slowly, dangerously*)   And you, Antigonê,
You with your head hanging,—do you confess this thing?
ANTIGONÊ   I do. I deny nothing.

20   KREON (*to* SENTRY)   You may go.

(*Exit* SENTRY.)

(*To* ANTIGONÊ.) Tell me, tell me briefly:
Had you heard my proclamation touching this matter?
ANTIGONÊ   It was public. Could I help hearing it?

25   KREON   And yet you dared defy the law.
ANTIGONÊ   I dared.
It was not God's proclamation. That final Justice
That rules the world below makes no such laws.

Your edict, King, was strong,
30   But all your strength is weakness itself against
The immortal unrecorded laws of God.
They are not merely now: they were, and shall be,
Operative for ever, beyond man utterly.

I knew I must die, even without your decree:
35   I am only mortal. And if I must die
Now, before it is my time to die,
Surely this is no hardship: can anyone
Living, as I live, with evil all about me,
Think Death less than a friend? This death of mine
40   Is of no importance; but if I had left my brother
Lying in death unburied, I should have suffered.

Now I do not.
You smile at me. Ah Kreon,

Think me a fool, if you like; but it may well be
That a fool convicts me of folly.

5 CHORAGOS   Like father, like daughter: both headstrong,
deaf to reason!
She has never learned to yield:
KREON   She has much to learn.
The inflexible heart breaks first, the toughest iron
10 Cracks first, and the wildest horses bend their necks
At the pull of the smallest curb.
Pride? In a slave?

This girl is guilty of a double insolence,
Breaking the given laws and boasting of it.
15 Who is the man here,
She or I, if this crime goes unpunished?
Sister's child, or more than sister's child,
Or closer yet in blood—she and her sister
Win bitter death for this!
20 (*To* SERVANTS.)   Go, some of you,
Arrest Ismenê. I accuse her equally.
Bring her: you will find her sniffling in the house there.

Her mind's a traitor: crimes kept in the dark
Cry for light, and the guardian brain shudders;
25 But how much worse than this
Is brazen boasting of barefaced anarchy!
ANTIGONÊ   Kreon, what more do you want than my death?
KREON   Nothing.
That gives me everything.
30 ANTIGONÊ   Then I beg you: kill me.
This talking is a great weariness: your words
Are distasteful to me, and I am sure that mine
Seem so to you. And yet they should not seem so:
I should have praise and honor for what I have done.
35 All these men here would praise me
Were their lips not frozen shut with fear of you.
(*Bitterly.*) Ah the good fortune of kings,
Licensed to say and do whatever they please!
KREON   You are alone here in that opinion.
40 ANTIGONÊ   No, they are with me. But they keep their tongues
in leash.
KREON   Maybe. But you are guilty, and they are not.
ANTIGONÊ   There is no guilt in reverence for the dead.
KREON   But Eteoclês—was he not your brother too?

ANTIGONÊ   My brother too.

KREON   And you insult his memory?

ANTIGONÊ (*softly*)   The dead man would not say that I insult it.

KREON   He would: for you honor a traitor as much as him.

5   ANTIGONÊ   His own brother, traitor or not, and equal in blood.

KREON   He made war on his country. Eteoclês defended it.

ANTIGONÊ   Nevertheless, there are honors due all the dead.

KREON   But not the same for the wicked as for the just.

ANTIGONÊ   Ah Kreon, Kreon,

10   Which of us can say what the gods hold wicked?

KREON   An enemy is an enemy, even dead.

ANTIGONÊ   It is my nature to join in love, not hate.

KREON (*finally losing patience*)   Go join them then; if you must
    have your love,

15   Find it in hell!

CHORAGOS   But see, Ismenê comes:

(*Enter* ISMENÊ, *guarded.*)

Those tears are sisterly, the cloud
That shadows her eyes rains down gentle sorrow.

20   KREON   You too, Ismenê,
Snake in my ordered house, sucking my blood
Stealthily—and all the time I never knew
That these two sisters were aiming at my throne!

                                        Ismenê

25   Do you confess your share in this crime, or deny it?
Answer me.

ISMENÊ   Yes, if she will let me say so. I am guilty.

ANTIGONÊ (*coldly*)   No, Ismenê. You have no right to say so.
You would not help me, and I will not have you help me.

30   ISMENÊ   But now I know what you meant; and I am here
To join you, to take my share of punishment.

ANTIGONÊ   The dead man and the gods who rule the dead
Know whose act this was. Words are not friends.

ISMENÊ   Do you refuse me, Antigonê? I want to die with you:

35   I too have a duty that I must discharge to the dead.

ANTIGONÊ   You shall not lessen my death by sharing it.

ISMENÊ   What do I care for life when you are dead?

ANTIGONÊ   Ask Kreon. You're always hanging on his opinions.

ISMENÊ   You are laughing at me. Why, Antigonê?

40   ANTIGONÊ   It's a joyless laughter, Ismenê.

ISMENÊ   But can I do nothing?

ANTIGONÊ   Yes. Save yourself. I shall not envy you.
There are those who will praise you; I shall have honor, too.

ISMENÊ   But we are equally guilty!

ANTIGONÊ　　　　　　　　No more, Ismenê.
You are alive, but I belong to Death.

KREON (*to the* CHORUS)　Gentlemen, I beg you to observe these
　　girls:

5　Onc has just now lost her mind; the other,
It seems, has never had a mind at all.

ISMENÊ　Grief teaches the steadiest minds to waver, King.

KREON　Yours certainly did, when you assumed guilt with the guilty!

ISMENÊ　But how could I go on living without her?

10　KREON　　　　　　　　　　　　　　　You are.
She is already dead.

ISMENÊ　　　　　　But your own son's bride!

KREON　There are places enough for him to push his plow.
I want no wicked women for my sons!

15　ISMENÊ　O dearest Haimon, how your father wrongs you!

KREON　I've had enough of your childish talk of marriage!

CHORAGOS　Do you really intend to steal this girl from your son?

KREON　No; Death will do that for me.

CHORAGOS　　　　　　　　　Then she must die?

20　KREON (*ironically*)　You dazzle me.
　　　　　　　　　　　　　But enough of this talk!
(*To* GUARDS.) You, there, take them away and guard them well:
For they are but women, and even brave men run
When they see Death coming.

25　(*Exeunt* ISMENÊ, ANTIGONÊ, *and* GUARDS.)

ODE II

Strophe 1

CHORUS　Fortunate is the man who has never tasted God's
　　vengeance!

30　Where once the anger of heaven has struck, that house is
　　shaken
For ever: damnation rises behind each child
Like a wave cresting out of the black northeast,
When the long darkness under sea roars up

35　And bursts drumming death upon the windwhipped sand.

Antistrophe 1

I have seen this gathering sorrow from time long past
Loom upon Oedipus' children: generation from generation
Takes the compulsive rage of the enemy god.

40　So lately this last flower of Oedipus' line

Drank the sunlight; but now a passionate word
And a handful of dust have closed up all its beauty.

Strophe 2

What mortal arrogance
5 Transcends the wrath of Zeus?
Sleep cannot lull him nor the effortless long months
Of the timeless gods: but he is young for ever,
And his house is the shining day of high Olympos.
All that is and shall be,
10 And all the past, is his.
No pride on earth is free of the curse of heaven.

Antistrophe 2

The straying dreams of men
May bring them ghosts of joy:
15 But as they drowse, the waking embers burn them;
Or they walk with fixed eyes, as blind men walk.
But the ancient wisdom speaks for our own time:
Fate works most for woe
With Folly's fairest show.
20 Man's little pleasure is the spring of sorrow.

SCENE III

CHORAGOS   But here is Haimon, King, the last of all your sons.
Is it grief for Antigonê that brings him here,
And bitterness at being robbed of his bride?

25 (*Enter* HAIMON.)

KREON   We shall soon see, and no need of diviners.
—Son,
You have heard my final judgment on that girl:
Have you come here hating me, or have you come
30 With deference and with love, whatever I do?
HAIMON   I am your son, father. You are my guide.
You make things clear for me, and I obey you.
No marriage means more to me than your continuing
wisdom.
35 KREON   Good. That is the way to behave: subordinate
Everything else, my son, to your father's will.
This is what a man prays for, that he may get
Sons attentive and dutiful in his house,
Each one hating his father's enemies,
40 Honoring his father's friends. But if his sons

Fail him, if they turn out unprofitably,
What has he fathered but trouble for himself
And amusement for the malicious?
                                    So you are right
5   Not to lose your head over this woman.
Your pleasure with her would soon grow cold, Haimon,
And then you'd have a hellcat in bed and elsewhere.
Let her find her husband in Hell!
Of all the people in this city, only she
10   Has had contempt for my law and broken it.

Do you want me to show myself weak before the people?
Or to break my sworn word? No, and I will not.
The woman dies.
I suppose she'll plead "family ties." Well, let her.
15   If I permit my own family to rebel,
How shall I earn the world's obedience?
Show me the man who keeps his house in hand,
He's fit for public authority.
                                    I'll have no dealings
20   With lawbreakers, critics of the government:
Whoever is chosen to govern should be obeyed—
Must be obeyed, in all things, great and small,
Just and unjust! O Haimon,
The man who knows how to obey, and that man only,
25   Knows how to give commands when the time comes.
You can depend on him, no matter how fast
The spears come: he's a good soldier, he'll stick it out.

Anarchy, anarchy! Show me a greater evil!
This is why cities tumble and the great houses rain down,
30   This is what scatters armies!
No, no: good lives are made so by discipline.
We keep the laws then, and the lawmakers,
And no woman shall seduce us. If we must lose,
Let's lose to a man, at least! Is a woman stronger than we?
35   CHORAGOS   Unless time has rusted my wits,
What you say, King, is said with point and dignity.
        HAIMON (*boyishly earnest*)   Father:
Reason is God's crowning gift to man, and you are right
To warn me against losing mine. I cannot say—
40   I hope that I shall never want to say!—that you
Have reasoned badly. Yet there are other men
Who can reason, too; and their opinions might be helpful.
You are not in a position to know everything

That people say or do, or what they feel:
Your temper terrifies—everyone
Will tell you only what you like to hear.
But I, at any rate, can listen; and I have heard them
5   Muttering and whispering in the dark about this girl.
They say no woman has ever, so unreasonably,
Died so shameful a death for a generous act:
"She covered her brother's body. Is this indecent?
She kept him from dogs and vultures. Is this a crime?
10   Death?—She should have all the honor that we can give her!"

This is the way they talk out there in the city.

You must believe me:
Nothing is closer to me than your happiness.
What could be closer? Must not any son
15   Value his father's fortune as his father does his?
I beg you, do not be unchangeable:
Do not believe that you alone can be right.
The man who thinks that,
The man who maintains that only he has the power
20   To reason correctly, the gift to speak, the soul—
A man like that, when you know him, turns out empty.

It is not reason never to yield to reason!

In flood time you can see how some trees bend,
And because they bend, even their twigs are safe,
25   While stubborn trees are torn up, roots and all.
And the same thing happens in sailing:
Make your sheet fast, never slacken,—and over you go,
Head over heels and under: and there's your voyage.
Forget you are angry! Let yourself be moved!
30   I know I am young; but please let me say this:
The ideal condition
Would be, I admit, that men should be right by instinct;
But since we are all too likely to go astray,
The reasonable thing is to learn from those who can teach.
35   CHORAGOS   You will do well to listen to him, King,
If what he says is sensible. And you, Haimon,
Must listen to your father.—Both speak well.
    KREON   You consider it right for a man of my years
       and experience
40   To go to school to a boy?

HAIMON   It is not right
If I am wrong. But if I am young, and right,
What does my age matter?
KREON   You think it right to stand up for an anarchist?
5 HAIMON   Not at all. I pay no respect to criminals.
KREON   Then she is not a criminal?
HAIMON   The City would deny it, to a man.
KREON   And the City proposes to teach me how to rule?
HAIMON   Ah. Who is it that's talking like a boy now?
10 KREON   My voice is the one voice giving orders in this City!
HAIMON   It is no City if it takes orders from one voice.
KREON   The State is the King!
HAIMON   Yes, if the State is a desert.

Pause.

15 KREON   This boy, it seems, has sold out to a woman.
HAIMON   If you are a woman: my concern is only for you.
KREON   So? Your "concern"! In a public brawl with your
    father!
HAIMON   How about you, in a public brawl with justice?
20 KREON   With justice, when all that I do is within my rights?
HAIMON   You have no right to trample on God's right.
KREON (*completely out of control*)   Fool, adolescent fool! Taken
    in by a woman!
HAIMON   You'll never see me taken in by anything vile.
25 KREON   Every word you say is for her!
HAIMON (*quietly, darkly*)   And for you.
    And for me. And for the gods under the earth.
KREON   You'll never marry her while she lives.
HAIMON   Then she must die.—But her death will cause another.
30 KREON   Another?
    Have you lost your senses? Is this an open threat?
HAIMON   There is no threat in speaking to emptiness.
KREON   I swear you'll regret this superior tone of yours!
    You are the empty one!
35 HAIMON   If you were not my father,
    I'd say you were perverse.
KREON   You girlstruck fool, don't play at words with me!
HAIMON   I am sorry. You prefer silence.
KREON   Now, by God—!
40 I swear, by all the gods in heaven above us,
    You'll watch it, I swear you shall!
    (*To the* SERVANTS.)   Bring her out!
    Bring the woman out! Let her die before his eyes!
    Here, this instant, with her bridegroom beside her!

HAIMON   Not here, no; she will not die here, King.
And you will never see my face again.
Go on raving as long as you've a friend to endure you.

(*Exit* HAIMON.)

5   CHORAGOS   Gone, gone.
Kreon, a young man in a rage is dangerous!
KREON   Let him do, or dream to do, more than a man can.
He shall not save these girls from death.
CHORAGOS   These girls?
10   You have sentenced them both?
KREON   No, you are right.
I will not kill the one whose hands are clean.
CHORAGOS   But Antigonê?
KREON (*somberly*)   I will carry her far away
15   Out there in the wilderness, and lock her
Living in a vault of stone. She shall have food,
As the custom is, to absolve the State of her death.
And there let her pray to the gods of hell:
They are her only gods:
20   Perhaps they will show her an escape from death,
Or she may learn,
                    though late,
That piety shown the dead is pity in vain.

(*Exit* KREON.)

25   ## ODE III

Strophe

CHORUS   Love, unconquerable
Waster of rich men, keeper
Of warm lights and all-night vigil
30   In the soft face of a girl:
Sea-wanderer, forest-visitor!
Even the pure Immortals cannot escape you,
And mortal man, in his one day's dusk,
Trembles before your glory.

35   ### Antistrophe

Surely you swerve upon ruin
The just man's consenting heart,
As here you have made bright anger
Strike between father and son—

And none has conquered but Love!
A girl's glance working the will of heaven:
Pleasure to her alone who mocks us,
Merciless Aphroditê.[1]

5 SCENE IV

CHORAGOS (*as* ANTIGONÊ *enters guarded*)   But I can no longer
stand in awe of this,
Nor, seeing what I see, keep back my tears.
Here is Antigonê, passing to that chamber
10   Where all find sleep at last.

Strophe 1

ANTIGONÊ   Look upon me, friends, and pity me
Turning back at the night's edge to say
Good-by to the sun that shines for me no longer;
15   Now sleepy Death
Summons me down to Acheron,[2] that cold shore:
There is no bridesong there, nor any music.
CHORUS   Yet not unpraised, not without a kind of honor,
You walk at last into the underworld;
20   Untouched by sickness, broken by no sword.
What woman has ever found your way to death?

Antistrophe 1

ANTIGONÊ   How often I have heard the story
of Niobê,[3]
25   Tantalos' wretched daughter, how the stone
Clung fast about her, ivy-close: and they say
The rain falls endlessly
And sifting soft snow; her tears are never done.
I feel the loneliness of her death in mine.
30   CHORUS   But she was born of heaven, and you
Are woman, woman-born. If her death is yours,
A mortal woman's, is this not for you
Glory in our world and in the world beyond?

---

[1] *Aphroditê* goddess of love
[2] *Acheron* a river in the underworld
[3] *Niobê* Niobê, the daughter of Tantalos, was turned into a stone on Mount
Sipylus while bemoaning the destruction of her many children by Leto, the
mother of Apollo.

Strophe 2

ANTIGONÊ   You laugh at me. Ah, friends, friends,
Can you not wait until I am dead? O Thebes,
O men many-charioted, in love with Fortune,
5   Dear springs of Dircê, sacred Theban grove,
Be witnesses for me, denied all pity,
Unjustly judged! and think a word of love
For her whose path turns
Under dark earth, where there are no more tears.
10   CHORUS   You have passed beyond human daring and come at last
Into a place of stone where Justice sits.
I cannot tell
What shape of your father's guilt appears in this.

Antistrophe 2

15   ANTIGONÊ   You have touched it at last:
that bridal bed
Unspeakable, horror of son and mother mingling:
Their crime, infection of all our family!
O Oedipus, father and brother!
20   Your marriage strikes from the grave to murder mine.
I have been a stranger here in my own land:
All my life
The blasphemy of my birth has followed me.
CHORUS   Reverence is a virtue, but strength
25   Lives in established law: that must prevail.
You have made your choice,
Your death is the doing of your conscious hand.

Epode

ANTIGONÊ   Then let me go, since all your words are bitter,
30   And the very light of the sun is cold to me.
Lead me to my vigil, where I must have
Neither love nor lamentation; no song, but silence.

(KREON *interrupts impatiently.*)

KREON   If dirges and planned lamentations could put off death,
35   Men would be singing for ever.
(*To the* SERVANTS)   Take her, go!
You know your orders: take her to the vault
And leave her alone there. And if she lives or dies,
That's her affair, not ours: our hands are clean.

40   ANTIGONÊ   O tomb, vaulted bride-bed in eternal rock,
Soon I shall be with my own again

Where Persephonê[1] welcomes the thin ghosts
   underground:
And I shall see my father again, and you, mother,
And dearest Polyneicês—
dearest indeed

5   To me, since it was my hand
That washed him clean and poured the ritual wine:
And my reward is death before my time!

And yet, as men's hearts know, I have done no wrong,
10   I have not sinned before God. Or if I have,
I shall know the truth in death. But if the guilt
Lies upon Kreon who judged me, then, I pray,
May his punishment equal my own.

CHORAGOS   O passionate heart,
15   Unyielding, tormented still by the same winds!

KREON   Her guards shall have good cause to regret their delaying.

ANTIGONÊ   Ah! That voice is like the voice of death!

KREON   I can give you no reason to think you are mistaken.

ANTIGONÊ   Thebes, and you my fathers' gods,
20   And rulers of Thebes, you see me now, the last
Unhappy daughter of a line of kings,
Your kings, led away to death. You will remember
What things I suffer, and at what men's hands,
Because I would not transgress the laws of heaven.
25   (*To the* GUARDS, *simply.*) Come: let us wait no longer.

(*Exit* ANTIGONÊ, *left, guarded.*)

ODE IV

Strophe 1

CHORUS   All Danaê's[2] beauty was locked away
30   In a brazen cell where the sunlight could not come:
A small room still as any grave, enclosed her.
Yet she was a princess too,
And Zeus in a rain of gold poured love upon her.
O child, child,
35   No power in wealth or war

---

1 *Persephonê* queen of the underworld
2 *Danaê* the mother of Perseus by Zeus, who visited her during her imprisonment in the form of a golden rain

Or tough sea-blackened ships
Can prevail against untiring Destiny!

Antistrophe 1

And Dryas' son[1] also, that furious king,
5   Bore the god's prisoning anger for his pride:
Sealed up by Dionysos in deaf stone,
His madness died among echoes.
So at the last he learned what dreadful power
His tongue had mocked:
10   For he had profaned the revels,
And fired the wrath of the nine
Implacable Sisters[2] that love the sound of the flute.

Strophe 2

And old men tell a half-remembered tale
15   Of horror where a dark ledge splits the sea
And a double surf beats on the gráy shóres:
How a king's new woman,[3] sick
With hatred for the queen he had imprisoned,
Ripped out his two sons' eyes with her bloody hands
20   While grinning Arês[4] watched the shuttle plunge
Four times: four blind wounds crying for revenge.

Antistrophe 2

Crying, tears and blood mingled.—Piteously born,
Those sons whose mother was of heavenly birth!
25   Her father was the god of the North Wind
And she was cradled by gales,
She raced with young colts on the glittering hills
And walked untrammeled in the open light:
But in her marriage deathless Fate found means
30   To build a tomb like yours for all her joy.

SCENE V

(*Enter blind* TEIRESIAS, *led by a boy. The opening speeches of* TEIRE-
SIAS *should be in singsong contrast to the realistic lines of* KREON.)

TEIRESIAS   This is the way the blind man comes, Princes, Princes,
35   Lock-step, two heads lit by the eyes of one.

---

[1] *Dryas' son* Lycurgus, king of Thrace
[2] *Sisters* the Muses
[3] *king's new woman* Eidothea, King Phineus' second wife, blinded her step-
sons.
[4] *Arês* god of war

KREON   What new thing have you to tell us, old Teiresias?

TEIRESIAS   I have much to tell you: listen to the prophet, Kreon.

KREON   I am not aware that I have ever failed to listen.

TEIRESIAS   Then you have done wisely, King, and ruled well.

5   KREON   I admit my debt to you. But what have you to say?

TEIRESIAS   This, Kreon: you stand once more on the edge of fate.

KREON   What do you mean? Your words are a kind of dread.

TEIRESIAS   Listen, Kreon:

I was sitting in my chair of augury, at the place

10   Where the birds gather about me. They were all a-chatter,

As is their habit, when suddenly I heard

A strange note in their jangling, a scream, a

Whirring fury; I knew that they were fighting,

Tearing each other, dying

15   In a whirlwind of wings clashing. And I was afraid.

I began the rites of burnt-offering at the altar,

But Hephaistos[1] failed me: instead of bright flame,

There was only the sputtering slime of the fat thigh-flesh

Melting: the entrails dissolved in gray smoke,

20   The bare bone burst from the welter. And no blaze!

This was a sign from heaven. My boy described it,

Seeing for me as I see for others.

I tell you, Kreon, you yourself have brought

This new calamity upon us. Our hearths and altars

25   Are stained with the corruption of dogs and carrion birds

That glut themselves on the corpse of Oedipus' son.

The gods are deaf when we pray to them, their fire

Recoils from our offering, their birds of omen

Have no cry of comfort, for they are gorged

30   With the thick blood of the dead.

O my son,

These are no trifles! Think: all men make mistakes,

But a good man yields when he knows his course is wrong,

And repairs the evil. The only crime is pride.

35   Give in to the dead man, then: do not fight with a corpse—

What glory is it to kill a man who is dead?

Think, I beg you:

---

[1] *Hephaistos* god of fire

It is for your own good that I speak as I do.
You should be able to yield for your own good.
KREON   It seems that prophets have made me their especial
 province.
5   All my life long
I have been a kind of butt for the dull arrows
Of doddering fortune-tellers!
                            No, Teiresias:
If your birds—if the great eagles of God himself
10   Should carry him stinking bit by bit to heaven,
I would not yield. I am not afraid of pollution:
No man can defile the gods.
                           Do what you will,
Go into business, make money, speculate
15   In India gold or that synthetic gold from Sardis,
Get rich otherwise than by my consent to bury him.
Teiresias, it is a sorry thing when a wise man
Sells his wisdom, lets out his words for hire!
TEIRESIAS   Ah Kreon! Is there no man left in the world—
20   KREON   To do what?—Come, let's have the aphorism!
TEIRESIAS   No man who knows that wisdom outweighs any wealth?
KREON   As surely as bribes are baser than any baseness.
TEIRESIAS   You are sick, Kreon! You are deathly sick!
KREON   As you say: it is not my place to challenge a prophet.
25   TEIRESIAS   Yet you have said my prophecy is for sale.
KREON   The generation of prophets has always loved gold.
TEIRESIAS   The generation of kings has always loved brass.
KREON   You forget yourself! You are speaking to your King.
TEIRESIAS   I know it. You are a king because of me.
30   KREON   You have a certain skill; but you have sold out.
TEIRESIAS   King, you will drive me to words that—
KREON   Say them, say them!
Only remember: I will not pay you for them.
TEIRESIAS   No, you will find them too costly,
35   KREON   No doubt. Speak:
Whatever you say, you will not change my will.
TEIRESIAS   Then take this, and take it to heart!
The time is not far off when you shall pay back
Corpse for corpse, flesh of your own flesh.
40   You have thrust the child of this world into living night,
You have kept from the gods below the child that is theirs:
The one in a grave before her death, the other,
Dead, denied the grave. This is your crime:
And the Furies and the dark gods of Hell
45   Are swift with terrible punishment for you.

Do you want to buy me now, Kreon?

                          Not many days,
And your house will be full of men and women weeping,
And curses will be hurled at you from far
5   Cities grieving for sons unburied, left to rot
Before the walls of Thebes.

These are my arrows, Kreon: they are all for you.

(*To* BOY.) But come, child: lead me home.
Let him waste his fine anger upon younger men.
10   Maybe he will learn at last
To control a wiser tongue in a better head.

(*Exit* TEIRESIAS.)

CHORAGOS   The old man has gone, King, but his words
Remain to plague us. I am old, too,
15   But I cannot remember that he was ever false.
KREON   That is true. . . . It troubles me.
Oh it is hard to give in! but it is worse
To risk everything for stubborn pride.
CHORAGOS   Kreon: take my advice.
20   KREON   What shall I do?
CHORAGOS   Go quickly: free Antigonê from her vault
And build a tomb for the body of Polyneicês.
KREON   You would have me do this!
CHORAGOS   Kreon, yes!
25   And it must be done at once: God moves
Swiftly to cancel the folly of stubborn men.
KREON   It is hard to deny the heart! But I
Will do it: I will not fight with destiny.
CHORAGOS   You must go yourself, you cannot leave it to others.
30   KREON   I will go.
                  —Bring axes, servants:
Come with me to the tomb. I buried her, I
Will set her free.
                  Oh quickly!
35   My mind misgives—
The laws of the gods are mighty, and a man must serve them
To the last day of his life!

(*Exit* KREON.)

PAEAN [1]

Strophe 1

CHORAGOS   God of many names

CHORUS   O Iacchos[2]

5   son
of Kadmeian Sémelê[3]
                         O born of the Thunder!
Guardian of the West
                         Regent
10   of Eleusis' plain
                         O Prince of maenad Thebes
and the Dragon Field by rippling Ismenós:[4]

Antistrophe 1

CHORAGOS   God of many names

15 CHORUS   the flame of torches
flares on our hills
                         the nymphs of Iacchos
dance at the spring of Castalia:[5]
from the vine-close mountain
20   come ah come in ivy:
Evohé evohé! sings through the streets of Thebes

Strophe 2

CHORAGOS   God of many names

CHORUS   Iacchos of Thebes
25   heavenly Child
                         of Sémelê bride of the Thunderer!
The shadow of plague is upon us:
                                         come
with clement feet
30   oh come from Parnasos
down the long slopes
                         across the lamenting water

Antistrophe 2

CHORAGOS   Iô Fire! Chorister of the throbbing stars!
35   O purest among the voices of the night!
Thou son of God, blaze for us!

---

[1] *Paean* a hymn of praise
[2] *Iacchos* another name for Dionysos (Bacchus)
[3] *Sémelê* the daughter of Kadmos, the founder of Thebes
[4] *Ismenós* a river east of Thebes. The ancestors of the Theban nobility sprang from dragon's teeth sown by the Ismenós.
[5] *Castalia* a spring on Mount Parnasos

CHORUS　Come with choric rapture of circling Maenads[1]
Who cry *Iô Iacche!*
　　God of many names!

EXODOS

5　(*Enter* MESSENGER *from left.*)

MESSENGER　Men of the line of Kadmos, you who live
Near Amphion's citadel,[2]
　　　　　　I cannot say
Of any condition of human life "This is fixed,
10　This is clearly good, or bad." Fate raises up,
And Fate casts down the happy and unhappy alike:
No man can foretell his Fate.
　　　　　　Take the case of Kreon:
Kreon was happy once, as I count happiness:
15　Victorious in battle, sole governor of the land,
Fortunate father of children nobly born.
And now it has all gone from him! Who can say
That a man is still alive when his life's joy fails?
He is a walking dead man. Grant him rich,
20　Let him live like a king in his great house:
If his pleasure is gone, I would not give
So much as the shadow of smoke for all he owns.
CHORAGOS　Your words hint at sorrow: what is your news for us?
MESSENGER　They are dead. The living are guilty of their death.
25　CHORAGOS　Who is guilty? Who is dead? Speak!
MESSENGER　　　　　　　　　　　　　Haimon.
Haimon is dead; and the hand that killed him
Is his own hand.
CHORAGOS　His father's? or his own?
30　MESSENGER　His own, driven mad by the murder his father had
done.
CHORAGOS　Teiresias, Teiresias, how clearly you saw it all!
MESSENGER　This is my news: you must draw what conclusions
you can from it.
35　CHORAGOS　But look: Eurydicê, our Queen:
Has she overheard us?

(*Enter* EURYDICÊ *from the palace, center.*)

---

[1] *Maenads* the worshippers of Dionysos
[2] *Amphion's citadel* Amphion used the music of his magic lyre to lure stones to form a wall around Thebes.

EURYDICÊ   I have heard something, friends:
As I was unlocking the gate of Pallas' [1] shrine,
For I needed her help today, I heard a voice
Telling of some new sorrow. And I fainted
5   There at the temple all my maidens about me.
But speak again: whatever it is, I can bear it:
Grief and I are no strangers.

MESSENGER   Dearest Lady,
I will tell you plainly all that I have seen.
10   I shall not try to comfort you: what is the use,
Since comfort could lie only in what is not true?
The truth is always best.

                          I went with Kreon
To the outer plain where Polyneicês was lying,
15   No friend to pity him, his body shredded by dogs.
We made our prayers in that place to Hecatê
And Pluto,[2] that they would be merciful. And we bathed
The corpse with holy water, and we brought
Fresh-broken branches to burn what was left of it,
20   And upon the urn we heaped up a towering barrow
Of the earth of his own land.

                          When we were done, we ran
To the vault where Antigonê lay on her couch of stone.
One of the servants had gone ahead,
25   And while he was yet far off he heard a voice
Grieving within the chamber, and he came back
And told Kreon. And as the King went closer,
The air was full of wailing, the words lost,
And he begged us to make all haste. "Am I a prophet?"
30   He said, weeping, "And must I walk this road,
The saddest of all that I have gone before?
My son's voice calls me on. Oh quickly, quickly!
Look through the crevice there, and tell me
If it is Haimon, or some deception of the gods!"

35   We obeyed; and in the cavern's farthest corner
We saw her lying:
She had made a noose of her fine linen veil
And hanged herself. Haimon lay beside her,
His arms about her waist, lamenting her,

---

[1] *Pallas* Pallas Athena, the goddess of wisdom
[2] *Hecatê . . . Pluto* the ruling deities of the underworld

His love lost under ground, crying out
That his father had stolen her away from him.

When Kreon saw him the tears rushed to his eyes
And he called to him: "What have you done, child?
5   Speak to me.
What are you thinking that makes your eyes so strange?
O my son, my son, I come to you on my knees!"
But Haimon spat in his face. He said not a word,
Staring—
10   And suddenly drew his sword
And lunged. Kreon shrank back, the blade missed; and the
      boy,
Desperate against himself, drove it half its length
Into his own side, and fell. And as he died
15 He gathered Antigonê close in his arms again,
Choking, his blood bright red on her white cheek.
And now he lies dead with the dead, and she is his
At last, his bride in the house of the dead.

(*Exit* EURYDICÊ *into the palace.*)

20 CHORAGOS   She has left us without a word. What can this mean?
MESSENGER   It troubles me, too; yet she knows what is best,
Her grief is too great for public lamentation,
And doubtless she has gone to her chamber to weep
For her dead son, leading her maidens in his dirge.

25   (*Pause.*)

CHORAGOS   It may be so: but I fear this deep silence.
MESSENGER   I will see what she is doing. I will go in.

(*Exit* MESSENGER *into the palace. Enter* KREON *with attendants, bearing* HAIMON's *body.*)

30 CHORAGOS   But here is the king himself: oh look at him,
Bearing his own damnation in his arms.
KREON   Nothing you say can touch me any more.
My own blind heart has brought me
From darkness to final darkness. Here you see
35 The father murdering, the murdered son—
And all my civic wisdom!

Haimon my son, so young, so young to die,
I was the fool, not you; and you died for me.
CHORAGOS   That is the truth; but you were late in learning it.

KREON   This truth is hard to bear. Surely a god
Has crushed me beneath the hugest weight of heaven,
And driven me headlong a barbaric way
To trample out the thing I held most dear.

5   The pains that men will take to come to pain!

(*Enter* MESSENGER *from the palace.*)

MESSENGER   The burden you carry in your hands is heavy,
But it is not all: you will find more in your house.
KREON   What burden worse than this shall I find there?
10   MESSENGER   The Queen is dead.
KREON   O port of death, deaf world,
Is there no pity for me? And you, Angel of evil,
I was dead, and your words are death again.
Is it true, boy? Can it be true?
15   Is my wife dead? Has death bred death?
MESSENGER   You can see for yourself.

(*The doors are opened and the body of* EURYDICÊ *is disclosed within.*)

KREON   Oh pity!
All true, all true, and more than I can bear!
20   O my wife, my son!
MESSENGER   She stood before the altar, and her heart
Welcomed the knife her own hand guided,
And a great cry burst from her lips for Megareus[1] dead,
And for Haimon dead, her sons; and her last breath
25   Was a curse for their father, the murderer of her sons.
And she fell, and the dark flowed in through her closing eyes.
KREON   O God, I am sick with fear.
Are there no swords here? Has no one a blow for me?
MESSENGER   Her curse is upon you for the deaths of both.
30   KREON   It is right that it should be. I alone am guilty.
I know it, and I say it. Lead me in,
Quickly, friends.
I have neither life nor substance. Lead me in.
CHORAGOS   You are right, if there can be right in so much wrong.
35   The briefest way is best in a world of sorrow.
KREON   Let it come,
Let death come quickly, and be kind to me.
I would not ever see the sun again.
CHORAGOS   All that will come when it will; but we, meanwhile,

---

[1] *Megareus* Megareus, brother of Haimon, had died in the assault on Thebes.

Have much to do. Leave the future to itself.

KREON   All my heart was in that prayer!

CHORAGOS   Then do not pray any more: the sky is deaf.

KREON   Lead me away. I have been rash and foolish.

5   I have killed my son and my wife.

I look for comfort; my comfort lies here dead.

Whatever my hands have touched has come to nothing.

Fate has brought all my pride to a thought of dust.

10   (*As* KREON *is being led into the house, the* CHORAGOS *advances and speaks directly to the audience.*)

CHORAGOS   There is no happiness where there is no wisdom;

No wisdom but in submission to the gods.

Big words are always punished,

And proud men in old age learn to be wise.

QUESTIONS

1. One might argue that in *Antigonê* each of the major characters undergoes his or her own moment of "recognition" and subsequent reversal of fortune. For instance, one can say that the play opens on Antigonê's recognition of Kreon's edict—both because she has just learned of the edict and because she here expresses her realization of how she must react to it and of what retaliation her reaction is likely to draw.
   a. Arguing along these lines, identify the scenes, events, and speeches that mark Kreon's recognition. What reversal would you say follows from it?
   b. Would you also want to argue for recognitions for Haimon, Eurydicê, and Ismenê? If so, where would you place them, and what reversals would you say follow them?
   c. Write an essay that (1) discusses each of these recognitions and their significance to the characters involved, and (2) demonstrates how the placement and cumulative effect of these several recognitions and reversals give the play its shape and dramatic impact. (Remember that you must define the structure and movement of the play as you see it, to ensure that you and your reader are working from the same basic understanding.)
2. How would you balance the claims of "thought" and "character" as the more important element in *Antigonê*? (In other words, is it the questions argued or the character and fate of the debaters that you feel provide the strongest source of the play's appeal?) Would either element alone suffice? Why or why not?
3. Antigonê and Kreon are, of course, the major antagonists in *Antigonê*. But each has another opponent as well. Ismenê argues against Antigonê's actions, and Haimon argues against Kreon. What do the presence and actions of these two characters add to the play?

3 Hamlet *and* Elizabethan *Tragedy*

Origins of English Drama

English drama can be traced back to two origins, one in tenth-century England and one in ancient Greece. The two beginnings differed greatly in style and content but did have one important thing in common: both formed parts of religious rituals.

Medieval Drama

Drama in medieval Europe seems to have begun as part of the Easter services. At some appropriate point during the Mass or the matins service, one or two men would unobtrusively position themselves near the altar or near some representation of a tomb. There, they would be approached by three other men, whose heads were covered to look like women and who moved slowly, as if seeking something. Singing in the Latin of the church service, the "angel" at the tomb would question the "women," "Whom seek you in the tomb, O followers of Christ?" The women would then sing the answer of the three Mary's, "Jesus of Nazareth, who was crucified, O heavenly one." The angel then would sing again, "He is not here; he is risen, just as he foretold. Go, announce that he is risen from the tomb."

The dramatization might stop there, or it might continue with the showing of the empty tomb to the women, their song of joy, and the spreading of the good news to the disciples. In either case, the culmination of the drama would mark a return to the service itself with the singing of the Mass's *Ressurexi* ("I have risen") or the matins' final *Te deum, laudamus* ("We praise thee, Lord").

One medieval manuscript in particular emphasizes the closeness of the connection. It describes the singers of the *Te Deum* as rejoicing with the three women at Christ's triumph over death and commands that all the church bells be rung together as soon as the hymn of praise has begun. Drama and service thus celebrate the same event. The joy expressed by the women at the news of the resurrection is the same joy felt by the worshippers in the congregation.

Latin drama continued to develop within the church services. Manuscripts still survive, not only of Easter and Christmas plays but of plays dealing with prophets and saints as well. They show the plays growing longer and more elaborate than the early one just described, but they still emphasize the close ties between the plays and the services at which they are performed. Thus, one Christmas pageant of the shepherds calls for many boys dressed as angels to sit in the roof of the church and sing in loud voices the angels' song, "Glory to God." But it also directs that, at the end of the pageant, the shepherds must return into the choir and there act as choir leaders for the Mass that follows.

By the fourteenth century, however, drama had also moved outside the church. There it was spoken almost wholly in the vernacular, though some bits of Latin, and a good deal of singing, remained. The plays were acted by laymen (including some professional actors) rather than by clerics, and they were developing modes of performance that might encompass up to three days of playing and involve most of the citizens of the towns where they were performed.

These were the Corpus Christi plays, also known as the "cycle plays" or the "mystery plays." Performed in celebration of Corpus Christi day, they comprised a series of pageants beginning with the creation of the world, proceeding through the history of the Old and New Testaments, and ending with the Last Judgment. Each pageant was performed on its own movable stage—its "pageant wagon." Mounted on four or six wheels, two stories high, the wagons provided facilities for some surprisingly complex stage effects and allowed each pageant to be presented several times at several different locations. One after another, the pageants would move through a town, usually stopping at three or four prearranged places to repeat their performances, so that everyone in town might see all of the twenty to fifty plays that made up the cycle.

The presentation of these cycles was undertaken by the towns themselves, with the town authorities ordering the performances. But the individual pageants were produced by the local trade and craft guilds. Ordinarily each guild would present one pageant, but sometimes several small guilds would team up to perform a single pageant or share the cost of a wagon that each could use. It is easy to imagine the competition this could produce, with each guild trying to outdo the next. But the plays were still religious in subject and import. They often spoke directly to the audience and always emphasized how the events they depicted pertained to each viewer's salvation.

Early English Dramatic Forms

As we suggested in the last chapter, Greek drama carefully labeled and segregated its forms. Tragedy dealt with noble persons and heroic actions. Comedy dealt with everyday affairs.

Medieval drama did not so carefully distinguish its forms. It had one central sacrificial subject: the death of Christ for the salvation of mankind. This sacrifice was always treated seriously; neither Christ nor Mary were ever burlesqued. But the world that Christ entered at his birth was the world of thin clothes and bad weather, of thieves and tricksters and con men, with the Devil himself, the arch-trickster, as Christ's opponent. It was, in short, the world of comedy. A drama that dealt with the history of man's fall and salvation would thus have to be both comic and tragic. There would be no way of separating the two.

Nor would medieval writers have wanted to separate them. Medieval art always seems to have preferred inclusiveness to exclusiveness. The great Gothic cathedrals themselves, with their profusion of sculpture and stained glass, would give their most prominent and most beautiful art to scenes of Christ, the Virgin, and the saints. But less prominent carvings would be likely to show small boys stealing apples, or people quarreling; while, in other places, comically or frighteningly grotesque demons would round out the portrayals.

A Corpus Christi cycle, therefore, would contain both serious and humorous elements. Some plays would be wholly serious; others would mix the serious with the comic. "The Sacrifice of Isaac," for instance, was always serious. The dilemma of the father, the emotions of the son as he realized what was happening, combined to produce plays that could virtually be described as tragedies with happy endings. "Noah's Flood," on the other hand, was usually given a comic treatment. (What would you do if your husband suddenly started building a giant boat in your front yard?) In some of the plays, Noah's wife thinks her husband has gone crazy. In others, she joins in the building until it is time to get on board, then rebels against leaving the world she knows and loves. In either case, a physical fight ensues before Noah can get her on board, and Noah's prophecies of doom are mixed with his complaints about marriage. Crucifixion plays, meanwhile, generally mixed the solemnity of the highest sacrifice with a certain amount of low comedy centering on the executioners. There was no thought of separating the two. Both were parts of the same event.

In this way, seeking to mirror life and to emphasize its mixture of noble and ignoble, sacred and mundane, the medieval drama provided Elizabethan playwrights a heritage of flexible, all-inclusive drama, capable at its best of seeing both sides of a subject at once, always insistent that both must be recognized. By mixing this heritage with the more single-minded Greek tragic tradition, Elizabethan dramatists produced a tragic form of their own as rich and compelling as any that has existed.

In this chapter, we shall study one of the most highly praised and frequently acted Elizabethan tragedies—William Shakespeare's *Hamlet*.

Hamlet and *Oedipus Rex*

In many ways, *Hamlet* is similar to *Oedipus Rex*. Both were written at times when tragedy was just coming to its full maturity in their playwrights' cultures. Both were written by the most influential playwrights of their time. Both helped set the shape of tragedy for their own period's drama and for the drama of future ages.

Both plays have heroes who dominate the action, catching the audience's attention early in the play and holding their attention and their sympathy throughout. (Hamlet, in fact, can even address the audience in soliloquies and "asides" that no one on stage is meant to hear.) Princely in nature and position, both men seem born to rule. The heroes are somewhat alike in their situations, as well. Both must avenge their father's murder and thus remove a pollution from their land. To do so, however, they must first find out who the murderer is; and they must pursue their search among people who want the truth to remain hidden.

Here, however, the situations diverge. Oedipus' companions want to conceal the truth for Oedipus' own sake. Hamlet's opponent, Claudius, wants the truth to remain hidden because he is the murderer. The element of active, willed evil, which is absent from *Oedipus Rex*, is thus present in *Hamlet*. Hamlet must not only destroy his father's murderer; he must do so before the murderer destroys him.

Hamlet, as we suggested earlier, is a play derived from both Greek and medieval drama. From Greek tragedy, it has taken the tragic hero—dominant, strong-willed, determined to accomplish his desires. From Greek tragedy also it has taken a certain elevation of tone and insistence on the dignity of human beings. From medieval drama, it has taken the medieval desire for inclusiveness and the medieval love of significant detail. *Hamlet* is much longer than *Oedipus Rex*. It has more characters, a more complex plot, and a generous amount of comedy.

Let us look at each of these elements in turn. Regarding characters, we notice that Oedipus is unique, but that Hamlet sees himself reflected in two other characters: first in Fortinbras, another son of a warrior king whose father has died and whose uncle has seized the throne, leaving him practically powerless; and later in Laertes, another son determined to avenge himself on his father's murderer. The deeds of Laertes and Fortinbras contrast with and comment on the actions of Hamlet himself, thus enriching our view of Hamlet and his dilemma. At the same time, the actions of the three men intertwine to create three of the play's major themes: fathers and sons, honor, and thought versus action.

Regarding plot, we can be sure that the affairs of three families will create a more complex plot than the affairs of one family. Thus critics sometimes speak of the Fortinbras "overplot" (which is mostly concerned with war and kingship) and the Laertes "underplot" (concerned with private family relationships), while discussing how these two "subplots" complement the "main plot" (which deals with Hamlet's familial and princely concerns). But the English inclusiveness goes even beyond this, adding also a love story between Hamlet and Laertes' sister, Ophelia, a study of true versus false friendship in the persons of Horatio and Rosencrantz and Guildenstern, and a few comments on the contemporary theater by a troupe of strolling players. There are also glimpses of three purely comic characters: two gravediggers and one intolerably affected courtier. Again, all these themes and characters are interwoven to illuminate Hamlet's character and dilemma. (The gravediggers, for instance, who seem at first wildly irrelevant, ultimately serve to bring Hamlet to a new understanding of mortality, an understanding that is crucial to his ability to face his own death.)

In *Hamlet* comedy is not separate from tragedy. Rather, it is used as a means to create a fuller awareness of tragedy. Hamlet himself is a master of comic wordplay. His first speech turns on a pun; and puns and bitter quips mark his speech to Claudius and his courtiers throughout the play. Many of these quips are spoken under the guise of pretended madness; and here the audience shares secrets with Hamlet. We know he is not really mad. But those on stage think he is. (The exception is Claudius, who suspects that Hamlet is not mad but who cannot reveal Hamlet's sanity without revealing his own crimes.) Pretending madness, therefore, Hamlet makes speeches that sound like nonsense to the courtiers but that we recognize as referring to his father's murder and his recognition of treachery in those around him. We are thus let into Hamlet's secrets and feelings as no single character in the play is let into them. Hamlet's use of jesting speech thus becomes not merely a weapon in his fight against Claudius, but also a means of winning the sympathetic partnership of the audience. In comic speech and tragic soliloquy alike, Hamlet reveals himself to us. By the play's end, we know Hamlet as we know few other stage characters.

Adding to our sense of knowledge is the fact that Hamlet is a complex and changing character. In this he differs markedly from Oedipus, whose character remains firm and fixed until it changes so drastically in his final scene. The essentially fixed character is typical of Greek drama, which seems to have been more interested in the clash of character against character (or of character against fate) than it was in the changes within or the development of a single character. It is far less typical of Elizabethan tragedy.

This emphasis on Hamlet's developing character is an indication of the influence of medieval Christian drama, with its concern for salvation and the dangers and triumphs of the soul. English drama was secular drama by Shakespeare's time, being performed regularly by professional troupes for paying audiences. Concern for the soul, however, remained one of its major concerns. When Elizabethan dramatists wrote tragedies, therefore, they tended to make the hero's inner concerns—his passions, his temptations, his spiritual triumphs or defeats—the central focus of their plays. Even the ghost in *Hamlet,* coming to call for revenge, warns Hamlet to "taint not thy mind, nor let thy soul contrive/Against thy mother aught." Hamlet must avenge his father and free Denmark from the polluting rule of Claudius; but he must do so in a manner that will imperil neither his own nor his mother's salvation.

When the play opens, Hamlet is a bitter man. So far from being at peace with himself or his surroundings is he that he seems to have little chance of fulfilling the ghost's demands. So close does he come to flinging away his own soul in pursuit of Claudius, in fact, that some critics have refused to believe that Hamlet's speeches in Act III, Scene 3, mean what they say. In fact, they mean exactly what they say. Hamlet in this scene is on the brink of disaster.

In the next scene, the "closet scene," the unexpected happens. Hamlet is caught in the wrong, realizes it, and begins the painful process of returning from his bitterness and hatreds to a reconciliation with himself, his mother, and humanity in general. Throughout the rest of the play, we watch Hamlet's speeches on human nature become gentler, his attitude more compassionate; we hear a new acceptance of his fate, a new trust in providence, revealed. By the play's end, when Hamlet gets his one chance at Claudius, he is fully ready for the task and its consequences. And so the play ends in mingled triumph and loss: a loss to Denmark and to us in the death of Hamlet, a joy that Hamlet has nobly achieved his purpose.

One final word must be said about the language of *Hamlet,* which is like the language of no other play we will read in this book. Seeking some meter in English that would match the beauty and dignity of the meters in which classical tragedy had been written, the sixteenth century dramatists had created **blank verse.** Blank verse does not rhyme. It usually has ten syllables to a line (though lines may be shorter or longer by a few syllables), and the second, fourth, sixth, eighth, and tenth syllables are generally accented more strongly than the rest. This meter was easily spoken. It was dignified and flexible. And it could slip neatly into prose (for comic scenes) or into rhymed couplets to mark a scene's end.

Blank verse was fairly new when Shakespeare began writing. In some of his early plays, it still sounds stiff and awkward. By the time he wrote

Hamlet, however, Shakespeare was entering into a mastery of blank verse that no one has ever surpassed. The rhythms and imagery of Hamlet's language warn us of every change in his moods, from pretended madness to honest friendship to bitter passion. By the modulation of Hamlet's language, as well as by his actions, Shakespeare shows us the battle within Hamlet's soul.

If you can see *Hamlet*—live or on film—or if you can hear recordings of it, do so. If not, read as much of it aloud as you can. For readers unfamiliar with Shakespearean language, *Hamlet* is not an easy play to read. Nearly every word of it counts; so every word must be attended to. But the play is well worth the effort it takes, for it is truly one of the finest plays of all time.

WILLIAM SHAKESPEARE (1564–1616)

Hamlet

CHARACTERS

CLAUDIUS, *King of Denmark*
HAMLET, *son to the late, and nephew to the present, King*
POLONIUS, *Lord Chamberlain*
HORATIO, *friend to Hamlet*
LAERTES, *son to Polonius*

VOLTEMAND
CORNELIUS
ROSENCRANTZ
GUILDENSTERN   *courtiers*
OSRIC
A GENTLEMAN

A PRIEST

MARCELLUS
BERNARDO   *officers*

FRANCISCO, *a soldier*
REYNALDO, *servant to Polonius*
PLAYERS
TWO CLOWNS, *gravediggers*
FORTINBRAS, *Prince of Norway*
A NORWEGIAN CAPTAIN
ENGLISH AMBASSADORS
GERTRUDE, *Queen of Denmark, mother to Hamlet*
OPHELIA, *daughter to Polonius*
GHOST OF HAMLET'S FATHER
LORDS, LADIES, OFFICERS, SOLDIERS, SAILORS, MESSENGERS,
    ATTENDANTS

633

ACT I

Scene I

Elsinore Castle: a sentry-post

(*Enter* BERNARDO *and* FRANCISCO, *two sentinels*)

5   BERNARDO   Who's there?

FRANCISCO   Nay, answer me. Stand and unfold yourself.

BERNARDO   Long live the king!

FRANCISCO   Bernardo?

BERNARDO   He.

10   FRANCISCO   You come most carefully upon your hour.

BERNARDO   'Tis now struck twelve. Get thee to bed, Francisco.

FRANCISCO   For this relief much thanks. 'Tis bitter cold,
And I am sick at heart.

BERNARDO   Have you had quiet guard?

15   FRANCISCO   Not a mouse stirring.

BERNARDO   Well, good night.
If you do meet Horatio and Marcellus,
The rivals[1] of my watch, bid them make haste.

(*Enter* HORATIO *and* MARCELLUS)

20   FRANCISCO   I think I hear them. Stand, ho! Who is there?

HORATIO   Friends to this ground.

MARCELLUS   And liegemen to the Dane.[2]

FRANCISCO   Give you good night.

MARCELLUS   O, farewell, honest soldier.

25   Who hath relieved you?

FRANCISCO   Bernardo hath my place.
Give you good night.

(*Exit* FRANCISCO)

MARCELLUS   Holla, Bernardo!

30   BERNARDO   Say—
What, is Horatio there?

HORATIO   A piece of him.

BERNARDO   Welcome, Horatio. Welcome, good Marcellus.

HORATIO   What, has this thing appeared again to-night?

35   BERNARDO   I have seen nothing.

MARCELLUS   Horatio says 'tis but our fantasy,
And will not let belief take hold of him

---

[1] *rivals* sharers   [2] *Dane* King of Denmark

Touching this dreaded sight twice seen of us.
Therefore I have entreated him along
With us to watch the minutes of this night,
That, if again this apparition come,
5   He may approve³ our eyes and speak to it.
HORATIO   Tush, tush, 'twill not appear.
BERNARDO   Sit down awhile,
And let us once again assail your ears,
That are so fortified against our story,
10 What we two nights have seen.
HORATIO   Well, sit we down,
And let us hear Bernardo speak of this.
BERNARDO   Last night of all,
When yond same star that's westward from the pole⁴
15 Had made his course t' illume that part of heaven
Where now it burns, Marcellus and myself,
The bell then beating one—

   (*Enter* GHOST)

MARCELLUS   Peace, break thee off. Look where it comes again.
20 BERNARDO   In the same figure like the king that's dead.
MARCELLUS   Thou art a scholar; speak to it, Horatio.
BERNARDO   Looks 'a not like the king? Mark it, Horatio.
HORATIO   Most like. It harrows me with fear and wonder.
BERNARDO   It would be spoke to.
25 MARCELLUS   Speak to it, Horatio.
HORATIO   What art thou that usurp'st this time of night
Together with that fair and warlike form
In which the majesty of buried Denmark⁵
Did sometimes⁶ march? By heaven I charge thee, speak.
30 MARCELLUS   It is offended.
BERNARDO   See, it stalks away.
HORATIO   Stay. Speak, speak. I charge thee, speak.

   (*Exit* GHOST)

MARCELLUS   'Tis gone and will not answer.
35 BERNARDO   How now, Horatio? You tremble and look pale.
Is not this something more than fantasy?
What think you on't?
HORATIO   Before my God, I might not this believe

---

³ *approve* confirm   ⁴ *pole* polestar   ⁵ *buried Denmark* the buried King of
Denmark   ⁶ *sometimes* formerly

Without the sensible and true avouch
Of mine own eyes.

MARCELLUS   Is it not like the king?

HORATIO   As thou art to thyself.

5   Such was the very armor he had on
When he th' ambitious Norway[7] combated.
So frowned he once when, in an angry parle,[8]
He smote the sledded Polacks on the ice.
'Tis strange.

10   MARCELLUS   Thus twice before, and jump[9] at this dead hour,
With martial stalk hath he gone by our watch.

HORATIO   In what particular thought to work I know not;
But, in the gross and scope[10] of my opinion,
This bodes some strange eruption to our state.

15   MARCELLUS   Good now, sit down, and tell me he that knows,
Why this same strict and most observant watch
So nightly toils the subject[11] of the land,
And why such daily cast of brazen cannon
And foreign mart[12] for implements of war,

20   Why such impress[13] of shipwrights, whose sore task
Does not divide the Sunday from the week.
What might be toward [14] that this sweaty haste
Doth make the night joint-laborer with the day?
Who is't that can inform me?

25   HORATIO   That can I.
At least the whisper goes so. Our last king,
Whose image even but now appeared to us,
Was as you know by Fortinbras of Norway,
Thereto pricked on by a most emulate[15] pride,

30   Dared to the combat; in which our valiant Hamlet
(For so this side of our known world esteemed him)
Did slay this Fortinbras; who, by a sealed compact
Well ratified by law and heraldry,[16]
Did forfeit, with his life, all those his lands

35   Which he stood seized [17] of to the conqueror;
Against the which a moiety competent[18]
Was gagèd [19] by our king, which had returned
To the inheritance of Fortinbras

---

[7] *Norway* King of Norway   [8] *parle* parley   [9] *jump* just, exactly   [10] *gross and scope* gross scope, general view   [11] *toils* makes toil; *subject* subjects   [12] *mart* trading   [13] *impress* conscription   [14] *toward* in preparation   [15] *emulate* jealously rivalling   [16] *law and heraldry* law of heralds regulating combat   [17] *seized* possessed   [18] *moiety competent* sufficient portion   [19] *gagèd* engaged, staked

Had he been vanquisher, as, by the same comart[20]
And carriage[21] of the article designed,
His fell to Hamlet. Now, sir, young Fortinbras,
Of unimprovèd [22] mettle hot and full,
5   Hath in the skirts of Norway here and there
Sharked [23] up a list of lawless resolutes[24]
For food and diet to some enterprise
That hath a stomach[25] in't; which is no other,
As it doth well appear unto our state,
10   But to recover of us by strong hand
And terms compulsatory those foresaid lands
So by his father lost; and this, I take it,
Is the main motive of our preparations,
The source of this our watch, and the chief head [26]
15   Of this posthaste and romage[27] in the land.

BERNARDO   I think it be no other but e'en so.
Well may it sort[28] that this portentous figure
Comes armèd through our watch so like the king
That was and is the question of these wars.

20   HORATIO   A mote[29] it is to trouble the mind's eye.
In the most high and palmy state of Rome,
A little ere the mightiest Julius fell,
The graves stood tenantless and the sheeted [30] dead
Did squeak and gibber in the Roman streets;
25   As stars with trains of fire and dews of blood,
Disasters[31] in the sun; and the moist star[32]
Upon whose influence Neptune's empire stands
Was sick almost to doomsday with eclipse.
And even the like precurse[33] of feared events,
30   As harbingers[34] preceding still [35] the fates
And prologue to the omen[36] coming on,
Have heaven and earth together demonstrated
Unto our climatures[37] and countrymen.

(*Enter* GHOST)

35   But soft, behold, lo where it comes again!

---

[20] *comart* joint bargain   [21] *carriage* purport   [22] *unimprovèd* unused
[23] *Sharked* snatched indiscriminately as the shark takes prey   [24] *resolutes*
desperadoes   [25] *stomach* show of venturesomeness   [26] *head* fountainhead,
source   [27] *romage* intense activity   [28] *sort* suit   [29] *mote* speck of dust
[30] *sheeted* in shrouds   [31] *Disasters* ominous signs   [32] *moist star* moon   [33] *precurse* foreshadowing   [34] *harbingers* forerunners   [35] *still* constantly   [36] *omen*
calamity   [37] *climatures* regions

I'll cross it,[38] though it blast me.—Stay, illusion.

(*He spreads his arms*)

If thou hast any sound or use of voice,
Speak to me.
5   If there be any good thing to be done
That may to thee do ease and grace to me,
Speak to me.
If thou art privy to thy country's fate,
Which happily[39] foreknowing may avoid,
10   O, speak!
Or if thou hast uphoarded in thy life
Extorted treasure in the womb of earth,
For which, they say, you spirits oft walk in death,

(*The cock crows*)

15   Speak of it. Stay and speak. Stop it, Marcellus.
MARCELLUS   Shall I strike at it with my partisan? [40]
HORATIO   Do, if it will not stand.
BERNARDO   'Tis here.
HORATIO   'Tis here.

20   (*Exit* GHOST)

MARCELLUS   'Tis gone.
We do it wrong, being so majestical,
To offer it the show of violence,
For it is as the air invulnerable,
25   And our vain blows malicious mockery.
BERNARDO   It was about to speak when the cock crew.
HORATIO   And then it started, like a guilty thing
Upon a fearful summons. I have heard
The cock, that is the trumpet to the morn,
30   Doth with his lofty and shrill-sounding throat
Awake the god of day, and at his warning,
Whether in sea or fire, in earth or air,
Th' extravagant[41] and erring[42] spirit hies
To his confine; and of the truth herein
35   This present object made probation.[43]

---

38 *cross it* cross its path   39 *happily* haply, perchance   40 *partisan* pike   41 *extravagant* wandering beyond bounds   42 *erring* wandering   43 *probation* proof

MARCELLUS   It faded on the crowing of the cock.
Some say that ever 'gainst[44] that season comes
Wherein our Saviour's birth is celebrated,
This bird of dawning singeth all night long,
5   And then, they say, no spirit dare stir abroad,
The nights are wholesome, then no planets strike,[45]
No fairy takes,[46] nor witch hath power to charm.
So hallowed and so gracious is that time.
HORATIO   So have I heard and do in part believe it.
10   But look, the morn in russet mantle clad
Walks o'er the dew of yon high eastward hill.
Break we our watch up, and by my advice
Let us impart what we have seen to-night
Unto young Hamlet, for upon my life
15   This spirit, dumb to us, will speak to him.
Do you consent we shall acquaint him with it,
As needful in our loves, fitting our duty?
MARCELLUS   Let's do't, I pray, and I this morning know
Where we shall find him most conveniently.

20   (*Exeunt*)

Act I, Scene II

Elsinore Castle: a room of state

Flourish. Enter CLAUDIUS, *King of Denmark,* GERTRUDE *the Queen,* COUN-
CILLORS, POLONIUS *and his son* LAERTES, HAMLET, *cum aliis*[1] [*including*
25   VOLTEMAND *and* CORNELIUS]

KING   Though yet of Hamlet our dear brother's death
The memory be green, and that it us befitted
To bear our hearts in grief, and our whole kingdom
To be contracted in one brow of woe,
30   Yet so far hath discretion fought with nature
That we with wisest sorrow think on him
Together with remembrance of ourselves.
Therefore our sometime sister, now our queen,
Th' imperial jointress[2] to this warlike state,
35   Have we, as 'twere with a defeated joy,
With an auspicious and a dropping eye,

---

[44] *'gainst* just before   [45] *strike* work evil by influence   [46] *takes* bewitches
[1] *cum aliis* with others   [2] *jointress* a woman who has a jointure, or joint ten-
ancy of an estate

With mirth in funeral and with dirge in marriage,
In equal scale weighing delight and dole,
Taken to wife. Nor have we herein barred [3]
Your better wisdoms, which have freely gone
5   With this affair along. For all, our thanks.
Now follows, that you know, young Fortinbras,
Holding a weak supposal of our worth,
Or thinking by our late dear brother's death
Our state to be disjoint and out of frame,
10   Colleaguèd [4] with this dream of his advantage,
He hath not failed to pester us with message
Importing the surrender of those lands
Lost by his father, with all bands of law,
To our most valiant brother. So much for him.
15   Now for ourself and for this time of meeting.
Thus much the business is: we have here writ
To Norway, uncle of young Fortinbras—
Who, impotent and bedrid, scarcely hears
Of this his nephew's purpose—to suppress
20   His further gait[5] herein, in that the levies,
The lists, and full proportions[6] are all made
Out of his subject; and we here dispatch
You, good Cornelius, and you, Voltemand,
For bearers of this greeting to old Norway,
25   Giving to you no further personal power
To business with the king, more than the scope
Of these delated [7] articles allow.
Farewell, and let your haste commend your duty.
    CORNELIUS, VOLTEMAND   In that, and all things, will we show our
30   duty.
    KING   We doubt it nothing. Heartily farewell.

    (*Exeunt* VOLTEMAND *and* CORNELIUS)

And now, Laertes, what's the news with you?
You told us of some suit. What is't, Laertes?
35   You cannot speak of reason to the Dane[8]
And lose your voice.[9] What wouldst thou beg, Laertes,
That shall not be my offer, not thy asking?
The head is not more native[10] to the heart,

---

[3] *barred* excluded   [4] *Colleaguèd* united   [5] *gait* going   [6] *proportions* amounts
of forces and supplies   [7] *delated* detailed   [8] *Dane* King of Denmark   [9] *lose
your voice* speak in vain   [10] *native* joined by nature

The hand more instrumental [11] to the mouth,
Than is the throne of Denmark to thy father.
What wouldst thou have, Laertes?

LAERTES   My dread lord,
5 Your leave and favor to return to France,
From whence though willingly I came to Denmark
To show my duty in your coronation,
Yet now I must confess, that duty done,
My thoughts and wishes bend again toward France
10 And bow them to your gracious leave and pardon.

KING Have you your father's leave? What says Polonius?

POLONIUS He hath, my lord, wrung from me my slow leave
By laborsome petition, and at last
Upon his will I sealed my hard consent.
15 I do beseech you give him leave to go.

KING Take thy fair hour, Laertes. Time be thine,
And thy best graces spend it at thy will.
But now, my cousin [12] Hamlet, and my son—

HAMLET (*aside*) A little more than kin, [13] and less than kind! [14]
20 KING How is it that the clouds still hang on you?

HAMLET Not so, my lord. I am too much in the sun. [15]

QUEEN Good Hamlet, cast thy nighted color off,
And let thine eye look like a friend on Denmark.
Do not for ever with thy vailèd [16] lids
25 Seek for thy noble father in the dust.
Thou know'st 'tis common. All that lives must die,
Passing through nature to eternity.

HAMLET Ay, madam, it is common.

QUEEN   If it be,
30 Why seems it so particular with thee?

HAMLET Seems, madam? Nay, it is. I know not "seems."
'Tis not alone my inky cloak, good mother,
Nor customary suits of solemn black,
Nor windy suspiration of forced breath,
35 No, nor the fruitful [17] river in the eye,
Nor the dejected havior of the visage,
Together with all forms, moods, shapes of grief,

---

11 *instrumental* serviceable   12 *cousin* kinsman more distant than parent, child, brother, or sister   13 *kin* related as nephew   14 *kind* kindly in feeling, as by kind, or nature, a son would be to his father   15 *sun* sunshine of the king's undesired favor (with the punning additional meaning of "place of a son")   16 *vailèd* downcast   17 *fruitful* copious

That can denote me truly. These indeed seem,
For they are actions that a man might play,
But I have that within which passeth show—
These but the trappings and the suits of woe.

5 KING 'Tis sweet and commendable in your nature, Hamlet,
To give these mourning duties to your father,
But you must know your father lost a father,
That father lost, lost his, and the survivor bound
In filial obligation for some term

10 To do obsequious[18] sorrow. But to persever[19]
In obstinate condolement is a course
Of impious stubbornness. 'Tis unmanly grief.
It shows a will most incorrect to heaven,
A heart unfortified, a mind impatient,

15 An understanding simple and unschooled.
For what we know must be and is as common
As any the most vulgar thing to sense,
Why should we in our peevish opposition
Take it to heart? Fie, 'tis a fault to heaven,

20 A fault against the dead, a fault to nature,
To reason most absurd, whose common theme
Is death of fathers, and who still hath cried,
From the first corse till he that died to-day,
"This must be so." We pray you throw to earth

25 This unprevailing woe, and think of us
As a father, for let the world take note
You are the most immediate to our throne,
And with no less nobility of love
Than that which dearest father bears his son

30 Do I impart toward you. For your intent
In going back to school in Wittenberg,
It is most retrograde[20] to our desire,
And we beseech you, bend you to remain
Here in the cheer and comfort of our eye,

35 Our chiefest courtier, cousin, and our son.
QUEEN Let not thy mother lose her prayers, Hamlet.
I pray thee stay with us, go not to Wittenberg.
HAMLET I shall in all my best obey you, madam.
KING Why, 'tis a loving and a fair reply.

40 Be as ourself in Denmark. Madam, come.

---

[18] *obsequious* proper to obsequies or funerals   [19] *persever* persevere (accented
on the second syllable, as always in Shakespeare)   [20] *retrograde* contrary

This gentle and unforced accord of Hamlet
Sits smiling to my heart, in grace whereof
No jocund health that Denmark drinks to-day
But the great cannon to the clouds shall tell,

5   And the king's rouse[21] the heaven shall bruit[22] again,
Respeaking earthly thunder. Come away.

(*Flourish. Exeunt all but* HAMLET)

HAMLET   O that this too too sullied flesh would melt,
Thaw, and resolve itself into a dew,

10   Or that the Everlasting had not fixed
His canon[23] gainst self-slaughter. O God, God,
How weary, stale, flat, and unprofitable
Seem to me all the uses of this world!
Fie on't, ah, fie, 'tis an unweeded garden

15   That grows to seed. Things rank and gross in nature
Possess it merely.[24] That it should come to this,
But two months dead, nay, not so much, not two,
So excellent a king, that was to this
Hyperion[25] to a satyr, so loving to my mother

20   That he might not beteem[26] the winds of heaven
Visit her face too roughly. Heaven and earth,
Must I remember? Why, she would hang on him
As if increase of appetite had grown
By what it fed on, and yet within a month —

25   Let me not think on't; frailty, thy name is woman—
A little month, or ere those shoes were old
With which she followed my poor father's body
Like Niobe,[27] all tears, why she, even she—
O God, a beast that wants discourse[28] of reason

30   Would have mourned longer—married with my uncle,
My father's brother, but no more like my father
Than I to Hercules. Within a month,
Ere yet the salt of most unrighteous tears
Had left the flushing in her gallèd [29] eyes,

35   She married. O, most wicked speed, to post
With such dexterity to incestuous sheets!

---

[21] *rouse* toast drunk in wine   [22] *bruit* echo   [23] *canon* law   [24] *merely* completely   [25] *Hyperion* the sun god   [26] *beteem* allow   [27] *Niobe* the proud mother who boasted of having more children than Leto and was punished when they were slain by Apollo and Artemis, children of Leto; the grieving Niobe was changed by Zeus into a stone, which continually dropped tears   [28] *discourse* logical power or process   [29] *gallèd* irritated

It is not nor it cannot come to good.
But break my heart, for I must hold my tongue.

(*Enter* Horatio, Marcellus, *and* Bernardo)

HORATIO   Hail to your lordship!
5   HAMLET   I am glad to see you well.
Horatio—or I do forget myself.
HORATIO   The same, my lord, and your poor servant ever.
HAMLET   Sir, my good friend, I'll change[30] that name with you.
And what make[31] you from Wittenberg, Horatio?
10   Marcellus?
MARCELLUS   My good lord!
HAMLET   I am very glad to see you. (*to* Bernardo) Good even, sir.
But what, in faith, make you from Wittenberg?
HORATIO   A truant disposition, good my lord.
15   HAMLET   I would not hear your enemy say so,
Nor shall you do my ear that violence
To make it truster of your own report
Against yourself. I know you are no truant.
But what is your affair in Elsinore?
20   We'll teach you to drink deep ere you depart.
HORATIO   My lord, I came to see your father's funeral.
HAMLET   I prithee do not mock me, fellow student.
I think it was to see my mother's wedding.
HORATIO   Indeed, my lord, it followed hard upon.
25   HAMLET   Thrift, thrift, Horatio. The funeral baked meats
Did coldly furnish forth the marriage tables.
Would I had met my dearest[32] foe in heaven
Or ever I had seen that day, Horatio!
My father—methinks I see my father.
30   HORATIO   Where, my lord?
HAMLET   In my mind's eye, Horatio.
HORATIO   I saw him once. 'A was a goodly king.
HAMLET   'A was a man, take him for all in all,
I shall not look upon his like again.
35   HORATIO   My lord, I think I saw him yesternight.
HAMLET   Saw? who?
HORATIO   My lord, the king your father.
HAMLET   The king my father?
HORATIO   Season your admiration[33] for a while

---

[30] *change* exchange   [31] *make* do   [32] *dearest* direst, bitterest   [33] *Season your admiration* control your wonder

With an attent ear till I may deliver
Upon the witness of these gentlemen
This marvel to you.

HAMLET   For God's love let me hear!

5   HORATIO   Two nights together had these gentlemen,
Marcellus and Bernardo, on their watch
In the dead waste and middle of the night
Been thus encountered. A figure like your father,
Armèd at point[34] exactly, cap-a-pe,[35]
10   Appears before them and with solemn march
Goes slow and stately by them. Thrice he walked
By their oppressed and fear-surprisèd eyes
Within his truncheon's[36] length, whilst they, distilled
Almost to jelly with the act of fear,
15   Stand dumb and speak not to him. This to me
In dreadful secrecy impart they did,
And I with them the third night kept the watch,
Where, as they had delivered, both in time,
Form of the thing, each word made true and good,
20   The apparition comes. I knew your father.
These hands are not more like.

HAMLET   But where was this?

MARCELLUS   My lord, upon the platform where we watched.

HAMLET   Did you not speak to it?

25   HORATIO   My lord, I did,
But answer made it none. Yet once methought
It lifted up it[37] head and did address
Itself to motion like as it would speak.
But even then the morning cock crew loud,
30   And at the sound it shrunk in haste away
And vanished from our sight.

HAMLET   'Tis very strange.

HORATIO   As I do live, my honored lord, 'tis true,
And we did think it writ down in our duty
35   To let you know of it.

HAMLET   Indeed, indeed, sirs, but this troubles me.
Hold you the watch to-night?

ALL   We do, my lord.

HAMLET   Armed, say you?

40   ALL   Armed, my lord.

---

[34] *at point* completely   [35] *cap-a-pe* from head to foot   [36] *truncheon* military
commander's baton   [37] *it* its

	HAMLET	From top to toe?
	ALL	My lord, from head to foot.
	HAMLET	Then saw you not his face?
	HORATIO	O, yes, my lord. He wore his beaver[38] up.
5	HAMLET	What, looked he frowningly?
	HORATIO	A countenance more in sorrow than in anger.
	HAMLET	Pale or red?
	HORATIO	Nay, very pale.
	HAMLET	And fixed his eyes upon you?
10	HORATIO	Most constantly.
	HAMLET	I would I had been there.
	HORATIO	It would have much amazed you.
	HAMLET	Very like, very like. Stayed it long?
	HORATIO	While one with moderate haste might tell [39] a hundred.
15	BOTH	Longer, longer.
	HORATIO	Not when I saw't.
	HAMLET	His beard was grizzled,[40] no?
	HORATIO	It was as I have seen it in his life,

A sable silvered.[41]

20	HAMLET	I will watch to-night.

Perchance 'twill walk again.

	HORATIO	I warr'nt it will.
	HAMLET	If it assume my noble father's person,

I'll speak to it though hell itself should gape
25 And bid me hold my peace. I pray you all,
If you have hitherto concealed this sight,
Let it be tenable[42] in your silence still,
And whatsomever else shall hap to-night,
Give it an understanding but no tongue.
30 I will requite your loves. So fare you well.
Upon the platform, 'twixt eleven and twelve
I'll visit you.

	ALL	Our duty to your honor.
	HAMLET	Your loves, as mine to you. Farewell.

35   (*Exeunt all but* HAMLET)

My father's spirit—in arms? All is not well.
I doubt[43] some foul play. Would the night were come!

---

[38] *beaver* visor or movable faceguard of the helmet   [39] *tell* count   [40] *grizzled* grey   [41] *sable silvered* black mixed with white   [42] *tenable* held firmly   [43] *doubt* suspect, fear

Till then sit still, my soul. Foul deeds will rise,
Though all the earth o'erwhelm them, to men's eyes.

(*Exit*)

Act I, Scene III

5   *Elsinore Castle: the chambers of* POLONIUS

    (*Enter* LAERTES *and* OPHELIA, *his sister*)

LAERTES   My necessaries are embarked. Farewell.
And, sister, as the winds give benefit
And convoy[1] is assistant, do not sleep,
10   But let me hear from you.
OPHELIA   Do you doubt that?
LAERTES   For Hamlet, and the trifling of his favor,
Hold it a fashion and a toy in blood,
A violet in the youth of primy[2] nature,
15   Forward, not permanent, sweet, not lasting,
The perfume and suppliance[3] of a minute,
No more.
OPHELIA   No more but so?
LAERTES   Think it no more.
20   For nature crescent[4] does not grow alone
In thews and bulk, but as this temple[5] waxes
The inward service of the mind and soul
Grows wide withal. Perhaps he loves you now,
And now no soil nor cautel [6] doth besmirch
25   The virtue of his will,[7] but you must fear,
His greatness weighed,[8] his will is not his own.
(For he himself is subject to his birth.)
He may not, as unvalued persons do,
Carve for himself, for on his choice depends
30   The safety and health of this whole state,
And therefore must his choice be circumscribed
Unto the voice and yielding[9] of that body
Whereof he is the head. Then if he says he loves you,
It fits your wisdom so far to believe it
35   As he in his particular act and place

---

[1] *convoy* means of transport   [2] *primy* of the springtime   [3] *perfume and suppliance* filling sweetness   [4] *crescent* growing   [5] *this temple* the body   [6] *cautel* deceit   [7] *will* desire   [8] *greatness weighed* high position considered   [9] *yielding* assent

May give his saying deed, which is no further
Than the main voice of Denmark goes withal.
Then weigh what loss your honor may sustain
If with too credent[10] ear you list his songs,

5   Or lose your heart, or your chaste treasure open
To his unmastered importunity.
Fear it, Ophelia, fear it, my dear sister,
And keep you in the rear of your affection,[11]
Out of the shot and danger of desire.

10   The chariest maid is prodigal enough
If she unmask her beauty to the moon.
Virtue itself scapes not calumnious strokes.
The canker[12] galls[13] the infants of the spring
Too oft before their buttons[14] be disclosed,

15   And in the morn and liquid dew of youth
Contagious blastments[15] are most imminent.
Be wary then; best safety lies in fear.
Youth to itself rebels, though none else near.

OPHELIA   I shall the effect of this good lesson keep

20   As watchman to my heart, but, good my brother,
Do not as some ungracious pastors do,
Show me the steep and thorny way to heaven,
Whiles like a puffed and reckless libertine
Himself the primrose path of dalliance treads

25   And recks[16] not his own rede.[17]

(*Enter* POLONIUS)

LAERTES   O, fear me not.
I stay too long. But here my father comes.
A double blessing is a double grace;

30   Occasion smiles upon a second leave.

POLONIUS   Yet here, Laertes? Aboard, aboard, for shame!
The wind sits in the shoulder of your sail,
And you are stayed for. There—my blessing with thee,
And these few precepts in thy memory

35   Look thou character.[18] Give thy thoughts no tongue,
Nor any unproportioned[19] thought his act.

---

[10] *credent* credulous   [11] *affection* feelings, which rashly lead forward into dangers   [12] *canker* rose worm   [13] *galls* injures   [14] *buttons* buds   [15] *blastments* blights   [16] *recks* regards   [17] *rede* counsel   [18] *character* inscribe   [19] *unproportioned* unadjusted to what is right

Be thou familiar, but by no means vulgar.
Those friends thou hast, and their adoption tried,
Grapple them unto thy soul with hoops of steel,
But do not dull thy palm with entertainment
5 Of each new-hatched, unfledged courage.[20] Beware
Of entrance to a quarrel; but being in,
Bear't that th' opposèd may beware of thee.
Give every man thine ear, but few thy voice;
Take each man's censure,[21] but reserve thy judgment.
10 Costly thy habit as thy purse can buy,
But not expressed in fancy; rich, not gaudy,
For the apparel oft proclaims the man,
And they in France of the best rank and station
Are of a most select and generous chief [22] in that.
15 Neither a borrower nor a lender be,
For loan oft loses both itself and friend,
And borrowing dulleth edge of husbandry.[23]
This above all, to thine own self be true,
And it must follow as the night the day
20 Thou canst not then be false to any man.
Farewell. My blessing season[24] this in thee!

LAERTES   Most humbly do I take my leave, my lord.

POLONIUS   The time invites you. Go, your servants tend.[25]

LAERTES   Farewell, Ophelia, and remember well
25 What I have said to you.

OPHELIA   'Tis in my memory locked,
And you yourself shall keep the key of it.

LAERTES   Farewell.

(*Exit* LAERTES)

30 POLONIUS   What is't, Ophelia, he hath said to you?

OPHELIA   So please you, something touching the Lord Hamlet.

POLONIUS   Marry,[26] well bethought.
'Tis told me he hath very oft of late
Given private time to you, and you yourself
35 Have of your audience been most free and bounteous.
If it be so—as so 'tis put on me,
And that in way of caution— I must tell you

---

[20] *courage* man of spirit, young blood   [21] *censure* judgment   [22] *chief* eminence   [23] *husbandry* thriftiness   [24] *season* ripen and make fruitful   [25] *tend* wait   [26] *Marry* by Mary

You do not understand yourself so clearly
As it behooves my daughter and your honor.
What is between you? Give me up the truth.

OPHELIA   He hath, my lord, of late made many tenders[27]
5   Of his affection to me.

POLONIUS   Affection? Pooh! You speak like a green girl,
Unsifted [28] in such perilous circumstance.
Do you believe his tenders, as you call them?

OPHELIA   I do not know, my lord, what I should think.

10 POLONIUS   Marry, I will teach you. Think yourself a baby
That you have ta'en these tenders[29] for true pay
Which are not sterling. Tender yourself more dearly,
Or (not to crack the wind of [30] the poor phrase,
Running it thus) you'll tender me a fool.

15 OPHELIA   My lord, he hath importuned me with love
In honorable fashion.

POLONIUS   Ay, fashion you may call it. Go to, go to.[31]

OPHELIA   And hath given countenance to his speech, my lord,
With almost all the holy vows of heaven.

20 POLONIUS   Ay, springes[32] to catch woodcocks.[33] I do know,
When the blood burns, how prodigal the soul
Lends the tongue vows. These blazes, daughter,
Giving more light than heat, extinct in both
Even in their promise, as it is a-making,
25   You must not take for fire. From this time
Be something scanter of your maiden presence.
Set your entreatments[34] at a higher rate
Than a command to parley.[35] For Lord Hamlet,
Believe so much in him that he is young,
30   And with a larger tether may he walk
Than may be given you. In few, Ophelia,
Do not believe his vows, for they are brokers,[36]
Not of that dye which their investments[37] show,

---

27 *tenders* offers   28 *Unsifted* untested   29 *tenders . . . Tender . . . tender* offers . . . hold in regard . . . present (a word play going through three meanings, the last use of the word yielding further complexity with its valid implications that she will show herself to him as a fool, will show him to the world as a fool, and may go so far as to present him with a baby, which would be a fool because "fool" was an Elizabethan term of endearment especially applicable to an infant as a "little innocent")   30 *crack . . . of* make wheeze like a horse driven too hard   31 *Go to* go away, go on (expressing impatience)   32 *springes* snares   33 *woodcocks* birds believed foolish   34 *entreatments* military negotiations for surrender   35 *parley* confer with a besieger   36 *brokers* middlemen, panders   37 *investments* clothes

But mere implorators of unholy suits,
Breathing like sanctified and pious bawds,
The better to beguile. This is for all:
I would not, in plain terms, from this time forth
5 Have you so slander[38] any moment[39] leisure
As to give words or talk with the Lord Hamlet.
Look to't, I charge you. Come your ways.
OPHELIA   I shall obey, my lord.

(*Exeunt*)

10 **Act I, Scene IV**

The sentry-post

(*Enter* HAMLET, HORATIO, *and* MARCELLUS)

HAMLET   The air bites shrewdly[1]; it is very cold.
HORATIO   It is a nipping and an eager[2] air.
15 HAMLET   What hour now?
HORATIO   I think it lacks of twelve.
MARCELLUS   No, it is struck.
HORATIO   Indeed? I heard it not. It then draws near the season
Wherein the spirit held his wont to walk.

20   (*A flourish of trumpets, and two pieces goes off*)

What does this mean, my lord?
HAMLET   The king doth wake to-night and takes his rouse,[3]
Keeps wassail, and the swaggering upspring[4] reels,
And as he drains his draughts of Rhenish[5] down
25 The kettledrum and trumpet thus bray out
The triumph[6] of his pledge.
HORATIO   Is it a custom?
HAMLET   Ay, marry, is't,
But to my mind, though I am native here
30 And to the manner born, it is a custom
More honored in the breach than the observance.[7]
This heavy-headed revel east and west
Makes us traduced and taxed of [8] other nations.
They clepe[9] us drunkards and with swinish phrase

---

38 *slander* use disgracefully   39 *moment* momentary
1 *shrewdly* wickedly   2 *eager* sharp   3 *rouse* carousal   4 *upspring* a German
dance   5 *Rhenish* Rhine wine   6 *triumph* achievement, feat (in downing a
cup of wine at one draught)   7 *More . . . observance* better broken than observed   8 *taxed of* censured by   9 *clepe* call

Soil our addition,[10] and indeed it takes
From our achievements, though performed at height,
The pith and marrow of our attribute.[11]
So oft it chances in particular men
5   That (for some vicious mole[12] of nature in them,
As in their birth, wherein they are not guilty,
Since nature cannot choose his[13] origin)
By the o'ergrowth of some complexion,[14]
Oft breaking down the pales[15] and forts of reason,
10   Or by some habit that too much o'erleavens[16]
The form of plausive[17] manners—that (these men
Carrying, I say, the stamp of one defect,
Being nature's livery,[18] or fortune's star)[19]
Their virtues else, be they as pure as grace,
15   As infinite as man may undergo,
Shall in the general censure take corruption
From that particular fault. The dram of evil
Doth all the noble substance of a doubt,
To his own scandal.

20   (*Enter* GHOST)

HORATIO   Look, my lord, it comes.
HAMLET   Angels and ministers of grace defend us!
Be thou a spirit of health[20] or goblin[21] damned,
Bring with thee airs from heaven or blasts from hell,
25   Be thy intents wicked or charitable,
Thou com'st in such a questionable shape
That I will speak to thee. I'll call thee Hamlet,
King, father, royal Dane. O, answer me!
Let me not burst in ignorance, but tell
30   Why thy canonized [22] bones, hearsèd in death,
Have burst their cerements,[23] why the sepulchre
Wherein we saw thee quietly interred
Hath oped his ponderous and marble jaws
To cast thee up again. What may this mean

---

[10] *addition* reputation, title added as a distinction   [11] *attribute* reputation, what is attributed   [12] *mole* blemish, flaw   [13] *his* its   [14] *complexion* part of the make-up, combination of humors   [15] *pales* barriers, fences   [16] *o'erleavens* works change throughout, as yeast ferments dough   [17] *plausive* pleasing   [18] *livery* characteristic equipment or provision   [19] *star* make-up as formed by stellar influence   [20] *of health* sound, good   [21] *goblin* fiend   [22] *canonized* buried with the established rites of the Church   [23] *cerements* waxed gravecloths

That thou, dead corse, again in complete steel,
Revisits thus the glimpses of the moon,
Making night hideous, and we fools of nature[24]
So horridly to shake our disposition
5　With thoughts beyond the reaches of our souls?
Say, why is this? wherefore? what should we do?

(GHOST *beckons*)

HORATIO　It beckons you to go away with it,
As if it some impartment did desire
10　To you alone.
MARCELLUS　Look with what courteous action
It waves you to a more removèd ground.
But do not go with it.
HORATIO　　　　　　No, by no means.
15　HAMLET　It will not speak. Then will I follow it.
HORATIO　Do not, my lord.
HAMLET　　　　　　　Why, what should be the fear?
I do not set my life at a pin's fee,
And for my soul, what can it do to that,
20　Being a thing immortal as itself?
It waves me forth again. I'll follow it.
HORATIO　What if it tempt you toward the flood, my lord,
Or to the dreadful summit of the cliff
That beetles[25] o'er his base into the sea,
25　And there assume some other horrible form,
Which might deprive[26] your sovereignty of reason[27]
And draw you into madness? Think of it.
The very place puts toys[28] of desperation,
Without more motive, into every brain
30　That looks so many fathoms to the sea
And hears it roar beneath.
HAMLET　　　　　　　　It waves me still.
Go on. I'll follow thee.
MARCELLUS　You shall not go, my lord.
35　HAMLET　　　　　　　　　Hold off your hands
HORATIO　Be ruled. You shall not go.
HAMLET　　　　　　　　　My fate cries out
And makes each petty artere[29] in this body

---

[24] *fools of nature* men made conscious of natural limitations by a supernatural manifestation　[25] *beetles* juts out　[26] *deprive* take away　[27] *sovereignty of reason* state of being ruled by reason　[28] *toys* fancies　[29] *artere* artery

As hardy as the Nemean lion's [30] nerve.[31]
Still am I called. Unhand me, gentlemen.
By heaven, I'll make a ghost of him that lets[32] me!
I say, away! Go on. I'll follow thee.

5   (*Exit* GHOST, *and* HAMLET)

HORATIO   He waxes desperate with imagination.
MARCELLUS   Let's follow. 'Tis not fit thus to obey him.
HORATIO   Have after. To what issue will this come?
MARCELLUS   Something is rotten in the state of Denmark.
10   HORATIO   Heaven will direct it.
MARCELLUS   Nay, let's follow him.

(*Exeunt*)

Act I, Scene V

Another part of the fortifications

15   (*Enter* GHOST *and* HAMLET)

HAMLET   Whither wilt thou lead me? Speak. I'll go no further.
GHOST   Mark me.
HAMLET   I will.
GHOST   My hour is almost come,
20   When I to sulph'rous and tormenting flames[1]
Must render up myself.
HAMLET   Alas, poor ghost!
GHOST   Pity me not, but lend thy serious hearing
To what I shall unfold.
25   HAMLET   Speak. I am bound to hear.
GHOST   So art thou to revenge, when thou shalt hear.
HAMLET   What?
GHOST   I am thy father's spirit,
Doomed for a certain term to walk the night,
30   And for the day confined to fast[2] in fires,
Till the foul crimes done in my days of nature
Are burnt and purged away. But that I am forbid
To tell the secrets of my prison house,
I could a tale unfold whose lightest word
35   Would harrow up thy soul, freeze thy young blood,

---

30 *Nemean lion* a lion slain by Hercules in the performance of one of his
twelve labors   31 *nerve* sinew   32 *lets* hinders
1 *flames* sufferings in purgatory (not hell)   2 *fast* do penance

Make thy two eyes like stars start from their spheres,[3]
Thy knotted and combinèd locks to part,
And each particular hair to stand an[4] end
Like quills upon the fretful porpentine.[5]

5 But this eternal blazon[6] must not be
To ears of flesh and blood. List, list, O, list!
If thou didst ever thy dear father love—

HAMLET   O God!

GHOST   Revenge his foul and most unnatural murder.

10 HAMLET   Murder?

GHOST   Murder most foul, as in the best it is,
But this most foul, strange, and unnatural.

HAMLET   Haste me to know't, that I, with wings as swift
As meditation[7] or the thoughts of love,

15 May sweep to my revenge.

GHOST   I find thee apt,
And duller shouldst thou be than the fat weed
That roots itself in ease on Lethe[8] wharf,
Wouldst thou not stir in this. Now, Hamlet, hear.

20 'Tis given out that, sleeping in my orchard,
A serpent stung me. So the whole ear of Denmark
Is by a forgèd process[9] of my death
Rankly abused. But know, thou noble youth,
The serpent that did sting thy father's life

25 Now wears his crown.

HAMLET   O my prophetic soul!
My uncle?

GHOST   Ay, that incestuous, that adulterate[10] beast,
With witchcraft of his wit, with traitorous gifts—

30 O wicked wit and gifts, that have the power
So to seduce!—won to this shameful lust
The will of my most seeming-virtuous queen.
O Hamlet, what a falling-off was there,
From me, whose love was of that dignity

35 That it went hand in hand even with the vow
I made to her in marriage, and to decline

---

[3] *spheres* transparent revolving shells in each of which, according to the Ptolemaic astronomy, a planet or other heavenly body was placed   [4] *an* on   [5] *porpentine* porcupine   [6] *eternal blazon* revelation of eternity   [7] *meditation* thought   [8] *Lethe* the river in Hades which brings forgetfulness of past life to a spirit who drinks of it   [9] *forgèd process* falsified official report   [10] *adulterate* adulterous

Upon a wretch whose natural gifts were poor
To those of mine!
But virtue, as it never will be moved,
Though lewdness court it in a shape of heaven,[11]
5   So lust, though to a radiant angel linked,
Will sate itself in a celestial bed
And prey on garbage.
But soft, methinks I scent the morning air.
Brief let me be. Sleeping within my orchard,
10   My custom always of the afternoon,
Upon my secure[12] hour thy uncle stole
With juice of cursed hebona[13] in a vial,
And in the porches of my ears did pour
The leperous distilment, whose effect
15   Holds such an enmity with blood of man
That swift as quicksilver it courses through
The natural gates and alleys of the body,
And with a sudden vigor it doth posset[14]
And curd, like eager[15] droppings into milk,
20   The thin and wholesome blood. So did it mine,
And a most instant tetter[16] barked [17] about
Most lazar-like[18] with vile and loathsome crust
All my smooth body.
Thus was I sleeping by a brother's hand
25   Of life, of crown, of queen at once dispatched,
Cut off even in the blossoms of my sin,
Unhouseled,[19] disappointed,[20] unaneled,[21]
No reck'ning made, but sent to my account
With all my imperfections on my head.
30   O, horrible! O, horrible! most horrible!
If thou hast nature in thee, bear it not.
Let not the royal bed of Denmark be
A couch for luxury[22] and damnèd incest.
But howsomever thou pursues this act,
35   Taint not thy mind, nor let thy soul contrive
Against thy mother aught. Leave her to heaven
And to those thorns that in her bosom lodge

---

[11] *shape of heaven* angelic disguise   [12] *secure* carefree, unsuspecting   [13] *hebona* some poisonous plant   [14] *posset* curdle   [15] *eager* sour   [16] *tetter* eruption   [17] *barked* covered as with a bark   [18] *lazar-like* leper-like   [19] *Unhouseled* without the Sacrament   [20] *disappointed* unprepared spiritually   [21] *unaneled* without extreme unction   [22] *luxury* lust

To prick and sting her. Fare thee well at once.
The glowworm shows the matin[23] to be near
And gins to pale his uneffectual fire.
Adieu, adieu, adieu. Remember me.

5   (*Exit*)

    HAMLET   O all you host of heaven! O earth! What else?
And shall I couple hell? O fie! Hold, hold, my heart,
And you, my sinews, grow not instant old,
But bear me stiffly up. Remember thee?
10   Ay, thou poor ghost, while memory holds a seat
In this distracted globe.[24] Remember thee?
Yea, from the table[25] of my memory
I'll wipe away all trivial fond records,
All saws[26] of books, all forms,[27] all pressures[28] past
15   That youth and observation copied there,
And thy commandment all alone shall live
Within the book and volume of my brain,
Unmixed with baser matter. Yes, by heaven!
O most pernicious woman!
20   O villain, villain, smiling, damnèd villain!
My tables—meet it is I set it down
That one may smile, and smile, and be a villain.
At least I am sure it may be so in Denmark.

    (*Writes*)

25   So, uncle, there you are. Now to my word:
It is "Adieu, adieu, remember me."
I have sworn't.

    (*Enter* HORATIO *and* MARCELLUS)

    HORATIO   My lord, my lord!
30   MARCELLUS   Lord Hamlet!
    HORATIO   Heavens secure him!
    HAMLET   So be it!
    MARCELLUS   Illo, ho, ho,[29] my lord!
    HAMLET   Hillo, ho, ho, boy! Come, bird, come.
35   MARCELLUS   How is't, my noble lord?
    HORATIO   What news, my lord?

---

[23] *matin* morning   [24] *globe* head   [25] *table* writing tablet, record book
[26] *saws* wise sayings   [27] *forms* mental images, concepts   [28] *pressures* impressions   [29] *Illo, ho, ho* cry of the falconer to summon his hawk

HAMLET   O, wonderful!

HORATIO   Good my lord, tell it.

HAMLET   No, you will reveal it.

HORATIO   Not I, my lord, by heaven.

5   MARCELLUS   Nor I, my lord.

HAMLET   How say you then? Would heart of man once think it?
But you'll be secret?

BOTH   Ay, by heaven, my lord.

HAMLET   There's never a villain dwelling in all Denmark

10   But he's an arrant knave.

HORATIO   There needs no ghost, my lord, come from the grave
To tell us this.

HAMLET   Why, right, you are in the right,
And so, without more circumstance[30] at all,

15   I hold it fit that we shake hands and part:
You, as your business and desires shall point you,
For every man hath business and desire
Such as it is, and for my own poor part,
Look you, I'll go pray.

20   HORATIO   These are but wild and whirling words, my lord.

HAMLET   I am sorry they offend you, heartily;
Yes, faith, heartily.

HORATIO   There's no offense, my lord.

HAMLET   Yes, by Saint Patrick, but there is, Horatio,

25   And much offense too. Touching this vision here,
It is an honest[31] ghost, that let me tell you.
For your desire to know what is between us,
O'ermaster't as you may. And now, good friends,
As you are friends, scholars, and soldiers,

30   Give me one poor request.

HORATIO   What is't, my lord? We will.

HAMLET   Never make known what you have seen to-night.

BOTH   My lord, we will not.

HAMLET   Nay, but swear't.

35   HORATIO   In faith,
My lord, not I.

MARCELLUS   Nor I, my lord—in faith.

HAMLET   Upon my sword.[32]

MARCELLUS   We have sworn, my lord, already.

---

[30] *circumstance* ceremony   [31] *honest* genuine (not a disguised demon)
[32] *sword* i.e. upon the cross formed by the sword hilt

HAMLET   Indeed, upon my sword, indeed.

(GHOST *cries under the stage*)

GHOST   Swear.

HAMLET   Ha, ha, boy, say'st thou so? Art thou there, truepenny? [33]

5 Come on. You hear this fellow in the cellarage.

Consent to swear.

HORATIO   Propose the oath, my lord.

HAMLET   Never to speak of this that you have seen,

Swear by my sword.

10 GHOST (*beneath*)   Swear.

HAMLET   Hic et ubique? [34] Then we'll shift our ground.

Come hither, gentlemen,

And lay your hands again upon my sword.

Swear by my sword

15 Never to speak of this that you have heard.

GHOST (*beneath*)   Swear by his sword.

HAMLET   Well said, old mole! Canst work i' th' earth so fast?

A worthy pioner! [35] Once more remove, good friends.

HORATIO   O day and night, but this is wondrous strange!

20 HAMLET   And therefore as a stranger give it welcome.

There are more things in heaven and earth, Horatio,

Than are dreamt of in your philosophy. [36]

But come:

Here as before, never, so help you mercy,

25 How strange or odd some'er I bear myself

(As I perchance hereafter shall think meet

To put an antic[37] disposition on),

That you, at such times seeing me, never shall,

With arms encumb'red [38] thus, or this head-shake,

30 Or by pronouncing of some doubtful phrase,

As "Well, well, we know," or "We could, an if [39] we would,"

Or "If we list to speak," or "There be, an if they might,"

Or such ambiguous giving out, to note

That you know aught of me—this do swear,

35 So grace and mercy at your most need help you.

GHOST (*beneath*)   Swear.

(*They swear*)

---

[33] *truepenny* honest old fellow   [34] *Hic et ubique* here and everywhere   [35] *pi-oner* pioneer, miner   [36] *your philosophy* this philosophy one hears about   [37] *antic* grotesque, mad   [38] *encumb'red* folded   [39] *an if* if

HAMLET   Rest, rest, perturbèd spirit! So, gentlemen,
With all my love I do commend [40] me to you,
And what so poor a man as Hamlet is
May do t' express his love and friending to you,
5   God willing, shall not lack. Let us go in together,
And still [41] your fingers on your lips, I pray.
The time is out of joint. O cursèd spite
That ever I was born to set it right!
Nay, come, let's go together.

10   (*Exeunt*)

ACT II

Scene I

The chambers of POLONIUS

(*Enter old* POLONIUS, *with his man* [REYNALDO])

15   POLONIUS   Give him this money and these notes, Reynaldo.
REYNALDO   I will, my lord.
POLONIUS   You shall do marvellous wisely, good Reynaldo,
Before you visit him, to make inquire
Of his behavior.
20   REYNALDO   My lord, I did intend it.
POLONIUS   Marry, well said, very well said. Look you, sir,
Enquire me first what Danskers[1] are in Paris,
And how, and who, what means,[2] and where they keep,[3]
What company, at what expense; and finding
25   By this encompassment[4] and drift of question
That they do know my son, come you more nearer
Than your particular demands[5] will touch it.
Take you as 'twere some distant knowledge of him,
As thus, "I know his father and his friends,
30   And in part him"—do you mark this, Reynaldo?
REYNALDO   Ay, very well, my lord.
POLONIUS   "And in part him, but," you may say, "not well,
But if't be he I mean, he's very wild
Addicted so and so." And there put on him
35   What forgeries[6] you please; marry, none so rank

---

[40] *commend* entrust   [41] *still* always
[1] *Danskers* Danes   [2] *what means* what their wealth   [3] *keep* dwell   [4] *encompassment* circling about   [5] *particular demands* definite questions   [6] *forgeries* invented wrongdoings

As may dishonor him—take heed of that—
But, sir, such wanton, wild, and usual slips
As are companions noted and most known
To youth and liberty.

5 REYNALDO As gaming, my lord.

POLONIUS Ay, or drinking, fencing, swearing, quarrelling,
Drabbing.[7] You may go so far.

REYNALDO My lord, that would dishonor him.

POLONIUS Faith, no, as you may season[8] it in the charge.

10 You must not put another scandal on him,
That he is open to incontinency.[9]
That's not my meaning. But breathe his faults so quaintly[10]
That they may seem the taints of liberty,
The flash and outbreak of a fiery mind,

15 A savageness in unreclaimèd [11] blood,
Of general assault.[12]

REYNALDO But, my good lord—

POLONIUS Wherefore should you do this?

REYNALDO Ay, my lord,

20 I would know that.

POLONIUS Marry, sir, here's my drift,
And I believe it is a fetch of warrant.[13]
You laying these slight sullies on my son
As 'twere a thing a little soiled i' th' working,

25 Mark you,
Your party in converse, him you would sound,
Having ever[14] seen in the prenominate[15] crimes
The youth you breathe of guilty, be assured
He closes with you[16] in this consequence:[17]

30 "Good sir," or so, or "friend," or "gentleman"—
According to the phrase or the addition[18]
Of man and country—

REYNALDO Very good, my lord.

POLONIUS And then, sir, does 'a this—'a does—

35 What was I about to say? By the mass, I was about to say something! Where did I leave?

---

[7] *Drabbing* whoring [8] *season* soften [9] *incontinency* extreme sensuality
[10] *quaintly* expertly, gracefully [11] *unreclaimèd* untamed [12] *Of general assault* assailing all young men [13] *fetch of warrant* allowable trick [14] *Having ever* if he has ever [15] *prenominate* aforementioned [16] *closes with you* follows your lead to a conclusion [17] *consequence* following way [18] *addition* title

REYNALDO   At "closes in the consequence," at "friend or so," and
     "gentleman."
POLONIUS   At "closes in the consequence"—Ay, marry!
     He closes thus: "I know the gentleman;
5   I saw him yesterday, or t' other day,
     Or then, or then, with such or such, and, as you say,
     There was 'a gaming, there o'ertook[19] in's rouse,[20]
     There falling[21] out at tennis"; or perchance,
     "I saw him enter such a house of sale,"
10   Videlicet,[22] a brothel, or so forth.
     See you now—
     Your bait of falsehood takes this carp of truth,
     And thus do we of wisdom and of reach,[23]
     With windlasses[24] and with assays of bias,[25]
15   By indirections find directions[26] out.
     So, by my former lecture and advice,
     Shall you my son. You have me, have you not?
REYNALDO   My lord, I have.
POLONIUS   God bye ye,[27] fare ye well.
20 REYNALDO   Good my lord.
POLONIUS   Observe his inclination in yourself.
REYNALDO   I shall, my lord.
POLONIUS   And let him ply his music.
REYNALDO   Well, my lord.
25 POLONIUS   Farewell.

     (*Exit* REYNALDO)

     (*Enter* OPHELIA)

                         How now, Ophelia, what's the matter?
OPHELIA   O my lord, my lord, I have been so affrighted!
30 POLONIUS   With what, i' th' name of God?
OPHELIA   My lord, as I was sewing in my closet,[28]
     Lord Hamlet, with his doublet[29] all unbraced,[30]
     No hat upon his head, his stockings fouled,
     Ungartered, and down-gyvèd [31] to his ankle,
35   Pale as his shirt, his knees knocking each other,

---

[19] *o'ertook* overcome with drunkenness   [20] *rouse* carousal   [21] *falling out* quarrelling   [22] *Videlicet* namely   [23] *reach* far-reaching comprehension   [24] *wind-
lasses* roundabout courses   [25] *assays of bias* devious attacks   [26] *directions*
ways of procedure   [27] *God bye ye* God be with you, good-bye   [28] *closet* private living-room   [29] *doublet* jacket   [30] *unbraced* unlaced   [31] *down-gyvèd*
fallen down like gyves or fetters on a prisoner's legs

And with a look so piteous in purport
As if he had been loosèd out of hell
To speak of horrors—he comes before me.
POLONIUS   Mad for thy love?

5   OPHELIA   My lord, I do not know,
But truly I do fear it.
POLONIUS   What said he?
OPHELIA   He took me by the wrist and held me hard,
Then goes he to the length of all his arm,

10   And with his other hand thus o'er his brow
He falls to such perusal of my face
As 'a would draw it. Long stayed he so.
At last, a little shaking of mine arm
And thrice his head thus waving up and down,

15   He raised a sigh so piteous and profound
As it did seem to shatter all his bulk
And end his being. That done, he lets me go,
And with his head over his shoulder turned
He seemed to find his way without his eyes,

20   For out o' doors he went without their helps
And to the last bended their light on me.
POLONIUS   Come, go with me. I will go seek the king.
This is the very ecstasy³² of love,
Whose violent property³³ fordoes³⁴ itself

25   And leads the will to desperate undertakings
As oft as any passion under heaven
That does afflict our natures. I am sorry.
What, have you given him any hard words of late?
OPHELIA   No, my good lord; but as you did command

30   I did repel his letters and denied
His access to me.
POLONIUS   That hath made him mad.
I am sorry that with better heed and judgment
I had not quoted ³⁵ him. I feared he did but trifle

35   And meant to wrack thee; but beshrew³⁶ my jealousy.
By heaven, it is as proper to our age
To cast beyond ourselves³⁷ in our opinions
As it is common for the younger sort
To lack discretion. Come, go we to the king.

---

³² *ecstasy* madness   ³³ *property* quality   ³⁴ *fordoes* destroys   ³⁵ *quoted* observed   ³⁶ *beshrew* curse   ³⁷ *cast beyond ourselves* find by calculation more significance in something than we ought to

This must be known, which, being kept close,[38] might move[39]
More grief to hide than hate to utter love.[40]
Come.

(Exeunt)

5   **Act II, Scene II**

A chamber in the castle

(Flourish. Enter KING *and* QUEEN, ROSENCRANTZ, *and* GUILDENSTERN
[*with others*])

KING   Welcome, dear Rosencrantz and Guildenstern.
10   Moreover that[1] we much did long to see you,
The need we have to use you did provoke
Our hasty sending. Something have you heard
Of Hamlet's transformation—so call it,
Sith[2] nor th' exterior nor the inward man
15   Resembles that it was. What it should be,
More than his father's death, that thus hath put him
So much from th' understanding of himself,
I cannot dream of. I entreat you both
That, being of so young days brought up with him,
20   And sith so neighbored to his youth and havior,[3]
That you vouchsafe your rest here in our court
Some little time, so by your companies
To draw him on to pleasures, and to gather
So much as from occasion you may glean,
25   Whether aught to us unknown afflicts him thus,
That opened [4] lies within our remedy.
QUEEN   Good gentlemen, he hath much talked of you,
And sure I am two men there are not living
To whom he more adheres.[5] If it will please you
30   To show us so much gentry[6] and good will
As to expend your time with us awhile
For the supply and profit of our hope,
Your visitation shall receive such thanks
As fits a king's remembrance.

---

[38] *close* secret   [39] *move* cause   [40] *to hide . . . love* by such hiding of love than
there would be hate moved by a revelation of it (a violently condensed
putting of the case which is a triumph of special statement for Polonius)
[1] *Moreover that* besides the fact that   [2] *Sith* since   [3] *youth and havior*
youthful ways of life   [4] *opened* revealed   [5] *more adheres* is more attached
[6] *gentry* courtesy

ROSENCRANTZ   Both your majesties
   Might, by the sovereign power you have of us,
   Put your dread pleasures more into command
   Than to entreaty.
5 GUILDENSTERN   But we both obey,
   And here give up ourselves in the full bent[7]
   To lay our service freely at your feet,
   To be commanded.
  KING   Thanks, Rosencrantz and gentle Guildenstern.
10 QUEEN   Thanks, Guildenstern and gentle Rosencrantz.
   And I beseech you instantly to visit
   My too much changèd son.—Go, some of you,
   And bring these gentlemen where Hamlet is.
  GUILDENSTERN   Heavens make our presence and our practices
15   Pleasant and helpful to him!
  QUEEN   Ay, amen!

  (*Exeunt* ROSENCRANTZ *and* GUILDENSTERN [*with some* ATTENDANTS])

  (*Enter* POLONIUS)

POLONIUS   Th' ambassadors from Norway, my good lord,
20   Are joyfully returned.
  KING   Thou still [8] hast been the father of good news.
  POLONIUS   Have I, my lord? Assure you, my good liege,
   I hold my duty as I hold my soul,
   Both to my God and to my gracious king,
25   And I do think—or else this brain of mine
   Hunts not the trail of policy so sure
   As it hath used to do—that I have found
   The very cause of Hamlet's lunacy.
  KING   O, speak of that! That do I long to hear.
30 POLONIUS   Give first admittance to th' ambassadors.
   My news shall be the fruit[9] to that great feast.
  KING   Thyself do grace[10] to them and bring them in.

  (*Exit* POLONIUS)

  He tells me, my dear Gertrude, he hath found
35   The head and source of all your son's distemper.
  QUEEN   I doubt[11] it is no other but the main,
   His father's death and our o'erhasty marriage.

---

[7] *in the full bent* at the limit of bending (of a bow), to full capacity   [8] *still*
always   [9] *fruit* dessert   [10] *grace* honor   [11] *doubt* suspect

KING   Well, we shall sift him.

(*Enter* AMBASSADORS [VOLTEMAND *and* CORNELIUS, *with* POLONIUS])

Welcome, my good friends.

Say, Voltemand, what from our brother Norway?

5   VOLTEMAND   Most fair return of greetings and desires.
Upon our first,[12] he sent out to suppress
His nephew's levies, which to him appeared
To be a preparation 'gainst the Polack,
But better looked into, he truly found
10   It was against your highness, whereat grieved,
That so his sickness, age, and impotence
Was falsely borne in hand,[13] sends out arrests
On Fortinbras; which he in brief obeys,
Receives rebuke from Norway, and in fine[14]
15   Makes vow before his uncle never more
To give th' assay[15] of arms against your majesty.
Whereon old Norway, overcome with joy,
Gives him threescore thousand crowns in annual fee
And his commission to employ those soldiers,
20   So levied as before, against the Polack,
With an entreaty, herein further shown,

(*Gives a paper*)

That it might please you to give quiet pass
Through your dominions for this enterprise,
25   On such regards[16] of safety and allowance
As therein are set down.

KING   It likes us well;
And at our more considered time[17] we'll read,
Answer, and think upon this business.
30   Meantime we thank you for your well-took labor.
Go to your rest; at night we'll feast together.
Most welcome home!

(*Exeunt* AMBASSADORS)

POLONIUS   This business is well ended.
35   My liege and madam, to expostulate[18]
What majesty should be, what duty is,

---

12 *our first* our first words about the matter   13 *borne in hand* deceived   14 *in fine* in the end   15 *assay* trial   16 *regards* terms   17 *considered time* convenient time for consideration   18 *expostulate* discuss

Why day is day, night night, and time is time,
Were nothing but to waste night, day, and time.
Therefore, since brevity is the soul of wit,[19]
And tediousness the limbs and outward flourishes,
5   I will be brief. Your noble son is mad.
Mad call I it, for, to define true madness,
What is't but to be nothing else but mad?
But let that go.
QUEEN   More matter, with less art.
10   POLONIUS   Madam, I swear I use no art at all.
That he is mad, 'tis true: 'tis true 'tis pity,
And pity 'tis 'tis true—a foolish figure.[20]
But farewell it, for I will use no art.
Mad let us grant him then, and now remains
15   That we find out the cause of this effect—
Or rather say, the cause of this defect,
For this effect defective comes by cause.
Thus it remains, and the remainder thus.
Perpend.[21]
20   I have a daughter (have while she is mine),
Who in her duty and obedience, mark,
Hath given me this. Now gather, and surmise.

(*Reads the letter*)

"To the celestial, and my soul's idol, the most beautified
25   Ophelia,"—
That's an ill phrase, a vile phrase; "beautified" is a vile phrase.
    But you shall hear. Thus:

(*Reads*)

"In her excellent white bosom, these, &c."
30   QUEEN   Came this from Hamlet to her?
POLONIUS   Good madam, stay awhile. I will be faithful.

(*Reads*)

    "Doubt thou the stars are fire;
      Doubt that the sun doth move;
35   Doubt[22] truth to be a liar;
      But never doubt I love.
O dear Ophelia, I am ill at these numbers.[23] I have not art to

---

[19] *wit* understanding   [20] *figure* figure in rhetoric   [21] *Perpend* ponder
[22] *Doubt* suspect   [23] *numbers* verses

reckon my groans, but that I love thee best, O most best, believe it.
Adieu.
                    Thine evermore, most dear lady,
                        whilst this machine²⁴ is to²⁵ him, Hamlet."

5   This in obedience hath my daughter shown me,
       And more above²⁶ hath his solicitings,
       As they fell out by time, by means, and place,
       All given to mine ear.
       KING   But how hath she
10   Received his love?
       POLONIUS   What do you think of me?
       KING   As of a man faithful and honorable.
       POLONIUS   I would fain prove so. But what might you think,
       When I had seen this hot love on the wing
15   (As I perceived it, I must tell you that,
       Before my daughter told me), what might you,
       Or my dear majesty your queen here, think,
       If I had played the desk or table book,²⁷
       Or given my heart a winking,²⁸ mute and dumb,
20   Or looked upon this love with idle sight?
       What might you think? No, I went round ²⁹ to work
       And my young mistress thus I did bespeak:
       "Lord Hamlet is a prince, out of thy star.³⁰
       This must not be." And then I prescripts³¹ gave her,
25   That she should lock herself from his resort,
       Admit no messengers, receive no tokens.
       Which done, she took the fruits of my advice,
       And he, repellèd, a short tale to make,
       Fell into a sadness, then into a fast,
30   Thence to a watch,³² thence into a weakness,
       Thence to a lightness,³³ and, by this declension,
       Into the madness wherein now he raves,
       And all we mourn for.
       KING   Do you think 'tis this?
35   QUEEN   It may be, very like.
       POLONIUS   Hath there been such a time—I would fain know that—

---

²⁴ *machine* body   ²⁵ *to* attached to   ²⁶ *above* besides   ²⁷ *desk or table book*
i.e. silent receiver   ²⁸ *winking* closing of the eyes   ²⁹ *round* roundly, plainly
³⁰ *star* condition determined by stellar influence   ³¹ *prescripts* instructions
³² *watch* sleepless state   ³³ *lightness* lightheadedness

That I have positively said " 'Tis so,"
When it proved otherwise?

KING   Not that I know.

POLONIUS (*pointing to his head and shoulder*)

5   Take this from this, if this be otherwise.
If circumstances lead me, I will find
Where truth is hid, though it were hid indeed
Within the center.[34]

KING   How may we try it further?

10 POLONIUS   You know sometimes he walks four hours together
Here in the lobby.

QUEEN   So he does indeed.

POLONIUS   At such a time I'll loose my daughter to him.
Be you and I behind an arras[35] then.

15 Mark the encounter. If he love her not,
And be not from his reason fallen thereon,[36]
Let me be no assistant for a state
But keep a farm and carters.

KING   We will try it.

20 (*Enter* HAMLET [*reading on a book*])

QUEEN   But look where sadly the poor wretch comes reading.

POLONIUS   Away, I do beseech you both, away.

(*Exit* KING *and* QUEEN [*with* ATTENDANTS])

I'll board [37] him presently.[38] O, give me leave.

25 How does my good Lord Hamlet?

HAMLET   Well, God-a-mercy.[39]

POLONIUS   Do you know me, my lord?

HAMLET   Excellent well. You are a fishmonger.[40]

POLONIUS   Not I, my lord.

30 HAMLET   Then I would you were so honest a man.

POLONIUS   Honest, my lord?

HAMLET   Ay, sir. To be honest, as this world goes, is to be one man
picked out of ten thousand.

POLONIUS   That's very true, my lord.

---

[34] *center* center of the earth and also of the Ptolemaic universe   [35] *arras* hanging tapestry   [36] *thereon* on that account   [37] *board* accost   [38] *presently* at once   [39] *God-a-mercy* thank you (literally, "God have mercy!")   [40] *fishmonger* seller of harlots, procurer (a cant term used here with a glance at the fishing Polonius is doing when he offers Ophelia as bait)

HAMLET   For if the sun breed maggots in a dead dog, being a good kissing carrion[41]—Have you a daughter?

POLONIUS   I have, my lord.

HAMLET   Let her not walk i' th' sun. Conception is a blessing, but
5   as your daughter may conceive, friend, look to't.

POLONIUS   (*aside*)   How say you by that? Still harping on my daughter. Yet he knew me not at first. 'A said I was a fishmonger. 'A is far gone, far gone. And truly in my youth I suffered much extremity for love, very near this. I'll speak to him again.—What do
10   you read, my lord?

HAMLET   Words, words, words.

POLONIUS   What is the matter, my lord?

HAMLET   Between who? [42]

POLONIUS   I mean the matter that you read, my lord.

15   HAMLET   Slanders, sir, for the satirical rogue says here that old men have grey beards, that their faces are wrinkled, their eyes purging thick amber and plum-tree gum, and that they have a plentiful lack of wit, together with most weak hams. All which, sir, though I most powerfully and potently believe, yet I hold it not honesty
20   to have it thus set down, for you yourself, sir, should be old as I am if, like a crab, you could go backward.

POLONIUS   (*aside*)   Though this be madness, yet there is method in't.
—Will you walk out of the air, my lord?

HAMLET   Into my grave?

25   POLONIUS   Indeed, that's out of the air. (*aside*) How pregnant[43] sometimes his replies are! a happiness[44] that often madness hits on, which reason and sanity could not so prosperously be delivered of. I will leave him and suddenly contrive the means of meeting between him and my daughter.—My honorable lord, I will most
30   humbly take my leave of you.

HAMLET   You cannot, sir, take from me anything that I will more willingly part withal [45]—except my life, except my life, except my life.

(*Enter* GUILDENSTERN *and* ROSENCRANTZ)

35   POLONIUS   Fare you well, my lord.

HAMLET   These tedious old fools!

POLONIUS   You go to seek the Lord Hamlet. There he is.

---

[41] *good kissing carrion* good bit of flesh for kissing   [42] *Between who* matter for a quarrel between what persons (Hamlet's willful misunderstanding) [43] *pregnant* full of meaning   [44] *happiness* aptness of expression   [45] *withal* with

ROSENCRANTZ (*to* POLONIUS)   God save you, sir!

(*Exit* POLONIUS)

GUILDENSTERN   My honored lord!

ROSENCRANTZ   My most dear lord!

5   HAMLET   My excellent good friends! How dost thou, Guildenstern? Ah, Rosencrantz! Good lads, how do ye both?

ROSENCRANTZ   As the indifferent[46] children of the earth.

GUILDENSTERN   Happy in that we are not over-happy. On Fortune's cap we are not the very button.

10   HAMLET   Nor the soles of her shoe?

ROSENCRANTZ   Neither, my lord.

HAMLET   Then you live about her waist, or in the middle of her favors?

GUILDENSTERN   Faith, her privates[47] we.

15   HAMLET   In the secret parts of Fortune? O, most true! she is a strumpet. What news?

ROSENCRANTZ   None, my lord, but that the world's grown honest.

HAMLET   Then is doomsday near. But your news is not true. (Let me question more in particular.) What have you, my good friends,

20   deserved at the hands of Fortune that she sends you to prison hither?

GUILDENSTERN   Prison, my lord?

HAMLET   Denmark 's a prison.

ROSENCRANTZ   Then is the world one.

25   HAMLET   A goodly one; in which there are many confines,[48] wards,[49] and dungeons, Denmark being one o' th' worst.

ROSENCRANTZ   We think not so, my lord.

HAMLET   Why, then 'tis none to you, for there is nothing either good or bad but thinking makes it so. To me it is a prison.

30   ROSENCRANTZ   Why, then your ambition makes it one. 'Tis too narrow for your mind.

HAMLET   O God, I could be bounded in a nutshell and count myself a king of infinite space, were it not that I have bad dreams.

GUILDENSTERN   Which dreams indeed are ambition, for the very

35   substance of the ambitious is merely the shadow of a dream.

HAMLET   A dream itself is but a shadow.

ROSENCRANTZ   Truly, and I hold ambition of so airy and light a quality that it is but a shadow's shadow.

---

[46] *indifferent* average   [47] *privates* ordinary men in private, not public, life (with obvious play upon the sexual term "private parts")   [48] *confines* places of imprisonment   [49] *wards* cells

HAMLET   Then are our beggars bodies,[50] and our monarchs and outstretched [51] heroes the beggars' shadows. Shall we to th' court?
for, by my fay,[52] I cannot reason.

BOTH   We'll wait upon[53] you.

5   HAMLET   No such matter. I will not sort you with the rest of my
servants, for, to speak to you like an honest man, I am most dreadfully attended. But in the beaten way of friendship, what make[54]
you at Elsinore?

ROSENCRANTZ   To visit you, my lord; no other occasion.

10   HAMLET   Beggar that I am, I am even poor in thanks, but I thank
you; and sure, dear friends, my thanks are too dear a halfpenny.[55]
Were you not sent for? Is it your own inclining? Is it a free visitation? Come, come, deal justly with me. Come, come. Nay, speak.

GUILDENSTERN   What should we say, my lord?

15   HAMLET   Why, anything—but to th' purpose. You were sent for,
and there is a kind of confession in your looks, which your modes-
ties have not craft enough to color. I know the good king and
queen have sent for you.

ROSENCRANTZ   To what end, my lord?

20   HAMLET   That you must teach me. But let me conjure you by the
rights of our fellowship, by the consonancy[56] of our youth, by the
obligation of our ever-preserved love, and by what more dear a
better proposer[57] can charge you withal,[58] be even[59] and direct
with me whether you were sent for or no.

25   ROSENCRANTZ   (*aside to* GUILDENSTERN)   What say you?

HAMLET   (*aside*)   Nay then, I have an eye of you.—If you love me,
hold not off.

GUILDENSTERN   My lord, we were sent for.

HAMLET   I will tell you why. So shall my anticipation prevent[60]
30   your discovery,[61] and your secrecy to the king and queen moult no
feather.[62] I have of late—but wherefore I know not—lost all my
mirth, forgone all custom of exercises; and indeed, it goes so heavily with my disposition that this goodly frame the earth seems to
me a sterile promontory; this most excellent canopy, the air, look
35   you, this brave o'erhanging firmament,[63] this majestical roof

---

[50] *bodies* solid substances, not shadows (because beggars lack ambition)
[51] *outstretched* elongated as shadows (with a corollary implication of far-
reaching with respect to the ambitions that make both heroes and monarchs
into shadows)   [52] *fay* faith   [53] *wait upon* attend   [54] *make* do   [55] *a halfpenny* at a halfpenny   [56] *consonancy* accord (in sameness of age)   [57] *proposer* propounder   [58] *withal* with   [59] *even* straight   [60] *prevent* forestall
[61] *discovery* disclosure   [62] *moult no feather* be left whole   [63] *firmament* sky

fretted [64] with golden fire— why, it appeareth nothing to me but
a foul and pestilent congregation of vapors. What a piece of work
is a man, how noble in reason, how infinite in faculties; in form
and moving how express[65] and admirable, in action how like an
angel, in apprehension how like a god: the beauty of the world,
the paragon of animals! And yet to me what is this quintessence[66]
of dust? Man delights not me— nor woman neither, though by
your smiling you seem to say so.

ROSENCRANTZ   My lord, there was no such stuff in my thoughts.

HAMLET   Why did ye laugh then, when I said "Man delights not
me"?

ROSENCRANTZ   To think, my lord, if you delight not in man, what
lenten[67] entertainment the players shall receive from you. We
coted [68] them on the way, and hither are they coming to offer you
service.

HAMLET   He that plays the king shall be welcome—his majesty shall
have tribute of me—, the adventurous knight shall use his foil and
target,[69] the lover shall not sigh gratis, the humorous man[70] shall
end his part in peace, the clown shall make those laugh whose
lungs are tickle o' th' sere,[71] and the lady shall say her mind freely,
or the blank verse shall halt[72] for't. What players are they?

ROSENCRANTZ   Even those you were wont to take such delight in,
the tragedians of the city.

HAMLET   How chances it they travel? Their residence,[73] both in
reputation and profit, was better both ways.

ROSENCRANTZ   I think their inhibition[74] comes by the means of the
late innovation.[75]

HAMLET   Do they hold the same estimation they did when I was in
the city? Are they so followed?

ROSENCRANTZ   No indeed, are they not.

HAMLET   How comes it? Do they grow rusty?

ROSENCRANTZ   Nay, their endeavor keeps in the wonted pace, but
there is, sir, an eyrie[76] of children, little eyases,[77] that cry out on

---

[64] *fretted* decorated with fretwork   [65] *express* well framed   [66] *quintessence*
fifth or last and finest essence (an alchemical term)   [67] *lenten* scanty
[68] *coted* overtook   [69] *foil and target* sword and shield   [70] *humorous man*
eccentric character dominated by one of the humours   [71] *tickle o' th' sere*
hair-triggered for the discharge of laughter ("sere": part of a gunlock)
[72] *halt* go lame   [73] *residence* residing at the capital   [74] *inhibition* impedi-
ment to acting in residence (formal prohibition?)   [75] *innovation* new fashion
of having companies of boy actors play on the "private" stage (?), political
upheaval (?)   [76] *eyrie* nest   [77] *eyases* nestling hawks

the top of question[78] and are most tyranically clapped for't. These are now the fashion, and so berattle[79] the common stages[80] (so they call them) that many wearing rapiers are afraid of goose-quills[81] and dare scarce come thither.

5 HAMLET What, are they children? Who maintains 'em? How are they escoted? [82] Will they pursue the quality[83] no longer than they can sing? [84] Will they not say afterwards, if they should grow themselves to common players (as it is most like, if their means are no better), their writers do them wrong to make them exclaim

10 against their own succession?

ROSENCRANTZ Faith, there has been much to do on both sides, and the nation holds it no sin to tarre[85] them to controversy. There was, for a while, no money bid for argument[86] unless the poet and the player went to cuffs in the question.

15 HAMLET Is't possible?

GUILDENSTERN O, there has been much throwing about of brains.

HAMLET Do the boys carry it away?

ROSENCRANTZ Ay, that they do, my lord—Hercules and his load [87] too.

20 HAMLET It is not very strange, for my uncle is King of Denmark, and those that would make mows[88] at him while my father lived give twenty, forty, fifty, a hundred ducats apiece for his picture in little. 'Sblood,[89] there is something in this more than natural, if philosophy could find it out.

25 *A flourish*

GUILDENSTERN There are the players.

HAMLET Gentlemen, you are welcome to Elsinore. Your hands, come then. Th' appurtenance of welcome is fashion and cere-mony. Let me comply with you in this garb,[90] lest my extent[91] to

30 the players (which I tell you must show fairly outwards) should more appear like entertainment than yours. You are welcome. But my uncle-father and aunt-mother are deceived.

---

[78] *on the top of question* above others on matter of dispute   [79] *berattle* be-rate   [80] *common stages* "public" theatres of the "common" players, who were organized in companies mainly composed of adult actors (allusion being made to the "War of the Theatres" in Shakespeare's London)   [81] *goosequills* pens (of satirists who made out that the London public stage showed low taste)   [82] *escoted* supported   [83] *quality* profession of acting   [84] *sing* i.e. with unchanged voices   [85] *tarre* incite   [86] *argument* matter of a play   [87] *load* i.e. the whole word (with a topical reference to the sign of the Globe Theatre, a representation of Hercules bearing the world on his shoulders)   [88] *mows* grimaces   [89] *'Sblood* by God's blood   [90] *garb* fashion   [91] *extent* showing of welcome

GUILDENSTERN   In what, my dear lord?

HAMLET   I am but mad north-north-west. When the wind is south-
erly I know a hawk from a handsaw.[92]

(*Enter* POLONIUS)

5   POLONIUS   Well be with you, gentlemen.

HAMLET   Hark you, Guildenstern—and you too—at each ear a
hearer. That great baby you see there is not yet out of his swad-
dling clouts.[93]

ROSENCRANTZ   Happily[94] he is the second time come to them, for
10   they say an old man is twice a child.

HAMLET   I will prophesy he comes to tell me of the players. Mark
it.— You say right, sir; a Monday morning, 'twas then indeed.

POLONIUS   My lord, I have news to tell you.

HAMLET   My lord, I have news to tell you. When Roscius[95] was an
15   actor in Rome—

POLONIUS   The actors are come hither, my lord.

HAMLET   Buzz, buzz.

POLONIUS   Upon my honor—

HAMLET   Then came each actor on his ass—

20   POLONIUS   The best actors in the world, either for tragedy, comedy,
history, pastoral, pastoral-comical, historical-pastoral, tragical-
historical, tragical-comical-historical-pastoral; scene individable,[96]
or poem unlimited.[97] Seneca[98] cannot be too heavy, nor Plautus[99]
too light. For the law of writ[100] and the liberty,[101] these are the
25   only men.

HAMLET   O Jephthah,[102] judge of Israel, what a treasure hadst
thou!

POLONIUS   What treasure had he, my lord?

HAMLET   Why,
30   "One fair daughter, and no more,
             The which he lovèd passing[103] well."

---

92 *hawk* mattock or pickaxe (also called "hack"; here used apparently with
a play on "hawk": a bird) ; *handsaw* carpenter's tool (apparently with a play
on some corrupt form of "hernshaw"; heron, a bird often hunted with the
hawk)   93 *clout*s clothes   94 *Happily* haply, perhaps   95 *Roscius* the greatest
of Roman comic actors   96 *scene individable* drama observing the unities
97 *poem unlimited* drama not observing the unities   98 *Seneca* Roman writer
of tragedies   99 *Plautus* Roman writer of comedies   100 *law of writ* orthodoxy determined by critical rules of the drama   101 *liberty* freedom from
such orthodoxy   102 *Jephthah* the compelled sacrificer of a dearly beloved
daughter (Judges xi)   103 *passing* surpassingly (verses are from a ballad on
Jephthah)

POLONIUS (*aside*)   Still on my daughter.

HAMLET   Am I not i' th' right, old Jephthah?

POLONIUS   If you call me Jephthah, my lord, I have a daughter that I love passing well.

5   HAMLET   Nay, that follows not.

POLONIUS   What follows then, my lord?

HAMLET   Why,

      "As by lot, God wot,"

and then, you know,

10   "It came to pass, as most like it was."

The first row[104] of the pious chanson[105] will show you more, for look where my abridgment[106] comes.

(*Enter the* PLAYERS)

You are welcome, masters, welcome, all.—I am glad to see thee

15   well.—Welcome, good friends.—O, old friend, why, thy face is valanced [107] since I saw thee last. Com'st thou to beard me in Denmark?—What, my young lady[108] and mistress? By'r Lady, your ladyship is nearer to heaven than when I saw you last by the altitude of a chopine.[109] Pray God your voice, like a piece of un-

20   current[110] gold, be not cracked within the ring.[111]—Masters, you are all welcome. We'll e'en to't like French falconers, fly at anything we see. We'll have a speech straight. Come, give us a taste of your quality. Come, a passionate speech.

PLAYER   What speech, my good lord?

25   HAMLET   I heard thee speak me a speech once, but it was never acted, or if it was, not above once, for the play, I remember, pleased not the million; 'twas caviary[112] to the general,[113] but it was (as I received it, and others, whose judgments in such matters cried in the top of [114] mine) an excellent play, well digested in the

30   scenes, set down with as much modesty as cunning. I remember one said there were no sallets[115] in the lines to make the matter savory, nor no matter in the phrase that might indict the author of affectation, but called it an honest method, as wholesome as sweet, and by very much more handsome than fine. One speech

---

104 *row* stanza   105 *chanson* song   106 *my abridgment* that which shortens my talk   107 *valanced* fringed (with a beard)   108 *young lady* boy who plays women's parts   109 *chopine* women's thick-soled shoe   110 *uncurrent* not legal tender   111 *within the ring* from the edge through the line circling the design on the coin (with a play on "ring": a sound)   112 *caviary* caviare   113 *general* multitude   114 *in the top of* more authoritatively than   115 *sallets* salads, highly seasoned passages

in't I chiefly loved. 'Twas Aeneas' tale to Dido, and thereabout of
it especially where he speaks of Priam's[116] slaughter. If it live in
your memory, begin at this line—let me see, let me see:
"The rugged Pyrrhus, like th' Hyrcanian beast[117]—"

5   'Tis not so; it begins with Pyrrhus:
"The rugged Pyrrhus, he whose sable[118] arms,
Black as his purpose, did the night resemble
When he lay couchèd in the ominous[119] horse,[120]
Hath now this dread and black complexion smeared

10   With heraldry more dismal.[121] Head to foot
Now is he total gules,[122] horridly tricked [123]
With blood of fathers, mothers, daughters, sons,
Baked and impasted with the parching[124] streets,
That lend a tyrannous and a damnèd light

15   To their lord's murder. Roasted in wrath and fire,
And thus o'ersizèd [125] with coagulate[126] gore,
With eyes like carbuncles, the hellish Pyrrhus
Old grandsire Priam seeks."
So, proceed you.

20   POLONIUS   Fore God, my lord, well spoken, with good accent and
good discretion.
PLAYER   "Anon he finds him,
Striking too short at Greeks. His antique sword,
Rebellious to his arms, lies where it falls,

25   Repugnant to command. Unequal matched,
Pyrrhus at Priam drives, in rage strikes wide,
But with the whiff and wind of his fell [127] sword
Th' unnervèd father falls. Then senseless[128] Ilium,
Seeming to feel this blow, with flaming top

30   Stoops to his[129] base, and with a hideous crash
Takes prisoner Pyrrhus' ear. For lo! his sword,
Which was declining on the milky head
Of reverend Priam, seemed i' th' air to stick.
So as a painted [130] tyrant Pyrrhus stood,

---

116 *Priam's slaughter* i.e. at the fall of Troy (Aeneid II, 506 ff.)   117 *Hyrcanian beast* tiger   118 *sable* black   119 *ominous* fateful   120 *horse* the wooden horse by which the Greeks gained entrance to Troy   121 *dismal* ill-omened   122 *gules* red (heraldic term)   123 *tricked* decorated in color (heraldic term)   124 *parching* i.e. because Troy was burning   125 *o'ersizèd* covered as with size, a glutinous material used for filling pores of plaster, etc.   126 *coagulate* clotted   127 *fell* cruel   128 *senseless* without feeling   129 *his* its   130 *painted* pictured

And like a neutral to his will and matter[131]
Did nothing.
But as we often see, against[132] some storm,
A silence in the heavens, the rack[133] stand still,

5 The bold winds speechless, and the orb below
As hush as death, anon the dreadful thunder
Doth rend the region,[134] so after Pyrrhus' pause,
Arousèd vengeance sets him new awork,
And never did the Cyclops'[135] hammers fall

10 On Mars' armor, forged for proof eterne,[136]
With less remorse than Pyrrhus' bleeding sword
Now falls on Priam.
Out, out, thou strumpet Fortune! All you gods,
In general synod take away her power,

15 Break all the spokes and fellies[137] from her wheel,
And bowl the round nave[138] down the hill of heaven,
As low as to the fiends."
POLONIUS   This is too long.
HAMLET   It shall to the barber's, with your beard.—Prithee say on.

20 He's for a jig[139] or a tale of bawdry, or he sleeps. Say on; come to
Hecuba.
PLAYER   "But who (ah woe!) had seen the mobled[140] queen—"
HAMLET   "The mobled queen"?
POLONIUS   That's good. "Mobled queen" is good.

25 PLAYER   "Run barefoot up and down, threat'ning the flames
With bisson rheum;[141] a clout[142] upon that head
Where late the diadem stood, and for a robe,
About her lank and all o'erteemèd[143] loins,
A blanket in the alarm of fear caught up—

30 Who this had seen, with tongue in venom steeped
'Gainst Fortune's state[144] would treason have pronounced.
But if the gods themselves did see her then,
When she saw Pyrrhus make malicious sport
In mincing with his sword her husband's limbs,

35 The instant burst of clamor that she made

---

[131] *will and matter* purpose and its realization (between which he stands motionless) [132] *against* just before [133] *rack* clouds [134] *region* sky [135] *Cyclops* giant workmen who made armor in the smithy of Vulcan [136] *proof eterne* eternal protection [137] *fellies* segments of the rim [138] *nave* hub [139] *jig* short comic piece with singing and dancing often presented after a play [140] *mobled* muffled [141] *bisson rheum* blinding tears [142] *clout* cloth [143] *o'erteemèd* overproductive of children [144] *state* government of worldly events

(Unless things mortal move them not at all)
Would have made milch[145] the burning eyes[146] of heaven
And passion in the gods."

POLONIUS Look, whe'r[147] he has not turned his color, and has tears
5 in's eyes. Prithee no more.

HAMLET 'Tis well. I'll have thee speak out the rest of this soon.—
Good my lord, will you see the players well bestowed?[148] Do you
hear? Let them be well used, for they are the abstract and brief
chronicles of the time. After your death you were better have a
10 bad epitaph than their ill report while you live.

POLONIUS My lord, I will use them according to their desert.

HAMLET God's bodkin,[149] man, much better! Use every man after
his desert, and who shall scape whipping? Use them after your
own honor and dignity. The less they deserve, the more merit is
15 in your bounty. Take them in.

POLONIUS Come, sirs.

HAMLET Follow him, friends. We'll hear a play tomorrow. (*aside
to* PLAYER) Dost thou hear me, old friend? Can you play "The
Murder of Gonzago"?

20 PLAYER Ay, my lord.

HAMLET We'll ha't to-morrow night. You could for a need study a
speech of some dozen or sixteen lines which I would set down and
insert in't, could you not?

PLAYER Ay, my lord.

25 HAMLET Very well. Follow that lord, and look you mock him not.
—My good friends, I'll leave you till night. You are welcome to
Elsinore.

(*Exeunt* POLONIUS *and* PLAYERS)

ROSENCRANTZ Good my lord.

30 (*Exeunt* ROSENCRANTZ *and* GUILDENSTERN)

HAMLET Ay, so, God bye to you.—Now I am alone.
O, what a rogue and peasant slave am I!
Is it not monstrous that this player here,
But in a fiction, in a dream of passion,
35 Could force his soul so to his own conceit[150]
That from her working all his visage wanned,
Tears in his eyes, distraction in his aspect.

---

[145] *milch* tearful (milk-giving) [146] *eyes* i.e. stars [147] *whe'r* whether [148] *bestowed* lodged [149] *God's bodkin* by God's little body [150] *conceit* conception, idea

A broken voice, and his whole function[151] suiting
With forms to his conceit? And all for nothing,
For Hecuba!
What's Hecuba to him, or he to Hecuba,
5   That he should weep for her? What would he do
Had he the motive and the cue for passion
That I have? He would drown the stage with tears
And cleave the general ear with horrid speech,
Make mad the guilty and appal the free,
10   Confound the ignorant, and amaze indeed
The very faculties of eyes and ears.
Yet I,
A dull and muddy-mettled [152] rascal, peak[153]
Like John-a-dreams,[154] unpregnant[155] of my cause,
15   And can say nothing. No, not for a king,
Upon whose property and most dear life
A damned defeat was made. Am I a coward?
Who calls me villain? breaks my pate across?
Plucks off my beard and blows it in my face?
20   Tweaks me by the nose? gives me the lie i' th' throat
As deep as to the lungs? Who does me this?
Ha, 'swounds,[156] I should take it, for it cannot be
But I am pigeon-livered [157] and lack gall
To make oppression bitter, or ere this
25   I should ha' fatted all the region kites[158]
With this slave's offal.[159] Bloody, bawdy villain!
Remorseless, treacherous, lecherous, kindless[160] villain!
O, vengeance!
Why, what an ass am I! This is most brave,
30   That I, the son of a dear father murdered,
Prompted to my revenge by heaven and hell,
Must like a whore unpack my heart with words
And fall a-cursing like a very drab,
A stallion! [161] Fie upon't, foh! About, my brains.
35   Hum—
I have heard that guilty creatures sitting at a play
Have by the very cunning of the scene

---

151 *function* action of bodily powers   152 *muddy-mettled* dull-spirited
153 *peak* mope 154 *John-a-dreams* a sleepy dawdler 155 *unpregnant* barren
of realization 156 *'swounds* by God's wounds 157 *pigeon-livered* of dove-like
gentleness 158 *region kites* kites of the air 159 *offal* guts 160 *kindless* unnatural 161 *stallion* prostitute (male or female)

Been struck so to the soul that presently[162]
They have proclaimed their malefactions.
For murder, though it have no tongue, will speak
With most miraculous organ. I'll have these players
5   Play something like the murder of my father
Before mine uncle. I'll observe his looks.
I'll tent[163] him to the quick. If 'a do blench,[164]
I know my course. The spirit that I have seen
May be a devil, and the devil hath power
10   T' assume a pleasing shape, yea, and perhaps
Out of my weakness and my melancholy,
As he is very potent with such spirits,
Abuses[165] me to damn me. I'll have grounds
More relative[166] than this. The play 's the thing
15   Wherein I'll catch the conscience of the king.

(*Exit*)

ACT III

Scene I

A chamber in the castle

20   (*Enter* KING, QUEEN, POLONIUS, OPHELIA, ROSENCRANTZ, GUILDEN-
STERN, LORDS)

KING   And can you by no drift of conference[1]
Get from him why he puts on this confusion,
Grating so harshly all his days of quiet
25   With turbulent and dangerous lunacy?
ROSENCRANTZ   He does confess he feels himself distracted,
But from what cause 'a will by no means speak.
GUILDENSTERN   Nor do we find him forward to be sounded,
But with a crafty madness keeps aloof
30   When we would bring him on to some confession
Of his true state.
QUEEN   Did he receive you well?
ROSENCRANTZ   Most like a gentleman.
GUILDENSTERN   But with much forcing of his disposition.
35   ROSENCRANTZ   Niggard of question, but of our demands
Most free in his reply.

---

162 *presently* immediately   163 *tent* probe   164 *blench* flinch   165 *Abuses* de-
ludes   166 *relative* pertinent
1 *drift of conference* direction of conversation

QUEEN   Did you assay[2] him
    To any pastime?
ROSENCRANTZ   Madam, it so fell out that certain players
    We o'erraught[3] on the way. Of these we told him,
5   And there did seem in him a kind of joy
    To hear of it. They are here about the court,
    And, as I think, they have already order
    This night to play before him.
POLONIUS   'Tis most true,
10   And he beseeched me to entreat your majesties
    To hear and see the matter.
KING   With all my heart, and it doth much content me
    To hear him so inclined.
    Good gentlemen, give him a further edge[4]
15   And drive his purpose into these delights.
ROSENCRANTZ   We shall, my lord.

    (*Exeunt* ROSENCRANTZ *and* GUILDENSTERN)

KING   Sweet Gertrude, leave us too,
    For we have closely[5] sent for Hamlet hither,
20   That he, as 'twere by accident, may here
    Affront[6] Ophelia.
    Her father and myself (lawful espials[7])
    Will so bestow ourselves that, seeing unseen,
    We may of their encounter frankly judge
25   And gather by him, as he is behaved,
    If't be th' affliction of his love or no
    That thus he suffers for.
QUEEN   I shall obey you.—
    And for your part, Ophelia, I do wish
30   That your good beauties be the happy cause
    Of Hamlet's wildness. So shall I hope your virtues
    Will bring him to his wonted way again,
    To both your honors.
OPHELIA   Madam, I wish it may.

35   (*Exit* QUEEN)

POLONIUS   Ophelia, walk you here.—Gracious, so please you,
    We will bestow ourselves.—

---

[2] *assay* try to win   [3] *o'erraught* overtook   [4] *edge* keenness of desire   [5] *closely* privately   [6] *Affront* come face to face with   [7] *espials* spies

(*To* OPHELIA)

Read on this book,
That show of such an exercise[8] may color[9]
Your loneliness. We are oft to blame in this,
5   'Tis too much proved, that with devotion's visage
And pious action we do sugar o'er
The devil himself.

KING (*aside*)   O, 'tis too true.
How smart a lash that speech doth give my conscience!
10   The harlot's cheek, beautied with plast'ring art,
Is not more ugly to[10] the thing that helps it
Than is my deed to my most painted word.
O heavy burthen!

POLONIUS   I hear him coming. Let's withdraw, my lord.

15   (*Exeunt* KING *and* POLONIUS)

(*Enter* HAMLET)

HAMLET   To be, or not to be—that is the question:
Whether 'tis nobler in the mind to suffer
The slings and arrows of outrageous fortune
20   Or to take arms against a sea of troubles
And by opposing end them. To die, to sleep—
No more—and by a sleep to say we end
The heartache, and the thousand natural shocks
That flesh is heir to. 'Tis a consummation
25   Devoutly to be wished. To die, to sleep—
To sleep—perchance to dream: ay, there's the rub,[11]
For in that sleep of death what dreams may come
When we have shuffled off [12] this mortal coil,[13]
Must give us pause. There's the respect[14]
30   That makes calamity of so long life.[15]
For who would bear the whips and scorns of time,
Th' oppressor's wrong, the proud man's contumely
The pangs of despised love, the law's delay,
The insolence of office, and the spurns
35   That patient merit of th' unworthy takes,
When he himself might his quietus[16] make

---

[8] *exercise* religious exercise (the book being obviously one of devotion)
[9] *color* give an appearance of naturalness to   [10] *to* compared to   [11] *rub* obstacle (literally, obstruction encountered by a bowler's ball)   [12] *shuffled off* cast off as an encumbrance   [13] *coil* to-do, turmoil   [14] *respect* consideration   [15] *of so long life* so long-lived   [16] *quietus* settlement (literally, release from debt)

With a bare bodkin? [17] Who would fardels[18] bear,
To grunt and sweat under a weary life,
But that the dread of something after death,
The undiscovered country, from whose bourn[19]

5   No traveller returns, puzzles the will,
And makes us rather bear those ills we have
Than fly to others that we know not of?
Thus conscience does make cowards of us all,
And thus the native hue of resolution

10   Is sicklied o'er with the pale cast of thought,
And enterprises of great pitch[20] and moment
With this regard [21] their currents turn awry
And lose the name of action.—Soft you now,
The fair Ophelia!—Nymph, in thy orisons[22]

15   Be all my sins remembered.

OPHELIA   Good my lord,
How does your honor for this many a day?

HAMLET   I humbly thank you, well, well, well.

OPHELIA   My lord, I have remembrances of yours

20   That I have longèd long to re-deliver.
I pray you, now receive them.

HAMLET   No, not I,
I never gave you aught.

OPHELIA   My honored lord, you know right well you did,

25   And with them words of so sweet breath composed
As made the things more rich. Their perfume lost,
Take these again, for to the noble mind
Rich gifts wax poor when givers prove unkind.
There, my lord.

30   HAMLET   Ha, ha! Are you honest? [23]

OPHELIA   My lord?

HAMLET   Are you fair?

OPHELIA   What means your lordship?

HAMLET   That if you be honest and fair, your honesty should admit

35   no discourse to your beauty.

OPHELIA   Could beauty, my lord, have better commerce[24] than
with honesty?

HAMLET   Ay, truly; for the power of beauty will sooner transform

---

[17] *bodkin* dagger   [18] *fardels* burdens   [19] *bourn* confine, region   [20] *pitch* height (of a soaring falcon's flight)   [21] *regard* consideration   [22] *orisons* prayers (because of the book of devotion she reads)   [23] *honest* chaste   [24] *commerce* intercourse

honesty from what it is to a bawd than the force of honesty can translate beauty into his likeness. This was sometime a paradox,[25] but now the time gives it proof. I did love you once.

OPHELIA   Indeed, my lord, you made me believe so.

5   HAMLET   You should not have believed me, for virtue cannot so inoculate[26] our old stock but we shall relish[27] of it. I loved you not.

OPHELIA   I was the more deceived.

HAMLET   Get thee to a nunnery. Why wouldst thou be a breeder
10   of sinners? I am myself indifferent honest,[28] but yet I could accuse me of such things that it were better my mother had not borne me: I am very proud, revengeful, ambitious, with more offenses at my beck than I have thoughts to put them in, imagination to give them shape, or time to act them in. What should
15   such fellows as I do crawling between earth and heaven? We are arrant knaves all; believe none of us. Go thy ways to a nunnery. Where's your father?

OPHELIA   At home, my lord.

HAMLET   Let the doors be shut upon him, that he may play the
20   fool nowhere but in's own house. Farewell.

OPHELIA   O, help him, you sweet heavens!

HAMLET   If thou dost marry, I'll give thee this plague for thy dowry: be thou as chaste as ice, as pure as snow, thou shalt not escape calumny. Get thee to a nunnery. Go, farewell. Or if thou
25   wilt needs marry, marry a fool, for wise men know well enough what monsters[29] you make of them. To a nunnery, go, and quickly too. Farewell.

OPHELIA   O heavenly powers, restore him!

HAMLET   I have heard of your paintings too, well enough. God
30   hath given you one face, and you make yourselves another. You jig, you amble, and you lisp; you nickname God's creatures and make your wantonness[30] your ignorance.[31] Go to, I'll no more on't; it hath made me mad. I say we will have no more marriage. Those that are married already—all but one—shall live. The rest
35   shall keep as they are. To a nunnery, go.

(*Exit*)

OPHELIA   O, what a noble mind is here o'erthrown!

---

[25] *paradox* idea contrary to common opinion   [26] *inoculate* graft   [27] *relish* have a flavor (because of original sin)   [28] *indifferent honest* moderately respectable   [29] *monsters* i.e. unnatural combinations of wisdom and uxorious folly   [30] *wantonness* affectation   [31] *your ignorance* a matter for which you offer the excuse that you don't know any better

The courtier's, soldier's, scholar's, eye, tongue, sword,
Th' expectancy and rose[32] of the fair state,
The glass[33] of fashion and the mould of form,
Th' observed of all observers, quite, quite down!
5   And I, of ladies most deject and wretched,
That sucked the honey of his music vows,
Now see that noble and most sovereign reason
Like sweet bells jangled, out of time and harsh,
That unmatched form and feature of blown youth
10 Blasted with ecstasy.[34] O, woe is me
T' have seen what I have seen, see what I see!

(*Enter* KING *and* POLONIUS)

KING   Love? his affections[35] do not that way tend,
Nor what he spake, though it lacked form a little,
15 Was not like madness. There's something in his soul
O'er which his melancholy sits on brood,
And I do doubt[36] the hatch and the disclose
Will be some danger; which for to prevent,
I have in quick determination
20 Thus set it down: he shall with speed to England
For the demand of our neglected tribute.
Haply the seas, and countries different,
With variable objects, shall expel
This something-settled [37] matter in his heart,
25 Whereon his brains still beating puts him thus
From fashion of himself. What think you on't?
POLONIUS   It shall do well. But yet do I believe
The origin and commencement of his grief
Sprung from neglected love.—How now, Ophelia?
30 You need not tell us what Lord Hamlet said.
We heard it all.—My lord, do as you please,
But if you hold it fit, after the play
Let his queen mother all alone entreat him
To show his grief. Let her be round [38] with him,
35 And I'll be placed, so please you, in the ear
Of all their conference. If she find him not,
To England send him, or confine him where
Your wisdom best shall think.

---

[32] *expectancy and rose* fair hope   [33] *glass* mirror   [34] *ecstasy* madness   [35] *affections* emotions   [36] *doubt* fear   [37] *something-settled* somewhat settled   [38] *round* plain-spoken

KING   It shall be so.
Madness in great ones must not unwatched go.

(*Exeunt*)

Act III, Scene II

5 *The hall of the castle*

(*Enter* HAMLET *and three of the* PLAYERS)

HAMLET   Speak the speech, I pray you, as I pronounced it to you,
trippingly[1] on the tongue. But if you mouth it, as many of our
players do, I had as lief the town crier spoke my lines. Nor do
10 not saw the air too much with your hand, thus, but use all gently,
for in the very torrent, tempest, and (as I may say) whirlwind of
your passion, you must acquire and beget a temperance that may
give it smoothness. O, it offends me to the soul to hear a robustious[2] periwig-pated [3] fellow tear a passion to tatters, to very rags,
15 to split the ears of the groundlings,[4] who for the most part are
capable of nothing but inexplicable dumb shows[5] and noise. I
would have such a fellow whipped for o'erdoing Termagant.[6] It
out-herods Herod.[7] Pray you avoid it.
PLAYER   I warrant your honor.
20 HAMLET   Be not too tame neither, but let your own discretion be
your tutor. Suit the action to the word, the word to the action,
with this special observance, that you o'erstep not the modesty of
nature. For anything so overdone is from[8] the purpose of playing,
whose end, both at the first and now, was and is, to hold, as
25 'twere, the mirror up to nature, to show virtue her own feature,
scorn her own image, and the very age and body of the time his
form and pressure.[9] Now this overdone, or come tardy off,[10]
though it make the unskillful laugh, cannot but make the judicious grieve, the censure of the which one[11] must in your allow-
30 ance o'erweigh a whole theatre of others. O, there be players that
I have seen play, and heard others praise, and that highly (not to

---

[1] *trippingly* easily   [2] *robustious* boisterous   [3] *periwig-pated* wig-wearing (after the custom of actors)   [4] *groundlings* spectators who paid least and stood on
the ground in the pit or yard of the theatre   [5] *dumb shows* brief actions
without words, forecasting dramatic matter to follow (the play presented
later in this scene giving an old-fashioned example)   [6] *Termagant* a Saracen
"god" in medieval romance and drama   [7] *Herod* the raging tyrant of old
Biblical plays   [8] *from* apart from   [9] *pressure* impressed or printed character
[10] *come tardy off* brought off slowly and badly   [11] *the censure of the which
one* the judgment of even one of whom

speak it profanely), that neither having th' accent of Christians, nor the gait of Christian, pagan, nor man, have so strutted and bellowed that I have thought some of Nature's journeymen[12] had made men, and not made them well, they imitated humanity so

5 abominably.

PLAYER   I hope we have reformed that indifferently[13] with us, sir.

HAMLET   O, reform it altogether! And let those that play your clowns speak no more than is set down for them, for there be of them[14] that will themselves laugh, to set on some quantity of

10 barren spectators to laugh too, though in the mean time some necessary question of the play be then to be considered. That's villainous and shows a most pitiful ambition in the fool that uses it. Go make you ready.

(*Exeunt* PLAYERS)

15 (*Enter* POLONIUS, GUILDENSTERN, *and* ROSENCRANTZ)

How now, my lord? Will the king hear this piece of work?

POLONIUS   And the queen too, and that presently.[15]

HAMLET   Bid the players make haste.

(*Exit* POLONIUS)

20 Will you two help to hasten them?

ROSENCRANTZ   Ay, my lord.

(*Exeunt they two*)

HAMLET   What, ho, Horatio!

(*Enter* HORATIO)

25 HORATIO   Here, sweet lord, at your service.

HAMLET   Horatio, thou art e'en as just a man
As e'er my conversation coped withal.[16]

HORATIO   O, my dear lord—

HAMLET   Nay, do not think I flatter.

30 For what advancement may I hope from thee,
That no revenue hast but thy good spirits
To feed and clothe thee? Why should the poor be flattered?
No, let the candied tongue lick absurd pomp,
And crook the pregnant[17] hinges of the knee

---

[12] *journeymen* workmen not yet masters of their trade   [13] *indifferently* fairly well   [14] *of them* some of them   [15] *presently* at once   [16] *conversation coped withal* intercourse with men encountered   [17] *pregnant* quick to move

Where thrift[18] may follow fawning. Dost thou hear?
Since my dear soul was mistress of her choice
And could of men distinguish her election,
S' hath sealed [19] thee for herself, for thou hast been
5   As one in suff'ring all that suffers nothing,
A man that Fortune's buffets and rewards
Hast ta'en with equal thanks; and blest are those
Whose blood [20] and judgment are so well commeddled [21]
That they are not a pipe for Fortune's finger
10   To sound what stop she please. Give me that man
That is not passion's slave, and I will wear him
In my heart's core, ay, in my heart of heart,
As I do thee. Something too much of this—
There is a play to-night before the king.
15   One scene of it comes near the circumstance
Which I have told thee, of my father's death.
I prithee, when thou seest that act afoot,
Even with the very comment of thy soul [22]
Observe my uncle. If his occulted [23] guilt
20   Do not itself unkennel in one speech,
It is a damnèd ghost[24] that we have seen,
And my imaginations are as foul
As Vulcan's stithy.[25] Give him heedful note,
For I mine eyes will rivet to his face,
25   And after we will both our judgments join
In censure of [26] his seeming.
HORATIO   Well, my lord.
If 'a steal aught the while this play is playing,
And scape detecting, I will pay the theft.

30   (*Enter* TRUMPETS *and* KETTLEDRUMS, KING, QUEEN, POLONIUS, OPHE-
LIA, [ROSENCRANTZ, GUILDENSTERN, *and other* LORDS *attendant*])

HAMLET   They are coming to the play. I must be idle.[27]
Get you a place.
KING   How fares our cousin[28] Hamlet?
35   HAMLET   Excellent, i' faith, of the chameleon's dish.[29] I eat the air,
promise-crammed. You cannot feed capons so.

---

18 *thrift* profit   19 *sealed* marked   20 *blood* passion   21 *commeddled* mixed
together   22 *the very . . . soul* thy deepest sagacity   23 *occulted* hidden
24 *damnèd ghost* evil spirit, devil   25 *stithy* smithy   26 *censure of* sentence
upon   27 *be idle* be foolish, act the madman   28 *cousin* nephew   29 *chameleon's dish* i.e. air (which was believed the chameleon's food; Hamlet willfully takes *fares* in the sense of "feeds")

KING   I have nothing with this answer, Hamlet. These words are not mine.[30]

HAMLET   No, nor mine now. (*to Polonius*) My lord, you played once i' th' university, you say?

5   POLONIUS   That did I, my lord, and was accounted a good actor.

HAMLET   What did you enact?

POLONIUS   I did enact Julius Caesar. I was killed i' th' Capitol; Brutus killed me.

HAMLET   It was a brute part of him to kill so capital a calf there.

10   Be the players ready?

ROSENCRANTZ   Ay, my lord. They stay upon your patience.[31]

QUEEN   Come hither, my dear Hamlet, sit by me.

HAMLET   No, good mother. Here's metal more attractive.

POLONIUS (*to the King*)   O ho! do you mark that?

15   HAMLET   Lady, shall I lie in your lap?

He lies at OPHELIA's *feet*

OPHELIA   No, my lord.

HAMLET   I mean, my head upon your lap?

OPHELIA   Ay, my lord.

20   HAMLET   Do you think I meant country matters? [32]

OPHELIA   I think nothing, my lord.

HAMLET   That's a fair thought to lie between maids' legs.

OPHELIA   What is, my lord?

HAMLET   Nothing.

25   OPHELIA   You are merry, my lord.

HAMLET   Who, I?

OPHELIA   Ay, my lord.

HAMLET   O God, your only jig-maker! [33] What should a man do but be merry? For look you how cheerfully my mother looks, and

30   my father died within's two hours.

OPHELIA   Nay, 'tis twice two months, my lord.

HAMLET   So long? Nay then, let the devil wear black, for I'll have a suit of sables.[34] O heavens! die two months ago, and not forgotten yet? Then there's hope a great man's memory may out-

35   live his life half a year. But, by'r Lady, 'a must build churches then, or else shall 'a suffer not thinking on, with the hobby-

---

[30] *not mine* not for me as the asker of my question   [31] *stay upon your patience* await your indulgence   [32] *country matters* rustic goings-on, barnyard mating (with a play upon a sexual term)   [33] *jig-maker* writer of jigs   [34] *sables* black furs (luxurious garb, not for mourning)

horse,[35] whose epitaph is "For O, for O, the hobby-horse is forgot!"

The trumpets sound. Dumb show follows:
Enter a KING *and a* QUEEN [*very lovingly*], *the* QUEEN *embracing him, and*
5   *he her.* [*She kneels; and makes show of protestation unto him.*] *He takes*
her up, and declines his head upon her neck. He lies him down upon a
bank of flowers. She, seeing him asleep, leaves him. Anon come in another
man: takes off his crown, kisses it, pours poison in the sleeper's ears, and
leaves him. The QUEEN *returns, finds the* KING *dead, makes passionate*
10 *action. The poisoner, with some three or four, come in again, seem to*
condole with her. The dead body is carried away. The poisoner woos the
QUEEN *with gifts; she seems harsh awhile, but in the end accepts love.*

(*Exeunt*)

OPHELIA   What means this, my lord?
15   HAMLET   Marry, this is miching mallecho;[36] it means mischief.
OPHELIA   Belike this show imports the argument of the play.

(*Enter* PROLOGUE)

HAMLET   We shall know by this fellow. The players cannot keep
counsel; they'll tell all.
20   OPHELIA   Will 'a tell us what this show meant?
HAMLET   Ay, or any show that you'll show him. Be not you
ashamed to show, he'll not shame to tell you what it means.
OPHELIA   You are naught, you are naught.[37] I'll mark the play.
PROLOGUE   For us and for our tragedy,
25   Here stooping to your clemency,
We beg your hearing patiently.

(*Exit*)

HAMLET   Is this a prologue, or the posy[38] of a ring? [39]
OPHELIA   'Tis brief, my lord.
30   HAMLET   As woman's love.

(*Enter* [*two* PLAYERS *as*] KING *and* QUEEN)

[P.] KING   Full thirty times hath Phoebus' cart[40] gone round
Neptune's salt wash and Tellus' [41] orbèd ground,
And thirty dozen moons with borrowed [42] sheen

---

[35] *hobby-horse* traditional figure strapped round the waist of a performer
in May games and morris dances   [36] *miching mallecho* sneaking iniquity
[37] *naught* indecent   [38] *posy* brief motto in rhyme ("poesy")   [39] *ring* finger
ring   [40] *Phoebus' cart* the sun's chariot   [41] *Tellus* Roman goddess of the
earth   [42] *borrowed* i.e. taken from the sun

About the world have times twelve thirties been,
Since love our hearts, and Hymen[43] did our hands,
Unite commutual [44] in most sacred bands.

[P.] QUEEN   So many journeys may the sun and moon
5   Make us again count o'er ere love be done!
But woe is me, you are so sick of late,
So far from cheer and from your former state,
That I distrust you.[45] Yet, though I distrust,
Discomfort you, my lord, it nothing must.
10   For women fear too much, even as they love,
And women's fear and love hold quantity,[46]
In neither aught, or in extremity.
Now what my love is, proof hath made you know,
And as my love is sized, my fear is so.
15   Where love is great, the littlest doubts are fear;
Where little fears grow great, great love grows there.

[P.] KING   Faith, I must leave thee, love, and shortly too;
My operant powers[47] their functions leave to do.
And thou shalt live in this fair world behind,
20   Honored, beloved, and haply one as kind
For husband shalt thou—

[P.] QUEEN   O, confound the rest!
Such love must needs be treason in my breast.
In second husband let me be accurst!
25   None wed the second but who killed the first.

HAMLET (*aside*)   That's wormwood.[48]

[P.] QUEEN   The instances[49] that second marriage move
Are base respects of thrift, but none of love.
A second time I kill my husband dead
30   When second husband kisses me in bed.

[P.] KING   I do believe you think what now you speak,
But what we do determine oft we break.
Purpose is but the slave to[50] memory,
Of violent birth, but poor validity,[51]
35   Which now like fruit unripe sticks on the tree,
But fall unshaken when they mellow be.
Most necessary 'tis that we forget
To pay ourselves what to ourselves is debt.

---

[43] *Hymen* Greek god of marriage   [44] *commutual* mutually   [45] *distrust you*
fear for you   [46] *quantity* proportion   [47] *operant powers* active bodily forces
[48] *wormwood* a bitter herb   [49] *instances* motives   [50] *slave to* i.e. dependent
upon for life   [51] *validity* strength

What to ourselves in passion we propose,
The passion ending, doth the purpose lose.
The violence of either grief or joy
Their own enactures[52] with themselves destroy.
5 Where joy most revels, grief doth most lament;
Grief joys, joy grieves, on slender accident.
This world is not for aye, nor 'tis not strange
That even our loves should with our fortunes change,
For 'tis a question left us yet to prove,
10 Whether love lead fortune, or else fortune love.
The great man down, you mark his favorite flies,
The poor advanced makes friends of enemies;
And hitherto doth love on fortune tend,
For who not needs shall never lack a friend,
15 And who in want a hollow friend doth try,
Directly seasons him[53] his enemy.
But, orderly to end where I begun,
Our wills and fates do so contrary run
That our devices still [54] are overthrown;
20 Our thoughts are ours, their ends none of our own.
So think thou wilt no second husband wed,
But die thy thoughts when thy first lord is dead.
[P.] QUEEN   Nor earth to me give food, nor heaven light,
Sport and repose lock from me day and night,
25 To desperation turn my trust and hope,
An anchor's[55] cheer in prison be my scope,
Each opposite that blanks[56] the face of joy
Meet what I would have well, and it destroy,
Both here and hence[57] pursue me lasting strife,
30 If, once a widow, ever I be wife!
HAMLET   If she should break it now!
[P.] KING   'Tis deeply sworn. Sweet, leave me here awhile.
My spirits grow dull, and fain I would beguile
The tedious day with sleep.
35 [P.] QUEEN   Sleep rock thy brain,

(*He sleeps*)

And never come mischance between us twain!

(*Exit*)

---

[52] *enactures* fulfillments   [53] *seasons him* ripens him into   [54] *still* always   [55] *anchor's* hermit's   [56] *blanks* blanches, makes pale   [57] *hence* in the next world.

HAMLET   Madam, how like you this play?

QUEEN   The lady doth protest too much, methinks.

HAMLET   O, but she'll keep her word.

KING   Have you heard the argument? [58] Is there no offense in't?

5   HAMLET   No, no, they do but jest, poison in jest; no offense i' th' world.

KING   What do you call the play?

HAMLET   "The Mousetrap." Marry, how? Tropically.[59] This play is the image of a murder done in Vienna. Gonzago is the duke's

10   name; his wife, Baptista. You shall see anon. 'Tis a knavish piece of work, but what o' that? Your majesty, and we that have free[60] souls, it touches us not. Let the galled [61] jade[62] winch;[63] our withers[64] are unwrung.

(*Enter* LUCIANUS)

15   This is one Lucianus, nephew to the king.

OPHELIA   You are as good as a chorus,[65] my lord.

HAMLET   I could interpret between you and your love, if I could see the puppets[66] dallying.

OPHELIA   You are keen, my lord, you are keen.

20   HAMLET   It would cost you a groaning to take off my edge.

OPHELIA   Still better, and worse.

HAMLET   So you must take your husbands.—Begin, murderer. Leave thy damnable faces and begin. Come, the croaking raven doth bellow for revenge.

25   LUCIANUS   Thoughts black, hands apt, drugs fit, and time agreeing,

Confederate season,[67] else no creature seeing,

Thou mixture rank, of midnight weeds collected,

With Hecate's[68] ban[69] thrice blasted, thrice infected,

Thy natural magic and dire property

30   On wholesome life usurps immediately.

(*Pours the poison in his ears*)

HAMLET   'A poisons him i' th' garden for his estate. His name's Gonzago. The story is extant, and written in very choice Italian. You shall see anon how the murderer gets the love of Gonzago's

35   wife.

---

[58] *argument* plot summary   [59] *Tropically* in the way of a trope or figure (with a play on "trapically")   [60] *free* guiltless   [61] *galled* sore-backed   [62] *jade* horse   [63] *winch* wince   [64] *withers* shoulders   [65] *chorus* one in a play who explains the action   [66] *puppets* i.e. you and your lover as in a puppet show   [67] *Confederate season* the occasion being my ally   [68] *Hecate* goddess of witchcraft and black magic   [69] *ban* curse

OPHELIA   The king rises.

HAMLET   What, frighted with false fire? [70]

QUEEN   How fares my lord?

POLONIUS   Give o'er the play.

5   KING   Give me some light. Away!

POLONIUS   Lights, lights, lights!

(*Exeunt all but* HAMLET *and* HORATIO)

HAMLET   Why, let the strucken deer go weep,
    The hart ungallèd play.

10   For some must watch, while some must sleep;
    Thus runs the world away.
Would not this, sir, and a forest of feathers[71]—if the rest of my
fortunes turn Turk[72] with me—with two Provincial roses[73] on my
razed [74] shoes, get me a fellowship in a cry[75] of players, sir?

15   HORATIO   Half a share.

HAMLET   A whole one, I.
    For thou dost know, O Damon dear,
    This realm dismantled was
    Of Jove himself; and now reigns here

20   A very, very—peacock.

HORATIO   You might have rhymed.

HAMLET   O good Horatio, I'll take the ghost's word for a thousand
pound. Didst perceive?

HORATIO   Very well, my lord.

25   HAMLET   Upon the talk of the poisoning?

HORATIO   I did very well note him.

HAMLET   Aha! Come, some music! Come, the recorders! [76]
    For if the king like not the comedy,
    Why then, belike he likes it not, perdy.[77]

30   Come, some music!

(*Enter* ROSENCRANTZ *and* GUILDENSTERN)

GUILDENSTERN   Good my lord, vouchsafe me a word with you.

HAMLET   Sir, a whole history.

GUILDENSTERN   The king, sir—

35   HAMLET   Ay, sir, what of him?

---

[70] *false fire* a firing of a gun charged with powder but no shot, a blank-dis-
charge   [71] *feathers* plumes for actors' costumes   [72] *turn Turk* turn renegade,
like a Christian turning Mohammedan   [73] *Provincial roses* ribbon rosettes
[74] *razed* decorated with cut patterns   [75] *cry* pack   [76] *recorders* musical instruments of the flute class   [77] *perdy* by God ("*par dieu*")

GUILDENSTERN   Is in his retirement marvellous distempered.[78]

HAMLET   With drink, sir?

GUILDENSTERN   No, my lord, with choler.[79]

HAMLET   Your wisdom should show itself more richer to signify this
5   to the doctor, for for me to put him to his purgation would perhaps plunge him into more choler.

GUILDENSTERN   Good my lord, put your discourse into some
frame,[80] and start not so wildly from my affair.

HAMLET   I am tame, sir; pronounce.

10   GUILDENSTERN   The queen, your mother, in most great affliction of
spirit hath sent me to you.

HAMLET   You are welcome.

GUILDENSTERN   Nay, good my lord, this courtesy is not of the right
breed. If it shall please you to make me a wholesome answer, I
15   will do your mother's commandment. If not, your pardon and my
return shall be the end of my business.

HAMLET   Sir, I cannot.

ROSENCRANTZ   What, my lord?

HAMLET   Make you a wholesome answer; my wit's diseased. But,
20   sir, such answer as I can make, you shall command, or rather, as
you say, my mother. Therefore no more, but to the matter. My
mother, you say—

ROSENCRANTZ   Then thus she says: your behavior hath struck her
into amazement and admiration.[81]

25   HAMLET   O wonderful son, that can so stonish a mother! But is
there no sequel at the heels of this mother's admiration? Impart.

ROSENCRANTZ   She desires to speak with you in her closet[82] ere you
go to bed.

HAMLET   We shall obey, were she ten times our mother. Have you
30   any further trade with us?

ROSENCRANTZ   My lord, you once did love me.

HAMLET   And do still, by these pickers and stealers.[83]

ROSENCRANTZ   Good my lord, what is your cause of distemper?
You do surely bar the door upon your own liberty, if you deny
35   your griefs to your friend.

HAMLET   Sir, I lack advancement.

ROSENCRANTZ   How can that be, when you have the voice of the
king himself for your succession in Denmark?

---

78 *distempered* out of temper, vexed (twisted by Hamlet into "deranged")
79 *choler* anger (twisted by Hamlet into "biliousness")   80 *frame* logical order
81 *admiration* wonder   82 *closet* private room   83 *pickers and stealers* i.e.
hands

HAMLET   Ay, sir, but "while the grass grows" [84] the proverb is something musty.

(*Enter the* PLAYER *with recorders*)

5   O, the recorders. Let me see one. To withdraw[85] with you—why do you go about to recover the wind [86] of me, as if you would drive me into a toil? [87]

GUILDENSTERN   O my lord, if my duty be too bold, my love is too unmannerly.[88]

HAMLET   I do not well understand that. Will you play upon this
10   pipe?

GUILDENSTERN   My lord, I cannot.

HAMLET   I pray you.

GUILDENSTERN   Believe me, I cannot.

HAMLET   I do beseech you.

15   GUILDENSTERN   I know no touch of it, my lord.

HAMLET   It is as easy as lying. Govern these ventages[89] with your fingers and thumb, give it breath with your mouth, and it will discourse most eloquent music. Look you, these are the stops.

GUILDENSTERN   But these cannot I command to any utt'rance of
20   harmony. I have not the skill.

HAMLET   Why, look you now, how unworthy a thing you make of me! You would play upon me, you would seem to know my stops, you would pluck out the heart of my mystery, you would sound me from my lowest note to the top of my compass; and there is
25   much music, excellent voice, in this little organ, yet cannot you make it speak. 'Sblood, do you think I am easier to be played on than a pipe? Call me what instrument you will, though you can fret[90] me, you cannot play upon me.

(*Enter* POLONIUS)

30   God bless you, sir!

POLONIUS   My lord, the queen would speak with you, and presently.[91]

HAMLET   Do you see yonder cloud that's almost in shape of a camel?

35   POLONIUS   By th' mass and 'tis, like a camel indeed.

---

[84] *while the grass grows* (a proverb, ending: "the horse starves")   [85] *withdraw* step aside   [86] *recover the wind* come up to windward like a hunter   [87] *toil* snare   [88] *is too unmannerly* leads me beyond the restraint of good manners   [89] *ventages* holes, vents   [90] *fret* irritate (with a play on the fret-fingering of certain stringed musical instruments)   [91] *presently* at once

HAMLET   Methinks it is like a weasel.
POLONIUS   It is backed like a weasel.
HAMLET   Or like a whale.
POLONIUS   Very like a whale.
5   HAMLET   Then I will come to my mother by and by.[92]   (*aside*)
They fool me to the top of my bent.—I will come by and by.
POLONIUS   I will say so.

(*Exit*)

HAMLET   "By and by" is easily said. Leave me, friends.

10   (*Exeunt all but* HAMLET)

'Tis now the very witching time of night,
When churchyards yawn, and hell itself breathes out
Contagion to this world. Now could I drink hot blood
And do such bitter business as the day
15   Would quake to look on. Soft, now to my mother.
O heart, lose not thy nature; let not ever
The soul of Nero[93] enter this firm bosom.
Let me be cruel, not unnatural;
I will speak daggers to her, but use none.
20   My tongue and soul in this be hypocrites:
How in my words somever she be shent,[94]
To give them seals[95] never, my soul, consent!

(*Exit*)

Act III, Scene III

25   *A chamber in the castle*

(*Enter* KING, ROSENCRANTZ, *and* GUILDENSTERN)

KING   I like him not, nor stands it safe with us
To let his madness range. Therefore prepare you.
I your commission will forthwith dispatch,
30   And he to England shall along with you.
The terms[1] of our estate[2] may not endure
Hazard so near's as doth hourly grow
Out of his brows.[3]

---

92 *by and by* immediately   93 *Nero* murderer of his mother   94 *shent* reproved
95 *seals* authentications in actions
1 *terms* circumstances   2 *estate* royal position   3 *brows* effronteries (apparently with an implication of knitted brows)

GUILDENSTERN   We will ourselves provide.
Most holy and religious fear it is
To keep those many many bodies safe
That live and feed upon your majesty.

5   ROSENCRANTZ   The single and peculiar[4] life is bound
With all the strength and armor of the mind
To keep itself from noyance,[5] but much more
That spirit upon whose weal depends and rests
The lives of many. The cess[6] of majesty

10   Dies not alone, but like a gulf [7]doth draw
What's near it with it; or 'tis a massy wheel
Fixed on the summit of the highest mount,
To whose huge spokes ten thousand lesser things
Are mortised and adjoined, which when it falls,

15   Each small annexment, petty consequence,
Attends[8] the boist'rous ruin. Never alone
Did the king sigh, but with a general groan.

KING   Arm[9] you, I pray you, to this speedy voyage,
For we will fetters put upon this fear,

20   Which now goes too free-footed.

ROSENCRANTZ   We will haste us.

(*Exeunt* GENTLEMEN)

(*Enter* POLONIUS)

POLONIUS   My lord, he's going to his mother's closet.

25   Behind the arras I'll convey myself
To hear the process.[10] I'll warrant she'll tax him home,[11]
And, as you said, and wisely was it said,
'Tis meet that some more audience than a mother,
Since nature makes them partial, should o'erhear

30   The speech, of vantage.[12] Fare you well, my liege.
I'll call upon you ere you go to bed
And tell you what I know.

KING   Thanks, dear my lord.

(*Exit* POLONIUS)

35   O, my offense is rank, it smells to heaven;
It hath the primal eldest curse[13] upon't,

---

[4] *peculiar* individual   [5] *noyance* harm   [6] *cess* cessation, decease   [7] *gulf*
whirlpool   [8] *Attends* joins in (like a royal attendant)   [9] *Arm* prepare
[10] *process* proceedings   [11] *tax him home* thrust home in reprimanding him
[12] *of vantage* from an advantageous position   [13] *primal eldest curse* that of
Cain, who also murdered a brother

A brother's murder. Pray can I not,
Though inclination be as sharp as will.
My stronger guilt defeats my strong intent,
And like a man to double business bound
5   I stand in pause where I shall first begin,
And both neglect. What if this cursèd hand
Were thicker than itself with brother's blood,
Is there not rain enough in the sweet heavens
To wash it white as snow? Whereto serves mercy
10   But to confront the visage of offense? [14]
And what's in prayer but this twofold force,
To be forestallèd ere we come to fall,
Or pardoned being down? Then I'll look up.
My fault is past. But, O, what form of prayer
15   Can serve my turn? "Forgive me my foul murder"?
That cannot be, since I am still possessed
Of those effects[15] for which I did the murder,
My crown, mine own ambition, and my queen.
May one be pardoned and retain th' offense?
20   In the corrupted currents of this world
Offense's gilded [16] hand may shove by justice,
And oft 'tis seen the wicked prize itself
Buys out the law. But 'tis not so above.
There is no shuffling;[17] there the action[18] lies
25   In his true nature, and we ourselves compelled,
Even to the teeth and forehead [19] of our faults,
To give in evidence. What then? What rests?
Try what repentance can. What can it not?
Yet what can it when one cannot repent?
30   O wretched state! O bosom black as death!
O limèd [20] soul, that struggling to be free
Art more engaged! [21] Help, angels! Make assay.[22]
Bow, stubborn knees, and, heart with strings of steel,
Be soft as sinews of the new-born babe.
35   All may be well.

He kneels

    (*Enter* HAMLET)

---

[14] *offense* sin   [15] *effects* things acquired   [16] *gilded* gold-laden   [17] *shuffling* sharp practice, double-dealing   [18] *action* legal proceeding (in heaven's court)   [19] *teeth and forehead* face-to-face recognition   [20] *limèd* caught in birdlime, a gluey material spread as a bird-snare   [21] *engaged* embedded   [22] *assay* an attempt

HAMLET   Now might I do it pat,[23] now 'a is a-praying,
And now I'll do't. And so 'a goes to heaven,
And so am I revenged. That would be scanned.
A villain kills my father, and for that
5   I, his sole son, do this same villain send
To heaven.
Why, this is hire and salary, not revenge.
'A took my father grossly,[24] full of bread,[25]
With all his crimes broad blown,[26] as flush[27] as May;
10   And how his audit[28] stands, who knows save heaven?
But in our circumstance and course of thought,
'Tis heavy with him; and am I then revenged,
To take him in the purging of his soul,
When he is fit and seasoned for his passage?
15   No.
Up, sword, and know thou a more horrid hent.[29]
When he is drunk asleep, or in his rage,
Or in th' incestuous pleasure of his bed,
At game a-swearing, or about some act
20   That has no relish[30] of salvation in't—
Then trip him, that his heels may kick at heaven,
And that his soul may be as damned and black
As hell, whereto it goes. My mother stays.
This physic but prolongs thy sickly days.

25   (*Exit*)

KING (*rises*)   My words fly up, my thoughts remain below.
Words without thoughts never to heaven go.

(*Exit*)

Act III, Scene IV

30   *The private chamber of the* QUEEN

(*Enter* [QUEEN] GERTRUDE *and* POLONIUS)

POLONIUS   'A will come straight. Look you lay[1] home to him.
Tell him his pranks have been too broad [2] to bear with,
And that your grace hath screened and stood between

---

[23] *pat* opportunely [24] *grossly* in a state of gross unpreparedness [25] *bread*
i.e. worldly sense gratification [26] *broad blown* fully blossomed [27] *flush* vigorous [28] *audit* account [29] *more horrid hent* grasping by me on a more
horrid occasion [30] *relish* flavor
[1] *lay* thrust [2] *broad* unrestrained

Much heat and him. I'll silence me even here.
Pray you be round ³ with him.   .
[HAMLET (*within*)   Mother, mother, mother!]
QUEEN   I'll warrant you; fear me not. Withdraw; I hear him
5   coming.

(POLONIUS *hides behind the arras*)

(*Enter* HAMLET)

HAMLET   Now, mother, what's the matter?
QUEEN   Hamlet, thou hast thy father much offended.
10 HAMLET   Mother, you have my father much offended.
QUEEN   Come, come, you answer with an idle⁴ tongue.
HAMLET   Go, go, you question with a wicked tongue.
QUEEN   Why, how now, Hamlet?
HAMLET   What's the matter now?
15 QUEEN   Have you forgot me?
HAMLET   No, by the rood,⁵ not so!
You are the queen, your husband's brother's wife,
And (would it were not so) you are my mother.
QUEEN   Nay, then I'll set those to you that can speak.
20 HAMLET   Come, come, and sit you down. You shall not budge.
You go not till I set you up a glass
Where you may see the inmost part of you.
QUEEN   What wilt thou do? Thou wilt not murder me?
Help, ho!
25 POLONIUS (*behind*)   What, ho! help!
HAMLET (*draws*)   How now? a rat? Dead for a ducat, dead!

(*Makes a pass through the arras and kills* POLONIUS)

POLONIUS (*behind*)   O, I am slain!
QUEEN   O me, what hast thou done?
30 HAMLET   Nay, I know not. Is it the king?
QUEEN   O, what a rash and bloody deed is this!
HAMLET   A bloody deed—almost as bad, good mother,
As kill a king, and marry with his brother.
QUEEN   As kill a king?
35 HAMLET   Ay, lady, it was my word.

(*Lifts up the arras and sees* POLONIUS)

Thou wretched, rash, intruding fool, farewell!

---

³ *round* plain-spoken   ⁴ *idle* foolish   ⁵ *rood* cross

I took thee for thy better. Take thy fortune.
Thou find'st to be too busy is some danger.—
Leave wringing of your hands. Peace, sit you down
And let me wring your heart, for so I shall

5   If it be made of penetrable stuff,
If damnèd custom[6] have not brazed [7] it so
That it is proof [8] and bulwark against sense.[9]
QUEEN   What have I done that thou dar'st wag thy tongue
In noise so rude against me?

10   HAMLET   Such an act
That blurs the grace and blush of modesty,
Calls virtue hypocrite, takes off the rose
From the fair forehead of an innocent love,
And sets a blister[10] there, makes marriage vows

15   As false as dicers' oaths. O, such a deed
As from the body of contraction[11] plucks
The very soul, and sweet religion[12] makes
A rhapsody of words! Heaven's face does glow,
And this solidity and compound mass,[13]

20   With heated visage, as against[14] the doom,[15]
Is thought-sick at the act.

QUEEN   Ay me, what act,
That roars so loud and thunders in the index? [16]

HAMLET   Look here upon this picture, and on this,

25   The counterfeit presentment[17] of two brothers.
See what a grace was seated on this brow:
Hyperion's[18] curls, the front[19] of Jove himself,
An eye like Mars, to threaten and command,
A station[20] like the herald Mercury

30   New lighted on a heaven-kissing hill—
A combination and a form indeed
Where every god did seem to set his seal
To give the world assurance of a man.
This was your husband. Look you now what follows.

35   Here is your husband, like a mildewed ear
Blasting his wholesome brother. Have you eyes?

---

6 *custom* habit   7 *brazed* hardened like brass   8 *proof* armor   9 *sense* feeling   10 *blister* brand (of degradation)   11 *contraction* the marriage contract   12 *religion* i.e. sacred marriage vows   13 *compound mass* the earth as compounded of the four elements   14 *against* in expectation of   15 *doom* Day of Judgment   16 *index* table of contents preceding the body of a book   17 *counterfeit presentment* portrayed representation   18 *Hyperion* the sun god   19 *front* forehead   20 *station* attitude in standing

Could you on this fair mountain leave to feed,
And batten[21] on this moor? Ha! have you eyes?
You cannot call it love, for at your age
The heyday[22] in the blood is tame, it's humble,
5   And waits upon[23] the judgment, and what judgment
Would step from this to this? Sense[24] sure you have,
Else could you not have motion,[25] but sure that sense
Is apoplexed,[26] for madness would not err,
Nor sense to ecstasy[27] was ne'er so thralled
10   But it reserved some quantity of choice
To serve in such a difference. What devil was't
That thus hath cozened [28] you at hoodman-blind? [29]
Eyes without feeling, feeling without sight,
Ears without hands or eyes, smelling sans[30] all,
15   Or but a sickly part of one true sense
Could not so mope.[31]
O shame, where is thy blush? Rebellious hell,
If thou canst mutine[32] in a matron's bones,
To flaming youth let virtue be as wax
20   And melt in her own fire. Proclaim no shame
When the compulsive[33] ardor gives the charge,[34]
Since frost itself as actively doth burn,
And reason panders will.[35]
QUEEN   O Hamlet, speak no more.
25   Thou turn'st mine eyes into my very soul,
And there I see such black and grainèd [36] spots
As will not leave their tinct.[37]
HAMLET   Nay, but to live
In the rank sweat of an enseamèd [38] bed,
30   Stewed in corruption, honeying and making love
Over the nasty sty—
QUEEN   O, speak to me no more.
These words like daggers enter in mine ears.
No more, sweet Hamlet.
35   HAMLET   A murderer and a villain,
A slave that is not twentieth part the tithe[39]

---

21 *batten* feed greedily   22 *heyday* excitement of passion   23 *waits upon* yields
to   24 *Sense* feeling   25 *motion* desire, impulse   26 *apoplexed* paralyzed
27 *ecstasy* madness   28 *cozened* cheated   29 *hoodman-blind* blindman's buff
30 *sans* without   31 *mope* be stupid   32 *mutine* mutiny   33 *compulsive* compelling   34 *gives the charge* delivers the attack   35 *panders will* acts as procurer for desire   36 *grainèd* dyed in grain   37 *tinct* color   38 *enseamèd*
grease-laden   39 *tithe* tenth part

Of your precedent lord, a vice[40] of kings,
A cutpurse[41] of the empire and the rule,
That from a shelf the precious diadem stole
And put it in his pocket—

5 QUEEN   No more.

(*Enter* [*the*] GHOST [*in his nightgown*[42]])

HAMLET   A king of shreds and patches—
Save me and hover o'er me with your wings,
You heavenly guards? What would your gracious figure?
10 QUEEN   Alas, he's mad.
HAMLET   Do you not come your tardy son to chide,
That, lapsed in time and passion,[43] lets go by
Th' important acting of your dread command?
O, say!
15 GHOST   Do not forget. This visitation
Is but to whet thy almost blunted purpose.
But look, amazement on thy mother sits.
O, step between her and her fighting soul!
Conceit[44] in weakest bodies strongest works.
20 Speak to her, Hamlet.
HAMLET   How is it with you, lady?
QUEEN   Alas, how is't with you,
That you do bend your eye on vacancy,
And with th' incorporal [45] air do hold discourse?
25 Forth at your eyes your spirits wildly peep,
And as the sleeping soldiers in th' alarm
Your bedded hairs like life in excrements[46]
Start up and stand an[47] end. O gentle son,
Upon the heat and flame of thy distemper[48]
30 Sprinkle cool patience. Whereon do you look?
HAMLET   On him, on him! Look you, how pale he glares!
His form and cause conjoined, preaching to stones,
Would make them capable.[49]—Do not look upon me,
Lest with his piteous action you convert
35 My stern effects.[50] Then what I have to do
Will want true color—tears perchance for blood.

---

[40] *vice* clownish rogue (like the Vice of the morality plays)   [41] *cutpurse* skulking thief   [42] *nightgown* dressing gown   [43] *lapsed . . . passion* having let the moment slip and passion cool   [44] *Conceit* imagination   [45] *incorporal* bodiless   [46] *excrements* outgrowths   [47] *an* on   [48] *distemper* mental disorder   [49] *capable* susceptible   [50] *effects* manifestations of emotion and purpose

QUEEN   To whom do you speak this?

HAMLET   Do you see nothing there?

QUEEN   Nothing at all; yet all that is I see.

HAMLET   Nor did you nothing hear?

5 QUEEN   No, nothing but ourselves.

HAMLET   Why, look you there! Look how it steals away!
My father, in his habit as he lived!
Look where he goes even now out at the portal!

(*Exit* GHOST)

10 QUEEN   This is the very coinage of your brain.
This bodiless creation ecstasy[51]
Is very cunning in.

HAMLET   Ecstasy?
My pulse as yours doth temperately keep time

15   And makes as healthful music. It is not madness
That I have uttered. Bring me to the test,
And I the matter will reword, which madness
Would gambol [52] from. Mother, for love of grace,
Lay not that flattering unction[53] to your soul,

20   That not your trespass but my madness speaks.
It will but skin and film the ulcerous place
Whiles rank corruption, mining[54] all within,
Infects unseen. Confess yourself to heaven,
Repent what's past, avoid what is to come,

25   And do not spread the compost[55] on the weeds
To make them ranker. Forgive me this my virtue.
For in the fatness[56] of these pursy[57] times
Virtue itself of vice must pardon beg,
Yea, curb[58] and woo for leave to do him good.

30 QUEEN   O Hamlet, thou hast cleft my heart in twain.

HAMLET   O, throw away the worser part of it,
And live the purer with the other half.
Good night—but go not to my uncle's bed.
Assume a virtue, if you have it not.

35   That monster custom, who all sense doth eat,
Of habits devil, is angel yet in this,
That to the use of actions fair and good

---

[51] *ecstasy* madness   [52] *gambol* shy (like a startled horse)   [53] *unction* ointment   [54] *mining* undermining   [55] *compost* fertilizing mixture   [56] *fatness* gross slackness   [57] *pursy* corpulent   [58] *curb* bow to

He likewise gives a frock or livery[59]
That aptly is put on. Refrain to-night,
And that shall lend a kind of easiness
To the next abstinence; the next more easy;
5 For use[60] almost can change the stamp[61] of nature,
And either [. . .] [62] the devil, or throw him out
With wondrous potency. Once more, good night,
And when you are desirous to be blest,
I'll blessing beg of you.—For this same lord,
10 I do repent; but heaven hath pleased it so,
To punish me with this, and this with me,
That I must be their scourge and minister.
I will bestow[63] him and will answer well
The death I gave him. So again, good night.
15 I must be cruel only to be kind.
Thus bad begins, and worse remains behind.[64]
One word more, good lady.

QUEEN   What shall I do?

HAMLET   Not this, by no means, that I bid you do:
20 Let the bloat[65] king tempt you again to bed,
Pinch wanton on your cheek, call you his mouse,
And let him, for a pair of reechy[66] kisses,
Or paddling in your neck with his damned fingers,
Make you to ravel all this matter out,[67]
25 That I essentially am not in madness,
But mad in craft. 'Twere good you let him know,
For who that's but a queen, fair, sober, wise,
Would from a paddock,[68] from a bat, a gib,[69]
Such dear concernings[70] hide? Who would do so?
30 No, in despite of sense and secrecy,
Unpeg the basket on the house's top,
Let the birds fly, and like the famous ape,[71]
To try conclusions,[72] in the basket creep
And break your own neck down.

35 QUEEN   Be thou assured, if words be made of breath,
And breath of life, I have no life to breathe

---

[59] *livery* characteristic dress (accompanying the suggestion of "garb" in *habits*) [60] *use* habit [61] *stamp* impression, form [62] A word is apparently omitted here [63] *bestow* stow, hide [64] *behind* to come [65] *bloat* bloated with sense gratification [66] *reechy* filthy [67] *ravel . . . out* disentangle [68] *paddock* toad [69] *gib* tomcat [70] *dear concernings* matters of great personal significance [71] *famous ape* (one in a story now unknown) [72] *conclusions* experiments

What thou hast said to me.
HAMLET   I must to England; you know that?
QUEEN   Alack,
I had forgot. 'Tis so concluded on.
5   HAMLET   There's letters sealed, and my two schoolfellows,
Whom I will trust as I will adders fanged,
They bear the mandate;[73] they must sweep my way
And marshal me to knavery. Let it work.
For 'tis the sport to have the enginer[74]
10 Hoist[75] with his own petar,[76] and 't shall go hard
But I will delve one yard below their mines
And blow them at the moon. O, 'tis most sweet
When in one line two crafts directly meet.
This man shall set me packing.[77]
15 I'll lug the guts into the neighbor room.
Mother, good night. Indeed, this counsellor
Is now most still, most secret, and most grave,
Who was in life a foolish prating knave.
Come, sir, to draw toward an end with you.
20 Good night, mother.

(*Exit the* QUEEN. *Then exit* HAMLET, *tugging in* POLONIUS)

ACT IV

Scene I

A chamber in the castle

25 (*Enter* KING *and* QUEEN, *with* ROSENCRANTZ *and* GUILDENSTERN)

KING   There's matter in these sighs. These profound heaves
You must translate; 'tis fit we understand them.
Where is your son?
QUEEN   Bestow this place on us a little while.

30 (*Exeunt* ROSENCRANTZ *and* GUILDENSTERN)

Ah, mine own lord, what have I seen to-night!
KING   What, Gertrude? How does Hamlet?

---

[73] *mandate* order   [74] *enginer* engineer, constructor of military engines or works   [75] *Hoist* blown up   [76] *petar* petard, bomb or mine   [77] *packing* travelling in a hurry (with a play upon his "packing" or shouldering of Polonius' body and also upon his "packing" in the sense of "plotting" or "contriving")

QUEEN   Mad as the sea and wind when both contend
    Which is the mightier. In his lawless fit,
    Behind the arras hearing something stir,
    Whips out his rapier, cries, "A rat, a rat!"
5   And in this brainish apprehension[1] kills
    The unseen good old man.
KING   O heavy deed!
    It had been so with us, had we been there.
    His liberty is full of threats to all,
10   To you yourself, to us, to every one.
    Alas, how shall this bloody deed be answered?
    It will be laid to us, whose providence[2]
    Should have kept short, restrained, and out of haunt[3]
    This mad young man. But so much was our love
15   We would not understand what was most fit,
    But, like the owner of a foul disease,
    To keep it from divulging,[4] let it feed
    Even on the pith of life. Where is he gone?
QUEEN   To draw apart the body he hath killed;
20   O'er whom his very madness, like some ore[5]
    Among a mineral [6] of metals base,
    Shows itself pure. 'A weeps for what is done.
KING   O Gertrude, come away!
    The sun no sooner shall the mountains touch
25   But we will ship him hence, and this vile deed
    We must with all our majesty and skill
    Both countenance and excuse. Ho, Guildenstern!

(*Enter* ROSENCRANTZ *and* GUILDENSTERN)

    Friends both, go join you with some further aid.
30   Hamlet in madness hath Polonius slain,
    And from his mother's closet hath he dragged him.
    Go seek him out; speak fair, and bring the body
    Into the chapel. I pray you haste in this.

(*Exeunt* ROSENCRANTZ *and* GUILDENSTERN)

35   Come, Gertrude, we'll call up our wisest friends
    And let them know both what we mean to do
    And what's untimely done [. . .] [7]

---

[1] *brainish apprehension* headstrong conception   [2] *providence* foresight
[3] *haunt* association with others   [4] *divulging* becoming known   [5] *ore* vein of
gold   [6] *mineral* mine   [7] Incomplete line; Capell suggests "So, haply, slander"

Whose whisper o'er the world's diameter,
As level [8] as the cannon to his blank[9]
Transports his poisoned shot, may miss our name
And hit the woundless air. O, come away!

5   My soul is full of discord and dismay.

(*Exeunt*)

Act IV, Scene II

A passage in the castle

(*Enter* HAMLET)

10 HAMLET   Safely stowed.

GENTLEMEN (*within*)   Hamlet! Lord Hamlet!

HAMLET   But soft, what noise? Who calls on Hamlet? O, here they
come.

(*Enter* ROSENCRANTZ, GUILDENSTERN, *and others*)

15 ROSENCRANTZ   What have you done, my lord, with the dead body?

HAMLET   Compounded it with dust, whereto 'tis kin.

ROSENCRANTZ   Tell us where 'tis, that we may take it thence
And bear it to the chapel.

HAMLET   Do not believe it.

20 ROSENCRANTZ   Believe what?

HAMLET   That I can keep your counsel and not mine own. Besides,
to be demanded of a sponge, what replication[1] should be made
by the son of a king?

ROSENCRANTZ   Take you me for a sponge, my lord?

25 HAMLET   Ay, sir, that soaks up the king's countenance,[2] his rewards, his authorities. But such officers do the king best service in
the end. He keeps them, like an ape, in the corner of his jaw, first
mouthed, to be last swallowed. When he needs what you have
gleaned, it is but squeezing you and, sponge, you shall be dry

30 again.

ROSENCRANTZ   I understand you not, my lord.

HAMLET   I am glad of it. A knavish speech sleeps in[3] a foolish ear.

ROSENCRANTZ   My lord, you must tell us where the body is and go
with us to the king.

35 HAMLET   The body is with the king, but the king is not with the
body. The king is a thing—

---

8 *As level* with as direct aim   9 *blank* mark, central white spot on a target
1 *replication* reply   2 *countenance* favor   3 *sleeps in* means nothing to

GUILDENSTERN   A thing, my lord?

HAMLET   Of nothing.[4] Bring me to him. Hide fox, and all after.[5]

(*Exeunt*)

Act IV, Scene III

5   *A chamber in the castle*

(*Enter* KING, *and two or three*)

KING   I have sent to seek him and to find the body.
How dangerous is it that this man goes loose!
Yet must not we put the strong law on him;
10   He's loved of the distracted [1] multitude,
Who like not in their judgment, but their eyes,
And where 'tis so, th' offender's scourge[2] is weighed,
But never the offense. To bear all smooth and even,
This sudden sending him away must seem
15   Deliberate pause.[3] Diseases desperate grown
By desperate appliance are relieved,
Or not at all.

(*Enter* ROSENCRANTZ, GUILDENSTERN, *and all the rest*)

How now? What hath befallen?

20   ROSENCRANTZ   Where the dead body is bestowed, my lord,
We cannot get from him.

KING   But where is he?

ROSENCRANTZ   Without, my lord; guarded, to know your pleasure.

KING   Bring him before us.

25   ROSENCRANTZ   Ho! Bring in the lord.

(*They enter [with* HAMLET]*)*

KING   Now, Hamlet, where's Polonius?

HAMLET   At supper.

KING   At supper? Where?

30   HAMLET   Not where he eats, but where 'a is eaten. A certain convocation of politic worms[4] are e'en at him. Your worm is your

---

[4] *Of nothing* (cf. Prayer Book, Psalm cxliv, 4, "Man is like a thing of naught:
his time passeth away like a shadow")   [5] *Hide ... after* (apparently well-
known words from some game of hide-and-seek)
[1] *distracted* confused   [2] *scourge* punishment   [3] *Deliberate pause* something
done with much deliberation   [4] *politic worms* political and craftily scheming
worms (such as Polonius might well attract)

only emperor for diet.[5] We fat all creatures else to fat us, and we fat ourselves for maggots. Your fat king and your lean beggar is but variable service[6]—two dishes, but to one table. That's the end.

KING   Alas, alas!

5   HAMLET   A man may fish with the worm that hath eat of a king, and eat of the fish that hath fed of that worm.

KING   What dost thou mean by this?

HAMLET   Nothing but to show you how a king may go a progress[7] through the guts of a beggar.

10   KING   Where is Polonius?

HAMLET   In heaven. Send thither to see. If your messenger find him not there, seek him i' th' other place yourself. But if indeed you find him not within this month, you shall nose him as you go up the stairs into the lobby.

15   KING   (*to* ATTENDANTS)   Go seek him there.

HAMLET   'A will stay till you come.

(*Exeunt* ATTENDANTS)

KING   Hamlet, this deed, for thine especial safety,
Which we do tender[8] as we dearly[9] grieve
20   For that which thou hast done, must send thee hence
With fiery quickness. Therefore prepare thyself.
The bark is ready and the wind at help,
Th' associates tend,[10] and everything is bent[11]
For England.

25   HAMLET   For England?

KING   Ay, Hamlet.

HAMLET   Good.

KING   So is it, if thou knew'st our purposes.

HAMLET   I see a cherub[12] that sees them. But come, for England!
30   Farewell, dear mother.

KING   Thy loving father, Hamlet.

HAMLET   My mother—father and mother is man and wife, man and wife is one flesh, and so, my mother. Come, for England!

(*Exit*)

---

[5] *diet* food and drink (perhaps with a play upon a famous "convocation," the Diet of Worms opened by the Emperor Charles V on January 28, 1521, before which Luther appeared)   [6] *variable service* different servings of one food   [7] *progress* royal journey of state   [8] *tender* hold dear   [9] *dearly* intensely   [10] *tend* wait   [11] *bent* set in readiness (like a bent bow)   [12] *cherub* one of the cherubim (angels with a distinctive quality of knowledge)

KING   Follow him at foot;[13] tempt him with speed aboard.
Delay it not; I'll have him hence to-night.
Away! for everything is sealed and done
That else leans on[14] th' affair. Pray you make haste.

5   (*Exeunt all but the* KING)

And, England,[15] if my love thou hold'st at aught—
As my great power thereof may give thee sense,
Since yet thy cicatrice looks raw and red
After the Danish sword, and thy free awe[16]
10   Pays homage to us—thou mayst not coldly set[17]
Our sovereign process,[18] which imports at full
By letters congruing[19] to that effect
The present[20] death of Hamlet. Do it, England,
For like the hectic[21] in my blood he rages,
15   And thou must cure me. Till I know 'tis done,
Howe'er my haps,[22] my joys were ne'er begun.

(*Exit*)

Act IV, Scene IV

A coastal highway

20   (*Enter* FORTINBRAS *with his* ARMY *over the stage*)

FORTINBRAS   Go, captain, from me greet the Danish king.
Tell him that by his license Fortinbras
Craves the conveyance[1] of a promised march
Over his kingdom. You know the rendezvous.
25   If that his majesty would aught with us,
We shall express our duty in his eye;[2]
And let him know so.
CAPTAIN   I will do't, my lord.
FORTINBRAS   Go softly[3] on.

30   (*Exeunt all but the* CAPTAIN)

(*Enter* HAMLET, ROSENCRANTZ, GUILDENSTERN, *and others*)

HAMLET   Good sir, whose powers[4] are these?

---

13 *at foot* at heel, close   14 *leans on* is connected with   15 *England* King of
England   16 *free awe* voluntary show of respect   17 *set* esteem   18 *process*
formal command   19 *congruing* agreeing   20 *present* instant   21 *hectic* a
continuous fever   22 *haps* fortunes
1 *conveyance* escort   2 *eye* presence   3 *softly* slowly   4 *powers* forces

    CAPTAIN   They are of Norway, sir.

    HAMLET   How purposed, sir, I pray you?

    CAPTAIN   Against some part of Poland.

    HAMLET   Who commands them, sir?

5   CAPTAIN   The nephew to old Norway, Fortinbras.

    HAMLET   Goes it against the main[5] of Poland, sir,
Or for some frontier?

    CAPTAIN   Truly to speak, and with no addition,[6]
We go to gain a little patch of ground

10   That hath in it no profit but the name.
To pay[7] five ducats, five, I would not farm it,
Nor will it yield to Norway or the Pole
A ranker[8] rate, should it be sold in fee.[9]

    HAMLET   Why, then the Polack never will defend it.

15   CAPTAIN   Yes, it is already garrisoned.

    HAMLET   Two thousand souls and twenty thousand ducats
Will not debate the question of this straw.
This is th' imposthume[10] of much wealth and peace,
That inward breaks, and shows no cause without

20   Why the man dies. I humbly thank you, sir.

    CAPTAIN   God bye you, sir.

    (*Exit*)

    ROSENCRANTZ   Will't please you go, my lord?

    HAMLET   I'll be with you straight. Go a little before.

25   (*Exeunt all but* HAMLET)

    How all occasions do inform[11] against me
And spur my dull revenge! What is a man,
If his chief good and market of [12] his time
Be but to sleep and feed? A beast, no more.

30   Sure he that made us with such large discourse,[13]
Looking before and after, gave us not
That capability and godlike reason
To fust[14] in us unused. Now, whether it be
Bestial oblivion,[15] or some craven scruple

35   Of thinking too precisely on th' event—[16]

---

5 *main* main body   6 *addition* exaggeration   7 *To pay* i.e. for a yearly rental of   8 *ranker* more abundant   9 *in fee* outright   10 *imposthume* abscess   11 *inform* take shape   12 *market of* compensation for   13 *discourse* power of thought   14 *fust* grow mouldy   15 *oblivion* forgetfulness   16 *event* outcome

A thought which, quartered, hath but one part wisdom
And ever three parts coward—I do not know
Why yet I live to say, "This thing 's to do,"
Sith I have cause, and will, and strength, and means
5 To do't. Examples gross[17] as earth exhort me.
Witness this army of such mass and charge,[18]
Led by a delicate and tender prince,
Whose spirit, with divine ambition puffed,
Makes mouths[19] at the invisible event,
10 Exposing what is mortal and unsure
To all that fortune, death, and danger dare,
Even for an eggshell. Rightly to be great
Is not to stir without great argument,
But greatly to find quarrel in a straw[20]
15 When honor 's at the stake. How stand I then,
That have a father killed, a mother stained,
Excitements of my reason and my blood,
And let all sleep, while to my shame I see
The imminent death of twenty thousand men
20 That for a fantasy[21] and trick[22] of fame
Go to their graves like beds, fight for a plot
Whereon the numbers cannot try the cause,[23]
Which is not tomb enough and continent[24]
To hide the slain? O, from this time forth,
25 My thoughts be bloody, or be nothing worth!

(*Exit*)

Act IV, Scene V

A chamber in the castle

(*Enter* HORATIO, [QUEEN] GERTRUDE, *and a* GENTLEMAN)

30 QUEEN   I will not speak with her.
GENTLEMAN   She is importunate, indeed distract.[1]
Her mood will needs be pitied.
QUEEN   What would she have?
GENTLEMAN   She speaks much of her father, says she hears

---

[17] *gross* large and evident   [18] *charge* expense   [19] *Makes mouths* makes faces
scornfully   [20] *greatly . . . straw* to recognize the great argument even in some
small matter   [21] *fantasy* fanciful image   [22] *trick* toy   [23] *try the cause* find
space in which to settle the issue by battle   [24] *continent* receptacle
[1] *distract* insane

There's tricks[2] i' th' world, and hems, and beats her heart,
Spurns enviously[3] at straws,[4] speaks things in doubt
That carry but half sense. Her speech is nothing,
Yet the unshapèd use[5] of it doth move
5   The hearers to collection;[6] they aim[7] at it,
And botch[8] the words up fit to their own thoughts,
Which, as her winks and nods and gestures yield them,
Indeed would make one think there might be thought,
Though nothing sure, yet much unhappily.
10   HORATIO   'Twere good she were spoken with, for she may strew
Dangerous conjectures in ill-breeding minds.
QUEEN   Let her come in.

(*Exit* GENTLEMAN)

(*Aside*)

15   To my sick soul (as sin's true nature is)
Each toy[9] seems prologue to some great amiss.[10]
So full of artless[11] jealousy[12] is guilt
It spills[13] itself in fearing to be spilt.

(*Enter* OPHELIA [*distracted*])

20   OPHELIA   Where is the beauteous majesty of Denmark?
QUEEN   How now, Ophelia?
OPHELIA (*She sings.*)
        How should I your true-love know
            From another one?
25   By his cockle hat[14] and staff
            And his sandal shoon.[15]
QUEEN   Alas, sweet lady, what imports this song?
OPHELIA   Say you? Nay, pray you mark.

Song

30   He is dead and gone, lady,
            He is dead and gone;
        At his head a grass-green turf,
            At his heels a stone.
        O, ho!

---

2 *tricks* deceits   3 *Spurns enviously* kicks spitefully, takes offense   4 *straws* trifles   5 *unshapèd use* disordered manner   6 *collection* attempts at shaping meaning   7 *aim* guess   8 *botch* patch   9 *toy* trifle   10 *amiss* calamity   11 *artless* unskillfully managed   12 *jealousy* suspicion   13 *spills* destroys   14 *cockle hat* hat bearing a cockle shell, worn by a pilgrim who had been to the shrine of St James of Compostela   15 *shoon* shoes

QUEEN   Nay, but Ophelia—
OPHELIA   Pray you mark.
(*Sings*) White his shroud as the mountain snow—

(*Enter* KING)

5   QUEEN   Alas, look here, my lord.
OPHELIA

Song

Larded [16] all with sweet flowers;
Which bewept to the grave did not go
10   With true-love showers.
KING   How do you, pretty lady?
OPHELIA   Well, God dild [17] you! They say the owl [18] was a baker's
daughter. Lord, we know what we are, but know not what we
may be. God be at your table!
15   KING   Conceit[19] upon her father.
OPHELIA   Pray let's have no words of this, but when they ask you
what it means, say you this:

Song

To-morrow is Saint Valentine's day.
20   All in the morning betime,[20]
And I a maid at your window,
To be your Valentine.
Then up he rose and donned his clo'es
And dupped [21] the chamber door,
25   Let in the maid, that out a maid
Never departed more.
KING   Pretty Ophelia!
OPHELIA   Indeed, la, without an oath, I'll make an end on't:
(*Sings*)   By Gis[22] and by Saint Charity,
30   Alack, and fie for shame!
Young men will do't if they come to't.
By Cock,[23] they are to blame.
Quoth she, "Before you tumbled me,
You promised me to wed."

---

[16] *Larded* garnished   [17] *dild* yield, repay   [18] *the owl* an owl into which, according to a folk-tale, a baker's daughter was transformed because of her failure to show whole-hearted generosity when Christ asked for bread in the
baker's shop   [19] *Conceit* thought   [20] *betime* early   [21] *dupped* opened   [22] *Gis*
Jesus   [23] *Cock* God (with a perversion of the name not uncommon in oaths)

He answers:
"So would I 'a' done, by yonder sun,
And thou hadst not come to my bed."
KING   How long hath she been thus?
5   OPHELIA   I hope all will be well. We must be patient, but I cannot
choose but weep to think they would lay him i' th' cold ground.
My brother shall know of it; and so I thank you for your good
counsel. Come, my coach! Good night, ladies, good night. Sweet
ladies, good night, good night.

10   (*Exit*)

KING   Follow her close; give her good watch, I pray you.

(*Exit* HORATIO)

O, this is the poison of deep grief; it springs
All from her father's death—and now behold!
15   O Gertrude, Gertrude,
When sorrows come, they come not single spies,
But in battalions: first, her father slain;
Next, your son gone, and he most violent author
Of his own just remove; the people muddied,[24]
20   Thick and unwholesome in their thoughts and whispers
For good Polonius' death, and we have done but greenly[25]
In hugger-mugger[26] to inter him; poor Ophelia
Divided from herself and her fair judgment,
Without the which we are pictures or mere beasts;
25   Last, and as much containing as all these,
Her brother is in secret come from France,
Feeds on his wonder, keeps himself in clouds,[27]
And wants[28] not buzzers[29] to infect his ear
With pestilent speeches of his father's death,
30   Wherein necessity, of matter beggared,[30]
Will nothing stick[31] our person to arraign[32]
In ear and ear. O my dear Gertrude, this,
Like to a murd'ring piece,[33] in many places
Gives me superfluous death.

35   *A noise within*

---

[24] *muddied* stirred up and confused   [25] *greenly* foolishly   [26] *hugger-mugger*
secrecy and disorder   [27] *clouds* obscurity   [28] *wants* lacks   [29] *buzzers* whispering tale-bearers   [30] *of matter beggared* unprovided with facts   [31] *nothing
stick* in no way hesitate   [32] *arraign* accuse   [33] *murd'ring piece* cannon loaded
with shot meant to scatter

(Enter a MESSENGER*)*

QUEEN   Alack, what noise is this?
KING   Attend, where are my Switzers?[34] Let them guard the door.
   What is the matter?
5   MESSENGER   Save yourself, my lord.
   The ocean, overpeering of [35] his list,[36]
   Eats not the flats with more impiteous[37] haste
   Than young Laertes, in a riotous head,[38]
   O'erbears your officers. The rabble call him lord,
10   And, as the world were now but to begin,
   Antiquity forgot, custom not known,
   The ratifiers and props of every word,[39]
   They cry, "Choose we! Laertes shall be king!"
   Caps, hands, and tongues applaud it to the clouds,
15   "Laertes shall be king! Laertes king!"

A noise within

QUEEN   How cheerfully on the false trail they cry!
   O, this is counter,[40] you false Danish dogs!
KING   The doors are broke.

20   *(Enter* LAERTES *with others)*

LAERTES   Where is this king?—Sirs, stand you all without.
ALL   No, let's come in.
LAERTES   I pray you give me leave.
ALL   We will, we will.
25   LAERTES   I thank you. Keep the door.

   (Exeunt his FOLLOWERS*)*

                                 O thou vile king,
   Give me my father.
QUEEN   Calmly, good Laertes.
30   LAERTES   That drop of blood that's calm proclaims me bastard,
   Cries cuckold to my father, brands the harlot
   Even here between the chaste unsmirchèd brows
   Of my true mother.
KING   What is the cause, Laertes,
35   That thy rebellion looks so giant-like?
   Let him go, Gertrude. Do not fear[41] our person.

---

[34] *Switzers* hired Swiss guards   [35] *overpeering of* rising to look over and pass
beyond   [36] *list* boundary   [37] *impiteous* pitiless   [38] *head* armed force   [39] *word*
promise   [40] *counter* hunting backward on the trail   [41] *fear* fear for

There's such divinity doth hedge a king
That treason can but peep to[42] what it would,
Acts little of his will. Tell me, Laertes,
Why thou art thus incensed. Let him go, Gertrude.

5   Speak, man.

LAERTES   Where is my father?

KING   Dead.

QUEEN   But not by him.

KING   Let him demand his fill.

10   LAERTES   How came he dead? I'll not be juggled with.
To hell allegiance, vows to the blackest devil,
Conscience and grace to the profoundest pit!
I dare damnation. To this point I stand,
That both the worlds[43] I give to negligence,[44]

15   Let come what comes, only I'll be revenged
Most throughly[45] for my father.

KING   Who shall stay you?

LAERTES   My will, not all the world's.
And for my means, I'll husband them so well

20   They shall go far with little.

KING   Good Laertes,
If you desire to know the certainty
Of your dear father, is't writ in your revenge
That swoopstake[46] you will draw both friend and foe,

25   Winner and loser?

LAERTES   None but his enemies.

KING   Will you know them then?

LAERTES   To his good friends thus wide I'll ope my arms
And like the kind life-rend'ring[47] pelican

30   Repast them with my blood.

KING   Why, now you speak
Like a good child and a true gentleman.
That I am guiltless of your father's death,
And am most sensibly[48] in grief for it,

35   It shall as level [49] to your judgment 'pear
As day does to your eye.

          A noise within: "Let her come in!"

---

[42] *peep to* i.e. through the barrier   [43] *both the worlds* whatever may result in
this world or the next   [44] *give to negligence* disregard   [45] *throughly* thoroughly   [46] *swoopstake* sweepstake, taking all stakes on the gambling table
[47] *life-rend'ring* life-yielding (because the mother pelican supposedly took
blood from her breast with her bill to feed her young)   [48] *sensibly* feelingly
[49] *level* plain

LAERTES   How now? What noise is that?

(*Enter* OPHELIA)

O heat, dry up my brains; tears seven times salt
Burn out the sense and virtue of mine eye!
5   By heaven, thy madness shall be paid by weight
Till our scale turn the beam.[50] O rose of May,
Dear maid, kind sister, sweet Ophelia!
O heavens, is't possible a young maid's wits
Should be as mortal as an old man's life?
10   Nature is fine[51] in love, and where 'tis fine,
It sends some precious instance[52] of itself
After the thing it loves.

OPHELIA

Song

15   They bore him barefaced on the bier
    Hey non nony, nony, hey nony
    And in his grave rained many a tear—
Fare you well, my dove!

LAERTES   Hadst thou thy wits, and didst persuade revenge,
20   It could not move thus.

OPHELIA   You must sing "A-down a-down, and you call him
a-down-a." O, how the wheel[53] becomes it! It is the false steward, that stole his master's daughter.

LAERTES   This nothing 's more than matter.[54]

25   OPHELIA   There's rosemary, that's for remembrance. Pray you, love,
remember. And there is pansies, that's for thoughts.

LAERTES   A document[55] in madness, thoughts and remembrance
fitted.

OPHELIA   There's fennel[56] for you, and columbines.[57] There's rue[58]
30   for you, and here's some for me. We may call it herb of grace o'
Sundays. O, you must wear your rue with a difference. There's
a daisy.[59] I would give you some violets,[60] but they withered all
when my father died. They say 'a made a good end.
(*Sings*)   For bonny sweet Robin is all my joy.

35   LAERTES   Thought and affliction, passion, hell itself,
She turns to favor[61] and to prettiness.

---

[50] *beam* bar of a balance   [51] *fine* refined to purity   [52] *instance* token   [53] *wheel*
burden, refrain   [54] *more than matter* more meaningful than sane speech
[55] *document* lesson   [56] *fennel* symbol of flattery   [57] *columbines* symbol of
thanklessness   [58] *rue* symbol of repentance   [59] *daisy* symbol of dissembling
[60] *violets* symbol of faithfulness   [61] *favor* charm

OPHELIA

Song

And will 'a not come again?
And will 'a not come again?
    No, no, he is dead;
    Go to thy deathbed;
He never will come again.
His beard was as white as snow,
All flaxen was his poll.[62]
    He is gone, he is gone,
    And we cast away moan.
God 'a' mercy on his soul!
And of [63] all Christian souls, I pray God. God bye you.

(Exit)

5

10

15 LAERTES Do you see this, O God?
KING Laertes, I must commune with your grief,
Or you deny me right. Go but apart,
Make choice of whom your wisest friends you will,
And they shall hear and judge 'twixt you and me.
20 If by direct or by collateral [64] hand
They find us touched,[65] we will our kingdom give,
Our crown, our life, and all that we call ours,
To you in satisfaction; but if not,
Be you content to lend your patience to us,
25 And we shall jointly labor with your soul
To give it due content.
LAERTES   Let this be so.
His means of death, his obscure funeral—
No trophy,[66] sword, nor hatchment[67] o'er his bones,
30 No noble rite nor formal ostentation[68]—
Cry to be heard, as 'twere from heaven to earth,
That[69] I must call't in question.
KING   So you shall;
And where th' offense is, let the great axe fall.
35 I pray you go with me.

(Exeunt)

---

[62] *poll* head   [63] *of* on   [64] *collateral* indirect   [65] *touched* i.e. with the crime
[66] *trophy* memorial   [67] *hatchment* coat of arms   [68] *ostentation* ceremony
[69] *That* so that

Act IV, Scene VI

A chamber in the castle

(*Enter* HORATIO *and others*)

HORATIO   What are they that would speak with me?

5 GENTLEMAN   Seafaring men, sir. They say they have letters for you.

HORATIO   Let them come in.

(*Exit* ATTENDANT)

I do not know from what part of the world
I should be greeted, if not from Lord Hamlet.

10 (*Enter* SAILORS)

SAILOR   God bless you, sir.

HORATIO   Let him bless thee too.

SAILOR   'A shall, sir, an't please him. There's a letter for you, sir—
it came from th' ambassador that was bound for England—if
15 your name be Horatio, as I am let to know it is.

HORATIO (*reads the letter*)   "Horatio, when thou shalt have overlooked [1] this, give these fellows some means[2] to the king. They
have letters for him. Ere we were two days old at sea, a pirate of
very warlike appointment[3] gave us chase. Finding ourselves too
20 slow of sail, we put on a compelled valor, and in the grapple I
boarded them. On the instant they got clear of our ship; so I
alone became their prisoner. They have dealt with me like thieves
of mercy,[4] but they knew what they did: I am to do a good turn
for them. Let the king have the letters I have sent, and repair
25 thou to me with as much speed as thou wouldest fly death. I have
words to speak in thine ear will make thee dumb; yet are they
much too light for the bore[5] of the matter. These good fellows
will bring thee where I am. Rosencrantz and Guildenstern hold
their course for England. Of them I have much to tell thee.
30 Farewell.

                    He that thou knowest thine, Hamlet."

Come, I will give you way for these your letters,
And do't the speedier that you may direct me
To him from whom you brought them.

35 (*Exeunt*)

---

[1] *overlooked* surveyed, scanned   [2] *means* i.e. of access   [3] *appointment* equipment   [4] *thieves of mercy* merciful thieves   [5] *bore* caliber (as of a gun)

Act IV, Scene VII

A chamber in the castle

(*Enter* KING *and* LAERTES)

KING   Now must your conscience my acquittance seal,
5   And you must put me in your heart for friend,
Sith you have heard, and with a knowing ear,
That he which hath your noble father slain
Pursued my life.

LAERTES   It well appears. But tell me
10   Why you proceeded not against these feats[1]
So crimeful and so capital[2] in nature,
As by your safety, wisdom, all things else,
You mainly[3] were stirred up.

KING   O, for two special reasons,
15   Which may to you perhaps seem much unsinewed,
But yet to me they're strong. The queen his mother
Lives almost by his looks, and for myself—
My virtue or my plague, be it either which—
She is so conjunctive[4] to my life and soul
20   That, as the star moves not but in his sphere,
I could not but by her. The other motive
Why to a public count[5] I might not go
Is the great love the general gender[6] bear him,
Who, dipping all his faults in their affection,
25   Would, like the spring that turneth wood to stone,
Convert his gyves[7] to graces; so that my arrows,
Too slightly timbered for so loud a wind,
Would have reverted to my bow again,
And not where I had aimed them.

30 LAERTES   And so have I a noble father lost,
A sister driven into desp'rate terms,[8]
Whose worth, if praises may go back again,[9]
Stood challenger on mount[10] of all the age
For her perfections. But my revenge will come.

35 KING   Break not your sleeps for that. You must not think
That we are made of stuff so flat and dull
That we can let our beard be shook with danger,

---

[1] *feats* deeds   [2] *capital* punishable by death   [3] *mainly* powerfully   [4] *conjunctive* closely united   [5] *count* trial, accounting   [6] *general gender* common people   [7] *gyves* fetters   [8] *terms* circumstances   [9] *back again* i.e. to her better circumstances   [10] *on mount* on a height

And think it pastime. You shortly shall hear more.
I loved your father, and we love ourself,
And that, I hope, will teach you to imagine—

(*Enter a* MESSENGER *with letters*)

5   How now? What news?
MESSENGER   Letters, my lord, from Hamlet:
These to your majesty, this to the queen.
KING   From Hamlet? Who brought them?
MESSENGER   Sailors, my lord, they say; I saw them not.
10   They were given me by Claudio; he received them
Of him that brought them.
KING   Laertes, you shall hear them.—
Leave us.

(*Exit* MESSENGER)

15   (*Reads*) "High and mighty, you shall know I am set naked [11]
on your kingdom. To-morrow shall I beg leave to see your kingly
eyes; when I shall (first asking your pardon thereunto) recount
the occasion of my sudden and more strange return.   Hamlet."
What should this mean? Are all the rest come back?
20   Or is it some abuse,[12] and no such thing?
LAERTES   Know you the hand?
KING   'Tis Hamlet's character.[13] "Naked"!
And in a postscript here, he says "alone."
Can you devise[14] me?
25   LAERTES   I am lost in it, my lord. But let him come.
It warms the very sickness in my heart
That I shall live and tell him to his teeth,
"Thus diddest thou."
KING   If it be so, Laertes,
30   (As how should it be so? how otherwise?)
Will you be ruled by me?
LAERTES   Ay, my lord,
So you will not o'errule me to a peace.
KING   To thine own peace. If he be now returned,
35   As checking at[15] his voyage, and that he means
No more to undertake it, I will work him

---

[11] *naked* destitute   [12] *abuse* imposture   [13] *character* handwriting   [14] *devise*
explain to   [15] *checking at* turning aside from (like a falcon turning from its
quarry for other prey)

To an exploit now ripe in my device,
Under the which he shall not choose but fall;
And for his death no wind of blame shall breathe,
But even his mother shall uncharge the practice[16]

5   And call it accident.
LAERTES   My lord, I will be ruled;
The rather if you could devise it so
That I might be the organ.[17]

KING   It falls right.

10   You have been talked of since your travel much,
And that in Hamlet's hearing, for a quality
Wherein they say you shine. Your sum of parts
Did not together pluck such envy from him
As did that one, and that, in my regard,

15   Of the unworthiest siege.[18]

LAERTES   What part is that, my lord?

KING   A very riband [19] in the cap of youth,
Yet needful too, for youth no less becomes
The light and careless livery[20] that it wears

20   Than settled age his sables[21] and his weeds,[22]
Importing health[23] and graveness. Two months since
Here was a gentleman of Normandy.
I have seen myself, and served against, the French,
And they can well [24] on horseback, but this gallant

25   Had witchcraft in't. He grew unto his seat,
And to such wondrous doing brought his horse
As had he been incorpsed [25] and demi-natured [26]
With the brave beast. So far he topped [27] my thought[28]
That I, in forgery[29] of shapes and tricks,

30   Come short of what he did.

LAERTES   A Norman was't?

KING   A Norman.

LAERTES   Upon my life, Lamord.

KING   The very same.

35   LAERTES   I know him well. He is the brooch[30] indeed

And gem of all the nation.
KING   He made confession[31] of you,
And gave you such a masterly report
For art and exercise in your defense,
5   And for your rapier most especial,
That he cried out 'twould be a sight indeed
If one could match you. The scrimers[32] of their nation
He swore had neither motion, guard, nor eye,
If you opposed them. Sir, this report of his
10   Did Hamlet so envenom with his envy
That he could nothing do but wish and beg
Your sudden coming o'er to play with you.
Now, out of this—
LAERTES   What out of this, my lord?
15   KING   Laertes, was your father dear to you?
Or are you like the painting of a sorrow,
A face without a heart?
LAERTES   Why ask you this?
KING   Not that I think you did not love your father,
20   But that I know love is begun by time,
And that I see, in passages of proof,[33]
Time qualifies[34] the spark and fire of it.
There lives within the very flame of love
A kind of wick or snuff [35] that will abate it,
25   And nothing is at a like goodness still,[36]
For goodness, growing to a plurisy,[37]
Dies in his own too-much. That we would do
We should do when we would, for this "would" changes,
And hath abatements and delays as many
30   As there are tongues, are hands, are accidents,
And then this "should" is like a spendthrift sigh,
That hurts[38] by easing. But to the quick[39] o' th' ulcer—
Hamlet comes back; what would you undertake
To show yourself your father's son in deed
35   More than in words?
LAERTES   To cut his throat i' th' church!

---

[31] *made confession* admitted the rival accomplishments   [32] *scrimers* fencers
[33] *passages of proof* incidents of experience   [34] *qualifies* weakens   [35] *snuff*
unconsumed portion of the burned wick   [36] *still* always   [37] *plurisy* excess
[38] *hurts* i.e. shortens life by drawing blood from the heart (as was believed)
[39] *quick* sensitive flesh

KING   No place indeed should murder sanctuarize;[40]
Revenge should have no bounds. But, good Laertes,
Will you do this? Keep close within your chamber.
Hamlet returned shall know you are come home.
5   We'll put on[41] those shall praise your excellence
And set a double varnish on the fame
The Frenchman gave you, bring you in fine[42] together
And wager on your heads. He, being remiss,[43]
Most generous, and free from all contriving,
10   Will not peruse[44] the foils, so that with ease,
Or with a little shuffling, you may choose
A sword unbated,[45] and, in a pass of practice,[46]
Requite him for your father.

LAERTES   I will do't,
15   And for that purpose I'll anoint my sword.
I bought an unction[47] of a mountebank,[48]
So mortal that, but dip a knife in it,
Where it draws blood no cataplasm[49] so rare,
Collected from all simples[50] that have virtue
20   Under the moon, can save the thing from death
That is but scratched withal.[51] I'll touch my point
With this contagion, that, if I gall [52] him slightly,
It may be death.

KING   Let's further think of this,
25   Weigh what convenience both of time and means
May fit us to our shape.[53] If this should fail,
And that our drift[54] look[55] through our bad performance,
'Twere better not assayed. Therefore this project
Should have a back or second, that might hold
30   If this did blast in proof.[56] Soft, let me see.
We'll make a solemn wager on your cunnings—
I ha't!
When in your motion you are hot and dry—
As make your bouts more violent to that end—
35   And that he calls for drink, I'll have preferred [57] him
A chalice for the nonce,[58] whereon but sipping,

---

40 *sanctuarize* protect from punishment, give sanctuary to   41 *put on* instigate
42 *in fine* finally   43 *remiss* negligent   44 *peruse* scan   45 *unbated* not blunted
46 *pass of practice* thrust made effective by trickery   47 *unction* ointment
48 *mountebank* quack-doctor   49 *cataplasm* poultice   50 *simples* herbs   51 *withal*
with it   52 *gall* scratch   53 *shape* plan   54 *drift* intention   55 *look* show
56 *blast in proof* burst during trial (like a faulty cannon)   57 *preferred* offered
58 *nonce* occasion

If he by chance escape your venomed stuck,[59]
Our purpose may hold there.—But stay, what noise?

(*Enter* QUEEN)

QUEEN   One woe doth tread upon another's heel,
5   So fast they follow. Your sister's drowned, Laertes.
LAERTES   Drowned! O, where?
QUEEN   There is a willow grows askant[60] the brook,
That shows his hoar[61] leaves in the glassy stream.
Therewith fantastic garlands did she make
10   Of crowflowers, nettles, daisies, and long purples,
That liberal[62] shepherds give a grosser name,
But our cold maids do dead men's fingers call them.
There on the pendent boughs her crownet[63] weeds
Clamb'ring to hang, an envious sliver broke,
15   When down her weedy trophies and herself
Fell in the weeping brook. Her clothes spread wide,
And mermaid-like awhile they bore her up,
Which time she chanted snatches of old lauds,[64]
As one incapable of[65] her own distress,
20   Or like a creature native and indued[66]
Unto that element. But long it could not be
Till that her garments, heavy with their drink,
Pulled the poor wretch from her melodious lay
To muddy death.
25   LAERTES   Alas, then she is drowned?
QUEEN   Drowned, drowned.
LAERTES   Too much of water hast thou, poor Ophelia,
And therefore I forbid my tears; but yet
It is our trick;[67] nature her custom holds,
30   Let shame say what it will. When these are gone,
The woman[68] will be out. Adieu, my lord.
I have a speech o' fire, that fain would blaze
But that this folly drowns it.

(*Exit*)

35   KING   Let's follow, Gertrude.
How much I had to do to calm his rage!

---

[59] *stuck* thrust   [60] *askant* alongside   [61] *hoar* grey   [62] *liberal* free-spoken, licentious   [63] *crownet* coronet   [64] *lauds* hymns   [65] *incapable of* insensible to   [66] *indued* endowed   [67] *trick* way (i.e. to shed tears when sorrowful)
[68] *woman* unmanly part of nature.

Now fear I this will give it start again;
Therefore let's follow.

(*Exeunt*)

ACT V

5 **Scene I**

A churchyard

(*Enter two* CLOWNS[1])

CLOWN   Is she to be buried in Christian burial [2] when she willfully
seeks her own salvation?

10 OTHER   I tell thee she is. Therefore make her grave straight.[3] The
crowner[4] hath sate on her, and finds it Christian burial.

CLOWN   How can that be, unless she drowned herself in her own
defense?

OTHER   Why, 'tis found so.

15 CLOWN   It must be *se offendendo*;[5] it cannot be else. For here lies
the point: if I drown myself wittingly, it argues an act, and an act
hath three branches—it is to act, to do, and to perform. Argal,[6]
she drowned herself wittingly.

OTHER   Nay, but hear you, Goodman Delver.[7]

20 CLOWN   Give me leave. Here lies the water—good. Here stands the
man—good. If the man go to this water and drown himself, it is,
will he nill he,[8] he goes, mark you that. But if the water come to
him and drown him, he drowns not himself. Argal, he that is not
guilty of his own death shortens not his own life.

25 OTHER   But is this law?

CLOWN   Ay marry, is't—crowner's quest[9] law.

OTHER   Will you ha' the truth on't? If this had not been a gentle-
woman, she should have been buried out o' Christian burial.

CLOWN   Why, there thou say'st.[10] And the more pity that great folk

30 should have count'nance[11] in this world to drown or hang themselves more than their even-Christen.[12] Come, my spade. There

---

[1] *Clowns* rustics   [2] *in Christian burial* in consecrated ground with the prescribed service of the Church (a burial denied to suicides)   [3] *straight*
straightway, at once   [4] *crowner* coroner   [5] *se offendendo* a clownish transformation of *"se defendendo,"* "in self-defense"   [6] *Argal* for *"ergo,"* "therefore"   [7] *Delver* Digger   [8] *will he nill he* willy-nilly   [9] *quest* inquest   [10] *thou
say'st* you have it right   [11] *count'nance* privilege   [12] *even-Christen* fellow
Christian

is no ancient gentlemen but gard'ners, ditchers, and grave-makers.
They hold up Adam's profession.

OTHER   Was he a gentleman?

CLOWN   'A was the first that ever bore arms.

5   OTHER   Why, he had none.[13]

CLOWN   What, art a heathen? How dost thou understand the
Scripture? The Scripture says Adam digged. Could he dig without arms? I'll put another question to thee. If thou answerest me
not to the purpose, confess thyself—

10   OTHER   Go to.

CLOWN   What is he that builds stronger than either the mason, the
shipwright, or the carpenter?

OTHER   The gallows-maker, for that frame outlives a thousand
tenants.

15   CLOWN   I like thy wit well, in good faith. The gallows does well.
But how does it well? It does well to those that do ill. Now thou
dost ill to say the gallows is built stronger than the church. Argal,
the gallows may do well to thee. To't again, come.

OTHER   Who builds stronger than a mason, a shipwright, or a car-
20   penter?

CLOWN   Ay, tell me that, and unyoke.[14]

OTHER   Marry, now I can tell.

CLOWN   To't.

OTHER   Mass,[15] I cannot tell.

25   CLOWN   Cudgel thy brains no more about it, for your dull ass will
not mend his pace with beating. And when you are asked this
question next, say "a grave-maker." The houses he makes last till
doomsday. Go, get thee in, and fetch me a stoup[16] of liquor.

(*Exit* OTHER CLOWN)

30   (*Enter* HAMLET *and* HORATIO [*as* CLOWN *digs and sings*])

Song

In youth when I did love, did love,
   Methought it was very sweet
To contract—O—the time for—a—my behove,[17]
35   O, methought there—a—was nothing—a—meet.

HAMLET   Has this fellow no feeling of his business, that 'a sings at
grave-making?

---

[13] *had none* i.e. had no gentleman's coat of arms   [14] *unyoke* i.e. unharness
your powers of thought after a good day's work   [15] *Mass* by the Mass   [16] *stoup*
large mug   [17] *behove* behoof, benefit

HORATIO Custom hath made it in him a property[18] of easiness.[19]

HAMLET 'Tis e'en so. The hand of little employment hath the daintier sense.[20]

CLOWN

5   **Song**

> But age with his stealing steps
> Hath clawed me in his clutch,
> And hath shipped me intil [21] the land,
> As if I had never been such.

10   (*Throws up a skull*)

HAMLET That skull had a tongue in it, and could sing once. How the knave jowls[22] it to the ground, as if 'twere Cain's jawbone, that did the first murder! This might be the pate of a politician,[23] which this ass now o'erreaches;[24] one that would circumvent

15   God, might it not?

HORATIO It might, my lord.

HAMLET Or of a courtier, which could say "Good morrow, sweet lord! How dost thou, sweet lord?" This might be my Lord Such-a-one, that praised my Lord Such-a-one's horse when 'a meant to

20   beg it, might it not?

HORATIO Ay, my lord.

HAMLET Why, e'en so, and now my Lady Worm's, chapless,[25] and knocked about the mazzard [26] with a sexton's spade. Here's fine revolution, an we had the trick to see't. Did these bones cost no

25   more the breeding but to play at loggets[27] with 'em? Mine ache to think on't.

CLOWN

Song

30
> A pickaxe and a spade, a spade,
> For and [28] a shrouding sheet;
> O, a pit of clay for to be made
> For such a guest is meet.

(*Throws up another skull*)

---

[18] *property* peculiarity   [19] *easiness* easy acceptability   [20] *daintier sense* more delicate feeling (because the hand is less calloused)   [21] *intil* into   [22] *jowls* hurls   [23] *politician* crafty schemer   [24] *o'erreaches* gets the better of (with a play upon the literal meaning)   [25] *chapless* lacking the lower chap or jaw   [26] *mazzard* head   [27] *loggets* small pieces of wood thrown in a game   [28] *For and* and

HAMLET   There's another. Why may not that be the skull of a lawyer? Where be his quiddities[29] now, his quillities,[30] his cases, his
tenures,[31] and his tricks? Why does he suffer this mad knave now
to knock him about the sconce[32] with a dirty shovel, and will not
5   tell him of his action of battery? Hum! This fellow might be in's
time a great buyer of land, with his statutes, his recognizances,[33]
his fines,[34] his double vouchers,[35] his recoveries. Is this the fine[36]
of his fines, and the recovery of his recoveries, to have his fine
pate full of fine dirt? Will his vouchers vouch him no more of his
10   purchases, and double ones too, than the length and breadth of
a pair of indentures? [37] The very conveyances[38] of his lands will
scarcely lie in this box, and must th' inheritor himself have no
more, ha?

HORATIO   Not a jot more, my lord.

15   HAMLET   Is not parchment made of sheepskins?

HORATIO   Ay, my lord, and of calveskins too.

HAMLET   They are sheep and calves which seek out assurance in
that. I will speak to this fellow. Whose grave 's this, sirrah?

CLOWN   Mine, sir.

20   (*Sings*)   O, a pit of clay for to be made
For such a guest is meet.

HAMLET   I think it be thine indeed, for thou liest in't.

CLOWN   You lie out on't, sir, and therefore 'tis not yours. For my
part, I do not lie in't, yet it is mine.

25   HAMLET   Thou dost lie in't, to be in't and say it is thine. 'Tis for
the dead, not for the quick;[39] therefore thou liest.

CLOWN   'Tis a quick lie, sir; 'twill away again from me to you.

HAMLET   What man dost thou dig it for?

CLOWN   For no man, sir.

30   HAMLET   What woman then?

CLOWN   For none neither.

HAMLET   Who is to be buried in't?

CLOWN   One that was a woman, sir; but, rest her soul, she's dead.

HAMLET   How absolute[40] the knave is! We must speak by the

---

[29] *quiddities* subtleties (from scholastic *"quidditas,"* meaning the distinctive
nature of anything)   [30] *quillities* nice distinctions   [31] *tenures* holdings of
property   [32] *sconce* head   [33] *statutes, recognizances* legal documents or bonds
acknowledging debt   [34] *fines, recoveries* modes of converting estate tail into
fee simple   [35] *vouchers* persons vouched or called on to warrant a title
[36] *fine* end (introducing a word play involving four meanings of "fine")
[37] *pair of indentures* deed or legal agreement in duplicate   [38] *conveyances*
deeds   [39] *quick* living   [40] *absolute* positive

card,[41] or equivocation[42] will undo us. By the Lord, Horatio, this three years I have taken note of it, the age is grown so picked [43] that the toe of the peasant comes so near the heel of the courtier he galls[44] his kibe.[45]—How long hast thou been a grave-maker?

5   CLOWN   Of all the days i' th' year, I came to't that day that our last king Hamlet overcame Fortinbras.

HAMLET   How long is that since?

CLOWN   Cannot you tell that? Every fool can tell that. It was the very day that young Hamlet was born—he that is mad, and sent
10   •into England.

HAMLET   Ay, marry, why was he sent into England?

CLOWN   Why, because 'a was mad. 'A shall recover his wits there; or, if 'a do not, 'tis no great matter there.

HAMLET   Why?

15   CLOWN   'Twill not be seen in him there. There the men are as mad as he.

HAMLET   How came he mad?

CLOWN   Very strangely, they say.

HAMLET   How strangely?

20   CLOWN   Faith, e'en with losing his wits.

HAMLET   Upon what ground?

CLOWN   Why, here in Denmark. I have been sexton here, man and boy, thirty years.

HAMLET   How long will a man lie i' th' earth ere he rot?

25   CLOWN   Faith, if 'a be not rotten before 'a die (as we have many pocky[46] corses now-a-days that will scarce hold the laying in), 'a will last you some eight year or nine year. A tanner will last you nine year.

HAMLET   Why he more than another?

30   CLOWN   Why, sir, his hide is so tanned with his trade that 'a will keep out water a great while, and your water is a sore decayer of your whoreson dead body. Here's a skull now hath lien you i' th' earth three-and-twenty years.

HAMLET   Whose was it?

35   CLOWN   A whoreson mad fellow's it was. Whose do you think it was?

HAMLET   Nay, I know not.

---

[41] *by the card* by the card on which the points of the mariner's compass are marked, absolutely to the point   [42] *equivocation* ambiguity   [43] *picked* refined, spruce   [44] *galls* chafes   [45] *kibe* chilblain   [46] *pocky* rotten (literally, corrupted by pox, or syphilis)

CLOWN   A pestilence on him for a mad rogue! 'A poured a flagon
of Rhenish[47] on my head once. This same skull, sir, was—sir—
Yorick's skull, the king's jester.

HAMLET   This?

5   CLOWN   E'en that.

HAMLET   Let me see. (*Takes the skull.*) Alas, poor Yorick! I knew
him, Horatio, a fellow of infinite jest, of most excellent fancy. He
hath borne me on his back a thousand times. And now how ab-
horred in my imagination it is! My gorge rises at it. Here hung

10   those lips that I have kissed I know not how oft. Where be your
gibes now? Your gambols, your songs, your flashes of merriment
that were wont to set the table on a roar? Not one now to mock
your own grinning? Quite chapfall'n?[48] Now get you to my lady's
chamber, and tell her, let her paint an inch thick, to this favor[49]

15   she must come. Make her laugh at that. Prithee, Horatio, tell me
one thing.

HORATIO   What's that, my lord?

HAMLET   Dost thou think Alexander looked o' this fashion i' th'
earth?

20   HORATIO   E'en so.

HAMLET   And smelt so? Pah!

(*Puts down the skull*)

HORATIO   E'en so, my lord.

HAMLET   To what base uses we may return, Horatio! Why may

25   not imagination trace the noble dust of Alexander till 'a find it
stopping a bunghole?

HORATIO   'Twere to consider too curiously,[50] to consider so.

HAMLET   No, faith, not a jot, but to follow him thither with modesty[51] enough, and likelihood to lead it; as thus: Alexander died,

30   Alexander was buried, Alexander returneth to dust; the dust is
earth; of earth we make loam; and why of that loam whereto he
was converted might they not stop a beer barrel?
Imperious[52] Caesar, dead and turned to clay,
Might stop a hole to keep the wind away.

35   O, that that earth which kept the world in awe
Should patch a wall t' expel the winter's flaw![53]

---

[47] *Rhenish* Rhine wine   [48] *chapfall'n* lacking the lower chap, or jaw (with a
play on the sense "down in the mouth," "dejected")   [49] *favor* countenance,
aspect   [50] *curiously* minutely   [51] *modesty* moderation   [52] *Imperious* imperial
[53] *flaw* gust of wind

But soft, but soft awhile! Here comes the king—

(*Enter* KING, QUEEN, LAERTES, *and the* CORSE [*with* LORDS *attendant and a* DOCTOR OF DIVINITY *as* PRIEST])

The queen, the courtiers. Who is this they follow?
5   And with such maimèd rites? This doth betoken
The corse they follow did with desp'rate hand
Fordo[54] it[55] own life. 'Twas of some estate.[56]
Couch[57] we awhile, and mark.

(*Retires with* HORATIO)

10   LAERTES   What ceremony else?
     HAMLET   That is Laertes,
     A very noble youth. Mark.
     LAERTES   What ceremony else?
     DOCTOR   Her obsequies have been as far enlarged
15   As we have warranty. Her death was doubtful,
     And, but that great command o'ersways the order,
     She should in ground unsanctified have lodged
     Till the last trumpet. For charitable prayers,
     Shards,[58] flints, and pebbles should be thrown on her.
20   Yet here she is allowed her virgin crants,[59]
     Her maiden strewments,[60] and the bringing home[61]
     Of bell and burial.
     LAERTES   Must there no more be done?
     DOCTOR   No more be done.
25   We should profane the service of the dead
     To sing a requiem and such rest to her
     As to peace-parted souls.
     LAERTES   Lay her i' th' earth,
     And from her fair and unpolluted flesh
30   May violets spring! I tell thee, churlish priest,
     A minist'ring angel shall my sister be
     When thou liest howling.
     HAMLET   What, the fair Ophelia?
     QUEEN   Sweets to the sweet! Farewell.

35   (*Scatters flowers*)

I hoped thou shouldst have been my Hamlet's wife.

---

[54] *Fordo* destroy   [55] *it* its   [56] *estate* rank   [57] *Couch* hide   [58] *Shards* broken pieces of pottery   [59] *crants* garland   [60] *strewments* strewings of the grave with flowers   [61] *bringing home* laying to rest

I thought thy bride-bed to have decked, sweet maid,
And not have strewed thy grave.

LAERTES   O, treble woe
Fall ten times treble on that cursèd head
5   Whose wicked deed thy most ingenious[62] sense
Deprived thee of! Hold off the earth awhile,
Till I have caught her once more in mine arms.

(Leaps in the grave)

Now pile your dust upon the quick and dead
10   Till of this flat a mountain you have made
T' o'ertop old Pelion[63] or the skyish head
Of blue Olympus.

HAMLET *(coming forward)*   What is he whose grief
Bears such an emphasis? whose phrase of sorrow
15   Conjures[64] the wand'ring stars,[65] and makes them stand
Like wonder-wounded hearers? This is I,
Hamlet the Dane.

(Leaps in after LAERTES*)*

LAERTES   The devil take thy soul!

20   *(Grapples with him)*

HAMLET   Thou pray'st not well.
I prithee take thy fingers from my throat,
For, though I am not splenitive[66] and rash,
Yet have I in me something dangerous,
25   Which let thy wisdom fear. Hold off thy hand.
KING   Pluck them asunder.
QUEEN   Hamlet, Hamlet!
ALL   Gentlemen!
HORATIO   Good my lord, be quiet.

30   *(ATTENDANTS part them, and they come out of the grave)*

HAMLET   Why, I will fight with him upon this theme
Until my eyelids will no longer wag.
QUEEN   O my son, what theme?

---

[62] *most ingenious* of quickest apprehension   [63] *Pelion* a mountain in Thessaly,
like Olympus and also Ossa (the allusion being to the war in which the Titans
fought the gods and attempted to heap Ossa and Olympus on Pelion, or
Pelion and Ossa on Olympus, in order to scale heaven)   [64] *Conjures* charms,
puts a spell upon   [65] *wand'ring stars* planets   [66] *splenitive* of fiery temper
(the spleen being considered the seat of anger)

HAMLET   I loved Ophelia. Forty thousand brothers
Could not with all their quantity of love
Make up my sum. What wilt thou do for her?
KING   O, he is mad, Laertes.
5   QUEEN   For love of God, forbear him.
HAMLET   'Swounds, show me what thou't do.
Woo't [67] weep? woo't fight? woo't fast? woo't tear thyself?
Woo't drink up esill? [68] eat a crocodile?
I'll do't. Dost thou come here to whine?
10   To outface me with leaping in her grave?
Be buried quick[69] with her, and so will I.
And if thou prate of mountains, let them throw
Millions of acres on us, till our ground,
Singeing his pate against the burning zone,
15   Make Ossa like a wart! Nay, an thou'lt mouth,
I'll rant as well as thou.
QUEEN   This is mere[70] madness;
And thus a while the fit will work on him.
Anon, as patient as the female dove
20   When that her golden couplets[71] are disclosed,[72]
His silence will sit drooping.
HAMLET   Hear you, sir.
What is the reason that you use me thus?
I loved you ever. But it is no matter.
25   Let Hercules himself do what he may,
The cat will mew, and dog will have his day.
KING   I pray thee, good Horatio, wait upon him.

(*Exit* HAMLET *and* HORATIO)

(*To* LAERTES)

30   Strengthen your patience in[73] our last night's speech.
We'll put the matter to the present push.[74]
Good Gertrude, set some watch over your son.—
This grave shall have a living monument.
An hour of quiet shortly shall we see;
35   Till then in patience our proceeding be.

(*Exeunt*)

---

[67] *Woo't* wilt (thou)   [68] *esill* vinegar   [69] *quick* alive   [70] *mere* absolute
[71] *couplets* pair of fledglings   [72] *disclosed* hatched   [73] *in* by calling to mind
[74] *present push* immediate trial

Act V, Scene II

The hall of the castle

(*Enter* HAMLET *and* HORATIO)

HAMLET So much for this, sir; now shall you see the other.
5   You do remember all the circumstance?

HORATIO Remember it, my lord!

HAMLET Sir, in my heart there was a kind of fighting
That would not let me sleep. Methought I lay
Worse than the mutines[1] in the bilboes.[2] Rashly,
10   And praised be rashness for it—let us know,
Our indiscretion sometime serves us well
When our deep plots do pall,[3] and that should learn us
There's a divinity that shapes our ends,
Rough-hew[4] them how we will—

15 HORATIO   That is most certain.

HAMLET Up from my cabin,
My sea-gown scarfed about me, in the dark
Groped I to find out them, had my desire,
Fingered [5] their packet, and in fine[6] withdrew
20   To mine own room again, making so bold,
My fears forgetting manners, to unseal
Their grand commission; where I found, Horatio—
Ah, royal knavery!—an exact command,
Larded [7] with many several sorts of reasons,
25   Importing[8] Denmark's health, and England's too,
With, ho! such bugs[9] and goblins in my life,[10]
That on the supervise,[11] no leisure bated,[12]
No, not to stay the grinding of the axe,
My head should be struck off.

30 HORATIO   Is't possible?

HAMLET Here's the commission; read it at more leisure.
But wilt thou hear me how I did proceed?

HORATIO I beseech you.

HAMLET Being thus benetted round with villainies,
35   Or[13] I could make a prologue to my brains,
They had begun the play. I sat me down,

---

[1] *mutines* mutineers [2] *bilboes* fetters [3] *pall* fail [4] *Rough-hew* shape roughly in trial form [5] *Fingered* filched [6] *in fine* finally [7] *Larded* enriched [8] *Importing* relating to [9] *bugs* bugbears [10] *in my life* to be encountered as dangers if I should be allowed to live [11] *supervise* perusal [12] *bated* deducted, allowed [13] *Or* ere

Devised a new commission, wrote it fair.
I once did hold it, as our statists[14] do,
A baseness to write fair,[15] and labored much
How to forget that learning, but, sir, now
5 It did me yeoman's service.[16] Wilt thou know
Th' effect[17] of what I wrote?

HORATIO   Ay, good my lord.

HAMLET An earnest conjuration from the king,
As England was his faithful tributary,
10 As love between them like the palm might flourish,
As peace should still her wheaten garland [18] wear
And stand a comma[19] 'tween their amities,
And many such-like as's of great charge,[20]
That on the view and knowing of these contents,
15 Without debatement further, more or less,
He should the bearers put to sudden death,
Not shriving time[21] allowed.

HORATIO   How was this sealed?

HAMLET Why, even in that was heaven ordinant.[22]
20 I had my father's signet in my purse,
Which was the model [23] of that Danish seal,
Folded the writ up in the form of th' other,
Subscribed it, gave't th' impression,[24] placed it safely,
The changeling never known. Now, the next day
25 Was our sea-fight, and what to this was sequent[25]
Thou know'st already.

HORATIO So Guildenstern and Rosencrantz go to't.

HAMLET Why, man, they did make love to this employment.
They are not near my conscience; their defeat
30 Does by their own insinuation[26] grow.
'Tis dangerous when the baser nature comes
Between the pass[27] and fell [28] incensèd points
Of mighty opposites.

---

[14] *statists* statesmen   [15] *fair* with professional clarity (like a clerk or a scrivener, not like a gentleman)   [16] *yeoman's service* stout service such as yeomen footsoldiers gave as archers   [17] *effect* purport   [18] *wheaten garland* adornment of fruitful agriculture   [19] *comma* connective (because it indicates continuity of thought in a sentence)   [20] *charge* burden (with a double meaning to fit a play that makes *as's* into "asses"   [21] *shriving time* time for confession and absolution   [22] *ordinant* controlling   [23] *model* counterpart   [24] *impression* i.e. of the signet   [25] *sequent* subsequent   [26] *insinuation* intrusion   [27] *pass* thrust   [28] *fell* fierce

HORATIO   Why, what a king is this!

HAMLET   Does it not, think thee, stand [29] me now upon—

He that hath killed my king, and whored my mother,

Popped in between th' election[30] and my hopes,

5   Thrown out his angle[31] for my proper[32] life,

And with such coz'nage[33]   is't not perfect conscience

To quit[34] him with this arm? And is't not to be damned

To let this canker[35] of our nature come

In further evil?

10   HORATIO   It must be shortly known to him from England

What is the issue of the business there.

HAMLET   It will be short; the interim is mine,

And a man's life 's no more than to say "one."

But I am very sorry, good Horatio,

15   That to Laertes I forgot myself,

For by the image of my cause I see

The portraiture of his. I'll court his favors.

But sure the bravery[36] of his grief did put me

Into a tow'ring passion.

20   HORATIO   Peace, who comes here?

(*Enter* OSRIC, *a courtier*)

OSRIC   Your lordship is right welcome back to Denmark.

HAMLET   I humbly thank you, sir. (*aside to* HORATIO) Dost know
this waterfly?

25   HORATIO (*aside to* HAMLET)   No, my good lord.

HAMLET (*aside to* HORATIO)   Thy state is the more gracious, for
'tis a vice to know him. He hath much land, and fertile. Let a
beast be lord of beasts, and his crib shall stand at the king's
mess.[37] 'Tis a chough,[38] but, as I say, spacious in the possession

30   of dirt.

OSRIC   Sweet lord, if your lordship were at leisure, I should impart
a thing to you from his majesty.

HAMLET   I will receive it, sir, with all diligence of spirit. Put your
bonnet to his right use. 'Tis for the head.

35   OSRIC   I thank your lordship, it is very hot.

HAMLET   No, believe me, 'tis very cold; the wind is northerly.

OSRIC   It is indifferent[39] cold, my lord, indeed.

---

[29] *stand* rest incumbent   [30] *election* i.e. to the kingship (the Danish kingship
being elective)   [31] *angle* fishing line   [32] *proper* own   [33] *coz'nage* cozenage,
trickery   [34] *quit* repay   [35] *canker* cancer, ulcer   [36] *bravery* ostentatious display   [37] *mess* table   [38] *chough* jackdaw, chatterer   [39] *indifferent* somewhat

HAMLET   But yet methinks it is very sultry and hot for my complexion.[40]

OSRIC   Exceedingly, my lord; it is very sultry, as 'twere—I cannot
tell how. But, my lord, his majesty bade me signify to you that
5   'a has laid a great wager on your head. Sir, this is the matter—

HAMLET   I beseech you remember.[41]

(HAMLET *moves him to put on his hat*)

OSRIC   Nay, good my lord; for mine ease,[42] in good faith. Sir, here
is newly come to court Laertes—believe me, an absolute gentle-
10   man, full of most excellent differences,[43] of very soft society[44]
and great showing.[45] Indeed, to speak feelingly[46] of him, he is the
card [47] or calendar[48] of gentry,[49] for you shall find in him the
continent[50] of what part a gentleman would see.

HAMLET   Sir, his definement[51] suffers no perdition[52] in you, though,
15   I know, to divide him inventorially would dozy[53] th' arithmetic
of memory, and yet but yaw[54] neither[55] in respect of [56] his quick
sail. But, in the verity of extolment, I take him to be a soul of
great article,[57] and his infusion[58] of such dearth[59] and rareness as,
to make true diction of him, his semblable[60] is his mirror, and
20   who else would trace[61] him, his umbrage,[62] nothing more.

OSRIC   Your lordship speaks most infallibly of him.

HAMLET   The concernancy,[63] sir? Why do we wrap the gentleman
in our more rawer[64] breath?

OSRIC   Sir?

25   HORATIO   Is't not possible to understand in another tongue? You
will to't,[65] sir, really.

HAMLET   What imports the nomination[66] of this gentleman?

OSRIC   Of Laertes?

---

[40] *complexion* temperament   [41] *remember* i.e. remember you have done all
that courtesy demands   [42] *for mine ease* i.e. I keep my hat off just for comfort (a conventional polite phrase)   [43] *differences* differentiating characteristics, special qualities   [44] *soft society* gentle manners   [45] *great showing* noble
appearance   [46] *feelingly* appropriately   [47] *card* map   [48] *calendar* guide
[49] *gentry* gentlemanliness   [50] *continent* all-containing embodiment (with an
implication of geographical continent to go with *card*)   [51] *definement* definition   [52] *perdition* loss   [53] *dozy* dizzy, stagger   [54] *yaw* hold to a course unsteadily like a ship that steers wild   [55] *neither* for all that   [56] *in respect of*
in comparison with   [57] *article* scope, importance   [58] *infusion* essence   [59] *dearth*
scarcity   [60] *semblable* likeness (i.e. only true likeness)   [61] *trace* follow
[62] *umbrage* shadow   [63] *concernancy* relevance   [64] *rawer breath* cruder speech
[65] *to't* i.e. get to an understanding   [66] *nomination* mention

HORATIO (*aside to* HAMLET) His purse is empty already. All's golden words are spent.

HAMLET Of him, sir.

OSRIC I know you are not ignorant—

5 HAMLET I would you did, sir; yet, in faith, if you did, it would not much approve me.[67] Well, sir?

OSRIC You are not ignorant of what excellence Laertes is—

HAMLET I dare not confess that, lest I should compare[68] with him in excellence; but to know a man well were to know himself.

10 OSRIC I mean, sir, for his weapon; but in the imputation laid on him by them, in his meed [69] he's unfellowed.

HAMLET What's his weapon?

OSRIC Rapier and dagger.

HAMLET That's two of his weapons—but well.

15 OSRIC The king, sir, hath wagered with him six Barbary horses, against the which he has impawned,[70] as I take it, six French rapiers and poniards, with their assigns,[71] as girdle, hangers,[72] and so. Three of the carriages, in faith, are very dear to fancy,[73] very responsive[74] to the hilts, most delicate carriages, and of very

20 liberal conceit.[75]

HAMLET What call you the carriages?

HORATIO (*aside to* HAMLET) I knew you must be edified by the margent[76] ere you had done.

OSRIC The carriages, sir, are the hangers.

25 HAMLET The phrase would be more germane to the matter if we could carry a cannon by our sides. I would it might be hangers till then. But on! Six Barbary horses against six French swords, their assigns, and three liberal-conceited carriages—that's the French bet against the Danish. Why is this all impawned, as you

30 call it?

OSRIC The king, sir, hath laid, sir, that in a dozen passes between yourself and him he shall not exceed you three hits; he hath laid on twelve for nine, and it would come to immediate trial if your lordship would vouchsafe the answer.

35 HAMLET How if I answer no?

OSRIC I mean, my lord, the opposition of your person in trial.

---

[67] *approve me* be to my credit   [68] *compare* compete   [69] *meed* worth   [70] *impawned* staked   [71] *assigns* appurtenances   [72] *hangers* straps by which the sword hangs from the belt   [73] *dear to fancy* finely designed   [74] *responsive* corresponding closely   [75] *liberal conceit* tasteful design, refined conception   [76] *margent* margin (i.e. explanatory notes there printed)

HAMLET   Sir, I will walk here in the hall. If it please his majesty, it is the breathing time[77] of day with me. Let the foils be brought, the gentleman willing, and the king hold his purpose, I will win for him an[78] I can; if not, I will gain nothing but my shame and
5   the odd hits.

OSRIC   Shall I redeliver you e'en so?

HAMLET   To this effect, sir, after what flourish your nature will.

OSRIC   I commend my duty to your lordship.

HAMLET   Your, yours. (*Exit* OSRIC) He does well to commend it
10   himself; there are no tongues else for's turn.

HORATIO   This lapwing[79] runs away with the shell on his head.

HAMLET   'A did comply,[80] sir, with his dug[81] before 'a sucked it. Thus has he, and many more of the same bevy[82] that I know the drossy[83] age dotes on, only got the tune of the time and, out of
15   an habit of encounter, a kind of yeasty collection, which carries them through and through the most fanned and winnowed [84] opinions; and do but blow them to their trial, the bubbles are out.

(*Enter a* LORD)

20   LORD   My lord, his majesty commended him to you by young Osric, who brings back to him that you attend him in the hall. He sends to know if your pleasure hold to play with Laertes, or that you will take longer time.

HAMLET   I am constant to my purposes; they follow the king's
25   pleasure. If his fitness speaks, mine is ready; now or whensoever, provided I be so able as now.

LORD   The king and queen and all are coming down.

HAMLET   In happy time.[85]

LORD   The queen desires you to use some gentle entertainment[86] to
30   Laertes before you fall to play.

HAMLET   She well instructs me.

(*Exit* LORD)

HORATIO   You will lose this wager, my lord.

HAMLET   I do not think so. Since he went into France I have been
35   in continual practice. I shall win at the odds. But thou wouldst not think how ill all's here about my heart. But it is no matter.

---

[77] *breathing time* exercise hour   [78] *an* if   [79] *lapwing* a bird reputed to be so precocious as to run as soon as hatched   [80] *comply* observe formalities of courtesy   [81] *dug* mother's nipple   [82] *bevy* company   [83] *drossy* frivolous   [84] *fanned and winnowed* select and refined   [85] *In happy time* I am happy (a polite response)   [86] *entertainment* words of reception or greeting

HORATIO Nay, good my lord —

HAMLET It is but foolery, but it is such a kind of gaingiving[87] as
would perhaps trouble a woman.

HORATIO If your mind dislike anything, obey it. I will forestall
5   their repair hither and say you are not fit.

HAMLET Not a whit, we defy augury. There is special providence
in the fall of a sparrow. If it be now, 'tis not to come; if it be
not to come, it will be now; if it be not now, yet it will come.
The readiness is all.[88] Since no man of aught he leaves knows,
10   what is't to leave betimes? Let be.

A table prepared. Enter TRUMPETS, DRUMS, *and* OFFICERS *with cushions;*
KING, QUEEN, OSRIC, *and all the* STATE, *with foils, daggers, and stoups of
wine borne in; and* LAERTES

KING Come, Hamlet, come, and take this hand from me.

15   (*The* KING *puts* LAERTES' *hand into* HAMLET'S)

HAMLET Give me your pardon, sir. I have done you wrong,
But pardon't, as you are a gentleman.
This presence[89] knows, and you must needs have heard,
How I am punished with a sore distraction.
20   What I have done
That might your nature, honor, and exception[90]
Roughly awake, I here proclaim was madness.
Was't Hamlet wronged Laertes? Never Hamlet.
If Hamlet from himself be ta'en away,
25   And when he's not himself does wrong Laertes,
Then Hamlet does it not, Hamlet denies it.
Who does it then? His madness. If't be so,
Hamlet is of the faction[91] that is wronged;
His madness is poor Hamlet's enemy.
30   Sir, in this audience,
Let my disclaiming from a purposed evil
Free me so far in your most generous thoughts
That I have shot my arrow o'er the house
And hurt my brother.

35   LAERTES   I am satisfied in nature,[92]
Whose motive in this case should stir me most
To my revenge. But in my terms of honor[93]

---

[87] *gaingiving* misgiving   [88] *all* all that matters   [89] *presence* assembly   [90] *exception* disapproval   [91] *faction* body of persons taking a side in a contention
[92] *nature* natural feeling as a person   [93] *terms of honor* position as a man of
honor

I stand aloof, and will no reconcilement
Till by some elder masters of known honor
I have a voice[94] and precedent of peace
To keep my name ungored.[95] But till that time
5   I do receive your offered love like love,
And will not wrong it.
    HAMLET   I embrace it freely,
And will this brother's wager frankly play.
Give us the foils. Come on.
10   LAERTES   Come, one for me.
    HAMLET   I'll be your foil,[96] Laertes. In mine ignorance
Your skill shall, like a star i' th' darkest night,
Stick fiery off [97] indeed.
    LAERTES   You mock me, sir.
15   HAMLET   No, by this hand.
    KING   Give them the foils, young Osric. Cousin Hamlet,
You know the wager?
    HAMLET   Very well, my lord.
Your grace has laid the odds o' the' weaker side.
20   KING   I do not fear it, I have seen you both;
But since he is bettered, we have therefore odds.
    LAERTES   This is too heavy; let me see another.
    HAMLET   This likes me well. These foils have all a length?

Prepare to play

25   OSRIC   Ay, my good lord.
    KING   Set me the stoups of wine upon that table.
If Hamlet give the first or second hit,
Or quit[98] in answer of the third exchange,
Let all the battlements their ordnance fire.
30   The king shall drink to Hamlet's better breath,
And in the cup an union[99] shall he throw
Richer than that which four successive kings
In Denmark's crown have worn. Give me the cups,
And let the kettle[100] to the trumpet speak,
35   The trumpet to the cannoneer without,
The cannons to the heavens, the heaven to earth,

---

[94] *voice* authoritative statement   [95] *ungored* uninjured   [96] *foil* setting that displays a jewel advantageously (with a play upon the meaning "weapon")   [97] *Stick fiery off* show in brilliant relief   [98] *quit* repay by a hit   [99] *union* pearl   [100] *kettle* kettledrum

"Now the king drinks to Hamlet." Come, begin.

Trumpets the while

And you, the judges, bear a wary eye.

HAMLET   Come on, sir.

5 LAERTES   Come, my lord.

They play

HAMLET   One.

LAERTES   No.

HAMLET   Judgment?

10 OSRIC   A hit, a very palpable hit.

DRUM, TRUMPETS, *and* SHOT. *Flourish; a piece goes off*

LAERTES   Well, again.

KING   Stay, give me drink. Hamlet, this pearl is thine.
Here's to thy health. Give him the cup.

15 HAMLET   I'll play this bout first; set it by awhile.
Come. (*They play*) Another hit. What say you?

LAERTES   A touch, a touch; I do confess't.

KING   Our son shall win.

QUEEN   He's fat,[101] and scant of breath.

20 Here, Hamlet, take my napkin,[102] rub thy brows.
The queen carouses[103] to thy fortune, Hamlet.

HAMLET   Good madam!

KING   Gertrude, do not drink.

QUEEN   I will, my lord; I pray you pardon me.

25 *Drinks*

KING (*aside*)   It is the poisoned cup; it is too late.

HAMLET   I dare not drink yet, madam—by and by.

QUEEN   Come, let me wipe thy face.

LAERTES   My lord, I'll hit him now.

30 KING   I do not think't.

LAERTES (*aside*)   And yet it is almost against my conscience.

HAMLET   Come for the third, Laertes. You but dally.
I pray you pass with your best violence;
I am afeard you make a wanton[104] of me.

---

[101] *fat* not physically fit, out of training [102] *napkin* handkerchief [103] *carouses* drinks a toast [104] *wanton* pampered child

LAERTES   Say you so? Come on.

They play

OSRIC   Nothing neither way.
LAERTES   Have at you now!

5   *In scuffling they change rapiers, and both are wounded with the poisoned weapon*

KING   Part them. They are incensed.
HAMLET   Nay, come—again!

The QUEEN *falls*

10   OSRIC   Look to the queen there, ho!
HORATIO   They bleed on both sides. How is it, my lord?
OSRIC   How is't, Laertes?
LAERTES   Why, as a woodcock[105] to mine own springe,[106] Osric.
I am justly killed with mine own treachery.
15   HAMLET   How does the queen?
KING   She sounds[107] to see them bleed.
QUEEN   No, no, the drink, the drink! O my dear Hamlet!
The drink, the drink! I am poisoned.

Dies

20   HAMLET   O villainy! Ho! let the door be locked.
Treachery! Seek it out.

LAERTES *falls*

LAERTES   It is here, Hamlet. Hamlet, thou art slain;
No med'cine in the world can do thee good.
25   In thee there is not half an hour's life.
The treacherous instrument is in thy hand,
Unbated [108] and envenomed. The foul practice[109]
Hath turned itself on me. Lo, here I lie,
Never to rise again. Thy mother's poisoned.
30   I can no more. The king, the king's to blame.
HAMLET   The point envenomed too?
Then venom, to thy work.

Hurts the KING

ALL   Treason! treason!

---

[105] *woodcock* a bird reputed to be stupid and easily trapped   [106] *springe* trap
[107] *sounds* swoons   [108] *Unbated* unblunted   [109] *practice* stratagem

KING   O, yet defend me, friends. I am but hurt.

HAMLET   Here, thou incestuous, murd'rous, damnèd Dane,
Drink off this potion. Is thy union here?
Follow my mother.

5   KING *dies*

LAERTES   He is justly served.
It is a poison tempered [110] by himself.
Exchange forgiveness with me, noble Hamlet.
Mine and my father's death come not upon thee,
10   Nor thine on me!

Dies

HAMLET   Heaven make thee free of it! I follow thee.
I am dead, Horatio. Wretched queen, adieu!
You that look pale and tremble at this chance,
15   That are but mutes[111] or audience to this act,
Had I but time—as this fell sergeant,[112] Death,
Is strict in his arrest—O, I could tell you —
But let it be. Horatio, I am dead;
Thou livest; report me and my cause aright
20   To the unsatisfied.

HORATIO   Never believe it.
I am more an antique Roman than a Dane.
Here's yet some liquor left.

HAMLET   As th' art a man,
25   Give me the cup. Let go. By heaven, I'll ha't!
O God, Horatio, what a wounded name,
Things standing thus unknown, shall live behind me!
If thou didst ever hold me in thy heart,
Absent thee from felicity awhile,
30   And in this harsh world draw thy breath in pain,
To tell my story.

A march afar off

                What warlike noise is this?

OSRIC   Young Fortinbras, with conquest come from Poland,
35   To the ambassadors of England gives
This warlike volley.

HAMLET   O, I die, Horatio!

---

[110] *tempered* mixed   [111] *mutes* actors in a play who speak no lines   [112] *sergeant* sheriff's officer

The potent poison quite o'ercrows[113] my spirit.
I cannot live to hear the news from England,
But I do prophesy th' election[114] lights
On Fortinbras. He has my dying voice.[115]
5   So tell him, with th' occurrents,[116] more and less,
Which have solicited [117]—the rest is silence.

Dies

HORATIO   Now cracks a noble heart. Good night, sweet prince,
And flights of angels sing thee to thy rest!

10   *March within*

Why does the drum come hither?

(*Enter* FORTINBRAS, *with the* AMBASSADORS [*and with his train of* DRUM,
COLORS, *and* ATTENDANTS])

FORTINBRAS   Where is this sight?
15   HORATIO   What is it you would see?
If aught of woe or wonder, cease your search.
FORTINBRAS   This quarry[118] cries on[119] havoc.[120] O proud Death,
What feast is toward [121] in thine eternal cell
That thou so many princes at a shot
20   So bloodily hast struck?
AMBASSADOR   The sight is dismal;
And our affairs from England come too late.
The ears are senseless that should give us hearing
To tell him his commandment is fulfilled,
25   That Rosencrantz and Guildenstern are dead.
Where should we have our thanks?
HORATIO   Not from his mouth,
Had it th' ability of life to thank you.
He never gave commandment for their death.
30   But since, so jump[122] upon this bloody question,
You from the Polack wars, and you from England,
Are here arrived, give order that these bodies
High on a stage[123] be placèd to the view,

---

[113] *o'ercrows* triumphs over (like a victor in a cockfight)   [114] *election* i.e. to
the throne [115] *voice* vote [116] *occurrents* occurrences [117] *solicited* incited,
provoked [118] *quarry* pile of dead (literally, of dead deer gathered after the
hunt) [119] *cries on* proclaims loudly [120] *havoc* indiscriminate killing and
destruction such as would follow the order "havoc," or "pillage," given to
an army [121] *toward* forthcoming [122] *jump* precisely [123] *stage* platform

And let me speak to th' yet unknowing world
How these things came about. So shall you hear
Of carnal, bloody, and unnatural acts,
Of accidental judgments,[124] casual [125] slaughters,
5   Of deaths put on[126] by cunning and forced cause,
And, in this upshot, purposes mistook
Fall'n on th' inventors' heads. All this can I
Truly deliver.

FORTINBRAS   Let us haste to hear it,
10   And call the noblest to the audience.
For me, with sorrow I embrace my fortune.
I have some rights of memory[127] in this kingdom,
Which now to claim my vantage[128] doth invite me.

HORATIO   Of that I shall have also cause to speak,
15   And from his mouth whose voice will draw on more.[129]
But let this same be presently[130] performed,
Even while men's minds are wild, lest more mischance
On[131] plots and errors happen.

FORTINBRAS   Let four captains
20   Bear Hamlet like a soldier to the stage,
For he was likely, had he been put on,[132]
To have proved most royal; and for his passage[133]
The soldiers' music and the rites of war
Speak loudly for him.
25   Take up the bodies. Such a sight as this
Becomes the field, but here shows much amiss.
Go, bid the soldiers shoot.

(Exeunt [marching; after the which a peal of ordinance are shot off])

QUESTIONS

1. The climax in *Hamlet* extends over several scenes. Which ones do you think they are?
2. What states does Hamlet pass through within these scenes?
3. How do his actions after the climax contrast with his actions before it?
4. What changes in Hamlet's outlook, or in your reaction to him, begin during these climactic scenes and develop during the latter part of the play?
5. Choose some topic that shows how the climax functions as a turning point in *Hamlet* and develop it as fully as possible, making use of specific examples not only from the climactic scenes but from earlier and later scenes as well.

---

[124] *judgments* retributions   [125] *casual* not humanly planned (reinforcing *accidental*)   [126] *put on* instigated   [127] *of memory* traditional and kept in mind   [128] *vantage* advantageous opportunity   [129] *more* i.e. more voices, or votes, for the kingship   [130] *presently* immediately   [131] *On* on the basis of   [132] *put on* set to perform in office   [133] *passage* death

4 Tartuffe *and the Comedy of Manners*

Our study of Hamlet brought us from the early Greek drama to the first great age of professional drama in England. Now we move ahead another half-century to the flowering of French drama and the comic genius of one of France's outstanding playwrights, Molière.

In 1643, Molière (whose real name was Jean-Baptiste Poquelin) broke away from a middle-class upbringing to found a troupe of players, which he called "the Illustrious Theatre." At school, he had acted in the Latin comedies of Plautus and Terence. As he toured the French provinces with his troupe, he became acquainted both with contemporary French tragedies and with the extremely popular Italian "commedia dell'arte." Commedia players extemporised their comedies. Working with stock characters and a rough plot sketch, they created action and dialogue as they went along, enlivening their plays with references to local contemporary events at will.

In 1659, the Illustrious Theatre came to Paris, presenting one of Molière's own comedies to great success. Working under the patronage first of the king's brother "Monsieur" and later of the king himself, the troupe settled in Paris, where Molière became simultaneously a controversial figure and the outstanding comedian of the time.

Molière's success and his controversial nature arose from the same cause. Discarding many of the stock figures of earlier comedies, Molière replaced them with contemporary character studies, satirizing people who might well be in his own audience. The height of the controversy was reached with

Tartuffe. The initial version of this comedy against hypocrisy and gullibility aroused such anger from church and critics that the play was prohibited for five years. Not until 1669 did the king allow the performance of a substantially rewritten version of the comedy.

Molière's Comic Vision

Comedy takes for its subject humans, the social beings. Tragedy studies kings and princes who are involved in dilemmas that will separate them from their fellows or from the normal concerns of society. (Thus, Oedipus dooms himself to blindness and exile, while Hamlet accepts death as the price for freeing Denmark from Claudius.) Comedy studies middle-class or lower-class citizens involved in the concerns of everyday life. The typical end of tragedy is death, with its total separation from the affairs of the world, frequently ameliorated by a hope for future healing of the hero's nation. (Now that Hamlet has removed the specific "rottenness" that was plaguing Denmark, Fortinbras may be able to return that nation to a healthier state.) The typical ending of comedy is marriage, with its commitment to wordly affairs. Thus, a typical final scene in a comedy acts out healing at the domestic level: families that have been split by loss or discord are reunited; new families are formed through the marriage of true lovers.

In Molière's plays, society is particularly important. The norm, for Molière, is a well-ordered society in which people, under the rule of a wise and benevolent monarch, act under the guidance of common sense and of their natural affection for friends and family. Discord comes when individuals, ignoring those two key guides, develop some unbalancing enthusiasm, follow its lead into ill-judged excesses, and thus become victims of their own folly and of those parasites who prey on others' folly.

The key figure in a Molière comedy, therefore, is generally a person who has forsaken truth and reason for the sake of some false goal. On one side of this central character stands a clear-sighted friend who tries to return the hero to more sensible conduct. On the other side stand those who seek to profit from the hero's foolishness, and so encourage him to continue in his wrong course.

In *Tartuffe*, the main character's flaw is gullibility. With considerable concern for religious conduct, Orgon has fallen prey to Tartuffe, a hypocrite and con man who pretends to religious virtue solely as a means towards money and sexual conquest. Attempts by Orgon's family to convince him of Tartuffe's falseness and to explain the difference between true religion and hypocrisy fall on deaf ears.

Two tensions are thus at work within the play. Orgon, in his obsession with Tartuffe, sees a rivalry between religion and worldliness. The other characters, clearer-sighted, see a battle between hypocrisy on the one hand and honest concern for one's fellow man on the other.

We can recognize in Orgon a man whose concern with a worthwhile value, linked with a weakness in judgment, have led him into trouble, and whose persistent refusal to admit his error lead him from folly nearly to disaster. We simultaneously rage at him and pity him for his folly. Which of us, after all, has not sometimes been guilty of bad judgment?

For Tartuffe, on the other hand, there is no pity. As the man who takes advantage of other men's aspirations towards holiness to deceive them and injure them, Tartuffe represents vice rather than folly. His destruction of Orgon, even granted the degree of Orgon's folly, is excessive. When that destruction threatens Orgon's family as well, it goes beyond the bounds of anything society can accept; and so society, in the person of its head, the king, steps forward to bring things back into order, and to allow the happy ending of comedy to take place.

MOLIÈRE (JEAN-BAPTISTE POQUELIN) (1622–1673)

Tartuffe

Translated by Richard Wilbur

CHARACTERS

MADAME PERNELLE, *Orgon's mother*
ORGON, *Elmire's husband*
ELMIRE, *Orgon's wife*
DAMIS, *Orgon's son, Elmire's stepson*
MARIANE, *Orgon's daughter, Elmire's stepdaughter, in love with Valère*
VALÈRE, *in love with Mariane*
CLÉANTE, *Orgon's brother-in-law*
TARTUFFE, *a hypocrite*
DORINE, *Mariane's lady's-maid*
MONSIEUR LOYAL, *a bailiff*
A POLICE OFFICER
FLIPOTE, *Madame Pernelle's maid*

The Scene throughout: ORGON'S *house in Paris.*

ACT I

Scene I (MADAME PERNELLE *and* FLIPOTE, *her maid,* ELMIRE, MARI-
ANE, DORINE, DAMIS, CLÉANTE)

MADAME PERNELLE Come, come, Flipote; it's time I left this place.
ELMIRE I can't keep up, you walk at such a pace.
MADAME PERNELLE Don't trouble, child; no need to show me out.
    It's not your manners I'm concerned about.
5 ELMIRE We merely pay you the respect we owe.
    But Mother, why this hurry? Must you go?
MADAME PERNELLE I must. This house appalls me. No one in it
    Will pay attention for a single minute.
    Children, I take my leave much vexed in spirit.
10   I offer good advice, but you won't hear it.
    You all break in and chatter on and on.
    It's like a madhouse with the keeper gone.

DORINE If . . .

MADAME PERNELLE

15   Girl, you talk too much, and I'm afraid
         You're far too saucy for a lady's-maid.
         You push in everywhere and have your say.

DAMIS But . . .

MADAME PERNELLE

20   You, boy, grow more foolish every day.
         To think my grandson should be such a dunce!
         I've said a hundred times, if I've said it once,
         That if you keep the course on which you've started,
         You'll leave your worthy father broken-hearted.

25 MARIANE I think . . .

MADAME PERNELLE   And you, his sister, seem so pure,
         So shy, so innocent, and so demure.
         But you know what they say about still waters.
         I pity parents with secretive daughters.

30 ELMIRE Now, Mother . . .

MADAME PERNELLE And as for you, child, let me add
         That your behavior is extremely bad,
         And a poor example for these children, too.
         Their dear, dead mother did far better than you.

35   You're much too free with money, and I'm distressed
         To see you so elaborately dressed.
         When it's one's husband that one aims to please,
         One has no need of costly fripperies.

CLÉANTE Oh, Madam, really . . .

40 MADAME PERNELLE   You are her brother, Sir,
         And I respect and love you; yet if I were
         My son, this lady's good and pious spouse,
         I wouldn't make you welcome in my house.
         You're full of worldly counsels which, I fear,

45   Aren't suitable for decent folk to hear.
         I've spoken bluntly, Sir; but it behooves us
         Not to mince words when righteous fervor moves us.

DAMIS Your man Tartuffe is full of holy speeches . . .

MADAME PERNELLE And practices precisely what he preaches.

50   He's a fine man, and should be listened to.
         I will not hear him mocked by fools like you.

DAMIS Good God! Do you expect me to submit
         To the tyranny of that carping hypocrite?
         Must we forgo all joys and satisfactions

55   Because that bigot censures all our actions?

DORINE To hear him talk—and he talks all the time—
         There's nothing one can do that's not a crime.
         He rails at everything, your dear Tartuffe.

MADAME PERNELLE   Whatever he reproves deserves reproof.
60   He's out to save your souls, and all of you
     Must love him, as my son would have you do.
   DAMIS   Ah no, Grandmother, I could never take
     To such a rascal, even for my father's sake.
     That's how I feel, and I shall not dissemble.
65   His every action makes me seethe and tremble
     With helpless anger, and I have no doubt
     That he and I will shortly have it out.
   DORINE   Surely it is a shame and a disgrace
     To see this man usurp the master's place—
70   To see this beggar who, when first he came,
     Had not a shoe or shoestring to his name
     So far forget himself that he behaves
     As if the house were his, and we his slaves.
   MADAME PERNELLE   Well, mark my words, your souls would fare far
75   better
     If you obeyed his precepts to the letter.
   DORINE   You see him as a saint. I'm far less awed;
     In fact, I see right through him. He's a fraud.
   MADAME PERNELLE   Nonsense!
80 DORINE   His man Laurent's the same, or worse;
     I'd not trust either with a penny purse.
   MADAME PERNELLE   I can't say what his servant's morals may be;
     His own great goodness I can guarantee.
     You all regard him with distaste and fear
85   Because he tells you what you're loath to hear,
     Condemns your sins, points out your moral flaws,
     And humbly strives to further Heaven's cause.
   DORINE   If sin is all that bothers him, why is it
     He's so upset when folk drop in to visit?
90   Is Heaven so outraged by a social call
     That he must prophesy against us all?
     I'll tell you what I think: if you ask me,
     He's jealous of my mistress' company.
   MADAME PERNELLE
95   Rubbish! (*To* ELMIRE) He's not alone, child, in complaining
     Of all of your promiscuous entertaining.
     Why, the whole neighborhood's upset, I know,
     By all these carriages that come and go,
     With crowds of guests parading in and out
100   And noisy servants loitering about.
     In all of this, I'm sure there's nothing vicious;
     But why give people cause to be suspicious?
   CLÉANTE   They need no cause; they'll talk in any case.
     Madam, this world would be a joyless place

105 If, fearing what malicious tongues might say,
We locked our doors and turned our friends away.
And even if one did so dreary a thing,
D'you think those tongues would cease their chattering?
One can't fight slander; it's a losing battle;
110 Let us instead ignore their tittle-tattle.
Let's strive to live by conscience' clear decrees,
And let the gossips gossip as they please.
    DORINE If there is talk against us, I know the source:
    It's Daphne and her little husband, of course.
115 Those who have greatest cause for guilt and shame
Are quickest to besmirch a neighbor's name.
When there's a chance for libel, they never miss it;
When something can be made to seem illicit
They're off at once to speak the joyous news,
120 Adding to fact what fantasies they choose.
By talking up their neighbor's indiscretions
They seek to camouflage their own transgressions,
Hoping that others' innocent affairs
Will lend a hue of innocence to theirs,
125 Or that their own black guilt will come to seem
Part of a general shady color-scheme.
    MADAME PERNELLE All that is quite irrelevant. I doubt
    That anyone's more virtuous and devout
    Than dear Orante; and I'm informed that she
130 Condemns your mode of life most vehemently.
    DORINE Oh, yes, she's strict, devout, and has no taint
    Of worldliness; in short, she seems a saint.
    But it was time which taught her that disguise;
    She's thus because she can't be otherwise.
135 So long as her attractions could enthrall,
She flounced and flirted and enjoyed it all,
But now that they're no longer what they were
She quits a world which fast is quitting her,
And wears a veil of virtue to conceal
140 Her bankrupt beauty and her lost appeal.
That's what becomes of old coquettes today:
Distressed when all their lovers fall away,
They see no recourse but to play the prude,
And so confer a style on solitude.
145 Thereafter, they're severe with everyone,
Condemning all our actions, pardoning none,
And claiming to be pure, austere, and zealous
When, if the truth were known, they're merely jealous,
And cannot bear to see another know
150 The pleasures time has forced them to forgo.

MADAME PERNELLE   (*initially to* ELMIRE)

That sort of talk is what you like to hear;
Therefore you'd have us all keep still, my dear,
While Madam rattles on the livelong day.
155   Nevertheless, I mean to have my say.
I tell you that you're blest to have Tartuffe
Dwelling, as my son's guest, beneath this roof;
That Heaven has sent him to forestall its wrath
By leading you, once more, to the true path;
160   That all he reprehends is reprehensible,
And that you'd better heed him, and be sensible.
These visits, balls, and parties in which you revel
Are nothing but inventions of the Devil.
One never hears a word that's edifying;
165   Nothing but chaff and foolishness and lying,
As well as vicious gossip in which one's neighbor
Is cut to bits with epee, foil, and saber.
People of sense are driven half-insane
At such affairs, where noise and folly reign
170   And reputations perish thick and fast.
As a wise preacher said on Sunday last,
Parties are Towers of Babylon, because
The guests all babble on with never a pause;
And then he told a story which, I think . . .

(*To* CLÉANTE)

175   I heard that laugh, Sir, and I saw that wink!
Go find your silly friends and laugh some more!
Enough; I'm going; don't show me to the door.
I leave this household much dismayed and vexed;
I cannot say when I shall see you next.

(*Slapping* FLIPOTE)

180   Wake up, don't stand there gaping into space!
I'll slap some sense into that stupid face.
Move, move, you slut.

Scene II (CLÉANTE, DORINE)

CLÉANTE

                I think I'll stay behind;
I want no further pieces of her mind.
How that old lady . . .
5 DORINE

                Oh, what wouldn't she say
If she could hear you speak of her that way!

> She'd thank you for the *lady,* but I'm sure
> She'd find the *old* a little premature.
> 10 CLÉANTE   My, what a scene she made, and what a din!
> And how this man Tartuffe has taken her in!
> DORINE   Yes, but her son is even worse deceived;
> His folly must be seen to be believed.
> In the late troubles, he played an able part
> 15 And served his king with wise and loyal heart,
> But he's quite lost his senses since he fell
> Beneath Tartuffe's infatuating spell.
> He calls him brother, and loves him as his life,
> Preferring him to mother, child, or wife.
> 20 In him and him alone will he confide;
> He's made him his confessor and his guide;
> He pets and pampers him with love more tender
> Than any pretty maiden could engender,
> Gives him the place of honor when they dine,
> 25 Delights to see him gorging like a swine,
> Stuffs him with dainties till his guts distend,
> And when he belches, cries "God bless you, friend!"
> In short, he's mad; he worships him; he dotes;
> His deeds he marvels at, his words he quotes,
> 30 Thinking each act a miracle, each word
> Oracular as those that Moses heard.
> Tartuffe, much pleased to find so easy a victim,
> Has in a hundred ways beguiled and tricked him,
> Milked him of money, and with his permission
> 35 Established here a sort of Inquisition.
> Even Laurent, his lackey, dares to give
> Us arrogant advice on how to live;
> He sermonizes us in thundering tones
> And confiscates our ribbons and colognes.
> 40 Last week he tore a kerchief into pieces
> Because he found it pressed in a *Life of Jesus:*
> He said it was a sin to juxtapose
> Unholy vanities and holy prose.

Scene III (ELMIRE, MARIANE, DAMIS, CLÉANTE, DORINE)

> ELMIRE (*to* CLÉANTE)   You did well not to follow; she stood in the door
> And said *verbatim* all she'd said before.
> I saw my husband coming. I think I'd best
> 5 Go upstairs now, and take a little rest.
> CLÉANTE   I'll wait and greet him here; then I must go.
> I've really only time to say hello.

DAMIS   Sound him about my sister's wedding, please.
   I think Tartuffe's against it, and that he's
10 Been urging Father to withdraw his blessing.
   As you well know, I'd find that most distressing.
   Unless my sister and Valère can marry,
   My hopes to wed *his* sister will miscarry,
   And I'm determined . . .
15 DORINE   He's coming.

Scene IV (ORGON, CLÉANTE, DORINE)

ORGON   Ah, Brother, good-day.
CLÉANTE   Well, welcome back. I'm sorry I can't stay.
   How was the country? Blooming, I trust, and green?
ORGON   Excuse me, Brother; just one moment.

(*To* DORINE)

5   Dorine . . .

(*To* CLÉANTE)

To put my mind at rest, I always learn
The household news the moment I return.

(*To* DORINE)

Has all been well, these two days I've been gone?
How are the family? What's been going on?
10 DORINE   Your wife, two days ago, had a bad fever,
   And a fierce headache which refused to leave her.
ORGON   Ah. And Tartuffe?
DORINE   Tartuffe? Why, he's round and red,
   Bursting with health, and excellently fed.
15 ORGON   Poor fellow!
DORINE   That night, the mistress was unable
   To take a single bite at the dinner-table.
   Her headache-pains, she said, were simply hellish.
ORGON   Ah. And Tartuffe?
20 DORINE   He ate his meal with relish,
   And zealously devoured in her presence
   A leg of mutton and a brace of pheasants.
ORGON   Poor fellow!
DORINE   Well, the pains continued strong,
25 And so she tossed and tossed the whole night long,
   Now icy-cold, now burning like a flame.
   We sat beside her bed till morning came.
ORGON   Ah. And Tartuffe?
DORINE   Why, having eaten, he rose

30   And sought his room, already in a doze,
      Got into his warm bed, and snored away
      In perfect peace until the break of day.
ORGON   Poor fellow!
DORINE   After much ado, we talked her
35   Into dispatching someone for the doctor.
      He bled her, and the fever quickly fell.
ORGON   Ah. And Tartuffe?
DORINE   He bore it very well.
      To keep his cheerfulness at any cost,
40   And make up for the blood *Madame* had lost,
      He drank, at lunch, four beakers full of port.
ORGON   Poor fellow!
DORINE   Both are doing well, in short.
      I'll go and tell *Madame* that you've expressed
45   Keen sympathy and anxious interest.

Scene V (ORGON, CLÉANTE)

CLÉANTE   That girl was laughing in your face, and though
      I've no wish to offend you, even so
      I'm bound to say that she had some excuse.
      How can you possibly be such a goose?
5   Are you so dazed by this man's hocus-pocus
      That all the world, save him, is out of focus?
      You've given him clothing, shelter, food, and care;
      Why must you also . . .
ORGON   Brother, stop right there.
10   You do not know the man of whom you speak.
CLÉANTE   I grant you that. But my judgment's not so weak
      That I can't tell, by his effect on others . . .
ORGON   Ah, when you meet him, you two will be like brothers!
      There's been no loftier soul since time began.
15   He is a man who . . . a man who . . . an excellent man.
      To keep his precepts is to be reborn,
      And view this dunghill of a world with scorn.
      Yes, thanks to him I'm a changed man indeed.
      Under his tutelage my soul's been freed
20   From earthly loves, and every human tie:
      My mother, children, brother, and wife could die,
      And I'd not feel a single moment's pain.
CLÉANTE   That's a fine sentiment, Brother; most humane.
ORGON   Oh, had you seen Tartuffe as I first knew him,
25   Your heart, like mine, would have surrendered to him.

He used to come into our church each day
And humbly kneel nearby, and start to pray.
He'd draw the eyes of everybody there
By the deep fervor of his heartfelt prayer;
30   He'd sigh and weep, and sometimes with a sound
Of rapture he would bend and kiss the ground;
And when I rose to go, he'd run before
To offer me holy-water at the door.
His serving-man, no less devout than he,
35   Informed me of his master's poverty;
I gave him gifts, but in his humbleness
He'd beg me every time to give him less.
"Oh, that's too much," he'd cry, "too much by twice!
I don't deserve it. The half, Sir, would suffice."
40   And when I wouldn't take it back, he'd share
Half of it with the poor, right then and there.
At length, Heaven prompted me to take him in
To dwell with us, and free our souls from sin.
He guides our lives, and to protect my honor
45   Stays by my wife, and keeps an eye upon her;
He tells me whom she sees, and all she does,
And seems more jealous than I ever was!
And how austere he is! Why, he can detect
A mortal sin where you would least suspect;
50   In smallest trifles, he's extremely strict.
Last week, his conscience was severely pricked
Because, while praying, he had caught a flea
And killed it, so he felt, too wrathfully.
CLÉANTE   Good God, man! Have you lost your common sense—
55   Or is this all some joke at my expense?
How can you stand there and in all sobriety . . .
ORGON   Brother, your language savors of impiety.
Too much free-thinking's made your faith unsteady,
And as I've warned you many times already,
60   'Twill get you into trouble before you're through.
CLÉANTE   So I've been told before by dupes like you:
Being blind, you'd have all others blind as well;
The clear-eyed man you call an infidel,
And he who sees through humbug and pretense
65   Is charged, by you, with want of reverence.
Spare me your warnings, Brother; I have no fear
Of speaking out, for you and Heaven to hear,
Against affected zeal and pious knavery.
There's true and false in piety, as in bravery,
70   And just as those whose courage shines the most

In battle, are the least inclined to boast,
So those whose hearts are truly pure and lowly
Don't make a flashy show of being holy.
There's a vast difference, so it seems to me,
75 Between true piety and hypocrisy:
How do you fail to see it, may I ask?
Is not a face quite different from a mask?
Cannot sincerity and cunning art,
Reality and semblance, be told apart?
80 Are scarecrows just like men, and do you hold
That a false coin is just as good as gold?
Ah, Brother, man's a strangely fashioned creature
Who seldom is content to follow Nature,
But recklessly pursues his inclination
85 Beyond the narrow bounds of moderation,
And often, by transgressing Reason's laws,
Perverts a lofty aim or noble cause.
A passing observation, but it applies.
   ORGON I see, dear Brother, that you're profoundly wise;
90 You harbor all the insight of the age.
You are our one clear mind, our only sage,
The era's oracle, its Cato too,
And all mankind are fools compared to you.
   CLÉANTE Brother, I don't pretend to be a sage,
95 Nor have I all the wisdom of the age.
There's just one insight I would dare to claim:
I know that true and false are not the same;
And just as there is nothing I more revere
Than a soul whose faith is steadfast and sincere,
100 Nothing that I more cherish and admire
Than honest zeal and true religious fire,
So there is nothing that I find more base
Than specious piety's dishonest face—
Than these bold mountebanks, these histrios
105 Whose impious mummeries and hollow shows
Exploit our love of Heaven, and make a jest
Of all that men think holiest and best;
These calculating souls who offer prayers
Not to their Maker, but as public wares,
110 And seek to buy respect and reputation
With lifted eyes and sighs of exaltation;
These charlatans, I say, whose pilgrim souls
Proceed, by way of Heaven, toward earthly goals,
Who weep and pray and swindle and extort,
115 Who preach the monkish life, but haunt the court,

Who make their zeal the partner of their vice—
Such men are vengeful, sly, and cold as ice,
And when there is an enemy to defame
They cloak their spite in fair religion's name,
120   Their private spleen and malice being made
To seem a high and virtuous crusade,
Until, to mankind's reverent applause,
They crucify their foe in Heaven's cause.
Such knaves are all too common; yet, for the wise,
125   True piety isn't hard to recognize,
And, happily, these present times provide us
With bright examples to instruct and guide us.
Consider Ariston and Périandre;
Look at Oronte, Alcidamas, Clitandre;
130   Their virtue is acknowledged; who could doubt it?
But you won't hear them beat the drum about it.
They're never ostentatious, never vain,
And their religion's moderate and humane;
It's not their way to criticize and chide:
135   They think censoriousness a mark of pride,
And therefore, letting others preach and rave,
They show, by deeds, how Christians should behave.
They think no evil of their fellow man,
But judge of him as kindly as they can.
140   They don't intrigue and wangle and conspire;
To lead a good life is their one desire;
The sinner wakes no rancorous hate in them;
It is the sin alone which they condemn;
Nor do they try to show a fiercer zeal
145   For Heaven's cause than Heaven itself could feel.
These men I honor, these men I advocate
As models for us all to emulate.
Your man is not their sort at all, I fear:
And, while your praise of him is quite sincere,
150   I think that you've been dreadfully deluded.
ORGON   Now then, dear Brother, is your speech concluded?
CLÉANTE   Why, yes.
ORGON   Your servant, Sir. (*He turns to go.*)
CLÉANTE   No, Brother; wait.
155   There's one more matter. You agreed of late
That young Valère might have your daughter's hand.
ORGON   I did.
CLÉANTE   And set the date, I understand.
ORGON   Quite so.
160   CLÉANTE   You've now postponed it; is that true?

ORGON   No doubt.
CLÉANTE   The match no longer pleases you?
ORGON   Who knows?
CLÉANTE   D'you mean to go back on your word?
165 ORGON   I won't say that.
CLÉANTE   Has anything occurred
Which might entitle you to break your pledge?
ORGON   Perhaps.
CLÉANTE   Why must you hem, and haw, and hedge?
170   The boy asked me to sound you in this affair . . .
ORGON   It's been a pleasure.
CLÉANTE   But what shall I tell Valère?
ORGON   Whatever you like.
CLÉANTE   But what have you decided?
175   What are your plans?
ORGON   I plan, Sir, to be guided
By Heaven's will.
CLÉANTE   Come, Brother, don't talk rot.
You've given Valère your word; will you keep it, or not?
180 ORGON   Good day.
CLÉANTE   This looks like poor Valère's undoing;
I'll go and warn him that there's trouble brewing.

ACT II

Scene I (ORGON, MARIANE)

ORGON   Mariane.
MARIANE   Yes, father?
ORGON   A word with you; come here.
MARIANE   What are you looking for?
5 ORGON (*peering into a small closet*)   Eavesdroppers, dear.
I'm making sure we shan't be overheard.
Someone in there could catch our every word.
Ah, good, we're safe. Now, Mariane, my child,
You're a sweet girl who's tractable and mild,
10   Whom I hold dear, and think most highly of.
MARIANE   I'm deeply grateful, Father, for your love.
ORGON   That's well said, Daughter; and you can repay me
If, in all things, you'll cheerfully obey me.
MARIANE   To please you, Sir, is what delights me best.
15 ORGON   Good, good. Now, what d'you think of Tartuffe, our guest?
MARIANE   I, Sir?
ORGON   Yes. Weigh your answer; think it through.
MARIANE   Oh, dear. I'll say whatever you wish me to.
ORGON   That's wisely said, my Daughter. Say of him, then,

20   That he's the very worthiest of men,
And that you're fond of him, and would rejoice
In being his wife, if that should be my choice.
Well?
MARIANE   What?
25 ORGON   What's that?
MARIANE   I . . .
ORGON   Well?
MARIANE   Forgive me, pray.
ORGON   Did you not hear me?
30 MARIANE   Of *whom*, Sir, must I say
That I am fond of him, and would rejoice
In being his wife, if that should be your choice?
ORGON   Why, of Tartuffe.
MARIANE   But, Father, that's false, you know.
35   Why would you have me say what isn't so?
ORGON   Because I am resolved it shall be true.
That it's my wish should be enough for you.
MARIANE   You can't mean, Father . . .
ORGON   Yes, Tartuffe shall be
40   Allied by marriage to this family,
And he's to be your husband, is that clear?
It's a father's privilege . . .

Scene II (DORINE, ORGON, MARIANE)

ORGON (*to* DORINE)   What are you doing in here?
Is curiosity so fierce a passion
With you, that you must eavesdrop in this fashion?
DORINE   There's lately been a rumor going about—
5   Based on some hunch or chance remark, no doubt—
That you mean Mariane to wed Tartuffe.
I've laughed it off, of course, as just a spoof.
ORGON   You find it so incredible?
DORINE   Yes, I do.
10   I won't accept that story, even from you.
ORGON   Well, you'll believe it when the thing is done.
DORINE   Yes, yes, of course. Go on and have your fun.
ORGON   I've never been more serious in my life.
DORINE   Ha!
15 ORGON   Daughter, I mean it; you're to be his wife.
DORINE   No, don't believe your father; it's all a hoax.
ORGON   See here, young woman . . .
DORINE   Come, Sir, no more jokes;
You can't fool us.

20 ORGON   How dare you talk that way?
    DORINE   All right, then; we believe you, sad to say.
        But how a man like you, who looks so wise
        And wears a moustache of such splendid size,
        Can be so foolish as to . . .
25 ORGON   Silence, please!
        My girl, you take too many liberties.
        I'm master here, as you must not forget.
    DORINE   Do let's discuss this calmly; don't be upset.
        You can't be serious, Sir, about this plan.
30   What should that bigot want with Mariane?
        Praying and fasting ought to keep him busy.
        And then, in terms of wealth and rank, what is he?
        Why should a man of property like you
        Pick out a beggar son-in-law?
35 ORGON   That will do.
        Speak of his poverty with reverence.
        His is a pure and saintly indigence
        Which far transcends all worldly pride and pelf.
        He lost his fortune, as he says himself,
40   Because he cared for Heaven alone, and so
        Was careless of his interests here below.
        I mean to get him out of his present straits
        And help him to recover his estates—
        Which, in his part of the world, have no small fame.
45   Poor though he is, he's a gentleman just the same.
    DORINE   Yes, so he tells us; and, Sir, it seems to me
        Such pride goes very ill with piety.
        A man whose spirit spurns this dungy earth
        Ought not to brag of lands and noble birth;
50   Such worldly arrogance will hardly square
        With meek devotion and the life of prayer.
        . . . But this approach, I see, has drawn a blank;
        Let's speak, then, of his person, not his rank.
        Doesn't it seem to you a trifle grim
55   To give a girl like her to a man like him?
        When two are so ill-suited, can't you see
        What the sad consequence is bound to be?
        A young girl's virtue is imperiled, Sir,
        When such a marriage is imposed on her;
60   For if one's bridegroom isn't to one's taste,
        It's hardly an inducement to be chaste,
        And many a man with horns upon his brow
        Has made his wife the thing that she is now.
        It's hard to be a faithful wife, in short,

65   To certain husbands of a certain sort,
      And he who gives his daughter to a man she hates
      Must answer for her sins at Heaven's gates.
      Think, Sir, before you play so risky a role.
      ORGON   This servant-girl presumes to save my soul!
70   DORINE   You would do well to ponder what I've said.
      ORGON   Daughter, we'll disregard this dunderhead.
      Just trust your father's judgment. Oh, I'm aware
      That I once promised you to young Valère;
      But now I hear he gambles, which greatly shocks me;
75   What's more, I've doubts about his orthodoxy.
      His visits to church, I note, are very few.
      DORINE   Would you have him go at the same hours as you,
      And kneel nearby, to be sure of being seen?
      ORGON   I can dispense with such remarks, Dorine.

                    (*To* MARIANE)

80   Tartuffe, however, is sure of Heaven's blessing,
      And that's the only treasure worth possessing.
      This match will bring you joys beyond all measure;
      Your cup will overflow with every pleasure;
      You two will interchange your faithful loves
85   Like two sweet cherubs, or two turtle-doves.
      No harsh word shall be heard, no frown be seen,
      And he shall make you happy as a queen.
      DORINE   And she'll make him a cuckold, just wait and see.
      ORGON   What language!
90   DORINE   Oh, he's a man of destiny;
      He's *made* for horns, and what the stars demand
      Your daughter's virtue surely can't withstand.
      ORGON   Don't interrupt me further. Why can't you learn
      That certain things are none of your concern?
95   DORINE   It's for your own sake that I interfere.

(*She repeatedly interrupts* ORGON *just as he is turning to speak to his daughter:*)

      ORGON   Most kind of you. Now, hold your tongue, d'you hear?
      DORINE   If I didn't love you . . .
      ORGON   Spare me your affection.
      DORINE   I'll love you, Sir, in spite of your objection.
100   ORGON   Blast!
      DORINE   I can't bear, Sir, for your honor's sake,
      To let you make this ludicrous mistake.
      ORGON   You mean to go on talking?
      DORINE   If I didn't protest
105   This sinful marriage, my conscience couldn't rest.

ORGON If you don't hold your tongue, you little shrew . . .
DORINE What, lost your temper? A pious man like you?
ORGON Yes! Yes! You talk and talk. I'm maddened by it.
    Once and for all, I tell you to be quiet.
110 DORINE Well, I'll be quiet. But I'll be thinking hard.
ORGON Think all you like, but you had better guard
    That saucy tongue of yours, or I'll . . .

(Turning back to MARIANE:*)*

                          Now, child,
    I've weighed this matter fully.
115 DORINE *(aside)*   It drives me wild
    That I can't speak.

*(*ORGON *turns his head, and she is silent.)*

ORGON   Tartuffe is no young dandy,
    But, still, his person . . .
DORINE *(aside)*   Is as sweet as candy.
120 ORGON Is such that, even if you shouldn't care
    For his other merits . . .

(He turns and stands facing DORINE, *arms crossed.)*

DORINE *(aside)*   They'll make a lovely pair.
    If I were she, no man would marry me
    Against my inclination, and go scot-free.
125 He'd learn, before the wedding-day was over,
    How readily a wife can find a lover.
ORGON *(to* DORINE) It seems you treat my orders as a joke.
DORINE Why, what's the matter? 'Twas not to you I spoke.
ORGON What *were* you doing?
130 DORINE   Talking to myself, that's all.
ORGON Ah! *(aside)* One more bit of impudence and gall,
    And I shall give her a good slap in the face.

(He puts himself in position to slap her; DORINE, *whenever he glances at her,*
                  stands immobile and silent:)

    Daughter, you shall accept, and with good grace,
    The husband I've selected . . . Your wedding day . . .

(To DORINE:*)*

135 Why don't you talk to yourself?
DORINE   I've nothing to say.
ORGON Come, just one word.
DORINE   No thank you, Sir. I pass.
ORGON Come, speak; I'm waiting.
140 DORINE   I'd not be such an ass.

ORGON (*turning to* MARIANE)   In short, dear Daughter, I mean to be
   obeyed,
And you must bow to the sound choice I've made.

DORINE (*moving away*)   I'd not wed such a monster, even in jest.

(ORGON *attempts to slap her, but misses.*)

145 ORGON   Daughter, that maid of yours is a thorough pest;
   She makes me sinfully annoyed and nettled.
   I can't speak further; my nerves are too unsettled.
   She's so upset me by her insolent talk,
   I'll calm myself by going for a walk.

Scene III (DORINE, MARIANE)

DORINE (*returning*)   Well, have you lost your tongue, girl? Must I play
   Your part, and say the lines you ought to say?
   Faced with a fate so hideous and absurd,
   Can you not utter one dissenting word?

5 MARIANE   What good would it do? A father's power is great.

DORINE   Resist him now, or it will be too late.

MARIANE   But . . .

DORINE   Tell him one cannot love at a father's whim;
   That you shall marry for yourself, not him;
10   That since it's you who are to be the bride,
   It's you, not he, who must be satisfied;
   And that if his Tartuffe is so sublime,
   He's free to marry him at any time.

MARIANE   I've bowed so long to Father's strict control,
15   I couldn't oppose him now, to save my soul.

DORINE   Come, come, Mariane. Do listen to reason, won't you?
   Valère has asked your hand. Do you love him, or don't you?

MARIANE   Oh, how unjust of you! What can you mean
   By asking such a question, dear Dorine?
20   You know the depth of my affection for him;
   I've told you a hundred times how I adore him.

DORINE   I don't believe in everything I hear;
   Who knows if your professions were sincere?

MARIANE   They were, Dorine, and you do me wrong to doubt it;
25   Heaven knows that I've been all too frank about it.

DORINE   You love him, then?

MARIANE   Oh, more than I can express.

DORINE   And he, I take it, cares for you no less?

MARIANE   I think so.

30 DORINE   And you both, with equal fire,
   Burn to be married?

MARIANE   That is our one desire.

DORINE   What of Tartuffe, then? What of your father's plan?

MARIANE   I'll kill myself, if I'm forced to wed that man.

35 DORINE   I hadn't thought of that recourse. How splendid!
Just die, and all your troubles will be ended!
A fine solution. Oh, it maddens me
To hear you talk in that self-pitying key.

MARIANE   Dorine, how harsh you are! It's most unfair.

40 You have no sympathy for my despair.

DORINE   I've none at all for people who talk drivel
And, faced with difficulties, whine and snivel.

MARIANE   No doubt I'm timid, but it would be wrong . . .

DORINE   True love requires a heart that's firm and strong.

45 MARIANE   I'm strong in my affection for Valère,
But coping with my father is his affair.

DORINE   But if your father's brain has grown so cracked
Over his dear Tartuffe that he can retract
His blessing, though your wedding day was named,

50 It's surely not Valère who's to be blamed.

MARIANE   If I defied my father, as you suggest,
Would it not seem unmaidenly, at best?
Shall I defend my love at the expense
Of brazenness and disobedience?

55 Shall I parade my heart's desires, and flaunt . . .

DORINE   No, I ask nothing of you. Clearly you want
To be Madame Tartuffe, and I feel bound
Not to oppose a wish so very sound.
What right have I to criticize the match?

60 Indeed, my dear, the man's a brilliant catch.
Monsieur Tartuffe! Now, there's a man of weight!
Yes, yes, Monsieur Tartuffe, I'm bound to state,
Is quite a person; that's not to be denied;
'Twill be no little thing to be his bride.

65 The world already rings with his renown;
He's a great noble—in his native town;
His ears are red, he has a pink complexion,
And all in all, he'll suit you to perfection.

MARIANE   Dear God!

70 DORINE   Oh, how triumphant you will feel
At having caught a husband so ideal!

MARIANE   Oh, do stop teasing, and use your cleverness
To get me out of this appalling mess.
Advise me, and I'll do whatever you say.

DORINE   Ah no, a dutiful daughter must obey

75 Her father, even if he weds her to an ape.

You've a bright future; why struggle to escape?
Tartuffe will take you back where his family lives,
To a small town aswarm with relatives—
80 Uncles and cousins whom you'll be charmed to meet.
You'll be received at once by the elite,
Calling upon the bailiff's wife, no less—
Even, perhaps, upon the mayoress,
Who'll sit you down in the *best* kitchen chair.
85 Then, once a year, you'll dance at the village fair
To the drone of bagpipes—two of them, in fact—
And see a puppet-show, or an animal act.
Your husband . . .

MARIANE   Oh, you turn my blood to ice!
90 Stop torturing me, and give me your advice.

DORINE (*threatening to go*)   Your servant, Madam.

MARIANE   Dorine, I beg of you . . .

DORINE   No, you deserve it; this marriage must go through.

MARIANE   Dorine!

95 DORINE   No.

MARIANE   Not Tartuffe! You know I think him . . .

DORINE   Tartuffe's your cup of tea, and you shall drink him.

MARIANE   I've told you everything, and relied . . .

DORINE   No. You deserve to be tartuffified.

100 MARIANE   Well, since you mock me and refuse to care,
I'll henceforth seek my solace in despair:
Despair shall be my counsellor and friend,
And help me bring my sorrows to an end.

                    (*She starts to leave.*)
105
DORINE   There, now, come back; my anger has subsided.
You do deserve some pity, I've decided.

MARIANE   Dorine, if Father makes me undergo
This dreadful martyrdom, I'll die, I know.

110 DORINE   Don't fret; it won't be difficult to discover
Some plan of action . . . But here's Valère, your lover.

Scene IV (VALÈRE, MARIANE, DORINE)

VALÈRE   Madam, I've just received some wondrous news
Regarding which I'd like to hear your views.

MARIANE   What news?

VALÈRE   You're marrying Tartuffe.

5 MARIANE   I find
That Father does have such a match in mind.

VALÈRE   Your father, Madam . . .

MARIANE   . . . has just this minute said
    That it's Tartuffe he wishes me to wed.
10 VALÈRE   Can he be serious?
MARIANE   Oh, indeed he can;
    He's clearly set this heart upon the plan.
VALÈRE   And what position do you propose to take,
    Madam?
15 MARIANE   Why—I don't know.
VALÈRE   For heaven's sake—
    You don't know?
MARIANE   No.
VALÈRE   Well, well!
20 MARIANE   Advise me, do.
VALÈRE   Marry the man. That's my advice to you.
MARIANE   That's your advice?
VALÈRE   Yes.
MARIANE   Truly?
25 VALÈRE   Oh, absolutely.
    You couldn't choose more wisely, more astutely.
MARIANE   Thanks for this counsel; I'll follow it, of course.
VALÈRE   Do, do; I'm sure 'twill cost you no remorse.
MARIANE   To give it didn't cause your heart to break.
30 VALÈRE   I gave it, Madam, only for your sake.
MARIANE   And it's for your sake that I take it, Sir.
DORINE (*withdrawing to the rear of the stage*)
    Let's see which fool will prove the stubborner.
VALÈRE   So! I am nothing to you, and it was flat
35   Deception when you . . .
MARIANE   Please, enough of that.
    You've told me plainly that I should agree
    To wed the man my father's chosen for me,
    And since you've deigned to counsel me so wisely,
40   I promise, Sir, to do as you advise me.
VALÈRE   Ah, no, 'twas not by me that you were swayed.
    No, your decision was already made;
    Though now, to save appearances, you protest
    That you're betraying me at my behest.
45 MARIANE   Just as you say.
VALÈRE   Quite so. And I now see
    That you were never truly in love with me.
MARIANE   Alas, you're free to think so if you choose.
VALÈRE   I choose to think so, and here's a bit of news:
50   You've spurned my hand, but I know where to turn
    For kinder treatment, as you shall quickly learn.
MARIANE   I'm sure you do. Your noble qualities
    Inspire affection . . .

VALÈRE	Forget my qualities, please.

55 They don't inspire you overmuch, I find.
But there's another lady I have in mind
Whose sweet and generous nature will not scorn
To compensate me for the loss I've borne.

MARIANE I'm no great loss, and I'm sure that you'll transfer
60 Your heart quite painlessly from me to her.

VALÈRE I'll do my best to take it in my stride.
The pain I feel at being cast aside
Time and forgetfulness may put an end to.
Or if I can't forget, I shall pretend to.
65 No self-respecting person is expected
To go on loving once he's been rejected.

MARIANE Now, that's a fine, high-minded sentiment.

VALÈRE One to which any sane man would assent.
Would you prefer it if I pined away
70 In hopeless passion till my dying day?
Am I to yield you to a rival's arms
And not console myself with other charms?

MARIANE Go then, console yourself; don't hesitate.
I wish you to; indeed, I cannot wait.

75 VALÈRE You wish me to?

MARIANE   Yes.

VALÈRE   That's the final straw.
Madam, farewell. Your wish shall be my law.

(He starts to leave, and then returns: this repeatedly:)

MARIANE Splendid.

80 VALÈRE *(coming back again)*
                        This breach, remember, is of your making;
It's you who've driven me to the step I'm taking.

MARIANE Of course.

VALÈRE *(coming back again)*
85   Remember, too, that I am merely
Following your example.

MARIANE   I see that clearly

VALÈRE Enough. I'll go and do your bidding, then.

MARIANE Good.

90 VALÈRE *(coming back again)*
                        You shall never see my face again.

MARIANE Excellent.

VALÈRE *(walking to the door, then turning about)*
                        Yes?

95 MARIANE   What?

VALÈRE   What's that? What did you say?

MARIANE Nothing. You're dreaming.

VALÈRE   Ah. Well, I'm on my way.
Farewell, *Madame.*

(*He moves slowly away.*)

100 MARIANE   Farewell.
DORINE (*to* MARIANE)   If you ask me,
Both of you are as mad as mad can be.
Do stop this nonsense, now. I've only let you
Squabble so long to see where it would get you.
105 Whoa there, Monsieur Valère!

(*She goes and seizes* VALÈRE *by the arm; he makes a great show of resistance.*)

VALÈRE   What's this, Dorine?
DORINE   Come here.
VALÈRE   No, no, my heart's too full of spleen.
Don't hold me back; her wish must be obeyed.
110 DORINE   Stop!
VALÈRE   It's too late now; my decision's made.
DORINE   Oh, pooh!
MARIANE (*aside*)   He hates the sight of me, that's plain.
I'll go, and so deliver him from pain.
115 DORINE (*leaving* VALÈRE, *running after* MARIANE)
And now *you* run away! Come back.
MARIANE   No, no.
Nothing you say will keep me here. Let go!
VALÈRE (*aside*) She cannot bear my presence, I perceive.
120 To spare her further torment, I shall leave.
DORINE   (*leaving* MARIANE, *running after* VALÈRE)
Again! You'll not escape, Sir; don't you try it.
Come here, you two. Stop fussing, and be quiet.

(*She takes* VALÈRE *by the hand, then* MARIANE, *and draws them together.*)

VALÈRE (*to* DORINE)   What do you want of me?
125 MARIANE (*to* DORINE)   What is the point of
this?
DORINE   We're going to have a little armistice.

(*To* VALÈRE:)

Now, weren't you silly to get so overheated?
VALÈRE   Didn't you see how badly I was treated?
130 DORINE (*to* MARIANE)   Aren't you a simpleton, to have lost your
head?
MARIANE   Didn't you hear the hateful things he said?
DORINE (*to* VALÈRE)   You're both great fools. Her sole desire, Valère,
Is to be yours in marriage. To that I'll swear.

(*To* MARIANE)

135 He loves you only, and he wants no wife
     But you, Mariane. On that I'll stake my life.
     MARIANE (*to* VALÈRE)   Then why you advised me so, I cannot see.
     VALÈRE (*to* MARIANE)   On such a question, why ask advice of *me?*
     DORINE Oh, you're impossible. Give me your hands, you two.

(*To* VALÈRE)

140 Yours first.
     VALÈRE (*giving* DORINE *his hand*)
                But why?
     DORINE (*to* MARIANE)   And now a hand from you.
     MARIANE (*also giving* DORINE *her hand*)
145 What are you doing?
     DORINE   There: a perfect fit.
     You suit each other better that you'll admit.

(VALÈRE *and* MARIANE *hold hands for some time without looking at each other.*)

     VALÈRE (*turning toward* MARIANE)
     Ah, come, don't be so haughty. Give a man
150 A look of kindness, won't you, Mariane?

(MARIANE *turns toward* VALÈRE *and smiles.*)

     DORINE I tell you, lovers are completely mad!
     VALÈRE (*to* MARIANE)   Now come, confess that you were very bad
     To hurt my feelings as you did just now.
     I have a just complaint, you must allow.
155 MARIANE *You* must allow that you were most unpleasant . . .
     DORINE Let's table that discussion for the present;
     Your father has a plan which must be stopped.
     MARIANE Advise us, then; what means must we adopt?
     DORINE We'll use all manner of means, and all at once.

(*To* MARIANE)

160 Your father's addled; he's acting like a dunce.
     Therefore you'd better humor the old fossil.
     Pretend to yield to him, be sweet and docile,
     And then postpone, as often as necessary,
     The day on which you have agreed to marry.
165 You'll thus gain time, and time will turn the trick.
     Sometimes, for instance, you'll be taken sick,
     And that will seem good reason for delay;
     Or some bad omen will make you change the day—
     You'll dream of muddy water, or you'll pass
170 A dead man's hearse, or break a looking-glass.

If all else fails, no man can marry you
Unless you take his ring and say "I do."
But now, let's separate. If they should find
Us talking here, our plot might be divined.

(*To* VALÈRE)

175   Go to your friends, and tell them what's occurred,
And have them urge her father to keep his word.
Meanwhile, we'll stir her brother into action,
And get Elmire, as well, to join our faction.
Good-bye.
180   VALÈRE (*to* MARIANE)
                    Though each of us will do his best,
It's your true heart on which my hopes shall rest.
MARIANE (*to* VALÈRE)   Regardless of what Father may decide,
    · None but Valère shall claim me as his bride.
185   VALÈRE   Oh, how those words content me! Come what will . . .
DORINE   Oh, lovers, lovers! Their tongues are never still.
Be off, now.
VALÈRE (*turning to go, then turning back*)
                    One last word . . .
190   DORINE   No time to chat:
You leave by this door; and *you* leave by that.

(DORINE *pushes them, by the shoulders, toward opposing doors.*)

ACT III

Scene I (DAMIS, DORINE)

DAMIS   May lightning strike me even as I speak,
May all men call me cowardly and weak,
If any fear or scruple holds me back
From settling things, at once, with that great quack!
5   DORINE   Now, don't give way to violent emotion.
Your father's merely talked about this notion,
And words and deeds are far from being one.
Much that is talked about is never done.
DAMIS   No, I must stop that scoundrel's machinations;
10   I'll go and tell him off; I'm out of patience.
DORINE   Do calm down and be practical. I had rather
My mistress dealt with him—and with your father.
She has some influence with Tartuffe, I've noted.
He hangs upon her words, seems most devoted,
15   And may, indeed, be smitten by her charm.
Pray Heaven it's true! 'Twould do our cause no harm.

She sent for him, just now, to sound him out
On this affair you're so incensed about;
She'll find out where he stands, and tell him too,
20   What dreadful strife and trouble will ensue
If he lends countenance to your father's plan.
I couldn't get in to see him, but his man
Says that he's almost finished with his prayers.
Go, now. I'll catch him when he comes downstairs.

25 DAMIS   I want to hear this conference, and I will.

DORINE   No, they must be alone.

DAMIS   Oh, I'll keep still.

DORINE   Not you. I know your temper. You'd start a brawl,
And shout and stamp your foot and spoil it all.
30   Go on.

DAMIS   I won't; I have a perfect right . . .

DORINE   Lord, you're a nuisance! He's coming; get out of sight.

     (DAMIS *conceals himself in a closet at the rear of the stage.*)

Scene II (TARTUFFE, DORINE)

TARTUFFE (*observing* DORINE, *and calling to his manservant offstage*)
Hang up my hair-shirt, put my scourge in place,
And pray, Laurent, for Heaven's perpetual grace.
I'm going to the prison now, to share
5   My last few coins with the poor wretches there.

DORINE (*aside*)   Dear God, what affectation! What a fake!

TARTUFFE   You wished to see me?

DORINE   Yes . . .

TARTUFFE (*taking a handkerchief from his pocket*) For mercy's sake,
10   Please take this handkerchief, before you speak.

DORINE   What?

TARTUFFE   Cover that bosom, girl. The flesh is weak,
And unclean thoughts are difficult to control.
Such sights as that can undermine the soul.

15 DORINE   Your soul, it seems, has very poor defenses,
And flesh makes quite an impact on your senses.
It's strange that you're so easily excited;
My own desires are not so soon ignited,
And if I saw you naked as a beast,
20   Not all your hide would tempt me in the least.

TARTUFFE   Girl, speak more modestly; unless you do,
I shall be forced to take my leave of you.

DORINE   Oh, no, it's I who must be on my way;
I've just one little message to convey.
25   *Madame* is coming down, and begs you, Sir,
To wait and have a word or two with her.

TARTUFFE   Gladly.

DORINE *(aside)*   *That* had a softening effect!
    I think my guess about him was correct.

20 TARTUFFE   Will she be long?

DORINE   No: that's her step I hear.
    Ah, here she is, and I shall disappear.

Scene III (ELMIRE, TARTUFFE)

TARTUFFE   May Heaven, whose infinte goodness we adore,
    Preserve your body and soul forevermore,
    And bless your days, and answer thus the plea
    Of one who is its humblest votary.

5 ELMIRE   I thank you for that pious wish, but please,
    Do take a chair and let's be more at ease.

                          (They sit down.)

TARTUFFE   I trust that you are once more well and strong?

ELMIRE   Oh, yes: the fever didn't last for long.

TARTUFFE   My prayers are too unworthy, I am sure,

10   To have gained from Heaven this most gracious cure;
    But lately, Madam, my every supplication
    Has had for object your recuperation.

ELMIRE   You shouldn't have troubled so. I don't deserve it.

TARTUFFE   Your health is priceless, Madam, and to preserve it

15   I'd gladly give my own, in all sincerity.

ELMIRE   Sir, you outdo us all in Christian charity.
    You've been most kind. I count myself your debtor.

TARTUFFE   'Twas nothing, Madam. I long to serve you better.

ELMIRE   There's a private matter I'm anxious to discuss.

20   I'm glad there's no one here to hinder us.

TARTUFFE   I too am glad; it floods my heart with bliss
    To find myself alone with you like this.
    For just this chance I've prayed with all my power—
    But prayed in vain, until this happy hour.

25 ELMIRE   This won't take long, Sir, and I hope you'll be
    Entirely frank and unconstrained with me.

TARTUFFE   Indeed, there's nothing I had rather do
    Than bare my inmost heart and soul to you.
    First, let me say that what remarks I've made

30   About the constant visits you are paid
    Were prompted not by any mean emotion,
    But rather by a pure and deep devotion,
    A fervent zeal . . .

ELMIRE   No need for explanation.

35   Your sole concern, I'm sure, was my salvation.

TARTUFFE (*taking* ELMIRE'S *hand and pressing her fingertips*)
Quite so; and such great fervor do I feel . . .
ELMIRE Ooh! Please! You're pinching!
TARTUFFE   'Twas from excess of zeal.
40 I never meant to cause you pain, I swear.
I'd rather . . .
                    (*He places his hand on* ELMIRE'S *knee*)
ELMIRE   What can your hand be doing there?
TARTUFFE Feeling your gown: what soft, fine-woven stuff!
45 ELMIRE Please, I'm extremely ticklish. That's enough.

            (*She draws her chair away;* TARTUFFE *pulls his after her.*)

TARTUFFE (*fondling the lace collar of her gown*)
My, my, what lovely lacework on your dress!
The workmanship's miraculous, no less.
50 I've not seen anything to equal it.
ELMIRE Yes, quite. But let's talk business for a bit.
They say my husband means to break his word
And give his daughter to you, Sir. Had you heard?
TARTUFFE He did once mention it. But I confess
55 I dream of quite a different happiness.
It's elsewhere, Madam, that my eyes discern
The promise of that bliss for which I yearn.
ELMIRE I see: you care for nothing here below.
TARTUFFE Ah, well—my heart's not made of stone, you know.
60 ELMIRE All your desires mount heavenward, I'm sure,
In scorn of all that's earthly and impure.
TARTUFFE A love of heavenly beauty does not preclude
A proper love for earthly pulchritude;
Our senses are quite rightly captivated
65 By perfect works our Maker has created.
Some glory clings to all that Heaven has made;
In you, all Heaven's marvels are displayed.
On that fair face, such beauties have been lavished,
The eyes are dazzled and the heart is ravished;
70 How could I look on you, O flawless creature,
And not adore the Author of all Nature,
Feeling a love both passionate and pure
For you, his triumph of self-portraiture?
At first, I trembled lest that love should be
75 A subtle snare that Hell had laid for me;
I vowed to flee the sight of you, eschewing
A rapture that might prove my soul's undoing;
But soon, fair being, I became aware
That my deep passion could be made to square
80 With rectitude, and with my bounden duty.

I thereupon surrendered to your beauty.
It is, I know, presumptuous on my part
To bring you this poor offering of my heart,
And it is not my merit, Heaven knows,
85 But your compassion on which my hopes repose.
You are my peace, my solace, my salvation;
On you depends my bliss—or desolation;
I bide your judgment and, as you think best,
I shall be either miserable or blest.
90 ELMIRE Your declaration is most gallant, Sir,
But don't you think it's out of character?
You'd have done better to restrain your passion
And think before you spoke in such a fashion.
It ill becomes a pious man like you . . .
95 TARTUFFE I may be pious, but I'm human too:
With your celestial charms before his eyes,
A man has not the power to be wise.
I know such words sound strangely, coming from me,
But I'm no angel, nor was meant to be,
100 And if you blame my passion, you must needs
Reproach as well the charms on which it feeds.
Your loveliness I had no sooner seen
Than you became my soul's unrivalled queen;
Before your seraph glance, divinely sweet,
105 My heart's defenses crumbled in defeat,
And nothing fasting, prayer, or tears might do
Could stay my spirit from adoring you.
My eyes, my sighs have told you in the past
What now my lips make bold to say at last,
110 And if, in your great goodness, you will deign
To look upon your slave, and ease his pain,—
If, in compassion for my soul's distress,
You'll stoop to comfort my unworthiness,
I'll raise to you, in thanks for that sweet manna,
115 An endless hymn, an infinite hosanna.
With me, of course, there need be no anxiety,
No fear of scandal or of notoriety.
These young court gallants, whom all the ladies fancy,
Are vain in speech, in action rash and chancy;
120 When they succeed in love, the world soon knows it;
No favor's granted them but they disclose it
And by the looseness of their tongues profane
The very altar where their hearts have lain.
Men of my sort, however, love discreetly,
125 And one may trust our reticence completely.

My keen concern for my good name insures
The absolute security of yours;
In short, I offer you, my dear Elmire,
Love without scandal, pleasure without fear.
130 ELMIRE   I've heard your well-turned speeches to the end,
And what you urge I clearly apprehend.
Aren't you afraid that I may take a notion
To tell my husband of your warm devotion,
And that, supposing he were duly told,
135   His feelings toward you might grow rather cold?
TARTUFFE   I know, dear lady, that your exceeding charity
Will lead your heart to pardon my temerity;
That you'll excuse my violent affection
As human weakness, human imperfection;
140   And that—O fairest!—you will bear in mind
That I'm but flesh and blood, and am not blind.
ELMIRE   Some women might do otherwise, perhaps,
But I shall be discreet about your lapse;
I'll tell my husband nothing of what's occurred
145   If, in return, you'll give your solemn word
To advocate as forcefully as you can
The marriage of Valère and Mariane,
Renouncing all desire to dispossess
Another of his rightful happiness,
150   And . . .

Scene IV (DAMIS, ELMIRE, TARTUFFE)

DAMIS (*emerging from the closet where he has been hiding*)
          No! We'll not hush up this vile affair;
I heard it all inside that closet there,
Where Heaven, in order to confound the pride
5   Of this great rascal, prompted me to hide.
Ah, now I have my long-awaited chance
To punish his deceit and arrogance,
And give my father clear and shocking proof
Of the black character of his dear Tartuffe.
10 ELMIRE   Ah no, Damis! I'll be content if he
Will study to deserve my leniency.
I've promised silence—don't make me break my word;
To make a scandal would be too absurd.
Good wives laugh off such trifles, and forget them;
15   Why should they tell their husbands, and upset them?
DAMIS   You have your reasons for taking such a course,
And I have reasons, too, of equal force.

To spare him now would be insanely wrong.
I've swallowed my just wrath for far too long
20 And watched this insolent bigot bringing strife
And bitterness into our family life.
Too long he's meddled in my father's affairs,
Thwarting my marriage-hopes, and poor Valère's.
It's high time that my father was undeceived,
25 And now I've proof that can't be disbelieved—
Proof that was furnished me by Heaven above.
It's too good not to take advantage of.
This is my chance, and I deserve to lose it
If, for one moment, I hesitate to use it.
30 ELMIRE   Damis . . .
DAMIS   No, I must do what I think right.
Madam, my heart is bursting with delight,
And, say whatever you will, I'll not consent
To lose the sweet revenge on which I'm bent.
35 I'll settle matters without more ado;
And here, most opportunely, is my cue.

Scene V (ORGON, DAMIS, TARTUFFE, ELMIRE)

DAMIS   Father, I'm glad you've joined us. Let us advise you
Of some fresh news which doubtless will surprise you.
You've just now been repaid with interest
40 For all your loving-kindness to our guest.
He's proved his warm and grateful feelings toward you;
It's with a pair of horns he would reward you.
Yes, I surprised him with your wife, and heard
His whole adulterous offer, every word.
45 She, with her all too gentle disposition,
Would not have told you of his proposition;
But I shall not make terms with brazen lechery,
And feel that not to tell you would be treachery.
ELMIRE   And I hold that one's husband's peace of mind
50 Should not be spoilt by tattle of this kind.
One's honor doesn't require it: to be proficient
In keeping men at bay is quite sufficient.
These are my sentiments, and I wish, Damis,
That you had heeded me and held your peace.

Scene VI (ORGON, DAMIS, TARTUFFE)

55 ORGON   Can it be true, this dreadful thing I hear?
TARTUFFE   Yes, Brother, I'm a wicked man, I fear:

A wretched sinner, all depraved and twisted,
The greatest villain that has ever existed.
My life's one heap of crimes, which grows each minute;
60 There's naught but foulness and corruption in it;
And I perceive that Heaven, outraged by me,
Has chosen this occasion to mortify me.
Charge me with any deed you wish to name;
I'll not defend myself, but take the blame.
65 Believe what you are told, and drive Tartuffe
Like some base criminal from beneath your roof;
Yes, drive me hence, and with a parting curse:
I shan't protest, for I deserve far worse.

ORGON (*to* DAMIS) Ah, you deceitful boy, how dare you try
70 To stain his purity with so foul a lie?

DAMIS What! Are you taken in by such a bluff?
Did you not hear . . . ?

ORGON   Enough, you rogue, enough!

TARTUFFE Ah, Brother, let him speak: you're being unjust.
75 Believe his story; the boy deserves your trust.
Why, after all, should you have faith in me?
How can you know what I might do, or be?
Is it on my good actions that you base
Your favor? Do you trust my pious face?
80 Ah, no, don't be deceived by hollow shows;
I'm far, alas, from being what men suppose;
Though the world takes me for a man of worth,
I'm truly the most worthless man on earth.

(*To* DAMIS)

Yes, my dear son, speak out now: call me the chief
85 Of sinners, a wretch, a murderer, a thief;
Load me with all the names men most abhor;
I'll not complain; I've earned them all, and more;
I'll kneel here while you pour them on my head
As a just punishment for the life I've led.

90 ORGON (*to* TARTUFFE) This is too much, dear Brother.

(*To* DAMIS)

                                                    Have you no heart?

DAMIS Are you so hoodwinked by this rascal's art . . . ?

ORGON Be still, you monster.

(*To* TARTUFFE)

Brother, I pray you, rise.

(*To* DAMIS)

95   Villain!
DAMIS   But . . .
ORGON   Silence!
DAMIS   Can't you realize . . . ?
ORGON   Just one word more, and I'll tear you limb from limb.
100 TARTUFFE   In God's name, Brother, don't be harsh with him.
        I'd rather far be tortured at the stake
        Than see him bear one scratch for my poor sake.
        ORGON (*to* DAMIS)   Ingrate!
        TARTUFFE   If I must beg you, on bended knee,
105 To pardon him . . .
        ORGON (*falling to his knees, addressing* TARTUFFE)
                            Such goodness cannot be!

                    (*To* DAMIS)

        Now, *there's* true charity!
        DAMIS   What, you . . . ?
110 ORGON   Villain, be still!
        I know your motives; I know you wish him ill:
        Yes, all of you—wife, children, servants, all—
        Conspire against him and desire his fall,
        Employing every shameful trick you can
115 To alienate me from this saintly man.
        Ah, but the more you seek to drive him away,
        The more I'll do to keep him. Without delay,
        I'll spite this household and confound its pride
        By giving him my daughter as his bride.
120 DAMIS   You're going to force her to accept his hand?
        ORGON   Yes, and this very night, d'you understand?
        I shall defy you all, and make it clear
        That I'm the one who gives the orders here.
        Come, wretch, kneel down and clasp his blessed feet,
125 And ask his pardon for your black deceit.
        DAMIS   I ask that swindler's pardon? Why, I'd rather . . .
        ORGON   So! You insult him, and defy your father!
        A stick! A stick! (*To* TARTUFFE)   No, no—release me, do.

                    (*To* DAMIS)

        Out of my house this minute! Be off with you,
130 And never dare set foot in it again.
        DAMIS   Well, I shall go, but . . .
        ORGON   Well, go quickly, then.
        I disinherit you; an empty purse
        Is all you'll get from me—except my curse!

Scene VII (ORGON, TARTUFFE)

ORGON   How he blasphemed your goodness! What a son!
TARTUFFE   Forgive him, Lord, as I've already done.

(To ORGON*)*

You can't know how it hurts when someone tries
To blacken me in my dear Brother's eyes.
5 ORGON   Ahh!
TARTUFFE   The mere thought of such ingratitude
Plunges my soul into so dark a mood . . .
Such horror grips my heart . . . I gasp for breath,
And cannot speak, and feel myself near death.
10 ORGON   (*He runs, in tears, to the door through which he has just driven his
son.*)
You blackguard! Why did I spare you? Why did I not
Break you in little pieces on the spot?
Compose yourself, and don't be hurt, dear friend.
15 TARTUFFE   These scenes, these dreadful quarrels, have got to end.
I've much upset your household, and I perceive
That the best thing will be for me to leave.
ORGON   What are you saying!
TARTUFFE   They're all against me here;
20 They'd have you think me false and insincere.
ORGON   Ah, what of that? Have I ceased believing in you?
TARTUFFE   Their adverse talk will certainly continue,
And charges which you now repudiate
You may find credible at a later date.
25 ORGON   No, Brother, never.
TARTUFFE   Brother, a wife can sway
Her husband's mind in many a subtle way.
ORGON   No, no.
TARTUFFE   To leave at once is the solution;
30 Thus only can I end their persecution.
ORGON   No, no, I'll not allow it; you shall remain.
TARTUFFE   Ah, well; 'twill mean much martyrdom and pain,
But if you wish it . . .
ORGON   Ah!
35 TARTUFFE   Enough; so be it.
But one thing must be settled, as I see it.
For your dear honor, and for our friendship's sake,
There's one precaution I feel bound to take.
I shall avoid your wife, and keep away . . .
40 ORGON   No, you shall not, whatever they may say.
It pleases me to vex them, and for spite

I'd have them see you with her day and night.
What's more, I'm going to drive them to despair
By making you my only son and heir;
45   This very day, I'll give to you alone
Clear deed and title to everything I own.
A dear, good friend and son-in-law-to-be
Is more than wife, or child, or kin to me,
Will you accept my offer, dearest son?
50   TARTUFFE   In all things, let the will of Heaven be done.
ORGON   Poor fellow! Come, we'll go draw up the deed.
Then let them burst with disappointed greed!

ACT IV

Scene I (CLÉANTE, TARTUFFE)

CLÉANTE   Yes, all the town's discussing it, and truly,
Their comments do not flatter you unduly.
I'm glad we've met, Sir, and I'll give my view
Of this sad matter in a word or two.
5   As for who's guilty, that I shan't discuss;
Let's say it was Damis who caused the fuss;
Assuming, then, that you have been ill-used
By young Damis, and groundlessly accused,
Ought not a Christian to forgive, and ought
10   He not to stifle every vengeful thought?
Should you stand by and watch a father make
His only son an exile for your sake?
Again I tell you frankly, be advised:
The whole town, high and low, is scandalized;
15   This quarrel must be mended, and my advice is
Not to push matters to a further crisis.
No, sacrifice your wrath to God above,
And help Damis regain his father's love.
TARTUFFE   Alas, for my part I should take great joy
20   In doing so. I've nothing against the boy.
I pardon all, I harbor no resentment;
To serve him would afford me much contentment.
But Heaven's interest will not have it so:
If he comes back, then I shall have to go.
25   After his conduct—so extreme, so vicious—
Our further intercourse would look suspicious.
God knows what people would think! Why, they'd describe
My goodness to him as a sort of bribe;
They'd say that out of guilt I made pretense

30 Of loving-kindness and benevolence—
   That, fearing my accuser's tongue, I strove
   To buy his silence with a show of love.
  CLÉANTE Your reasoning is badly warped and stretched,
   And these excuses, Sir, are most far-fetched.
35 Why put yourself in charge of Heaven's cause?
   Does Heaven need our help to enforce its laws?
   Leave vengeance to the Lord, Sir; while we live,
   Our duty's not to punish, but forgive;
   And what the Lord commands, we should obey
40 Without regard to what the world may say.
   What! Shall the fear of being misunderstood
   Prevent our doing what is right and good?
   No, no: let's simply do what Heaven ordains,
   And let no other thoughts perplex our brains.
45 TARTUFFE Again, Sir, let me say that I've forgiven
   Damis, and thus obeyed the laws of Heaven;
   But I am not commanded by the Bible
   To live with one who smears my name with libel.
  CLÉANTE Were you commanded, Sir, to indulge the whim
50 Of poor Orgon, and to encourage him
   In suddenly transferring to your name
   A large estate to which you have no claim?
  TARTUFFE T'would never occur to those who know me best
   To think I acted from self-interest.
55 The treasures of this world I quite despise;
   Their specious glitter does not charm my eyes;
   And if I have resigned myself to taking
   The gift which my dear Brother insists on making,
   I do so only, as he well understands,
60 Lest so much wealth fall into wicked hands,
   Lest those to whom it might descend in time
   Turn it to purposes of sin and crime,
   And not, as I shall do, make use of it
   For Heaven's glory and mankind's benefit.
65 CLÉANTE Forget these trumped-up fears. Your argument
   Is one the rightful heir might well resent;
   It *is* a moral burden to inherit
   Such wealth, but give Damis a chance to bear it.
   And would it not be worse to be accused
70 Of swindling, than to see that wealth misused?
   I'm shocked that you allowed Orgon to broach
   This matter, and that you feel no self-reproach:
   Does true religion teach that lawful heirs
   May freely be deprived of what is theirs?

75   And if the Lord has told you in your heart
     That you and young Damis must dwell apart,
     Would it not be the decent thing to beat
     A generous and honorable retreat,
     Rather than let the son of the house be sent,
80   For your convenience, into banishment?
     Sir, if you wish to prove the honesty
     Of your intentions . . .
     TARTUFFE   Sir, it is half-past three.
     I've certain pious duties to attend to,
85   And hope my prompt departure won't offend you.
     CLÉANTE (*alone*)   Damn.

Scene II (ELMIRE, MARIANE, CLÉANTE, DORINE)

DORINE   Stay, Sir, and help Mariane, for Heaven's sake!
     She's suffering so, I fear her heart will break.
     Her father's plan to marry her off tonight
     Has put the poor child in a desperate plight.
5   I hear him coming. Let's stand together, now,
     And see if we can't change his mind, somehow,
     About this match we all deplore and fear.

Scene III (ORGON, ELMIRE, MARIANE, CLÉANTE, DORINE)

ORGON   Hah! Glad to find you all assembled here.

                    (*To* MARIANE:)

     This contract, child, contains your happiness,
     And what it says I think your heart can guess.
     MARIANE (*falling to her knees*)
5   Sir, by that Heaven which sees me here distressed,
     And by whatever else can move your breast,
     Do not employ a father's power, I pray you,
     To crush my heart and force it to obey you,
     Nor by your harsh commands oppress me so
10   That I'll begrudge the duty which I owe—
     And do not so embitter and enslave me
     That I shall hate the very life you gave me.
     If my sweet hopes must perish, if you refuse
     To give me to the one I've dared to choose,
15   Spare me at least—I beg you, I implore—
     The pain of wedding one whom I abhor;
     And do not, by a heartless use of force,
     Drive me to contemplate some desperate course.
     ORGON (*feeling himself touched by her*)
20   Be firm, my soul. No human weakness, now.

MARIANE   I don't resent your love for him. Allow
   Your heart free rein, Sir; give him your property,
   And if that's not enough, take mine from me;
   He's welcome to my money; take it, do,
25   But don't, I pray, include my person too.
   Spare me, I beg you; and let me end the tale
   Of my sad days behind a convent veil.
ORGON   A convent! Hah! When crossed in their amours,
   All lovesick girls have the same thought as yours.
30   Get up! The more you loathe the man, and dread him,
   The more ennobling it will be to wed him.
   Marry Tartuffe, and mortify your flesh!
   Enough; don't start that whimpering afresh.
DORINE   But why . . . ?
35 ORGON   Be still, there. Speak when you're spoken to.
   Not one more bit of impudence out of you.
CLÉANTE   If I may offer a word of counsel here . . .
ORGON   Brother, in counseling you have no peer;
   All your advice is forceful, sound, and clever;
40   I don't propose to follow it, however.
ELMIRE (*to* ORGON)   I am amazed, and don't know what to say;
   Your blindness simply takes my breath away.
   You are indeed bewitched, to take no warning
   From our account of what occurred this morning.
45 ORGON   Madam, I know a few plain facts, and one
   Is that you're partial to my rascal son;
   Hence, when he sought to make Tartuffe the victim
   Of a base lie, you dared not contradict him.
   Ah, but you underplayed your part, my pet;
50   You should have looked more angry, more upset.
ELMIRE   When men make overtures, must we reply
   With righteous anger and a battle-cry?
   Must we turn back their amorous advances
   With sharp reproaches and with fiery glances?
55   Myself, I find such offers merely amusing,
   And make no scenes and fusses in refusing;
   My taste is for good-natured rectitude,
   And I dislike the savage sort of prude
   Who guards her virtue with her teeth and claws,
60   And tears men's eyes out for the slightest cause:
   The Lord preserve me from such honor as that,
   Which bites and scratches like an alley-cat!
   I've found that a polite and cool rebuff
   Discourages a lover quite enough.
65 ORGON   I know the facts, and I shall not be shaken.
ELMIRE   I marvel at your power to be mistaken.

Would it, I wonder, carry weight with you
If I could *show* you that our tale was true?

ORGON   Show me?

70 ELMIRE   Yes.

ORGON   Rot.

ELMIRE   Come, what if I found a way
To make you see the facts as plain as day?

ORGON   Nonsense.

75 ELMIRE   Do answer me; don't be absurd.
I'm not now asking you to trust our word.
Suppose that from some hiding-place in here
You learned the whole sad truth by eye and ear—
What would you say of your good friend, after that?

80 ORGON   Why, I'd say . . . nothing, by Jehoshaphat!
It can't be true.

ELMIRE   You've been too long deceived,
And I'm quite tired of being disbelieved.
Come now: let's put my statements to the test,

85   And you shall see the truth made manifest.

ORGON   I'll take that challenge. Now do your uttermost.
We'll see how you make good your empty boast.

ELMIRE *(to* DORINE*)*   Send him to me.

DORINE   He's crafty; it may be hard

90   To catch the cunning scoundrel off his guard.

ELMIRE   No, amorous men are gullible. Their conceit
So blinds them that they're never hard to cheat.
Have him come down

(To CLÉANTE *and* MARIANE*)*

Please leave us, for a bit.

Scene IV (ELMIRE, ORGON)

ELMIRE   Pull up this table, and get under it.

ORGON   What?

ELMIRE   It's essential that you be well-hidden.

ORGON   Why there?

5 ELMIRE   Oh, Heavens! Just do as you are bidden.
I have my plans; we'll soon see how they fare.
Under the table, now; and once you're there,
Take care that you are neither seen nor heard.

ORGON   Well, I'll indulge you, since I gave my word

10   To see you through this infantile charade.

ELMIRE   Once it is over, you'll be glad we played.

(To her husband, who is now under the table)

I'm going to act quite strangely, now, and you
Must not be shocked at anything I do.
Whatever I may say, you must excuse
15 As part of that deceit I'm forced to use.
I shall employ sweet speeches in the task
Of making that imposter drop his mask;
I'll give encouragement to his bold desires,
And furnish fuel to his amorous fires.
20 Since it's for your sake, and for his destruction,
That I shall seem to yield to his seduction,
I'll gladly stop whenever you decide
That all your doubts are fully satisfied.
I'll count on you, as soon as you have seen
25 What sort of man he is, to intervene,
And not expose me to his odious lust
One moment longer than you feel you must.
Remember: you're to save me from my plight
Whenever . . . He's coming! Hush! Keep out of sight!

Scene V (TARTUFFE, ELMIRE, ORGON)

TARTUFFE You wish to have a word with me, I'm told.
ELMIRE Yes. I've a little secret to unfold.
Before I speak, however, it would be wise
To close that door, and look about for spies.

(TARTUFFE *goes to the door, closes it, and returns.*)

5 The very last thing that must happen now
Is a repetition of this morning's row.
I've never been so badly caught off guard.
Oh, how I feared for you! You saw how hard
I tried to make that troublesome Damis
10 Control his dreadful temper, and hold his peace.
In my confusion, I didn't have the sense
Simply to contradict his evidence;
But as it happened, that was for the best,
And all has worked out in our interest.
15 This storm has only bettered your position;
My husband doesn't have the least suspicion,
And now, in mockery of those who do,
He bids me be continually with you.
And that is why, quite fearless of reproof,
20 I now can be alone with my Tartuffe,
And why my heart—perhaps too quick to yield—
Feels free to let its passion be revealed.

TARTUFFE   Madam, your words confuse me. Not long ago,
You spoke in quite a different style, you know.
25 ELMIRE   Ah, Sir, if that refusal made you smart,
It's little that you know of woman's heart,
Or what that heart is trying to convey
When it resists in such a feeble way!
Always, at first, our modesty prevents
30   The frank avowal of tender sentiments;
However high the passion which inflames us,
Still, to confess its power somehow shames us.
Thus we reluct, at first, yet in a tone
Which tells you that our heart is overthrown,
35   That what our lips deny, our pulse confesses,
And that, in time, all noes will turn to yesses.
I fear my words are all too frank and free,
And a poor proof of woman's modesty;
But since I'm started, tell me, if you will—
40   Would I have tried to make Damis be still,
Would I have listened, calm and unoffended,
Until your lengthy offer of love was ended,
And been so very mild in my reaction,
Had your sweet words not given me satisfaction?
45   And when I tried to force you to undo
The marriage-plans my husband has in view,
What did my urgent pleading signify
If not that I admired you, and that I
Deplored the thought that someone else might own
50   Part of a heart I wished for mine alone?
   TARTUFFE   Madam, no happiness is so complete
As when, from lips we love, come words so sweet;
Their nectar floods my every sense, and drains
In honeyed rivulets through all my veins.
55   To please you is my joy, my only goal;
Your love is the restorer of my soul;
And yet I must beg leave, now, to confess
Some lingering doubts as to my happiness.
Might not this be a trick? Might not the catch
60   Be that you wish me to break off the match
With Mariane, and so have feigned to love me?
I shan't quite trust your fond opinion of me
Until the feelings you've expressed so sweetly
Are demonstrated somewhat more concretely,
65   And you have shown, by certain kind concessions,
That I may put my faith in your professions.
ELMIRE   (*She coughs, to warn her husband.*)
Why be in such a hurry? Must my heart

Exhaust its bounty at the very start?
70   To make that sweet admission cost me dear,
But you'll not be content, it would appear,
Unless my store of favors is disbursed
To the last farthing, and at the very first.
TARTUFFE   The less we merit, the less we dare to hope,
75   And with our doubts, mere words can never cope.
We trust no promised bliss till we receive it;
Not till a joy is ours can we believe it.
I, who so little merit your esteem,
Can't credit this fulfillment of my dream,
80   And shan't believe it, Madam, until I savor
Some palpable assurance of your favor.
ELMIRE   My, how tyrannical your love can be,
And how it flusters and perplexes me!
How furiously you take one's heart in hand,
85   And make your every wish a fierce command!
Come, must you hound and harry me to death?
Will you not give me time to catch my breath?
Can it be right to press me with such force,
Give me no quarter, show me no remorse,
90   And take advantage, by your stern insistence,
Of the fond feelings which weaken my resistance?
TARTUFFE   Well, if you look with favor upon my love,
Why, then, begrudge me some clear proof thereof?
ELMIRE   But how can I consent without offense
95   To Heaven, toward which you feel such reverence?
TARTUFFE   If Heaven is all that holds you back, don't worry.
I can remove that hindrance in a hurry.
Nothing of that sort need obstruct our path.
ELMIRE   Must one not be afraid of Heaven's wrath?
100   TARTUFFE   Madam, forget such fears, and be my pupil,
And I shall teach you how to conquer scruple.
Some joys, it's true, are wrong in Heaven's eyes;
Yet Heaven is not averse to compromise;
There is a science, lately formulated,
105   Whereby one's conscience may be liberated,
And any wrongful act you care to mention
May be redeemed by purity of intention.
I'll teach you, Madam, the secrets of that science;
Meanwhile, just place on me your full reliance.
110   Assuage my keen desires, and feel no dread:
The sin, if any, shall be on my head.

(ELMIRE *coughs, this time more loudly.*)

You've a bad cough.

ELMIRE   Yes, yes. It's bad indeed.

TARTUFFE (*producing a little paper bag*)

115   A bit of licorice may be what you need.

ELMIRE   No, I've a stubborn cold, it seems. I'm sure it
Will take much more than licorice to cure it.

TARTUFFE   How aggravating.

ELMIRE   Oh, more than I can say.

120 TARTUFFE   If you're still troubled, think of things this way:
No one shall know our joys, save us alone,
And there's no evil till the act is known;
It's scandal, Madam, which makes it an offense,
And it's no sin to sin in confidence.

125 ELMIRE (*having coughed once more*)   Well, clearly I must do as you re-
quire,
And yield to your importunate desire.
It is apparent, now, that nothing less
Will satisfy you, and so I acquiesce.

130   To go so far is much against my will;
I'm vexed that it should come to this; but still,
Since you are so determined on it, since you
Will not allow mere language to convince you,
And since you ask for concrete evidence, I

135   See nothing for it, now, but to comply.
If this is sinful, if I'm wrong to do it,
So much the worse for him who drove me to it.
The fault can surely not be charged to me.

TARTUFFE   Madam, the fault is mine, if fault there be,

140   And . . .

ELMIRE   Open the door a little, and peek out;
I wouldn't want my husband poking about.

TARTUFFE   Why worry about the man? Each day he grows
More gullible; one can lead him by the nose.

145   To find us here would fill him with delight,
And if he saw the worst, he'd doubt his sight.

ELMIRE   Nevertheless, do step out for a minute
Into the hall, and see that no one's in it.

Scene VI (ORGON, ELMIRE)

ORGON (*coming out from under the table*)
That man's a perfect monster, I must admit!
I'm simply stunned. I can't get over it.

ELMIRE   What, coming out so soon? How premature!

5   Get back in hiding, and wait until you're sure.
Stay till the end, and be convinced completely;
We mustn't stop till things are proved concretely.

ORGON   Hell never harbored anything so vicious!

ELMIRE   Tut, don't be hasty. Try to be judicious.

10   Wait, and be certain that there's no mistake.

No jumping to conclusions, for Heaven's sake!

(She places ORGON *behind her, as* TARTUFFE *re-enters.)*

Scene VII (TARTUFFE, ELMIRE, ORGON)

TARTUFFE *(not seeing* ORGON)

Madam, all things have worked out to perfection;

I've given the neighboring rooms a full inspection;

No one's about; and now I may at last . . .

5   ORGON *(intercepting him)*   Hold on, my passionate fellow, not so fast!

I should advise a little more restraint.

Well, so you thought you'd fool me, my dear saint!

How soon you wearied of the saintly life—

Wedding my daughter, and coveting my wife!

10   I've long suspected you, and had a feeling

That soon I'd catch you at your double-dealing.

Just now, you've given me the evidence galore;

It's quite enough; I have no wish for more.

ELMIRE *(to* TARTUFFE)   I'm sorry to have treated you so slyly,

15   But circumstances forced me to be wily.

TARTUFFE   Brother, you can't think . . .

ORGON: No more talk from you:

Just leave this household, without more ado.

TARTUFFE   What I intended . . .

20   ORGON   That seems fairly clear.

Spare me your falsehoods and get out of here.

TARTUFFE   No, I'm the master, and you're the one to go!

This house belongs to me, I'll have you know,

And I shall show you that you can't hurt *me*

25   By this contemptible conspiracy,

That those who cross me know not what they do,

And that I've means to expose and punish you,

Avenge offended Heaven, and make you grieve

That ever you dared order me to leave.

Scene VIII (ELMIRE, ORGON)

ELMIRE   What was the point of all that angry chatter?

ORGON   Dear God, I'm worried. This is no laughing matter.

ELMIRE   How so?

ORGON   I fear I understood his drift.

5   I'm much disturbed about that deed of gift.

ELMIRE   You gave him . . . ?

ORGON   Yes, it's all been drawn and signed.
But one thing more is weighing on my mind.
ELMIRE   What's that?
10 ORGON   I'll tell you; but first let's see if there's
A certain strong-box in his room upstairs.

ACT V

Scene I (ORGON, CLÉANTE)

CLÉANTE   Where are you going so fast?
ORGON   God knows!
CLÉANTE   Then wait;
    Let's have a conference, and deliberate
5   On how this situation's to be met.
ORGON   That strong-box has me utterly upset;
This is the worst of many, many shocks.
CLÉANTE   Is there some fearful mystery in that box?
ORGON   My poor friend Argas brought that box to me
10   With his own hands, in utmost secrecy;
'Twas on the very morning of his flight.
It's full of papers which, if they came to light,
Would ruin him—or such is my impression.
CLÉANTE   Then why did you let it out of your possession?
15 ORGON   Those papers vexed my conscience, and it seemed best
To ask the counsel of my pious guest.
The cunning scoundrel got me to agree
To leave the strong-box in his custody,
So that, in case of an investigation,
20   I could employ a slight equivocation
And swear I didn't have it, and thereby,
At no expense to conscience, tell a lie.
CLÉANTE   It looks to me as if you're out on a limb.
Trusting him with that box, and offering him
25   That deed of gift, were actions of a kind
Which scarcely indicate a prudent mind.
With two such weapons, he has the upper hand,
And since you're vulnerable, as matters stand,
You erred once more in bringing him to bay.
30   You should have acted in some subtler way.
ORGON   Just think of it: behind that fervent face,
A heart so wicked, and a soul so base!
I took him in, a hungry beggar, and then . . .
Enough, by God! I'm through with pious men:
35   Henceforth I'll hate the whole false brotherhood,
And persecute them worse than Satan could.

CLÉANTE   Ah, there you go—extravagant as ever!
Why can you not be rational? You never
Manage to take the middle course, it seems,
40   But jump, instead, between absurd extremes.
You've recognized your recent grave mistake
In falling victim to a pious fake;
Now, to correct that error, must you embrace
An even greater error in its place,
45   And judge our worthy neighbors as a whole
By what you've learned of one corrupted soul?
Come, just because one rascal made you swallow
A show of zeal which turned out to be hollow,
Shall you conclude that all men are deceivers,
50   And that, today, there are no true believers?
Let atheists make that foolish inference;
Learn to distinguish virtue from pretense,
Be cautious in bestowing admiration,
And cultivate a sober moderation.
55   Don't humor fraud, but also don't asperse
True piety; the latter fault is worse,
And it is best to err, if err one must,
As you have done, upon the side of trust.

Scene II (DAMIS, ORGON, CLÉANTE)

DAMIS   Father, I hear that scoundrel's uttered threats
Against you; that he pridefully forgets
How, in his need, he was befriended by you,
And means to use your gifts to crucify you.
5   ORGON   It's true, my boy. I'm too distressed for tears.
DAMIS   Leave it to me, Sir; let me trim his ears.
Faced with such insolence, we must not waver.
I shall rejoice in doing you the favor
Of cutting short his life, and your distress.
10   CLÉANTE   What a display of young hotheadedness!
Do learn to moderate your fits of rage.
In this just kingdom, this enlightened age,
One does not settle things by violence.

Scene III (MADAME PERNELLE, MARIANE, ELMIRE, DORINE, DAMIS, ORGON, CLÉANTE)

MADAME PERNELLE   I hear strange tales of very strange events.
ORGON   Yes, strange events which these two eyes beheld.
The man's ingratitude is unparalleled.

I save a wretched pauper from starvation,
5   House him, and treat him like a blood relation,
Shower him every day with my largesse,
Give him my daughter, and all that I possess;
And meanwhile the unconscionable knave
Tries to induce my wife to misbehave;
10   And not content with such extreme rascality,
Now threatens me with my own liberality,
And aims, by taking base advantage of
The gifts I gave him out of Christian love,
To drive me from my house, a ruined man,
15   And make me end a pauper, as he began.
DORINE   Poor fellow!
MADAME PERNELLE   No, my son, I'll never bring
Myself to think him guilty of such a thing.
ORGON   How's that?
20   MADAME PERNELLE   The righteous always were maligned.
ORGON   Speak clearly, Mother. Say what's on your mind.
MADAME PERNELLE   I mean that I can smell a rat, my dear.
You know how everybody hates him, here.
ORGON   That has no bearing on the case at all.
25   MADAME PERNELLE   I told you a hundred times, when you were
     small,
That virtue in this world is hated ever;
Malicious men may die, but malice never.
ORGON   No doubt that's true, but how does it apply?
30   MADAME PERNELLE   They've turned you against him by a clever lie.
ORGON   I've told you, I was there and saw it done.
MADAME PERNELLE   Ah, slanderers will stop at nothing, Son.
ORGON   Mother, I'll lose my temper . . . For the last time,
I tell you I was witness to the crime.
35   MADAME PERNELLE   The tongues of spite are busy night and noon,
And to their venom no man is immune.
ORGON   You're talking nonsense. Can't you realize
I saw it; saw it; saw it with my eyes?
Saw, do you understand me? Must I shout it
40   Into your ears before you'll cease to doubt it?
MADAME PERNELLE   Appearances can deceive, my son. Dear me,
We cannot always judge by what we see.
ORGON   Drat! Drat!
MADAME PERNELLE   One often interprets things awry;
45   Good can seem evil to a suspicious eye.
ORGON   Was I to see his pawing at Elmire
As an act of charity?
MADAME PERNELLE   Till his guilt is clear,

A man deserves the benefit of the doubt.
50 You should have waited, to see how things turned out.
ORGON   Great God in Heaven, what more proof did I need?
Was I to sit there, watching, until he'd . . .
You drive me to the brink of impropriety.
MADAME PERNELLE   No, no, a man of such surpassing piety
55 Could not do such a thing. You cannot shake me.
I don't believe it, and you shall not make me.
ORGON   You vex me so that, if you weren't my mother,
I'd say to you . . . some dreadful thing or other.
DORINE   It's your turn now, Sir, not to be listened to;
60 You'd not trust us, and now she won't trust you.
CLÉANTE   My friends, we're wasting time which should be spent
In facing up to our predicament.
I fear that scoundrel's threats weren't made in sport.
DAMIS   Do you think he'd have the nerve to go to court?
65 ELMIRE   I'm sure he won't; they'd find it all too crude
A case of swindling and ingratitude.
CLÉANTE   Don't be too sure. He won't be at a loss
To give his claims a high and righteous gloss;
And clever rogues with far less valid cause
70 Have trapped their victims in a web of laws.
I say again that to antagonize
A man so strongly armed was most unwise.
ORGON   I know it; but the man's appalling cheek
Outraged me so, I couldn't control my pique.
75 CLÉANTE   I wish to Heaven that we could devise
Some truce between you, or some compromise.
ELMIRE   If I had known what cards he held, I'd not
Have roused his anger by my little plot.
ORGON (*to* DORINE, *as* M. LOYAL *enters*)
80 What is that fellow looking for? Who is he?
Go talk to him—and tell him that I'm busy.

Scene IV (MONSIEUR LOYAL, MADAME PERNELLE, ORGON, DAMIS, MARIANE, DORINE, ELMIRE, CLÉANTE)

MONSIEUR LOYAL   Good day, dear sister. Kindly let me see
Your master.
DORINE   He's involved with company,
And cannot be disturbed just now, I fear.
5 MONSIEUR LOYAL   I hate to intrude; but what has brought me here
Will not disturb your master, in any event.
Indeed, my news will make him most content.

DORINE   Your name?

MONSIEUR LOYAL   Just say that I bring greetings from
10   Monsieur Tartuffe, on whose behalf I've come.

DORINE (*to* ORGON)   Sir, he's a very gracious man, and bears
     A message from Tartuffe, which, he declares,
     Will make you most content.

CLÉANTE   Upon my word,
15   I think this man had best be seen, and heard.

ORGON   Perhaps he has some settlement to suggest.
     How shall I treat him? What manner would be best?

CLÉANTE   Control your anger, and if he should mention
     Some fair adjustment, give him your full attention.

20 MONSIEUR LOYAL   Good health to you, good Sir. May Heaven con-
     found
     Your enemies, and may your joys abound.

ORGON (*aside, to* CLÉANTE)   A gentle salutation: it confirms
     My guess that he is here to offer terms.

25 MONSIEUR LOYAL   I've always held your family most dear;
     I served your father, Sir, for many a year.

ORGON   Sir, I must ask your pardon; to my shame,
     I cannot now recall your face or name.

MONSIEUR LOYAL   Loyal's my name; I come from Normandy,
30   And I'm a bailiff, in all modesty.
     For forty years, praise God, it's been my boast
     To serve with honor in that vital post,
     And I am here, Sir, if you will permit
     The liberty, to serve you with this writ . . .

35 ORGON   To—*what?*

MONSIEUR LOYAL   Now, please, Sir, let us have no friction:
     It's nothing but an order of eviction.
     You are to move your goods and family out
     And make way for new occupants, without
40   Deferment or delay, and give the keys . . .

ORGON   I? Leave this house?

MONSIEUR LOYAL   Why yes, Sir, if you please.
     This house, Sir, from the cellar to the roof,
     Belongs now to the good Monsieur Tartuffe,
45   And he is lord and master of your estate
     By virtue of a deed of present date,
     Drawn in due form, with clearest legal phrasing . . .

DAMIS   Your insolence is utterly amazing!

MONSIEUR LOYAL   Young man, my business here is not with you,
50   But with your wise and temperate father, who,
     Like every worthy citizen, stands in awe
     Of justice, and would never obstruct the law.

ORGON   But . . .

MONSIEUR LOYAL   Not for a million, Sir, would you rebel
55   Against authority; I know that well.
You'll not make trouble, Sir, or interfere
With the execution of my duties here.

DAMIS   Someone may execute a smart tattoo
On that black jacket of yours, before you're through.

60 MONSIEUR LOYAL   Sir, bid your son be silent. I'd much regret
Having to mention such a nasty threat
Of violence, in writing my report.

DORINE (*aside*)   This man Loyal's a most disloyal sort!

MONSIEUR LOYAL   I love all men of upright character,
65   And when I agreed to serve these papers, Sir,
It was your feelings that I had in mind.
I couldn't bear to see the case assigned
To someone else, who might esteem you less
And so subject you to unpleasantness.

70 ORGON   What's more unpleasant than telling a man to leave
His house and home?

MONSIEUR LOYAL   You'd like a short reprieve?
If you desire it, Sir, I shall not press you,
But wait until tomorrow to dispossess you.
75   Splendid. I'll come and spend the night here, then,
Most quietly, with half a score of men.
For form's sake, you might bring me, just before
You go to bed, the keys to the front door.
My men, I promise, will be on their best
80   Behavior, and will not disturb your rest.
But bright and early, Sir, you must be quick
And move out all your furniture, every stick:
The men I've chosen are both young and strong,
And with their help it shouldn't take you long.
85   In short, I'll make things pleasant and convenient,
And since I'm being so extremely lenient,
Please show me, Sir, a like consideration,
And give me your entire cooperation.

ORGON (*aside*)   I may be all but bankrupt, but I vow
90   I'd give a hundred louis, here and now,
Just for the pleasure of landing one good clout
Right on the end of that complacent snout.

CLÉANTE   Careful; don't make things worse.

DAMIS   My bootsole itches
95   To give that beggar a good kick in the breeches.

DORINE   Monsieur Loyal, I'd love to hear the whack
Of a stout stick across your fine broad back.

MONSIEUR LOYAL   Take care: a woman too may go to jail if
   She uses threatening language to a bailiff.
100 CLÉANTE   Enough, enough, Sir. This must not go on.
   Give me that paper, please, and then begone.
MONSIEUR LOYAL   Well, *au revoir*. God give you all good cheer!
ORGON   May God confound you, and him who sent you here!

Scene V (ORGON, CLÉANTE, MARIANE, ELMIRE, MADAME PERNELLE, DORINE, DAMIS)

ORGON   Now, Mother, was I right or not? This writ
   Should change your notion of Tartuffe a bit.
   Do you perceive his villainy at last?
MADAME PERNELLE   I'm thunderstruck. I'm utterly aghast.
5 DORINE   Oh, come, be fair. You mustn't take offense
   At this new proof of his benevolence.
   He's acting out of selfless love, I know.
   Material things enslave the soul, and so
   He kindly has arranged your liberation
10   From all that might endanger your salvation.
ORGON   Will you not ever hold your tongue, you dunce?
CLÉANTE   Come, you must take some action, and at once.
ELMIRE   Go tell the world of the low trick he's tried.
   The deed of gift is surely nullified
15   By such behavior, and public rage will not
   Permit the wretch to carry out his plot.

Scene VI (VALÈRE, ORGON, CLÉANTE, ELMIRE, MARIANE, MADAME PERNELLE, DAMIS, DORINE)

VALÈRE   Sir, though I hate to bring you more bad news,
   Such is the danger that I cannot choose.
   A friend who is extremely close to me
   And knows my interest in your family
5   Has, for my sake, presumed to violate
   The secrecy that's due to things of state,
   And sends me word that you are in a plight
   From which your one salvation lies in flight,
   That scoundrel who's imposed upon you so
10   Denounced you to the King an hour ago
   And, as supporting evidence, displayed
   The strong-box of a certain renegade
   Whose secret papers, so he testified,
   You had disloyally agreed to hide.
15   I don't know just what charges may be pressed,

But there's a warrant out for your arrest;
Tartuffe has been instructed, furthermore,
To guide the arresting officer to your door.

CLÉANTE   He's clearly done this to facilitate
20   His seizure of your house and your estate.

ORGON   That man, I must say, is a vicious beast!

VALÈRE   You can't afford to delay, Sir, in the least.
My carriage is outside, to take you hence,
This thousand louis should cover all expense.
25   Let's lose no time, or you shall be undone;
The sole defense, in this case, is to run.
I shall go with you all the way, and place you
In a safe refuge to which they'll never trace you.

ORGON   Alas, dear boy, I wish that I could show you
30   My gratitude for everything I owe you.
But now is not the time; I pray the Lord
That I may live to give you your reward.
Farewell, my dears; be careful . . .

CLÉANTE   Brother, hurry.
35   We shall take care of things; you needn't worry.

Scene VII (The Officer, Tartuffe, Valère, Orgon, Elmire, Mariane, Madame Pernelle, Dorine, Cléante, Damis)

TARTUFFE   Gently, Sir, gently; stay right where you are.
No need for haste; your lodging isn't far.
You're off to prison, by order of the Prince.

ORGON   This is the crowning blow, you wretch; and since
5   It means my total ruin and defeat,
Your villainy is now at last complete.

TARTUFFE   You needn't try to provoke me; it's no use.
Those who serve Heaven must expect abuse.

CLÉANTE   You are indeed most patient, sweet, and blameless.
10   DORINE   How he exploits the name of Heaven! It's shameless.

TARTUFFE   Your taunts and mockeries are all for naught;
To do my duty is my only thought.

MARIANE   Your love of duty is most meritorious,
And what you've done is little short of glorious.

15   TARTUFFE   All deeds are glorious, Madam, which obey
The sovereign prince who sent me here today.

ORGON   I rescued you when you were destitute;
Have you forgotten that, you thankless brute?

TARTUFFE   No, no, I well remember everything;
20   But my first duty is to serve my King.
That obligation is so paramount

That other claims, beside it, do not count;
And for it I would sacrifice my wife,
My family, my friend, or my own life.

25 ELMIRE   Hypocrite!

DORINE   All that we most revere, he uses
To cloak his plots and camouflage his ruses.

CLÉANTE   If it is true that you are animated
By pure and loyal zeal, as you have stated,

30 Why was this zeal not roused until you'd sought
To make Orgon a cuckold, and been caught?
Why weren't you moved to give your evidence
Until your outraged host had driven you hence?
I shan't say that the gift of all his treasure

35 Ought to have damped your zeal in any measure;
But if he is a traitor, as you declare,
How could you condescend to be his heir?

TARTUFFE (*to the* OFFICER)
Sir, spare me all this clamor; it's growing shrill.

40 Please carry out your orders, if you will.

OFFICER   Yes, I've delayed too long, Sir. Thank you kindly.
You're just the proper person to remind me.
Come, you are off to join the other boarders
In the King's prison, according to his orders.

45 TARTUFFE   Who? I, Sir?

OFFICER   Yes.

TARTUFFE   To prison? This can't be true!

OFFICER   I owe an explanation, but not to you.

(*To* ORGON)

Sir, all is well; rest easy, and be grateful.

50 We serve a Prince to whom all sham is hateful,
A Prince who sees into our inmost hearts,
And can't be fooled by any trickster's arts.
His royal soul, though generous and human,
Views all things with discernment and acumen;

55 His sovereign reason is not lightly swayed,
And all his judgments are discreetly weighed.
He honors righteous men of every kind,
And yet his zeal for virtue is not blind,
Nor does his love of piety numb his wits

60 And make him tolerant of hypocrites.
'Twas hardly likely that this man could cozen
A King who's foiled such liars by the dozen.
With one keen glance, the King perceived the whole
Perverseness and corruption of his soul,

65 And thus high Heaven's justice was displayed:
 Betraying you, the rogue stood self-betrayed.
 The King soon recognized Tartuffe as one
 Notorious by another name, who'd done
 So many vicious crimes that one could fill
70 Ten volumes with them, and be writing still.
 But to be brief: our sovereign was appalled
 By this man's treachery toward you, which he called
 The last, worst villainy of a vile career,
 And bade me follow the imposter here
75 To see how gross his impudence could be,
 And force him to restore your property.
 Your private papers, by the King's command,
 I hereby seize and give into your hand.
 The King, by royal order, invalidates
80 The deed which gave this rascal your estates,
 And pardons, furthermore, your grave offense
 In harboring an exile's documents.
 By these decrees, our Prince rewards you for
 Your loyal deeds in the late civil war,
85 And shows how heartfelt is his satisfaction
 In recompensing any worthy action,
 How much he prizes merit, and how he makes
 More of men's virtues than of their mistakes.
 DORINE Heaven be praised!
90 MADAME PERNELLE   I breathe again, at last.
 ELMIRE We're safe.
 MARIANE   I can't believe the danger's past.
 ORGON (*to* TARTUFFE)
 Well, traitor, now you see . . .
95 CLÉANTE   Ah, Brother, please,
 Let's not descend to such indignities.
 Leave the poor wretch to his unhappy fate,
 And don't say anything to aggravate
 His present woes; but rather hope that he
100 Will soon embrace an honest piety,
 And mend his ways, and by a true repentance
 Move our just King to moderate his sentence.
 Meanwhile, go kneel before your sovereign's throne
 And thank him for the mercies he has shown.
105 ORGON Well said: let's go at once and, gladly kneeling,
 Express the gratitude which all are feeling.
 Then, when that first great duty has been done,
 We'll turn with pleasure to a second one,
 And give Valère, whose love has proven so true,
110 The wedded happiness which is his due.

QUESTIONS

Note: Any of these questions, treated in depth, can be a suitable topic for a paper.

1. Discuss the development of Tartuffe's character throughout the play. (Note that we hear about Tartuffe for two acts, and see him only in the last three.)
2. Discuss the relationship of Orgon with his son. What does this relationship contribute to the play?
3. Act IV, Scenes 4–7, which contain the exposure of Tartuffe and the reversal of Orgon's feelings about him, mark a turning-point in the play. Discuss the content of these scenes: why are they an appropriate climax for this comedy?
4. Discuss the roles and characterization of Mariane and Valère. What does their love relationship add to the comedy? How is it worked into the main plot?

5 *Realism*

The late nineteenth and early twentieth centuries mark another period of notable theatrical growth and development throughout Europe—the age of realism. Realism was an international style, popular from Norway and Russia through England, Ireland, and America.

Realism was, of course, a literary style; but it was a style of production as well. Look, for instance, at the opening of *A Doll's House*. Not only does Ibsen carefully list the placement of the four doors and the furniture used in the action; he even details the "copperplate etchings on the walls" and the "deluxe editions" that are to fill the "small bookcase."

Note, too, that Ibsen speaks of the "rear wall," "left wall," and "right wall" of the room. To most of us, this seems quite natural. Of course a room has four walls. Of course three of them are shown onstage and the fourth is imagined to be at the front of the stage. Of course characters enter and exit through doors in these walls; how else does one enter or leave a room? In fact, however, this form of stage setting, known as the "box set," was a new form of stage setting. The box set was far more realistic than the older "wings"; but it was more cumbersome as well, requiring long intermissions between acts to allow for scene changes. Thus, it may have helped to promote the popularity, not only of realistic drama, but also of the one-act play, which is often set in one scene and thus requires no change of scenery.

Realism in production, then, meant sets and costumes as like those of everyday life as possible. In playwriting, it meant plots, characters, and language drawn from everyday life, as well. (Comedy, as usual, retained the right of exaggeration in all these areas.)

In addition, realism implied a new approach to drama. The realistic play hoped to make two impacts on its audience. First, of course, it sought to make the audience sympathize with the plight of its characters. But it also strove to raise in the minds of its audience questions as to the rightness of some aspect of social order, and the desire to change what the dramatist perceived as evil or wrong.

From these goals came a new form of play known as the **realistic drama:** a serious play, usually on a domestic or semi-domestic theme, featuring middle-class (or sometimes lower-class) characters, a contemporary setting, and a plot that questions some aspect or dictate of society.

Take, for example, *A Doll's House* by Henrik Ibsen, a Norwegian playwright who was one of the earliest and most admired of the realists. We see in *A Doll's House,* one of Ibsen's most popular plays, the mixture of elements described above. The scene is unrelievedly domestic. Money and marriage (normally the concerns of comedy) are both major concerns in this play. Yet the movement within the play is more like that of tragedy, being, in general, "from happiness to unhappiness." Comedy usually ends in the making of a marriage. *A Doll's House* details the breakup of one. In line with the domesticity of the scene, we notice a new concern with detail: the clothes Nora wears, the ornaments she puts on her Christmas tree, the macaroons she eats or does not eat all reflect her struggle for self-identity. We see, too, her concern with upbringing: what effect has Nora's father had on her? What effect is she having on her own children? Finally, we observe how the domestic nature of the realistic drama heightens the disparity between what the play's main characters perceive and feel and what is perceived of them by those around them. The onlookers in *Œdipus Rex* and *Antigonê* recognize the magnitude of the struggles they are watching. The onlookers in *A Doll's House* see only a peaceful, prosperous, well-ordered household.

Today, *A Doll's House* is most frequently read as a complaint against the undervaluation and suppression of women. But strong arguments can be made for the theory that Ibsen is showing men and women as equal victims of society's insistence on "respectability." Notice, as you read this play, how the characters are grouped in this regard, how each sins and is sinned against. Consider, too, the ending, which is of a type impossible for both tragedy and comedy. What effect does it have on your response to the play?

Realism and Comedy

Comedy was a favorite form in the nineteenth century, both before and during the age of realism, if only because nineteenth-century theatre and comedy are both strongly oriented towards middle-class characters and dilemmas. Nineteenth-century drama, following the theory that people are creatures of their society, saw its role as portraying and commenting on that society. Comedy, too, sees people in their roles as social beings, and has, since the ancient Greeks, been willing to comment on individuals and society alike.

Sometimes, as in *Tartuffe*, comedy sets the folly of an individual against the good sense of society at large. At other times, a rebellious hero and/or heroine fight on the side of love and nature, against the follies of society. In either case, society is usually the victor. No matter how hard comic characters may struggle to escape the bonds of society—no matter what unusual methods they may use to outwit other characters or to solve some particular conflict between society's dictates and their own desires—at the play's end they return to the very society they've been fighting. The conflict has been solved, the goal or the marriage won; and society promises to go on exactly as it did before.

Seldom is this game of struggle and surrender more clearly played out than in Oscar Wilde's *The Importance of Being Earnest*. The lovers in this comedy belong to Society with a capital S—a carefully defined world admitting only those who can claim proper birth, breeding, and behavior. Lady Bracknell epitomizes the protocols of this world and seeks to govern (that is, to manipulate the lovers) in its name. The young men, Jack and Algernon, try to manipulate the rules of social behavior, escaping their responsibilities whenever possible; the young women, Cecily and Gwendolyn, manipulate social rules and individuals alike in order to attain their desires. And the entire comedy of maneuver and counter-maneuver is accompanied by Algernon's relentless commentary on social pretense and psychological realities.

In contrast to the seriousness of *Tartuffe*, *The Importance of Being Earnest* is a farce. It contains a patently absurd plot, and makes no pretense to depth of characterization. The characters perform the plot's ridiculous actions with verve, however, even while mocking them, and seem to turn themselves into actors of their own extemporaneous plots, admiring their own wit and postures as they do so. Everything seems to center on pretense and dialogue; most of the characters are devoted practitioners of the verbal arts of epigram and paradox, witty speech and polished writing. Thus, Algernon defends a witticism by claiming that "It is perfectly phrased! and quite as true as any observation in civilized life should be"; Cecily describes her diary as "simply a very young girl's record of her own thoughts and impressions, and consequently meant for publication"; Jack, as a baby, is mistakenly substituted not for another baby (which would be a normal comic error), but for "a three-volume novel of more than usually revolting sentimentality."

Like his greater contemporary, George Bernard Shaw, Oscar Wilde uses outrageous yet witty dialogue to create an ironic view that illuminates and dismisses the surface conventions of life. Each jest, pun, or paradox by itself may seem trifling; but their cumulative effect, built as they are around a plot that takes nothing except eating seriously, is that of a distinctive and thorough-going social criticism.

Realism and Tragedy

Tragedy did not fare well during the nineteenth century, for several reasons. First, tragedy took kings and princes for its heroes, not members of the middle class. Second, it tended to insist that these kings and princes speak poetry, a speech form not well suited to discussion of everyday matters. Third, tragedy traditionally portrayed its heroes as people who have power over their societies: Oedipus, Hamlet, and Claudius are directly responsible for the physical and moral health of Thebes and of Denmark. And this characteristic of tragedy did not fit well with the trend of nineteenth-century drama to depict people as beings shaped by the society in which they had been born and reared. The thrust towards realism was thus antithetical to the grand tragedies of the classic and Renaissance styles; and attempts by nineteenth-century playwrights to reproduce some of that grandeur were generally failures.

Once realism was firmly established, however, the twentieth century could try variations on its theme; and some of these variations recreated tragedy as a newly effective form. Some of these new tragedies were written in poetry, but most were in prose—though in some few cases the prose is so artfully handled that it almost becomes poetry.

Glaspell's *Trifles* is a gripping blend of the realistic and tragic. It achieves this effect by presenting two sets of characters: five realistic ones, who carry all the speech and action of the play; and two tragic ones, who never appear onstage but whose actions form the focus of concern for the other five. When the play begins, the tragic roles have already been played out: the antagonist has been murdered, and the protagonist is in jail, charged with the crime. The play thus functions largely as a detective story, as its five characters puzzle out the possible whys and wherefores of the murder, sifting through the extremely realistic "trifles" of everyday rural life in search of the answers. Almost like the two halves of a Greek chorus, these three men and two women seek to understand, in practical terms, the forces that have moved the protagonist into her current fearful isolation and led to her husband's death. The successive discoveries that unveil the mystery, and the tensions within and between the characters as their search progresses, create the power and movement of the play. The working-out of the realistic "puzzle" thus exposes the finality and inevitability of the tragic situation. For the women in the play, the result becomes a new dilemma. For the audience, equally faced with a blend of intellectual challenge and emotional demand, there is a similar demand for judgment: how do we judge all seven characters, the five onstage and the two off?

The layering of action and reaction in this play, the mixture of judgment and sympathy asked first of Mrs. Hale and Mrs. Peters and then of us, produces a play well worth seeing and reading. (It's also a good play to read aloud, or to act out.) In addition, the types of questions this play asks and the complexity of response that they demand illustrate one of the major trends (one might almost say, philosophies) of twentieth-century American literature.

HENRIK IBSEN (1828–1906)

A Doll's House

A new translation by Otto Reinert

C H A R A C T E R S

___

Torvald Helmer, *a lawyer*
Nora, *his wife*
Dr. Rank
Mrs. Linde
Krogstad
The Helmers' three small children
Anne-Marie, *the children's nurse*
A Housemaid
A Porter

scene. *The Helmers' living room.*

ACT I

A pleasant, tastefully but not expensively furnished, living room. A door on the rear wall, right, leads to the front hall, another door, left, to Helmer's *study. Between the two doors a piano. A third door in the middle of the left wall; further front a window. Near the window a round table and a small couch. Towards the rear of the right wall a fourth door; further front a tile stove with a rocking chair and a couple of armchairs in front of it. Between the stove and the door a small table. Copperplate etchings on the walls. A whatnot with porcelain figurines and other small objects. A small bookcase with de luxe editions. A rug on the floor; fire in the stove. Winter day.*

The doorbell rings, then the sound of the front door opening. Nora, *dressed for outdoors, enters, humming cheerfully. She carries several packages, which she puts down on the table, right. She leaves the door to the front hall open; there a* Porter *is seen holding a Christmas tree and a basket. He gives them to the* Maid *who has let them in.*

nora Be sure to hide the Christmas tree, Helene. The children mustn't see it before tonight when we've trimmed it. (*Opens her purse; to the* Porter.) How much?

PORTER   Fifty ore.

NORA   Here's a crown. No, keep the change. (*The* PORTER *thanks her, leaves.* NORA *closes the door. She keeps laughing quietly to herself as she takes off her coat, etc. She takes a bag of macaroons from her pocket and eats a couple. She walks cautiously over to the door to the study and listens.*) Yes, he's home. (*Resumes her humming, walks over to the table, right.*)

HELMER   (*in his study*)   Is that my little lark twittering out there?

NORA   (*opening some packages*)   That's right.

HELMER   My squirrel bustling about?

NORA   Yes.

HELMER   When did squirrel come home?

NORA   Just now. (*Puts the bag of macaroons back in her pocket, wipes her mouth.*) Come out here, Torvald. I want to show you what I've bought.

HELMER   I'm busy! (*After a little while he opens the door and looks in, pen in hand.*) Bought, eh? All that? So little wastrel has been throwing money around again?

NORA   Oh but Torvald, this Christmas we can be a little extravagant, can't we? It's the first Christmas we don't have to scrimp.

HELMER   I don't know about that. We certainly don't have money to waste.

NORA   Yes, Torvald, we do. A little, anyway. Just a tiny little bit? Now that you're going to get that big salary and make lots and lots of money.

HELMER   Starting at New Year's, yes. But payday isn't till the end of the quarter.

NORA   That doesn't matter. We can always borrow.

HELMER   Nora! (*Goes over to her and playfully pulls her ear.*) There you go being irresponsible again. Suppose I borrowed a thousand crowns today and you spent it all for Christmas and on New Year's Eve a tile hit me in the head and laid me out cold.

NORA   (*putting her hand over his mouth*)   I won't have you say such horrid things.

HELMER   But suppose it happened. Then what?

NORA   If it did, I wouldn't care whether we owed money or not.

HELMER   But what about the people I had borrowed from?

NORA   Who cares about them! They are strangers.

HELMER   Nora, Nora, you *are* a woman! No, really! You know how I feel about that. No debts! A home in debt isn't a free home, and if it isn't free it isn't beautiful. We've managed nicely so far, you and I, and that's the way we'll go on. It won't be for much longer.

NORA (*walks over toward the stove*)   All right, Torvald. Whatever you say.

HELMER (*follows her*)   Come, come, my little songbird mustn't droop her wings. What's this? Can't have a pouty squirrel in the house, you know. (*Takes out his wallet.*) Nora, what do you think I have here?

NORA (*turns around quickly*)   Money!

HELMER   Here. (*Gives her some bills.*) Don't you think I know Christmas is expensive?

NORA (*counting*)   Ten—twenty—thirty—forty. Thank you, thank you, Torvald. This helps a lot.

HELMER   I certainly hope so.

NORA   It does, it does. But I want to show you what I got. It was cheap, too. Look. New clothes for Ivar. And a sword. And a horse and trumpet for Bob. And a doll and a little bed for Emmy. It isn't any good, but it wouldn't last, anyway. And here's some dress material and scarves for the maids. I feel bad about old Anne-Marie, though. She really should be getting much more.

HELMER   And what's in here?

NORA (*cries*)   Not till tonight!

HELMER   I see. But now what does my little prodigal have in mind for herself?

NORA   Oh, nothing. I really don't care.

HELMER   Of course you do. Tell me what you'd like. Within reason.

NORA   Oh, I don't know. Really, I don't. The only thing—

HELMER   Well?

NORA (*fiddling with his buttons, without looking at him*)   If you really want to give me something, you might—you could—

HELMER   All right, let's have it.

NORA (*quickly*)   Some money, Torvald. Just as much as you think you can spare. Then I'll buy myself something one of these days.

HELMER   No, really Nora—

NORA   Oh yes, please, Torvald. Please? I'll wrap the money in pretty gold paper and hang it on the tree. Won't that be nice?

HELMER   What's the name for little birds that are always spending money?

NORA   Wastrels, I know. But please let's do it my way, Torvald. Then I'll have time to decide what I need most. Now that's sensible, isn't it?

HELMER (*smiling*)   Oh, very sensible. That is, if you really bought yourself something you could use. But it all disappears in the household expenses or you buy things you don't need. And then you come back to me for more.

NORA   Oh, but Torvald—

HELMER   That's the truth, dear little Nora, and you know it. (*Puts his arm around her.*) My wastrel is a little sweetheart, but she *does* go through an awful lot of money awfully fast. You've no idea how expensive it is for a man to keep a wastrel.

NORA   That's not fair, Torvald. I really save all I can.

HELMER (*laughs*)   Oh, I believe that. All you can. Meaning, exactly nothing!

NORA (*hums, smiles mysteriously*)   You don't know all the things we songbirds and squirrels need money for, Torvald.

HELMER   You know, you're funny. Just like your father. You're always looking for ways to get money, but as soon as you do it runs through your fingers and you can never say what you spent it for. Well, I guess I'll just have to take you the way you are. It's in your blood. Yes, that sort of thing is hereditary, Nora.

NORA   In that case, I wish I had inherited many of Daddy's qualities.

HELMER   And I don't want you any different from just what you are—my own sweet little songbird. Hey!—I think I just noticed something. Aren't you looking—what's the word?—a little—sly—?

NORA   I am?

HELMER   You definitely are. Look at me.

NORA (*looks at him*)   Well?

HELMER (*wagging a finger*)   Little sweet-tooth hasn't by any chance been on a rampage today, has she?

NORA   Of course not. Whatever makes you think that?

HELMER   A little detour by the pastryshop maybe?

NORA   No, I assure you, Torvald—

HELMER   Nibbled a little jam?

NORA   Certainly not!

HELMER   Munched a macaroon or two?

NORA   No, really, Torvald, I honestly—

HELMER   All right. Of course I was only joking.

NORA (*walks toward the table, right*)   You know I wouldn't do anything to displease you.

HELMER   I know. And I have your promise. (*Over to her.*) All right, keep your little Christmas secrets to yourself, Nora darling. They'll all come out tonight, I suppose, when we light the tree.

NORA   Did you remember to invite Rank?

HELMER   No, but there's no need to. He knows he'll have dinner with us. Anyway, I'll see him later this morning. I'll ask him then. I did order some good wine. Oh Nora, you've no idea how much I'm looking forward to tonight!

NORA   Me, too. And the children Torvald! They'll have such a good time!

HELMER   You know, it *is* nice to have a good, safe job and a comfortable income. Feels good just thinking about it. Don't you agree?

NORA   Oh, it's wonderful!

HELMER   Remember last Christmas? For three whole weeks you shut yourself up every evening till long after midnight making ornaments for the Christmas tree and I don't know what else. Some big surprise for all of us, anyway. I'll be damned if I've ever been so bored in my whole life!

NORA   I wasn't bored at all!

HELMER   (*smiling*)   But you've got to admit you didn't have much to show for it in the end.

NORA   Oh, don't tease me again about that! Could I help it that the cat got in and tore up everything?

HELMER   Of course you couldn't, my poor little Nora. You just wanted to please the rest of us, and that's the important thing. But I *am* glad the hard times are behind us. Aren't you?

NORA   Oh yes. I think it's just wonderful.

HELMER   This year, I won't be bored and lonely. And you won't have to strain your dear eyes and your delicate little hands—

NORA   (*claps her hands*)   No I won't, will I Torvald? Oh, how wonderful, how lovely, to hear you say that! (*Puts her arm under his.*) Let me tell you how I think we should arrange things, Torvald. Soon as Christmas is over—(*The doorbell rings.*) Someone's at the door. (*Straightens things up a bit.*) A caller, I suppose. Bother!

HELMER   Remember, I'm not home for visitors.

THE MAID   (*in the door to the front hall*)   Ma'am, there's a lady here—

NORA   All right. Ask her to come in.

THE MAID   (*to* HELMER)   And the Doctor just arrived.

HELMER   Is he in the study?

THE MAID   Yes, sir.

(HELMER *exits into his study.* THE MAID *shows* MRS. LINDE *in and closes the door behind her as she leaves.* MRS. LINDE *is in travel dress.*)

MRS. LINDE   (*timid and a little hesitant*)   Good morning, Nora.

NORA   (*uncertainly*)   Good morning.

MRS. LINDE   I don't believe you know who I am.

NORA   No—I'm not sure—Though I know I should— Of course! Kristine! It's you!

MRS. LINDE   Yes, it's me.

NORA   And I didn't even recognize you! I had no idea (*In a lower voice.*) You've changed, Kristine.

MRS. LINDE   I'm sure I have. It's been nine or ten long years.

NORA   Has it really been that long? Yes, you're right. I've been so happy these last eight years. And now you're here. Such a long trip in the middle of winter. How brave!

MRS. LINDE   I got in on the steamer this morning.

NORA   To have some fun over the holidays, of course. That's lovely. For we are going to have fun. But take off your coat! You aren't cold, are you? (*Helps her.*) There, now! Let's sit down here by the fire and just relax and talk. No, you sit there. I want the rocking chair. (*Takes her hands.*) And now you've got your old face back. It was just for a minute, right at first—Though you are a little more pale, Kristine. And maybe a little thinner.

MRS. LINDE   And much, much older, Nora.

NORA   Maybe a little older. Just a teeny-weeny bit, not much. (*Interrupts herself, serious.*) Oh, but how thoughtless of me, chatting away like this! Sweet, good Kristine, can you forgive me?

MRS. LINDE   Forgive you what, Nora?

NORA   (*in a low voice*) You poor dear, you lost your husband, didn't you?

MRS. LINDE   Three years ago, yes.

NORA   I know. I saw it in the paper. Oh please believe me, Kristine. I really meant to write you, but I never got around to it. Something was always coming up.

MRS. LINDE   Of course, Nora. I understand.

NORA   No, that wasn't very nice of me. You poor thing, all you must have been through. And he didn't leave you much, either, did he?

MRS. LINDE   No.

NORA   And no children?

MRS. LINDE   No.

NORA   Nothing at all, in other words?

MRS. LINDE   Not so much as a sense of loss—a grief to live on—

NORA   (*incredulous*) But Kristine, how can that *be*?

MRS. LINDE   (*with a sad smile, strokes* NORA's *hair*) That's the way it sometimes is, Nora.

NORA   All alone. How awful for you. I have three darling children. You can't see them right now, though; they're out with their nurse. But now you must tell me everything—

MRS. LINDE   No, no; I'd rather listen to you.

NORA   No, you begin. Today I won't be selfish. Today I'll think only of you. Except there's one thing I've just got to tell you first. Something marvelous that's happened to us just these last few days. You haven't heard, have you?

MRS. LINDE   No; tell me.

NORA Just think. My husband's been made manager of the Mutual Bank.

MRS. LINDE Your husband —! Oh, I'm so glad!

NORA Yes, isn't that great? You see, private law practice is so uncertain, especially when you won't have anything to do with cases that aren't—you know—quite nice. And of course Torvald won't do that and I quite agree with him. Oh, you've no idea how delighted we are! He takes over at New Year's, and he'll be getting a big salary and all sorts of extras. From now on we'll be able to live in quite a different way—exactly as we like. Oh, Kristine! I feel so carefree and happy! It's lovely to have lots and lots of money and not have to worry about a thing! Don't you agree?

MRS. LINDE It would be nice to have enough at any rate.

NORA No, I don't mean just enough. I mean lots and lots!

MRS. LINDE (*smiles*) Nora, Nora, when are you going to be sensible? In school you spent a great deal of money.

NORA (*quietly laughing*) Yes, and Torvald says I still do. (*Raises her finger at* MRS. LINDE.) But "Nora, Nora" isn't so crazy as you all think. Believe me, we've had nothing to be extravagant with. We've both had to work.

MRS. LINDE You too?

NORA Yes. Oh, it's been little things, mostly—sewing, crocheting, embroidery—that sort of thing. (*Casually.*) And other things too. You know, of course, that Torvald left government service when we got married? There was no chance of promotion in his department, and of course he had to make more money than he had been making. So for the first few years he worked altogether too hard. He had to take jobs on the side and work night and day. It turned out to be too much for him. He became seriously ill. The doctors told him he needed to go south.

MRS. LINDE That's right; you spent a year in Italy, didn't you?

NORA Yes, we did. But you won't believe how hard it was to get away. Ivar had just been born. But of course we had to go. Oh, it was a wonderful trip. And it saved Torvald's life. But it took a lot of money, Kristine.

MRS. LINDE I'm sure it did.

NORA Twelve hundred specie dollars. Four thousand eight hundred crowns. That's a lot of money.

MRS. LINDE Yes. So it's lucky you have it when something like that happens.

NORA Well, actually we got the money from Daddy.

MRS. LINDE I see. That was about the time your father died, I believe.

NORA   Yes, just about then. And I couldn't even go and take care of him. I was expecting little Ivar any day. And I had poor Torvald to look after, desperately sick and all. My dear, good Daddy! I never saw him again, Kristine. That's the saddest thing that's happened to me since I got married.

MRS. LINDE   I know you were very fond of him. But then you went to Italy?

NORA   Yes, for now we had the money, and the doctors urged us to go. So we left about a month later.

MRS. LINDE   And when you came back your husband was well again?

NORA   Healthy as a horse!

MRS. LINDE   But—the doctor?

NORA   What do you mean?

MRS. LINDE   I thought the maid said it was the doctor, that gentleman who came the same time I did.

NORA   Oh, that's Dr. Rank. He doesn't come as a doctor. He's our closest friend. He looks in at least once every day. No, Torvald hasn't been sick once since then. And the children are strong and healthy, too, and so am I. (*Jumps up and claps her hands.*) Oh God, Kristine! Isn't it wonderful to be alive and happy! Isn't it just lovely!—But now I'm being mean again, talking only about myself and my things. (*Sits down on a footstool close to* MRS. LINDE *and puts her arm on her lap.*) Please don't be angry with me! Tell me, is it really true that you didn't care for your husband? Then why did you marry him?

MRS. LINDE   Mother was still alive then, but she was bedridden and helpless. And I had my two younger brothers to look after. I didn't think I had the right to turn him down.

NORA   No, I suppose not. So he had money then?

MRS. LINDE   He was quite well off, I think. But it was an uncertain business, Nora. When he died, the whole thing collapsed and there was nothing left.

NORA   And then—?

MRS. LINDE   Well, I had to manage as best I could. With a little store and a little school and anything else I could think of. The last three years have been one long work day for me, Nora, without any rest. But now it's over. My poor mother doesn't need me any more. She's passed away. And the boys are on their own too. They've both got jobs and support themselves.

NORA   What a relief for you—

MRS. LINDE   No, not relief. Just a great emptiness. Nobody to live for any more. (*Gets up restlessly.*) That's why I couldn't stand it any longer in that little hole. Here in town it has to be easier to find something to keep me busy and occupy my thoughts. With a little luck I should be able to find a permanent job, something in an office—

NORA   Oh but Kristine, that's exhausting work, and you look worn out already. It would be much better for you to go to a resort.

MRS. LINDE (*walks over to the window*)   I don't have a Daddy who can give me the money, Nora.

NORA (*getting up*)   Oh, don't be angry with me.

MRS. LINDE (*over to her*)   Dear Nora, don't *you* be angry with *me*. That's the worst thing about my kind of situation: you become so bitter. You've nobody to work for, and yet you have to look out for yourself, somehow. You've got to keep on living, and so you become selfish. Do you know—when you told me about your husband's new position I was delighted not so much for your sake as for my own.

NORA   Why was that? Oh, I see. You think maybe Torvald can give you a job?

MRS. LINDE   That's what I had in mind.

NORA   And he will too, Kristine. Just leave it to me. I'll be ever so subtle about it. I'll think of something nice to tell him, something he'll like. Oh I so much want to help you.

MRS. LINDE   That's very good of you, Nora—making an effort like that for me. Especially since you've known so little trouble and hardship in your own life.

NORA   I—?—have known so little—?

MRS. LINDE (*smiling*)   Oh well, a little sewing or whatever it was. You're still a child, Nora.

NORA (*with a toss of her head, walks away*)   You shouldn't sound so superior.

MRS. LINDE   I shouldn't?

NORA   You're just like all the others. None of you think I'm good for anything really serious.

MRS. LINDE   Well, now—

NORA   That I've never been through anything difficult.

MRS. LINDE   But Nora! You just told me all your troubles!

NORA   That's nothing! (*Lowers her voice.*) I haven't told you about *it*.

MRS. LINDE   It? What's that? What do you mean?

NORA   You patronize me, Kristine, and that's not fair. You're proud that you worked so long and so hard for your mother.

MRS. LINDE   I don't think I patronize anyone. But it *is* true that I'm both proud and happy that I could make mother's last years comparatively easy.

NORA   And you're proud of all you did for your brothers.

MRS. LINDE   I think I have the right to be.

NORA   And so do I. But now I want to tell you something, Kristine. I have something to be proud and happy about too.

MRS. LINDE   I don't doubt that for a moment. But what exactly do you mean?

NORA   Not so loud! Torvald mustn't hear—not for anything in the world. Nobody must know about this, Kristine. Nobody but you.

MRS. LINDE   But what is it?

NORA   Come here. (*Pulls her down on the couch beside her.*) You see, I *do* have something to be proud and happy about. I've saved Torvald's life.

MRS. LINDE   Saved—? How do you mean—"saved"?

NORA   I told you about our trip to Italy. Torvald would have died if he hadn't gone.

MRS. LINDE   I understand that. And so your father gave you the money you needed.

NORA   (*smiles*)   Yes, that's what Torvald and all the others think. But—

MRS. LINDE   But what?

NORA   Daddy didn't give us a penny. *I* raised that money.

MRS. LINDE   *You* did? That whole big amount?

NORA   Twelve hundred specie dollars. Four thousand eight hundred crowns. *Now* what do you say?

MRS. LINDE   But Nora, how could you? Did you win in the state lottery?

NORA   (*contemptuously*)   State lottery! (*Snorts.*) What is so great about that?

MRS. LINDE   Where did it come from then?

NORA   (*humming and smiling, enjoying her secret*)   Hmmm. Tra-la-la-la-la!

MRS. LINDE   You certainly couldn't have borrowed it.

NORA   Oh? And why not?

MRS. LINDE   A wife can't borrow money without her husband's consent.

NORA   (*with a toss of her head*)   Oh, I don't know—take a wife with a little bit of a head for business—a wife who knows how to manage things—

MRS. LINDE   But Nora, I don't understand at all—

NORA   You don't have to. I didn't say I borrowed the money, did I? I could have gotten it some other way. (*Leans back.*) An admirer may have given it to me. When you're as tolerably good-looking as I am—

MRS. LINDE   Oh, you're crazy.

NORA   I think you're dying from curiosity, Kristine.

MRS. LINDE   I'm beginning to think you've done something very foolish, Nora.

NORA (*sits up*)   Is it foolish to save your husband's life?

MRS. LINDE   I say it's foolish to act behind his back.

NORA   But don't you see: he couldn't be told! You're missing the whole point, Kristine. We couldn't even let him know how seriously ill he was. The doctors came to *me* and told me his life was in danger, that nothing could save him but a stay in the south. Don't you think I tried to work on him? I told him how lovely it would be if I could go abroad like other young wives. I cried and begged. I said he'd better remember what condition I was in, that he had to be nice to me and do what I wanted. I even hinted he could borrow the money. But that almost made him angry with me. He told me I was being irresponsible and that it was his duty as my husband not to give in to my moods and whims—I think that's what he called it. All right, I said to myself, you've got to be saved somehow, and so I found a way—

MRS. LINDE   And your husband never learned from your father that the money didn't come from him?

NORA   Never. Daddy died that same week. I thought of telling him all about it and ask him not to say anything. But since he was so sick—It turned out I didn't have to—

MRS. LINDE   And you've never told your husband?

NORA   Of course not! Good heavens, how could I? He, with his strict principles! Besides, you know how men are. Torvald would find it embarrassing and humiliating to learn that he owed me anything. It would upset our whole relationship. Our happy, beautiful home would no longer be what it is.

MRS. LINDE   Aren't you ever going to tell him?

NORA (*reflectively, half smiling*)   Yes—one day, maybe. Many, many years from now, when I'm no longer young and pretty. Don't laugh! I mean when Torvald no longer feels about me the way he does now, when he no longer thinks it's fun when I dance for him and put on costumes and recite for him. Then it will be good to have something in reserve—(*Interrupts herself.*) Oh, I'm just being silly! That day will never come.—Well, now, Kristine, what do you think of my great secret? Don't you think I'm good for something too?—By the way, you wouldn't believe all the worry I've had because of it. It's been very hard to meet my obligations on schedule. You see, in business there's something called quarterly interest and something called installments on the principal, and those are terribly hard to come up with. I've had to save a little here and a little there, whenever I could. I couldn't use much of the housekeeping money, for Torvald has to eat well.

And I couldn't use what I got for clothes for the children. They have to look nice, and I didn't think it would be right to spend less than I got—the sweet little things!

MRS. LINDE   Poor Nora! So you had to take it from your own allowance!

NORA   Yes, of course. After all, it was my affair. Every time Torvald gave me money for a new dress and things like that, I never used more than half of it. I always bought the cheapest, simplest things for myself. Thank God, everything looks good on me, so Torvald never noticed. But it was hard many times, Kristine, for it's fun to have pretty clothes. Don't you think?

MRS. LINDE   Certainly.

NORA   Anyway, I had other ways of making money too. Last winter I was lucky enough to get some copying work. So I locked the door and sat up writing every night till quite late. God! I often got so tired—! But it was great fun, too, working and making money. It was almost like being a man.

MRS. LINDE   But how much have you been able to pay off this way?

NORA   I couldn't tell you exactly. You see, it's very difficult to keep track of business like that. All I know is I have been paying off as much as I've been able to scrape together. Many times I just didn't know what to do. (*Smiles.*) Then I used to imagine a rich old gentleman had fallen in love with me—

MRS. LINDE   What! What old gentleman?

NORA   Phooey! And now he was dead and they were reading his will, and there it said in big letters, "All my money is to be paid in cash immediately to the charming Mrs. Nora Helmer."

MRS. LINDE   But dearest Nora—who *was* this old gentleman?

NORA   For heaven's sake, Kristine, don't you see? There *was* no old gentleman. He was just somebody I made up when I couldn't think of any way to raise the money. But never mind him. The old bore can be anyone he likes to for all I care. I have no use for him or his last will, for now I don't have a single worry in the world. (*Jumps up.*) Dear God, what a lovely thought this is! To be able to play and have fun with the children, to have everything nice and pretty in the house, just the way Torvald likes it! Not a care! And soon spring will be here, and the air will be blue and high. Maybe we can travel again. Maybe I'll see the ocean again! Oh, yes, yes!—it's wonderful to be alive and happy!

The doorbell rings.

MRS. LINDE   (*getting up*) There's the doorbell. Maybe I better be going.

NORA   No, please stay. I'm sure it's just someone for Torvald—

THE MAID (*in the hall door*) Excuse me, ma'am. There's a gentleman here who'd like to see Mr. Helmer.

NORA You mean the bank manager.

THE MAID Sorry, ma'am; the bank manager. But I didn't know—since the Doctor is with him—

NORA Who is the gentleman?

KROGSTAD (*appearing in the door*) It's just me, Mrs. Helmer.

MRS. LINDE *starts, looks, turns away toward the window.*

NORA (*takes a step toward him, tense, in a low voice*) You? What do you want? What do you want with my husband?

KROGSTAD Bank business—in a way. I have a small job in the Mutual, and I understand your husband is going to be our new boss—

NORA So it's just—

KROGSTAD Just routine business, ma'am. Nothing else.

NORA All right. In that case, why don't you go through the door to the office.

Dismisses him casually as she closes the door. Walks over to the stove and tends the fire.

MRS. LINDE Nora—who was that man?

NORA His name's Krogstad. He's a lawyer.

MRS. LINDE So it *was* him.

NORA Do you know him?

MRS. LINDE I used to—many years ago. For a while he clerked in our part of the country.

NORA Right. He did.

MRS. LINDE He has changed a great deal.

NORA I believe he had a very unhappy marriage.

MRS. LINDE And now he's a widower, isn't he?

NORA With many children. There now; it's burning nicely again. (*Closes the stove and moves the rocking chair a little to the side.*)

MRS. LINDE They say he's into all sorts of business.

NORA Really? Maybe so. I wouldn't know. But let's not think about business. It's such a bore.

DR. RANK (*appears in the door to* HELMER'S *study.*) No. I don't want to be in the way. I'd rather talk to your wife a bit. (*Closes the door and notices* MRS. LINDE.) Oh, I beg your pardon. I believe I'm in the way here too.

NORA No, not at all. (*Introduces them.*) Dr. Rank. Mrs. Linde.

RANK Aha. A name often heard in this house. I believe I passed you on the stairs coming up.

MRS. LINDE Yes. I'm afraid I climb stairs very slowly. They aren't good for me.

RANK   I see. A slight case of inner decay, perhaps?

MRS. LINDE   Overwork, rather.

RANK   Oh, is that all? And now you've come to town to relax at all the parties?

MRS. LINDE   I have come to look for a job.

RANK   A proven cure for overwork, I take it?

MRS. LINDE   One has to live, Doctor.

RANK   Yes, that seems to be the common opinion.

NORA   Come on, Dr. Rank—you want to live just as much as the rest of us.

RANK   Of course I do. Miserable as I am, I prefer to go on being tortured as long as possible. All my patients feel the same way. And that's true of the moral invalids too. Helmer is talking with a specimen right this minute.

MRS. LINDE   (*in a low voice*)   Ah!

NORA   What do you mean?

RANK   Oh, this lawyer, Krogstad. You don't know him. The roots of his character are decayed. But even he began by saying something about having *to live*—as if it were a matter of the highest importance.

NORA   Oh? What did he want with Torvald?

RANK   I don't really know. All I heard was something about the bank.

NORA   I didn't know that Krog—that this Krogstad had anything to do with the Mutual Bank.

RANK   Yes, he seems to have some kind of job there. (*To* MRS. LINDE.) I don't know if you are familiar in your part of the country with the kind of person who is always running around trying to sniff out cases of moral decrepitude and as soon as he finds one puts the individual under observation in some excellent position or other. All the healthy ones are left out in the cold.

MRS. LINDE   I should think it's the sick who need looking after the most.

RANK   (*shrugs his shoulders*)   There we are. That's the attitude that turns society into a hospital.

(NORA, *absorbed in her own thoughts, suddenly starts giggling and clapping her hands.*)

RANK   What's so funny about that? Do you even know what society is?

NORA   What do I care about your stupid society! I laughed at something entirely different—something terribly amusing. Tell me, Dr. Rank—all the employees in the Mutual Bank, from now on they'll all be dependent on Torvald, right?

RANK   Is that what you find so enormously amusing?

NORA   (*smiles and hums*)   That's my business, that's my business!
(*Walks around.*) Yes, I do think it's fun that we—that Torvald
is going to have so much influence on so many people's lives.
(*Brings out the bag of macaroons.*) Have a macaroon, Dr. Rank.

RANK   Well, well—macaroons. I thought they were banned around
here.

NORA   Yes, but these were some that Kristine gave me.

MRS. LINDE   What! I?

NORA   That's all right. Don't look so scared. You couldn't know that
Torvald won't let me have them. He's afraid they'll ruin my teeth.
But who cares! Just once in a while—! Right, Dr. Rank? Have
one! (*Puts a macaroon into his mouth.*) You too, Kristine. And
one for me. A very small one. Or at most two. (*Walks around
again.*) Yes, I really feel very, very happy. Now there's just one
thing I'm dying to do.

RANK   Oh, And what's that?

NORA   Something I'm dying to say so Torvald could hear.

RANK   And why can't you?

NORA   I don't dare to, for it's not nice.

MRS. LINDE   Not nice?

RANK   In that case, I guess you'd better not. But surely to the two
of us—? What is it you'd like to say for Helmer to hear?

NORA   I want to say, "Goddammit!"

RANK   Are you out of your mind!

MRS. LINDE   For heaven's sake, Nora!

RANK   Say it. Here he comes.

NORA   (*hiding the macaroons*).   Shhh!

(*HELMER enters from his study, carrying his hat and overcoat.*)

NORA   (*going to him*)   Well, dear, did you get rid of him?

HELMER   Yes, he just left.

NORA   Torvald, I want you to meet Kristine. She's just come to
town.

HELMER   Kristine—? I'm sorry; I don't think—

NORA   Mrs. Linde, Torvald dear. Mrs. Kristine Linde.

HELMER   Ah, yes. A childhood friend of my wife's, I suppose.

MRS. LINDE   Yes, we've known each other for a long time.

NORA   Just think; she has come all this way just to see you.

HELMER   I'm not sure I understand—

MRS. LINDE   Well, not really—

NORA   You see, Kristine is an absolutely fantastic secretary, and she
would so much like to work for a competent executive and learn
more than she knows already—

HELMER   Very sensible, I'm sure, Mrs. Linde.

NORA   So when she heard about your appointment—there was a wire—she came here as fast as she could. How about it, Torvald? Couldn't you do something for Kristine? For my sake. Please?

HELMER   Quite possibly. I take it you're a widow, Mrs. Linde?

MRS. LINDE   Yes.

HELMER   And you've had office experience?

MRS. LINDE   Some—yes.

HELMER   In that case I think it's quite likely that I'll be able to find you a position.

NORA   (*claps her hands*)   I knew it! I knew it!

HELMER   You've arrived at a most opportune time, Mrs. Linde.

MRS. LINDE   Oh, how can I ever thank you—

HELMER   Not at all, not at all. (*Puts his coat on.*) But today you'll have to excuse me—

RANK   Wait a minute; I'll come with you. (*Gets his fur coat from the front hall, warms it by the stove.*)

NORA   Don't be long, Torvald.

HELMER   An hour or so; no more.

NORA   Are you leaving, too, Kristine?

MRS. LINDE   (*putting on her things*)   Yes, I'd better go and find a place to stay.

HELMER   Good. Then we'll be going the same way.

NORA   (*helping her*)   I'm sorry this place is so small, but I don't think we very well could—

MRS. LINDE   Of course! Don't be silly, Nora. Goodbye, and thank you for everything.

NORA   Goodbye. We'll see you soon. You'll be back this evening, of course. And you too, Dr. Rank; right? If you feel well enough? Of course you will. Just wrap yourself up.

(*General small talk as all exit into the hall. Children's voices are heard on the stairs.*)

NORA   There they are! There they are! (*She runs and opens the door. The nurse* ANNE-MARIE *enters with the children.*)

NORA   Come in! Come in! (*Bends over and kisses them.*) Oh, you sweet, sweet darlings! Look at them, Kristine! Aren't they beautiful?

RANK   No standing around in the draft!

HELMER   Come along, Mrs. Linde. This place isn't fit for anyone but mothers right now.

(DR. RANK, HELMER, *and* MRS. LINDE *go down the stairs. The* NURSE *enters the living room with the children.* NORA *follows, closing the door behind her.*)

NORA My, how nice you all look! Such red cheeks! Like apples and roses. (*The children all talk at the same time.*) You've had so much fun? I bet you have. Oh, isn't that nice! You pulled both Emmy and Bob on your sleigh? Both at the same time? That's very good, Ivar. Oh, let me hold her for a minute, Anne-Marie. My sweet little doll baby! (*Takes the smallest of the children from the* NURSE *and dances with her.*) Yes, yes, of course; Mama'll dance with you too, Bob. What? You threw snowballs? Oh, I wish I'd been there! No, no; *I* want to take their clothes off, Anne-Marie. Please let me; I think it's so much fun. You go on in. You look frozen. There's hot coffee on the stove.

(*The* NURSE *exits into the room to the left.* NORA *takes the children's wraps off and throws them all around. They all keep telling her things at the same time.*)

NORA Oh, really? A big dog ran after you? But it didn't bite you. Of course not. Dogs don't bite sweet little doll babies. Don't peek at the packages, Ivar! What's in them? Wouldn't you like to know! No, no; that's something terrible! Play? You want to play? What do you want to play? Okay, let's play hide-and-seek. Bob hides first. You want me to? All right. I'll go first.

(*Laughing and shouting,* NORA *and the children play in the living room and in the adjacent room, right. Finally,* NORA *hides herself under the table; the children rush in, look for her, can't find her. They hear her low giggle, run to the table, lift the rug that covers it, see her. General hilarity. She crawls out, pretends to scare them. New delight. In the meantime there has been a knock on the door between the living room and the front hall, but nobody has noticed. Now the door is opened halfway;* KROGSTAD *appears. He waits a little. The play goes on.*)

KROGSTAD Pardon me, Mrs. Helmer—

NORA (*with a muted cry turns around, jumps up*) Ah! What do you want?

KROGSTAD I'm sorry. The front door was open. Somebody must have forgotten to close it—

NORA (*standing up*) My husband isn't here, Mr. Krogstad.

KROGSTAD I know.

NORA So what do you want?

KROGSTAD I'd like a word with you.

NORA With—? (*To the children.*) Go in to Anne-Marie. What? No, the strange man won't do anything bad to Mama. When he's gone we'll play some more.

(*She takes the children into the room to the left and closes the door.*)

NORA (*tense, troubled*) You want to speak with me?

KROGSTAD Yes I do.

NORA   Today—? It isn't the first of the month yet.

KROGSTAD   No, it's Christmas Eve. It's up to you what kind of holiday you'll have.

NORA   What do you want? I can't possibly—

KROGSTAD   Let's not talk about that just yet. There's something else. You do have a few minutes, don't you?

NORA   Yes. Yes, of course. That is,—

KROGSTAD   Good. I was sitting in Olsen's restaurant when I saw your husband go by.

NORA   Yes—?

KROGSTAD   —with a lady.

NORA   What of it?

KROGSTAD   May I be so free as to ask: wasn't that lady Mrs. Linde?

NORA   Yes.

KROGSTAD   Just arrived in town?

NORA   Yes, today.

KROGSTAD   She's a good friend of yours, I understand?

NORA   Yes, she is. But I fail to see—

KROGSTAD   I used to know her myself.

NORA   I know that.

KROGSTAD   So you know about that. I thought as much. In that case, let me ask you a simple question. Is Mrs. Linde going to be employed in the bank?

NORA   What makes you think you have the right to cross-examine me like this, Mr. Krogstad—you, one of my husband's employees? But since you ask, I'll tell you. Yes, Mrs. Linde is going to be working in the bank. And it was I who recommended her, Mr. Krogstad. Now you know.

KROGSTAD   So I was right.

NORA   (*walks up and down*)   After all, one does have a little influence, you know. Just because you're a woman, it doesn't mean that—Really, Mr. Krogstad, people in a subordinate position should be careful not to offend someone who—oh well—

KROGSTAD   —has influence?

NORA   Exactly.

KROGSTAD   (*changing his tone*)   Mrs. Helmer, I must ask you to be good enough to use your influence on my behalf.

NORA   What do you mean?

KROGSTAD   I want you to make sure that I am going to keep my subordinate position in the bank.

NORA   I don't understand. Who is going to take your position away from you?

KROGSTAD   There's no point in playing ignorant with me, Mrs. Helmer. I can very well appreciate that your friend would find it unpleasant to run into me. So now I know who I can thank for my dismissal.

NORA But I assure you—

KROGSTAD Never mind. Just want to say you still have time. I advise you to use your influence to prevent it.

NORA But Mr. Krogstad, I don't have any influence—none at all.

KROGSTAD No? I thought you just said—

NORA Of course I didn't mean it that way. I! Whatever makes you think that I have any influence of that kind on my husband?

KROGSTAD I went to law school with your husband. I have no reason to think that the bank manager is less susceptible than other husbands.

NORA If you're going to insult my husband, I'll ask you to leave.

KROGSTAD You're brave, Mrs. Helmer.

NORA I'm not afraid of you any more. After New Year's I'll be out of this thing with you.

KROGSTAD (*more controlled*) Listen, Mrs. Helmer. If necessary I'll fight as for my life to keep my little job in the bank.

NORA So it seems.

KROGSTAD It isn't just the money; that's really the smallest part of it. There is something else—Well, I guess I might as well tell you. It's like this. I'm sure you know, like everybody else, that some years ago I committed—an impropriety.

NORA I believe I've heard it mentioned.

KROGSTAD The case never came to court, but from that moment all doors were closed to me. So I took up the kind of business you know about. I had to do something, and I think I can say about myself that I have not been among the worst. But now I want to get out of all that. My sons are growing up. For their sake I must get back as much of my good name as I can. This job in the bank was like the first rung on the ladder. And now your husband wants to kick me down and leave me back in the mud again.

NORA But I swear to you, Mr. Krogstad; it's not at all in my power to help you.

KROGSTAD That's because you don't want to. But I have the means to force you.

NORA You don't mean you're going to tell my husband I owe you money?

KROGSTAD And if I did?

NORA That would be a mean thing to do. (*Almost crying.*) That secret, which is my joy and my pride—for him to learn about it in such a coarse and ugly manner—to learn it from *you*—! It would be terribly unpleasant for me.

KROGSTAD   Just unpleasant?

NORA (*heatedly*)   But go ahead! Do it! It will be worse for you than for me. When my husband realizes what a bad person you are, you'll be sure to lose your job.

KROGSTAD   I asked you if it was just domestic unpleasantness you were afraid of?

NORA   When my husband finds out, of course he'll pay off the loan, and then we won't have anything more to do with you.

KROGSTAD (*stepping closer*)   Listen, Mrs. Helmer—either you have a very bad memory, or you don't know much about business. I think I had better straighten you out on a few things.

NORA   What do you mean?

KROGSTAD   When your husband was ill, you came to me to borrow twelve hundred dollars.

NORA   I knew nobody else.

KROGSTAD   I promised to get you the money—

NORA   And you did.

KROGSTAD   I promised to get you the money on certain conditions. At the time you were so anxious about your husband's health and so set on getting him away that I doubt very much that you paid much attention to the details of our transaction. That's why I remind you of them now. Anyway, I promised to get you the money if you would sign an I.O.U., which I drafted.

NORA   And which I signed.

KROGSTAD   Good. But below your signature I added a few lines, making your father security for the loan. Your father was supposed to put his signature to those lines.

NORA   Supposed to—? He did.

KROGSTAD   I had left the date blank. That is, your father was to date his own signature. You recall that, don't you, Mrs. Helmer?

NORA   I guess so—

KROGSTAD   I gave the note to you. You were to mail it to your father. Am I correct?

NORA   Yes.

KROGSTAD   And of course you did so right away, for no more than five or six days later you brought the paper back to me, signed by your father. Then I paid you the money.

NORA   Well? And haven't I been keeping up with the payments?

KROGSTAD   Fairly well, yes. But to get back to what we were talking about—those were difficult days for you, weren't they, Mrs. Helmer?

NORA   Yes, they were.

KROGSTAD   Your father was quite ill, I believe.

NORA   He was dying.

KROGSTAD   And died shortly afterwards?

NORA   That's right.

KROGSTAD   Tell me, Mrs. Helmer; do you happen to remember the date of your father's death? I mean the exact day of the month?

NORA   Daddy died on September 29.

KROGSTAD   Quite correct. I have ascertained that fact. That's why there is something peculiar about this (*takes out a piece of paper*), which I can't account for.

NORA   Peculiar? How? I don't understand—

KROGSTAD   It seems very peculiar, Mrs. Helmer, that your father signed this promissory note three days after his death.

NORA   How so? I don't see what—

KROGSTAD   Your father died on September 29. Now look. He has dated his signature October 2. Isn't that odd?

(NORA *remains silent.*)

KROGSTAD   Can you explain it?

(NORA *is still silent.*)

KROGSTAD   I also find it striking that the date and the month and the year are not in your father's handwriting but in a hand I think I recognize. Well, that might be explained. Your father may have forgotten to date his signature and somebody else may have done it here, guessing at the date before he had learned of your father's death. That's all right. It's only the signature itself that matters. And that is genuine, isn't it, Mrs. Helmer? Your father *did* put his name to this note?

NORA   (*after a brief silence tosses her head back and looks defiantly at him*)   No, he didn't. *I* wrote Daddy's name.

KROGSTAD   Mrs. Helmer—do you realize what a dangerous admission you just made?

NORA   Why? You'll get your money soon.

KROGSTAD   Let me ask you something. Why didn't you mail this note to your father?

NORA   Because it was impossible. Daddy was sick—you know that. If I had asked him to sign it, I would have had to tell him what the money was for. But I couldn't tell him, as sick as he was, that my husband's life was in danger. That was impossible. Surely you can see that.

KROGSTAD   Then it would have been better for you if you had given up your trip abroad.

NORA   No, that was impossible! That trip was to save my husband's life. I couldn't give it up.

KROGSTAD   But didn't you realize that what you did amounted to fraud against me?

NORA   I couldn't let that make any difference. I didn't care about you at all. I hated the way you made all those difficulties for me, even though you knew the danger my husband was in. I thought you were cold and unfeeling.

KROGSTAD   Mrs. Helmer, obviously you have no clear idea of what you have done. Let me tell you that what I did that time was no more and no worse. And it ruined my name and reputation.

NORA   You! Are you trying to tell me that you did something brave once in order to save your wife's life?

KROGSTAD   The law doesn't ask about motives.

NORA   Then it's a bad law.

KROGSTAD   Bad or not—if I produce this note in court you'll be judged according to the law.

NORA   I refuse to believe you. A daughter shouldn't have the right to spare her dying old father worry and anxiety? A wife shouldn't have the right to save her husband's life? I don't know the laws very well, but I'm sure that somewhere they make allowance for cases like that. And you, a lawyer, don't know that? I think you must be a bad lawyer, Mr. Krogstad.

KROGSTAD   That may be. But business—the kind of business you and I have with one another—don't you think I know something about that? Very well. Do what you like. But let me tell you this: if I'm going to be kicked out again, you'll keep me company. (*He bows and exits through the front hall.*)

NORA   (*pauses thoughtfully; then, with a defiant toss of her head*) Oh, nonsense! Trying to scare me like that! I'm not all that silly. (*Starts picking up the children's clothes; soon stops.*) But—? No! That's impossible! I did it for love!

THE CHILDREN   (*in the door to the left*) Mama, the strange man just left. We saw him.

NORA   Yes, yes; I know. But don't tell anybody about the strange man. Do you hear? Not even Daddy.

THE CHILDREN   We won't. But now you'll play with us again, won't you, Mama?

NORA   No, not right now.

THE CHILDREN   But Mama—you promised.

NORA   I know, but I can't just now. Go to your own room. I've so much to do. Be nice now, my little darlings. Do as I say. (*She nudges them gently into the other room and closes the door. She sits down on the couch, picks up a piece of embroidery, makes a few stitches, then stops.*) No! (*Throws the embroidery down, goes to the hall door and calls out.*) Helene! Bring the Christmas tree

in here, please! (*Goes to the table, left, opens the drawer, halts.*)
No—that's impossible!

THE MAID (*with the Christmas tree*)   Where do you want it, ma'am?

NORA   There. The middle of the floor.

THE MAID   You want anything else?

NORA   No, thanks. I have everything I need. (THE MAID *goes out.*
NORA *starts trimming the tree.*) I want candles—and flowers—
That awful man! Oh, nonsense! There's nothing wrong. This will
be a lovely tree. I'll do everything you want me to, Torvald. I'll
sing for you—dance for you—

(*Helmer, a bundle of papers under his arm, enters from outside.*)

NORA   Ah—you're back already?

HELMER   Yes. Has anybody been here?

NORA   Here? No.

HELMER   That's funny. I saw Krogstad leaving just now.

NORA   Oh? Oh yes, that's right. Krogstad was here for just a
moment.

HELMER   I can tell from your face that he came to ask you to put
in a word for him.

NORA   Yes.

HELMER   And it was supposed to be your own idea, wasn't it? You
were not to tell me he'd been here. He asked you that too, didn't
he?

NORA   Yes, Torvald, but—

HELMER   Nora, Nora, how could you! Talk to a man like that and
make him promises! And lying to me about it afterwards—!

NORA   Lying—?

HELMER   Didn't you say nobody had been here? (*Shakes his finger
at her.*) My little songbird must never do that again. Songbirds
are supposed to have clean beaks to chirp with—no false notes.
(*Puts his arms around her waist.*) Isn't that so? Of course it is.
(*Lets her go.*) And that's enough about that. (*Sits down in front
of the fireplace.*) Ah, it's nice and warm in here. (*Begins to leaf
through his papers.*)

NORA (*busy with the tree; after a brief pause*)   Torvald.

HELMER   Yes.

NORA   I'm looking forward so much to the Stenborgs' costume party
day after tomorrow.

HELMER   And I can't wait to find out what you're going to surprise
me with.

NORA   Oh, that silly idea!

HELMER   Oh?

NORA   I can't think of anything. It all seems so foolish and pointless.

HELMER   Ah, my little Nora admits that?

NORA   (*behind his chair, her arms on the back of the chair*)   Are you very busy, Torvald?

HELMER   Well—

NORA   What are all those papers?

HELMER   Bank business.

NORA   Already?

HELMER   I've asked the board to give me the authority to make certain changes in organization and personnel. That's what I'll be doing over the holidays. I want it all settled before New Year's.

NORA   So that's why this poor Krogstad—

HELMER   Hm.

NORA   (*leisurely playing with the hair on his neck*)   If you weren't so busy, Torvald, I'd ask you for a great big favor.

HELMER   Let's hear it, anyway.

NORA   I don't know anyone with better taste than you, and I want so much to look nice at the party. Couldn't you sort of take charge of me, Torvald, and decide what I'll wear—Help me with my costume?

HELMER   Aha! Little Lady Obstinate is looking for someone to rescue her?

NORA   Yes, Torvald. I won't get anywhere without your help.

HELMER   All right. I'll think about it. We'll come up with something.

NORA   Oh, you *are* nice! (*Goes back to the Christmas tree. A pause.*) Those red flowers look so pretty.—Tell me, was it really all that bad what this Krogstad fellow did?

HELMER   He forged signatures. Do you have any idea what that means?

NORA   Couldn't it have been because he felt he had to?

HELMER   Yes, or like so many others he may simply have been thoughtless. I'm not so heartless as to condemn a man absolutely because of a single imprudent act.

NORA   Of course not, Torvald!

HELMER   People like him can redeem themselves morally by openly confessing their crime and taking their punishment.

NORA   Punishment—?

HELMER   But that was not the way Krogstad chose. He got out of it with tricks and evasions. That's what has corrupted him.

NORA   So you think that if—?

HELMER   Can't you imagine how a guilty person like that has to lie and fake and dissemble wherever he goes—putting on a mask before everybody he's close to, even his own wife and children. It's this thing with the children that's the worst part of it, Nora.

NORA   Why is that?

HELMER   Because when a man lives inside such a circle of stinking lies he brings infection into his own home and contaminates his whole family. With every breath of air his children inhale the germs of something ugly.

NORA   (*moving closer behind him*)   Are you so sure of that?

HELMER   Of course I am. I have seen enough examples of that in my work. Nearly all young criminals have had mothers who lied.

NORA   Why mothers—particularly?

HELMER   Most often mothers. But of course fathers tend to have the same influence. Every lawyer knows that. And yet, for years this Krogstad has been poisoning his own children in an atmosphere of lies and deceit. That's why I call him a lost soul morally. (*Reaches out for her hands.*) And that's why my sweet little Nora must promise me never to take his side again. Let's shake on that.—What? What's this? Give me your hand. There! Now that's settled. I assure you, I would find it impossible to work in the same room with that man. I feel literally sick when I'm around people like that.

NORA   (*withdraws her hand and goes to the other side of the Christmas tree*)   It's so hot in here. And I have so much to do.

HELMER   (*gets up and collects his papers*)   Yes, and I really should try to get some of this reading done before dinner. I must think about your costume too. And maybe just possibly I'll have something to wrap in gilt paper and hang on the Christmas tree. (*Puts his hand on her head.*) Oh my adorable little songbird! (*Enters his study and closes the door.*)

NORA   (*after a pause, in a low voice*)   It's all a lot of nonsense. It's not that way at all. It's impossible. It has to be impossible.

THE NURSE   (*in the door, left*)   The little ones are asking ever so nicely if they can't come in and be with their mama.

NORA   No, no no! Don't let them in here! You stay with them, Anne-Marie.

THE NURSE   If you say so, ma'am. (*Closes the door.*)

NORA   (*pale with terror*)   Corrupt my little children—! Poison my home—? (*Brief pause; she lifts her head.*) That's not true. Never. Never in a million years.

ACT II

The same room. The Christmas tree is in the corner by the piano, stripped, shabby-looking, with burnt-down candles. NORA's outside clothes are on the couch. NORA is alone. She walks around restlessly. She stops by the couch and picks up her coat.

NORA (*drops the coat again*)   There's somebody now! (*Goes to the door, listens.*) No. Nobody. Of course not—not on Christmas. And not tomorrow either.[1]—But perhaps—(*Opens the door and looks.*) No, nothing in the mailbox. All empty. (*Comes forward.*) How silly I am! Of course he isn't serious. Nothing like that could happen. After all, I have three small children.

(*The* NURSE *enters from the room, left, carrying a big carton.*)

THE NURSE   Well, at last I found it—the box with your costume.
NORA   Thanks. Just put it on the table.
NURSE (*does so*)   But it's all a big mess, I'm afraid.
NORA   Oh, I wish I could tear the whole thing to little pieces!
NURSE   Heavens! It's not as bad as all that. It can be fixed all right. All it takes is a little patience.
NORA   I'll go over and get Mrs. Linde to help me.
NURSE   Going out again? In this awful weather? You'll catch a cold.
NORA   That might not be such a bad thing. How are the children?
NURSE   The poor little dears are playing with their presents, but—
NORA   Do they keep asking for me?
NURSE   Well, you know, they're used to being with their mamma.
NORA   I know. But Anne-Marie, from now on I can't be with them as much as before.
NURSE   Oh well. Little children get used to everything.
NORA   You think so? Do you think they'll forget their mamma if I were gone altogether?
NURSE   Goodness me—gone altogether?
NORA   Listen, Anne-Marie—something I've wondered about. How could you bring yourself to leave your child with strangers?
NURSE   But I had to, if I were to nurse you.
NORA   Yes, but how could you *want* to?
NURSE   When I could get such a nice place? When something like that happens to a poor young girl, she'd better be grateful for whatever she gets. For *he* didn't do a thing for me—the louse!
NORA   But your daughter has forgotten all about you, hasn't she?
NURSE   Oh no! Not at all! She wrote to me both when she was confirmed and when she got married.
NORA (*putting her arms around her neck*)   You dear old thing— you were a good mother to me when I was little.
NURSE   Poor little Nora had no one else, you know.
NORA   And if my little ones didn't, I know you'd—oh, I'm be-

---

[1] In Norway both December 25 and 26 are legal holidays.

ing silly! (*Opens the carton.*) Go in to them, please. I really should—. Tomorrow you'll see how pretty I'll be.

NURSE   I know. There won't be anybody at that party half as pretty as you, ma'am. (*Goes out, left.*)

NORA   (*begins to take clothes out of the carton; in a moment she throws it all down*) If only I dared to go out. If only I knew nobody would come. That nothing would happen while I was gone.—How silly! Nobody'll come. Just don't think about it. Brush the muff. Beautiful gloves. Beautiful gloves. Forget it. Forget it. One, two, three, four, five, six—(*Cries out.*) There they are! (*Moves toward the door, stops irresolutely.*)

(MRS. LINDE *enters from the hall. She has already taken off her coat.*)

NORA   Oh, it's you, Kristine. There's no one else out there, is there? I'm so glad you're here.

MRS. LINDE   They told me you'd asked for me.

NORA   I just happened to walk by. I need your help with something—badly. Let's sit here on the couch. Look. Torvald and I are going to a costume party tomorrow night—at Consul Stenborg's upstairs—and Torvald wants me to go as a Neapolitan fisher girl and dance the tarantella. I learned it when we were on Capri.

MRS. LINDE   Well, well! So you'll be putting on a whole show?

NORA   Yes. Torvald thinks I should. Look, here's the costume. Torvald had it made for me while we were there. But it's all so torn and everything. I just don't know—

MRS. LINDE   Oh, that can be fixed. It's not that much. The trimmings have come loose in a few places. Do you have needle and thread? Ah, here we are. All set.

NORA   I really appreciate it, Kristine.

MRS. LINDE   (*sewing*).   So you'll be in disguise tomorrow night, eh? You know—I may come by for just a moment, just to look at you. — Oh dear. I haven't even thanked you for the nice evening last night.

NORA   (*gets up, moves around*).   Oh, I don't know. I don't think last night was as nice as it usually is.—You should have come to town a little earlier, Kristine.—Yes, Torvald knows how to make it nice and pretty around here.

MRS. LINDE   You too, I should think. After all, you're your father's daughter. By the way, is Dr. Rank always as depressed as he was last night?

NORA   No, last night was unusual. He's a very sick man, you know —very sick. Poor Rank, his spine is rotting away. Tuberculosis, I think. You see, his father was a nasty old man with mistresses and all that sort of thing. Rank has been sickly ever since he was a little boy.

MRS. LINDE (*dropping her sewing to her lap*) But dearest, Nora, where have you learned about things like that?

NORA (*still walking about*) Oh, you know—with three children you sometimes get to talk with—other wives. Some of them know quite a bit about medicine. So you pick up a few things.

MRS. LINDE (*resumes her sewing; after a brief pause*) Does Dr. Rank come here every day?

NORA Every single day. He's Torvald's oldest and best friend, after all. And my friend too, for that matter. He's part of the family, almost.

MRS. LINDE But tell me, is he quite sincere? I mean, isn't he the kind of man who likes to say nice things to people?

NORA No, not at all. Rather the opposite, in fact. What makes you say that?

MRS. LINDE When you introduced us yesterday, he told me he'd often heard my name mentioned in this house. But later on it was quite obvious that your husband really had no idea who I was. So how could Dr. Rank—?

NORA You're right, Kristine, but I can explain that. You see, Torvald loves me so very much that he wants me all to himself. That's what he says. When we were first married he got almost jealous when I as much as mentioned anybody from back home that I was fond of. So of course I soon stopped doing that. But with Dr. Rank I often talk about home. You see, he likes to listen to me.

MRS. LINDE Look here, Nora. In many ways you're still a child. After all, I'm quite a bit older than you and have had more experience. I want to give you a piece of advice. I think you should get out of this thing with Dr. Rank.

NORA Get out of what thing?

MRS. LINDE Several things in fact, if you want my opinion. Yesterday you said something about a rich admirer who was going to give you money—

NORA One who doesn't exist, unfortunately. What of it?

MRS. LINDE Does Dr. Rank have money?

NORA Yes, he does.

MRS. LINDE And no dependents?

NORA No. But—?

MRS. LINDE And he comes here every day?

NORA Yes, I told you that already.

MRS. LINDE But how can that sensitive man be so tactless?

NORA I haven't the slightest idea what you're talking about.

MRS. LINDE   Don't play games with me, Nora. Don't you think I know who you borrowed the twelve hundred dollars from?

NORA   Are you out of your mind! The very idea—! A friend of both of us who sees us every day—! What a dreadfully uncomfortable position that would be!

MRS. LINDE   So it really isn't Dr. Rank?

NORA   Most certainly not! I would never have dreamed of asking him—not for a moment. Anyway, he didn't have any money then. He inherited it afterwards.

MRS. LINDE   Well, I still think it may have been lucky for you, Nora dear.

NORA   The idea! It would never have occurred to me to ask Dr. Rank—. Though I'm sure that if I *did* ask him—

MRS. LINDE   But of course you wouldn't.

NORA   Of course not. I can't imagine that that would ever be necessary. But I am quite sure that if I told Dr. Rank——

MRS. LINDE   Behind your husband's back?

NORA   I must get out of—this other thing. That's also behind his back. I *must* get out of it.

MRS. LINDE   That's what I told you yesterday. But—

NORA   (*walking up and down*)   A man manages these things so much better than a woman—

MRS. LINDE   One's husband, yes.

NORA   Silly, silly! (*Stops.*) When you've paid off all you owe, you get your I.O.U. back; right?

MRS. LINDE   Yes, of course.

NORA   And you can tear it into a hundred thousand little pieces and burn it—that dirty, filthy, paper!

MRS. LINDE   (*looks hard at her, puts down her sewing, rises slowly*)   Nora—you're hiding something from me.

NORA   Can you tell?

MRS. LINDE   Something's happened to you, Nora, since yesterday morning. What is it?

NORA   (*going to her*)   Kristine! (*Listens.*) Shhh. Torvald just came back. Listen. Why don't you go in to the children for a while. Torvald can't stand having sewing around. Get Anne-Marie to help you.

MRS. LINDE   (*gathers some of the sewing things together*)   All right, but I'm not leaving here till you and I have talked.

(*She goes out left, as* HELMER *enters from the front hall.*)

NORA   (*towards him*)   I have been waiting and waiting for you, Torvald.

HELMER   Was that the dressmaker?

NORA   No, it was Kristine. She's helping me with my costume. Oh Torvald, just wait till you see how nice I'll look!

HELMER   I told you. Pretty good idea I had, wasn't it?

NORA   Lovely! And wasn't it nice of me to go along with it?

HELMER   (*his hands under her chin*)   Nice? To do what your husband tells you? All right, you little rascal; I know you didn't mean it that way. But don't let me interrupt you. I suppose you want to try it on.

NORA   And you'll be working?

HELMER   Yes. (*Shows her a pile of papers.*) Look. I've been down to the bank. (*Is about to enter his study.*)

NORA   Torvald.

HELMER   (*halts*)   Yes?

NORA   What if your little squirrel asked you ever so nicely—

HELMER   For what?

NORA   Would you do it?

HELMER   Depends on what it is.

NORA   Squirrel would run around and do all sorts of fun tricks if you'd be nice and agreeable.

HELMER   All right. What is it?

NORA   Lark would chirp and twitter in all the rooms, up and down—

HELMER   So what? Lark does that anyway.

NORA   I'll be your elfmaid and dance for you in the moonlight, Torvald.

HELMER   Nora, don't tell me it's the same thing you mentioned this morning?

NORA   (*closer to him*)   Yes, Torvald. I beg you!

HELMER   You really have the nerve to bring that up again?

NORA   Yes. You've just got to do as I say. You *must* let Krogstad keep his job.

HELMER   My dear Nora. It's his job I intend to give to Mrs. Linde.

NORA   I know. And that's ever so nice of you. But can't you just fire somebody else?

HELMER   This is incredible! You just don't give up do you? Because you make some foolish promise, *I* am supposed to—!

NORA   That's not the reason, Torvald. It's for your own sake. That man writes for the worst newspapers. You've said so yourself. There's no telling what he may do to you. I'm scared to death of him.

HELMER   Ah, I understand. You're afraid because of what happened before.

NORA   What do you mean?

HELMER   You're thinking of your father, of course.

NORA   Yes. Yes, you're right. Remember the awful things they wrote about Daddy in the newspapers. I really think they might have forced him to resign if the ministry hadn't sent you to look into the charges and if you hadn't been so helpful and understanding.

HELMER   My dear little Nora, there is a world of difference between your father and me. Your father's official conduct was not above reproach. Mine is, and I intend for it to remain that way as long as I hold my position.

NORA   Oh, but you don't know what vicious people like that may think of. Oh, Torvald! Now all of us could be so happy together here in our own home, peaceful and carefree. Such a good life, Torvald, for you and me and the children! That's why I implore you—

HELMER   And it's exactly because you plead for him that you make it impossible for me to keep him. It's already common knowledge in the bank that I intend to let Krogstad go. If it gets out that the new manager has changed his mind because of his wife—

NORA   Yes? What then?

HELMER   No, of course, that wouldn't matter at all as long as little Mrs. Pighead here got her way! Do you want me to make myself look ridiculous before my whole staff—make people think I can be swayed by just anybody—by outsiders? Believe me, I would soon enough find out what the consequences would be! Besides, there's another thing that makes it absolutely impossible for Krogstad to stay on in the bank now that I'm in charge.

NORA   What's that?

HELMER   I suppose in a pinch I could overlook his moral shortcomings—

NORA   Yes, you could; couldn't you, Torvald?

HELMER   And I understand he's quite a good worker, too. But we've known each other for a long time. It's one of those imprudent relationships you get into when you're young that embarrass you for the rest of your life. I guess I might as well be frank with you: he and I are on a first name basis. And that tactless fellow never hides the fact even when other people are around. Rather, he seems to think it entitles him to be familiar with me. Every chance he gets he comes out with his damn "Torvald, Torvald." I'm telling you, I find it most awkward. He would make my position in the bank intolerable.

NORA   You don't really mean any of this, Torvald.

HELMER   Oh? I don't? And why not?

NORA   No, for it's all so petty.

HELMER   What! Petty? You think I'm being petty!

NORA   No, I *don't* think you are petty, Torvald dear. That's exactly why I—

HELMER   Never mind. You think my reasons are petty, so it follows that I must be petty too. Petty! Indeed! By God, I'll put an end to this right now! (*Opens the door to the front hall and calls out.*) Helene!

NORA   What are you doing?

HELMER   (*searching among his papers*)   Making a decision. (THE MAID *enters.*) Here. Take this letter. Go out with it right away. Find somebody to deliver it. But quick. The address is on the envelope. Wait. Here's money.

THE MAID   Very good sir. (*She takes the letter and goes out.*)

HELMER   (*collecting his papers*)   There now, little Mrs. Obstinate!

NORA   (*breathless*)   Torvald—what was that letter?

HELMER   Krogstad's dismissal.

NORA   Call it back, Torvald! There's still time! Oh Torvald, please —call it back! For my sake, for your own sake, for the sake of the children! Listen to me, Torvald! Do it! You don't know what you're doing to all of us!

HELMER   Too late.

NORA   Yes. Too late.

HELMER   Dear Nora, I forgive you this fear you're in, although it really is an insult to me. Yes, it is! It's an insult to think that I am scared of a shabby scrivener's revenge. But I forgive you, for it's such a beautiful proof how much you love me. (*Takes her in his arms.*) And that's the way it should be, my sweet darling. Whatever happens, you'll see that when things get really rough I have both strength and courage. You'll find out that I am man enough to shoulder the whole burden.

NORA   (*terrified*)   What do you mean by that?

HELMER   All of it, I tell you—

NORA   (*composed*)   You'll never have to do that.

HELMER   Good. Then we'll share the burden, Nora—like husband and wife, the way it ought to be. (*Caresses her.*) Now are you satisfied? There, there, there. Not that look in your eyes—like a frightened dove. It's all your own foolish imagination.—Why don't you practice the tarantella—and your tambourine, too. I'll be in the inner office and close both doors, so I won't hear you. You can make as much noise as you like. (*Turning in the doorway.*) And when Rank comes, tell him where to find me. (*He nods to her, enters his study carrying his papers, and closes the door.*)

NORA   (*transfixed by terror, whispers*)   He would do it. He'll do it. He'll do it in spite of the whole world.—No, this mustn't happen.

Anything rather than that! There must be a way—! (*The door-bell rings.*) Dr. Rank! Anything rather than that! Anything—anything at all!

(*She passes her hand over her face, pulls herself together, and opens the door to the hall.* DR. RANK *is out there, hanging up his coat. Darkness begins to fall during the following scene.*)

NORA Hello there, Dr. Rank. I recognized your ringing. Don't go in to Torvald yet. I think he's busy.

RANK And you?

NORA (*as he enters and she closes the door behind him*) You know I always have time for you.

RANK Thanks. I'll make use of that as long as I can.

NORA What do you mean by that—As long as you can?

RANK Does that frighten you?

NORA Well, it's a funny expression. As if something was going to happen.

RANK Something is going to happen that I've long been expecting. But I admit I hadn't thought it would come quite so soon.

NORA (*seizes his arm*) What is it you've found out? Dr. Rank—tell me!

RANK (*sits down by the stove*) I'm going downhill fast. There's nothing to do about that.

NORA (*with audible relief*) So it's *you*—

RANK Who else? No point in lying to myself. I'm in worse shape than any of my other patients, Mrs. Helmer. These last few days I've been making up my inner status. Bankrupt. Chances are that within a month I'll be rotting up in the cemetery.

NORA Shame on you! Talking that horrid way!

RANK The thing itself is horrid—damn horrid. The worst of it, though, is all that other horror that comes first. There is only one more test I need to make. After that I'll have a pretty good idea when I'll start coming apart. There is something I want to say to you. Helmer's refined nature can't stand anything hideous. I don't want him in my sick room.

NORA Oh, but Dr. Rank—

RANK I don't want him there. Under no circumstances. I'll close my door to him. As soon as I have full certainty that the worst is about to begin I'll give you my card with a black cross on it. Then you'll know the last horror of destruction has started.

NORA Today you're really quite impossible. And I had hoped you'd be in a particularly good mood.

RANK With death on my hands? Paying for someone else's sins? Is there justice in that? And yet there isn't a single family that isn't ruled by the same law of ruthless retribution, in one way or another.

NORA (*puts her hands over her ears*) Poppycock! Be fun! Be fun!

RANK Well, yes. You may just as well laugh at the whole thing. My poor, innocent spine is suffering from my father's frolics as a young lieutenant.

NORA (*over by the table, left*) Right. He was addicted to asparagus and goose liver paté, wasn't he?

RANK And truffles.

NORA Of course. Truffles. And oysters too, I think.

RANK And oysters. Obviously.

NORA And all the port and champagne that go with it. It's really too bad that goodies like that ruin your backbone.

RANK Particularly an unfortunate backbone that never enjoyed any of it.

NORA Ah yes, that's the saddest part of it all.

RANK (*looks searchingly at her*) Hm—

NORA (*after a brief pause*) Why did you smile just then?

RANK No, it was you that laughed.

NORA No, it was you that smiled, Dr. Rank!

RANK (*gets up*) You're more of a mischief-maker than I thought.

NORA I feel in the mood for mischief today.

RANK So it seems.

NORA (*with both her hands on his shoulders*) Dear, dear Dr. Rank, don't you go and die and leave Torvald and me.

RANK Oh, you won't miss me for very long. Those who go away are soon forgotten.

NORA (*with an anxious look*) Do you believe that?

RANK You'll make new friends, and then—

NORA Who'll make new friends?

RANK Both you and Helmer, once I'm gone. You yourself seem to have made a good start already. What was this Mrs. Linde doing here last night?

NORA Aha—Don't tell me you're jealous of poor Kristine?

RANK Yes, I am. She'll be my successor in this house. As soon as I have made my excuses, that woman is likely to—

NORA Shh—not so loud. She's in there.

RANK Today too? There you are!

NORA She's mending my costume. My God, you really *are* unreasonable. (*Sits down on the couch*). Now be nice, Dr. Rank. Tomorrow you'll see how beautifully I'll dance, and then you are to pretend I'm dancing just for you—and for Torvald too, of course. (*Takes several items out of the carton.*) Sit down, Dr. Rank; I want to show you something.

RANK (*sitting down*)   What?

NORA   Look.

RANK   Silk stockings.

NORA   Flesh-colored. Aren't they lovely? Now it's getting dark in here, but tomorrow—No, no. You only get to see the foot. Oh well, you might as well see all of it.

RANK   Hmm.

NORA   Why do you look so critical? Don't you think they'll fit?

RANK   That's something I can't possibly have a reasoned opinion about.

NORA (*looks at him for a moment*)   Shame on you. (*Slaps his ear lightly with the stocking.*) That's what you get. (*Puts the things back in the carton.*)

RANK   And what other treasures are you going to show me?

NORA   Nothing at all, because you're naughty. (*She hums a little and rummages in the carton.*)

RANK (*after a brief silence*)   When I sit here like this, talking confidently with you, I can't imagine—I can't possibly imagine what would have become of me if I hadn't had you and Helmer.

NORA (*smiles*)   Well, yes—I do believe you like being with us.

RANK (*in a lower voice, lost in thought*)   And then to have to go away from it all—

NORA   Nonsense. You are not going anywhere.

RANK (*as before*)   —and not to leave behind as much as a poor little token of gratitude, hardly a brief memory of someone missed, nothing but a vacant place that anyone can fill.

NORA   And what if I were to ask you—? No—

RANK   Ask me what?

NORA   For a great proof of your friendship—

RANK   Yes, yes—?

NORA   No, I mean— for an enormous favor—

RANK   Would you really for once make me as happy as all that?

NORA   But you don't even know what it is.

RANK   Well, then; tell me.

NORA   Oh, but I can't, Dr. Rank. It's altogether too much to ask— It's advice and help and a favor—

RANK   So much the better. I can't even begin to guess what it is you have in mind. So for heaven's sake tell me! Don't you trust me?

NORA   Yes, I trust you more than anyone else I know. You are my best and most faithful friend. I know that. So I will tell you. All right, Dr. Rank. There is something you can help me prevent. You know how much Torvald loves me—beyond all words. Never for a moment would he hesitate to give his life for me.

RANK (*leaning over to her*)   Nora—do you really think he's the only one—?

NORA (*with a slight start*)   Who—?

RANK   —would gladly give his life for you.

NORA (*heavily*)   I see.

RANK   I have sworn an oath to myself to tell you before I go. I'll never find a better occasion.—All right, Nora; now you know. And now you also know that you can confide in me more than in anyone else.

NORA (*gets up; in a calm, steady voice*)   Let me get by.

RANK (*makes room for her but remains seated*)   Nora—

NORA (*in the door to the front hall*)   Helene, bring the lamp in here, please. (*Walks over to the stove.*) Oh, dear Dr. Rank. That really wasn't very nice of you.

RANK (*gets up*)   That I have loved you as much as anybody—was that not nice?

NORA   No; not that. But that you told me. There was no need for that.

RANK   What do you mean? Have you known—?

(THE MAID *enters with the lamp, puts it on the table, and goes out.*)

RANK   Nora—Mrs. Helmer—I'm asking you: did you know?

NORA   Oh, how can I tell what I knew and didn't know! I really can't say—But that you could be so awkward, Dr. Rank! Just when everything was so comfortable.

RANK   Well, anyway, now you know that I'm at your service with my life and soul. And now you must speak.

NORA (*looks at him*)   After what just happened?

RANK   I beg of you—let me know what it is.

NORA   There is nothing I can tell you now.

RANK   Yes, yes. You mustn't punish me this way. Please let me do for you whatever anyone *can* do.

NORA   Now there is nothing you can do. Besides, I don't think I really need any help, anyway. It's probably just my imagination. Of course that's all it is. I'm sure of it! (*Sits down in the rocking chair, looks at him, smiles.*) Well, well, well, Dr. Rank! What a fine gentleman you turned out to be! Aren't you ashamed of yourself, now that we have light?

RANK   No, not really. But perhaps I ought to leave—and not come back?

NORA   Don't be silly; of course not! You'll come here exactly as you have been doing. You know perfectly well that Torvald can't do without you.

RANK   Yes, but what about you?

NORA   Oh, I always think it's perfectly delightful when you come.

RANK   That's the very thing that misled me. You are a riddle to
me. It has often seemed to me that you'd just as soon be with me
as with Helmer.

NORA   Well, you see, there are people you love, and then there are
other people you'd almost rather be with.

RANK   Yes, there is something in that.

NORA   When I lived at home with Daddy, of course I loved him
most. But I always thought it was so much fun to sneak off down
to the maids' room, for they never gave me good advice and they
always talked about such fun things.

RANK   Aha! So it's *their* place I have taken.

NORA   (*jumps up and goes over to him*)   Oh dear, kind Dr. Rank,
you know very well I didn't mean it that way. Can't you see that
with Torvald it is the way it used to be with Daddy?

(THE MAID *enters from the front hall.*)

THE MAID   Ma'am! (*Whispers to her and gives her a caller's card.*)

NORA (*glances at the card*)   Ah! (*Puts it in her pocket*).

RANK   Anything wrong?

NORA   No, no; not at all. It's nothing—just my new costume—

RANK   But your costume is lying right there!

NORA   Oh yes, that one. But this is another one. I ordered it. Torvald mustn't know—

RANK   Aha. So that's the great secret.

NORA   That's it. Why don't you go in to him, please. He's in the
inner office. And keep him there for a while—

RANK   Don't worry. He won't get away. (*Enters* HELMER's *study.*)

NORA (*to* THE MAID)   You say he's waiting in the kitchen?

THE MAID   Yes. He came up the back stairs.

NORA   But didn't you tell him there was somebody with me?

THE MAID   Yes, but he wouldn't listen.

NORA   He won't leave?

THE MAID   No, not till he's had a word with you, ma'am.

NORA   All right. But try not to make any noise. And, Helene—
don't tell anyone he's here. It's supposed to be a surprise for my
husband.

THE MAID   I understand, ma'am—(*She leaves.*)

NORA   The terrible is happening. It's happening, after all. No, no,
no. It can't happen. It won't happen. (*She bolts the study door.*)

(THE MAID *opens the front hall door for* KROGSTAD *and closes the door
behind him. He wears a fur coat for traveling, boots, and a fur hat.*)

NORA (*toward him*) Keep your voice down. My husband's home.

KROGSTAD That's all right.

NORA What do you want?

KROGSTAD To find out something.

NORA Be quick, then. What is it?

KROGSTAD I expect you know I've been fired.

NORA I couldn't prevent it, Mr. Krogstad. I fought for you as long and as hard as I could but it didn't do any good.

KROGSTAD Your husband doesn't love you any more than that? He knows what I can do to you, and yet he runs the risk—

NORA Surely you didn't think I'd tell him?

KROGSTAD No, I really didn't. It wouldn't be like Torvald Helmer to show that kind of guts—

NORA Mr. Krogstad, I insist that you show respect for my husband.

KROGSTAD By all means. All due respect. But since you're so anxious to keep this a secret, may I assume that you are a little better informed than yesterday about exactly what you have done?

NORA Better than *you* could ever teach me.

KROGSTAD Of course. Such a bad lawyer as I am—

NORA What do you want of me?

KROGSTAD I just wanted to find out how you are, Mrs. Helmer. I've been thinking about you all day. You see, even a bill collector, a pen pusher, a—anyway, someone like me—even he has a little of what they call a heart.

NORA Then show it. Think of my little children.

KROGSTAD Have you and your husband thought of mine? Never mind. All I want to tell you is that you don't need to take this business too seriously. I have no intention of bringing charges right away.

NORA Oh no, you wouldn't; would you? I knew you wouldn't.

KROGSTAD The whole thing can be settled quite amiably. Nobody else needs to know anything. It will be between the three of us.

NORA My husband must never find out about this.

KROGSTAD How are you going to prevent that? Maybe you can pay me the balance on the loan?

NORA No, not right now.

KROGSTAD Or do you have a way of raising the money one of these next few days?

NORA None I intend to make use of.

KROGSTAD It wouldn't do you any good, anyway. Even if you had the cash in your hand right this minute, I wouldn't give you your note back. It wouldn't make any difference *how* much money you offered me.

NORA Then you'll have to tell me what you plan to use the note *for*.

KROGSTAD Just keep it; that's all. Have it on hand, so to speak. I won't say a word to anybody else. So if you've been thinking about doing something desperate—

NORA I have.

KROGSTAD —like leaving house and home—

NORA I have!

KROGSTAD —or even something worse—

NORA How did you know?

KROGSTAD —then: don't.

NORA How did you know I was thinking of *that?*

KROGSTAD Most of us do, right at first. I did, too, but when it came down to it I didn't have the courage—

NORA (*tonelessly*) Nor do I.

KROGSTAD (*relieved*) See what I mean? I thought so. You don't either.

NORA I don't. I don't.

KROGSTAD Besides, it would be very silly of you. Once that first domestic blowup is behind you—. Here in my pocket is a letter for your husband.

NORA Telling him everything?

KROGSTAD As delicately as possible.

NORA (*quickly*) He mustn't get that letter. Tear it up. I'll get you the money somehow.

KROGSTAD Excuse me, Mrs. Helmer, I thought I just told you—

NORA I'm not talking about the money I owe you. Just let me know how much money you want from my husband, and I'll get it for you.

KROGSTAD I want no money from your husband.

NORA Then, what *do* you want?

KROGSTAD I'll tell you, Mrs. Helmer. I want to rehabilitate myself; I want to get up in the world; and your husband is going to help me. For a year and a half I haven't done anything disreputable. All that time I have been struggling with the most miserable circumstances. I was content to work my way up step by step. Now I've been kicked out, and I'm no longer satisfied just getting my old job back. I want more than that; I want to get to the top. I'm being quite serious. I want the bank to take me back but in a higher position. I want your husband to create a new job for me—

NORA He'll never do that!

KROGSTAD He will. I know him. He won't dare not to. And once I'm back inside and he and I are working together, you'll see! Within a year I'll be the manager's right hand. It will be Nils

Krogstad and not Torvald Helmer who'll be running the Mutual Bank!

NORA   You'll never see that happen!

KROGSTAD   Are you thinking of—?

NORA   Now I *do* have the courage.

KROGSTAD   You can't scare me. A fine, spoiled lady like you—

NORA   You'll see, you'll see!

KROGSTAD   Under the ice, perhaps? Down into that cold, black water? Then spring comes, and you float up again—hideous, can't be identified, hair all gone—

NORA   You don't frighten me.

KROGSTAD   Nor you me. One doesn't do that sort of thing, Mrs. Helmer. Besides, what good would it do? He'd still be in my power.

NORA   Afterwards? When I'm no longer—?

KROGSTAD   Aren't you forgetting that your reputation would be in my hands?

(NORA *stares at him, speechless.*)

KROGSTAD   All right; now I've told you what to expect. So don't do anything foolish. When Helmer gets my letter I expect to hear from him. And don't you forget that it's your husband himself who forces me to use such means again. That I'll never forgive him. Goodbye, Mrs. Helmer. (*Goes out through the hall.*)

NORA   (*at the door, opens it a little, listens*) He's going. And no letter. Of course not! That would be impossible. (*Opens the door more.*) What's he doing? He's still there. Doesn't go down. Having second thoughts—? Will he—?

(*The sound of a letter dropping into the mailbox. Then* KROGSTAD's *steps are heard going down the stairs, gradually dying away.*)

NORA   (*with a muted cry runs forward to the table by the couch; brief pause*) In the mailbox. (*Tiptoes back to the door to the front hall.*) There it is. Torvald, Torvald—now we're lost!

MRS. LINDE   (*enters from the left, carrying* NORA's *Capri costume*) There now. I think it's all fixed. Why don't we try it on you—

NORA   (*in a low, hoarse voice*) Kristine, come here.

MRS. LINDE   What's wrong with you? You look quite beside yourself.

NORA   Come over here. Do you see that letter? There, look— through the glass in the mailbox.

MRS. LINDE   Yes, yes; I see it.

NORA   That letter is from Krogstad.

MRS. LINDE   Nora—it was Krogstad who lent you the money!

NORA   Yes, and now Torvald will find out about it.

MRS. LINDE   Oh believe me, Nora. That's the best thing for both of you.

NORA   There's more to it than you know. I forged a signature—

MRS. LINDE   Oh my God—!

NORA   I just want to tell you this, Kristine, that you must be my witness.

MRS. LINDE   Witness? How? Witness to what?

NORA   If I lose my mind—and that could very well happen—

MRS. LINDE   Nora!

NORA   —or if something were to happen to me—something that made it impossible for me to be here—

MRS. LINDE   Nora, Nora! You're not yourself!

NORA   —and if someone were to take all the blame, assume the whole responsibility—Do you understand—?

MRS. LINDE   Yes, yes; but how can you think—!

NORA   Then you are to witness that that's not so, Kristine. I am not beside myself. I am perfectly rational, and what I'm telling you is that nobody else has known about this. I've done it all by myself, the whole thing. Just remember that.

MRS. LINDE   I will. But I don't understand any of it.

NORA   Oh, how could you! For it's the wonderful that's about to happen.

MRS. LINDE   The wonderful?

NORA   Yes, the wonderful. But it's so terrible, Kristine. It mustn't happen for anything in the whole world!

MRS. LINDE   I'm going over to talk to Krogstad right now.

NORA   No, don't. Don't go to him. He'll do something bad to you.

MRS. LINDE   There was a time when he would have done anything for me.

NORA   He!

MRS. LINDE   Where does he live?

NORA   Oh, I don't know—Yes, wait a minute—(*Reaches into her pocket.*)   here's his card.—But the letter, the letter—!

HELMER   (*in his study, knocks on the door*)   Nora!

NORA   (*cries out in fear*)   Oh, what is it? What do you want?

HELMER   That's all right. Nothing to be scared about. We're not coming in. For one thing, you've bolted the door, you know. Are you modeling your costume?

NORA   Yes, yes; I am. I'm going to be so pretty, Torvald.

MRS. LINDE   (*having looked at the card*)   He lives just around the corner.

NORA   Yes, but it's no use. Nothing can save us now. The letter is in the mailbox.

MRS. LINDE   And your husband has the key?

NORA   Yes. He always keeps it with him.

MRS. LINDE   Krogstad must ask for his letter back, unread. He's got to think up some pretext or other—

NORA   But this is just the time of day when Torvald—

MRS. LINDE   Delay him. Go in to him. I'll be back as soon as I can. (*She hurries out through the hall door.*)

NORA (*walks over to* HELMER'*s door, opens it, and peeks in*)   Torvald.

HELMER (*still offstage*)   Well, well! So now one's allowed in one's own living room again. Come on, Rank. Now we'll see—(*In the doorway.*) But what's this?

NORA   What, Torvald dear?

HELMER   Rank prepared me for a splendid metamorphosis.

RANK (*in the doorway*)   That's how I understood it. Evidently I was mistaken.

NORA   Nobody gets to admire me in my costume before tomorrow.

HELMER   But, dearest Nora—you look all done in. Have you been practicing too hard?

NORA   No, I haven't practiced at all.

HELMER   But you'll have to, you know.

NORA   I know it, Torvald. I simply must. But I can't do a thing unless you help me. I have forgotten everything.

HELMER   Oh it will all come back. We'll work on it.

NORA   Oh yes, please, Torvald. You just have to help me. Promise? I am so nervous. That big party—. You mustn't do anything else tonight. Not a bit of business. Don't even touch a pen. Will you promise, Torvald?

HELMER   I promise. Tonight I'll be entirely at your service—you helpless little thing.—Just a moment, though. First I want to— (*Goes to the door to the front hall.*)

NORA   What are you doing out there?

HELMER   Just looking to see if there's any mail.

NORA   No, no! Don't, Torvald!

HELMER   Why not?

NORA   Torvald, I beg you. There is no mail.

HELMER   Let me just look, anyway. (*Is about to go out.*)

(NORA *by the piano, plays the first bars of the tarantella dance.*)

HELMER (*halts at the door*)   Aha!

NORA   I won't be able to dance tomorrow if I don't get to practice with you.

HELMER (*goes to her*)   Are you really all that scared, Nora dear?

NORA   Yes, so terribly scared. Let's try it right now. There's still time before we eat. Oh please, sit down and play for me, Torvald. Teach me, coach me, the way you always do.

HELMER   Of course I will, my darling, if that's what you want. (*Sits down at the piano.*)

(NORA *takes the tambourine out of the carton, as well as a long, many-colored shawl. She quickly drapes the shawl around herself, then leaps into the middle of the floor.*)

NORA   Play for me! I want to dance!

(HELMER *plays and* NORA *dances.* DR. RANK *stands by the piano behind* HELMER *and watches.*)

HELMER (*playing*)   Slow down, slow down!
NORA   Can't!
HELMER   Not so violent, Nora!
NORA   It has to be this way.
HELMER (*stops playing*)   No, no. This won't do at all.
NORA (*laughing, swinging her tambourine*)   What did I tell you?
RANK   Why don't you let me play?
HELMER (*getting up*)   Good idea. Then I can direct her better.

(RANK *sits down at the piano and starts playing.* NORA *dances more and more wildly.* HELMER *stands over by the stove, repeatedly correcting her. She doesn't seem to hear. Her hair comes loose and falls down over her shoulders. She doesn't notice but keeps on dancing.* MRS. LINDE *enters.*)

MRS. LINDE (*stops by the door, dumbfounded*)   Ah—!
NORA (*dancing*)   We're having such fun, Kristine!
HELMER   My dearest Nora, you're dancing as if it were a matter of life and death!
NORA   It is! It is!
HELMER   Rank, stop. This is sheer madness. Stop, I say!

(RANK *stops playing;* NORA *suddenly stops dancing.*)

HELMER (*goes over to her*)   If I hadn't seen it I wouldn't have believed it. You've forgotten every single thing I ever taught you.
NORA (*tosses away the tambourine*)   See? I told you.
HELMER   Well! You certainly need coaching.
NORA   Didn't I tell you I did? Now you've seen for yourself. I'll need your help till the very minute we're leaving for the party. Will you promise, Torvald?
HELMER   You can count on it.
NORA   You're not to think of anything except me—not tonight and

not tomorrow. You're not to read any letters—not to look in the mailbox—

HELMER   Ah, I see. You're still afraid of that man.

NORA   Yes—yes, that too.

HELMER   Nora, I can tell from looking at you. There's a letter from him out there.

NORA   I don't know. I think so. But you're not to read it now. I don't want anything ugly to come between us before it's all over.

RANK   (*to* HELMER *in a low voice*)   Better not argue with her.

HELMER   (*throws his arm around her*)   The child shall have her way. But tomorrow night, when you've done your dance—

NORA   Then you'll be free.

THE MAID   (*in the door, right*)   Dinner can be served any time, ma'am.

NORA   We want champagne, Helene.

THE MAID   Very good, ma'am. (*Goes out.*)

HELMER   Aha! Having a party, eh?

NORA   Champagne from now till sunrise! (*Calls out.*) And some macaroons, Helene. Lots!—just this once.

HELMER   (*taking her hands*)   There, there—I don't like this wild— frenzy—Be my own sweet little lark again, the way you always are.

NORA   Oh, I will. But you go on in. You too, Dr. Rank. Kristine, please help me put up my hair.

RANK   (*in a low voice to* HELMER *as they go out*)   You don't think she is—you know—expecting—?

HELMER   Oh no. Nothing like that. It's just this childish fear I was telling you about. (*They go out, right.*)

NORA   Well?

MRS. LINDE   Left town.

NORA   I saw it in your face.

MRS. LINDE   He'll be back tomorrow night. I left him a note.

NORA   You shouldn't have. I don't want you to try to stop anything. You see, it's a kind of ecstasy, too, this waiting for the wonderful.

MRS. LINDE   But what is it you're waiting *for*?

NORA   You wouldn't understand. Why don't you go in to the others. I'll be there in a minute.

(MRS. LINDE *enters the dining room, right.*)

NORA   (*stands still for a little while, as if collecting herself; she looks at her watch*)   Five o'clock. Seven hours till midnight. Twenty-four more hours till next midnight. Then the tarantella is over. Twenty-four plus seven—thirty-one more hours to live.

HELMER   (*in the door, right*)   What's happening to my little lark?

NORA   (*to him, with open arms*)   Here's your lark!

ACT III

The same room. The table by the couch and the chairs around it have been moved to the middle of the floor. A lighted lamp is on the table. The door to the front hall is open. Dance music is heard from upstairs. MRS. LINDE *is seated by the table, idly leafing through the pages of a book. She tries to read but seems unable to concentrate. Once or twice she turns her head in the direction of the door, anxiously listening.*)

MRS. LINDE (*looks at her watch*)   Not yet. It's almost too late. If only he hasn't—(*Listens again.*) Ah! There he is. (*She goes to the hall and opens the front door carefully. Quiet footsteps on the stairs. She whispers.*)   Come in. There's nobody here.

KROGSTAD (*in the door*)   I found your note when I got home. What's this all about?

MRS. LINDE   I've got to talk to you.

KROGSTAD   Oh? And it has to be here?

MRS. LINDE   It couldn't be at my place. My room doesn't have a separate entrance. Come in. We're quite alone. The maid is asleep and the Helmers are at a party upstairs.

KROGSTAD (*entering*)   Really? The Helmers are dancing tonight, are they?

MRS. LINDE   And why not?

KROGSTAD   You're right. Why not, indeed.

MRS. LINDE   All right, Krogstad. Let's talk, you and I.

KROGSTAD   I didn't know we had anything to talk about.

MRS. LINDE   We have much to talk about.

KROGSTAD   I didn't think so.

MRS. LINDE   No, because you've never really understood me.

KROGSTAD   What was there to understand? What happened was perfectly commonplace. A heartless woman jilts a man when she gets a more attractive offer.

MRS. LINDE   Do you think I'm all that heartless? And do you think it was easy for me to break with you?

KROGSTAD   No?

MRS. LINDE   You really thought it was?

KROGSTAD   If it wasn't, why did you write the way you did that time?

MRS. LINDE   What else could I do? If I had to make a break, I also had the duty to destroy whatever feelings you had for me.

KROGSTAD (*clenching his hands*)   So that's the way it was. And you did—*that*—just for money!

MRS. LINDE   Don't forget I had a helpless mother and two small brothers. We couldn't wait for you, Krogstad. You know yourself how uncertain your prospects were then.

KROGSTAD   All right. But you still didn't have the right to throw me over for somebody else.

MRS. LINDE   I don't know. I have asked myself that question many times. Did I have that right?

KROGSTAD (*in a lower voice*)   When I lost you I lost my footing. Look at me now. A shipwrecked man on a raft.

MRS. LINDE   Rescue may be near.

KROGSTAD   It *was* near. Then you came between.

MRS. LINDE   I didn't know that, Krogstad. Only today did I find out it's your job I'm taking over in the bank.

KROGSTAD   I believe you when you say so. But now that you *do* know, aren't you going to step aside?

MRS. LINDE   No, for it wouldn't do you any good.

KROGSTAD   Whether it would or not—*I* would do it.

MRS. LINDE   I have learned common sense. Life and hard necessity have taught me that.

KROGSTAD   And life has taught me not to believe in pretty speeches.

MRS. LINDE   Then life has taught you a very sensible thing. But you do believe in actions, don't you?

KROGSTAD   How do you mean?

MRS. LINDE   You referred to yourself just now as a shipwrecked man.

KROGSTAD   It seems to me I had every reason to do so.

MRS. LINDE   And I am a shipwrecked woman. No one to grieve for, no one to care for.

KROGSTAD   You made your choice.

MRS. LINDE   I had no other choice that time.

KROGSTAD   Let's say you didn't. What then?

MRS. LINDE   Krogstad, how would it be if we two shipwrecked people got together?

KROGSTAD   What's this!

MRS. LINDE   Two on one wreck are better off than each on his own.

KROGSTAD   Kristine!

MRS. LINDE   Why do you think I came to town?

KROGSTAD   Surely not because of me?

MRS. LINDE   If I'm going to live at all I must work. All my life, for as long as I can remember, I have worked. That's been my one and only pleasure. But now that I'm all alone in the world I feel nothing but this terrible emptiness and desolation. There is no joy in working just for yourself. Krogstad—give me someone and something to work for.

KROGSTAD   I don't believe this. Only hysterical females go in for that kind of high-minded self-sacrifice.

MRS. LINDE   Did you ever know me to be hysterical?

KROGSTAD   You really could do this? Listen—do you know about my past? All of it?

MRS. LINDE   Yes, I do.

KROGSTAD   Do you also know what people think of me around here?

MRS. LINDE   A little while ago you sounded as if you thought that together with me you might have become a different person.

KROGSTAD   I'm sure of it.

MRS. LINDE   Couldn't that still be?

KROGSTAD   Kristine—do you know what you are doing? Yes, I see you do. And you think you have the courage—?

MRS. LINDE   I need someone to be a mother to, and your children need a mother. You and I need one another. Nils, I believe in you—in the real you. Together with you I dare to do anything.

KROGSTAD   (*seizes her hands*)   Thanks, thanks, Kristine—Now I know I'll raise myself in the eyes of others—Ah, but I forget—!

MRS. LINDE   (*listening*)   Shh!—there's the tarantella. You must go; hurry!

KROGSTAD   Why? What is it?

MRS. LINDE   Do you hear what they're playing up there? When that dance is over they'll be down.

KROGSTAD   All right. I'm leaving. The whole thing is pointless, anyway. Of course you don't know what I'm doing to the Helmers.

MRS. LINDE   Yes, Krogstad; I do know.

KROGSTAD   Still, you're brave enough—?

MRS. LINDE   I very well understand to what extremes despair can drive a man like you.

KROGSTAD   If only it could be undone!

MRS. LINDE   It could, for your letter is still out there in the mailbox.

KROGSTAD   Are you sure?

MRS. LINDE   Quite sure. But—

KROGSTAD   (*looks searchingly at her*)   Maybe I'm beginning to understand. You want to save your friend at any cost. Be honest with me. That's it, isn't it?

MRS. LINDE   Krogstad, you may sell yourself once for somebody else's sake, but you don't do it twice.

KROGSTAD   I'll demand my letter back.

MRS. LINDE   No, no.

KROGSTAD   Yes, of course. I'll wait here till Helmer comes down. Then I'll ask him for my letter. I'll tell him it's just about my dismissal—that he shouldn't read it.

MRS. LINDE   No, Krogstad. You are not to ask for that letter back.

KROGSTAD   But tell me—wasn't that the real reason you wanted to meet me here?

MRS. LINDE   At first it was, because I was so frightened. But that was yesterday. Since then I have seen the most incredible things going on in this house. Helmer must learn the whole truth. This miserable secret must come out in the open; those two must come to a full understanding. They simply can't continue with all this concealment and evasion.

KROGSTAD   All right; if you want to take that chance. But there is one thing I *can* do, and I'll do that right now.

MRS. LINDE   (*listening*)   But hurry! Go! The dance is over. We aren't safe another minute.

KROGSTAD   I'll be waiting for you downstairs.

MRS. LINDE   Yes, do. You must see me home.

KROGSTAD   I've never been so happy in my whole life. (*He leaves through the front door. The door between the living room and the front hall remains open.*)

MRS. LINDE   (*straightens up the room a little and gets her things ready*)   What a change! Oh yes!—what a change! People to work for—to live for—a home to bring happiness to. I can't wait to get to work—! If only they'd come soon—(*Listens.*) Ah, there they are. Get my coat on—(*Puts on her coat and hat.*)

(HELMER's *and* NORA's *voices are heard outside. A key is turned in the lock, and* HELMER *almost forces* NORA *into the hall. She is dressed in her Italian costume, with a big black shawl over her shoulders. He is in evening dress under an open black cloak.*)

NORA   (*in the door, still resisting*)   No, no, no! I don't want to! I want to go back upstairs. I don't want to leave so early.

HELMER   But dearest Nora—

NORA   Oh please, Torvald—please! I'm asking you as nicely as I can—just another hour!

HELMER   Not another minute, sweet. You know we agreed. There now. Get inside. You'll catch a cold out here. (*She still resists, but he guides her gently into the room.*)

MRS. LINDE   Good evening.

NORA   Kristine!

HELMER   Ah, Mrs. Linde. Still here?

MRS. LINDE   I know. I really should apologize, but I so much wanted to see Nora in her costume.

NORA   You've been waiting up for me?

MRS. LINDE   Yes, unfortunately I didn't get here in time. You were already upstairs, but I just didn't feel like leaving till I had seen you.

HELMER   (*removing* NORA's *shawl*)   Yes, do take a good look at her, Mrs. Linde. I think I may say she's worth looking at. Isn't she lovely?

MRS. LINDE   She certainly is—

HELMER   Isn't she a miracle of loveliness, though? That was the general opinion at the party, too. But dreadfully obstinate—that she is, the sweet little thing. What can we do about that? Will you believe it—I practically had to use force to get her away.

NORA   Oh Torvald, you're going to be sorry you didn't give me even half an hour more.

HELMER   See what I mean, Mrs. Linde? She dances the tarantella —she is a tremendous success—quite deservedly so, though perhaps her performance was a little too natural—I mean, more than could be reconciled with the rules of art. But all right! The point is: she's a success, a tremendous success. So should I let her stay after that? Weaken the effect? Of course not. So I take my lovely little Capri girl—I might say, my capricious little Capri girl— under my arm—a quick turn around the room—a graceful bow in all directions, and—as they say in the novels—the beautiful apparition is gone. A finale should always be done for effect, Mrs. Linde, but there doesn't seem to be any way of getting that into Nora's head. Poooh—! It's hot in here. (*Throws his cloak down on a chair and opens the door to his room.*) Why, it's dark in here! Of course. Excuse me—(*Goes inside and lights a couple of candles.*)

NORA   (*in a hurried, breathless whisper*)   Well?

MRS. LINDE   (*in a low voice*)   I have talked to him.

NORA   And ?

MRS. LINDE   Nora—you've got to tell your husband everything.

NORA   (*no expression in her voice*)   I knew it.

MRS. LINDE   You have nothing to fear from Krogstad. But you must speak.

NORA   I'll say nothing.

MRS. LINDE   Then the letter will.

NORA   Thank you, Kristine. Now I know what I have to do. Shh!

HELMER   (*returning*)   Well, Mrs. Linde, have you looked your fill?

MRS. LINDE   Yes. And now I'll say goodnight.

HELMER   So soon? Is that your knitting?

MRS. LINDE   (*takes it*)   Yes, thank you. I almost forgot.

HELMER   So you knit, do you?

MRS. LINDE   Oh yes.

HELMER   You know—you ought to take up embroidery instead.

MRS. LINDE   Oh? Why?

HELMER   Because it's so much more beautiful. Look. You hold the embroidery so—in your left hand. Then with your right you move the needle—like this—in an easy, elongated arc—you see?

MRS. LINDE   Maybe you're right—

HELMER   Knitting, on the other hand, can never be anything but ugly. Look here: arms pressed close to the sides—the needles going up and down—there's something Chinese about it somehow—. That really was an excellent champagne they served us tonight.

MRS. LINDE   Well, goodnight! Nora. And don't be obstinate any more.

HELMER   Well said, Mrs. Linde!

MRS. LINDE   Goodnight, sir.

HELMER   (*sees her to the front door*)   Goodnight, goodnight. I hope you'll get home all right? I'd be very glad to—but of course you don't have far to walk, do you? Goodnight, goodnight. (*She leaves. He closes the door behind her and returns to the living room.*) There! At last we got rid of her. She really is an incredible bore, that woman.

NORA   Aren't you very tired, Torvald?

HELMER   No, not in the least.

NORA   Not sleepy either?

HELMER   Not at all. Quite the opposite. I feel enormously—animated. How about you? Yes, you do look tired and sleepy.

NORA   Yes, I am very tired. Soon I'll be asleep.

HELMER   What did I tell you? I was right, wasn't I? Good thing I didn't let you stay any longer.

NORA   Everything you do is right.

HELMER   (*kissing her forehead*)   Now my little lark is talking like a human being. But did you notice what splended spirits Rank was in tonight?

NORA   Was he? I didn't notice. I didn't get to talk with him.

HELMER   Nor did I—hardly. But I haven't seen him in such a good mood for a long time. (*Looks at her, comes closer to her.*) Ah! It does feel good to be back in our own home again, to be quite alone with you—my young, lovely, ravishing woman!

NORA   Don't look at me like that, Torvald!

HELMER   Am I not to look at my most precious possession? All that loveliness that is mine, nobody's but mine, all of it mine.

NORA   (*walks to the other side of the table*)   I won't have you talk to me like that tonight.

HELMER   (*follows her*)   The Tarantella is still in your blood. I can tell. That only makes you all the more alluring. Listen! The guests are beginning to leave. (*Softly.*) Nora—soon the whole house will be quiet.

NORA   Yes, I hope so.

HELMER   Yes, don't you, my darling? Do you know—when I'm at a party with you, like tonight—do you know why I hardly ever talk to you, why I keep away from you, only look at you once in

a while—a few stolen glances—do you know why I do that? It's
because I pretend that you are my secret love, my young, secret
bride-to-be, and nobody has the slightest suspicion that there is
anything between us.

NORA   Yes, I know. All your thoughts are with me.

HELMER   Then when we're leaving and I lay your shawl around
your delicate young shoulders—around that wonderful curve of
your neck—then I imagine you're my young bride, that we're
coming away from the wedding, that I am taking you to my home
for the first time—that I am alone with you for the first time—
quite alone with you, you young, trembling beauty! I have desired
you all evening—there hasn't been a longing in me that hasn't
been for you. When you were dancing the tarantella, chasing,
inviting—my blood was on fire; I couldn't stand it any longer—
that's why I brought you down so early—

NORA   Leave me now, Torvald. Please! I don't want all this.

HELMER   What do you mean? You're only playing your little teasing bird game with me; aren't you, Nora? Don't want to? I'm
your husband, aren't I?

(*There is a knock on the front door.*)

NORA (*with a start*)   Did you hear that—?

HELMER (*on his way to the hall*)   Who is it?

RANK (*outside*)   It's me. May I come in for a moment?

HELMER (*in a low voice, annoyed*)   Oh, what does he want now?
(*Aloud.*) Just a minute. (*Opens the door.*) Well! How good of
you not to pass by our door.

RANK   I thought I heard your voice, so I felt like saying hello.
(*Looks around.*) Ah yes—this dear, familiar room. What a cozy,
comfortable place you have here, you two.

HELMER   Looked to me as if you were quite comfortable upstairs
too.

RANK   I certainly was. Why not? Why not enjoy all you can in
this world? As much as you can for as long as you can, anyway.
Excellent wine.

HELMER   The champagne, particularly.

RANK   You noticed that too? Incredible how much I managed to
put away.

NORA   Torvald drank a lot of champagne tonight, too.

RANK   Did he?

NORA   Yes, he did, and then he's always so much fun afterwards.

RANK   Well, why not have some fun in the evening after a well
spent day?

HELMER   Well spent? I'm afraid I can't claim that.

RANK (*slapping him lightly on the shoulder*)   But you see, I can!

NORA   Dr. Rank, I believe you must have been conducting a scientific test today.

RANK   Exactly.

HELMER   What do you know—little Nora talking about scientific tests!

NORA   May I congratulate you on the result?

RANK   You may indeed.

NORA   It was a good one?

RANK   The best possible for both doctor and patient—certainty.

NORA (*a quick query*)   Certainty?

RANK   Absolute certainty. So why shouldn't I have myself an enjoyable evening afterwards?

NORA   I quite agree with you, Dr. Rank. You should.

HELMER   And so do I. If only you don't pay for it tomorrow.

RANK   Oh well—you get nothing for nothing in this world.

NORA   Dr. Rank—you are fond of costume parties, aren't you?

RANK   Yes, particularly when there is a reasonable number of amusing disguises.

NORA   Listen—what are the two of us going to be the next time?

HELMER   You frivolous little thing! Already thinking about the next party!

RANK   You and I? That's easy. You'll be Fortune's Child.

HELMER   Yes, but what is a fitting costume for that?

RANK   Let your wife appear just the way she always is.

HELMER   Beautiful. Very good indeed. But how about yourself? Don't you know what you'll go as?

RANK   Yes, my friend. I know precisely what I'll be.

HELMER   Yes?

RANK   At the next masquerade I'll be invisible.

HELMER   That's a funny idea.

RANK   There's a certain black hat—you've heard about the hat that makes you invisible, haven't you? You put that on, and nobody can see you.

HELMER (*suppressing a smile*)   I guess that's right.

RANK   But I'm forgetting what I came for. Helmer, give me a cigar —one of your dark Havanas.

HELMER   With the greatest pleasure. (*Offers him his case.*)

RANK (*takes one and cuts off the tip*)   Thanks.

NORA (*striking a match*)   Let me give you a light.

RANK   Thanks. (*She holds the match; he lights his cigar.*) And now goodbye!

HELMER   Goodbye, goodbye, my friend.

NORA   Sleep well, Dr. Rank.

RANK I thank you.

NORA Wish me the same.

RANK You? Well, if you really want me to—. Sleep well. And thanks for the light. (*He nods to both of them and goes out.*)

HELMER (*in a low voice*) He had had quite a bit to drink.

NORA (*absently*) Maybe so.

(HELMER *takes out his keys and goes out into the hall.*)

NORA Torvald—what are you doing out there?

HELMER Emptying the mailbox. It is quite full. There wouldn't be room for the newspapers in the morning—

NORA Are you going to work tonight?

HELMER You know very well I won't.—Say! What's this? Somebody's been at the lock.

NORA The lock—?

HELMER Yes. Why, I wonder. I hate to think that any of the maids—. Here's a broken hairpin. It's one of yours. Nora.

NORA (*quickly*) Then it must be one of the children.

HELMER You better make damn sure they stop that. Hm, hm.— There! I got it open, finally. (*Gathers up the mail, calls out to the kitchen.*) Helene?—Oh Helene—turn out the light here in the hall, will you? (*He comes back into the living room and closes the door.*) Look how it's been piling up. (*Shows her the bundle of letters. Starts leafing through it.*) What's this?

NORA (*by the window*) The letter! Oh no, no, Torvald!

HELMER Two calling cards—from Rank.

NORA From Dr. Rank?

HELMER (*looking at them*) "Doctor medicinae Rank." They were on top. He must have put them there when he left just now.

NORA Anything written on them?

HELMER A black cross above the name. What a macabre idea. Like announcing his own death.

NORA That's what it is.

HELMER Hm? You know about this? Has he said anything to you?

NORA That card means he has said goodbye to us. He'll lock himself up to die.

HELMER My poor friend. I knew of course he wouldn't be with me very long. But so soon—. And hiding himself away like a wounded animal—

NORA When it has to be, it's better it happens without words. Don't you think so, Torvald?

HELMER (*walking up and down*) He'd grown so close to us. I find it hard to think of him as gone. With his suffering and loneliness he was like a clouded background for our happy sunshine.

Well, it may be better this way. For him, at any rate. (*Stops.*) And perhaps for us, too, Nora. For now we have nobody but each other. (*Embraces her.*) Oh you—my beloved wife! I feel I just can't hold you close enough. Do you know, Nora—many times I have wished some great danger threatened you, so I could risk my life and blood and everything—everything, for your sake.

NORA (*frees herself and says in a strong and firm voice*)   I think you should go and read your letters now, Torvald.

HELMER   No, no—not tonight. I want to be with you, my darling.

NORA   With the thought of your dying friend—?

HELMER   You are right. This has shaken both of us. Something not beautiful has come between us. Thoughts of death and dissolution. We must try to get over it—out of it. Till then—we'll each go to our own room.

NORA (*her arms around his neck*)   Torvald—goodnight! Goodnight!

HELMER (*kisses her forehead*)   Goodnight, my little songbird. Sleep well, Nora. Now I'll read my letters. (*He goes into his room, carrying the mail. Closes the door.*)

NORA (*her eyes desperate, her hands groping, finds Helmer's black cloak and throws it around her; she whispers, quickly, brokenly, hoarsely*)   Never see him again. Never. Never. Never. (*Puts her shawl over her head.*) And never see the children again, either. Never; never.—The black, icy water—fathomless—this—! If only it was all over.—Now he has it. Now he's reading it. No, no; not yet. Torvald—goodbye—you—the children—

(*She is about to hurry through the hall, when* HELMER *flings open the door to his room and stands there with an open letter in his hand.*)

HELMER   Nora!

NORA (*cries out*)   Ah—!

HELMER   What is it? You know what's in this letter?

NORA   Yes, I do! Let me go! Let me out!

HELMER (*holds her back*).   Where do you think you're going?

NORA (*trying to tear herself loose from him*)   I won't let you save me, Torvald!

HELMER (*tumbles back*).   True! Is it true what he writes? Oh my God! No, no—this can't possibly be true.

NORA   It is true. I have loved you more than anything else in the whole world.

HELMER   Oh, don't give me any silly excuses.

NORA (*taking a step towards him*)   Torvald—!

HELMER   You wretch! What have you done!

NORA   Let me go. You are not to sacrifice yourself for me. You are
not to take the blame.

HELMER   No more playacting. (*Locks the door to the front hall.*)
You'll stay here and answer me. Do you understand what you
have done? Answer me! Do you understand?

NORA (*gazes steadily at him with an increasingly frozen expression*)
Yes. Now I'm beginning to understand.

HELMER (*walking up and down*)   What a dreadful awakening. All
these years—all these eight years—she, my pride and my joy—a
hypocrite, a liar—oh worse! worse!—a criminal! Oh, the bottom-
less ugliness in all this! Damn! Damn! Damn!

(NORA, *silent, keeps gazing at him.*)

HELMER (*stops in front of her*)   I ought to have guessed that something like this would happen. I should have expected it. All your
father's loose principles—Silence! You have inherited every one
of your father's loose principles. No religion, no morals, no sense
of duty—. Now I am being punished for my leniency with him.
I did it for your sake, and this is how you pay me back.

NORA   Yes. This is how.

HELMER   You have ruined all my happiness. My whole future—
that's what you have destroyed. Oh, it's terrible to think about.
I am at the mercy of an unscrupulous man. He can do with me
whatever he likes, demand anything of me, command me and
dispose of me just as he pleases—I dare not say a word! To go
down so miserably, to be destroyed—all because of an irresponsible woman!

NORA   When I am gone from the world, you'll be free.

HELMER   No noble gestures, please. Your father was always full of
such phrases too. What good would it do me if you were gone
from the world, as you put it? Not the slightest good at all. He
could still make the whole thing public, and if he did, people
would be likely to think I had been your accomplice. They might
even think it was my idea—that it was I who urged you to do it!
And for all this I have you to thank—you, whom I've borne on
my hands through all the years of our marriage. *Now* do you
understand what you've done to me?

NORA (*with cold calm*)   Yes.

HELMER   I just can't get it into my head that this is happening; it's
all so incredible. But we have to come to terms with it somehow.
Take your shawl off. Take it off, I say! I have to satisfy him one
way or another. The whole affair must be kept quiet at whatever
cost.—And as far as you and I are concerned, nothing must seem
to have changed. I'm talking about appearances, of course. You'll

go on living here; that goes without saying. But I won't let you bring up the children; I dare not trust you with them. —Oh! Having to say this to one I have loved so much, and whom I still—! But all that is past. It's not a question of happiness any more but of hanging on to what can be salvaged—pieces, appearances—(*The doorbell rings.*)

HELMER (*jumps*) What's that? So late. Is the worst—? Has he—! Hide, Nora! Say you're sick.

NORA *doesn't move.* HELMER *opens the door to the hall.*

THE MAID (*half dressed, out in the hall*) A letter for your wife, sir.

HELMER Give it to me. (*Takes the letter and closes the door.*) Yes, it's from him. But I won't let you have it. I'll read it myself.

NORA Yes—you read it.

HELMER (*by the lamp*) I hardly dare. Perhaps we're lost, both you and I. No; I've got to know. (*Tears the letter open, glances through it, looks at an enclosure; a cry of joy.*) Nora!

(NORA *looks at him with a question in her eyes.*)

HELMER Nora!—No, I must read it again.—Yes, yes; it is so! I'm saved! Nora, I'm saved!

NORA And I?

HELMER You too, of course; we're both saved, both you and I. Look! He's returning your note. He writes that he's sorry, he regrets, a happy turn in his life—oh, it doesn't matter what he writes. We're saved, Nora! Nobody can do anything to you now. Oh Nora, Nora—. No, I want to get rid of this disgusting thing first. Let me see—(*Looks at the signature.*) No, I don't want to see it. I don't want it to be more than a bad dream, the whole thing. (*Tears up the note and both letters, throws the pieces in the stove, and watches them burn.*) There! Now it's gone.—He wrote that ever since Christmas Eve—. Good God, Nora, these must have been three terrible days for you.

NORA I have fought a hard fight these last three days.

HELMER And been in agony and seen no other way out than—. No, we won't think of all that ugliness. We'll just rejoice and tell ourselves it's over, it's all over! Oh, listen to me, Nora. You don't seem to understand. It's over. What *is* it? Why do you look like that—that frozen expression on your face? Oh my poor little Nora, don't you think I know what it is? You can't make yourself believe that I have forgiven you. But I have, Nora; I swear to you, I have forgiven you for everything. Of course I know that what you did was for love of me.

NORA   That is true.

HELMER   You have loved me the way a wife ought to love her husband. You just didn't have the wisdom to judge the means. But do you think I love you any less because you don't know how to act on your own? Of course not. Just lean on me. I'll advise you; I'll guide you. I wouldn't be a man if I didn't find you twice as attractive because of your womanly helplessness. You mustn't pay any attention to the hard words I said to you right at first. It was just that first shock when I thought everything was collapsing all around me. I have forgiven you, Nora. I swear to you—I really have forgiven you.

NORA   I thank you for your forgiveness. (*She goes out through the door, right.*)

HELMER   No, stay—(*Looks into the room she entered.*) What are you doing in there?

NORA   (*within*)   Getting out of my costume.

HELMER   (*by the open door*)   Good, good. Try to calm down and compose yourself, my poor little frightened songbird. Rest safely; I have broad wings to cover you with. (*Walks around near the door.*) What a nice and cozy home we have, Nora. Here's shelter for you. Here I'll keep you safe like a hunted dove I have rescued from the hawk's talons. Believe me: I'll know how to quiet your beating heart. It will happen by and by, Nora; you'll see. Why, tomorrow you'll look at all this in quite a different light. And soon everything will be just the way it was before. I won't need to keep reassuring you that I have forgiven you; you'll feel it yourself. Did you really think I could have abandoned you, or even reproached you? Oh, you don't know a real man's heart, Nora. There is something unspeakably sweet and satisfactory for a man to know deep in himself that he has forgiven his wife—forgiven her in all the fullness of his honest heart. You see, that way she becomes his very own all over again—in a double sense, you might say. He has, so to speak, given her a second birth; it is as if she had become his wife and his child, both. From now on that's what you'll be to me, you lost and helpless creature. Don't worry about a thing, Nora. Only be frank with me, and I'll be your will and your conscience.—What's this? You're not in bed? You've changed your dress—!

NORA   (*in an everyday dress*)   Yes, Torvald. I have changed my dress.

HELMER   But why—now—this late—?

NORA   I'm not going to sleep tonight.

HELMER   But my dear Nora—

NORA   (*looks at her watch*)   It isn't all that late. Sit down here with me, Torvald. You and I have much to talk about. (*Sits down at the table.*)

HELMER   Nora—what is this all about? That rigid face—

NORA   Sit down. This will take a while. I have much to say to you.

HELMER   (*sits down, facing her across the table*)   You worry me, Nora. I don't understand you.

NORA   No, that's just it. You don't understand me. And I have never understood you—not till tonight. No, don't interrupt me. Just listen to what I have to say.—This is a settling of accounts, Torvald.

HELMER   What do you mean by that?

NORA   (*after a brief silence*)   Doesn't one thing strike you, now that we are sitting together like this?

HELMER   What would that be?

NORA   We have been married for eight years. Doesn't it occur to you that this is the first time that you and I, husband and wife, are having a serious talk?

HELMER   Well—serious—. What do you mean by that?

NORA   For eight whole years—longer, in fact—ever since we first met, we have never talked seriously to each other about a single serious thing.

HELMER   You mean I should forever have been telling you about worries you couldn't have helped me with anyway?

NORA   I am not talking about worries. I'm saying we have never tried seriously to get to the bottom of anything together.

HELMER   But dearest Nora, I hardly think that would have been something *you*—

NORA   That's the whole point. You have never understood me. Great wrong has been done to me, Torvald. First by Daddy and then by you.

HELMER   What! By us two? We who have loved you more deeply than anyone else?

NORA   (*shakes her head*)   You never loved me—neither Daddy nor you. You only thought it was fun to be in love with me.

HELMER   But, Nora—what an expression to use!

NORA   That's the way it has been, Torvald. When I was home with Daddy, he told me all his opinions, and so they became my opinions too. If I disagreed with him I kept it to myself, for he wouldn't have liked that. He called me his little doll baby, and he played with me the way I played with my dolls. Then I came to your house—

HELMER   What a way to talk about our marriage!

NORA   (*imperturbably*)   I mean that I passed from Daddy's hands into yours. You arranged everything according to your taste, and so I came to share it—or I pretended to; I'm not sure which. I think it was a little of both, now one and now the other. When I look back on it now, it seems to me I've been living here like a pauper—just a hand-to-mouth kind of existence. I have earned my keep by doing tricks for you, Torvald. But that's the way you wanted it. You have great sins against me to answer for, Daddy and you. It's your fault that nothing has become of me.

HELMER Nora, you're being both unreasonable and ungrateful. Haven't you been happy here?

NORA No, never. I thought I was, but I wasn't.

HELMER Not—not happy!

NORA No; just having fun. And you have always been very good to me. But our home has never been more than a playroom. I have been your doll wife here, just the way I used to be Daddy's doll child. And the children have been my dolls. I thought it was fun when you played with me, just as they thought it was fun when I played with them. That's been our marriage, Torvald.

HELMER There is something in what you are saying—exaggerated and hysterical though it is. But from now on things will be different. Playtime is over; it's time for growing up.

NORA Whose growing up—mine or the children's?

HELMER Both yours and the children's, Nora darling.

NORA Oh Torvald, you're not the man to bring me up to be the right kind of wife for you.

HELMER How can you say that?

NORA And I—? What qualifications do I have for bringing up the children?

HELMER Nora!

NORA You said so yourself a minute ago—that you didn't dare to trust me with them.

HELMER In the first flush of anger, yes. Surely, you're not going to count that.

NORA But you were quite right. I am *not* qualified. Something else has to come first. Somehow I have to grow up myself. And you are not the man to help me do that. That's a job I have to do by myself. And that's why I'm leaving you.

HELMER (*jumps up*) What did you say!

NORA I have to be by myself if I am to find out about myself and about all the other things too. So I can't stay here with you any longer.

HELMER Nora, Nora!

NORA I'm leaving now. I'm sure Kristine will put me up for tonight.

HELMER You're out of your mind! I won't let you! I forbid you!

NORA   You can't forbid me anything any more; it won't do any good. I'm taking my own things with me. I won't accept anything from you, either now or later.

HELMER   But this is madness!

NORA   Tomorrow I'm going home—I mean back to my old home town. It will be easier for me to find some kind of job there.

HELMER   Oh, you blind, inexperienced creature—!

NORA   I must see to it that I get experience, Torvald.

HELMER   Leaving your home, your husband, your children! Not a thought of what people will say!

NORA   I can't worry about that. All I know is that I have to leave.

HELMER   Oh, this is shocking! Betraying your most sacred duties like this!

NORA   And what do you consider my most sacred duties?

HELMER   Do I need to tell you that? They are your duties to your husband and your children.

NORA   I have other duties equally sacred.

HELMER   You do not. What duties would they be?

NORA   My duties to myself.

HELMER   You are a wife and a mother before you are anything else.

NORA   I don't believe that any more. I believe I am first of all a human being, just as much as you—or at any rate that I must try to become one. Oh, I know very well that most people agree with you, Torvald, and that it says something like that in all the books. But what people say and what the books say is no longer enough for me. I have to think about these things myself and see if I can't find the answers.

HELMER   You mean to tell me you don't know what your proper place in your own home is? Don't you have a reliable guide in such matters? Don't you have religion?

NORA   Oh but Torvald—I don't really know what religion is.

HELMER   What are you saying!

NORA   All I know is what the Reverend Hansen told me when he prepared me for confirmation. He said that religion was *this* and it was *that*. When I get by myself, away from here, I'll have to look into that, too. I have to decide if what the Reverend Hansen said was right, or anyway if it is right for *me*.

HELMER   Oh, this is unheard of in a young woman! If religion can't guide you, let me appeal to your conscience. For surely you have moral feelings? Or—answer me—maybe you don't?

NORA   Well, you see, Torvald, I don't really know what to say. I just don't know. I am confused about these things. All I know is that my ideas are quite different from yours. I have just found out that the laws are different from what I thought they were, but in no way can I get it into my head that those laws are right. A woman shouldn't have the right to spare her dying old father or save her husband's life! I just can't believe that.

HELMER   You speak like a child. You don't understand the society you live in.

NORA   No, I don't. But I want to find out about it. I have to make up my mind who is right, society or I.

HELMER   You are sick, Nora; you have a fever. I really don't think you are in your right mind.

NORA   I have never felt so clearheaded and sure of myself as I do tonight.

HELMER   And clearheaded and sure of yourself you're leaving your husband and children?

NORA   Yes.

HELMER   Then there is only one possible explanation.

NORA   What?

HELMER   You don't love me any more.

NORA   No, that's just it.

HELMER   Nora! Can you say that?

NORA   I am sorry, Torvald, for you have always been so good to me. But I can't help it. I don't love you any more.

HELMER   (*with forced composure*)   And this too is a clear and sure conviction?

NORA   Completely clear and sure. That's why I don't want to stay here any more.

HELMER   And are you ready to explain to me how I came to forfeit your love?

NORA   Certainly I am. It was tonight, when the wonderful didn't happen. That was when I realized you were not the man I thought you were.

HELMER   You have to explain. I don't understand.

NORA   I have waited patiently for eight years, for I wasn't such a fool that I thought the wonderful is something that happens any old day. Then this—thing—came crashing in on me, and then there wasn't a doubt in my mind that now—now comes the wonderful. When Krogstad's letter was in that mailbox, never for a moment did it even occur to me that you would submit to his conditions. I was so absolutely certain that you would say to him: make the whole thing public—tell everybody. And when that had happened—

HELMER   Yes, then what? When I had surrendered my wife to shame and disgrace—!

NORA   When that had happened, I was absolutely certain that you would stand up and take the blame and say, "I'm the guilty one."

HELMER   Nora!

NORA   You mean I never would have accepted such a sacrifice from you? Of course not. But what would my protests have counted against yours. *That* was the wonderful I was hoping for in terror. And to prevent that I was going to kill myself.

HELMER   I'd gladly work nights and days for you, Nora—endure sorrow and want for your sake. But nobody sacrifices his *honor* for his love.

NORA   A hundred thousand women have done so.

HELMER   Oh, you think and talk like a silly child.

NORA   All right. But you don't think and talk like the man I can live with. When you had gotten over your fright—not because of what threatened *me* but because of the risk to *you*—and the whole danger was past, then you acted as if nothing at all had happened. Once again I was your little songbird, your doll, just as before, only now you had to handle her even more carefully, because she was so frail and weak. (*Rises.*) Torvald—that moment I realized that I had been living here for eight years with a stranger and had borne him three children—Oh, I can't stand thinking about it! I feel like tearing myself to pieces!

HELMER   (*heavily*)   I see it, I see it. An abyss has opened up between us.—Oh but Nora—surely it can be filled?

NORA   The way I am now I am no wife for you.

HELMER   I have it in me to change.

NORA   Perhaps—if your doll is taken from you.

HELMER   To part—to part from you! No, no, Nora! I can't grasp that thought!

NORA   (*goes out, right*)   All the more reason why it has to be. (*She returns with her outdoor clothes and a small bag, which she sets down on the chair by the table.*)

HELMER   Nora, Nora! Not now! Wait till tomorrow.

NORA   (*putting on her coat*)   I can't spend the night in a stranger's rooms.

HELMER   But couldn't we live here together like brother and sister—?

NORA   (*tying on her hat*)   You know very well that wouldn't last long—. (*Wraps her shawl around her.*) Goodbye, Torvald. I don't want to see the children. I know I leave them in better hands than mine. The way I am now I can't be anything to them.

HELMER   But some day, Nora—some day—?

NORA   How can I tell? I have no idea what's going to become of me.

HELMER   But you're still my wife, both as you are now and as you will be.

NORA   Listen, Torvald—when a wife leaves her husband's house, the way I am doing now, I have heard he has no more legal responsibilities for her. At any rate, I now release you from all responsibility. You are not to feel yourself obliged to me for anything, and I have no obligations to you. There has to be full freedom on both sides. Here is your ring back. Now give me mine.

HELMER   Even this?

NORA   Even this.

HELMER   Here it is.

NORA   There. So now it's over. I'm putting the keys here. The maids know everything about the house—better than I. Tomorrow, after I'm gone, Kristine will come over and pack my things from home. I want them sent after me.

HELMER   Over! It's all over! Nora, will you never think of me?

NORA   I'm sure I'll often think of you and the children and this house.

HELMER   May I write to you, Nora?

NORA   No—never. I won't have that.

HELMER   But send you things—? You must let me.

NORA   Nothing, nothing.

HELMER   —help you, when you need help—?

NORA   I told you, no; I won't have it. I'll accept nothing from strangers.

HELMER   Nora—can I never again be more to you than a stranger?

NORA   (*picks up her bag*)   Oh Torvald—then the most wonderful of all would have to happen—

HELMER   Tell me what that would be—!

NORA   For that to happen, both you and I would have to change so that—Oh Torvald, I no longer believe in the wonderful.

HELMER   But I *will* believe. Tell me! Change, so that—?

NORA   So that our living together would become a true marriage. Goodbye. (*She goes out through the hall.*)

HELMER   (*sinks down on a chair near the door and covers his face with his hands*)   Nora! Nora! (*Looks around him and gets up.*)   All empty. She's gone. (*With sudden hope.*)   The most wonderful—?!

(*From downstairs comes the sound of a heavy door slamming shut.*)

QUESTIONS

1. The action of *A Doll's House* centers on the development and the alterations of the relationships among Nora, Helmer, Krogstad, and Mrs. Linde. How does Ibsen portray these characters? How do their relationships illuminate their personalities and their actions? How do they emphasize the themes and social comments of the play?

2. Both Nora and Antigonê are women who place moral principles above legal values. What happens to each character in consequence, in terms of her play's plot? Other characters' reactions to her action? Her view of their reaction, and of herself?

3. Discuss the play's ending. Do you find it successful? What is its effect? What do you think is "the most wonderful of all"?

OSCAR WILDE (1854–1900)

The Importance of Being Earnest

CHARACTERS

JOHN WORTHING, J.P.
ALGERNON MONCRIEFF
REV. CANON CHASUBLE, D.D.
MERRIMAN, butler
LANE, manservant
LADY BRACKNELL
HON. GWENDOLEN FAIRFAX
CECILY CARDEW
MISS PRISM, governess

THE SCENES OF THE PLAY

ACT I. *Algernon Moncrieff's Flat in Half-Moon Street, W.*
ACT II. *The Garden at the Manor House, Woolton.*
ACT III. *Drawing-Room of the Manor House, Woolton.*

TIME—*The Present.*
PLACE—*London.*

ACT I

SCENE. *Morning-room in* ALGERNON'S *flat in Half-Moon Street. The room is luxuriously and artistically furnished. The sound of a piano is heard in the adjoining room.*

(LANE *is arranging afternoon tea on the table, and after the music has ceased,* ALGERNON *enters.*)

ALGERNON   Did you hear what I was playing, Lane?
LANE   I didn't think it polite to listen, sir.
ALGERNON   I'm sorry for that, for your sake. I don't play accurately—any one can play accurately—but I play with wonderful expression. As far as the piano is concerned, sentiment is my forte. I keep science for Life.
LANE   Yes, sir.

ALGERNON   And, speaking of the science of Life, have you got the cucumber sandwiches cut for Lady Bracknell?

LANE   Yes, sir. (*Hands them on a salver.*)

ALGERNON (*inspects them, takes two, and sits down on the sofa*)   Oh! . . . by the way, Lane, I see from your book that on Thursday night, when Lord Shoreman and Mr. Worthing were dining with me, eight bottles of champagne are entered as having been consumed.

LANE   Yes, sir; eight bottles and a pint.

ALGERNON   Why is it that at a bachelor's establishment the servants invariably drink the champagne? I ask merely for information.

LANE   I attribute it to the superior quality of the wine, sir. I have often observed that in married households the champagne is rarely of a first-rate brand.

ALGERNON   Good Heavens! Is marriage so demoralizing as that?

LANE   I believe it *is* a very pleasant state, sir. I have had very little experience of it myself up to the present. I have only been married once. That was in consequence of a misunderstanding between myself and a young woman.

ALGERNON (*languidly*)   I don't know that I am much interested in your family life, Lane.

LANE   No, sir; it is not a very interesting subject. I never think of it myself.

ALGERNON   Very natural, I am sure. That will do, Lane, thank you.

LANE   Thank you, sir. (LANE *goes out.*)

ALGERNON   Lane's views on marriage seem somewhat lax. Really, if the lower orders don't set us a good example, what on earth is the use of them? They seem, as a class, to have absolutely no sense of moral responsibility.

Enter LANE.

. LANE   Mr. Ernest Worthing.

Enter JACK. LANE *goes out.*

ALGERNON   How are you, my dear Ernest? What brings you up to town?

JACK   Oh, pleasure, pleasure! What else should bring one anywhere? Eating as usual, I see, Algy!

ALGERNON (*stiffly*)   I believe it is customary in good society to take some slight refreshment at five o'clock. Where have you been since last Thursday?

JACK (*sitting down on the sofa*)   In the country.

ALGERNON   What on earth do you do there?

JACK (*pulling off his gloves*)   When one is in town one amuses oneself. When one is in the country one amuses other people. It is excessively boring.

ALGERNON   And who are the people you amuse?

JACK (*airily*)   Oh, neighbors, neighbors.

ALGERNON   Got nice neighbors in your part of Shropshire?

JACK   Perfectly horrid! Never speak to one of them.

ALGERNON   How immensely you must amuse them! (*Goes over and takes sandwich.*) By the way, Shropshire is your county, is it not?

JACK   Eh? Shropshire? Yes, of course. Hallo! Why all these cups? Why cucumber sandwiches? Why such reckless extravagance in one so young? Who is coming to tea?

ALGERNON   Oh! merely Aunt Augusta and Gwendolen.

JACK   How perfectly delightful!

ALGERNON   Yes, that is all very well; but I am afraid Aunt Augusta won't quite approve of your being here.

JACK   May I ask why?

ALGERNON   My dear fellow, the way you flirt with Gwendolen is perfectly disgraceful. It is almost as bad as the way Gwendolen flirts with you.

JACK   I am in love with Gwendolen. I have come up to town expressly to propose to her.

ALGERNON   I thought you had come up for pleasure? . . . I call that business.

JACK   How utterly unromantic you are!

ALGERNON   I really don't see anything romantic in proposing. It is very romantic to be in love. But there is nothing romantic about a definite proposal. Why, one may be accepted. One usually is, I believe. Then the excitement is all over. The very essence of romance is uncertainty. If ever I get married, I'll certainly try to forget the fact.

JACK   I have no doubt about that, dear Algy. The Divorce Court was specially invented for people whose memories are so curiously constituted.

ALGERNON   Oh! there is no use speculating on that subject. Divorces are made in Heaven—(JACK *puts out his hand to take a sandwich.* ALGERNON *at once interferes.*) Please don't touch the cucumber sandwiches. They are ordered specially for Aunt Augusta. (*Takes one and eats it.*)

JACK   Well, you have been eating them all the time.

ALGERNON   That is quite a different matter. She is my aunt. (*Takes plate from below.*) Have some bread and butter. The bread and butter is for Gwendolen. Gwendolen is devoted to bread and butter.

JACK (*advancing to table and helping himself*)   And very good bread and butter it is, too.

ALGERNON   Well, my dear fellow, you need not eat as if you were going to eat it all. You behave as if you were married to her already. You are not married to her already, and I don't think you ever will be.

JACK   Why on earth do you say that?

ALGERNON   Well, in the first place girls never marry the men they flirt with. Girls don't think it right.

JACK   Oh, that is nonsense!

ALGERNON   It isn't. It is a great truth. It accounts for the extraordinary number of bachelors that one sees all over the place. In the second place, I don't give my consent.

JACK   Your consent!

ALGERNON   My dear fellow, Gwendolen is my first cousin. And before I allow you to marry her, you will have to clear up the whole question of Cecily. (*Rings bell.*)

JACK   Cecily! What on earth do you mean? What do you mean, Algy, by Cecily? I don't know any one of the name of Cecily.

Enter LANE.

ALGERNON   Bring me that cigarette case Mr. Worthing left in the smoking-room the last time he dined here.

LANE   Yes, sir. (LANE *goes out.*)

JACK   Do you mean to say you have had my cigarette case all this time? I wish to goodness you had let me know. I have been writing frantic letters to Scotland Yard about it. I was very nearly offering a large reward.

ALGERNON   Well, I wish you would offer one. I happen to be more than usually hard up.

JACK   There is no good offering a large reward now that the thing is found.

Enter LANE *with the cigarette case on a salver.* ALGERNON *takes it at once.* LANE *goes out.*

ALGERNON   I think that is rather mean of you, Ernest, I must say. (*Opens case and examines it.*) However, it makes no matter, for, now that I look at the inscription, I find that the thing isn't yours after all.

JACK   Of course it's mine. (*Moving to him.*) You have seen me with it a hundred times, and you have no right whatsoever to read what is written inside. It is a very ungentlemanly thing to read a private cigarette case.

ALGERNON   Oh! it is absurd to have a hard-and-fast rule about what one should read and what one shouldn't. More than half of modern culture depends on what one shouldn't read.

JACK   I am quite aware of the fact, and I don't propose to discuss modern culture. It isn't the sort of thing one should talk of in private. I simply want my cigarette case back.

ALGERNON   Yes; but this isn't your cigarette case. This cigarette case is a present from some one of the name of Cecily, and you said you didn't know any one of that name.

JACK   Well, if you want to know, Cecily happens to be my aunt.

ALGERNON   Your aunt!

JACK   Yes. Charming old lady she is, too. Lives at Tunbridge Wells. Just give it back to me, Algy.

ALGERNON (*retreating to back of sofa*) But why does she call herself little Cecily if she is your aunt and lives at Tunbridge Wells? (*Reading.*) "From little Cecily with her fondest love."

JACK (*moving to sofa and kneeling upon it*) My dear fellow, what on earth is there in that? Some aunts are tall, some aunts are not tall. That is a matter that surely an aunt may be allowed to decide for herself. You seem to think that every aunt should be exactly like your aunt! That is absurd! For Heaven's sake give me back my cigarette case. (*Follows* ALGERNON *round the room.*)

ALGERNON Yes. But why does your aunt call you her uncle? "From little Cecily, with her fondest love to her dear Uncle Jack." There is no objection, I admit, to an aunt being a small aunt, but why an aunt, no matter what her size may be, should call her own nephew her uncle, I can't quite make out. Besides, your name isn't Jack at all; it is Ernest.

JACK It isn't Ernest; it's Jack.

ALGERNON You have always told me it was Ernest. I have introduced you to every one as Ernest. You answer to the name of Ernest. You look as if your name was Ernest. You are the most earnest looking person I ever saw in my life. It is perfectly absurd your saying that your name isn't Ernest. It's on your cards. Here is one of them. (*Taking it from case.*) "Mr. Ernest Worthing, B 4, The Albany." I'll keep this as a proof your name is Ernest if ever you attempt to deny it to me, or to Gwendolen, or to any one else. (*Puts the card in his pocket.*)

JACK Well, my name is Ernest in town and Jack in the country, and the cigarette case was given to me in the country.

ALGERNON Yes, but that does not account for the fact that your small Aunt Cecily, who lives at Tunbridge Wells, calls you her dear uncle. Come, old boy, you had much better have the thing out at once.

JACK My dear Algy, you talk exactly as if you were a dentist. It is very vulgar to talk like a dentist when one isn't a dentist. It produces a false impression.

ALGERNON Well, that is exactly what dentists always do. Now, go on! Tell me the whole thing, I may mention that I have always suspected you of being a confirmed and secret Bunburyist; and I am quite sure of it now.

JACK Bunburyist? What on earth do you mean by a Bunburyist?

ALGERNON I'll reveal to you the meaning of that incomparable expression as soon as you are kind enough to inform me why you are Ernest in town and Jack in the country.

JACK Well, produce my cigarette case first.

ALGERNON Here it is. (*Hands cigarette case.*) Now produce your explanation, and pray make it improbable. (*Sits on sofa.*)

JACK My dear fellow, there is nothing improbable about my explanation at all. In fact it's perfectly ordinary. Old Mr. Thomas Cardew, who adopted me when I was a little boy, made me in his will guardian to his grand-daughter, Miss Cecily Cardew. Cecily, who addresses me as her uncle from motives of respect that you could not possibly appreciate, lives at my place in the country under the charge of her admirable governess, Miss Prism.

ALGERNON   Where is that place in the country, by the way?

JACK   That is nothing to you, dear boy. You are not going to be invited. . . . I may tell you candidly that the place is not in Shropshire.

ALGERNON   I suspected that, my dear fellow! I have Bunburyed all over Shropshire on two separate occasions. Now, go on. Why are you Ernest in town and Jack in the country?

JACK   My dear Algy, I don't know whether you will be able to understand my real motives. You are hardly serious enough. When one is placed in the position of guardian, one has to adopt a very high moral tone on all subjects. It's one's duty to do so. And as a high moral tone can hardly be said to conduce very much to either one's health or one's happiness, in order to get up to town I have always pretended to have a younger brother of the name of Ernest, who lives in the Albany, and gets into the most dreadful scrapes. That, my dear Algy, is the whole truth pure and simple.

ALGERNON   The truth is rarely pure and never simple. Modern life would be very tedious if it were either, and modern literature a complete impossibility!

JACK   That wouldn't be at all a bad thing.

ALGERNON   Literary criticism is not your forte, my dear fellow. Don't try it. You should leave that to people who haven't been at a University. They do it so well in the daily papers. What you really are is a Bunburyist. I was quite right in saying you were a Bunburyist. You are one of the most advanced Bunburyists I know.

JACK   What on earth do you mean?

ALGERNON   You have invented a very useful younger brother called Ernest, in order that you may be able to come up to town as often as you like. I have invented an invaluable permanent invalid called Bunbury, in order that I may be able to go down into the country whenever I choose. Bunbury is perfectly invaluable. If it wasn't for Bunbury's extraordinary bad health, for instance, I wouldn't be able to dine with you at Willis's to-night, for I have been really engaged to Aunt Augusta for more than a week.

JACK   I haven't asked you to dine with me anywhere tonight.

ALGERNON   I know. You are absolutely careless about sending out invitations. It is very foolish of you. Nothing annoys people so much as not receiving invitations.

JACK   You had much better dine with your Aunt Augusta.

ALGERNON   I haven't the smallest intention of doing anything of the kind. To begin with, I dined there on Monday, and once a week is quite enough to dine with one's own relatives. In the second place, whenever I do dine there I am always treated as a member of the family, and sent down with either no woman at all, or two. In the third place, I know perfectly well whom she will place me next to, tonight. She will place me next Mary Farquhar, who always flirts with her own husband across the dinner-table. That is not very pleasant. Indeed, it is not even decent . . . and that sort of thing is enormously on the increase. The amount of women in London who flirt with their own husbands is perfectly scandalous. It looks so bad. It is simply washing one's clean linen in public. Besides, now that I know you to be a confirmed Bunburyist I naturally want to talk to you about Bunburying. I want to tell you the rules.

JACK   I'm not a Bunburyist at all. If Gwendolen accepts me, I am going to kill my brother, indeed I think I'll kill him in any case. Cecily is a little too much interested in him. It is rather a bore. So I am going to get rid of Ernest. And I strongly advise you to do the same with Mr. ———— with your invalid friend who has the absurd name.

ALGERNON   Nothing will induce me to part with Bunbury, and if you ever get married, which seems to me extremely problematic, you will be very glad to know Bunbury. A man who marries without knowing Bunbury has a very tedious time of it.

JACK   That is nonsense. If I marry a charming girl like Gwendolen, and she is the only girl I ever saw in my life that I would marry, I certainly won't want to know Bunbury.

ALGERNON   Then your wife will. You don't seem to realize, that in married life three is company and two is none.

JACK (*sententiously*)   That, my dear young friend, is the theory that the corrupt French Drama has been propounding for the last fifty years.

ALGERNON   Yes; and that the happy English home has proved in half the time.

JACK   For heaven's sake, don't try to be cynical. It's perfectly easy to be cynical.

ALGERNON   My dear fellow, it isn't easy to be anything now-a-days. There's such a lot of beastly competition about. (*The sound of an electric bell is heard.*) Ah! that must be Aunt Augusta. Only relatives, or creditors, ever ring in that Wagnerian manner. Now, if I get her out of the way for ten minutes, so that you can have an opportunity for proposing to Gwendolen, may I dine with you to-night at Willis's?

JACK   I suppose so, if you want to.

ALGERNON   Yes, but you must be serious about it. I have people who are not serious about meals. It is so shallow of them.

Enter LANE.

LANE   Lady Bracknell and Miss Fairfax. (ALGERNON *goes forward to meet them. Enter* LADY BRACKNELL *and* GWENDOLEN.)

LADY BRACKNELL   Good afternoon, dear Algernon, I hope you are behaving very well.

ALGERNON   I'm feeling very well, Aunt Augusta.

LADY BRACKNELL   That's not quite the same thing. In fact the two things rarely go together. (*Sees* JACK *and bows to him with icy coldness.*)

ALGERNON (*to* GWENDOLEN)   Dear me, you are smart!

GWENDOLEN   I am always smart! Aren't I, Mr. Worthing?

JACK   You're quite perfect, Miss Fairfax.

GWENDOLEN   Oh! I hope I am not that. It would leave no room for developments, and I intend to develop in many directions. (GWENDOLEN *and* JACK *sit down together in the corner.*)

LADY BRACKNELL   I'm sorry if we are a little late, Algernon, but I was obliged to call on dear Lady Harbury. Hadn't been there since her poor husband's death. I never saw a woman so altered; she looks quite twenty years younger. And now I'll have a cup of tea, and one of those nice cucumber sandwiches you promised me.

ALGERNON   Certainly, Aunt Augusta. (*Goes over to tea-table.*)

LADY BRACKNELL   Won't you come and sit here, Gwendolen?

GWENDOLEN   Thanks, mamma, I'm quite comfortable where I am.

ALGERNON (*picking up empty plate in horror*)   Good heavens! Lane! Why are there no cucumber sandwiches? I ordered them specially.

LANE (*gravely*)   There were no cucumbers in the market this morning, sir. I went down twice.

ALGERNON   No cucumbers!

LANE   No, sir. Not even for ready money.

ALGERNON   That will do, Lane, thank you.

LANE   Thank you, sir. (*Goes out.*)

ALGERNON   I am greatly distressed, Aunt Augusta, about there being no cucumbers, not even for ready money.

LADY BRACKNELL   It really makes no matter, Algernon. I had some crumpets with Lady Harbury, who seems to me to be living entirely for pleasure now.

ALGERNON   I hear her hair has turned quite gold from grief.

LADY BRACKNELL   It certainly has changed its color. From what cause I, of course, cannot say. (ALGERNON *crosses and hands tea.*) Thank you. I've quite a treat for you to-night, Algernon. I am going to send you down with Mary Farquhar. She is such a nice woman, and so attentive to her husband. It's delightful to watch them.

ALGERNON   I am afraid, Aunt Augusta, I shall have to give up the pleasure of dining with you to-night after all.

LADY BRACKNELL (*frowning*)   I hope not, Algernon. It would put my table completely out. Your uncle would have to dine upstairs. Fortunately he is accustomed to that.

ALGERNON   It is a great bore, and, I need hardly say, a terrible disappointment to me, but the fact is I have just had a telegram to say that my poor friend Bunbury is very ill again. (*Exchanges glances with* JACK.) They seem to think I should be with him.

LADY BRACKNELL   It is very strange. This Mr. Bunbury seems to suffer from curiously bad health.

ALGERNON   Yes; poor Bunbury is a dreadful invalid.

LADY BRACKNELL   Well, I must say, Algernon, that I think it is high time that Mr. Bunbury made up his mind whether he was going to live or to die. This shilly-shallying with the question is absurd. Nor do I in any way approve of the modern sympathy with invalids. I consider it morbid. Illness of any kind is hardly a thing to be encouraged in others. Health is the primary duty of life. I am always telling that to your poor uncle, but he never seems to take much notice . . . as far as any improvement in his ailments goes. I should be much obliged if you would ask Mr. Bunbury, from me, to be kind enough not to have a relapse on Saturday, for I rely on you to arrange my music for me. It is my last reception and one wants something that will encourage conversation, particularly at the end of the season when every one has practically said whatever they had to say, which, in most cases, was probably not much.

ALGERNON   I'll speak to Bunbury, Aunt Augusta, if he is still conscious, and I think I can promise you he'll be all right by Saturday. Of course the music is a great difficulty. You see, if one plays good music, people don't listen, and if one plays bad music, people don't talk. But I'll run over the program I've drawn out, if you will kindly come into the next room for a moment.

LADY BRACKNELL   Thank you, Algernon. It is very thoughtful of you. (*Rising, and following* ALGERNON.) I'm sure the program will be delightful, after a few expurgations. French songs I cannot possibly allow. People always seem to think that they are improper, and either look shocked, which is vulgar, or laugh, which is worse. But German sounds a thoroughly respectable language, and indeed, I believe is so. Gwendolen, you will accompany me.

GWENDOLEN   Certainly, mamma. (LADY BRACKNELL *and* ALGERNON *go into the music-room;* GWENDOLEN *remains behind.*)

JACK   Charming day it has been, Miss Fairfax.

GWENDOLEN   Pray don't talk to me about the weather, Mr. Worthing. Whenever people talk to me about the weather, I always feel quite certain that they mean something else. And that makes me so nervous.

JACK   I do mean something else.

GWENDOLEN   I thought so. In fact, I am never wrong.

JACK   And I would like to be allowed to take advantage of Lady Bracknell's temporary absence . . .

GWENDOLEN   I would certainly advise you to do so. Mamma has a way of coming back suddenly into a room that I have often had to speak to her about.

JACK (*nervously*)   Miss Fairfax, ever since I met you I have admired you more than any girl . . . I have ever met since . . . I met you.

GWENDOLEN   Yes, I am quite aware of the fact. And I often wish that in public, at any rate, you had been more demonstrative. For me you have always had an irresistible fascination. Even before I met you I was far from indifferent to you. (JACK *looks at her in amazement.*) We live, as I hope you know, Mr. Worthing, in an age of ideals. The fact is constantly mentioned in the more expensive monthly magazines, and has reached the provincial pulpits I am told: and my ideal has always been to love some one of the name of Ernest. There is something in that name that inspires absolute confidence. The moment Algernon first mentioned to me that he had a friend called Ernest, I knew I was destined to love you.

JACK   You really love me, Gwendolen?

GWENDOLEN   Passionately!

JACK   Darling! You don't know how happy you've made me.

GWENDOLEN   My own Ernest!

JACK   But you don't really mean to say that you couldn't love me if my name wasn't Ernest?

GWENDOLEN   But your name is Ernest.

JACK   Yes, I know it is. But supposing it was something else? Do you mean to say you couldn't love me then?

GWENDOLEN (*glibly*)   Ah! that is clearly a metaphysical speculation, and like most metaphysical speculations has very little reference at all to the actual facts of real life, as we know them.

JACK   Personally, darling, to speak quite candidly, I don't much care about the name of Ernest . . . I don't think that name suits me at all.

GWENDOLEN   It suits you perfectly. It is a divine name. It has a music of its own. It produces vibrations.

JACK   Well, really, Gwendolen, I must say that I think there are lots of other much nicer names. I think, Jack, for instance, a charming name.

GWENDOLEN   Jack? . . . No, there is very little music in the name Jack, if any at all, indeed. It does not thrill. It produces absolutely no vibrations. . . . I have known several Jacks, and they all, without exception, were more than usually plain. Besides, Jack is a notorious domesticity for John! And I pity any woman who is married to a man called John. She would probably never be allowed to know the entrancing pleasure of a single moment's solitude. The only really safe name is Ernest.

JACK   Gwendolen, I must get christened at once—I mean we must get married at once. There is no time to be lost.

GWENDOLEN   Married, Mr. Worthing?

JACK (*astounded*)   Well . . . surely. You know that I love you, and you led me to believe, Miss Fairfax, that you were not absolutely indifferent to me.

GWENDOLEN   I adore you. But you haven't proposed to me yet. Nothing has been said at all about marriage. The subject has not even been touched on.

JACK   Well . . . may I propose to you now?

GWENDOLEN   I think it would be an admirable opportunity. And to spare you any possible disappointment, Mr. Worthing, I think it only fair to tell you quite frankly beforehand that I am fully determined to accept you.

JACK   Gwendolen!

GWENDOLEN   Yes, Mr. Worthing, what have you got to say to me?

JACK   You know what I have got to say to you.

GWENDOLEN   Yes, but you don't say it.

JACK   Gwendolen, will you marry me? (*Goes on his knees.*)

GWENDOLEN   Of course I will, darling. How long you have been about it! I am afraid you have had very little experience in how to propose.

JACK   My own one, I have never loved any one in the world but you.

GWENDOLEN   Yes, but men often propose for practice. I know my brother Gerald does. All my girl-friends tell me so. What wonderfully blue eyes you have, Ernest! They are quite, quite blue. I hope you will always look at me just like that, especially when there are other people present.

Enter LADY BRACKNELL.

LADY BRACKNELL   Mr. Worthing! Rise, sir, from this semi-recumbent posture. It is most indecorous.

GWENDOLEN   Mamma! (*He tries to rise; she restrains him.*) I must beg you to retire. This is no place for you. Besides, Mr. Worthing has not quite finished yet.

LADY BRACKNELL   Finished what, may I ask?

GWENDOLEN   I am engaged to Mr. Worthing, mamma. (*They rise together.*)

LADY BRACKNELL   Pardon me, you are not engaged to any one. When you do become engaged to some one, I, or your father, should his health permit him, will inform you of the fact. An engagement should come on a young girl as a surprise, pleasant or unpleasant, as the case may be. It is hardly a matter that she could be allowed to arrange for herself. . . . And now I have a few questions to put to you, Mr. Worthing. While I am making these inquiries, you, Gwendolen, will wait for me below in the carriage.

GWENDOLEN (*reproachfully*)   Mamma!

LADY BRACKNELL   In the carriage, Gwendolen! (GWENDOLEN *goes to the door. She and* JACK *blow kisses to each other behind* LADY BRACKNELL'S *back.* LADY BRACKNELL *looks vaguely about as if she could not understand what the noise was. Finally turns round.*) Gwendolen, the carriage!

GWENDOLEN   Yes, mamma. (*Goes out, looking back at* JACK.)

LADY BRACKNELL (*sitting down*) You can take a seat, Mr. Worthing. (*Looks in her pocket for note-book and pencil.*)

JACK   Thank you, Lady Bracknell, I prefer standing.

LADY BRACKNELL (*pencil and note-book in hand*) I feel bound to tell you that you are not down on my list of eligible young men, although I have the same list as the dear Duchess of Bolton has. We work together, in fact. However, I am quite ready to enter your name, should your answers be what a really affectionate mother requires. Do you smoke?

JACK   Well, yes, I must admit I smoke.

LADY BRACKNELL   I am glad to hear it. A man should always have an occupation of some kind. There are far too many idle men in London as it is. How old are you?

JACK   Twenty-nine.

LADY BRACKNELL   A very good age to be married at. I have always been of the opinion that a man who desires to get married should know either everything or nothing. Which do you know?

JACK (*after some hesitation*) I know nothing, Lady Bracknell.

LADY BRACKNELL   I am pleased to hear it. I do not approve of anything that tampers with natural ignorance. Ignorance is like a delicate exotic fruit; touch it and the bloom is gone. The whole theory of modern education is radically unsound. Fortunately in England, at any rate, education produces no effect whatsoever. If it did, it would prove a serious danger to the upper classes, and probably lead to acts of violence in Grosvenor Square. What is your income?

JACK   Between seven and eight thousand a year.

LADY BRACKNELL (*makes a note in her book*) In land, or in investments?

JACK   In investments, chiefly.

LADY BRACKNELL   That is satisfactory. What between the duties expected of one during one's life-time, and the duties exacted from one after one's death, land has ceased to be either a profit or a pleasure. It gives one position, and prevents one from keeping it up. That's all that can be said about land.

JACK   I have a country house with some land, of course, attached to it, about fifteen hundred acres, I believe; but I don't depend on that for my real income. In fact, as far as I can make out, the poachers are the only people who make anything out of it.

LADY BRACKNELL   A country house! How many bedrooms? Well, that point can be cleared up afterwards. You have a town house, I hope? A girl with a simple, unspoiled nature, like Gwendolen, could hardly be expected to reside in the country.

JACK   Well, I own a house in Belgrave Square, but it is let by the year to Lady Bloxham. Of course, I can get it back whenever I like, at six months' notice.

LADY BRACKNELL   Lady Bloxham? I don't know her.

JACK   Oh, she goes about very little. She is a lady considerably advanced in years.

LADY BRACKNELL   Ah, now-a-days that is no guarantee of respectability of character. What number in Belgrave Square?

JACK   149.

LADY BRACKNELL (*shaking her head*)   The unfashionable side. I thought there was something. However, that could easily be altered.

JACK   Do you mean the fashion, or the side?

LADY BRACKNELL (*sternly*)   Both, if necessary, I presume. What are your politics?

JACK   Well, I am afraid I really have none. I am a Liberal Unionist.

LADY BRACKNELL   Oh, they count as Tories. They dine with us. Or come in the evening, at any rate. Now to minor matters. Are your parents living?

JACK   I have lost both my parents.

LADY BRACKNELL   Both? . . . That seems like carelessness. Who was your father? He was evidently a man of some wealth. Was he born in what the Radical papers call the purple of commerce, or did he rise from the ranks of the aristocracy?

JACK   I am afraid I really don't know. The fact is, Lady Bracknell, I said I had lost my parents. It would be nearer the truth to say that my parents seem to have lost me . . . I don't actually know who I am by birth. I was . . . well, I was found.

LADY BRACKNELL   Found!

JACK   The late Mr. Thomas Cardew, an old gentleman of a very charitable and kindly disposition, found me, and gave me the name of Worthing, because he happened to have a first-class ticket for Worthing in his pocket at the time. Worthing is a place in Sussex. It is a seaside resort.

LADY BRACKNELL   Where did the charitable gentleman who had a first-class ticket for this seaside resort find you?

JACK (*gravely*)   In a hand-bag.

LADY BRACKNELL   A hand-bag?

JACK (*very seriously*)   Yes, Lady Bracknell. I was in a hand-bag—a somewhat large, black leather hand-bag, with handles to it—an ordinary hand-bag in fact.

LADY BRACKNELL   In what locality did this Mr. James, or Thomas, Cardew come across this ordinary hand-bag?

JACK   In the cloak-room at Victoria Station. It was given to him in mistake for his own.

LADY BRACKNELL   The cloak-room at Victoria Station?

JACK   Yes. The Brighton line.

LADY BRACKNELL   The line is immaterial. Mr. Worthing, I confess I feel somewhat bewildered by what you have just told me. To be born, or at any rate bred, in a handbag, whether it had handles or not, seems to me to display a contempt for the ordinary decencies of family life that remind one of the worst excesses of the French Revolution. And I presume you know what that unfortunate movement led to? As for the particular locality in which the hand-bag was found, a cloak-room at a railway station might serve to conceal a social indiscretion—has probably, indeed, been used for that purpose before now—but it could hardly be regarded as an assured basis for a recognized position in good society.

JACK   May I ask you then what you would advise me to do? I need hardly say I would do anything in the world to ensure Gwendolen's happiness.

LADY BRACKNELL   I would strongly advise you, Mr. Worthing, to try and acquire some relations as soon as possible, and to make a definite effort to produce at any rate one parent, of either sex, before the season is quite over.

JACK   Well, I don't see how I could possibly manage to do that. I can produce the hand-bag at any moment. It is in my dressing-room at home. I really think that should satisfy you, Lady Bracknell.

LADY BRACKNELL   Me, sir! What has it to do with me? You can hardly imagine that I and Lord Bracknell would dream of allowing our only daughter—a girl brought up with the utmost care—to marry into a cloak-room, and form an alliance with a parcel? Good morning, Mr. Worthing! (LADY BRACKNELL *sweeps out in majestic indignation.*)

JACK   Good morning! (ALGERNON, *from the other room, strikes up the Wedding March.* JACK *looks perfectly furious, and goes to the door.*) For goodness' sake don't play that ghastly tune, Algy! How idiotic you are! (*The music stops, and* ALGERNON *enters cheerily.*)

ALGERNON   Didn't it go off all right, old boy? You don't mean to say Gwendolen refused you? I know it is a way she has. She is always refusing people. I think it is most ill-natured of her.

JACK   Oh, Gwendolen is as right as a trivet. As far as she is concerned, we are engaged. Her mother is perfectly unbearable. Never met such a Gorgon . . . I don't really know what a Gorgon is like, but I am quite sure that Lady Bracknell is one. In any case, she is a monster, without being a myth, which is rather unfair. . . . I beg your pardon, Algy, I suppose I shouldn't talk about your own aunt in that way before you.

ALGERNON   My dear boy, I love hearing my relations abused. It is the only thing that makes me put up with them at all. Relations are simply a tedious pack of people, who haven't got the remotest knowledge of how to live, nor the smallest instinct about when to die.

JACK   Oh, that is nonsense!

ALGERNON   It isn't!

JACK   Well, I won't argue about the matter. You always want to argue about things.

ALGERNON   That is exactly what things were originally made for.

JACK　Upon my word, if I thought that, I'd shoot myself . . . (*A pause.*) You don't think there is any chance of Gwendolen becoming like her mother in about a hundred and fifty years, do you, Algy?

ALGERNON　All women become like their mothers. That is their tragedy. No man does. That's his.

JACK　Is that clever?

ALGERNON　It is perfectly phrased! and quite as true as any observation in civilized life should be.

JACK　I am sick to death of cleverness. Everybody is clever now-a-days. You can't go anywhere without meeting clever people. The thing has become an absolute public nuisance. I wish to goodness we had a few fools left.

ALGERNON　We have.

JACK　I should extremely like to meet them. What do they talk about?

ALGERNON　The fools? Oh! about the clever people, of course.

JACK　What fools!

ALGERNON　By the way, did you tell Gwendolen the truth about your being Ernest in town, and Jack in the country?

JACK　(*in a very patronizing manner*)　My dear fellow, the truth isn't quite the sort of thing one tells to a nice, sweet, refined girl. What extraordinary ideas you have about the way to behave to a woman!

ALGERNON　The only way to behave to a woman is to make love to her, if she is pretty, and to some one else if she is plain.

JACK　Oh, that is nonsense.

ALGERNON　What about your brother? What about the profligate Ernest?

JACK　Oh, before the end of the week I shall have got rid of him. I'll say he died in Paris of apoplexy. Lots of people die of apoplexy, quite suddenly, don't they?

ALGERNON　Yes, but it's hereditary, my dear fellow. It's a sort of thing that runs in families. You had much better say a severe chill.

JACK　You are sure a severe chill isn't hereditary, or anything of that kind?

ALGERNON　Of course it isn't!

JACK　Very well, then. My poor brother Ernest is carried off suddenly in Paris, by a severe chill. That gets rid of him.

ALGERNON　But I thought you said that . . . Miss Cardew was a little too much interested in your poor brother Ernest? Won't she feel his loss a good deal?

JACK　Oh, that is all right. Cecily is not a silly, romantic girl, I am glad to say. She has got a capital appetite, goes for long walks, and pays no attention at all to her lessons.

ALGERNON　I would rather like to see Cecily.

JACK　I will take very good care you never do. She is excessively pretty, and she is only just eighteen.

ALGERNON   Have you told Gwendolen yet that you have an excessively pretty ward who is only just eighteen?

JACK   Oh, one doesn't blurt these things out to people. Cecily and Gwendolen are perfectly certain to be extremely great friends. I'll bet you anything you like that half an hour after they have met, they will be calling each other sister.

ALGERNON   Women only do that when they have called each other a lot of other things first. Now, my dear boy, if we want to get a good table at Willis's, we really must go and dress. Do you know it is nearly seven?

JACK (*irritably*)   Oh! it always is nearly seven.

ALGERNON   Well, I'm hungry.

JACK   I never knew you when you weren't. . . .

ALGERNON   What shall we do after dinner? Go to a theater?

JACK   Oh, no! I loathe listening.

ALGERNON   Well, let us go to the Club?

JACK   Oh, no! I hate talking.

ALGERNON   Well, we might trot round to the Empire at ten?

JACK   Oh, no! I can't bear looking at things. It is so silly.

ALGERNON   Well, what shall we do?

JACK   Nothing!

ALGERNON   It is awfully hard work doing nothing. However, I don't mind hard work where there is no definite object of any kind.

Enter LANE.

LANE   Miss Fairfax.

Enter GWENDOLEN. LANE *goes out.*

ALGERNON   Gwendolen, upon my word!

GWENDOLEN   Algy, kindly turn your back. I have something very particular to say to Mr. Worthing.

ALGERNON   Really, Gwendolen, I don't think I can allow this at all.

GWENDOLEN   Algy, you always adopt a strictly immoral attitude towards life. You are not quite old enough to do that. (ALGERNON *retires to the fireplace.*)

JACK   My own darling!

GWENDOLEN   Ernest, we may never be married. From the expression on mamma's face I fear we never shall. Few parents now-a-days pay any regard to what their children say to them. The old-fashioned respect for the young is fast dying out. Whatever influence I ever had over mamma, I lost at the age of three. But although she may prevent us from becoming man and wife, and I may marry some one else, and marry often, nothing that she can possibly do can alter my eternal devotion to you.

JACK   Dear Gwendolen.

GWENDOLEN   The story of your romantic origin, as related to me by mamma, with unpleasing comments, has naturally stirred the deeper fibers of my nature. Your Christian name has an irresistible fascination. The simplicity of your character makes you exquisitely incomprehensible to me. Your town address at the Albany I have. What is your address in the country?

JACK   The Manor House, Woolton, Hertfordshire. (ALGERNON, *who has been carefully listening, smiles to himself, and writes the address on his shirt-cuff. Then picks up the Railway Guide.*)

GWENDOLEN   There is a good postal service, I suppose? It may be necessary to do something desperate. That, of course, will require serious consideration. I will communicate with you daily.

JACK   My own one!

GWENDOLEN   How long do you remain in town?

JACK   Till Monday.

GWENDOLEN   Good! Algy, you may turn round now.

ALGERNON   Thanks, I've turned round already.

GWENDOLEN   You may also ring the bell.

JACK   You will let me see you to your carriage, my own darling?

GWENDOLEN   Certainly.

JACK (*to* LANE, *who now enters*)   I will see Miss Fairfax out.

LANE   Yes, sir. (JACK *and* GWENDOLEN *go off.* LANE *presents several letters on a salver to* ALGERNON. *It is to be surmised that they are bills, as* ALGERNON, *after looking at the envelopes, tears them up.*)

ALGERNON   A glass of sherry, Lane.

LANE   Yes, sir.

ALGERNON   To-morrow, Lane. I'm going Bunburying.

LANE   Yes, sir.

ALGERNON   I shall probably not be back till Monday. You can put up my dress clothes, my smoking jacket, and all the Bunbury suits . . .

LANE   Yes, sir. (*Handing sherry.*)

ALGERNON   I hope to-morrow will be a fine day, Lane.

LANE   It never is, sir.

ALGERNON   Lane, you're a perfect pessimist.

LANE   I do my best to give satisfaction, sir.

Enter JACK. LANE *goes off.*

JACK   There's a sensible, intellectual girl! the only girl I ever cared for in my life. (ALGERNON *is laughing immoderately.*) What on earth are you so amused at?

ALGERNON   Oh, I'm a little anxious about poor Bunbury, that's all.

JACK   If you don't take care, your friend Bunbury will get you into a serious scrape some day.

ALGERNON   I love scrapes. They are the only things that are never serious.

JACK   Oh, that's nonsense, Algy. You never talk anything but nonsense.

ALGERNON   Nobody ever does. (JACK *looks indignantly at him, and leaves the room.* ALGERNON *lights a cigarette, reads his shirt-cuff and smiles.*)

Curtain

ACT II

SCENE   *Garden at the Manor House. A flight of gray stone steps leads up to the house. The garden, an old-fashioned one, full of roses. Time of year, July. Basket chairs, and a table covered with books, are set under a large yew tree.*

(MISS PRISM *discovered seated at the table.* CECILY *is at the back watering flowers.*)

MISS PRISM (*calling*)   Cecily, Cecily! Surely such a utilitarian occupation as the watering of flowers is rather Moulton's duty than yours? Especially at a moment when intellectual pleasures await you. Your German grammar is on the table. Pray open it at page fifteen. We will repeat yesterday's lesson.

CECILY (*coming over very slowly*)   But I don't like German. It isn't at all a becoming language. I know perfectly well that I look quite plain after my German lesson.

MISS PRISM   Child, you know how anxious your guardian is that you should improve yourself in every way. He laid particular stress on your German, as he was leaving for town yesterday. Indeed, he always lays stress on your German when he is leaving for town.

CECILY   Dear Uncle Jack is so very serious! Sometimes he is so serious that I think he cannot be quite well.

MISS PRISM (*drawing herself up*)   Your guardian enjoys the best of health, and his gravity of demeanor is especially to be commended in one so comparatively young as he is. I know no one who has a higher sense of duty and responsibility.

CECILY   I suppose that is why he often looks a little bored when we three are together.

MISS PRISM   Cecily! I am surprised at you. Mr. Worthing has many troubles in his life. Idle merriment and triviality would be out of place in his conversation. You must remember his constant anxiety about that unfortunate young man, his brother.

CECILY   I wish Uncle Jack would allow that unfortunate young man, his brother, to come down here sometimes. We might have a good influence over him, Miss Prism. I am sure you certainly would. You know German, and geology, and things of that kind influence a man very much. (CECILY *begins to write in her diary.*)

MISS PRISM (*shaking her head*)   I do not think that even I could produce any effect on a character that, according to his own brother's admission, is irretrievably weak and vacillating. Indeed, I am not sure that I would desire to reclaim him. I am not in favor of this modern mania for turning bad people into good people at a moment's notice. As a man sows so let him reap. You must put away your diary, Cecily. I really don't see why you should keep a diary at all.

CECILY   I keep a diary in order to enter the wonderful secrets of my life. If I didn't write them down I should probably forget all about them.

MISS PRISM   Memory, my dear Cecily, is the diary that we all carry about with us.

CECILY   Yes, but it usually chronicles the things that have never happened, and couldn't possibly have happened. I believe that Memory is responsible for nearly all the three-volume novels that Mudie sends us.

MISS PRISM   Do not speak slightingly of the three-volume novel, Cecily. I wrote one myself in earlier days.

CECILY   Did you really, Miss Prism? How wonderfully clever you are! I hope it did not end happily? I don't like novels that end happily. They depress me so much.

MISS PRISM   The good ended happily, and the bad unhappily. That is what Fiction means.

CECILY   I suppose so. But it seems very unfair. And was your novel ever published?

MISS PRISM   Alas! no. The manuscript unfortunately was abandoned. I use the word in the sense of lost or mislaid. To your work, child, these speculations are profitless.

CECILY (*smiling*)   But I see dear Dr. Chasuble coming up through the garden.

MISS PRISM (*rising and advancing*)   Dr. Chasuble! This is indeed a pleasure.

Enter CANON CHASUBLE.

CHASUBLE   And how are we this morning? Miss Prism, you are, I trust, well?

CECILY   Miss Prism has just been complaining of a slight headache. I think it would do her so much good to have a short stroll with you in the park, Dr. Chasuble.

MISS PRISM   Cecily, I have not mentioned anything about a headache.

CECILY   No, dear Miss Prism, I know that, but I felt instinctively that you had a headache. Indeed I was thinking about that, and not about my German lesson, when the Rector came in.

CHASUBLE   I hope, Cecily, you are not inattentive.

CECILY   Oh, I am afraid I am.

CHASUBLE   That is strange. Were I fortunate enough to be Miss Prism's pupil, I would hang upon her lips. (MISS PRISM *glares*.) I spoke metaphorically.—My metaphor was drawn from bees. Ahem! Mr. Worthing, I suppose, has not returned from town yet?

MISS PRISM   We do not expect him till Monday afternoon.

CHASUBLE   Ah, yes, he usually likes to spend his Sunday in London. He is not one of those whose sole aim is enjoyment, as, by all accounts, that unfortunate young man, his brother, seems to be. But I must not disturb Egeria and her pupil any longer.

MISS PRISM   Egeria? My name is Laetitia, Doctor.

CHASUBLE (*bowing*)   A classical allusion merely, drawn from the Pagan authors. I shall see you both no doubt at Evensong.

MISS PRISM   I think, dear Doctor, I will have a stroll with you. I find I have a headache after all, and a walk might do it good.

CHASUBLE   With pleasure, Miss Prism, with pleasure. We might go as far as the schools and back.

MISS PRISM   That would be delightful. Cecily, you will read your Political Economy in my absence. The chapter on the Fall of the Rupee you may omit. It is somewhat too sensational. Even these metallic problems have their melodramatic side. (*Goes down the garden with* DR. CHASUBLE.)

CECILY (*picks up books and throws them back on table*)   Horrid Political Economy! Horrid Geography! Horrid, horrid German!

Enter MERRIMAN *with a card on a salver.*

MERRIMAN   Mr. Ernest Worthing has just driven over from the station. He has brought his luggage with him.

CECILY (*takes the card and reads it*)   "Mr. Ernest Worthing, B4, The Albany, W." Uncle Jack's brother! Did you tell him Mr. Worthing was in town?

MERRIMAN   Yes, Miss. He seemed very much disappointed. I mentioned that you and Miss Prism were in the garden. He said he was anxious to speak to you privately for a moment.

CECILY   Ask Mr. Ernest Worthing to come here. I suppose you had better talk to the housekeeper about a room for him.

MERRIMAN   Yes, Miss. (MERRIMAN *goes off.*)

CECILY   I have never met any really wicked person before. I feel rather frightened. I am so afraid he will look just like every one else.

Enter ALGERNON, *very gay and debonair.*

He does!

ALGERNON (*raising his hat*)   You are my little cousin Cecily, I'm sure.

CECILY   You are under some strange mistake. I am not little. In fact, I am more than usually tall for my age. (ALGERNON *is rather taken aback.*) But I am your cousin Cecily. You, I see from your card, are Uncle Jack's brother, my cousin Ernest, my wicked cousin Ernest.

ALGERNON   Oh! I am not really wicked at all, cousin Cecily. You mustn't think that I am wicked.

CECILY   If you are not, then you have certainly been deceiving us all in a very inexcusable manner. I hope you have not been leading a double life, pretending to be wicked and being really good all the time. That would be hypocrisy.

ALGERNON (*looks at her in amazement*)   Oh! of course I have been rather reckless.

CECILY   I am glad to hear it.

ALGERNON   In fact, now you mention the subject, I have been very bad in my own small way.

CECILY   I don't think you should be so proud of that, though I am sure it must have been very pleasant.

ALGERNON   It is much pleasanter being here with you.

CECILY   I can't understand how you are here at all. Uncle Jack won't be back till Monday afternoon.

ALGERNON   That is a great disappointment. I am obliged to go up by the first train on Monday morning. I have a business appointment that I am anxious . . . to miss.

CECILY   Couldn't you miss it anywhere but in London?

ALGERNON   No; the appointment is in London.

CECILY   Well, I know, of course, how important it is not to keep a business engagement, if one wants to retain any sense of the beauty of life, but still I think you had better wait till Uncle Jack arrives. I know he wants to speak to you about your emigrating.

ALGERNON   About my what?

CECILY   Your emigrating. He has gone up to buy your outfit.

ALGERNON   I certainly wouldn't let Jack buy my outfit. He has no taste in neckties at all.

CECILY   I don't think you will require neckties. Uncle Jack is sending you to Australia.

ALGERNON   Australia! I'd sooner die.

CECILY   Well, he said at dinner on Wednesday night, that you would have to choose between this world, the next world, and Australia.

ALGERNON   Oh, well! The accounts I have received of Australia and the next world, are not particularly encouraging. This world is good enough for me, cousin Cecily.

CECILY   Yes, but are you good enough for it?

ALGERNON   I'm afraid I'm not that. That is why I want you to reform me. You might make that your mission, if you don't mind, cousin Cecily.

CECILY   I'm afraid I've not time, this afternoon.

ALGERNON   Well, would you mind my reforming myself this afternoon?

CECILY   That is rather Quixotic of you. But I think you should try.

ALGERNON   I will. I feel better already.

CECILY   You are looking a little worse.

ALGERNON   That is because I am hungry.

CECILY   How thoughtless of me. I should have remembered that when one is going to lead an entirely new life, one requires regular and wholesome meals. Won't you come in?

ALGERNON   Thank you. Might I have a button-hole first? I never have any appetite unless I have a button-hole first.

CECILY   A Maréchal Niel? (*Picks up scissors.*)

ALGERNON   No, I'd sooner have a pink rose.

CECILY   Why? (*Cuts a flower.*)

ALGERNON   Because you are like a pink rose, cousin Cecily.

CECILY   I don't think it can be right for you to talk to me like that. Miss Prism never says such things to me.

ALGERNON   Then Miss Prism is a short-sighted old lady. (CECILY *puts the rose in his button-hole.*) You are the prettiest girl I ever saw.

CECILY   Miss Prism says that all good looks are a snare.

ALGERNON   They are a snare that every sensible man would like to be caught in.

CECILY   Oh! I don't think I would care to catch a sensible man. I shouldn't know what to talk to him about. (*They pass into the house.* MISS PRISM *and* DR. CHASUBLE *return.*)

MISS PRISM   You are too much alone, dear Dr. Chasuble. You should get married. A misanthrope I can understand—a womanthrope, never!

CHASUBLE (*with a scholar's shudder*)   Believe me, I do not deserve so neologistic a phrase. The precept as well as the practice of the Primitive Church was distinctly against matrimony.

MISS PRISM (*sententiously*)   That is obviously the reason why the Primitive Church has not lasted up to the present day. And you do not seem to realize, dear Doctor, that by persistently remaining single, a man converts himself into a permanent public temptation. Men should be careful; this very celibacy leads weaker vessels astray.

CHASUBLE   But is a man not equally attractive when married?

MISS PRISM   No married man is ever attractive except to his wife.

CHASUBLE   And often, I've been told, not even to her.

MISS PRISM   That depends on the intellectual sympathies of the woman. Maturity can always be depended on. Ripeness can be trusted. Young women are green. (DR. CHASUBLE *starts.*) I spoke horticulturally. My metaphor was drawn from fruits. But where is Cecily?

CHASUBLE   Perhaps she followed us to the schools.

Enter JACK *slowly from the back of the garden. He is dressed in the deepest mourning, with crape hatband and black gloves.*

MISS PRISM   Mr. Worthing!

CHASUBLE   Mr. Worthing?

MISS PRISM This is indeed a surprise. We did not look for you till Monday afternoon.

JACK (*shakes* MISS PRISM'S *hand in a tragic manner*) I have returned sooner than I expected. Dr. Chasuble, I hope you are well?

CHASUBLE Dear Mr. Worthing, I trust this garb of woe does not betoken some terrible calamity?

JACK My brother.

MISS PRISM More shameful debts and extravagance?

CHASUBLE Still leading his life of pleasure?

JACK (*shaking his head*) Dead!

CHASUBLE Your brother Ernest dead?

JACK Quite dead.

MISS PRISM What a lesson for him! I trust he will profit by it.

CHASUBLE Mr. Worthing, I offer you my sincere condolence. You have at least the consolation of knowing that you were always the most generous and forgiving of brothers.

JACK Poor Ernest! He had many faults, but it is a sad, sad blow.

CHASUBLE Very sad indeed. Were you with him at the end?

JACK No. He died abroad; in Paris, in fact. I had a telegram last night from the manager of the Grand Hotel.

CHASUBLE Was the cause of death mentioned?

JACK A severe chill, it seems.

MISS PRISM As a man sows, so shall he reap.

CHASUBLE (*raising his hand*) Charity, dear Miss Prism, charity! None of us are perfect. I myself am peculiarly susceptible to draughts. Will the interment take place here?

JACK No. He seems to have expressed a desire to be buried in Paris.

CHASUBLE In Paris! (*Shakes his head.*) I fear that hardly points to any very serious state of mind at the last. You would no doubt wish me to make some slight allusion to this tragic domestic affliction next Sunday. (JACK *presses his hand convulsively.*) My sermon on the meaning of the manna in the wilderness can be adapted to almost any occasion, joyful, or, as in the present case, distressing. (*All sigh.*) I have preached it at harvest celebrations, christenings, confirmations, on days of humiliation and festal days. The last time I delivered it was in the Cathedral, as a charity sermon on behalf of the Society for the Prevention of Discontentment among the Upper Orders. The Bishop, who was present, was much struck by some of the analogies I drew.

JACK Ah, that reminds me, you mentioned christenings I think, Dr. Chasuble? I suppose you know how to christen all right? (DR. CHASUBLE *looks astounded.*) I mean, of course, you are continually christening, aren't you?

MISS PRISM It is, I regret to say, one of the Rector's most constant duties in this parish. I have often spoken to the poorer classes on the subject. But they don't seem to know what thrift is.

CHASUBLE   But is there any particular infant in whom you are interested, Mr. Worthing? Your brother was, I believe, unmarried, was he not?

JACK   Oh, yes.

MISS PRISM   (*bitterly*)   People who live entirely for pleasure usually are.

JACK   But it is not for any child, dear Doctor. I am very fond of children. No! the fact is, I would like to be christened myself, this afternoon, if you have nothing better to do.

CHASUBLE   But surely, Mr. Worthing, you have been christened already?

JACK   I don't remember anything about it.

CHASUBLE   But have you any grave doubts on the subject?

JACK   I certainly intend to have. Of course, I don't know if the thing would bother you in any way, or if you think I am a little too old now.

CHASUBLE   Not at all. The sprinkling, and, indeed, the immersion of adults is a perfectly canonical practice.

JACK   Immersion!

CHASUBLE   You need have no apprehensions. Sprinkling is all that is necessary, or indeed I think advisable. Our weather is so changeable. At what hour would you wish the ceremony performed?

JACK   Oh, I might trot around about five if that would suit you.

CHASUBLE   Perfectly, perfectly! In fact I have two similar ceremonies to perform at that time. A case of twins that occurred recently in one of the outlying cottages on your own estate. Poor Jenkins the carter, a most hard-working man.

JACK   Oh! I don't see much fun in being christened along with other babies. It would be childish. Would half-past five do?

CHASUBLE   Admirably! Admirably! (*Takes out watch.*) And now, dear Mr. Worthing, I will not intrude any longer into a house of sorrow. I would merely beg you not to be too much bowed down by grief. What seem to us bitter trials at the moment are often blessings in disguise.

MISS PRISM   This seems to me a blessing of an extremely obvious kind.

Enter CECILY *from the house.*

CECILY   Uncle Jack! Oh, I am pleased to see you back. But what horrid clothes you have on! Do go and change them.

MISS PRISM   Cecily!

CHASUBLE   My child! my child! (CECILY *goes towards* JACK; *he kisses her brow in a melancholy manner.*)

CECILY   What is the matter, Uncle Jack? Do look happy! You look as if you had a toothache and I have such a surprise for you. Who do you think is in the dining-room? Your brother!

JACK   Who?

CECILY Your brother Ernest. He arrived about half an hour ago.

JACK What nonsense! I haven't got a brother.

CECILY Oh, don't say that. However badly he may have behaved to you in the past he is still your brother. You couldn't be so heartless as to disown him. I'll tell him to come out. And you will shake hands with him, won't you, Uncle Jack? (*Runs back into the house.*)

CHASUBLE These are very joyful tidings.

MISS PRISM After we had all been resigned to his loss, his sudden return seems to me peculiarly distressing.

JACK My brother is in the dining-room? I don't know what it all means. I think it is perfectly absurd.

Enter ALGERNON *and* CECILY *hand in hand. They come slowly up to* JACK.

JACK Good heavens! (*Motions* ALGERNON *away.*)

ALGERNON Brother John, I have come down from town to tell you that I am very sorry for all the trouble I have given you, and that I intend to lead a better life in the future. (JACK *glares at him and does not take his hand.*)

CECILY Uncle Jack, you are not going to refuse your own brother's hand?

JACK Nothing will induce me to take his hand. I think his coming down here disgraceful. He knows perfectly well why.

CECILY Uncle Jack, do be nice. There is some good in every one. Ernest has just been telling me about his poor invalid friend, Mr. Bunbury, whom he goes to visit so often. And surely there must be much good in one who is kind to an invalid, and leaves the pleasures of London to sit by a bed of pain.

JACK Oh, he has been talking about Bunbury, has he?

CECILY Yes, he has told me all about poor Mr. Bunbury, and his terrible state of health.

JACK Bunbury! Well, I won't have him talk to you about Bunbury or about anything else. It is enough to drive one perfectly frantic.

ALGERNON Of course I admit that the faults were all on my side. But I must say that I think that Brother John's coldness to me is peculiarly painful. I expected a more enthusiastic welcome, especially considering it is the first time I have come here.

CECILY Uncle Jack, if you don't shake hands with Ernest I will never forgive you.

JACK Never forgive me?

CECILY Never, never, never!

JACK Well, this is the last time I shall ever do it. (*Shakes hands with* ALGERNON *and glares.*)

CHASUBLE It's pleasant, is it not, to see so perfect a reconciliation? I think we might leave the two brothers together.

MISS PRISM Cecily, you will come with us.

CECILY   Certainly, Miss Prism. My little task of reconciliation is over.
CHASUBLE   You have done a beautiful action to-day, dear child.
MISS PRISM   We must not be premature in our judgments.
CECILY   I feel very happy. (*They all go off.*)
JACK   You young scoundrel, Algy, you must get out of this place as soon as possible. I don't allow any Bunburying here.

Enter MERRIMAN.

MERRIMAN   I have put Mr. Ernest's things in the room next to yours, sir. I suppose that is all right?
JACK   What?
MERRIMAN   Mr. Ernest's luggage, sir. I have unpacked it and put it in the room next to your own.
JACK   His luggage?
MERRIMAN   Yes, sir. Three portmanteaus, a dressing-case, two hat-boxes, and a large luncheon-basket.
ALGERNON   I am afraid I can't stay more than a week this time.
JACK   Merriman, order the dog-cart at once. Mr. Ernest has been suddenly called back to town.
MERRIMAN   Yes, sir. (*Goes back into the house.*)
ALGERNON   What a fearful liar you are, Jack. I have not been called back to town at all.
JACK   Yes, you have.
ALGERNON   I haven't heard any one call me.
JACK   Your duty as a gentleman calls you back.
ALGERNON   My duty as a gentleman has never interfered with my pleasures in the smallest degree.
JACK   I can quite understand that.
ALGERNON   Well, Cecily is a darling.
JACK   You are not to talk of Miss Cardew like that. I don't like it.
ALGERNON   Well, I don't like your clothes. You look perfectly ridiculous in them. Why on earth don't you go up and change? It is perfectly childish to be in deep mourning for a man who is actually staying for a whole week with you in your house as a guest. I call it grotesque.
JACK   You are certainly not staying with me for a whole week as a guest or anything else. You have got to leave . . . by the four-five train.
ALGERNON   I certainly won't leave you so long as you are in mourning. It would be most unfriendly. If I were in mourning you would stay with me, I suppose. I should think it very unkind if you didn't.
JACK   Well, will you go if I change my clothes?
ALGERNON   Yes, if you are not too long. I never saw anybody take so long to dress, and with such little result.
JACK   Well, at any rate, that is better than being always over-dressed as you are.

ALGERNON　If I am occasionally a little over-dressed, I make up for it by being always immensely over-educated.

JACK　Your vanity is ridiculous, your conduct an outrage, and your presence in my garden utterly absurd. However, you have got to catch the four-five, and I hope you will have a pleasant journey back to town. This Bunburying, as you call it, has not been a great success for you. (*Goes into the house.*)

ALGERNON　I think it has been a great success. I'm in love with Cecily, and that is everything. (*Enter* CECILY *at the back of the garden. She picks up the can and begins to water the flowers.*) But I must see her before I go, and make arrangements for another Bunbury. Ah, there she is.

CECILY　Oh, I merely came back to water the roses. I thought you were with Uncle Jack.

ALGERNON　He's gone to order the dog-cart for me.

CECILY　Oh, is he going to take you for a nice drive?

ALGERNON　He's going to send me away.

CECILY　Then have we got to part?

ALGERNON　I am afraid so. It's a very painful parting.

CECILY　It is always painful to part from people whom one has known for a very brief space of time. The absence of old friends one can endure with equanimity. But even a momentary separation from any one to whom one has just been introduced is almost unbearable.

ALGERNON　Thank you.

Enter MERRIMAN.

MERRIMAN　The dog-cart is at the door, sir. (ALGERNON *looks appealingly at* CECILY.)

CECILY　It can wait, Merriman . . . for . . . five minutes.

MERRIMAN　Yes, miss.

Exit MERRIMAN.

ALGERNON　I hope, Cecily, I shall not offend you if I state quite frankly and openly that you seem to me to be in every way the visible personification of absolute perfection.

CECILY　I think your frankness does you great credit, Ernest. If you will allow me I will copy your remarks into my diary. (*Goes over to table and begins writing in diary.*)

ALGERNON　Do you really keep a diary? I'd give anything to look at it. May I?

CECILY　Oh, no. (*Puts her hand over it.*) You see it is simply a very young girl's record of her own thoughts and impressions, and consequently meant for publication. When it appears in volume form I hope you will order a copy. But pray, Ernest, don't stop. I delight in taking down from dictation. I have reached "absolute perfection." You can go on. I am quite ready for more.

ALGERNON (*somewhat taken aback*)   Ahem! Ahem!

CECILY   Oh, don't cough, Ernest. When one is dictating one should speak fluently and not cough. Besides, I don't know how to spell a cough. (*Writes as* ALGERNON *speaks.*)

ALGERNON (*speaking very rapidly*)   Cecily, ever since I first looked upon your wonderful and incomparable beauty, I have dared to love you wildly, passionately, devotedly, hopelessly.

CECILY   I don't think that you should tell me that you love me wildly, passionately, devotedly, hopelessly. Hopelessly doesn't seem to make much sense, does it?

ALGERNON   Cecily!

Enter MERRIMAN.

MERRIMAN   The dog-cart is waiting, sir.

ALGERNON   Tell it to come round next week, at the same hour.

MERRIMAN (*looks at* CECILY, *who makes no sign*)   Yes, sir.

MERRIMAN *retires.*

CECILY   Uncle Jack would be very much annoyed if he knew you were staying on till next week, at the same hour.

ALGERNON   Oh, I don't care about Jack. I don't care for anybody in the whole world but you. I love you, Cecily. You will marry me, won't you?

CECILY   You silly you! Of course. Why, we have been engaged for the last three months.

ALGERNON   For the last three months?

CECILY   Yes, it will be exactly three months on Thursday.

ALGERNON   But how did we become engaged?

CECILY   Well, ever since dear Uncle Jack first confessed to us that he had a younger brother who was very wicked and bad, you of course have formed the chief topic of conversation between myself and Miss Prism. And of course a man who is much talked about is always very attractive. One feels there must be something in him after all. I daresay it was foolish of me, but I fell in love with you, Ernest.

ALGERNON   Darling! And when was the engagement actually settled?

CECILY   On the 4th of February last. Worn out by your entire ignorance of my existence, I determined to end the matter one way or the other, and after a long struggle with myself I accepted you under this dear old tree here. The next day I bought this little ring in your name, and this is the little bangle with the true lovers' knot I promised you always to wear.

ALGERNON   Did I give you this? It's very pretty, isn't it?

CECILY   Yes, you've wonderfully good taste, Ernest. It's the excuse I've always given for your leading such a bad life. And this is the box in which I keep all your dear letters. (*Kneels at table, opens box, and produces letters tied up with blue ribbon.*)

ALGERNON   My letters! but my own sweet Cecily, I have never written you any letters.

CECILY   You need hardly remind me of that, Ernest. I remember only too well that I was forced to write your letters for you. I wrote always three times a week, and sometimes oftener.

ALGERNON   Oh, do let me read them, Cecily?

CECILY   Oh, I couldn't possibly. They would make you far too conceited. (*Replaces box.*) The three you wrote me after I had broken off the engagement are so beautiful, and so badly spelled, that even now I can hardly read them without crying a little.

ALGERNON   But was our engagement ever broken off?

CECILY   Of course it was. On the 22nd of last March. You can see the entry if you like. (*Shows diary.*) "To-day I broke off my engagement with Ernest. I feel it is better to do so. The weather still continues charming."

ALGERNON   But why on earth did you break it off? What had I done? I had done nothing at all. Cecily, I am very much hurt indeed to hear you broke it off. Particularly when the weather was so charming.

CECILY   It would hardly have been a really serious engagement if it hadn't been broken off at least once. But I forgave you before the week was out.

ALGERNON (*crossing to her, and kneeling*)   What a perfect angel you are, Cecily.

CECILY   You dear romantic boy. (*He kisses her, she puts her fingers through his hair.*) I hope your hair curls naturally, does it?

ALGERNON   Yes, darling, with a little help from others.

CECILY   I am so glad.

ALGERNON   You'll never break off our engagement again, Cecily?

CECILY   I don't think I could break it off now that I have actually met you. Besides, of course, there is the question of your name.

ALGERNON   Yes, of course. (*Nervously.*)

CECILY   You must not laugh at me, darling, but it had always been a girlish dream of mine to love some one whose name was Ernest. (ALGERNON *rises*, CECILY *also.*) There is something in that name that seems to inspire absolute confidence. I pity any poor married woman whose husband is not called Ernest.

ALGERNON   But, my dear child, do you mean to say you could not love me if I had some other name?

CECILY   But what name?

ALGERNON   Oh, any name you like—Algernon, for instance. . . .

CECILY   But I don't like the name of Algernon.

ALGERNON   Well, my own dear, sweet, loving little darling, I really can't see why you should object to the name of Algernon. It is not at all a bad name. In fact, it is rather an aristocratic name. Half of the chaps who get into the Bankruptcy Court are called Algernon. But seriously, Cecily . . . (*moving to her*) . . . if my name was Algy, couldn't you love me?

CECILY (*rising*)   I might respect you, Ernest, I might admire your character, but I fear that I should not be able to give you my undivided attention.

ALGERNON   Ahem! Cecily! (*Picking up hat.*) Your Rector here is, I suppose, thoroughly experienced in the practice of all the rites and ceremonials of the church?

CECILY   Oh, yes. Dr. Chasuble is a most learned man. He has never written a single book, so you can imagine how much he knows.

ALGERNON   I must see him at once on a most important christening—I mean on most important business.

CECILY   Oh!

ALGERNON   I sha'n't be away more than half an hour.

CECILY   Considering that we have been engaged since February the 14th, and that I only met you to-day for the first time, I think it is rather hard that you should leave me for so long a period as half an hour. Couldn't you make it twenty minutes?

ALGERNON   I'll be back in no time. (*Kisses her and rushes down the garden.*)

CECILY   What an impetuous boy he is. I like his hair so much. I must enter his proposal in my diary.

Enter MERRIMAN.

MERRIMAN   A Miss Fairfax has just called to see Mr. Worthing. On very important business, Miss Fairfax states.

CECILY   Isn't Mr. Worthing in his library?

MERRIMAN   Mr. Worthing went over in the direction of the Rectory some time ago.

CECILY   Pray ask the lady to come out here; Mr. Worthing is sure to be back soon. And you can bring tea.

MERRIMAN   Yes, miss. (*Goes out.*)

CECILY   Miss Fairfax! I suppose one of the many good elderly women who are associated with Uncle Jack in some of his philanthropic work in London. I don't quite like women who are interested in philanthropic work. I think it is so forward of them.

Enter MERRIMAN.

MERRIMAN   Miss Fairfax.

Enter GWENDOLEN. *Exit* MERRIMAN.

CECILY (*advancing to meet her*)   Pray let me introduce myself to you. My name is Cecily Cardew.

GWENDOLEN   Cecily Cardew? (*Moving to her and shaking hands.*) What a very sweet name! Something tells me that we are going to be great friends. I like you already more than I can say. My first impressions of people are never wrong.

CECILY How nice of you to like me so much after we have known each other such a comparatively short time. Pray sit down.

GWENDOLEN (*still standing up*) I may call you Cecily, may I not?

CECILY With pleasure!

GWENDOLEN And you will always call me Gwendolen, won't you?

CECILY If you wish.

GWENDOLEN Then that is all quite settled, is it not?

CECILY I hope so. (*A pause; they both sit down together.*)

GWENDOLEN Perhaps this might be a favorable opportunity for my mentioning who I am. My father is Lord Bracknell. You have never heard of papa, I suppose?

CECILY I don't think so.

GWENDOLEN Outside the family circle, papa, I am glad to say, is entirely unknown. I think that is quite as it should be. The home seems to me to be the proper sphere for the man. And certainly once a man begins to neglect his domestic duties he becomes painfully effeminate, does he not? And I don't like that. It makes men so very attractive. Cecily, mamma, whose views on education are remarkably strict, has brought me up to be extremely short-sighted; it is part of her system; so do you mind my looking at you through my glasses?

CECILY Oh, not at all, Gwendolen. I am very fond of being looked at.

GWENDOLEN (*after examining* CECILY *carefully through a lorgnette*) You are here on a short visit, I suppose.

CECILY Oh, no, I live here.

GWENDOLEN (*severely*) Really? Your mother, no doubt, or some female relative of advanced years, resides here also?

CECILY Oh, no. I have no mother, nor, in fact, any relations.

GWENDOLEN Indeed?

CECILY My dear guardian, with the assistance of Miss Prism, has the arduous task of looking after me.

GWENDOLEN Your guardian?

CECILY Yes, I am Mr. Worthing's ward.

GWENDOLEN Oh! It is strange he never mentioned to me that he had a ward. How secretive of him! He grows more interesting hourly. I am not sure, however, that the news inspires me with feelings of unmixed delight. (*Rising and going to her.*) I am very fond of you, Cecily; I have liked you ever since I met you. But I am bound to state that now that I know that you are Mr. Worthing's ward, I cannot help expressing a wish you were—well, just a little older than you seem to be— and not quite so very alluring in appearance. In fact, if I may speak candidly—

CECILY Pray do! I think that whenever one has anything unpleasant to say, one should always be quite candid.

GWENDOLEN Well, to speak with perfect candor, Cecily, I wish that you were fully forty-two, and more than usually plain for your age. Ernest has a strong upright nature. He is the very soul of truth and honor.

Disloyalty would be as impossible to him as deception. But even men of the noblest possible moral character are extremely susceptible to the influence of the physical charms of others. Modern, no less than Ancient History, supplies us with many most painful examples of what I refer to. If it were not so, indeed, History would be quite unreadable.

CECILY   I beg your pardon, Gwendolen, did you say Ernest?

GWENDOLEN   Yes.

CECILY   Oh, but it is not Mr. Ernest Worthing who is my guardian. It is his brother—his elder brother.

GWENDOLEN (*sitting down again*)   Ernest never mentioned to me that he had a brother.

CECILY   I am sorry to say they have not been on good terms for a long time.

GWENDOLEN   Ah! that accounts for it. And now that I think of it I have never heard any man mention his brother. The subject seems distasteful to most men. Cecily, you have lifted a load from my mind. I was growing almost anxious. It would have been terrible if any cloud had come across a friendship like ours, would it not? Of course you are quite, quite sure that it is not Mr. Ernest Worthing who is your guardian?

CECILY   Quite sure. (*A pause.*) In fact, I am going to be his.

GWENDOLEN (*enquiringly*)   I beg your pardon?

CECILY (*rather shy and confidingly*)   Dearest Gwendolen, there is no reason why I should make a secret of it to you. Our little county newspaper is sure to chronicle the fact next week. Mr. Ernest Worthing and I are engaged to be married.

GWENDOLEN (*quite politely, rising*)   My darling Cecily, I think there must be some slight error. Mr. Ernest Worthing is engaged to me. The announcement will appear in the *Morning Post* on Saturday at the latest.

CECILY (*very politely, rising*)   I am afraid you must be under some misconception. Ernest proposed to me exactly ten minutes ago. (*Shows diary.*)

GWENDOLEN (*examines diary through her lorgnette carefully*)   It is certainly very curious, for he asked me to be his wife yesterday afternoon at 5:30. If you would care to verify the incident, pray do so. (*Produces diary of her own.*) I never travel without my diary. One should always have something sensational to read in the train. I am so sorry, dear Cecily, if it is any disappointment to you, but I'm afraid *I* have the prior claim.

CECILY   It would distress me more than I can tell you, dear Gwendolen, if it caused you any mental or physical anguish, but I feel bound to point out that since Ernest proposed to you he clearly has changed his mind.

GWENDOLEN (*meditatively*)   If the poor fellow has been entrapped into any foolish promise I shall consider it my duty to rescue him at once, and with a firm hand.

CECILY (*thoughtfully and sadly*)   Whatever unfortunate entanglement my dear boy may have got into, I will never reproach him with it after we are married.

GWENDOLEN   Do you allude to me, Miss Cardew, as an entanglement? You are presumptuous. On an occasion of this kind it becomes more than a moral duty to speak one's mind. It becomes a pleasure.

CECILY   Do you suggest, Miss Fairfax, that I entrapped Ernest into an engagement? How dare you? This is no time for wearing the shallow mask of manners. When I see a spade I call it a spade.

GWENDOLEN (*satirically*)   I am glad to say that I have never seen a spade. It is obvious that our social spheres have been widely different.

Enter MERRIMAN, *followed by the footman. He carries a salver, table-cloth, and plate-stand.* CECILY *is about to retort. The presence of the servants exercises a restraining influence, under which both girls chafe.*

MERRIMAN   Shall I lay tea here as usual, miss?

CECILY (*sternly, in a calm voice*)   Yes, as usual. (MERRIMAN *begins to clear and lay cloth. A long pause.* CECILY *and* GWENDOLEN *glare at each other.*)

GWENDOLEN   Are there many interesting walks in the vicinity, Miss Cardew?

CECILY   Oh, yes, a great many. From the top of one of the hills quite close one can see five counties.

GWENDOLEN   Five counties! I don't think I should like that. I hate crowds.

CECILY (*sweetly*)   I suppose that is why you live in town? (GWENDOLYN *bites her lip, and beats her foot nervously with her parasol.*)

GWENDOLEN (*looking round*)   Quite a well-kept garden this is, Miss Cardew.

CECILY   So glad you like it, Miss Fairfax.

GWENDOLEN   I had no idea there were any flowers in the country.

CECILY   Oh, flowers are as common here, Miss Fairfax, as people are in London.

GWENDOLEN   Personally I cannot understand how anybody manages to exist in the country, if anybody who is anybody does. The country always bores me to death.

CECILY   Ah! This is what the newspapers call agricultural depression, is it not? I believe the aristocracy are suffering very much from it just at present. It is almost an epidemic amongst them, I have been told. May I offer you some tea, Miss Fairfax?

GWENDOLEN (*with elaborate politeness*)   Thank you. (*Aside.*) Detestable girl! But I require tea!

CECILY (*sweetly*)   Sugar?

GWENDOLEN (*superciliously*)   No, thank you. Sugar is not fashionable any more. (CECILY *looks angrily at her, takes up the tongs and puts four lumps of sugar into the cup.*)

CECILY (*severely*)   Cake or bread and butter?

GWENDOLEN (*in a bored manner*)   Bread and butter, please. Cake is rarely seen at the best houses now-a-days.

CECILY (*cuts a very large slice of cake, and puts it on the tray*).   Hand that to Miss Fairfax. (MERRIMAN *does so, and goes out with footman.* GWENDOLEN *drinks the tea and makes a grimace. Puts down cup at once, reaches out her hand to the bread and butter, looks at it, and finds it is cake. Rises in indignation.*)

GWENDOLEN   You have filled my tea with lumps of sugar, and though I asked most distinctly for bread and butter, you have given me cake. I am known for the gentleness of my disposition, and the extraordinary sweetness of my nature, but I warn you, Miss Cardew, you may go too far.

CECILY (*rising*)   To save my poor, innocent, trusting boy from the machinations of any other girl there are no lengths to which I would not go.

GWENDOLEN   From the moment I saw you I distrusted you. I felt that you were false and deceitful. I am never deceived in such matters. My first impressions of people are invariably right.

CECILY   It seems to me, Miss Fairfax, that I am trespassing on your valuable time. No doubt you have many other calls of a similar character to make in the neighborhood.

Enter JACK.

GWENDOLEN (*catching sight of him*)   Ernest! My own Ernest!

JACK   Gwendolen! Darling! (*Offers to kiss her.*)

GWENDOLEN (*drawing back*)   A moment! May I ask if you are engaged to be married to this young lady? (*Points to* CECILY.)

JACK (*laughing*)   To dear little Cecily! Of course not! What could have put such an idea into your pretty little head?

GWENDOLEN   Thank you. You may. (*Offers her cheek.*)

CECILY (*very sweetly*)   I knew there must be some misunderstanding, Miss Fairfax. The gentleman whose arm is at present around your waist is my dear guardian, Mr. John Worthing.

GWENDOLEN   I beg your pardon?

CECILY   This is Uncle Jack.

GWENDOLEN (*receding*)   Jack! Oh!

Enter ALGERNON.

CECILY   Here is Ernest.

ALGERNON (*goes straight over to* CECILY *without noticing any one else*)   My own love! (*Offers to kiss her.*)

CECILY (*drawing back*) A moment, Ernest! May I ask you—are you engaged to be married to this young lady?

ALGERNON (*looking round*) To what young lady? Good heavens! Gwendolen!

CECILY Yes, to good heavens, Gwendolen, I mean to Gwendolen.

ALGERNON (*laughing*) Of course not! What could have put such an idea into your pretty little head?

CECILY Thank you. (*Presenting her cheek to be kissed.*) You may (ALGERNON *kisses her.*)

GWENDOLEN I felt there was some slight error, Miss Cardew. The gentleman who is now embracing you is my cousin, Mr. Algernon Moncrieff.

CECILY (*breaking away from* ALGERNON) Algernon Moncrieff! Oh! (*The two girls move towards each other and put their arms round each other's waists as if for protection.*)

CECILY Are you called Algernon?

ALGERNON I cannot deny it.

CECILY Oh!

GWENDOLEN Is your name really John?

JACK (*standing rather proudly*) I could deny it if I liked. I could deny anything if I liked. But my name certainly is John. It has been John for years.

CECILY (*to* GWENDOLEN) A gross deception has been practiced on both of us.

GWENDOLEN My poor wounded Cecily!

CECILY My sweet, wronged Gwendolen!

GWENDOLEN (*slowly and seriously*) You will call me sister, will you not? (*They embrace.* JACK *and* ALGERNON *groan and walk up and down.*)

CECILY (*rather brightly*) There is just one question I would like to be allowed to ask my guardian.

GWENDOLEN An admirable idea! Mr. Worthing, there is just one question I would like to be permitted to put to you. Where is your brother Ernest? We are both engaged to be married to your brother Ernest, so it is a matter of some importance to us to know where your brother Ernest is at present.

JACK (*slowly and hesitatingly*) Gwendolen—Cecily—it is very painful for me to be forced to speak the truth. It is the first time in my life that I have ever been reduced to such a painful position, and I am really quite inexperienced in doing anything of the kind. However I will tell you quite frankly that I have no brother Ernest. I have no brother at all. I never had a brother in my life, and I certainly have not the smallest intention of ever having one in the future.

CECILY (*surprised*) No brother at all?

JACK (*cheerily*) None!

GWENDOLEN (*severely*) Had you never a brother of any kind?

JACK (*pleasantly*)   Never. Not even of any kind.

GWENDOLEN   I am afraid it is quite clear, Cecily, that neither of us is engaged to be married to any one.

CECILY   It is not a very pleasant position for a young girl suddenly to find herself in. Is it?

GWENDOLEN   Let us go into the house. They will hardly venture to come after us there.

CECILY   No, men are so cowardly, aren't they? (*They retire into the house with scornful looks.*)

JACK   This ghastly state of things is what you call Bunburying, I suppose?

ALGERNON   Yes, and a perfectly wonderful Bunbury it is. The most wonderful Bunbury I have ever had in my life.

JACK   Well, you've no right whatsoever to Bunbury here.

ALGERNON   That is absurd. One has a right to Bunbury anywhere one chooses. Every serious Bunburyist knows that.

JACK   Serious Bunburyist! Good heavens!

ALGERNON   Well, one must be serious about something, if one wants to have any amusement in life. I happen to be serious about Bunburying. What on earth you are serious about I haven't got the remotest idea. About everything, I should fancy. You have such an absolutely trivial nature.

JACK   Well, the only small satisfaction I have in the whole of this wretched business is that your friend Bunbury is quite exploded. You won't be able to run down to the country quite so often as you used to do, dear Algy. And a very good thing, too.

ALGERNON   Your brother is a little off color, isn't he, dear Jack? You won't be able to disappear to London quite so frequently as your wicked custom was. And not a bad thing, either.

JACK   As for your conduct towards Miss Cardew, I must say that your taking in a sweet, simple, innocent girl like that is quite inexcusable. To say nothing of the fact that she is my ward.

ALGERNON   I can see no possible defense at all for your deceiving a brilliant, clever, thoroughly experienced young lady like Miss Fairfax. To say nothing of the fact that she is my cousin.

JACK   I wanted to be engaged to Gwendolen, that is all. I love her.

ALGERNON   Well, I simply wanted to be engaged to Cecily. I adore her.

JACK   There is certainly no chance of your marrying Miss Cardew.

ALGERNON   I don't think there is much likelihood, Jack, of you and Miss Fairfax being united.

JACK   Well, that is no business of yours.

ALGERNON   If it was my business, I wouldn't talk about it. (*Begins to eat muffins.*) It is very vulgar to talk about one's business. Only people like stock-brokers do that, and then merely at dinner parties.

JACK   How you can sit there, calmly eating muffins, when we are in this horrible trouble, I can't make out. You seem to me to be perfectly heartless.

ALGERNON   Well, I can't eat muffins in an agitated manner. The butter would probably get on my cuffs. One should always eat muffins quite calmly. It is the only way to eat them.

JACK   I say it's perfectly heartless your eating muffins at all, under the circumstances.

ALGERNON   When I am in trouble, eating is the only thing that consoles me. Indeed, when I am in really great trouble, as any one who knows me intimately will tell you, I refuse everything except food and drink. At the present moment I am eating muffins because I am unhappy. Besides, I am particularly fond of muffins. (*Rising.*)

JACK (*rising*)   Well, that is no reason why you should eat them all in that greedy way. (*Takes muffins from* ALGERNON.)

ALGERNON (*offering tea-cake*)   I wish you would have tea-cake instead. I don't like tea-cake.

JACK   Good heavens! I suppose a man may eat his own muffins in his own garden.

ALGERNON   But you have just said it was perfectly heartless to eat muffins.

JACK   I said it was perfectly heartless of you, under the circumstances. That is a very different thing.

ALGERNON   That may be. But the muffins are the same. (*He seizes the muffin-dish from* JACK.)

JACK   Algy, I wish to goodness you would go.

ALGERNON   You can't possibly ask me to go without having some dinner. It's absurd. I never go without my dinner. No one ever does, except vegetarians, and people like that. Besides I have just made arrangements with Dr. Chasuble to be christened at a quarter to six under the name of Ernest.

JACK   My dear fellow, the sooner you give up that nonsense the better. I made arrangements this morning with Dr. Chasuble to be christened myself at 5:30, and I naturally will take the name of Ernest. Gwendolen would wish it. We can't both be christened Ernest. It's absurd. Besides, I have a perfect right to be christened if I like. There is no evidence at all that I ever have been christened by anybody. I should think it extremely probable I never was, and so does Dr. Chasuble. It is entirely different in your case. You have been christened already.

ALGERNON   Yes, but I have not been christened for years.

JACK   Yes, but you have been christened. That is the important thing.

ALGERNON   Quite so. So I know my constitution can stand it. If you are not quite sure about your ever having been christened, I must say I think it rather dangerous your venturing on it now. It might make you very unwell. You can hardly have forgotten that some one very closely connected with you was very nearly carried off this week in Paris by a severe chill.

JACK   Yes, but you said yourself that a severe chill was not hereditary.

ALGERNON   It usedn't to be, I know—but I daresay it is now. Science is always making wonderful improvements in things.

JACK (*picking up the muffin-dish*)   Oh, that is nonsense, you are always talking nonsense.

ALGERNON   Jack, you are at the muffins again! I wish you wouldn't. There are only two left. (*Takes them.*) I told you I was particularly fond of muffins.

JACK   But I hate tea-cake.

ALGERNON   Why on earth then do you allow tea-cake to be served up for your guests? What ideas you have of hospitality!

JACK   Algernon! I have already told you to go. I don't want you here. Why don't you go?

ALGERNON   I haven't quite finished my tea yet, and there is still one muffin left. (JACK *groans, and sinks into a chair.* ALGERNON *still continues eating.*)

Curtain

ACT III

SCENE   *Morning-room at the Manor House.* GWENDOLEN *and* CECILY *are at the window, looking out into the garden.*

GWENDOLEN   The fact that they did not follow us at once into the house, as any one else would have done, seems to me to show that they have some sense of shame left.

CECILY   They have been eating muffins. That looks like repentance.

GWENDOLEN (*after a pause*)   They don't seem to notice us at all. Couldn't you cough?

GWENDOLEN   They're looking at us. What effrontery!

CECILY   They're approaching. That's very forward of them.

GWENDOLEN   Let us preserve a dignified silence.

CECILY   Certainly. It's the only thing to do now.

Enter JACK, *followed by* ALGERNON. *They whistle some dreadful popular air from a British opera.*

GWENDOLEN   This dignified silence seems to produce an unpleasant effect.

CECILY   A most distasteful one.

GWENDOLEN   But we will not be the first to speak.

CECILY   Certainly not.

GWENDOLEN   Mr. Worthing, I have something very particular to ask you. Much depends on your reply.

CECILY   Gwendolen, your common sense is invaluable. Mr. Moncrieff, kindly answer me the following question. Why did you pretend to be my guardian's brother?

ALGERNON   In order that I might have an opportunity of meeting you.

CECILY (*to* GWENDOLEN)   That certainly seems a satisfactory explanation, does it not?

GWENDOLEN   Yes, dear, if you can believe him.

CECILY   I don't. But that does not affect the wonderful beauty of his answer.

GWENDOLEN   True. In matters of grave importance, style, not sincerity, is the vital thing. Mr. Worthing, what explanation can you offer to me for pretending to have a brother? Was it in order that you might have an opportunity of coming up to town to see me as often as possible?

JACK   Can you doubt it, Miss Fairfax?

GWENDOLEN   I have the gravest doubts upon the subject. But I intend to crush them. This is not the moment for German skepticism. (*Moving to* CECILY.) Their explanations appear to be quite satisfactory, especially Mr. Worthing's. That seems to me to have the stamp of truth upon it.

CECILY   I am more than content with what Mr. Moncrieff said. His voice alone inspires one with absolute credulity.

GWENDOLEN   Then you think we should forgive them?

CECILY   Yes. I mean no.

GWENDOLEN   True! I had forgotten. There are principles at stake that one cannot surrender. Which of us should tell them? The task is not a pleasant one.

CECILY   Could we not both speak at the same time?

GWENDOLEN   An excellent idea! I nearly always speak at the same time as other people. Will you take the time from me?

CECILY   Certainly. (GWENDOLEN *beats time with uplifted finger.*)

GWENDOLEN *and* CECILY (*speaking together*)   Your Christian names are still an insuperable barrier. That is all!

JACK and ALGERNON (*speaking together*)   Our Christian names! Is that all? But we are going to be christened this afternoon.

GWENDOLEN (*to* JACK)   For my sake you are prepared to do this terrible thing?

JACK   I am.

CECILY (*to* ALGERNON)   To please me you are ready to face this fearful ordeal?

ALGERNON   I am!

GWENDOLEN   How absurd to talk of the equality of the sexes! Where questions of self-sacrifice are concerned, men are infinitely beyond us.

JACK   We are. (*Clasps hands with* ALGERNON.)

CECILY   They have moments of physical courage of which we women know absolutely nothing.

GWENDOLEN (*to* JACK)   Darling!

ALGERNON (*to* CECILY)   Darling! (*They fall into each other's arms.*)

Enter MERRIMAN. *When he enters he coughs loudly, seeing the situation.*

MERRIMAN   Ahem! Ahem! Lady Bracknell!
JACK   Good heavens!

Enter LADY BRACKNELL. *The couples separate in alarm. Exit* MERRIMAN.

LADY BRACKNELL   Gwendolen! What does this mean?
GWENDOLEN   Merely that I am engaged to be married to Mr. Worthing, mamma.
LADY BRACKNELL   Come here. Sit down. Sit down immediately. Hesitation of any kind is a sign of mental decay in the young, of physical weakness in the old. (*Turns to* JACK.) Apprised, sir, of my daughter's sudden flight by her trusty maid, whose confidence I purchased by means of a small coin, I followed her at once by a luggage train. Her unhappy father is, I am glad to say, under the impression that she is attending a more than usually lengthy lecture by the University Extension Scheme on the Influence of a Permanent Income on Thought. I do not propose to undeceive him. Indeed I have never undeceived him on any question. I would consider it wrong. But of course you will clearly understand that all communication between yourself and my daughter must cease immediately from this moment. On this point, as indeed on all points, I am firm.
JACK   I am engaged to be married to Gwendolen, Lady Bracknell!
LADY BRACKNELL   You are nothing of the kind, sir. And now, as regards Algernon! . . . Algernon!
ALGERNON   Yes, Aunt Augusta.
LADY BRACKNELL   May I ask if it is in this house that your invalid friend Mr. Bunbury resides?
ALGERNON (*stammering*)   Oh, no! Bunbury doesn't live here. Bunbury is somewhere else at present. In fact, Bunbury is dead.
LADY BRACKNELL   Dead! When did Mr. Bunbury die? His death must have been extremely sudden.
ALGERNON (*airily*)   Oh, I killed Bunbury this afternoon. I mean poor Bunbury died this afternoon.
LADY BRACKNELL   What did he die of?
ALGERNON   Bunbury? Oh, he was quite exploded.
LADY BRACKNELL   Exploded! Was he the victim of a revolutionary outrage? I was not aware that Mr. Bunbury was interested in social legislation. If so, he is well punished for his morbidity.
ALGERNON   My dear Aunt Augusta, I mean he was found out! The doctors found out that Bunbury could not live, that is what I mean— so Bunbury died.
LADY BRACKNELL   He seems to have had great confidence in the opinion of his physicians. I am glad, however, that he made up his mind at

the last to some definite course of action, and acted under proper medical advice. And now that we have finally got rid of this Mr. Bunbury, may I ask, Mr. Worthing, who is that young person whose hand my nephew Algernon is now holding in what seems to me a peculiarly unnecessary manner?

JACK   That lady is Miss Cecily Cardew, my ward. (LADY BRACKNELL *bows coldly to* CECILY.)

ALGERNON   I am engaged to be married to Cecily, Aunt Augusta.

LADY BRACKNELL   I beg your pardon?

CECILY   Mr. Moncrieff and I are engaged to be married, Lady Bracknell.

LADY BRACKNELL (*with a shiver, crossing to the sofa and sitting down*)   I do not know whether there is anything peculiarly exciting in the air of this particular part of Hertfordshire, but the number of engagements that go on seems to me considerably above the proper average that statistics have laid down for our guidance. I think some preliminary enquiry on my part would not be out of place. Mr. Worthing, is Miss Cardew at all connected with any of the larger railway stations in London? I merely desire information. Until yesterday I had no idea that there were any families or persons whose origin was a Terminus. (JACK *looks perfectly furious, but restrains himself.*)

JACK (*in a clear, cold voice*)   Miss Cardew is the granddaughter of the late Mr. Thomas Cardew of 149, Belgrave Square, S.W.; Gervase Park, Dorking, Surrey; and the Sporran, Fifeshire, N.B.

LADY BRACKNELL   That sounds not unsatisfactory. Three addresses always inspire confidence, even in tradesmen. But what proof have I of their authenticity?

JACK   I have carefully preserved the Court Guides of the period. They are open to your inspection, Lady Bracknell.

LADY BRACKNELL (*grimly*)   I have known strange errors in that publication.

JACK   Miss Cardew's family solicitors are Messrs. Markby, Markby, and Markby.

LADY BRACKNELL   Markby, Markby, and Markby? A firm of the very highest position in their profession. Indeed I am told that one of the Mr. Markbys is occasionally to be seen at dinner parties. So far I am satisfied.

JACK (*very irritably*)   How extremely kind of you, Lady Bracknell! I have also in my possession, you will pleased to hear, certificates of Miss Cardew's birth, baptism, whooping cough, registration, vaccination, confirmation, and the measles; both the German and the English variety.

LADY BRACKNELL   Ah! A life crowded with incident, I see; though perhaps somewhat too exciting for a young girl. I am not myself in favor of premature experiences. (*Rises, looks at her watch.*) Gwendolen! the time approaches for our departure. We have not a moment to lose. As a matter of form, Mr. Worthing, I had better ask you if Miss Cardew has any little fortune?

JACK   Oh, about a hundred and thirty thousand pounds in the Funds. That is all. Goodby, Lady Bracknell. So pleased to have seen you.

LADY BRACKNELL (*sitting down again*)   A moment, Mr. Worthing. A hundred and thirty thousand pounds! And in the Funds! Miss Cardew seems to me a most attractive young lady, now that I look at her. Few girls of the present day have any really solid qualities, any of the qualities that last, and improve with time. We live, I regret to say, in an age of surfaces. (*To* CECILY.) Come over here, dear. (CECILY *goes across.*) Pretty child! your dress is sadly simple, and your hair seems almost as Nature might have left it. But we can soon alter all that. A thoroughly experienced French maid produces a really marvelous result in a very brief space of time. I remember recommending one to young Lady Lancing, and after three months her own husband did not know her.

JACK (*aside*)   And after six months nobody knew her.

LADY BRACKNELL (*glares at* JACK *for a few moments, then bends, with a practiced smile, to* CECILY)   Kindly turn round, sweet child. (CECILY *turns completely round.*) No, the side view is what I want. (CECILY *presents her profile.*) Yes, quite as I expected. There are distinct social possibilities in your profile. The two weak points in our age are its want of principle and its want of profile. The chin a little higher, dear. Style largely depends on the way the chin is worn. They are worn very high, just at present. Algernon!

ALGERNON   Yes, Aunt Augusta!

LADY BRACKNELL   There are distinct social possibilities in Miss Cardew's profile.

ALGERNON   Cecily is the sweetest, dearest, prettiest girl in the whole world. And I don't care twopence about social possibilities.

LADY BRACKNELL   Never speak disrespectfully of society, Algernon. Only people who can't get into it do that. (*To* CECILY.) Dear child, of course you know that Algernon has nothing but his debts to depend upon. But I do not approve of mercenary marriages. When I married Lord Bracknell I had no fortune of any kind. But I never dreamed for a moment of allowing that to stand in my way. Well, I suppose I must give my consent.

ALGERNON   Thank you, Aunt Augusta.

LADY BRACKNELL   Cecily, you may kiss me!

CECILY (*kisses her*)   Thank you, Lady Bracknell.

LADY BRACKNELL   You may address me as Aunt Augusta for the future.

CECILY   Thank you, Aunt Augusta.

LADY BRACKNELL   The marriage, I think, had better take place quite soon.

ALGERNON   Thank you, Aunt Augusta.

CECILY   Thank you, Aunt Augusta.

LADY BRACKNELL   To speak frankly, I am not in favor of long engagements. They give people the opportunity of finding out each other's character before marriage, which I think is never advisable.

JACK   I beg your pardon for interrupting you, Lady Bracknell, but this engagement is quite out of the question. I am Miss Cardew's guardian, and she cannot marry without my consent until she comes of age. That consent I absolutely decline to give.

LADY BRACKNELL   Upon what grounds, may I ask? Algernon is an extremely, I may almost say an ostentatiously, eligible young man. He has nothing, but he looks everything. What more can one desire?

JACK   It pains me very much to have to speak frankly to you, Lady Bracknell, about your nephew, but the fact is that I do not approve at all of his moral character. I suspect him of being untruthful. (ALGERNON and CECILY *look at him in indignant amazement.*)

LADY BRACKNELL   Untruthful! My nephew Algernon? Impossible! He is an Oxonian.

JACK   I fear there can be no possible doubt about the matter. This afternoon, during my temporary absence in London on an important question of romance, he obtained admission to my house by means of the false pretense of being my brother. Under an assumed name he drank, I've just been informed by my butler, an entire pint bottle of my Perrier-Jouet, Brut, '89; a wine I was specially reserving for myself. Continuing his disgraceful deception, he succeeded in the course of the afternoon in alienating the affections of my only ward. He subsequently stayed to tea, and devoured every single muffin. And what makes his conduct all the more heartless is, that he was perfectly well aware from the first that I have no brother, that I never had a brother, and that I don't intend to have a brother, not even of any kind. I distinctly told him so myself yesterday afternoon.

LADY BRACKNELL   Ahem! Mr. Worthing, after careful consideration I have decided entirely to overlook my nephew's conduct to you.

JACK   That is very generous of you, Lady Bracknell. My own decision, however, is unalterable. I decline to give my consent.

LADY BRACKNELL   (*to* CECILY)   Come here, sweet child. (CECILY *goes over.*) How old are you, dear?

CECILY   Well, I am really only eighteen, but I always admit to twenty when I go to evening parties.

LADY BRACKNELL   You are perfectly right in making some slight alteration. Indeed, no woman should ever be quite accurate about her age. It looks so calculating. . . . (*In meditative manner.*) Eighteen, but admitting to twenty at evening parties. Well, it will not be very long before you are of age and free from the restraints of tutelage. So I don't think your guardian's consent is, after all, a matter of any importance.

JACK   Pray excuse me, Lady Bracknell, for interrupting you again, but it is only fair to tell you that according to the terms of her grandfather's will Miss Cardew does not come legally of age till she is thirty-five.

LADY BRACKNELL   That does not seem to me to be a grave objection. Thirty-five is a very attractive age. London society is full of women of the very highest birth who have, of their own free choice, remained thirty-five for years. Lady Dumbleton is an instance in point. To my own knowledge she has been thirty-five ever since she arrived at the age of forty, which was many years ago now. I see no reason why our dear Cecily should not be even still more attractive at the age you mention than she is at present. There will be a large accumulation of property.

CECILY   Algy, could you wait for me till I was thirty-five?

ALGERNON   Of course I could, Cecily. You know I could.

CECILY   Yes, I felt it instinctively, but I couldn't wait all that time. I hate waiting even five minutes for anybody. It always makes me rather cross. I am not punctual myself, I know, but I do like punctuality in others, and waiting, even to be married, is quite out of the question.

ALGERNON   Then what is to be done, Cecily?

CECILY   I don't know, Mr. Moncrieff.

LADY BRACKNELL   My dear Mr. Worthing, as Miss Cardew states positively that she cannot wait till she is thirty-five—a remark which I am bound to say seems to me to show a somewhat impatient nature—I would beg of you to reconsider your decision.

JACK   But, my dear Lady Bracknell, the matter is entirely in your own hands. The moment you consent to my marriage with Gwendolen, I will most gladly allow your nephew to form an alliance with my ward.

LADY BRACKNELL   (*rising and drawing herself up*)   You must be quite aware that what you propose is out of the question.

JACK   Then a passionate celibacy is all that any of us can look forward to.

LADY BRACKNELL   That is not the destiny I propose for Gwendolen. Algernon, of course, can choose for himself. (*Pulls out her watch.*) Come, dear (GWENDOLEN *rises*), we have already missed five, if not six, trains. To miss any more might expose us to comment on the platform.

Enter DR. CHASUBLE.

CHASUBLE   Everything is quite ready for the christenings.

LADY BRACKNELL   The christenings, sir! Is not that somewhat premature?

CHASUBLE (*looking rather puzzled, and pointing to* JACK *and* ALGERNON)
Both these gentlemen have expressed a desire for immediate baptism.

LADY BRACKNELL   At their age? The idea is grotesque and irreligious!
Algernon, I forbid you to be baptized. I will not hear of such excesses. Lord Bracknell would be highly displeased if he learned that that
was the way in which you wasted your time and money.

CHASUBLE   Am I to understand then that there are to be no christenings at all this afternoon?

JACK   I don't think that, as things are now, it would be of much practi
cal value to either of us, Dr. Chasuble.

CHASUBLE   I am grieved to hear such sentiments from you, Mr. Worthing. They savor of the heretical views of the Anabaptists, views that I
have completely refuted in four of my unpublished sermons. However, as your present mood seems to be one peculiarly secular, I will
return to the church at once. Indeed, I have just been informed by
the pewopener that for the last hour and a half Miss Prism has been
waiting for me in the vestry.

LADY BRACKNELL (*starting*)   Miss Prism! Did I hear you mention a Miss
Prism?

CHASUBLE   Yes, Lady Bracknell. I am on my way to join her.

LADY BRACKNELL   Pray allow me to detain you for a moment. This
matter may prove to be one of vital importance to Lord Bracknell and
myself. Is this Miss Prism a female of repellent aspect, remotely connected with education?

CHASUBLE (*somewhat indignantly*)   She is the most cultivated of ladies,
and the very picture of respectability.

LADY BRACKNELL   It is obviously the same person. May I ask what position she holds in your household?

CHASUBLE (*severely*)   I am a celibate, madam.

JACK (*interposing*)   Miss Prism, Lady Bracknell, has been for the last
three years Miss Cardew's esteemed governess and valued companion.

LADY BRACKNELL   In spite of what I hear of her, I must see her at once.
Let her be sent for.

CHASUBLE (*looking off*)   She approaches; she is nigh.

Enter MISS PRISM *hurriedly.*

MISS PRISM   I was told you expected me in the vestry, dear Canon. I
have been waiting for you there for an hour and three-quarters.
(*Catches sight of* LADY BRACKNELL, *who has fixed her with a stony glare.*
MISS PRISM *grows pale and quails. She looks anxiously round as if desirous to
escape.*)

LADY BRACKNELL (*in a severe, judicial voice*)   Prism! (MISS PRISM *bows her head in shame.*) Come here, Prism! (MISS PRISM *approaches in a humble manner.*) Prism! Where is that baby? (*General consternation. The Canon starts back in horror.* ALGERNON *and* JACK *pretend to be anxious to shield* CECILY *and* GWENDOLEN *from hearing the details of a terrible public scandal.*) Twenty-eight years ago, Prism, you left Lord Bracknell's house, Number 104, Upper Grosvenor Street, in charge of a perambulator that contained a baby, of the male sex. You never returned. A few weeks later, through the elaborate investigations of the Metropolitan police, the perambulator was discovered at midnight, standing by itself in a remote corner of Bayswater. It contained the manuscript of a three-volume novel of more than usually revolting sentimentality. (MISS PRISM *starts in involuntary indignation.*) But the baby was not there! (*Every one looks at* MISS PRISM.) Prism, where is that baby? (*A pause.*)

MISS PRISM   Lady Bracknell, I admit with shame that I do not know. I only wish I did. The plain facts of the case are these. On the morning of the day you mention, a day that is forever branded on my memory, I prepared as usual to take the baby out in its perambulator. I had also with me a somewhat old but capacious hand-bag in which I had intended to place the manuscript of a work of fiction that I had written during my few unoccupied hours. In a moment of mental abstraction, for which I never can forgive myself, I deposited the manuscript in the bassinet, and placed the baby in the hand-bag.

JACK (*who has been listening attentively*)   But where did you deposit the hand-bag?

MISS PRISM   Do not ask me, Mr. Worthing.

JACK   Miss Prism, this is a matter of no small importance to me. I insist on knowing where you deposited the hand-bag that contained that infant.

MISS PRISM   I left it in the cloak-room of one of the larger railway stations in London.

JACK   What railway station?

MISS PRISM (*quite crushed*)   Victoria. The Brighton line. (*Sinks into a chair.*)

JACK   I must retire to my room for a moment. Gwendolen, wait here for me.

GWENDOLEN   If you are not too long, I will wait here for you all my life.

Exit JACK *in great excitement.*

CHASUBLE   What do you think this means, Lady Bracknell?

LADY BRACKNELL   I dare not even suspect, Dr. Chasuble. I need hardly tell you that in families of high position strange coincidences are not supposed to occur. They are hardly considered the thing. (*Noises heard overhead as if some one was throwing trunks about. Everybody looks up.*)

CECILY Uncle Jack seems strangely agitated.

CHASUBLE Your guardian has a very emotional nature.

LADY BRACKNELL This noise is extremely unpleasant. It sounds as if he was having an argument. I dislike arguments of any kind. They are always vulgar, and often convincing.

CHASUBLE (*looking up*) It has stopped now. (*The noise is redoubled.*)

LADY BRACKNELL I wish he would arrive at some conclusion.

GWENDOLEN This suspense is terrible. I hope it will last.

Enter JACK *with a hand-bag of black leather in his hand.*

JACK (*rushing over to* MISS PRISM) Is this the hand-bag, Miss Prism? Examine it carefully before you speak. The happiness of more than one life depends on your answer.

MISS PRISM (*calmly*) It seems to be mine. Yes, here is the injury it received through the upsetting of a Gower Street omnibus in younger and happier days. Here is the stain on the lining caused by the explosion of a temperance beverage, an incident that occurred at Leamington. And here, on the lock, are my initials. I had forgotten that in an extravagant mood I had had them placed there. The bag is undoubtedly mine. I am delighted to have it so unexpectedly restored to me. It has been a great inconvenience being without it all these years.

JACK (*in a pathetic voice*) Miss Prism, more is restored to you than this hand-bag. I was the baby you placed in it.

MISS PRISM (*amazed*) You?

JACK (*embracing her*) Yes . . . mother!

MISS PRISM (*recoiling in indignant astonishment*) Mr. Worthing! I am unmarried!

JACK Unmarried! I do not deny that is a serious blow. But after all, who has the right to cast a stone against one who has suffered? Cannot repentance wipe out an act of folly? Why should there be one law for men and another for women? Mother, I forgive you. (*Tries to embrace her again.*)

MISS PRISM (*still more indignant*) Mr. Worthing, there is some error. (*Pointing to* LADY BRACKNELL.) There is the lady who can tell you who you really are.

JACK (*after a pause*) Lady Bracknell, I hate to seem inquisitive, but would you kindly inform me who I am?

LADY BRACKNELL I am afraid that the news I have to give you will not altogether please you. You are the son of my poor sister, Mrs. Moncrieff, and consequently Algernon's elder brother.

JACK Algy's elder brother! Then I have a brother after all. I knew I had a brother! I always said I had a brother! Cecily,—how could you have ever doubted that I had a brother? (*Seizes hold of* ALGERNON.) Dr. Chasuble, my unfortunate brother. Miss Prism, my unfortunate brother. Gwendolen, my unfortunate brother. Algy, you young scoundrel, you will have to treat me with more respect in the future. You have never behaved to me like a brother in all your life.

ALGERNON   Well, not till to-day, old boy, I admit. I did my best, however, though I was out of practice. (*Shakes hands.*)

GWENDOLEN (*to* JACK)   My own! but what own are you? What is your Christian name, now that you have become some one else?

JACK   Good heavens! . . . I had quite forgotten that point. Your decision on the subject of my name is irrevocable, I suppose?

GWENDOLEN   I never change, except in my affections.

CECILY   What a noble nature you have, Gwendolen!

JACK   Then the question had better be cleared up at once. Aunt Augusta, a moment. At the time when Miss Prism left me in the handbag, had I been christened already?

LADY BRACKNELL   Every luxury that money could buy, including christening, had been lavished on you by your fond and doting parents.

JACK   Then I was christened! That is settled. Now, what name was I given? Let me know the worst.

LADY BRACKNELL   Being the eldest son you were naturally christened after your father.

JACK (*irritably*)   Yes, but what was my father's Christian name?

LADY BRACKNELL (*meditatively*)   I cannot at the present moment recall what the General's Christian name was. But I have no doubt he had one. He was eccentric, I admit. But only in later years. And that was the result of the Indian climate, and marriage, and indigestion, and other things of that kind.

JACK   Algy! Can't you recollect what our father's Christian name was?

ALGERNON   My dear boy, we were never even on speaking terms. He died before I was a year old.

JACK   His name would appear in the Army Lists of the period, I suppose, Aunt Augusta?

LADY BRACKNELL   The General was essentially a man of peace, except in his domestic life. But I have no doubt his name would appear in any military directory.

JACK   The Army Lists of the last forty years are here. These delightful records should have been my constant study. (*Rushes to bookcase and tears the books out.*) M. Generals . . . Mallam, Maxbohm, Magley, what ghastly names they have—Markby, Migsby, Mobbs, Moncrieff! Lieutenant 1840, Captain, Lieutenant-Colonel, Colonel, General 1869, Christian names, Ernest John. (*Puts book very quietly down and speaks quite calmly.*) I always told you, Gwendolen, my name was Ernest, didn't I? Well, it is Ernest after all. I mean it naturally is Ernest.

LADY BRACKNELL   Yes, I remember that the General was called Ernest. I knew I had some particular reason for disliking the name.

GWENDOLEN   Ernest! My own Ernest! I felt from the first that you could have no other name!

JACK   Gwendolen, it is a terrible thing for a man to find out suddenly that all his life he has been speaking nothing but the truth. Can you forgive me?

GWENDOLEN   I can. For I feel that you are sure to change

JACK   My own one!

CHASUBLE (*to* MISS PRISM)   Laetitia! (*Embraces her.*)

MISS PRISM (*enthusiastically*)   Frederick! At last!

ALGERNON   Cecily! (*Embraces her.*) At last!

JACK   Gwendolen! (*Embraces her.*) At last!

LADY BRACKNELL   My nephew, you seem to be displaying signs of triviality.

JACK   On the contrary, Aunt Augusta, I've now realized for the first time in my life the vital Importance of Being Earnest.

Tableau

Curtain

QUESTIONS

1. This comedy has been called one of the wittiest plays in the English language. What might you say about the play, or what lines from it might you quote, in support of this statement?
2. Compare and contrast the town and country milieus depicted in *The Importance of Being Earnest*. Why might Wilde have used both in the play?
3. It's hard not to notice the amount of eating and drinking that occurs in this play. Discuss how Wilde uses this to support particular themes and characterizations.
4. Do you think a production of *The Importance of Being Earnest* would be a success at your school? Why or why not?
5. Discuss the subject of marriage in *Tartuffe* and *The Importance of Being Earnest*.

SUSAN GLASPELL   (1882–1948)

Trifles

CHARACTERS

SHERIFF PETERS
MRS. PETERS
HALE
MRS. HALE
COUNTY ATTORNEY HENDERSON

SCENE.   *The kitchen in the now abandoned farmhouse of John Wright, a gloomy kitchen, and left without having been put in order—the walls covered with a faded wall paper. Down right is a door leading to the parlor. On the right wall above this door is a built-in kitchen cupboard with shelves in the upper portion and drawers below. In the rear wall at right, up two steps is a door opening onto stairs leading to the second floor. In the rear wall at left is a door to the shed and from there to the outside. Between these two doors is an old-fashioned black iron stove. Running along the left wall from the shed door is an old iron sink and sink shelf, in which is set a hand pump. Downstage of the sink is an uncurtained window. Near the window is an old wooden rocker. Center stage is an unpainted wooden kitchen table with straight chairs on either side. There is a small chair down right. Unwashed pans under the sink, a loaf of bread outside the breadbox, a dish towel on the table—other signs of incompleted work. At the rear the shed door opens and the* SHERIFF *comes in followed by the* COUNTY ATTORNEY *and* HALE. *The* SHERIFF *and* HALE *are men in middle life, the* COUNTY ATTORNEY *is a young man; all are much bundled up and go at once to the stove. They are followed by the two women—the* SHERIFF's *wife,* MRS. PETERS, *first; she is a slight wiry woman, a thin nervous face.* MRS. HALE *is larger and would ordinarily be called more comfortable looking, but she is disturbed now and looks fearfully about as she enters. The women have come in slowly, and stand close together near the door.*

COUNTY ATTORNEY (*at stove rubbing his hands*)   This feels good. Come up to the fire, ladies.

MRS. PETERS (*after taking a step forward*)   I'm not—cold.

SHERIFF (*unbuttoning his overcoat and stepping away from the stove to right of table as if to mark the beginning of official business*)   Now, Mr. Hale, before we move things about, you explain to Mr. Henderson just what you saw when you came here yesterday morning.

COUNTY ATTORNEY (*crossing down to left of the table*)   By the way, has anything been moved? Are things just as you left them yesterday?

SHERIFF (*looking about*)   It's just about the same. When it dropped below zero last night I thought I'd better send Frank out this morning to make a fire for us—(*sits right of center table*) no use getting pneumonia with a big case on, but I told him not to touch anything except the stove—and you know Frank.

COUNTY ATTORNEY Somebody should have been left here yesterday.

SHERIFF Oh—yesterday. When I had to send Frank to Morris Center for that man who went crazy—I want you to know I had my hands full yesterday. I knew you could get back from Omaha by today and as long as I went over everything here myself——

COUNTY ATTORNEY Well, Mr. Hale, tell just what happened when you came here yesterday morning.

HALE (*crossing down to above table*) Harry and I had started to town with a load of potatoes. We came along the road from my place and as I got here I said, "I'm going to see if I can't get John Wright to go in with me on a party telephone." I spoke to Wright about it once before and he put me off, saying folks talked too much anyway, and all he asked was peace and quiet—I guess you know about how much he talked himself; but I thought maybe if I went to the house and talked about it before his wife, though I said to Harry that I didn't know as what his wife wanted made much difference to John——

COUNTY ATTORNEY Let's talk about that later, Mr. Hale. I do want to talk about that, but tell now just what happened when you got to the house.

HALE I didn't hear or see anything; I knocked at the door, and still it was all quiet inside. I knew they must be up, it was past eight o'clock. So I knocked again, and I thought I heard somebody say, "Come in." I wasn't sure, I'm not sure yet, but I opened the door—this door (*indicating the door by which the two women are still standing*) and there in that rocker—(*pointing to it*) sat Mrs. Wright. (*They all look at the rocker down left.*)

COUNTY ATTORNEY What—was she doing?

HALE She was rockin' back and forth. She had her apron in her hand and was kind of—pleating it.

COUNTY ATTORNEY And how did she—look?

HALE Well, she looked queer.

COUNTY ATTORNEY How do you mean—queer?

HALE Well, as if she didn't know what she was going to do next. And kind of done up.

COUNTY ATTORNEY (*takes out notebook and pencil and sits left of center table*) How did she seem to feel about your coming?

HALE Why, I don't think she minded—one way or other. She didn't pay much attention. I said, "How do, Mrs. Wright, it's cold, ain't it?" And she said, "Is it?"—and went on kind of pleating at her apron. Well, I was surprised; she didn't ask me to come up to the stove, or to set down, but just sat there, not even looking at me, so I said, "I want to see John." And then she—laughed. I guess you would call it a laugh. I thought of Harry and the team outside, so I said a little sharp: "Can't I see John?" "No," she says, kind o' dull like. "Ain't he home?" says I. "Yes," says she, "he's home." "Then why can't I see him?" I asked her, out of patience. " 'Cause he's dead," says she. "*Dead?*" says I. She just nodded her head, not getting a bit excited, but rockin' back and forth. "Why—where is he?" says I, not knowing what to say. She just pointed upstairs—like that. (*Himself pointing to the room above.*) I started for the stairs, with the idea of going up there. I walked from there to here—then I says, "Why, what did he die of?" "He died of a rope round his neck," says she, and just went on pleatin' at her apron. Well, I went out and called Harry. I thought I might— need help. We went upstairs and there he was lyin'——

COUNTY ATTORNEY   I think I'd rather have you go into that upstairs, where you can point it all out. Just go on now with the rest of the story.

HALE   Well, my first thought was to get that rope off. It looked . . . (*stops, his face twitches*) . . . but Harry, he went up to him, and he said, "No, he's dead all right, and we'd better not touch anything." So we went back downstairs. She was still sitting that same way. "Has anybody been notified?" I asked. "No," says she, unconcerned. "Who did this, Mrs. Wright?" said Harry. He said it business-like—and she stopped pleatin' of her apron. "I don't know," she says. "You don't *know?*" says Harry. "No," says she. "Weren't you sleepin' in the bed with him?" says Harry. "Yes," says she, "but I was on the inside." "Somebody slipped a rope round his neck and strangled him and you didn't wake up?" says Harry. "I didn't wake up," she said after him. We must 'a' looked as if we didn't see how that could be, for after a minute she said, "I sleep sound." Harry was going to ask her more questions but I said maybe we ought to let her tell her story first to the coroner, or the sheriff, so Harry went fast as he could to Rivers' place, where there's a telephone.

COUNTY ATTORNEY   And what did Mrs. Wright do when she knew that you had gone for the coroner?

HALE   She moved from the rocker to that chair over there (*pointing to a small chair in the down right corner*)   and just sat there with her hands held together and looking down. I got a feeling that I ought to make some conversation, so I said I had come in to see if John wanted to put in a telephone, and at that she started to laugh, and then she stopped and looked at me—scared. (*The* COUNTY ATTORNEY, *who has had his notebook out, makes a note.*) I dunno, maybe it wasn't scared. I wouldn't like to say it was. Soon Harry got back, and then Dr. Lloyd came and you, Mr. Peters, and so I guess that's all I know that you don't.

COUNTY ATTORNEY (*rising and looking around*)   I guess we'll go upstairs first—and then out to the barn and around there. (*To the* SHERIFF.) You're convinced that there was nothing important here—nothing that would point to any motive?

SHERIFF Nothing here but kitchen things. (*The* COUNTY ATTORNEY, *after again looking around the kitchen, opens the door of a cupboard closet in right wall. He brings a small chair from right—gets on it and looks on a shelf. Pulls his hand away, sticky.*)

COUNTY ATTORNEY Here's a nice mess. (*The women draw nearer up center.*)

MRS. PETERS (*to the other woman*) Oh, her fruit; it did freeze. (*To the Lawyer.*) She worried about that when it turned so cold. She said the fire'd go out and her jars would break.

SHERIFF (*rises*) Well, can you beat the woman! Held for murder and worryin' about her preserves.

COUNTY ATTORNEY (*getting down from chair*) I guess before we're through she may have something more serious than preserves to worry about. (*Crosses down right center.*)

HALE Well, women are used to worrying over trifles. (*The two women move a little closer together.*)

COUNTY ATTORNEY (*with the gallantry of a young politician*) And yet, for all their worries, what would we do without the ladies? (*The women do not unbend. He goes below the center table to the sink, takes a dipperful of water from the pail and pouring it into a basin, washes his hands. While he is doing this the* SHERIFF *and* HALE *cross to cupboard, which they inspect. The* COUNTY ATTORNEY *starts to wipe his hands on the roller towel, turns it for a cleaner place.*) Dirty towels! (*Kicks his foot against the pans under the sink.*) Not much of a housekeeper, would you say, ladies?

MRS. HALE (*stiffly*) There's a great deal of work to be done on a farm.

COUNTY ATTORNEY To be sure. And yet (*with a little bow to her*) I know there are some Dickson County farmhouses which do not have such roller towels (*He gives it a pull to expose its full length again.*)

MRS. HALE Those towels get dirty awful quick. Men's hands aren't always as clean as they might be.

COUNTY ATTORNEY Ah, loyal to your sex, I see. But you and Mrs. Wright were neighbors. I suppose you were friends, too.

MRS. HALE (*shaking her head*) I've not seen much of her of late years. I've not been in this house—it's more than a year.

COUNTY ATTORNEY (*crossing to women up center*) And why was that? You didn't like her?

MRS. HALE I liked her all well enough. Farmers' wives have their hands full, Mr. Henderson. And then——

COUNTY ATTORNEY Yes ——?

MRS. HALE (*looking about*) It never seemed a very cheerful place.

COUNTY ATTORNEY No—it's not cheerful. I shouldn't say she had the homemaking instinct.

MRS. HALE Well, I don't know as Wright had, either.

COUNTY ATTORNEY You mean that they didn't get on very well?

MRS. HALE No, I don't mean anything. But I don't think a place'd be any cheerfuller for John Wright's being in it.

COUNTY ATTORNEY   I'd like to talk more of that a little later. I want to get the lay of things upstairs now. (*He goes past the women to up right where steps lead to a stair door.*)

SHERIFF   I suppose anything Mrs. Peters does'll be all right. She was to take in some clothes for her, you know, and a few little things. We left in such a hurry yesterday.

COUNTY ATTORNEY   Yes, but I would like to see what you take, Mrs. Peters, and keep an eye out for anything that might be of use to us.

MRS. PETERS   Yes, Mr. Henderson. (*The men leave by up right door to stairs. The women listen to the men's steps on the stairs, then look about the kitchen.*)

MRS. HALE   (*crossing left to sink*)   I'd hate to have men coming into my kitchen, snooping around and criticizing. (*She arranges the pans under sink which the* LAWYER *had shoved out of place.*)

MRS. PETERS   Of course it's no more than their duty. (*Crosses to cupboard up right.*)

MRS. HALE   Duty's all right, but I guess that deputy sheriff that came out to make the fire might have got a little of this on. (*Gives the roller towel a pull.*) Wish I'd thought of that sooner. Seems mean to talk about her for not having things slicked up when she had to come away in such a hurry. (*Crosses right to* MRS. PETERS *at cupboard.*)

MRS. PETERS   (*who has been looking through cupboard, lifts one end of towel that covers a pan*)   She had bread set. (*Stands still.*)

MRS. HALE   (*eyes fixed on a loaf of bread beside the breadbox, which is on a low shelf of the cupboard.*)   She was going to put this in there. (*Picks up loaf, then abruptly drops it. In a manner of returning to familiar things.*) It's a shame about her fruit. I wonder if it's all gone. (*Gets up on the chair and looks.*) I think there's some here that's all right, Mrs. Peters. Yes— here; (*holding it toward the window*) this is cherries, too. (*Looking again.*) I declare I believe that's the only one. (*Gets down, jar in her hand. Goes to the sink and wipes it off on the outside.*) She'll feel awful bad after all her hard work in the hot weather. I remember the afternoon I put up my cherries last summer. (*She puts the jar on the big kitchen table, center of the room. With a sigh, is about to sit down in the rocking chair. Before she is seated realizes what chair it is; with a slow look at it, steps back. The chair which she has touched rocks back and forth.* MRS. PETERS *moves to center table and they both watch the chair rock for a moment or two.*)

MRS. PETERS   (*shaking off the mood which the empty rocking chair has evoked. Now in a businesslike manner she speaks.*)   Well I must get those things from the front room closet. (*She goes to the door at the right but, after looking into the other room, steps back.*) You coming with me, Mrs. Hale? You could help me carry them. (*They go in the other room; reappear,* MRS. PETERS *carrying a dress, petticoat and skirt,* MRS. HALE *following with a pair of shoes.*) My, it's cold in there. (*She puts the clothes on the big table, and hurries to the stove.*)

MRS. HALE   (*right of center table examining the skirt*)   Wright was close. I think maybe that's why she kept so much to herself. She didn't even belong to the Ladies' Aid. I suppose she felt she couldn't do her part, and then you don't enjoy things when you feel shabby. I heard she used to wear pretty clothes and be lively, when she was Minnie Foster, one of the town girls singing in the choir. But that —oh, that was thirty years ago. This all you want to take in?

MRS. PETERS   She said she wanted an apron. Funny thing to want, for there isn't much to get you dirty in jail, goodness knows. But I suppose just to make her feel more natural. (*Crosses to cupboard.*) She said they was in the top drawer in this cupboard. Yes, here. And then her little shawl that always hung behind the door. (*Opens stair door and looks.*) Yes, here it is. (*Quickly shuts door leading upstairs.*)

MRS. HALE (*abruptly moving toward her*)   Mrs. Peters?

MRS. PETERS   Yes, Mrs. Hale? (*At up right door.*)

MRS. HALE   Do you think she did it?

MRS. PETERS (*in a frightened voice*)   Oh, I don't know.

MRS. HALE   Well, I don't think she did. Asking for an apron and her little shawl. Worrying about her fruit.

MRS. PETERS (*starts to speak, glances up, where footsteps are heard in the room above. In a low voice*)   Mr. Peters says it looks bad for her. Mr. Henderson is awful sarcastic in a speech and he'll make fun of her sayin' she didn't wake up.

MRS. HALE   Well, I guess John Wright didn't wake when they was slipping that rope under his neck.

MRS. PETERS (*crossing slowly to table and placing shawl and apron on table with other clothing*)   No, it's strange. It must have been done awful crafty and still. They say it was such a—funny way to kill a man, rigging it all up like that.

MRS. HALE (*crossing to left of MRS. PETERS at table*)   That's just what Mr. Hale said. There was a gun in the house. He says that's what he can't understand.

MRS. PETERS   Mr. Henderson said coming out that what was needed for the case was a motive; something to show anger, or—sudden feeling.

MRS. HALE (*who is standing by the table*)   Well, I don't see any signs of anger around here. (*She puts her hand on the dish towel which lies on the table, stands looking down at table, one-half of which is clean, the other half messy.*) It's wiped to here. (*Makes a move as if to finish work, then turns and looks at loaf of bread outside the breadbox. Drops towel. In that voice of coming back to familiar things.*) Wonder how they are finding things upstairs. (*Crossing below table to down right.*) I hope she had it a little more red-up up there. You know, it seems kind of *sneaking*. Locking her up in town and then coming out here and trying to get her own house to turn against her!

MRS. PETERS   But, Mrs. Hale, the law is the law.

MRS. HALE   I s'pose 'tis. (*Unbuttoning her coat.*) Better loosen up your things, Mrs. Peters. You won't feel them when you go out. (MRS.

PETERS *takes off her fur tippet, goes to hang it on chair back left of table, stands looking at the work basket on floor near down left window.*)

MRS. PETERS   She was piecing a quilt. (*She brings the large sewing basket to the center table and they look at the bright pieces,* MRS. HALE *above the table and* MRS. PETERS *left of it.*)

MRS. HALE   It's a log cabin pattern. Pretty, isn't it? I wonder if she was goin' to quilt it or just knot it? (*Footsteps have been heard coming down the stairs. The* SHERIFF *enters followed by* HALE *and the* COUNTY ATTORNEY.)

SHERIFF   They wonder if she was going to quilt it or just knot it! (*The men laugh, the women look abashed.*)

COUNTY ATTORNEY (*rubbing his hands over the stove*)   Frank's fire didn't do much up there, did it? Well, let's go out to the barn and get that cleared up. (*The men go outside by up left door.*)

MRS. HALE (*resentfully*)   I don't know as there's anything so strange, our takin' up our time with little things while we're waiting for them to get the evidence. (*She sits in chair right of table smoothing out a block with decision.*) I don't see as it's anything to laugh about.

MRS. PETERS (*apologetically*)   Of course they've got awful important things on their minds. (*Pulls up a chair and joins* MRS. HALE *at the left of the table.*)

MRS. HALE (*examining another block*)   Mrs. Peters, look at this one. Here, this is the one she was working on, and look at the sewing! All the rest of it has been so nice and even. And look at this! It's all over the place! Why, it looks as if she didn't know what she was about! (*After she has said this they look at each other, then start to glance back at the door. After an instant* MRS. HALE *has pulled at a knot and ripped the sewing.*)

MRS. PETERS   Oh, what are you doing, Mrs. Hale?

MRS. HALE (*mildly*)   Just pulling out a stitch or two that's not sewed very good. (*Threading a needle.*) Bad sewing always made me fidgety.

MRS. PETERS (*with a glance at door, nervously*)   I don't think we ought to touch things.

MRS. HALE   I'll just finish up this end. (*Suddenly stopping and leaning forward.*) Mrs. Peters?

MRS. PETERS   Yes, Mrs. Hale?

MRS. HALE   What do you suppose she was so nervous about?

MRS. PETERS   Oh—I don't know. I don't know as she was nervous. I sometimes sew awful queer when I'm just tired. (*Mrs.* HALE *starts to say something, looks at* MRS. PETERS, *then goes on sewing.*) Well, I must get these things wrapped up. They may be through sooner than we think. (*Putting apron and other things together.*) I wonder where I can find a piece of paper, and string. (*Rises.*)

MRS. HALE   In that cupboard, maybe.

MRS. PETERS (*crosses right looking in cupboard*)   Why, here's a bird-cage. (*Holds it up.*) Did she have a bird, Mrs. Hale?

MRS. HALE   Why, I don't know whether she did or not—I've not been here for so long. There was a man around last year selling canaries cheap, but I don't know as she took one; maybe she did. She used to sing real pretty herself.

MRS. PETERS (*glancing around*)   Seems funny to think of a bird here. But she must have had one, or why would she have a cage? I wonder what happened to it.

MRS. HALE   I s'pose maybe the cat got it.

MRS. PETERS   No, she didn't have a cat. She's got that feeling some people have about cats—being afraid of them. My cat got in her room and she was real upset and asked me to take it out.

MRS. HALE   My sister Bessie was like that. Queer, ain't it?

MRS. PETERS (*examining the cage*)   Why, look at this door. It's broke. One hinge is pulled apart. (*Takes a step down to* MRS. HALE'*s right.*)

MRS. HALE (*looking too*)   Looks as if someone must have been rough with it.

MRS. PETERS   Why, yes. (*She brings the cage forward and puts it on the table.*)

MRS. HALE (*glancing toward up left door*)   I wish if they're going to find any evidence they'd be about it. I don't like this place.

MRS. PETERS   But I'm awful glad you came with me, Mrs. Hale. It would be lonesome for me sitting here alone.

MRS. HALE   It would, wouldn't it? (*Dropping her sewing.*) But I tell you what I do wish, Mrs. Peters. I wish I had come over sometimes when *she* was here. I—(*looking around the room*)—wish I had.

MRS. PETERS   But of course you were awful busy, Mrs. Hale—your house and your children.

MRS. HALE (*rises and crosses left*)   I could've come. I stayed away because it weren't cheerful—and that's why I ought to have come. I—(*looking out left window*)—I've never liked this place. Maybe because it's down in a hollow and you don't see the road. I dunno what it is, but it's a lonesome place and always was. I wish I had come over to see Minnie Foster sometimes. I can see now—(*Shakes her head.*)

MRS. PETERS (*left of table and above it*)   Well, you mustn't reproach yourself, Mrs. Hale. Somehow we just don't see how it is with other folks until—something turns up.

MRS. HALE   Not having children makes less work—but it makes a quiet house, and Wright out to work all day, and no company when he did come in. (*Turning from window.*) Did you know John Wright, Mrs. Peters?

MRS. PETERS   Not to know him; I've seen him in town. They say he was a good man.

MRS. HALE   Yes—good; he didn't drink, and kept his word as well as most, I guess, and paid his debts. But he was a hard man, Mrs. Peters. Just to pass the time of day with him——(*Shivers.*) Like a raw wind that gets to the bone. (*Pauses, her eye falling on the cage.*) I should think she would 'a' wanted a bird. But what do you suppose went with it?

MRS. PETERS   I don't know, unless it got sick and died. (*She reaches over and swings the broken door, swings it again, both women watch it.*)

MRS. HALE   You weren't raised round here, were you? (MRS. PETERS *shakes her head.*) You didn't know—her?

MRS. PETERS   Not till they brought her yesterday.

MRS. HALE   She—come to think of it, she was kind of like a bird herself—real sweet and pretty, but kind of timid and—fluttery. How—she—did—change. (*Silence: then as if struck by a happy thought and relieved to get back to everyday things. Crosses right above* MRS. PETERS *to cupboard, replaces small chair used to stand on to its original place down right.*) Tell you what, Mrs. Peters, why don't you take the quilt in with you? It might take up her mind.

MRS. PETERS   Why, I think that's a real nice idea, Mrs. Hale. There couldn't possibly be any objection to it could there? Now, just what would I take? I wonder if her patches are in here—and her things. (*They look in the sewing basket.*)

MRS. HALE (*crosses to right of table*)   Here's some red. I expect this has got sewing things in it. (*Brings out a fancy box.*) What a pretty box. Looks like something somebody would give you. Maybe her scissors are in here. (*Opens box. Suddenly puts her hand to her nose.*) Why——(MRS. PETERS *bends nearer, then turns her face away.*) There's something wrapped up in this piece of silk.

MRS. PETERS   Why, this isn't her scissors.

MRS. HALE (*lifting the silk*)   Oh, Mrs. Peters—it's——(MRS. PETERS *bends closer.*)

MRS. PETERS   It's the bird.

MRS. HALE   But, Mrs. Peters—look at it! Its neck! Look at its neck! It's all—other side *to.*

MRS. PETERS   Somebody—wrung—its—neck. (*Their eyes meet. A look of growing comprehension, of horror. Steps are heard outside.* MRS. HALE *slips box under quilt pieces, and sinks into her chair. Enter* SHERIFF *and* COUNTY ATTORNEY. MRS. PETERS *steps down left and stands looking out of window.*)

COUNTY ATTORNEY (*as one turning from serious things to little pleasantries*)   Well, ladies, have you decided whether she was going to quilt it or knot it? (*Crosses to center above table.*)

MRS. PETERS   We think she was going to—knot it. (SHERIFF *crosses to right of stove, lifts stove lid and glances at fire, then stands warming hands at stove.*)

COUNTY ATTORNEY   Well, that's interesting, I'm sure. (*Seeing the birdcage.*) Has the bird flown?

MRS. HALE (*putting more quilt pieces over the box*)   We think the—cat got it.

COUNTY ATTORNEY (*preoccupied*)   Is there a cat? (MRS. HALE *glances in a quick covert way at* MRS. PETERS.)

MRS. PETERS   Well, not *now.* They're superstitious, you know. They leave.

COUNTY ATTORNEY (*to* SHERIFF PETERS, *continuing an interrupted conversation*) No sign at all of anyone having come from the outside. Their own rope. Now let's go up again and go over it piece by piece. (*They start upstairs.*) It would have to have been someone who knew just the—— (MRS. PETERS *sits down left of table. The two women sit there not looking at one another, but as if peering into something and at the same time holding back. When they talk now it is in the manner of feeling their way over strange ground, as if afraid of what they are saying, but as if they cannot help saying it.*)

MRS. HALE She liked the bird. She was going to bury it in that pretty box.

MRS. PETERS (*in a whisper*) When I was a girl—my kitten –there was a boy took a hatchet, and before my eyes—and before I could get there—— (*Covers her face an instant.*) If they hadn't held me back I would have—(*catches herself, looks upstairs where steps are heard, falters weakly*)—hurt him.

MRS. HALE (*with a slow look around her*) I wonder how it would seem never to have had any children around. (*Pause.*) No, Wright wouldn't like the bird—a thing that sang. She used to sing. He killed that, too.

MRS. PETERS (*moving uneasily*) We don't know who killed the bird.

MRS. HALE I knew John Wright.

MRS. PETERS It was an awful thing was done in this house that night, Mrs. Hale. Killing a man while he slept, slipping a rope around his neck that choked the life out of him.

MRS. HALE His neck. Choked the life out of him. (*Her hand goes out and rests on the bird-cage.*)

MRS. PETERS (*with rising voice*) We don't know who killed him. We don't know.

MRS. HALE (*her own feeling not interrupted*) If there'd been years and years of nothing, then a bird to sing to you, it would be awful—still, after the bird was still.

MRS. PETERS (*something within her speaking*) I know what stillness is. When we homesteaded in Dakota, and my first baby died—after he was two years old, and me with no other then——

MRS. HALE (*moving*) How soon do you suppose they'll be through looking for the evidence?

MRS. PETERS I know what stillness is. (*Pulling herself back.*) The law has got to punish crime, Mrs. Hale.

MRS. HALE (*not as if answering that*) I wish you'd seen Minnie Foster when she wore a white dress with blue ribbons and stood up there in the choir and sang. (*A look around the room.*) Oh, I *wish* I'd come over here once in a while! That was a crime! That was a crime! Who's going to punish that?

MRS. PETERS (*looking upstairs*) We mustn't—take on.

MRS. HALE I might have known she needed help! I know how things can be—for women. I tell you, it's queer, Mrs. Peters. We live close together and we live far apart. We all go through the same things— it's all just a different kind of the same thing. (*Brushes her eyes, noticing the jar of fruit, reaches out for it.*) If I was you I wouldn't tell her her fruit was gone. Tell her it *ain't.* Tell her it's all right. Take this in to prove it to her. She—she may never know whether it was broke or not.

MRS. PETERS (*takes the jar, looks about for something to wrap it in; takes petticoat from the clothes brought from the other room, very nervously begins winding this around the jar. In a false voice*) My, it's a good thing the men couldn't hear us. Wouldn't they just laugh! Getting all stirred up over a little thing like a—dead canary. As if that could have anything to do with—with—wouldn't they *laugh!* (*The men are heard coming downstairs.*)

MRS. HALE (*under her breath*) Maybe they would—maybe they wouldn't.

COUNTY ATTORNEY No, Peters, it's all perfectly clear except a reason for doing it. But you know juries when it comes to women. If there was some definite thing. (*Crosses slowly to above table.* SHERIFF *crosses down right.* MRS. HALE *and* MRS. PETERS *remain seated at either side of table.*) Something to show—something to make a story about—a thing that would connect up with this strange way of doing it——(*The women's eyes meet for an instant. Enter* HALE *from outer door.*)

HALE (*remaining by door*) Well, I've got the team around. Pretty cold out there.

COUNTY ATTORNEY I'm going to stay awhile by myself. (*To the* SHERIFF.) You can send Frank out for me, can't you? I want to go over everything. I'm not satisfied that we can't do better.

SHERIFF Do you want to see what Mrs. Peters is going to take in? (*The* LAWYER *picks up the apron, laughs.*)

COUNTY ATTORNEY Oh, I guess they're not very dangerous things the ladies have picked out. (*Moves a few things about, disturbing the quilt pieces which cover the box. Steps back.*) No, Mrs. Peters doesn't need supervising. For that matter a sheriff's wife is married to the law. Ever think of it that way, Mrs. Peters?

MRS. PETERS Not—just that way.

SHERIFF (*chuckling*) Married to the law. (*Moves to down right door to the other room.*) I just want you to come in here a minute, George. We ought to take a look at these windows.

COUNTY ATTORNEY (*scoffingly*) Oh, windows!

SHERIFF We'll be right out, Mr. Hale. (HALE *goes outside. The* SHERIFF *follows the* COUNTY ATTORNEY *into the room. Then* MRS. HALE *rises, hands tight together, looking intensely at* MRS. PETERS, *whose eyes make a slow turn, finally meeting* MRS. HALE's. *A moment* MRS. HALE *holds her, then her own eyes point the way to where the box is concealed. Suddenly* MRS. PETERS *throws back quilt pieces and tries to put the box in the bag she is carrying. It is too big. She opens box, starts to take bird out, cannot touch it, goes to pieces,*

stands there helpless. Sound of a knob turning in the other room. MRS. HALE
snatches the box and puts it in the pocket of her big coat. Enter COUNTY
ATTORNEY *and* SHERIFF, *who remains down right.*)

COUNTY ATTORNEY (*crosses to up left door facetiously*)   Well, Henry, at least
we found out that she was not going to quilt it. She was going to—
what is it you call it, ladies?

MRS. HALE (*standing center below table facing front, her hand against her
pocket*)   We call it—knot it, Mr. Henderson.

Curtain

QUESTIONS

1. What does *Trifles* say about men? about women? about the ways in which they
   act toward each other? In how many different ways does Glaspell touch on
   this theme? (Notice the speech patterns of the men and the women. How do
   they differ? What themes and concerns do you hear from each?)
2. Discuss the use of "trifles" in the play.
3. Discuss the characterization of Mrs. Hale and Mrs. Peters. How are they
   contrasted in the early part of the play? What happens to them during the
   course of the play?
4. With which of the characters in this play do your sympathies lie? Why? To
   what extent do you approve of their actions?

6 Contemporary Drama

By the middle of the twentieth century, new trends in drama were noticeable. Comedies, tragedies, and the hard-to-classify "dramas" alike often moved beyond realism into surrealism, beyond social comment to psychological portraiture. In stage settings, language, and refusal to follow a straightforward course of time, twentieth-century playwrights often pushed towards new forms of expression, hoping to evoke fresh responses from their audiences.

The study of humans as social beings, and of the way in which social pressures shape people, similarly modulates into the study of individual beings isolated in the midst of (often overwhelming) social demands. Thus, physical and spiritual isolation was a key theme in an early twentieth-century play, *Trifles;* and spiritual (and sometimes physical) isolation remains an important theme in the three plays we study in this chapter: *The Glass Menagerie, Desire under the Elms,* and *A Raisin in the Sun.* Yet, as we will see, these plays study isolation in no cold or clinical sense. Rather, they use the drama's traditional role as social critic to call for a more caring society, a society that can accommodate dreams and dreamers as well as the realistic and practical.

Isolation, depicted and set off by failed tenderness, is a notable theme in Tennessee Williams' *The Glass Menagerie.* Amanda lives half in a semi-illusory past, half in a present of unpalatable truths that she ignores whenever possible; Laura is isolated by her physical disability and by her great shyness; and Tom has isolated himself from everything except his memories.

The play is performed as a series of remembered scenes, with Tom sometimes narrator and sometimes actor. This device allows for great differences in stagecraft between this play and the realistic plays against which it rebels. The episodic structure; the lyrical, beautifully modulated language that defines each character and differentiates each from his or her companions; the unrealistic stage setting, with its use of lighting and music to set moods and scenes; and the symbolic value of props such as the glass unicorn: all work together to create, in the narrator's words, "truth in the pleasant disguise of illusion."

Eugene O'Neill's *Desire under the Elms* is set in rural New England in the nineteenth century. The drama revolves around the classic struggle between father and son. Ephraim Cabot and his son Eben compete for both the father's young wife and the ancestral farm. This confrontation achieves tragic proportions.

In contrast to the experimental stagecraft of *The Glass Menagerie*, Lorraine Hansberry's *A Raisin in the Sun* reverts to an older form of stagecraft. The unity of place and action, the steady flow of time, parallel those of the eighteenth- and nineteenth-century "well made play," while the play's emphasis on "the virtues of private life" are reminiscent of eighteenth-century sentimental comedy.[1] It is perhaps not surprising that this should be so; like the rationalists of the eighteenth century, Hansberry unabashedly celebrates the spirit of mankind. (Asked by an interviewer, "You believe in a kind of increase in moral and philosophical strength by the use of reason, don't you?" she replied "Oh, yes. Yes. I don't think the time will ever come when we will dismiss the human spirit."[2])

This faith in the human spirit, whether rational, religious, or a blend of both, illumines *A Raisin in the Sun*. Where *The Glass Menagerie* looks primarily backwards, asking "how did these characters come to be this way?," *A Raisin in the Sun* looks primarily forward. Conflicts there certainly are within the play, both within the Younger family and between the Youngers and the outside world. But in each case the conflict is seen as a challenge for further growth. And though the play presents us with as open an ending as we have seen since *The Doll's House*, the ending is strongly optimistic. We may see further problems ahead for the Youngers as they move into a potentially hostile neighborhood, as Walter strives to learn to lead his family (and Lena to be a less assertive leader), as Beneatha chooses among her various potential roads to adulthood. But we have seen also the strengths and loves that will help them meet their challenges, and thrive by so doing.

---

[1] Oliver Goldsmith, in his 1773 "Essay on the Theatre," defined sentimental comedy as a form "in which the virtues of private life are exhibited, rather than the vices exposed; and the distresses rather than the faults of mankind make our interest in the piece."

[2] *To Be Young, Gifted, and Black* (Prentice-Hall, 1969), pp. 185–86.

A Raisin in the Sun is very much a black play. As such, it won immense acceptance and praise when it appeared in 1959, and placed Hansberry among the best twentieth-century dramatists. Paradoxically, the strength of the portrayal of what it means to be black allows the play to be something more, as well. As Hansberry herself said, "in order to create the universal, you must pay very great attention to the specific. . . . I think people, to the extent we accept them and believe them as who they're supposed to be, to that extent they can become everybody."[3] *Raisin* illustrates the truth of this belief. With a firm and unwavering insistence on the truth of her characters and their actions as a black Southside Chicago family in the 1950's, Hansberry has created not only a new Everyman, but a new Everywoman as well.

---

[3] *To Be Young, Gifted, and Black,* p. 114.

TENNESSEE WILLIAMS (1911–1983)

The Glass Menagerie

CHARACTERS

AMANDA WINGFIELD, *the mother.*
  A little woman of great but confused vitality clinging frantically to another time and place. Her characterization must be carefully created, not copied from type. She is not paranoiac, but her life is paranoia. There is much to admire in AMANDA, *and as much to love and pity as there is to laugh at. Certainly she has endurance and a kind of heroism, and though her foolishness makes her unwittingly cruel at times, there is tenderness in her slight person.*

LAURA WINGFIELD, *her daughter.*
  AMANDA, *having failed to establish contact with reality, continues to live vitally in her illusions, but* LAURA's *situation is even graver. A childhood*

illness has left her crippled, one leg slightly shorter than the other, and held in a brace. This defect need not be more than suggested on the stage. Stemming from this, LAURA's *separation increases till she is like a piece of her own glass collection, too exquisitely fragile to move from the shelf.*

TOM WINGFIELD, *her son, and the narrator of the play.*
  A poet with a job in a warehouse. His nature is not remorseless, but to escape from a trap he has to act without pity.

JIM O'CONNOR, *the gentleman caller.*
  A nice, ordinary, young man.

SCENE: *An alley in St. Louis.*
PART I: *Preparation for a Gentleman Caller.*
PART II: *The Gentleman Calls.*
TIME: *Now and the Past.*

SCENE I

The Wingfield apartment is in the rear of the building, one of those vast hive-like conglomerations of cellular living-units that flower as warty growths in overcrowded urban centers of lower middle-class population and are symptomatic of the impulse of this largest and fundamentally enslaved section of American society to avoid fluidity and differentiation and to exist and function as one interfused mass of automatism.

The apartment faces an alley and is entered by a fire-escape, a structure whose name is a touch of accidental poetic truth, for all of these huge buildings are always burning with the slow and implacable fires of human desperation. The fire-escape is included in the set—that is, the landing of it and steps descending from it.

The scene is memory and is therefore nonrealistic. Memory takes a lot of poetic license. It omits some details; others are exaggerated, according to the emotional value of the articles it touches, for memory is seated predominantly in the heart. The interior is therefore rather dim and poetic.

At the rise of the curtain, the audience is faced with the dark, grim rear wall of the Wingfield tenement. This building, which runs parallel to the footlights, is flanked on both sides by dark, narrow alleys which run into murky canyons of tangled clotheslines, garbage cans and the sinister lattice-work of neighboring fire-escapes. It is up and down these side alleys that exterior entrances and exits are made, during the play. At the end of Tom's *opening commentary, the dark tenement wall slowly reveals (by means of a transparency) the interior of the ground floor Wingfield apartment.*

Downstage is the living room, which also serves as a sleeping room for Laura, *the sofa unfolding to make her bed. Upstage, center, and divided by a wide arch or second proscenium with transparent faded portieres (or second curtain), is the dining room. In an old-fashioned what-not in the living room are seen scores of transparent glass animals. A blown-up photograph of the father hangs on the wall of the living room, facing the audience, to the left of the archway. It is the face of a very handsome young man in a doughboy's First World War cap. He is gallantly smiling, ineluctably smiling, as if to say, "I will be smiling forever."*

The audience hears and sees the opening scene in the dining room through both the transparent fourth wall of the building and the transparent gauze portieres of the dining-room arch. It is during this revealing scene that the fourth wall slowly ascends, out of sight. This transparent exterior wall is not brought down again until the very end of the play, during Tom's *final speech.*

The narrator is an undisguised convention of the play. He takes whatever license with dramatic convention as is convenient to his purposes.

Tom *enters dressed as a merchant sailor from alley, stage left, and strolls across the front of the stage to the fire-escape. There he stops and lights a cigarette. He addresses the audience.*

TOM   Yes, I have tricks in my pocket, I have things up my sleeve. But I am the opposite of a stage magician. He gives you illusion that has the appearance of truth. I give you truth in the pleasant disguise of illusion. To begin with, I turn back time. I reverse it to that quaint period, the thirties, when the huge middle class of America was matriculating in a school for the blind. Their eyes had failed them, or they had failed their eyes, and so they were having their fingers pressed forcibly down on the fiery Braille alphabet of a dissolving economy. In Spain there was revolution.

Here there was only shouting and confusion. In Spain there was Guernica. Here there were disturbances of labor, sometimes pretty violent, in otherwise peaceful cities such as Chicago, Cleveland, Saint Louis. . . . This is the social background of the play.

(MUSIC.)

The play is memory. Being a memory play, it is dimly lighted, it is sentimental, it is not realistic. In memory everything seems to happen to music. That explains the fiddle in the wings. I am the narrator of the play, and also a character in it. The other characters are my mother, Amanda, my sister, Laura, and a gentleman caller who appears in the final scenes. He is the most realistic character in the play, being an emissary from a world of reality that we were somehow set apart from. But since I have a poet's weakness for symbols, I am using this character also as a symbol; he is the long delayed but always expected something that we live for. There is a fifth character in the play who doesn't appear except in this larger-than-life photograph over the mantel. This is our father who left us a long time ago. He was a telephone man who fell in love with long distances; he gave up his job with the telephone company and skipped the light fantastic out of town . . . The last we heard of him was a picture post-card from Mazatlan, on the Pacific coast of Mexico, containing a message of two words—"Hello—Goodbye!" and an address. I think the rest of the play will explain itself. . . .

Amanda's voice becomes audible through the portieres.

(LEGEND ON SCREEN: "où sont les neiges.")

He divides the portieres and enters the upstage area.
 AMANDA *and* LAURA *are seated at a drop-leaf table. Eating is indicated by gestures without food or utensils.* AMANDA *faces the audience.* TOM *and* LAURA *are seated in profile.*
 The interior has lit up softly and through the scrim we see AMANDA *and* LAURA *seated at the table in the upstage area.*

AMANDA (*calling*) Tom?
TOM Yes, Mother.
AMANDA We can't say grace until you come to the table!
TOM Coming, Mother. (*He bows slightly and withdraws, reappearing a few moments later in his place at the table.*)
AMANDA (*to her son*) Honey, don't *push* with your *fingers*. If you have to push with something, the thing to push with is a crust of bread. And chew—chew! Animals have sections in their stomachs which enable them to digest food without mastication, but human

beings are supposed to chew their food before they swallow it down. Eat food leisurely, son, and really enjoy it. A well-cooked meal has lots of delicate flavors that have to be held in the mouth for appreciation. So chew your food and give your salivary glands a chance to function!

TOM *deliberately lays his imaginary fork down and pushes his chair back from the table.*

TOM   I haven't enjoyed one bite of this dinner because of your constant directions on how to eat it. It's you that makes me rush through meals with your hawk-like attention to every bite I take. Sickening—spoils my appetite—all this discussion of animals' secretion—salivary glands—mastication!

AMANDA *(lightly)*   Temperament like a Metropolitan star! *(He rises and crosses downstage.)* You're not excused from the table.

TOM   I am getting a cigarette.

AMANDA   You smoke too much.

LAURA *rises.*

LAURA   I'll bring in the blanc mange.

He remains standing with his cigarette by the portieres during the following.

AMANDA *(rising)*   No, sister, no, sister—you be the lady this time and I'll be the darky.

LAURA   I'm already up.

AMANDA   Resume your seat, little sister—I want you to stay fresh and pretty—for gentlemen callers!

LAURA   I'm not expecting any gentlemen callers.

AMANDA *(crossing out to kitchenette. Airily)*   Sometimes they come when they are least expected! Why, I remember one Sunday afternoon in Blue Mountain—*(Enters kitchenette.)*

TOM   I know what's coming!

LAURA   Yes. But let her tell it.

TOM   Again?

LAURA   She loves to tell it.

AMANDA *returns with bowl of dessert.*

AMANDA   One Sunday afternoon in Blue Mountain—your mother received—*seventeen!*—gentlemen callers! Why, sometimes there weren't chairs enough to accommodate them all. We had to send the nigger over to bring in folding chairs from the parish house.

TOM *(remaining at portieres)*   How did you entertain those gentlemen callers?

AMANDA   I understood the art of conversation!

TOM   I bet you could talk.

AMANDA   Girls in those days *knew* how to talk, I can tell you.

TOM   Yes?

(IMAGE: AMANDA AS A GIRL ON A PORCH GREETING CALLERS.)

AMANDA   They knew how to entertain their gentlemen callers. It wasn't enough for a girl to be possessed of a pretty face and a graceful figure—although I wasn't slighted in either respect. She also needed to have a nimble wit and a tongue to meet all occasions.

TOM   What did you talk about?

AMANDA   Things of importance going on in the world! Never anything coarse or common or vulgar. (*She addresses* TOM *as though he were seated in the vacant chair at the table though he remains by portieres. He plays this scene as though he held the book.*) My callers were gentlemen—all! Among my callers were some of the most prominent young planters of the Mississippi Delta—planters and sons of planters!

TOM *motions for music and a spot of light on* AMANDA.
Her eyes lift, her face glows, her voice becomes rich and elegiac.

(SCREEN LEGEND: "OÙ SONT LES NEIGES.")

There was young Champ Laughlin who later became vice-president of the Delta Planters Bank. Hadley Stevenson who was drowned in Moon Lake and left his widow one hundred and fifty thousand in Government bonds. There were the Cutrere brothers, Wesley and Bates. Bates was one of my bright particular beaux! He got in a quarrel with that wild Wainright boy. They shot it out on the floor of Moon Lake Casino. Bates was shot through the stomach. Died in the ambulance on his way to Memphis. His widow was also well-provided for, came into eight or ten thousand acres, that's all. She married him on the rebound—never loved her—carried my picture on him the night he died! And there was that boy that every girl in the Delta had set her cap for! That beautiful, brilliant young Fitzhugh boy from Green County!

TOM   What did he leave his widow?

AMANDA   He never married! Gracious, you talk as though all of my old admirers had turned up their toes to the daisies!

TOM   Isn't this the first you mentioned that still survives?

AMANDA   That Fitzhugh boy went North and made a fortune— came to be known as the Wolf of Wall Street! He had the Midas touch, whatever he touched turned to gold! And I could have been Mrs. Duncan J. Fitzhugh, mind you! But—I picked your *father!*

LAURA (*rising*)   Mother, let me clear the table.

AMANDA   No, dear, you go in front and study your typewriter chart. Or practice your shorthand a little. Stay fresh and pretty—It's almost time for our gentlemen callers to start arriving. (*She flounces girlishly toward the kitchenette.*) How many do you suppose we're going to entertain this afternoon?

TOM *throws down the paper and jumps up with a groan.*

LAURA (*alone in the dining room*)   I don't believe we're going to receive any, Mother.

AMANDA (*reappearing, airily*)   What? No one—not one? You must be joking! (LAURA *nervously echoes her laugh. She slips in a fugitive manner through the half-open portieres and draws them gently behind her. A shaft of very clear light is thrown on her face against the faded tapestry of the curtains.* MUSIC: "THE GLASS MENAGERIE" UNDER FAINTLY. *Lightly.*) Not one gentleman caller? It can't be true! There must be a flood, there must have been a tornado!

LAURA   It isn't a flood, it's not a tornado, Mother. I'm just not popular like you were in Blue Mountain.... (TOM *utters another groan.* LAURA *glances at him with a faint, apologetic smile. Her voice catching a little.*) Mother's afraid I'm going to be an old maid.

(THE SCENE DIMS OUT WITH "GLASS MENAGERIE" MUSIC.)

SCENE II

"Laura, Haven't You Ever Liked Some Boy?"

On the dark stage the screen is lighted with the image of blue roses. Gradually LAURA's figure becomes apparent and the screen goes out. The music subsides.

LAURA *is seated in the delicate ivory chair at the small clawfoot table.*

She wears a dress of soft violet material for a kimono—her hair tied back from her forehead with a ribbon.

She is washing and polishing her collection of glass.

AMANDA *appears on the fire-escape steps. At the sound of her ascent,* LAURA *catches her breath, thrusts the bowl of ornaments away and seats herself stiffly before the diagram of the typewriter keyboard as though it held her spellbound. Something has happened to* AMANDA. *It is written in her face as she climbs to the landing: a look that is grim and hopeless and a little absurd.*

She has on one of those cheap or imitation velvety-looking cloth coats with imitation fur collar. Her hat is five or six years old, one of those dreadful cloche hats that were worn in the late twenties and she is clasping an enormous black patent-leather pocket-book with nickel clasp and initials. This is her full-dress outfit, the one she usually wears to the D.A.R. Before entering she looks through the door.

She purses her lips, opens her eyes wide, rolls them upward, and shakes her head.

Then she slowly lets herself in the door. Seeing her mother's expression LAURA *touches her lips with a nervous gesture.*

LAURA   Hello, Mother, I was—(*She makes a nervous gesture toward the chart on the wall.* AMANDA *leans against the shut door and stares at* LAURA *with a martyred look.*)

AMANDA   Deception? Deception? (*She slowly removes her hat and gloves, continuing the swift suffering stare. She lets the hat and gloves fall on the floor—a bit of acting.*)

LAURA   (*shakily*)   How was the D.A.R. meeting? (AMANDA *slowly opens her purse and removes a dainty white handkerchief which she shakes out delicately and delicately touches to her lips and nostrils.*) Didn't you go to the D.A.R. meeting, Mother?

AMANDA   (*faintly, almost inaudibly*)   —No.—No. (*Then more forcibly.*) I did not have the strength—to go to the D.A.R. In fact, I did not have the courage! I wanted to find a hole in the ground and hide myself in it forever! (*She crosses slowly to the wall and removes the diagram of the typewriter keyboard. She holds it in front of her for a second, staring at it sweetly and sorrowfully—then bites her lips and tears it in two pieces.*)

LAURA   (*faintly*)   Why did you do that, Mother? (AMANDA *repeats the same procedure with the chart of the Gregg Alphabet.*) Why are you—

AMANDA   Why? Why? How old are you, Laura?

LAURA   Mother, you know my age.

AMANDA   I thought that you were an adult; it seems that I was mistaken. (*She crosses slowly to the sofa and sinks down and stares at* LAURA.)

LAURA   Please don't stare at me, Mother.

AMANDA *closes her eyes and lowers her head. Count ten.*

AMANDA   What are we going to do, what is going to become of us, what is the future?

Count ten.

LAURA   Has something happened, Mother? (AMANDA *draws a long breath and takes out the handkerchief again. Dabbing process.*) Mother, has—something happened?

AMANDA   I'll be all right in a minute. I'm just bewildered—(*Count five.*)—by life. . . .

LAURA   Mother, I wish that you would tell me what's happened.

AMANDA   As you know, I was supposed to be inducted into my office at the D.A.R. this afternoon. (IMAGE: A SWARM OF TYPEWRITERS.) But I stopped off at Rubicam's Business College to speak to your teachers about your having a cold and ask them what progress they thought you were making down there.

LAURA   Oh. . . .

AMANDA   I went to the typing instructor and introduced myself as your mother. She didn't know who you were. Wingfield, she said. We don't have any such student enrolled at the school! I assured her she did, that you had been going to classes since early in January. "I wonder," she said, "if you could be talking about that terribly shy little girl who dropped out of school after only a few days' attendance?" "No," I said, "Laura, my daughter, has been going to school every day for the past six weeks!" "Excuse me," she said. She took the attendance book out and there was your name, unmistakably printed, and all the dates you were absent until they decided that you had dropped out of school. I still said, "No, there must have been some mistake! There must have been some mix-up in the records!" And she said, "No—I remember her perfectly now. Her hand shook so that she couldn't hit the right keys! The first time we gave a speed-test, she broke down completely—was sick at the stomach and almost had to be carried into the wash-room! After that morning she never showed up any more. We phoned the house but never got any answer—while I was working at Famous and Barr, I suppose, demonstrating those—Oh!" I felt so weak I could barely keep on my feet! I had to sit down while they got me a glass of water! Fifty dollars' tuition, all of our plans—my hopes and ambitions for you—just gone up the spout, just gone up the spout like that. (LAURA *draws a long breath and gets awkwardly to her feet. She crosses to the victrola and winds it up.*) What are you doing?

LAURA   Oh! (*She releases the handle and returns to her seat.*)

AMANDA   Laura, where have you been going when you've gone out pretending that you were going to business college?

LAURA   I've just been going out walking.

AMANDA   That's not true.

LAURA   It is. I just went walking.

AMANDA   Walking? Walking? In winter? Deliberately courting pneumonia in that light coat? Where did you walk to, Laura?

LAURA   All sorts of places—mostly in the park.

AMANDA   Even after you'd started catching that cold?

LAURA It was the lesser of two evils, Mother. (IMAGE: WINTER SCENE IN PARK.) I couldn't go back up. I—threw up—on the floor!

AMANDA From half past seven till after five every day you mean to tell me you walked around in the park, because you wanted to make me think that you were still going to Rubicam's Business College?

LAURA It wasn't as bad as it sounds. I went inside places to get warmed up.

AMANDA Inside where?

LAURA I went in the art museum and the bird-houses at the Zoo. I visited the penguins every day! Sometimes I did without lunch and went to the movies. Lately I've been spending most of my afternoons in the Jewel-box, that big glass house where they raise the tropical flowers.

AMANDA You did all this to deceive me, just for the deception? (LAURA *looks down.*) Why?

LAURA Mother, when you're disappointed, you get that awful suffering look on your face, like the picture of Jesus' mother in the museum!

AMANDA Hush!

LAURA I couldn't face it.

Pause. A whisper of strings.

(LEGEND: "THE CRUST OF HUMILITY.")

AMANDA (*hopelessly fingering the huge pocketbook*) So what are we going to do the rest of our lives? Stay home and watch the parades go by? Amuse ourselves with the glass menagerie, darling? Eternally play those worn-out phonograph records your father left as a painful reminder of him? We won't have a business career—we've given that up because it gave us nervous indigestion! (*Laughs wearily.*) What is there left but dependency all our lives? I know so well what becomes of unmarried women who aren't prepared to occupy a position. I've seen such pitiful cases in the South—barely tolerated spinsters living upon the grudging patronage of sister's husband or brother's wife!—stuck away in some little mouse-trap of a room—encouraged by one in-law to visit another—little birdlike women without any nest—eating the crust of humility all their life! Is that the future that we've mapped out for ourselves? I swear it's the only alternative I can think of! It isn't a very pleasant alternative, is it? Of course—some girls *do marry.* (LAURA *twists her hands nervously.*) Haven't you ever liked some boy?

LAURA   Yes. I liked one once. (*Rises.*) I came across his picture a while ago.

AMANDA (*with some interest*)   He gave you his picture?

LAURA   No, it's in the year-book.

AMANDA (*disappointed*)   Oh—a high-school boy.

(SCREEN IMAGE: JIM AS A HIGH-SCHOOL HERO BEARING A SILVER CUP.)

LAURA   Yes. His name was Jim. (LAURA *lifts the heavy annual from the claw-foot table.*) Here he is in *The Pirates of Penzance.*

AMANDA (*absently*)   The what?

LAURA   The operetta the senior class put on. He had a wonderful voice and we sat across the aisle from each other Mondays, Wednesdays and Fridays in the Aud. Here he is with the silver cup for debating! See his grin?

AMANDA (*absently*)   He must have had a jolly disposition.

LAURA   He used to call me—Blue Roses.

(IMAGE: BLUE ROSES.)

AMANDA   Why did he call you such a name as that?

LAURA   When I had that attack of pleurosis—he asked me what was the matter when I came back. I said pleurosis—he thought that I said Blue Roses! So that's what he always called me after that. Whenever he saw me, he'd holler, "Hello, Blue Roses!" I didn't care for the girl that he went out with. Emily Meisenbach. Emily was the best-dressed girl at Soldan. She never struck me, though, as being sincere . . . It says in the Personal Section—they're engaged. That's—six years ago! They must be married by now.

AMANDA   Girls that aren't cut out for business careers usually wind up married to some nice man. (*Gets up with a spark of revival.*) Sister, that's what you'll do!

LAURA *utters a startled, doubtful laugh. She reaches quickly for a piece of glass.*

LAURA   But, Mother—

AMANDA   Yes? (*Crossing to photograph.*)

LAURA (*in a tone of frightened apology*)   I'm—crippled!

(IMAGE: SCREEN.)

AMANDA   Nonsense! Laura, I've told you never, never to use that word. Why, you're not crippled, you just have a little defect—hardly noticeable, even! When people have some slight disadvantage like that, they cultivate other things to make up for it—develop charm—and vivacity—and—*charm!* That's all you have to do! (*She turns again to the photograph.*) One thing your father had *plenty of*—was *charm!*

TOM *motions to the fiddle in the wings.*

(THE SCENE FADES OUT WITH MUSIC.)

SCENE III

(LEGEND ON SCREEN: "AFTER THE FIASCO—")

TOM *speaks from the fire-escape landing.*

TOM   After the fiasco at Rubicam's Business College, the idea of getting a gentleman caller for Laura began to play a more important part in Mother's calculations. It became an obsession. Like some archetype of the universal unconscious, the image of the gentleman caller haunted our small apartment.... (IMAGE: YOUNG MAN AT DOOR WITH FLOWERS.) An evening at home rarely passed without some allusion to this image, this spectre, this hope.... Even when he wasn't mentioned, his presence hung in Mother's preoccupied look and in my sister's frightened, apologetic manner—hung like a sentence passed upon the Wingfields! Mother was a woman of action as well as words. She began to take logical steps in the planned direction. Late that winter and in the early spring—realizing that extra money would be needed to properly feather the nest and plume the bird—she conducted a vigorous campaign on the telephone, roping in subscribers to one of those magazines for matrons called *The Home-maker's Companion,* the type of journal that features the serialized sublimations of ladies of letters who think in terms of delicate cup-like breasts, slim, tapering waists, rich, creamy thighs, eyes like woodsmoke in autumn, fingers that soothe and caress like strains of music, bodies as powerful as Etruscan sculpture.

(SCREEN IMAGE: GLAMOR MAGAZINE COVER.)

AMANDA *enters with phone on long extension cord. She is spotted in the dim stage.*

AMANDA   Ida Scott? This is Amanda Wingfield! We *missed* you at the D.A.R. last Monday! I said to myself: She's probably suffering with that sinus condition! How is that sinus condition? Horrors! Heaven have mercy!—You're a Christian martyr, yes, that's what you are, a Christian martyr! Well, I just now happened to notice that your subscription to the *Companion's* about to expire!

Yes, it expires with the next issue, honey!—just when that wonderful new serial by Bessie Mae Hopper is getting off to such an
exciting start. Oh, honey, it's something that you can't miss! You
remember how *Gone with the Wind* took everybody by storm?
You simply couldn't go out if you hadn't read it. All everybody
talked was Scarlett O'Hara. Well, this is a book that critics already compare to *Gone with the Wind*. It's the *Gone with the
Wind* of the post-World War generation!—What?—Burning?—
Oh, honey, don't let them burn, go take a look in the oven and
I'll hold the wire! Heavens—I think she's hung up!

(DIM OUT.)

(LEGEND ON SCREEN: "YOU THINK I'M IN LOVE WITH CONTINENTAL
SHOEMAKERS?")

Before the stage is lighted, the violent voices of TOM *and* AMANDA *are
heard.*
    They are quarreling behind the portieres. In front of them stands LAURA
with clenched hands and panicky expression.
    A clear pool of light on her figure throughout this scene.

TOM   What in Christ's name am I—
AMANDA (*shrilly*) Don't you use that—
TOM   Supposed to do!
AMANDA   Expression! Not in my—
TOM   Ohhh!
AMANDA   Presence! Have you gone out of your senses?
TOM   I have, that's true, *driven* out!
AMANDA   What is the matter with you, you—big—big—IDIOT!
TOM   Look—I've got *no thing,* no single thing—
AMANDA   Lower your voice!
TOM   In my life here that I can call my OWN! Everything is—
AMANDA   Stop that shouting!
TOM   Yesterday you confiscated my books! You had the nerve to—
AMANDA   I took that horrible novel back to the library—yes! That
    hideous book by that insane Mr. Lawrence. (TOM *laughs wildly.*)
    I cannot control the output of diseased minds or people who cater
    to them—(TOM *laughs still more wildly.*) BUT I WON'T ALLOW
    SUCH FILTH BROUGHT INTO MY HOUSE! No, no, no, no, no!
TOM   House, house! Who pays rent on it, who makes a slave of
    himself to—
AMANDA (*fairly screeching*) Don't you DARE to—
TOM   No, no, *I* mustn't say things! *I've* got to just—
AMANDA   Let me tell you—

TOM   I don't want to hear any more! (*He tears the portieres open. The upstage area is lit with a turgid smoky red glow.*)

AMANDA's *hair is in metal curlers and she wears a very old bathrobe, much too large for her slight figure, a relic of the faithless Mr. Wingfield.*
   An upright typewriter and a wild disarray of manuscripts is on the drop-leaf table. The quarrel was probably precipitated by AMANDA's *interruption of his creative labor. A chair lying overthrown on the floor.*
   Their gesticulating shadows are cast on the ceiling by the fiery glow.

AMANDA   You *will* hear more, you—
TOM   No, I won't hear more, I'm going out!
AMANDA   You come right back in—
TOM   Out, out out! Because I'm—
AMANDA   Come back here, Tom Wingfield! I'm not through talking to you!
TOM   Oh, go—
LAURA (*desperately*)   —Tom!
AMANDA   You're going to listen, and no more insolence from you! I'm at the end of my patience! (*He comes back toward her.*)
TOM   What do you think I'm at? Aren't I supposed to have any patience to reach the end of, Mother? I know, I know. It seems unimportant to you, what I'm *doing*—what I *want* to do—having a little *difference* between them! You don't think that—
AMANDA   I think you've been doing things that you're ashamed of. That's why you act like this. I don't believe that you go every night to the movies. Nobody goes to the movies night after night. Nobody in their right minds goes to the movies as often as you pretend to. People don't go to the movies at nearly midnight, and movies don't let out at two A.M. Come in stumbling. Muttering to yourself like a maniac! You get three hours sleep and then go to work. Oh, I can picture the way you're doing down there. Moping, doping, because you're in no condition.
TOM (*wildly*)   No, I'm in no condition!
AMANDA   What right have you got to jeopardize your job? Jeopardize the security of us all? How do you think we'd manage if you were—
TOM   Listen! You think I'm crazy *about* the *warehouse?* (*He bends fiercely toward her slight figure.*) You think I'm in love with the Continental Shoemakers? You think I want to spend fifty-five *years* down there in that—*celotex interior!* with—*fluorescent—tubes!* Look! I'd rather somebody picked up a crowbar and battered out my brains—than go back mornings! I *go!* Every time you come in yelling that God damn *"Rise and Shine!" "Rise and*

Shine!" I say to myself "How *lucky dead* people are!" But I get up. I *go!* For sixty-five dollars a month I give up all that I dream of doing and being *ever!* And you say self—*self's* all I ever think of. Why, listen, if self is what I thought of, Mother, I'd be where he is—GONE! (*Pointing to father's picture.*) As far as the system of transportation reaches! (*He starts past her. She grabs his arm.*) Don't grab me, Mother!

AMANDA   Where are you going?

TOM   I'm going to the *movies!*

AMANDA   I don't believe that lie!

TOM (*crouching toward her, overtowering her tiny figure. She backs away, gasping*)   I'm going to opium dens! Yes, opium dens, dens of vice and criminals' hang-outs, Mother. I've joined the Hogan gang, I'm a hired assassin, I carry a tommy-gun in a violin case! I run a string of cat-houses in the Valley! They call me Killer, Killer Wingfield, I'm leading a double-life, a simple, honest ware-house worker by day, by night, a dynamic *czar* of the *underworld, Mother.* I go to gambling casinos, I spin away fortunes on the roulette table! I wear a patch over one eye and a false mustache, sometimes I put on green whiskers. On those occasions they call me—*El Diablo!* Oh, I could tell you things to make you sleepless! My enemies plan to dynamite this place. They're going to blow us all sky-high some night! I'll be glad, very happy, and so will you! You'll go up, up on a broomstick, over Blue Mountain with seven-teen gentlemen callers! You ugly—babbling old—*witch....* (*He goes through a series of violent, clumsy movements, seizing his overcoat, lunging to the door, pulling it fiercely open. The women watch him, aghast. His arm catches in the sleeve of the coat as he struggles to pull it on. For a moment he is pinioned by the bulky garment. With an outraged groan he tears the coat off again, splitting the shoulders of it, and hurls it across the room. It strikes against the shelf of* LAURA'S *glass collection, there is a tinkle of shattering glass.* LAURA *cries out as if wounded.*)

(MUSIC LEGEND: "THE GLASS MENAGERIE.")

LAURA (*shrilly*)   My *glass!*—menagerie.... (*She covers her face and turns away.*)

But AMANDA *is still stunned and stupefied by the "ugly witch" so that she barely notices this occurrence. Now she recovers her speech.*

AMANDA (*in an awful voice*)   I won't speak to you—until you apol-ogize! (*She crosses through portieres and draws them together behind her.* TOM *is left with* LAURA. LAURA *clings weakly to the mantel with her face averted.* TOM *stares at her stupidly for a moment. Then he crosses to shelf. Drops awkwardly to his knees to collect the fallen glass, glancing at* LAURA *as if he would speak but couldn't.*

"The Glass Menagerie" steals in as

(THE SCENE DIMS OUT.)

SCENE IV

The interior is dark. Faint light in the alley.

A deep-voiced bell in a church is tolling the hour of five as the scene commences.

TOM *appears at the top of the alley. After each solemn boom of the bell in the tower, he shakes a little noise-maker or rattle as if to express the tiny spasm of man in contrast to the sustained power and dignity of the Almighty. This and the unsteadiness of his advance make it evident that he has been drinking.*

As he climbs the few steps to the fire-escape landing light steals up inside. LAURA *appears in night-dress, observing* TOM'S *empty bed in the front room.*

TOM *fishes in his pockets for the door-key, removing a motley assortment of articles in the search, including a perfect shower of movie-ticket stubs and an empty bottle. At last he finds the key, but just as he is about to insert it, it slips from his fingers. He strikes a match and crouches below the door.*

TOM (*bitterly*) One crack—and it falls through!

LAURA *opens the door.*

LAURA Tom! Tom, what are you doing?

TOM Looking for a door-key.

LAURA Where have you been all this time?

TOM I have been to the movies.

LAURA All this time at the movies?

TOM There was a very long program. There was a Garbo picture and a Mickey Mouse and a travelogue and a newsreel and a preview of coming attractions. And there was an organ solo and a collection for the milk-fund—simultaneously—which ended up in a terrible fight between a fat lady and an usher!

LAURA (*innocently*) Did you have to stay through everything?

TOM Of course! And, oh, I forgot! There was a big stage show! The headliner on this stage show was Malvolio the Magician. He performed wonderful tricks, many of them, such as pouring water back and forth between pitchers. First it turned to wine and then it turned to beer and then it turned to whiskey. I know it was whiskey it finally turned into because he needed somebody to come up out of the audience to help him, and I came up—both shows! It was Kentucky Straight Bourbon. A very generous fellow, he gave souvenirs. (*He pulls from his back pocket a shimmering rainbow-colored scarf.*) He gave me this. This is his magic scarf. You can have it, Laura. You wave it over a canary cage and you get a bowl of gold-fish. You wave it over the gold-fish bowl and they fly away canaries. . . . But the wonderfullest trick of all was the coffin trick. We nailed him into a coffin and he got out of the coffin without removing one nail. (*He has come inside.*) There is a trick that would come in handy for me—get me out of this 2 by 4 situation! (*Flops onto bed and starts removing shoes.*)

LAURA   Tom—Shhh!

TOM   What you shushing me for?

LAURA   You'll wake up Mother.

TOM   Goody, goody! Pay 'er back for all those "Rise an' Shines." (*Lies down, groaning.*) You know it don't take much intelligence to get yourself into a nailed-up coffin, Laura. But who in hell ever got himself out of one without removing one nail?

As if in answer, the father's grinning photograph lights up.

(SCENE DIMS OUT.)

Immediately following: The church bell is heard striking six. At the sixth stroke the alarm clock goes off in AMANDA'S *room, and after a few moments we hear her calling: "Rise and Shine! Rise and Shine! Laura, go tell your brother to rise and shine!"*

TOM   (*Sitting up slowly*)   I'll rise—but I won't shine.

The light increases.

AMANDA   Laura, tell your brother his coffee is ready.

LAURA *slips into front room.*

LAURA   Tom! it's nearly seven. Don't make Mother nervous. (*He stares at her stupidly. Beseechingly.*) Tom, speak to Mother this morning. Make up with her, apologize, speak to her!

TOM   She won't to me. It's her that started not speaking.

LAURA   If you just say you're sorry she'll start speaking.

TOM   Her not speaking—is that such a tragedy?

LAURA   Please—please!

AMANDA   (*calling from kitchenette*)   Laura, are you going to do what I asked you to do, or do I have to get dressed and go out myself?

LAURA   Going, going—soon as I get on my coat! (*She pulls on a shapeless felt hat with nervous, jerky movement, pleadingly glancing at* TOM. *Rushes awkwardly for coat. The coat is one of* AMANDA's, *inaccurately made-over, the sleeves too short for* LAURA.) Butter and what else?

AMANDA (*entering upstage*)   Just butter. Tell them to charge it.

LAURA   Mother, they make such faces when I do that.

AMANDA   Sticks and stones may break my bones, but the expression on Mr. Garfinkel's face won't harm us! Tell your brother his coffee is getting cold.

LAURA (*at door*)   Do what I asked you, will you, will you, Tom?

He looks sullenly away.

AMANDA   Laura, go now or just don't go at all!

LAURA (*rushing out*)   Going—going! (*A second later she cries out.* TOM *springs up and crosses to the door.* AMANDA *rushes anxiously in.* TOM *opens the door.*)

TOM   Laura?

LAURA   I'm all right. I slipped, but I'm all right.

AMANDA (*peering anxiously after her*)   If anyone breaks a leg on those fire-escape steps, the landlord ought to be sued for every cent he possesses! (*She shuts door. Remembers she isn't speaking and returns to other room.*)

As TOM *enters listlessly for his coffee, she turns her back to him and stands rigidly facing the window on the gloomy gray vault of the areaway. Its light on her face with its aged but childish features is cruelly sharp, satirical as a Daumier print.*

(MUSIC UNDER: "AVE MARIA.")

TOM *glances sheepishly but sullenly at her averted figure and slumps at the table. The coffee is scalding hot; he sips it and gasps and spits it back in the cup. At his gasp,* AMANDA *catches her breath and half turns. Then catches herself and turns back to window.*

TOM *blows on his coffee, glancing sidewise at his mother. She clears her throat.* TOM *clears his. He starts to rise. Sinks back down again, scratches his head, clears his throat again.* AMANDA *coughs.* TOM *raises his cup in both hands to blow on it, his eyes staring over the rim of it at his mother for several moments. Then he slowly sets the cup down and awkwardly and hesitantly rises from the chair.*

TOM (*hoarsely*)   Mother. I—I apologize. Mother. (AMANDA *draws a quick, shuddering breath. Her face works grotesquely. She breaks into childlike tears.*) I'm sorry for what I said, for everything that I said, I didn't mean it.

AMANDA (*sobbingly*)   My devotion has made me a witch and so I make myself hateful to my children!

TOM   No, you *don't.*

AMANDA   I worry so much, don't sleep, it makes me nervous!

TOM (*gently*)   I understand that.

AMANDA   I've had to put up a solitary battle all these years. But you're my right-hand bower! Don't fall down, don't fail!

TOM (*gently*)   I try, Mother.

AMANDA (*with great enthusiasm*)   Try and you will SUCCEED! (*The notion makes her breathless.*) Why, you—you're just *full* of natural endowments! Both of my children—they're *unusual* children! Don't you think I know it? I'm so—*proud!* Happy and—feel I've —so much to be thankful for but—Promise me one thing, son!

TOM   What, Mother?

AMANDA   Promise, son, you'll—never be a drunkard!

TOM (*turns to her grinning*)   I will never be a drunkard, Mother.

AMANDA   That's what frightened me so, that you'd be drinking! Eat a bowl of Purina!

TOM   Just coffee, Mother.

AMANDA   Shredded wheat biscuit?

TOM   No. No, Mother, just coffee.

AMANDA   You can't put in a day's work on an empty stomach. You've got ten minutes—don't gulp! Drinking too-hot liquids makes cancer of the stomach. . . . Put cream in.

TOM   No, thank you.

AMANDA   To cool it.

TOM   No! No, thank you, I want it black.

AMANDA   I know, but it's not good for you. We have to do all that we can to build ourselves up. In these trying times we live in, all that we have to cling to is—each other. . . . That's why it's so important to—Tom, I—I sent out your sister so I could discuss something with you. If you hadn't spoken I would have spoken to you. (*Sits down.*)

TOM (*gently*)   What is it, Mother, that you want to discuss?

AMANDA   Laura!

TOM *puts his cup down slowly.*

(LEGEND ON SCREEN: "LAURA.")

(MUSIC: "THE GLASS MENAGERIE.")

TOM   —Oh.—Laura . . .

AMANDA (*touching his sleeve*)   You know how Laura is. So quiet but—still water runs deep! She notices things and I think she—

broods about them. (TOM *looks up.*) A few days ago I came in and she was crying.

TOM   What about?

AMANDA   You.

TOM   Me?

AMANDA   She has an idea that you're not happy here.

TOM   What gave her that idea?

AMANDA   What gives her any idea? However, you do act strangely. I—I'm not criticizing, understand *that!* I know your ambitions do not lie in the warehouse, that like everybody in the whole wide world—you've had to—make sacrifices, but—Tom—Tom —life's not easy, it calls for— Spartan endurance! There's so many things in my heart that I cannot describe to you! I've never told you but I—*loved* your father. . . .

TOM (*gently*)   I know that, Mother.

AMANDA   And you— when I see you taking after his ways! Staying out late—and—well, you *had* been drinking the night you were in that—terrifying condition! Laura says that you hate the apartment and that you go out nights to get away from it! Is that true, Tom?

TOM   No. You say there's so much in your heart that you can't describe to me. That's true of me, too. There's so much in my heart that I can't describe to *you!* So let's respect each other's—

AMANDA   But, why—*why,* Tom—are you always so *restless?* Where do you go to, nights?

TOM   I—go to the movies.

AMANDA   Why do you go to the movies so much, Tom?

TOM   I go to the movies because—I like adventure. Adventure is something I don't have much of at work, so I go to the movies.

AMANDA   But, Tom, you go to the movies *entirely* too *much!*

TOM   I like a lot of adventure.

AMANDA *looks baffled, then hurt. As the familiar inquisition resumes he becomes hard and impatient again.* AMANDA *slips back into her querulous attitude toward him.*

(IMAGE ON SCREEN: SAILING VESSEL WITH JOLLY ROGER.)

AMANDA   Most young men find adventure in their careers.

TOM   Then most young men are not employed in a warehouse.

AMANDA   The world is full of young men employed in warehouses and offices and factories.

TOM   Do all of them find adventure in their careers?

AMANDA   They do or they do without it! Not everybody has a craze for adventure.

TOM   Man is by instinct a lover, a hunter, a fighter, and none of those instincts are given much play at the warehouse!

AMANDA   Man is by instinct! Don't quote instinct to me! Instinct is something that people have got away from! It belongs to animals! Christian adults don't want it!

TOM   What do Christian adults want, then, Mother?

AMANDA   Superior things! Thinks of the mind and the spirit! Only animals have to satisfy instincts! Surely your aims are somewhat higher than theirs! Than monkeys—pigs—

TOM   I reckon they're not.

AMANDA   You're joking. However, that isn't what I wanted to discuss.

TOM   (*rising*)   I haven't much time.

AMANDA   (*pushing his shoulders*)   Sit down.

TOM   You want me to punch in red at the warehouse, Mother?

AMANDA   You have five minutes. I want to talk about Laura.

(LEGEND: "PLANS AND PROVISIONS.")

TOM   All right! What about Laura?

AMANDA   We have to be making plans and provisions for her. She's older than you, two years, and nothing has happened. She just drifts along doing nothing. It frightens me terribly how she just drifts along.

TOM   I guess she's the type that people call home girls.

AMANDA   There's no such type, and if there is, it's a pity! That is unless the home is hers, with a husband!

TOM   What?

AMANDA   Oh, I can see the handwriting on the wall as plain as I see the nose in front of my face! It's terrifying! More and more you remind me of your father! He was out all hours without explanation—Then *left! Goodbye!* And me with a bag to hold. I saw that letter you got from the Merchant Marine. I know what you're dreaming of. I'm not standing here blindfolded. Very well, then. Then *do* it! But not till there's somebody to take your place.

TOM   What do you mean?

AMANDA   I mean that as soon as Laura has got somebody to take care of her, married, a home of her own, independent—why, then you'll be free to go wherever you please, on land, on sea, whichever way the wind blows! But until that time you've got to look out for your sister. I don't say me because I'm old and don't matter! I say for your sister because she's young and dependent. I put her in business college—a dismal failure! Frightened her so it made her sick to her stomach. I took her over to the Young People's League at the church. Another fiasco. She spoke to nobody,

nobody spoke to her. Now all she does is fool with those pieces of glass and play those worn-out records. What kind of a life is that for a girl to lead?

TOM   What can I do about it?

AMANDA   Overcome selfishness! Self, self, self is all that you ever think of! (TOM *springs up and crosses to get his coat. It is ugly and bulky. He pulls on a cap with earmuffs.*) Where is your muffler? Put your wool muffler on! (*He snatches it angrily from the closet and tosses it around his neck and pulls both ends tight.*) Tom! I haven't said what I had in mind to ask you.

TOM   I'm too late to—

AMANDA   (*catching his arm—very importunately. Then shyly*). Down at the warehouse, aren't there some—nice young men?

TOM   No!

AMANDA   There *must* be—*some* . . .

TOM   Mother—

Gesture.

AMANDA   Find out one that's clean-living—doesn't drink and—ask him out for sister!

TOM   What?

AMANDA   For *sister!* To *meet!* Get *acquainted!*

TOM   (*stamping to door*)   Oh, my *go-osh!*

AMANDA   Will you? (*He opens door. Imploringly.*) Will you? (*He starts down.*) Will you? *Will* you, dear?

TOM   (*calling back*)   YES!

AMANDA *closes the door hesitantly and with a troubled but faintly hopeful expression.*

(SCREEN IMAGE: GLAMOR MAGAZINE COVER.)

Spot AMANDA *at phone.*

AMANDA   Ella Cartwright? This is Amanda Wingfield! How are you, honey? How is that kidney condition? (*Count five.*) Horrors! (*Count five.*) You're a Christian martyr, yes, honey, that's what you are, a Christian martyr! Well, I just happened to notice in my little red book that your subscription to the *Companion* has just run out! I knew that you wouldn't want to miss out on the wonderful serial starting in this new issue. It's by Bessie Mae Hopper, the first thing she's written since *Honeymoon for Three.* Wasn't that a strange and interesting story? Well, this one is even lovelier, I believe. It has a sophisticated society background. It's all about the horsey set on Long Island!

(FADE OUT.)

SCENE V

(LEGEND ON SCREEN: "ANNUNCIATION.")

Fade with music.

It is early dusk of a spring evening. Supper has just been finished in the Wingfield apartment. AMANDA *and* LAURA *in light colored dresses are removing dishes from the table, in the upstage area, which is shadowy, their movements formalized almost as a dance or ritual, their moving forms as pale and silent as moths.*

Tom, in white shirt and trousers, rises from the table and crosses toward the fire-escape.

AMANDA (*as he passes her*)   Son, will you do me a favor?

TOM   What?

AMANDA   Comb your hair! You look so pretty when your hair is combed! (TOM *slouches on sofa with evening paper. Enormous caption "Franco Triumphs."*) There is only one respect in which I would like you to emulate your father.

TOM   What respect is that?

AMANDA   The care he always took of his appearance. He never allowed himself to look untidy. (*He throws down the paper and crosses to fire-escape.*) Where are you going?

TOM   I'm going out to smoke.

AMANDA   You smoke too much. A pack a day at fifteen cents a pack. How much would that amount to in a month? Thirty times fifteen is how much, Tom? Figure it out and you will be astounded at what you could save. Enough to give you a night-school course in accounting at Washington U! Just think what a wonderful thing that would be for you, son!

TOM *is unmoved by the thought.*

TOM   I'd rather smoke. (*He steps out on landing, letting the screen door slam.*)

AMANDA (*sharply*)   I know! That's the tragedy of it.... (*Alone, she turns to look at her husband's picture.*)

(DANCE MUSIC: "ALL THE WORLD IS WAITING FOR THE SUNRISE!")

TOM (*to the audience*)   Across the alley from us was the Paradise Dance Hall. On evenings in spring the windows and doors were open and the music came outdoors. Sometimes the lights were turned out except for a large glass sphere that hung from the ceiling. It would turn slowly about and filter the dusk with delicate rainbow colors. Then the orchestra played a waltz or a tango, something that had a slow and sensuous rhythm. Couples would come outside, to the relative privacy of the alley. You could see them kissing behind ash-pits and telephone poles. This was the compensation for lives that passed like mine, without any change or adventure. Adventure and change were imminent in this year. They were waiting around the corner for all these kids. Suspended in the mist over Berchtesgaden, caught in the folds of Chamberlain's umbrella—In Spain there was Guernica! But here there was only hot swing music and liquor, dance halls, bars, and movies, and sex that hung in the gloom like a chandelier and flooded the world with brief, deceptive rainbows. . . . All the world was waiting for bombardments!

AMANDA *turns from the picture and comes outside.*

AMANDA (*sighing*) A fire-escape landing's a poor excuse for a porch. (*She spreads a newspaper on a step and sits down, gracefully and demurely as if she were settling into a swing on a Mississippi veranda.*) What are you looking at?

TOM The moon.

AMANDA Is there a moon this evening?

TOM It's rising over Garfinkel's Delicatessen.

AMANDA So it is! A little silver slipper of a moon. Have you made a wish on it yet?

TOM Um-hum.

AMANDA What did you wish for?

TOM That's a secret.

AMANDA A secret, huh? Well, I won't tell mine either. I will be just as mysterious as you.

TOM I bet I can guess what yours is.

AMANDA Is my head so transparent?

TOM You're not a sphinx.

AMANDA No, I don't have secrets. I'll tell you what I wished for on the moon. Success and happiness for my precious children! I wish for that whenever there's a moon, and when there isn't a moon, I wish for it, too.

TOM I thought perhaps you wished for a gentleman caller.

AMANDA Why do you say that?

TOM Don't you remember asking me to fetch one?

AMANDA I remember suggesting that it would be nice for your sister if you brought home some nice young man from the warehouse. I think I've made that suggestion more than once.

TOM Yes, you have made it repeatedly.

AMANDA Well?

TOM   We are going to have one.

AMANDA   *What?*

TOM   A gentleman caller!

(THE ANNUNCIATION IS CELEBRATED WITH MUSIC.)

AMANDA *rises.*

(IMAGE ON SCREEN: CALLER WITH BOUQUET.)

AMANDA   You mean you have asked some nice young man to come over?

TOM   Yep. I've asked him to dinner.

AMANDA   You really did?

TOM   I did!

AMANDA   You did, and did he—*accept?*

TOM   He did!

AMANDA   Well, well—well, well! That's—lovely!

TOM   I thought that you would be pleased.

AMANDA   It's definite, then?

TOM   Very definite.

AMANDA   Soon?

TOM   Very soon.

AMANDA   For heaven's sake, stop putting on and tell me some things, will you?

TOM   What things do you want me to tell you?

AMANDA   *Naturally* I would like to know when he's *coming!*

TOM   He's coming tomorrow.

AMANDA   *Tomorrow?*

TOM   Yep. Tomorrow.

AMANDA   But, Tom!

TOM   Yes, Mother?

AMANDA   Tomorrow gives me no time!

TOM   Time for what?

AMANDA   Preparations! Why didn't you phone me at once, as soon as you asked him, the minute that he accepted? Then, don't you see, I could have been getting ready!

TOM   You don't have to make any fuss.

AMANDA   Oh, Tom, Tom, Tom, of course I have to make a fuss! I want things nice, not sloppy! Not thrown together. I'll certainly have to do some fast thinking, won't I?

TOM   I don't see why you have to think at all.

AMANDA   You just don't know. We can't have a gentleman caller in a pig-sty! All my wedding silver has to be polished, the monogrammed table linen ought to be laundered! The windows have to be washed and fresh curtains put up. And how about clothes? We have to *wear* something, don't we?

TOM Mother, this boy is no one to make a fuss over!

AMANDA Do you realize he's the first young man we've introduced to your sister? It's terrible, dreadful, disgraceful that poor little sister has never received a single gentleman caller! Tom, come inside! (*She opens the screen door.*)

TOM What for?

AMANDA I want to ask you some things.

TOM If you're going to make such a fuss, I'll call it off, I'll tell him not to come.

AMANDA You certainly won't do anything of the kind. Nothing offends people worse than broken engagements. It simply means I'll have to work like a Turk! We won't be brilliant, but we'll pass inspection. Come on inside. (TOM *follows, groaning.*) Sit down.

TOM Any particular place you would like me to sit?

AMANDA Thank heavens I've got that new sofa! I'm also making payments on a floor lamp I'll have sent out! And put the chintz covers on, they'll brighten things up! Of course I'd hoped to have these walls re-papered. . . . What is the young man's name?

TOM His name is O'Connor.

AMANDA That, of course, means fish—tomorrow is Friday! I'll have that salmon loaf—with Durkee's dressing! What does he do? He works at the warehouse?

TOM Of course! How else would I—

AMANDA Tom, he—doesn't drink?

TOM Why do you ask me that?

AMANDA Your father *did!*

TOM Don't get started on that!

AMANDA He *does* drink, then?

TOM Not that I know of!

AMANDA Make sure, be certain! The last thing I want for my daughter's a boy who drinks!

TOM Aren't you being a little premature? Mr. O'Connor has not yet appeared on the scene!

AMANDA But will tomorrow. To meet your sister, and what do I know about his character? Nothing! Old maids are better off than wives of drunkards!

TOM Oh, my God!

AMANDA Be still!

TOM (*leaning forward to whisper*) Lots of fellows meet girls whom they don't marry!

AMANDA   Oh, talk sensibly, Tom—and don't be sarcastic! (*She has gotten a hairbrush.*)

TOM   What are you doing?

AMANDA   I'm brushing that cow-lick down! What is this young man's position at the warehouse?

TOM   (*submitting grimly to the brush and the interrogation*)   This young man's position is that of a shipping clerk, Mother.

AMANDA   Sounds to me like a fairly responsible job, the sort of a job *you* would be in if you just had more *get-up*. What is his salary? Have you got any idea?

TOM   I would judge it to be approximately eighty-five dollars a month.

AMANDA   Well—not princely, but—

TOM   Twenty more than I make.

AMANDA   Yes, how well I know! But for a family man, eighty-five dollars a month is not much more than you can just get by on. . . .

TOM   Yes, but Mr. O'Connor is not a family man.

AMANDA   He might be, mightn't he? Some time in the future?

TOM   I see. Plans and provisions.

AMANDA   You are the only young man that I know of who ignores the fact that the future becomes the present, the present the past, and the past turns into everlasting regret if you don't plan for it!

TOM   I will think that over and see what I can make of it.

AMANDA   Don't be supercilious with your mother! Tell me some more about this—what do you call him?

TOM   James D. O'Connor. The D. is for Delaney.

AMANDA   Irish on *both* sides! *Gracious!* And doesn't drink?

TOM   Shall I call him up and ask him right this minute?

AMANDA   The only way to find out about those things is to make discreet inquiries at the proper moment. When I was a girl in Blue Mountain and it was suspected that a young man drank, the girl whose attentions he had been receiving, if any girl *was,* would sometimes speak to the minister of his church, or rather her father would if her father was living, and sort of feel him out on the young man's character. That is the way such things are discreetly handled to keep a young woman from making a tragic mistake!

TOM   Then how did you happen to make a tragic mistake?

AMANDA   That innocent look of your father's had everyone fooled! He *smiled*—the world was *enchanted!* No girl can do worse than put herself at the mercy of a handsome appearance! I hope that Mr. O'Connor is not too good-looking.

TOM   No, he's not too good-looking. He's covered with freckles and hasn't too much of a nose.

AMANDA   He's not right-down homely, though?

TOM   Not right-down homely. Just medium homely. I'd say.

AMANDA   Character's what to look for in a man.

TOM   That's what I've always said, Mother.

AMANDA   You've never said anything of the kind and I suspect you would never give it a thought.

TOM   Don't be suspicious of me.

AMANDA   At least I hope he's the type that's up and coming.

TOM   I think he really goes in for self-improvement.

AMANDA   What reason have you to think so?

TOM   He goes to night school.

AMANDA   (*beaming*)   Splendid! What does he do, I mean study?

TOM   Radio engineering and public speaking!

AMANDA   Then he has visions of being advanced in the world! Any young man who studies public speaking is aiming to have an executive job some day! And radio engineering? A thing for the future! Both of these facts are very illuminating. Those are the sort of things that a mother should know concerning any young man who comes to call on her daughter. Seriously or—not.

TOM   One little warning. He doesn't know about Laura. I didn't let on that we had dark ulterior motives. I just said, why don't you come have dinner with us? He said okay and that was the whole conversation.

AMANDA   I bet it was! You're eloquent as an oyster. However, he'll know about Laura when he gets here. When he sees how lovely and sweet and pretty she is, he'll thank his lucky stars he was asked to dinner.

TOM   Mother, you mustn't expect too much of Laura.

AMANDA   What do you mean?

TOM   Laura seems all those things to you and me because she's ours and we love her. We don't even notice she's crippled any more.

AMANDA   Don't say crippled! You know that I never allow that word to be used!

TOM   But face facts, Mother. She is and—that's not all—

AMANDA   What do you mean "not all"?

TOM   Laura is very different from other girls.

AMANDA   I think the difference is all to her advantage.

TOM   Not quite all—in the eyes of others—strangers—she's terribly shy and lives in a world of her own and those things make her seem a little peculiar to people outside the house.

AMANDA   Don't say peculiar.

TOM   Face the facts. She is.

(THE DANCE-HALL MUSIC CHANGES TO A TANGO THAT HAS A MINOR AND SOMEWHAT OMINOUS TONE.)

AMANDA   In what way is she peculiar—may I ask?

TOM   (*gently*)   She lives in a world of her own—a world of—little glass ornaments, Mother. . . . (*Gets up.* AMANDA *remains holding brush, looking at him, troubled.*) She plays old phonograph records and—that's about all—(*He glances at himself in the mirror and crosses to door.*)

AMANDA   (*sharply*)   Where are you going?

TOM   I'm going to the movies. (*Out screen door.*)

AMANDA   Not to the movies, every night to the movies! (*Follows quickly to screen door.*) I don't believe you always go to the movies! (*He is gone.* AMANDA *looks worriedly after him for a moment. Then vitality and optimism return and she turns from the door. Crossing to portieres.*) Laura! Laura! (LAURA *answers from kitchenette.*)

LAURA   Yes, Mother.

AMANDA   Let those dishes go and come in front! (LAURA *appears with dish towel. Gaily.*) Laura, come here and make a wish on the moon!

LAURA   (*entering*)   Moon—moon?

AMANDA   A little silver slipper of a moon. Look over your left shoulder, Laura, and make a wish! (LAURA *looks faintly puzzled as if called out of sleep.* AMANDA *seizes her shoulders and turns her at an angle by the door.*) No! Now, darling, *wish!*

LAURA   What shall I wish for, Mother?

AMANDA   (*her voice trembling and her eyes suddenly filling with tears*)   Happiness! Good Fortune!

The violin rises and the stage dims out.

SCENE VI

(IMAGE: HIGH SCHOOL HERO.)

TOM   And so the following evening I brought Jim home to dinner. I had known Jim slightly in high school. In high school Jim was a hero. He had tremendous Irish good nature and vitality with the scrubbed and polished look of white chinaware. He seemed to move in a continual spotlight. He was a star in basketball, captain of the debating club, president of the senior class and the glee club and he sang the male lead in the annual light operas. He was always running or bounding, never just walking. He seemed always at the point of defeating the law of gravity. He was shooting with such velocity through his adolescence that you would logically expect him to arrive at nothing short of the White House by the time he was thirty. But Jim apparently ran into more in-

terference after his graduation from Soldan. His speed had definitely slowed. Six years after he left high school he was holding a
job that wasn't much better than mine.

(IMAGE: CLERK.)

He was the only one at the warehouse with whom I was on
friendly terms. I was valuable to him as someone who could remember his former glory, who had seen him win basketball games
and the silver cup in debating. He knew of my secret practice of
retiring to a cabinet of the washroom to work on poems when
business was slack in the warehouse. He called me Shakespeare.
And while the other boys in the warehouse regarded me with suspicious hostility, Jim took a humorous attitude toward me. Gradually his attitude affected the others, their hostility wore off and
they also began to smile at me as people smile at an oddly fashioned dog who trots across their path at some distance.

I knew that Jim and Laura had known each other at Soldan,
and I had heard Laura speak admiringly of his voice. I didn't
know if Jim remembered her or not. In high school Laura had
been as unobtrusive as Jim had been astonishing. If he did remember Laura, it was not as my sister, for when I asked him to
dinner, he grinned and said, "You know, Shakespeare, I never
thought of you as having folks!"

He was about to discover that I did. . . .

(LIGHT UP STAGE.)

(LEGEND ON SCREEN: "THE ACCENT OF A COMING FOOT.")

*Friday evening. It is about five o'clock of a late spring evening which
comes "scattering poems in the sky."*

A delicate lemony light is in the Wingfield apartment.

AMANDA *has worked like a Turk in preparation for the gentleman
caller. The results are astonishing. The new floor lamp with its rose-silk
shade is in place, a colored paper lantern conceals the broken light fixture
in the ceiling, new billowing white curtains are at the windows, chintz
covers are on chairs and sofa, a pair of new sofa pillows make their
initial appearance.*

Open boxes and tissue paper are scattered on the floor.

LAURA *stands in the middle with lifted arms while* AMANDA *crouches
before her, adjusting the hem of the new dress, devout and ritualistic.
The dress is colored and designed by memory. The arrangement of* LAURA's
*hair is changed; it is softer and more becoming. A fragile, unearthly
prettiness has come out in* LAURA: *she is like a piece of translucent glass
touched by light, given a momentary radiance, not actual, not lasting.*

AMANDA (*impatiently*)   Why are you trembling?

LAURA   Mother, you've made me so nervous!

AMANDA   How have I made you nervous?

LAURA   By all this fuss! You make it seem so important!

AMANDA   I don't understand you, Laura. You couldn't be satisfied with just sitting home, and yet whenever I try to arrange something for you, you seem to resist it. (*She gets up.*) Now take a look at yourself. No, wait! Wait just a moment—I have an idea!

LAURA   What is it now?

AMANDA *produces two powder puffs which she wraps in handkerchiefs and stuffs in* LAURA'S *bosom.*

LAURA   Mother, what are you doing?

AMANDA   They call them "Gay Deceivers"!

LAURA   I won't wear them!

AMANDA   You will!

LAURA   Why should I?

AMANDA   Because, to be painfully honest, your chest is flat.

LAURA   You make it seem like we were setting a trap.

AMANDA   All pretty girls are a trap, a pretty trap, and men expect them to be. (LEGEND: "A PRETTY TRAP.") Now look at yourself, young lady. This is the prettiest you will ever be! I've got to fix myself now! You're going to be surprised by your mother's appearance! (*She crosses through portieres, humming gaily.*)

LAURA *moves slowly to the long mirror and stares solemnly at herself.*
  A wind blows the white curtains inward in a slow, graceful motion and with a faint, sorrowful sighing.

AMANDA (*off stage*)   It isn't dark enough yet. (*She turns slowly before the mirror with a troubled look.*)

(LEGEND ON SCREEN: "THIS IS MY SISTER: CELEBRATE HER WITH STRINGS!" MUSIC.)

AMANDA (*laughing, off*)   I'm going to show you something. I'm going to make a spectacular appearance!

LAURA   What is it, mother?

AMANDA   Possess your soul in patience—you will see! Something I've resurrected from that old trunk! Styles haven't changed so terribly much after all.... (*She parts the portieres.*) Now just look at your mother! (*She wears a girlish frock of yellowed voile with a blue silk sash. She carries a bunch of jonquils—the legend of her youth is nearly revived. Feverishly.*) This is the dress in which I led the cotillion. Won the cakewalk twice at Sunset Hill, wore one spring to the Governor's ball in Jackson! See how I sashayed around the ballroom, Laura? (*She raises her skirt and does a mincing step around the room.*) I wore it on Sundays for my gentlemen callers! I had it on the day I met your father—I had malaria fever all that spring. The change of climate from East Tennessee to the Delta—weakened resistance—I had a little temperature all the time—not enough to be serious—just enough to make me restless and giddy! Invitations poured in—parties all over the Delta!—"Stay in bed," said Mother, "you have fever!" —but I just wouldn't.—I took quinine but kept on going, going! —Evenings, dances!—Afternoons, long, long rides! Picnics— lovely!—So lovely, that country in May.—All lacy with dogwood, literally flooded with jonquils!—That was the spring I had the craze for jonquils. Jonquils became an absolute obsession. Mother said, "Honey, there's no more room for jonquils." And still I kept bringing in more jonquils. Whenever, wherever I saw them, I'd say, "Stop! Stop! I see jonquils!" I made the young men help me gather the jonquils! It was a joke, Amanda and her jonquils! Finally there were no more vases to hold them, every available space was filled with jonquils. No vases to hold them? All right, I'll hold them myself! And then I—(*She stops in front of the picture.* MUSIC.) met your father! Malaria fever and jonquils and then—this—boy.... (*She switches on the rose-colored lamp.*) I hope they get here before it starts to rain. (*She crosses upstage and places the jonquils in bowl on table.*) I gave your brother a little extra change so he and Mr. O'Connor could take the service car home.

LAURA (*with altered look*)   What did you say his name was?
AMANDA   O'Connor.
LAURA   What is his first name?
AMANDA   I don't remember. Oh, yes, I do. It was—Jim!

LAURA *sways slightly and catches hold of a chair.*

(LEGEND ON SCREEN: "NOT JIM!")

LAURA (*faintly*)   Not—Jim!
AMANDA   Yes, that was it, it was Jim! I've never known a Jim that wasn't nice!

(MUSIC: OMINOUS.)

LAURA   Are you sure his name is Jim O'Connor?
AMANDA   Yes. Why?
LAURA   Is he the one that Tom used to know in high school?
AMANDA   He didn't say so. I think he just got to know him at the warehouse.
LAURA   There was a Jim O'Connor we both knew in high school—

(*Then, with effort.*) If that is the one that Tom is bringing to dinner—you'll have to excuse me, I won't come to the table.

AMANDA   What sort of nonsense is this?

LAURA   You asked me once if I'd ever liked a boy. Don't you remember I showed you this boy's picture?

AMANDA   You mean the boy you showed me in the year book?

LAURA   Yes, that boy.

AMANDA   Laura, Laura, were you in love with that boy?

LAURA   I don't know, Mother. All I know is I couldn't sit at the table if it was him!

AMANDA   It won't be him! It isn't the least bit likely. But whether it is or not, you will come to the table. You will not be excused.

LAURA   I'll have to be, Mother.

AMANDA   I don't intend to humor your silliness, Laura. I've had too much from you and your brother, both! So just sit down and compose yourself till they come. Tom has forgotten his key so you'll have to let them in, when they arrive.

LAURA (*panicky*)   Oh, Mother—*you* answer the door!

AMANDA (*lightly*)   I'll be in the kitchen—busy!

LAURA   Oh, Mother, please answer the door, don't make me do it!

AMANDA (*crossing into kitchenette*)   I've got to fixe the dressing for the salmon. Fuss, fuss—silliness!—over a gentleman caller!

Door swings shut. LAURA *is left alone.*

(LEGEND: "TERROR!")

She utters a low moan and turns off the lamp—sits stiffly on the edge of the sofa, knotting her fingers together.

(LEGEND ON SCREEN: "THE OPENING OF A DOOR!")

TOM *and* JIM *appear on the fire-escape steps and climb to landing. Hearing their approach,* LAURA *rises with a panicky gesture. She retreats to the portieres.*
   The doorbell. LAURA *catches her breath and touches her throat. Low drums.*

AMANDA (*calling*)   Laura, sweetheart! The door!

LAURA *stares at it without moving.*

JIM   I think we just beat the rain.

TOM   Uh-huh. (*He rings again, nervously.* JIM *whistles and fishes for a cigarette.*)

AMANDA (*very, very gaily*)   Laura, that is your brother and Mr. O'Connor! Will you let them in, darling?

LAURA *crosses toward kitchenette door.*

LAURA (*breathlessly*) Mother—you go to the door!

AMANDA *steps out of kitchenette and stares furiously at* LAURA. *She points imperiously at the door.*

LAURA Please, please!

AMANDA (*in a fierce whisper*) What is the matter with you, you silly thing?

LAURA (*desperately*) Please, you answer It, *please!*

AMANDA I told you I wasn't going to humor you, Laura. Why have you chosen this moment to lose your mind?

LAURA Please, please, please, you go!

AMANDA You'll have to go to the door because I can't!

LAURA (*despairingly*) I can't either!

AMANDA Why?

LAURA I'm *sick!*

AMANDA I'm sick, too—of your nonsense! Why can't you and your brother be normal people? Fantastic whims and behavior! (TOM *gives a long ring.*) Preposterous goings on! Can you give me one reason—(*Calls out lyrically.*) COMING! JUST ONE SECOND!—why should you be afraid to open a door? Now you answer it, Laura!

LAURA Oh, oh, oh . . . (*She returns through the portieres. Darts to the victrola and winds it frantically and turns it on.*)

AMANDA Laura Wingfield, you march right to that door!

LAURA Yes—yes, Mother!

A faraway, scratchy rendition of "Dardanella" softens the air and gives her strength to move through it. She slips to the door and draws it cautiously open.
Tom enters with the caller, JIM O'CONNOR.

TOM Laura, this is Jim. Jim, this is my sister, Laura.

JIM (*stepping inside*) I didn't know that Shakespeare had a sister!

LAURA (*retreating stiff and trembling from the door*) How—how do you do?

JIM (*heartily extending his hand*) Okay!

LAURA *touches it hesitantly with hers.*

JIM Your hand's *cold,* Laura!

LAURA Yes, well—I've been playing the victrola. . . .

JIM Must have been playing classical music on it! You ought to play a little hot swing music to warm you up!

LAURA Excuse me—I haven't finished playing the victrola. . . .

She turns awkwardly and hurries into the front room. She pauses a second by the victrola. Then catches her breath and darts through the portieres like a frightened deer.

JIM (*grinning*)   What was the matter?

TOM   Oh—with Laura? Laura is—terribly shy.

JIM   Shy, huh? It's unusual to meet a shy girl nowadays. I don't believe you ever mentioned you had a sister.

TOM   Well, now you know. I have one. Here is the *Post Dispatch.* You want a piece of it?

JIM   Uh-huh.

TOM   What piece? The comics?

JIM   Sports! (*Glances at it.*) Ole Dizzy Dean is on his bad behavior.

TOM (*disinterest*)   Yeah? (*Lights cigarette and crosses back to fire-escape door.*)

JIM   Where are *you* going?

TOM   I'm going out on the terrace.

JIM (*goes after him*)   You know, Shakespeare—I'm going to sell you a bill of goods!

TOM   What goods?

JIM   A course I'm taking.

TOM   Huh?

JIM   In public speaking! You and me, we're not the warehouse type.

TOM   Thanks—that's good news. But what has public speaking got to do with it?

JIM   It fits you for—executive positions!

TOM   Awww.

JIM   I tell you it's done a helluva lot for me.

(IMAGE: EXECUTIVE AT DESK.)

TOM   In what respect?

JIM   In every! Ask yourself what is the difference between you an' me and men in the office down front? Brains?—No!—Ability?—No! Then what? Just one little thing—

TOM   What is that one little thing?

JIM   Primarily it amounts to—social poise! Being able to square up to people and hold your own on any social level!

AMANDA (*off stage*)   Tom?

TOM   Yes, Mother?

AMANDA   Is that you and Mr. O'Connor?

TOM   Yes, Mother.

AMANDA   Well, you just make yourselves comfortable in there.

TOM   Yes, Mother.

AMANDA   Ask Mr. O'Connor if he would like to wash his hands.

JIM   Aw—no—no—thank you—I took care of that at the warehouse. Tom—

TOM   Yes?

JIM   Mr. Mendoza was speaking to me about you.

TOM   Favorably?

JIM   What do you think?

TOM   Well—

JIM   You're going to be out of a job if you don't wake up.

TOM   I am waking up—

JIM   You show no signs.

TOM   The signs are interior.

(IMAGE ON SCREEN: THE SAILING VESSEL WITH JOLLY ROGER AGAIN.)

TOM   I'm planning to change. (*He leans over the rail speaking with quiet exhilaration. The incandescent marquees and signs of the first-run movie houses light his face from across the alley. He looks like a voyager.*) I'm right at the point of committing myself to a future that doesn't include the warehouse and Mr. Mendoza or even a night-school course in public speaking.

JIM   What are you gassing about?

TOM   I'm tired of the movies.

JIM   Movies!

TOM   Yes, movies! Look at them—(*A wave toward the marvels of Grand Avenue.*) All of those glamorous people—having adventures—hogging it all, gobbling the whole thing up! You know what happens? People go to the *movies* instead of *moving!* Hollywood characters are supposed to have all the adventures for everybody in America, while everybody in America sits in a dark room and watches them have them! Yes, until there's a war. That's when adventure becomes available to the masses! *Everyone's* dish, not only Gable's! Then the people in the dark room come out of the dark room to have some adventures themselves— Goody, goody!—It's our turn now, to go to the South Sea Island —to make a safari—to be exotic, far-off!—But I'm not patient. I don't want to wait till then. I'm tired of the *movies* and I am *about* to *move!*

JIM   (*incredulously*)   Move?

TOM   Yes.

JIM   When?

TOM   Soon!

JIM   Where? Where?

(THEME THREE MUSIC SEEMS TO ANSWER THE QUESTION, WHILE TOM THINKS IT OVER. HE SEARCHES AMONG HIS POCKETS.)

TOM   I'm starting to boil inside. I know I seem dreamy, but inside —well, I'm boiling! Whenever I pick up a shoe, I shudder a little thinking how short life is and what I am doing!—Whatever that means. I know it doesn't mean shoes—except as something to wear on a traveler's feet! (*Finds paper.*) Look—

JIM   What?

TOM   I'm a member.

JIM   (*reading*)   The Union of Merchant Seamen.

TOM   I paid my dues this month, instead of the light bill.

JIM   You will regret it when they turn the lights off.

TOM   I won't be here.

JIM   How about your mother?

TOM   I'm like my father. The bastard son of a bastard! See how he grins? And he's been absent going on sixteen years!

JIM   You're just talking, you drip. How does your mother feel about it?

TOM   Shhh!—Here comes Mother! Mother is not acquainted with my plans!

AMANDA   (*enters portieres*)   Where are you all?

TOM   On the terrace, Mother.

They start inside. She advances to them. TOM is distinctly shocked at her appearance. Even JIM blinks a little. He is making his first contact with girlish Southern vivacity and in spite of the night-school course in public speaking is somewhat thrown off the beam by the unexpected outlay of social charm.

Certain responses are attempted by JIM but are swept aside by AMANDA's gay laughter and chatter. TOM is embarrassed but after the first shock JIM reacts very warmly. Grins and chuckles, is altogether won over.

(IMAGE: AMANDA AS A GIRL.)

AMANDA   (*coyly smiling, shaking her girlish ringlets*)   Well, well, well, so this is Mr. O'Connor. Introductions entirely unnecessary. I've heard so much about you from my boy. I finally said to him, Tom—good gracious!—why don't you bring this paragon to supper? I'd like to meet this nice young man at the warehouse!— Instead of just hearing him sing your praises so much! I don't know why my son is so stand-offish—that's not Southern behavior! Let's sit down and—I think we could stand a little more air in here! Tom, leave the door open. I felt a nice fresh breeze a moment ago. Where has it gone? Mmm, so warm already! And not quite summer, even. We're going to burn up when summer really gets started. However, we're having—we're having a very light supper. I think light things are better fo' this time of year. The same as light clothes are. Light clothes an' light food are what warm weather calls fo'. You know our blood gets so thick during th' winter—it takes a while fo' us to *adjust* ou'selves!—

when the season changes . . . It's come so quick this year. I wasn't prepared. All of a sudden—heavens! Already summer!—I ran to the trunk an' pulled out this light dress—Terribly old! Historical almost! But feels so good—so good an' co-ol, y'know. . . .

TOM Mother—

AMANDA Yes, honey?

TOM How about—supper?

AMANDA Honey, you go ask Sister if supper is ready! You know that Sister is in full charge of supper! Tell her you hungry boys are waiting for it. (*To* JIM.) Have you met Laura?

JIM She—

AMANDA Let you in? Oh, good, you've met already! It's rare for a girl as sweet an' pretty as Laura to be domestic! But Laura is, thank heavens, not only pretty but also very domestic. I'm not at all. I never was a bit. I never could make a thing but angel-food cake. Well, in the South we had so many servants. Gone, gone, gone. All vestige of gracious living! Gone completely! I wasn't prepared for what the future brought me. All of my gentlemen callers were sons of planters and so of course I assumed that I would be married to one and raise my family on a large piece of land with plenty of servants. But man proposes—and woman accepts the proposal!—To vary that old, old saying a little bit—I married no planter! I married a man who worked for the telephone company!—That gallantly smiling gentleman over there! (*Points to the picture.*) A telephone man who—fell in love with long-distance! Now he travels and I don't even know where!— But what am I going on for about my—tribulations? Tell me yours— I hope you don't have any! Tom?

TOM (*returning*) Yes, Mother?

AMANDA Is supper nearly ready?

TOM It looks to me like supper is on the table.

AMANDA Let me look—(*She rises prettily and looks through portieres.*) Oh, lovely!—But where is Sister?

TOM Laura is not feeling well and she says that she thinks she'd better not come to the table.

AMANDA What?—Nonsense!—Laura? Oh, Laura!

LAURA (*off stage, faintly*) Yes, Mother.

AMANDA You really must come to the table. We won't be seated until you come to the table! Come in, Mr. O'Connor. You sit over there and I'll—Laura? Laura Wingfield! You're keeping us waiting, honey! We can't say grace until you come to the table!

The back door is pushed weakly open and LAURA *comes in. She is obviously quite faint, her lips trembling, her eyes wide and staring. She moves unsteadily toward the table.*

(LEGEND: "TERROR!")

Outside a summer storm is coming abruptly. The white curtains billow inward at the windows and there is a sorrowful murmur and deep blue dusk.
LAURA *suddenly stumbles—she catches at a chair with a faint moan.*

TOM   Laura!

AMANDA   Laura! (*There is a clap of thunder.*) (LEGEND: "AH!") (*Despairingly.*) Why, Laura, you *are* sick, darling! Tom, help your sister into the living room, dear! Sit in the living room, Laura —rest on the sofa. Well! (*To the gentleman caller.*) Standing over the hot stove made her ill!—I told her that it was just too warm this evening, but—(TOM *comes back in.* LAURA *is on the sofa.*) Is Laura all right now?

TOM   Yes.

AMANDA   What *is* that? Rain? A nice cool rain has come up! (*She gives the gentleman caller a frightened look.*) I think we may— have grace—now . . . (TOM *looks at her stupidly.*) Tom, honey— you say grace!

TOM   Oh . . . "For these and all thy mercies—" (*They bow their heads,* AMANDA *stealing a nervous glance at* JIM. *In the living room* LAURA, *stretched on the sofa, clenches her hand to her lips, to hold back a shuddering sob.*) God's Holy Name be praised—

(THE SCENE DIMS OUT.)

SCENE VII

(LEGEND: "A SOUVENIR.")

Half an hour later. Dinner is just being finished in the upstage area which is concealed by the drawn portieres.
As the curtain rises LAURA *is still huddled upon the sofa, her feet drawn under her, her head resting on a pale blue pillow, her eyes wide and mysteriously watchful. The new floor lamp with its shade of rose-colored silk gives a soft, becoming light to her face, bringing out the fragile, unearthly prettiness which usually escapes attention. There is a steady murmur of rain, but it is slackening and stops soon after the scene begins; the air outside becomes pale and luminous as the moon breaks out.*
A moment after the curtain rises, the lights in both rooms flicker and go out.

JIM   Hey, there, Mr. Light Bulb!

AMANDA *laughs nervously.*

(LEGEND: "SUSPENSION OF A PUBLIC SERVICE.")

AMANDA Where was Moses when the lights went out? Ha-ha. Do
you know the answer to that one, Mr. O'Connor?

JIM No, Ma'am, what's the answer?

AMANDA In the dark! (JIM *laughs appreciably.*) Everybody sit still.
I'll light the candles. Isn't it lucky we have them on the table?
Where's a match? Which of you gentlemen can provide a match?

JIM Here.

AMANDA Thank you, sir.

JIM Not at all, Ma'am!

AMANDA I guess the fuse has burnt out. Mr. O'Connor, can you
tell a burnt out fuse? I know I can't and Tom is a total loss when
it comes to mechanics. (SOUND: GETTING UP: VOICES RECEDE A
LITTLE TO KITCHENETTE.) Oh, be careful you don't bump into
something. We don't want our gentleman caller to break his neck.
Now wouldn't that be a fine howdy-do?

JIM Ha-ha! Where is the fuse-box?

AMANDA Right here next to the stove. Can you see anything?

JIM Just a minute.

AMANDA Isn't electricity a mysterious thing? Wasn't it Benjamin
Franklin who tied a key to a kite? We live in such a mysterious
universe, don't we? Some people say that science clears up all the
mysteries for us. In my opinion it only creates more! Have you
found it yet?

JIM No, Ma'am. All these fuses look okay to me.

AMANDA Tom!

TOM Yes, Mother?

AMANDA That light bill I gave you several days ago. The one I told
you we got the notices about?

TOM Oh.— Yeah.

(LEGEND: "HA!")

AMANDA You didn't neglect to pay it by any chance?

TOM Why, I—

AMANDA Didn't! I might have known it!

JIM Shakespeare probably wrote a poem on that light bill, Mrs.
Wingfield.

AMANDA I might have known better than to trust him with it!
There's such a high price for negligence in this world!

JIM Maybe the poem will win a ten-dollar prize.

AMANDA We'll just have to spend the remainder of the evening in
the nineteenth century, before Mr. Edison made the Mazda lamp!

JIM Candlelight is my favorite kind of light.

AMANDA That shows you're romantic! But that's no excuse for

Tom. Well, we got through dinner. Very considerate of them to let us get through dinner before they plunged us into everlasting darkness, wasn't it, Mr. O'Connor?

JIM   Ha-ha!

AMANDA   Tom, as a penalty for your carelessness you can help me with the dishes.

JIM   Let me give you a hand.

AMANDA   Indeed you will not!

JIM   I ought to be good for something.

AMANDA   Good for something? (*Her tone is rhapsodic.*) *You?* Why, Mr. O'Connor, nobody, *nobody's* given me this much entertainment in years—as you have!

JIM   Aw, now, Mrs. Wingfield!

AMANDA   I'm not exaggerating, not one bit! But Sister is all by her lonesome. You go keep her company in the parlor! I'll give you this lovely old candelabrum that used to be on the altar at the church of the Heavenly Rest. It was melted a little out of shape when the church burnt down. Lightning struck it one spring. Gypsy Jones was holding a revival at the time and he intimated that the church was destroyed because the Episcopalians gave card parties.

JIM   Ha-ha.

AMANDA   And how about coaxing Sister to drink a little wine? I think it would be good for her! Can you carry both at once?

JIM   Sure. I'm Superman!

AMANDA   Now, Thomas, get into this apron!

The door of kitchenette swings closed on AMANDA's *gay laughter; the flickering light approaches the portieres.*

LAURA *sits up nervously as he enters. Her speech at first is low and breathless from the almost intolerable strain of being alone with a stranger.*

(THE LEGEND: "I DON'T SUPPOSE YOU REMEMBER ME AT ALL!")

In her first speeches in this scene, before JIM's *warmth overcomes her paralyzing shyness,* LAURA's *voice is thin and breathless as though she has just run up a steep flight of stairs.*

JIM's *attitude is gently humorous. In playing this scene it should be stressed that while the incident is apparently unimportant, it is to* LAURA *the climax of her secret life.*

JIM   Hello, there, Laura.

LAURA (*faintly*)   Hello (*She clears her throat.*)

JIM   How are you feeling now? Better?

LAURA   Yes. Yes, thank you.

JIM   This is for you. A little dandelion wine. (*He extends it toward her with extravagant gallantry.*)

LAURA   Thank you.

JIM   Drink it—but don't get drunk! (*He laughs heartily.* LAURA *takes the glass uncertainly; laughs shyly.*) Where shall I set the candles?

LAURA   Oh—oh, anywhere . . .

JIM   How about here on the floor? Any objections?

LAURA   No.

JIM   I'll spread a newspaper under to catch the drippings. I like to sit on the floor. Mind if I do?

LAURA   Oh, no.

JIM   Give me a pillow?

LAURA   What?

JIM   A pillow!

LAURA   Oh . . . (*Hands him one quickly.*)

JIM   How about you? Don't you like to sit on the floor?

LAURA   Oh—yes.

JIM   Why don't you, then?

LAURA   I—will.

JIM   Take a pillow! (LAURA *does. Sits on the other side of the candelabrum.* JIM *crosses his legs and smiles engagingly at her.*) I can't hardly see you sitting way over there.

LAURA   I can—see you.

JIM   I know, but that's not fair, I'm in the limelight. (LAURA *moves her pillow closer.*) Good! Now I can see you! Comfortable?

LAURA   Yes.

JIM   So am I. Comfortable as a cow. Will you have some gum?

LAURA   No, thank you.

JIM   I think that I will indulge, with your permission. (*Musingly unwraps it and holds it up.*) Think of the fortune made by the guy that invented the first piece of chewing gum. Amazing, huh? The Wrigley Building is one of the sights of Chicago.—I saw it summer before last when I went up to the Century of Progress. Did you take in the Century of Progress?

LAURA   No, I didn't.

JIM   Well, it was quite a wonderful exposition. What impressed me most was the Hall of Science. Gives you an idea of what the future will be in America, even more wonderful than the present time is! (*Pause. Smiling at her.*) Your brother tells me you're shy. Is that right, Laura?

LAURA   I—don't know.

JIM   I judge you to be an old-fashioned type of girl. Well, I think that's a pretty good type to be. Hope you don't think I'm being too personal—do you?

LAURA   (*hastily, out of embarrassment*)   I believe I *will* take a piece of gum, if you—don't mind. (*Clearing her throat.*) Mr. O'Connor, have you—kept up with your singing?

JIM   Singing? Me?

LAURA   Yes. I remember what a beautiful voice you had.

JIM   When did you hear me sing?

(VOICE OFF STAGE IN THE PAUSE.)

VOICE (*off stage*)

> O blow, ye winds, heigh-ho,
> A-roving I will go!
> I'm off to my love
> With a boxing glove—
> Ten thousand miles away!

JIM   You say you've heard me sing?

LAURA   Oh, yes! Yes, very often . . . I—don't suppose you remember me—at all?

JIM   (*smiling doubtfully*)   You know I have an idea I've seen you before. I had that idea soon as you opened the door. It seemed almost like I was about to remember your name. But the name that I started to call you—wasn't a name! And so I stopped myself before I said it.

LAURA   Wasn't it—Blue Roses?

JIM   (*springs up, grinning*)   Blue Roses! My gosh, yes—Blue Roses! That's what I had on my tongue when you opened the door! Isn't it funny what tricks your memory plays? I didn't connect you with the high school somehow or other. But that's where it was; it was high school. I didn't even know you were Shakespeare's sister! Gosh, I'm sorry.

LAURA   I didn't expect you to. You—barely knew me!

JIM   But we did have a speaking acquaintance, huh?

LAURA   Yes, we—spoke to each other.

JIM   When did you recognize me?

LAURA   Oh, right away!

JIM   Soon as I came in the door?

LAURA   When I heard your name I thought it was probably you. I knew that Tom used to know you a little in high school. So when you came in the door—Well, then I was—sure.

JIM   Why didn't you *say* something, then?

LAURA   (*breathlessly*)   I didn't know what to say, I was—too surprised!

JIM   For goodness' sakes! You know, this sure is funny!

LAURA   Yes! Yes, isn't it, though . . .

JIM   Didn't we have a class in something together?

LAURA   Yes, we did.

JIM   What class was that?

LAURA   It was—singing—Chorus!

JIM   Aw!

LAURA   I sat across the aisle from you in the Aud.

JIM   Aw.

LAURA   Mondays, Wednesdays and Fridays.

JIM   Now I remember—you always came in late.

LAURA   Yes, it was so hard for me, getting upstairs. I had that brace on my leg—it clumped so loud!

JIM   I never heard any clumping.

LAURA   (*wincing at the recollection*)   To me it sounded like—thunder!

JIM   Well, well, well. I never even noticed.

LAURA   And everybody was seated before I came in. I had to walk in front of all those people. My seat was in the back row. I had to go clumping all the way up the aisle with everyone watching!

JIM   You shouldn't have been self-conscious.

LAURA   I know, but I was. It was always such a relief when the singing started.

JIM   Aw, yes. I've placed you now! I used to call you Blue Roses. How was it that I got started calling you that?

LAURA   I was out of school a little while with pleurosis. When I came back you asked me what was the matter. I said I had pleurosis—you thought I said Blue Roses. That's what you always called me after that!

JIM   I hope you didn't mind.

LAURA   Oh, no—I liked it. You see, I wasn't acquainted with many —people. . . .

JIM   As I remember you sort of stuck by yourself.

LAURA   I—I—never had much luck at—making friends.

JIM   I don't see why you wouldn't.

LAURA   Well, I—started out badly.

JIM   You mean being—

LAURA   Yes, it sort of—stood between me—

JIM   You shouldn't have let it!

LAURA   I know, but it did, and—

JIM   You were shy with people!

LAURA   I tried not to be but never could—

JIM   Overcome it?

LAURA   No, I—I never could!

JIM   I guess being shy is something you have to work out of kind of gradually.

LAURA   (*sorrowfully*)   Yes—I guess it—

JIM   Takes time!

LAURA   Yes—

JIM   People are not so dreadful when you know them. That's what you have to remember! And everybody has problems, not just you, but practically everybody has got some problems. You think of yourself as having the only problems, as being the only one who is disappointed. But just look around you and you will see lots of people as disappointed as you are. For instance, I hoped when I was going to high school that I would be further along at this time, six years later, than I am now—You remember that wonderful write-up I had in *The Torch?*

LAURA   Yes! (*She rises and crosses to table.*)

JIM   It said I was bound to succeed in anything I went into! (LAURA *returns with the annual.*) Holy Jeez! *The Torch!* (*He accepts it reverently. They smile across it with mutual wonder. LAURA crouches beside him and they begin to turn through it. LAURA's shyness is dissolving in his warmth.*)

LAURA   Here you are in *Pirates of Penzance!*

JIM   (*wistfully*)   I sang the baritone lead in that operetta.

LAURA   (*rapidly*)   So—*beautifully!*

JIM   (*protesting*)   Aw—

LAURA   Yes, yes—beautifully—beautifully!

JIM   You heard me?

LAURA   All three times!

JIM   No!

LAURA   Yes!

JIM   All three performances?

LAURA   (*looking down*)   Yes.

JIM   Why?

LAURA   I—wanted to ask you to—autograph my program.

JIM   Why didn't you ask me to.

LAURA   You were always surrounded by your own friends so much that I never had a chance to.

JIM   You should have just—

LAURA   Well, I—thought you might think I was—

JIM   Thought I might think you was—what?

LAURA   Oh—

JIM   (*with reflective relish*)   I was beleaguered by females in those days.

LAURA   You were terribly popular!

JIM   Yeah—

LAURA   You had such a—friendly way—

JIM   I was spoiled in high school.

LAURA   Everybody—liked you!

JIM Including you?

LAURA I—yes, I—I did, too—(*She gently closes the book in her lap.*)

JIM Well, well, well!—Give me that program, Laura. (*She hands it to him. He signs it with a flourish.*) There you are—better late than never!

LAURA Oh, I—what a—surprise!

JIM My signature isn't worth very much right now. But some day —maybe—it will increase in value! Being disappointed is one thing and being discouraged is something else. I am disappointed but I am not discouraged. I'm twenty-three years old. How old are you?

LAURA I'll be twenty-four in June.

JIM That's not old age!

LAURA No, but—

JIM You finished high school?

LAURA (*with difficulty*) I didn't go back.

JIM You mean you dropped out?

LAURA I made bad grades in my final examinations. (*She rises and replaces the book and the program. Her voice strained.*) How is—Emily Meisenbach getting along?

JIM Oh, that kraut-head!

LAURA Why do you call her that?

JIM That's what she was.

LAURA You're not still— going with her?

JIM I never see her.

LAURA It said in the Personal Section that you were—engaged!

JIM I know, but I wasn't impressed by that—propaganda!

LAURA It wasn't—the truth?

JIM Only in Emily's optimistic opinion!

LAURA Oh—

(LEGEND: "WHAT HAVE YOU DONE SINCE HIGH SCHOOL?")

JIM *lights a cigarette and leans indolently back on his elbows smiling at* LAURA *with a warmth and charm which lights her inwardly with altar candles. She remains by the table and turns in her hands a piece of glass to cover her tumult.*

JIM (*after several reflective puffs on a cigarette*) What have you done since high school? (*She seems not to hear him.*) Huh? (LAURA *looks up.*) I said what have you done since high school, Laura?

LAURA Nothing much.

JIM You must have been doing something these six long years.

LAURA Yes.

JIM   Well, then, such as what?

LAURA   I took a business course at business college—

JIM   How did that work out?

LAURA   Well, not very—well—I had to drop out, it gave me—in-digestion—

JIM *laughs gently.*

JIM   What are you doing now?

LAURA   I don't do anything—much. Oh, please don't think I sit around doing nothing! My glass collection takes up a good deal of my time. Glass is something you have to take good care of.

JIM   What did you say—about glass?

LAURA   Collection I said—I have one—(*She clears her throat and turns away again, acutely shy.*)

JIM   (*abruptly*)   You know what I judge to be the trouble with you? Inferiority complex! Know what that is? That's what they call it when someone low-rates himself! I understand it because I had it, too. Although my case was not so aggravated as yours seems to be. I had it until I took up public speaking, developed my voice, and learned that I had an aptitude for science. Before that time I never thought of myself as being outstanding in any way whatsoever! Now I've never made a regular study of it, but I have a friend who says I can analyze people better than doctors that make a profession of it. I don't claim that to be necessarily true, but I can sure guess a person's psychology, Laura! (*Takes out his gum.*) Excuse me, Laura. I always take it out when the flavor is gone. I'll use this scrap of paper to wrap it in. I know how it is to get it stuck on a shoe. Yep—that's what I judge to be your principal trouble. A lack of confidence in yourself as a person. You don't have the proper amount of faith in yourself. I'm basing that fact on a number of your remarks and also on certain observations I've made. For instance that clumping you thought was so awful in high school. You say that you even dreaded to walk into class. You see what you did? You dropped out of school, you gave up an education because of a clump, which as far as I know was practically non-existent! A little physical defect is what you have. Hardly noticeable even! Magnified thousands of times by imagination! You know what my strong advice to you is? Think of yourself as *superior* in some way!

LAURA   In what way would I think?

JIM   Why, man alive, Laura! Just look about you a little. What do you see? A world full of common people! All of 'em born and all of 'em going to die! Which of them has one-tenth of your good points! Or mine! Or anyone else's, as far as that goes—Gosh!

Everybody excels in some one thing. Some in many! (*Unconsciously glances at himself in the mirror.*) All you've got to do is discover in *what!* Take me, for instance. (*He adjusts his tie at the mirror.*) My interest happens to lie in electro-dynamics. I'm taking a course in radio engineering at night school, Laura, on top of a fairly responsible job at the warehouse. I'm taking that course and studying public speaking.

LAURA　Ohhhh.

JIM　Because I believe in the future of television! (*Turning back to her.*) I wish to be ready to go up right along with it. Therefore I'm planning to get in on the ground floor. In fact, I've already made the right connections and all that remains is for the industry itself to get under way! Full steam—(*His eyes are starry.*) Knowledge—Zzzzzp! Money -Zzzzzzp!—Power! That's the cycle democracy is built on! (*His attitude is convincingly dynamic. LAURA stares at him, even her shyness eclipsed in her absolute wonder. He suddenly grins.*) I guess you think I think a lot of myself!

LAURA　No—o-o-o, I—

JIM　Now how about you? Isn't there something you take more interest in than anything else?

LAURA　Well, I do—as I said—have my—glass collection—

A peal of girlish laughter from the kitchen.

JIM　I'm not right sure I know what you're talking about. What kind of glass is it?

LAURA　Little articles of it, they're ornaments mostly! Most of them are little animals made out of glass, the tiniest little animals in the world. Mother calls them a glass menagerie! Here's an example of one, if you'd like to see it! This one is one of the oldest. It's nearly thirteen. (*He stretches out his hand.*) (MUSIC: "THE GLASS MENAGERIE.") Oh, be careful—if you breathe, it breaks!

JIM　I'd better not take it. I'm pretty clumsy with things.

LAURA　Go on, I trust you with him! (*Places it in his palm.*) There now—you're holding him gently! Hold him over the light, he loves the light! You see how the light shines through him?

JIM　It sure does shine!

LAURA　I shouldn't be partial, but he is my favorite one.

JIM　What kind of a thing is this one supposed to be?

LAURA　Haven't you noticed the single horn on his forehead?

JIM　A unicorn, huh?

LAURA　Mmm-hmmm!

JIM　Unicorns, aren't they extinct in the modern world?

LAURA　I know!

JIM   Poor little fellow, he must feel sort of lonesome.

LAURA (*smiling*) Well, if he does he doesn't complain about it. He stays on a shelf with some horses that don't have horns and all of them seem to get along nicely together.

JIM   How do you know?

LAURA (*lightly*) I haven't heard any arguments among them!

JIM (*grinning*) No arguments, huh? Well, that's a pretty good sign! Where shall I set him?

LAURA   Put him on the table. They all like a change of scenery once in a while!

JIM (*stretching*) Well, well, well, well—Look how big my shadow is when I stretch!

LAURA   Oh, oh, yes—it stretches across the ceiling!

JIM (*crossing to door*) I think it's stopped raining. (*Opens fire-escape door.*) Where does the music come from?

LAURA   From the Paradise Dance Hall across the alley.

JIM   How about cutting the rug a little, Miss Wingfield?

LAURA   Oh, I—

JIM   Or is your program filled up? Let me have a look at it. *Grasps imaginary card.*) Why, every dance is taken! I'll just have to scratch some out. (WALTZ MUSIC: "LA GOLONDRINA.") Ahhh, a waltz! (*He executes some sweeping turns by himself, then holds his arms toward* LAURA.)

LAURA (*breathlessly*) I—can't dance!

JIM   There you go, that inferiority stuff!

LAURA   I've never danced in my life!

JIM   Come on, try!

LAURA   Oh, but I'd step on you!

JIM   I'm not made out of glass.

LAURA   How—how—how do we start?

JIM   Just leave it to me. You hold your arms out a little.

LAURA   Like this?

JIM   A little bit higher. Right. Now don't tighten up, that's the main thing about it—relax.

LAURA (*laughing breathlessly*) It's hard not to.

JIM   Okay.

LAURA   I'm afraid you can't budge me.

JIM   What do you bet I can't? (*He swings her into motion.*)

LAURA   Goodness, yes, you can!

JIM   Let yourself go, now, Laura, just let yourself go.

LAURA   I'm—

JIM   Come on!

LAURA   Trying!

JIM   Not so stiff—Easy does it!

LAURA I know but I'm—

JIM Loosen th' backbone! There now, that's a lot better.

LAURA Am I?

JIM Lots, lots better! (*He moves her about the room in a clumsy waltz.*)

LAURA Oh, my!

JIM Ha-ha!

LAURA Goodness, yes you can!

JIM Ha-ha-ha! (*They suddenly bump into the table. JIM stops.*) What did we hit on?

LAURA Table.

JIM Did something fall off it? I think—

LAURA Yes.

JIM I hope that it wasn't the little glass horse with the horn!

LAURA Yes.

JIM Aw, aw, aw. Is it broken?

LAURA Now it is just like all the other horses.

JIM It's lost its—

LAURA Horn! It doesn't matter. Maybe it's a blessing in disguise.

JIM You'll never forgive me. I bet that that was your favorite piece of glass.

LAURA I don't have favorites much. It's no tragedy, Freckles. Glass breaks so easily. No matter how careful you are. The traffic jars the shelves and things fall off them.

JIM Still I'm awfully sorry that I was the cause.

LAURA (*smiling*) I'll just imagine he had an operation. The horn was removed to make him feel less- -freakish! (*They both laugh.*) Now he will feel more at home with the other horses, the ones that don't have horns . . .

JIM Ha-ha, that's very funny! (*Suddenly serious.*) I'm glad to see that you have a sense of humor. You know—you're—well—very different! Surprisingly different from anyone else I know! (*His voice becomes soft and hesitant with a genuine feeling.*) Do you mind me telling you that? (*LAURA is abashed beyond speech.*) You make me feel sort of—I don't know how to put it! I'm usually pretty good at expressing things, but—This is something that I don't know how to say! (*LAURA touches her throat and clears it- -turns the broken unicorn in her hands.*) (*Even softer.*) Has anyone ever told you that you were pretty? (PAUSE: MUSIC.) (*LAURA looks up slowly, with wonder, and shakes her head.*) Well, you are! In a very different way from anyone else. And all the nicer because of the difference, too. (*His voice becomes low and husky. LAURA turns away, nearly faint with the novelty of her emotions.*) I wish that you were my sister. I'd teach you to have some confidence in yourself. The different people are not like other people, but being different is nothing to be ashamed of. Because other people are not such wonderful people. They're one hundred times one thousand. You're one times one! They walk all over the earth. You just stay here. They're common as—weeds, but—you—well, you're—*Blue Roses!*

(IMAGE ON SCREEN: BLUE ROSES.)

(MUSIC CHANGES.)

LAURA   But blue is wrong for—roses . . .
JIM   It's right for you—You're—pretty!
LAURA   In what respect am I pretty?
JIM   In all respects—believe me! Your eyes—your hair—are pretty! Your hands are pretty! (*He catches hold of her hand.*) You think I'm making this up because I'm invited to dinner and have to be nice. Oh, I could do that! I could put on an act for you, Laura, and say lots of things without being very sincere. But this time I am. I'm talking to you sincerely. I happened to notice you had this inferiority complex that keeps you from feeling comfortable with people. Somebody needs to build your confidence up and make you proud instead of shy and turning away and—blushing —Somebody ought to—Ought to—*kiss* you, Laura! (*His hand slips slowly up her arm to her shoulder.*) (MUSIC SWELLS TUMULTUOUSLY.) (*He suddenly turns her about and kisses her on the lips. When he releases her* LAURA *sinks on the sofa with a bright, dazed look.* JIM *backs away and fishes in his pocket for a cigarette.*) (LEGEND ON SCREEN: "SOUVENIR.") Stumble-john! (*He lights the cigarette, avoiding her look. There is a peal of girlish laughter from* AMANDA *in the kitchen.* LAURA *slowly raises and opens her hand. It still contains the little broken glass animal. She looks at it with a tender, bewildered expression.*) Stumble-john! I shouldn't have done that—That was way off the beam. You don't smoke, do you? (*She looks up, smiling, not hearing the question. He sits beside her a little gingerly. She looks at him speechlessly —waiting. He coughs decorously and moves a little farther aside as he considers the situation and senses her feelings, dimly, with perturbation. Gently.*) Would you—care for a—mint? (*She doesn't seem to hear him but her look grows brighter even.*) Peppermint—Life Saver? My pocket's a regular drug store—wherever I go . . . (*He pops a mint in his mouth. Then gulps and decides to make a clean breast of it. He speaks slowly and gingerly.*) Laura, you know, if I had a sister like you, I'd do the same thing

as Tom. I'd bring out fellows—introduce her to them. The right type of boys of a type to—appreciate her. Only—well—he made a mistake about me. Maybe I've got no call to be saying this. That may not have been the idea in having me over. But what if it was? There's nothing wrong about that. The only trouble is that in my case—I'm not in a situation to—do the right thing. I can't take down your number and say I'll phone. I can't call up next week and—ask for a date. I thought I had better explain the situation in case you misunderstood it and—hurt your feelings. . . . (*Pause. Slowly, very slowly,* LAURA's *look changes, her eyes returning slowly from his to the ornament in her palm.*)

AMANDA *utters another gay laugh in the kitchen.*

LAURA (*faintly*) You—won't—call again?

JIM No, Laura, I can't. (*He rises from the sofa.*) As I was just explaining, I've—got strings on me, Laura, I've—been going steady! I go out all the time with a girl named Betty. She's a home-girl like you, and Catholic, and Irish, and in a great many ways we—get along fine. I met her last summer on a moonlight boat trip up the river to Alton, on the *Majestic.* Well—right away from the start it was—love! (LEGEND: LOVE!) (LAURA *sways slightly forward and grips the arm of the sofa. He fails to notice, now enrapt in his own comfortable being.*) Being in love has made a new man of me! (*Leaning stiffly forward, clutching the arm of the sofa,* LAURA *struggles visibly with her storm. But* JIM *is oblivious, she is a long way off.*) The power of love is really pretty tremendous! Love is something that—changes the whole world, Laura! (*The storm abates a little and* LAURA *leans back. He notices her again.*) It happened that Betty's aunt took sick, she got a wire and had to go to Centralia. So Tom—when he asked me to dinner—I naturally just accepted the invitation, not knowing that you—that he—that I—(*He stops awkwardly.*) Huh—I'm a stumble-john! (*He flops back on the sofa. The holy candles in the altar of* LAURA's *face have been snuffed out! There is a look of almost infinite desolation.* JIM *glances at her uneasily.*) I wish that you would—say something. (*She bites her lip which was trembling and then bravely smiles. She opens her hand again on the broken glass ornament. Then she gently takes his hand and raises it level with her own. She carefully places the unicorn in the palm of his hand, then pushes his fingers closed upon it.*) What are you—doing that for? You want me to have him?—Laura? (*She nods.*) What for?

LAURA A—souvenir . . .

She rises unsteadily and crouches beside the victrola to wind it up.

(LEGEND ON SCREEN: "THINGS HAVE A WAY OF TURNING OUT SO BADLY.")

(OR IMAGE: "GENTLEMAN CALLER WAVING GOODBYE!—GAILY.")

At this moment AMANDA *rushes brightly back in the front room. She bears a pitcher of fruit punch in an old-fashioned cut-glass pitcher and a plate of macaroons. The plate has a gold border and poppies painted on it.*

AMANDA　Well, well, well! Isn't the air delightful after the shower? I've made you children a little liquid refreshment. (*Turns gaily to the gentleman caller.*) Jim, do you know that song about lemonade?

> "Lemonade, lemonade
> Made in the shade and stirred with a spade—
> Good enough for any old maid!"

JIM　(*uneasily*)　Ha-ha! No—I never heard it.

AMANDA　Why, Laura! You look so serious!

JIM　We were having a serious conversation.

AMANDA　Good! Now you're better acquainted!

JIM　(*uncertainly*)　Ha-ha! Yes.

AMANDA　You modern young people are much more serious-minded than my generation. I was so gay as a girl!

JIM　You haven't changed, Mrs. Wingfield.

AMANDA　Tonight I'm rejuvenated! The gaiety of the occasion, Mr. O'Connor! (*She tosses her head with a peal of laughter. Spills lemonade.*) Oooo! I'm baptizing myself!

JIM　Here—let me—

AMANDA　(*setting the pitcher down*)　There now. I discovered we had some maraschino cherries. I dumped them in, juice and all!

JIM　You shouldn't have gone to that trouble, Mrs. Wingfield.

AMANDA　Trouble, trouble? Why it was loads of fun! Didn't you hear me cutting up in the kitchen? I bet your ears were burning! I told Tom how outdone with him I was for keeping you to himself so long a time! He should have brought you over much, much sooner! Well, now that you've found your way, I want you to be a very frequent caller! Not just occasional but all the time. Oh, we're going to have a lot of gay times together! I see them coming! Mmm, just breathe that air! So fresh, and the moon's so pretty! I'll skip back out—I know where my place is when young folks are having a—serious conversation!

JIM　Oh, don't go out, Mrs. Wingfield. The fact of the matter is I've got to be going.

AMANDA   Going, now? You're joking! Why, it's only the shank of the evening, Mr. O'Connor!

JIM   Well, you know how it is.

AMANDA   You mean you're a young workingman and have to keep workingmen's hours. We'll let you off early tonight. But only on the condition that next time you stay later. What's the best night for you? Isn't Saturday night the best night for you workingmen?

JIM   I have a couple of time-clocks to punch, Mrs. Wingfield. One at morning, another one at night!

AMANDA   My, but you *are* ambitious! You work at night, too?

JIM   No, Ma'am, not work but—Betty! (*He crosses deliberately to pick up his hat. The band at the Paradise Dance Hall goes into a tender waltz.*)

AMANDA   Betty? Betty? Who's—Betty! (*There is an ominous cracking sound in the sky.*)

JIM   Oh, just a girl. The girl I go steady with! (*He smiles charmingly. The sky falls.*)

(LEGEND: "THE SKY FALLS.")

AMANDA   (*a long-drawn exhalation*)   Ohhhh . . . Is it a serious romance, Mr. O'Connor?

JIM   We're going to be married the second Sunday in June.

AMANDA   Ohhhh—how nice! Tom didn't mention that you were engaged to be married.

JIM   The cat's not out of the bag at the warehouse yet. You know how they are. They call you Romeo and stuff like that. (*He stops at the oval mirror to put on his hat. He carefully shapes the brim and the crown to give a discreetly dashing effect.*) It's been a wonderful evening, Mrs. Wingfield. I guess this is what they mean by Southern hospitality.

AMANDA   It really wasn't anything at all.

JIM   I hope it don't seem like I'm rushing off. But I promised Betty I'd pick her up at the Wabash depot, an' by the time I get my jalopy down there her train'll be in. Some women are pretty upset if you keep 'em waiting.

AMANDA   Yes, I know—The tyranny of women! (*Extends her hand.*) Goodbye, Mr. O'Connor. I wish you luck—and happiness —and success! All three of them, and so does Laura!—Don't you, Laura?

LAURA   Yes!

JIM   (*taking her hand*)   Good-bye, Laura. I'm certainly going to treasure that souvenir. And don't you forget the good advice I gave you. (*Raises his voice to a cheery shout.*) So long, Shakespeare! Thanks again, ladies—Good night!

He grins and ducks jauntily out.
Still bravely grimacing, AMANDA *closes the door on the gentleman caller.*
Then she turns back to the room with a puzzled expression. She and LAURA
don't dare to face each other. LAURA *crouches beside the victrola to wind it.*

AMANDA (*faintly*) Things have a way of turning out so badly. I
don't believe that I would play the victrola. Well, well—well—
Our gentleman caller was engaged to be married! Tom!

TOM (*from back*) Yes, Mother?

AMANDA Come in here a minute. I want to tell you something awfully funny.

TOM (*enters with a macaroon and a glass of the lemonade*) Has
the gentleman caller gotten away already?

AMANDA The gentleman caller has made an early departure. What
a wonderful joke you played on us!

TOM How do you mean?

AMANDA You didn't mention that he was engaged to be married.

TOM Jim? Engaged?

AMANDA That's what he just informed us.

TOM I'll be jiggered! I didn't know about that.

AMANDA That seems very peculiar.

TOM What's peculiar about it?

AMANDA Didn't you call him your best friend down at the warehouse?

TOM He is, but how did I know?

AMANDA It seems extremely peculiar that you wouldn't know your
best friend was going to be married!

TOM The warehouse is where I work, not where I know things
about people!

AMANDA You don't know things anywhere! You live in a dream;
you manufacture illusions! (*He crosses to door.*) Where are you
going?

TOM I'm going to the movies.

AMANDA That's right, now that you've had us make such fools of
ourselves. The effort, the preparations, all the expense! The new
floor lamp, the rug, the clothes for Laura! All for what? To entertain some other girl's fiancé! Go to the movies, go! Don't think
about us, a mother deserted, an unmarried sister who's crippled
and has no job! Don't let anything interfere with your selfish
pleasure! Just go, go, go—to the movies!

TOM All right, I will! The more you shout about my selfishness to
me the quicker I'll go, and I won't go to the movies!

AMANDA Go, then! Then go to the moon—you selfish dreamer!

Tom *smashes his glass on the floor. He plunges out on the fire-escape, slamming the door,* Laura *screams—cut off by the door.*

Dance-hall music up. Tom *goes to the rail and grips it desperately, lifting his face in the chill white moonlight penetrating the narrow abyss of the alley.*

(legend on screen: "and so good-bye . . .")

Tom's *closing speech is timed with the interior pantomime. The interior scene is played as though viewed through soundproof glass.* Amanda *appears to be making a comforting speech to* Laura *who is huddled upon the sofa. Now that we cannot hear the mother's speech, her silliness is gone and she has dignity and tragic beauty.* Laura's *dark hair hides her face until at the end of the speech she lifts it to smile at her mother.* Amanda's *gestures are slow and graceful, almost dancelike, as she comforts the daughter. At the end of her speech she glances a moment at the father's picture—then withdraws through the portieres. At close of* Tom's *speech,* Laura *blows out the candles, ending the play.*

tom   I didn't go to the moon, I went much further—for time is the longest distance between two places—Not long after that I was fired for writing a poem on the lid of a shoe-box. I left Saint Louis. I descended the steps of this fire-escape for a last time and followed, from then on, in my father's footsteps, attempting to find in motion what was lost in space—I traveled around a great deal. The cities swept about me like dead leaves, leaves that were brightly colored but torn away from the branches. I would have stopped, but I was pursued by something. It always came upon me unawares, taking me altogether by surprise. Perhaps it was a familiar bit of music. Perhaps it was only a piece of transparent glass—Perhaps I am walking along a street at night, in some strange city, before I have found companions. I pass the lighted window of a shop where perfume is sold. The window is filled with pieces of colored glass, tiny transparent bottles in delicate colors, like bits of a shattered rainbow. Then all at once my sister touches my shoulder. I turn around and look into her eyes . . . Oh, Laura, Laura, I tried to leave you behind me, but I am more faithful than I intended to be! I reach for a cigarette, I cross the street, I run into the movies or a bar, I buy a drink, I speak to the nearest stranger—anything that can blow your candles out! (Laura *bends over the candles.*)—for nowadays the world is lit by lightning! Blow out your candles, Laura—and so good-bye. . . .

She blows the candles out.

(the scene dissolves.)

QUESTIONS

1. What elements of plot and characterization do you see in *The Glass Menagerie* that remind you of tragedy? of comedy? of realism? What elements will not fit into any of these categories?
2. Consider the play's characters.
   What strengths and weaknesses does each have?
   What illusions?
   What themes are associated with each?
   What development (if any) does each demonstrate in the play?
   How do the characterizations reinforce or contrast with each other?
3. Discuss the use Williams makes of the glass menagerie, and especially of the glass unicorn.
4. Discuss the use of candles as a symbol in the play.
5. Discuss the language of the play. How does it differ from the language of other plays you've read?
6. Discuss the device of having the play presented as a set of remembered scenes. How, in particular, does this affect the play's ending and our sense of any future the characters might have beyond the end of the play?

POSSIBLE ESSAY TOPIC

Discuss the relative importance of plot, character, and "thought" (both in terms of language and of symbolism) within *The Glass Menagerie*.

EUGENE O'NEILL (1888–1953)

Desire under the Elms

CHARACTERS

EPHRAIM CABOT
SIMEON ⎫
PETER ⎬ *his sons*
EBEN ⎭
ABBIE PUTNAM

YOUNG GIRL, TWO FARMERS, THE FIDDLER, THE SHERIFF, OTHER FOLK
from the neighboring farms

*The action of the entire play takes place in, and immediately outside of,
the* CABOT *farmhouse in New England, in the year 1850. The south end
of the house faces front to a stone wall with a wooden gate at center
opening on a country road. The house is in good condition but in need of
paint. Its walls are a sickly grayish, the green of the shutters faded. Two
enormous elms are on each side of the house. They bend their trailing
branches down over the roof. They appear to protect and at the same
time subdue. There is a sinister maternity in their aspect, a crushing,
jealous absorption. They have developed from their intimate contact with
the life of man in the house an appalling humaneness. They brood op-
pressively over the house. They are like exhausted women resting their
sagging breasts and hands and hair on its roof, and when it rains their
tears trickle down monotonously and rot on the shingles.*
*There is a path running from the gate around the right corner of the
house to the front door. A narrow porch is on this side. The end wall
facing us has two windows in its upper story, two larger ones on the floor
below. The two upper are those of the father's bedroom and that of the
brothers. On the left, ground floor, is the kitchen—on the right, the parlor,
the shades of which are always drawn down.*

PART I

Scene 1

*Exterior of the farmhouse. It is sunset of a day at the beginning of summer
in the year 1850. There is no wind and everything is still. The sky above*

the roof is suffused with deep colors, the green of the elms glows, but the house is in shadow, seeming pale and washed out by contrast.

A door opens and EBEN CABOT *comes to the end of the porch and stands looking down the road to the right. He has a large bell in his hand and this he swings mechanically, awakening a deafening clangor. Then he puts his hands on his hips and stares up at the sky. He sighs with a puzzled awe and blurts out with halting appreciation.*

EBEN   God! Purty! (*His eyes fall and he stares about him frowningly. He is twenty-five, tall and sinewy. His face is well-formed, good-looking, but its expression is resentful and defensive. His defiant, dark eyes remind one of a wild animal's in captivity. Each day is a cage in which he finds himself trapped but inwardly unsubdued. There is a fierce repressed vitality about him. He has black hair, mustache, a thin curly trace of beard. He is dressed in rough farm clothes.*

He spits on the ground with intense disgust, turns and goes back into the house.

SIMEON *and* PETER *come in from their work in the fields. They are tall men, much older than their half-brother* [SIMEON *is thirty-nine and* PETER *thirty-seven*], *built on a squarer, simpler model, fleshier in body, more bovine and homelier in face, shrewder and more practical. Their shoulders stoop a bit from years of farm work. They clump heavily along in their clumsy thick-soled boots caked with earth. Their clothes, their faces, hands, bare arms and throats are earth-stained. They smell of earth. They stand together for a moment in front of the house and, as if with the one impulse, stare dumbly up at the sky, leaning on their hoes. Their faces have a compressed, unresigned expression. As they look upward, this softens.*)

SIMEON (*grudgingly*)   Purty.

PETER   Ay-eh.

SIMEON (*suddenly*)   Eighteen year ago.

PETER   What?

SIMEON   Jenn. My woman. She died.

PETER   I'd fergot.

SIMEON   I rec'lect—now an' agin. Makes it lonesome. She'd hair long's a hoss' tail—an' yaller like gold!

PETER   Waal—she's gone. (*This with indifferent finality—then after a pause*) They's gold in the West, Sim.

SIMEON (*still under the influence of sunset—vaguely*)   In the sky?

PETER   Waal—in a manner o' speakin'—thar's the promise. (*growing excited*) Gold in the sky—in the West—Golden Gate—Californi-a!—Goldest West!—fields o' gold!

SIMEON (*excited in his turn*)   Fortunes layin' just atop o' the ground waitin' t' be picked! Solomon's mines, they says! (*For a moment they continue looking up at the sky—then their eyes drop.*)

PETER (*with sardonic bitterness*) Here— it's stones atop o' the ground—stones atop o' stones—makin' stone walls—year atop o' year—him 'n' yew 'n' me 'n' then Eben—makin' stone walls fur him to fence us in!

SIMEON We've wuked. Give our strength. Give our years. Plowed 'em under in the ground—(*he stamps rebelliously*)—rottin'— makin' soil for his crops! (*a pause*) Waal—the farm pays good for hereabouts.

PETER If we plowed in Californi-a, they'd be lumps o' gold in the furrow!

SIMEON Californi-a's t'other side o' earth, a'most. We got t' calc'-late—

PETER (*after a pause*) 'Twould be hard fur me, too, to give up what we've 'arned here by our sweat. (*A pause,* EBEN *sticks his head out of the dining-room window, listening.*)

SIMEON Ay-eh. (*a pause*) Mebbe—he'll die soon.

PETER (*doubtfully*) Mebbe.

SIMEON Mebbe—fur all we knows—he's dead now.

PETER Ye'd need proof.

SIMEON He's been gone two months—with no word.

PETER Left us in the fields an evenin' like this. Hitched up an' druv off into the West. That's plum onnateral. He hain't never been off this farm 'ceptin' t' the village in thirty year or more, not since he married Eben's maw. (*A pause. Shrewdly*) I calc'late we might git him declared crazy by the court.

SIMEON He skinnned 'em too slick. He got the best o' all on 'em. They'd never b'lieve him crazy. (*a pause*) We got t' wait—till he's under ground.

EBEN (*with a sardonic chuckle*) Honor thy father! (*They turn, startled, and stare at him. He grins, then scowls.*) I pray he's died. (*They stare at him. He continues matter-of-factly*) Supper's ready.

SIMEON *and* PETER (*together*) Ay-eh.

EBEN (*gazing up at the sky*) Sun's downin' purty.

SIMEON *and* PETER (*together*) Ay-eh. They's gold in the West.

EBEN Ay-eh. (*pointing*) Yonder atop o' the hill pasture, ye mean?

SIMEON *and* PETER (*together*) In Californi-a!

EBEN Hunh? (*Stares at them indifferently for a second, then drawls*) Waal—supper's gittin' cold. (*He turns back into kitchen.*)

SIMEON (*startled—smacks his lips*) I air hungry!

PETER (*sniffing*) I smells bacon!

SIMEON (*with hungry appreciation*)   Bacon's good!

PETER (*in same tone*)   Bacon's bacon! (*They turn, shouldering each other, their bodies bumping and rubbing together as they hurry clumsily to their food, like two friendly oxen toward their evening meal. They disappear around the right corner of house and can be heard entering the door.*)

Scene 2

The color fades from the sky. Twilight begins. The interior of the kitchen is now visible. A pine table is at center, a cookstove in the right rear corner, four rough wooden chairs, a tallow candle on the table. In the middle of the rear wall is fastened a big advertising poster with a ship in full sail and the word "California" in big letters. Kitchen utensils hang from nails. Everything is neat and in order but the atmosphere is of a men's camp kitchen rather than that of a home.

Places for three are laid. EBEN *takes boiled potatoes and bacon from the stove and puts them on the table, also a loaf of bread and a crock of water.* SIMEON *and* PETER *shoulder in, slump down in their chairs without a word.* EBEN *joins them. The three eat in silence·for a moment, the two elder as naturally unrestrained as beasts of the field,* EBEN *picking at his food without appetite, glancing at them with a tolerant dislike.*

SIMEON (*suddenly turns to* EBEN)   Looky here! Ye'd oughtn't t' said that, Eben.

PETER   'Twa'n't righteous.

EBEN   What?

SIMEON   Ye prayed he'd died.

EBEN   Waal—don't yew pray it? (*a pause*)

PETER   He's our Paw.

EBEN (*violently*)   Not mine!

SIMEON (*dryly*)   Ye'd not let no one else say that about yer Maw! Ha! (*He gives one abrupt sardonic guffaw.* PETER *grins.*)

EBEN (*very pale*)   I meant—I hain't his'n—I hain't like him—he hain't me!

PETER (*dryly*)   Wait till ye've growed his age!

EBEN (*intensely*)   I'm Maw—every drop o' blood! (*A pause. They stare at him with indifferent curiosity.*)

PETER (*reminiscently*)   She was good t' Sim 'n' me. A good step-maw's scurse.

SIMEON   She was good t' everyone.

EBEN (*greatly moved, gets to his feet and makes an awkward bow to each of them—stammering*)   I be thankful t' ye. I'm her—her heir. (*He sits down in confusion.*)

PETER (*after a pause—judicially*)   She was good even t' him.

EBEN (*fiercely*)   An' fur thanks he killed her!

SIMEON (*after a pause*)   No one never kills nobody. It's allus somethin'. That's the murderer.

EBEN   Didn't he slave Maw t' death?

PETER   He's slaved himself t' death. He's slaved Sim 'n' me 'n' yew t' death—on'y none o' us hain't died—yit.

SIMEON   It's somethin'—drivin' him—t' drive us!

EBEN (*vengefully*)   Waal—I hold him t' jedgment! (*then scornfully*) Somethin'! What's somethin'?

SIMEON   Dunno.

EBEN (*sardonically*)   What's drivin' yew to Californi-a, mebbe? (*They look at him in surprise.*) Oh, I've heerd ye! (*then, after a pause*) But ye'll never go t' the gold fields!

PETER (*assertively*)   Mebbe!

EBEN   Whar'll ye git the money?

PETER   We kin walk. It's an a'mighty ways—Californi-a—but if yew was t' put all the steps we've walked on this farm end t' end we'd be in the moon!

EBEN   The Injuns'll skulp ye on the plains.

SIMEON (*with grim humor*)   We'll mebbe make 'em pay a hair fur a hair!

EBEN (*decisively*)   But t'ain't that. Ye won't never go because ye'll wait here fur yer share o' the farm, thinkin' allus he'll die soon.

SIMEON (*after a pause*)   We've a right.

PETER   Two-thirds belongs t'us.

EBEN (*jumping to his feet*)   Ye've no right! She wa'n't yewr Maw! It was her farm! Didn't he steal it from her? She's dead. It's my farm.

SIMEON (*sardonically*)   Tell that t' Paw—when he comes! I'll bet ye a dollar he'll laugh—fur once in his life. Ha! (*He laughs himself in one single mirthless bark.*)

PETER (*amused in turn, echoes his brother*)   Ha!

SIMEON (*after a pause*)   What've ye got held agin us, Eben? Year arter year it's skulked in yer eye—somethin'.

PETER   Ay-eh.

EBEN   Ay-eh. They's somethin'. (*suddenly exploding*) Why didn't ye never stand between him 'n' my Maw when he was slavin' her to her grave—t' pay her back fur the kindness she done t' yew? (*There is a long pause. They stare at him in surprise.*)

SIMEON   Waal—the stock'd got t' be watered.

PETER   'R they was woodin' t' do.

SIMEON   'R plowin'.

PETER   'R hayin'.

SIMEON   'R spreadin' manure.

PETER   'R weedin'.

SIMEON   'R prunin'.

PETER   'R milkin'.

EBEN   (*breaking in harshly*)   An' makin' walls—stone atop o' stone —makin' walls till yer heart's a stone ye heft up out o' the way o' growth onto a stone wall t' wall in yer heart!

SIMEON   (*matter-of-factly*)   We never had no time t' meddle.

PETER   (*to* EBEN)   Yew was fifteen afore yer Maw died—an' big fur yer age. Why didn't ye never do nothin'?

EBEN   (*harshly*)   They was chores t' do, wa'n't they? (*a pause—then slowly*) It was on'y arter she died I come to think o' it. Me cookin'—doin' her work—that made me know her, suffer her suf-ferin'—she'd come back t' help—come back t' bile potatoes—come back t' fry bacon—come back t' bake biscuits—come back all cramped up t' shake the fire, an' carry ashes, her eyes weepin' an' bloody with smoke an' cinders same's they used t' be. She still comes back—stands by the stove thar in the evenin'—she can't find it nateral sleepin' an' restin' in peace. She can't git used t' bein' free—even in her grave.

SIMEON   She never complained none.

EBEN   She'd got too tired. She'd got too used t' being' too tired. That was what he done. (*with vengeful passion*) An' sooner'r later, I'll meddle. I'll say the thin's I didn't say then t' him! I'll yell 'em at the top o' my lungs. I'll see t' it my Maw gits some rest an' sleep in her grave! (*He sits down again, relapsing into a brooding silence. They look at him with a queer indifferent curi-osity.*)

PETER   (*after a pause*)   Whar in tarnation d'ye s'pose he went, Sim?

SIMEON   Dunno. He druv off in the buggy, all spick an' span, with the mare all breshed an' shiny, druv off clackin' his tongue an' wavin' his whip. I remember it right well. I was finishin' plowin', it was spring an' May an' sunset, an' gold in the West, an' he druv off into it. I yells "Whar ye goin', Paw?" an' he hauls up by the stone wall a jiffy. His old snake's eyes was glitterin' in the sun like he'd been drinkin' a jugful an' he says with a mule's grin: "Don't ye run away till I come back!"

PETER   Wonder if he knowed we was wantin' fur Californi-a?

SIMEON   Mebbe. I didn't say nothin' and he says, lookin' kinder queer an' sick: "I been hearin' the hens cluckin' an' the roosters crowin' all the durn day. I been listenin' t' the cows lowin' an' everythin' else kickin' up till I can't stand it no more. It's spring an' I'm feelin' damned," he says. "Damned like an old bare hick-ory tree fit on'y fur burnin'," he says. An' then I calc'late I must've looked a mite hopeful, fur he adds real spry and vicious:

"But don't git no fool idee I'm dead. I've sworn t' live a hundred an' I'll do it, if on'y t' spite yer sinful greed! An' now I'm ridin' out t' learn God's message t' me in the spring, like the prophets done. An' yew git back t' yer plowin'," he says. An' he druv off singin' a hymn. I thought he was drunk—'r I'd stopped him goin'.

EBEN (*scornfully*) No, ye wouldn't! Ye're scared o' him. He's stronger—inside—than both o' ye put together!

PETER (*sardonically*) An' yew—he yew Samson?

EBEN I'm gittin' stronger. I kin feel it growin' in me—growin' an' growin'—till it'll bust out—! (*He gets up and puts on his coat and a hat. They watch him, gradually breaking into grins.* EBEN *avoids their eyes sheepishly.*) I'm goin' out fur a spell—up the road.

PETER T' the village?

SIMEON T' see Minnie?

EBEN (*defiantly*) Ay-eh!

PETER (*jeeringly*) The Scarlet Woman!

SIMEON Lust—that's what's growin' in ye!

EBEN Waal—she's purty!

PETER She's been purty fur twenty year!

SIMEON A new coat o' paint'll make a heifer out of forty.

EBEN She hain't forty!

PETER If she hain't, she's teeterin' on the edge.

EBEN (*desperately*) What d'yew know—

PETER All they is . . . Sim knew her—an' then me arter—

SIMEON An' Paw kin tell yew somethin' too! He was fust!

EBEN D'ye mean t' say he . . . ?

SIMEON (*with a grin*) Ay-eh! We air his heirs in everythin'!

EBEN (*intensely*) That's more to it! That grows on it! It'll bust soon! (*then violently*) I'll go smash my fist in her face! (*He pulls open the door in rear violently.*)

SIMEON (*with a wink at* PETER—*drawlingly*) Mebbe—but the night's wa'm—purty—by the time ye git thar mebbe ye'll kiss her instead!

PETER Sart'n he will! (*They both roar with coarse laughter.* EBEN *rushes out and slams the door—then the outside front door—comes around the corner of the house and stands still by the gate, staring up at the sky.*)

SIMEON (*looking after him*) Like his Paw.

PETER Dead spit an' image!

SIMEON Dog'll eat dog!

PETER Ay-eh. (*Pause. With yearning*) Mebbe a year from now we'll be in Californi-a.

SIMEON   Ay-eh. (*A pause. Both yawn.*) Let's git t'bed. (*He blows out the candle. They go out door in rear. EBEN stretches his arms up to the sky—rebelliously.*)

EBEN   Waal—thar's a star, an' somewhar's they's him, an' here's me, an' thar's Min up the road—in the same night. What if I does kiss her? She's like t'night, she's soft 'n' wa'm, her eyes kin wink like a star, her mouth's wa'm, her arms're wa'm, she smells like a wa'm plowed field, she's purty . . . Ay-eh! By God A'mighty she's purty, an' I don't give a damn how many sins she's sinned afore mine or who she's sinned 'em with, my sin's as purty as any one on 'em! (*He strides off down the road to the left.*)

Scene 3

It is the pitch darkness just before dawn. EBEN comes in from the left and goes around to the porch, feeling his way, chuckling bitterly and cursing half-aloud to himself.

EBEN   The cussed old miser! (*He can be heard going in the front door. There is a pause as he goes upstairs, then a loud knock on the bedroom door of the brothers.*) Wake up!

SIMEON   (*startedly*)   Who's thar?

EBEN   (*pushing open the door and coming in, a lighted candle in his hand. The bedroom of the brothers is revealed. Its ceiling is the sloping roof. They can stand upright only close to the center dividing wall of the upstairs. SIMEON and PETER are in a double bed, front. EBEN's cot is to the rear. EBEN has a mixture of silly grin and vicious scowl on his face*)   I be!

PETER   (*angrily*)   What in hell's-fire . . . ?

EBEN   I got news fur ye! Ha! (*He gives one abrupt sardonic guffaw.*)

SIMEON   (*angrily*)   Couldn't ye hold it 'til we'd got our sleep?

EBEN   It's nigh sunup. (*then explosively*) He's gone an' married agen!

SIMEON *and* PETER   (*explosively*)   Paw?

EBEN   Got himself hitched to a female 'bout thirty-five—an' purty, they says . . .

SIMEON   (*aghast*)   It's a durn lie!

PETER   Who says?

SIMEON   They been stringin' ye!

EBEN   Think I'm a dunce, do ye? The hull village says. The preacher from New Dover, he brung the news—told it t'our preacher—New Dover, that's whar the old loon got himself hitched—that's whar the woman lived—

PETER   (*no longer doubting—stunned*)   Waal . . . !

SIMEON (*the same*) Waal ... !

EBEN (*sitting down on a bed—with vicious hatred*) Ain't he a devil out o' hell? It's jest t' spite us—the damned old mule!

PETER (*after a pause*) Everythin'll go t' her now.

SIMEON Ay-eh. (*A pause—dully*) Waal—if it's done—

PETER It's done us. (*pause—then persuasively*) They's gold in the fields o' Californi-a, Sim. No good a-stayin' here now.

SIMEON Jest what I was a-thinkin'. (*then with decision*) S'well fust's last! Let's light out and git this mornin'.

PETER Suits me.

EBEN Ye must like walkin'.

SIMEON (*sardonically*) If ye'd grow wings on us we'd fly thar!

EBEN Ye'd like ridin' better—on a boat, wouldn't ye? (*Fumbles in his pocket and takes out a crumpled sheet of foolscap.*) Waal, if ye sign this ye kin ride on a boat. I've had it writ out an' ready in case ye'd ever go. It says fur three hundred dollars t' each ye agree yewr shares o' the farm is sold t' me. (*They look suspiciously at the paper. A pause.*)

SIMEON (*wonderingly*) But if he's hitched agen—

PETER An' whar'd yew git that sum o' money, anyways?

EBEN (*cunningly*) I know whar it's hid. I been waitin'—Maw told me. She knew whar it lay fur years, but she was waitin' ... It's her'n—the money he hoarded from her farm an' hid from Maw. It's my money by rights now.

PETER Whar's it hid?

EBEN (*cunningly*) Whar yew won't never find it without me. Maw spied on him—'r she'd never knowed. (*A pause. They look at him suspiciously, and he at them.*) Waal, is it fa'r trade?

SIMEON Dunno.

PETER Dunno.

SIMEON (*looking at window*) Sky's grayin'.

PETER Ye better start the fire, Eben.

SIMEON An' fix some vittles.

EBEN Ay-eh. (*Then with a forced jocular heartiness*) I'll git ye a good one. If ye're startin' t' hoof it t' Californi-a ye'll need somethin' that'll stick t' yer ribs. (*He turns to the door, adding meaningly*) But ye kin ride on a boat if ye'll swap. (*He stops at the door and pauses. They stare at him.*)

SIMEON (*suspiciously*) Whar was ye all night?

EBEN (*defiantly*) Up t' Min's. (*then slowly*) Walkin' thar, fust I felt 's if I'd kiss her; then I got a-thinkin' on' what ye'd said o' him an' her an' I says, I'll bust her nose fur that! Then I got t' the village an' heerd the news an' I got madder'n hell an' run all the way t' Min's not knowin' what I'd do—(*He pauses—then*

sheepishly but more defiantly) Waal—when I seen her, I didn't
hit her—nor I didn't kiss her nuther—I begun t' beller like a calf
an' cuss at the same time, I was so durn mad—an' she got scared
—an' I jest grabbed holt an' tuk her! (*Proudly*) Yes, sirree! I tuk
her. She may've been his'n—an' your'n, too—but she's mine now!

SIMEON (*dryly*) In love, air yew?

EBEN (*with lofty scorn*) Love! I don't take no stock in sech slop!

PETER (*winking at* SIMEON) Mebbe Eben's aimin' t' marry, too.

SIMEON Min'd make a true faithful he'pmeet! (*They snicker.*)

EBEN What do I care fur her—'ceptin' she's round an' wa'm? The
p'int is she was his'n—an' now she belongs t' me! (*He goes to the
door—then turns—rebelliously.*) An' Min hain't sech a bad un.
They's worse'n Min in the world, I'll bet ye! Wait'll we see this
cow the Old Man's hitched t'! She'll beat Min, I got a notion!
(*He starts to go out.*)

SIMEON (*suddenly*) Mebbe ye'll try t' make her your'n, too?

PETER Ha! (*He gives a sardonic laugh of relish at this idea.*)

EBEN (*spitting with disgust*) Her—here—sleepin' with him—
stealin' my Maw's farm! I'd as soon pet a skunk 'r kiss a snake!
(*He goes out. The two stare after him suspiciously. A pause. They
listen to his steps receding.*)

PETER He's startin' the fire.

SIMEON I'd like t' ride t' Californi-a—but—

PETER Min might o' put some scheme in his head.

SIMEON Mebbe it's all a lie 'bout Paw marryin'. We'd best wait
an' see the bride.

PETER An' don't sign nothin' till we does!

SIMEON Nor till we've tested it's good money! (*then with a grin*)
But if Paw's hitched we'd be sellin' Eben somethin' we'd never git
nohow!

PETER We'll wait an' see. (*then with sudden vindictive anger*) An'
till he comes, let's yew 'n' me not wuk a lick, let Eben tend to
thin's if he's a mind t', let's us jest sleep an' eat an' drink likker,
an' let the hull damned farm go t' blazes!

SIMEON (*excitedly*) By God, we've 'arned a rest! We'll play rich
fur a change. I hain't a-going to stir outa bed till breakfast's
ready.

PETER An' on the table!

SIMEON (*after a pause—thoughtfully*) What d'ye calc'late she'll be
like—our new Maw? Like Eben thinks?

PETER More'n likely.

SIMEON (*vindictively*) Waal—I hope she's a she-devil that'll make
him wish he was dead an' livin' in the pit o' hell fur comfort!

PETER (*fervently*) Amen!

SIMEON (*imitating his father's voice*) "I'm ridin' out t' learn God's message t' me in the spring like the prophets done," he says. I'll bet right then an' thar he knew plumb well he was goin' whorin', the stinkin' old hypocrite!

Scene 4

Same as SCENE 2 *shows the interior of the kitchen with a lighted candle on table. It is gray dawn outside.* SIMEON *and* PETER *are just finishing their breakfast.* EBEN *sits before his plate of untouched food, brooding frowningly.*

PETER (*glancing at him rather irritably*) Lookin' glum don't help none.

SIMEON (*sarcastically*) Sorrowin' over his lust o' the flesh!

PETER (*with a grin*) Was she yer fust?

EBEN (*angrily*) None o' yer business. (*a pause*) I was thinkin' o' him. I got a notion he's gittin' near—I kin feel him comin' on like yew kin feel malaria chill afore it takes ye.

PETER It's too early yet.

SIMEON Dunno. He'd like t' catch us nappin'—jest t' have somethin' t' hoss us 'round over.

PETER (*mechanically gets to his feet.* SIMEON *does the same*) Waal —let's git t' wuk. (*They both plod mechanically toward the door before they realize. Then they stop short.*)

SIMEON (*grinning*) Ye're a cussed fool, Pete and I be wuss! Let him see we hain't wukin'! We don't give a durn!

PETER (*as they go back to the table*) Not a damned durn! It'll serve t' show him we're done with him. (*They sit down again.* EBEN *stares from one to the other with surprise.*)

SIMEON (*grins at him*) We're aimin' t' start bein' lilies o' the field.

PETER Nary a toil 'r spin 'r lick o' wuk do we put in!

SIMEON Ye're sole owner—till he comes—that's what ye wanted. Waal, ye got t' be sole hand, too.

PETER The cows air bellerin'. Ye better hustle at the milkin'.

EBEN (*with excited joy*) Ye mean ye'll sign the paper?

SIMEON (*dryly*) Mebbe.

PETER Mebbe.

SIMEON We're considerin'. (*peremptorily*) Ye better git t' wuk.

EBEN (*with queer excitement*) It's Maw's farm agen! It's my farm! Them's my cows! I'll milk my durn fingers off fur cows o' mine! (*He goes out door in rear, they stare after him indifferently.*)

SIMEON Like his Paw.

PETER Dead spit 'n' image!

SIMEON   Waal—let dog eat dog! (EBEN *comes out of front door and around the corner of the house. The sky is beginning to grow flushed with sunrise.* EBEN *stops by the gate and stares around him with glowing, possessive eyes. He takes in the whole farm with his embracing glance of desire.*)

EBEN   It's purty! It's damned purty! It's mine! (*He suddenly throws his head back boldly and glares with hard, defiant eyes at the sky.*) Mine, d'ye hear? Mine! (*He turns and walks quickly off left, rear, toward the barn. The two brothers light their pipes.*)

SIMEON   (*putting his muddy boots up on the table, tilting back his chair, and puffing defiantly*)   Waal—this air solid comfort—fur once.

PETER   Ay-eh. (*He follows suit. A pause. Unconsciously they both sigh.*)

SIMEON   (*suddenly*)   He never was much o' a hand at milkin', Eben wa'n't.

PETER   (*with a snort*)   His hands air like hoofs! (*a pause*)

SIMEON   Reach down the jug thar! Let's take a swaller. I'm feelin' kind o' low.

PETER   Good idee! (*He does so—gets two glasses—they pour out drinks of whisky.*) Here's t' the gold in Californi-a!

SIMEON   An' luck t' find it! (*They drink—puff resolutely—sigh—take their feet down from the table.*)

PETER   Likker don't pear t' sot right.

SIMEON   We hain't used t' it this early. (*A pause. They become very restless.*)

PETER   Gittin' close in this kitchen.

SIMEON   (*with immense relief*)   Let's git a breath o' air. (*They arise briskly and go out rear—appear around house and stop by the gate. They stare up at the sky with a numbed appreciation.*)

PETER   Purty!

SIMEON   Ay-eh. Gold's t' the East now.

PETER   Sun's startin' with us fur the Golden West.

SIMEON   (*staring around the farm, his compressed face tightened, unable to conceal his emotion*)   Waal—it's our last mornin'—mebbe.

PETER   (*the same*)   Ay-eh.

SIMEON   (*stamps his foot on the earth and addresses it desperately*)   Waal—ye've thirty year o' me buried in ye—spread out over ye —blood an' bone an' sweat—rotted away—fertilizin' ye—richin' yer soul—prime manure, by God, that's what I been t' ye!

PETER   Ay-eh! An' me!

SIMEON   An' yew, Peter. (*He sighs—then spits.*) Waal—no use'n cryin' over spilt milk.

PETER They's gold in the West—an' freedom, mebbe. We been slaves t' stone walls here.

SIMEON (*defiantly*) We hain't nobody's slaves from this out—nor nothin's slaves nuther. (*a pause—restlessly*) Speakin' o' milk, wonder how Eben's managin'?

PETER I s'pose he's managin'.

SIMEON Mebbe we'd ought t' help—this once.

PETER Mebbe. The cows knows us.

SIMEON An' likes us. They don't know him much.

PETER An' the hosses, an' pigs, an' chickens. They don't know him much.

SIMEON They knows us like brothers—an' likes us! (*proudly*) Hain't we raised 'em t' be fust-rate, number one prize stock?

PETER We hain't—not no more.

SIMEON (*dully*) I was fergittin'. (*then resignedly*) Waal, let's go help Eben a spell an' git waked up.

PETER Suits me. (*They are starting off down left, rear, for the barn when* EBEN *appears from there hurrying toward them, his face excited.*)

EBEN (*breathlessly*) Waal—har they be! The old mule an' the bride! I seen 'em from the barn down below at the turnin'.

PETER How could ye tell that far?

EBEN Hain't I as far-sight as he's near-sight? Don't I know the mare 'n' buggy, an' two people settin' in it? Who else . . . ? An' I tell ye I kin feel 'em a-comin', too! (*He squirms as if he had the itch.*)

PETER (*beginning to be angry*) Waal—let him do his own un-hitchin'!

SIMEON (*angry in his turn*) Let's hustle in an' git our bundles an' be a-goin' as he's a-comin'. I don't want never t' step inside the door agen arter he's back. (*They both start back around the corner of the house.* EBEN *follows them.*)

EBEN (*anxiously*) Will ye sign it afore ye go?

PETER Let's see the color o' the old skinflint's money an' we'll sign. (*They disappear left. The two brothers clump upstairs to get their bundles.* EBEN *appears in the kitchen, runs to the window, peers out, comes back and pulls up a strip of flooring in under stove, takes out a canvas bag and puts it on table, then sets the floor-board back in place. The two brothers appear a moment after. They carry old carpet bags.*)

EBEN (*puts his hand on bag guardingly*) Have ye signed?

SIMEON (*shows paper in his hand*) Ay-eh. (*greedily*) Be that the money?

EBEN (*opens bag and pours out pile of twenty-dollar gold pieces*)

Twenty-dollar pieces—thirty on 'em. Count 'em. (PETER *does so, arranging them in stacks of five, biting one or two to test them.*)

PETER   Six hundred. (*He puts them in bag and puts it inside his shirt carefully.*)

SIMEON (*handing paper to* EBEN)   Har ye be.

EBEN (*after a glance, folds it carefully and hides it under his shirt— gratefully*)   Thank yew.

PETER   Thank yew fur the ride.

SIMEON   We'll send ye a lump o' gold fur Christmas. (*A pause.* EBEN *stares at them and they at him.*)

PETER (*awkwardly*)   Waal—we're a-goin'.

SIMEON   Comin' out t' the yard?

EBEN   No. I'm waitin' in here a spell. (*Another silence. The brothers edge awkwardly to door in rear—then turn and stand.*)

SIMEON   Waal—good-by.

PETER   Good-by.

EBEN   Good-by. (*They go out. He sits down at the table, faces the stove and pulls out the paper. He looks from it to the stove. His face, lighted up by the shaft of sunlight from the window, has an expression of trance. His lips move. The two brothers come out to the gate.*)

PETER (*looking off toward barn*)   Thar he be—unhitchin'.

SIMEON (*with a chuckle*)   I'll bet ye he's riled!

PETER   An' thar she be.

SIMEON   Let's wait 'n' see what our new Maw looks like.

PETER (*with a grin*)   An' give him our partin' cuss!

SIMEON (*grinning*)   I feel like raisin' fun. I feel light in my head an' feet.

PETER   Me, too. I feel like laffin' till I'd split up the middle.

SIMEON   Reckon it's the likker?

PETER   No. My feet feel itchin' t' walk an' walk—an' jump high over thin's—an' . . . .

SIMEON   Dance? (*a pause*)

PETER (*puzzled*)   It's plumb onnateral.

SIMEON (*a light coming over his face*)   I calc'late it's 'cause school's out. It's holiday. Fur once we're free!

PETER (*dazedly*)   Free?

SIMEON   The halter's broke—the harness is busted—the fence bars is down—the stone walls air crumblin' an' tumblin'! We'll be kickin' up an' tearin' away down the road!

PETER (*drawing a deep breath—oratorically*)   Anybody that wants this stinkin' old rock-pile of a farm kin hev it. 'Tain't our'n, no sirree!

SIMEON (*takes the gate off its hinges and puts it under his arm*) We harby 'bolishes shet gates an' open gates, an' all gates, by thunder!

PETER We'll take it with us fur luck an' let 'er sail free down some river.

SIMEON (*as a sound of voices comes from left, rear*) Har they comes! (*The two brothers congeal into two stiff, grim-visaged statues.* EPHRAIM CABOT *and* ABBIE PUTNAM *come in.* CABOT *is seventy-five, tall and gaunt, with great, wiry, concentrated power, but stoop-shouldered from toil. His face is as hard as if it were hewn out of a boulder, yet there is a weakness in it, a pretty pride in its own narrow strength. His eyes are small, close together, and extremely near-sighted, blinking continually in the effort to focus on objects, their stare having a straining, ingrowing quality. He is dressed in his dismal black Sunday suit.* ABBIE *is thirty-five, buxom, full of vitality. Her round face is pretty but marred by its rather gross sensuality. There is strength and obstinacy in her jaw, a hard determination in her eyes, and about her whole personality the same unsettled, untamed, desperate quality which is so apparent in* EBEN.)

CABOT (*as they enter—a queer strangled emotion in his dry cracking voice*) Har we be t' hum, Abbie.

ABBIE (*with lust for the word*) Hum! (*Her eyes gloating on the house without seeming to see the two stiff figures at the gate.*) It's purty—purty! I can't b'lieve it's r'ally mine.

CABOT (*sharply*) Yewr'n? Mine! (*He stares at her penetratingly. She stares back. He adds relentingly.*) Our'n—mebbe! It was lonesome too long. I was growin' old in the spring. A hum's got t' hev a woman.

ABBIE (*her voice taking possession*) A woman's got t' hev a hum!

CABOT (*nodding uncertainly*) Ay-eh. (*then irritably*) Whar be they? Ain't thar nobody about— 'r wukin'—'r nothin'?

ABBIE (*sees the brothers. She returns their stare of cold appraising contempt with interest—slowly*) Thar's two men loafin' at the gate an' starin' at me like a couple o' strayed hogs.

CABOT (*straining his eyes*) I kin see 'em—but I can't make out. . . .

SIMEON It's Simeon.

PETER It's Peter.

CABOT (*exploding*) Why hain't ye wukin'?

SIMEON (*dryly*) We're waitin' t' welcome ye hum—yew an' the bride!

CABOT (*confusedly*) Huh? Waal—this be yer new Maw, boys. (*She stares at them and they at her.*)

SIMEON (*turns away and spits contemptuously*)   I see her!

PETER (*spits also*)   An' I see her!

ABBIE (*with the conqueror's conscious superiority*)   I'll go in an' look at *my* house. (*She goes slowly around to porch.*)

SIMEON (*with a snort*)   *Her* house!

PETER (*calls after her*)   Ye'll find Eben inside. Ye better not tell him it's *yewr* house.

ABBIE (*mouthing the name*)   Eben. (*then quietly*)   I'll tell Eben.

CABOT (*with a contemptuous sneer*)   Ye needn't heed Eben. Eben's a dumb fool—like his Maw—soft an' simple!

SIMEON (*with his sardonic burst of laughter*)   Ha! Eben's a chip o' yew—spit 'n' image—hard 'n' bitter's a hickory tree! Dog'll eat dog. He'll eat ye yet, old man!

CABOT (*commandingly*)   Ye git t' wuk!

SIMEON (*as* ABBIE *disappears in house—winks at* PETER *and says tauntingly*)   So that thar's our new Maw, be it? Whar in hell did ye dig her up? (*He and* PETER *laugh.*)

PETER   Ha! Ye'd better turn her in the pen with the other sows. (*They laugh uproariously, slapping their thighs.*)

CABOT (*so amazed at their effrontery that he stutters in confusion*)   Simeon! Peter! What's come over ye? Air ye drunk?

SIMEON   We're free, old man—free o' yew an' the hull damned farm! (*They grow more and more hilarious and excited.*)

PETER   An' we're startin' out fur the gold fields o' Californi-a!

SIMEON   Ye kin take this place an' burn it!

PETER   An' bury it—fur all we cares!

SIMEON   We're free, old man! (*He cuts a caper.*)

PETER   Free! (*He gives a kick in the air.*)

SIMEON (*in a frenzy*)   Whoop!

PETER   Whoop! (*They do an absurd Indian war dance about the old man who is petrified between rage and the fear that they are insane.*)

SIMEON   We're free as Injuns! Lucky we don't sculp ye!

PETER   An' burn yer barn an' kill the stock!

SIMEON   An' rape yer new woman! Whoop! (*He and* PETER *stop their dance, holding their sides, rocking with wild laughter.*)

CABOT (*edging away*)   Lust fur gold—fur the sinful, easy gold o' Californi-a! It's made ye mad!

SIMEON (*tauntingly*)   Wouldn't ye like us to send ye back some sinful gold, ye old sinner?

PETER   They's gold besides what's in Californi-a! (*He retreats back beyond the vision of the old man and takes the bag of money and flaunts it in the air above his head, laughing.*)

SIMEON   And sinfuller, too!

PETER   We'll be voyagin' on the sea! Whoop! (*He leaps up and down.*)

SIMEON   Livin' free! Whoop! (*He leaps in turn.*)

CABOT (*suddenly roaring with rage*)   My cuss on ye!

SIMEON   Take our'n in trade fur it! Whoop!

CABOT   I'll hev ye both chained up in the asylum!

PETER   Ye old skinflint! Good-by!

SIMEON   Ye old blood sucker! Good-by!

CABOT   Go afore I . . . !

PETER   Whoop! (*He picks a stone from the road.* SIMEON *does the same.*)

SIMEON   Maw'll be in the parlor.

PETER   Ay-eh! One! Two!

CABOT (*frightened*)   What air ye . . . ?

PETER   Three! (*They both throw, the stones hitting the parlor window with a crash of glass, tearing the shade.*)

SIMEON   Whoop!

PETER   Whoop!

CABOT (*in a fury now, rushing toward them*)   If I kin lay hands on ye—I'll break yer bones fur ye! (*But they beat a capering retreat before him,* SIMEON *with the gate still under his arm.* CABOT *comes back, panting with impotent rage. Their voices as they go off take up the song of the gold-seekers to the old tune of "Oh, Susannah!"*)

> "I jumped aboard the Liza ship,
> And traveled on the sea,
> And every time I thought of home
> I wished it wasn't me!
> Oh! Californi-a,
> That's the land fur me!
> I'm off to Californi-a!
> With my wash bowl on my knee."

(*In the meantime, the window of the upper bedroom on right is raised and* ABBIE *sticks her head out. She looks down at* CABOT— *with a sigh of relief.*)

ABBIE   Waal—that's the last o' them two, hain't it? (*He doesn't answer. Then in possessive tones*) This here's a nice bedroom, Ephraim. It's a r'al nice bed. Is it my room, Ephraim?

CABOT (*grimly—without looking up*)   Our'n! (*She cannot control a grimace of aversion and pulls back her head slowly and shuts the window. A sudden horrible thought seems to enter* CABOT's *head.*) They been up to somethin'! Mebbe—mebbe they've pizened the stock—'r somethin'! (*He almost runs off down toward the barn. A moment later the kitchen door is slowly pushed open and* ABBIE *enters. For a moment she stands looking at* EBEN. *He does not notice her at first. Her eyes take him in penetratingly with a calculating appraisal of his strength as against hers. But under this her desire is dimly awakened by his youth and good looks. Suddenly he becomes conscious of her presence and looks up. Their eyes meet. He leaps to his feet, glowering at her speechlessly.*)

ABBIE (*in her most seductive tones which she uses all through this scene*)   Be you—Eben? I'm Abbie—(*She laughs.*) I mean, I'm yer new Maw.

EBEN (*viciously*)   No, damn ye!

ABBIE (*as if she hadn't heard—with a queer smile*)   Yer Paw's spoke a lot o' yew. . . .

EBEN   Ha!

ABBIE   Ye mustn't mind him. He's an old man. (*A long pause. They stare at each other.*) I don't want t' pretend playin' Maw t' ye, Eben. (*admiringly*) Ye're too big an' too strong fur that. I want t' be frens with ye. Mebbe with me fur a fren ye'd find ye'd like livin' here better. I kin make it easy fur ye with him, mebbe. (*with a scornful sense of power*) I calc'late I kin git him t' do most anythin' fur me.

EBEN (*with bitter scorn*)   Ha! (*They stare again,* EBEN *obscurely moved, physically attracted to her—in forced stilted tones*) Yew kin go t' the devil!

ABBIE (*calmly*)   If cussin' me does ye good, cuss all ye've a mind t'. I'm all prepared t' have ye agin me—at fust. I don't blame ye nuther. I'd feel the same at any stranger comin' t' take my Maw's place. (*He shudders. She is watching him carefully.*) Yew must've cared a lot fur yewr Maw, didn't ye? My Maw died afore I'd growed. I don't remember her none. (*A pause.*) But yew won't hate me long, Eben. I'm not the wust in the world—an' yew an' me've got a lot in common. I kin tell that by lookin' at ye. Waal —I've had a hard life, too—oceans o' trouble an' nuthin' but wuk fur reward. I was a orphan early an' had t' wuk fur others in other folks' hums. Then I married an' he turned out a drunken spreer an' so he had to wuk fur others an' me too agen in other folks' hums, an' the baby died, an' my husband got sick an' died too, an' I was glad sayin' now I'm free fur once, on'y I diskivered right away all I was free fur was t' wuk agen in other folks' hums, doin' other folks' wuk till I'd most give up hope o' ever doin' my own wuk in my own hum, an' then your Paw come. . . . (CABOT *appears returning from the barn. He comes to the gate and looks down the road the brothers have gone. A faint strain of their re-treating voices is heard: "Oh, Californi-a! That's the place for me." He stands glowering, his fist clenched, his face grim with rage.*)

EBEN (*fighting against his growing attraction and sympathy— harshly*) An' bought yew—like a harlot! (*She is stung and flushes angrily. She has been sincerely moved by the recital of her troubles. He adds furiously*) An' the price he's payin' ye—this farm —was my Maw's, damn ye!—an' mine now!

ABBIE (*with a cool laugh of confidence*) Yewr'n? We'll see 'bout that! (*then strongly*) Waal—what if I did need a hum? What else'd I marry an old man like him fur?

EBEN (*maliciously*) I'll tell him ye said that!

ABBIE (*smiling*) I'll say ye're lyin' a-purpose—an' he'll drive ye off the place!

EBEN Ye devil!

ABBIE (*defying him*) This be my farm—this be my hum—this be my kitchen—!

EBEN (*furiously, as if he were going to attack her*) Shut up, damn ye!

ABBIE (*walks up to him—a queer coarse expression of desire in her face and body—slowly*) An' upstairs—that be my bedroom— an' my bed! (*He stares into her eyes, terribly confused and torn. She adds softly*) I hain't bad nor mean—'ceptin' fur an enemy —but I got t' fight fur what's due me out o' life, if I ever 'spect t' git it. (*Then putting her hand on his arm—seductively*) Let's yew 'n' me be frens, Eben.

EBEN (*stupidly—as if hypnotized*) Ay-eh. (*Then furiously flinging off her arm*) No, ye durned old witch! I hate ye! (*He rushes out the door.*)

ABBIE (*looks after him smiling satisfiedly—then half to herself, mouthing the word*) Eben's nice. (*She looks at the table, proudly.*) I'll wash up my dishes now. (EBEN *appears outside, slamming the door behind him. He comes around corner, stops on seeing his father, and stands staring at him with hate.*)

CABOT (*raising his arms to heaven in the fury he can no longer control*) Lord God o' Hosts, smite the undutiful sons with Thy wust cuss!

EBEN (*breaking in violently*) Yew 'n' yewr God! Allus cussin' folks —allus naggin' 'em!

CABOT (*oblivious to him—summoningly*) God o' the old! God o' the lonesome!

EBEN (*mockingly*) Naggin' His sheep t' sin! T' hell with yewr God! (CABOT *turns. He and* EBEN *glower at each other.*)

CABOT (*harshly*) So it's yew. I might've knowed it. (*shaking his finger threateningly at him*) Blasphemin' fool! (*then quickly*) Why hain't ye t' wuk?

EBEN Why hain't yew? They've went. I can't wuk it all alone.

CABOT (*contemptuously*) Nor noways! I'm wuth ten o' ye yit, old's I be! Ye'll never be more'n half a man! (*then, matter-of-factly*) Waal—let's git t' the barn. (*They go. A last faint note of the "Californi-a" song is heard from the distance.* ABBIE *is washing her dishes.*)

PART II

Scene 1

The exterior of the farmhouse, as in PART I—*a hot Sunday afternoon two months later.* ABBIE, *dressed in her best, is discovered sitting in a rocker at the end of the porch. She rocks listlessly, enervated by the heat, staring in front of her with bored, half-closed eyes.*

EBEN *sticks his head out of his bedroom window. He looks around furtively and tries to see—or hear—if anyone is on the porch, but although he has been careful to make no noise,* ABBIE *has sensed his movement. She stops rocking, her face grows animated and eager, she waits attentively.* EBEN *seems to feel her presence, he scowls back his thoughts of her and spits with exaggerated disdain—then withdraws back into the room.* ABBIE *waits, holding her breath as she listens with passionate eagerness for every sound within the house.*

EBEN *comes out. Their eyes meet; his falter. He is confused, he turns away and slams the door resentfully. At this gesture,* ABBIE *laughs tantalizingly, amused but at the same time piqued and irritated. He scowls, strides off the porch to the path and starts to walk past her to the road with a grand swagger of ignoring her existence. He is dressed in his store suit, spruced up, his face shines from soap and water.* ABBIE *leans forward on her chair, her eyes hard and angry now, and, as he passes her, gives a sneering, taunting chuckle.*

EBEN (*stung—turns on her furiously*) What air yew cacklin' 'bout?

ABBIE (*triumphant*) Yew!

EBEN What about me?

ABBIE Ye look all slicked up like a prize bull.

EBEN (*with a sneer*) Waal—ye hain't so durned purty yourself, be ye? (*They stare into each other's eyes, his held by hers in spite of himself, hers glowingly possessive. Their physical attraction becomes a palpable force quivering in the hot air.*)

ABBIE (*softly*) Ye don't mean that, Eben. Ye may think ye mean it, mebbe, but ye don't. Ye can't. It's agin nature, Eben. Ye been fightin' yer nature ever since the day I come—tryin' t' tell yerself I hain't purty t'ye. (*She laughs a low humid laugh without taking her eyes from his. A pause—her body squirms desirously —she murmurs languorously.*) Hain't the sun strong an' hot? Ye kin feel it burnin' into the earth—Nature—makin' thin's grow— bigger 'n' bigger—burnin' inside ye—makin' ye want t' grow— into somethin' else—till ye're jined with it—an' it's your'n—but it owns ye, too—an' makes ye grow bigger—like a tree—like them elums— (*She laughs again softly, holding his eyes. He takes a step toward her, compelled against his will.*) Nature'll beat ye, Eben. Ye might's well own up t' it fust 's last.

EBEN (*trying to break from her spell—confusedly*) If Paw'd hear ye goin' on.... (*resentfully*) But ye've made such a damned idjit out o' the old devil . . . ! (ABBIE *laughs.*)

ABBIE   Waal—hain't it easier fur yew with him changed softer?

EBEN (*defiantly*)   No. I'm fightin' him—fightin' yew—fightin' fur Maw's right t' her hum! (*This breaks her spell for him. He glowers at her.*) An' I'm onto ye. Ye hain't foolin' me a mite. Ye're aimin' t' swaller up everythin' an' make it your'n. Waal, you'll find I'm a heap sight bigger hunk nor yew kin chew! (*He turns from her with a sneer.*)

ABBIE (*trying to regain her ascendancy—seductively*)   Eben!

EBEN   Leave me be! (*He starts to walk away.*)

ABBIE (*more commandingly*)   Eben!

EBEN (*stops—resentfully*)   What d'ye want?

ABBIE (*trying to conceal a growing excitement*)   Whar air ye goin'?

EBEN (*with malicious nonchalance*)   Oh—up the road a spell.

ABBIE   T' the village?

EBEN (*airly*)   Mebbe.

ABBIE (*excitedly*)   T' see that Min, I s'pose?

EBEN   Mebbe.

ABBIE (*weakly*)   What d'ye want t' waste time on her fur?

EBEN (*revenging himself now—grinning at her*)   Ye can't beat Nature, didn't ye say? (*He laughs and again starts to walk away.*)

ABBIE (*bursting out*)   An ugly old hake!

EBEN (*with a tantalizing sneer*)   She's purtier'n yew be!

ABBIE   That every wuthless drunk in the country has. . . .

EBEN (*tauntingly*)   Mebbe—but she's better'n yew. She owns up fa'r 'n' squar' t' her doin's.

ABBIE (*furiously*)   Don't ye dare compare. . . .

EBEN   She don't go sneakin' an' stealin'—what's mine.

ABBIE (*savagely seizing on his weak point*)   Your'n? Yew mean— my farm?

EBEN   I mean the farm yew sold yerself fur like any other old whore—my farm!

ABBIE (*stung—fiercely*)   Ye'll never live t' see the day when even a stinkin' weed on it 'll belong t' ye! (*then in a scream*) Git out o' my sight! Go on t' yer slut—disgracin' yer Paw 'n' me! I'll git yer Paw t' horsewhip ye off the place if I want t'! Ye're only livin' here 'cause I tolerate ye! Git along! I hate the sight o' ye! (*She stops, panting and glaring at him.*)

EBEN (*returning her glance in kind*)   An' I hate the sight o' yew! (*He turns and strides off up the road. She follows his retreating figure with concentrated hate. Old* CABOT *appears coming up from the barn. The hard, grim expression of his face has changed. He seems in some queer way softened, mellowed. His eyes have taken on a strange, incongruous dreamy quality. Yet there is no hint of physical weakness about him—rather he looks more robust and younger.* ABBIE *sees him and turns away quickly with unconcealed aversion. He comes slowly up to her.*)

CABOT (*mildly*)   War yew an' Eben quarrelin' agen?

ABBIE (*shortly*)   No.

CABOT   Ye was talkin' a'mighty loud. (*He sits down on the edge of porch.*)

ABBIE (*snappishly*)   If ye heerd us they hain't no need askin' questions.

CABOT   I didn't hear what ye said.

ABBIE (*relieved*)   Waal—it wa'n't nothin' t' speak on.

CABOT (*after a pause*)   Eben's queer.

ABBIE (*bitterly*)   He's the dead spit 'n' image o' yew!

CABOT (*queerly interested*)   D'ye think so, Abbie? (*After a pause, ruminatingly*) Me 'n' Eben's allus fit 'n' fit. I never could b'ar him noways. He's so thunderin' soft—like his Maw.

ABBIE (*scornfully*)   Ay-eh! 'Bout as soft as yew be!

CABOT (*as if he hadn't heard*)   Mebbe I been too hard on him.

ABBIE (*jeeringly*)   Waal—ye're gittin' soft now—soft as slop! That's what Eben was sayin'.

CABOT (*his face instantly grim and ominous*)   Eben was sayin'? Waal, he'd best not do nothin' t' try me 'r he'll soon diskiver.... (*A pause. She keeps her face turned away. His gradually softens. He stares up at the sky.*) Purty, hain't it?

ABBIE (*crossly*)   I don't see nothin' purty.

CABOT   The sky. Feels like a wa'm field up thar.

ABBIE (*sarcastically*)   Air yew aimin' t' buy up over the farm too? (*She snickers contemptuously.*)

CABOT (*strangely*)   I'd like t' own my place up thar. (*a pause*) I'm gittin' old, Abbie. I'm gittin' ripe on the bough. (*A pause. She stares at him mystified. He goes on.*) It's allus lonesome cold in the house—even when it's bilin' hot outside. Hain't yew noticed?

ABBIE   No.

CABOT   It's wa'm down t' the barn—nice smellin' an' warm—with the cows. (*a pause*) Cows is queer.

ABBIE   Like yew?

CABOT   Like Eben. (*a pause*) I'm gittin' t' feel resigned t' Eben— jest as I got t' feel 'bout his Maw. I'm gittin' t' learn to b'ar his softness—jest like her'n. I calc'late I c'd a'most take t' him—if he wa'n't sech a dumb fool! (*a pause*) I s'pose it's old age a-creepin' in my bones.

ABBIE   (*indifferently*)   Waal—ye hain't dead yet.

CABOT   (*roused*)   No, I hain't, yew bet—not by a hell of a sight— I'm sound 'n' tough as hickory! (*then moodily*) But arter three score and ten the Lord warns ye t' prepare. (*a pause*) That's why Eben's come in my head. Now that his cussed sinful brothers is gone their path t' hell, they's no one left but Eben.

ABBIE   (*resentfully*)   They's me, hain't they? (*Agitatedly*) What's all this sudden likin' ye tuk to Eben? Why don't ye say nothin' 'bout me? Hain't I yer lawful wife?

CABOT   (*simply*)   Ay-eh. Ye be. (*A pause—he stares at her de- sirously—his eyes grow avid—then with a sudden movement he seizes her hands and squeezes them, declaiming in a queer camp meeting preacher's tempo*) Yew air my Rose o' Sharon! Behold, yew air fair; yer eyes air doves; yer lips air like scarlet; yer two breasts air like two fawns; yer navel be like a round goblet; yer belly be like a heap o' wheat.... (*He covers her hand with kisses. She does not seem to notice. She stares before her with hard angry eyes.*)

ABBIE   (*jerking her hands away—harshly*)   So ye're plannin' t' leave the farm t' Eben, air ye?

CABOT   (*dazedly*)   Leave...? (*then with resentful obstinacy*) I hain't a-givin' it t' no one!

ABBIE   (*remorselessly*)   Ye can't take it with ye.

CABOT   (*thinks a moment—then reluctantly*)   No, I calc'late not. (*after a pause—with a strange passion*) But if I could, I would, by the Eternal! 'R if I could, in my dyin' hour, I'd set it afire an' watch it burn—this house an' every ear o' corn an' every tree down t' the last blade o' hay! I'd sit an' know it was all a-dying with me an' no one else'd ever own what was mine, what I'd made out o' nothin' with my own sweat 'n' blood! (*a pause— then he adds with a queer affection*) 'Ceptin' the cows. Them I'd turn free.

ABBIE   (*harshly*)   An' me?

CABOT (*with a queer smile*)   Ye'd be turned free, too.

ABBIE (*furiously*)   So that's the thanks I git fur marryin' ye—t' have ye change kind to Eben who hates ye, an' talk o' turnin' me out in the road.

CABOT (*hastily*)   Abbie! Ye know I wa'n't. . . .

ABBIE (*vengefully*)   Just let me tell ye a thing or two 'bout Eben! Whar's he gone? T' see that harlot, Min! I tried fur t' stop him. Disgracin' yew an' me—on the Sabbath, too!

CABOT (*rather guiltily*)   He's a sinner—nateral-born. It's lust eatin' his heart.

ABBIE (*enraged beyond endurance—wildly vindictive*)   An' his lust fur me! Kin ye find excuses fur that?

CABOT (*stares at her—after a dead pause*)   Lust—fur yew?

ABBIE (*defiantly*)   He was tryin' t' make love t' me—when ye heerd us quarrelin'.

CABOT (*stares at her—then a terrible expression of rage comes over his face—he springs to his feet shaking all over*)   By the A'mighty God—I'll end him!

ABBIE (*frightened now for* EBEN)   No! Don't ye!

CABOT (*violently*)   I'll git the shotgun an' blow his soft brains t' the top o' them elums!

ABBIE (*throwing her arms around him*)   No, Ephraim!

CABOT (*pushing her away violently*)   I will, by God!

ABBIE (*in a quieting tone*)   Listen, Ephraim. 'Twa'n't nothin' bad —on'y a boy's foolin'—'twa'n't meant serious—jest jokin' an' teasin'. . . .

CABOT   Then why did ye say—lust?

ABBIE   It must hev sounded wusser'n I meant. An' I was mad at thinkin'—ye'd leave him the farm.

CABOT (*quieter but still grim and cruel*)   Waal then, I'll horsewhip him off the place if that much'll content ye.

ABBIE (*reaching out and taking his hand*)   No. Don't think o' me! Ye mustn't drive him off. 'Tain't sensible. Who'll ye get to help ye on the farm? They's no one hereabouts.

CABOT (*considers this—then nodding his appreciation*)   Ye got a head on ye. (*then irritably*) Waal, let them stay. (*He sits down on the edge of the porch. She sits beside him. He murmurs contemptuously*) I oughtn't t' git riled so—at that 'ere fool calf. (*a pause*) But har's the p'int. What son o' mine'll keep on here t' the farm—when the Lord does call me? Simeon an' Peter air gone t' hell—an' Eben's follerin' 'em.

ABBIE   They's me.

CABOT   Ye're on'y a woman.

ABBIE   I'm yewr wife.

CABOT   That hain't me. A son is me—my blood—mine. Mine ought t' git mine. An' then it's still mine—even though I be six foot under. D'ye see?

ABBIE   (*giving him a look of hatred*)   Ay-eh. I see. (*She becomes very thoughtful, her face growing shrewd, her eyes studying* CABOT *craftily.*)

CABOT   I'm gittin' old—ripe on the bough. (*then with a sudden forced reassurance*) Not but what I hain't a hard nut t' crack even yet—an' fur many a year t' come! By the Etarnal, I kin break most o' the young fellers' backs at any kind o' work any day o' the year!

ABBIE   (*suddenly*)   Mebbe the Lord'll give *us* a son.

CABOT   (*turns and stares at her eagerly*)   Ye mean—a son –t' me 'n' yew?

ABBIE   (*with a cajoling smile*)   Ye're a strong man yet, hain't ye? 'Tain't noways impossible, be it? We know that. Why d'ye stare so? Hain't ye never thought o' that afore? I been thinkin' o' it all along. Ay-eh –an' I been prayin' it'd happen, too.

CABOT   (*his face growing full of joyous pride and a sort of religious ecstasy*)   Ye been prayin', Abbie?—fur a son?—t' us?

ABBIE   Ay-eh. (*with a grim resolution*) I want a son now.

CABOT   (*excitedly clutching both of her hands in his*)   It'd be the blessin' o' God, Abbie—the blessin' o' God A'mighty on me—in my old age- -in my lonesomeness! They hain't nothin' I wouldn't do fur ye then, Abbie. Ye'd hev on'y ask it—anythin' ye'd a mind t'!

ABBIE   (*interrupting*)   Would ye will the farm t' me then—t' me an' it . .?

CABOT   (*vehemently*)   I'd do anythin' ye axed, I tell ye! I swar it! May I be everlastin' damned t' hell if I wouldn't! (*He sinks to his knees pulling her down with him. He trembles all over with the fervor of his hopes.*) Pray t' the Lord agen, Abbie. It's the Sabbath! I'll jine ye! Two prayers air better nor one. "An' God hearkened unto Rachel"! An' God hearkened unto Abbie! Pray, Abbie! Pray fur him to hearken! (*He bows his head, mumbling. She pretends to do likewise but gives him a side glance of scorn and triumph.*)

Scene 2

*About eight in the evening. The interior of the two bedrooms on the top floor is shown—*EBEN *is sitting on the side of his bed in the room on the left. On account of the heat he has taken off everything but his undershirt and pants. His feet are bare. He faces front, brooding moodily, his chin propped on his hands, a desperate expression on his face.*

In the other room CABOT *and* ABBIE *are sitting side by side on the edge of their bed, an old four-poster with feather mattress. He is in his night shirt, she in her nightdress. He is still in the queer, excited mood into which the notion of a son has thrown him. Both rooms are lighted dimly and flickeringly by tallow candles.*

CABOT   The farm needs a son.

ABBIE   I need a son.

CABOT   Ay-eh. Sometimes ye air the farm an' sometimes the farm be yew. That's why I clove t' ye in my lonesomeness. (*A pause. He pounds his knee with his fist.*) Me an' the farm has got t' beget a son!

ABBIE   Ye'd best go t' sleep. Ye're gittin' thin's all mixed.

CABOT (*with an impatient gesture*) No, I hain't. My mind's clear's a bell. Ye don't know me, that's it. (*He stares hopelessly at the floor.*)

ABBIE (*indifferently*)   Mebbe. (*In the next room* EBEN *gets up and paces up and down distractedly.* ABBIE *hears him. Her eyes fasten on the intervening wall with concentrated attention.* EBEN *stops and stares. Their hot glances seem to meet through the wall. Unconsciously he stretches out his arms for her and she half rises. Then aware, he mutters a curse at himself and flings himself face downward on the bed, his clenched fists above his head, his face buried in the pillow.* ABBIE *relaxes with a faint sigh but her eyes remain fixed on the wall; she listens with all her attention for some movement from* EBEN.)

CABOT (*suddenly raises his head and looks at her—scornfully*)   Will ye ever know me—'r will any man 'r woman? (*Shaking his head*) No. I calc'late 't wa'n't t' be. (*He turns away.* ABBIE *looks at the wall. Then, evidently unable to keep silent about his thoughts, without looking at his wife, he puts out his hand and clutches her knee. She starts violently, looks at him, sees he is not watching her, concentrates again on the wall and pays no attention to what he says.*) Listen, Abbie. When I come here fifty odd year ago—I was jest twenty an' the strongest an' hardest ye ever seen—ten times as strong an' fifty times as hard as Eben. Waal—this place was nothin' but fields o' stones. Folks laughed when I tuk it. They couldn't know what I knowed. When he kin make corn sprout out o' stones, God's livin' in yew! They wa'n't strong enuf fur that! They reckoned God was easy. They laughed. They don't laugh no more. Some died hereabouts. Some went West an' died. They're all under ground—fur follerin' arter an easy God. God hain't easy. (*He shakes his head slowly.*) An' I growed hard. Folks kept allus sayin' he's a hard man like 'twas sinful t' be hard, so's at last I said back at 'em: Waal then, by thunder, ye'll git me hard an' see how ye like it! (*Then suddenly*) But I give in t' weakness once. 'Twas arter I'd been here two year. I got weak—despairful—they was so many stones. They was a party leavin', givin' up, goin' West. I jined 'em. We tracked on 'n' on. We come t' broad medders, plains, whar the soil was black an' rich as gold. Nary a stone, Easy. Ye'd on'y to plow an' sow an' then set an' smoke yer pipe an' watch thin's grow. I could o' been a rich man—but somethin' in me fit me an' fit me—the voice o' God sayin': "This hain't wuth nothin' t' Me. Get ye back t' hum!" I got afeerd o' that voice an' I lit out back t' hum here, leavin' my claim an' crops t' whoever'd a mind t' take 'em. Ay-eh. I actoolly give up what was rightful mine! God's hard, not easy! God's in the stones! Build my church on a rock—out o' stones an' I'll be in them! That's what He meant t' Peter! (*He sighs heavily —a pause*) Stones. I picked 'em up an' piled 'em into walls. Ye kin read the years o' my life in them walls, every day a hefted stone, climbin' over the hills up and down, fencin' in the fields that was mine, whar I'd made thin's grow out o' nothin'—like the will o' God, like the servant o' His hand. It wa'n't easy. It was hard an' He made me hard fur it. (*He pauses.*) All the time I kept gittin' lonesomer. I tuk a wife. She bore Simeon an' Peter. She was a good woman. She wuked hard. We was married twenty year. She never knowed me. She helped but she never knowed what she was helpin'. I was allus lonesome. She died. After that it wa'n't so lonesome fur a spell. (*a pause*) I lost count o' the years. I had no time t' fool away countin' 'em. Sim an' Peter helped. The farm growed. It was all mine! When I thought o' that I didn't feel lonesome. (*a pause*) But ye can't hitch yer mind t' one thin' day an' night. I tuk another wife—Eben's Maw. Her folks was contestin' me at law over my deeds t' the farm—my farm! That's why Eben keeps a'talkin' his fool talk o' this bein' his Maw's farm. She bore Eben. She was purty—but soft. She tried t' be hard. She couldn't. She never knowed me nor nothin'. It was lonesomer 'n hell with her. After a matter o' sixteen odd years, she died. (*a pause*) I lived with the boys. They hated me 'cause I was hard. I hated them 'cause they was soft. They coveted the farm without knowin' what it meant. It made me bitter 'n wormwood. It aged me—them coveting what I'd made fur mine. Then this spring the call come—the voice o' God cryin' in my wilderness, in my lonesomeness—t' go out an' seek an' find! (*Turning to her with strange passion*) I sought ye an' I found ye! Yew air my Rose o' Sharon! Yer eyes air like.... (*She has turned a*

*blank face, resentful eyes to his. He stares at her for a moment—
then harshly*) Air ye any the wiser fur all I've told ye?

ABBIE (*confusedly*)   Mebbe.

CABOT (*pushing her away from him—angrily*)   Ye don't know
nothin'—nor never will. If ye don't hev a son t' redeem ye ...
(*this in a tone of cold threat*)

ABBIE (*resentfully*)   I've prayed, hain't I?

CABOT (*bitterly*)   Pray agen—fur understandin'!

ABBIE (*a veiled threat in her tone*)   Ye'll have a son out o' me, I
promise ye.

CABOT   How kin ye promise?

ABBIE   I got second-sight mebbe. I kin foretell. (*She gives a queer
smile.*)

CABOT   I believe ye have. Ye give me the chills sometimes. (*He
shivers.*) It's cold in this house. It's oneasy. They's thin's pokin'
about in the dark—in the corners. (*He pulls on his trousers, tuck-
ing in his night shirt, and pulls on his boots.*)

ABBIE (*surprised*)   Whar air ye goin'?

CABOT (*queerly*)   Down whar it's restful—whar it's warm—down
t' the barn. (*bitterly*) I kin talk t' the cows. They know. They
know the farm an' me. They'll give me peace. (*He turns to go
out the door.*)

ABBIE (*a bit frightenedly*)   Air ye ailin' tonight, Ephraim?

CABOT   Growin'. Growin' ripe on the bough. (*He turns and goes,
his boots clumping down the stairs.* EBEN *sits up with a start,
listening.* ABBIE *is conscious of his movement and stares at the
wall.* CABOT *comes out of the house around the corner and stands
by the gate, blinking at the sky. He stretches up his hands in a
tortured gesture*) God A'mighty, call from the dark! (*He listens
as if expecting an answer. Then his arms drop, he shakes his head
and plods off toward the barn.* EBEN *and* ABBIE *stare at each
other through the wall.* EBEN *sighs heavily and* ABBIE *echoes it.
Both become terribly nervous, uneasy. Finally* ABBIE *gets up and
listens, her ear to the wall. He acts as if he saw every move she
was making, he becomes resolutely still. She seems driven into a
decision—goes out the door in rear determinedly. His eyes follow
her. Then as the door of his room is opened softly, he turns away,
waits in an attitude of strained fixity.* ABBIE *stands for a second
staring at him, her eyes burning with desire. Then with a little
cry she runs over and throws her arms about his neck, she pulls
his head back and covers his mouth with kisses. At first, he sub-
mits dumbly; then he puts his arms about her neck and returns
her kisses, but finally, suddenly aware of his hatred, he hurls her*

away from him, springing to his feet. They stand speechless and breathless, panting like two animals.)

ABBIE (*at last—painfully*) Ye shouldn't, Eben—ye shouldn't—I'd make ye happy!

EBEN (*harshly*) I don't want t' be happy— from yew!

ABBIE (*helplessly*) Ye do, Eben! Ye do! Why d'ye lie?

EBEN (*viciously*) I don't take t'ye, I tell ye! I hate the sight o' ye!

ABBIE (*with an uncertain troubled laugh*) Waal, I kissed ye anyways—an' ye kissed back—yer lips was burnin'—ye can't lie 'bout that! (*intensely*) If ye don't care, why did ye kiss me back —why was yer lips burnin'?

EBEN (*wiping his mouth*) It was like pizen on 'em (*then tauntingly*) When I kissed ye back, mebbe I thought 'twas someone else.

ABBIE (*wildly*) Min?

EBEN Mebbe.

ABBIE (*torturedly*) Did ye go t' see her? Did ye r'ally go? I thought ye mightn't. Is that why ye throwed me off jest now?

EBEN (*sneeringly*) What if it be?

ABBIE (*raging*) Then ye're a dog, Eben Cabot!

EBEN (*threateningly*) Ye can't talk that way t' me!

ABBIE (*with a shrill laugh*) Can't I? Did ye think I was in love with ye—a weak thin' like yew? Not much! I on'y wanted ye fur a purpose o' my own—an' I'll hev ye fur it yet 'cause I'm stronger'n yew be!

EBEN (*resentfully*) I knowed well it was on'y part o' yer plan t' swaller everythin'!

ABBIE (*tauntingly*) Mebbe!

EBEN (*furious*) Git out o' my room!

ABBIE This air my room an' ye're on'y hired help!

EBEN (*threateningly*) Git out afore I murder ye!

ABBIE (*quite confident now*) I hain't a mite afeerd. Ye want me, don't ye? Yes, ye do! An' yer Paw's son'll never kill what he wants! Look at yer eyes! They's lust fur me in 'em, burnin' 'em up! Look at yer lips now! They're tremblin' an' longin' t' kiss me, an' yer teeth t'bite! (*He is watching her now with a horrible fascination. She laughs a crazy triumphant laugh.*) I'm a-goin' t' make all o' this hum my hum! They's one room hain't mine yet, but it's a-goin' t' be tonight. I'm a-goin' down now an' light up! (*She makes him a mocking bow.*) Won't ye come courtin' me in the best parlor, Mister Cabot?

EBEN (*staring at her—horribly confused—dully*) Don't ye dare! It hain't been opened since Maw died an' was laid out thar! Don't ye . . . ! (*But her eyes are fixed on his so burningly that his will seems to wither before hers. He stands swaying toward her helplessly.*)

ABBIE (*holding his eyes and putting all her will into her words as she backs out the door*) I'll expect ye afore long, Eben.

EBEN (*stares after her for a while, walking toward the door. A light appears in the parlor window. He murmurs*) In the parlor? (*This seems to arouse connotations for he comes back and puts on his white shirt, collar, half ties the tie mechanically, puts on coat, takes his hat, stands barefooted looking about him in bewilderment, mutters wonderingly*) Maw! Whar air yew? (*Then goes slowly toward the door in rear.*)

Scene 3

A few minutes later. The interior of the parlor is shown. A grim, repressed room like a tomb in which the family has been interred alive. ABBIE sits on the edge of the horsehair sofa. She has lighted all the candles and the room is revealed in all its preserved ugliness. A change has come over the woman. She looks awed and frightened now, ready to run away.

The door is opened and EBEN appears. His face wears an expression of obsessed confusion. He stands staring at her, his arms hanging disjointedly from his shoulders, his feet bare, his hat in his hand.

ABBIE (*after a pause—with a nervous, formal politeness*) Won't ye set?

EBEN (*dully*) Ay-eh. (*Mechanically he places his hat carefully on the floor near the door and sits stiffly beside her on the edge of the sofa. A pause. They both remain rigid, looking straight ahead with eyes full of fear.*)

ABBIE When I fust came in—in the dark—they seemed somethin' here.

EBEN (*simply*) Maw.

ABBIE I kin still feel—somethin'. . . .

EBEN It's Maw.

ABBIE At fust I was feered o' it. I wanted t' yell an' run. Now—since yew come—seems like it's growin' soft an' kind t' me. (*Addressing the air—queerly*) Thank yew.

EBEN Maw allus loved me.

ABBIE Mebbe it knows I love yew too. Mebbe that makes it kind t' me.

EBEN (*dully*) I dunno. I should think she'd hate ye.

ABBIE (*with certainty*) No. I kin feel it don't—not no more.

EBEN Hate yer fur stealin' her place—here in her hum—settin' in her parlor whar she was laid— (*He suddenly stops, staring stupidly before him.*)

ABBIE   What is it, Eben?

EBEN   (*in a whisper*)   Seems like Maw didn't want me t' remind ye.

ABBIE   (*excitedly*)   I knowed, Eben! It's kind t' me! It don't b'ar me no grudges fur what I never knowed an' couldn't help!

EBEN   Maw b'ars him a grudge.

ABBIE   Waal, so does all o' us.

EBEN   Ay-ch. (*with passion*)   I does, by God!

ABBIE   (*taking one of his hands in hers and patting it*)   Thar! Don't git riled thinkin' o' him. Think o' yer Maw who's kind t' us. Tell me about yer Maw, Eben.

EBEN   They hain't nothin' much. She was kind. She was good.

ABBIE   (*putting one arm over his shoulder. He does not seem to notice—passionately*)   I'll be kind an' good t' ye!

EBEN   Sometimes she used t' sing fur me.

ABBIE   I'll sing fur ye!

EBEN   This was her hum. This was her farm.

ABBIE   This is my hum! This is my farm!

EBEN   He married her t' steal 'em. She was soft an' easy. He couldn't 'preciate her.

ABBIE   He can't 'preciate me!

EBEN   He murdered her with his hardness.

ABBIE   He's murderin' me!

EBEN   She died. (*a pause*) Sometimes she used to sing fur me. (*He bursts into a fit of sobbing.*)

ABBIE   (*both arms around him—with wild passion*)   I'll sing fur ye! I'll die fur ye! (*In spite of her overwhelming desire for him, there is a sincere maternal love in her manner and voice—a horribly frank mixture of lust and mother love.*) Don't cry, Eben! I'll take yer Maw's place! I'll be everythin' she was t' ye! Let me kiss ye, Eben! (*She pulls his head around. He makes a bewildered pretense of resistance. She is tender.*) Don't be afeered! I'll kiss ye pure, Eben—same 's if I was a Maw t' ye—an' ye kin kiss me back 's if yew was my son—my boy— sayin' goodnight t' me! Kiss me, Eben. (*They kiss in restrained fashion. Then suddenly wild passion overcomes her. She kisses him lustfully again and again and he flings his arms about her and returns her kisses. Suddenly, as in the bedroom, he frees himself from her violently and springs to his feet. He is trembling all over, in a strange state of terror. Abbie strains her arms toward him with fierce pleading.*) Don't ye leave me, Eben! Can't ye see it hain't enuf— lovin' ye like a Maw —can't ye see it's got t' be that an' more—much more—a hundred times more—fur me t' be happy—fur yew t' be happy?

EBEN   (*to the presence he feels in the room*)   Maw! Maw! What d'ye want? What air ye tellin' me?

ABBIE   She's tellin' ye t' love me. She knows I love ye an' I'll be good t' ye. Can't ye feel it? Don't ye know? She's tellin' ye t' love me, Eben!

EBEN   Ah-eh. I feel—mebbe she—but—I can't figger out—why—when ye've stole her place—here in her hum—in the parlor whar she was—

ABBIE   (*fiercely*)   She knows I love ye!

EBEN   (*his face suddenly lighting up with a fierce triumphant grin*) I see it! I sees why. It's her vengeance on him—so's she kin rest quiet in her grave!

ABBIE   (*wildly*)   Vengeance o' God on the hull o' us! What d'we give a durn? I love ye, Eben! God knows I love ye! (*She stretches out her arms for him.*)

EBEN   (*throws himself on his knees beside the sofa and grabs her in his arms—releasing all his pent-up passion*)   An' I love yew, Abbie!—now I kin say it! I been dyin' fur want o' ye—every hour since ye come! I love ye! (*Their lips meet in a fierce, bruising kiss.*)

Scene 4

Exterior of the farmhouse. It is just dawn. The front door at right is opened.

Eben comes out and walks around to the gate. He is dressed in his working clothes. He seems changed. His face wears a bold and confident expression, he is grinning to himself with evident satisfaction. As he gets near the gate, the window of the parlor is heard opening and the shutters are flung back and ABBIE *sticks her head out. Her hair tumbles over her shoulders in disarray, her face is flushed, she looks at* EBEN *with tender, languorous eyes and calls softly.*

ABBIE   Eben. (*As he turns—playfully*) Jest one more kiss afore ye go. I'm goin' to miss ye fearful all day.

EBEN   An' me yew, ye kin bet! (*He goes to her. They kiss several times. He draws away, laughingly.*) Thar. That's enuf, hain't it? Ye won't hev none left fur next time.

ABBIE   I got a million o' 'em left fur yew! (*then a bit anxiously*) D'ye r'ally love me, Eben?

EBEN   (*emphatically*)   I like ye better'n any gal I ever knowed! That's gospel!

ABBIE   Likin' hain't lovin'.

EBEN   Waal then—I love ye. Now air yew satisfied?

ABBIE   Ay-eh, I be. (*She smiles at him adoringly.*)

EBEN   I better git t' the barn. The old critter's liable t' suspicion an' come sneakin' up.

ABBIE (*with a confident laugh*)   Let him! I kin allus pull the wool over his eyes. I'm goin' t' leave the shutters open and let in the sun 'n' air. This room's been dead long enuf. Now it's goin' t' be my room!

EBEN (*frowning*) Ay-eh.

ABBIE   We made it our'n last night, didn't we? We give it life— our lovin' did. (*a pause*)

EBEN (*with a strange look*)   Maw's gone back t' her grave. She kin sleep now.

ABBIE   May she rest in peace! (*then tenderly rebuking*) Ye oughtn't t' talk o' sad thin's—this mornin'.

EBEN   It jest come up in my mind o' itself.

ABBIE   Don't let it. (*He doesn't answer. She yawns.*) Waal, I'm a-goin' t' steal a wink o' sleep. I'll tell the Old Man I hain't feelin' pert. Let him git his own vittles.

EBEN   I see him comin' from the barn. Ye better look smart an' git upstairs.

ABBIE   Ay-eh. Good-by. Don't fergit me. (*She throws him a kiss. He grins—then squares his shoulders and awaits his father confidently. CABOT walks slowly up from the left, staring up at the sky with a vague face.*)

EBEN (*jovially*)   Mornin', Paw. Star-gazin' in daylight?

CABOT   Purty, hain't it?

EBEN (*looking around him possessively*)   It's a durned purty farm.

CABOT   I mean the sky.

EBEN (*grinning*)   How d'ye know? Them eyes o' your'n can't see that fur. (*This tickles his humor and he slaps his thigh and laughs.*) Ho-ho! That's a good un!

CABOT (*grimly sarcastic*)   Ye're feelin' right chipper, hain't ye? Whar'd ye steal the likker?

EBEN (*good-naturedly*)   'Taint likker. Jest life. (*Suddenly holding out his hand—soberly*)   Yew 'n' me is quits. Let's shake hands.

CABOT (*suspiciously*)   What's come over ye?

EBEN   Then don't. Mebbe it's jest as well. (*a moment's pause*) What's come over me? (*queerly*) Didn't ye feel her passin'— goin' back t' her grave?

CABOT (*dully*)   Who?

EBEN   Maw. She kin rest now an' sleep content. She's quit with ye.

CABOT (*confusedly*)   I rested. I slept good—down with the cows. They know how t' sleep. They're teachin' me.

EBEN (*suddenly jovial again*)   Good fur the cows! Waal—ye better git t' work.

CABOT (*grimly amused*)   Air yew bossin' me, ye calf?

EBEN (*beginning to laugh*)   Ah-eh! I'm bossin' yew! Ha-ha-ha! see how ye like it! Ha-ha-ha! I'm the prize rooster o' this roost. Ha-ha-ha! (*He goes off toward the barn laughing.*)

CABOT (*looks after him with scornful pity*)   Soft-headed. Like his Maw. Dead spit 'n' image. No hope in him! (*He spits with contemptuous disgust.*) A born fool! (*Then matter-of-factly*) Waal —I'm gittin' peckish. (*He goes toward door.*)

PART III

Scene 1

A night in late spring the following year. The kitchen and the two bedrooms upstairs are shown. The two bedrooms are dimly lighted by a tallow candle in each. EBEN *is sitting on the side of the bed in his room, his chin propped on his fists, his face a study of the struggle he is making to understand his conflicting emotions. The noisy laughter and music from below where a kitchen dance is in progress annoy and distract him. He scowls at the floor. In the next room a cradle stands beside the double bed.*

In the kitchen all is festivity. The stove has been taken down to give more room to the dancers. The chairs, with wooden benches added, have been pushed back against the walls. On these are seated, squeezed in tight against one another, farmers and their wives and their young folks of both sexes from the neighboring farms. They are all chattering and laughing loudly. They evidently have some secret joke in common. There is no end of winking, of nudging, of meaning nods of the head toward CABOT *who, in a state of extreme hilarious excitement increased by the amount he has drunk, is standing near the rear door where there is a small keg of whisky and serving drinks to all the men. In the left corner, front, dividing the attention with her husband,* ABBIE *is sitting in a rocking chair, a shawl wrapped about her shoulders. She is very pale, her face is thin and drawn, her eyes are fixed anxiously on the open door in rear as if waiting for someone.*

The MUSICIAN *is tuning up his fiddle, seated in the far right corner. He is a lanky young fellow with a long, weak face. His pale eyes blink incessantly and he grins about him slyly with a greedy malice.*

ABBIE (*suddenly turning to a young girl on her right*)   Whar's Eben?

YOUNG GIRL (*eying her scornfully*)   I dunno, Mrs. Cabot. I hain't seen Eben in ages. (*meaningly*) Seems like he's spent most o' his time t' hum since yew come.

ABBIE (*vaguely*)   I tuk his Maw's place.

YOUNG GIRL   Ay-eh. So I've heerd. (*She turns away to retail this bit of gossip to her mother sitting next to her.* ABBIE *turns to her left to a big stoutish middle-aged man whose flushed face and staring eyes show the amount of "likker" he has consumed.*)

ABBIE   Ye hain't seen Eben, hev ye?

MAN   No, I hain't. (*then he adds with a wink*) If yew hain't, who would?

ABBIE   He's the best dancer in the county. He'd ought t' come an' dance.

MAN   (*with a wink*)   Mebbe he's doin' the dutiful an' walkin' the kid t' sleep. It's a boy, hain't it?

ABBIE   (*nodding vaguely*)   Ay-eh—born two weeks back—purty's a picter.

MAN   They all is—t' their Maws. (*then in a whisper, with a nudge and a leer*) Listen, Abbie—if ye ever git tired o' Eben, remember me! Don't fergit now! (*He looks at her uncomprehending face for a second—then grunts disgustedly.*) Waal—guess I'll likker agin. (*He goes over and joins* CABOT *who is arguing noisily with an old farmer over cows. They all drink.*)

ABBIE   (*this time appealing to nobody in particular*)   Wonder what Eben's a-doin'? (*Her remark is repeated down the line with many a guffaw and titter until it reaches the fiddler. He fastens his blinking eyes on* ABBIE.)

FIDDLER   (*raising his voice*)   Bet I kin tell ye, Abbie, what Eben's doin'! He's down t' the church offerin' up prayers o' thanksgivin'. (*They all titter expectantly.*)

MAN   What fur? (*Another titter.*)

FIDDLER   'Cause unto him a— (*He hesitates just long enough.*)— brother is born! (*A roar of laughter. They all look from* ABBIE *to* CABOT. *She is oblivious, staring at the door.* CABOT, *although he hasn't heard the words, is irritated by the laughter and steps forward, glaring about him. There is an immediate silence.*)

CABOT   What're ye all bleatin' about—like a flock o' goats? Why don't ye dance, damn ye? I axed ye here t' dance—t' eat, drink an' be merry—an' thar ye set cacklin' like a lot o' wet hens with the pip! Ye've swilled my likker an' guzzled my vittles like hogs, hain't ye? Then dance fur me, can't ye? That's fa'r an' squar', hain't it? (*A grumble of resentment goes around but they are all evidently in too much awe of him to express it openly.*)

FIDDLER   (*slyly*)   We're waitin' fur Eben. (*a suppressed laugh*)

CABOT   (*with a fierce exultation*)   T'hell with Eben! Eben's done fur now! I got a new son! (*his mood switching with drunken suddenness*) But ye needn't t' laugh at Eben, none o' ye! He's my blood, if he be a dumb fool. He's better nor any o' yew! He kin do a day's work a'most up t' what I kin—an' that'd put any o' yew pore critters t' shame!

FIDDLER   An' he kin do a good night's work, too! (*a roar of laughter*)

CABOT   Laugh, ye damn fools! Ye're right jist the same, Fiddler. He kin work day an' night too, like I kin, if need be!

OLD FARMER   (*from behind the keg where he is weaving drunkenly back and forth—with great simplicity*)   They hain't many t' touch ye, Ephraim—a son at seventy-six. That's a hard man fur ye! I be on'y sixty-eight an' I couldn't do it. (*a roar of laughter in which* CABOT *joins uproariously*)

CABOT   (*slapping him on the back*)   I'm sorry fur ye, Hi. I'd never suspicion sech weakness from a boy like yew!

OLD FARMER   An' I never reckoned yew had it in ye nuther, Ephraim. (*There is another laugh.*)

CABOT   (*suddenly grim*)   I got a lot in me—a hell of a lot—folks don't know on. (*turning to the* FIDDLER) Fiddle 'er up, durn ye! Give 'em somethin' t' dance t'! What air ye, an ornament? Hain't this a celebration? Then grease yer elbow an' go it!

FIDDLER   (*seizes a drink which the* OLD FARMER *holds out to him and downs it*)   Here goes! (*He starts to fiddle "Lady of the Lake." Four young fellows and four girls form in two lines and dance a square dance. The* FIDDLER *shouts directions for the different movements, keeping his words in the rhythm of the music and interspersing them with jocular personal remarks to the dancers themselves. The people seated along the walls stamp their feet and clap their hands in unison.* CABOT *is especially active in this respect. Only* ABBIE *remains apathetic, staring at the door as if she were alone in a silent room.*)

FIDDLER   Swing your partner t' the right! That's it, Jim! Give her a b'ar hug! Her Maw hain't lookin'. (*laughter*) Change partners! That suits ye, don't it, Essie, now ye got Reub afore ye? Look at her redden up, will ye! Waal, life is short an' so's love, as the feller says. (*laughter*)

CABOT   (*excitedly, stamping his foot*)   Go it, boys! Go it, gals!

FIDDLER   (*with a wink at the others*)   Ye're the spryest seventy-six ever I sees, Ephraim! Now if ye'd on'y good eye-sight . . . ! (*Suppressed laughter. He gives* CABOT *no chance to retort but roars*) Promenade! Ye're walkin' like a bride down the aisle, Sarah! Waal, while they's life they's allus hope, I've heerd tell. Swing your partner to the left! Gosh A'mighty, look at Johnny Cook high-steppin'! They hain't goin' t'be much strength left fur howin' in the corn lot t'morrow. (*laughter*)

CABOT   Go it! Go it! (*Then suddenly, unable to restrain himself any longer, he prances into the midst of the dancers, scattering them, waving his arms about wildly.*) Ye're all hoofs! Git out o' my road! Give me room! I'll show ye dancin'. Ye're all too soft!

(*He pushes them roughly away. They crowd back toward the walls, muttering, looking at him resentfully.*)

FIDDLER (*jeeringly*) Go it, Ephraim! Go it! (*He starts "Pop Goes the Weasel," increasing the tempo with every verse until at the end he is fiddling crazily as fast as he can go.*)

CABOT (*starts to dance, which he does very well and with tremendous vigor. Then he begins to improvise, cuts incredibly grotesque capers, leaping up and cracking his heels together, prancing around in a circle with body bent in an Indian war dance, then suddenly straightening up and kicking as high as he can with both legs. He is like a monkey on a string. And all the while he intersperses his antics with shouts and derisive comments*) Whoop! Here's dancin' fur ye! Whoop! See that! Seventy-six, if I'm a day! Hard as iron yet! Beatin' the young 'uns like I allus done! Look at me! I'd invite ye t' dance on my hundredth birthday on'y ye'll all be dead by then. Ye're a sickly generation! Yer hearts air pink, not red! Yer veins is full o' mud an' water! I be the on'y man in the county! Whoop! See that! I'm a Injun! I've killed Injuns in the West afore ye was born—an' skulped 'em too! They's a arrer wound on my backside I c'd show ye! The hull tribe chased me. I outrun 'em all—with the arrer stuck in me! An' I tuk vengeance on 'em. Ten eyes fur an eye, that was my motter! Whoop! Look at me! I kin kick the ceilin' off the room! Whoop!

FIDDLER (*stops playing—exhaustedly*) God A'mighty, I got enuf. Ye got the devil's strength in ye.

CABOT (*delightedly*) Did I beat yew, too? Wa'al, ye played smart. Hev a swig. (*He pours whisky for himself and* FIDDLER. *They drink. The others watch* CABOT *silently with cold, hostile eyes. There is a dead pause. The* FIDDLER *rests.* CABOT *leans against the keg, panting, glaring around him confusedly. In the room above,* EBEN *gets to his feet and tiptoes out the door in rear, appearing a moment later in the other bedroom. He moves silently, even frightenedly, toward the cradle and stands there looking down at the baby. His face is as vague as his reactions are confused, but there is a trace of tenderness, of interested discovery. At the same moment that he reaches the cradle,* ABBIE *seems to sense something. She gets up weakly and goes to* CABOT.)

ABBIE I'm goin' up t' the baby.

CABOT (*with real solicitude*) Air ye able fur the stairs? D'ye want me t' help ye, Abbie?

ABBIE No. I'm able. I'll be down agen soon.

CABOT Don't ye git wore out! He needs ye, remember—our son

does! (*He grins affectionately, patting her on the back. She shrinks from his touch.*)

ABBIE (*dully*) Don't—tech me. I'm goin'—up. (*She goes.* CABOT *looks after her. A whisper goes around the room.* CABOT *turns. It ceases. He wipes his forehead streaming with sweat. He is breathing pantingly.*)

CABOT I'm a-goin' out t' git fresh air. I'm feelin' a mite dizzy. Fiddle up thar! Dance, all o' ye! Here's likker fur them as wants it. Enjoy yerselves. I'll be back. (*He goes, closing the door behind him.*)

FIDDLER (*sarcastically*) Don't hurry none on our account! (*A suppressed laugh. He imitates* ABBIE.) Whar's Eben? (*more laughter*)

A WOMAN (*loudly*) What's happened in this house is plain as the nose on yer face! (ABBIE *appears in the doorway upstairs and stands looking in surprise and adoration at* EBEN *who does not see her.*)

A MAN Ssshh! He's li'ble t' be listenin' at the door. That'd be like him. (*Their voices die to an intensive whispering. Their faces are concentrated on this gossip. A noise as of dead leaves in the wind comes from the room.* CABOT *has come out from the porch and stands by the gate, leaning on it, staring at the sky blinkingly.* ABBIE *comes across the room silently.* EBEN *does not notice her until quite near.*)

EBEN (*starting*) Abbie!

ABBIE Ssshh! (*She throws her arms around him. They kiss—then bend over the cradle together.*) Ain't he purty?—dead spit 'n' image o' yew!

EBEN (*pleased*) Air he? I can't tell none.

ABBIE E-zactly like!

EBEN (*frowningly*) I don't like this. I don't like lettin' on what's mine's his'n. I been doin' that all my life. I'm gittin' t' the end o' b'arin' it!

ABBIE (*putting her finger on his lips*) We're doin' the best we kin. We got t' wait. Somethin's bound t' happen. (*She puts her arms around him.*) I got t' go back.

EBEN I'm goin' out. I can't b'ar it with the fiddle playin' an' the laughin'.

ABBIE Don't git feelin' low. I love ye, Eben. Kiss me. (*He kisses her. They remain in each other's arms.*)

CABOT (*at the gate, confusedly*) Even the music can't drive it out —somethin'. Ye kin feel it droppin' off the elums, climbin' up the roof, sneakin' down the chimney, pokin' in the corners! They's no peace in houses, they's no rest livin' with folks. Somethin's always

livin' with ye. (*with a deep sigh*) I'll go t' the barn an' rest a
spell. (*He goes wearily toward the barn.*)

FIDDLER (*tuning up*) Let's celebrate the old skunk gittin' fooled!
We kin have some fun now he's went. (*He starts to fiddle "Turkey in the Straw." There is real merriment now. The young folks
get up to dance.*)

Scene 2

A half hour later—exterior.

EBEN *is standing by the gate looking up at the sky, an expression of
dumb pain bewildered by itself on his face.* CABOT *appears, returning from
the barn, walking wearily, his eyes on the ground. He sees* EBEN *and his
whole mood immediately changes. He becomes excited, a cruel, triumphant
grin comes to his lips, he strides up and slaps* EBEN *on the back. From
within comes the whining of the fiddle and the noise of stamping feet
and laughing voices.*

CABOT So har ye be!

EBEN (*startled, stares at him with hatred for a moment—then dully*)
Ay-eh.

CABOT (*surveying him jeeringly*) Why hain't ye been in t' dance?
They was all axin' fur ye.

EBEN Let 'em ax!

CABOT They's a hull pasel o' purty gals.

EBEN T' hell with 'em!

CABOT Ye'd ought t' be marryin' one o' 'em soon.

EBEN I hain't marryin' no one.

CABOT Ye might 'arn a share o' a farm that way.

EBEN (*with a sneer*) Like yew did, ye mean? I hain't that kind.

CABOT (*stung*) Ye lie! 'Twas yer Maw's folks aimed t' steal my
farm from me.

EBEN Other folks don't say so. (*after a pause—defiantly*) An' I
got a farm, anyways!

CABOT (*derisively*) Whar?

EBEN (*stamps a foot on the ground*) Har!

CABOT (*throws his head back and laughs coarsely*) Ho-ho! Ye hev,
hev ye? Waal, that's a good un!

EBEN (*controlling himself—grimly*) Ye'll see!

CABOT (*stares at him suspiciously, trying to make him out—a pause
—then with scornful confidence*) Ay-eh. I'll see. So'll ye. It's ye
that's blind—blind as a mole underground. (EBEN *suddenly
laughs, one short sardonic bark: "Ha." A pause.* CABOT *peers at
him with renewed suspicion.*) Whar air ye hawin' 'bout? (EBEN
turns away without answering. CABOT *grows angry.*) God

A'mighty, yew air a dumb dunce! They's nothin' in that thick
skull o' your'n but noise—like a empty keg it be! (EBEN *doesn't
seem to hear*—CABOT's *rage grows.*) Yewr farm! God A'mighty!
If ye wa'n't a born donkey ye'd know ye'll never own stick nor
stone on it, specially now arter him bein' born. It's his'n, I tell ye
—his'n arter I die—but I'll live a hundred jest t' fool ye all—an'
he'll be growed then—yewr age a'most! (EBEN *laughs again his
sardonic "Ha." This drives* CABOT *into a fury.*) Ha? Ye think ye
kin git 'round that someways, do ye? Waal, it'll be her'n, too—
Abbie's—ye won't git 'round her—she knows yer tricks—she'll
be too much fur ye—she wants the farm her'n—she was afeerd
o' ye—she told me ye was sneakin' 'round tryin' t' make love t'
her t' git her on yer side . . . ye . . . ye mad fool, ye! (*He raises his
clenched fists threateningly.*)

EBEN (*is confronting him choking with rage*)   Ye lie, ye old skunk!
Abbie never said no sech thing!

CABOT (*suddenly triumphant when he sees how shaken* EBEN *is*)
She did. An' I says, I'll blow his brains t' the top o' them elums—
an' she says no, that hain't sense, who'll ye git t'help ye on the
farm in his place—an' then she says yew'n me ought t' have a
son—I know we kin, she says—an' I says, if we do, ye kin have
anythin' I've got ye've a mind t'. An' she says, I wants Eben cut
off so's this farm'll be mine when ye die! (*with terrible gloating*)
An' that's what's happened, hain't it? An' the farm's her'n! An'
the dust o' the road—that's you'rn! Ha! Now who's hawin'?

EBEN (*has been listening, petrified with grief and rage—suddenly
laughs wildly and brokenly*)   Ha-ha-ha! So that's her sneakin'
game—all along!—like I suspicioned at fust—t' swaller it all—
an' me, too . . . ! (*madly*) I'll murder her! (*He springs toward
the porch but* CABOT *is quicker and gets in between.*)

CABOT   No, ye don't!

EBEN   Git out o' my road! (*He tries to throw* CABOT *aside. They
grapple in what becomes immediately a murderous struggle. The
old man's concentrated strength is too much for* EBEN. CABOT
*gets one hand on his throat and presses him back across the stone
wall. At the same moment,* ABBIE *comes out on the porch. With
a stifled cry she runs toward them.*)

ABBIE   Eben! Ephraim! (*She tugs at the hand on* EBEN's *throat.*)
Let go, Ephraim! Ye're chokin' him!

CABOT (*removes his hand and flings* EBEN *sideways full length on
the grass, gasping and choking. With a cry,* ABBIE *kneels beside
him, trying to take his head on her lap, but he pushes her away.*
CABOT *stands looking down with fierce triumph*)   Ye needn't t've
fret, Abbie, I wa'n't aimin' t' kill him. He hain't wuth hangin' fur

—not by a hell of a sight! (*more and more triumphantly*) Seventy-six an' him not thirty yit— an' look whar he be fur thinkin' his Paw was easy! No, by God, I hain't easy! An' him upstairs, I'll raise him t' be like me! (*He turns to leave them.*) I'm goin' in an' dance!—sing an' celebrate! (*He walks to the porch—then turns with a great grin.*) I don't calc'late it's left in him, but if he gits pesky, Abbie, ye jest sing out. I'll come a-runnin' an' by the Etarnal, I'll put him across my knee an' birch him! Ha-ha ha! (*He goes into the house laughing. A moment later his loud "whoop" is heard.*)

ABBIE (*tenderly*) Eben. Air ye hurt? (*She tries to kiss him but he pushes her violently away and struggles to a sitting position.*)

EBEN (*gaspingly*) T'hell—with ye!

ABBIE (*not believing her ears*) It's me, Eben—Abbie—don't ye know me?

EBEN (*glowering at her with hatred*) Ay-eh—I know ye—now! (*He suddenly breaks down, sobbing weakly.*)

ABBIE (*fearfully*) Eben—what's happened t' ye—why did ye look at me 's if ye hated me?

EBEN (*violently, between sobs and gasps*) I do hate ye! Ye're a whore—a damn trickin' whore!

ABBIE (*shrinking back horrified*) Eben! Ye don't know what ye're sayin'!

EBEN (*scrambling to his feet and following her—accusingly*) Ye're nothin' but a stinkin' passel o' lies! Ye've been lyin' t' me every word ye spoke, day an' night, since we fust—done it. Ye've kept sayin' ye loved me. . . .

ABBIE (*frantically*) I do love ye! (*She takes his hand but he flings hers away.*)

EBEN (*unheeding*) Ye've made a fool o' me—a sick, dumb fool—a-purpose! Ye've been on'y playin' yer sneakin', stealin' game all along—gittin' me t' lie with ye so's ye'd hev a son he'd think was his'n, an' makin' him promise he'd give ye the farm and let me eat dust, if ye did git him a son! (*staring at her with anguished, bewildered eyes*) They must be a devil livin' in ye! 'Tain't human t' be as bad as that be!

ABBIE (*stunned—dully*) He told yew . . . ?

EBEN Hain't it true? It hain't no good in yew lyin'.

ABBIE (*pleadingly*) Eben, listen—ye must listen—it was long ago —afore we done nothin'—yew was scornin' me—goin' t' see Min —when I was lovin' ye—an' I said it t' him t' git vengeance on ye!

EBEN (*unheedingly. With tortured passion*) I wish ye was dead! I wish I was dead along with ye afore this come! (*ragingly*) But

I'll git my vengeance too! I'll pray Maw t' come back t' help me
—t' put her cuss on yew an' him!

ABBIE (*brokenly*)   Don't ye, Eben! Don't ye! (*She throws herself
on her knees before him, weeping.*) I didn't mean t' do bad t'ye!
Fergive me, won't ye?

EBEN (*not seeming to hear her—fiercely*)   I'll git squar' with the
old skunk—an' yew! I'll tell him the truth 'bout the son he's so
proud o'! Then I'll leave ye here t' pizen each other—with Maw
comin' out o' her grave at nights—an' I'll go t' the gold fields
o' Californi-a whar Sim an' Peter be!

ABBIE (*terrified*)   Ye won't—leave me? Ye can't!

EBEN (*with fierce determination*)   I'm a-goin', I tell ye! I'll git
rich thar an' come back an' fight him fur the farm he stole—an'
I'll kick ye both out in the road—t' beg an' sleep in the woods—
an' yer son along with ye—t' starve an' die! (*He is hysterical at
the end.*)

ABBIE (*with a shudder—humbly*)   He's yewr son, too, Eben.

EBEN (*torturedly*)   I wish he never was born! I wish he'd die this
minit! I wish I'd never sot eyes on him! It's him—yew havin' him
—a-purpose t' steal—that's changed everythin'!

ABBIE (*gently*)   Did ye believe I loved ye—afore he come?

EBEN   Ay-eh—like a dumb ox!

ABBIE   An' ye don't believe no more?

EBEN   B'lieve a lyin' thief! Ha!

ABBIE (*shudders—then humbly*)   An did ye r'ally love me afore?

EBEN (*brokenly*)   Ay-eh—an' ye was trickin' me!

ABBIE   An' ye don't love me now!

EBEN (*violently*)   I hate ye, I tell ye!

ABBIE   An' ye're truly goin' West—goin' t' leave me—all account o'
him being born?

EBEN   I'm a-goin' in the mornin'—or may God strike me t' hell!

ABBIE (*after a pause—with a dreadful cold intensity—slowly*)   If
that's what his comin's done t' me—killin' yewr love—takin' yew
away—my on'y joy—the on'y joy I've ever knowed—like heaven
t' me—purtier'n heaven—then I hate him, too, even if I be his
Maw!

EBEN (*bitterly*)   Lies! Ye love him! He'll steal the farm fur ye!
(*brokenly*) But 'tain't the farm so much—not no more—it's yew
foolin' me—gittin' me t' love ye—lyin' yew loved me—jest t' git
a son t' steal!

ABBIE (*distractedly*)   He won't steal! I'd kill him fust! I do love
ye! I'll prove t' ye . . . !

EBEN (*harshly*)   'Tain't no use lyin' no more. I'm deaf t' ye! (*He
turns away.*) I hain't seein' ye agen. Good-by!

ABBIE (*pale with anguish*)   Hain't ye even goin' t' kiss me—not once—arter all we loved?

EBEN (*in a hard voice*)   I hain't wantin' t' kiss ye never agen! I'm wantin' t' forgit I ever sot eyes on ye!

ABBIE   Eben!—ye mustn't—wait a spell—I want t' tell ye. . . .

EBEN   I'm a-goin' in t' git drunk. I'm a-goin' t' dance.

ABBIE (*clinging to his arm—with passionate earnestness*)   If I could make it—'s if he'd never come up between us—if I could prove t' ye I wa'n't schemin' t' steal from ye—so's everythin' could be jest the same with us, lovin' each other jest the same, kissin' an' happy the same's we've been happy afore he come— if I could do it—ye'd love me agen, wouldn't ye? Ye'd kiss me agen? Ye wouldn't never leave me, would ye?

EBEN (*moved*)   I calc'late not. (*Then shaking her hand off his arm —with a bitter smile*) But ye hain't God, be ye?

ABBIE (*exultantly*)   Remember ye've promised! (*Then with strange intensity*) Mebbe I kin take back one thin' God does!

EBEN (*peering at her*)   Ye're gittin' cracked, hain't ye? (*Then going towards door*) I'm a-goin' t' dance.

ABBIE (*calls after him intensely*)   I'll prove t' ye! I'll prove I love ye better'n. . . . (*He goes in the door, not seeming to hear. She remains standing where she is, looking after him—then she finishes desperately*) Better'n everythin' else in the world!

Scene 3

Just before dawn in the morning—shows the kitchen and CABOT's *bedroom.*

In the kitchen, by the light of a tallow candle on the table, EBEN *is sitting, his chin propped on his hands, his drawn face blank and expressionless. His carpetbag is on the floor beside him. In the bedroom, dimly lighted by a small whale-oil lamp,* CABOT *lies asleep.* ABBIE *is bending over the cradle, listening, her face full of terror yet with an undercurrent of desperate triumph. Suddenly, she breaks down and sobs, appears about to throw herself on her knees beside the cradle; but the old man turns restlessly, groaning in his sleep, and she controls herself, and shrinking away from the cradle with a gesture of horror, backs swiftly toward the door in rear and goes out. A moment later she comes into the kitchen and, running to* EBEN, *flings her arms about his neck and kisses him wildly. He hardens himself; he remains unmoved and cold, he keeps his eyes straight ahead.*

ABBIE (*hysterically*)   I done it, Eben! I told ye I'd do it! I've proved I love ye—better'n everythin'—so's ye can't never doubt me no more!

EBEN (*dully*) Whatever ye done, it hain't no good now.

ABBIE (*wildly*) Don't ye say that! Kiss me, Eben, won't ye? I need ye t' kiss me arter what I done! I need ye t' say ye love me!

EBEN (*kisses her without emotion—dully*) That's fur good-by. I'm a-goin' soon.

ABBIE No! No! Ye won't go—not now!

EBEN (*going on with his own thoughts*) I been a-thinkin'—an' I hain't goin' t' tell Paw nothin'. I'll leave Maw t' take vengeance on ye. If I told him, the old skunk'd jest be stinkin' mean enuf to take it out on that baby. (*His voice showing emotion in spite of him*) An' I don't want nothin' bad t' happen t' him. He hain't t' blame fur yew. (*He adds with a certain queer pride*) An' he looks like me! An' by God, he's mine! An' some day I'll be a-comin' back an' . . . !

ABBIE (*too absorbed in her own thoughts to listen to him—pleadingly*) They's no cause fur ye t' go now—they's no sense—it's all the same's it was—they's nothin' come b'tween us now—arter what I done!

EBEN (*something in her voice arouses him. He stares at her a bit frightenedly*) Ye look mad, Abbie. What did ye do?

ABBIE I—I killed him, Eben.

EBEN (*amazed*) Ye killed him?

ABBIE (*dully*) Ay-eh.

EBEN (*recovering from his astonishment—savagely*) An' serves him right! But we got t' do somethin' quick t' make it look s'if the old skunk'd killed himself when he was drunk. We kin prove by 'em all how drunk he got.

ABBIE (*wildly*) No! No! Not him! (*Laughing distractedly*) But that's what I ought t' done, hain't it? I oughter killed him instead! Why didn't ye tell me?

EBEN (*appalled*) Instead? What d'ye mean?

ABBIE Not him.

EBEN (*his face grown ghastly*) Not—not that baby!

ABBIE (*dully*) Ay-eh!

EBEN (*falls to his knees as if he'd been struck—his voice trembling with horror*) Oh, God A'mighty! A'mighty God! Maw, whar was ye, why didn't ye stop her?

ABBIE (*simply*) She went back t' her grave that night we fust done it, remember? I hain't felt her about since. (*A pause. EBEN hides his head in his hands, trembling all over as if he had the ague. She goes on dully*) I left the piller over his little face. Then he killed himself. He stopped breathin'. (*She begins to weep softly.*)

EBEN (*rage beginning to mingle with grief*) He looked like me. He was mine, damn ye!

ABBIE (*slowly and brokenly*) I didn't want t' do it. I hated myself

fur doin' it. I loved him. He was so purty—dead spit 'n' image o'
yew. But I loved yew more—an' yew was goin' away—far off
whar I'd never see ye agen, never kiss ye, never feel ye pressed
agin me agen—an' ye said ye hated me fur havin' him—ye said
ye hated him an' wished he was dead—ye said if it hadn't been fur
him comin' it'd be the same's afore between us.

EBEN (*unable to endure this, springs to his feet in a fury, threatening her, his twitching fingers seeming to reach out for her throat*)
Ye lie! I never said—I never dreamed ye'd—I'd cut off my head
afore I'd hurt his finger!

ABBIE (*piteously, sinking on her knees*)   Eben, don't ye look at me
like that—hatin' me—not after what I done fur ye—fur us—so's
we could be happy agen—

EBEN (*furiously now*)   Shut up, or I'll kill ye! I see yer game now
—the same old sneakin' trick—ye're aimin' t' blame me fur the
murder ye done!

ABBIE (*moaning—putting her hands over her ears*)   Don't ye, Eben!
Don't ye! (*She grasps his legs.*)

EBEN (*his mood suddenly changing to horror, shrinks away from
her*)   Don't ye tech me! Ye're pizen! How could ye—t' murder
a pore little critter—Ye must've swapped yer soul t' hell! (*suddenly raging*) Ha! I kin see why ye done it! Not the lies ye jest
told—but 'cause ye wanted t' steal agen—steal the last thin' ye'd
left me—my part o' him—no, the hull o' him—ye saw he looked
like me—ye knowed he was all mine—an' ye couldn't b'ar it—I
know ye! Ye killed him fur bein' mine! (*All this has driven him
almost insane. He makes a rush past her for the door—then turns
—shaking both fists at her, violently.*) But I'll take vengeance
now! I'll git the Sheriff! I'll tell him everythin'! Then I'll sing
"I'm off to Californi-a!" an' go—gold—Golden Gate—gold sun
—fields o' gold in the West! (*This last he half shouts, half croons
incoherently, suddenly breaking off passionately.*) I'm a-goin' fur
the Sheriff t' come an' git ye! I want ye tuk away, locked up
from me! I can't stand t'luk at ye! Murderer an' thief 'r not, ye
still tempt me! I'll give ye up t' the Sheriff! (*He turns and runs
out, around the corner of house, panting and sobbing, and breaks
into a swerving sprint down the road.*)

ABBIE (*struggling to her feet, runs to the door, calling after him*)   I
love ye, Eben! I love ye! (*She stops at the door weakly, swaying,
about to fall.*) I don't care what ye do—if ye'll on'y love me
agen—(*She falls limply to the floor in a faint.*)

Scene 4

About an hour later. Same as SCENE 3. *Shows the kitchen and* CABOT'S
bedroom. It is after dawn. The sky is brilliant with the sunrise.

In the kitchen, ABBIE sits at the table, her body limp and exhausted, her head bowed down over her arms, her face hidden. Upstairs, CABOT is still asleep but awakens with a start. He looks toward the window and gives a snort of surprise and irritation—throws back the covers and begins hurriedly pulling on his clothes. Without looking behind him, he begins talking to ABBIE whom he supposes beside him.

CABOT   Thunder 'n' lightnin', Abbie! I hain't slept this late in fifty year! Looks 's if the sun was full riz a'most. Must've been the dancin' an' likker. Must be gittin' old. I hope Eben's t' wuk. Ye might've tuk the trouble t' rouse me, Abbie. (*He turns—sees no one there—surprised.*) Waal—whar air she? Gittin' vittles, I calc'late. (*He tiptoes to the cradle and peers down—proudly*) Mornin', sonny. Purty's a picter! Sleepin' sound. He don't beller all night like most o' 'em. (*He goes quietly out the door in rear —a few moments later enters kitchen—sees ABBIE—with satisfaction*) So thar ye be. Ye got any vittles cooked?

ABBIE   (*without moving*)   No.

CABOT   (*coming to her, almost sympathetically*)   Ye feelin' sick?

ABBIE   No.

CABOT   (*pats her on shoulder. She shudders*)   Ye'd best lie down a spell. (*half jocularly*) Yer son'll be needin' ye soon. He'd ought t' wake up with a gnashin' appetite, the sound way he's sleepin'.

ABBIE   (*shudders—then in a dead voice*)   He ain't never goin' to wake up.

CABOT   (*jokingly*)   Takes after me this mornin'. I ain't slept so late in . . .

ABBIE   He's dead.

CABOT   (*stares at her—bewilderedly*)   What . . .

ABBIE   I killed him.

CABOT   (*stepping back from her—aghast*)   Air ye drunk—'r crazy —'r . . . !

ABBIE   (*suddenly lifts her head and turns on him—wildly*)   I killed him, I tell ye! I smothered him. Go up an' see if ye don't b'lieve me! (*CABOT stares at her a second, then bolts out the rear door, can be heard bounding up the stairs, and rushes into the bedroom and over to the cradle. ABBIE has sunk back lifelessly into her former position. CABOT puts his hand down on the body in the crib. An expression of fear and horror comes over his face.*)

CABOT   (*shrinking away—tremblingly*)   God A'mighty! God A'mighty. (*He stumbles out the door—in a short while returns to the kitchen—comes to ABBIE, the stunned expression still on his face—hoarsely*) Why did ye do it? Why? (*As she doesn't answer, he grabs her violently by the shoulder and shakes her.*) I ax ye why ye done it! Ye'd better tell me 'r . . . !

ABBIE (*gives him a furious push which sends him staggering back and springs to her feet—with wild rage and hatred*) Don't ye dare tech me! What right hev ye t' question me 'bout him? He wa'n't yewr son! Think I'd have a son by yew? I'd die fust! I hate the sight o' ye an' allus did! It's yew I should've murdered, if I'd had good sense! I hate ye! I love Eben. I did from the fust. An' he was Eben's son—mine an' Eben's—not your'n!

CABOT (*stands looking at her dazedly—a pause—finding his words with an effort—dully*) That was it—what I felt—pokin' round the corners—while ye lied—holdin' herself from me—sayin' ye'd a'ready conceived—(*He lapses into crushed silence—then with a strange emotion*) He's dead, sart'n. I felt his heart. Pore little critter! (*He blinks back one tear, wiping his sleeve across his nose.*)

ABBIE (*hysterically*) Don't ye! Don't ye! (*She sobs unrestrainedly.*)

CABOT (*with a concentrated effort that stiffens his body into a rigid line and hardens his face into a stony mask—through his teeth to himself*) I got t' be—like a stone—a rock o' jedgment! (*A pause. He gets complete control over himself—harshly*) If he was Eben's, I be glad he air gone! An' mebbe I suspicioned it all along. I felt they was somethin' onnateral—somewhars—the house got so lonesome—an' cold—drivin' me down t' the barn—t' the beasts o' the field. . . . Ay-eh. I must've suspicioned—somethin'. Ye didn't fool me—not altogether, leastways—I'm too old a bird —growin' ripe on the bough. . . . (*He becomes aware he is wandering, straightens again, looks at* ABBIE *with a cruel grin.*) So ye'd liked t' hev murdered me 'stead o' him, would ye? Waal, I'll live to a hundred! I'll live t' see ye hung! I'll deliver ye up t' the jedgment o' God an' the law! I'll git the Sheriff now. (*Starts for the door.*)

ABBIE (*dully*) Ye needn't. Eben's gone fur him.

CABOT (*amazed*) Eben—gone fur the Sheriff?

ABBIE Ay-eh.

CABOT T' inform agen ye?

ABBIE Ay-eh.

CABOT (*considers this—a pause—then in a hard voice*) Waal, I'm thankful fur him savin' me the trouble. I'll git t' wuk. (*He goes to the door—then turns—in a voice full of strange emotion*) He'd ought t' been my son, Abbie. Ye'd ought t' loved me. I'm a man. If ye'd loved me, I'd never told no Sheriff on ye no matter what ye did, if they was t' brile me alive!

ABBIE (*defensively*) They's more to it nor yew know, makes him tell.

CABOT (*dryly*) Fur yewr sake, I hope they be. (*He goes out—

comes around to the gate—stares up at the sky. His control re-
laxes. For a moment he is old and weary. He murmurs despair-
ingly) God A'mighty, I be lonesomer'n ever! (*He hears running*
footsteps from the left, immediately is himself again. EBEN *runs*
in, panting exhaustedly, wild-eyed and mad looking. He lurches
through the gate. CABOT *grabs him by the shoulder.* EBEN *stares*
at him dumbly.) Did ye tell the Sheriff?

EBEN (*nodding stupidly*)   Ay-eh.

CABOT (*gives him a push away that sends him sprawling—laughing*
with withering contempt)   Good fur ye! A prime chip o' yer
Maw ye be! (*He goes toward the barn, laughing harshly.* EBEN
scrambles to his feet. Suddenly CABOT *turns—grimly threatening*)
Git off this farm when the Sheriff takes her—or, by God, he'll
have t' come back an' git me fur murder, too! (*He stalks off.*
EBEN *does not appear to have heard him. He runs to the door*
and comes into the kitchen. ABBIE *looks up with a cry of an-*
guished joy. EBEN *stumbles over and throws himself on his knees*
beside her—sobbing brokenly.)

EBEN   Fergive me!

ABBIE (*happily*)   Eben! (*She kisses him and pulls his head over*
against her breast.)

EBEN   I love ye! Fergive me!

ABBIE (*ecstatically*)   I'd fergive ye all the sins in hell fur sayin'
that! (*She kisses his head, pressing it to her with a fierce passion*
of possession.)

EBEN (*brokenly*)   But I told the Sheriff. He's comin' fur ye!

ABBIE   I kin b'ar what happens t' me—now!

EBEN   I woke him up. I told him. He says, wait 'til I git dressed. I
was waiting. I got to thinkin' o' yew. I got to thinkin' how I'd loved
ye. It hurt like somethin' was bustin' in my chest an' head. I got
t' cryin'. I knowed sudden I loved ye yet, an' allus would love ye!

ABBIE (*caressing his hair—tenderly*)   My boy, hain't ye?

EBEN   I begun t' run back. I cut across the fields an' through the
woods. I thought ye might have time t' run away—with me—
an' . . .

ABBIE (*shaking her head*)   I got t' take my punishment—t' pay fur
my sin.

EBEN   Then I want t' share it with ye.

ABBIE   Ye didn't do nothin'.

EBEN   I put it in yer head. I wisht he was dead! I as much as urged
ye t' do it!

ABBIE   No. It was me alone!

EBEN   I'm as guilty as yew be! He was the child o' our sin.

ABBIE (*lifting her head as if defying God*)   I don't repent that sin! I hain't askin' God t' fergive that!

EBEN   Nor me—but it led up t' the other—an' the murder ye did, ye did 'count o' me   an' it's my murder, too, I'll tell the Sheriff — an' if ye deny it, I'll say we planned it t'gether—an' they'll all b'lieve me, fur they suspicion everythin' we've done, an' it'll seem likely an' true to 'em. An' it is true—way down. I did help ye— somehow.

ABBIE (*laying her head on his—sobbing*)   No! I don't want ye t' suffer!

EBEN   I got t' pay fur my part o' the sin! An' I'd suffer wuss leavin' ye, goin' West, thinkin' o' ye day an' night, bein' out when yew was in—(*lowering his voice*)—'r bein' alive when yew was dead. (*a pause*) I want t' share with ye, Abbie—prison 'r death 'r hell 'r anythin'! (*He looks into her eyes and forces a trembling smile.*) If I'm sharin' with ye, I won't feel lonesome, leastways.

ABBIE (*weakly*)   Eben! I won't let ye! I can't let ye!

EBEN (*kissing her—tenderly*)   Ye can't he'p yerself. I got ye beat fur once!

ABBIE (*forcing a smile—adoringly*)   I hain't beat—s'long's I got ye!

EBEN (*hears the sound of feet outside*)   Ssshh! Listen! They've come t' take us!

ABBIE   No, it's him. Don't give him no chance to fight ye, Eben. Don't say nothin'—no matter what he says. An' I won't neither. (*It is* CABOT. *He comes up from the barn in a great state of excitement and strides into the house and then into the kitchen.* EBEN *is kneeling beside* ABBIE, *his arm around her, hers around him. They stare straight ahead.*)

CABOT (*stares at them, his face hard. A long pause—vindictively*)   Ye make a slick pair o' murderin' turtle doves! Ye'd ought t' be both hung on the same limb an' left thar t' swing in the breeze an' rot—a warnin' t' old fools like me t' b'ar their lonesomeness alone —an' fur young fools like ye t' hobble their lust. (*A pause. The excitement returns to his face, his eyes snap, he looks a bit crazy.*) I couldn't work today. I couldn't take no interest. T' hell with the farm! I'm leavin' it! I've turned the cows an' other stock loose! I've druv 'em into the woods whar they kin be free! By freein' 'em, I'm freein' myself! I'm quittin' here today! I'll set fire t' house an' barn an' watch 'em burn, an' I'll leave yer Maw t' haunt the ashes, an' I'll will the fields back t' God, so that nothin' human kin never touch 'em! I'll be a-goin' to Californi-a—t' jine Simeon an' Peter—true sons o' mine if they be dumb fools—an' the Cabots'll find Solomon's Mines t'gether! (*He suddenly cuts*

a mad caper.) Whoop! What was the song they sung? "Oh, Californi-a! That's the land fur me." (*He sings this—then gets on his
knees by the floorboard under which the money was hid.*) An'
I'll sail thar on one o' the finest clippers I kin find! I've got the
money! Pity ye didn't know whar this was hidden so's ye could
steal... (*He has pulled up the board. He stares—feels—stares
again. A pause of dead silence. He slowly turns, slumping into a
sitting position on the floor, his eyes like those of a dead fish, his
face the sickly green of an attack of nausea. He swallows painfully several times—forces a weak smile at last.*) So—ye did steal
it!

EBEN (*emotionlessly*)   I swapped it t' Sim an' Peter fur their share
o' the farm—t' pay their passage t' Californi-a.

CABOT (*with one sardonic*)   Ha! (*He begins to recover. Gets slowly
to his feet—strangly*) I calc'late God give it to 'em—not yew!
God's hard, not easy! Mebbe they's easy gold in the West but it
hain't God's gold. It hain't fur me. I kin hear His voice warnin'
me agen t' be hard an' stay on my farm. I kin see his hand usin'
Eben t' steal t' keep me from weakness. I kin feel I be in the palm
o' His hand, His fingers guidin' me. (*A pause—then he mutters
sadly*)   It's a-goin' t' be lonesomer now than ever it war afore—
an' I'm gittin' old, Lord—ripe on the bough.... (*Then stiffening*) Waal—what d'ye want? God's lonesome, hain't He? God's
hard an' lonesome! (*A pause. The SHERIFF with two men comes
up the road from the left. They move cautiously to the door. The
SHERIFF knocks on it with the butt of his pistol.*)

SHERIFF   Open in the name o' the law! (*They start.*)

CABOT   They've come fur ye. (*He goes to the rear door.*) Come in,
Jim! (*The three men enter. CABOT meets them in doorway.*) Jest
a minit, Jim. I got 'em safe here. (*The SHERIFF nods. He and his
companions remain in the doorway.*)

EBEN (*suddenly calls*)   I lied this mornin', Jim. I helped her to do
it. Ye kin take me, too.

ABBIE (*brokenly*)   No!

CABOT   Take 'em both. (*He comes forward—stares at EBEN with a
trace of grudging admiration*) Purty good—fur yew! Waal, I got
t' round up the stock. Good-by.

EBEN   Good-by.

ABBIE   Good-by. (*CABOT turns and strides past the men—comes out
and around the corner of the house, his shoulders squared, his
face stony, and stalks grimly toward the barn. In the meantime
the SHERIFF and men have come into the room.*)

SHERIFF (*embarrassedly*)   Waal—we'd best start.

ABBIE   Wait. (*Turns to EBEN*)   I love ye, Eben.

EBEN   I love ye, Abbie. (*They kiss. The three men grin and shuffle embarrassedly.* EBEN *takes* ABBIE's *hand. They go out the door in rear, the men following, and come from the house, walking hand in hand to the gate.* EBEN *stops there and points to the sunrise sky.*) Sun's a-rizin'. Purty, hain't it?

ABBIE   Ay-eh. (*They both stand for a moment looking up raptly in attitudes strangely aloof and devout.*)

SHERIFF (*looking around at the farm enviously to his companion*) It's a jim-dandy farm, no denyin'. Wished I owned it!

QUESTIONS

1. Why is there such a detailed description of the trees surrounding the farmhouse? Explain how this description does or does not set the mood for the play.
2. Discuss the significance and role of the nature images that occur throughout *Desire under the Elms.*
3. Do you find O'Neill's use of dialect effective? Why or why not?
4. Are Eben and Abbie a classical tragic hero and heroine? Discuss.
5. Compare and contrast this tragedy with another in this anthology.

LORRAINE HANSBERRY (1930–1965)

A Raisin in the Sun

To Mama: in gratitude for the dream

CHARACTERS

RUTH YOUNGER
TRAVIS YOUNGER
WALTER LEE YOUNGER (*Brother*)
BENEATHA YOUNGER
LENA YOUNGER (*Mama*)
JOSEPH ASAGAI
GEORGE MURCHISON
KARL LINDNER
BOBO
MOVING MEN

The action of the play is set in Chicago's Southside, sometime between World War II and the present.

ACT I

Scene I.
Friday morning

Scene II.
The following morning

ACT II

Scene I.
Later, the same day

Scene II.
Friday night, a few weeks later

Scene III.
Saturday, moving day, one week later

ACT III

An hour later

What happens to a dream deferred?
Does it dry up
Like a raisin in the sun?
Or fester like a sore—

And then run?
Does it stink like rotten meat?
Or crust and sugar over—
Like a syrupy sweet?

Maybe it just sags
Like a heavy load.

Or does it explode?

Langston Hughes[1]

ACT I

Scene I

The YOUNGER *living room would be a comfortable and well-ordered room if it were not for a number of indestructible contradictions to this state of being. Its furnishings are typical and undistinguished and their primary feature now is that they have clearly had to accommodate the living of too many people for too many years—and they are tired. Still, we can see that at some time, a time probably no longer remembered by the family (except perhaps for* MAMA), *the furnishings of this room were actually selected with care and love and even hope—and brought to this apartment and arranged with taste and pride.*

That was a long time ago. Now the once loved pattern of the couch upholstery has to fight to show itself from under acres of crocheted doilies and couch covers which have themselves finally come to be more important than the upholstery. And here a table or a chair has been moved to disguise the worn places in the carpet; but the carpet has fought back by showing its weariness, with depressing uniformity, elsewhere on its surface.

Weariness has, in fact, won in this room. Everything has been polished, washed, sat on, used, scrubbed too often. All pretenses but living itself have long since vanished from the very atmosphere of this room.

Moreover, a section of this room, for it is not really a room unto itself, though the landlord's lease would make it seem so, slopes backward to

---

[1] From "Dream Deferred." Copyright 1951 by Langston Hughes. Reprinted from *The Panther and the Lash* by Langston Hughes, by permission of Alfred A. Knopf, Inc.

provide a small kitchen area, where the family prepares the meals that are eaten in the living room proper, which must also serve as dining room. The single window that has been provided for these "two" rooms is located in this kitchen area. The sole natural light the family may enjoy in the course of a day is only that which fights its way through this little window.

At left, a door leads to a bedroom which is shared by MAMA *and her daughter,* BENEATHA. *At right, opposite, is a second room (which in the beginning of the life of this apartment was probably a breakfast room), which serves as a bedroom for* WALTER *and his wife,* RUTH.

Time: Sometime between World War II and the present.

Place: Chicago's Southside.

At rise: It is morning dark in the living room. TRAVIS *is asleep on the make-down bed at center. An alarm clock sounds from within the bedroom at right, and presently* RUTH *enters from that room and closes the door behind her. She crosses sleepily toward the window. As she passes her sleeping son she reaches down and shakes him a little. At the window she raises the shade and a dusky Southside morning light comes in feebly. She fills a pot with water and puts it on to boil. She calls to the boy, between yawns, in a slightly muffled voice.*

RUTH *is about thirty. We can see that she was a pretty girl, even exceptionally so, but now it is apparent that life has been little that she expected, and disappointment has already begun to hang in her face. In a few years, before thirty-five even, she will be known among her people as a "settled woman."*

She crosses to her son and gives him a good, final, rousing shake.

RUTH   Come on now, boy, it's seven thirty! (*Her son sits up at last, in a stupor of sleepiness.*) I say hurry up, Travis! You ain't the only person in the world got to use a bathroom! (*The child, a sturdy, handsome little boy of ten or eleven, drags himself out of the bed and almost blindly takes his towels and "today's clothes" from drawers and a closet and goes out to the bathroom, which is in an outside hall and which is shared by another family or families on the same floor.* RUTH *crosses to the bedroom door at right and opens it and calls in to her husband.*) Walter Lee! . . . It's after seven thirty! Lemme see you do some waking up in there now! (*She waits.*) You better get up from there, man! It's after seven thirty I tell you. (*She waits again.*) All right, you just go ahead and lay there and next thing you know Travis be finished and Mr. Johnson'll be in there and you'll be fussing and cussing round here like a mad man! And be late too! (*She waits, at the end of patience.*) Walter Lee—it's time for you to get up!

(*She waits another second and then starts to go into the bedroom, but is apparently satisfied that her husband has begun to get up. She stops, pulls the door to, and returns to the kitchen area. She wipes her face with a moist cloth and runs her fingers through her sleep-disheveled hair*

*in a vain effort and ties an apron around her housecoat. The bedroom
door at right opens and her husband stands in the doorway in his pajamas, which are rumpled and mismated. He is a lean, intense young
man in his middle thirties, inclined to quick nervous movements and
erratic speech habits—and always in his voice there is a quality of
indictment.)*

WALTER   Is he out yet?

RUTH   What you mean *out*? He ain't hardly got in there good yet

WALTER   (*wandering in, still more oriented to sleep than to a new
day*)   Well, what was you doing all that yelling for if I can't even
get in there yet? (*Stopping and thinking*) Check coming today?

RUTH   They *said* Saturday and this is just Friday and I hopes to
God you ain't going to get up here first thing this morning and
start talking to me 'bout no money—'cause I 'bout don't want to
hear it.

WALTER   Something the matter with you this morning?

RUTH   No—I'm just sleepy as the devil. What kind of eggs you
want?

WALTER   Not scrambled. (RUTH *starts to scramble eggs.*)   Paper
come? (RUTH *points impatiently to the rolled up* Tribune *on the
table, and he gets it and spreads it out and vaguely reads the front
page.*)   Set off another bomb yesterday.

RUTH   (*maximum indifference*)   Did they?

WALTER   (*looking up*)   What's the matter with you?

RUTH   Ain't nothing the matter with me. And don't keep asking
me that this morning.

WALTER   Ain't nobody bothering you. (*Reading the news of the day
absently again*) Say Colonel McCormick is sick.

RUTH   (*affecting tea-party interest*)   Is he now? Poor thing.

WALTER   (*sighing and looking at his watch*)   Oh, me. (*He waits.*)
Now what is that boy doing in that bathroom all this time? He
just going to have to start getting up earlier. I can't be being late
to work on account of him fooling around in there.

RUTH   (*turning on him*)   Oh, no he ain't going to be getting up no
earlier no such thing! It ain't his fault that he can't get to bed
no earlier nights 'cause he got a bunch of crazy good-for-nothing
clowns sitting up running their mouths in what is supposed to be
his bedroom after ten o'clock at night. . . .

WALTER   That's what you mad about, ain't it? The things I want
to talk about with my friends just couldn't be important in your
mind, could they?

*He rises and finds a cigarette in her handbag on the table and crosses to
the little window and looks out, smoking and deeply enjoying this first one.*

RUTH (*almost matter of factly, a complaint too automatic to deserve emphasis*)   Why you always got to smoke before you eat in the morning?

WALTER (*at the window*)   Just look at 'em down there. . . . Running and racing to work . . . (*he turns and faces his wife and watches her a moment at the stove, and then, suddenly*) You look young this morning, baby.

RUTH (*indifferently*)   Yeah?

WALTER   Just for a second—stirring them eggs. It's gone now—just for a second it was—you looked real young again. (*Then, drily*) It's gone now—you look like yourself again.

RUTH   Man, if you don't shut up and leave me alone.

WALTER (*looking out to the street again*)   First thing a man ought to learn in life is not to make love to no colored woman first thing in the morning. You all some evil people at eight o'clock in the morning.

(TRAVIS *appears in the hall doorway, almost fully dressed and quite wide awake now, his towels and pajamas across his shoulders. He opens the door and signals for his father to make the bathroom in a hurry.*)

TRAVIS (*watching the bathroom*)   Daddy, come on!

(WALTER *gets his bathroom utensils and flies out to the bathroom.*)

RUTH   Sit down and have your breakfast, Travis.

TRAVIS   Mama, this is Friday. (*Gleefully*) Check coming tomorrow, huh?

RUTH   You get your mind off money and eat your breakfast.

TRAVIS (*eating*)   This is the morning we supposed to bring the fifty cents to school.

RUTH   Well, I ain't got no fifty cents this morning.

TRAVIS   Teacher say we have to.

RUTH   I don't care what teacher say. I ain't got it. Eat your breakfast, Travis.

TRAVIS   I *am* eating.

RUTH   Hush up now and just eat!

The boy gives her an exasperated look for her lack of understanding, and eats grudgingly.

TRAVIS   You think Grandmama would have it?

RUTH   No! And I want you to stop asking your grandmother for money, you hear me?

TRAVIS (*outraged*)   Gaaaleee! I don't ask her, she just gimme it sometimes!

RUTH   Travis Willard Younger—I got too much on me this morning to be—

TRAVIS   Maybe Daddy—

RUTH   *Travis!*

The boy hushes abruptly. They are both quiet and tense for several seconds.

TRAVIS   (*presently*)   Could I maybe go carry some groceries in front of the supermarket for a little while after school then?

RUTH   Just hush, I said. (TRAVIS *jabs his spoon into his cereal bowl viciously, and rests his head in anger upon his fists.*) If you through eating, you can get over there and make up your bed.

(The boy obeys stiffly and crosses the room, almost mechanically, to the bed and more or less carefully folds the covering. He carries the bedding into his mother's room and returns with his books and cap.)

TRAVIS   (*sulking and standing apart from her unnaturally*)   I'm gone.

RUTH   (*looking up from the stove to inspect him automatically*) Come here. (*He crosses to her and she studies his head.*) If you don't take this comb and fix this here head, you better! (TRAVIS *puts down his books with a great sigh of oppression, and crosses to the mirror. His mother mutters under her breath about his "slubbornness."*) 'Bout to march out of here with that head looking just like chickens slept in it! I just don't know where you get your slubborn ways. . . . And get your jacket, too. Looks chilly out this morning.

TRAVIS   (*with conspicuously brushed hair and jacket*)   I'm gone.

RUTH   Get carfare and milk money—(*waving one finger*)—and not a single penny for no caps, you hear me?

TRAVIS   (*with sullen politeness*)   Yes'm.

He turns in outrage to leave. His mother watches after him as in his frustration he approaches the door almost comically. When she speaks to him her voice has become a very gentle tease.

RUTH   (*mocking; as she thinks he would say it*)   Oh, Mama makes me so mad sometimes, I don't know what to do! (*She waits and continues to his back as he stands stock-still in front of the door.*) I wouldn't kiss that woman good-bye for nothing in this world this morning! (*The boy finally turns around and rolls his eyes at her, knowing the mood has changed and he is vindicated; he does not, however, move toward her yet.*) Not for nothing in this world! (*She finally laughs aloud at him and holds out her arms to him and we see that it is a way between them, very old and practiced. He crosses to her and allows her to embrace him warmly but keeps his face fixed with masculine rigidity. She holds him back from her presently and looks at him and runs her fingers over the features of his face. With utter gentleness—)* Now— whose little old angry man are you?

TRAVIS *(the masculinity and gruffness start to fade at last)*   Aw gaalee—Mama . . .

RUTH *(mimicking)*   Aw—gaaaaalleeeee, Mama! *(She pushes him, with rough playfulness and finality, toward the door.)* Get on out of here or you going to be late.

TRAVIS *(in the face of love, new aggressiveness)*   Mama, could I *please* go carry groceries?

RUTH   Honey, it's starting to get so cold evenings.

WALTER *(coming in from the bathroom and drawing a make-believe gun from a make-believe holster and shooting at his son)*   What is it he wants to do?

RUTH   Go carry groceries after school at the supermarket.

WALTER   Well, let him go . . .

TRAVIS *(quickly, to the ally)*   I *have* to—she won't gimme the fifty cents. . . .

WALTER *(to his wife only)*   Why not?

RUTH *(simply, and with flavor)*   'Cause we don't have it.

WALTER *(to* RUTH *only)*   What you tell the boy things like that for? *(Reaching down into his pants with a rather important gesture)* Here, son—

He hands the boy the coin, but his eyes are directed to his wife's. TRAVIS *takes the money happily.*

TRAVIS   Thanks, Daddy.

He starts out. RUTH *watches both of them with murder in her eyes.* WALTER *stands and stares back at her with defiance, and suddenly reaches into his pocket again on an afterthought.*

WALTER *(without even looking at his son, still staring hard at his wife)*   In fact, here's another fifty cents. . . . Buy yourself some fruit today—or take a taxicab to school or something!

TRAVIS   Whoopee—

He leaps up and clasps his father around the middle with his legs, and they face each other in mutual appreciation; slowly WALTER LEE *peeks around the boy to catch the violent rays from his wife's eyes and draws his head back as if shot.*

WALTER   You better get down now—and get to school, man.

TRAVIS *(at the door)*   O.K. Good-bye. *(He exits.)*

WALTER *(after him, pointing with pride)*   That's *my* boy. *(She looks at him in disgust and turns back to her work.*) You know what I was thinking 'bout in the bathroom this morning?

RUTH No.

WALTER How come you always try to be so pleasant!

RUTH What is there to be pleasant 'bout!

WALTER You want to know what I was thinking 'bout in the bathroom or not!

RUTH I know what you thinking 'bout.

WALTER (*ignoring her*) 'Bout what me and Willy Harris was talking about last night.

RUTH (*immediately—a refrain*) Willy Harris is a good-for-nothing loud mouth.

WALTER Anybody who talks to me has got to be a good-for-nothing loud mouth, ain't he? And what you know about who is just a good-for-nothing loud mouth? Charlie Atkins was just a "good-for-nothing loud mouth" too, wasn't he! When he wanted me to go in the dry-cleaning business with him. And now—he's grossing a hundred thousand a year. A hundred thousand dollars a year! You still call *him* a loud mouth!

RUTH (*bitterly*) Oh, Walter Lee. . . . (*She folds her head on her arms over the table.*)

WALTER (*rising and coming to her and standing over her*) You tired, ain't you? Tired of everything. Me, the boy, the way we live—this beat-up hole—everything. Ain't you? (*She doesn't look up, doesn't answer.*) So tired—moaning and groaning all the time, but you wouldn't do nothing to help, would you? You couldn't be on my side that long for nothing, could you?

RUTH Walter, please leave me alone.

WALTER A man needs for a woman to back him up. . . .

RUTH Walter—

WALTER Mama would listen to you. You know she listen to you more than she do me and Bennie. She think more of you. All you have to do is just sit down with her when you drinking your coffee one morning and talking 'bout things like you do and—(*he sits down beside her and demonstrates graphically what he thinks her methods and tone should be*)—you just sip your coffee, see, and say easy like that you been thinking 'bout that deal Walter Lee is so interested in, 'bout the store and all, and sip some more coffee, like what you saying ain't really that important to you— And the next thing you know, she be listening good and asking you questions and when I come home—I can tell her the details. This ain't no fly-by-night proposition, baby. I mean we figured it out, me and Willy and Bobo.

RUTH (*with a frown*) Bobo?

WALTER   Yeah. You see, this little liquor store we got in mind cost seventy-five thousand and we figured the initial investment on the place be 'bout thirty thousand, see. That be ten thousand each. Course, there's a couple of hundred you got to pay so's you don't spend your life just waiting for them clowns to let your license get approved—

RUTH   You mean graft?

WALTER   *(frowning impatiently)*   Don't call it that. See there, that just goes to show you what women understand about the world. Baby, don't *nothing* happen for you in this world 'less you pay *somebody* off!

RUTH   Walter, leave me alone! *(She raises her head and stares at him vigorously—then says, more quietly)* Eat your eggs, they gonna be cold.

WALTER   *(straightening up from her and looking off)* That's it. There you are. Man say to his woman: I got me a dream. His woman say: Eat your eggs. *(Sadly, but gaining in power)* Man say: I got to take hold of this here world, baby! And a woman will say: Eat your eggs and go to work. *(Passionately now)* Man say: I got to change my life, I'm choking to death, baby! And his woman say—*(in utter anguish as he brings his fists down on his thighs)*—Your eggs is getting cold!

RUTH   *(softly)*   Walter, that ain't none of our money.

WALTER   *(not listening at all or even looking at her)*   This morning, I was lookin' in the mirror and thinking about it. . . . I'm thirty-five years old; I been married eleven years and I got a boy who sleeps in the living room—*(very, very quietly)*—and all I got to give him is stories about how rich white people live. . . .

RUTH   Eat your eggs, Walter.

WALTER   *Damn my eggs . . . damn all the eggs that ever was!*

RUTH   Then go to work.

WALTER   *(looking up at her)*   See—I'm trying to talk to you 'bout myself—*(shaking his head with the repetition)*—and all you can say is eat them eggs and go to work.

RUTH   *(wearily)*   Honey, you never say nothing new. I listen to you every day, every night and every morning, and you never say nothing new. *(Shrugging.)* So you would rather *be* Mr. Arnold than be his chauffeur. So— I would *rather* be living in Buckingham Palace.

WALTER   That is just what is wrong with the colored woman in this world. . . . Don't understand about building their men up and making 'em feel like they somebody. Like they can do something.

RUTH   *(drily, but to hurt)*   There *are* colored men who do things.

WALTER   No thanks to the colored woman.

RUTH   Well, being a colored woman, I guess I can't help myself none.

She rises and gets the ironing board and sets it up and attacks a huge pile of rough-dried clothes, sprinkling them in preparation for the ironing and then rolling them into tight fat balls.

WALTER   (*mumbling*)   We one group of men tied to a race of women with small minds.

His sister BENEATHA *enters. She is about twenty, as slim and intense as her brother. She is not as pretty as her sister-in-law, but her lean, almost intellectual face has a handsomeness of its own. She wears a bright-red flannel nightie, and her thick hair stands wildly about her head. Her speech is a mixture of many things; it is different from the rest of the family's insofar as education has permeated her sense of English—and perhaps the Midwest rather than the South has finally—at last—won out in her inflection; but not altogether, because over all of it is a soft slurring and transformed use of vowels which is the decided influence of the Southside. She passes through the room without looking at either* RUTH *or* WALTER *and goes to the outside door and looks, a little blindly, out to the bathroom. She sees that it has been lost to the Johnsons. She closes the door with a sleepy vengeance and crosses to the table and sits down a little defeated.*

BENEATHA   I am going to start timing those people.

WALTER   You should get up earlier.

BENEATHA   (*her face in her hands; she is still fighting the urge to go back to bed*)   Really—would you suggest dawn? Where's the paper?

WALTER   (*pushing the paper across the table to her as he studies her almost clinically, as though he has never seen her before*)   You a horrible-looking chick at this hour.

BENEATHA   (*drily*)   Good morning, everybody.

WALTER   (*senselessly*)   How is school coming?

BENEATHA   (*in the same spirit*)   Lovely. Lovely. And you know, biology is the greatest. (*Looking up at him.*) I dissected something that looked just like you yesterday.

WALTER   I just wondered if you've made up your mind and everything.

BENEATHA   (*gaining in sharpness and impatience*)   And what did I answer yesterday morning—and the day before that?

RUTH   (*from the ironing board, like someone disinterested and old*)   Don't be so nasty, Bennie.

BENEATHA   (*still to her brother*)   And the day before that and the day before that!

WALTER (*defensively*)   I'm interested in you. Something wrong with that? Ain't many girls who decide—

WALTER and BENEATHA (*in unison*)   —"to be a doctor."

Silence.

WALTER   Have we figured out yet just exactly how much medical school is going to cost?

RUTH   Walter Lee, why don't you leave that girl alone and get out of here to work?

BENEATHA (*exits to the bathroom and bangs on the door*)   Come on out of there, please! (*She comes back into the room.*)

WALTER (*looking at his sister intently*)   You know the check is coming tomorrow.

BENEATHA (*turning on him with a sharpness all her own*)   That money belongs to Mama, Walter, and it's for her to decide how she wants to use it. I don't care if she wants to buy a house or a rocket ship or just nail it up somewhere and look at it. It's hers. Not ours—*hers.*

WALTER (*bitterly*)   Now ain't that fine! You just got your mother's interest at heart, ain't you, girl? You such a nice girl—but if Mama got that money she can always take a few thousand and help you through school too—can't she?

BENEATHA   I have never asked anyone around here to do anything for me!

WALTER   No! And the line between asking and just accepting when the time comes is big and wide—ain't it!

BENEATHA (*with fury*)   What do you want from me, Brother—that I quit school or just drop dead, which!

WALTER   I don't want nothing but for you to stop acting holy 'round here. Me and Ruth done made some sacrifices for you—why can't you do something for the family?

RUTH   Walter, don't be dragging me in it.

WALTER   You are in it—Don't you get up and go work in somebody's kitchen for the last three years to help put clothes on her back?

RUTH   Oh, Walter—that's not fair. . . .

WALTER   It ain't that nobody expects you to get on your knees and say thank you, Brother; thank you, Ruth; thank you, Mama— and thank you, Travis, for wearing the same pair of shoes for two semesters—

BENEATHA (*dropping to her knees*)   Well—I *do*—all right?—thank everybody . . . and forgive me for ever wanting to be anything at all . . . forgive me, forgive me!

RUTH   Please stop it! Your mama'll hear you.

WALTER   Who the hell told you you had to be a doctor? If you so crazy 'bout messing 'round with sick people—then go be a nurse like other women—or just get married and be quiet. . . .

BENEATHA   Well—you finally got it said. . . . It took you three years but you finally got it said. Walter, give up; leave me alone—it's Mama's money.

WALTER   *He was my father, too!*

BENEATHA   So what? He was mine, too—and Travis' grandfather— but the insurance money belongs to Mama. Picking on me is not going to make her give it to you to invest in any liquor stores— (*underbreath, dropping into a chair*)—and I for one say, God bless Mama for that!

WALTER (*to* RUTH)   See—did you hear? Did you hear!

RUTH   Honey, please go to work.

WALTER   Nobody in this house is ever going to understand me.

BENEATHA   Because you're a nut.

WALTER   Who's a nut?

BENEATHA   You—you are a nut. Thee is mad, boy.

WALTER (*looking at his wife and his sister from the door, very sadly*)   The world's most backward race of people, and that's a fact.

BENEATHA (*turning slowly in her chair*)   And then there are all those prophets who would lead us out of the wilderness—(WALTER *slams out of the house*)—into the swamps!

RUTH   Bennie, why you always gotta be pickin' on your brother? Can't you be a little sweeter sometimes?

(*Door opens.* WALTER *walks in.*)

WALTER (*to* RUTH)   I need some money for carfare.

RUTH (*looks at him, then warms; teasing, but tenderly*)   Fifty cents? (*She goes to her bag and gets money.*) Here, take a taxi.

(WALTER *exits.* MAMA *enters. She is a woman in her early sixties, full-bodied and strong. She is one of those women of a certain grace and beauty who wear it so unobtrusively that it takes a while to notice. Her dark-brown face is surrounded by the total whiteness of her hair, and, being a woman who has adjusted to many things in life and overcome many more, her face is full of strength. She has, we can see, wit and faith of a kind that keep her eyes lit and full of interest and expectancy. She is, in a word, a beautiful woman. Her bearing is perhaps most like the noble bearing of the women of the Hereros of Southwest Africa— rather as if she imagines that as she walks she still bears a basket or a vessel upon her head. Her speech, on the other hand, is as careless as her carriage is precise—she is inclined to slur everything—but her voice is perhaps not so much quiet as simply soft.*)

MAMA   Who that 'round here slamming doors at this hour?

She crosses through the room, goes to the window, opens it, and brings in a feeble little plant growing doggedly in a small pot on the window sill. She feels the dirt and puts it back out.

RUTH   That was Walter Lee. He and Bennie was at it again.

MAMA   My children and they tempers. Lord, if this little old plant don't get more sun than it's been getting it ain't never going to see spring again. (*She turns from the window.*) What's the matter with you this morning, Ruth? You looks right peaked. You aiming to iron all them things? Leave some for me. I'll get to 'em this afternoon. Bennie honey, it's too drafty for you to be sitting 'round half dressed. Where's your robe?

BENEATHA   In the cleaners.

MAMA   Well, go get mine and put it on.

BENEATHA   I'm not cold, Mama, honest.

MAMA   I know—but you so thin. . . .

BENEATHA (*irritably*)   Mama, I'm not cold.

MAMA (*seeing the make-down bed as* TRAVIS *has left it*)   Lord have mercy, look at that poor bed. Bless his heart—he tries, don't he? (*She moves to the bed* TRAVIS *has sloppily made up.*)

RUTH   No—he don't half try at all 'cause he knows you going to come along behind him and fix everything. That's just how come he don't know how to do nothing right now—you done spoiled that boy so.

MAMA   Well—he's a little boy. Ain't supposed to know 'bout housekeeping. My baby, that's what he is. What you fix for his breakfast this morning?

RUTH (*angrily*)   I feed my son, Lena!

MAMA   I ain't meddling—(*underbreath; busy bodyish*)—I just noticed all last week he had cold cereal, and when it starts getting this chilly in the fall a child ought to have some hot grits or something when he goes out in the cold—

RUTH (*furious*)   I gave him hot oats—is that all right!

MAMA   I ain't meddling. (*Pause.*) Put a lot of nice butter on it? (RUTH *shoots her an angry look and does not reply.*) He likes lots of butter.

RUTH (*exasperated*)   Lena—

MAMA (*to* BENEATHA; MAMA *is inclined to wander conversationally sometimes*)   What was you and your brother fussing 'bout this morning?

BENEATHA   It's not important, Mama.

(*She gets up and goes to look out at the bathroom, which is apparently free, and she picks up her towels and rushes out.*)

MAMA   What was they fighting about?

RUTH   Now you know as well as I do.

MAMA   (*shaking her head*)   Brother still worrying his self sick about that money?

RUTH   You know he is.

MAMA   You had breakfast?

RUTH   Some coffee.

MAMA   Girl, you better start eating and looking after yourself better. You almost thin as Travis.

RUTH   Lena—

MAMA   Un-hunh?

RUTH   What are you going to do with it?

MAMA   Now don't you start, child. It's too early in the morning to be talking about money. It ain't Christian.

RUTH   It's just that he got his heart set on that store—

MAMA   You mean that liquor store that Willy Harris want him to invest in?

RUTH   Yes—

MAMA   We ain't no business people, Ruth. We just plain working folks.

RUTH   Ain't nobody business people till they go into business. Walter Lee say colored people ain't never going to start getting ahead till they start gambling on some different kinds of things in the world—investments and things.

MAMA   What done got into you, girl? Walter Lee done finally sold you on investing.

RUTH   No. Mama, something is happening between Walter and me. I don't know what it is— but he needs something—something I can't give him any more. He needs this chance, Lena.

MAMA   (*frowning deeply*)   But liquor, honey—

RUTH   Well—like Walter say—I spec people going to always be drinking themselves some liquor.

MAMA   Well—whether they drinks it or not ain't none of my business. But whether I go into business selling it to 'em *is,* and I don't want that on my ledger this late in life. (*Stopping suddenly and studying her daughter-in-law*) Ruth Younger, what's the matter with you today? You look like you could fall over right there.

RUTH   I'm tired.

MAMA   Then you better stay home from work today.

RUTH   I can't stay home. She'd be calling up the agency and screaming at them, "My girl didn't come in today—send me somebody! My girl didn't come in!" Oh, she just have a fit. . . .

MAMA   Well, let her have it. I'll just call her up and say you got the flu—

RUTH (*laughing*)   Why the flu?

MAMA   'Cause it sounds respectable to 'em. Something white people get, too. They know 'bout the flu. Otherwise they think you been cut up or something when you tell 'em you sick.

RUTH   I got to go in. We need the money.

MAMA   Somebody would of thought my children done all but starved to death the way they talk about money here late. Child, we got a great big old check coming tomorrow.

RUTH (*sincerely, but also self-righteously*)   Now that's your money. It ain't got nothing to do with me. We all feel like that—Walter and Bennie and me—even Travis.

MAMA (*thoughtfully, and suddenly very far away*)   Ten thousand dollars—

RUTH   Sure is wonderful.

MAMA   Ten thousand dollars.

RUTH   You know what you should do, Miss Lena? You should take yourself a trip somewhere. To Europe or South America or someplace—

MAMA (*throwing up her hands at the thought*)   Oh, child!

RUTH   I'm serious. Just pack up and leave! Go on away and enjoy yourself some. Forget about the family and have yourself a ball for once in your life—

MAMA (*drily*)   You sound like I'm just about ready to die. Who'd go with me? What I look like wandering 'round Europe by myself?

RUTH   Shoot—these here rich white women do it all the time. They don't think nothing of packing up they suitcases and piling on one of them big steamships and—swoosh!—they gone, child.

MAMA   Something always told me I wasn't no rich white woman.

RUTH   Well—what are you going to do with it then?

MAMA   I ain't rightly decided. (*Thinking. She speaks now with emphasis.*) Some of it got to be put away for Beneatha and her schoolin'—and ain't nothing going to touch that part of it. Nothing. (*She waits several seconds, trying to make up her mind about something, and looks at* RUTH *a little tentatively before going on.*) Been thinking that we maybe could meet the notes on a little old two-story somewhere, with a yard where Travis could play in the summertime, if we use part of the insurance for a down payment and everybody kind of pitch in. I could maybe take on a little day work again, few days a week—

RUTH (*studying her mother-in-law furtively and concentrating on her ironing, anxious to encourage without seeming to*)   Well, Lord knows, we've put enough rent into this here rat trap to pay for four houses by now. . . .

MAMA (*looking up at the words "rat trap" and then looking around*

and leaning back and sighing—in a suddenly reflective mood—)
"Rat trap"—yes, that's all it is. (*Smiling*) I remember just as well
the day me and Big Walter moved in here. Hadn't been married
but two weeks and wasn't planning on living here no more than
a year. (*She shakes her head at the dissolved dream.*) We was
going to set away, little by little, don't you know, and buy a little
place out in Morgan Park. We had even picked out the house.
(*Chuckling a little*) Looks right dumpy today. But Lord, child,
you should know all the dreams I had 'bout buying that house
and fixing it up and making me a little garden in the back—
(*She waits and stops smiling.*) And didn't none of it happen.
(*Dropping her hands in a futile gesture*)

RUTH (*keeps her head down, ironing*) Yes, life can be a barrel of
disappointments, sometimes.

MAMA Honey, Big Walter would come in here some nights back
then and slump down on that couch there and just look at the
rug, and look at me and look at the rug and then back at me—
and I'd know he was down then... really down. (*After a second
very long and thoughtful pause; she is seeing back to times that
only she can see.*) And then, Lord, when I lost that baby—little
Claude—I almost thought I was going to lose Big Walter too.
Oh, that man grieved hisself! He was one man to love his children.

RUTH Ain't nothin' can tear at you like losin' your baby.

MAMA I guess that's how come that man finally worked hisself to
death like he done. Like he was fighting his own war with this
here world that took his baby from him.

RUTH He sure was a fine man, all right. I always liked Mr.
Younger.

MAMA Crazy 'bout his children! God knows there was plenty wrong
with Walter Younger—hard-headed, mean, kind of wild with
women—plenty wrong with him. But he sure loved his children.
Always wanted them to have something—be something. That's
where Brother gets all these notions, I reckon. Big Walter used
to say, he'd get right wet in the eyes sometimes, lean his head
back with the water standing in his eyes and say, "Seem like God
didn't see fit to give the black man nothing but dreams—but He
did give us children to make them dreams seem worth while."
(*She smiles.*) He could talk like that, don't you know.

RUTH Yes, he sure could. He was a good man, Mr. Younger.

MAMA Yes, a fine man—just couldn't never catch up with his
dreams, that's all.

(BENEATHA *comes in, brushing her hair and looking up to the ceiling,
where the sound of a vacuum cleaner has started up.*)

BENEATHA   What could be so dirty on that woman's rugs that she has to vacuum them every single day?

RUTH   I wish certain young women 'round here who I could name would take inspiration about certain rugs in a certain apartment I could also mention.

BENEATHA (*shrugging*)   How much cleaning can a house need, for Christ's sakes.

MAMA (*not liking the Lord's name used thus*)   Bennie!

RUTH   Just listen to her—just listen!

BENEATHA   Oh, God!

MAMA   If you use the Lord's name just one more time—

BENEATHA (*a bit of a whine*)   Oh, Mama—

RUTH   Fresh—just fresh as salt, this girl!

BENEATHA (*drily*)   Well—if the salt loses its savor—

MAMA   Now that will do. I just ain't going to have you 'round here reciting the scriptures in vain—you hear me?

BENEATHA   How did I manage to get on everybody's wrong side by just walking into a room?

RUTH   If you weren't so fresh—

BENEATHA   Ruth, I'm twenty years old.

MAMA   What time you be home from school today?

BENEATHA   Kind of late. (*With enthusiasm*) Madeline is going to start my guitar lessons today.

MAMA *and* RUTH *look up with the same expression.*

MAMA   Your *what* kind of lessons?

BENEATHA   Guitar.

RUTH   Oh, Father!

MAMA   How come you done taken it in your mind to learn to play the guitar?

BENEATHA   I just want to, that's all.

MAMA (*smiling*)   Lord, child, don't you know what to do with yourself? How long it going to be before you get tired of this now—like you got tired of that little play-acting group you joined last year? (*Looking at* RUTH) And what was it the year before that?

RUTH   The horseback-riding club for which she bought that fifty-five-dollar riding habit that's been hanging in the closet ever since!

MAMA (*to* BENEATHA)   Why you got to flit so from one thing to another, baby?

BENEATHA (*sharply*)   I just want to learn to play the guitar. Is there anything wrong with that?

MAMA   Ain't nobody trying to stop you. I just wonders sometimes why you has to flit so from one thing to another all the time. You ain't never done nothing with all that camera equipment you brought home—

BENEATHA I don't flit! I—I experiment with different forms of expression—

RUTH Like riding a horse?

BENEATHA —People have to express themselves one way or another.

MAMA What is it you want to express?

BENEATHA (*angrily*) Me! (MAMA *and* RUTH *look at each other and burst into raucous laughter.*) Don't worry—I don't expect you to understand.

MAMA (*to change the subject*) Who you going out with tomorrow night?

BENEATHA (*with displeasure*) George Murchison again.

MAMA (*pleased*) Oh—you getting a little sweet on him?

RUTH You ask me, this child ain't sweet on nobody but herself—(*Underbreath*) Express herself!

They laugh.

BENEATHA Oh—I like George all right, Mama. I mean I like him enough to go out with him and stuff, but—

RUTH (*for devilment*) What does *and stuff* mean?

BENEATHA Mind your own business.

MAMA Stop picking at her now, Ruth. (*A thoughtful pause, and then a suspicious sudden look at her daughter as she turns in her chair for emphasis*) What *does* it mean?

BENEATHA (*wearily*) Oh, I just mean I couldn't ever really be serious about George. He's—he's so shallow.

RUTH Shallow—what do you mean he's shallow? He's *rich!*

MAMA Hush, Ruth.

BENEATHA I know he's rich. He knows he's rich, too.

RUTH Well—what other qualities a man got to have to satisfy you, little girl?

BENEATHA You wouldn't even begin to understand. Anybody who married Walter could not possibly understand.

MAMA (*outraged*) What kind of way is that to talk about your brother?

BENEATHA Brother is a flip—let's face it.

MAMA (*to* RUTH, *helplessly*) What's a flip?

RUTH (*glad to add kindling*) She's saying he's crazy.

BENEATHA Not crazy. Brother isn't really crazy yet—he—he's an elaborate neurotic.

MAMA Hush your mouth!

BENEATHA As for George. Well. George looks good—he's got a beautiful car and he takes me to nice places and, as my sister-in-law says, he is probably the richest boy I will ever get to know and I even like him sometimes—but if the Youngers are sitting around waiting to see if their little Bennie is going to tie up the family with the Murchisons, they are wasting their time.

RUTH   You mean you wouldn't marry George Murchison if he asked you someday? That pretty, rich thing? Honey, I knew you was odd—

BENEATHA   No I would not marry him if all I felt for him was what I feel now. Besides, George's family wouldn't really like it.

MAMA   Why not?

BENEATHA   Oh, Mama—The Murchisons are honest-to-God-real-*live*-rich colored people, and the only people in the world who are more snobbish than rich white people are rich colored people. I thought everybody knew that. I've met Mrs. Murchison. She's a scene!

MAMA   You must not dislike people 'cause they well off, honey.

BENEATHA   Why not? It makes just as much sense as disliking people 'cause they are poor, and lots of people do that.

RUTH   (*a wisdom-of-the-ages manner; to* MAMA)   Well, she'll get over some of this—

BENEATHA   Get over it? What are you talking about, Ruth? Listen, I'm going to be a doctor. I'm not worried about who I'm going to marry yet—if I ever get married.

MAMA *and* RUTH   *If!*

MAMA   Now, Bennie—

BENEATHA   Oh, I probably will . . . but first I'm going to be a doctor, and George, for one, still think's that's pretty funny. I couldn't be bothered with that, I am going to be a doctor and everybody around here better understand that!

MAMA   (*kindly*)   'Course you going to be a doctor, honey, God willing.

BENEATHA   (*drily*)   God hasn't got a thing to do with it.

MAMA   Beneatha—that just wasn't necessary.

BENEATHA   Well—neither is God. I get sick of hearing about God.

MAMA   Beneatha!

BENEATHA   I mean it! I'm just tired of hearing about God all the time. What has He got to do with anything? Does He pay tuition?

MAMA   You 'bout to get your fresh little jaw slapped!

RUTH   That's just what she needs, all right!

BENEATHA   Why? Why can't I say what I want to around here, like everybody else?

MAMA   It don't sound nice for a young girl to say things like that— you wasn't brought up that way. Me and your father went to trouble to get you and Brother to church every Sunday.

BENEATHA   Mama, you don't understand. It's all a matter of ideas, and God is just one idea I don't accept. It's not important, I am not going out and be immoral or commit crimes because I don't believe in God. I don't even think about it. It's just that I get tired of Him getting credit for all the things the human race achieves through its own stubborn effort. There simply is no blasted God—there is only man and it is he who makes miracles!

MAMA *absorbs this speech, studies her daughter and rises slowly and crosses to* BENEATHA *and slaps her powerfully across the face. After, there is only silence and the daughter drops her eyes from her mother's face, and* MAMA *is very tall before her.*

MAMA   Now—you say after me, in my mother's house there is still God. (*There is a long pause and* BENEATHA *stares at the floor wordlessly.* MAMA *repeats the phrase with precision and cool emotion.*) In my mother's house there is still God.

BENEATHA   In my mother's house there is still God.

A long pause.

MAMA (*walking away from* BENEATHA, *too disturbed for triumphant posture; stopping and turning back to her daughter*)   There are some ideas we ain't going to have in this house. Not long as I am at the head of this family.

BENEATHA   Yes, ma'am.

(MAMA *walks out of the room.*)

RUTH (*almost gently, with profound understanding*)   You think you a woman, Bennie—but you still a little girl. What you did was childish—so you got treated like a child.

BENEATHA   I see. (*Quietly*) I also see that everybody thinks it's all right for Mama to be a tyrant. But all the tyranny in the world will never put a God in the heavens! (*She picks up her books and goes out.*)

RUTH (*goes to* MAMA's *door*)   She said she was sorry.

MAMA (*coming out, going to her plant*)   They frightens me, Ruth. My children.

RUTH   You got good children, Lena. They just a little off sometimes—but they're good.

MAMA   No—there's something come down between me and them that don't let us understand each other and I don't know what it is. One done almost lost his mind thinking 'bout money all the time and the other done commence to talk about things I can't seem to understand in no form or fashion. What is it that's changing, Ruth?

RUTH (*soothingly, older than her years*)   Now . . . you taking it all too seriously. You just got strong-willed children and it takes a strong woman like you to keep 'em in hand.

MAMA (*looking at her plant and sprinkling a little water on it*) They spirited all right, my children. Got to admit they got spirit— Bennie and Walter. Like this little old plant that ain't never had enough sunshine or nothing—and look at it. . . .

She has her back to RUTH, *who has had to stop ironing and lean against something and put the back of her hand to her forehead.*

RUTH (*trying to keep* MAMA *from noticing*)   You . . . sure . . . loves that little old thing, don't you? . . .

MAMA   Well, I always wanted me a garden like I used to see some-times at the back of the houses down home. This plant is close as I ever got to having one. (*She looks out of the window as she replaces the plant.*) Lord, ain't nothing as dreary as the view from this window on a dreary day, is there? Why ain't you singing this morning, Ruth? Sing that "No Ways Tired." That song always lifts me up so—(*She turns at last to see that* RUTH *has slipped quietly into a chair, in a state of semiconsciousness.*) Ruth! Ruth honey—what's the matter with you . . . Ruth!

Curtain

Scene II

It is the following morning; a Saturday morning, and house cleaning is in progress at the YOUNGERS. *Furniture has been shoved hither and yon and* MAMA *is giving the kitchen-area walls a washing down.* BENEATHA, *in dungarees, with a handkerchief tied around her face, is spraying insecticide into the cracks in the walls. As they work, the radio is on and a Southside disc-jockey program is inappropriately filling the house with a rather exotic saxophone blues.* TRAVIS, *the sole idle one, is leaning on his arms, looking out of the window.*

TRAVIS   Grandmama, that stuff Bennie is using smells awful. Can I go downstairs, please?

MAMA   Did you get all them chores done already? I ain't see you doing much.

TRAVIS   Yes'm—finished early. Where did Mama go this morning?

MAMA (*looking at* BENEATHA)   She had to go on a little errand.

TRAVIS   Where?

MAMA   To tend to her business.

TRAVIS   Can I go outside then?

MAMA   Oh, I guess so. You better stay right in front of the house, though . . . and keep a good lookout for the postman.

TRAVIS   Yes'm. (*He starts out and decides to give his* AUNT BE-
NEATHA *a good swat on the legs as he passes her.*) Leave them
poor little old cockroaches alone, they ain't bothering you none.

(*He runs as she swings the spray gun at him both viciously and playfully.* WALTER *enters from the bedroom and goes to the phone.*)

MAMA   Look out there, girl, before you be spilling some of that stuff
on that child!

TRAVIS   (*teasing*)   That's right—look out now! (*He exits.*)

BENEATHA   (*drily*)   I can't imagine that it would hurt him—it has
never hurt the roaches.

MAMA   Well, little boys' hides ain't as tough as Southside roaches.

WALTER   (*into phone*)   Hello—Let me talk to Willy Harris.

MAMA   You better get over there behind the bureau. I seen one
marching out of there like Napoleon yesterday.

WALTER   Hello. Willy? It ain't come yet. It'll be here in a few minutes. Did the lawyer give you the papers?

BENEATHA   There's really only one way to get rid of them, Mama –

MAMA   How?

BENEATHA   Set fire to this building.

WALTER   Good. Good. I'll be right over.

BENEATHA   Where did Ruth go, Walter?

WALTER   I don't know. (*He exits abruptly.*)

BENEATHA   Mama, where did Ruth go?

MAMA   (*looking at her with meaning*)   To the doctor, I think.

BENEATHA   The doctor? What's the matter? (*They exchange
glances.*) You don't think—

MAMA   (*with her sense of drama*)   Now I ain't saying what I think.
But I ain't never been wrong 'bout a woman neither.

The phone rings.

BENEATHA   (*at the phone*)   Hay-lo ... (*Pause, and a moment of
recognition*) Well—when did you get back! ... And how was it?
... Of course I've missed you—in my way.... This morning?
No ... house cleaning and all that and Mama hates it if I let
people come over when the house is like this.... You *have*?
Well, that's different.... What is it— Oh, what the hell, come
on over.... Right, see you then. (*She hangs up.*)

MAMA   (*who has listened vigorously, as is her habit*)   Who is that
you inviting over here with this house looking like this? You ain't
got the pride you was born with!

BENEATHA   Asagai doesn't care how houses look, Mama—he's an
intellectual.

MAMA   *Who?*

BENEATHA Asagai—Joseph Asagai. He's an African boy I met on campus. He's been studying in Canada all summer.

MAMA What's his name?

BENEATHA Asagai, Joseph. Ah-sah-guy . . . He's from Nigeria.

MAMA Oh, that's the little country that was founded by slaves way back. . . .

BENEATHA No, Mama—that's Liberia.

MAMA I don't think I never met no African before.

BENEATHA Well, do me a favor and don't ask him a whole lot of ignorant questions about Africans. I mean, do they wear clothes and all that—

MAMA Well, now, I guess if you think we so ignorant 'round here maybe you shouldn't bring your friends here—

BENEATHA It's just that people ask such crazy things. All anyone seems to know about when it comes to Africa is Tarzan—

MAMA (*indignantly*) Why should I know anything about Africa?

BENEATHA Why do you give money at church for the missionary work?

MAMA Well, that's to help save people.

BENEATHA You mean to save them from *heathenism*—

MAMA (*innocently*) Yes.

BENEATHA I'm afraid they need more salvation from the British and the French.

(RUTH *comes in forlornly and pulls off her coat with dejection. They both turn to look at her.*)

RUTH (*dispiritedly*) Well, I guess from all the happy faces—everybody knows.

BENEATHA You pregnant?

MAMA Lord have mercy, I sure hope it's a little old girl. Travis ought to have a sister.

BENEATHA *and* RUTH *give her a hopeless look for this grandmotherly enthusiasm.*

BENEATHA How far along are you?

RUTH Two months.

BENEATHA Did you mean to? I mean did you plan it or was it an accident?

MAMA What do you know about planning or not planning?

BENEATHA Oh, Mama.

RUTH (*wearily*) She's twenty years old, Lena.

BENEATHA Did you plan it, Ruth?

RUTH Mind your own business.

BENEATHA It is my business—where is he going to live, on the *roof?*

(There is silence following the remark as the three women react to the sense of it.) Gee—I didn't mean that, Ruth, honest. Gee, I don't feel like that at all. I—I think it is wonderful.

RUTH *(dully)* Wonderful.

BENEATHA Yes—really.

MAMA *(looking at* RUTH, *worried)* Doctor say everything going to be all right?

RUTH *(far away)* Yes—she says everything is going to be fine. . . .

MAMA *(immediately suspicious)* "She"—What doctor you went to?

RUTH *folds over, near hysteria.*

MAMA *(worriedly hovering over* RUTH*)* Ruth honey—what's the matter with you—you sick?

RUTH *has her fists clenched on her thighs and is fighting hard to suppress a scream that seems to be rising in her.*

BENEATHA What's the matter with her, Mama?

MAMA *(working her fingers in* RUTH's *shoulder to relax her)* She be all right. Women gets right depressed sometimes when they get her way. *(Speaking softly, expertly, rapidly)* Now you just relax. That's right . . . just lean back, don't think 'bout nothing at all . . . nothing at all—

RUTH I'm all right. . . .

The glassy-eyed look melts and then she collapses into a fit of heavy sobbing. The bell rings.

BENEATHA Oh, my God— that must be Asagai.

MAMA *(to* RUTH*)* Come on now, honey. You need to lie down and rest awhile . . . then have some nice hot food.

(They exit, RUTH's *weight on her mother-in-law.* BENEATHA, *herself profoundly disturbed, opens the door to admit a rather dramatic-looking young man with a large package.)*

ASAGAI Hello, Alaiyo—

BENEATHA *(holding the door open and regarding him with pleasure)* Hello . . . *(Long pause)* Well—come in. And please excuse everything. My mother was very upset about my letting anyone come here with the place like this.

ASAGAI *(coming into the room)* You look disturbed too. . . . Is something wrong?

BENEATHA *(still at the door, absently)* Yes . . . we've all got acute ghetto-itis. *(She smiles and comes toward him, finding a cigarette and sitting.)* So—sit down! How was Canada?

ASAGAI (*a sophisticate*)   Canadian.

BENEATHA (*looking at him*)   I'm very glad you are back.

ASAGAI (*looking back at her in turn*)   Are you really?

BENEATHA   Yes—very.

ASAGAI   Why—you were quite glad when I went away. What happened?

BENEATHA   You went away.

ASAGAI   Ahhhhhhhh.

BENEATHA   Before—you wanted to be so serious before there was time.

ASAGAI   How much time must there be before one knows what one feels?

BENEATHA (*stalling this particular conversation; her hands pressed together, in a deliberately childish gesture*)   What did you bring me?

ASAGAI (*handing her the package*)   Open it and see.

BENEATHA (*eagerly opening the package and drawing out some records and the colorful robes of a Nigerian woman*)   Oh, Asagai! . . . You got them for me! . . . How beautiful . . . and the records too! (*She lifts out the robes and runs to the mirror with them and holds the drapery up in front of herself.*)

ASAGAI (*coming to her at the mirror*)   I shall have to teach you how to drape it properly. (*He flings the material about her for the moment and stands back to look at her.*) Ah—*Oh-pay-gay-day, oh-gbah-mu-shay.* (*A Yoruba exclamation for admiration*) You wear it well . . . very well . . . mutilated hair and all.

BENEATHA (*turning suddenly*)   My hair—what's wrong with my hair?

ASAGAI (*shrugging*)   Were you born with it like that?

BENEATHA (*reaching up to touch it*)   No . . . of course not. (*She looks back to the mirror, disturbed.*)

ASAGAI (*smiling*)   How then?

BENEATHA   You know perfectly well how . . . as crinkly as yours . . . that's how.

ASAGAI   And it is ugly to you that way?

BENEATHA (*quickly*)   Oh, no—not ugly . . . (*More slowly, apologetically*) But it's so hard to manage when it's well—raw.

ASAGAI   And so to accommodate that—you mutilate it every week?

BENEATHA   It's not mutilation!

ASAGAI (*laughing aloud at her seriousness*)   Oh . . . please! I am only teasing you because you are so very serious about these things. (*He stands back from her and folds his arms across his chest as he watches her pulling at her hair and frowning in the mirror.*) Do you remember the first time you met me at school? . . . (*He *laughs.*) You came up to me and you said—and I thought you were the most serious little thing I had ever seen—you said: (*He imitates her.*) "Mr. Asagai—I want very much to talk with you. About Africa. You see, Mr. Asagai, I am looking for my *identity!*" (*He laughs.*)

BENEATHA (*turning to him, not laughing*) Yes—(*Her face is quizzical, profoundly disturbed.*)

ASAGAI (*still teasing and reaching out and taking her face in his hands and turning her profile to him*) Well . . . it is true that this is not so much a profile of a Hollywood queen as perhaps a queen of the Nile—(*A mock dismissal of the importance of the question*) But what does it matter? Assimilationism is so popular in your country.

BENEATHA (*wheeling, passionately, sharply*) I am not an assimilationist!

ASAGAI (*the protest hangs in the room for a moment and* ASAGAI *studies her, his laughter fading*) Such a serious one. (*There is a pause.*) So—you like the robes? You must take excellent care of them—they are from my sister's personal wardrobe.

BENEATHA (*with incredulity*) You—you sent all the way home—for me?

ASAGAI (*with charm*) For you—I would do much more. . . . Well, that is what I came for. I must go.

BENEATHA Will you call me Monday?

ASAGAI Yes . . . We have a great deal to talk about. I mean about identity and time and all that.

BENEATHA Time?

ASAGAI Yes. About how much time one needs to know what one feels.

BENEATHA You never understood that there is more than one kind of feeling which can exist between a man and a woman—or, at least, there should be.

ASAGAI (*shaking his head negatively but gently*) No. Between a man and a woman there need be only one kind of feeling. I have that for you. . . . Now even . . . right this moment. . . .

BENEATHA I know—and by itself—it won't do. I can find that anywhere.

ASAGAI For a woman it should be enough.

BENEATHA I know—because that's what it says in all the novels that men write. But it isn't. Go ahead and laugh—but I'm not interested in being someone's little episode in America or—(*with feminine vengeance*)—one of them! (ASAGAI *has burst into laughter again.*) That's funny as hell, huh!

ASAGAI It's just that every American girl I have known has said that to me. White—black—in this you are all the same. And the same speech, too!

BENEATHA (*angrily*)   Yuk, yuk, yuk!

ASAGAI   It's how you can be sure that the world's most liberated women are not liberated at all. You all talk about it too much!

(MAMA *enters and is immediately all social charm because of the presence of a guest.*)

BENEATHA   Oh—Mama—this is Mr. Asagai.

MAMA   How do you do?

ASAGAI (*total politeness to an elder*)   How do you do, Mrs. Younger. Please forgive me for coming at such an outrageous hour on a Saturday.

MAMA   Well, you are quite welcome. I just hope you understand that our house don't always look like this. (*Chatterish*) You must come again. I would love to hear all about—(*not sure of the name*)—your country. I think it's so sad the way our American Negroes don't know nothing about Africa 'cept Tarzan and all that. And all that money they pour into these churches when they ought to be helping you people over there drive out them French and Englishmen done taken away your land.

The mother flashes a slightly superior look at her daughter upon completion of the recitation.

ASAGAI (*taken aback by this sudden and acutely unrelated expression of sympathy*)   Yes . . . yes. . . .

MAMA (*smiling at him suddenly and relaxing and looking him over*)   How many miles is it from here to where you come from?

ASAGAI   Many thousands.

MAMA (*looking at him as she would* WALTER)   I bet you don't half look after yourself, being away from your mama either. I spec you better come 'round here from time to time and get yourself some decent home-cooked meals. . . .

ASAGAI (*moved*)   Thank you. Thank you very much. (*They are all quiet, then—*) Well . . . I must go. I will call you Monday, Alaiyo.

MAMA   What's that he call you?

ASAGAI   Oh—"Alaiyo." I hope you don't mind. It is what you would call a nickname, I think. It is a Yoruba word. I am a Yoruba.

MAMA (*looking at* BENEATHA)   I—I thought he was from—

ASAGAI (*understanding*)   Nigeria is my country. Yoruba is my tribal origin—

BENEATHA   You didn't tell us what Alaiyo means . . . for all I know, you might be calling me Little Idiot or something. . . .

ASAGAI   Well . . . let me see . . . I do not know how just to explain it.

... The sense of a thing can be so different when it changes languages.

BENEATHA You're evading.

ASAGAI No—really it is difficult. ... (*Thinking*) It means ... it means One for Whom Bread—Food—Is Not Enough. (*He looks at her.*) Is that all right?

BENEATHA (*understanding, softly*) Thank you.

MAMA (*looking from one to the other and not understanding any of it*) Well ... that's nice. ... You must come see us again—Mr.—

ASAGAI Ah-sah-guy ...

MAMA Yes ... Do come again.

ASAGAI Good-bye. (*He exits.*)

MAMA (*after him*) Lord, that's a pretty thing just went out here! (*Insinuatingly, to her daughter*) Yes, I guess I see why we done commence to get so interested in Africa 'round here. Missionaries my aunt Jenny! (*She exits.*)

BENEATHA Oh, Mama! ...

(*She picks up the Nigerian dress and holds it up to her in front of the mirror again. She sets the headdress on haphazardly and then notices her hair again and clutches at it and then replaces the headdress and frowns at herself. Then she starts to wriggle in front of the mirror as she thinks a Nigerian woman might.* TRAVIS *enters and regards her.*)

TRAVIS You cracking up?

BENEATHA Shut up.

She pulls the headdress off and looks at herself in the mirror and clutches at her hair again and squinches her eyes as if trying to imagine something. Then, suddenly, she gets her raincoat and kerchief and hurriedly prepares for going out.

MAMA (*coming back into the room*) She's resting now. Travis, baby, run next door and ask Miss Johnson to please let me have a little kitchen cleanser. This here can is empty as Jacob's kettle.

TRAVIS I just come in.

MAMA Do as you told. (*He exits and she looks at her daughter.*) Where you going?

BENEATHA (*halting at the door*) To become a queen of the Nile!

(*She exits in a breathless blaze of glory.* RUTH *appears in the bedroom doorway.*)

MAMA Who told you to get up?

RUTH Ain't nothing wrong with me to be lying in no bed for. Where did Bennie go?

MAMA (*drumming her fingers*) Far as I could make out—to Egypt. (RUTH *just looks at her.*) What time is it getting to?

RUTH   Ten twenty. And the mailman going to ring that bell this morning just like he done every morning for the last umpteen years.

(TRAVIS *comes in with the cleanser can.*)

TRAVIS   She say to tell you that she don't have much.

MAMA (*angrily*)   Lord, some people I could name sure is tight-fisted! (*Directing her grandson*) Mark two cans of cleanser down on the list there. If she that hard up for kitchen cleanser, I sure don't want to forget to get her none!

RUTH   Lena—maybe the woman is just short on cleanser—

MAMA (*not listening*)   —Much baking powder as she done borrowed from me all these years, she could of done gone into the baking business!

The bell sounds suddenly and sharply and all three are stunned—serious and silent—mid-speech. In spite of all the other conversations and distractions of the morning, this is what they have been waiting for, even TRAVIS, *who looks helplessly from his mother to his grandmother.* RUTH *is the first to come to life again.*

RUTH (*to* TRAVIS)   *Get down them steps, boy!*

(TRAVIS *snaps to life and flies out to get the mail.*)

MAMA (*her eyes wide, her hand to her breast*)   You mean it done really come?

RUTH (*excitedly*)   Oh, Miss Lena!

MAMA (*collecting herself*)   Well . . . I don't know what we all so excited about 'round here for. We known it was coming for months.

RUTH   That's a whole lot different from having it come and being able to hold it in your hands . . . a piece of paper worth ten thousand dollars. . . . (TRAVIS *bursts back into the room. He holds the envelope high above his head, like a little dancer, his face is radiant and he is breathless. He moves to his grandmother with sudden slow ceremony and puts the envelope into her hands. She accepts it, and then merely holds it and looks at it.*) Come on! Open it . . . Lord have mercy, I wish Walter Lee was here!

TRAVIS   Open it, Grandmama!

MAMA (*staring at it*)   Now you all be quiet. It's just a check.

RUTH   *Open it. . . .*

MAMA (*still staring at it*)   Now don't act silly. . . . We ain't never been no people to act silly 'bout no money—

RUTH (*swiftly*)   We ain't never had none before—*open it!*

MAMA *finally makes a good strong tear and pulls out the thin blue slice of paper and inspects it closely. The boy and his mother study it raptly over* MAMA'S *shoulders.*

MAMA   *Travis! (She is counting off with doubt.)* Is that the right number of zeros.

TRAVIS   Yes'm . . . ten thousand dollars. Gaalee, Grandmama, you rich.

MAMA   *(She holds the check away from her, still looking at it. Slowly her face sobers into a mask of unhappiness)* Ten thousand dollars. *(She hands it to* RUTH.) Put it away somewhere, Ruth. *(She does not look at* RUTH; *her eyes seem to be seeing something somewhere very far off.)* Ten thousand dollars they give you. Ten thousand dollars.

TRAVIS   *(to his mother, sincerely)* What's the matter with Grandmama—don't she want to be rich?

RUTH   *(distractedly)* You go on out and play now, baby. *(*TRAVIS *exits.* MAMA *starts wiping dishes absently, humming intently to herself.* RUTH *turns to her, with kind exasperation.)* You're gone and got yourself upset.

MAMA   *(not looking at her)* I spec if it wasn't for you all . . . I would just put that money away or give it to the church or something.

RUTH   Now what kind of talk is that. Mr. Younger would just be plain mad if he could hear you talking foolish like that.

MAMA   *(stopping and staring off)* Yes . . . he sure would. *(Sighing)* We got enough to do with that money, all right. *(She halts then, and turns and looks at her daughter-in-law hard;* RUTH *avoids her eyes and* MAMA *wipes her hands with finality and starts to speak firmly to* RUTH.) Where did you go today, girl?

RUTH   To the doctor.

MAMA   *(impatiently)* Now, Ruth . . . you know better than that. Old Doctor Jones is strange enough in his way but there ain't nothing 'bout him make somebody slip and call him "she"—like you done this morning.

RUTH   Well, that's what happened—my tongue slipped.

MAMA   You went to see that woman, didn't you?

RUTH   *(defensively, giving herself away)* What woman you talking about?

MAMA   *(angrily)* That woman who—

*(*WALTER *enters in great excitement.)*

WALTER   Did it come?

MAMA   *(quietly)* Can't you give people a Christian greeting before you start asking about money?

WALTER (*to* RUTH) Did it come? (RUTH *unfolds the check and lays it quietly before him, watching him intently with thoughts of her own.* WALTER *sits down and grasps it close and counts off the zeros.*) Ten thousand dollars—(*He turns suddenly, frantically to his mother and draws some papers out of his breast pocket.*) Mama—look. Old Willy Harris put everything on paper—

MAMA Son—I think you ought to talk to your wife. . . . I'll go on out and leave you alone if you want—

WALTER I can talk to her later—Mama, look—

MAMA Son—

WALTER WILL SOMEBODY PLEASE LISTEN TO ME TO-DAY!

MAMA (*quietly*) I don't 'low no yellin' in this house, Walter Lee, and you know it—(WALTER *stares at them in frustration and starts to speak several times.*) And there ain't going to be no investing in no liquor stores. I don't aim to have to speak on that again.

A long pause.

WALTER Oh—so you don't aim to have to speak on that again? So *you* have decided. . . . (*Crumpling his papers*) Well, *you* tell that to my boy tonight when you put him to sleep on the living-room couch. . . . (*Turning to* MAMA *and speaking directly to her*) Yeah —and tell it to my wife, MAMA, tomorrow when she has to go out of here to look after somebody else's kids. And tell it to *me,* Mama, every time we need a new pair of curtains and I have to watch *you* go out and work in somebody's kitchen. Yeah, you tell me then!

(WALTER *starts out.*)

RUTH Where you going?

WALTER I'm going out!

RUTH Where?

WALTER Just out of this house somewhere—

RUTH (*getting her coat*) I'll come too.

WALTER I don't want you to come!

RUTH I got something to talk to you about, Walter.

WALTER That's too bad.

MAMA (*still quietly*) Walter Lee—(*She waits and he finally turns and looks at her.*) Sit down.

WALTER I'm a grown man, Mama.

MAMA Ain't nobody said you wasn't grown. But you still in my house and my presence. And as long as you are—you'll talk to your wife civil. Now sit down.

RUTH (*suddenly*)   Oh, let him go on out and drink himself to death! He makes me sick to my stomach! (*She flings her coat against him.*)

WALTER (*violently*)   And you turn mine too, baby! (RUTH *goes into their bedroom and slams the door behind her.*) That was my greatest mistake—

MAMA (*still quietly*)   Walter, what is the matter with you?

WALTER   Matter with me? Ain't nothing the matter with *me!*

MAMA   Yes there is. Something eating you up like a crazy man. Something more than me not giving you this money. The past few years I been watching it happen to you. You get all nervous acting and kind of wild in the eyes—(WALTER *jumps up impatiently at her words.*) I said sit there now, I'm talking to you!

WALTER   Mama—I don't need no nagging at me today.

MAMA   Seem like you getting to a place where you always tied up in some kind of knot about something. But if anybody ask you 'bout it you just yell at 'em and bust out the house and go out and drink somewheres. Walter Lee, people can't live with that. Ruth's a good, patient girl in her way—but you getting to be too much. Boy, don't make the mistake of driving that girl away from you.

WALTER   Why—what she do for me?

MAMA   She loves you.

WALTER   Mama—I'm going out. I want to go off somewhere and be by myself for a while.

MAMA   I'm sorry 'bout your liquor store, son. It just wasn't the thing for us to do. That's what I want to tell you about—

WALTER   I got to go out, Mama—(*He rises.*)

MAMA   It's dangerous, son.

WALTER   What's dangerous?

MAMA   When a man goes outside his home to look for peace.

WALTER (*beseechingly*)   Then why can't there never be no peace in this house then?

MAMA   You done found it in some other house?

WALTER   No—there ain't no woman! Why do women always think there's a woman somewhere when a man gets restless. (*Coming to her*) Mama—Mama—I want so many things. . . .

MAMA   Yes, son—

WALTER   I want so many things that they are driving me kind of crazy. . . . Mama—look at me.

MAMA   I'm looking at you. You a good-looking boy. You got a job, a nice wife, a fine boy and—

WALTER   A job. (*Looks at her*) Mama, a job? I open and close car doors all day long. I drive a man around in his limousine and I say, "Yes, sir; no, sir; very good, sir; shall I take the Drive, sir?" Mama, that ain't no kind of job ... that ain't nothing at all. (*Very quietly*) Mama, I don't know if I can make you understand.

MAMA   Understand what, baby?

WALTER (*quietly*)   Sometimes it's like I can see the future stretched out in front of me—just plain as day. The future, Mama. Hanging over there at the edge of my days. Just waiting for me—a big, looming blank space—full of *nothing*. Just waiting for *me*. (*Pause*) Mama—sometimes when I'm downtown and I pass them cool, quiet-looking restaurants where them white boys are sitting back and talking 'bout things ... sitting there turning deals worth millions of dollars ... sometimes I see guys don't look much older than me—

MAMA   Son—how come you talk so much 'bout money?

WALTER (*with immense passion*)   Because it is life, Mama!

MAMA (*quietly*)   Oh—(*Very quietly*) So now it's life. Money is life. Once upon a time freedom used to be life—now it's money. I guess the world really do change. . . .

WALTER   No—it was always money, Mama. We just didn't know about it.

MAMA   No ... something has changed. (*She looks at him.*) You something new, boy. In my time we was worried about not being lynched and getting to the North if we could and how to stay alive and still have a pinch of dignity too. . . . Now here come you and Beneatha—talking 'bout things we ain't never even thought about hardly, me and your daddy. You ain't satisfied or proud of nothing we done. I mean that you had a home; that we kept you out of trouble till you was grown; that you don't have to ride to work on the back of nobody's streetcar—You my children—but how different we done become.

WALTER   You just don't understand, Mama, you just don't understand.

MAMA   Son—do you know your wife is expecting another baby? (WALTER *stands, stunned, and absorbs what his mother has said.*) That's what she wanted to talk to you about. (WALTER *sinks down into a chair.*) This ain't for me to be telling—but you ought to know. (*She waits.*) I think Ruth is thinking 'bout getting rid of that child.

WALTER (*slowly understanding*)   No—no—Ruth wouldn't do that.

MAMA   When the world gets ugly enough—a woman will do anything for her family. *The part that's already living.*

WALTER   You don't know Ruth, Mama, if you think she would do that.

(RUTH *opens the bedroom door and stands there a little limp.*)

RUTH (*beaten*) Yes I would too, Walter. (*Pause*) I gave her a five-dollar down payment.

There is total silence as the man stares at his wife and the mother stares at her son.

MAMA (*presently*) Well—(*Tightly*) Well—son, I'm waiting to hear you say something.... I'm waiting to hear how you be your father's son. Be the man he was.... (*Pause*) Your wife say she going to destroy your child. And I'm waiting to hear you talk like him and say we a people who give children life, not who destroys them—(*She rises.*) I'm waiting to see you stand up and look like your daddy and say we done give up one baby to poverty and that we ain't going to give up nary another one.... I'm waiting.

WALTER Ruth—

MAMA If you a son of mine, tell her! (WALTER *turns, looks at her and can say nothing. She continues, bitterly.*) You ... you are a disgrace to your father's memory. Somebody get me my hat.

Curtain

ACT II

Scene I

Time: Later the same day.
At rise: RUTH *is ironing again. She has the radio going. Presently BE-*NEATHA's *bedroom door opens and* RUTH's *mouth falls and she puts down the iron in fascination.*

RUTH What have we got on tonight!

BENEATHA (*emerging grandly from the doorway so that we can see her thoroughly robed in the costume* ASAGAI *brought*) You are looking at what a well-dressed Nigerian woman wears—(*She parades for* RUTH, *her hair completely hidden by the headdress; she is coquettishly fanning herself with an ornate oriental fan, mistakenly more like Butterfly than any Nigerian that ever was.*) Isn't it beautiful? (*She promenades to the radio and, with an arrogant flourish, turns off the good loud blues that is playing.*) Enough of this assimilationist junk! (RUTH *follows her with her eyes as she goes to the phonograph and puts on a record and turns and waits ceremoniously for the music to come up. Then, with a shout—*) OCOMOGOSIAY!

RUTH *jumps. The music comes up, a lovely Nigerian melody.* BENEATHA *listens, enraptured, her eyes far away—"back to the past." She begins to dance.* RUTH *is dumfounded.*

RUTH   What kind of dance is that?

BENEATHA   A folk dance.

RUTH (*Pearl Bailey*)   What kind of folks do that, honey?

BENEATHA   It's from Nigeria. It's a dance of welcome.

RUTH   Who you welcoming?

BENEATHA   The men back to the village.

RUTH   Where they been?

BENEATHA   How should I know—out hunting or something. Anyway, they are coming back now. . . .

RUTH   Well, that's good.

BENEATHA (*with the record*)

Alundi, alundi
Alundi alunya
Jop pu a jeepua
Ang gu soooooooooo

Ai yai yae . . .
Ayehaye—alundi . . .

(WALTER *comes in during this performance; he has obviously been drinking. He leans against the door heavily and watches his sister, at first with distaste. Then his eyes look off—"back to the past"—as he lifts both his fists to the roof, screaming.*)

WALTER   YEAH . . . AND ETHIOPIA STRETCH FORTH HER HANDS AGAIN! . . .

RUTH (*drily, looking at him*)   Yes—and Africa sure is claiming her own tonight. (*She gives them both up and starts ironing again.*)

WALTER (*all in a drunken, dramatic shout*)   Shut up! . . . I'm digging them drums . . . them drums move me! . . . (*He makes his weaving way to his wife's face and leans in close to her.*) In my heart of hearts—(*he thumps his chest*)—I am much warrior!

RUTH (*without even looking up*)   In your heart of hearts you are much drunkard.

WALTER (*coming away from her and starting to wander around the room, shouting*)   Me and Jomo . . . (*Intently, in his sister's face. She has stopped dancing to watch him in this unknown mood.*) That's my man, Kenyatta. (*Shouting and thumping his chest*) FLAMING SPEAR! HOT DAMN! (*He is suddenly in possession of an imaginary spear and actively spearing enemies all over the room.*) OCOMOGOSIAY . . . THE LION IS WAKING . . . . OWIMOWEH! (*He pulls his shirt open and leaps up on a table and gestures with his spear. The bell rings.* RUTH *goes to answer.*)

BENEATHA (*to encourage* WALTER, *thoroughly caught up with this side of him*) OCOMOGOSIAY, FLAMING SPEAR!

WALTER (*on the table, very far gone, his eyes pure glass sheets; he sees what we cannot, that he is a leader of his people, a great chief, a descendant of Chaka, and that the hour to march has come*) Listen, my black broth—ers—

BENEATHA OCOMOGOSIAY!

WALTER —Do you hear the waters rushing against the shores of the coastlands—

BENEATHA OCOMOGOSIAY!

WALTER —Do you hear the screeching of the cocks in yonder hills beyond where the chiefs meet in council for the coming of the mighty war—

BENEATHA OCOMOGOSIAY!

WALTER — Do you hear the beating of the wings of the birds flying low over the mountains and the low places of our land—

(RUTH *opens the door.* GEORGE MURCHISON *enters.*)

BENEATHA OCOMOGOSIAY!

WALTER —Do you hear the singing of the women, singing the war songs of our fathers to the babies in the great houses . . . singing the sweet war songs? OH, DO YOU HEAR, MY BLACK BROTHERS!

BENEATHA (*completely gone*) We hear you, Flaming Spear—

WALTER Telling us to prepare for the greatness of the time—(*To* GEORGE) Black Brother! (*He extends his hand for the fraternal clasp.*)

GEORGE Black Brother, hell!

RUTH (*having had enough, and embarrassed for the family*) Beneatha, you got company—what's the matter with you? Walter Lee Younger, get down off that table and stop acting like a fool. . . .

(WALTER *comes down off the table suddenly and makes a quick exit to the bathroom.*)

RUTH He's had a little to drink. . . . I don't know what her excuse is.

GEORGE (*to* BENEATHA) Look honey, we're going *to* the theater— we're not going to be *in* it . . . so go change, huh?

RUTH You expect this boy to go out with you looking like that?

BENEATHA (*looking at* GEORGE) That's up to George. If he's ashamed of his heritage—

GEORGE Oh, don't be so proud of yourself, Bennie—just because you look eccentric.

BENEATHA　How can something that's natural be eccentric?

GEORGE　That's what being eccentric means—being natural. Get dressed.

BENEATHA　I don't like that, George.

RUTH　Why must you and your brother make an argument out of everything people say?

BENEATHA　Because I hate assimilationist Negroes!

RUTH　Will somebody please tell me what assimila-whoever means!

GEORGE　Oh, it's just a college girl's way of calling people Uncle Toms—but that isn't what it means at all.

RUTH　Well, what does it mean?

BENEATHA　(*cutting* GEORGE *off and staring at him as she replies to* RUTH)　It means someone who is willing to give up his own culture and submerge himself completely in the dominant, and in this case, *oppressive* culture!

GEORGE　Oh, dear, dear, dear! Here we go! A lecture on the African past! On our Great West African Heritage! In one second we will hear all about the great Ashanti empires; the great Songhay civilizations; and the great sculpture of Bénin—and then some poetry in the Bantu—and the whole monologue will end with the word *heritage!* (*Nastily*) Let's face it, baby, your heritage is nothing but a bunch of raggedy-assed spirituals and some grass huts!

BENEATHA　*Grass huts!* (RUTH *crosses to her and forcibly pushes her toward the bedroom.*) See there ... you are standing there in your splendid ignorance talking about people who were the first to smelt iron on the face of the earth! (RUTH *is pushing her through the door.*) The Ashanti were performing surgical operations when the English—(RUTH *pulls the door to, with* BENEATHA *on the other side, and smiles graciously at* GEORGE. BENEATHA *opens the door and shouts the end of the sentence defiantly at* GEORGE)—were still tattooing themselves with blue dragons.... (*She goes back inside.*)

RUTH　Have a seat, George. (*They both sit.* RUTH *folds her hands rather primly on her lap, determined to demonstrate the civilization of the family.*) Warm, ain't it? I mean for September. (*Pause*) Just like they always say about Chicago weather: If it's too hot or cold for you, just wait a minute and it'll change. (*She smiles happily at this cliché of clichés.*) Everybody say it's got to do with them bombs and things they keep setting off. (*Pause*) Would you like a nice cold beer?

GEORGE　No, thank you. I don't care for beer. (*He looks at his watch.*) I hope she hurries up.

RUTH　What time is the show?

GEORGE It's an eight-thirty curtain. That's just Chicago, though. In New York standard curtain time is eight forty. (*He is rather proud of this knowledge.*)

RUTH (*properly appreciating it*) You get to New York a lot?

GEORGE (*offhand*) Few times a year.

RUTH Oh—that's nice. I've never been to New York.

(WALTER *enters. We feel he has relieved himself, but the edge of unreality is still with him.*)

WALTER New York ain't got nothing Chicago ain't. Just a bunch of hustling people all squeezed up together—being "Eastern." (*He turns his face into a screw of displeasure.*)

GEORGE Oh—you've been?

WALTER *Plenty* of times.

RUTH (*shocked at the lie*) Walter Lee Younger!

WALTER (*staring her down*) Plenty! (*Pause*) What we got to drink in this house? Why don't you offer this man some refreshment? (*To* GEORGE) They don't know how to entertain people in this house, man.

GEORGE Thank you—I don't really care for anything.

WALTER (*feeling his head; sobriety coming*) Where's Mama?

RUTH She ain't come back yet.

WALTER (*looking* MURCHISON *over from head to toe, scrutinizing his carefully casual tweed sports jacket over cashmere V-neck sweater over soft eyelet shirt and tie, and soft slacks, finished off with white buckskin shoes*) Why all you college boys wear them fairyish-looking white shoes?

RUTH Walter Lee!

(GEORGE MURCHISON *ignores the remark.*)

WALTER (*to* RUTH) Well, they look crazy as hell—white shoes, cold as it is.

RUTH (*crushed*) You have to excuse him—

WALTER No he don't! Excuse me for what? What you always excusing me for! I'll excuse myself when I needs to be excused! (*A pause*) They look as funny as them black knee socks Beneatha wears out of here all the time.

RUTH It's the college *style,* Walter.

WALTER Style, hell. She looks like she got burnt legs or something!

RUTH Oh, Walter—

WALTER (*an irritable mimic*) Oh, Walter! Oh, Walter! (*To* MURCHISON) How's your old man making out? I understand you all going to buy that big hotel on the Drive? (*He finds a beer in the refrigerator, wanders over to* MURCHISON, *sipping and wiping his lips with the back of his hand, and straddling a chair back-*

wards to talk to the other man.) Shrewd move. Your old man is all right, man. (*Tapping his head and half winking for emphasis*) I mean he knows how to operate. I mean he thinks *big,* you know what I mean, I mean for a *home,* you know? But I think he's kind of running out of ideas now. I'd like to talk to him. Listen, man, I got some plans that could turn this city upside down. I mean I think like he does. *Big.* Invest big, gamble big, hell, lose *big* if you have to, you know what I mean. It's hard to find a man on this whole Southside who understands my kind of thinking—you dig? (*He scrutinizes* MURCHISON *again, drinks his beer, squints his eyes and leans in close, confidential, man to man.*) Me and you ought to sit down and talk sometimes, man. Man, I got me some ideas. . . .

MURCHISON (*with boredom*)   Yeah—sometimes we'll have to do that, Walter.

WALTER (*understanding the indifference, and offended*)   Yeah—well, when you get the time, man. I know you a busy little boy.

RUTH   Walter, please—

WALTER (*bitterly, hurt*)   I know ain't nothing in this world as busy as you colored college boys with your fraternity pins and white shoes. . . .

RUTH (*covering her face with humiliation*)   Oh, Walter Lee—

WALTER   I see you all all the time—with the books tucked under your arms—going to your (*British A—a mimic*) "clahsses." And for what! What the hell you learning over there? Filling up your heads—(*counting off on his fingers*)—with the sociology and the psychology—but they teaching you how to be a man? How to take over and run the world? They teaching you how to run a rubber plantation or a steel mill? Naw—just to talk proper and read books and wear white shoes. . . .

GEORGE (*looking at him with distaste, a little above it all*)   You're all wacked up with bitterness, man.

WALTER (*intently, almost quietly, between the teeth, glaring at the boy*)   And you—ain't you bitter, man? Ain't you just about had it yet? Don't you see no stars gleaming that you can't reach out and grab? You happy?—You contented son-of-a-bitch—you happy? You got it made? Bitter? Man, I'm a volcano. Bitter? Here I am a giant—surrounded by ants! Ants who can't even understand what it is the giant is talking about.

RUTH (*passionately and suddenly*)   Oh, Walter—ain't you with nobody!

WALTER (*violently*)   No! 'Cause ain't nobody with me! Not even my own mother!

RUTH   Walter, that's a terrible thing to say!

(BENEATHA *enters, dressed for the evening in a cocktail dress and earrings.*)

GEORGE   Well—hey, you look great.

BENEATHA   Let's go, George. See you all later.

RUTH   Have a nice time.

GEORGE   Thanks. Good night. (*To* WALTER, *sarcastically*) Good night, *Prometheus.* (BENEATHA *and* GEORGE *exit.*)

WALTER (*to* RUTH)   Who is Prometheus?

RUTH   I don't know. Don't worry about it.

WALTER (*in fury, pointing after* GEORGE)   See there—they get to a point where they can't insult you man to man—they got to talk about something ain't nobody never heard of!

RUTH   How do you know it was an insult? (*To humor him*) Maybe Prometheus is a nice fellow.

WALTER   Prometheus! I bet there ain't even no such thing! I bet that simple-minded clown—

RUTH   Walter—(*She stops what she is doing and looks at him.*)

WALTER (*yelling*)   Don't start!

RUTH   Start what?

WALTER   Your nagging! Where was I? Who was I with? How much money did I spend?

RUTH (*plaintively*)   Walter Lee—why don't we just try to talk about it. . . .

WALTER (*not listening*)   I been out talking with people who understand me. People who care about the things I got on my mind.

RUTH (*wearily*)   I guess that means people like Willy Harris.

WALTER   Yes, people like Willy Harris.

RUTH (*with a sudden flash of impatience*)   Why don't you all just hurry up and go into the banking business and stop talking about it!

WALTER   Why? You want to know why? 'Cause we all tied up in a race of people that don't know how to do nothing but moan, pray and have babies!

The line is too bitter even for him and he looks at her and sits down.

RUTH   Oh, Walter . . . (*Softly*) Honey, why can't you stop fighting me?

WALTER (*without thinking*)   Who's fighting you? Who even cares about you?

This line begins the retardation of his mood.

RUTH   Well—(*She waits a long time, and then with resignation starts to put away her things.*) I guess I might as well go on to bed. ... (*More or less to herself*) I don't know where we lost it ... but we have. ... (*Then, to him*) I—I'm sorry about this new baby, Walter. I guess maybe I better go on and do what I started ... I guess I just didn't realize how bad things was with us ... I guess I just didn't really realize—(*She starts out to the bedroom and stops.*) You want some hot milk?

WALTER   Hot milk?

RUTH   Yes—hot milk.

WALTER   Why hot milk?

RUTH   'Cause after all that liquor you come home with you ought to have something hot in your stomach.

WALTER   I don't want no milk.

RUTH   You want some coffee then?

WALTER   No, I don't want no coffee. I don't want nothing hot to drink. (*Almost plaintively*) Why you always trying to give me something to eat?

RUTH   (*standing and looking at him helplessly*)   What else can I give you, Walter Lee Younger?

She stands and looks at him and presently turns to go out again. He lifts his head and watches her going away from him in a new mood which began to emerge when he asked her "Who cares about you?"

WALTER   It's been rough, ain't it, baby? (*She hears and stops but does not turn around and he continues to her back.*) I guess between two people there ain't never as much understood as folks generally thinks there is. I mean like between me and you— (*She turns to face him.*) How we gets to the place where we scared to talk softness to each other. (*He waits, thinking hard himself.*) Why you think it got to be like that? (*He is thoughtful, almost as a child would be.*) Ruth, what is it gets into people ought to be close?

RUTH   I don't know, honey. I think about it a lot.

WALTER   On account of you and me, you mean? The way things are with us. The way something done come down between us.

RUTH   There ain't so much between us, Walter. ... Not when you come to me and try to talk to me. Try to be with me ... a little even.

WALTER   (*total honesty*)   Sometimes ... sometimes ... I don't even know how to try.

RUTH   Walter—

WALTER   Yes?

RUTH   (*coming to him, gently and with misgiving, but coming to him*)   Honey ... life don't have to be like this. I mean sometimes people can do things so that things are better. ... You remember how we used to talk when Travis was born . . . about the way we were going to live . . . the kind of house . . . (*She is stroking his head.*) Well, it's all starting to slip away from us. . . .

(MAMA *enters, and* WALTER *jumps up and shouts at her.*)

WALTER   Mama, where have you been?

MAMA   My—them steps is longer than they used to be. Whew! (*She sits down and ignores him.*) How you feeling this evening, Ruth?

RUTH *shrugs, disturbed some at having been prematurely interrupted and watching her husband knowingly.*

WALTER   Mama, where have you been all day?

MAMA (*still ignoring him and leaning on the table and changing to more comfortable shoes*)   Where's Travis?

RUTH   I let him go out earlier and he ain't come back yet. Boy, is he going to get it!

WALTER   Mama!

MAMA (*as if she has heard him for the first time*)   Yes, son?

WALTER   Where did you go this afternoon?

MAMA   I went downtown to tend to some business that I had to tend to.

WALTER   What kind of business?

MAMA   You know better than to question me like a child, Brother.

WALTER (*rising and bending over the table*)   Where were you, Mama? (*Bringing his fists down and shouting*) Mama, you didn't go do something with that insurance money, something crazy?

(*The front door opens slowly, interrupting him, and* TRAVIS *peeks his head in, less than hopefully.*)

TRAVIS (*to his mother*)   Mama, I—

RUTH   "Mama I" nothing! You're going to get it, boy! Get on in that bedroom and get yourself ready!

TRAVIS   But I—

MAMA   Why don't you all never let the child explain hisself.

RUTH   Keep out of it now, Lena.

MAMA *clamps her lips together, and* RUTH *advances toward her son menacingly.*

RUTH   A thousand times I have told you not to go off like that—

MAMA (*holding out her arms to her grandson*)   Well—at least let me tell him something. I want him to be the first one to hear. . . . Come here, Travis. (*The boy obeys, gladly.*) Travis—(*she takes him by the shoulder and looks into his face*)—you know that money we got in the mail this morning?

TRAVIS   Yes'm—

MAMA   Well—what do you think your grandmama gone and done with that money?

TRAVIS   I don't know, Grandmama.

MAMA   (*putting her finger on his nose for emphasis*)   She went out and she bought you a house! (*The explosion comes from* WALTER *at the end of the revelation and he jumps up and turns away from all of them in a fury.* MAMA *continues, to* TRAVIS) You glad about the house? It's going to be yours when you get to be a man.

TRAVIS   Yeah—I always wanted to live in a house.

MAMA   All right, gimme some sugar then—(TRAVIS *puts his arms around her neck as she watches her son over the boy's shoulder. Then, to* TRAVIS, *after the embrace*) Now when you say your prayers tonight, you thank God and your grandfather—'cause it was him who give you the house—in his way.

RUTH   (*taking the boy from* MAMA *and pushing him toward the bedroom*)   Now you get out of here and get ready for your beating.

TRAVIS   Aw, Mama—

RUTH   Get on in there—(*Closing the door behind him and turning radiantly to her mother-in-law*) So you went and did it!

MAMA   (*quietly, looking at her son with pain*)   Yes, I did.

RUTH   (*raising both arms classically*)   Praise God! (*Looks at* WALTER *a moment, who says nothing. She crosses rapidly to her husband.*) Please, honey—let me be glad . . . you be glad too. (*She has laid her hands on his shoulders, but he shakes himself free of her roughly, without turning to face her.*) Oh, Walter . . . a home . . . a home . . . a home. (*She comes back to* MAMA) Well—where is it? How big is it? How much it going to cost?

MAMA   Well—

RUTH   When we moving?

MAMA   (*smiling at her*)   First of the month.

RUTH   (*throwing back her head with jubilance*)   *Praise God!*

MAMA   (*tentatively, still looking at her son's back turned against her and* RUTH)   It's—it's a nice house too. . . . (*She cannot help speaking directly to him. An imploring quality in her voice, her manner, makes her almost like a girl now.*) Three bedrooms— nice big one for you and Ruth. . . . Me and Beneatha still have to share our room, but Travis have one of his own—and (*with difficulty*) I figure if the—new baby—is a boy, we could get one of them double-decker outfits. . . . And there's a yard with a little patch of dirt where I could maybe get to grow me a few flowers. . . . And a nice big basement. . . .

RUTH   Walter honey, be glad—

MAMA   (*still to his back, fingering things on the table*)   'Course I

don't want to make it sound fancier than it is.... It's just a plain
little old house—but it's made good and solid—and it will be *ours*.
Walter Lee—it makes a difference in a man when he can walk
on floors that belong to *him*....

RUTH   Where is it?

MAMA (*frightened at this telling*)   Well—well—it's out there in Clybourne Park—

RUTH's *radiance fades abruptly, and* WALTER *finally turns slowly to face
his mother with incredulity and hostility.*

RUTH   Where?

MAMA (*matter-of-factly*)   Four o six Clybourne Street, Clybourne
Park.

RUTH   Clybourne Park? Mama, there ain't no colored people living
in Clybourne Park.

MAMA (*almost idiotically*)   Well, I guess there's going to be some
now.

WALTER (*bitterly*)   So that's the peace and comfort you went out
and bought for us today!

MAMA (*raising her eyes to meet his finally*)   Son—I just tried to find
the nicest place for the least amount of money for my family.

RUTH (*trying to recover from the shock*)   Well—well—'course I
ain't one never been 'fraid of no crackers, mind you—but—well,
wasn't there no other houses nowhere?

MAMA   Them houses they put up for colored in them areas way out
all seem to cost twice as much as other houses. I did the best I
could.

RUTH (*struck senseless with the news, in its various degrees of goodness and trouble, she sits a moment, her fists propping her chin
in thought, and then she starts to rise, bringing her fists down
with vigor, the radiance spreading from cheek to cheek again*)
Well—well!—All I can say is—if this is my time in life—*my time*
—to say goodbye—(*and she builds with momentum as she starts
to circle the room with an exuberant, almost tearfully happy release*)—to these Goddamned cracking walls!—(*she pounds the
walls*)—and these marching roaches!—(*she wipes at an imaginary
army of marching roaches*)—and this cramped little closet which
ain't now or never was no kitchen!... then I say it loud and good,
Hallelujah! and good-bye misery.... I don't never want to see
your ugly face again! (*She laughs joyously, having practically
destroyed the apartment, and flings her arms up and lets them
come down happily, slowly, reflectively, over her abdomen, aware
for the first time perhaps that the life therein pulses with happiness and not despair.*) Lena?

MAMA (*moved, watching her happiness*)   Yes, honey?
RUTH (*looking off*)   Is there—is there a whole lot of sunlight?
MAMA (*understanding*)   Yes, child, there's a whole lot of sunlight.

Long pause.

RUTH (*collecting herself and going to the door of the room* TRAVIS *is in*)   Well—I guess I better see 'bout Travis. (*To* MAMA) Lord, I sure don't feel like whipping nobody today! (*She exits.*)
MAMA (*the mother and son are left alone now and the mother waits a long time, considering deeply, before she speaks*)   Son—you— you understand what I done, don't you? (WALTER *is silent and sullen.*) I—I just seen my family falling apart today . . . just falling to pieces in front of my eyes. . . . We couldn't of gone on like we was today. We was going backwards 'stead of forwards—talking 'bout killing babies and wishing each other was dead. . . . When it gets like that in life—you just got to do something different, push on out and do something bigger. . . . (*She waits.*) I wish you say something, son . . . I wish you'd say how deep inside you you think I done the right thing—
WALTER (*crossing slowly to his bedroom door and finally turning there and speaking measuredly*)   What you need me to say you done right for? *You* the head of this family. You run our lives like you want to. It was your money and you did what you wanted with it. So what you need for me to say it was all right for? (*Bitterly, to hurt her as deeply as he knows is possible*) So you butchered up a dream of mine—you—who always talking 'bout your children's dreams. . . .
MAMA   Walter Lee—

(*He just closes the door behind him.* MAMA *sits alone, thinking heavily.*)

Curtain

Scene II

Time: Friday night, a few weeks later.
At rise: Packing crates mark the intention of the family to move. BE- NEATHA *and* GEORGE *come in, presumably from an evening out again.*

GEORGE   O.K. . . . O.K., whatever you say. . . . (*They both sit on the couch. He tries to kiss her. She moves away.*) Look, we've had a nice evening; let's not spoil it, huh? . . .

He again turns her head and tries to nuzzle in and she turns away from him, not with distaste but with momentary lack of interest; in a mood to pursue what they were talking about.

BENEATHA   I'm *trying* to talk to you.

GEORGE   We always talk.

BENEATHA   Yes—and I love to talk.

GEORGE *(exasperated; rising)*   I know it and I don't mind it sometimes . . . I want you to cut it out, see—The moody stuff. I mean.
I don't like it. You're a nice-looking girl . . . all over. That's all
you need, honey, forget the atmosphere. Guys aren't going to go
for the atmosphere—they're going to go for what they see. Be
glad for that. Drop the Garbo routine. It doesn't go with you. As
for myself, I want a nice—*(groping)*—simple *(thoughtfully)*—
sophisticated girl . . . not a poet—O.K.?

She rebuffs him again and he starts to leave.

BENEATHA   Why are you angry?

GEORGE   Because this is stupid! I don't go out with you to discuss
the nature of "quiet desperation" or to hear all about your
thoughts—because the world will go on thinking what it thinks
regardless—

BENEATHA   Then why read books? Why go to school?

GEORGE *(with artificial patience, counting on his fingers)*   It's simple. You read books—to learn facts—to get grades—to pass the
course—to get a degree. That's all—it has nothing to do with
thoughts.

A long pause.

BENEATHA   I see. *(A longer pause as she looks at him)* Good night,
George.

GEORGE *looks at her a little oddly, and starts to exit. He meets* MAMA
coming in.

GEORGE   Oh—hello, Mrs. Younger.

MAMA   Hello, George, how you feeling?

GEORGE   Fine—fine, how are you?

MAMA   Oh, a little tired. You know them steps can get you after a
day's work. You all have a nice time tonight?

GEORGE   Yes—a fine time. Well, good night.

MAMA   Good night. *(He exits.* MAMA *closes the door behind her.)*
Hello, honey. What you sitting like that for?

BENEATHA   I'm just sitting.

MAMA   Didn't you have a nice time?

BENEATHA   No.

MAMA   No? What's the matter?

BENEATHA   Mama, George is a fool—honest. *(She rises.)*

MAMA (*hustling around unloading the packages she has entered with; she stops*) Is he, baby?
BENEATHA Yes.

BENEATHA *makes up* TRAVIS' *bed as she talks.*

MAMA You sure?
BENEATHA Yes.
MAMA Well—I guess you better not waste your time with no fools.

BENEATHA *looks up at her mother, watching her put groceries in the refrigerator. Finally she gathers up her things and starts into the bedroom. At the door she stops and looks back at her mother.*

BENEATHA Mama—
MAMA Yes, baby—
BENEATHA Thank you.
MAMA For what?
BENEATHA For understanding me this time.

(*She exits quickly and the mother stands, smiling a little, looking at the place where* BENEATHA *just stood.* RUTH *enters.*)

RUTH Now don't you fool with any of this stuff, Lena—
MAMA Oh, I just thought I'd sort a few things out.

The phone rings. RUTH *answers.*

RUTH (*at the phone*) Hello—Just a minute. (*Goes to the door*) Walter, it's Mrs. Arnold. (*Waits. Goes back to the phone. Tense*) Hello. Yes, this is his wife speaking . . . He's lying down now. Yes . . . well, he'll be in tomorrow. He's been very sick. Yes—I know we should have called, but we were so sure he'd be able to come in today. Yes—yes, I'm very sorry. Yes . . . Thank you very much. (*She hangs up.* WALTER *is standing in the doorway of the bedroom behind her.*) That was Mrs. Arnold.
WALTER (*indifferently*) Was it?
RUTH She said if you don't come in tomorrow that they are getting a new man. . . .
WALTER Ain't that sad—ain't that crying sad.
RUTH She said Mr. Arnold has had to take a cab for three days. . . . Walter, you ain't been to work for three days! (*This is a revelation to her.*) Where you been, Walter Lee Younger? (WALTER *looks at her and starts to laugh.*) You're going to lose your job.
WALTER That's right . . .
RUTH Oh, Walter, and with your mother working like a dog every day—
WALTER That's sad too—Everything is sad.

MAMA   What you been doing for these three days, son?

WALTER   Mama—you don't know all the things a man what got leisure can find to do in this city.... What's this—Friday night? Well Wednesday I borrowed Willy Harris' car and I went for a drive ... just me and myself and I drove and drove ... Way out ... way past South Chicago, and I parked the car and I sat and looked at the steel mills all day long. I just sat in the car and looked at them big black chimneys for hours. Then I drove back and I went to the Green Hat. (*Pause*) And Thursday— Thursday I borrowed the car again and I got in it and I pointed it the other way and I drove the other way—for hours—way, way up to Wisconsin, and I looked at the farms. I just drove and looked at the farms. Then I drove back and I went to the Green Hat. (*Pause*) And today—today I didn't get the car. Today I just walked. All over the South side. And I looked at the Negroes and they looked at me and finally I just sat down on the curb at Thirty-ninth and South Parkway and I just sat there and watched the Negroes go by. And then I went to the Green Hat. You all sad? You all depressed? And you know where I am going right now—

(RUTH *goes out quietly.*)

MAMA   Oh, Big Walter, is this the harvest of our days?

WALTER   You know what I like about the Green Hat? (*He turns the radio on and a steamy, deep blues pours into the room.*) I like this little cat they got there who blows a sax.... He blows. He talks to me. He ain't but 'bout five feet tall and he's got a conked head and his eyes is always closed and he's all music—

MAMA   (*rising and getting some papers out of her handbag*) Walter—

WALTER   And there's this other guy who plays the piano ... and they got a sound. I mean they can work on some music.... They got the best little combo in the world in the Green Hat.... You can just sit there and drink and listen to them three men play and you realize that don't nothing matter worth a damn, but just being there—

MAMA   I've helped do it to you, haven't I, son? Walter, I been wrong.

WALTER   Naw—you ain't never been wrong about nothing, Mama.

MAMA   Listen to me, now. I say I been wrong, son. That I been doing to you what the rest of the world been doing to you. (*She stops and he looks up slowly at her and she meets his eyes pleadingly.*) Walter—what you ain't never understood is that I ain't got nothing, don't own nothing, ain't never really wanted nothing that wasn't for you. There ain't nothing as precious to me. . . . There ain't nothing worth holding on to, money, dreams, nothing else—if it means—if it means it's going to destroy my boy. (*She puts her papers in front of him and he watches her without speaking or moving.*) I paid the man thirty-five hundred dollars down on the house. That leaves sixty-five hundred dollars. Monday morning I want you to take this money and take three thousand dollars and put it in a savings account for Beneatha's medical schooling. The rest you put in a checking account—with your name on it. And from now on any penny that come out of it or that go in it is for you to look after. For you to decide. (*She drops her hands a little helplessly.*) It ain't much, but it's all I got in the world and I'm putting it in your hands. I'm telling you to be the head of this family from now on like you supposed to be.

WALTER (*stares at the money*)   You trust me like that, Mama?

MAMA   I ain't never stop trusting you. Like I ain't never stop loving you.

(*She goes out, and* WALTER *sits looking at the money on the table as the music continues in its idiom, pulsing in the room. Finally, in a decisive gesture, he gets up, and, in mingled joy and desperation, picks up the money. At the same moment,* TRAVIS *enters for bed.*)

TRAVIS   What's the matter, Daddy? You drunk?

WALTER (*sweetly, more sweetly than we have ever known him*)   No, Daddy ain't drunk. Daddy ain't going to never be drunk again. . . .

TRAVIS   Well, good night, Daddy.

The Father has come from behind the couch and leans over, embracing his son.

WALTER   Son, I feel like talking to you tonight.

TRAVIS   About what?

WALTER   Oh, about a lot of things. About you and what kind of man you going to be when you grow up. . . . Son—son, what do you want to be when you grow up?

TRAVIS   A bus driver.

WALTER (*laughing a little*)   A what? Man, that ain't nothing to want to be!

TRAVIS   Why not?

WALTER   'Cause, man—it ain't big enough—you know what I mean.

TRAVIS   I don't know then. I can't make up my mind. Sometimes Mama asks me that too. And sometimes when I tell her I just want to be like you—she says she don't want me to be like that and sometimes she says she does. . . .

WALTER (*gathering him up in his arms*) You know what, Travis? In seven years you going to be seventeen years old. And things is going to be very different with us in seven years, Travis. . . . One day when you are seventeen I'll come home—home from my office downtown somewhere—

TRAVIS You don't work in no office, Daddy.

WALTER No—but after tonight. After what your daddy gonna do tonight, there's going to be offices—a whole lot of offices. . . .

TRAVIS What you gonna do tonight, Daddy?

WALTER You wouldn't understand yet, son, but your daddy's gonna make a transaction . . . a business transaction that's going to change our lives. . . . That's how come one day when you 'bout seventeen years old I'll come home and I'll be pretty tired, you know what I mean, after a day of conferences and secretaries getting things wrong the way they do . . . 'cause an executive's life is hell, man—(*The more he talks, the farther away he gets.*) And I'll pull the car up on the driveway . . . just a plain black Chrysler, I think, with white walls—no—black tires. More elegant. Rich people don't have to be flashy . . . though I'll have to get something a little sportier for Ruth—maybe a Cadillac convertible to do her shopping in. . . . And I'll come up the steps to the house and the gardener will be clipping away at the hedges and he'll say, "Good evening, Mr. Younger." And I'll say, "Hello, Jefferson, how are you this evening?" And I'll go inside and Ruth will come downstairs and meet me at the door and we'll kiss each other and she'll take my arm and we'll go up to your room to see you sitting on the floor with the catalogues of all the great schools in America around you. . . . All the great schools in the world! And—and I'll say, all right son—it's your seventeenth birthday, what is it you've decided? . . . Just tell me where you want to go to school and you'll *go*. Just tell me, what it is you want to be—and you'll *be* it. . . . Whatever you want to be— Yessir! (*He holds his arms open for* TRAVIS.) You just name it, son . . . (TRAVIS *leaps into them.*) and I hand you the world!

WALTER's *voice has risen in pitch and hysterical promise and on the last line he lifts* TRAVIS *high.*

Blackout

Scene III

Time: Saturday, moving day, one week later.

Before the curtain rises, RUTH's *voice, a strident, dramatic church alto cuts through the silence.*

It is, in the darkness a triumphant surge, a penetrating statement of ex-

pectation: "*Oh, Lord, I don't feel no ways tired! Children, oh, glory halle-lujah!*"

    As the curtain rises we see that RUTH *is alone in the living room, finish-ing up the family's packing. It is moving day. She is nailing crates and tying cartons.* BENEATHA *enters, carrying a guitar case, and watches her exuberant sister-in-law.*

RUTH   Hey!

BENEATHA (*putting away the case*)   Hi.

RUTH (*pointing at a package*)   Honey—look in that package there and see what I found on sale this morning at the South Center. (RUTH *gets up and moves to the package and draws out some curtains.*) Lookahere—hand-turned hems!

BENEATHA   How do you know the window size out there?

RUTH (*who hadn't thought of that*)   Oh—Well, they bound to fit something in the whole house. Anyhow, they was too good a bar-gain to pass up. (RUTH *slaps her head, suddenly remembering something.*) Oh, Bennie—I meant to put a special note on that carton over there. That's your mamma's good china and she wants 'em to be very careful with it.

BENEATHA   I'll do it.

BENEATHA *finds a piece of paper and starts to draw large letters on it.*

RUTH   You know what I'm going to do soon as I get in that new house?

BENEATHA   What?

RUTH   Honey—I'm going to run me a tub of water up to here.... (*With her fingers practically up to her nostrils*) And I'm going to get in it—and I am going to sit ... and sit ... and sit in that hot water and the first person who knocks to tell *me* to hurry up and come out—

BENEATHA   Gets shot at sunrise.

RUTH (*laughing happily*)   You said it, sister! (*Noticing how large* BENEATHA *is absent-mindedly making the note*) Honey, they ain't going to read that from no airplane.

BENEATHA (*laughing herself*)   I guess I always think things have more emphasis if they are big, somehow.

RUTH (*looking up at her and smiling*)   You and your brother seem to have that as a philosophy of life. Lord, that man—done changed so 'round here. You know—you know what we did last night? Me and Walter Lee?

BENEATHA   What?

RUTH (*smiling to herself*)   We went to the movies. (*Looking at* BENEATHA *to see if she understands*) We went to the movies. You

know the last time me and Walter went to the movies together?
BENEATHA   No.
RUTH   Me neither. That's how long it been. (*Smiling again*) But
we went last night. The picture wasn't much good, but that didn't
seem to matter. We went—and we held hands.
BENEATHA   Oh, Lord!
RUTH   We held hands—and you know what?
BENEATHA   What?
RUTH   When we come out of the show it was late and dark and all
the stores and things was closed up . . . and it was kind of chilly
and there wasn't many people on the streets . . . and we was still
holding hands, me and Walter.
BENEATHA   You're killing me.

(WALTER *enters with a large package. His happiness is deep in him; he
cannot keep still with his new-found exuberance. He is singing and
wiggling and snapping his fingers. He puts his package in a corner and
puts a phonograph record, which he has brought in with him, on the
record player. As the music comes up he dances over to* RUTH *and tries
to get her to dance with him. She gives in at last to his raunchiness and
in a fit of giggling allows herself to be drawn into his mood and together they deliberately burlesque an old social dance of their youth.*)

BENEATHA   (*regarding them a long time as they dance, then drawing in her breath for a deeply exaggerated comment which she
does not particularly mean*)   Talk about—olddddddddddd-fash-
ionedddddddd—Negroes!
WALTER   (*stopping momentarily*)   What kind of Negroes?

*He says this in fun. He is not angry with her today, nor with anyone. He
starts to dance with his wife again.*

BENEATHA   Old-fashioned.
WALTER   (*as he dances with* RUTH)   You know, when these *New
Negroes* have their convention—(*pointing at his sister*)—that is
going to be the chairman of the Committee on Unending Agitation. (*He goes on dancing, then stops.*) Race, race, race! . . . Girl,
I do believe you are the first person in the history of the entire
human race to successfully brainwash yourself. (BENEATHA *breaks
up and he goes on dancing. He stops again, enjoying his tease.*)
Damn, even the N double A C P takes a holiday sometimes!
(BENEATHA *and* RUTH *laugh. He dances with* RUTH *some more
and starts to laugh and stops and pantomimes someone over an
operating table.*) I can just see that chick someday looking down
at some poor cat on an operating table before she starts to slice
him, saying . . . (*pulling his sleeves back maliciously*) "By the
way, what are your views on civil rights down there? . . ."

He laughs at her again and starts to dance happily. The bell sounds.

BENEATHA   Sticks and stones may break my bones but . . . words will never hurt me!

(BENEATHA *goes to the door and opens it as* WALTER *and* RUTH *go on with the clowning.* BENEATHA *is somewhat surprised to see a quiet-looking middle-aged white man in a business suit holding his hat and a briefcase in his hand and consulting a small piece of paper.*)

MAN   Uh—how do you do, miss. I am looking for a Mrs.—(*he looks at the slip of paper*) Mrs. Lena Younger?

BENEATHA   (*smoothing her hair with slight embarrassment*)   Oh—yes, that's my mother. Excuse me. (*She closes the door and turns to quiet the other two.*) Ruth! Brother! Somebody's here. (*Then she opens the door. The man casts a curious quick glance at all of them.*) Uh—come in please.

MAN   (*coming in*)   Thank you.

BENEATHA   My mother isn't here just now. Is it business?

MAN   Yes . . . well, of a sort.

WALTER   (*freely, the Man of the House*)   Have a seat. I'm Mrs. Younger's son. I look after most of her business matters.

RUTH *and* BENEATHA *exchange amused glances.*

MAN   (*regarding* WALTER, *and sitting*)   Well—my name is Karl Lindner . . .

WALTER   (*stretching out his hand*)   Walter Younger. This is my wife—(RUTH *nods politely*)—and my sister.

LINDNER   How do you do.

WALTER   (*amiably, as he sits himself easily on a chair, leaning with interest forward on his knees and looking expectantly into the newcomer's face*)   What can we do for you, Mr. Lindner!

LINDNER   (*some minor shuffling of the hat and briefcase on his knees*)   Well—I am a representative of the Clybourne Park Improvement Association—

WALTER   (*pointing*)   Why don't you sit your things on the floor?

LINDNER   Oh—yes. Thank you. (*He slides the briefcase and hat under the chair.*) And as I was saying—I am from the Clybourne Park Improvement Association and we have had it brought to our attention at the last meeting that you people—or at least your mother—has bought a piece of residential property at—(*he digs for the slip of paper again*)—four o six Clybourne Street. . . .

WALTER   That's right. Care for something to drink? Ruth, get Mr. Lindner a beer.

LINDNER   (*upset for some reason*)   Oh—no, really. I mean thank you very much, but no thank you.

RUTH (*innocently*)   Some coffee?

LINDNER   Thank you, nothing at all.

BENEATHA *is watching the man carefully.*

LINDNER   Well, I don't know how much you folks know about our organization. (*He is a gentle man; thoughtful and somewhat labored in his manner.*) It is one of those community organizations set up to look after—oh, you know, things like block upkeep and special projects and we also have what we call our New Neighbors Orientation Committee. . . .

BENEATHA (*drily*)   Yes—and what do they do?

LINDNER (*turning a little to her and then returning the main force to* WALTER)   Well—it's what you might call a sort of welcoming committee, I guess. I mean they, we, I'm the chairman of the committee—go around and see the new people who move into the neighborhood and sort of give them the lowdown on the way we do things out in Clybourne Park.

BENEATHA (*with appreciation of the two meanings, which escape* RUTH *and* WALTER)   Uh-huh.

LINDNER   And we also have the category of what the association calls—(*he looks elsewhere*)—uh—special community problems. . . .

BENEATHA   Yes—and what are some of those?

WALTER   Girl, let the man talk.

LINDNER (*with understated relief*)   Thank you. I would sort of like to explain this thing in my own way. I mean I want to explain to you in a certain way.

WALTER   Go ahead.

LINDNER   Yes. Well. I'm going to try to get right to the point. I'm sure we'll all appreciate that in the long run.

BENEATHA   Yes.

LINDNER   Well—

WALTER   Be still now!

LINDNER   Well —

RUTH (*still innocently*)   Would you like another chair— you don't look comfortable.

LINDNER (*more frustrated than annoyed*)   No, thank you very much. Please. Well—to get right to the point I—(*a great breath, and he is off at last*) I am sure you people must be aware of some of the incidents which have happened in various parts of the city when colored people have moved into certain areas—(BENEATHA *exhales heavily and starts tossing a piece of fruit up and down in the air.*) Well—because we have what I think is going to be a unique type of organization in American community life —not only do we deplore that kind of thing—but we are trying to do something about it. (BENEATHA *stops tossing and turns with a new and quizzical interest to the man.*) We feel—(*gaining confidence in his mission because of the interest in the faces of the people he is talking to*)—we feel that most of the trouble in this world, when you come right down to it—(*he hits his knee for emphasis*)—most of the trouble exists because people just don't sit down and talk to each other.

RUTH   (*nodding as she might in church, pleased with the remark*) You can say that again, mister.

LINDNER   (*more encouraged by such affirmation*)   That we don't try hard enough in this world to understand the other fellow's problem. The other guy's point of view.

RUTH   Now that's right.

BENEATHA *and* WALTER *merely watch and listen with genuine interest.*

LINDNER   Yes—that's the way we feel out in Clybourne Park. And that's why I was elected to come here this afternoon and talk to you people. Friendly like, you know, the way people should talk to each other and see if we couldn't find some way to work this thing out. As I say, the whole business is a matter of *caring* about the other fellow. Anybody can see that you are a nice family of folks, hard-working and honest I'm sure. (BENEATHA *frowns slightly, quizzically, her head tilted regarding him.*) Today everybody knows what it means to be on the outside of *something*. And of course, there is always somebody who is out to take the advantage of people who don't always understand.

WALTER   What do you mean?

LINDNER   Well—you see our community is made up of people who've worked hard as the dickens for years to build up that little community. They're not rich and fancy people; just hard-working, honest people who don't really have much but those little homes and a dream of the kind of community they want to raise their children in. Now, I don't say we are perfect and there is a lot wrong in some of the things they want. But you've got to admit that a man, right or wrong, has the right to want to have the neighborhood he lives in a certain kind of way. And at the moment the overwhelming majority of our people out there feel that people get along better, take more of a common interest in the life of the community, when they share a common background. I want you to believe me when I tell you that race prejudice simply doesn't enter into it. It is a matter of the people of Clybourne Park believing, rightly or wrongly, as I say, that for the happiness of all concerned that our Negro families are happier when they live in their *own* communities.

BENEATHA (*with a grand and bitter gesture*) This, friends, is the Welcoming Committee!

WALTER (*dumbfounded, looking at* LINDNER) Is this what you came marching all the way over here to tell us?

LINDNER Well, now we've been having a fine conversation. I hope you'll hear me all the way through.

WALTER (*tightly*) Go ahead, man.

LINDNER You see—in the face of all things I have said, we are prepared to make your family a very generous offer. . . .

BENEATHA Thirty pieces and not a coin less!

WALTER Yeah?

LINDNER (*putting on his glasses and drawing a form out of the briefcase*) Our association is prepared, through the collective effort of our people, to buy the house from you at a financial gain to your family.

RUTH Lord have mercy, ain't this the living gall!

WALTER All right, you through?

LINDNER Well, I want to give you the exact terms of the financial arrangement—

WALTER We don't want to hear no exact terms of no arrangements. I want to know if you got any more to tell us 'bout getting together?

LINDNER (*taking off his glasses*) Well—I don't suppose that you feel. . . .

WALTER Never mind how I feel—you got any more to say 'bout how people ought to sit down and talk to each other? . . . Get out of my house, man. (*He turns his back and walks to the door.*)

LINDNER (*looking around at the hostile faces and reaching and assembling his hat and briefcase*) Well—I don't understand why you people are reacting this way. What do you think you are going to gain by moving into a neighborhood where you just aren't wanted and where some elements—well—people can get awful worked up when they feel that their whole way of life and everything they've ever worked for is threatened.

WALTER Get out.

LINDNER (*at the door, holding a small card*) Well—I'm sorry it went like this.

WALTER Get out.

LINDNER (*almost sadly, regarding* WALTER) You just can't force people to change their hearts, son.

(*He turns and puts his card on a table and exits.* WALTER *pushes the door to with stinging hatred, and stands looking at it.* RUTH *just sits and* BENEATHA *just stands. They say nothing.* MAMA *and* TRAVIS *enter.*)

MAMA   Well—this all the packing got done since I left out of here this morning. I testify before God that my children got all the energy of the dead. What time the moving men due?

BENEATHA   Four o'clock. You had a caller, Mama. (*She is smiling, teasingly.*)

MAMA   Sure enough—who?

BENEATHA   (*her arms folded saucily*)   The Welcoming Committee.

WALTER *and* RUTH *giggle.*

MAMA   (*innocently*)   Who?

BENEATHA   The Welcoming Committee. They said they're sure going to be glad to see you when you get there.

WALTER   (*devilishly*)   Yeah, they said they can't hardly wait to see your face.

Laughter.

MAMA   (*sensing their facetiousness*)   What's the matter with you all?

WALTER   Ain't nothing the matter with us. We just telling you 'bout the gentleman who came to see you this afternoon. From the Clybourne Park Improvement Association.

MAMA   What he want?

RUTH   (*in the same mood as* BENEATHA *and* WALTER)   To welcome you, honey.

WALTER   He said they can't hardly wait. He said the one thing they don't have, that they just *dying* to have out there is a fine family of colored people! (*To* RUTH *and* BENEATHA) Ain't that right!

RUTH *and* BENEATHA   (*mockingly*)   Yeah! He left his card in case—

They indicate the card, and MAMA *picks it up and throws it on the floor —understanding and looking off as she draws her chair up to the table on which she has put her plant and some sticks and some cord.*

MAMA   Father, give us strength. (*Knowingly—and without fun*) Did he threaten us?

BENEATHA   Oh—Mama—they don't do it like that any more. He talked Brotherhood. He said everybody ought to learn how to sit down and hate each other with good Christian fellowship.

She and WALTER *shake hands to ridicule the remark.*

MAMA   (*sadly*)   Lord, protect us. . . .

RUTH   You should hear the money those folks raised to buy the house from us. All we paid and then some.

BENEATHA   What they think we going to do—eat 'em?

RUTH   No, honey, marry 'em.

MAMA   (*shaking her head*)   Lord, Lord, Lord. . . .

RUTH   Well—that's the way the crackers crumble. Joke.

BENEATHA   (*laughingly noticing what her mother is doing*)   Mama, what are you doing?

MAMA   Fixing my plant so it won't get hurt none on the way. . . .

BENEATHA   Mama, you going to take *that* to the new house?

MAMA   Uh-huh—

BENEATHA   That raggedy-looking old thing?

MAMA   (*stopping and looking at her*)   It expresses *me*.

RUTH   (*with delight, to* BENEATHA)   So there, Miss Thing!

WALTER *comes to* MAMA *suddenly and bends down behind her and squeezes her in his arms with all his strength. She is overwhelmed by the suddenness of it and, though delighted, her manner is like that of* RUTH *with* TRAVIS.

MAMA   Look out now, boy! You make me mess up my thing here!

WALTER   (*his face lit, he slips down on his knees beside her, his arms still about her*)   Mama . . . you know what it means to climb up in the chariot?

MAMA   (*gruffly, very happy*)   Get on away from me now. . . .

RUTH   (*near the gift-wrapped package, trying to catch* WALTER's *eye*)   Psst—

WALTER   What the old song say, Mama. . . .

RUTH   Walter—Now? (*She is pointing at the package.*)

WALTER   (*speaking the lines, sweetly, playfully, in his mother's face*)

I got wings . . . you got wings . . .
All God's children got wings . . .

MAMA   Boy—get out of my face and do some work. . . .

WALTER

When I get to heaven gonna put on my wings.
Gonna fly all over God's heaven . . .

BENEATHA   (*teasingly, from across the room*)   Everybody talking 'bout heaven ain't going there!

WALTER   (*to* RUTH, *who is carrying the box across to them*)   I don't know, you think we ought to give her that. . . . Seems to me she ain't been very appreciative around here.

MAMA   (*eying the box, which is obviously a gift*)   What is that?

WALTER   (*taking it from* RUTH *and putting it on the table in front of* MAMA)   Well—what you all think? Should we give it to her?

RUTH   Oh—she was pretty good today.

MAMA   I'll good you—(*She turns her eyes to the box again.*)
BENEATHA   Open it, Mama.

She stands up, looks at it, turns and looks at all of them, and then presses her hands together and does not open the package.

WALTER (*sweetly*)   Open it, Mama. It's for you. (MAMA *looks in his eyes. It is the first present in her life without its being Christmas. Slowly she opens her package and lifts out, one by one, a brand-new sparkling set of gardening tools.* WALTER *continues, prodding*) Ruth made up the note— read it . . .
MAMA (*picking up the card and adjusting her glasses*)   "To our own Mrs. Miniver—Love from Brother, Ruth and Beneatha." Ain't that lovely. . . .
TRAVIS (*tugging at his father's sleeve*)   Daddy, can I give her mine now?
WALTER   All right, son. (TRAVIS *flies to get his gift*) Travis didn't want to go in with the rest of us, Mama. He got his own. (*Somewhat amused*) We don't know what it is. . . .
TRAVIS (*racing back in the room with a large hatbox and putting it in front of his grandmother*)   Here!
MAMA   Lord have mercy, baby. You done gone and bought your grandmother a hat?
TRAVIS (*very proud*)   Open it!

She does and lifts out an elaborate, but very elaborate, wide gardening hat, and all the adults break up at the sight of it.

RUTH   Travis, honey, what is that?
TRAVIS (*who thinks it is beautiful and appropriate*)   It's a gardening hat! Like the ladies always have on in the magazines when they work in their gardens.
BENEATHA (*giggling fiercely*)   Travis—we were trying to make MAMA Mrs. Miniver—not Scarlett O'Hara!
MAMA (*indignantly*)   What's the matter with you all! This here is a beautiful hat! (*Absurdly*) I always wanted me one just like it!

She pops it on her head to prove it to her grandson, and the hat is ludicrous and considerably oversized.

RUTH   Hot dog! Go, Mama!
WALTER (*doubled over with laughter*)   I'm sorry, Mama—but you look like you ready to go out and chop you some cotton sure enough!

They all laugh except MAMA, out of deference to TRAVIS' feelings.

MAMA (*gathering the boy up to her*) Bless your heart—this is the prettiest hat I ever owned—(WALTER, RUTH, *and* BENEATHA *chime in noisily, festively and insincerely congratulating* TRAVIS *on his gift.*) What are we all standing around here for? We ain't finished packin' yet. Bennie, you ain't packed one book.

The bell rings.

BENEATHA That couldn't be the movers . . . it's not hardly two good yet—

(BENEATHA *goes into her room.* MAMA *starts for door.*)

WALTER (*turning, stiffening*) Wait—wait—I'll get it. (*He stands and looks at the door.*)

MAMA You expecting company, son?

WALTER (*just looking at the door*) Yeah—yeah. . . .

MAMA *looks at* RUTH, *and they exchange innocent and unfrightened glances.*

MAMA (*not understanding*) Well, let them in, son.

BENEATHA (*from her room*) We need some more string.

MAMA Travis—you run to the hardware and get me some string cord.

(MAMA *goes out and* WALTER *turns and looks at* RUTH. TRAVIS *goes to a dish for money.*)

RUTH Why don't you answer the door, man?

WALTER (*suddenly bounding across the floor to her*) 'Cause some times it hard to let the future begin! (*Stooping down in her face*)

I got wings! You got wings!
All God's children got wings!

(*He crosses to the door and throws it open. Standing there is a very slight little man in a not too prosperous business suit and with haunted frightened eyes and a hat pulled down tightly, brim up, around his forehead.* TRAVIS *passes between the men and exits.* WALTER *leans deep in the man's face, still in his jubilance.*)

When I get to heaven gonna put on my wings.
Gonna fly all over God's heaven . . .

The little man just stares at him.

Heaven—

(*Suddenly he stops and looks past the little man into the empty hall-way.*) Where's Willy, man?

BOBO   He ain't with me.

WALTER (*not disturbed*)   Oh—come on in. You know my wife.

BOBO (*dumbly, taking off his hat*)   Yes—h'you, Miss Ruth.

RUTH (*quietly, a mood apart from her husband already, seeing* BOBO)   Hello, Bobo.

WALTER   You right on time today. . . . Right on time. That's the way! (*He slaps* BOBO *on his back.*) Sit down . . . lemme hear.

RUTH *stands stiffly and quietly in back of them, as though somehow she senses death, her eyes fixed on her husband.*

BOBO (*his frightened eyes on the floor, his hat in his hands*)   Could I please get a drink of water, before I tell you about it, Walter Lee?

WALTER *does not take his eyes off the man.* RUTH *goes blindly to the tap and gets a glass of water and brings it to* BOBO.

WALTER   There ain't nothing wrong, is there?

BOBO   Lemme tell you—

WALTER   Man—didn't nothing go wrong?

BOBO   Lemme tell you—Walter Lee. (*Looking at* RUTH *and talking to her more than to* WALTER) You know how it was. I got to tell you how it was. I mean first I got tell you how it was all the way . . . I mean about the money I put in, Walter Lee. . . .

WALTER (*with taut agitation*)   What about the money you put in?

BOBO   Well—it wasn't much as we told you—me and Willy—(*He stops.*) I'm sorry, Walter. I got a bad feeling about it. I got a real bad feeling about it. . . .

WALTER   Man, what you telling me about all this for? . . . Tell me what happened in Springfield. . . .

BOBO   Springfield.

RUTH (*like a dead woman*)   What was supposed to happen in Springfield?

BOBO (*to her*)   This deal that me and Walter went into with Willy —Me and Willy was going to go down to Springfield and spread some money 'round so's we wouldn't have to wait so long for the liquor license. . . . That's what we were going to do. Everybody said that was the way you had to do, you understand, Miss Ruth?

WALTER   Man—what happened down there?

BOBO (*a pitiful man, near tears*)   I'm trying to tell you, Walter.

WALTER (*screaming at him suddenly*)   THEN TELL ME, GOD-DAMMIT . . . WHAT'S THE MATTER WITH YOU?

BOBO   Man . . . I didn't go to no Springfield, yesterday.

WALTER (*halted, life hanging in the moment*)   Why not?

BOBO (*the long way, the hard way to tell*)　'Cause I didn't have no reasons to. . . .

WALTER　Man, what are you talking about!

BOBO　I'm talking about the fact that when I got to the train station yesterday morning—eight o'clock like we planned . . . Man—*Willy didn't never show up.*

WALTER　Why . . . where was he . . . where is he?

BOBO　That's what I'm trying to tell you . . . I don't know . . . I waited six hours . . . I called his house . . . and I waited . . . six hours . . . I waited in that train station six hours . . . (*Breaking into tears*) That was all the extra money I had in the world. . . . (*Looking up at* WALTER *with the tears running down his face*) Man, *Willy is gone.*

WALTER　Gone, what you mean Willy is gone? Gone where? You mean he went by himself. You mean he went off to Springfield by himself—to take care of getting the license—(*Turns and looks anxiously at* RUTH) You mean maybe he didn't want too many people in on the business down there? (*Looks to* RUTH *again, as before*) You know Willy got his own ways. (*Looks back to* BOBO) Maybe you was late yesterday and he just went on down there without you. Maybe—maybe—he's been callin' you at home tryin' to tell you what happened or something. Maybe—maybe—he just got sick. He's somewhere—he's got to be somewhere. We just got to find him—me and you got to find him. (*Grabs* BOBO *senselessly by the collar and starts to shake him*) We got to!

BOBO (*in sudden angry, frightened agony*)　What's the matter with you, Walter! *When a cat take off with your money he don't leave you no maps!*

WALTER (*turning madly, as though he is looking for* WILLY *in the very room*)　Willy! . . . Willy . . . don't do it. . . . Please don't do it . . . Man, not with that money . . . Man, please not with that money . . . Oh, God . . . Don't let it be true. . . . (*He is wandering around, crying out for* WILLY *and looking for him or perhaps for help from God.*) Man . . . I trusted you . . . Man, I put my life in your hands. . . . (*He starts to crumple down on the floor as* RUTH *just covers her face in horror.* MAMA *opens the door and comes into the room, with* BENEATHA *behind her.*) Man . . . (*He starts to pound the floor with his fists, sobbing wildly.*) That money is made out of my father's flesh. . . .

BOBO (*standing over him helplessly*)　I'm sorry, Walter. . . . (*Only* WALTER'S *sobs reply.* BOBO *puts on his hat.*) I had my life staked on this deal, too. . . . (*He exits.*)

MAMA (*to* WALTER)　Son—(*She goes to him, bends down to him, talks to his bent head.*) Son . . . Is it gone? Son, I gave you sixty-

five hundred dollars. Is it gone? All of it? Beneatha's money too?
WALTER *(lifting his head slowly)*   Mama . . . I never . . . went to
the bank at all. . . .
MAMA *(not wanting to believe him)*   You mean . . . your sister's
school money . . . you used that too . . . Walter? . . .
WALTER   Yessss! . . . All of it. . . . It's all gone. . . .

There is total silence. RUTH *stands with her face covered with her hands;*
BENEATHA *leans forlornly against a wall, fingering a piece of red ribbon
from the mother's gift.* MAMA *stops and looks at her son without recognition and then, quite without thinking about it, starts to beat him senselessly in the face.* BENEATHA *goes to them and stops it.*

BENEATHA   Mama!

MAMA *stops and looks at both of her children and rises slowly and wanders vaguely, aimlessly away from them.*

MAMA   I seen . . . him . . . night after night . . . come in . . . and look
at that rug . . . and then look at me . . . the red showing in his
eyes . . . the veins moving in his head. . . . I seen him grow thin
and old before he was forty . . . working and working and working like somebody's old horse . . . killing himself . . . and you—you
give it all away in a day. . . .
BENEATHA   Mama—
MAMA   Oh, God. . . . *(She looks up to Him.)* Look down here—and
show me the strength.
BENEATHA   Mama—
MAMA *(plaintively)*   Strength. . . .
BENEATHA *(plaintively)*   Mama. . . .
MAMA   Strength!

Curtain

ACT   III

An hour later.
*At curtain, there is a sullen light of gloom in the living room, gray light
not unlike that which began the first scene of Act I. At left we can see*
WALTER *within his room, alone with himself. He is stretched out on the
bed, his shirt out and open, his arms under his head. He does not smoke,
he does not cry out, he merely lies there, looking up at the ceiling, much
as if he were alone in the world.*
In the living room BENEATHA *sits at the table, still surrounded by the
now almost ominous packing crates. She sits looking off. We feel that this
is a mood struck perhaps an hour before, and it lingers now, full of the
empty sound of profound disappointment. We see on a line from her
brother's bedroom the sameness of their attitudes. Presently the bell rings*

and BENEATHA *rises without ambition or interest in answering. It is* ASAGAI, *smiling broadly, striding into the room with energy and happy expectation and conversation.*

ASAGAI   I came over ... I had some free time. I thought I might help with the packing. Ah, I like the look of packing crates! A household in preparation for a journey! It depresses some people ... but for me ... it is another feeling. Something full of the flow of life, do you understand? Movement, progress ... It makes me think of Africa.

BENEATHA   Africa!

ASAGAI   What kind of a mood is this? Have I told you how deeply you move me?

BENEATHA   He gave away the money, Asagai. ...

ASAGAI   Who gave away what money?

BENEATHA   The insurance money. My brother gave it away.

ASAGAI   Gave it away?

BENEATHA   He made an investment! With a man even Travis wouldn't have trusted.

ASAGAI   And it's gone?

BENEATHA   Gone!

ASAGAI   I'm very sorry. ... And you, now?

BENEATHA   Me? ... Me? ... Me I'm nothing. ... Me. When I was very small ... we used to take our sleds out in the wintertime and the only hills we had were the ice-covered stone steps of some houses down the street. And we used to fill them in with snow and make them smooth and slide down them all day ... and it was very dangerous you know ... far too steep ... and sure enough one day a kid named Rufus came down too fast and hit the sidewalk ... and we saw his face just split open right there in front of us. ... And I remember standing there looking at his bloody open face thinking that was the end of Rufus. But the ambulance came and they took him to the hospital and they fixed the broken bones and they sewed it all up ... and the next time I saw Rufus he just had a little line down the middle of his face. ... I never got over that. ...

WALTER *sits up, listening on the bed. Throughout this scene it is important that we feel his reaction at all times, that he visibly respond to the words of his sister and* ASAGAI.

ASAGAI   What?

BENEATHA   That was what one person could do for another, fix him up—sew up the problem, make him all right again. That was the most marvelous thing in the world. ... I wanted to do that. I always thought it was the one concrete thing in the world that a human being could do. Fix up the sick, you know—and make them whole again. This was truly being God. . . .

ASAGAI   You wanted to be God?

BENEATHA   No—I wanted to cure. It used to be so important to me. I wanted to cure. It used to matter. I used to care. I mean about people and how their bodies hurt. . . .

ASAGAI   And you've stopped caring?

BENEATHA   Yes—I think so.

ASAGAI   Why?

WALTER *rises, goes to the door of his room and is about to open it, then stops and stands listening, leaning on the door jamb.*

BENEATHA   Because it doesn't seem deep enough, close enough to what ails mankind—I mean this thing of sewing up bodies or administering drugs. Don't you understand? It was a child's reaction to the world. I thought that doctors had the secret to all the hurts. . . . That's the way a child sees things—or an idealist.

ASAGAI   Children see things very well sometimes—and idealists even better.

BENEATHA   I know that's what you think. Because you are still where I left off—you still care. This is what you see for the world, for Africa. You with the dreams of the future will patch up all Africa—you are going to cure the Great Sore of colonialism with Independence—

ASAGAI   Yes!

BENEATHA   Yes—and you think that one word is the penicillin of the human spirit: "Independence!" But then what?

ASAGAI   That will be the problem for another time. First we must get there.

BENEATHA   And where does it end?

ASAGAI   End? Who even spoke of an end? To life? To living?

BENEATHA   An end to misery!

ASAGAI (*smiling*)   You sound like a French intellectual.

BENEATHA   No! I sound like a human being who just had her future taken right out of her hands! While I was sleeping in my bed in there, things were happening in this world that directly concerned me—and nobody asked me, consulted me—they just went out and did things—and changed my life. Don't you see there isn't any real progress, Asagai, there is only one large circle that we march in, around and around, each of us with our own little picture—in front of us—our own little mirage that we think is the future.

ASAGAI   That is the mistake.

BENEATHA   What?

ASAGAI   What you just said—about the circle. It isn't a circle—it
is simply a long line—as in geometry, you know, one that reaches
into infinity. And because we cannot see the end—we also cannot
see how it changes. And it is very odd but those who see the
changes are called "idealists"—and those who cannot, or refuse
to think, they are the "realists." It is very strange, and amusing
too, I think.

BENEATHA   You   you are almost religious.

ASAGAI   Yes . . . I think I have the religion of doing what is necessary in the world—and of worshipping man—because he is so
marvelous, you see.

BENEATHA   Man is foul! And the human race deserves its misery!

ASAGAI   You see: *you* have become the religious one in the old
sense. Already, and after such a small defeat, you are worshipping despair.

BENEATHA   From now on, I worship the truth—and the truth is
that people are puny, small and selfish. . . .

ASAGAI   Truth? Why is it that you despairing ones always think
that only you have the truth? I never thought to see *you* like
that. You! Your brother made a stupid, childish mistake—and
you are grateful to him. So that now you can give up the ailing
human race on account of it. You talk about what good is struggle;
what good is anything? Where are we all going? And why are
we bothering?

BENEATHA   *And you cannot answer it!* All your talk and dreams
about Africa and Independence. Independence and then what?
What about all the crooks and petty thieves and just plain idiots
who will come into power to steal and plunder the same as before
—only now they will be black and do it in the name of the new
Independence—You cannot answer that.

ASAGAI   (*shouting over her*)   *I live the answer!* (*Pause.*) In my village at home it is the exceptional man who can even read a newspaper . . . or who ever *sees* a book at all. I will go home and much
of what I will have to say will seem strange to the people of my
village. . . . But I will teach and work and things will happen,
slowly and swiftly. At times it will seem that nothing changes at
all . . . and then again . . . the sudden dramatic events which make
history leap into the future. And then quiet again. Retrogression
even. Guns, murder, revolution. And I even will have moments
when I wonder if the quiet was not better than all that death
and hatred. But I will look about my village at the illiteracy and
disease and ignorance and I will not wonder long. And perhaps
. . . perhaps I will be a great man. . . . I mean perhaps I will hold
on to the substance of truth and find my way always with the

right course . . . and perhaps for it I will be butchered in my bed some night by the servants of the empire. . . .

BENEATHA   *The martyr!*

ASAGAI   . . . or perhaps I shall live to be a very old man, respected and esteemed in my new nation. . . . And perhaps I shall hold office and this is what I'm trying to tell you, Alaiyo; perhaps the things I believe now for my country will be wrong and outmoded, and I will not understand and do terrible things to have things my way or merely to keep my power. Don't you see that there will be young men and women, not British soldiers then, but my own black countrymen . . . to step out of the shadows some evening and slit my then useless throat? Don't you see they have always been there . . . that they always will be. And that such a thing as my own death will be an advance? They who might kill me even . . . actually replenish me!

BENEATHA   Oh, Asagai, I know all that.

ASAGAI   Good! Then stop moaning and groaning and tell me what you plan to do.

BENEATHA   Do?

ASAGAI   I have a bit of a suggestion.

BENEATHA   What?

ASAGAI   (*rather quietly for him*)   That when it is all over—that you come home with me—

BENEATHA   (*slapping herself on the forehead with exasperation born of misunderstanding*)   Oh—Asagai—at this moment you decide to be romantic!

ASAGAI   (*quickly understanding and misunderstanding*)   My dear, young creature of the New World—I do not mean across the city—I mean across the ocean; home—to Africa.

BENEATHA   (*slowly understanding and turning to him with murmured amazement*)   To—to Nigeria?

ASAGAI   Yes! . . . (*Smiling and lifting his arms playfully*)   Three hundred years later the African Prince rose up out of the seas and swept the maiden back across the middle passage over which her ancestors had come—

BENEATHA   (*unable to play*)   Nigeria?

ASAGAI   Nigeria. Home. (*Coming to her with genuine romantic flippancy.*)   I will show you our mountains and our stars; and give you cool drinks from gourds and teach you the old songs and the ways of our people—and, in time, we will pretend that—(*very softly*)—you have only been away for a day—

She turns her back to him, thinking. He swings her around and takes her full in his arms in a long embrace which proceeds to passion.

BENEATHA (*pulling away*)   You're getting me all mixed up—
ASAGAI   Why?
BENEATHA   Too many things—too many things have happened today. I must sit down and think. I don't know what I feel about
anything right this minute. (*She promptly sits down and props
her chin on her fist.*)
ASAGAI (*charmed*)   All right, I shall leave you. No—don't get up.
(*Touching her, gently, sweetly*) Just sit awhile and think. . . .
Never be afraid to sit awhile and think. (*He goes to door and
looks at her.*) How often I have looked at you and said, "Ah—
so this is what the New World hath finally wrought. . . ."

(*He exits. BENEATHA sits on alone. Presently WALTER enters from his
room and starts to rummage through things, feverishly looking for something. She looks up and turns in her seat.*)

BENEATHA (*hissingly*)   Yes—just look at what the New World hath
wrought! . . . Just look! (*She gestures with bitter disgust.*) There
he is! *Monsieur le petit bourgeois noir*—himself! There he is—
Symbol of a Rising Class! Entrepreneur! Titan of the system!
(*WALTER ignores her completely and continues frantically and
destructively looking for something and hurling things to floor
and tearing things out of their place in his search. BENEATHA
ignores the eccentricity of his actions and goes on with the monologue of insult.*) Did you dream of yachts on Lake Michigan,
Brother? Did you see yourself on that Great Day sitting down at
the Conference Table, surrounded by all the mighty bald-headed
men in America? All halted, waiting, breathless, waiting for your
pronouncements on industry? Waiting for you—Chairman of the
Board? (*WALTER finds what he is looking for—a small piece of
white paper—and pushes it in his pocket and puts on his coat
and rushes out without even having looked at her. She shouts
after him.*) I look at you and I see the final triumph of stupidity
in the world!

(*The door slams and she returns to just sitting again. RUTH comes
quickly out of MAMA's room.*)

RUTH   Who was that?
BENEATHA   Your husband.
RUTH   Where did he go?
BENEATHA   Who knows—maybe he has an appointment at U.S.
Steel.
RUTH (*anxiously, with frightened eyes*)   You didn't say nothing
bad to him, did you?

BENEATHA   Bad? Say anything bad to him? No—I told him he was a sweet boy and full of dreams and everything is strictly peachy keen, as the ofay kids say!

(MAMA *enters from her bedroom. She is lost, vague, trying to catch hold, to make some sense of her former command of the world, but it still eludes her. A sense of waste overwhelms her gait; a measure of apology rides on her shoulders. She goes to her plant, which has remained on the table, looks at it, picks it up and takes it to the window sill and sits it outside, and she stands and looks at it a long moment. Then she closes the window, straightens her body with effort and turns around to her children.*)

MAMA   Well—ain't it a mess in here, though? (*A false cheerfulness, a beginning of something*) I guess we all better stop moping around and get some work done. All this unpacking and everything we got to do. (RUTH *raises her head slowly in response to the sense of the line; and* BENEATHA *in similar manner turns very slowly to look at her mother.*) One of you all better call the moving people and tell 'em not to come.

RUTH   Tell 'em not to come?

MAMA   Of course, baby. Ain't no need in 'em coming all the way here and having to go back. They charges for that too. (*She sits down, fingers to her brow, thinking.*) Lord, ever since I was a little girl, I always remembers people saying, "Lena—Lena Eggleston, you aims too high all the time. You needs to slow down and see life a little more like it is. Just slow down some." That's what they always used to say down home—"Lord, that Lena Eggleston is a high-minded thing. She'll get her due one day!"

RUTH   No, Lena. . . .

MAMA   Me and Big Walter just didn't never learn right.

RUTH   Lena, no! We gotta go. Bennie—tell her. . . . (*She rises and crosses to* BENEATHA *with her arms outstretched.* BENEATHA *doesn't respond.*) Tell her we can still move . . . the notes ain't but a hundred and twenty-five a month. We got four grown people in this house—we can work. . . .

MAMA (*to herself*)   Just aimed too high all the time—

RUTH (*turning and going to* MAMA *fast—the words pouring out with urgency and desperation*)   Lena—I'll work. . . . I'll work twenty hours a day in all the kitchens in Chicago. . . . I'll strap my baby on my back if I have to and scrub all the floors in America and wash all the sheets in America if I have to—but we got to move. . . . We got to get out of here. . . .

MAMA *reaches out absently and pats* RUTH's *hand.*

MAMA   No—I see things differently now. Been thinking 'bout some of the things we could do to fix this place up some. I seen a second-hand bureau over on Maxwell Street just the other day that could fit right there. (*She points to where the new furniture might go.* RUTH *wanders away from her.*) Would need some new handles on it and then a little varnish and then it look like something brand-new. And—we can put up them new curtains in the kitchen.... Why this place be looking fine. Cheer us all up so that we forget trouble ever came.... (*To* RUTH) And you could get some nice screens to put up in your room round the baby's bassinet.... (*She looks at both of them, pleadingly.*) Sometimes you just got to know when to give up some things ... and hold on to what you got.

(WALTER *enters from the outside, looking spent and leaning against the door, his coat hanging from him.*)

MAMA   Where you been, son?

WALTER   (*breathing hard*)   Made a call.

MAMA   To who, son?

WALTER   To The Man.

MAMA   What man, baby?

WALTER   The Man, Mama. Don't you know who The Man is?

RUTH   Walter Lee?

WALTER   *The Man.* Like the guys in the streets say—The Man. Captain Boss—Mistuh Charley ... Old Captain Please Mr. Boss-man ...

BENEATHA   (*suddenly*)   Lindner!

WALTER   That's right! That's good. I told him to come right over.

BENEATHA   (*fiercely, understanding*)   For what? What do you want to see him for!

WALTER   (*looking at his sister*)   We going to do business with him.

MAMA   What you talking 'bout, son?

WALTER   Talking 'bout life, Mama. You all always telling me to see life like it is. Well—I laid in there on my back today ... and I figured it out. Life just like it is. Who gets and who don't get. (*He sits down with his coat on and laughs.*) Mama, you know it's all divided up. Life is. Sure enough. Between the takers and the "tooken." (*He laughs.*) I've figured it out finally. (*He looks around at them.*) Yeah. Some of us always getting "tooken." (*He laughs.*) People like Willy Harris, they don't never get "tooken." And you know why the rest of us do? 'Cause we all mixed up. Mixed up bad. We get to looking 'round for the right and the wrong; and we worry about it and cry about it and stay up nights trying to figure out 'bout the wrong and the right of things all the time. . . . And all the time, man, them takers is out there operating, just taking and taking. Willy Harris? Shoot— Willy Harris don't even count. He don't even count in the big scheme of things. But I'll say one thing for old Willy Harris . . . he's taught me something. He's taught me to keep my eye on what counts in this world. Yeah—(*shouting out a little*). Thanks, Willy!

RUTH   What did you call that man for, Walter Lee?

WALTER   Called him to tell him to come on over to the show. Gonna put on a show for the man. Just what he wants to see. You see, Mama, the man came here today and he told us that them people out there where you want us to move—well they so upset they willing to pay us not to move out there. (*He laughs again.*) And—and oh, Mama—you would of been proud of the way me and Ruth and Bennie acted. We told him to get out . . . Lord have mercy! We told the man to get out. Oh, we was some proud folks this afternoon, yeah. (*He lights a cigarette.*) We were still full of that old-time stuff. . . .

RUTH   (*coming toward him slowly*)   You talking 'bout taking them people's money to keep us from moving in that house?

WALTER   I ain't just talking 'bout it, baby—I'm telling you that's what's going to happen.

BENEATHA   Oh, God! Where is the bottom! Where is the real honest-to-God bottom so he can't go any farther!

WALTER   See—that's old stuff. You and that boy that was here today. You all want everybody to carry a flag and a spear and sing some marching songs, huh? You wanna spend your life looking into things and trying to find the right and the wrong part, huh? Yeah. You know what's going to happen to that boy someday—he'll find himself sitting in a dungeon, locked in forever—and the takers will have the key! Forget it, baby! There ain't no causes—there ain't nothing but taking in this world, and he who takes most is smartest—and it don't make a damn bit of difference *how*.

MAMA   You making something inside me cry, son. Some awful pain inside me.

WALTER   Don't cry, Mama. Understand. That white man is going to walk in that door able to write checks for more money than we ever had. It's important to him and I'm going to help him . . . I'm going to put on the show, Mama.

MAMA   Son—I come from five generations of people who was slaves and sharecroppers—but ain't nobody in my family never let nobody pay 'em no money that was a way of telling us we wasn't fit to walk the earth. We ain't never been that poor. (*Raising her eyes and looking at him*) We ain't never been that dead inside.

BENEATHA Well—we are dead now. All the talk about dreams and sunlight that goes on in this house. All dead.

WALTER What's the matter with you all! I didn't make this world! It was give to me this way! Hell, yes, I want me some yachts someday! Yes, I want to hang some real pearls 'round my wife's neck. Ain't she supposed to wear no pearls? Somebody tell me—tell me, who decides which women is suppose to wear pearls in this world. I tell you I am a *man*—and I think my wife should wear some pearls in this world!

This last line hangs a good while and WALTER *begins to move about the room. The word "Man" has penetrated his consciousness; he mumbles it to himself repeatedly between strange agitated pauses as he moves about.*

MAMA Baby, how you going to feel on the inside?

WALTER Fine! ... Going to feel fine ... a man. ...

MAMA You won't have nothing left then, Walter Lee.

WALTER (*coming to her*) I'm going to feel fine, Mama. I'm going to look that son-of-a-bitch in the eyes and say—(*he falters*)—and say, "All right, Mr. Lindner—(*he falters even more*)—that's your neighborhood out there. You got the right to keep it like you want. You got the right to have it like you want. Just write the check and—the house is yours." And, and I am going to say—(*His voice almost breaks.*) And you—you people just put the money in my hand and you won't have to live next to this bunch of stinking niggers! ... (*He straightens up and moves away from his mother, walking around the room.*) Maybe—maybe I'll just get down on my black knees. ... (*He does so;* RUTH *and* BENNIE *and* MAMA *watch him in frozen horror.*) Captain, Mistuh, Bossman. (*He starts crying.*) A-hee-hee-hee! (*Wringing his hands in profoundly anguished imitation*) Yassssuh! Great White Father, just gi' ussen de money, fo' God's sake, and we's ain't gwine come out deh and dirty up yo' white folks neighborhood. ...

(He breaks down completely, then gets up and goes into the bedroom.)

BENEATHA That is not a man. That is nothing but a toothless rat.

MAMA Yes—death done come in this here house. (*She is nodding, slowly, reflectively.*) Done come walking in my house. On the lips of my children. You what supposed to be my beginning again. You—what supposed to be my harvest. (*To* BENEATHA) You—you mourning your brother?

BENEATHA He's no brother of mine.

MAMA What you say?

BENEATHA I said that that individual in that room is no brother of mine.

MAMA   That's what I thought you said. You feeling like you better than he is today? (BENEATHA *does not answer.*) Yes? What you tell him a minute ago? That he wasn't a man? Yes? You give him up for me? You done wrote his epitaph too—like the rest of the world? Well, who give you the privilege?

BENEATHA   Be on my side for once! You saw what he just did, Mama! You saw him—down on his knees. Wasn't it you who taught me—to despise any man who would do that. Do what he's going to do.

MAMA   Yes—I taught you that. Me and your daddy. But I thought I taught you something else too . . . I thought I taught you to love him.

BENEATHA   Love him? There is nothing left to love.

MAMA   There is always something left to love. And if you ain't learned that, you ain't learned nothing. (*Looking at her*) Have you cried for that boy today? I don't mean for yourself and for the family 'cause we lost the money. I mean for him; what he been through and what it done to him. Child, when do you think is the time to love somebody the most; when they done good and made things easy for everybody? Well then, you ain't through learning—because that ain't the time at all. It's when he's at his lowest and can't believe in hisself 'cause the world done whipped him so. When you starts measuring somebody, measure him right, child, measure him right. Make sure you done taken into account what hills and valleys he come through before he got to wherever he is.

(TRAVIS *bursts into the room at the end of the speech, leaving the door open.*)

TRAVIS   Grandmama—the moving men are downstairs! The truck just pulled up.

MAMA (*turning and looking at him*)   Are they, baby? They downstairs?

(*She sighs and sits.* LINDNER *appears in the doorway. He peers in and knocks lightly, to gain attention, and comes in. All turn to look at him.*)

LINDNER (*hat and briefcase in hand*)   Uh—hello . . .

RUTH *crosses mechanically to the bedroom door and opens it and lets it swing open freely and slowly as the lights come up on* WALTER *within, still in his coat, sitting at the far corner of the room. He looks up and out through the room to* LINDNER.

RUTH   He's here.

A long minute passes and WALTER *slowly gets up.*

LINDNER (*coming to the table with efficiency, putting his briefcase on the table and starting to unfold papers and unscrew fountain pens*) Well, I certainly was glad to hear from you people. (WALTER *has begun the trek out of the room, slowly and awkwardly, rather like a small boy, passing the back of his sleeve across his mouth from time to time.*) Life can really be so much simpler than people let it be most of the time. Well—with whom do I negotiate? You, Mrs. Younger, or your son here? (MAMA *sits with her hands folded on her lap and her eyes closed as* WALTER *advances.* TRAVIS *goes close to* LINDNER *and looks at the papers curiously.*) Just some official papers, sonny.

RUTH Travis, you go downstairs.

MAMA (*opening her eyes and looking into* WALTER'S) No. Travis, you stay right here. And you make him understand what you doing, Walter Lee. You teach him good. Like Willy Harris taught you. You show where our five generations done come to. Go ahead, son—

WALTER (*looks down into his boy's eyes;* TRAVIS *grins at him merrily and* WALTER *draws him beside him with his arm lightly around his shoulders*) Well, Mr. Lindner. (BENEATHA *turns away.*) We called you—(*there is a profound, simple groping quality in his speech*)—because, well, me and my family—(*He looks around and shifts from one foot to the other.*) Well—we are very plain people. . . .

LINDNER Yes—

WALTER I mean—I have worked as a chauffeur most of my life— and my wife here, she does domestic work in people's kitchens. So does my mother. I mean—we are plain people. . . .

LINDNER Yes, Mr. Younger—

WALTER (*really like a small boy, looking down at his shoes and then up at the man*) And—uh—well, my father, well, he was a laborer most of his life.

LINDNER (*absolutely confused*) Uh, yes—

WALTER (*looking down at his toes once again*) My father almost beat a man to death once because this man called him a bad name or something, you know what I mean?

LINDNER No, I'm afraid I don't.

WALTER (*finally straightening up*) Well, what I mean is that we come from people who had a lot of pride. I mean—we are very proud people. And that's my sister over there and she's going to be a doctor—and we are very proud—

LINDNER Well— I am sure that is very nice, but—

WALTER (*starting to cry and facing the man eye to eye*) What I am telling you is that we called you over here to tell you that we are very proud and that this is—this is my son, who makes the sixth generation of our family in this country, and that we have all thought about your offer and we have decided to move into our house because my father—my father—he earned it. (*MAMA has her eyes closed and is rocking back and forth as though she were in church, with her head nodding the amen yes.*) We don't want to make no trouble for nobody or fight no causes—but we will try to be good neighbors. That's all we got to say. (*He looks the man absolutely in the eyes.*) We don't want your money. (*He turns and walks away from the man.*)

LINDNER (*looking around at all of them*)   I take it then that you have decided to occupy.

BENEATHA   That's what the man said.

LINDNER (*to MAMA in her reverie*)   Then I would like to appeal to you, Mrs. Younger. You are older and wiser and understand things better I am sure . . .

MAMA (*rising*)   I am afraid you don't understand. My son said we was going to move and there ain't nothing left for me to say. (*Shaking her head with double meaning*) You know how these young folks is nowadays, mister. Can't do a thing with 'em. Good-bye.

LINDNER (*folding up his materials*)   Well—if you are that final about it. . . . There is nothing left for me to say. (*He finishes. He is almost ignored by the family, who are concentrating on WALTER LEE. At the door LINDNER halts and looks around.*) I sure hope you people know what you're doing. (*He shakes his head and exits.*)

RUTH (*looking around and coming to life*)   Well, for God's sake— if the moving men are here—LET'S GET THE HELL OUT OF HERE!

MAMA (*into action*)   Ain't it the truth! Look at all this here mess. Ruth, put Travis' good jacket on him. . . . Walter Lee, fix your tie and tuck your shirt in, you look just like somebody's hoodlum. Lord have mercy, where is my plant? (*She flies to get it amid the general bustling of the family, who are deliberately trying to ignore the nobility of the past moment.*) You all start on down. . . . Travis child, don't go empty-handed. . . . Ruth, where did I put that box with my skillets in it? I want to be in charge of it myself. . . . I'm going to make us the biggest dinner we ever ate tonight. . . . Beneatha, what's the matter with them stockings? Pull them things up, girl. . . .

(*The family starts to file out as two moving men appear and begin to carry out the heavier pieces of furniture, bumping into the family as they move about.*)

BENEATHA   Mama, Asagai—asked me to marry him today and go to Africa—

MAMA (*in the middle of her getting-ready activity*)   He did? You ain't old enough to marry nobody—(*Seeing the moving men lifting one of her chairs precariously*) Darling, that ain't no bale of cotton, please handle it so we can sit in it again. I had that chair twenty-five years. . . .

The movers sigh with exasperation and go on with their work.

BENEATHA (*girlishly and unreasonably trying to pursue the conversation*)   To go to Africa, Mama—be a doctor in Africa. . . .

MAMA (*distracted*)   Yes, baby—

WALTER   Africa! What he want you to go to Africa for?

BENEATHA   To practice there. . . .

WALTER   Girl, if you don't get all them silly ideas out your head! You better marry yourself a man with some loot. . . .

BENEATHA (*angrily, precisely as in the first scene of the play*)   What have you got to do with who I marry!

WALTER   Plenty. Now I think George Murchison—

(*He and* BENEATHA *go out yelling at each other vigorously;* BENEATHA *is heard saying that she would not marry* GEORGE MURCHISON *if he were Adam and she were Eve, etc. The anger is loud and real till their voices diminish.* RUTH *stands at the door and turns to* MAMA *and smiles knowingly.*)

MAMA (*fixing her hat at last*)   Yeah—they something all right, my children. . . .

RUTH   Yeah—they're something. Let's go, Lena.

MAMA (*stalling, starting to look around at the house*)   Yes—I'm coming. Ruth—

RUTH   Yes?

MAMA (*quietly, woman to woman*)   He finally come into his manhood today, didn't he? Kind of like a rainbow after the rain. . . .

RUTH (*biting her lip lest her own pride explode in front of* MAMA)   Yes, Lena.

WALTER'S *voice calls for them raucously.*

MAMA (*waving* RUTH *out vaguely*)   All right, honey—go on down. I be down directly.

(RUTH *hesitates, then exits.* MAMA *stands, at last alone in the living room, her plant on the table before her as the lights start to come down. She looks around at all the walls and ceilings and suddenly, despite*

*herself, while the children call below, a great heaving thing rises in her
and she puts her fist to her mouth, takes a final desperate look, pulls
her coat about her, pats her hat and goes out. The lights dim down.
The door opens and she comes back in, grabs her plant, and goes out
for the last time.)*

Curtain

QUESTIONS

1. *A Raisin in the Sun* uses many comic devices in its plot: for instance, the young
   girl trying to choose between two suitors (shall she accept one, the other, or
   neither?), and the gullible man who, through obsession and folly, falls prey
   to a con man, a representative of vice.
   How are these two plots worked out in this play? How do they contrast with
   and support one another? What is their role in the play's overall plot?
2. Discuss the use of Lena's plant. What does it symbolize? How does it help
   emphasize Lena's role in the play?

POSSIBLE ESSAY TOPICS

1. Lorraine Hansberry wrote in a letter

   There is . . . a great deal to be fought in America—but, at the same time,
   there is so much that begs to be re-affirmed and cherished with sweet defiance. . . . There is simply no reason why dreams should dry up like raisins
   or prunes or anything else in America. If you will permit me to say so, I
   believe that we can impose beauty on our future . . ." (*To Be Young, Gifted,
   and Black,* p. 115).
   Discuss how *A Raisin in the Sun* dramatizes this thesis.
2. Compare and contrast *A Raisin in the Sun* and *Tartuffe.*
3. Discuss *A Raisin in the Sun* in conjunction with the Langston Hughes poems
   "Harlem" (from which the play got its title) and "A Mother to Her Son"
   (from which Hansberry was considering a title, *The Crystal Stair*).

Index of Terms

Index of Authors and Titles

Index of First Lines